Yearbook of Tourism Statistics

Data 2002-2006

2008 Edition

Copyright © 2008 World Tourism Organization
Calle Capitán Haya, 42
28020 Madrid, Spain

Yearbook of Tourism Statistics – Data 2002–2006, 2008 Edition
ISBN 13: 978-92-844-1249-5

Published and printed by the World Tourism Organization, Madrid, Spain
First printing: 2008
All rights reserved

The designations employed and the presentation of material in this publication do not imply the expression of any opinions whatsoever on the part of the Secretariat of the World Tourism Organization concerning the legal status of any country, territory, city or area, or of its authorities or concerning the delimitation of its frontiers or boundaries.

World Tourism Organization
Calle Capitán Haya, 42
28020 Madrid, Spain
Tel.: (+34) 915 678 100
Fax: (+34) 915 713 733
Website: www.unwto.org
Email: omt@unwto.org

TABLE OF CONTENTS

Pages   Pages

TABLE OF CONTENTS

Pages   Pages

TABLE OF CONTENTS

TABLE OF CONTENTS

Pages   Pages

TABLE OF CONTENTS

Pages   Pages

INTRODUCTION

The present Yearbook of Tourism Statistics, has been prepared by the UNWTO Department of Statistics and Economic Measurement of Tourism. It is the 60 edition in a series initiated in 1947. It presents for 204 countries and territories data on total arrivals and overnight stays associated to inbound tourism with breakdown by country of origin.

In the present Yearbook, the titles of the tables are in English only. Notes are given in English, French and Spanish. Names of countries, regions and sub-regions as well as the classification included on the tables are in English only. Countries are classified in accordance with English alphabetical order.

The statistical data published are those officially received from national tourism administrations and national statistical offices.

All the data received are subject to different kind of controls and any discrepancies observed are consulted with the informing unit that confirms or rectifies, if necessary, the data previously sent.

Due to the rounding in the partial figures, the totals shown in the different tables of the Yearbook of Tourism Statistics may not coincide with the totals shown in the basic indicators of the Compendium of Tourism Statistics.

Consequently, **the data included in this Yearbook have an official character and have been entered in the UNWTO database as of 31 March 2008**. Therefore, any corrections or changes in the tables received after this date will be included in the next edition of the Yearbook.

The Yearbook contains data of total arrivals and overnight stays of international inbound tourism with breakdown by country of origin:

> Arrivals

    A.   Border statistics
- Table 1. Arrivals of non-resident tourists at national borders
- Table 2. Arrivals of non-resident visitors at national borders

    B.   Statistics on accommodation establishments
- Table 3. Arrivals of non-resident tourists in hotels and similar establishments
- Table 4. Arrivals of non-resident tourists in all types of accommodation establishments.

When a person visits the same country several times a year, each visit by the same person is counted as a separate arrival. If a person visits several countries during the course of a single trip, his/her arrival in each country is recorded separately. Consequently, *arrivals* are not necessarily equal to the number of different persons travelling.

Arrivals data correspond to international visitors to the economic territory of the country of reference and include both tourists and same-day non-resident visitors.

Data may be obtained from different sources: border statistics derived from administrative records (police, immigration, traffic counts, and other types of controls), border surveys and registrations at accommodation establishments.

➢   Overnight stays

- Table 5.   Overnight stays of non-resident tourists in hotels and similar establishments
- Table 6.   Overnight stays of non-resident tourists in all types of accommodation establishments.

Overnight stays refers to the number of nights spent by non-resident tourists in accommodation establishments (*guests*). If one person travels to a country and spends five nights there, that makes five tourist overnight stays (or person-nights).

The World Tourism Organization wishes to express its gratitude to the national tourism administrations and national statistical offices of the various countries and territories for their valuable co-operation.

Madrid, April 2008

INTRODUCTION

La Section Statistiques et mesure économique du tourisme de l'OMT est chargée d'élaborer l'Annuaire des Statistiques du Tourisme. Le présent Annuaire, constitue la 60e édition d'une qui a débuté en 1947. Il contient pour 204 pays et territoires des données détaillées sur la ventilation par pays d'origine des totaux des arrivées et des nuitées associées au tourisme récepteur.

Dans le présent Annuaire les titres des tableaux sont publiés en anglais uniquement. Les notes sont fournies en anglais, français et espagnol. Le nom des pays, régions et sous-régions ainsi que les classifications incluses dans les divers tableaux des arrivées et des nuitées sont publiés uniquement en anglais. Les pays ont été classés par ordre alphabétique anglais.

Les données publiées sont celles officiellement reçues des administrations nationales du tourisme et des instituts nationaux de la statistique.

Toutes les données reçues sont soumises à différents types de contrôle et les anomalies éventuellement relevées sont consultées avec l'unité chargée de l'information qui confirme ou, au besoin, rectifie les données envoyées.

Etant donné l'arrondissement des données partielles, les totaux qui apparaissent dans les différents tableaux de l'Annuaire des statistiques du tourisme peuvent ne pas correspondre aux totaux des Indicateurs de base du Compendium des statistiques du tourisme.

En conséquence, **les données figurant dans le présent Annuaire ont un caractère officiel et ont été introduites dans la base de données de l'OMT jusqu'à la date limite du 31 mars 2008.** Toute correction ou modification reçue après cette date sera incorporée à la prochaine édition de l'Annuaire.

L'Annuaire contient des données détaillées sur la ventilation par pays d'origine des totaux des arrivées et des nuitées du tourisme international récepteur:

> Arrivées

A. Statistiques de frontière
  - Tableau 1. Arrivées de touristes non résidents aux frontières nationales
  - Tableau 2. Arrivées de visiteurs non résidents aux frontières nationales

B. Statistiques dans les établissements d'hébergement
  - Tableau 3. Arrivées de touristes non résidents dans les hôtels et établissements assimilés
  - Tableau 4. Arrivées de touristes non résidents dans tous les types d'établissements d'hébergement

Lorsqu'une personne visite le même pays plusieurs fois dans l'année, chacune de ses visites est comptée séparément comme une arrivée. Si une personne visite plusieurs pays au cours d'un seul et même voyage, son arrivée dans chaque pays est enregistrée séparément. Par conséquent, le nombre d'arrivées n'est pas forcément égal au nombre de personnes qui voyagent.

Les données des arrivées correspondent aux visiteurs internationaux du territoire économique du pays dont il s'agit, visiteurs qui comprennent à la fois les touristes et les visiteurs de la journée (excursionnistes) non résidents.

Ces données peuvent être obtenues de différentes sources : statistiques des frontières tirées des registres administratifs (police, immigration, comptages de véhicules et autre types de contrôle), enquêtes aux frontières et registres des établissements d'hébergement.

> ➤ <u>Nuitées</u>

- • Tableau 5. Nuitées de touristes non résidents dans les hôtels et établissements assimilés
- • Tableau 6. Nuitées de touristes non résidents dans tous les types d'établissements d'hébergement

Nuitées indique le nombre de nuits que les touristes non résidents ont passées dans les établissements d'hébergement (en qualité de clients). Si une personne se rend dans un pays et y passe cinq nuits, on enregistre cinq nuitées de touriste (ou nuits-personne).

L'Organisation mondiale du tourisme tient à exprimer sa gratitude aux administrations nationales du tourisme et aux instituts nationaux de la statistique des divers pays et territoires pour leur précieuse coopération.

Madrid, avril 2008

INTRODUCCION

La Sección de Estadísticas y Evaluación Económica del Turismo de la OMT es la encargada de elaborar el Anuario de Estadísticas de Turismo. La presente edición del Anuario, constituye la 60 edición de una serie que comenzó en 1947. Contiene para 204 países y territorios, datos detallados sobre el desglose por país de origen de los totales de llegadas y pernoctaciones asociadas al turismo receptor.

En el presente Anuario los títulos de los cuadros aparecen en inglés únicamente. Las notas figuran en inglés, francés y español. Se publica únicamente en inglés el nombre de los países, las regiones y subregiones así como las clasificaciones incluidas en los diversos cuadros. Se han clasificado los países por orden alfabético inglés.

Los datos publicados son los remitidos oficialmente por las administraciones nacionales de turismo y los institutos nacionales de estadística.

Todos los datos recibidos están sujetos a diversos controles y se consultan todas las discrepancias con la unidad informante, la cual confirma o rectifica, si es necesario, los datos remitidos.

Debido al redondeo de las cifras parciales, los totales que aparecen en los distintos cuadros del Anuario de Estadísticas de Turismo, pueden no coincidir con los totales que aparecen en los Indicadores Básicos del Compendio de Estadísticas de Turismo.

Así pues, **las cifras incluidas en este Anuario tienen carácter oficial y han sido introducidas en la base de datos de la OMT al 31 de marzo de 2008.** Por consiguiente, cualquier corrección o cambio recibido después de esta fecha aparecerá en la próxima edición del Anuario.

El Anuario contiene datos detallados sobre el desglose por país de origen de las tablas de llegadas y pernoctaciones del turismo internacional receptor:

> Llegadas

  A. Estadísticas de fronteras
    • Cuadro 1. Llegadas de turistas no residentes en las fronteras nacionales
    • Cuadro 2. Llegadas de visitantes no residentes en las fronteras nacionales

  B. Estadísticas en establecimientos de alojamiento
    • Cuadro 3. Llegadas de turistas no residentes a los hoteles y establecimientos asimilados
    • Cuadro 4. Llegadas de turistas no residentes en todo tipo de establecimientos de alojamiento

Cuando una persona visita un mismo país varias veces en un año, cada una de esas visitas se cuenta como una llegada. Si una persona visita varios países en el transcurso de un mismo viaje, cada llegada a uno de esos países se registra por separado. Por lo tanto, el número de llegadas no tiene que ser igual al número de personas que viajan.

Los datos de llegadas se refieren a las llegadas de visitantes internacionales en el territorio económico del país de referencia, sean turistas o visitantes del día no residentes.

Los datos pueden proceder de diversas fuentes: estadísticas de fronteras basadas en registros administrativos (policía, inmigración, recuentos de circulación y otros tipos de controles), encuestas en las fronteras e inscripciones en establecimientos de alojamiento.

▷   <u>Pernoctaciones</u>

- Cuadro 5.   Pernoctaciones de turistas no residentes en hoteles y establecimientos asimilados
- Cuadro 6.   Pernoctaciones de turistas no residentes en todo tipo de establecimientos de alojamiento

Las *pernoctaciones* se refieren al número de noches que pasan los turistas no residentes en establecimientos de alojamiento. Si una persona viaja a un país y pasa en él cinco noches, se contarán cinco pernoctaciones turísticas (o pernoctaciones/persona).

La Organización Mundial del Turismo desea expresar su agradecimiento a las administraciones nacionales de turismo y a los institutos nacionales de estadística de los diversos países y territorios por su valiosa cooperación.

Madrid, abril de 2008

Country tables
2002-2006

➢ <u>Arrivals</u>

    A.   Border statistics

- Table 1.   Arrivals of non-resident tourists at national borders

- Table 2.   Arrivals of non-resident visitors at national borders

    B.   Statistics on accommodation establishments

- Table 3.   Arrivals of non-resident tourists in hotels and similar establishments

- Table 4.   Arrivals of non-resident tourists in all types of accommodation establishments

➢ <u>Overnight stays</u>

- Table 5.   Overnight stays of non-resident tourists in hotels and similar establishments

- Table 6.   Overnight stays of non-resident tourists in all types of accommodation establishments

ALBANIA

2. Arrivals of non-resident visitors at national borders, by nationality

	2002	2003	2004	2005	2006	Market share 06	% Change 06-05
TOTAL	469,691	557,210	645,409	747,837	937,038	100.00	25.30
AFRICA	75	233	174	174	220	0.02	26.44
Central Africa	12	8	6	4	11		175.00
Democratic Republic of the Congo	12	8	6	4	11		175.00
North Africa	53	52	83	69	130	0.01	88.41
Morocco	35	28	44	33	49	0.01	48.48
Sudan					63	0.01	
Tunisia	18	24	39	36	18		-50.00
Southern Africa	10	173	85	101	79	0.01	-21.78
South Africa	10	173	85	101	79	0.01	-21.78
AMERICAS	15,790	18,895	25,519	34,816	42,241	4.51	21.33
Caribbean				22	37		68.18
Dominican Republic					5		
Saint Lucia				22	32		45.45
Central America	32	3					
Honduras	32	3					
North America	15,468	18,554	25,138	34,336	41,752	4.46	21.60
Canada	1,424	2,046	3,043	4,176	5,653	0.60	35.37
Mexico	7	11	35	52	42		-19.23
United States	14,037	16,497	22,060	30,108	36,057	3.85	19.76
South America	290	338	381	458	452	0.05	-1.31
Argentina	99	95	82	81	108	0.01	33.33
Brazil	173	167	197	200	175	0.02	-12.50
Colombia	3	32	42	82	45		-45.12
Peru	13	29	28	52	63	0.01	21.15
Uruguay	2	5	23	37	47	0.01	27.03
Venezuela		10	9	6	14		133.33
EAST ASIA AND THE PACIFIC	2,901	3,805	4,288	5,444	7,592	0.81	39.46
North-East Asia	1,267	1,830	2,049	2,304	2,320	0.25	0.69
China	688	562	1,189	1,233	1,005	0.11	-18.49
Japan	275	897	596	673	753	0.08	11.89
Korea, Republic of	304	371	264	398	562	0.06	41.21
South-East Asia	169	306	316	291	363	0.04	24.74
Malaysia	94	200	230	193	177	0.02	-8.29
Philippines	74	92	68	78	138	0.01	76.92
Singapore					34		
Thailand	1	14	18	20	14		-30.00
Australasia	1,465	1,669	1,923	2,849	4,909	0.52	72.31
Australia	1,217	1,386	1,669	2,470	4,155	0.44	68.22
New Zealand	248	283	254	379	754	0.08	98.94
EUROPE	439,151	531,927	609,821	703,205	857,358	91.50	21.92
Central/Eastern Europe	7,779	11,139	15,073	22,319	30,171	3.22	35.18
Bulgaria	3,335	4,989	5,694	7,593	8,395	0.90	10.56
Czech Republic	888	1,084	2,141	3,578	4,252	0.45	18.84
Estonia	8	95	121	225	326	0.03	44.89
Hungary	1,127	1,338	1,965	3,087	3,866	0.41	25.23
Lithuania	2	97	249	260	588	0.06	126.15
Republic of Moldova	97	99	84	130	2		-98.46

ALBANIA

2. Arrivals of non-resident visitors at national borders, by nationality

	2002	2003	2004	2005	2006	Market share 06	% Change 06-05
Poland	867	1,190	2,064	3,523	5,787	0.62	64.26
Romania	868	1,211	1,569	1,760	2,894	0.31	64.43
Russian Federation	536	680	557	728	1,682	0.18	131.04
Slovakia	51	227	444	770	1,496	0.16	94.29
Ukraine		129	185	665	883	0.09	32.78
Northern Europe	**28,778**	**32,905**	**39,578**	**44,829**	**61,426**	**6.56**	**37.02**
Denmark	1,985	1,200	1,611	1,672	1,449	0.15	-13.34
Finland	787	801	891	1,933	2,425	0.26	25.45
Iceland	80	79	128	89	332	0.04	273.03
Ireland	1,175	1,610	1,531	1,956	2,324	0.25	18.81
Norway	1,580	1,770	1,482	1,953	2,110	0.23	8.04
Sweden	1,565	2,206	2,749	4,063	3,900	0.42	-4.01
United Kingdom	21,606	25,239	31,186	33,163	48,886	5.22	47.41
Southern Europe	**360,006**	**440,437**	**498,948**	**564,333**	**681,084**	**72.68**	**20.69**
Bosnia and Herzegovina	309	597	932	1,320	1,464	0.16	10.91
Croatia	1,595	1,978	2,771	4,065	6,018	0.64	48.04
Greece	30,315	34,266	40,541	47,776	56,219	6.00	17.67
Italy	51,615	49,984	51,703	62,520	68,240	7.28	9.15
Malta	216	180	216	229	1,336	0.14	483.41
Portugal	31	116	210	196	601	0.06	206.63
Slovenia	696	1,263	1,946	2,591	4,776	0.51	84.33
Spain	799	983	1,304	1,807	2,169	0.23	20.03
TFYR of Macedonia	75,759	79,012	99,837	141,160	187,554	20.02	32.87
Serbia and Montenegro	198,671	272,058	299,488	302,669	352,707	37.64	16.53
Western Europe	**32,240**	**37,267**	**44,206**	**56,271**	**69,147**	**7.38**	**22.88**
Austria	3,100	3,575	5,079	6,230	7,796	0.83	25.14
Belgium	2,530	2,417	3,197	4,713	5,908	0.63	25.36
France	4,321	9,213	7,399	9,984	12,608	1.35	26.28
Germany	14,791	15,169	18,420	23,391	27,364	2.92	16.99
Luxembourg	56	106	92	125	1,409	0.15	1,027.20
Netherlands	3,848	3,288	4,413	5,678	6,718	0.72	18.32
Switzerland	3,594	3,499	5,606	6,150	7,344	0.78	19.41
East Mediterranean Europe	**10,348**	**10,179**	**12,016**	**15,453**	**15,530**	**1.66**	**0.50**
Cyprus	77	120	197	163	372	0.04	128.22
Israel	407	325	417	695	872	0.09	25.47
Turkey	9,864	9,734	11,402	14,595	14,286	1.52	-2.12
MIDDLE EAST	**752**	**896**	**775**	**837**	**1,068**	**0.11**	**27.60**
Middle East	**752**	**896**	**775**	**837**	**1,068**	**0.11**	**27.60**
Palestine	12	10	23	13	12		-7.69
Iraq	14	19	9	6	21		250.00
Jordan	2	45	59	69	88	0.01	27.54
Kuwait	1	7	10	15	24		60.00
Libyan Arab Jamahiriya	40	20	40	43	111	0.01	158.14
Saudi Arabia	92	169	74	156	113	0.01	-27.56
Syrian Arab Republic	65	80	60	53	64	0.01	20.75
Egypt	526	546	500	482	635	0.07	31.74
SOUTH ASIA	**351**	**424**	**410**	**354**	**376**	**0.04**	**6.21**
South Asia	**351**	**424**	**410**	**354**	**376**	**0.04**	**6.21**
Bangladesh	3	11	16	18	13		-27.78
India	185	239	185	202	176	0.02	-12.87
Iran, Islamic Republic of	124	104	118	78	111	0.01	42.31
Nepal	1	21	14	6	16		166.67

ALBANIA

2. Arrivals of non-resident visitors at national borders, by nationality

	2002	2003	2004	2005	2006	Market share 06	% Change 06-05
Pakistan	38	49	77	50	60	0.01	20.00
REGION NOT SPECIFIED	**10,671**	**1,030**	**4,422**	**3,007**	**28,183**	**3.01**	**837.25**
Not Specified	**10,671**	**1,030**	**4,422**	**3,007**	**28,183**	**3.01**	**837.25**
Other countries of the World	10,671	1,030	4,422	3,007	28,183	3.01	837.25

Source: World Tourism Organization (UNWTO)

ALGERIA

2. Arrivals of non-resident visitors at national borders, by nationality

	2002	2003	2004	2005	2006	Market share 06	% Change 06-05
TOTAL (*)	988,060	1,166,287	1,233,719	1,443,090	1,637,582	100.00	13.48
AFRICA	72,041	111,941	131,066	161,182	159,869	9.76	-0.81
North Africa	51,553	90,211	109,017	138,749	133,691	8.16	-3.65
Morocco	3,849	4,186	5,424	9,984	13,213	0.81	32.34
Tunisia	47,704	86,025	103,593	128,765	120,478	7.36	-6.44
West Africa	16,012	17,392	15,459	17,107	19,917	1.22	16.43
Mali	11,387	14,453	11,520	12,817	13,703	0.84	6.91
Mauritania	2,591	1,596	1,914	3,028	4,121	0.25	36.10
Niger	2,034	1,343	2,025	1,262	2,093	0.13	65.85
Other Africa	4,476	4,338	6,590	5,326	6,261	0.38	17.56
Other countries of Africa	4,476	4,338	6,590	5,326	6,261	0.38	17.56
AMERICAS	4,626	4,949	6,830	8,117	9,724	0.59	19.80
North America	3,877	4,438	6,126	7,081	8,349	0.51	17.91
Canada	1,941	2,255	2,655	3,305	4,015	0.25	21.48
Mexico	62	85	150	227	248	0.02	9.25
United States	1,874	2,098	3,321	3,549	4,086	0.25	15.13
South America	187	201	255	433	630	0.04	45.50
Argentina	83	118	111	200	236	0.01	18.00
Brazil	104	83	144	233	394	0.02	69.10
Other Americas	562	310	449	603	745	0.05	23.55
Other countries of the Americas	562	310	449	603	745	0.05	23.55
EAST ASIA AND THE PACIFIC	9,491	8,260	9,401	15,157	19,207	1.17	26.72
North-East Asia	1,004	1,236	1,435	1,721	2,325	0.14	35.10
Japan	1,004	1,236	1,435	1,721	2,325	0.14	35.10
Australasia	285	374	378	501	736	0.04	46.91
Australia	230	281	333	420	664	0.04	58.10
New Zealand	55	93	45	81	72		-11.11
Other East Asia and the Pacific	8,202	6,650	7,588	12,935	16,146	0.99	24.82
Other countries of Asia	8,202	6,650	7,588	12,935	16,146	0.99	24.82
EUROPE	140,844	157,093	198,230	227,618	252,553	15.42	10.95
Northern Europe	4,430	6,482	9,198	10,935	11,154	0.68	2.00
Denmark	277	458	592	513	454	0.03	-11.50
Finland	199	239	202	245	345	0.02	40.82
Norway	185	291	464	776	982	0.06	26.55
Sweden	642	945	984	1,275	1,209	0.07	-5.18
United Kingdom	3,127	4,549	6,956	8,126	8,164	0.50	0.47
Southern Europe	16,091	20,615	22,976	29,772	35,185	2.15	18.18
Greece	359	395	384	518	549	0.03	5.98
Italy	9,763	10,571	10,642	13,676	15,055	0.92	10.08
Portugal	501	1,049	920	1,571	2,154	0.13	37.11
Spain	5,468	8,600	11,030	14,007	17,427	1.06	24.42
Western Europe	113,240	122,007	155,148	173,613	188,857	11.53	8.78
Austria	1,292	959	665	900	959	0.06	6.56
Belgium	3,126	3,801	4,769	5,393	6,926	0.42	28.43
France	96,626	106,042	138,473	153,398	161,090	9.84	5.01
Germany	8,182	7,049	7,306	9,392	14,771	0.90	57.27
Luxembourg	101	73	94	89	118	0.01	32.58
Netherlands	1,159	1,525	1,496	1,536	2,106	0.13	37.11

ALGERIA

2. Arrivals of non-resident visitors at national borders, by nationality

	2002	2003	2004	2005	2006	Market share 06	% Change 06-05
Switzerland	2,754	2,558	2,345	2,905	2,887	0.18	-0.62
East Mediterranean Europe	**3,622**	**3,741**	**6,013**	**7,548**	**9,929**	**0.61**	**31.54**
Turkey	3,622	3,741	6,013	7,548	9,929	0.61	31.54
Other Europe	**3,461**	**4,248**	**4,895**	**5,750**	**7,428**	**0.45**	**29.18**
Other countries of Europe	3,461	4,248	4,895	5,750	7,428	0.45	29.18
MIDDLE EAST	**24,143**	**22,671**	**23,035**	**29,132**	**37,005**	**2.26**	**27.03**
Middle East	**24,143**	**22,671**	**23,035**	**29,132**	**37,005**	**2.26**	**27.03**
Libyan Arab Jamahiriya	7,671	9,391	10,007	11,803	13,353	0.82	13.13
Other countries of Middle East	16,472	13,280	13,028	17,329	23,652	1.44	36.49
REGION NOT SPECIFIED	**736,915**	**861,373**	**865,157**	**1,001,884**	**1,159,224**	**70.79**	**15.70**
Not Specified	**736,915**	**861,373**	**865,157**	**1,001,884**	**1,159,224**	**70.79**	**15.70**
Nationals Residing Abroad	736,915	861,373	865,157	1,001,884	1,159,224	70.79	15.70

Source: World Tourism Organization (UNWTO)

AMERICAN SAMOA

1. Arrivals of non-resident tourists at national borders, by nationality

	2002	2003	2004	2005	2006	Market share 06	% Change 06-05
TOTAL				24,496	25,347	100.00	3.47
AFRICA				11	7	0.03	-36.36
Other Africa				11	7	0.03	-36.36
All countries of Africa				11	7	0.03	-36.36
AMERICAS				6,899	7,205	28.43	4.44
Central America				5	6	0.02	20.00
All countries of Central America				5	6	0.02	20.00
North America				6,836	7,161	28.25	4.75
Canada				66	121	0.48	83.33
Mexico				13	3	0.01	-76.92
United States				6,757	7,037	27.76	4.14
South America				58	38	0.15	-34.48
All countries of South America				58	38	0.15	-34.48
EAST ASIA AND THE PACIFIC				16,933	17,640	69.59	4.18
North-East Asia				631	604	2.38	-4.28
China				501	439	1.73	-12.38
Japan				54	108	0.43	100.00
Korea, Republic of				76	57	0.22	-25.00
South-East Asia				366	260	1.03	-28.96
Indonesia				17	12	0.05	-29.41
Malaysia				15	6	0.02	-60.00
Philippines				317	230	0.91	-27.44
Singapore				8	5	0.02	-37.50
Thailand				9	7	0.03	-22.22
Australasia				3,893	4,174	16.47	7.22
Australia				755	950	3.75	25.83
New Zealand				3,138	3,224	12.72	2.74
Melanesia				282	371	1.46	31.56
Solomon Islands				10	13	0.05	30.00
Fiji				264	345	1.36	30.68
Vanuatu				3	4	0.02	33.33
Papua New Guinea				5	9	0.04	80.00
Micronesia				26	14	0.06	-46.15
Kiribati				4	4	0.02	
Micronesia (Federated States of)				22	10	0.04	-54.55
Polynesia				11,662	11,763	46.41	0.87
Tonga				385	450	1.78	16.88
Samoa				11,277	11,313	44.63	0.32
Other East Asia and the Pacific				73	454	1.79	521.92
Other countries of Oceania				73	454	1.79	521.92
EUROPE				382	358	1.41	-6.28
Central/Eastern Europe				6	2	0.01	-66.67
Russian Federation					2	0.01	
All countries Central/East Europe				6			
Northern Europe				171	173	0.68	1.17
Denmark				6	2	0.01	-66.67
Finland				6			

AMERICAN SAMOA

1. Arrivals of non-resident tourists at national borders, by nationality

	2002	2003	2004	2005	2006	Market share 06	% Change 06-05
Norway				17	4	0.02	-76.47
Sweden				16	19	0.07	18.75
United Kingdom				126	148	0.58	17.46
Southern Europe				**60**	**56**	**0.22**	**-6.67**
Italy				19	24	0.09	26.32
Portugal				37	23	0.09	-37.84
Spain				4	9	0.04	125.00
Western Europe				**143**	**121**	**0.48**	**-15.38**
Austria				4			
Belgium				9	12	0.05	33.33
France				48	37	0.15	-22.92
Germany				64	60	0.24	-6.25
Netherlands				14	12	0.05	-14.29
Switzerland				4			
Other Europe				**2**	**6**	**0.02**	**200.00**
Other countries of Europe				2	6	0.02	200.00
MIDDLE EAST				**8**	**5**	**0.02**	**-37.50**
Middle East				**8**	**5**	**0.02**	**-37.50**
All countries of Middle East				8	5	0.02	-37.50
SOUTH ASIA				**37**	**49**	**0.19**	**32.43**
South Asia				**37**	**49**	**0.19**	**32.43**
Sri Lanka				13	6	0.02	-53.85
India				24	42	0.17	75.00
Pakistan					1		
REGION NOT SPECIFIED				**226**	**83**	**0.33**	**-63.27**
Not Specified				**226**	**83**	**0.33**	**-63.27**
Other countries of the World				226	83	0.33	-63.27

Source: World Tourism Organization (UNWTO)

ANDORRA

1. Arrivals of non-resident tourists at national borders, by country of residence

	2002	2003	2004	2005	2006	Market share 06	% Change 06-05
TOTAL	3,387,586	3,137,738	2,791,116	2,418,409	2,226,922	100.00	-7.92
EUROPE	3,387,586	3,137,738	2,791,116	2,418,409	2,226,922	100.00	-7.92
Southern Europe	2,333,793	2,266,051	2,011,304	1,762,882	1,625,893	73.01	-7.77
Spain	2,333,793	2,266,051	2,011,304	1,762,882	1,625,893	73.01	-7.77
Western Europe	846,626	719,163	637,953	529,521	485,183	21.79	-8.37
France	846,626	719,163	637,953	529,521	485,183	21.79	-8.37
Other Europe	207,167	152,524	141,859	126,006	115,846	5.20	-8.06
Other countries of Europe	207,167	152,524	141,859	126,006	115,846	5.20	-8.06

Source: World Tourism Organization (UNWTO)

ANGOLA

1. Arrivals of non-resident tourists at national borders, by country of residence

	2002	2003	2004	2005	2006	Market share 06	% Change 06-05
TOTAL	90,532	106,625	194,329	209,956	121,426	100.00	-42.17
AFRICA	16,618	30,915	41,873	43,138	18,921	15.58	-56.14
East Africa	1,488			6,050	2,358	1.94	-61.02
Burundi	29			9	31	0.03	244.44
Ethiopia	69			180	128	0.11	-28.89
Eritrea	8			73	98	0.08	34.25
Djibouti					2		
Kenya	120			101	139	0.11	37.62
Madagascar	6			26	17	0.01	-34.62
Malawi	51			41	45	0.04	9.76
Mauritius				19	74	0.06	289.47
Mozambique	552			2,227	830	0.68	-62.73
Rwanda	63			66	52	0.04	-21.21
Seychelles	3			2	3		50.00
Somalia	1			9	6		-33.33
Zimbabwe	295			1,837	355	0.29	-80.68
Uganda	35			207	43	0.04	-79.23
United Republic of Tanzania	92			158	101	0.08	-36.08
Zambia	164			1,095	434	0.36	-60.37
Central Africa	2,775			13,788	2,799	2.31	-79.70
Cameroon	127			1,030	266	0.22	-74.17
Central African Republic	31			716	16	0.01	-97.77
Chad	17			28	43	0.04	53.57
Congo	945			4,191	588	0.48	-85.97
Democratic Republic of the Congo	821			4,147	694	0.57	-83.27
Equatorial Guinea	5			810	146	0.12	-81.98
Gabon	140			990	157	0.13	-84.14
Sao Tome and Principe	689			1,876	889	0.73	-52.61
North Africa	135			2,474	345	0.28	-86.05
Algeria	45			779	127	0.10	-83.70
Morocco	42			906	87	0.07	-90.40
Sudan	6			45	15	0.01	-66.67
Tunisia	42			744	116	0.10	-84.41
Southern Africa	10,270			14,879	10,551	8.69	-29.09
Botswana	47			42	125	0.10	197.62
Lesotho	38			23	33	0.03	43.48
Namibia	482			1,429	700	0.58	-51.01
South Africa	9,674			13,294	9,648	7.95	-27.43
Swaziland	29			91	45	0.04	-50.55
West Africa	1,950			5,947	2,859	2.35	-51.93
Cape Verde	307			1,788	497	0.41	-72.20
Benin	53			98	45	0.04	-54.08
Gambia	85			85	85	0.07	
Ghana	159			262	216	0.18	-17.56
Guinea	242			604	265	0.22	-56.13
Cote D'Ivoire	131			246	139	0.11	-43.50
Liberia	6			7	17	0.01	142.86
Mali	84			182	130	0.11	-28.57
Mauritania	110			306	187	0.15	-38.89
Niger	11			8	9	0.01	12.50
Nigeria	311			1,799	902	0.74	-49.86
Guinea-Bissau	168			192	132	0.11	-31.25
Senegal	216			276	163	0.13	-40.94

ANGOLA

1. Arrivals of non-resident tourists at national borders, by country of residence

	2002	2003	2004	2005	2006	Market share 06	% Change 06-05
Sierra Leone	24			44	27	0.02	-38.64
Togo	15			14	25	0.02	78.57
Burkina Faso	28			36	20	0.02	-44.44
Other Africa		**30,915**	**41,873**		**9**	**0.01**	
Other countries of Africa					9	0.01	
All countries of Africa		30,915	41,873				
AMERICAS	**15,044**	**14,770**	**34,045**	**36,140**	**20,847**	**17.17**	**-42.32**
Caribbean	**914**			**3,813**	**735**	**0.61**	**-80.72**
Barbados	11			1	1		
Cuba	761			3,673	570	0.47	-84.48
Dominica					5		
Dominican Republic	27			6	8	0.01	33.33
Grenada					1		
Guadeloupe	4						
Haiti	9			21	2		-90.48
Jamaica	34			14	16	0.01	14.29
Martinique	6			6	3		-50.00
Puerto Rico	17			6	6		
Trinidad and Tobago	45			86	123	0.10	43.02
Central America	**189**			**42**	**100**	**0.08**	**138.10**
Belize	2						
Costa Rica	9			2	7	0.01	250.00
El Salvador	26			1	4		300.00
Guatemala	25			13	4		-69.23
Honduras	65			22	57	0.05	159.09
Nicaragua	46			2	11	0.01	450.00
Panama	16			2	17	0.01	750.00
North America	**6,274**			**17,001**	**8,298**	**6.83**	**-51.19**
Canada	759			1,566	1,250	1.03	-20.18
Mexico	106			1,539	81	0.07	-94.74
United States	5,409			13,896	6,967	5.74	-49.86
South America	**7,667**			**15,284**	**11,714**	**9.65**	**-23.36**
Argentina	231			868	258	0.21	-70.28
Bolivia	46			877	37	0.03	-95.78
Brazil	6,859			11,053	10,589	8.72	-4.20
Chile	149			803	103	0.08	-87.17
Colombia	95			921	277	0.23	-69.92
Ecuador	4			21	20	0.02	-4.76
French Guiana	3						
Guyana				12	38	0.03	216.67
Paraguay	74			23	18	0.01	-21.74
Peru	104			268	103	0.08	-61.57
Uruguay	78			57	64	0.05	12.28
Venezuela	24			381	207	0.17	-45.67
Other Americas		**14,770**	**34,045**				
All countries of the Americas		14,770	34,045				
EAST ASIA AND THE PACIFIC	**4,746**	**5,396**	**16,061**	**15,358**	**15,248**	**12.56**	**-0.72**
North-East Asia	**1,534**			**8,214**	**11,044**	**9.10**	**34.45**
China	712			5,849	9,352	7.70	59.89
Taiwan (Province of China)	40			4	15	0.01	275.00
Hong Kong, China	15						
Japan	372			1,661	380	0.31	-77.12

ANGOLA

1. Arrivals of non-resident tourists at national borders, by country of residence

	2002	2003	2004	2005	2006	Market share 06	% Change 06-05
Korea, Republic of	330			700	1,296	1.07	85.14
Macao, China	50						
Mongolia	15				1		
South-East Asia	**2,057**			**6,444**	**3,180**	**2.62**	**-50.65**
Myanmar				20			
Cambodia	10						
Indonesia	128			136	229	0.19	68.38
Malaysia	110			197	165	0.14	-16.24
Philippines	1,034			4,697	2,143	1.76	-54.38
Timor-Leste				12	7	0.01	-41.67
Singapore	73			38	67	0.06	76.32
Viet Nam	667			1,322	545	0.45	-58.77
Thailand	35			22	24	0.02	9.09
Australasia	**1,151**			**700**	**747**	**0.62**	**6.71**
Australia	976			541	579	0.48	7.02
New Zealand	175			159	168	0.14	5.66
Melanesia	**4**						
Fiji	4						
Other East Asia and the Pacific		**5,396**	**16,061**		**277**	**0.23**	
Other countries of Asia					277	0.23	
All countries of Asia		4,613	14,556				
All countries of Oceania		783	1,505				
EUROPE	**52,169**	**55,190**	**101,180**	**110,025**	**63,459**	**52.26**	**-42.32**
Central/Eastern Europe	**3,342**			**5,460**	**4,379**	**3.61**	**-19.80**
Azerbaijan	49			163	48	0.04	-70.55
Armenia	3			146	40	0.03	-72.60
Bulgaria	101			191	108	0.09	-43.46
Belarus	33			248	127	0.10	-48.79
Czech Republic	75			122	264	0.22	116.39
Estonia	28			55	18	0.01	-67.27
Georgia	25			73	30	0.02	-58.90
Hungary	11			25	26	0.02	4.00
Kazakhstan	5			85	41	0.03	-51.76
Kyrgyzstan				4	1		-75.00
Latvia	34				6		
Lithuania	287			109	119	0.10	9.17
Republic of Moldova	10			45			
Poland	198			527	592	0.49	12.33
Romania	178			324	553	0.46	70.68
Russian Federation	1,748			2,788	1,634	1.35	-41.39
Slovakia	110			52	51	0.04	-1.92
Turkmenistan	13			3	6		100.00
Ukraine	428			488	705	0.58	44.47
Uzbekistan	6			12	10	0.01	-16.67
Northern Europe	**8,674**			**22,829**	**13,926**	**11.47**	**-39.00**
Denmark	337			1,686	380	0.31	-77.46
Finland	81			1,436	104	0.09	-92.76
Iceland	28			81	14	0.01	-82.72
Ireland	159			2,257	322	0.27	-85.73
Norway	874			3,747	1,907	1.57	-49.11
Sweden	367			2,465	462	0.38	-81.26
United Kingdom	6,828			11,157	10,737	8.84	-3.76
Southern Europe	**22,341**			**42,884**	**29,935**	**24.65**	**-30.20**

ANGOLA

1. Arrivals of non-resident tourists at national borders, by country of residence

	2002	2003	2004	2005	2006	Market share 06	% Change 06-05
Albania	2			48	9	0.01	-81.25
Bosnia and Herzegovina	2				2		
Croatia	323			347	456	0.38	31.41
Greece	46			217	52	0.04	-76.04
Italy	2,431			5,250	1,747	1.44	-66.72
Malta	8			30	26	0.02	-13.33
Portugal	17,182			29,527	25,984	21.40	-12.00
Slovenia	66			16	51	0.04	218.75
Spain	2,005			7,368	1,605	1.32	-78.22
TFYR of Macedonia	2			2	3		50.00
Serbia and Montenegro	274			79			
Western Europe	**17,253**			**34,888**	**13,832**	**11.39**	**-60.35**
Austria	151			720	109	0.09	-84.86
Belgium	2,162			7,459	1,016	0.84	-86.38
France	12,125			17,658	10,103	8.32	-42.79
Germany	2,272			3,399	1,161	0.96	-65.84
Luxembourg				134			
Netherlands	345			4,530	1,142	0.94	-74.79
Switzerland	198			988	301	0.25	-69.53
East Mediterranean Europe	**559**			**3,964**	**1,293**	**1.06**	**-67.38**
Cyprus	11						
Israel	522			3,886	1,246	1.03	-67.94
Turkey	26			78	47	0.04	-39.74
Other Europe		55,190	101,180		94	0.08	
Other countries of Europe					94	0.08	
All countries of Europe		55,190	101,180				
MIDDLE EAST	**1,127**	**354**	**1,170**	**3,151**	**896**	**0.74**	**-71.56**
Middle East	**1,127**	**354**	**1,170**	**3,151**	**896**	**0.74**	**-71.56**
Palestine	73			436			
Iraq				11	16	0.01	45.45
Jordan	73			32	46	0.04	43.75
Lebanon	815			580	467	0.38	-19.48
Libyan Arab Jamahiriya	2			890	13	0.01	-98.54
Oman	8						
Qatar				10	23	0.02	130.00
Saudi Arabia	2			11	4		-63.64
Syrian Arab Republic	2			12	55	0.05	358.33
United Arab Emirates	43			20	15	0.01	-25.00
Egypt	103			1,072	244	0.20	-77.24
Yemen	6			12	6		-50.00
Other countries of Middle East				65	7	0.01	-89.23
All countries of Middle East		354	1,170				
SOUTH ASIA	**828**			**2,144**	**2,055**	**1.69**	**-4.15**
South Asia	**828**			**2,144**	**2,055**	**1.69**	**-4.15**
Afghanistan	9			1	2		100.00
Bangladesh	30			56	26	0.02	-53.57
Sri Lanka	34			35	17	0.01	-51.43
India	653			1,642	1,852	1.53	12.79
Iran, Islamic Republic of	2			54	8	0.01	-85.19
Nepal	23			15	12	0.01	-20.00
Pakistan	77			341	138	0.11	-59.53

Source: World Tourism Organization (UNWTO)

ANGUILLA

1. Arrivals of non-resident tourists at national borders, by country of residence

		2002	2003	2004	2005	2006	Market share 06	% Change 06-05
TOTAL	(*)	43,969	46,915	53,987	62,084	72,962	100.00	17.52
AMERICAS		37,479	39,295	44,799	52,054	61,746	84.63	18.62
Caribbean		7,423	7,362	7,499	8,529	15,280	20.94	79.15
Puerto Rico			837	591	590	848	1.16	43.73
Other countries of the Caribbean			6,525	6,908	7,939	14,432	19.78	81.79
All countries of the Caribbean		7,423						
North America		30,056	31,933	37,300	43,525	46,466	63.69	6.76
Canada		1,301	1,289	1,549	1,792	1,977	2.71	10.32
United States		28,755	30,644	35,751	41,733	44,489	60.98	6.60
EUROPE		5,415	6,308	7,667	8,113	9,218	12.63	13.62
Northern Europe		2,529	2,962	3,198	3,834	4,344	5.95	13.30
United Kingdom		2,529	2,962	3,198	3,834	4,344	5.95	13.30
Southern Europe		707	945	1,086	1,199	1,301	1.78	8.51
Italy		707	945	1,086	1,199	1,301	1.78	8.51
Western Europe		537	1,096	1,303	654	2,221	3.04	239.60
Austria			135	65	65	144	0.20	121.54
Belgium						68	0.09	
France						1,306	1.79	
Germany		537	649	1,019	410	461	0.63	12.44
Luxembourg						2		
Switzerland			312	219	179	240	0.33	34.08
Other Europe		1,642	1,305	2,080	2,426	1,352	1.85	-44.27
Other countries of Europe		1,642	1,305	2,080	2,426	1,352	1.85	-44.27
REGION NOT SPECIFIED		1,075	1,312	1,521	1,917	1,998	2.74	4.23
Not Specified		1,075	1,312	1,521	1,917	1,998	2.74	4.23
Other countries of the World		1,075	1,312	1,521	1,917	1,998	2.74	4.23

Source: World Tourism Organization (UNWTO)

ANGUILLA

2. Arrivals of non-resident visitors at national borders, by country of residence

	2002	2003	2004	2005	2006	Market share 06	% Change 06-05
TOTAL	111,118	109,282	120,788	143,186	167,245	100.00	16.80
AMERICAS	91,359	88,538	95,695	113,860	133,442	79.79	17.20
Caribbean	27,373	27,250	28,701	30,217	32,713	19.56	8.26
Puerto Rico		1,137	977	1,079	1,178	0.70	9.18
Other countries of the Caribbean		26,113	27,724	29,138	31,535	18.86	8.23
All countries of the Caribbean	27,373						
North America	63,986	61,288	66,994	83,643	100,729	60.23	20.43
Canada	4,425	4,296	4,782	6,856	7,485	4.48	9.17
United States	59,561	56,992	62,212	76,787	93,244	55.75	21.43
EUROPE	16,540	17,492	21,416	24,584	28,628	17.12	16.45
Northern Europe	4,847	5,081	5,581	7,084	7,952	4.75	12.25
United Kingdom	4,847	5,081	5,581	7,084	7,952	4.75	12.25
Southern Europe	1,903	2,115	2,204	2,585	2,562	1.53	-0.89
Italy	1,903	2,115	2,204	2,585	2,562	1.53	-0.89
Western Europe	1,376	2,097	2,614	1,828	12,019	7.19	557.49
Austria		212	148	159	236	0.14	48.43
Belgium					353	0.21	
France					9,260	5.54	
Germany	1,376	1,424	2,029	1,249	1,686	1.01	34.99
Luxembourg					12	0.01	
Switzerland		461	437	420	472	0.28	12.38
Other Europe	8,414	8,199	11,017	13,087	6,095	3.64	-53.43
Other countries of Europe	8,414	8,199	11,017	13,087	6,095	3.64	-53.43
REGION NOT SPECIFIED	3,219	3,252	3,677	4,742	5,175	3.09	9.13
Not Specified	3,219	3,252	3,677	4,742	5,175	3.09	9.13
Other countries of the World	3,219	3,252	3,677	4,742	5,175	3.09	9.13

Source: World Tourism Organization (UNWTO)

ANTIGUA AND BARBUDA

1. Arrivals of non-resident tourists at national borders, by country of residence

		2002	2003	2004	2005	2006	Market share 06	% Change 06-05
TOTAL	(*)	198,085	224,032	245,797	238,804	253,669	100.00	6.22
AMERICAS		108,235	121,563	129,316	126,096	138,547	54.62	9.87
Caribbean		37,371	43,584	45,540	45,760	49,951	19.69	9.16
Barbados			4,150	4,129	4,903	5,548	2.19	13.16
Jamaica			4,516	4,407	4,315	5,195	2.05	20.39
Netherlands Antilles			1,753	1,962	2,343	2,010	0.79	-14.21
Puerto Rico			1,305	1,291	1,472	1,455	0.57	-1.15
Trinidad and Tobago			6,040	6,042	7,037	8,417	3.32	19.61
United States Virgin Islands			2,859	3,304	3,168	2,578	1.02	-18.62
Other countries of the Caribbean			22,961	24,405	22,522	24,748	9.76	9.88
All countries of the Caribbean		37,371						
North America		70,864	72,966	79,983	76,215	83,550	32.94	9.62
Canada		10,184	8,603	9,452	9,571	10,053	3.96	5.04
United States		60,680	64,363	70,531	66,644	73,497	28.97	10.28
South America			5,013	3,793	4,121	5,046	1.99	22.45
Guyana			4,004	3,053	3,251	4,037	1.59	24.18
Other countries of South America			1,009	740	870	1,009	0.40	15.98
EUROPE		81,907	98,665	113,033	105,735	106,538	42.00	0.76
Northern Europe		72,401	83,447	97,829	90,568	89,563	35.31	-1.11
United Kingdom		72,401	83,447	97,829	90,568	89,563	35.31	-1.11
Southern Europe			5,520	6,116	5,525	5,994	2.36	8.49
Italy			5,520	6,116	5,525	5,994	2.36	8.49
Western Europe			4,254	4,474	4,681	5,330	2.10	13.86
France			1,354	1,177	1,203	1,382	0.54	14.88
Germany			2,100	2,344	2,586	3,025	1.19	16.98
Switzerland			800	953	892	923	0.36	3.48
Other Europe		9,506	5,444	4,614	4,961	5,651	2.23	13.91
Other countries of Europe		9,506	5,444	4,614	4,961	5,651	2.23	13.91
REGION NOT SPECIFIED		7,943	3,804	3,448	6,973	8,584	3.38	23.10
Not Specified		7,943	3,804	3,448	6,973	8,584	3.38	23.10
Other countries of the World		7,943	3,804	3,448	6,973	8,584	3.38	23.10

Source: World Tourism Organization (UNWTO)

ARGENTINA

1. Arrivals of non-resident tourists at national borders, by nationality

	2002	2003	2004	2005	2006	Market share 06	% Change 06-05
TOTAL (*)	2,820,039	2,995,271	3,456,526	3,822,666	4,155,921	100.00	8.72
AMERICAS	2,419,591	2,424,735	2,721,888	2,983,895	3,271,292	78.71	9.63
North America	152,620	224,472	302,255	369,753	400,354	9.63	8.28
All countries of North America	152,620	224,472	302,255	369,753	400,354	9.63	8.28
South America	2,094,468	1,970,633	2,128,965	2,259,545	2,475,248	59.56	9.55
Bolivia	119,121	59,678	145,244	151,510	155,169	3.73	2.42
Brazil	345,038	350,298	418,865	452,663	559,219	13.46	23.54
Chile	749,036	767,758	848,162	915,508	933,140	22.45	1.93
Paraguay	518,310	429,792	346,266	302,150	313,313	7.54	3.69
Uruguay	362,963	363,107	370,428	437,714	514,407	12.38	17.52
Other Americas	172,503	229,630	290,668	354,597	395,690	9.52	11.59
Other countries of the Americas	172,503	229,630	290,668	354,597	395,690	9.52	11.59
EUROPE	323,729	455,998	546,184	630,888	658,160	15.84	4.32
Other Europe	323,729	455,998	546,184	630,888	658,160	15.84	4.32
All countries of Europe	323,729	455,998	546,184	630,888	658,160	15.84	4.32
REGION NOT SPECIFIED	76,719	114,538	188,454	207,883	226,469	5.45	8.94
Not Specified	76,719	114,538	188,454	207,883	226,469	5.45	8.94
Other countries of the World	76,719	114,538	188,454	207,883	226,469	5.45	8.94

Source: World Tourism Organization (UNWTO)

ARMENIA

1. Arrivals of non-resident tourists at national borders, by country of residence

	2002	2003	2004	2005	2006	Market share 06	% Change 06-05
TOTAL	162,089	206,094	262,959	318,563	381,136	100.00	19.64
AFRICA	89	133	184	335	396	0.10	18.21
East Africa	25	34	44	48	52	0.01	8.33
Ethiopia	13	19	26	28	31	0.01	10.71
Zimbabwe	12	15	18	20	21	0.01	5.00
Central Africa	15	19	22	35	40	0.01	14.29
Cameroon	15	19	22	35	40	0.01	14.29
North Africa	34	52	70	230	282	0.07	22.61
Algeria	20	32	42	154	168	0.04	9.09
Morocco	14	20	28	76	114	0.03	50.00
Southern Africa	5	10	19		3		
All countries of Southern Africa	5	10	19		3		
West Africa	10	18	29	22	19		-13.64
Liberia	10	18	29	22	19		-13.64
AMERICAS	46,088	58,258	75,496	85,994	96,525	25.33	12.25
Caribbean			8	50	38	0.01	-24.00
Cuba			8	45	35	0.01	-22.22
Puerto Rico				5	3		-40.00
Central America		10	19	47	64	0.02	36.17
Guatemala			2	5	12		140.00
Honduras		5	7	11	13		18.18
Nicaragua		5	10	31	39	0.01	25.81
North America	34,681	43,144	54,173	60,518	66,340	17.41	9.62
Canada	9,375	11,895	13,588	15,795	19,840	5.21	25.61
Mexico	280	405	620	854	965	0.25	13.00
United States	25,026	30,844	39,965	43,869	45,535	11.95	3.80
South America	11,407	15,104	21,296	25,379	30,083	7.89	18.54
Argentina	6,674	9,855	14,935	17,560	21,500	5.64	22.44
Brazil	4,214	4,609	5,412	6,465	7,014	1.84	8.49
Chile	97	103	120	170	150	0.04	-11.76
Colombia	15	27	32	25	28	0.01	12.00
Peru	25	45	72	111	128	0.03	15.32
Uruguay	307	368	599	791	905	0.24	14.41
Venezuela	75	97	126	257	358	0.09	39.30
EAST ASIA AND THE PACIFIC	3,369	5,669	9,355	13,592	15,557	4.08	14.46
North-East Asia	2,298	4,467	6,964	9,800	11,640	3.05	18.78
China	305	345	968	1,685	3,020	0.79	79.23
Taiwan (Province of China)	98	103	135	105	120	0.03	14.29
Japan	1,790	3,850	5,585	7,681	8,125	2.13	5.78
Korea, Republic of	105	169	207	198	250	0.07	26.26
Mongolia			69	131	125	0.03	-4.58
South-East Asia	125	187	312	213	229	0.06	7.51
Malaysia	15	22	63		15		
Philippines	48	65	110	95	89	0.02	-6.32
Viet Nam	40	75	98	80	80	0.02	
Thailand	22	25	41	38	45	0.01	18.42
Australasia	946	1,015	2,079	3,579	3,688	0.97	3.05
Australia	934	1,007	2,064	3,562	3,678	0.97	3.26

ARMENIA

1. Arrivals of non-resident tourists at national borders, by country of residence

	2002	2003	2004	2005	2006	Market share 06	% Change 06-05
New Zealand	12	8	15	17	10		-41.18
EUROPE	**79,761**	**98,884**	**127,242**	**160,479**	**203,539**	**53.40**	**26.83**
Central/Eastern Europe	**54,146**	**61,576**	**76,999**	**94,837**	**128,120**	**33.62**	**35.09**
Bulgaria	305	739	980	1,260	2,569	0.67	103.89
Czech Republic	130	268	558	763	1,045	0.27	36.96
Estonia	125	274	290	185	206	0.05	11.35
Hungary	160	243	310	425	604	0.16	42.12
Latvia	150	249	289	384	450	0.12	17.19
Lithuania	30	37	80	111	119	0.03	7.21
Poland	277	648	965	1,098	1,135	0.30	3.37
Romania	244	287	378	438	631	0.17	44.06
Slovakia	30	87	153	205	397	0.10	93.66
Commonwealth Independent State	52,695	58,744	72,996	89,968	120,964	31.74	34.45
Northern Europe	**2,701**	**6,408**	**7,789**	**10,566**	**11,258**	**2.95**	**6.55**
Denmark	310	487	545	679	750	0.20	10.46
Finland	142	170	205	343	420	0.11	22.45
Iceland	14	75	102	86	65	0.02	-24.42
Ireland	57	107	145	122	130	0.03	6.56
Norway	362	508	610	825	790	0.21	-4.24
Sweden	91	168	194	387	544	0.14	40.57
United Kingdom	1,725	4,893	5,988	8,124	8,559	2.25	5.35
Southern Europe	**4,789**	**7,210**	**10,903**	**15,759**	**17,349**	**4.55**	**10.09**
Bosnia and Herzegovina	470	625	783	1,084	988	0.26	-8.86
Croatia	65	77	93	86	55	0.01	-36.05
Greece	1,810	2,795	4,002	6,588	7,356	1.93	11.66
Italy	1,750	2,840	4,189	5,244	5,920	1.55	12.89
Malta	8						
Portugal	290	340	668	866	891	0.23	2.89
Slovenia	85	128	145	209	351	0.09	67.94
Spain	191	235	795	1,377	1,400	0.37	1.67
Serbia and Montenegro	120	170	228	305	388	0.10	27.21
Western Europe	**16,423**	**21,398**	**28,854**	**36,092**	**43,220**	**11.34**	**19.75**
Austria	783	985	1,853	2,866	3,159	0.83	10.22
Belgium	896	1,118	1,756	3,025	3,261	0.86	7.80
France	7,925	9,754	12,368	14,294	18,699	4.91	30.82
Germany	5,170	7,771	10,688	12,966	14,666	3.85	13.11
Netherlands	854	875	1,102	1,753	2,080	0.55	18.65
Switzerland	795	895	1,087	1,188	1,355	0.36	14.06
East Mediterranean Europe	**1,702**	**2,292**	**2,697**	**3,225**	**3,592**	**0.94**	**11.38**
Cyprus	390	505	720	864	967	0.25	11.92
Israel	572	807	982	1,495	1,684	0.44	12.64
Turkey	740	980	995	866	941	0.25	8.66
MIDDLE EAST	**13,692**	**19,155**	**23,131**	**28,182**	**32,621**	**8.56**	**15.75**
Middle East	**13,692**	**19,155**	**23,131**	**28,182**	**32,621**	**8.56**	**15.75**
Iraq	25	50	62	85	112	0.03	31.76
Jordan	27						
Lebanon	7,480	9,875	11,556	13,411	15,490	4.06	15.50
Qatar	25	45	49	61	84	0.02	37.70
Saudi Arabia	29	35	41	55	20	0.01	-63.64
Syrian Arab Republic	5,790	8,790	10,985	13,941	16,119	4.23	15.62
United Arab Emirates	126	150	183	285	307	0.08	7.72
Egypt	190	210	255	344	489	0.13	42.15

ARMENIA

1. Arrivals of non-resident tourists at national borders, by country of residence

	2002	2003	2004	2005	2006	Market share 06	% Change 06-05
SOUTH ASIA	**19,090**	**23,995**	**27,551**	**29,981**	**32,498**	**8.53**	**8.40**
South Asia	**19,090**	**23,995**	**27,551**	**29,981**	**32,498**	**8.53**	**8.40**
Afghanistan	220	335	365	351	547	0.14	55.84
Bangladesh	48	55	67	50	64	0.02	28.00
Sri Lanka	36						
India	470	780	1,380	1,967	2,340	0.61	18.96
Iran, Islamic Republic of	18,256	22,750	25,650	27,458	29,347	7.70	6.88
Pakistan	60	75	89	155	200	0.05	29.03

Source: World Tourism Organization (UNWTO)

ARUBA

1. Arrivals of non-resident tourists at national borders, by country of residence

	2002	2003	2004	2005	2006	Market share 06	% Change 06-05
TOTAL	642,627	641,906	728,157	732,514	694,372	100.00	-5.21
AMERICAS	595,350	584,651	665,489	666,454	629,925	90.72	-5.48
Caribbean	27,275	29,973	29,187	25,583	26,759	3.85	4.60
Dominican Republic	986	921	1,338	1,269	1,448	0.21	14.11
Curacao	16,381	17,061	16,649	15,047	15,645	2.25	3.97
Puerto Rico	3,754	4,225	3,846	3,096	2,846	0.41	-8.07
Trinidad and Tobago	1,554	2,168	1,487	1,201	1,668	0.24	38.88
Other countries of the Caribbean	4,600	5,598	5,867	4,970	5,152	0.74	3.66
North America	451,566	478,368	552,787	554,732	516,913	74.44	-6.82
Canada	17,601	17,218	20,560	21,350	22,590	3.25	5.81
Mexico	1,059	909	940	1,030	1,038	0.15	0.78
United States	432,906	460,241	531,287	532,352	493,285	71.04	-7.34
South America	116,509	76,310	83,515	86,139	86,253	12.42	0.13
Argentina	1,727	1,761	2,071	2,569	3,526	0.51	37.25
Brazil	2,314	2,785	4,762	6,067	6,667	0.96	9.89
Chile	592	325	416	428	517	0.07	20.79
Colombia	23,362	11,397	10,648	9,863	11,598	1.67	17.59
Ecuador	520	611	723	679	1,190	0.17	75.26
Peru	3,685	1,055	1,087	946	925	0.13	-2.22
Suriname	1,111	1,515	2,084	2,336	1,626	0.23	-30.39
Venezuela	81,665	54,554	59,218	59,928	57,105	8.22	-4.71
Other countries of South America	1,533	2,307	2,506	3,323	3,099	0.45	-6.74
EAST ASIA AND THE PACIFIC	209	162	211	191	199	0.03	4.19
North-East Asia	209	162	211	191	199	0.03	4.19
Japan	209	162	211	191	199	0.03	4.19
EUROPE	43,970	54,711	60,428	63,181	61,993	8.93	-1.88
Central/Eastern Europe	141	105	159	161	213	0.03	32.30
Russian Federation	141	105	159	161	213	0.03	32.30
Northern Europe	5,885	8,294	10,385	12,309	12,652	1.82	2.79
Denmark	174	201	204	586	587	0.08	0.17
Finland	125	286	257	664	1,164	0.17	75.30
Norway	295	337	434	575	523	0.08	-9.04
Sweden	489	748	1,680	3,472	2,872	0.41	-17.28
United Kingdom	4,802	6,722	7,810	7,012	7,506	1.08	7.05
Southern Europe	2,525	2,062	2,201	2,603	2,973	0.43	14.21
Italy	1,244	1,223	1,319	1,664	1,644	0.24	-1.20
Portugal	501	156	158	119	252	0.04	111.76
Spain	780	683	724	820	1,077	0.16	31.34
Western Europe	33,178	42,074	44,794	45,652	43,681	6.29	-4.32
Austria	374	452	609	600	655	0.09	9.17
Belgium	1,148	1,536	1,820	1,858	1,617	0.23	-12.97
Germany	2,765	2,905	3,090	3,333	3,271	0.47	-1.86
Netherlands	27,992	36,415	38,122	38,667	37,130	5.35	-3.97
Switzerland	899	766	1,153	1,194	1,008	0.15	-15.58
Other Europe	2,241	2,176	2,889	2,456	2,474	0.36	0.73
Other countries of Europe	2,241	2,176	2,889	2,456	2,474	0.36	0.73
REGION NOT SPECIFIED	3,098	2,382	2,029	2,688	2,255	0.32	-16.11
Not Specified	3,098	2,382	2,029	2,688	2,255	0.32	-16.11
Other countries of the World	3,098	2,382	2,029	2,688	2,255	0.32	-16.11

ARUBA

3. Arrivals of non-resident tourists in hotels and similar establishments, by country of residence

	2002	2003	2004	2005	2006	Market share 06	% Change 06-05
TOTAL	567,475	567,615	647,163	653,379	619,062	100.00	-5.25
AMERICAS	539,548	529,679	602,472	606,781	574,170	92.75	-5.37
Caribbean	13,194	13,672	12,582	10,726	11,763	1.90	9.67
Dominican Republic	373	365	403	311	723	0.12	132.48
Netherlands Antilles	10,059	11,140	10,674	9,158	9,732	1.57	6.27
Trinidad and Tobago	822	1,121	873	664	828	0.13	24.70
Other countries of the Caribbean	1,940	1,046	632	593	480	0.08	-19.06
North America	432,465	458,392	526,146	529,486	493,471	79.71	-6.80
Canada	15,597	16,072	19,301	20,010	21,186	3.42	5.88
United States	416,868	442,320	506,845	509,476	472,285	76.29	-7.30
South America	92,020	55,347	61,623	66,569	68,936	11.14	3.56
Argentina	1,550	1,615	1,896	2,416	3,310	0.53	37.00
Brazil	2,085	2,591	4,442	5,656	5,953	0.96	5.25
Chile	555	296	397	388	459	0.07	18.30
Colombia	15,547	7,594	7,476	7,155	9,503	1.54	32.82
Ecuador	362	355	430	356	855	0.14	140.17
Peru	3,061	652	749	660	756	0.12	14.55
Suriname	317	607	776	904	539	0.09	-40.38
Venezuela	68,543	41,637	45,457	46,345	45,170	7.30	-2.54
Other countries of South America				2,689	2,391	0.39	-11.08
Other Americas	1,869	2,268	2,121				
Other countries of the Americas	1,869	2,268	2,121				
EAST ASIA AND THE PACIFIC	186	151	180	175	172	0.03	-1.71
North-East Asia	186	151	180	175	172	0.03	-1.71
Japan	186	151	180	175	172	0.03	-1.71
EUROPE	27,160	35,964	39,935	42,309	41,034	6.63	-3.01
Central/Eastern Europe				75	148	0.02	97.33
Russian Federation				75	148	0.02	97.33
Northern Europe	5,021	7,425	10,047	11,086	11,458	1.85	3.36
Denmark				492	517	0.08	5.08
Finland				601	1,068	0.17	77.70
Norway				442	383	0.06	-13.35
Sweden				3,202	2,618	0.42	-18.24
United Kingdom	4,181	6,131	7,186	6,349	6,872	1.11	8.24
Scandinavia	840	1,294	2,861				
Southern Europe	859	973	1,046	1,958	2,250	0.36	14.91
Italy	859	973	1,046	1,218	1,292	0.21	6.08
Portugal				101	175	0.03	73.27
Spain				639	783	0.13	22.54
Western Europe	17,569	23,775	24,392	27,375	25,241	4.08	-7.80
Austria				542	581	0.09	7.20
Belgium				1,387	1,182	0.19	-14.78
Germany	2,244	2,312	2,532	2,691	2,758	0.45	2.49
Netherlands	14,573	20,796	20,912	21,768	19,888	3.21	-8.64
Switzerland	752	667	948	987	832	0.13	-15.70
Other Europe	3,711	3,791	4,450	1,815	1,937	0.31	6.72
Other countries of Europe	3,711	3,791	4,450	1,815	1,937	0.31	6.72
REGION NOT SPECIFIED	581	1,821	4,576	4,114	3,686	0.60	-10.40

ARUBA

3. Arrivals of non-resident tourists in hotels and similar establishments, by country of residence

	2002	2003	2004	2005	2006	Market share 06	% Change 06-05
Not Specified	581	1,821	4,576	4,114	3,686	0.60	-10.40
Other countries of the World	581	1,821	4,576	4,114	3,686	0.60	-10.40

Source: World Tourism Organization (UNWTO)

ARUBA

5. Overnight stays of non-resident tourists in hotels and similar establishments, by country of residence

	2002	2003	2004	2005	2006	Market share 06	% Change 06-05
TOTAL	3,945,472	4,059,145	4,615,338	4,735,380	4,515,022	100.00	-4.65
AMERICAS	3,691,355	3,708,580	4,207,992	4,294,975	4,087,155	90.52	-4.84
Caribbean	49,342	59,341	47,936	39,277	53,487	1.18	36.18
Dominican Republic	1,833	2,193	2,111	1,475	12,866	0.28	772.27
Netherlands Antilles	33,736	40,803	37,474	30,923	33,730	0.75	9.08
Trinidad and Tobago	3,970	8,899	4,615	4,052	4,676	0.10	15.40
Other countries of the Caribbean	9,803	7,446	3,736	2,827	2,215	0.05	-21.65
North America	3,105,644	3,275,703	3,759,234	3,845,121	3,598,783	79.71	-6.41
Canada	131,476	136,324	162,208	174,295	180,815	4.00	3.74
United States	2,974,168	3,139,379	3,597,026	3,670,826	3,417,968	75.70	-6.89
South America	526,583	361,315	388,925	410,577	434,885	9.63	5.92
Argentina	14,195	14,905	16,733	20,669	29,778	0.66	44.07
Brazil	13,625	16,666	29,411	37,514	37,575	0.83	0.16
Chile	4,425	2,096	2,755	2,736	3,458	0.08	26.39
Colombia	91,877	52,238	51,886	49,610	60,561	1.34	22.07
Ecuador	2,075	1,999	2,184	2,206	4,089	0.09	85.36
Peru	17,074	4,842	5,918	5,176	5,293	0.12	2.26
Suriname	1,687	3,347	3,994	4,240	3,690	0.08	-12.97
Venezuela	381,625	265,222	276,044	273,149	275,260	6.10	0.77
Other countries of South America				15,277	15,181	0.34	-0.63
Other Americas	9,786	12,221	11,897				
Other countries of the Americas	9,786	12,221	11,897				
EAST ASIA AND THE PACIFIC	819	648	698	719	738	0.02	2.64
North-East Asia	819	648	698	719	738	0.02	2.64
Japan	819	648	698	719	738	0.02	2.64
EUROPE	252,087	341,335	385,907	417,565	414,144	9.17	-0.82
Central/Eastern Europe				664	1,321	0.03	98.95
Russian Federation				664	1,321	0.03	98.95
Northern Europe	44,542	78,649	110,905	119,010	125,908	2.79	5.80
Denmark				4,691	4,813	0.11	2.60
Finland				5,507	9,706	0.21	76.25
Norway				4,132	3,773	0.08	-8.69
Sweden				30,711	26,359	0.58	-14.17
United Kingdom	37,722	66,917	83,475	73,969	81,257	1.80	9.85
Scandinavia	6,820	11,732	27,430				
Southern Europe	7,678	8,463	9,301	15,032	18,502	0.41	23.08
Italy	7,678	8,463	9,301	10,019	12,087	0.27	20.64
Portugal				743	1,378	0.03	85.46
Spain				4,270	5,037	0.11	17.96
Western Europe	171,613	220,389	227,860	266,997	251,031	5.56	-5.98
Austria				5,784	6,546	0.14	13.17
Belgium				12,736	11,382	0.25	-10.63
Germany	22,189	26,416	28,913	29,381	31,407	0.70	6.90
Netherlands	141,838	186,499	188,713	209,196	193,545	4.29	-7.48
Switzerland	7,586	7,474	10,234	9,900	8,151	0.18	-17.67
Other Europe	28,254	33,834	37,841	15,862	17,382	0.38	9.58
Other countries of Europe	28,254	33,834	37,841	15,862	17,382	0.38	9.58
REGION NOT SPECIFIED	1,211	8,582	20,741	22,121	12,985	0.29	-41.30

ARUBA

5. Overnight stays of non-resident tourists in hotels and similar establishments, by country of residence

	2002	2003	2004	2005	2006	Market share 06	% Change 06-05
Not Specified	1,211	8,582	20,741	22,121	12,985	0.29	-41.30
Other countries of the World	1,211	8,582	20,741	22,121	12,985	0.29	-41.30

Source: World Tourism Organization (UNWTO)

ARUBA

6. Overnight stays of non-resident tourists in all types of accommodation establishments, by country of residence

	2002	2003	2004	2005	2006	Market share 06	% Change 06-05
TOTAL	4,862,548	5,097,571	5,639,869	5,694,501	5,470,542	100.00	-3.93
AMERICAS	4,302,530	4,425,765	4,919,123	4,929,531	4,697,153	85.86	-4.71
Caribbean	165,564	217,198	193,250	170,494	188,118	3.44	10.34
Dominican Republic	14,187	17,986	23,999	20,086	26,273	0.48	30.80
Curacao	77,659	85,447	79,239	75,024	81,446	1.49	8.56
Puerto Rico	17,576	16,875	16,500	14,421	13,224	0.24	-8.30
Trinidad and Tobago	20,475	48,967	21,871	14,265	22,477	0.41	57.57
Other countries of the Caribbean	35,667	47,923	51,641	46,698	44,698	0.82	-4.28
North America	3,306,265	3,515,097	4,019,131	4,069,226	3,824,294	69.91	-6.02
Canada	146,460	152,049	178,657	191,042	200,234	3.66	4.81
Mexico	6,978	5,891	6,249	6,701	6,646	0.12	-0.82
United States	3,152,827	3,357,157	3,834,225	3,871,483	3,617,414	66.13	-6.56
South America	830,701	693,470	706,742	689,811	684,741	12.52	-0.73
Argentina	16,475	17,121	19,299	22,650	32,581	0.60	43.85
Brazil	15,820	18,514	32,204	41,344	42,329	0.77	2.38
Chile	4,886	2,485	3,040	3,201	4,037	0.07	26.12
Colombia	226,333	151,574	155,586	137,137	123,145	2.25	-10.20
Ecuador	3,934	5,296	6,356	6,880	8,506	0.16	23.63
Peru	23,321	14,096	13,899	10,747	8,435	0.15	-21.51
Suriname	12,458	16,146	20,974	20,462	18,527	0.34	-9.46
Venezuela	514,325	444,578	425,211	411,539	408,526	7.47	-0.73
Other countries of South America	13,149	23,660	30,173	35,851	38,655	0.71	7.82
EAST ASIA AND THE PACIFIC	919	698	812	836	837	0.02	0.12
North-East Asia	919	698	812	836	837	0.02	0.12
Japan	919	698	812	836	837	0.02	0.12
EUROPE	518,541	635,356	700,888	738,209	752,584	13.76	1.95
Central/Eastern Europe	1,641	984	1,029	1,443	1,834	0.03	27.10
Russian Federation	1,641	984	1,029	1,443	1,834	0.03	27.10
Northern Europe	55,362	89,260	116,237	134,422	142,333	2.60	5.89
Denmark			1,753	5,832	5,711	0.10	-2.07
Finland			2,218	6,284	11,122	0.20	76.99
Norway			4,581	6,307	6,373	0.12	1.05
Sweden			16,381	33,924	29,596	0.54	-12.76
United Kingdom	46,211	73,921	91,304	82,075	89,531	1.64	9.08
Scandinavia	9,151	15,339					
Southern Europe	21,172	19,194	20,406	23,362	27,400	0.50	17.28
Italy	11,456	11,914	12,588	15,418	17,161	0.31	11.30
Portugal	3,790	1,247	1,363	936	2,493	0.05	166.35
Spain	5,926	6,033	6,455	7,008	7,746	0.14	10.53
Western Europe	422,918	505,388	538,416	557,498	558,306	10.21	0.14
Austria	3,278	4,853	6,419	6,571	7,496	0.14	14.08
Belgium	14,089	17,979	19,186	20,084	19,042	0.35	-5.19
Germany	29,980	33,894	37,305	37,135	39,222	0.72	5.62
Netherlands	366,146	439,916	463,299	481,015	481,391	8.80	0.08
Switzerland	9,425	8,746	12,207	12,693	11,155	0.20	-12.12
Other Europe	17,448	20,530	24,800	21,484	22,711	0.42	5.71
Other countries of Europe	17,448	20,530	24,800	21,484	22,711	0.42	5.71
REGION NOT SPECIFIED	40,558	35,752	19,046	25,925	19,968	0.37	-22.98

ARUBA

6. Overnight stays of non-resident tourists in all types of accommodation establishments, by country of residence

	2002	2003	2004	2005	2006	Market share 06	% Change 06-05
Not Specified	40,558	35,752	19,046	25,925	19,968	0.37	-22.98
Other countries of the World	40,558	35,752	19,046	25,925	19,968	0.37	-22.98

Source: World Tourism Organization (UNWTO)

AUSTRALIA

2. Arrivals of non-resident visitors at national borders, by country of residence

	2002	2003	2004	2005	2006	Market share 06	% Change 06-05
TOTAL (*)	4,841,152	4,745,855	5,214,981	5,499,050	5,532,435	100.00	0.61
AFRICA	68,244	69,535	67,711	70,877	77,615	1.40	9.51
East Africa	13,569	13,170	13,939	14,266	16,203	0.29	13.58
Burundi	3	22	17	4	5		25.00
Ethiopia	90	121	124	81	93		14.81
Eritrea	55	21	102	32	36		12.50
Djibouti				12	11		-8.33
Kenya	1,772	1,687	1,765	2,050	2,360	0.04	15.12
Madagascar	81	53	46	65	156		140.00
Malawi	231	309	233	161	134		-16.77
Mauritius	3,653	3,811	3,927	4,156	4,861	0.09	16.96
Mozambique	267	170	430	203	279	0.01	37.44
Reunion	1,446	1,536	2,136	2,381	2,769	0.05	16.30
Rwanda	51	9	58	29	17		-41.38
Seychelles	227	263	370	424	448	0.01	5.66
Somalia	75	82	64	45	183		306.67
Zimbabwe	3,857	3,658	3,280	2,848	2,702	0.05	-5.13
Uganda	489	259	325	390	444	0.01	13.85
United Republic of Tanzania	484	577	561	651	932	0.02	43.16
Zambia	788	592	501	734	773	0.01	5.31
Central Africa	217	250	97	161	259		60.87
Angola	132	125	28	68	130		91.18
Cameroon	32	30	30	29	71		144.83
Congo	48	88	27	61	52		-14.75
Gabon	5	7	12	3	6		100.00
North Africa	671	366	494	572	473	0.01	-17.31
Algeria	172	139	132	162	166		2.47
Morocco	206	78	117	178	114		-35.96
Sudan	93	119	133	162	138		-14.81
Tunisia	200	30	112	70	55		-21.43
Southern Africa	52,266	54,247	51,755	53,748	58,296	1.05	8.46
Botswana	589	912	833	786	648	0.01	-17.56
Lesotho	84	32	24	22	98		345.45
Namibia	408	482	389	339	447	0.01	31.86
South Africa	50,971	52,736	50,433	52,505	56,935	1.03	8.44
Swaziland	214	85	76	96	168		75.00
West Africa	1,449	1,469	1,321	1,890	2,288	0.04	21.06
Cape Verde	6	3	3	3	3		
Benin	15	30	3	5	6		20.00
Gambia	29	3	4	11	51		363.64
Ghana	521	320	329	572	409	0.01	-28.50
Guinea			95	19	37		94.74
Cote D'Ivoire	26	16	40	12	6		-50.00
Liberia	6	7	22	17	43		152.94
Mali	7	187	83	12	10		-16.67
Mauritania	264	10	43	200	206		3.00
Niger	32	27		18	40		122.22
Nigeria	500	767	575	859	1,349	0.02	57.04
Senegal	18	61	68	94	76		-19.15
Sierra Leone	16	17	46	55	39		-29.09
Togo	3	6	3	10	8		-20.00
Burkina Faso	6	15	7	3	5		66.67
Other Africa	72	33	105	240	96		-60.00

AUSTRALIA

2. Arrivals of non-resident visitors at national borders, by country of residence

	2002	2003	2004	2005	2006	Market share 06	% Change 06-05
Other countries of Africa	72	33	105	240	96		-60.00
AMERICAS	**556,186**	**537,494**	**561,454**	**584,395**	**611,140**	**11.05**	**4.58**
Caribbean	**2,424**	**2,068**	**2,171**	**2,318**	**3,250**	**0.06**	**40.21**
Antigua and Barbuda	69	11	6	82	81		-1.22
Bahamas	412	164	173	165	264		60.00
Barbados	178	95	173	245	243		-0.82
Bermuda	313	496	616	260	708	0.01	172.31
British Virgin Islands	25	83		142	37		-73.94
Cayman Islands	178	121	132	140	173		23.57
Cuba	99	64	125	142	136		-4.23
Dominica	53	34	23	23	55		139.13
Dominican Republic	14	11	20	44	16		-63.64
Grenada	230	96	28	68	75		10.29
Haiti	4		3	10	3		-70.00
Jamaica	192	335	303	222	361	0.01	62.61
Martinique	26	25	75	33	11		-66.67
Netherlands Antilles		15	30		19		
Puerto Rico	323	206	133	418	296	0.01	-29.19
Saint Kitts and Nevis	11			6	13		116.67
Saint Lucia	32	13	11	40	94		135.00
Saint Vincent and the Grenadines	3	10	3	8	37		362.50
Trinidad and Tobago	119	206	195	240	501	0.01	108.75
All countries of the Caribbean	143	83	122	30	127		323.33
Central America	**789**	**663**	**756**	**769**	**756**	**0.01**	**-1.69**
Belize	69	74	60	31	39		25.81
Costa Rica	168	201	218	220	220		
El Salvador	212	148	148	184	164		-10.87
Guatemala	153	83	139	153	100		-34.64
Honduras	49	27	72	31	60		93.55
Nicaragua	18	14	22	17	29		70.59
Panama	104	113	97	133	138		3.76
Other countries of Central America	16	3			6		
North America	**530,788**	**515,469**	**536,631**	**554,230**	**572,099**	**10.34**	**3.22**
Canada	90,874	87,929	98,189	102,504	109,871	1.99	7.19
Mexico	5,404	5,291	5,069	5,331	6,022	0.11	12.96
United States	434,470	422,136	433,329	446,308	456,142	8.24	2.20
Other countries of North America	40	113	44	87	64		-26.44
South America	**22,185**	**19,294**	**21,896**	**27,078**	**35,035**	**0.63**	**29.39**
Argentina	4,358	3,726	3,660	4,254	5,274	0.10	23.98
Bolivia	141	71	76	174	124		-28.74
Brazil	10,247	8,301	10,417	12,862	16,719	0.30	29.99
Chile	3,007	3,456	3,988	4,955	6,648	0.12	34.17
Colombia	1,614	1,420	1,394	1,968	2,756	0.05	40.04
Ecuador	242	135	243	280	357	0.01	27.50
Guyana	10	61	27	31	58		87.10
Paraguay	165	96	145	114	115		0.88
Peru	772	812	917	1,136	1,413	0.03	24.38
Suriname	8	21	27	12	31		158.33
Uruguay	772	609	426	568	700	0.01	23.24
Venezuela	773	443	485	634	813	0.01	28.23
Other countries of South America	76	143	91	90	27		-70.00
EAST ASIA AND THE PACIFIC	**2,924,158**	**2,811,834**	**3,205,477**	**3,374,765**	**3,314,747**	**59.91**	**-1.78**
North-East Asia	**1,345,495**	**1,230,047**	**1,411,761**	**1,493,952**	**1,471,721**	**26.60**	**-1.49**

AUSTRALIA

2. Arrivals of non-resident visitors at national borders, by country of residence

	2002	2003	2004	2005	2006	Market share 06	% Change 06-05
China	190,016	176,128	251,300	285,031	308,484	5.58	8.23
Taiwan (Province of China)	97,429	87,741	98,760	110,892	93,837	1.70	-15.38
Hong Kong, China	150,943	129,292	137,199	159,520	154,803	2.80	-2.96
Japan	715,458	627,737	710,351	685,330	651,046	11.77	-5.00
Korea, Dem. People's Republic of	15	36	30	35	18		-48.57
Korea, Republic of	189,729	207,281	211,872	250,518	260,778	4.71	4.10
Macao, China	1,698	1,641	1,851	2,207	2,326	0.04	5.39
Mongolia	207	191	398	419	429	0.01	2.39
South-East Asia	**673,772**	**625,298**	**638,692**	**654,079**	**632,145**	**11.43**	**-3.35**
Brunei Darussalam	7,182	7,757	6,905	7,179	6,411	0.12	-10.70
Myanmar	505	724	1,065	937	1,238	0.02	32.12
Cambodia	1,168	1,310	1,908	2,512	3,012	0.05	19.90
Indonesia	89,432	90,277	84,354	83,495	83,557	1.51	0.07
Lao People's Democratic Republic	815	779	998	992	1,128	0.02	13.71
Malaysia	158,990	155,613	166,841	165,972	150,277	2.72	-9.46
Philippines	28,453	27,020	31,235	33,656	37,471	0.68	11.34
Timor-Leste	8,436	5,847	2,743	1,874	2,621	0.05	39.86
Singapore	286,852	253,364	251,162	266,053	253,417	4.58	-4.75
Viet Nam	9,247	9,428	11,672	14,487	19,061	0.34	31.57
Thailand	82,671	73,179	79,809	76,922	73,952	1.34	-3.86
Other countries of South-East Asia	21						
Australasia	**790,068**	**839,092**	**1,032,749**	**1,098,850**	**1,075,809**	**19.45**	**-2.10**
New Zealand	790,068	839,092	1,032,749	1,098,850	1,075,809	19.45	-2.10
Melanesia	**96,496**	**98,677**	**103,307**	**108,086**	**114,364**	**2.07**	**5.81**
Solomon Islands	4,297	4,629	5,597	5,124	5,900	0.11	15.14
Fiji	23,168	25,485	25,800	28,373	29,608	0.54	4.35
New Caledonia	30,514	33,603	36,118	37,745	39,164	0.71	3.76
Vanuatu	5,275	5,243	6,975	7,194	6,999	0.13	-2.71
Norfolk Island	1,995	2,420	3,065	1,813	2,155	0.04	18.86
Papua New Guinea	31,247	27,297	25,752	27,837	30,538	0.55	9.70
Micronesia	**7,063**	**6,780**	**6,503**	**6,251**	**5,860**	**0.11**	**-6.25**
Kiribati	2,259	1,929	2,141	2,154	1,813	0.03	-15.83
Guam	1,338	2,072	1,815	1,938	1,981	0.04	2.22
Nauru	2,857	1,870	1,546	1,314	1,326	0.02	0.91
Northern Mariana Islands	80	138	30	32	16		-50.00
Micronesia (Federated States of)	233	353	471	210	291	0.01	38.57
Marshall Islands	60	162	199	372	291	0.01	-21.77
Palau	236	256	301	231	142		-38.53
Polynesia	**10,688**	**11,711**	**12,273**	**13,537**	**14,848**	**0.27**	**9.68**
American Samoa	15	27	44	6	82		1,266.67
Cook Islands	1,419	1,742	1,459	1,544	1,211	0.02	-21.57
French Polynesia	3,514	3,336	3,842	5,034	5,482	0.10	8.90
Niue	5	216	219	246	174		-29.27
Tokelau			3		88		
Tonga	2,794	2,998	2,660	2,544	3,146	0.06	23.66
Tuvalu	166	166	251	250	240		-4.00
Wallis and Futuna Islands	303	303	190	256	254		-0.78
Samoa	2,472	2,923	3,605	3,657	4,171	0.08	14.06
Other East Asia and the Pacific	**576**	**229**	**192**	**10**			
Other countries of Oceania	576	229	192	10			
EUROPE	**1,198,361**	**1,228,033**	**1,261,477**	**1,330,233**	**1,367,738**	**24.72**	**2.82**
Central/Eastern Europe	**28,504**	**24,973**	**28,544**	**31,049**	**33,286**	**0.60**	**7.20**
Azerbaijan	16	185	114	254	122		-51.97

AUSTRALIA

2. Arrivals of non-resident visitors at national borders, by country of residence

	2002	2003	2004	2005	2006	Market share 06	% Change 06-05
Armenia	74	49	45	109	95		-12.84
Bulgaria	351	536	472	552	716	0.01	29.71
Belarus	93	101	131	222	222		
Czech Republic/Slovakia	2,754	1,999	1,932	3,217	3,496	0.06	8.67
Czech Republic	2,178	3,124	3,349	2,362	1,782	0.03	-24.56
Estonia	555	382	561	651	993	0.02	52.53
Georgia	64	84	82	42	139		230.95
Hungary	3,166	3,243	3,556	3,443	3,567	0.06	3.60
Kazakhstan	121	263	165	411	495	0.01	20.44
Kyrgyzstan	31	13	57	96	30		-68.75
Latvia	761	476	614	681	928	0.02	36.27
Lithuania	441	178	358	465	539	0.01	15.91
Republic of Moldova	33	42	66	47	69		46.81
Poland	8,775	5,501	6,268	6,528	6,790	0.12	4.01
Romania	887	782	1,055	891	764	0.01	-14.25
Russian Federation	4,373	5,062	6,158	7,170	8,917	0.16	24.37
Slovakia	1,501	1,716	1,828	1,812	1,495	0.03	-17.49
Tajikistan	22	9	22	26	40		53.85
Turkmenistan		3	9	17	5		-70.59
Ukraine	831	836	1,262	1,572	1,795	0.03	14.19
Ussr (Former)	1,353	299	132	206	126		-38.83
Uzbekistan	124	90	308	275	161		-41.45
Northern Europe	**764,229**	**801,871**	**810,472**	**853,792**	**878,448**	**15.88**	**2.89**
Denmark	18,870	19,005	20,515	22,615	22,997	0.42	1.69
Faeroe Islands	20	52		139	61		-56.12
Finland	6,529	7,688	9,375	9,961	10,194	0.18	2.34
Iceland	294	377	478	683	676	0.01	-1.02
Ireland	48,048	52,961	53,670	59,831	59,091	1.07	-1.24
Norway	16,876	17,172	16,789	16,458	15,574	0.28	-5.37
Sweden	30,905	31,802	33,371	35,280	35,600	0.64	0.91
United Kingdom	640,782	671,164	674,664	707,517	732,585	13.24	3.54
Channel Islands	1,151	1,077	769	681	747	0.01	9.69
Isle of Man	734	573	801	577	893	0.02	54.77
Other countries of Northern Europe	20		40	50	30		-40.00
Southern Europe	**75,551**	**72,455**	**83,644**	**89,385**	**90,796**	**1.64**	**1.58**
Albania	268	112	100	124	177		42.74
Andorra	48	225	73	115	61		-46.96
Bosnia and Herzegovina	284	506	655	457	650	0.01	42.23
Croatia	1,634	2,192	2,089	2,211	1,832	0.03	-17.14
Gibraltar		82	84	91	82		-9.89
Greece	7,027	5,709	6,512	6,666	6,683	0.12	0.26
Italy	43,300	41,317	47,148	50,902	51,715	0.93	1.60
Malta	2,220	1,942	2,986	2,574	2,803	0.05	8.90
Portugal	4,324	3,677	3,072	4,048	3,399	0.06	-16.03
San Marino	38	43	44	27	32		18.52
Slovenia	2,196	1,891	2,080	2,429	2,075	0.04	-14.57
Spain	12,451	12,455	15,802	16,888	18,204	0.33	7.79
TFYR of Macedonia	637	981	1,191	1,137	1,216	0.02	6.95
Serbia and Montenegro	1,124	1,323	1,808	1,716	1,867	0.03	8.80
Western Europe	**310,334**	**311,146**	**319,092**	**333,674**	**342,998**	**6.20**	**2.79**
Austria	19,008	18,832	18,441	18,931	19,240	0.35	1.63
Belgium	10,803	9,860	11,048	11,892	12,934	0.23	8.76
France	49,557	51,391	58,077	63,752	67,379	1.22	5.69
Germany	134,806	137,873	140,554	146,521	148,239	2.68	1.17
Liechtenstein	206	132	76	88	99		12.50

AUSTRALIA

2. Arrivals of non-resident visitors at national borders, by country of residence

	2002	2003	2004	2005	2006	Market share 06	% Change 06-05
Luxembourg	863	691	1,135	858	978	0.02	13.99
Monaco	590	502	325	485	457	0.01	-5.77
Netherlands	52,992	50,959	48,235	49,685	51,168	0.92	2.98
Switzerland	41,509	40,906	41,201	41,462	42,504	0.77	2.51
East Mediterranean Europe	**19,691**	**17,575**	**19,718**	**22,313**	**22,183**	**0.40**	**-0.58**
Cyprus	1,848	1,502	2,068	2,498	2,710	0.05	8.49
Israel	15,072	13,334	14,388	15,594	15,017	0.27	-3.70
Turkey	2,771	2,739	3,262	4,221	4,456	0.08	5.57
Other Europe	**52**	**13**	**7**	**20**	**27**		**35.00**
Other countries of Europe	52	13	7	20	27		35.00
MIDDLE EAST	**30,962**	**34,432**	**43,484**	**49,195**	**52,401**	**0.95**	**6.52**
Middle East	**30,962**	**34,432**	**43,484**	**49,195**	**52,401**	**0.95**	**6.52**
Bahrain	1,432	2,179	2,281	3,068	3,216	0.06	4.82
Iraq	78	208	177	588	519	0.01	-11.73
Jordan	966	600	770	812	1,074	0.02	32.27
Kuwait	2,666	2,111	3,952	3,828	3,735	0.07	-2.43
Lebanon	3,219	4,350	4,988	5,019	4,872	0.09	-2.93
Libyan Arab Jamahiriya	50	173	138	201	235		16.92
Oman	1,669	2,119	2,261	2,157	2,472	0.04	14.60
Qatar	825	1,190	1,497	1,899	1,992	0.04	4.90
Saudi Arabia	4,074	4,042	4,836	6,042	6,611	0.12	9.42
Syrian Arab Republic	293	334	486	533	521	0.01	-2.25
United Arab Emirates	13,286	15,226	19,846	22,451	24,728	0.45	10.14
Egypt	2,340	1,797	2,069	2,356	2,333	0.04	-0.98
Yemen	24	40	183	129	29		-77.52
Other countries of Middle East	40	63		112	64		-42.86
SOUTH ASIA	**60,687**	**63,264**	**75,233**	**89,356**	**108,324**	**1.96**	**21.23**
South Asia	**60,687**	**63,264**	**75,233**	**89,356**	**108,324**	**1.96**	**21.23**
Afghanistan	41	59	37	183	281	0.01	53.55
Bangladesh	3,145	3,405	3,638	2,991	3,091	0.06	3.34
Bhutan	136	102	100	203	123		-39.41
Sri Lanka	7,185	8,562	9,864	10,105	11,656	0.21	15.35
India	45,022	45,597	55,603	67,930	83,771	1.51	23.32
Iran, Islamic Republic of	1,764	1,769	2,209	2,870	3,411	0.06	18.85
Maldives	415	338	405	416	425	0.01	2.16
Nepal	922	827	844	1,141	1,568	0.03	37.42
Pakistan	2,057	2,605	2,533	3,517	3,998	0.07	13.68
REGION NOT SPECIFIED	**2,554**	**1,263**	**145**	**229**	**470**	**0.01**	**105.24**
Not Specified	**2,554**	**1,263**	**145**	**229**	**470**	**0.01**	**105.24**
Other countries of the World	2,554	1,263	145	229	470	0.01	105.24

Source: World Tourism Organization (UNWTO)

AUSTRIA

3. Arrivals of non-resident tourists in hotels and similar establishments, by country of residence

		2002	2003	2004	2005	2006	Market share 06	% Change 06-05
TOTAL	(*)	**13,486,750**	**13,748,371**	**14,074,767**	**14,541,922**	**14,946,795**	**100.00**	**2.78**
AFRICA	.	**23,080**	**24,364**	**28,748**	**38,204**	**38,006**	**0.25**	**-0.52**
Southern Africa		**11,939**	**11,279**	**13,735**	**17,292**	**17,477**	**0.12**	**1.07**
South Africa		11,939	11,279	13,735	17,292	17,477	0.12	1.07
Other Africa		**11,141**	**13,085**	**15,013**	**20,912**	**20,529**	**0.14**	**-1.83**
Other countries of Africa		11,141	13,085	15,013	20,912	20,529	0.14	-1.83
AMERICAS		**593,439**	**544,856**	**616,659**	**628,696**	**704,832**	**4.72**	**12.11**
North America		**541,036**	**500,431**	**566,844**	**566,212**	**631,650**	**4.23**	**11.56**
Canada		54,506	56,689	62,757	62,543	73,202	0.49	17.04
Mexico		16,640						
United States		469,890	443,742	504,087	503,669	558,448	3.74	10.88
South America		**23,618**						
Argentina		6,402						
Brazil		17,216						
Other Americas		**28,785**	**44,425**	**49,815**	**62,484**	**73,182**	**0.49**	**17.12**
Other countries of the Americas		28,785	44,425	49,815	62,484	73,182	0.49	17.12
EAST ASIA AND THE PACIFIC		**571,241**	**576,817**	**708,203**	**741,161**	**740,782**	**4.96**	**-0.05**
North-East Asia		**239,560**	**214,667**	**477,810**	**518,681**	**537,895**	**3.60**	**3.70**
China				166,970	171,122	171,408	1.15	0.17
Taiwan (Province of China)				23,942	28,774	37,859	0.25	31.57
Japan		239,560	214,667	247,415	268,831	260,024	1.74	-3.28
Korea, Republic of				39,483	49,954	68,604	0.46	37.33
Australasia		**76,570**	**82,754**	**110,033**	**111,498**	**120,814**	**0.81**	**8.36**
Australia				99,164	99,518	108,631	0.73	9.16
New Zealand				10,869	11,980	12,183	0.08	1.69
Australia, New Zealand		76,570	82,754					
Other East Asia and the Pacific		**255,111**	**279,396**	**120,360**	**110,982**	**82,073**	**0.55**	**-26.05**
Other countries of Asia						40,943	0.27	
Other countries East Asia/Pacific		255,111	279,396	120,360	110,982	41,130	0.28	-62.94
EUROPE		**12,018,188**	**12,232,636**	**12,340,708**	**12,804,083**	**13,123,803**	**87.80**	**2.50**
Central/Eastern Europe		**644,765**	**621,659**	**667,945**	**870,409**	**1,033,754**	**6.92**	**18.77**
Bulgaria		20,039			25,603	33,074	0.22	29.18
Czech Republic		116,737	140,454	157,583	173,519	196,710	1.32	13.37
Hungary		161,364	186,928	215,751	237,800	262,946	1.76	10.57
Poland		123,049	116,017	111,625	125,815	138,711	0.93	10.25
Romania		47,998			79,289	124,608	0.83	57.16
Slovakia		35,544	40,517	48,986	51,862	58,571	0.39	12.94
Baltic countries		8,610			27,122	38,111	0.25	40.52
Commonwealth Independent State		131,424	137,743	134,000	149,399	181,023	1.21	21.17
Northern Europe		**979,511**	**964,773**	**1,036,707**	**1,112,935**	**1,205,097**	**8.06**	**8.28**
Denmark		133,552	139,454	144,377	161,715	184,503	1.23	14.09
Finland		42,283	43,891	49,773	56,701	58,127	0.39	2.51
Iceland		3,621	4,343	4,452	4,946	7,282	0.05	47.23
Ireland		30,707	33,857	38,883	45,407	60,020	0.40	32.18
Norway		44,058	43,389	42,203	47,679	55,709	0.37	16.84
Sweden		126,114	124,507	129,587	139,925	143,657	0.96	2.67
United Kingdom		599,176	575,332	627,432	656,562	695,799	4.66	5.98
Southern Europe		**1,231,124**	**1,316,148**	**1,360,853**	**1,411,989**	**1,469,301**	**9.83**	**4.06**

AUSTRIA

3. Arrivals of non-resident tourists in hotels and similar establishments, by country of residence

	2002	2003	2004	2005	2006	Market share 06	% Change 06-05
Croatia	52,510	54,830	58,531	63,580	72,533	0.49	14.08
Greece	58,310	63,242	61,721	70,486	81,685	0.55	15.89
Italy	865,002	933,346	937,928	940,199	950,732	6.36	1.12
Malta				3,629	4,984	0.03	37.34
Portugal	20,329	19,750	22,348	24,374	26,447	0.18	8.50
Slovenia	43,068	46,395	50,115	53,857	56,339	0.38	4.61
Spain	164,768	173,165	203,978	225,474	237,720	1.59	5.43
Serbia and Montenegro	27,137	25,420	26,232	30,390	38,861	0.26	27.87
Western Europe	**9,096,524**	**9,260,657**	**9,206,623**	**9,334,171**	**9,324,525**	**62.38**	**-0.10**
Belgium			305,262	325,205	337,965	2.26	3.92
France	340,583	362,412	385,755	373,218	399,586	2.67	7.07
Germany	6,975,268	7,024,935	6,919,705	7,005,322	6,895,399	46.13	-1.57
Luxembourg			35,590	38,268	41,538	0.28	8.54
Netherlands	759,155	778,118	786,735	819,831	846,257	5.66	3.22
Switzerland	707,351	765,522	773,576	772,327	803,780	5.38	4.07
Belgium / Luxembourg	314,167	329,670					
East Mediterranean Europe	**66,264**	**69,399**	**68,580**	**74,579**	**91,126**	**0.61**	**22.19**
Cyprus				3,844	5,515	0.04	43.47
Israel	44,531	45,411	44,102	44,199	53,113	0.36	20.17
Turkey	21,733	23,988	24,478	26,536	32,498	0.22	22.47
MIDDLE EAST	**28,081**	**35,512**	**40,652**	**64,633**	**70,975**	**0.47**	**9.81**
Middle East	**28,081**	**35,512**	**40,652**	**64,633**	**70,975**	**0.47**	**9.81**
All countries of Middle East	28,081	35,512	40,652	64,633	70,975	0.47	9.81
SOUTH ASIA	**38,884**	**28,747**	**38,947**	**37,857**	**48,169**	**0.32**	**27.24**
South Asia	**38,884**	**28,747**	**38,947**	**37,857**	**48,169**	**0.32**	**27.24**
All countries of South Asia	38,884	28,747	38,947	37,857	48,169	0.32	27.24
REGION NOT SPECIFIED	**213,837**	**305,439**	**300,850**	**227,288**	**220,228**	**1.47**	**-3.11**
Not Specified	**213,837**	**305,439**	**300,850**	**227,288**	**220,228**	**1.47**	**-3.11**
Other countries of the World	213,837	305,439	300,850	227,288	220,228	1.47	-3.11

Source: World Tourism Organization (UNWTO)

AUSTRIA

4. Arrivals of non-resident tourists in all types of accommodation establishments, by country of residence

	2002	2003	2004	2005	2006	Market share 06	% Change 06-05
TOTAL (*)	18,610,925	19,077,630	19,372,816	19,952,350	20,261,292	100.00	1.55
AFRICA	25,779	27,206	32,114	42,259	42,501	0.21	0.57
Southern Africa	14,574	13,552	16,355	20,202	20,776	0.10	2.84
South Africa	14,574	13,552	16,355	20,202	20,776	0.10	2.84
Other Africa	11,205	13,654	15,759	22,057	21,725	0.11	-1.51
Other countries of Africa	11,205	13,654	15,759	22,057	21,725	0.11	-1.51
AMERICAS	646,863	599,474	673,695	691,644	780,218	3.85	12.81
North America	593,795	550,600	618,479	620,702	693,369	3.42	11.71
Canada	64,724	65,949	72,534	72,326	85,504	0.42	18.22
Mexico	16,687						
United States	512,384	484,651	545,945	548,376	607,865	3.00	10.85
South America	23,696						
Argentina	6,423						
Brazil	17,273						
Other Americas	29,372	48,874	55,216	70,942	86,849	0.43	22.42
Other countries of the Americas	29,372	48,874	55,216	70,942	86,849	0.43	22.42
EAST ASIA AND THE PACIFIC	593,583	618,852	755,406	792,197	797,479	3.94	0.67
North-East Asia	293,001	287,420	500,323	543,375	565,418	2.79	4.06
China			172,361	176,777	176,704	0.87	-0.04
Taiwan (Province of China)	24,979	23,817	25,240	30,420	40,309	0.20	32.51
Japan	240,146	222,275	256,541	278,686	267,913	1.32	-3.87
Korea, Republic of	27,876	41,328	46,181	57,492	80,492	0.40	40.01
South-East Asia	95,594	73,315	72,126	58,596	43,418	0.21	-25.90
All countries of South-East Asia	95,594	73,315	72,126	58,596	43,418	0.21	-25.90
Australasia	97,273	104,172	131,103	133,386	144,547	0.71	8.37
Australia	88,157	91,443	117,353	118,128	128,894	0.64	9.11
New Zealand	9,116	12,729	13,750	15,258	15,653	0.08	2.59
Other East Asia and the Pacific	107,715	153,945	51,854	56,840	44,096	0.22	-22.42
Other countries of Asia	105,340	70,779	51,854	56,840	44,096	0.22	-22.42
Other countries East Asia/Pacific		83,166					
Other countries of Oceania	2,375						
EUROPE	16,983,956	17,386,722	17,445,939	18,030,663	18,257,289	90.11	1.26
Central/Eastern Europe	950,273	940,252	1,009,453	1,262,494	1,463,863	7.22	15.95
Bulgaria	26,663			28,965	37,578	0.19	29.74
Czech Republic	226,282	265,139	295,125	317,621	354,460	1.75	11.60
Hungary	247,772	286,649	325,426	363,105	392,605	1.94	8.12
Poland	193,430	184,560	174,061	192,025	207,937	1.03	8.29
Romania	55,640			90,404	141,498	0.70	56.52
Slovakia	49,381	54,892	66,146	70,010	78,007	0.39	11.42
Baltic countries	8,906			38,547	55,362	0.27	43.62
Commonwealth Independent State	142,199	149,012	148,695	161,817	196,416	0.97	21.38
Northern Europe	1,199,466	1,183,109	1,272,385	1,367,594	1,479,181	7.30	8.16
Denmark	207,338	213,970	221,119	249,629	280,760	1.39	12.47
Finland	52,936	53,132	59,883	66,697	68,070	0.34	2.06
Iceland	4,062	4,918	5,391	5,632	8,123	0.04	44.23
Ireland	36,053	39,666	49,930	56,830	73,832	0.36	29.92
Norway	53,400	51,404	50,486	56,280	66,203	0.33	17.63

AUSTRIA

4. Arrivals of non-resident tourists in all types of accommodation establishments, by country of residence

	2002	2003	2004	2005	2006	Market share 06	% Change 06-05
Sweden	160,838	157,280	163,646	175,555	179,927	0.89	2.49
United Kingdom	684,839	662,739	721,930	756,971	802,266	3.96	5.98
Southern Europe	**1,426,855**	**1,542,405**	**1,597,367**	**1,650,121**	**1,705,796**	**8.42**	**3.37**
Croatia	70,335	74,251	78,893	84,688	94,565	0.47	11.66
Greece	61,774	66,726	65,989	74,024	85,226	0.42	15.13
Italy	995,182	1,089,554	1,100,564	1,101,840	1,105,585	5.46	0.34
Malta				4,226	5,508	0.03	30.34
Portugal	22,987	22,412	25,652	27,289	29,737	0.15	8.97
Slovenia	62,833	68,139	72,293	77,224	80,716	0.40	4.52
Spain	183,220	193,258	225,061	247,709	261,804	1.29	5.69
Serbia and Montenegro	30,524	28,065	28,915	33,121	42,655	0.21	28.79
Western Europe	**13,331,914**	**13,642,132**	**13,488,197**	**13,666,641**	**13,505,831**	**66.66**	**-1.18**
Belgium	374,183	391,463	400,965	425,093	436,932	2.16	2.79
France	406,251	436,088	469,131	451,993	478,018	2.36	5.76
Germany	10,349,377	10,467,992	10,254,991	10,366,808	10,101,194	49.85	-2.56
Luxembourg	34,509	39,809	41,904	44,120	47,686	0.24	8.08
Netherlands	1,350,212	1,418,402	1,425,605	1,483,909	1,516,188	7.48	2.18
Switzerland	817,382	888,378	895,601	894,718	925,813	4.57	3.48
East Mediterranean Europe	**75,448**	**78,824**	**78,537**	**83,813**	**102,618**	**0.51**	**22.44**
Cyprus				4,177	6,232	0.03	49.20
Israel	52,419	53,396	52,675	51,849	61,908	0.31	19.40
Turkey	23,029	25,428	25,862	27,787	34,478	0.17	24.08
MIDDLE EAST	**28,524**	**37,667**	**43,202**	**67,833**	**75,217**	**0.37**	**10.89**
Middle East	**28,524**	**37,667**	**43,202**	**67,833**	**75,217**	**0.37**	**10.89**
All countries of Middle East	28,524	37,667	43,202	67,833	75,217	0.37	10.89
SOUTH ASIA	**39,011**	**29,619**	**39,882**	**39,204**	**49,684**	**0.25**	**26.73**
South Asia	**39,011**	**29,619**	**39,882**	**39,204**	**49,684**	**0.25**	**26.73**
All countries of South Asia	39,011	29,619	39,882	39,204	49,684	0.25	26.73
REGION NOT SPECIFIED	**293,209**	**378,090**	**382,578**	**288,550**	**258,904**	**1.28**	**-10.27**
Not Specified	**293,209**	**378,090**	**382,578**	**288,550**	**258,904**	**1.28**	**-10.27**
Other countries of the World	293,209	378,090	382,578	288,550	258,904	1.28	-10.27

Source: World Tourism Organization (UNWTO)

AUSTRIA

5. Overnight stays of non-resident tourists in hotels and similar establishments, by country of residence

	2002	2003	2004	2005	2006	Market share 06	% Change 06-05
TOTAL (*)	55,167,340	55,200,185	55,159,678	56,690,261	57,114,126	100.00	0.75
AFRICA	87,356	91,446	102,697	118,872	124,966	0.22	5.13
Southern Africa	51,465	48,738	55,712	65,672	72,226	0.13	9.98
South Africa	51,465	48,738	55,712	65,672	72,226	0.13	9.98
Other Africa	35,891	42,708	46,985	53,200	52,740	0.09	-0.86
Other countries of Africa	35,891	42,708	46,985	53,200	52,740	0.09	-0.86
AMERICAS	1,499,166	1,368,122	1,557,727	1,554,689	1,700,135	2.98	9.36
North America	1,383,416	1,266,999	1,440,499	1,414,131	1,540,520	2.70	8.94
Canada	142,618	145,180	157,062	162,099	182,173	0.32	12.38
Mexico	35,171						
United States	1,205,627	1,121,819	1,283,437	1,252,032	1,358,347	2.38	8.49
South America	52,770						
Argentina	15,225						
Brazil	37,545						
Other Americas	62,980	101,123	117,228	140,558	159,615	0.28	13.56
Other countries of the Americas	62,980	101,123	117,228	140,558	159,615	0.28	13.56
EAST ASIA AND THE PACIFIC	1,042,477	1,059,602	1,254,323	1,340,815	1,345,378	2.36	0.34
North-East Asia	557,547	521,521	819,075	894,650	913,888	1.60	2.15
China			224,312	238,535	241,258	0.42	1.14
Taiwan (Province of China)	37,459	33,116	35,269	43,044	56,097	0.10	30.32
Japan	478,549	437,105	504,965	540,859	521,155	0.91	-3.64
Korea, Republic of	41,539	51,300	54,529	72,212	95,378	0.17	32.08
South-East Asia	134,027	104,038	102,239	93,506	74,343	0.13	-20.49
All countries of South-East Asia	134,027	104,038	102,239	93,506	74,343	0.13	-20.49
Australasia	176,521	187,826	238,810	252,070	270,622	0.47	7.36
Australia	155,149	161,520	215,774	226,431	243,646	0.43	7.60
New Zealand	21,372	26,306	23,036	25,639	26,976	0.05	5.21
Other East Asia and the Pacific	174,382	246,217	94,199	100,589	86,525	0.15	-13.98
Other countries of Asia	168,575	132,674	94,199	100,589	86,525	0.15	-13.98
Other countries East Asia/Pacific		113,543					
Other countries of Oceania	5,807						
EUROPE	51,897,352	51,782,798	51,308,544	52,785,022	53,073,405	92.93	0.55
Central/Eastern Europe	2,027,820	2,088,816	2,230,283	2,828,331	3,325,135	5.82	17.57
Bulgaria	43,298			56,611	75,834	0.13	33.96
Czech Republic	361,970	431,133	486,162	541,867	597,878	1.05	10.34
Hungary	481,856	577,407	662,281	747,114	828,285	1.45	10.86
Poland	451,039	426,464	390,791	431,244	478,067	0.84	10.86
Romania	96,594			191,144	303,842	0.53	58.96
Slovakia	101,283	119,550	142,986	150,835	175,048	0.31	16.05
Baltic countries	22,796			92,145	133,856	0.23	45.27
Commonwealth Independent State	468,984	534,262	548,063	617,371	732,325	1.28	18.62
Northern Europe	4,329,127	4,275,964	4,534,784	4,875,786	5,250,252	9.19	7.68
Denmark	597,611	601,716	619,288	704,727	801,099	1.40	13.68
Finland	143,545	149,398	173,191	207,289	208,260	0.36	0.47
Iceland	11,653	15,907	16,462	20,563	28,281	0.05	37.53
Ireland	149,455	162,590	180,826	212,043	281,331	0.49	32.68
Norway	131,113	132,767	127,888	151,875	183,757	0.32	20.99

AUSTRIA

5. Overnight stays of non-resident tourists in hotels and similar establishments, by country of residence

	2002	2003	2004	2005	2006	Market share 06	% Change 06-05
Sweden	480,441	469,064	487,702	517,864	543,796	0.95	5.01
United Kingdom	2,815,309	2,744,522	2,929,427	3,061,425	3,203,728	5.61	4.65
Southern Europe	**3,212,077**	**3,405,565**	**3,505,334**	**3,720,093**	**3,884,371**	**6.80**	**4.42**
Croatia	151,762	163,773	167,783	180,833	206,128	0.36	13.99
Greece	162,603	180,020	177,382	208,781	237,444	0.42	13.73
Italy	2,289,540	2,419,300	2,418,866	2,483,189	2,534,928	4.44	2.08
Malta				13,712	23,045	0.04	68.06
Portugal	52,997	51,391	60,137	63,925	71,259	0.12	11.47
Slovenia	107,725	119,612	123,646	139,384	144,708	0.25	3.82
Spain	383,664	412,986	496,305	564,231	586,042	1.03	3.87
Serbia and Montenegro	63,786	58,483	61,215	66,038	80,817	0.14	22.38
Western Europe	**42,125,223**	**41,800,972**	**40,820,736**	**41,139,439**	**40,334,071**	**70.62**	**-1.96**
Belgium	1,585,942	1,620,177	1,642,182	1,736,613	1,772,135	3.10	2.05
France	1,263,804	1,300,552	1,394,105	1,336,810	1,416,514	2.48	5.96
Germany	32,355,981	31,716,151	30,666,483	30,854,121	29,754,144	52.10	-3.57
Luxembourg	165,542	192,416	202,797	209,517	223,478	0.39	6.66
Netherlands	4,070,347	4,082,012	4,009,578	4,135,337	4,225,750	7.40	2.19
Switzerland	2,683,607	2,889,664	2,905,591	2,867,041	2,942,050	5.15	2.62
East Mediterranean Europe	**203,105**	**211,481**	**217,407**	**221,373**	**279,576**	**0.49**	**26.29**
Cyprus				11,320	16,035	0.03	41.65
Israel	140,592	143,885	143,270	140,031	176,116	0.31	25.77
Turkey	62,513	67,596	74,137	70,022	87,425	0.15	24.85
MIDDLE EAST	**110,327**	**118,965**	**144,751**	**235,979**	**233,393**	**0.41**	**-1.10**
Middle East	**110,327**	**118,965**	**144,751**	**235,979**	**233,393**	**0.41**	**-1.10**
All countries of Middle East	110,327	118,965	144,751	235,979	233,393	0.41	-1.10
SOUTH ASIA	**57,570**	**46,682**	**58,191**	**66,963**	**82,912**	**0.15**	**23.82**
South Asia	**57,570**	**46,682**	**58,191**	**66,963**	**82,912**	**0.15**	**23.82**
All countries of South Asia	57,570	46,682	58,191	66,963	82,912	0.15	23.82
REGION NOT SPECIFIED	**473,092**	**732,570**	**733,445**	**587,921**	**553,937**	**0.97**	**-5.78**
Not Specified	**473,092**	**732,570**	**733,445**	**587,921**	**553,937**	**0.97**	**-5.78**
Other countries of the World	473,092	732,570	733,445	587,921	553,937	0.97	-5.78

Source: World Tourism Organization (UNWTO)

AUSTRIA

6. Overnight stays of non-resident tourists in all types of accommodation establishments, by country of residence

	2002	2003	2004	2005	2006	Market share 06	% Change 06-05
TOTAL (*)	85,791,658	86,347,992	85,917,026	87,740,632	87,240,855	100.00	-0.57
AFRICA	102,914	108,588	121,602	140,050	151,417	0.17	8.12
Southern Africa	66,733	62,535	70,601	82,517	94,233	0.11	14.20
South Africa	66,733	62,535	70,601	82,517	94,233	0.11	14.20
Other Africa	36,181	46,053	51,001	57,533	57,184	0.07	-0.61
Other countries of Africa	36,181	46,053	51,001	57,533	57,184	0.07	-0.61
AMERICAS	1,666,906	1,533,740	1,733,714	1,741,325	1,898,284	2.18	9.01
North America	1,548,667	1,422,854	1,605,052	1,582,566	1,714,000	1.96	8.31
Canada	171,798	173,545	187,783	193,311	216,507	0.25	12.00
Mexico	35,533						
United States	1,341,336	1,249,309	1,417,269	1,389,255	1,497,493	1.72	7.79
South America	53,214						
Argentina	15,393						
Brazil	37,821						
Other Americas	65,025	110,886	128,662	158,759	184,284	0.21	16.08
Other countries of the Americas	65,025	110,886	128,662	158,759	184,284	0.21	16.08
EAST ASIA AND THE PACIFIC	1,113,775	1,169,254	1,377,054	1,461,219	1,473,821	1.69	0.86
North-East Asia	562,327	556,402	871,280	945,776	966,825	1.11	2.23
China			237,208	248,594	252,700	0.29	1.65
Taiwan (Province of China)	37,759	37,089	38,010	46,460	60,876	0.07	31.03
Japan	482,252	457,055	530,566	565,637	539,269	0.62	-4.66
Korea, Republic of	42,316	62,258	65,496	85,085	113,980	0.13	33.96
South-East Asia	134,850	108,164	107,108	98,975	80,469	0.09	-18.70
All countries of South-East Asia	134,850	108,164	107,108	98,975	80,469	0.09	-18.70
Australasia	241,059	243,380	293,704	309,277	332,624	0.38	7.55
Australia	217,642	208,525	263,074	274,716	296,589	0.34	7.96
New Zealand	23,417	34,855	30,630	34,561	36,035	0.04	4.26
Other East Asia and the Pacific	175,539	261,308	104,962	107,191	93,903	0.11	-12.40
Other countries of Asia	169,728	141,412	104,962	107,191	93,903	0.11	-12.40
Other countries East Asia/Pacific		119,896					
Other countries of Oceania	5,811						
EUROPE	82,041,064	82,423,118	81,502,107	83,288,031	82,681,189	94.77	-0.73
Central/Eastern Europe	3,380,901	3,551,700	3,819,397	4,637,277	5,290,882	6.06	14.09
Bulgaria	60,585			68,452	88,905	0.10	29.88
Czech Republic	788,124	922,325	1,043,002	1,133,267	1,236,048	1.42	9.07
Hungary	859,900	1,009,437	1,150,045	1,295,882	1,398,386	1.60	7.91
Poland	840,660	830,366	764,368	819,743	893,938	1.02	9.05
Romania	116,066			230,462	363,082	0.42	57.55
Slovakia	164,560	184,576	220,119	232,178	263,125	0.30	13.33
Baltic countries	24,819			148,039	206,218	0.24	39.30
Commonwealth Independent State	526,187	604,996	641,863	709,254	841,180	0.96	18.60
Northern Europe	5,405,849	5,366,726	5,714,629	6,167,844	6,667,177	7.64	8.10
Denmark	980,480	988,497	1,026,264	1,158,661	1,309,473	1.50	13.02
Finland	180,242	182,944	210,522	246,408	250,885	0.29	1.82
Iceland	13,419	18,255	19,963	24,005	32,491	0.04	35.35
Ireland	170,344	184,795	214,538	252,636	332,433	0.38	31.59
Norway	171,308	165,300	159,257	189,576	229,507	0.26	21.06

AUSTRIA

6. Overnight stays of non-resident tourists in all types of accommodation establishments, by country of residence

	2002	2003	2004	2005	2006	Market share 06	% Change 06-05
Sweden	648,843	626,818	661,472	694,522	727,105	0.83	4.69
United Kingdom	3,241,213	3,200,117	3,422,613	3,602,036	3,785,283	4.34	5.09
Southern Europe	**4,023,567**	**4,294,214**	**4,458,926**	**4,688,714**	**4,852,315**	**5.56**	**3.49**
Croatia	256,733	277,505	284,137	298,895	330,401	0.38	10.54
Greece	178,654	195,782	195,303	224,878	254,299	0.29	13.08
Italy	2,812,364	3,003,822	3,056,260	3,119,101	3,153,338	3.61	1.10
Malta				15,891	24,924	0.03	56.84
Portugal	61,111	60,055	71,144	73,327	81,634	0.09	11.33
Slovenia	196,711	215,881	219,345	243,574	249,449	0.29	2.41
Spain	437,630	468,772	559,877	632,216	660,383	0.76	4.46
Serbia and Montenegro	80,364	72,397	72,860	80,832	97,887	0.11	21.10
Western Europe	**68,983,030**	**68,955,762**	**67,246,253**	**67,528,979**	**65,540,711**	**75.13**	**-2.94**
Belgium	2,185,364	2,249,672	2,267,663	2,389,054	2,421,348	2.78	1.35
France	1,561,654	1,612,031	1,736,268	1,664,253	1,751,023	2.01	5.21
Germany	53,521,157	52,804,677	50,982,759	51,027,523	48,764,882	55.90	-4.43
Luxembourg	203,598	231,676	242,131	248,199	262,714	0.30	5.85
Netherlands	8,226,126	8,517,981	8,453,710	8,685,713	8,762,901	10.04	0.89
Switzerland	3,285,131	3,539,725	3,563,722	3,514,237	3,577,843	4.10	1.81
East Mediterranean Europe	**247,717**	**254,716**	**262,902**	**265,217**	**330,104**	**0.38**	**24.47**
Cyprus				13,062	18,391	0.02	40.80
Israel	177,482	181,096	182,616	175,882	213,572	0.24	21.43
Turkey	70,235	73,620	80,286	76,273	98,141	0.11	28.67
MIDDLE EAST	**115,071**	**138,398**	**166,765**	**265,227**	**270,817**	**0.31**	**2.11**
Middle East	**115,071**	**138,398**	**166,765**	**265,227**	**270,817**	**0.31**	**2.11**
All countries of Middle East	115,071	138,398	166,765	265,227	270,817	0.31	2.11
SOUTH ASIA	**58,196**	**48,836**	**60,623**	**71,162**	**88,246**	**0.10**	**24.01**
South Asia	**58,196**	**48,836**	**60,623**	**71,162**	**88,246**	**0.10**	**24.01**
All countries of South Asia	58,196	48,836	60,623	71,162	88,246	0.10	24.01
REGION NOT SPECIFIED	**693,732**	**926,058**	**955,161**	**773,618**	**677,081**	**0.78**	**-12.48**
Not Specified	**693,732**	**926,058**	**955,161**	**773,618**	**677,081**	**0.78**	**-12.48**
Other countries of the World	693,732	926,058	955,161	773,618	677,081	0.78	-12.48

Source: World Tourism Organization (UNWTO)

AZERBAIJAN

1. Arrivals of non-resident tourists at national borders, by country of residence

	2002	2003	2004	2005	2006	Market share 06	% Change 06-05
TOTAL	834,351	1,013,811	1,348,655	1,177,277	1,193,742	100.00	1.40
AFRICA	108	320	661	544	807	0.07	48.35
East Africa	4	18	103	32	97	0.01	203.13
Comoros					2		
Ethiopia	4	1		3	15		400.00
Eritrea		2	3				
Djibouti			2		2		
Kenya		6	13	9			
Madagascar				2	1		-50.00
Mauritius				2	6		200.00
Mozambique				1	9		800.00
Rwanda			45				
Somalia			10	8	23		187.50
Zimbabwe		3	13	2	4		100.00
Uganda		4	7	2	8		300.00
United Republic of Tanzania		2	2		18		
Zambia			8	3	9		200.00
Central Africa		11	31	38	53		39.47
Angola			12	10	5		-50.00
Cameroon		2	6	18	32		77.78
Congo		9	13	7	5		-28.57
Gabon				3	11		266.67
North Africa	17	90	117	154	225	0.02	46.10
Algeria	2	36	39	60	62	0.01	3.33
Morocco	1	11	23	27	41		51.85
Sudan	2	24	30	23	51		121.74
Tunisia	12	19	25	44	71	0.01	61.36
Southern Africa	27	92	171	174	219	0.02	25.86
Botswana				1			
Namibia		1					
South Africa	27	91	171	173	219	0.02	26.59
West Africa	60	109	239	146	213	0.02	45.89
Gambia	1	3	3		4		
Ghana		7	11	6	11		83.33
Cote D'Ivoire		3	1	1	1		
Liberia		9		4	1		-75.00
Mali			4	2	7		250.00
Niger				12			
Nigeria	59	82	213	109	161	0.01	47.71
Guinea-Bissau			6	3	7		133.33
Senegal		3		1	19		1,800.00
Sierra Leone		2					
Togo				2			
Burkina Faso			1	6	2		-66.67
AMERICAS	6,532	7,951	12,358	11,272	10,133	0.85	-10.10
Caribbean	37	74	141	116	178	0.01	53.45
Barbados		2	8	3	1		-66.67
Cuba	15	11	40	5	22		340.00
Dominican Republic	4	2			68	0.01	
Grenada				1	1		
Haiti	3	10					
Trinidad and Tobago	15	49	93	107	86	0.01	-19.63

AZERBAIJAN

1. Arrivals of non-resident tourists at national borders, by country of residence

	2002	2003	2004	2005	2006	Market share 06	% Change 06-05
Central America	1	130	103	75	26		-65.33
Belize		2	7	3	2		-33.33
Costa Rica		14	25	24	5		-79.17
El Salvador		95	49	4	2		-50.00
Guatemala	1	2	9	8	4		-50.00
Honduras		2	1	7	1		-85.71
Nicaragua			7	4	1		-75.00
Panama		15	5	25	11		-56.00
North America	6,360	7,490	11,668	10,728	9,549	0.80	-10.99
Canada	833	1,075	1,465	985	1,238	0.10	25.69
Mexico	23	30	88	62	58		-6.45
United States	5,504	6,385	10,115	9,681	8,253	0.69	-14.75
South America	134	257	446	353	380	0.03	7.65
Argentina	23	59	104	72	62	0.01	-13.89
Bolivia	11	9	23	6	8		33.33
Brazil	16	45	110	83	65	0.01	-21.69
Chile		7	16	2	17		750.00
Colombia	16	23	54	81	118	0.01	45.68
Ecuador	4	10	15	21	3		-85.71
Guyana					1		
Paraguay		7					
Peru		16	7	10	13		30.00
Uruguay		2	1	2	3		50.00
Venezuela	64	79	116	76	90	0.01	18.42
EAST ASIA AND THE PACIFIC	2,748	4,271	6,051	6,825	7,205	0.60	5.57
North-East Asia	1,829	2,405	2,501	2,846	4,151	0.35	45.85
China	591	1,280	1,532	1,595	2,061	0.17	29.22
Taiwan (Province of China)		25	18	50	128	0.01	156.00
Hong Kong, China				15			
Japan	1,070	767	661	849	925	0.08	8.95
Korea, Dem. People's Republic of	98	63	198		3		
Korea, Republic of	70	247	68	286	1,016	0.09	255.24
Mongolia		23	24	51	18		-64.71
South-East Asia	453	1,285	2,296	2,906	2,227	0.19	-23.37
Brunei Darussalam			2	1	8		700.00
Myanmar	1	22	27	75	15		-80.00
Cambodia		3		2	1		-50.00
Indonesia	37	79	215	309	277	0.02	-10.36
Lao People's Democratic Republic			2				
Malaysia	106	274	447	673	473	0.04	-29.72
Philippines	179	527	1,076	1,060	816	0.07	-23.02
Singapore	82	154	232	329	321	0.03	-2.43
Viet Nam	28	25	49	55	46		-16.36
Thailand	20	201	246	402	270	0.02	-32.84
Australasia	466	581	1,254	1,073	827	0.07	-22.93
Australia	419	439	998	745	623	0.05	-16.38
New Zealand	47	142	256	328	204	0.02	-37.80
EUROPE	581,633	746,916	1,050,943	945,662	1,007,670	84.41	6.56
Central/Eastern Europe	504,987	653,009	941,840	829,681	894,125	74.90	7.77
Armenia		6					
Bulgaria	359	360	599	627	860	0.07	37.16
Belarus	1,547	1,609	1,475	3,552	2,678	0.22	-24.61

AZERBAIJAN

1. Arrivals of non-resident tourists at national borders, by country of residence

	2002	2003	2004	2005	2006	Market share 06	% Change 06-05
Czech Republic	54	195	468	627	406	0.03	-35.25
Estonia	116	148	296	350	337	0.03	-3.71
Georgia	252,317	209,698	405,500	396,391	386,180	32.35	-2.58
Hungary	60	180	277	206	277	0.02	34.47
Kazakhstan	5,180	5,673	6,924	7,697	8,027	0.67	4.29
Kyrgyzstan	426	692	1,032	1,230	1,588	0.13	29.11
Latvia	103	186	261	311	683	0.06	119.61
Lithuania	56	125	266	247	340	0.03	37.65
Republic of Moldova	417	591	698	669	643	0.05	-3.89
Poland	427	516	579	950	841	0.07	-11.47
Romania	82	298	650	2,781	3,483	0.29	25.24
Russian Federation	216,923	401,505	496,050	387,368	460,801	38.60	18.96
Slovakia	42	114	93	124	123	0.01	-0.81
Tajikistan	127	311	350	207	262	0.02	26.57
Turkmenistan	2,992	2,290	4,585	4,347	4,514	0.38	3.84
Ukraine	21,038	25,965	12,386	17,519	17,232	1.44	-1.64
Uzbekistan	2,721	2,547	9,351	4,478	4,850	0.41	8.31
Northern Europe	**12,358**	**14,164**	**21,987**	**24,329**	**23,515**	**1.97**	**-3.35**
Denmark	316	474	436	845	441	0.04	-47.81
Finland	167	398	299	409	328	0.03	-19.80
Iceland		85	247	476	607	0.05	27.52
Ireland	150	310	314	419	497	0.04	18.62
Norway	812	1,150	1,525	1,038	1,091	0.09	5.11
Sweden	380	468	846	951	886	0.07	-6.83
United Kingdom	10,533	11,279	18,320	20,191	19,665	1.65	-2.61
Southern Europe	**1,884**	**2,501**	**2,826**	**3,285**	**3,571**	**0.30**	**8.71**
Albania	35	32	52	27	29		7.41
Bosnia and Herzegovina		27	66	64	61	0.01	-4.69
Croatia	83	138	170	242	300	0.03	23.97
Greece	177	657	318	306	306	0.03	
Holy See				7	3		-57.14
Italy	1,268	1,045	1,000	1,180	1,644	0.14	39.32
Malta		17	55	12	15		25.00
Portugal	88	165	195	484	418	0.04	-13.64
Slovenia	30	37	164	217	217	0.02	
Spain	146	228	567	382	301	0.03	-21.20
TFYR of Macedonia	57	155	239	364	277	0.02	-23.90
Western Europe	**6,256**	**5,691**	**9,919**	**14,497**	**13,113**	**1.10**	**-9.55**
Austria	410	500	738	1,060	753	0.06	-28.96
Belgium	288	347	989	1,846	1,648	0.14	-10.73
France	1,522	195	2,418	3,344	2,472	0.21	-26.08
Germany	3,074	3,470	3,651	5,589	5,479	0.46	-1.97
Liechtenstein			1	1			
Luxembourg	10	48	185	493	760	0.06	54.16
Monaco				3			
Netherlands	752	700	1,499	1,203	1,382	0.12	14.88
Switzerland	200	431	438	958	619	0.05	-35.39
East Mediterranean Europe	**56,148**	**71,551**	**74,371**	**73,870**	**73,346**	**6.14**	**-0.71**
Cyprus		45	52	53	13		-75.47
Israel	2,173	2,406	2,710	3,062	3,359	0.28	9.70
Turkey	53,975	69,100	71,609	70,755	69,974	5.86	-1.10
MIDDLE EAST	**1,978**	**1,684**	**2,143**	**1,942**	**1,888**	**0.16**	**-2.78**
Middle East	**1,978**	**1,684**	**2,143**	**1,942**	**1,888**	**0.16**	**-2.78**
Bahrain	3	21	48	18	58		222.22

AZERBAIJAN

1. Arrivals of non-resident tourists at national borders, by country of residence

	2002	2003	2004	2005	2006	Market share 06	% Change 06-05
Palestine		30	57	13	19		46.15
Iraq	1,277	113	124	334	307	0.03	-8.08
Jordan	57	155	215	140	219	0.02	56.43
Kuwait	48	75	69	62	82	0.01	32.26
Lebanon	76	355	403	260	162	0.01	-37.69
Libyan Arab Jamahiriya	10	37	60	77	54		-29.87
Oman		39	11	7	10		42.86
Qatar		12	3	20	19		-5.00
Saudi Arabia	134	144	177	204	246	0.02	20.59
Syrian Arab Republic	195	318	267	377	273	0.02	-27.59
United Arab Emirates	92	137	408	198	151	0.01	-23.74
Egypt	86	159	219	164	225	0.02	37.20
Yemen		89	82	68	63	0.01	-7.35
SOUTH ASIA	**241,352**	**252,669**	**275,147**	**211,032**	**165,144**	**13.83**	**-21.74**
South Asia	**241,352**	**252,669**	**275,147**	**211,032**	**165,144**	**13.83**	**-21.74**
Afghanistan	88	365	350	270	300	0.03	11.11
Bangladesh	30	78	134	198	114	0.01	-42.42
Bhutan				1	1		
Sri Lanka		42	130	106	71	0.01	-33.02
India	1,008	1,545	2,695	2,034	1,969	0.16	-3.20
Iran, Islamic Republic of	239,694	249,700	270,657	207,105	161,504	13.53	-22.02
Maldives		3					
Nepal		27	36	23			
Pakistan	532	909	1,145	1,295	1,185	0.10	-8.49
REGION NOT SPECIFIED			**1,352**		**895**	**0.07**	
Not Specified			**1,352**		**895**	**0.07**	
Other countries of the World			1,352		895	0.07	

Source: World Tourism Organization (UNWTO)

BAHAMAS

1. Arrivals of non-resident tourists at national borders, by country of residence

	2002	2003	2004	2005	2006	Market share 06	% Change 06-05
TOTAL	1,513,151	1,510,169	1,561,312	1,608,153	1,600,112	100.00	-0.50
AFRICA	1,166	1,409	1,427	1,302	1,397	0.09	7.30
East Africa	75	126	124				
Burundi		1					
Comoros	1						
Ethiopia	2	15	8				
Djibouti		1					
Kenya	21	28	38				
Madagascar	1	1					
Malawi	4	3	7				
Mauritius	6	11	18				
Mozambique		2					
Seychelles	2	4	2				
Zimbabwe	21	36	36				
Uganda	5	8	6				
United Republic of Tanzania	1	6	6				
Zambia	11	10	3				
Central Africa	16	39	15				
Angola	4	2	4				
Cameroon	5	5	2				
Chad	3	7	2				
Congo	2		2				
Gabon	2	25	5				
North Africa	47	75	39				
Algeria	5	3					
Morocco	38	55	18				
Sudan	1	4					
Tunisia	3	13	21				
Southern Africa	952	1,069	1,124	1,261	1,345	0.08	6.66
Botswana		9	10				
Lesotho		3					
Namibia	1	5	18				
South Africa	832	896	1,032	1,205	1,285	0.08	6.64
Swaziland	119	156	64	56	60		7.14
West Africa	76	100	125	41	52		26.83
Benin		1					
Gambia	2		3				
Ghana	24	29	47				
Cote D'Ivoire	6	9	8				
Liberia		1	6				
Mali	5						
Nigeria	32	45	43	41	52		26.83
Senegal	5	11	8				
Sierra Leone		2	6				
Togo	2	2	4				
AMERICAS	1,406,458	1,392,578	1,455,375	1,484,921	1,484,485	92.77	-0.03
Caribbean	15,970	14,323	15,719	17,290	18,699	1.17	8.15
Antigua and Barbuda	147	135	121	148	157	0.01	6.08
Barbados	1,044	945	939	939	1,040	0.06	10.76
Bermuda	754	784	661	834	851	0.05	2.04
British Virgin Islands	121	37	61	113	95	0.01	-15.93
Cayman Islands	772	923	1,260	1,298	1,287	0.08	-0.85

BAHAMAS

1. Arrivals of non-resident tourists at national borders, by country of residence

	2002	2003	2004	2005	2006	Market share 06	% Change 06-05
Cuba	511	524	546	412	297	0.02	-27.91
Dominica	79	126	88	90	101	0.01	12.22
Dominican Republic	424	344	358	550	496	0.03	-9.82
Grenada	108	78	80	61	71		16.39
Haiti	1,240	1,243	1,291	1,322	1,816	0.11	37.37
Jamaica	7,199	5,444	5,835	6,599	7,060	0.44	6.99
Martinique	64	42	52	35	43		22.86
Montserrat	8	8	11	18	13		-27.78
Netherlands Antilles	91	28	25	38	41		7.89
Aruba	68	109	118	82	73		-10.98
Curacao	89	127	120	135	162	0.01	20.00
Puerto Rico	195	365	483	328	269	0.02	-17.99
Saint Eustatius	2	7	5	4	9		125.00
Saint Kitts and Nevis	64	94	94	118	120	0.01	1.69
Anguilla	66	29	40	66	47		-28.79
Saint Lucia	168	158	222	171	198	0.01	15.79
Saint Maarten	38	41	73	102	102	0.01	
Saint Vincent and the Grenadines	61	60	71	72	80		11.11
Trinidad and Tobago	1,249	1,328	1,212	1,417	1,776	0.11	25.34
Turks and Caicos Islands	1,389	1,295	1,920	2,299	2,433	0.15	5.83
United States Virgin Islands	18	46	32	21	19		-9.52
Other countries of the Caribbean	1	3	1	18	43		138.89
Central America	**1,785**	**1,352**	**1,547**	**1,701**	**1,696**	**0.11**	**-0.29**
Belize	138	124	97	112	145	0.01	29.46
Costa Rica	459	328	395	485	446	0.03	-8.04
El Salvador	91	106	135	116	146	0.01	25.86
Guatemala	225	224	245	281	295	0.02	4.98
Honduras	315	138	152	171	176	0.01	2.92
Nicaragua	46	57	97	56	69		23.21
Panama	511	375	426	480	419	0.03	-12.71
North America	**1,382,095**	**1,371,610**	**1,432,474**	**1,459,272**	**1,455,709**	**90.98**	**-0.24**
Canada	68,592	63,148	68,462	75,643	84,626	5.29	11.88
Greenland	6	1	6				
Mexico	3,357	3,126	3,094	3,546	6,615	0.41	86.55
United States	1,310,140	1,305,335	1,360,912	1,380,083	1,364,468	85.27	-1.13
South America	**6,608**	**5,293**	**5,635**	**6,658**	**8,381**	**0.52**	**25.88**
Argentina	877	838	926	955	1,167	0.07	22.20
Bolivia	71	52	57	38	120	0.01	215.79
Brazil	1,988	1,237	1,487	1,880	2,439	0.15	29.73
Chile	463	339	346	376	361	0.02	-3.99
Colombia	622	547	547	651	785	0.05	20.58
Ecuador	296	284	296	440	531	0.03	20.68
Guyana	344	272	243	362	343	0.02	-5.25
Paraguay	42	26	31	26	49		88.46
Peru	554	513	405	494	622	0.04	25.91
Suriname	40	37	53	46	83	0.01	80.43
Uruguay	131	135	167	187	119	0.01	-36.36
Venezuela	1,180	1,013	1,077	1,203	1,762	0.11	46.47
EAST ASIA AND THE PACIFIC	**8,080**	**6,285**	**6,890**	**7,145**	**6,907**	**0.43**	**-3.33**
North-East Asia	**4,741**	**3,021**	**3,210**	**3,227**	**3,066**	**0.19**	**-4.99**
China	155	279	345	290	278	0.02	-4.14
Taiwan (Province of China)	87	28	70	98	82	0.01	-16.33
Hong Kong, China	188	164	212	258	286	0.02	10.85
Japan	4,229	2,391	2,375	2,356	2,098	0.13	-10.95

BAHAMAS

1. Arrivals of non-resident tourists at national borders, by country of residence

	2002	2003	2004	2005	2006	Market share 06	% Change 06-05
Korea, Dem. People's Republic of	3	1	3				
Korea, Republic of	78	158	201	225	322	0.02	43.11
Mongolia	1		4				
South-East Asia	**766**	**566**	**628**	**655**	**615**	**0.04**	**-6.11**
Brunei Darussalam	2	1					
Myanmar	1	1	1				
Cambodia	15	19	6				
Indonesia	48	47	48				
Malaysia	62	46	56	96	69		-28.13
Philippines	430	275	266	282	261	0.02	-7.45
Singapore	149	124	212	206	185	0.01	-10.19
Viet Nam	13	9	10				
Thailand	46	44	29	71	100	0.01	40.85
Australasia	**2,553**	**2,684**	**3,023**	**3,263**	**3,226**	**0.20**	**-1.13**
Australia	1,979	2,162	2,381	2,597	2,551	0.16	-1.77
New Zealand	574	522	642	666	675	0.04	1.35
Melanesia	**5**	**6**	**23**				
Solomon Islands	1	3	4				
Fiji	2	2	13				
Vanuatu	2		5				
Papua New Guinea		1	1				
Micronesia	**1**	**2**	**5**				
Palau	1	2	5				
Polynesia		**6**	**1**				
French Polynesia		6	1				
Other East Asia and the Pacific	**14**						
Other countries of Asia	14						
EUROPE	**80,140**	**93,714**	**84,121**	**85,857**	**82,740**	**5.17**	**-3.63**
Central/Eastern Europe	**1,136**	**1,302**	**1,440**	**1,471**	**1,592**	**0.10**	**8.23**
Azerbaijan	2		2				
Bulgaria	45	56	85	67	91	0.01	35.82
Belarus	4	14	13	11	16		45.45
Czech Republic	148	113	116	127	159	0.01	25.20
Estonia	17	25	23	30	26		-13.33
Georgia		4	14	6	6		
Hungary	159	194	123	206	233	0.01	13.11
Kazakhstan	3		13				
Latvia	23	24	39	45	32		-28.89
Lithuania	37	54	25	26	21		-19.23
Republic of Moldova		2	4	6	2		-66.67
Poland	274	321	472	331	328	0.02	-0.91
Romania	108	134	125	176	149	0.01	-15.34
Russian Federation	222	253	283	269	374	0.02	39.03
Slovakia	38	38	37	81	63		-22.22
Ukraine	50	70	66	90	92	0.01	2.22
Uzbekistan	6						
Northern Europe	**50,322**	**47,739**	**45,520**	**50,262**	**49,559**	**3.10**	**-1.40**
Denmark	721	801	861	888	875	0.05	-1.46
Faeroe Islands	1	7	2	11	2		-81.82
Finland	214	330	472	487	435	0.03	-10.68
Iceland	69	114	134	205	158	0.01	-22.93
Ireland	549	1,407	1,411	1,446	1,310	0.08	-9.41

BAHAMAS

1. Arrivals of non-resident tourists at national borders, by country of residence

	2002	2003	2004	2005	2006	Market share 06	% Change 06-05
Norway	940	839	942	884	879	0.05	-0.57
Sweden	801	992	1,219	1,495	1,339	0.08	-10.43
United Kingdom	47,027	43,249	40,479	44,846	44,561	2.78	-0.64
Southern Europe	**6,312**	**8,759**	**10,848**	**9,323**	**8,386**	**0.52**	**-10.05**
Albania	8	7	49	10	12		20.00
Andorra	6	3	14	16	21		31.25
Bosnia and Herzegovina	1	6	5	3	5		66.67
Croatia	49	68	51	47	61		29.79
Greece	282	273	312	382	347	0.02	-9.16
Italy	3,961	6,057	8,386	6,775	5,720	0.36	-15.57
Malta	27	27	53	54	49		-9.26
Portugal	456	736	475	367	397	0.02	8.17
San Marino	7	2		5	9		80.00
Slovenia	21	23	51	54	44		-18.52
Spain	1,462	1,530	1,428	1,571	1,673	0.10	6.49
TFYR of Macedonia	9	7	9	8	8		
Serbia and Montenegro	23	20	15	31	40		29.03
Western Europe	**21,485**	**34,987**	**25,496**	**23,813**	**22,281**	**1.39**	**-6.43**
Austria	1,110	1,039	974	1,095	1,010	0.06	-7.76
Belgium	820	1,288	1,280	1,227	1,038	0.06	-15.40
France	7,545	20,649	11,408	9,830	8,788	0.55	-10.60
Germany	7,039	7,056	6,630	6,451	6,317	0.39	-2.08
Liechtenstein	19	22	21	34	14		-58.82
Luxembourg	58	125	184	146	160	0.01	9.59
Monaco	101	140	126	193	162	0.01	-16.06
Netherlands	1,491	1,721	1,949	1,682	1,644	0.10	-2.26
Switzerland	3,302	2,947	2,924	3,155	3,148	0.20	-0.22
East Mediterranean Europe	**885**	**927**	**817**	**988**	**922**	**0.06**	**-6.68**
Cyprus	43	88	90	92	68		-26.09
Israel	571	545	522	580	583	0.04	0.52
Turkey	271	294	205	316	271	0.02	-14.24
MIDDLE EAST	**347**	**346**	**616**	**361**	**452**	**0.03**	**25.21**
Middle East	**347**	**346**	**616**	**361**	**452**	**0.03**	**25.21**
Bahrain	12	14	18				
Iraq	1		1				
Jordan	6	8	10				
Kuwait	8	12	41				
Lebanon	20	8	16				
Libyan Arab Jamahiriya			5				
Oman	3	3	2				
Qatar	2		37				
Saudi Arabia	222	139	379	178	223	0.01	25.28
Syrian Arab Republic	2	1					
United Arab Emirates	31	133	88	105	163	0.01	55.24
Egypt	40	28	19	78	66		-15.38
SOUTH ASIA	**377**	**381**	**347**	**285**	**438**	**0.03**	**53.68**
South Asia	**377**	**381**	**347**	**285**	**438**	**0.03**	**53.68**
Bangladesh	10	2	9				
Bhutan		1	1				
Sri Lanka	13	24	14				
India	308	327	265	285	438	0.03	53.68
Iran, Islamic Republic of	13	6	14				
Maldives	6		4				

BAHAMAS

1. Arrivals of non-resident tourists at national borders, by country of residence

	2002	2003	2004	2005	2006	Market share 06	% Change 06-05
Nepal	3	8	21				
Pakistan	24	13	19				
REGION NOT SPECIFIED	**16,583**	**15,456**	**12,536**	**28,282**	**23,693**	**1.48**	**-16.23**
Not Specified	**16,583**	**15,456**	**12,536**	**28,282**	**23,693**	**1.48**	**-16.23**
Other countries of the World	16,583	15,456	12,536	28,282	23,693	1.48	-16.23

Source: World Tourism Organization (UNWTO)

50

BAHAMAS

6. Overnight stays of non-resident tourists in all types of accommodation establishments, by country of residence

	2002	2003	2004	2005	2006	Market share 06	% Change 06-05
TOTAL (*)	8,703,805	8,956,743	9,898,181	10,297,327	10,264,399	100.00	-0.32
AFRICA	15,588	18,501	18,587	18,465	17,463	0.17	-5.43
East Africa	1,002	1,632	991	347	390		12.39
Burundi		3					
Comoros	3						
Ethiopia	45	275	94				
Djibouti		3					
Kenya	269	297	356				
Madagascar	4	1					
Malawi	28	24	87				
Mauritius	111	610	118				
Mozambique		8					
Seychelles	11	25	10				
Zimbabwe	330	182	171	347	390		12.39
Uganda	30	79	61				
United Republic of Tanzania	8	96	70				
Zambia	163	29	24				
Central Africa	155	168	123				
Angola	34	28	34				
Cameroon	52	26	10				
Chad	37	43	11				
Congo	14		34				
Gabon	18	71	34				
North Africa	247	584	522				
Algeria	18	15					
Morocco	225	370	140				
Sudan	1	31					
Tunisia	3	168	382				
Southern Africa	13,501	15,213	15,917	18,118	17,073	0.17	-5.77
Botswana		152	137				
Lesotho		63					
Namibia	3	22	221				
South Africa	12,266	13,414	15,001	17,593	16,376	0.16	-6.92
Swaziland	1,232	1,562	558	525	697	0.01	32.76
West Africa	683	904	1,034				
Benin		5					
Gambia	15		17				
Ghana	379	270	477				
Cote D'Ivoire	89	81	73				
Liberia		15	27				
Mali	14						
Nigeria	140	335	321				
Senegal	35	142	37				
Sierra Leone		50	69				
Togo	11	6	13				
AMERICAS	7,722,342	7,857,967	8,831,985	9,060,180	9,088,383	88.54	0.31
Caribbean	114,941	111,901	135,907	142,203	158,747	1.55	11.63
Antigua and Barbuda	924	871	820	1,045	1,138	0.01	8.90
Barbados	5,984	5,344	6,132	6,803	6,621	0.06	-2.68
Bermuda	4,744	4,974	4,895	6,374	6,030	0.06	-5.40
British Virgin Islands	902	329	510	822	899	0.01	9.37

BAHAMAS

6. Overnight stays of non-resident tourists in all types of accommodation establishments, by country of residence

	2002	2003	2004	2005	2006	Market share 06	% Change 06-05
Cayman Islands	3,607	4,473	7,124	6,258	6,333	0.06	1.20
Cuba	5,115	7,998	9,286	6,546	5,643	0.05	-13.79
Dominica	796	799	581	811	881	0.01	8.63
Dominican Republic	2,388	2,052	1,883	3,017	3,884	0.04	28.74
Grenada	444	668	928	341	524	0.01	53.67
Haiti	8,799	9,972	12,215	12,626	20,073	0.20	58.98
Jamaica	54,353	48,589	57,894	65,602	73,270	0.71	11.69
Martinique	342	307	445	284	388		36.62
Montserrat	44	35	49	324	137		-57.72
Netherlands Antilles	668	228	410	525	523	0.01	-0.38
Aruba	348	565	763	534	375		-29.78
Curacao	908	893	827	835	750	0.01	-10.18
Puerto Rico	631	1,403	1,839	1,308	1,076	0.01	-17.74
Saint Eustatius	4	40	22	19	46		142.11
Saint Kitts and Nevis	427	714	1,443	622	961	0.01	54.50
Anguilla	780	464	289	568	277		-51.23
Saint Lucia	1,795	1,534	2,198	1,681	1,775	0.02	5.59
Saint Maarten	312	219	481	645	709	0.01	9.92
Saint Vincent and the Grenadines	366	455	813	548	596	0.01	8.76
Trinidad and Tobago	10,329	10,568	11,810	11,283	12,708	0.12	12.63
Turks and Caicos Islands	9,810	8,103	11,896	12,507	12,825	0.12	2.54
United States Virgin Islands	120	275	354	196	161		-17.86
Other countries of the Caribbean	1	29		79	144		82.28
Central America	**9,154**	**7,086**	**9,351**	**10,387**	**11,301**	**0.11**	**8.80**
Belize	846	1,470	1,541	1,257	969	0.01	-22.91
Costa Rica	2,656	1,937	2,577	2,882	2,891	0.03	0.31
El Salvador	414	405	522	609	760	0.01	24.79
Guatemala	1,691	989	1,339	1,732	1,771	0.02	2.25
Honduras	1,357	514	646	1,228	1,903	0.02	54.97
Nicaragua	161	246	377	300	411		37.00
Panama	2,029	1,525	2,349	2,379	2,596	0.03	9.12
North America	**7,563,850**	**7,706,781**	**8,650,417**	**8,865,549**	**8,866,575**	**86.38**	**0.01**
Canada	502,101	518,460	618,772	667,310	737,039	7.18	10.45
Greenland	44	12	62				
Mexico	16,253	15,478	19,519	21,854	37,461	0.36	71.41
United States	7,045,452	7,172,831	8,012,064	8,176,385	8,092,075	78.84	-1.03
South America	**34,397**	**32,199**	**36,310**	**42,041**	**51,760**	**0.50**	**23.12**
Argentina	4,373	5,312	5,507	5,650	6,690	0.07	18.41
Bolivia	509	194	307	271	783	0.01	188.93
Brazil	10,051	6,135	9,207	10,221	12,734	0.12	24.59
Chile	2,303	2,389	2,314	2,257	2,368	0.02	4.92
Colombia	2,928	2,894	3,163	4,159	5,977	0.06	43.71
Ecuador	1,518	1,906	1,695	2,661	3,423	0.03	28.64
Guyana	3,152	2,590	2,407	3,779	4,165	0.04	10.21
Paraguay	233	107	229	104	276		165.38
Peru	2,622	3,105	2,495	3,677	3,479	0.03	-5.38
Suriname	177	150	379	224	623	0.01	178.13
Uruguay	912	1,015	1,492	1,303	1,007	0.01	-22.72
Venezuela	5,619	6,402	7,115	7,735	10,235	0.10	32.32
EAST ASIA AND THE PACIFIC	**63,938**	**57,920**	**64,532**	**66,951**	**63,490**	**0.62**	**-5.17**
North-East Asia	**22,211**	**14,717**	**16,916**	**17,282**	**15,477**	**0.15**	**-10.44**
China	874	2,095	2,005	1,928	1,626	0.02	-15.66
Taiwan (Province of China)	559	213	359	514			

BAHAMAS

6. Overnight stays of non-resident tourists in all types of accommodation establishments, by country of residence

	2002	2003	2004	2005	2006	Market share 06	% Change 06-05
Hong Kong, China	1,395	1,104	2,674	1,648	1,842	0.02	11.77
Japan	19,053	10,567	10,818	12,114	10,500	0.10	-13.32
Korea, Dem. People's Republic of	27	3	13				
Korea, Republic of	302	735	1,025	1,078	1,509	0.01	39.98
Mongolia	1		22				
South-East Asia	**7,221**	**5,897**	**7,178**	**7,220**	**5,921**	**0.06**	**-17.99**
Myanmar	1		7				
Cambodia	128	122	163				
Indonesia	278	188	498				
Malaysia	720	256	501	742	388		-47.71
Philippines	4,262	3,856	4,534	4,545	3,679	0.04	-19.05
Singapore	1,340	953	1,162	1,348	974	0.01	-27.74
Viet Nam	145	53	66				
Thailand	347	469	247	585	880	0.01	50.43
Australasia	**34,272**	**37,133**	**40,026**	**42,449**	**42,092**	**0.41**	**-0.84**
Australia	25,678	29,964	29,819	32,517	30,865	0.30	-5.08
New Zealand	8,594	7,169	10,207	9,932	11,227	0.11	13.04
Melanesia	**38**	**70**	**200**				
Solomon Islands		50	25				
Fiji	16	17	111				
Vanuatu	22		47				
Papua New Guinea		3	17				
Micronesia	**93**	**35**	**205**				
Palau	93	35	205				
Polynesia		**68**	**7**				
French Polynesia		68	7				
Other East Asia and the Pacific	**103**						
Other countries of Asia	103						
EUROPE	**766,083**	**887,216**	**863,224**	**903,324**	**865,799**	**8.43**	**-4.15**
Central/Eastern Europe	**10,543**	**11,984**	**18,243**	**16,627**	**16,199**	**0.16**	**-2.57**
Azerbaijan	7		2				
Bulgaria	274	326	1,221	1,474	1,634	0.02	10.85
Belarus	49	129	137	100	139		39.00
Czech Republic	1,124	975	883	949	2,277	0.02	139.94
Estonia	99	140	173	353	101		-71.39
Georgia		24	162	32	24		-25.00
Hungary	1,503	1,577	1,258	2,067	1,997	0.02	-3.39
Kazakhstan	14	185	143				
Latvia	119	102	242	1,343	273		-79.67
Lithuania	373	371	713	508	173		-65.94
Republic of Moldova		6	41	58	25		-56.90
Poland	1,952	3,598	5,756	3,738	3,077	0.03	-17.68
Romania	1,442	1,331	3,490	1,761	2,367	0.02	34.41
Russian Federation	2,507	1,903	3,143	2,624	2,641	0.03	0.65
Slovakia	350	296	328	629	456		-27.50
Ukraine	691	943	551	991	1,015	0.01	2.42
Uzbekistan	39	78					
Northern Europe	**487,735**	**470,635**	**478,539**	**552,448**	**546,353**	**5.32**	**-1.10**
Denmark	7,159	6,867	8,040	8,630	7,797	0.08	-9.65
Faeroe Islands	33	32	21	152	3		-98.03
Finland	2,201	2,095	5,193	4,154	3,973	0.04	-4.36

BAHAMAS

6. Overnight stays of non-resident tourists in all types of accommodation establishments, by country of residence

	2002	2003	2004	2005	2006	Market share 06	% Change 06-05
Iceland	458	1,105	1,935	2,427	1,142	0.01	-52.95
Ireland	4,626	12,355	14,065	15,171	13,171	0.13	-13.18
Norway	10,341	9,058	7,792	7,161	7,821	0.08	9.22
Sweden	7,270	10,282	10,273	14,248	13,591	0.13	-4.61
United Kingdom	455,647	428,841	431,220	500,505	498,855	4.86	-0.33
Southern Europe	**51,113**	**71,833**	**93,691**	**81,547**	**67,712**	**0.66**	**-16.97**
Albania	46	64	316	76	70		-7.89
Andorra	21	8	99	106	299		182.08
Bosnia and Herzegovina	5	31	36	12	62		416.67
Croatia	286	412	324	792	529	0.01	-33.21
Greece	2,454	2,618	2,590	3,416	2,884	0.03	-15.57
Italy	32,112	47,816	72,429	59,552	46,613	0.45	-21.73
Malta	505	521	464	463	348		-24.84
Portugal	3,765	5,711	4,741	3,681	3,338	0.03	-9.32
San Marino	36	5		24	55		129.17
Slovenia	158	97	436	498	383		-23.09
Spain	11,463	14,366	12,112	12,495	12,751	0.12	2.05
TFYR of Macedonia	20	44	49	68	35		-48.53
Serbia and Montenegro	242	140	95	364	345		-5.22
Western Europe	**211,882**	**326,791**	**267,641**	**247,016**	**228,952**	**2.23**	**-7.31**
Austria	13,435	10,821	11,357	12,942	11,749	0.11	-9.22
Belgium	7,034	12,202	11,794	11,027	7,968	0.08	-27.74
France	66,384	170,788	106,087	91,857	81,575	0.79	-11.19
Germany	77,656	83,538	84,606	79,487	77,321	0.75	-2.72
Liechtenstein	213	218	222	394	116		-70.56
Luxembourg	509	1,330	2,017	1,669	2,033	0.02	21.81
Monaco	1,739	1,682	2,041	2,351	2,058	0.02	-12.46
Netherlands	12,532	16,172	19,064	16,232	15,394	0.15	-5.16
Switzerland	32,380	30,040	30,453	31,057	30,738	0.30	-1.03
East Mediterranean Europe	**4,810**	**5,973**	**5,110**	**5,686**	**6,583**	**0.06**	**15.78**
Cyprus	225	556	587	830	417		-49.76
Israel	3,550	3,773	3,422	3,073	4,771	0.05	55.26
Turkey	1,035	1,644	1,101	1,783	1,395	0.01	-21.76
MIDDLE EAST	**2,033**	**2,395**	**3,569**	**2,636**	**4,851**	**0.05**	**84.03**
Middle East	**2,033**	**2,395**	**3,569**	**2,636**	**4,851**	**0.05**	**84.03**
Bahrain	56	79	208				
Jordan	27	42	48				
Kuwait	46	65	166				
Lebanon	110	64	107				
Libyan Arab Jamahiriya			30				
Oman	33	24	6				
Qatar	4		156				
Saudi Arabia	1,424	1,406	2,334	1,661	3,314	0.03	99.52
Syrian Arab Republic	22		7				
United Arab Emirates	101	455	366	590	1,110	0.01	88.14
Egypt	210	260	141	385	427		10.91
SOUTH ASIA	**2,203**	**3,454**	**3,303**	**2,891**	**2,889**	**0.03**	**-0.07**
South Asia	**2,203**	**3,454**	**3,303**	**2,891**	**2,889**	**0.03**	**-0.07**
Bangladesh	52	9	66				
Bhutan		14	3				
Sri Lanka	25	270	192	74	472		537.84
India	1,874	3,007	2,726	2,817	2,417	0.02	-14.20

BAHAMAS

6. Overnight stays of non-resident tourists in all types of accommodation establishments, by country of residence

	2002	2003	2004	2005	2006	Market share 06	% Change 06-05
Iran, Islamic Republic of	76	25	63				
Maldives	17		33				
Nepal	21	27	129				
Pakistan	138	102	91				
REGION NOT SPECIFIED	**131,618**	**129,290**	**112,981**	**242,880**	**221,524**	**2.16**	**-8.79**
Not Specified	**131,618**	**129,290**	**112,981**	**242,880**	**221,524**	**2.16**	**-8.79**
Other countries of the World	131,618	129,290	112,981	242,880	221,524	2.16	-8.79

Source: World Tourism Organization (UNWTO)

BAHRAIN

2. Arrivals of non-resident visitors at national borders, by nationality

	2002	2003	2004	2005	2006	Market share 06	% Change 06-05
TOTAL (*)	4,830,943	4,844,497	5,667,331	6,313,232	7,288,716	100.00	15.45
AFRICA	46,663	59,989	76,325	82,121	98,749	1.35	20.25
East Africa	6,933	8,947	9,449	11,526	14,805	0.20	28.45
Burundi	2	1		1	2		100.00
Comoros	16	12	26	15	15		
Ethiopia	2,719	3,867	4,125	5,774	8,499	0.12	47.19
Eritrea	1,045	1,152	1,515	1,975	2,049	0.03	3.75
Djibouti	36	48	122	175	142		-18.86
Kenya	1,154	1,414	1,112	1,253	1,413	0.02	12.77
Madagascar	2	4	11	19	13		-31.58
Malawi	20	27	5	9	7		-22.22
Mauritius	63	91	314	321	339		5.61
Mozambique	5	7	21	20	41		105.00
Rwanda	7		10	3	2		-33.33
Seychelles	450	375	401	387	481	0.01	24.29
Somalia	592	704	899	1,084	1,183	0.02	9.13
Zimbabwe	101	124	281	167	183		9.58
Uganda	92	135	69	55	81		47.27
United Republic of Tanzania	615	980	515	237	309		30.38
Zambia	14	6	23	31	46		48.39
Central Africa	165	375	322	226	238		5.31
Angola		4	15		4		
Cameroon	44	48	76	85	79		-7.06
Central African Republic		2		3	2		-33.33
Chad	103	295	203	115	108		-6.09
Congo	10	22	23	21	32		52.38
Democratic Republic of the Congo	1	1	1	1	3		200.00
Equatorial Guinea	3	1					
Gabon	4	2	3		10		
Sao Tome and Principe			1	1			
North Africa	26,489	33,836	42,038	44,813	54,190	0.74	20.92
Algeria	942	1,004	1,452	2,047	3,167	0.04	54.71
Morocco	7,638	9,162	11,992	10,995	12,399	0.17	12.77
Sudan	15,390	20,646	25,397	28,084	34,608	0.47	23.23
Tunisia	2,519	3,024	3,197	3,687	4,016	0.06	8.92
Southern Africa	11,966	15,350	22,521	22,461	25,662	0.35	14.25
Botswana	7	6	2	9	34		277.78
Lesotho	2	2		1	23		2,200.00
Namibia	6	2	5	27	16		-40.74
South Africa	11,948	15,340	22,513	22,386	25,586	0.35	14.29
Swaziland	3		1	38	3		-92.11
West Africa	1,110	1,481	1,995	3,095	3,854	0.05	24.52
Cape Verde	3	1	3	3	3		
Benin	7	9	7	14	9		-35.71
Gambia	13	17	17	24	12		-50.00
Ghana	228	297	402	259	286		10.42
Guinea	48	76	42	40	25		-37.50
Cote D'Ivoire	53	36	44	39	54		38.46
Liberia	46	55	68	68	80		17.65
Mali	38	61	70	128	111		-13.28
Mauritania	60	54	45	55	93		69.09
Niger	28	36	33	84	149		77.38
Nigeria	509	719	1,133	2,052	2,719	0.04	32.50

BAHRAIN

2. Arrivals of non-resident visitors at national borders, by nationality

	2002	2003	2004	2005	2006	Market share 06	% Change 06-05
Guinea-Bissau			1	3	6		100.00
Senegal	58	88	71	275	202		-26.55
Sierra Leone	13	21	28	27	55		103.70
Togo		1	5	8	38		375.00
Burkina Faso	6	10	26	16	12		-25.00
AMERICAS	**177,089**	**192,206**	**200,481**	**189,778**	**234,467**	**3.22**	**23.55**
Caribbean	**591**	**910**	**984**	**1,164**	**1,708**	**0.02**	**46.74**
Antigua and Barbuda			1	1	1		
Bahamas	31	36		2	3		50.00
Barbados	5	3	3	8	17		112.50
Cayman Islands			1		3		
Cuba	22	26	36	28	38		35.71
Dominica	41	37	30	36	17		-52.78
Dominican Republic	28	36	46	60	38		-36.67
Grenada	5	9	12	7	18		157.14
Haiti	5	3	7	7	5		-28.57
Jamaica	50	44	40	44	53		20.45
Netherlands Antilles			1		1		
Saint Eustatius	3		2	1			
Saint Kitts and Nevis					1		
Saint Lucia	1	3	2	3	21		600.00
Saint Vincent and the Grenadines			8	3	4		33.33
Trinidad and Tobago	400	713	795	964	1,488	0.02	54.36
Central America	**355**	**442**	**422**	**355**	**481**	**0.01**	**35.49**
Belize	124	115	94	66	84		27.27
Costa Rica	99	128	143	78	112		43.59
El Salvador	5	2	1	7	16		128.57
Guatemala	15	18	18	29	52		79.31
Honduras	103	165	146	150	150		
Nicaragua		2	4	4	12		200.00
Panama	9	12	16	21	55		161.90
North America	**173,091**	**187,236**	**194,834**	**182,590**	**223,207**	**3.06**	**22.24**
Canada	33,419	37,307	45,008	44,829	54,267	0.74	21.05
Mexico	345	360	505	438	574	0.01	31.05
United States	139,327	149,569	149,321	137,323	168,366	2.31	22.61
South America	**3,052**	**3,618**	**4,241**	**5,669**	**9,071**	**0.12**	**60.01**
Argentina	694	638	870	995	1,313	0.02	31.96
Bolivia	36	65	83	49	143		191.84
Brazil	920	1,050	1,374	1,447	1,803	0.02	24.60
Chile	65	83	103	135	121		-10.37
Colombia	587	611	735	1,052	2,161	0.03	105.42
Ecuador	175	345	158	189	187		-1.06
French Guiana	1						
Guyana		5	3	9	11		22.22
Paraguay	2	5	8	25	13		-48.00
Peru	141	137	106	205	690	0.01	236.59
Suriname		1					
Uruguay	9	4	19	103	53		-48.54
Venezuela	422	674	782	1,460	2,576	0.04	76.44
EAST ASIA AND THE PACIFIC	**187,058**	**211,749**	**267,978**	**287,257**	**374,335**	**5.14**	**30.31**
North-East Asia	**26,192**	**25,851**	**32,435**	**36,041**	**41,022**	**0.56**	**13.82**
China	6,693	6,051	7,669	8,699	10,136	0.14	16.52
Hong Kong, China	1,812	3,013	6,324	7,433	4,989	0.07	-32.88

BAHRAIN

2. Arrivals of non-resident visitors at national borders, by nationality

	2002	2003	2004	2005	2006	Market share 06	% Change 06-05
Japan	13,482	12,430	12,749	14,158	17,050	0.23	20.43
Korea, Dem. People's Republic of	69	115	221	102	45		-55.88
Korea, Republic of	4,128	4,227	5,429	5,614	8,767	0.12	56.16
Macao, China	1	5	34	34	21		-38.24
Mongolia	7	10	9	1	14		1,300.00
South-East Asia	**137,247**	**159,778**	**199,045**	**209,814**	**286,901**	**3.94**	**36.74**
Brunei Darussalam	89	46	74	58	75		29.31
Myanmar	174	233	429	759	722	0.01	-4.87
Cambodia	5	17	67	50	102		104.00
Indonesia	23,865	30,379	34,776	29,648	42,525	0.58	43.43
Lao People's Democratic Republic	8	2	13	7	5		-28.57
Malaysia	4,335	4,670	8,071	9,132	12,638	0.17	38.39
Philippines	101,875	109,730	134,369	143,641	198,331	2.72	38.07
Timor-Leste					5		
Singapore	1,432	1,459	2,921	2,926	3,847	0.05	31.48
Viet Nam	39	48	55	65	134		106.15
Thailand	5,425	13,194	18,270	23,528	28,517	0.39	21.20
Australasia	**23,547**	**26,037**	**35,944**	**40,984**	**46,330**	**0.64**	**13.04**
Australia	18,099	19,990	28,293	33,906	38,188	0.52	12.63
New Zealand	5,448	6,047	7,651	7,078	8,142	0.11	15.03
Melanesia	**60**	**64**	**535**	**401**	**64**		**-84.04**
Solomon Islands		2			1		
Fiji	54	56	535	392	61		-84.44
Vanuatu	3	1					
Papua New Guinea	3	5		9	2		-77.78
Micronesia	**9**	**9**	**3**	**3**	**7**		**133.33**
Kiribati	7	6		1	4		300.00
Nauru	1	3	1	2	2		
Marshall Islands			2		1		
Palau	1						
Polynesia	**3**	**10**	**16**	**14**	**11**		**-21.43**
American Samoa		2	4	1			
French Polynesia	3	4	6	4	3		-25.00
Tonga			6	9	4		-55.56
Tuvalu		4			4		
EUROPE	**256,437**	**260,698**	**333,920**	**357,623**	**429,750**	**5.90**	**20.17**
Central/Eastern Europe	**8,399**	**7,660**	**11,507**	**12,399**	**14,699**	**0.20**	**18.55**
Azerbaijan	159	137	190	291	411	0.01	41.24
Armenia	72	34	46	56	53		-5.36
Bulgaria	949	1,162	1,207	1,197	1,660	0.02	38.68
Belarus	586	468	509	538	612	0.01	13.75
Czech Republic/Slovakia	21	27	72	37	21		-43.24
Czech Republic	546	622	830	688	936	0.01	36.05
Estonia	19	50	258	316	270		-14.56
Georgia	115	111	117	106	171		61.32
Hungary	571	477	682	551	611	0.01	10.89
Kazakhstan	141	87	193	220	394	0.01	79.09
Kyrgyzstan	98	135	182	120	141		17.50
Latvia	74	90	188	117	150		28.21
Lithuania	60	66	113	106	166		56.60
Republic of Moldova	90	87	119	114	149		30.70
Poland	886	984	1,209	1,207	1,533	0.02	27.01
Romania	873	783	1,214	1,135	1,790	0.02	57.71

BAHRAIN

2. Arrivals of non-resident visitors at national borders, by nationality

	2002	2003	2004	2005	2006	Market share 06	% Change 06-05
Russian Federation	1,123	1,170	2,072	2,935	3,180	0.04	8.35
Slovakia	217	159	288	383	475	0.01	24.02
Tajikistan	32	9	84	90	65		-27.78
Turkmenistan	48	43	54	59	89		50.85
Ukraine	758	685	865	1,093	1,102	0.02	0.82
Uzbekistan	961	274	1,015	1,040	720	0.01	-30.77
Northern Europe	**175,790**	**178,886**	**214,062**	**232,827**	**272,546**	**3.74**	**17.06**
Denmark	2,059	2,240	2,611	2,414	2,709	0.04	12.22
Finland	720	786	883	1,014	1,004	0.01	-0.99
Iceland	29	19	30	36	166		361.11
Ireland	10,692	10,714	13,314	13,297	15,903	0.22	19.60
Norway	2,009	1,968	2,299	2,335	3,439	0.05	47.28
Sweden	2,724	3,271	3,922	3,628	4,251	0.06	17.17
United Kingdom	157,557	159,888	191,003	210,103	245,074	3.36	16.64
Southern Europe	**12,783**	**12,636**	**20,916**	**23,573**	**28,548**	**0.39**	**21.10**
Albania	54	13	39	35	39		11.43
Andorra	1						
Bosnia and Herzegovina	126	132	129	315	267		-15.24
Croatia	317	443	556	566	743	0.01	31.27
Gibraltar	1						
Greece	2,114	1,804	5,705	7,436	7,856	0.11	5.65
Italy	7,907	7,886	10,837	11,395	14,078	0.19	23.55
Malta	140	150	218	130	169		30.00
Portugal	488	513	890	683	880	0.01	28.84
San Marino	3	2	3	6	5		-16.67
Slovenia	36	52	84	135	124		-8.15
Spain	1,386	1,473	2,150	2,489	4,011	0.06	61.15
TFYR of Macedonia	59	22	48	103	70		-32.04
Serbia and Montenegro	151	146	257	280	306		9.29
Western Europe	**44,499**	**47,380**	**70,468**	**72,162**	**93,930**	**1.29**	**30.17**
Austria	1,514	1,969	3,341	3,234	4,419	0.06	36.64
Belgium	2,710	2,875	4,490	4,225	5,044	0.07	19.38
France	16,372	16,979	21,277	21,819	27,516	0.38	26.11
Germany	13,393	14,251	24,930	26,498	34,775	0.48	31.24
Liechtenstein	8	15	27	16	18		12.50
Luxembourg	65	64	89	99	161		62.63
Monaco	1	1	7	2	8		300.00
Netherlands	8,415	9,158	13,262	13,279	17,249	0.24	29.90
Switzerland	1,954	2,043	2,978	2,978	4,724	0.06	58.63
Other countries of Western Europe	67	25	67	12	16		33.33
East Mediterranean Europe	**14,966**	**14,136**	**16,967**	**16,662**	**20,027**	**0.27**	**20.20**
Cyprus	2,514	1,927	2,662	2,522	2,760	0.04	9.44
Turkey	12,452	12,209	14,305	14,140	17,267	0.24	22.11
MIDDLE EAST	**3,641,900**	**3,558,805**	**4,140,624**	**4,676,446**	**5,209,825**	**71.48**	**11.41**
Middle East	**3,641,900**	**3,558,805**	**4,140,624**	**4,676,446**	**5,209,825**	**71.48**	**11.41**
Palestine	14,265	8,897	13,666	14,489	19,385	0.27	33.79
Iraq	3,472	3,600	6,506	9,804	10,906	0.15	11.24
Jordan	67,301	74,362	90,365	95,732	112,894	1.55	17.93
Kuwait	218,570	180,711	213,821	239,532	298,616	4.10	24.67
Lebanon	46,871	52,285	68,549	70,018	87,247	1.20	24.61
Libyan Arab Jamahiriya	439	457	664	742	768	0.01	3.50
Oman	25,820	25,593	29,089	32,482	38,347	0.53	18.06
Qatar	89,939	86,680	103,172	132,546	154,285	2.12	16.40
Saudi Arabia	3,030,039	2,963,641	3,415,008	3,864,624	4,225,623	57.97	9.34

BAHRAIN

2. Arrivals of non-resident visitors at national borders, by nationality

	2002	2003	2004	2005	2006	Market share 06	% Change 06-05
Syrian Arab Republic	28,346	35,178	42,670	45,236	57,332	0.79	26.74
United Arab Emirates	38,357	37,328	41,953	44,296	51,691	0.71	16.69
Egypt	53,719	60,651	79,913	88,040	106,470	1.46	20.93
Yemen	24,762	29,422	35,248	38,905	46,261	0.63	18.91
SOUTH ASIA	**521,796**	**561,050**	**648,003**	**720,007**	**941,590**	**12.92**	**30.78**
South Asia	**521,796**	**561,050**	**648,003**	**720,007**	**941,590**	**12.92**	**30.78**
Afghanistan	148	279	352	452	1,250	0.02	176.55
Bangladesh	46,847	43,171	47,975	51,679	78,854	1.08	52.58
Bhutan		1	12	16	4		-75.00
Sri Lanka	21,702	21,594	23,061	23,042	26,936	0.37	16.90
India	312,975	350,996	418,767	466,849	590,198	8.10	26.42
Iran, Islamic Republic of	10,880	16,161	20,304	21,934	27,640	0.38	26.01
Maldives	12	21	33	12	33		175.00
Nepal	30,887	21,104	12,977	17,974	44,417	0.61	147.12
Pakistan	98,345	107,723	124,522	138,049	172,258	2.36	24.78

Source: World Tourism Organization (UNWTO)

BANGLADESH

1. Arrivals of non-resident tourists at national borders, by nationality

	2002	2003	2004	2005	2006	Market share 06	% Change 06-05
TOTAL	207,246	244,509	271,270	207,662	200,311	100.00	-3.54
AFRICA	1,297	2,012	2,147	1,730	1,953	0.97	12.89
East Africa	364	670	572	378	341	0.17	-9.79
Burundi	1		1	5	3		-40.00
Ethiopia	55	103	86	59	62	0.03	5.08
Eritrea	1	2	9				
Djibouti	8	2	3	3			
Kenya	97	176	139	106	66	0.03	-37.74
Madagascar	2	5		1	1		
Malawi	1	1		2			
Mauritius	28	29	59	35	14	0.01	-60.00
Mozambique	18	7	19	18	19	0.01	5.56
Rwanda		2					
Somalia	53	90	47	36	19	0.01	-47.22
Zimbabwe	35	77	92	45	37	0.02	-17.78
Uganda	18	94	77	9	37	0.02	311.11
United Republic of Tanzania	26	55	13	41	22	0.01	-46.34
Zambia	21	27	27	18	61	0.03	238.89
Central Africa	16	26	32	37	45	0.02	21.62
Angola		10		2			
Cameroon	11	12	18	34	45	0.02	32.35
Chad	5	2					
Congo		2	14	1			
North Africa	273	220	434	172	316	0.16	83.72
Algeria	36	23	19		11	0.01	
Morocco	158	117	292	116	161	0.08	38.79
Western Sahara					1		
Sudan	42	40	91	17	99	0.05	482.35
Tunisia	37	40	32	39	44	0.02	12.82
Southern Africa	419	619	600	695	808	0.40	16.26
Botswana				3			
Namibia	3	11	6	1	8		700.00
South Africa	416	608	592	691	800	0.40	15.77
Swaziland			2				
West Africa	225	477	509	448	443	0.22	-1.12
Benin		37	27	17			
Gambia			7	31	8		-74.19
Ghana	22	19	23	12	8		-33.33
Guinea		2					
Cote D'Ivoire	2	1	9	5	62	0.03	1,140.00
Liberia				2	8		300.00
Mali	1		3	3			
Mauritania	18	38	53	106	111	0.06	4.72
Niger				22	80	0.04	263.64
Nigeria	163	307	182	214	152	0.08	-28.97
Saint Helena		3					
Senegal	15	28	27	23	14	0.01	-39.13
Sierra Leone	4	42	178	13			
AMERICAS	17,538	30,795	37,404	18,673	25,129	12.54	34.57
Caribbean	36	118	73	229	19	0.01	-91.70
Barbados	1	18	4				
Cuba		1	5	2	6		200.00

BANGLADESH

1. Arrivals of non-resident tourists at national borders, by nationality

	2002	2003	2004	2005	2006	Market share 06	% Change 06-05
Dominica	4	6					
Dominican Republic	1	6	16				
Haiti	2	17	25	227	13	0.01	-94.27
Jamaica	3	25	1				
Trinidad and Tobago	25	45	22				
Central America	**18**	**41**	**25**	**33**	**36**	**0.02**	**9.09**
Costa Rica		29	6	27	29	0.01	7.41
El Salvador	1	1		5	6		20.00
Guatemala	9	2	9	1			
Honduras	1	7	10		1		
Nicaragua	7						
Panama		2					
North America	**17,346**	**30,393**	**36,965**	**18,035**	**24,784**	**12.37**	**37.42**
Canada	3,603	5,847	8,964	4,519	5,085	2.54	12.52
Greenland					15	0.01	
Mexico	121	88	106	94	3,168	1.58	3,270.21
United States	13,622	24,458	27,895	13,422	16,516	8.25	23.05
South America	**138**	**243**	**341**	**376**	**290**	**0.14**	**-22.87**
Argentina	47	30	47	61	20	0.01	-67.21
Bolivia	2	1	3	1	8		700.00
Brazil	40	89	97	115	138	0.07	20.00
Chile	11	12	24	27	7		-74.07
Colombia	2	35	81	54	70	0.03	29.63
Ecuador	1	4	5	14	5		-64.29
Guyana	9	21	19				
Peru	19	27	52	102	37	0.02	-63.73
Uruguay		2					
Venezuela	7	22	13	2	5		150.00
EAST ASIA AND THE PACIFIC	**41,019**	**42,824**	**51,230**	**35,887**	**37,032**	**18.49**	**3.19**
North-East Asia	**22,524**	**23,311**	**26,610**	**20,752**	**17,398**	**8.69**	**-16.16**
China	6,681	7,021	9,238	6,892	6,955	3.47	0.91
Taiwan (Province of China)	1,621	1,988	2,655	2,127	1,662	0.83	-21.86
Hong Kong, China	332	310	270	103	264	0.13	156.31
Japan	7,325	6,523	7,857	6,269	4,370	2.18	-30.29
Korea, Republic of	6,511	7,465	6,575	5,332	4,135	2.06	-22.45
Mongolia	54	4	15	29	12	0.01	-58.62
South-East Asia	**14,271**	**14,562**	**16,080**	**9,961**	**13,656**	**6.82**	**37.09**
Brunei Darussalam	49	32	40	13	31	0.02	138.46
Myanmar	358	437	649	541	1,074	0.54	98.52
Cambodia	54	85	75	22	41	0.02	86.36
Indonesia	1,455	1,507	2,155	2,107	1,676	0.84	-20.46
Lao People's Democratic Republic	19	15	10	1	3		200.00
Malaysia	3,706	3,689	4,750	1,045	2,671	1.33	155.60
Philippines	1,550	1,650	1,648	1,627	1,930	0.96	18.62
Singapore	2,920	2,786	3,073	1,562	2,281	1.14	46.03
Viet Nam	163	173	304	88	480	0.24	445.45
Thailand	3,997	4,188	3,376	2,955	3,469	1.73	17.39
Australasia	**4,182**	**4,881**	**8,421**	**5,167**	**5,962**	**2.98**	**15.39**
Australia	3,409	3,787	6,815	3,686	4,878	2.44	32.34
New Zealand	773	1,094	1,606	1,481	1,084	0.54	-26.81
Melanesia	**22**	**55**	**117**	**4**	**15**	**0.01**	**275.00**
Fiji	22	45	51	4	15	0.01	275.00
Papua New Guinea		10	66				

BANGLADESH

1. Arrivals of non-resident tourists at national borders, by nationality

	2002	2003	2004	2005	2006	Market share 06	% Change 06-05
Micronesia				2			
Other countries of Micronesia				2			
Polynesia	20	15	2	1	1		
American Samoa		5					
Tonga	18	8	1		1		
Samoa	2	2	1	1			
EUROPE	46,641	63,749	77,307	48,961	56,709	28.31	15.82
Central/Eastern Europe	105	104	248	623	1,400	0.70	124.72
Azerbaijan	1			4	146	0.07	3,550.00
Armenia			1				
Bulgaria	1	4	62	121	104	0.05	-14.05
Belarus	1						
Czech Republic/Slovakia			1	2	31	0.02	1,450.00
Czech Republic	13	5	13	21	24	0.01	14.29
Estonia				3			
Georgia	6	1					
Hungary	5	7	16	9	8		-11.11
Kazakhstan		3	3	1	5		400.00
Kyrgyzstan	3	1	2	5	8		60.00
Latvia	1	1	33	14	11	0.01	-21.43
Lithuania			2				
Poland	12	23	10	184	21	0.01	-88.59
Romania		5	4	6	38	0.02	533.33
Russian Federation	26	33	17	198	723	0.36	265.15
Slovakia	10	1	24	17	52	0.03	205.88
Tajikistan					5		
Turkmenistan			4				
Ukraine	24	20	42	38	179	0.09	371.05
Uzbekistan	2		14		45	0.02	
Northern Europe	33,205	47,665	59,265	32,889	42,037	20.99	27.81
Denmark	1,248	1,408	1,930	1,137	1,268	0.63	11.52
Finland	292	378	376	318	425	0.21	33.65
Iceland	91	1	3		103	0.05	
Ireland	312	676	904	703	511	0.26	-27.31
Norway	821	1,002	1,282	1,025	725	0.36	-29.27
Sweden	1,536	2,062	2,360	2,414	1,869	0.93	-22.58
United Kingdom	28,905	42,138	52,410	27,292	37,136	18.54	36.07
Southern Europe	2,967	3,471	3,762	3,241	3,053	1.52	-5.80
Albania		6	2				
Bosnia and Herzegovina	4		8		14	0.01	
Croatia			2	3	2		-33.33
Gibraltar					6		
Greece	81	147	211	164	174	0.09	6.10
Holy See	1	5		10	7		-30.00
Italy	2,112	2,420	2,629	1,800	1,667	0.83	-7.39
Malta	1	11	5				
Portugal	71	45	108	167	220	0.11	31.74
San Marino	1						
Slovenia		7	4	5	2		-60.00
Spain	695	829	793	1,091	958	0.48	-12.19
Yugoslavia, Sfr (Former)	1	1			3		
Serbia and Montenegro				1			
Western Europe	9,956	11,928	13,432	11,520	9,382	4.68	-18.56

BANGLADESH

1. Arrivals of non-resident tourists at national borders, by nationality

	2002	2003	2004	2005	2006	Market share 06	% Change 06-05
Austria	87	115	354	881	286	0.14	-67.54
Belgium	795	1,089	1,203	1,080	838	0.42	-22.41
France	2,589	2,924	3,157	2,736	2,674	1.33	-2.27
Germany	3,297	4,184	4,812	3,128	3,190	1.59	1.98
Luxembourg		8	10				
Netherlands	2,524	2,735	2,939	2,431	1,416	0.71	-41.75
Switzerland	664	873	957	1,264	978	0.49	-22.63
East Mediterranean Europe	**408**	**580**	**600**	**688**	**837**	**0.42**	**21.66**
Cyprus	7	44	35	14	1		-92.86
Israel	26	26	6		16	0.01	
Turkey	375	510	559	674	820	0.41	21.66
Other Europe		1					
Other countries of Europe		1					
MIDDLE EAST	**3,128**	**2,626**	**3,243**	**2,861**	**4,021**	**2.01**	**40.55**
Middle East	**3,128**	**2,626**	**3,243**	**2,861**	**4,021**	**2.01**	**40.55**
Bahrain	40	38	24	55	43	0.02	-21.82
Palestine	31	130	458	322	599	0.30	86.02
Iraq	24	18	60	12	64	0.03	433.33
Jordan	236	383	373	206	238	0.12	15.53
Kuwait	249	265	268	194	206	0.10	6.19
Lebanon	54	65	118	153	185	0.09	20.92
Libyan Arab Jamahiriya	25	29	34	29	14	0.01	-51.72
Oman	101	63	78	153	164	0.08	7.19
Qatar	179	34	54	41	126	0.06	207.32
Saudi Arabia	1,468	1,167	1,134	731	1,078	0.54	47.47
Syrian Arab Republic	119	96	66	134	254	0.13	89.55
United Arab Emirates	343	120	94	33	18	0.01	-45.45
Egypt	208	170	294	663	756	0.38	14.03
Yemen	51	48	188	135	276	0.14	104.44
SOUTH ASIA	**97,623**	**102,503**	**99,939**	**99,458**	**75,467**	**37.67**	**-24.12**
South Asia	**97,623**	**102,503**	**99,939**	**99,458**	**75,467**	**37.67**	**-24.12**
Afghanistan	20	105	221	104	58	0.03	-44.23
Bhutan	1,241	1,228	847	1,187	1,422	0.71	19.80
Sri Lanka	2,524	2,831	2,826	2,322	2,410	1.20	3.79
India	80,415	84,704	80,469	86,231	60,516	30.21	-29.82
Iran, Islamic Republic of	411	311	337	345	266	0.13	-22.90
Maldives	150	182	98	220	693	0.35	215.00
Nepal	4,159	3,904	3,144	3,378	3,422	1.71	1.30
Pakistan	8,703	9,238	11,997	5,671	6,680	3.33	17.79
REGION NOT SPECIFIED					**92**		
Not Specified					**92**		
Other countries of the World					92		

Source: World Tourism Organization (UNWTO)

BARBADOS

1. Arrivals of non-resident tourists at national borders, by country of residence

		2002	2003	2004	2005	2006	Market share 06	% Change 06-05
TOTAL	(*)	497,899	531,211	551,502	547,534	562,558	100.00	2.74
AFRICA		626	668	753	1,117	988	0.18	-11.55
East Africa		102	96	154	177	152	0.03	-14.12
Ethiopia		3	2	6	3	7		133.33
Kenya		37	41	55	47	43	0.01	-8.51
Malawi		1	1	6	13	5		-61.54
Mauritius		2	5	20	15	22		46.67
Rwanda		2	1	6	6	3		-50.00
Seychelles		4	7	10	1	5		400.00
Zimbabwe		28	18	31	34	23		-32.35
Uganda		8	7	7	18	10		-44.44
United Republic of Tanzania		2	7	5	26	9		-65.38
Zambia		15	7	8	14	25		78.57
Central Africa		10	9	2	7	17		142.86
Angola		2	2	1		9		
Cameroon		4	1	1	7	2		-71.43
Congo		4	6			6		
North Africa		12	17	13	15	25		66.67
Morocco		5	6	5	8	11		37.50
Sudan		3	7	1	2	5		150.00
Tunisia		4	4	7	5	9		80.00
Southern Africa		378	397	414	720	475	0.08	-34.03
Botswana		43	36	34	51	27		-47.06
Lesotho			2	1	9	3		-66.67
Namibia		3	3	2	9	7		-22.22
South Africa		327	354	373	644	433	0.08	-32.76
Swaziland		5	2	4	7	5		-28.57
West Africa		124	149	170	198	319	0.06	61.11
Benin		1	2			4		
Gambia		1	6	1	6	6		
Ghana		9	24	23	30	31	0.01	3.33
Guinea		1	1		8	2		-75.00
Liberia		6	3	1	1	1		
Mali		2	1		1	4		300.00
Nigeria		103	111	143	131	265	0.05	102.29
Sierra Leone			1	2	21	3		-85.71
Burkina Faso		1				3		
AMERICAS		275,144	291,623	301,268	311,222	312,317	55.52	0.35
Caribbean		86,227	92,172	99,655	108,957	107,867	19.17	-1.00
Antigua and Barbuda		5,719	6,514	7,337	7,130	5,886	1.05	-17.45
Bahamas		1,081	1,116	1,067	1,173	1,231	0.22	4.94
Bermuda		1,591	1,509	1,660	1,595	1,296	0.23	-18.75
British Virgin Islands		1,995	2,288	2,472	2,513	2,665	0.47	6.05
Cayman Islands		875	820	787	758	839	0.15	10.69
Cuba		181	180	176	276	340	0.06	23.19
Dominica		3,465	3,907	4,770	5,245	5,590	0.99	6.58
Dominican Republic		335	274	281	297	434	0.08	46.13
Grenada		5,792	5,953	7,850	7,896	6,269	1.11	-20.61
Guadeloupe		683	982	1,485	1,778	1,049	0.19	-41.00
Haiti		132	128	245	264	123	0.02	-53.41
Jamaica		6,007	7,010	7,349	7,969	9,497	1.69	19.17
Martinique		1,306	1,068	1,439	1,816	1,872	0.33	3.08

BARBADOS

1. Arrivals of non-resident tourists at national borders, by country of residence

	2002	2003	2004	2005	2006	Market share 06	% Change 06-05
Montserrat	257	266	280	269	278	0.05	3.35
Netherlands Antilles	1,383	1,758	2,209	2,013	2,085	0.37	3.58
Aruba	96	152	111	98	176	0.03	79.59
Curacao	106	124	146	178	158	0.03	-11.24
Puerto Rico	1,365	1,187	969	1,019	950	0.17	-6.77
Saint Kitts and Nevis	2,267	2,479	3,610	4,179	3,962	0.70	-5.19
Anguilla	720	606	592	664	729	0.13	9.79
Saint Lucia	12,986	13,661	14,672	15,592	12,989	2.31	-16.69
Saint Vincent and the Grenadines	11,393	11,800	12,750	13,896	13,982	2.49	0.62
Trinidad and Tobago	25,559	27,530	26,492	30,889	34,480	6.13	11.63
Turks and Caicos Islands	209	163	202	204	207	0.04	1.47
United States Virgin Islands	724	697	704	703	780	0.14	10.95
Other countries of the Caribbean				543			
Central America	**1,003**	**1,090**	**1,037**	**1,076**	**1,222**	**0.22**	**13.57**
Belize	342	376	393	379	436	0.08	15.04
Costa Rica	136	189	164	157	123	0.02	-21.66
El Salvador	49	46	38	35	47	0.01	34.29
Guatemala	126	141	109	86	93	0.02	8.14
Honduras	60	37	28	44	22		-50.00
Nicaragua	35	24	16	32	31	0.01	-3.13
Panama	255	277	289	343	470	0.08	37.03
North America	**170,575**	**179,441**	**180,023**	**179,111**	**180,429**	**32.07**	**0.74**
Canada	46,754	49,641	50,032	47,690	49,198	8.75	3.16
Greenland				1			
Mexico	392	474	327	415	464	0.08	11.81
United States	123,429	129,326	129,664	131,005	130,767	23.25	-0.18
South America	**17,339**	**18,920**	**20,553**	**22,078**	**22,799**	**4.05**	**3.27**
Argentina	165	196	226	169	248	0.04	46.75
Bolivia	16	15	16	19	34	0.01	78.95
Brazil	371	478	359	429	452	0.08	5.36
Chile	76	90	124	78	93	0.02	19.23
Colombia	221	439	323	365	319	0.06	-12.60
Ecuador	36	56	39	22	64	0.01	190.91
French Guiana	74	81		119	88	0.02	-26.05
Guyana	13,589	15,063	16,862	18,698	19,312	3.43	3.28
Paraguay	20	6	4	1	3		200.00
Peru	86	92	55	80	69	0.01	-13.75
Suriname	500	528	540	532	601	0.11	12.97
Uruguay	32	53	53	26	32	0.01	23.08
Venezuela	2,153	1,823	1,952	1,540	1,484	0.26	-3.64
EAST ASIA AND THE PACIFIC	**2,103**	**4,027**	**2,679**	**2,710**	**2,758**	**0.49**	**1.77**
North-East Asia	**584**	**614**	**626**	**882**	**744**	**0.13**	**-15.65**
China	274	185	214	372	355	0.06	-4.57
Taiwan (Province of China)	22	40	37	25	37	0.01	48.00
Hong Kong, China	50	89	62	91	97	0.02	6.59
Japan	238	300	309	297	244	0.04	-17.85
Korea, Dem. People's Republic of			4	97	11		-88.66
South-East Asia	**359**	**461**	**536**	**529**	**589**	**0.10**	**11.34**
Brunei Darussalam	3	6	2	4	2		-50.00
Indonesia	39	46	25	30	49	0.01	63.33
Malaysia	26	48	44	34	65	0.01	91.18
Philippines	155	221	318	316	314	0.06	-0.63
Singapore	104	111	115	104	99	0.02	-4.81
Viet Nam	1			1	4		300.00

BARBADOS

1. Arrivals of non-resident tourists at national borders, by country of residence

	2002	2003	2004	2005	2006	Market share 06	% Change 06-05
Thailand	31	29	32	40	56	0.01	40.00
Australasia	**1,152**	**2,942**	**1,508**	**1,267**	**1,400**	**0.25**	**10.50**
Australia	862	2,752	1,178	1,037	1,116	0.20	7.62
New Zealand	290	190	330	230	284	0.05	23.48
Melanesia	**4**	**7**	**7**	**25**	**23**		**-8.00**
Fiji	3	7	5	16	21		31.25
Vanuatu	1		1	3	2		-33.33
Papua New Guinea			1	6			
Polynesia	**4**	**3**	**2**	**7**	**2**		**-71.43**
Tonga	3			4			
Samoa	1	3	2	3	2		-33.33
EUROPE	**219,006**	**233,791**	**245,919**	**230,167**	**241,141**	**42.87**	**4.77**
Central/Eastern Europe	**1,146**	**1,697**	**1,518**	**1,653**	**1,876**	**0.33**	**13.49**
Azerbaijan		6		2	9		350.00
Bulgaria	24	38	40	47	47	0.01	
Belarus	3	11	8	10	18		80.00
Czech Republic/Slovakia		1	1	1			
Czech Republic	223	209	231	236	288	0.05	22.03
Estonia	22	26	43	78	79	0.01	1.28
Georgia	1	1	22	7	4		-42.86
Hungary	80	118	110	114	69	0.01	-39.47
Kazakhstan	6	5	6	7	16		128.57
Latvia	47	30	43	55	81	0.01	47.27
Lithuania	8	26	24	29	41	0.01	41.38
Poland	242	394	194	181	216	0.04	19.34
Romania	28	68	76	78	49	0.01	-37.18
Russian Federation	371	644	569	659	703	0.12	6.68
Slovakia	47	32	68	50	71	0.01	42.00
Ukraine	44	88	83	99	185	0.03	86.87
Northern Europe	**199,733**	**210,785**	**223,798**	**209,285**	**219,343**	**38.99**	**4.81**
Denmark	787	1,456	991	1,230	985	0.18	-19.92
Finland	299	528	301	299	254	0.05	-15.05
Iceland	22	41	34	48	45	0.01	-6.25
Ireland	3,672	3,915	6,540	4,531	4,615	0.82	1.85
Norway	842	868	635	617	627	0.11	1.62
Sweden	1,505	1,413	1,352	1,124	1,294	0.23	15.12
United Kingdom	192,606	202,564	213,945	201,436	211,523	37.60	5.01
Southern Europe	**5,421**	**6,168**	**6,047**	**5,075**	**5,226**	**0.93**	**2.98**
Albania	3	2	1	4	1		-75.00
Andorra	9	2	8	2	1		-50.00
Bosnia and Herzegovina	8	8	3	3	3		
Croatia	30	34	49	44	40	0.01	-9.09
Gibraltar	10	19	22	29	40	0.01	37.93
Greece	94	89	100	161	116	0.02	-27.95
Italy	4,322	4,912	4,914	3,830	3,832	0.68	0.05
Malta	32	19	14	27	41	0.01	51.85
Portugal	279	407	227	139	186	0.03	33.81
San Marino	9	4	3	6	12		100.00
Slovenia	61	64	32	70	50	0.01	-28.57
Spain	564	608	674	760	904	0.16	18.95
Western Europe	**12,494**	**14,745**	**14,292**	**13,865**	**14,335**	**2.55**	**3.39**
Austria	531	640	586	591	598	0.11	1.18
Belgium	710	541	621	670	923	0.16	37.76

BARBADOS

1. Arrivals of non-resident tourists at national borders, by country of residence

	2002	2003	2004	2005	2006	Market share 06	% Change 06-05
France	2,447	2,820	2,272	2,343	2,679	0.48	14.34
Germany	5,931	7,612	6,970	6,995	7,478	1.33	6.90
Liechtenstein	8	5	21	11	13		18.18
Luxembourg	123	86	107	111	165	0.03	48.65
Monaco	105	75	68	107	109	0.02	1.87
Netherlands	1,339	1,557	2,209	1,603	854	0.15	-46.72
Switzerland	1,300	1,409	1,438	1,434	1,516	0.27	5.72
East Mediterranean Europe	**212**	**396**	**264**	**289**	**361**	**0.06**	**24.91**
Cyprus	35	43	37	51	40	0.01	-21.57
Israel	145	304	169	171	232	0.04	35.67
Turkey	32	49	58	67	89	0.02	32.84
MIDDLE EAST	**101**	**160**	**145**	**154**	**230**	**0.04**	**49.35**
Middle East	**101**	**160**	**145**	**154**	**230**	**0.04**	**49.35**
Bahrain	4	14	11	9	9		
Jordan	1	7	7	14	14		
Kuwait	7	12	13	19	11		-42.11
Lebanon	13	17	29	11	14		27.27
Oman	2		1	4	6		50.00
Saudi Arabia	42	44	18	29	31	0.01	6.90
Syrian Arab Republic	5	13	10	6	7		16.67
United Arab Emirates	19	30	39	45	115	0.02	155.56
Egypt	8	13	17	17	23		35.29
Yemen		10					
SOUTH ASIA	**503**	**466**	**627**	**756**	**784**	**0.14**	**3.70**
South Asia	**503**	**466**	**627**	**756**	**784**	**0.14**	**3.70**
Afghanistan					1		
Bangladesh	31	5	5	6	3		-50.00
Sri Lanka	21	56	10	5	27		440.00
India	433	373	564	644	629	0.11	-2.33
Iran, Islamic Republic of	4		1	13	2		-84.62
Maldives		2		4	5		25.00
Nepal	4	5	7	9	4		-55.56
Pakistan	10	25	40	75	113	0.02	50.67
REGION NOT SPECIFIED	**416**	**476**	**111**	**1,408**	**4,340**	**0.77**	**208.24**
Not Specified	**416**	**476**	**111**	**1,408**	**4,340**	**0.77**	**208.24**
Other countries of the World	416	476	111	1,408	4,340	0.77	208.24

Source: World Tourism Organization (UNWTO)

BELARUS

1. Arrivals of non-resident tourists at national borders, by nationality

	2002	2003	2004	2005	2006	Market share 06	% Change 06-05
TOTAL (*)	63,336	64,190	67,297	90,588	89,101	100.00	-1.64
AFRICA	58	65	47	399	148	0.17	-62.91
East Africa	1	3	7	12	7	0.01	-41.67
Ethiopia			2	1	5	0.01	400.00
Madagascar				1			
Mauritius			2				
Somalia		3		3			
Zimbabwe	1			5	2		-60.00
Uganda			3	2			
Central Africa	1			2	3		50.00
Angola				2	3		50.00
Congo	1						
North Africa	7	4	12	19	59	0.07	210.53
Algeria			4	6	1		-83.33
Morocco		2	1	5	8	0.01	60.00
Sudan	2	2	5	5	23	0.03	360.00
Tunisia	5		2	3	27	0.03	800.00
Southern Africa	30	45	12	51	44	0.05	-13.73
South Africa	30	45	12	51	44	0.05	-13.73
West Africa	19	13	16	315	35	0.04	-88.89
Ghana		1	1	43	7	0.01	-83.72
Guinea	1						
Nigeria	18	12	9	270	27	0.03	-90.00
Sierra Leone			6	1	1		
Togo				1			
AMERICAS	2,999	3,522	5,892	4,663	4,292	4.82	-7.96
Caribbean	2	6	4	4	15	0.02	275.00
Cuba		6	4	3	14	0.02	366.67
Dominican Republic	2			1	1		
Central America	1	2		1			
El Salvador				1			
Guatemala	1	1					
Nicaragua		1					
North America	2,925	3,447	5,796	4,581	4,193	4.71	-8.47
Canada	68	65	273	282	179	0.20	-36.52
Mexico	2	6	5	25	9	0.01	-64.00
United States	2,855	3,376	5,518	4,274	4,005	4.49	-6.29
South America	71	67	92	77	84	0.09	9.09
Argentina	55	45	11	17	10	0.01	-41.18
Brazil	15	15	72	44	27	0.03	-38.64
Chile			3	2	10	0.01	400.00
Colombia			2	3	2		-33.33
Ecuador				1	1		
Peru	1	1	2	7	1		-85.71
Uruguay		5		3	5	0.01	66.67
Venezuela		1	2		28	0.03	
EAST ASIA AND THE PACIFIC	2,766	1,833	2,150	1,860	1,815	2.04	-2.42
North-East Asia	1,033	874	1,169	961	1,270	1.43	32.15
China	399	361	323	375	343	0.38	-8.53

BELARUS

1. Arrivals of non-resident tourists at national borders, by nationality

	2002	2003	2004	2005	2006	Market share 06	% Change 06-05
Taiwan (Province of China)	130	96	185	124	120	0.13	-3.23
Hong Kong, China				10			
Japan	390	383	428	342	614	0.69	79.53
Korea, Dem. People's Republic of	72	30	7	33	48	0.05	45.45
Korea, Republic of	42	2	225	67	132	0.15	97.01
Mongolia		2	1	10	13	0.01	30.00
South-East Asia	**56**	**82**	**44**	**113**	**79**	**0.09**	**-30.09**
Indonesia			1	2	1		-50.00
Malaysia	1	3	2	94	4		-95.74
Philippines		1	3	10	10	0.01	
Singapore	1	1	15	6	32	0.04	433.33
Viet Nam	53	76	23		30	0.03	
Thailand	1	1		1	2		100.00
Australasia	**1,677**	**877**	**937**	**786**	**466**	**0.52**	**-40.71**
Australia	622	295	838	711	412	0.46	-42.05
New Zealand	1,055	582	99	75	54	0.06	-28.00
EUROPE	**56,833**	**57,916**	**58,524**	**82,247**	**80,956**	**90.86**	**-1.57**
Central/Eastern Europe	**32,936**	**34,339**	**29,833**	**48,606**	**52,658**	**59.10**	**8.34**
Azerbaijan	22	36	37	104	32	0.04	-69.23
Bulgaria	132	61	31	96	126	0.14	31.25
Czech Republic	152	389	148	277	267	0.30	-3.61
Estonia	268	727	840	732	1,647	1.85	125.00
Hungary	52	24	51	111	125	0.14	12.61
Kyrgyzstan	16	3	9	6	4		-33.33
Latvia	6,359	7,665	4,978	7,409	8,156	9.15	10.08
Lithuania	6,734	7,458	5,317	8,249	12,481	14.01	51.30
Republic of Moldova	74	108	206	102	136	0.15	33.33
Poland	11,028	10,287	5,563	2,983	3,329	3.74	11.60
Romania	11	51	2	44	42	0.05	-4.55
Russian Federation	7,343	6,801	11,681	27,097	24,859	27.90	-8.26
Slovakia	35	84	51	54	64	0.07	18.52
Ukraine	710	645	919	1,342	1,390	1.56	3.58
Northern Europe	**10,140**	**4,643**	**7,570**	**11,278**	**4,933**	**5.54**	**-56.26**
Denmark	247	535	529	307	280	0.31	-8.79
Finland	125	132	338	184	209	0.23	13.59
Iceland	29	8	1	4	7	0.01	75.00
Ireland	90	118	165	216	506	0.57	134.26
Norway	120	153	222	1,632	286	0.32	-82.48
Sweden	412	415	1,093	727	553	0.62	-23.93
United Kingdom	9,117	3,282	5,222	8,208	3,092	3.47	-62.33
Southern Europe	**2,457**	**4,885**	**5,388**	**6,063**	**5,980**	**6.71**	**-1.37**
Albania				1	3		200.00
Bosnia and Herzegovina		4	1	25	79	0.09	216.00
Croatia	91	123	21	27	12	0.01	-55.56
Greece	99	58	85	71	86	0.10	21.13
Italy	2,067	4,225	4,533	5,090	4,910	5.51	-3.54
Malta	1	4	30	2	5	0.01	150.00
Portugal	6	7	51	37	28	0.03	-24.32
Slovenia	3	43	34	263	199	0.22	-24.33
Spain	131	392	573	509	630	0.71	23.77
TFYR of Macedonia			4	17	5	0.01	-70.59
Serbia and Montenegro	59	29	56	21	23	0.03	9.52
Western Europe	**8,823**	**10,279**	**11,840**	**10,912**	**12,797**	**14.36**	**17.27**

BELARUS

1. Arrivals of non-resident tourists at national borders, by nationality

	2002	2003	2004	2005	2006	Market share 06	% Change 06-05
Austria	733	593	723	508	387	0.43	-23.82
Belgium	313	322	497	495	303	0.34	-38.79
France	581	486	759	1,176	1,037	1.16	-11.82
Germany	6,147	7,067	8,542	7,402	9,973	11.19	34.73
Liechtenstein		1	2				
Luxembourg	17	99	11	16	20	0.02	25.00
Netherlands	648	1,347	954	868	611	0.69	-29.61
Switzerland	384	364	352	447	466	0.52	4.25
East Mediterranean Europe	**2,477**	**3,770**	**3,893**	**5,388**	**4,588**	**5.15**	**-14.85**
Cyprus	1,258	2,602	1,179	940	956	1.07	1.70
Israel	1,119	755	2,515	3,120	1,829	2.05	-41.38
Turkey	100	413	199	1,328	1,803	2.02	35.77
MIDDLE EAST	**401**	**382**	**415**	**825**	**1,318**	**1.48**	**59.76**
Middle East	**401**	**382**	**415**	**825**	**1,318**	**1.48**	**59.76**
Iraq	31	35	9	153	29	0.03	-81.05
Jordan	17	12	25	36	34	0.04	-5.56
Kuwait	1	1	1		3		
Lebanon	60	149	140	227	331	0.37	45.81
Libyan Arab Jamahiriya	7	7	32	24	11	0.01	-54.17
Saudi Arabia	18	18	15	9	27	0.03	200.00
Syrian Arab Republic	160	76	44	92	130	0.15	41.30
United Arab Emirates	70	66	116	80	91	0.10	13.75
Egypt	37	18	32	203	662	0.74	226.11
Yemen				1	1		
SOUTH ASIA	**279**	**472**	**269**	**594**	**572**	**0.64**	**-3.70**
South Asia	**279**	**472**	**269**	**594**	**572**	**0.64**	**-3.70**
Afghanistan	1	4	3	12	5	0.01	-58.33
Bangladesh	9	42	8	14	6	0.01	-57.14
Sri Lanka		1	3	3	10	0.01	233.33
India	124	258	113	282	105	0.12	-62.77
Iran, Islamic Republic of	136	150	108	222	427	0.48	92.34
Nepal		1	2	2	2		
Pakistan	9	16	32	59	17	0.02	-71.19

Source: World Tourism Organization (UNWTO)

BELGIUM

3. Arrivals of non-resident tourists in hotels and similar establishments, by country of residence

	2002	2003	2004	2005	2006	Market share 06	% Change 06-05
TOTAL	5,322,521	5,261,182	5,385,214	5,409,064	5,664,940	100.00	4.73
AFRICA	55,865	58,467	57,115	57,812	60,945	1.08	5.42
East Africa	5,883	5,936	4,898	5,397	5,160	0.09	-4.39
British Indian Ocean Territory	82	61					
Burundi	625	599	566	593	534	0.01	-9.95
Comoros	37	43	31	31	17		-45.16
Ethiopia	385	525	594	1,031	905	0.02	-12.22
Eritrea	12	18	45	97	51		-47.42
Djibouti	74	79	58	48	81		68.75
Kenya	599	707	532	660	781	0.01	18.33
Madagascar	234	223	223	180	172		-4.44
Malawi	86	42	109	53	45		-15.09
Mauritius	1,121	1,346	489	281	189		-32.74
Mozambique	54	88	68	88	92		4.55
Rwanda	668	807	899	727	749	0.01	3.03
Seychelles	169	141	180	193	206		6.74
Somalia	68	73	116	85	148		74.12
Zimbabwe	1,109	569	340	632	479	0.01	-24.21
Uganda	230	265	260	292	303	0.01	3.77
United Republic of Tanzania	143	211	209	280	333	0.01	18.93
Zambia	187	139	179	126	75		-40.48
Central Africa	12,726	14,897	12,708	12,512	12,042	0.21	-3.76
Angola	1,059	970	887	713	981	0.02	37.59
Cameroon	1,893	4,129	2,151	2,347	2,130	0.04	-9.25
Central African Republic	215	132	250	409	316	0.01	-22.74
Chad	324	193	194	163	116		-28.83
Congo	3,448	3,400	3,299	2,883	2,460	0.04	-14.67
Democratic Republic of the Congo	4,270	4,210	4,407	5,006	4,902	0.09	-2.08
Equatorial Guinea	36	48	65	47	52		10.64
Gabon	1,438	1,776	1,393	885	1,046	0.02	18.19
Sao Tome and Principe	43	39	62	59	39		-33.90
North Africa	19,867	19,842	20,280	19,222	20,503	0.36	6.66
Algeria	3,515	2,891	3,331	3,294	3,490	0.06	5.95
Morocco	13,161	13,828	13,708	12,701	13,684	0.24	7.74
Sudan	424	316	336	392	246		-37.24
Tunisia	2,767	2,807	2,905	2,835	3,083	0.05	8.75
Southern Africa	6,889	6,631	7,173	8,011	9,985	0.18	24.64
Botswana	104	56	30	41	68		65.85
Lesotho	20	29	13	27	47		74.07
Namibia	154	226	111	202	183		-9.41
South Africa	6,407	6,058	6,710	7,422	9,325	0.16	25.64
Swaziland	204	262	309	319	362	0.01	13.48
West Africa	10,500	11,161	12,056	12,670	13,255	0.23	4.62
Cape Verde	40	86	60	86	47		-45.35
Benin	313	230	266	246	268		8.94
Gambia	422	425	263	287	231		-19.51
Ghana	518	567	441	481	563	0.01	17.05
Guinea	509	640	704	694	702	0.01	1.15
Cote D'Ivoire	1,177	1,529	1,821	1,421	1,603	0.03	12.81
Liberia	229	149	393	366	317	0.01	-13.39
Mali	555	805	671	708	896	0.02	26.55
Mauritania	234	308	318	401	374	0.01	-6.73

BELGIUM

3. Arrivals of non-resident tourists in hotels and similar establishments, by country of residence

	2002	2003	2004	2005	2006	Market share 06	% Change 06-05
Niger	2,012	1,566	1,536	1,845	2,597	0.05	40.76
Nigeria	1,906	2,177	2,623	2,556	2,101	0.04	-17.80
Guinea-Bissau	65	48	51	42	78		85.71
Saint Helena	8	16					
Senegal	1,148	1,228	1,011	1,138	961	0.02	-15.55
Sierra Leone	705	804	1,137	1,564	1,625	0.03	3.90
Togo	311	215	259	248	391	0.01	57.66
Burkina Faso	348	368	502	587	501	0.01	-14.65
AMERICAS	**346,659**	**322,188**	**337,218**	**343,485**	**370,042**	**6.53**	**7.73**
Caribbean	**4,441**	**4,691**	**1,995**	**2,426**	**2,974**	**0.05**	**22.59**
Antigua and Barbuda	54	97	108	334	450	0.01	34.73
Bahamas	218	279	188	197	474	0.01	140.61
Barbados	63	61	72	152	485	0.01	219.08
Bermuda	1,549	2,418					
British Virgin Islands	3	13					
Cayman Islands	16	20					
Cuba	635	319	914	756	465	0.01	-38.49
Dominica	254	234	58	78	267		242.31
Dominican Republic	195	190	173	376	309	0.01	-17.82
Grenada	52	21	23	25	42		68.00
Haiti	117	73	97	215	105		-51.16
Jamaica	392	202	232	162	207		27.78
Montserrat	10	12					
Netherlands Antilles	228	146					
Aruba	46	29					
Saint Kitts and Nevis	2	20	9	18	5		-72.22
Anguilla	140	170					
Saint Lucia	60	42	27	22	28		27.27
Saint Vincent and the Grenadines	11	12	13	7	18		157.14
Trinidad and Tobago	107	77	81	84	119		41.67
Turks and Caicos Islands	281	241					
United States Virgin Islands	8	15					
Central America	**2,186**	**2,245**	**2,501**	**2,700**	**4,239**	**0.07**	**57.00**
Belize	233	130	149	185	271		46.49
Costa Rica	585	742	773	940	1,689	0.03	79.68
El Salvador	420	480	516	517	1,013	0.02	95.94
Guatemala	265	205	245	269	232		-13.75
Honduras	161	156	163	164	189		15.24
Nicaragua	280	289	268	350	487	0.01	39.14
Panama	242	243	387	275	358	0.01	30.18
North America	**317,615**	**294,748**	**311,976**	**314,668**	**332,565**	**5.87**	**5.69**
Canada	28,320	29,623	32,278	32,868	39,044	0.69	18.79
Greenland	392	198					
Mexico	14,136	11,808	11,183	12,332	17,582	0.31	42.57
Saint Pierre and Miquelon	18	6					
United States	274,749	253,113	268,515	269,468	275,939	4.87	2.40
South America	**22,417**	**20,504**	**20,746**	**23,691**	**30,264**	**0.53**	**27.74**
Argentina	4,073	3,549	3,827	3,797	4,670	0.08	22.99
Bolivia	254	206	166	293	279		-4.78
Brazil	8,482	8,954	10,000	11,455	14,677	0.26	28.13
Chile	2,442	2,134	1,849	1,954	2,460	0.04	25.90
Colombia	1,997	2,222	1,973	2,539	3,275	0.06	28.99
Ecuador	1,930	1,024	585	550	997	0.02	81.27

BELGIUM

3. Arrivals of non-resident tourists in hotels and similar establishments, by country of residence

	2002	2003	2004	2005	2006	Market share 06	% Change 06-05
Falkland Islands (Malvinas)	19	8					
Guyana	62	50	40	65	64		-1.54
Paraguay	65	106	62	96	159		65.63
Peru	1,158	967	757	728	984	0.02	35.16
Suriname	144	145	123	138	203		47.10
Uruguay	351	288	333	788	1,029	0.02	30.58
Venezuela	1,440	851	1,031	1,288	1,467	0.03	13.90
EAST ASIA AND THE PACIFIC	**315,205**	**259,597**	**285,799**	**267,316**	**275,090**	**4.86**	**2.91**
North-East Asia	**276,242**	**225,474**	**245,048**	**226,433**	**226,128**	**3.99**	**-0.13**
China	111,384	105,699	112,685	106,345	104,239	1.84	-1.98
Taiwan (Province of China)	5,806	2,981	2,959	2,859	7,131	0.13	149.42
Hong Kong, China	4,802	1,954					
Japan	144,739	105,129	117,847	104,459	102,777	1.81	-1.61
Korea, Dem. People's Republic of	3,695	2,855	2,879	3,224	2,273	0.04	-29.50
Korea, Republic of	5,418	6,515	8,527	9,485	9,600	0.17	1.21
Macao, China	259	237					
Mongolia	139	104	151	61	108		77.05
South-East Asia	**18,743**	**13,711**	**15,567**	**15,789**	**18,613**	**0.33**	**17.89**
Brunei Darussalam	51	71	40	76	77		1.32
Myanmar	60	30	19	36	39		8.33
Cambodia	79	92	42	106	109		2.83
Indonesia	1,689	1,500	2,024	1,515	1,984	0.04	30.96
Lao People's Democratic Republic	132	182	149	204	245		20.10
Malaysia	2,381	2,150	2,640	3,109	3,419	0.06	9.97
Philippines	3,307	3,277	3,253	2,886	3,877	0.07	34.34
Timor-Leste			6	39	37		-5.13
Singapore	6,950	3,474	3,755	4,169	4,100	0.07	-1.66
Viet Nam	1,099	686	865	1,092	1,624	0.03	48.72
Thailand	2,995	2,249	2,774	2,557	3,102	0.05	21.31
Australasia	**18,460**	**18,773**	**22,272**	**24,162**	**28,681**	**0.51**	**18.70**
Australia	14,584	14,790	17,763	19,653	23,312	0.41	18.62
New Zealand	3,876	3,983	4,509	4,509	5,369	0.09	19.07
Melanesia	**655**	**822**	**2,246**	**488**	**937**	**0.02**	**92.01**
Solomon Islands	14	10	51	50	52		4.00
Fiji	480	729	2,125	309	791	0.01	155.99
New Caledonia	26	19					
Vanuatu	12	7	13	25	17		-32.00
Papua New Guinea	123	57	57	104	77		-25.96
Micronesia	**485**	**315**	**327**	**289**	**433**	**0.01**	**49.83**
Kiribati	26	69	63	28	52		85.71
Nauru	303	56	51	70	95		35.71
Northern Mariana Islands	4	7					
Micronesia (Federated States of)	4	3	1	6	21		250.00
Marshall Islands	6	1	6		6		
Palau	142	179	206	185	259		40.00
Polynesia	**271**	**156**	**339**	**155**	**298**	**0.01**	**92.26**
French Polynesia	134	50					
Pitcairn	9						
Tonga	18	18	43	36	36		
Tuvalu	11	13	30	46	114		147.83
Wallis and Futuna Islands	3	5					
Samoa	96	70	266	73	148		102.74

BELGIUM

3. Arrivals of non-resident tourists in hotels and similar establishments, by country of residence

	2002	2003	2004	2005	2006	Market share 06	% Change 06-05
Other East Asia and the Pacific	349	346					
Other countries of Oceania	349	346					
EUROPE	4,506,317	4,511,686	4,564,601	4,589,651	4,786,091	84.49	4.28
Central/Eastern Europe	141,515	147,868	179,207	206,253	243,244	4.29	17.93
Azerbaijan	325	290	307	353	463	0.01	31.16
Armenia	738	695	677	600	689	0.01	14.83
Bulgaria	6,272	6,113	7,611	8,394	10,751	0.19	28.08
Belarus	1,419	1,163	994	870	1,814	0.03	108.51
Czech Republic	14,182	16,064	20,181	20,572	23,865	0.42	16.01
Estonia	3,037	4,688	4,902	5,309	5,839	0.10	9.98
Georgia	2,909	2,019	3,161	2,288	2,746	0.05	20.02
Hungary	13,131	15,493	18,624	20,937	22,915	0.40	9.45
Kazakhstan	300	431	347	552	753	0.01	36.41
Kyrgyzstan	52	172	107	189	71		-62.43
Latvia	1,299	1,681	3,476	3,702	3,890	0.07	5.08
Lithuania	5,065	6,701	9,402	10,212	11,661	0.21	14.19
Republic of Moldova	307	261	293	362	336	0.01	-7.18
Poland	40,838	38,755	47,712	55,437	64,437	1.14	16.23
Romania	8,562	8,961	10,985	13,626	19,255	0.34	41.31
Russian Federation	31,381	32,818	36,580	48,051	56,309	0.99	17.19
Slovakia	4,718	5,210	6,322	6,915	7,260	0.13	4.99
Tajikistan	62	143	148	101	124		22.77
Turkmenistan	147	147	81	183	106		-42.08
Ukraine	6,319	5,600	6,305	6,949	9,229	0.16	32.81
Uzbekistan	452	463	992	651	731	0.01	12.29
Northern Europe	1,397,665	1,355,240	1,306,121	1,249,320	1,245,013	21.98	-0.34
Denmark	53,784	49,537	50,971	51,121	52,862	0.93	3.41
Faeroe Islands	1,001	1,125					
Finland	29,362	29,297	29,211	31,651	33,978	0.60	7.35
Iceland	3,821	4,217	6,094	4,993	4,888	0.09	-2.10
Ireland	39,817	47,471	46,544	39,658	38,287	0.68	-3.46
Norway	32,716	33,630	36,629	33,833	32,062	0.57	-5.23
Sweden	69,875	75,280	74,835	73,323	75,857	1.34	3.46
United Kingdom	1,167,289	1,114,683	1,061,837	1,014,741	1,007,079	17.78	-0.76
Southern Europe	475,569	493,901	500,876	514,871	541,868	9.57	5.24
Albania	5,497	8,165	10,081	11,168	11,236	0.20	0.61
Andorra	387	384	323	1,588	917	0.02	-42.25
Bosnia and Herzegovina	982	1,048	920	1,366	1,298	0.02	-4.98
Croatia	3,061	3,529	3,825	4,570	6,260	0.11	36.98
Gibraltar	97	80					
Greece	30,168	34,652	30,718	30,030	32,835	0.58	9.34
Holy See	74	20	59	30	73		143.33
Italy	207,691	214,451	205,907	202,054	215,321	3.80	6.57
Malta	2,287	2,792	3,320	3,945	4,684	0.08	18.73
Portugal	30,340	31,659	34,659	35,732	31,029	0.55	-13.16
San Marino	74	44	37	56	75		33.93
Slovenia	4,493	5,604	6,123	5,686	6,354	0.11	11.75
Spain	188,204	188,844	201,030	214,787	228,061	4.03	6.18
TFYR of Macedonia	1,079	1,235	2,101	1,743	1,544	0.03	-11.42
Serbia and Montenegro	1,135	1,394	1,773	2,116	2,181	0.04	3.07
Western Europe	2,445,615	2,466,502	2,527,075	2,561,599	2,690,985	47.50	5.05
Austria	26,902	28,061	27,801	27,543	32,893	0.58	19.42

BELGIUM

3. Arrivals of non-resident tourists in hotels and similar establishments, by country of residence

	2002	2003	2004	2005	2006	Market share 06	% Change 06-05
France	785,633	806,695	841,983	854,797	910,724	16.08	6.54
Germany	590,781	571,031	565,592	565,845	578,674	10.22	2.27
Liechtenstein	4,512	4,103	4,596	3,333	2,259	0.04	-32.22
Luxembourg	52,609	53,943	51,421	57,733	58,938	1.04	2.09
Monaco			60	297	347	0.01	16.84
Netherlands	931,607	949,482	978,326	992,340	1,043,757	18.42	5.18
Switzerland	53,571	53,187	57,296	59,711	63,393	1.12	6.17
East Mediterranean Europe	**45,953**	**48,175**	**51,322**	**57,608**	**64,981**	**1.15**	**12.80**
Cyprus	2,115	2,877	3,867	3,870	4,155	0.07	7.36
Israel	28,488	27,875	27,803	30,458	31,969	0.56	4.96
Turkey	15,350	17,423	19,652	23,280	28,857	0.51	23.96
MIDDLE EAST	**17,304**	**17,195**	**17,289**	**19,193**	**20,173**	**0.36**	**5.11**
Middle East	**17,304**	**17,195**	**17,289**	**19,193**	**20,173**	**0.36**	**5.11**
Bahrain	328	242	233	227	276		21.59
Palestine			33	61	57		-6.56
Iraq	301	226	296	353	367	0.01	3.97
Jordan	715	789	686	627	713	0.01	13.72
Kuwait	786	807	724	776	888	0.02	14.43
Lebanon	1,565	1,697	1,553	1,716	1,768	0.03	3.03
Libyan Arab Jamahiriya	661	639	949	1,151	973	0.02	-15.46
Oman	168	191	199	170	220		29.41
Qatar	571	491	578	506	637	0.01	25.89
Saudi Arabia	3,975	4,362	4,973	5,821	2,756	0.05	-52.65
Syrian Arab Republic	594	682	977	978	703	0.01	-28.12
United Arab Emirates	3,145	2,984	2,348	3,550	7,081	0.12	99.46
Egypt	4,299	3,961	3,666	3,170	3,635	0.06	14.67
Yemen	170	92	74	87	99		13.79
Other countries of Middle East	26	32					
SOUTH ASIA	**35,701**	**29,536**	**30,913**	**33,412**	**31,411**	**0.55**	**-5.99**
South Asia	**35,701**	**29,536**	**30,913**	**33,412**	**31,411**	**0.55**	**-5.99**
Afghanistan	1,665	1,823	1,534	1,376	1,073	0.02	-22.02
Bangladesh	4,466	4,422	3,730	6,422	1,653	0.03	-74.26
Bhutan	72	102	103	89	27		-69.66
Sri Lanka	347	261	251	240	325	0.01	35.42
India	22,956	17,453	19,479	19,572	21,683	0.38	10.79
Iran, Islamic Republic of	4,568	3,894	4,089	4,040	4,577	0.08	13.29
Maldives	24	25	14	35	33		-5.71
Nepal	139	113	99	151	239		58.28
Pakistan	1,464	1,443	1,614	1,487	1,801	0.03	21.12
REGION NOT SPECIFIED	**45,470**	**62,513**	**92,279**	**98,195**	**121,188**	**2.14**	**23.42**
Not Specified	**45,470**	**62,513**	**92,279**	**98,195**	**121,188**	**2.14**	**23.42**
Other countries of the World	45,470	62,513	92,279	98,195	121,188	2.14	23.42

Source: World Tourism Organization (UNWTO)

BELGIUM

4. Arrivals of non-resident tourists in all types of accommodation establishments, by country of residence

		2002	2003	2004	2005	2006	Market share 06	% Change 06-05
TOTAL	(*)	6,719,653	6,689,998	6,709,740	6,747,123	6,994,819	100.00	3.67
AFRICA		60,026	62,755	60,872	62,455	65,438	0.94	4.78
East Africa		6,150	6,142	5,262	5,725	5,311	0.08	-7.23
British Indian Ocean Territory		82	81					
Burundi		648	634	591	620	539	0.01	-13.06
Comoros		40	46	39	33	18		-45.45
Ethiopia		432	530	604	1,081	921	0.01	-14.80
Eritrea		20	18	63	109	52		-52.29
Djibouti		75	81	66	48	81		68.75
Kenya		629	726	632	696	796	0.01	14.37
Madagascar		248	232	286	187	177		-5.35
Malawi		87	42	110	61	49		-19.67
Mauritius		1,146	1,350	499	293	216		-26.28
Mozambique		54	100	69	94	93		-1.06
Rwanda		693	850	925	747	766	0.01	2.54
Seychelles		169	142	180	200	210		5.00
Somalia		82	73	119	94	150		59.57
Zimbabwe		1,150	596	403	705	506	0.01	-28.23
Uganda		232	281	279	342	311		-9.06
United Republic of Tanzania		156	214	215	285	348		22.11
Zambia		207	146	182	130	78		-40.00
Central Africa		13,217	15,449	13,089	13,017	12,436	0.18	-4.46
Angola		1,072	982	903	716	993	0.01	38.69
Cameroon		1,949	4,180	2,206	2,418	2,225	0.03	-7.98
Central African Republic		218	133	255	420	318		-24.29
Chad		327	193	194	168	241		43.45
Congo		3,734	3,736	3,451	2,952	2,497	0.04	-15.41
Democratic Republic of the Congo		4,340	4,323	4,532	5,320	5,007	0.07	-5.88
Equatorial Guinea		48	49	72	47	54		14.89
Gabon		1,486	1,807	1,410	911	1,062	0.02	16.58
Sao Tome and Principe		43	46	66	65	39		-40.00
North Africa		21,030	20,875	21,253	20,201	21,469	0.31	6.28
Algeria		3,755	3,089	3,564	3,619	3,816	0.05	5.44
Morocco		13,790	14,415	14,240	13,179	14,221	0.20	7.91
Sudan		430	318	348	406	256		-36.95
Tunisia		3,055	3,053	3,101	2,997	3,176	0.05	5.97
Southern Africa		8,100	7,734	7,971	10,031	11,652	0.17	16.16
Botswana		104	56	30	41	69		68.29
Lesotho		20	30	13	27	47		74.07
Namibia		206	262	127	264	450	0.01	70.45
South Africa		7,566	7,117	7,487	9,376	10,724	0.15	14.38
Swaziland		204	269	314	323	362	0.01	12.07
West Africa		11,529	12,555	13,297	13,481	14,570	0.21	8.08
Cape Verde		40	89	60	90	50		-44.44
Benin		345	257	273	263	278		5.70
Gambia		429	531	264	290	233		-19.66
Ghana		528	630	471	488	572	0.01	17.21
Guinea		525	682	720	721	728	0.01	0.97
Cote D'Ivoire		1,854	2,159	2,459	1,565	1,679	0.02	7.28
Liberia		230	154	396	371	320		-13.75
Mali		567	858	703	718	1,236	0.02	72.14
Mauritania		250	320	326	415	384	0.01	-7.47

BELGIUM

4. Arrivals of non-resident tourists in all types of accommodation establishments, by country of residence

	2002	2003	2004	2005	2006	Market share 06	% Change 06-05
Niger	2,032	1,600	1,593	2,087	3,107	0.04	48.87
Nigeria	1,941	2,269	2,760	2,644	2,166	0.03	-18.08
Guinea-Bissau	65	53	55	45	79		75.56
Saint Helena	8	17					
Senegal	1,282	1,422	1,229	1,294	1,119	0.02	-13.52
Sierra Leone	706	875	1,182	1,581	1,678	0.02	6.14
Togo	355	236	271	252	413	0.01	63.89
Burkina Faso	372	403	535	657	528	0.01	-19.63
AMERICAS	**399,576**	**368,814**	**382,249**	**390,160**	**407,403**	**5.82**	**4.42**
Caribbean	**4,553**	**4,916**	**2,176**	**2,672**	**3,061**	**0.04**	**14.56**
Antigua and Barbuda	54	99	111	337	451	0.01	33.83
Bahamas	220	281	205	200	491	0.01	145.50
Barbados	69	66	111	152	509	0.01	234.87
Bermuda	1,563	2,420					
British Virgin Islands	3	14					
Cayman Islands	16	22					
Cuba	658	432	939	904	469	0.01	-48.12
Dominica	267	241	66	87	279		220.69
Dominican Republic	215	215	192	384	320		-16.67
Grenada	52	22	40	63	51		-19.05
Haiti	126	89	121	247	108		-56.28
Jamaica	400	225	244	167	208		24.55
Montserrat	13	12					
Netherlands Antilles	229	148					
Aruba	46	33					
Saint Kitts and Nevis	2	22	14	18	5		-72.22
Anguilla	140	171					
Saint Lucia	61	42	27	22	28		27.27
Saint Vincent and the Grenadines	11	12	16	7	18		157.14
Trinidad and Tobago	115	77	90	84	124		47.62
Turks and Caicos Islands	285	254					
United States Virgin Islands	8	19					
Central America	**2,624**	**2,577**	**2,975**	**3,048**	**4,604**	**0.07**	**51.05**
Belize	237	141	173	243	373	0.01	53.50
Costa Rica	735	827	876	1,019	1,795	0.03	76.15
El Salvador	447	500	547	540	1,043	0.01	93.15
Guatemala	361	254	313	320	282		-11.88
Honduras	192	190	263	184	192		4.35
Nicaragua	392	408	399	456	536	0.01	17.54
Panama	260	257	404	286	383	0.01	33.92
North America	**362,917**	**334,117**	**349,486**	**353,522**	**362,223**	**5.18**	**2.46**
Canada	40,374	41,236	43,927	43,810	47,709	0.68	8.90
Greenland	400	200					
Mexico	20,837	17,766	16,850	17,662	21,690	0.31	22.81
Saint Pierre and Miquelon	26	9					
United States	301,280	274,906	288,709	292,050	292,824	4.19	0.27
South America	**29,482**	**27,204**	**27,612**	**30,918**	**37,515**	**0.54**	**21.34**
Argentina	5,230	4,366	4,894	5,157	6,238	0.09	20.96
Bolivia	320	265	283	432	365	0.01	-15.51
Brazil	11,673	12,579	13,843	15,181	18,048	0.26	18.89
Chile	3,388	2,961	2,455	2,718	3,076	0.04	13.17
Colombia	2,655	2,718	2,474	3,072	3,913	0.06	27.38
Ecuador	2,228	1,235	770	673	1,288	0.02	91.38

BELGIUM

4. Arrivals of non-resident tourists in all types of accommodation establishments, by country of residence

	2002	2003	2004	2005	2006	Market share 06	% Change 06-05
Falkland Islands (Malvinas)	21	16					
Guyana	62	50	42	83	64		-22.89
Paraguay	104	128	112	108	180		66.67
Peru	1,377	1,215	947	979	1,221	0.02	24.72
Suriname	148	169	134	154	205		33.12
Uruguay	645	526	518	992	1,200	0.02	20.97
Venezuela	1,631	976	1,140	1,369	1,717	0.02	25.42
EAST ASIA AND THE PACIFIC	**347,725**	**294,364**	**318,231**	**298,360**	**304,773**	**4.36**	**2.15**
North-East Asia	**292,361**	**243,809**	**263,454**	**243,308**	**243,308**	**3.48**	
China	112,652	107,016	114,456	108,702	107,380	1.54	-1.22
Taiwan (Province of China)	6,281	3,391	3,429	3,340	7,839	0.11	134.70
Hong Kong, China	4,900	2,082					
Japan	154,138	114,452	126,523	111,985	110,076	1.57	-1.70
Korea, Dem. People's Republic of	4,212	3,766	3,811	3,824	4,024	0.06	5.23
Korea, Republic of	9,778	12,752	15,078	15,386	13,862	0.20	-9.91
Macao, China	260	245					
Mongolia	140	105	157	71	127		78.87
South-East Asia	**20,268**	**15,122**	**16,861**	**17,088**	**19,887**	**0.28**	**16.38**
Brunei Darussalam	51	73	40	82	81		-1.22
Myanmar	60	31	20	37	39		5.41
Cambodia	79	99	47	106	114		7.55
Indonesia	1,954	1,769	2,094	1,598	2,161	0.03	35.23
Lao People's Democratic Republic	133	197	162	214	250		16.82
Malaysia	2,859	2,556	2,893	3,297	3,611	0.05	9.52
Philippines	3,405	3,334	3,318	2,987	3,955	0.06	32.41
Timor-Leste			6	39	37		-5.13
Singapore	7,244	3,743	3,954	4,299	4,321	0.06	0.51
Viet Nam	1,173	770	1,331	1,518	1,867	0.03	22.99
Thailand	3,310	2,550	2,996	2,911	3,451	0.05	18.55
Australasia	**33,265**	**33,748**	**34,955**	**36,992**	**39,826**	**0.57**	**7.66**
Australia	26,751	27,468	28,578	30,992	32,844	0.47	5.98
New Zealand	6,514	6,280	6,377	6,000	6,982	0.10	16.37
Melanesia	**684**	**839**	**2,285**	**495**	**945**	**0.01**	**90.91**
Solomon Islands	24	13	67	51	54		5.88
Fiji	480	732	2,136	313	791	0.01	152.72
New Caledonia	28	25					
Vanuatu	12	7	19	25	19		-24.00
Papua New Guinea	140	62	63	106	81		-23.58
Micronesia	**492**	**316**	**334**	**312**	**509**	**0.01**	**63.14**
Kiribati	26	70	63	28	52		85.71
Nauru	304	56	56	93	171		83.87
Northern Mariana Islands	8	7					
Micronesia (Federated States of)	4	3	1	6	21		250.00
Marshall Islands	8	1	6		6		
Palau	142	179	208	185	259		40.00
Polynesia	**278**	**159**	**342**	**165**	**298**		**80.61**
French Polynesia	135	50					
Pitcairn	9						
Tonga	18	18	43	44	36		-18.18
Tuvalu	16	13	30	47	114		142.55
Wallis and Futuna Islands	4	8					
Samoa	96	70	269	74	148		100.00

BELGIUM

4. Arrivals of non-resident tourists in all types of accommodation establishments, by country of residence

	2002	2003	2004	2005	2006	Market share 06	% Change 06-05
Other East Asia and the Pacific	377	371					
Other countries of Oceania	377	371					
EUROPE	5,798,298	5,846,966	5,800,440	5,835,628	6,035,866	86.29	3.43
Central/Eastern Europe	159,245	165,208	197,707	222,652	260,834	3.73	17.15
Azerbaijan	333	297	313	360	513	0.01	42.50
Armenia	796	701	694	634	701	0.01	10.57
Bulgaria	6,732	6,460	7,996	8,704	11,194	0.16	28.61
Belarus	1,541	1,275	1,142	908	1,931	0.03	112.67
Czech Republic	16,524	17,979	21,977	22,353	25,864	0.37	15.71
Estonia	3,278	4,905	5,168	5,519	6,090	0.09	10.35
Georgia	2,975	2,042	3,182	2,310	2,759	0.04	19.44
Hungary	15,204	20,347	23,928	24,758	25,840	0.37	4.37
Kazakhstan	389	481	418	586	775	0.01	32.25
Kyrgyzstan	52	206	118	189	72		-61.90
Latvia	1,573	2,048	3,728	3,977	4,522	0.06	13.70
Lithuania	5,694	7,480	9,963	10,708	12,066	0.17	12.68
Republic of Moldova	321	270	297	373	348		-6.70
Poland	48,756	44,334	53,532	61,425	71,666	1.02	16.67
Romania	9,487	9,873	12,917	14,800	20,393	0.29	37.79
Russian Federation	33,039	34,061	37,700	49,176	57,672	0.82	17.28
Slovakia	5,238	5,749	6,860	7,713	7,904	0.11	2.48
Tajikistan	62	151	152	103	124		20.39
Turkmenistan	201	155	115	189	108		-42.86
Ukraine	6,523	5,920	6,493	7,188	9,535	0.14	32.65
Uzbekistan	527	474	1,014	679	757	0.01	11.49
Northern Europe	1,506,968	1,460,483	1,396,189	1,335,805	1,328,256	18.99	-0.57
Denmark	62,956	59,161	58,528	60,186	60,762	0.87	0.96
Faeroe Islands	1,058	1,277					
Finland	31,960	32,989	31,838	34,220	36,088	0.52	5.46
Iceland	3,894	4,320	6,193	5,099	4,991	0.07	-2.12
Ireland	47,505	52,840	50,830	43,613	41,233	0.59	-5.46
Norway	34,710	35,402	38,346	35,622	34,170	0.49	-4.08
Sweden	74,587	79,371	80,230	78,573	79,517	1.14	1.20
United Kingdom	1,250,298	1,195,123	1,130,224	1,078,492	1,071,495	15.32	-0.65
Southern Europe	523,695	542,439	550,025	566,909	585,226	8.37	3.23
Albania	5,580	8,211	10,140	11,410	11,290	0.16	-1.05
Andorra	415	412	342	1,615	944	0.01	-41.55
Bosnia and Herzegovina	1,025	1,103	1,027	1,520	1,355	0.02	-10.86
Croatia	3,271	3,847	4,189	4,755	6,543	0.09	37.60
Gibraltar	101	83					
Greece	31,094	36,128	31,990	31,405	34,453	0.49	9.71
Holy See	74	20	61	31	77		148.39
Italy	223,363	231,085	220,976	216,169	227,951	3.26	5.45
Malta	2,367	2,836	3,377	3,976	4,735	0.07	19.09
Portugal	33,454	34,389	36,957	37,676	33,109	0.47	-12.12
San Marino	74	64	37	66	75		13.64
Slovenia	5,129	6,349	6,715	6,504	7,787	0.11	19.73
Spain	215,331	215,009	230,205	247,798	252,986	3.62	2.09
TFYR of Macedonia	1,188	1,350	2,162	1,781	1,636	0.02	-8.14
Serbia and Montenegro	1,229	1,553	1,847	2,203	2,285	0.03	3.72
Western Europe	3,560,612	3,628,787	3,603,388	3,650,605	3,794,570	54.25	3.94
Austria	30,122	30,842	30,639	35,420	35,610	0.51	0.54

BELGIUM

4. Arrivals of non-resident tourists in all types of accommodation establishments, by country of residence

	2002	2003	2004	2005	2006	Market share 06	% Change 06-05
France	908,596	940,628	985,341	1,011,482	1,075,643	15.38	6.34
Germany	815,359	780,911	753,131	748,295	749,710	10.72	0.19
Liechtenstein	4,531	4,105	4,614	3,358	2,271	0.03	-32.37
Luxembourg	65,962	67,856	65,411	74,803	73,682	1.05	-1.50
Monaco			60	299	347		16.05
Netherlands	1,677,462	1,746,093	1,701,337	1,711,355	1,788,707	25.57	4.52
Switzerland	58,580	58,352	62,855	65,593	68,600	0.98	4.58
East Mediterranean Europe	**47,778**	**50,049**	**53,131**	**59,657**	**66,980**	**0.96**	**12.28**
Cyprus	2,186	2,927	3,934	3,933	4,268	0.06	8.52
Israel	29,733	28,907	28,905	31,600	33,015	0.47	4.48
Turkey	15,859	18,215	20,292	24,124	29,697	0.42	23.10
MIDDLE EAST	**17,724**	**17,502**	**17,664**	**19,793**	**20,978**	**0.30**	**5.99**
Middle East	**17,724**	**17,502**	**17,664**	**19,793**	**20,978**	**0.30**	**5.99**
Bahrain	328	244	234	232	276		18.97
Palestine			45	80	112		40.00
Iraq	321	259	351	443	397	0.01	-10.38
Jordan	729	805	701	639	739	0.01	15.65
Kuwait	811	817	738	820	921	0.01	12.32
Lebanon	1,636	1,784	1,598	1,772	1,839	0.03	3.78
Libyan Arab Jamahiriya	682	665	975	1,175	983	0.01	-16.34
Oman	173	197	201	172	222		29.07
Qatar	633	498	661	557	695	0.01	24.78
Saudi Arabia	4,005	4,366	4,984	5,847	2,805	0.04	-52.03
Syrian Arab Republic	603	690	1,001	1,012	749	0.01	-25.99
United Arab Emirates	3,161	3,029	2,365	3,596	7,104	0.10	97.55
Egypt	4,440	4,021	3,733	3,361	4,032	0.06	19.96
Yemen	170	95	77	87	104		19.54
Other countries of Middle East	32	32					
SOUTH ASIA	**38,542**	**32,362**	**33,152**	**34,844**	**32,673**	**0.47**	**-6.23**
South Asia	**38,542**	**32,362**	**33,152**	**34,844**	**32,673**	**0.47**	**-6.23**
Afghanistan	1,701	1,836	1,565	1,384	1,114	0.02	-19.51
Bangladesh	4,495	4,440	3,757	6,435	1,661	0.02	-74.19
Bhutan	72	102	103	101	27		-73.27
Sri Lanka	358	419	287	244	336		37.70
India	25,452	19,790	21,390	20,624	22,589	0.32	9.53
Iran, Islamic Republic of	4,791	4,077	4,241	4,290	4,731	0.07	10.28
Maldives	24	25	14	50	34		-32.00
Nepal	151	176	132	172	281		63.37
Pakistan	1,498	1,497	1,663	1,544	1,900	0.03	23.06
REGION NOT SPECIFIED	**57,762**	**67,235**	**97,132**	**105,883**	**127,688**	**1.83**	**20.59**
Not Specified	**57,762**	**67,235**	**97,132**	**105,883**	**127,688**	**1.83**	**20.59**
Other countries of the World	57,762	67,235	97,132	105,883	127,688	1.83	20.59

Source: World Tourism Organization (UNWTO)

BELGIUM

5. Overnight stays of non-resident tourists in hotels and similar establishments, by country of residence

	2002	2003	2004	2005	2006	Market share 06	% Change 06-05
TOTAL	10,409,787	10,280,537	10,315,280	10,296,907	10,634,156	100.00	3.28
AFRICA	129,379	129,267	121,026	126,365	127,173	1.20	0.64
East Africa	15,188	13,583	11,415	14,644	14,016	0.13	-4.29
British Indian Ocean Territory	282	107					
Burundi	1,995	1,729	1,414	1,839	1,519	0.01	-17.40
Comoros	87	89	56	78	41		-47.44
Ethiopia	1,102	1,118	1,245	2,731	1,921	0.02	-29.66
Eritrea	29	40	118	181	105		-41.99
Djibouti	135	171	81	92	126		36.96
Kenya	1,815	1,743	1,553	2,204	2,916	0.03	32.30
Madagascar	1,219	452	556	375	435		16.00
Malawi	248	120	192	126	148		17.46
Mauritius	1,471	1,761	701	797	433		-45.67
Mozambique	236	531	194	211	317		50.24
Rwanda	1,859	2,392	1,970	2,091	1,740	0.02	-16.79
Seychelles	495	396	361	391	895	0.01	128.90
Somalia	139	117	299	158	351		122.15
Zimbabwe	2,614	1,265	851	1,474	1,140	0.01	-22.66
Uganda	544	598	657	781	842	0.01	7.81
United Republic of Tanzania	353	556	665	727	810	0.01	11.42
Zambia	565	398	502	388	277		-28.61
Central Africa	28,241	30,947	25,709	25,813	23,600	0.22	-8.57
Angola	1,727	2,066	1,530	1,536	1,994	0.02	29.82
Cameroon	3,987	6,869	4,395	4,039	3,851	0.04	-4.65
Central African Republic	416	243	549	795	534	0.01	-32.83
Chad	506	397	573	370	237		-35.95
Congo	8,924	8,001	6,578	5,401	4,995	0.05	-7.52
Democratic Republic of the Congo	9,762	9,077	8,654	11,488	9,921	0.09	-13.64
Equatorial Guinea	103	84	185	113	94		-16.81
Gabon	2,718	4,155	3,109	1,958	1,890	0.02	-3.47
Sao Tome and Principe	98	55	136	113	84		-25.66
North Africa	40,107	39,727	41,272	37,606	38,651	0.36	2.78
Algeria	9,092	6,736	8,343	9,585	9,543	0.09	-0.44
Morocco	19,766	24,652	24,741	21,027	21,949	0.21	4.38
Sudan	974	742	728	996	705	0.01	-29.22
Tunisia	10,275	7,597	7,460	5,998	6,454	0.06	7.60
Southern Africa	20,656	17,588	17,549	20,226	22,280	0.21	10.16
Botswana	1,460	148	92	100	234		134.00
Lesotho	85	108	30	79	169		113.92
Namibia	718	519	345	415	456		9.88
South Africa	17,987	16,281	16,519	18,888	20,645	0.19	9.30
Swaziland	406	532	563	744	776	0.01	4.30
West Africa	25,187	27,422	25,081	28,076	28,626	0.27	1.96
Cape Verde	103	140	173	286	126		-55.94
Benin	1,273	676	788	812	845	0.01	4.06
Gambia	1,383	1,023	627	633	635	0.01	0.32
Ghana	1,358	1,470	1,099	1,255	1,386	0.01	10.44
Guinea	1,245	1,694	1,613	1,445	1,548	0.01	7.13
Cote D'Ivoire	2,126	3,436	3,546	2,880	3,318	0.03	15.21
Liberia	639	405	616	566	570	0.01	0.71
Mali	1,751	3,929	1,896	1,770	1,929	0.02	8.98
Mauritania	426	597	568	914	677	0.01	-25.93

BELGIUM

5. Overnight stays of non-resident tourists in hotels and similar establishments, by country of residence

	2002	2003	2004	2005	2006	Market share 06	% Change 06-05
Niger	3,498	2,766	2,773	3,469	4,410	0.04	27.13
Nigeria	4,664	4,540	4,710	4,716	4,247	0.04	-9.94
Guinea-Bissau	111	127	107	135	221		63.70
Saint Helena	15	39					
Senegal	3,274	3,245	2,611	3,963	2,794	0.03	-29.50
Sierra Leone	1,499	1,846	2,336	3,149	3,888	0.04	23.47
Togo	826	407	559	663	921	0.01	38.91
Burkina Faso	996	1,082	1,059	1,420	1,111	0.01	-21.76
AMERICAS	**781,874**	**730,195**	**763,865**	**763,197**	**798,370**	**7.51**	**4.61**
Caribbean	**8,470**	**7,318**	**8,581**	**5,754**	**5,622**	**0.05**	**-2.29**
Antigua and Barbuda	124	210	199	782	641	0.01	-18.03
Bahamas	357	348	518	481	639	0.01	32.85
Barbados	234	128	217	383	807	0.01	110.70
Bermuda	1,608	2,522					
British Virgin Islands	3	17					
Cayman Islands	37	69					
Cuba	2,028	771	5,931	1,546	1,007	0.01	-34.86
Dominica	425	410	130	215	373		73.49
Dominican Republic	397	453	455	908	795	0.01	-12.44
Grenada	115	42	83	43	95		120.93
Haiti	304	160	235	673	277		-58.84
Jamaica	807	423	425	393	537	0.01	36.64
Montserrat	26	44					
Netherlands Antilles	582	442					
Aruba	83	76					
Saint Kitts and Nevis	2	55	14	52	24		-53.85
Anguilla	188	185					
Saint Lucia	152	107	84	57	77		35.09
Saint Vincent and the Grenadines	27	39	37	16	20		25.00
Trinidad and Tobago	321	212	253	205	330		60.98
Turks and Caicos Islands	641	577					
United States Virgin Islands	9	28					
Central America	**4,565**	**4,606**	**5,790**	**5,827**	**8,415**	**0.08**	**44.41**
Belize	711	282	271	386	385		-0.26
Costa Rica	1,207	1,458	1,852	2,008	3,125	0.03	55.63
El Salvador	648	877	1,006	1,022	2,083	0.02	103.82
Guatemala	550	462	530	672	618	0.01	-8.04
Honduras	317	368	311	326	473		45.09
Nicaragua	546	668	605	742	957	0.01	28.98
Panama	586	491	1,215	671	774	0.01	15.35
North America	**721,570**	**670,201**	**703,893**	**697,596**	**720,679**	**6.78**	**3.31**
Canada	70,426	72,165	78,118	76,722	86,723	0.82	13.04
Greenland	848	381					
Mexico	24,428	23,494	20,587	21,831	29,330	0.28	34.35
Saint Pierre and Miquelon	45	8					
United States	625,823	574,153	605,188	599,043	604,626	5.69	0.93
South America	**47,269**	**48,070**	**45,601**	**54,020**	**63,654**	**0.60**	**17.83**
Argentina	7,912	7,909	7,584	7,822	9,601	0.09	22.74
Bolivia	528	412	310	676	634	0.01	-6.21
Brazil	19,093	19,949	22,098	27,446	31,315	0.29	14.10
Chile	6,007	7,999	5,312	4,428	6,028	0.06	36.13
Colombia	4,348	4,293	3,477	4,713	5,538	0.05	17.50
Ecuador	2,902	1,883	1,275	1,385	1,814	0.02	30.97

BELGIUM

5. Overnight stays of non-resident tourists in hotels and similar establishments, by country of residence

	2002	2003	2004	2005	2006	Market share 06	% Change 06-05
Falkland Islands (Malvinas)	27	18					
Guyana	188	125	134	197	187		-5.08
Paraguay	135	252	178	213	477		123.94
Peru	1,929	2,338	1,765	1,820	2,035	0.02	11.81
Suriname	361	339	394	406	711	0.01	75.12
Uruguay	688	629	805	1,844	2,320	0.02	25.81
Venezuela	3,151	1,924	2,269	3,070	2,994	0.03	-2.48
EAST ASIA AND THE PACIFIC	**536,834**	**437,372**	**480,204**	**452,975**	**468,042**	**4.40**	**3.33**
North-East Asia	**447,355**	**363,360**	**394,822**	**365,852**	**365,646**	**3.44**	**-0.06**
China	138,376	132,410	142,788	137,945	141,952	1.33	2.90
Taiwan (Province of China)	8,518	5,114	5,375	5,764	10,167	0.10	76.39
Hong Kong, China	6,610	4,013					
Japan	276,962	205,441	227,804	200,806	194,166	1.83	-3.31
Korea, Dem. People's Republic of	6,260	4,940	4,852	5,404	3,735	0.04	-30.88
Korea, Republic of	9,829	10,797	13,762	15,772	15,461	0.15	-1.97
Macao, China	458	439					
Mongolia	342	206	241	161	165		2.48
South-East Asia	**46,647**	**32,560**	**35,344**	**36,293**	**42,732**	**0.40**	**17.74**
Brunei Darussalam	140	206	119	242	183		-24.38
Myanmar	98	56	52	69	60		-13.04
Cambodia	211	429	253	319	294		-7.84
Indonesia	4,973	3,910	5,529	4,037	4,654	0.04	15.28
Lao People's Democratic Republic	451	487	363	683	483		-29.28
Malaysia	5,343	4,933	5,093	6,089	6,525	0.06	7.16
Philippines	6,080	5,685	5,629	5,243	8,021	0.08	52.98
Timor-Leste			8	96	63		-34.38
Singapore	20,074	8,534	9,173	9,997	11,081	0.10	10.84
Viet Nam	2,476	1,467	2,077	2,288	3,657	0.03	59.83
Thailand	6,801	6,853	7,048	7,230	7,711	0.07	6.65
Australasia	**39,685**	**38,868**	**46,369**	**49,050**	**56,530**	**0.53**	**15.25**
Australia	30,996	30,285	36,895	39,843	44,964	0.42	12.85
New Zealand	8,689	8,583	9,474	9,207	11,566	0.11	25.62
Melanesia	**987**	**1,014**	**2,540**	**806**	**1,594**	**0.01**	**97.77**
Solomon Islands	22	15	105	96	117		21.88
Fiji	600	820	2,272	387	1,165	0.01	201.03
New Caledonia	60	34					
Vanuatu	30	20	42	53	31		-41.51
Papua New Guinea	275	125	121	270	281		4.07
Micronesia	**905**	**561**	**645**	**612**	**949**	**0.01**	**55.07**
Kiribati	37	118	102	65	105		61.54
Nauru	545	82	92	136	248		82.35
Northern Mariana Islands	14	9					
Micronesia (Federated States of)	7	3	2	9	51		466.67
Marshall Islands	20	1	12		6		
Palau	282	348	437	402	539	0.01	34.08
Polynesia	**556**	**335**	**484**	**362**	**591**	**0.01**	**63.26**
French Polynesia	371	151					
Pitcairn	16						
Tonga	34	38	72	132	55		-58.33
Tuvalu	12	22	64	118	216		83.05
Wallis and Futuna Islands	3	9					
Samoa	120	115	348	112	320		185.71

BELGIUM

5. Overnight stays of non-resident tourists in hotels and similar establishments, by country of residence

	2002	2003	2004	2005	2006	Market share 06	% Change 06-05
Other East Asia and the Pacific	699	674					
Other countries of Oceania	699	674					
EUROPE	8,723,953	8,740,562	8,646,434	8,638,832	8,889,735	83.60	2.90
Central/Eastern Europe	332,051	330,185	392,240	441,238	518,337	4.87	17.47
Azerbaijan	1,020	852	864	895	1,302	0.01	45.47
Armenia	1,697	1,609	1,604	1,574	1,456	0.01	-7.50
Bulgaria	15,842	15,504	21,272	19,309	24,406	0.23	26.40
Belarus	2,805	1,997	1,846	1,972	3,144	0.03	59.43
Czech Republic	33,661	40,648	41,960	45,606	48,584	0.46	6.53
Estonia	7,023	10,622	9,885	9,919	10,499	0.10	5.85
Georgia	5,181	3,936	5,932	4,583	5,471	0.05	19.38
Hungary	29,565	35,109	42,210	45,494	51,443	0.48	13.08
Kazakhstan	793	1,249	948	1,639	2,328	0.02	42.04
Kyrgyzstan	106	722	297	432	221		-48.84
Latvia	3,235	3,537	6,903	7,089	7,356	0.07	3.77
Lithuania	10,914	14,579	22,221	21,334	22,107	0.21	3.62
Republic of Moldova	809	669	636	1,041	913	0.01	-12.30
Poland	88,121	82,579	103,383	114,425	155,128	1.46	35.57
Romania	24,451	23,400	26,648	31,186	43,245	0.41	38.67
Russian Federation	76,320	65,945	75,640	99,506	104,939	0.99	5.46
Slovakia	11,004	12,137	12,797	17,601	15,514	0.15	-11.86
Tajikistan	175	482	307	218	310		42.20
Turkmenistan	303	254	176	936	158		-83.12
Ukraine	17,923	12,209	13,732	14,972	17,873	0.17	19.38
Uzbekistan	1,103	2,146	2,979	1,507	1,940	0.02	28.73
Northern Europe	2,838,240	2,738,994	2,590,061	2,453,962	2,425,244	22.81	-1.17
Denmark	106,188	96,917	97,326	94,629	98,239	0.92	3.81
Faeroe Islands	7,826	4,805					
Finland	59,526	62,404	57,818	65,477	66,244	0.62	1.17
Iceland	8,723	9,737	15,548	11,154	11,728	0.11	5.15
Ireland	82,249	95,816	94,982	80,766	74,101	0.70	-8.25
Norway	63,744	66,724	68,495	66,280	65,411	0.62	-1.31
Sweden	130,905	145,588	139,692	136,540	137,326	1.29	0.58
United Kingdom	2,379,079	2,257,003	2,116,200	1,999,116	1,972,195	18.55	-1.35
Southern Europe	946,289	1,031,930	986,695	1,047,877	1,089,563	10.25	3.98
Albania	9,660	14,793	19,427	20,467	21,342	0.20	4.28
Andorra	1,660	1,804	1,000	2,444	2,653	0.02	8.55
Bosnia and Herzegovina	2,279	2,190	2,442	2,948	3,087	0.03	4.72
Croatia	7,504	8,125	8,636	14,195	15,470	0.15	8.98
Gibraltar	187	284					
Greece	69,746	83,670	68,356	67,687	70,090	0.66	3.55
Holy See	150	34	107	66	229		246.97
Italy	412,632	455,836	406,121	413,316	427,786	4.02	3.50
Malta	6,476	8,395	9,234	10,764	11,230	0.11	4.33
Portugal	63,246	70,257	68,203	78,240	71,494	0.67	-8.62
San Marino	118	72	77	114	195		71.05
Slovenia	10,019	12,956	12,652	12,804	14,208	0.13	10.97
Spain	357,411	367,439	381,704	416,288	442,652	4.16	6.33
TFYR of Macedonia	2,433	2,937	4,561	3,840	4,213	0.04	9.71
Serbia and Montenegro	2,768	3,138	4,175	4,704	4,914	0.05	4.46
Western Europe	4,494,104	4,518,869	4,554,943	4,561,534	4,722,410	44.41	3.53
Austria	56,059	57,009	56,797	55,715	62,985	0.59	13.05

BELGIUM

5. Overnight stays of non-resident tourists in hotels and similar establishments, by country of residence

	2002	2003	2004	2005	2006	Market share 06	% Change 06-05
France	1,318,215	1,361,557	1,406,285	1,415,360	1,484,012	13.96	4.85
Germany	1,223,196	1,206,241	1,173,290	1,161,263	1,167,302	10.98	0.52
Liechtenstein	8,135	7,772	8,789	6,693	4,404	0.04	-34.20
Luxembourg	115,967	119,142	110,597	119,221	120,271	1.13	0.88
Monaco			99	649	596	0.01	-8.17
Netherlands	1,666,590	1,663,371	1,689,265	1,690,032	1,767,157	16.62	4.56
Switzerland	105,942	103,777	109,821	112,601	115,683	1.09	2.74
East Mediterranean Europe	**113,269**	**120,584**	**122,495**	**134,221**	**134,181**	**1.26**	**-0.03**
Cyprus	6,042	6,917	8,443	9,428	10,634	0.10	12.79
Israel	64,382	65,394	59,557	60,804	62,848	0.59	3.36
Turkey	42,845	48,273	54,495	63,989	60,699	0.57	-5.14
MIDDLE EAST	**60,085**	**58,388**	**57,301**	**62,341**	**64,053**	**0.60**	**2.75**
Middle East	**60,085**	**58,388**	**57,301**	**62,341**	**64,053**	**0.60**	**2.75**
Bahrain	887	783	637	647	867	0.01	34.00
Palestine			83	179	109		-39.11
Iraq	793	472	878	1,200	958	0.01	-20.17
Jordan	2,066	2,352	2,104	1,945	2,160	0.02	11.05
Kuwait	2,381	2,805	2,456	2,275	2,680	0.03	17.80
Lebanon	4,541	5,802	4,778	4,470	5,049	0.05	12.95
Libyan Arab Jamahiriya	2,858	2,423	2,318	3,047	2,487	0.02	-18.38
Oman	654	504	562	541	803	0.01	48.43
Qatar	3,235	3,197	4,202	3,998	3,291	0.03	-17.68
Saudi Arabia	9,509	11,839	12,872	14,137	8,971	0.08	-36.54
Syrian Arab Republic	1,658	1,885	2,687	2,975	1,969	0.02	-33.82
United Arab Emirates	18,578	15,836	13,662	16,498	24,709	0.23	49.77
Egypt	12,291	10,184	9,886	9,763	9,812	0.09	0.50
Yemen	550	235	176	666	188		-71.77
Other countries of Middle East	84	71					
SOUTH ASIA	**87,773**	**73,429**	**79,929**	**77,264**	**78,940**	**0.74**	**2.17**
South Asia	**87,773**	**73,429**	**79,929**	**77,264**	**78,940**	**0.74**	**2.17**
Afghanistan	3,167	3,286	2,975	2,817	1,919	0.02	-31.88
Bangladesh	13,270	12,719	10,663	9,423	2,885	0.03	-69.38
Bhutan	91	174	272	120	60		-50.00
Sri Lanka	798	682	645	648	843	0.01	30.09
India	56,078	41,971	51,970	51,626	58,516	0.55	13.35
Iran, Islamic Republic of	10,890	10,553	9,526	8,706	10,097	0.09	15.98
Maldives	60	63	46	101	90		-10.89
Nepal	249	228	152	337	419		24.33
Pakistan	3,170	3,753	3,680	3,486	4,111	0.04	17.93
REGION NOT SPECIFIED	**89,889**	**111,324**	**166,521**	**175,933**	**207,843**	**1.95**	**18.14**
Not Specified	**89,889**	**111,324**	**166,521**	**175,933**	**207,843**	**1.95**	**18.14**
Other countries of the World	89,889	111,324	166,521	175,933	207,843	1.95	18.14

Source: World Tourism Organization (UNWTO)

BELGIUM

6. Overnight stays of non-resident tourists in all types of accommodation establishments, by country of residence

		2002	2003	2004	2005	2006	Market share 06	% Change 06-05
TOTAL	(*)	15,895,417	15,929,415	15,544,514	15,553,279	16,039,960	100.00	3.13
AFRICA		142,180	142,395	130,763	137,897	140,905	0.88	2.18
East Africa		15,942	14,319	12,912	15,866	14,438	0.09	-9.00
British Indian Ocean Territory		282	161					
Burundi		2,111	1,898	1,616	2,050	1,567	0.01	-23.56
Comoros		90	140	64	80	43		-46.25
Ethiopia		1,150	1,125	1,257	2,870	1,964	0.01	-31.57
Eritrea		39	40	154	197	106		-46.19
Djibouti		166	175	268	92	126		36.96
Kenya		1,921	1,843	1,688	2,291	2,967	0.02	29.51
Madagascar		1,241	487	1,069	388	447		15.21
Malawi		251	120	193	150	153		2.00
Mauritius		1,511	1,765	712	811	515		-36.50
Mozambique		236	573	195	254	318		25.20
Rwanda		1,917	2,530	2,128	2,176	1,787	0.01	-17.88
Seychelles		495	401	361	408	905	0.01	121.81
Somalia		153	117	302	173	356		105.78
Zimbabwe		2,700	1,306	1,031	1,674	1,194	0.01	-28.67
Uganda		546	656	684	1,103	865	0.01	-21.58
United Republic of Tanzania		378	568	671	757	843	0.01	11.36
Zambia		755	414	519	392	282		-28.06
Central Africa		29,929	32,535	26,535	27,237	24,394	0.15	-10.44
Angola		1,750	2,159	1,571	1,542	2,007	0.01	30.16
Cameroon		4,135	7,186	4,499	4,221	3,987	0.02	-5.54
Central African Republic		424	244	560	817	536		-34.39
Chad		543	397	573	381	488		28.08
Congo		9,607	8,761	6,978	5,505	5,074	0.03	-7.83
Democratic Republic of the Congo		9,924	9,353	8,878	12,440	10,174	0.06	-18.22
Equatorial Guinea		306	85	192	113	96		-15.04
Gabon		3,142	4,213	3,140	2,097	1,948	0.01	-7.11
Sao Tome and Principe		98	137	144	121	84		-30.58
North Africa		43,574	42,849	44,510	40,874	41,765	0.26	2.18
Algeria		9,630	7,098	8,826	10,794	10,576	0.07	-2.02
Morocco		21,688	26,462	26,616	22,570	23,477	0.15	4.02
Sudan		983	753	748	1,010	721		-28.61
Tunisia		11,273	8,536	8,320	6,500	6,991	0.04	7.55
Southern Africa		24,544	20,708	18,967	23,179	25,286	0.16	9.09
Botswana		1,460	148	92	100	237		137.00
Lesotho		85	110	30	79	169		113.92
Namibia		1,170	693	386	683	859	0.01	25.77
South Africa		21,423	19,216	17,890	21,568	23,245	0.14	7.78
Swaziland		406	541	569	749	776		3.60
West Africa		28,191	31,984	27,839	30,741	35,022	0.22	13.93
Cape Verde		103	149	173	292	129		-55.82
Benin		1,965	924	798	1,014	866	0.01	-14.60
Gambia		1,483	1,377	628	636	638		0.31
Ghana		1,370	1,773	1,172	1,266	1,416	0.01	11.85
Guinea		1,312	1,813	1,637	1,530	1,648	0.01	7.71
Cote D'Ivoire		3,038	4,378	4,295	3,061	3,414	0.02	11.53
Liberia		640	411	619	583	578		-0.86
Mali		1,788	4,150	2,220	1,784	2,317	0.01	29.88
Mauritania		470	609	578	983	688		-30.01

BELGIUM

6. Overnight stays of non-resident tourists in all types of accommodation establishments, by country of residence

	2002	2003	2004	2005	2006	Market share 06	% Change 06-05
Niger	3,558	2,898	2,950	4,189	8,261	0.05	97.21
Nigeria	4,721	4,747	5,007	4,904	4,492	0.03	-8.40
Guinea-Bissau	111	151	113	138	228		65.22
Saint Helena	15	40					
Senegal	3,978	3,993	3,333	4,625	3,820	0.02	-17.41
Sierra Leone	1,503	2,841	2,410	3,166	4,219	0.03	33.26
Togo	1,009	491	629	668	1,062	0.01	58.98
Burkina Faso	1,127	1,239	1,277	1,902	1,246	0.01	-34.49
AMERICAS	**860,992**	**798,854**	**829,024**	**830,622**	**855,323**	**5.33**	**2.97**
Caribbean	**8,695**	**8,255**	**9,059**	**6,631**	**5,869**	**0.04**	**-11.49**
Antigua and Barbuda	124	214	206	787	642		-18.42
Bahamas	359	350	538	485	659		35.88
Barbados	242	138	308	383	915	0.01	138.90
Bermuda	1,624	2,524					
British Virgin Islands	3	18					
Cayman Islands	37	71					
Cuba	2,073	1,442	6,116	1,948	1,027	0.01	-47.28
Dominica	442	417	141	279	393		40.86
Dominican Republic	422	486	480	917	822	0.01	-10.36
Grenada	115	43	122	91	111		21.98
Haiti	375	263	282	1,009	289		-71.36
Jamaica	819	466	442	402	551		37.06
Montserrat	30	44					
Netherlands Antilles	584	447					
Aruba	83	83					
Saint Kitts and Nevis	2	75	19	52	24		-53.85
Anguilla	188	190					
Saint Lucia	153	107	84	57	77		35.09
Saint Vincent and the Grenadines	27	39	43	16	20		25.00
Trinidad and Tobago	338	212	278	205	339		65.37
Turks and Caicos Islands	646	594					
United States Virgin Islands	9	32					
Central America	**5,216**	**5,426**	**6,585**	**6,269**	**9,286**	**0.06**	**48.13**
Belize	724	297	338	454	725		59.69
Costa Rica	1,423	1,626	1,992	2,107	3,302	0.02	56.72
El Salvador	707	930	1,059	1,054	2,119	0.01	101.04
Guatemala	653	592	604	735	688		-6.39
Honduras	444	435	444	361	479		32.69
Nicaragua	661	1,026	911	872	1,156	0.01	32.57
Panama	604	520	1,237	686	817	0.01	19.10
North America	**788,439**	**727,847**	**756,919**	**752,775**	**765,708**	**4.77**	**1.72**
Canada	89,955	90,180	95,973	93,482	100,889	0.63	7.92
Greenland	877	386					
Mexico	32,967	31,003	27,847	28,038	34,481	0.21	22.98
Saint Pierre and Miquelon	53	13					
United States	664,587	606,265	633,099	631,255	630,338	3.93	-0.15
South America	**58,642**	**57,326**	**56,461**	**64,947**	**74,460**	**0.46**	**14.65**
Argentina	9,875	9,165	9,010	9,525	11,609	0.07	21.88
Bolivia	609	517	653	1,051	768		-26.93
Brazil	23,252	24,567	28,563	32,653	35,866	0.22	9.84
Chile	8,610	9,244	6,143	6,321	7,062	0.04	11.72
Colombia	5,211	4,936	4,073	5,435	6,599	0.04	21.42
Ecuador	3,480	2,211	1,609	1,546	2,247	0.01	45.34

BELGIUM

6. Overnight stays of non-resident tourists in all types of accommodation establishments, by country of residence

	2002	2003	2004	2005	2006	Market share 06	% Change 06-05
Falkland Islands (Malvinas)	29	26					
Guyana	188	125	144	215	187		-13.02
Paraguay	271	284	279	225	524		132.89
Peru	2,197	2,696	2,090	2,280	2,788	0.02	22.28
Suriname	371	366	416	425	715		68.24
Uruguay	1,121	1,078	1,055	2,099	2,577	0.02	22.77
Venezuela	3,428	2,111	2,426	3,172	3,518	0.02	10.91
EAST ASIA AND THE PACIFIC	**588,014**	**489,366**	**530,156**	**500,080**	**514,581**	**3.21**	**2.90**
North-East Asia	**473,723**	**390,561**	**422,320**	**390,457**	**390,684**	**2.44**	**0.06**
China	141,457	134,592	145,548	141,552	146,687	0.91	3.63
Taiwan (Province of China)	9,228	6,393	7,262	6,498	11,224	0.07	72.73
Hong Kong, China	6,779	4,481					
Japan	293,369	220,566	241,985	213,696	206,399	1.29	-3.41
Korea, Dem. People's Republic of	6,880	6,018	5,997	6,156	5,884	0.04	-4.42
Korea, Republic of	15,156	17,851	21,281	22,376	20,283	0.13	-9.35
Macao, China	459	451					
Mongolia	395	209	247	179	207		15.64
South-East Asia	**49,618**	**35,431**	**37,492**	**40,395**	**46,192**	**0.29**	**14.35**
Brunei Darussalam	140	208	119	254	247		-2.76
Myanmar	98	63	53	70	60		-14.29
Cambodia	211	440	262	319	303		-5.02
Indonesia	5,547	4,450	5,674	4,202	4,982	0.03	18.56
Lao People's Democratic Republic	453	503	383	768	501		-34.77
Malaysia	6,050	5,610	5,484	6,421	6,885	0.04	7.23
Philippines	6,258	5,761	5,713	5,465	8,184	0.05	49.75
Timor-Leste			8	96	63		-34.38
Singapore	20,608	9,073	9,517	10,275	11,390	0.07	10.85
Viet Nam	2,906	2,022	2,855	3,979	5,367	0.03	34.88
Thailand	7,347	7,301	7,424	8,546	8,210	0.05	-3.93
Australasia	**61,433**	**60,716**	**66,615**	**67,384**	**74,367**	**0.46**	**10.36**
Australia	48,474	47,727	53,639	55,721	58,923	0.37	5.75
New Zealand	12,959	12,989	12,976	11,663	15,444	0.10	32.42
Melanesia	**1,028**	**1,035**	**2,587**	**819**	**1,602**	**0.01**	**95.60**
Solomon Islands	34	18	125	100	119		19.00
Fiji	600	823	2,283	394	1,165	0.01	195.69
New Caledonia	70	40					
Vanuatu	30	20	48	53	33		-37.74
Papua New Guinea	294	134	131	272	285		4.78
Micronesia	**916**	**562**	**652**	**653**	**1,145**	**0.01**	**75.34**
Kiribati	37	119	102	65	105		61.54
Nauru	547	82	97	177	444		150.85
Northern Mariana Islands	19	9					
Micronesia (Federated States of)	7	3	2	9	51		466.67
Marshall Islands	24	1	12		6		
Palau	282	348	439	402	539		34.08
Polynesia	**565**	**338**	**490**	**372**	**591**		**58.87**
French Polynesia	373	151					
Pitcairn	16						
Tonga	34	38	72	140	55		-60.71
Tuvalu	17	22	64	119	216		81.51
Wallis and Futuna Islands	5	12					
Samoa	120	115	354	113	320		183.19

BELGIUM

6. Overnight stays of non-resident tourists in all types of accommodation establishments, by country of residence

	2002	2003	2004	2005	2006	Market share 06	% Change 06-05
Other East Asia and the Pacific	731	723					
Other countries of Oceania	731	723					
EUROPE	14,031,475	14,229,703	13,721,303	13,741,275	14,156,479	88.26	3.02
Central/Eastern Europe	383,150	377,272	440,778	489,799	583,965	3.64	19.23
Azerbaijan	1,062	861	877	914	1,403	0.01	53.50
Armenia	2,931	1,616	1,638	1,612	1,482	0.01	-8.06
Bulgaria	16,703	16,505	22,052	20,429	25,332	0.16	24.00
Belarus	3,128	2,362	2,766	2,214	4,216	0.03	90.42
Czech Republic	40,781	45,533	47,856	49,864	54,146	0.34	8.59
Estonia	7,604	10,967	10,511	10,267	11,393	0.07	10.97
Georgia	5,530	4,012	5,986	4,614	5,502	0.03	19.25
Hungary	35,757	43,936	50,402	51,441	57,539	0.36	11.85
Kazakhstan	2,254	1,542	1,101	1,714	2,416	0.02	40.96
Kyrgyzstan	106	1,035	312	432	222		-48.61
Latvia	3,884	4,582	8,448	8,034	8,971	0.06	11.66
Lithuania	12,966	19,394	23,941	23,031	23,069	0.14	0.16
Republic of Moldova	837	694	641	1,076	954	0.01	-11.34
Poland	106,220	96,270	122,908	138,233	193,258	1.20	39.81
Romania	27,322	28,186	29,990	34,492	46,594	0.29	35.09
Russian Federation	82,254	70,023	78,947	103,783	108,792	0.68	4.83
Slovakia	12,859	13,718	14,637	18,918	17,214	0.11	-9.01
Tajikistan	175	496	311	220	310		40.91
Turkmenistan	392	265	217	947	160		-83.10
Ukraine	18,468	13,088	14,164	15,981	18,703	0.12	17.03
Uzbekistan	1,917	2,187	3,073	1,583	2,289	0.01	44.60
Northern Europe	3,168,586	3,062,214	2,853,764	2,707,636	2,691,604	16.78	-0.59
Denmark	130,845	128,905	117,691	120,837	120,920	0.75	0.07
Faeroe Islands	8,183	6,527					
Finland	68,523	73,394	62,849	70,247	70,109	0.44	-0.20
Iceland	8,856	10,445	15,716	11,483	12,168	0.08	5.97
Ireland	96,290	105,805	103,543	88,679	80,416	0.50	-9.32
Norway	69,497	71,523	72,751	70,366	71,466	0.45	1.56
Sweden	141,134	156,374	151,462	146,735	146,094	0.91	-0.44
United Kingdom	2,645,258	2,509,241	2,329,752	2,199,289	2,190,431	13.66	-0.40
Southern Europe	1,041,575	1,138,482	1,092,590	1,172,217	1,204,223	7.51	2.73
Albania	10,105	14,859	19,530	20,835	21,433	0.13	2.87
Andorra	1,782	1,848	1,033	2,499	2,762	0.02	10.52
Bosnia and Herzegovina	2,339	2,322	3,020	3,574	3,249	0.02	-9.09
Croatia	8,052	8,928	9,307	14,746	16,386	0.10	11.12
Gibraltar	191	287					
Greece	72,752	95,703	81,996	86,906	99,077	0.62	14.00
Holy See	150	34	109	67	238		255.22
Italy	443,679	488,713	437,367	441,620	452,493	2.82	2.46
Malta	6,653	8,500	9,366	10,853	11,471	0.07	5.69
Portugal	70,119	78,565	72,364	83,385	76,904	0.48	-7.77
San Marino	118	130	77	136	195		43.38
Slovenia	11,596	14,949	14,510	16,715	22,192	0.14	32.77
Spain	407,273	416,576	434,701	482,007	488,029	3.04	1.25
TFYR of Macedonia	2,754	3,224	4,726	3,987	4,608	0.03	15.58
Serbia and Montenegro	4,012	3,844	4,484	4,887	5,186	0.03	6.12
Western Europe	9,320,212	9,526,560	9,206,942	9,231,963	9,536,944	59.46	3.30
Austria	63,929	64,199	63,053	82,477	69,013	0.43	-16.32

BELGIUM

6. Overnight stays of non-resident tourists in all types of accommodation establishments, by country of residence

	2002	2003	2004	2005	2006	Market share 06	% Change 06-05
France	1,702,696	1,786,424	1,882,048	1,941,152	2,066,796	12.89	6.47
Germany	2,227,918	2,118,726	1,981,742	1,952,157	1,925,213	12.00	-1.38
Liechtenstein	8,168	7,774	8,836	6,736	4,444	0.03	-34.03
Luxembourg	176,659	185,308	175,255	194,739	185,676	1.16	-4.65
Monaco			99	651	596		-8.45
Netherlands	5,022,770	5,246,444	4,973,469	4,924,745	5,156,292	32.15	4.70
Switzerland	118,072	117,685	122,440	129,306	128,914	0.80	-0.30
East Mediterranean Europe	**117,952**	**125,175**	**127,229**	**139,660**	**139,743**	**0.87**	**0.06**
Cyprus	6,125	7,053	8,638	9,553	10,903	0.07	14.13
Israel	67,944	68,648	62,818	64,336	66,518	0.41	3.39
Turkey	43,883	49,474	55,773	65,771	62,322	0.39	-5.24
MIDDLE EAST	**63,012**	**59,269**	**59,556**	**64,315**	**67,456**	**0.42**	**4.88**
Middle East	**63,012**	**59,269**	**59,556**	**64,315**	**67,456**	**0.42**	**4.88**
Bahrain	887	785	638	652	867	0.01	32.98
Palestine			130	219	269		22.83
Iraq	831	523	937	1,306	1,030	0.01	-21.13
Jordan	2,087	2,380	2,135	1,978	2,213	0.01	11.88
Kuwait	2,538	2,875	2,522	2,501	2,878	0.02	15.07
Lebanon	4,693	6,079	4,947	4,652	5,269	0.03	13.26
Libyan Arab Jamahiriya	2,880	2,453	2,360	3,080	2,501	0.02	-18.80
Oman	661	510	564	543	807	0.01	48.62
Qatar	4,677	3,216	5,560	4,442	4,982	0.03	12.16
Saudi Arabia	9,652	11,843	12,885	14,169	9,149	0.06	-35.43
Syrian Arab Republic	1,674	1,906	2,725	3,014	2,064	0.01	-31.52
United Arab Emirates	18,685	15,975	13,715	16,862	24,765	0.15	46.87
Egypt	13,082	10,412	10,259	10,231	10,469	0.07	2.33
Yemen	550	241	179	666	193		-71.02
Other countries of Middle East	115	71					
SOUTH ASIA	**92,806**	**77,998**	**83,011**	**79,378**	**81,278**	**0.51**	**2.39**
South Asia	**92,806**	**77,998**	**83,011**	**79,378**	**81,278**	**0.51**	**2.39**
Afghanistan	3,221	3,302	3,034	2,830	1,971	0.01	-30.35
Bangladesh	13,314	12,744	10,710	9,455	2,900	0.02	-69.33
Bhutan	91	174	272	132	60		-54.55
Sri Lanka	809	904	690	655	961	0.01	46.72
India	59,657	45,499	54,548	53,055	60,045	0.37	13.18
Iran, Islamic Republic of	12,144	11,036	9,752	9,181	10,467	0.07	14.01
Maldives	60	63	46	116	91		-21.55
Nepal	273	431	197	380	528		38.95
Pakistan	3,237	3,845	3,762	3,574	4,255	0.03	19.05
REGION NOT SPECIFIED	**116,938**	**131,830**	**190,701**	**199,712**	**223,938**	**1.40**	**12.13**
Not Specified	**116,938**	**131,830**	**190,701**	**199,712**	**223,938**	**1.40**	**12.13**
Other countries of the World	116,938	131,830	190,701	199,712	223,938	1.40	12.13

Source: World Tourism Organization (UNWTO)

BELIZE

1. Arrivals of non-resident tourists at national borders, by nationality

	2002	2003	2004	2005	2006	Market share 06	% Change 06-05
TOTAL	199,521	220,574	230,835	236,573	247,309	100.00	4.54
AFRICA	374	337	349	348	359	0.15	3.16
Other Africa	374	337	349	348	359	0.15	3.16
All countries of Africa	374	337	349	348	359	0.15	3.16
AMERICAS	154,321	174,784	185,254	190,301	199,315	80.59	4.74
Caribbean	1,941	2,055	2,210	2,086	2,319	0.94	11.17
Jamaica	719	846	735	729	704	0.28	-3.43
Other countries of the Caribbean	1,222	1,209	1,475	1,357	1,615	0.65	19.01
Central America	28,619	27,514	24,957	20,828	21,942	8.87	5.35
Guatemala	21,184	17,632	15,951	13,907	13,616	5.51	-2.09
Honduras	2,826	4,124	3,479	2,559	2,918	1.18	14.03
Other countries of Central America	4,609	5,758	5,527	4,362	5,408	2.19	23.98
North America	122,201	143,431	156,146	165,450	172,918	69.92	4.51
Canada	9,185	9,831	11,926	13,580	15,553	6.29	14.53
Mexico	8,413	6,312	6,853	5,893	5,855	2.37	-0.64
United States	104,603	127,288	137,367	145,977	151,510	61.26	3.79
South America	1,560	1,784	1,941	1,937	2,136	0.86	10.27
All countries of South America	1,560	1,784	1,941	1,937	2,136	0.86	10.27
EAST ASIA AND THE PACIFIC	3,411	3,754	4,285	4,384	4,516	1.83	3.01
Other East Asia and the Pacific	3,411	3,754	4,285	4,384	4,516	1.83	3.01
All countries of Asia	2,235	2,413	2,729	2,469	2,367	0.96	-4.13
All countries of Oceania	1,176	1,341	1,556	1,915	2,149	0.87	12.22
EUROPE	29,115	33,530	32,768	33,466	34,373	13.90	2.71
Northern Europe	10,130	10,102	10,827	10,982	10,852	4.39	-1.18
Sweden	686	784	836	993	1,053	0.43	6.04
United Kingdom	9,444	9,318	9,991	9,989	9,799	3.96	-1.90
Southern Europe	5,033	5,584	4,251	4,466	4,800	1.94	7.48
Italy	3,656	3,847	2,850	3,080	3,073	1.24	-0.23
Spain	1,377	1,737	1,401	1,386	1,727	0.70	24.60
Western Europe	9,916	12,492	12,190	12,190	12,255	4.96	0.53
France	2,218	3,115	3,308	3,803	3,167	1.28	-16.72
Germany	3,602	4,146	4,269	3,966	4,308	1.74	8.62
Netherlands	3,122	4,212	3,585	3,617	4,017	1.62	11.06
Switzerland	974	1,019	1,028	804	763	0.31	-5.10
Other Europe	4,036	5,352	5,500	5,828	6,466	2.61	10.95
Other countries of Europe	4,036	5,352	5,500	5,828	6,466	2.61	10.95
MIDDLE EAST	405	370	481	369	381	0.15	3.25
Middle East	405	370	481	369	381	0.15	3.25
All countries of Middle East	405	370	481	369	381	0.15	3.25
REGION NOT SPECIFIED	11,895	7,799	7,698	7,705	8,365	3.38	8.57
Not Specified	11,895	7,799	7,698	7,705	8,365	3.38	8.57
Nationals Residing Abroad	11,895	7,799	7,698	7,705	8,365	3.38	8.57

Source: World Tourism Organization (UNWTO)

BELIZE

2. Arrivals of non-resident visitors at national borders, by nationality

		2002	2003	2004	2005	2006	Market share 06	% Change 06-05
TOTAL	(*)	693,754	999,100	1,328,709				
AMERICAS		627,804	923,476	1,230,373				
Caribbean		4,283	5,090	6,452				
Cuba		573	758	1,019				
Jamaica		1,253	1,285	1,239				
Other countries of the Caribbean		2,457	3,047	4,194				
Central America		156,272	183,176	166,696				
Costa Rica		1,041	1,124	1,127				
El Salvador		4,834	6,197	5,654				
Guatemala		144,459	167,715	152,162				
Honduras		4,372	5,921	5,399				
Other countries of Central America		1,566	2,219	2,354				
North America		463,520	729,149	1,050,302				
Canada		22,742	28,645	48,078				
Mexico		32,256	39,144	37,978				
United States		408,522	661,360	964,246				
South America		3,729	6,061	6,923				
All countries of South America		3,729	6,061	6,923				
EAST ASIA AND THE PACIFIC		3,784	4,347	6,741				
Other East Asia and the Pacific		3,784	4,347	6,741				
All countries of Asia		3,784	4,347	6,741				
EUROPE		58,252	67,043	85,735				
Northern Europe		19,783	20,193	24,331				
United Kingdom		19,783	20,193	24,331				
Other Europe		38,469	46,850	61,404				
Other countries of Europe		38,469	46,850	61,404				
REGION NOT SPECIFIED		3,914	4,234	5,860				
Not Specified		3,914	4,234	5,860				
Other countries of the World		3,914	4,234	5,860				

Source: World Tourism Organization (UNWTO)

BENIN

1. Arrivals of non-resident tourists at national borders, by country of residence

	2002	2003	2004	2005	2006	Market share 06	% Change 06-05
TOTAL (*)	72,288	175,000	173,500	176,000	180,006	100.00	2.28
AFRICA	49,387	148,646	147,536	140,185	152,000	84.44	8.43
East Africa	633	10,287	10,122	9,755	10,615	5.90	8.82
Burundi	250	2,100	2,157	2,749	2,036	1.13	-25.94
Comoros		938	898	978	980	0.54	0.20
Ethiopia	90	688	677	141	130	0.07	-7.80
Eritrea			520	66	45	0.02	-31.82
Djibouti		21	33	99	105	0.06	6.06
Kenya	45	410	112	86	112	0.06	30.23
Madagascar	70	1,800	1,102	2,172	1,988	1.10	-8.47
Malawi	5	2,100	2,330	700	1,700	0.94	142.86
Mauritius	7	77	50	19	53	0.03	178.95
Mozambique	11	650	548	1,236	996	0.55	-19.42
Rwanda	100	884	987	991	1,750	0.97	76.59
Seychelles			11	2			
Zimbabwe	20				7		
Uganda		299	287	177	230	0.13	29.94
United Republic of Tanzania	20	187	190	208	344	0.19	65.38
Zambia	15	133	220	131	139	0.08	6.11
Central Africa	6,050	68,187	67,794	62,840	61,900	34.39	-1.50
Angola	110	8,592	9,613	10,540	10,880	6.04	3.23
Cameroon	2,200	9,814	10,599	11,500	12,500	6.94	8.70
Central African Republic	210	2,000	1,877	880	600	0.33	-31.82
Chad	370	1,870	2,110	1,950	2,400	1.33	23.08
Congo	2,000	37,781	36,376	35,320	32,114	17.84	-9.08
Democratic Republic of the Congo	150	1,125	1,221	996	1,330	0.74	33.53
Equatorial Guinea	10	87	52	21	19	0.01	-9.52
Gabon	1,000	6,830	5,878	1,600	2,050	1.14	28.13
Sao Tome and Principe		88	68	33	7		-78.79
North Africa	715	2,751	3,220	3,100	2,879	1.60	-7.13
Algeria	410	510	490	640	550	0.31	-14.06
Morocco	150	162	377	310	300	0.17	-3.23
Sudan	15	355	435	265	302	0.17	13.96
Tunisia	140	1,724	1,918	1,885	1,727	0.96	-8.38
Southern Africa	185	1,241	1,270	931	1,360	0.76	46.08
Botswana	45	15	22	18	35	0.02	94.44
Lesotho			44	6	44	0.02	633.33
Namibia	20	460	515	355	551	0.31	55.21
South Africa	120	766	689	543	712	0.40	31.12
Swaziland				9	18	0.01	100.00
West Africa	41,804	66,180	65,130	63,559	75,246	41.80	18.39
Cape Verde	10	133	120	300	255	0.14	-15.00
Gambia	35	799	633	850	1,054	0.59	24.00
Ghana	1,340	7,311	7,511	6,600	9,500	5.28	43.94
Guinea	1,010	730	1,810	1,320	620	0.34	-53.03
Cote D'Ivoire	7,600	12,000	10,705	10,900	15,800	8.78	44.95
Liberia	310	350	320	550	130	0.07	-76.36
Mali	2,310	1,300	1,210	900	1,470	0.82	63.33
Mauritania	210	200	210	244	198	0.11	-18.85
Niger	4,310	6,810	5,900	5,300	6,900	3.83	30.19
Nigeria	15,250	19,800	20,200	20,500	22,200	12.33	8.29
Guinea-Bissau	4	7	9	25	31	0.02	24.00
Senegal	1,915	3,800	1,100	1,339	1,586	0.88	18.45

BENIN

1. Arrivals of non-resident tourists at national borders, by country of residence

	2002	2003	2004	2005	2006	Market share 06	% Change 06-05
Sierra Leone	50	340	452	241	336	0.19	39.42
Togo	4,650	10,400	11,200	10,590	11,146	6.19	5.25
Burkina Faso	2,800	2,200	3,750	3,900	4,020	2.23	3.08
AMERICAS	**1,281**	**471**	**360**	**500**	**972**	**0.54**	**94.40**
Caribbean	**1**	**1**	**5**	**87**	**130**	**0.07**	**49.43**
Cuba				19	35	0.02	84.21
Dominican Republic		1		5	12	0.01	140.00
Guadeloupe					2		
Haiti	1			17	19	0.01	11.76
Jamaica			5	31	44	0.02	41.94
Netherlands Antilles				15	18	0.01	20.00
Central America			**1**	**4**	**6**		**50.00**
Honduras					2		
Nicaragua			1		4		
All countries of Central America				4			
North America	**1,280**	**460**	**338**	**289**	**681**	**0.38**	**135.64**
Canada	280	110	127	220	305	0.17	38.64
Mexico				48	99	0.05	106.25
United States	1,000	350	211	21	277	0.15	1,219.05
South America		**10**	**16**	**120**	**155**	**0.09**	**29.17**
Argentina			5	39	44	0.02	12.82
Bolivia				2	12	0.01	500.00
Brazil		10	7	53	61	0.03	15.09
Chile			1	15	8		-46.67
Colombia				3	11	0.01	266.67
Uruguay					9		
Venezuela			3	8	10	0.01	25.00
EAST ASIA AND THE PACIFIC	**220**	**225**	**261**	**321**	**633**	**0.35**	**97.20**
North-East Asia	**192**	**191**	**257**	**288**	**407**	**0.23**	**41.32**
China	89	100	124	209	266	0.15	27.27
Japan	100	87	133	47	105	0.06	123.40
Korea, Dem. People's Republic of	3	4		32	36	0.02	12.50
South-East Asia	**13**	**27**	**3**	**31**	**205**	**0.11**	**561.29**
Myanmar					12	0.01	
Indonesia		8		8	60	0.03	650.00
Malaysia				2	11	0.01	450.00
Philippines	5	7	2	5	14	0.01	180.00
Singapore	8	5		4	88	0.05	2,100.00
Viet Nam		7	1	5	17	0.01	240.00
Thailand				7	3		-57.14
Australasia	**10**	**7**		**1**	**21**	**0.01**	**2,000.00**
Australia	10	7		1	21	0.01	2,000.00
Melanesia	**5**		**1**	**1**			
Fiji	5		1	1			
EUROPE	**21,090**	**25,403**	**25,157**	**31,500**	**22,257**	**12.36**	**-29.34**
Northern Europe	**1,040**	**560**	**628**	**644**	**597**	**0.33**	**-7.30**
Denmark	500	450	477	350	230	0.13	-34.29
Finland	10	3		7	1		-85.71
Ireland		2		11	1		-90.91
Norway	30	8	4	19	33	0.02	73.68

BENIN

1. Arrivals of non-resident tourists at national borders, by country of residence

	2002	2003	2004	2005	2006	Market share 06	% Change 06-05
Sweden	500	97	147	257	332	0.18	29.18
Southern Europe	**550**	**1,113**	**1,014**	**1,065**	**966**	**0.54**	**-9.30**
Bosnia and Herzegovina					2		
Greece				2			
Italy	300	380	415	500	725	0.40	45.00
Portugal		458	322	364	66	0.04	-81.87
Slovenia					3		
Spain	250	275	277	199	170	0.09	-14.57
Western Europe	**19,000**	**23,460**	**23,410**	**28,477**	**20,483**	**11.38**	**-28.07**
Austria	5,000	4,000	3,000	2,500	1,308	0.73	-47.68
Belgium	3,000	3,500	3,125	4,630	3,360	1.87	-27.43
France	10,000	11,000	14,210	16,147	12,115	6.73	-24.97
Germany	500	2,500	1,520	1,900	1,700	0.94	-10.53
Luxembourg		320	20	140	104	0.06	-25.71
Netherlands	200	1,100	220	1,360	996	0.55	-26.76
Switzerland	300	1,040	1,315	1,800	900	0.50	-50.00
East Mediterranean Europe			**3**	**14**	**11**	**0.01**	**-21.43**
Israel			3	9	8		-11.11
Turkey				5	3		-40.00
Other Europe	**500**	**270**	**102**	**1,300**	**200**	**0.11**	**-84.62**
Other countries of Europe	500	270	102	1,300	200	0.11	-84.62
MIDDLE EAST	**185**	**112**	**61**	**518**	**644**	**0.36**	**24.32**
Middle East	**185**	**112**	**61**	**518**	**644**	**0.36**	**24.32**
Palestine				12	19	0.01	58.33
Iraq		1		7	11	0.01	57.14
Jordan					6		
Kuwait		4		22	7		-68.18
Lebanon	30	27	11	55	258	0.14	369.09
Libyan Arab Jamahiriya	150	51	25	189	144	0.08	-23.81
Saudi Arabia		20	19	166	22	0.01	-86.75
Syrian Arab Republic				12			
Egypt	5	9	6	55	177	0.10	221.82
SOUTH ASIA	**115**	**137**	**125**	**2,956**	**3,500**	**1.94**	**18.40**
South Asia	**115**	**137**	**125**	**2,956**	**3,500**	**1.94**	**18.40**
Afghanistan		2		177	89	0.05	-49.72
Bangladesh				2			
Sri Lanka					2		
India	100	110	99	1,300	1,225	0.68	-5.77
Iran, Islamic Republic of	5	8	7	810	1,215	0.67	50.00
Nepal				11			
Pakistan	10	17	19	656	969	0.54	47.71
REGION NOT SPECIFIED	**10**	**6**		**20**			
Not Specified	**10**	**6**		**20**			
Other countries of the World	10	6		20			

Source: World Tourism Organization (UNWTO)

BERMUDA

1. Arrivals of non-resident tourists at national borders, by country of residence

		2002	2003	2004	2005	2006	Market share 06	% Change 06-05
TOTAL	(*)	284,024	256,579	271,620	269,591	298,973	100.00	10.90
AMERICAS		243,793	222,396	235,546	232,661	255,400	85.43	9.77
North America		243,793	222,396	235,546	232,661	255,400	85.43	9.77
Canada		25,892	24,485	26,492	28,665	27,675	9.26	-3.45
United States		217,901	197,911	209,054	203,996	227,725	76.17	11.63
EAST ASIA AND THE PACIFIC		861	503	834	639	647	0.22	1.25
North-East Asia		346	229	419	227	175	0.06	-22.91
Japan		346	229	419	227	175	0.06	-22.91
Australasia		515	274	415	412	472	0.16	14.56
Australia		515	274	415	412	472	0.16	14.56
EUROPE		30,669	25,938	25,873	26,678	32,347	10.82	21.25
Northern Europe		25,871	21,887	21,670	22,714	27,323	9.14	20.29
Sweden		269	220	236	274	315	0.11	14.96
United Kingdom		25,602	21,667	21,434	22,440	27,008	9.03	20.36
Southern Europe		815	696	559	601	969	0.32	61.23
Italy		815	696	559	601	969	0.32	61.23
Western Europe		2,976	2,328	2,452	2,373	3,063	1.02	29.08
Austria		169	78	98	97	120	0.04	23.71
France		869	730	742	758	834	0.28	10.03
Germany		1,262	1,109	1,162	1,051	1,467	0.49	39.58
Switzerland		676	411	450	467	642	0.21	37.47
Other Europe		1,007	1,027	1,192	990	992	0.33	0.20
Other countries of Europe		1,007	1,027	1,192	990	992	0.33	0.20
REGION NOT SPECIFIED		8,701	7,742	9,367	9,613	10,579	3.54	10.05
Not Specified		8,701	7,742	9,367	9,613	10,579	3.54	10.05
Other countries of the World		8,701	7,742	9,367	9,613	10,579	3.54	10.05

Source: World Tourism Organization (UNWTO)

BERMUDA

6. Overnight stays of non-resident tourists in all types of accommodation establishments, by nationality

	2002	2003	2004	2005	2006	Market share 06	% Change 06-05
TOTAL (*)	**1,822,169**	**1,597,677**	**1,733,166**	**1,728,591**	**1,931,436**	**100.00**	**11.73**
AMERICAS	**1,424,337**	**1,237,079**	**1,355,968**	**1,335,308**	**1,469,369**	**76.08**	**10.04**
North America	**1,424,337**	**1,237,079**	**1,355,968**	**1,335,308**	**1,469,369**	**76.08**	**10.04**
Canada	224,757	212,261	261,007	271,650	267,276	13.84	-1.61
United States	1,199,580	1,024,818	1,094,961	1,063,658	1,202,093	62.24	13.01
EAST ASIA AND THE PACIFIC	**6,572**	**2,809**	**5,652**	**4,579**	**5,103**	**0.26**	**11.44**
North-East Asia	**1,665**	**768**	**1,938**	**1,357**	**1,156**	**0.06**	**-14.81**
Japan	1,665	768	1,938	1,357	1,156	0.06	-14.81
Australasia	**4,907**	**2,041**	**3,714**	**3,222**	**3,947**	**0.20**	**22.50**
Australia	4,907	2,041	3,714	3,222	3,947	0.20	22.50
EUROPE	**299,999**	**261,428**	**267,621**	**271,635**	**321,922**	**16.67**	**18.51**
Northern Europe	**257,410**	**225,788**	**230,024**	**235,480**	**277,152**	**14.35**	**17.70**
Sweden	2,016	1,976	1,852	2,281	2,683	0.14	17.62
United Kingdom	255,394	223,812	228,172	233,199	274,469	14.21	17.70
Southern Europe	**8,569**	**6,883**	**6,248**	**7,366**	**9,390**	**0.49**	**27.48**
Italy	8,569	6,883	6,248	7,366	9,390	0.49	27.48
Western Europe	**25,091**	**20,920**	**20,030**	**20,173**	**27,437**	**1.42**	**36.01**
Austria	1,758	960	1,163	1,309	1,720	0.09	31.40
France	6,643	6,561	5,337	5,716	7,388	0.38	29.25
Germany	11,598	10,412	10,240	9,655	13,084	0.68	35.52
Switzerland	5,092	2,987	3,290	3,493	5,245	0.27	50.16
Other Europe	**8,929**	**7,837**	**11,319**	**8,616**	**7,943**	**0.41**	**-7.81**
Other countries of Europe	8,929	7,837	11,319	8,616	7,943	0.41	-7.81
REGION NOT SPECIFIED	**91,261**	**96,361**	**103,925**	**117,069**	**135,042**	**6.99**	**15.35**
Not Specified	**91,261**	**96,361**	**103,925**	**117,069**	**135,042**	**6.99**	**15.35**
Other countries of the World	91,261	96,361	103,925	117,069	135,042	6.99	15.35

Source: World Tourism Organization (UNWTO)

BHUTAN

1. Arrivals of non-resident tourists at national borders, by nationality

	2002	2003	2004	2005	2006	Market share 06	% Change 06-05
TOTAL	5,599	6,261	9,249	13,626	17,348	100.00	27.32
AFRICA	17	14	14	45	88	0.51	95.56
North Africa				1	1	0.01	
Morocco				1	1	0.01	
Southern Africa	17	14	14	44	87	0.50	97.73
South Africa	17	14	14	44	47	0.27	6.82
Swaziland					40	0.23	
AMERICAS	2,154	2,034	3,607	5,168	5,627	32.44	8.88
Caribbean					3	0.02	
Cuba					3	0.02	
Central America	2						
Costa Rica	2						
North America	2,127	1,995	3,534	5,056	5,466	31.51	8.11
Canada	166	119	257	292	375	2.16	28.42
Mexico	38	72	34	83	73	0.42	-12.05
United States	1,923	1,804	3,243	4,681	5,018	28.93	7.20
South America	25	39	73	112	158	0.91	41.07
Argentina	4	7	7	13	39	0.22	200.00
Brazil	21	19	60	44	55	0.32	25.00
Chile				2	12	0.07	500.00
Colombia		7	4	24	14	0.08	-41.67
Peru		2		5	3	0.02	-40.00
Venezuela		4	2	24	35	0.20	45.83
EAST ASIA AND THE PACIFIC	1,310	1,415	1,680	2,759	4,317	24.88	56.47
North-East Asia	1,005	1,077	1,223	1,859	2,273	13.10	22.27
China	25	23	78	234	362	2.09	54.70
Taiwan (Province of China)	40	90	46	10	35	0.20	250.00
Hong Kong, China	4		2		1	0.01	
Japan	892	951	1,087	1,554	1,815	10.46	16.80
Korea, Republic of	44	13	10	61	60	0.35	-1.64
South-East Asia	59	136	92	366	1,154	6.65	215.30
Myanmar		5					
Cambodia					3	0.02	
Indonesia		10	6	22	61	0.35	177.27
Malaysia	2	27	17	72	49	0.28	-31.94
Philippines	3	8	21	21	72	0.42	242.86
Singapore	8	20	16	149	180	1.04	20.81
Viet Nam			2	6	13	0.07	116.67
Thailand	46	66	30	96	776	4.47	708.33
Australasia	246	202	365	534	890	5.13	66.67
Australia	214	165	315	458	774	4.46	69.00
New Zealand	32	37	50	76	116	0.67	52.63
EUROPE	2,094	2,774	3,905	5,619	7,267	41.89	29.33
Central/Eastern Europe	78	107	170	232	454	2.62	95.69
Belarus					1	0.01	
Czech Republic	5	10	17	29	49	0.28	68.97
Estonia		8		16	49	0.28	206.25
Hungary		11	36	19	37	0.21	94.74
Kazakhstan					2	0.01	

BHUTAN

1. Arrivals of non-resident tourists at national borders, by nationality

	2002	2003	2004	2005	2006	Market share 06	% Change 06-05
Latvia	2			9	14	0.08	55.56
Republic of Moldova					3	0.02	
Poland	41	11	47	52	133	0.77	155.77
Romania					1	0.01	
Russian Federation	25	56	63	87	125	0.72	43.68
Slovakia	3	1		6	27	0.16	350.00
Ukraine	2	10	7	14	13	0.07	-7.14
Northern Europe	**615**	**747**	**1,149**	**1,712**	**2,341**	**13.49**	**36.74**
Denmark	10	55	85	56	85	0.49	51.79
Finland	14	14	11	21	35	0.20	66.67
Iceland		2			13	0.07	
Ireland	7	14	24	31	51	0.29	64.52
Norway	25	9	10	58	104	0.60	79.31
Sweden	41	48	61	84	103	0.59	22.62
United Kingdom	518	605	958	1,462	1,950	11.24	33.38
Southern Europe	**253**	**462**	**699**	**798**	**1,065**	**6.14**	**33.46**
Greece	4	2	18	39	42	0.24	7.69
Italy	177	331	462	529	648	3.74	22.50
Portugal	4	25	21	45	64	0.37	42.22
Slovenia					27	0.16	
Spain	68	77	198	185	281	1.62	51.89
Yugoslavia, Sfr (Former)		27			3	0.02	
Western Europe	**1,082**	**1,402**	**1,795**	**2,726**	**3,310**	**19.08**	**21.42**
Austria	94	152	225	319	484	2.79	51.72
Belgium	75	104	124	134	220	1.27	64.18
France	194	286	434	532	708	4.08	33.08
Germany	357	497	671	1,042	1,074	6.19	3.07
Luxembourg	1	7	5	9	8	0.05	-11.11
Netherlands	197	179	163	327	389	2.24	18.96
Switzerland	164	177	173	363	427	2.46	17.63
East Mediterranean Europe	**66**	**56**	**92**	**147**	**97**	**0.56**	**-34.01**
Israel	5	47	37	98	46	0.27	-53.06
Turkey	61	9	55	49	51	0.29	4.08
Other Europe				**4**			
Other countries of Europe				4			
MIDDLE EAST	**3**			**7**	**12**	**0.07**	**71.43**
Middle East	**3**			**7**	**12**	**0.07**	**71.43**
Jordan					1	0.01	
Lebanon				2	10	0.06	400.00
Egypt	3			5	1	0.01	-80.00
SOUTH ASIA	**18**	**12**	**19**	**17**	**30**	**0.17**	**76.47**
South Asia	**18**	**12**	**19**	**17**	**30**	**0.17**	**76.47**
Afghanistan					4	0.02	
Sri Lanka	1		1	1	1	0.01	
Iran, Islamic Republic of	2	1	3				
Nepal	15	11	15	16	25	0.14	56.25
REGION NOT SPECIFIED	**3**	**12**	**24**	**11**	**7**	**0.04**	**-36.36**
Not Specified	**3**	**12**	**24**	**11**	**7**	**0.04**	**-36.36**
Other countries of the World	3	12	24	11	7	0.04	-36.36

Source: World Tourism Organization (UNWTO)

BOLIVIA

3. Arrivals of non-resident tourists in hotels and similar establishments, by nationality

		2002	2003	2004	2005	2006	Market share 06	% Change 06-05
TOTAL	(*)	380,202	367,036	390,888	413,267			
AFRICA		977	1,117	1,278	1,661			
Other Africa		977	1,117	1,278	1,661			
All countries of Africa		977	1,117	1,278	1,661			
AMERICAS		216,960	209,715	227,280	250,107			
North America		50,432	49,256	52,202	52,038			
Canada		7,873	7,429	8,120	8,297			
Mexico		4,070	5,026	6,016	5,983			
United States		38,489	36,801	38,066	37,758			
South America		161,582	155,903	170,847	193,161			
Argentina		35,185	31,242	36,320	41,610			
Brazil		26,185	23,810	29,745	32,400			
Chile		21,898	17,152	14,948	19,234			
Colombia		6,512	7,503	8,286	8,615			
Ecuador		4,270	6,106	4,788	5,315			
Paraguay		3,110	3,498	3,486	3,849			
Peru		59,674	62,164	68,739	77,380			
Uruguay		2,791	2,515	2,591	2,398			
Venezuela		1,957	1,913	1,944	2,360			
Other Americas		4,946	4,556	4,231	4,908			
Other countries of the Americas		4,946	4,556	4,231	4,908			
EAST ASIA AND THE PACIFIC		16,293	15,291	18,917	19,878			
North-East Asia		6,931	6,379	7,469	7,226			
Japan		6,931	6,379	7,469	7,226			
Other East Asia and the Pacific		9,362	8,912	11,448	12,652			
Other countries of Asia		3,901	2,787	3,870	4,063			
All countries of Oceania		5,461	6,125	7,578	8,589			
EUROPE		145,972	140,913	143,413	141,621			
Northern Europe		22,638	23,181	23,686	23,885			
Sweden		2,605	2,747	3,070	3,084			
United Kingdom		20,033	20,434	20,616	20,801			
Southern Europe		18,355	18,595	20,620	20,075			
Italy		7,623	7,631	8,480	8,101			
Spain		10,732	10,964	12,140	11,974			
Western Europe		69,021	62,469	62,515	62,619			
France		26,277	24,356	24,416	25,167			
Germany		21,592	19,056	19,804	20,308			
Netherlands		11,953	10,444	9,764	8,625			
Switzerland		9,199	8,613	8,531	8,519			
East Mediterranean Europe		10,702	12,003	12,149	9,405			
Israel		10,702	12,003	12,149	9,405			
Other Europe		25,256	24,665	24,443	25,637			
Other countries of Europe		25,256	24,665	24,443	25,637			

Source: World Tourism Organization (UNWTO)

BOLIVIA

5. Overnight stays of non-resident tourists in hotels and similar establishments, by nationality

		2002	2003	2004	2005	2006	Market share 06	% Change 06-05
TOTAL	(*)	969,118	1,005,581	1,030,479	1,099,027			
AFRICA		3,034	3,801	4,007	6,013			
Other Africa		3,034	3,801	4,007	6,013			
All countries of Africa		3,034	3,801	4,007	6,013			
AMERICAS		583,818	610,409	623,735	683,919			
North America		133,974	138,105	147,082	140,818			
Canada		19,328	18,599	20,395	21,046			
Mexico		10,424	12,523	15,089	15,526			
United States		104,222	106,983	111,598	104,246			
South America		431,709	454,643	459,138	520,799			
Argentina		106,165	107,444	105,751	121,406			
Brazil		76,176	71,951	84,666	91,425			
Chile		55,196	50,703	39,783	47,869			
Colombia		25,027	27,802	29,484	32,685			
Ecuador		14,640	25,554	18,686	16,208			
Paraguay		9,399	12,635	13,738	17,138			
Peru		129,715	139,944	151,483	178,006			
Uruguay		8,170	9,199	8,392	8,532			
Venezuela		7,221	9,411	7,155	7,530			
Other Americas		18,135	17,661	17,515	22,302			
Other countries of the Americas		18,135	17,661	17,515	22,302			
EAST ASIA AND THE PACIFIC		45,725	44,442	50,252	54,019			
North-East Asia		22,513	22,333	22,519	21,843			
Japan		22,513	22,333	22,519	21,843			
Other East Asia and the Pacific		23,212	22,109	27,733	32,176			
Other countries of Asia		11,232	8,374	10,912	12,686			
All countries of Oceania		11,980	13,735	16,821	19,490			
EUROPE		336,541	346,929	352,485	355,076			
Northern Europe		51,212	53,078	56,356	55,938			
Sweden		6,893	7,201	9,405	9,100			
United Kingdom		44,319	45,877	46,951	46,838			
Southern Europe		50,758	52,476	59,093	60,208			
Italy		18,659	19,466	20,901	21,208			
Spain		32,099	33,010	38,192	39,000			
Western Europe		147,939	142,566	140,847	143,012			
France		52,373	52,302	51,227	52,622			
Germany		48,885	46,253	45,903	46,955			
Netherlands		25,643	23,952	23,106	22,165			
Switzerland		21,038	20,059	20,611	21,270			
East Mediterranean Europe		27,412	37,184	38,668	33,484			
Israel		27,412	37,184	38,668	33,484			
Other Europe		59,220	61,625	57,521	62,434			
Other countries of Europe		59,220	61,625	57,521	62,434			

Source: World Tourism Organization (UNWTO)

BONAIRE

1. Arrivals of non-resident tourists at national borders, by country of residence

	2002	2003	2004	2005	2006	Market share 06	% Change 06-05
TOTAL	52,085	62,179	63,156	62,550	63,552	100.00	1.60
AMERICAS	33,548	32,771	34,576	32,244	35,093	55.22	8.84
Caribbean	2,891	3,178	3,172	2,572	3,161	4.97	22.90
Antigua and Barbuda			1				
Bahamas	4	2	15				
Barbados	6	7	6				
Dominica	1	10	4				
Dominican Republic	250	145	122				
Haiti	5	12	1				
Jamaica	66	71	49				
Montserrat	3						
Aruba	2,162	2,493	2,690	2,018	2,592	4.08	28.44
Puerto Rico	212	190	136				
Saint Lucia		2	1				
Trinidad and Tobago	70	70	47				
Turks and Caicos Islands	6	1					
United States Virgin Islands		31	29				
Other countries of the Caribbean	106	144	71	554	569	0.90	2.71
Central America	52	40	25				
Costa Rica	17	13	8				
Panama	18	18	17				
Other countries of Central America	17	9					
North America	27,123	26,083	27,842	26,520	28,301	44.53	6.72
Canada	593	843	1,175	1,157	1,511	2.38	30.60
Mexico	31	12	44				
United States	26,499	25,228	26,623	25,363	26,790	42.15	5.63
South America	3,482	3,470	3,537	3,152	3,631	5.71	15.20
Argentina	60	36	107				
Bolivia	3	1	5				
Brazil	246	234	479	415	834	1.31	100.96
Chile	27	42	11				
Colombia	437	235	222	222	228	0.36	2.70
Ecuador	262	280	396	251	189	0.30	-24.70
Guyana		17					
Peru	97	655	437	278	367	0.58	32.01
Suriname	175	179	138				
Uruguay	18	13	10				
Venezuela	2,150	1,725	1,633	1,632	1,642	2.58	0.61
Other countries of South America	7	53	99	354	371	0.58	4.80
EUROPE	18,152	29,079	27,973	30,066	28,202	44.38	-6.20
Northern Europe	1,535	3,333	3,565	3,861	3,897	6.13	0.93
Denmark	87	119	111				
Finland	122	157	153	274	229	0.36	-16.42
Norway	63	292	188	175	241	0.38	37.71
Sweden	122	460	572	622	656	1.03	5.47
United Kingdom	1,141	2,305	2,541	2,790	2,771	4.36	-0.68
Southern Europe	512	728	576	463	491	0.77	6.05
Greece	18	24	17				
Italy	287	475	413	463	491	0.77	6.05
Portugal	79	50	32				
Spain	128	179	114				
Western Europe	15,870	24,422	23,437	24,478	22,586	35.54	-7.73

BONAIRE

1. Arrivals of non-resident tourists at national borders, by country of residence

	2002	2003	2004	2005	2006	Market share 06	% Change 06-05
Austria	210	353	191				
Belgium	429	663	715	722	593	0.93	-17.87
France	231	292	304	294	327	0.51	11.22
Germany	1,602	2,236	1,868	2,072	1,709	2.69	-17.52
Luxembourg	14	22	7				
Netherlands	12,814	19,995	19,506	20,676	19,246	30.28	-6.92
Switzerland	570	861	846	714	711	1.12	-0.42
Other Europe	**235**	**596**	**395**	**1,264**	**1,228**	**1.93**	**-2.85**
Other countries of Europe	235	596	395	1,264	1,228	1.93	-2.85
REGION NOT SPECIFIED	**385**	**329**	**607**	**240**	**257**	**0.40**	**7.08**
Not Specified	**385**	**329**	**607**	**240**	**257**	**0.40**	**7.08**
Other countries of the World	385	329	607	240	257	0.40	7.08

Source: World Tourism Organization (UNWTO)

BONAIRE

6. Overnight stays of non-resident tourists in all types of accommodation establishments, by country of residence

	2002	2003	2004	2005	2006	Market share 06	% Change 06-05
TOTAL	**486,055**	**574,102**	**577,997**				
AMERICAS	**268,764**	**267,369**	**278,925**				
Caribbean	**15,150**	**16,992**	**15,571**				
All countries of the Caribbean	15,150	16,992	15,571				
North America	**228,843**	**224,083**	**238,028**				
Canada	8,016	9,813	11,521				
United States	220,827	214,270	226,507				
Other Americas	**24,771**	**26,294**	**25,326**				
Other countries of the Americas	24,771	26,294	25,326				
EUROPE	**213,883**	**303,493**	**293,930**				
Western Europe	**153,814**	**217,381**	**212,936**				
Netherlands	153,814	217,381	212,936				
Other Europe	**60,069**	**86,112**	**80,994**				
Other countries of Europe	60,069	86,112	80,994				
REGION NOT SPECIFIED	**3,408**	**3,240**	**5,142**				
Not Specified	**3,408**	**3,240**	**5,142**				
Other countries of the World	3,408	3,240	5,142				

Source: World Tourism Organization (UNWTO)

BOSNIA AND HERZEGOVINA

4. Arrivals of non-resident tourists in all types of accommodation establishments, by country of residence

	2002	2003	2004	2005	2006	Market share 06	% Change 06-05
TOTAL	159,763	165,465	190,300	217,273	255,764	100.00	17.72
AMERICAS	8,286	7,339	8,442	8,030	10,195	3.99	26.96
North America	8,286	7,339	8,442	8,030	10,195	3.99	26.96
Canada	1,058	793	1,082	1,064	1,502	0.59	41.17
United States	7,228	6,546	7,360	6,966	8,693	3.40	24.79
EAST ASIA AND THE PACIFIC	1,496	1,870	2,177	2,355	2,869	1.12	21.83
North-East Asia	958	1,308	1,413	1,212	1,383	0.54	14.11
China	307	315	276	308	194	0.08	-37.01
Japan	651	993	1,137	904	1,189	0.46	31.53
Australasia	538	562	764	1,143	1,486	0.58	30.01
Australia	469	425	621	980	1,294	0.51	32.04
New Zealand	69	137	143	163	192	0.08	17.79
EUROPE	145,883	152,246	176,588	203,564	238,976	93.44	17.40
Central/Eastern Europe	12,959	11,922	11,381	14,231	17,496	6.84	22.94
Bulgaria	1,365	513	888	634	720	0.28	13.56
Czech Republic	2,686	2,919	2,308	2,947	2,762	1.08	-6.28
Hungary	2,252	2,810	2,527	2,801	3,349	1.31	19.56
Poland	4,496	3,174	3,030	4,842	7,293	2.85	50.62
Romania	764	502	708	647	661	0.26	2.16
Russian Federation	695	652	673	897	1,120	0.44	24.86
Slovakia	701	1,352	1,247	1,463	1,591	0.62	8.75
Northern Europe	10,561	13,018	12,056	13,670	14,291	5.59	4.54
Denmark	1,136	1,582	1,002	1,142	1,284	0.50	12.43
Finland	530	495	607	1,103	1,013	0.40	-8.16
Iceland	86	1,192	68	144	68	0.03	-52.78
Ireland	764	771	782	1,043	1,235	0.48	18.41
Norway	1,306	1,419	1,533	1,707	1,706	0.67	-0.06
Sweden	2,352	2,680	2,788	2,869	3,432	1.34	19.62
United Kingdom	4,387	4,879	5,276	5,662	5,553	2.17	-1.93
Southern Europe	98,769	99,647	118,449	130,814	153,648	60.07	17.46
Albania	473	347	561	436	632	0.25	44.95
Croatia	23,536	28,032	29,867	31,854	38,009	14.86	19.32
Greece	951	884	1,049	828	1,225	0.48	47.95
Italy	7,362	7,693	12,083	13,888	15,131	5.92	8.95
Portugal	575	337	361	577	1,503	0.59	160.49
Slovenia	15,280	17,840	20,400	25,934	31,383	12.27	21.01
Spain	2,865	1,680	2,128	2,966	3,682	1.44	24.14
TFYR of Macedonia	2,232	2,567	2,788	3,493	4,019	1.57	15.06
Serbia and Montenegro	45,495	40,267	49,212	50,838	58,064	22.70	14.21
Western Europe	18,225	22,076	27,227	35,524	41,456	16.21	16.70
Austria	3,793	5,933	6,921	7,325	8,882	3.47	21.26
Belgium	661	1,003	1,154	1,238	2,089	0.82	68.74
France	2,523	3,217	4,461	10,049	8,612	3.37	-14.30
Germany	7,900	8,321	10,418	11,509	14,096	5.51	22.48
Luxembourg	68	136	82	151	163	0.06	7.95
Netherlands	2,024	2,200	2,728	3,283	3,674	1.44	11.91
Switzerland	1,256	1,266	1,463	1,969	3,940	1.54	100.10
East Mediterranean Europe	2,199	2,951	4,949	6,920	9,319	3.64	34.67
Israel	320	383	273	257	536	0.21	108.56

BOSNIA AND HERZEGOVINA

4. Arrivals of non-resident tourists in all types of accommodation establishments, by country of residence

	2002	2003	2004	2005	2006	Market share 06	% Change 06-05
Turkey	1,879	2,568	4,676	6,663	8,783	3.43	31.82
Other Europe	**3,170**	**2,632**	**2,526**	**2,405**	**2,766**	**1.08**	**15.01**
Other countries of Europe	3,170	2,632	2,526	2,405	2,766	1.08	15.01
MIDDLE EAST	**93**	**94**	**132**	**46**	**175**	**0.07**	**280.43**
Middle East	93	94	132	46	175	0.07	280.43
Egypt	93	94	132	46	175	0.07	280.43
SOUTH ASIA	**122**	**189**	**116**	**265**	**51**	**0.02**	**-80.75**
South Asia	122	189	116	265	51	0.02	-80.75
Iran, Islamic Republic of	122	189	116	265	51	0.02	-80.75
REGION NOT SPECIFIED	**3,883**	**3,727**	**2,845**	**3,013**	**3,498**	**1.37**	**16.10**
Not Specified	3,883	3,727	2,845	3,013	3,498	1.37	16.10
Other countries of the World	3,883	3,727	2,845	3,013	3,498	1.37	16.10

Source: World Tourism Organization (UNWTO)

BOSNIA AND HERZEGOVINA

6. Overnight stays of non-resident tourists in all types of accommodation establishments, by country of residence

	2002	2003	2004	2005	2006	Market share 06	% Change 06-05
TOTAL	392,354	419,343	459,600	484,545	594,380	100.00	22.67
AMERICAS	21,453	20,169	21,854	21,721	25,042	4.21	15.29
North America	21,453	20,169	21,854	21,721	25,042	4.21	15.29
Canada	2,879	1,993	2,852	2,755	3,342	0.56	21.31
United States	18,574	18,176	19,002	18,966	21,700	3.65	14.42
EAST ASIA AND THE PACIFIC	3,520	4,785	5,255	5,071	5,896	0.99	16.27
North-East Asia	2,360	3,598	3,597	2,734	3,053	0.51	11.67
China	969	513	453	741	530	0.09	-28.48
Japan	1,391	3,085	3,144	1,993	2,523	0.42	26.59
Australasia	1,160	1,187	1,658	2,337	2,843	0.48	21.65
Australia	998	854	1,303	2,038	2,447	0.41	20.07
New Zealand	162	333	355	299	396	0.07	32.44
EUROPE	357,539	372,348	423,469	448,515	552,866	93.02	23.27
Central/Eastern Europe	63,250	51,799	45,835	49,275	59,010	9.93	19.76
Bulgaria	1,721	1,399	1,935	2,052	2,187	0.37	6.58
Czech Republic	20,127	15,472	10,936	12,014	10,575	1.78	-11.98
Hungary	6,397	7,713	6,910	6,430	7,887	1.33	22.66
Poland	26,489	17,618	16,431	17,305	25,296	4.26	46.18
Romania	2,982	1,329	1,725	1,910	2,004	0.34	4.92
Russian Federation	3,482	1,942	1,869	2,987	4,323	0.73	44.73
Slovakia	2,052	6,326	6,029	6,577	6,738	1.13	2.45
Northern Europe	23,973	28,103	29,092	31,823	36,066	6.07	13.33
Denmark	2,499	3,766	2,375	2,765	3,745	0.63	35.44
Finland	997	1,099	1,403	1,939	2,249	0.38	15.99
Iceland	571	320	161	660	144	0.02	-78.18
Ireland	1,619	1,950	1,741	2,290	2,324	0.39	1.48
Norway	3,004	3,322	3,573	3,403	4,265	0.72	25.33
Sweden	4,780	6,562	7,345	8,240	9,693	1.63	17.63
United Kingdom	10,503	11,084	12,494	12,526	13,646	2.30	8.94
Southern Europe	224,373	233,148	269,333	268,374	328,030	55.19	22.23
Albania	773	1,189	3,419	1,214	1,512	0.25	24.55
Croatia	50,068	51,238	63,918	66,678	82,189	13.83	23.26
Greece	1,474	2,431	2,253	2,143	2,568	0.43	19.83
Italy	15,225	16,141	23,290	23,847	28,684	4.83	20.28
Portugal	522	492	695	1,061	2,397	0.40	125.92
Slovenia	44,216	48,513	46,181	52,918	62,537	10.52	18.18
Spain	4,109	3,372	4,495	5,012	7,396	1.24	47.57
TFYR of Macedonia	5,350	5,800	5,914	7,772	13,149	2.21	69.18
Serbia and Montenegro	102,636	103,972	119,168	107,729	127,598	21.47	18.44
Western Europe	36,004	46,229	61,504	74,488	99,958	16.82	34.19
Austria	7,332	12,049	11,563	13,551	16,307	2.74	20.34
Belgium	1,701	2,266	2,600	2,641	6,220	1.05	135.52
France	5,272	6,486	8,162	16,800	14,732	2.48	-12.31
Germany	14,687	17,483	29,691	29,535	40,732	6.85	37.91
Luxembourg	141	304	175	394	523	0.09	32.74
Netherlands	4,489	4,758	6,375	7,554	8,486	1.43	12.34
Switzerland	2,382	2,883	2,938	4,013	12,958	2.18	222.90
East Mediterranean Europe	4,526	7,646	12,755	18,856	23,492	3.95	24.59
Israel	544	904	588	809	1,046	0.18	29.30

BOSNIA AND HERZEGOVINA

6. Overnight stays of non-resident tourists in all types of accommodation establishments, by country of residence

	2002	2003	2004	2005	2006	Market share 06	% Change 06-05
Turkey	3,982	6,742	12,167	18,047	22,446	3.78	24.38
Other Europe	**5,413**	**5,423**	**4,950**	**5,699**	**6,310**	**1.06**	**10.72**
Other countries of Europe	5,413	5,423	4,950	5,699	6,310	1.06	10.72
MIDDLE EAST	**193**	**284**	**564**	**132**	**543**	**0.09**	**311.36**
Middle East	**193**	**284**	**564**	**132**	**543**	**0.09**	**311.36**
Egypt	193	284	564	132	543	0.09	311.36
SOUTH ASIA	**240**	**499**	**377**	**869**	**143**	**0.02**	**-83.54**
South Asia	**240**	**499**	**377**	**869**	**143**	**0.02**	**-83.54**
Iran, Islamic Republic of	240	499	377	869	143	0.02	-83.54
REGION NOT SPECIFIED	**9,409**	**21,258**	**8,081**	**8,237**	**9,890**	**1.66**	**20.07**
Not Specified	**9,409**	**21,258**	**8,081**	**8,237**	**9,890**	**1.66**	**20.07**
Other countries of the World	9,409	21,258	8,081	8,237	9,890	1.66	20.07

Source: World Tourism Organization (UNWTO)

BOTSWANA

1. Arrivals of non-resident tourists at national borders, by country of residence

	2002	2003	2004	2005	2006	Market share 06	% Change 06-05
TOTAL	1,273,784	1,405,535	1,522,807				
AFRICA	1,095,572	1,235,404	1,353,125				
East Africa	491,388	643,625	657,497				
Ethiopia	240	210	245				
Djibouti			10				
Kenya	2,832	2,107	1,910				
Madagascar	20	20	50				
Malawi	3,942	3,142	3,109				
Mauritius	930	480	481				
Mozambique	790	713	615				
Seychelles	30	190	20				
Zimbabwe	454,847	550,994	576,328				
Uganda	740	673	650				
United Republic of Tanzania	1,380	1,508	1,587				
Zambia	25,637	83,588	72,492				
Central Africa	910	460	410				
Angola	810	420	350				
Democratic Republic of the Congo	100	40	60				
North Africa	40		10				
Sudan	40		10				
Southern Africa	601,604	590,002	694,134				
Lesotho	5,053	3,193	5,474				
Namibia	64,001	69,587	57,542				
South Africa	527,505	514,708	626,207				
Swaziland	5,045	2,514	4,911				
West Africa	810	501	572				
Ghana	480	300	410				
Nigeria	330	201	162				
Other Africa	820	816	502				
Other countries of Africa	820	816	502				
AMERICAS	19,014	18,025	21,023				
North America	18,254	17,152	20,481				
Canada	1,932	2,065	2,811				
United States	16,322	15,087	17,670				
Other Americas	760	873	542				
Other countries of the Americas	760	873	542				
EAST ASIA AND THE PACIFIC	11,972	12,442	11,848				
North-East Asia	3,744	3,638	3,940				
China	1,203	934	1,062				
Taiwan (Province of China)	110	100	130				
Hong Kong, China	150	112	230				
Japan	2,281	2,492	2,518				
South-East Asia	320	361	342				
Malaysia	140	221	180				
Singapore	180	140	162				
Australasia	7,058	7,543	6,976				
Australia	5,728	5,708	5,595				
New Zealand	1,330	1,835	1,381				
Other East Asia and the Pacific	850	900	590				

BOTSWANA

1. Arrivals of non-resident tourists at national borders, by country of residence

	2002	2003	2004	2005	2006	Market share 06	% Change 06-05
Other countries of Asia	850	900	590				
EUROPE	**56,917**	**55,054**	**58,432**				
Central/Eastern Europe	**801**	**535**	**1,133**				
Czech Republic	361	284	568				
Poland	280	251	180				
Russian Federation	160		385				
Northern Europe	**24,500**	**21,836**	**27,897**				
Denmark	642	832	905				
Finland	252	197	263				
Ireland	1,136	940	945				
Norway	1,195	704	671				
Sweden	727	645	1,044				
United Kingdom	20,548	18,518	24,069				
Southern Europe	**6,019**	**6,727**	**5,825**				
Greece	350	300	63				
Italy	2,323	2,782	3,196				
Portugal	430	255	440				
Spain	2,546	3,210	1,956				
Serbia and Montenegro	370	180	170				
Western Europe	**24,564**	**25,280**	**23,165**				
Austria	463	1,000	930				
France	3,596	3,732	3,989				
Germany	9,985	10,444	9,685				
Netherlands	6,377	6,146	4,929				
Switzerland	2,070	1,856	1,846				
Belgium / Luxembourg	2,073	2,102	1,786				
East Mediterranean Europe	**600**	**302**	**172**				
Israel	600	302	172				
Other Europe	**433**	**374**	**240**				
Other countries of Europe	433	374	240				
MIDDLE EAST	**20**						
Middle East	**20**						
Iraq	20						
SOUTH ASIA	**4,542**	**1,889**	**2,223**				
South Asia	**4,542**	**1,889**	**2,223**				
Bangladesh	151	71	110				
Sri Lanka	570	142	102				
India	3,421	1,476	1,691				
Iran, Islamic Republic of	100	10					
Pakistan	300	190	320				
REGION NOT SPECIFIED	**85,747**	**82,721**	**76,156**				
Not Specified	**85,747**	**82,721**	**76,156**				
Other countries of the World	85,747	82,721	76,156				

Source: World Tourism Organization (UNWTO)

BRAZIL

1. Arrivals of non-resident tourists at national borders, by country of residence

	2002	2003	2004	2005	2006	Market share 06	% Change 06-05
TOTAL	3,784,898	4,132,847	4,793,703	5,358,170	5,018,991	100.00	-6.33
AFRICA	40,259	52,489	64,678	75,676	83,721	1.67	10.63
Central Africa	8,873	8,850	13,679	14,226	26,619	0.53	87.12
Angola	8,873	8,850	13,679	14,226	26,619	0.53	87.12
Southern Africa	20,798	26,963	32,415	36,139	30,486	0.61	-15.64
South Africa	20,798	26,963	32,415	36,139	30,486	0.61	-15.64
West Africa	1,848	1,230	1,611	13,645	8,495	0.17	-37.74
Cape Verde				11,826	6,592	0.13	-44.26
Nigeria	1,848	1,230	1,611	1,819	1,903	0.04	4.62
Other Africa	8,740	15,446	16,973	11,666	18,121	0.36	55.33
Other countries of Africa	8,740	15,446	16,973	11,666	18,121	0.36	55.33
AMERICAS	2,205,618	2,396,832	2,703,442	2,998,060	2,703,123	53.86	-9.84
Caribbean	6,495	4,188	2,751	3,595	1,999	0.04	-44.39
Puerto Rico	6,495	4,188	2,751	3,595	1,999	0.04	-44.39
Central America	17,596	25,348	33,079	36,486	43,013	0.86	17.89
Costa Rica	3,495	4,800	6,741	7,202	6,240	0.12	-13.36
Panama	6,396	7,217	9,586	10,516	10,365	0.21	-1.44
Other countries of Central America	7,705	13,331	16,752	18,768	26,408	0.53	40.71
North America	740,029	787,407	838,595	941,777	855,098	17.04	-9.20
Canada	62,721	63,183	66,895	75,100	62,603	1.25	-16.64
Mexico	48,896	55,556	65,707	73,118	70,862	1.41	-3.09
United States	628,412	668,668	705,993	793,559	721,633	14.38	-9.06
South America	1,441,498	1,579,889	1,829,017	2,016,202	1,803,013	35.92	-10.57
Argentina	698,465	786,568	922,484	992,299	921,061	18.35	-7.18
Bolivia	57,878	54,865	60,239	68,670	55,169	1.10	-19.66
Chile	113,507	126,591	155,026	169,953	148,327	2.96	-12.72
Colombia	38,828	36,283	42,163	47,230	50,103	1.00	6.08
Ecuador	11,375	11,990	13,343	15,149	19,293	0.38	27.35
French Guiana	11,663	12,227	14,244	17,372	9,208	0.18	-47.00
Guyana	2,114	2,321	3,221	3,248	3,849	0.08	18.50
Paraguay	226,011	198,170	204,762	249,030	198,958	3.96	-20.11
Peru	39,723	38,948	56,647	60,251	54,002	1.08	-10.37
Suriname	4,462	2,441	2,899	2,755	2,332	0.05	-15.35
Uruguay	195,384	270,251	309,732	341,647	290,240	5.78	-15.05
Venezuela	42,088	39,234	44,257	48,598	50,471	1.01	3.85
EAST ASIA AND THE PACIFIC	108,201	128,640	155,605	177,381	219,936	4.38	23.99
North-East Asia	71,723	81,599	98,464	110,398	136,113	2.71	23.29
China	13,981	10,714	16,305	18,017	37,656	0.75	109.00
Japan	42,829	51,387	60,806	68,066	74,638	1.49	9.66
Korea, Republic of	14,913	19,498	21,353	24,315	23,819	0.47	-2.04
Australasia	24,191	21,880	22,972	26,023	31,819	0.63	22.27
Australia	19,959	17,798	18,454	20,949	26,610	0.53	27.02
New Zealand	4,232	4,082	4,518	5,074	5,209	0.10	2.66
Other East Asia and the Pacific	12,287	25,161	34,169	40,960	52,004	1.04	26.96
Other countries of Asia	12,287	25,161	34,169	40,960	52,004	1.04	26.96
EUROPE	1,414,962	1,543,559	1,860,259	2,097,357	1,997,127	39.79	-4.78
Central/Eastern Europe				35,899	21,217	0.42	-40.90
Hungary				16,364	5,870	0.12	-64.13

BRAZIL

1. Arrivals of non-resident tourists at national borders, by country of residence

	2002	2003	2004	2005	2006	Market share 06	% Change 06-05
Poland				19,535	15,347	0.31	-21.44
Northern Europe	**215,959**	**200,573**	**227,260**	**296,714**	**290,100**	**5.78**	**-2.23**
Denmark	21,454	19,722	15,555	19,672	23,288	0.46	18.38
Finland				21,827	21,732	0.43	-0.44
Ireland				13,125	12,574	0.25	-4.20
Norway	24,383	15,631	23,560	26,812	26,761	0.53	-0.19
Sweden	33,073	26,939	37,809	45,764	36,118	0.72	-21.08
United Kingdom	137,049	138,281	150,336	169,514	169,627	3.38	0.07
Southern Europe	**522,537**	**580,438**	**779,675**	**846,603**	**829,500**	**16.53**	**-2.02**
Greece	7,720	7,013	10,703	12,106	13,340	0.27	10.19
Italy	197,641	221,190	276,563	303,878	291,898	5.82	-3.94
Portugal	203,126	229,594	336,988	357,640	312,521	6.23	-12.62
Spain	114,050	122,641	155,421	172,979	211,741	4.22	22.41
Western Europe	**634,844**	**693,587**	**754,325**	**827,223**	**771,217**	**15.37**	**-6.77**
Austria	17,581	16,745	21,034	22,558	17,147	0.34	-23.99
Belgium	23,574	28,237	28,549	32,741	30,037	0.60	-8.26
France	199,613	211,347	224,160	263,829	275,913	5.50	4.58
Germany	268,903	283,615	294,989	308,598	277,182	5.52	-10.18
Netherlands	62,331	83,999	102,480	109,708	86,122	1.72	-21.50
Switzerland	62,842	69,644	83,113	89,789	84,816	1.69	-5.54
East Mediterranean Europe	**20,784**	**20,865**	**26,095**	**28,136**	**28,289**	**0.56**	**0.54**
Israel	20,784	20,865	26,095	28,136	28,289	0.56	0.54
Other Europe	**20,838**	**48,096**	**72,904**	**62,782**	**56,804**	**1.13**	**-9.52**
Other countries of Europe	20,838	48,096	72,904	62,782	56,804	1.13	-9.52
MIDDLE EAST	**7,118**	**5,595**	**6,064**	**7,002**	**13,172**	**0.26**	**88.12**
Middle East	**7,118**	**5,595**	**6,064**	**7,002**	**13,172**	**0.26**	**88.12**
Iraq	250	96	95	134	133		-0.75
Saudi Arabia	815	653	800	881	747	0.01	-15.21
Other countries of Middle East	6,053	4,846	5,169	5,987	12,292	0.24	105.31
REGION NOT SPECIFIED	**8,740**	**5,732**	**3,655**	**2,694**	**1,912**	**0.04**	**-29.03**
Not Specified	**8,740**	**5,732**	**3,655**	**2,694**	**1,912**	**0.04**	**-29.03**
Other countries of the World	8,740	5,732	3,655	2,694	1,912	0.04	-29.03

Source: World Tourism Organization (UNWTO)

BRITISH VIRGIN ISLANDS

1. Arrivals of non-resident tourists at national borders, by country of residence

	2002	2003	2004	2005	2006	Market share 06	% Change 06-05
TOTAL	281,696	317,758					
AMERICAS	250,013	261,201					
Caribbean	31,908	69,102					
Antigua and Barbuda	1,442	1,273					
Barbados	940	918					
Dominica	1,456	2,648					
Dominican Republic	804	837					
Grenada	494	621					
Haiti	10	73					
Jamaica	1,177	2,179					
Puerto Rico	15,378	14,930					
Saint Kitts and Nevis	2,983	3,411					
Saint Lucia	662	905					
Saint Vincent and the Grenadines	1,584	2,091					
Trinidad and Tobago	1,499	1,572					
Other countries of the Caribbean	3,479	37,644					
North America	215,817	189,404					
Canada	6,307	8,961					
United States	209,510	180,443					
South America	887	1,080					
Guyana	887	1,080					
Other Americas	1,401	1,615					
Other countries of the Americas	1,401	1,615					
EUROPE	28,511	49,952					
Northern Europe	14,999	22,561					
Sweden	526	508					
United Kingdom	14,473	22,053					
Southern Europe	2,487	8,889					
Italy	1,998	7,502					
Spain	489	1,387					
Western Europe	7,223	13,800					
France	3,796	7,497					
Germany	2,463	5,209					
Netherlands	964	1,094					
Other Europe	3,802	4,702					
Other countries of Europe	3,802	4,702					
REGION NOT SPECIFIED	3,172	6,605					
Not Specified	3,172	6,605					
Other countries of the World	3,172	6,605					

Source: World Tourism Organization (UNWTO)

BRITISH VIRGIN ISLANDS

2. Arrivals of non-resident visitors at national borders, by country of residence

	2002	2003	2004	2005	2006	Market share 06	% Change 06-05
TOTAL	543,423	657,503	812,908	820,766			
AMERICAS	389,914	474,695	598,633	600,732			
Caribbean	19,354	25,616	28,395	28,948			
All countries of the Caribbean	19,354	25,616	28,395	28,948			
North America	366,127	444,456	562,689	564,337			
Canada	18,092	22,302	29,669	29,285			
United States	348,035	422,154	533,020	535,052			
South America	4,433	4,623	7,549	7,447			
All countries of South America	4,433	4,623	7,549	7,447			
EUROPE	148,150	169,928	199,790	203,004			
Other Europe	148,150	169,928	199,790	203,004			
All countries of Europe	148,150	169,928	199,790	203,004			
REGION NOT SPECIFIED	5,359	12,880	14,485	17,030			
Not Specified	5,359	12,880	14,485	17,030			
Other countries of the World	5,359	12,880	14,485	17,030			

Source: World Tourism Organization (UNWTO)

BRUNEI DARUSSALAM

1. Arrivals of non-resident tourists at national borders, by nationality

		2002	2003	2004	2005	2006	Market share 06	% Change 06-05
TOTAL	(*)				126,217	158,095	100.00	25.26
AMERICAS					3,313	3,943	2.49	19.02
North America					3,313	3,943	2.49	19.02
Canada					1,362	1,492	0.94	9.54
United States					1,951	2,451	1.55	25.63
EAST ASIA AND THE PACIFIC					75,781	100,160	63.35	32.17
North-East Asia					19,654	30,077	19.02	53.03
Taiwan (Province of China)					3,012	2,707	1.71	-10.13
Japan					1,607	3,319	2.10	106.53
Korea, Republic of					1,123	3,829	2.42	240.96
China + Hong Kong, China					13,912	20,222	12.79	45.36
South-East Asia					47,237	51,614	32.65	9.27
Malaysia					39,128	39,914	25.25	2.01
Singapore					8,109	11,700	7.40	44.28
Australasia					8,890	18,469	11.68	107.75
Australia, New Zealand					8,890	18,469	11.68	107.75
EUROPE					14,428	20,847	13.19	44.49
Central/Eastern Europe					231	410	0.26	77.49
Russian Federation					231	410	0.26	77.49
Northern Europe					10,747	13,856	8.76	28.93
United Kingdom/Ireland					10,298	13,013	8.23	26.36
Scandinavia					449	843	0.53	87.75
Southern Europe					850	1,500	0.95	76.47
All countries Southern Europe					850	1,500	0.95	76.47
Western Europe					2,600	5,081	3.21	95.42
Germany					1,584	3,432	2.17	116.67
Benelux					1,016	1,649	1.04	62.30
MIDDLE EAST					210	654	0.41	211.43
Middle East					210	654	0.41	211.43
Saudi Arabia					54	167	0.11	209.26
Other countries of Middle East					156	487	0.31	212.18
REGION NOT SPECIFIED					32,485	32,491	20.55	0.02
Not Specified					32,485	32,491	20.55	0.02
Other countries of the World					32,485	32,491	20.55	0.02

Source: World Tourism Organization (UNWTO)

BRUNEI DARUSSALAM

2. Arrivals of non-resident visitors at national borders, by nationality

	2002	2003	2004	2005	2006	Market share 06	% Change 06-05
TOTAL				815,054			
AMERICAS				3,530			
North America				3,313			
Canada				1,362			
United States				1,951			
Other Americas				217			
Other countries of the Americas				217			
EAST ASIA AND THE PACIFIC				791,190			
North-East Asia				12,429			
China				4,505			
Taiwan (Province of China)				834			
Hong Kong, China				263			
Japan				1,607			
Korea, Republic of				1,123			
Other countries of North-East Asia				4,097			
South-East Asia				773,525			
Myanmar				327			
Cambodia				64			
Indonesia				43,421			
Lao People's Democratic Republic				102			
Malaysia				667,692			
Philippines				46,853			
Singapore				8,109			
Viet Nam				198			
Thailand				6,759			
Australasia				5,236			
Australia				3,360			
New Zealand				1,876			
EUROPE				14,428			
Central/Eastern Europe				53			
Russian Federation				53			
Northern Europe				10,747			
Denmark				71			
Finland				40			
Ireland				169			
Norway				107			
Sweden				231			
United Kingdom				10,129			
Southern Europe				273			
Italy				193			
Spain				80			
Western Europe				3,081			
Austria				86			
Belgium				119			
France				481			
Germany				1,339			
Netherlands				897			
Switzerland				159			
Other Europe				274			

BRUNEI DARUSSALAM

2. Arrivals of non-resident visitors at national borders, by nationality

	2002	2003	2004	2005	2006	Market share 06	% Change 06-05
Other countries of Europe				274			
MIDDLE EAST				**695**			
Middle East				**695**			
Bahrain				4			
Kuwait				5			
Oman				90			
Saudi Arabia				54			
United Arab Emirates				52			
Other countries of Middle East				490			
SOUTH ASIA				**5,211**			
South Asia				**5,211**			
India				5,211			

Source: World Tourism Organization (UNWTO)

BULGARIA

2. Arrivals of non-resident visitors at national borders, by country of residence

	2002	2003	2004	2005	2006	Market share 06	% Change 06-05
TOTAL	5,562,917	6,240,932	6,981,597	7,282,455	7,499,117	100.00	2.98
AFRICA	3,778	3,848	2,937	2,774	2,668	0.04	-3.82
East Africa	40	54	45	47	40		-14.89
Ethiopia	40	54	45	47	40		-14.89
North Africa	3,359	3,165	2,417	2,418	2,272	0.03	-6.04
Algeria	1,849	1,851	1,732	1,680	1,482	0.02	-11.79
Morocco	468	461	340	377	343		-9.02
Sudan	98	75	69	87	87		
Tunisia	944	778	276	274	360		31.39
West Africa	379	629	475	309	356		15.21
Ghana	98	146	70	68	94		38.24
Nigeria	281	483	405	241	262		8.71
AMERICAS	46,934	54,701	67,605	76,514	85,158	1.14	11.30
Caribbean	218	206	254	306	253		-17.32
Cuba	218	206	254	306	253		-17.32
North America	45,465	53,368	65,976	74,827	82,592	1.10	10.38
Canada	5,641	6,826	8,442	10,064	12,313	0.16	22.35
Mexico	671	668	583	546	801	0.01	46.70
United States	39,153	45,874	56,951	64,217	69,478	0.93	8.19
South America	1,251	1,127	1,375	1,381	2,313	0.03	67.49
Argentina	393	368	372	427	611	0.01	43.09
Brazil	672	595	775	766	1,425	0.02	86.03
Venezuela	186	164	228	188	277		47.34
EAST ASIA AND THE PACIFIC	21,957	26,521	32,067	35,127	38,186	0.51	8.71
North-East Asia	11,671	16,127	19,180	20,520	21,730	0.29	5.90
China	3,570	3,408	4,125	4,108	4,637	0.06	12.88
Japan	7,184	7,575	9,682	11,273	11,833	0.16	4.97
Korea, Republic of	391	4,300	4,608	4,777	4,958	0.07	3.79
Mongolia	526	844	765	362	302		-16.57
South-East Asia	4,050	3,686	4,066	3,606	4,033	0.05	11.84
Indonesia	520	595	1,270	1,178	2,076	0.03	76.23
Viet Nam	3,530	3,091	2,796	2,428	1,957	0.03	-19.40
Australasia	6,236	6,708	8,821	11,001	12,423	0.17	12.93
Australia	5,055	5,423	7,228	9,021	10,001	0.13	10.86
New Zealand	1,181	1,285	1,593	1,980	2,422	0.03	22.32
EUROPE	5,426,164	6,088,039	6,806,650	7,087,954	7,286,509	97.16	2.80
Central/Eastern Europe	1,413,560	1,587,856	1,661,418	1,796,106	2,005,006	26.74	11.63
Belarus	16,946	14,997	15,517	18,924	24,829	0.33	31.20
Czech Republic	129,945	142,096	171,726	174,766	137,800	1.84	-21.15
Hungary	203,468	205,085	194,539	142,913	74,853	1.00	-47.62
Republic of Moldova	19,103	22,267	31,560	46,365	55,467	0.74	19.63
Poland	102,106	193,989	236,381	211,032	158,018	2.11	-25.12
Romania	571,525	606,572	612,630	783,563	1,117,297	14.90	42.59
Russian Federation	129,598	153,994	152,121	177,590	218,194	2.91	22.86
Slovakia	145,049	144,476	157,523	143,974	109,155	1.46	-24.18
Ukraine	95,820	104,380	89,421	96,979	109,393	1.46	12.80
Northern Europe	283,775	376,284	544,776	723,392	856,194	11.42	18.36
Denmark	35,794	47,434	59,594	77,966	94,089	1.25	20.68

BULGARIA

2. Arrivals of non-resident visitors at national borders, by country of residence

	2002	2003	2004	2005	2006	Market share 06	% Change 06-05
Finland	39,293	50,139	60,042	83,482	88,073	1.17	5.50
Iceland	689	648	919	1,045	6,678	0.09	539.04
Ireland	5,953	7,300	13,253	29,421	59,955	0.80	103.78
Norway	16,332	17,972	24,519	41,725	70,477	0.94	68.91
Sweden	61,332	79,026	107,626	109,632	110,981	1.48	1.23
United Kingdom	124,382	173,765	278,823	380,121	425,941	5.68	12.05
Southern Europe	**2,281,517**	**2,530,735**	**2,651,538**	**2,398,227**	**2,346,195**	**31.29**	**-2.17**
Albania	12,737	8,814	9,707	9,696	9,330	0.12	-3.77
Bosnia and Herzegovina	25,062	21,876	22,331	22,517	16,799	0.22	-25.39
Croatia	9,905	11,740	15,354	18,459	16,983	0.23	-8.00
Greece	486,750	644,512	803,311	714,239	648,546	8.65	-9.20
Italy	40,953	46,465	56,731	64,357	70,561	0.94	9.64
Portugal	2,251	2,270	3,632	4,864	8,197	0.11	68.52
Slovenia	4,500	10,345	15,527	14,255	12,962	0.17	-9.07
Spain	9,629	10,625	13,959	19,271	23,117	0.31	19.96
TFYR of Macedonia	848,849	886,939	857,885	755,286	712,941	9.51	-5.61
Serbia and Montenegro	840,881	887,149	853,101	775,283	826,759	11.02	6.64
Western Europe	**789,324**	**899,710**	**1,085,652**	**1,163,586**	**1,123,696**	**14.98**	**-3.43**
Austria	58,805	67,423	96,297	119,057	120,820	1.61	1.48
Belgium	45,279	52,733	63,308	67,958	68,965	0.92	1.48
France	43,238	49,795	71,230	91,790	103,470	1.38	12.72
Germany	562,239	631,448	719,825	728,878	663,767	8.85	-8.93
Luxembourg			2,950	3,035	2,771	0.04	-8.70
Netherlands	67,040	80,131	107,150	129,170	138,975	1.85	7.59
Switzerland	12,723	18,180	24,892	23,698	24,928	0.33	5.19
East Mediterranean Europe	**657,988**	**693,454**	**863,266**	**1,006,643**	**955,418**	**12.74**	**-5.09**
Cyprus	8,723	12,657	18,523	16,721	16,425	0.22	-1.77
Israel	67,974	72,883	83,830	103,804	89,703	1.20	-13.58
Turkey	581,291	607,914	760,913	886,118	849,290	11.33	-4.16
MIDDLE EAST	**14,144**	**15,132**	**16,124**	**17,569**	**14,284**	**0.19**	**-18.70**
Middle East	**14,144**	**15,132**	**16,124**	**17,569**	**14,284**	**0.19**	**-18.70**
Iraq	898	793	896	941	1,003	0.01	6.59
Jordan	1,009	1,764	2,062	2,283	1,799	0.02	-21.20
Kuwait	853	918	884	1,265	1,251	0.02	-1.11
Lebanon	3,698	3,861	3,522	3,731	2,212	0.03	-40.71
Libyan Arab Jamahiriya	841	764	597	711	532	0.01	-25.18
Saudi Arabia	165	190	175	196	134		-31.63
Syrian Arab Republic	5,243	5,076	5,870	6,284	5,882	0.08	-6.40
United Arab Emirates	122	158	185	483	212		-56.11
Egypt	1,315	1,608	1,933	1,675	1,259	0.02	-24.84
SOUTH ASIA	**9,498**	**11,613**	**12,199**	**11,396**	**13,267**	**0.18**	**16.42**
South Asia	**9,498**	**11,613**	**12,199**	**11,396**	**13,267**	**0.18**	**16.42**
Afghanistan	261	387	307	218	258		18.35
Bangladesh	85	79	99	144	95		-34.03
India	2,099	2,361	2,361	2,766	3,187	0.04	15.22
Iran, Islamic Republic of	6,691	8,420	9,041	7,823	9,302	0.12	18.91
Pakistan	362	366	391	445	425	0.01	-4.49
REGION NOT SPECIFIED	**40,442**	**41,078**	**44,015**	**51,121**	**59,045**	**0.79**	**15.50**
Not Specified	**40,442**	**41,078**	**44,015**	**51,121**	**59,045**	**0.79**	**15.50**
Other countries of the World	40,442	41,078	44,015	51,121	59,045	0.79	15.50

Source: World Tourism Organization (UNWTO)

BULGARIA

5. Overnight stays of non-resident tourists in hotels and similar establishments, by country of residence

	2002	2003	2004	2005	2006	Market share 06	% Change 06-05
TOTAL (*)	6,985,110	8,986,533	10,139,180	11,471,082	11,776,062	100.00	2.66
AMERICAS	85,750	93,166	92,576	103,262	96,182	0.82	-6.86
North America	85,750	93,166	92,576	103,262	96,182	0.82	-6.86
Canada	4,994	7,727	8,873				
United States	80,756	85,439	83,703	103,262	96,182	0.82	-6.86
EAST ASIA AND THE PACIFIC	16,587	15,861	23,815	30,813	32,378	0.27	5.08
North-East Asia	16,587	15,861	23,815	30,813	32,378	0.27	5.08
Japan	16,587	15,861	23,815	30,813	32,378	0.27	5.08
EUROPE	6,695,922	8,589,884	9,563,591	10,712,014	10,915,265	92.69	1.90
Central/Eastern Europe	788,471	1,106,033	1,243,306	1,625,837	2,134,470	18.13	31.28
Belarus	38,364	28,327					
Czech Republic	67,123	97,387	148,825	213,359	226,749	1.93	6.28
Hungary	16,251	20,969	28,700	40,587	76,471	0.65	88.41
Poland	81,483	94,442	189,073	241,902	248,040	2.11	2.54
Romania	24,584	32,547	35,405	83,144	250,308	2.13	201.05
Russian Federation	451,400	696,297	691,652	840,712	1,109,353	9.42	31.95
Slovakia	42,552	57,981	72,167	117,840	101,588	0.86	-13.79
Ukraine	66,714	78,083	77,484	88,293	121,961	1.04	38.13
Northern Europe	1,281,875	1,971,961	2,575,976	3,228,584	3,273,734	27.80	1.40
Denmark	114,166	207,696	247,911	354,875	383,403	3.26	8.04
Finland	190,414	245,289	273,113	348,739	344,998	2.93	-1.07
Norway	72,184	89,565	108,614	180,516	338,976	2.88	87.78
Sweden	239,551	395,442	457,929	463,833	446,167	3.79	-3.81
United Kingdom	665,560	1,033,969	1,488,409	1,880,621	1,760,190	14.95	-6.40
Southern Europe	330,444	437,358	510,659	548,873	546,519	4.64	-0.43
Greece	88,836	115,753	170,301	225,178	196,799	1.67	-12.60
Italy	59,192	67,545	88,332	101,948	117,200	1.00	14.96
Spain	19,029	22,516	32,880	50,551	51,497	0.44	1.87
TFYR of Macedonia	86,770	100,250	72,179	73,874	84,154	0.71	13.92
Serbia and Montenegro	76,617	131,294	146,967	97,322	96,869	0.82	-0.47
Western Europe	4,029,666	4,767,895	4,887,001	4,875,969	4,539,751	38.55	-6.90
Austria	114,573	98,575	111,435	152,080	161,829	1.37	6.41
Belgium	227,380	230,138	210,157	228,521	163,729	1.39	-28.35
France	164,192	164,729	202,262	247,969	292,439	2.48	17.93
Germany	3,403,454	4,116,941	4,163,546	4,008,846	3,643,347	30.94	-9.12
Netherlands	63,531	75,718	99,886	159,630	186,854	1.59	17.05
Switzerland	56,536	81,794	99,715	78,923	91,553	0.78	16.00
East Mediterranean Europe	265,466	306,637	346,649	432,751	420,791	3.57	-2.76
Israel	208,496	237,189	275,699	335,369	318,640	2.71	-4.99
Turkey	56,970	69,448	70,950	97,382	102,151	0.87	4.90
REGION NOT SPECIFIED	186,851	287,622	459,198	624,993	732,237	6.22	17.16
Not Specified	186,851	287,622	459,198	624,993	732,237	6.22	17.16
Other countries of the World	186,851	287,622	459,198	624,993	732,237	6.22	17.16

Source: World Tourism Organization (UNWTO)

BULGARIA

6. Overnight stays of non-resident tourists in all types of accommodation establishments, by country of residence

		2002	2003	2004	2005	2006	Market share 06	% Change 06-05
TOTAL	(*)	7,055,140	9,142,170	10,303,560	11,624,051	11,960,168	100.00	2.89
AMERICAS		86,007	93,225	93,131	103,696	97,665	0.82	-5.82
North America		86,007	93,225	93,131	103,696	97,665	0.82	-5.82
Canada		5,047	7,577	9,016				
United States		80,960	85,648	84,115	103,696	97,665	0.82	-5.82
EAST ASIA AND THE PACIFIC		16,708	15,908	23,867	31,027	32,509	0.27	4.78
North-East Asia		16,708	15,908	23,867	31,027	32,509	0.27	4.78
Japan		16,708	15,908	23,867	31,027	32,509	0.27	4.78
EUROPE		6,765,898	8,742,231	9,718,562	10,854,188	11,084,393	92.68	2.12
Central/Eastern Europe		833,013	1,146,771	1,288,429	1,683,557	2,210,372	18.48	31.29
Belarus		39,639	30,174					
Czech Republic		70,330	103,613	157,454	220,671	234,378	1.96	6.21
Hungary		19,664	24,123	31,598	43,647	82,056	0.69	88.00
Poland		83,705	98,811	198,031	247,695	256,798	2.15	3.68
Romania		24,911	32,897	36,158	84,808	253,676	2.12	199.12
Russian Federation		483,626	714,466	709,714	874,467	1,155,358	9.66	32.12
Slovakia		43,810	63,703	77,123	121,298	103,534	0.87	-14.64
Ukraine		67,328	78,984	78,351	90,971	124,572	1.04	36.94
Northern Europe		1,288,708	2,005,626	2,630,248	3,267,591	3,315,300	27.72	1.46
Denmark		115,036	209,890	249,378	357,022	385,790	3.23	8.06
Finland		192,193	247,105	275,866	350,891	346,544	2.90	-1.24
Norway		74,210	91,403	113,094	182,990	341,242	2.85	86.48
Sweden		241,433	404,042	463,137	468,259	449,753	3.76	-3.95
United Kingdom		665,836	1,053,186	1,528,773	1,908,429	1,791,971	14.98	-6.10
Southern Europe		333,601	443,210	516,996	554,526	557,868	4.66	0.60
Greece		88,897	115,914	171,144	226,398	198,246	1.66	-12.43
Italy		59,582	67,987	89,044	102,923	118,213	0.99	14.86
Spain		19,078	22,628	33,095	50,778	51,973	0.43	2.35
TFYR of Macedonia		88,238	103,281	74,924	76,119	87,193	0.73	14.55
Serbia and Montenegro		77,806	133,400	148,789	98,308	102,243	0.85	4.00
Western Europe		4,044,839	4,839,407	4,934,942	4,913,274	4,577,995	38.28	-6.82
Austria		114,679	99,269	112,755	153,200	163,076	1.36	6.45
Belgium		227,645	237,086	213,163	230,514	164,772	1.38	-28.52
France		166,031	167,480	205,359	251,569	295,984	2.47	17.66
Germany		3,415,367	4,173,328	4,199,652	4,033,607	3,671,655	30.70	-8.97
Netherlands		64,437	79,547	103,775	163,180	190,281	1.59	16.61
Switzerland		56,680	82,697	100,238	81,204	92,227	0.77	13.57
East Mediterranean Europe		265,737	307,217	347,947	435,240	422,858	3.54	-2.84
Israel		208,554	237,219	276,400	335,846	319,264	2.67	-4.94
Turkey		57,183	69,998	71,547	99,394	103,594	0.87	4.23
REGION NOT SPECIFIED		186,527	290,806	468,000	635,140	745,601	6.23	17.39
Not Specified		186,527	290,806	468,000	635,140	745,601	6.23	17.39
Other countries of the World		186,527	290,806	468,000	635,140	745,601	6.23	17.39

Source: World Tourism Organization (UNWTO)

BURKINA FASO

3. Arrivals of non-resident tourists in hotels and similar establishments, by nationality

	2002	2003	2004	2005	2006	Market share 06	% Change 06-05
TOTAL	**150,204**	**163,123**	**222,201**	**244,728**	**263,978**	**100.00**	**7.87**
AFRICA	**55,144**	**65,459**	**96,385**	**100,674**	**108,019**	**40.92**	**7.30**
West Africa	**42,532**	**52,387**	**80,313**	**77,928**	**88,310**	**33.45**	**13.32**
Benin	4,216	6,443	8,765	9,186	9,233	3.50	0.51
Ghana	2,804	3,831	5,456	4,914	5,819	2.20	18.42
Guinea	1,612	2,759	4,528	3,534	4,033	1.53	14.12
Cote D'Ivoire	6,840	9,229	14,924	14,454	15,659	5.93	8.34
Mali	4,388	7,785	12,411	12,018	14,103	5.34	17.35
Mauritania	1,028	1,652	1,834	1,854	2,188	0.83	18.02
Niger	7,172	7,016	11,455	10,836	13,044	4.94	20.38
Nigeria	4,236	2,328	4,097	3,366	4,653	1.76	38.24
Senegal	5,456	5,950	9,882	9,792	10,724	4.06	9.52
Togo	4,780	5,394	6,961	7,974	8,854	3.35	11.04
Other Africa	**12,612**	**13,072**	**16,072**	**22,746**	**19,709**	**7.47**	**-13.35**
Other countries of Africa	12,612	13,072	16,072	22,746	19,709	7.47	-13.35
AMERICAS	**9,840**	**10,025**	**12,991**	**14,724**	**15,814**	**5.99**	**7.40**
North America	**8,760**	**9,030**	**11,420**	**13,338**	**13,943**	**5.28**	**4.54**
Canada	2,820	3,000	4,548	6,048	6,088	2.31	0.66
United States	5,940	6,030	6,872	7,290	7,855	2.98	7.75
Other Americas	**1,080**	**995**	**1,571**	**1,386**	**1,871**	**0.71**	**34.99**
Other countries of the Americas	1,080	995	1,571	1,386	1,871	0.71	34.99
EAST ASIA AND THE PACIFIC	**3,760**	**3,271**	**4,550**	**6,582**	**6,387**	**2.42**	**-2.96**
North-East Asia	**872**	**910**	**1,473**	**1,830**	**1,520**	**0.58**	**-16.94**
China	872	910	1,473	1,830	1,520	0.58	-16.94
Other East Asia and the Pacific	**2,888**	**2,361**	**3,077**	**4,752**	**4,867**	**1.84**	**2.42**
Other countries of Asia	2,888	2,361	3,077	4,752	4,867	1.84	2.42
EUROPE	**73,076**	**76,743**	**99,742**	**113,496**	**123,426**	**46.76**	**8.75**
Northern Europe	**2,376**	**2,475**	**3,618**	**3,288**	**3,424**	**1.30**	**4.14**
United Kingdom	2,376	2,475	3,618	3,288	3,424	1.30	4.14
Southern Europe	**3,580**	**3,215**	**3,727**	**5,244**	**6,806**	**2.58**	**29.79**
Italy	3,580	3,215	3,727	5,244	6,806	2.58	29.79
Western Europe	**59,816**	**64,089**	**82,639**	**95,874**	**103,009**	**39.02**	**7.44**
Belgium	3,996	4,984	6,482	6,438	7,454	2.82	15.78
France	45,868	47,663	62,510	77,220	81,532	30.89	5.58
Germany	3,612	4,683	5,523	5,190	5,914	2.24	13.95
Netherlands	2,460	2,734	2,932	3,198	3,575	1.35	11.79
Switzerland	3,880	4,025	5,192	3,828	4,534	1.72	18.44
Other Europe	**7,304**	**6,964**	**9,758**	**9,090**	**10,187**	**3.86**	**12.07**
Other countries of Europe	7,304	6,964	9,758	9,090	10,187	3.86	12.07
MIDDLE EAST	**876**	**1,447**	**1,982**	**2,220**	**2,022**	**0.77**	**-8.92**
Middle East	**876**	**1,447**	**1,982**	**2,220**	**2,022**	**0.77**	**-8.92**
Lebanon	876	1,447	1,982	2,220	2,022	0.77	-8.92
REGION NOT SPECIFIED	**7,508**	**6,178**	**6,551**	**7,032**	**8,310**	**3.15**	**18.17**
Not Specified	**7,508**	**6,178**	**6,551**	**7,032**	**8,310**	**3.15**	**18.17**
Nationals Residing Abroad	7,508	6,178	6,551	7,032	8,310	3.15	18.17

Source: World Tourism Organization (UNWTO)

BURKINA FASO

5. Overnight stays of non-resident tourists in hotels and similar establishments, by nationality

	2002	2003	2004	2005	2006	Market share 06	% Change 06-05
TOTAL	526,822	553,740	632,340	788,914	794,152	100.00	0.66
AFRICA	210,775	246,060	271,508	359,310	357,759	45.05	-0.43
West Africa	159,465	181,195	197,719	274,056	281,401	35.43	2.68
Benin	19,170	22,905	23,368	33,138	27,712	3.49	-16.37
Ghana	9,265	11,696	12,129	14,784	16,909	2.13	14.37
Guinea	7,185	8,564	9,423	14,118	12,924	1.63	-8.46
Cote D'Ivoire	25,925	34,000	33,995	58,296	62,044	7.81	6.43
Mali	24,090	26,306	29,370	38,628	42,212	5.32	9.28
Mauritania	4,145	4,453	5,446	5,196	9,921	1.25	90.94
Niger	23,205	22,938	27,829	37,512	33,611	4.23	-10.40
Nigeria	7,285	8,058	8,180	9,000	14,778	1.86	64.20
Senegal	21,585	24,281	27,095	36,132	35,367	4.45	-2.12
Togo	17,610	17,994	20,884	27,252	25,923	3.26	-4.88
Other Africa	51,310	64,865	73,789	85,254	76,358	9.62	-10.43
Other countries of Africa	51,310	64,865	73,789	85,254	76,358	9.62	-10.43
AMERICAS	47,670	43,115	47,522	51,552	47,580	5.99	-7.70
North America	44,310	39,780	42,882	47,524	43,212	5.44	-9.07
Canada	12,755	12,466	21,525	19,762	19,439	2.45	-1.63
United States	31,555	27,314	21,357	27,762	23,773	2.99	-14.37
Other Americas	3,360	3,335	4,640	4,028	4,368	0.55	8.44
Other countries of the Americas	3,360	3,335	4,640	4,028	4,368	0.55	8.44
EAST ASIA AND THE PACIFIC	13,415	12,753	14,819	22,230	23,172	2.92	4.24
North-East Asia	4,200	4,490	5,636	7,434	5,318	0.67	-28.46
China	4,200	4,490	5,636	7,434	5,318	0.67	-28.46
Other East Asia and the Pacific	9,215	8,263	9,183	14,796	17,854	2.25	20.67
Other countries of Asia	9,215	8,263	9,183	14,796	17,854	2.25	20.67
EUROPE	229,305	230,557	275,849	331,880	340,047	42.82	2.46
Northern Europe	8,505	8,295	12,928	10,548	10,409	1.31	-1.32
United Kingdom	8,505	8,295	12,928	10,548	10,409	1.31	-1.32
Southern Europe	10,880	10,188	13,640	14,118	16,901	2.13	19.71
Italy	10,880	10,188	13,640	14,118	16,901	2.13	19.71
Western Europe	179,770	191,443	224,734	278,390	280,264	35.29	0.67
Belgium	14,400	18,148	21,238	22,212	25,053	3.15	12.79
France	134,715	141,156	170,956	216,708	212,305	26.73	-2.03
Germany	11,750	13,813	13,973	16,908	18,209	2.29	7.69
Netherlands	9,195	8,415	9,451	9,738	11,075	1.39	13.73
Switzerland	9,710	9,911	9,116	12,824	13,622	1.72	6.22
Other Europe	30,150	20,631	24,547	28,824	32,473	4.09	12.66
Other countries of Europe	30,150	20,631	24,547	28,824	32,473	4.09	12.66
MIDDLE EAST	2,945	4,392	5,330	5,184	5,095	0.64	-1.72
Middle East	2,945	4,392	5,330	5,184	5,095	0.64	-1.72
Lebanon	2,945	4,392	5,330	5,184	5,095	0.64	-1.72
REGION NOT SPECIFIED	22,712	16,863	17,312	18,758	20,499	2.58	9.28
Not Specified	22,712	16,863	17,312	18,758	20,499	2.58	9.28
Nationals Residing Abroad	22,712	16,863	17,312	18,758	20,499	2.58	9.28

Source: World Tourism Organization (UNWTO)

BURUNDI

1. Arrivals of non-resident tourists at national borders, by nationality

		2002	2003	2004	2005	2006	Market share 06	% Change 06-05
TOTAL	(*)	**74,406**	**74,116**	**133,228**	**148,418**	**201,241**	**100.00**	**35.59**
AFRICA		**24,802**	**24,706**	**1,333**	**49,473**	**140,868**	**70.00**	**184.74**
Other Africa		24,802	24,706	1,333	49,473	140,868	70.00	184.74
All countries of Africa		24,802	24,706	1,333	49,473	140,868	70.00	184.74
AMERICAS		**2,090**	**2,308**	**5,908**	**9,956**	**4,025**	**2.00**	**-59.57**
Other Americas		2,090	2,308	5,908	9,956	4,025	2.00	-59.57
All countries of the Americas		2,090	2,308	5,908	9,956	4,025	2.00	-59.57
EAST ASIA AND THE PACIFIC		**1,054**	**1,162**	**4,528**	**4,023**	**10,062**	**5.00**	**150.11**
Other East Asia and the Pacific		1,054	1,162	4,528	4,023	10,062	5.00	150.11
All countries of Asia		1,054	1,162	4,528	4,023	10,062	5.00	150.11
EUROPE		**6,156**	**7,620**	**29,409**	**29,486**	**32,199**	**16.00**	**9.20**
Other Europe		6,156	7,620	29,409	29,486	32,199	16.00	9.20
All countries of Europe		6,156	7,620	29,409	29,486	32,199	16.00	9.20
REGION NOT SPECIFIED		**40,304**	**38,320**	**92,050**	**55,480**	**14,087**	**7.00**	**-74.61**
Not Specified		40,304	38,320	92,050	55,480	14,087	7.00	-74.61
Other countries of the World		40,304	38,320	92,050	55,480	14,087	7.00	-74.61

Source: World Tourism Organization (UNWTO)

CAMBODIA

1. Arrivals of non-resident tourists at national borders, by country of residence

	2002	2003	2004	2005	2006	Market share 06	% Change 06-05
TOTAL	786,526	701,014	1,055,202	1,421,615	1,700,041	100.00	19.59
AMERICAS	113,144	88,662	122,169	152,328	159,429	9.38	4.66
North America	103,946	80,995	115,631	133,529	151,864	8.93	13.73
Canada	15,550	14,872	20,680	24,110	28,017	1.65	16.20
United States	88,396	66,123	94,951	109,419	123,847	7.28	13.19
Other Americas	9,198	7,667	6,538	18,799	7,565	0.44	-59.76
Other countries of the Americas	9,198	7,667	6,538	18,799	7,565	0.44	-59.76
EAST ASIA AND THE PACIFIC	409,489	412,245	589,230	786,506	1,022,181	60.13	29.96
North-East Asia	222,608	226,681	348,833	471,778	612,305	36.02	29.79
China	54,045	38,664	46,325	59,153	80,540	4.74	36.16
Taiwan (Province of China)	33,020	37,345	53,041	54,771	85,139	5.01	55.45
Hong Kong, China	2,889		2,887	3,421	2,920	0.17	-14.64
Japan	105,545	88,401	118,157	137,849	158,353	9.31	14.87
Korea, Republic of	27,109	62,271	128,423	216,584	285,353	16.79	31.75
South-East Asia	133,882	136,099	183,362	219,579	328,459	19.32	49.59
Brunei Darussalam	176	210	249	226	388	0.02	71.68
Myanmar	917	1,575	1,544	1,586	1,766	0.10	11.35
Indonesia	3,633	3,625	4,710	5,611	7,372	0.43	31.38
Lao People's Democratic Republic	3,083	1,716	1,658	2,780	7,082	0.42	154.75
Malaysia	17,942	26,285	32,864	36,876	77,028	4.53	108.88
Philippines	4,248	23,953	32,910	40,261	49,707	2.92	23.46
Singapore	12,700	14,407	17,830	18,966	30,639	1.80	61.55
Viet Nam	31,608	28,610	36,511	49,642	77,524	4.56	56.17
Thailand	59,575	35,718	55,086	63,631	76,953	4.53	20.94
Australasia	32,429	31,985	45,567	56,949	67,668	3.98	18.82
Australia	28,401	26,638	38,211	47,465	56,945	3.35	19.97
New Zealand	4,028	5,347	7,356	9,484	10,723	0.63	13.06
Other East Asia and the Pacific	20,570	17,480	11,468	38,200	13,749	0.81	-64.01
Other countries East Asia/Pacific	20,570	17,480	11,468	38,200	13,749	0.81	-64.01
EUROPE	218,950	183,353	242,811	310,006	314,194	18.48	1.35
Central/Eastern Europe			1,837	3,627	5,779	0.34	59.33
Russian Federation			1,837	3,627	5,779	0.34	59.33
Northern Europe	53,901	62,422	88,775	96,596	110,268	6.49	14.15
Denmark	2,735	3,574	4,556	5,519	6,592	0.39	19.44
Finland	1,179		2,370	3,145	3,565	0.21	13.35
Ireland			5,387	6,915	8,347	0.49	20.71
Norway	1,817	3,119	3,900	4,498	5,024	0.30	11.69
Sweden		5,463	8,433	9,984	12,973	0.76	29.94
United Kingdom	48,170	50,266	64,129	66,535	73,767	4.34	10.87
Southern Europe	13,800	6,657	17,116	22,837	28,055	1.65	22.85
Italy	13,800	6,657	10,034	11,408	13,899	0.82	21.84
Spain			7,082	11,429	14,156	0.83	23.86
Western Europe	113,609	91,041	119,015	142,253	155,877	9.17	9.58
Austria	2,860	2,385	3,690	4,092	5,046	0.30	23.31
Belgium	5,642	6,284	7,208	9,199	10,538	0.62	14.56
France	62,817	45,396	58,076	68,947	71,978	4.23	4.40
Germany	30,108	25,671	29,112	35,560	40,113	2.36	12.80
Netherlands	5,506	6,391	11,875	13,843	17,019	1.00	22.94
Switzerland	6,676	4,914	9,054	10,612	11,183	0.66	5.38

CAMBODIA

1. Arrivals of non-resident tourists at national borders, by country of residence

	2002	2003	2004	2005	2006	Market share 06	% Change 06-05
Other Europe	**37,640**	**23,233**	**16,068**	**44,693**	**14,215**	**0.84**	**-68.19**
Other countries of Europe	37,640	23,233	16,068	44,693	14,215	0.84	-68.19
SOUTH ASIA	**4,459**	**5,286**	**7,132**	**7,516**	**9,245**	**0.54**	**23.00**
South Asia	**4,459**	**5,286**	**7,132**	**7,516**	**9,245**	**0.54**	**23.00**
Sri Lanka	674		535	578	555	0.03	-3.98
India	3,785	5,286	6,597	6,938	8,690	0.51	25.25
REGION NOT SPECIFIED	**40,484**	**11,468**	**93,860**	**165,259**	**194,992**	**11.47**	**17.99**
Not Specified	**40,484**	**11,468**	**93,860**	**165,259**	**194,992**	**11.47**	**17.99**
Other countries of the World (*)	40,484	11,468	93,860	165,259	194,992	11.47	17.99

Source: World Tourism Organization (UNWTO)

CAMEROON

3. Arrivals of non-resident tourists in hotels and similar establishments, by nationality

	2002	2003	2004	2005	2006	Market share 06	% Change 06-05
TOTAL	226,019		189,856	176,372			
AFRICA	104,695		80,013	88,739			
Other Africa	104,695		80,013	88,739			
All countries of Africa	104,695		80,013	88,739			
AMERICAS	13,506		11,593	10,002			
North America	13,506		11,593	10,002			
Canada	2,600		2,399	2,760			
United States	10,906		9,194	7,242			
EAST ASIA AND THE PACIFIC	4,882		4,248	4,580			
Other East Asia and the Pacific	4,882		4,248	4,580			
All countries of Asia	4,882		4,248	4,580			
EUROPE	98,570		83,272	68,058			
Central/Eastern Europe	1,053		1,325	1,242			
Ussr (Former)	1,053		1,325	1,242			
Northern Europe	6,905		6,800	6,102			
Sweden	836		982	1,026			
United Kingdom	6,069		5,818	5,076			
Southern Europe	4,628		4,426	4,211			
Italy	4,628		4,426	4,211			
Western Europe	76,899		61,508	48,943			
Belgium	4,383		3,885	3,046			
France	53,167		40,611	33,650			
Germany	7,461		7,127	5,581			
Netherlands	3,214		4,217	2,951			
Switzerland	8,674		5,668	3,715			
Other Europe	9,085		9,213	7,560			
Other countries of Europe	9,085		9,213	7,560			
MIDDLE EAST	1,153		4,583	2,007			
Middle East	1,153		4,583	2,007			
All countries of Middle East	1,153		4,583	2,007			
REGION NOT SPECIFIED	3,213		6,147	2,986			
Not Specified	3,213		6,147	2,986			
Other countries of the World	3,213		6,147	2,986			

Source: World Tourism Organization (UNWTO)

CAMEROON

5. Overnight stays of non-resident tourists in hotels and similar establishments, by nationality

	2002	2003	2004	2005	2006	Market share 06	% Change 06-05
TOTAL	458,135		413,958	355,322			
AFRICA	155,197		149,369	155,109			
Other Africa	155,197		149,369	155,109			
All countries of Africa	155,197		149,369	155,109			
AMERICAS	43,071		33,329	27,697			
North America	43,071		33,329	27,697			
Canada	9,173		6,285	5,918			
United States	33,898		27,044	21,779			
EAST ASIA AND THE PACIFIC	13,490		9,983	10,643			
Other East Asia and the Pacific	13,490		9,983	10,643			
All countries of Asia	13,490		9,983	10,643			
EUROPE	239,091		201,603	152,979			
Central/Eastern Europe	2,413		2,961	3,123			
Ussr (Former)	2,413		2,961	3,123			
Northern Europe	18,750		18,360	13,857			
Sweden	1,746		1,948	2,239			
United Kingdom	17,004		16,412	11,618			
Southern Europe	9,475		9,792	8,915			
Italy	9,475		9,792	8,915			
Western Europe	188,427		139,359	111,924			
Belgium	9,989		8,236	6,454			
France	133,579		95,742	80,057			
Germany	13,489		14,018	11,266			
Netherlands	7,180		11,480	6,959			
Switzerland	24,190		9,883	7,188			
Other Europe	20,026		31,131	15,160			
Other countries of Europe	20,026		31,131	15,160			
MIDDLE EAST	2,096		8,493	4,157			
Middle East	2,096		8,493	4,157			
All countries of Middle East	2,096		8,493	4,157			
REGION NOT SPECIFIED	5,190		11,181	4,737			
Not Specified	5,190		11,181	4,737			
Other countries of the World	5,190		11,181	4,737			

Source: World Tourism Organization (UNWTO)

CANADA

1. Arrivals of non-resident tourists at national borders, by country of residence

	2002	2003	2004	2005	2006	Market share 06	% Change 06-05
TOTAL	20,057,024	17,534,329	19,144,810	18,770,444	18,265,071	100.00	-2.69
AFRICA	54,111	52,437	58,210	61,842	72,388	0.40	17.05
East Africa	11,078	10,046	11,136	11,617	15,208	0.08	30.91
Burundi	275	218	214	163	304		86.50
Comoros	14	73	140	99	36		-63.64
Ethiopia	755	679	590	747	1,133	0.01	51.67
Eritrea	154	100	143	186	301		61.83
Djibouti	55	75	123	79	90		13.92
Kenya	3,640	3,096	2,967	3,029	4,037	0.02	33.28
Madagascar	313	379	320	319	424		32.92
Malawi	202	180	213	200	372		86.00
Mauritius	1,159	946	1,324	1,357	1,479	0.01	8.99
Mozambique	201	188	148	214	324		51.40
Reunion	336	481	921	1,178	1,164	0.01	-1.19
Rwanda	227	232	292	280	389		38.93
Seychelles	170	103	66	83	55		-33.73
Somalia	87	75	53	69	50		-27.54
Zimbabwe	863	770	840	875	910		4.00
Uganda	858	674	944	735	1,376	0.01	87.21
United Republic of Tanzania	1,287	1,367	1,358	1,376	1,965	0.01	42.81
Zambia	482	410	480	628	799		27.23
Central Africa	2,389	2,451	2,536	2,418	3,250	0.02	34.41
Angola	288	307	328	247	352		42.51
Cameroon	738	880	878	998	1,377	0.01	37.98
Central African Republic	17	19	3	18	12		-33.33
Chad	130	107	61	71	82		15.49
Congo	82	99	257	157	174		10.83
Democratic Republic of the Congo	508	499	485	375	678		80.80
Equatorial Guinea	63	22	33	58	28		-51.72
Gabon	556	480	480	490	547		11.63
Sao Tome and Principe	7	38	11	4			
North Africa	12,491	12,813	14,058	14,747	17,654	0.10	19.71
Algeria	1,742	2,035	2,462	2,543	4,306	0.02	69.33
Morocco	7,733	7,808	8,733	8,747	9,571	0.05	9.42
Western Sahara			1		4		
Sudan	402	241	335	318	414		30.19
Tunisia	2,614	2,729	2,527	3,139	3,359	0.02	7.01
Southern Africa	19,096	17,728	20,466	22,312	23,463	0.13	5.16
Botswana	379	362	413	512	572		11.72
Lesotho	49	68	57	82	107		30.49
Namibia	266	295	229	312	377		20.83
South Africa	18,324	16,935	19,694	21,310	22,293	0.12	4.61
Swaziland	78	68	73	96	114		18.75
West Africa	9,046	9,341	9,973	10,710	12,764	0.07	19.18
Cape Verde	30	39	34	24	24		
Benin	346	378	433	411	564		37.23
Gambia	75	127	147	119	123		3.36
Ghana	1,294	1,172	1,449	1,606	1,641	0.01	2.18
Guinea	669	808	809	520	583		12.12
Cote D'Ivoire	921	558	544	478	695		45.40
Liberia	96	242	88	215	128		-40.47
Mali	564	527	484	547	634		15.90
Mauritania	170	165	210	222	221		-0.45

130

CANADA

1. Arrivals of non-resident tourists at national borders, by country of residence

	2002	2003	2004	2005	2006	Market share 06	% Change 06-05
Niger	91	105	206	162	273		68.52
Nigeria	2,927	3,305	3,374	4,395	5,694	0.03	29.56
Guinea-Bissau	13	9		14	12		-14.29
Saint Helena	2	6	2				
Senegal	1,093	1,208	1,286	1,297	1,257	0.01	-3.08
Sierra Leone	119	188	285	106	128		20.75
Togo	195	153	167	180	197		9.44
Burkina Faso	441	351	455	414	590		42.51
Other Africa	**11**	**58**	**41**	**38**	**49**		**28.95**
Other countries of Africa	11	58	41	38	49		28.95
AMERICAS	**16,576,480**	**14,588,822**	**15,518,243**	**14,867,460**	**14,372,244**	**78.69**	**-3.33**
Caribbean	**119,283**	**106,642**	**123,196**	**127,470**	**132,678**	**0.73**	**4.09**
Antigua and Barbuda	1,625	1,462	1,602	1,695	1,757	0.01	3.66
Bahamas	8,212	7,566	8,275	8,878	8,871	0.05	-0.08
Barbados	9,775	8,394	10,433	10,394	11,475	0.06	10.40
Bermuda	22,925	23,317	24,149	23,932	22,959	0.13	-4.07
British Virgin Islands	436	397	630	547	584		6.76
Cayman Islands	5,402	5,287	7,153	5,939	6,251	0.03	5.25
Cuba	4,004	3,792	3,819	4,811	5,284	0.03	9.83
Dominica	378	406	585	891	626		-29.74
Dominican Republic	4,254	2,718	3,128	3,404	3,777	0.02	10.96
Grenada	1,140	1,077	1,218	979	1,148	0.01	17.26
Guadeloupe	2,094	1,741	2,782	2,748	2,627	0.01	-4.40
Haiti	8,150	6,317	6,166	7,103	6,651	0.04	-6.36
Jamaica	18,350	15,977	21,034	20,493	23,424	0.13	14.30
Martinique	2,493	1,527	2,051	2,604	1,666	0.01	-36.02
Montserrat	35	29	14	24	20		-16.67
Netherlands Antilles	1,054	816	1,084	1,086	1,146	0.01	5.52
Puerto Rico	1,797	1,305	1,314	1,711	1,759	0.01	2.81
Saint Kitts and Nevis	594	631	692	716	766		6.98
Anguilla	159	145	140	119	177		48.74
Saint Lucia	2,176	2,144	2,272	2,495	2,335	0.01	-6.41
Saint Vincent and the Grenadines	3,028	2,758	2,729	3,275	3,088	0.02	-5.71
Trinidad and Tobago	19,750	17,725	20,688	22,239	24,780	0.14	11.43
Turks and Caicos Islands	1,316	1,051	1,150	1,260	1,416	0.01	12.38
United States Virgin Islands	136	60	88	127	91		-28.35
Central America	**18,720**	**16,554**	**15,603**	**15,333**	**16,076**	**0.09**	**4.85**
Belize	660	547	885	708	780		10.17
Costa Rica	8,452	8,901	6,565	5,128	4,912	0.03	-4.21
El Salvador	2,851	1,763	2,181	2,531	2,436	0.01	-3.75
Guatemala	2,475	2,328	2,713	3,084	3,686	0.02	19.52
Honduras	1,513	993	1,042	1,100	1,319	0.01	19.91
Nicaragua	916	601	546	754	876		16.18
Panama	1,850	1,419	1,671	2,028	2,067	0.01	1.92
Other countries of Central America	3	2					
North America	**16,343,151**	**14,389,218**	**15,276,810**	**14,596,074**	**14,083,037**	**77.10**	**-3.51**
Greenland	311	177	401	276	259		-6.16
Mexico	161,843	142,162	173,243	189,357	210,641	1.15	11.24
Saint Pierre and Miquelon	13,778	14,478	15,658	15,745	17,076	0.09	8.45
United States	16,167,219	14,232,401	15,087,508	14,390,696	13,855,061	75.86	-3.72
South America	**95,326**	**76,408**	**102,634**	**128,583**	**140,453**	**0.77**	**9.23**
Argentina	11,188	9,545	11,835	13,927	15,507	0.08	11.34
Bolivia	806	821	712	839	901		7.39
Brazil	36,393	31,140	49,840	61,118	65,169	0.36	6.63

CANADA

1. Arrivals of non-resident tourists at national borders, by country of residence

	2002	2003	2004	2005	2006	Market share 06	% Change 06-05
Chile	8,670	6,802	8,323	10,425	11,107	0.06	6.54
Colombia	9,314	7,585	8,366	11,149	14,145	0.08	26.87
Ecuador	3,474	2,400	2,543	2,845	3,332	0.02	17.12
Falkland Islands (Malvinas)	9	4	12	16	17		6.25
French Guiana	37	42	144	136	53		-61.03
Guyana	4,522	3,497	3,738	3,937	4,111	0.02	4.42
Paraguay	971	904	991	1,072	1,143	0.01	6.62
Peru	5,993	5,560	4,851	9,067	9,014	0.05	-0.58
Suriname	190	120	184	168	369		119.64
Uruguay	1,710	1,549	1,886	1,938	1,848	0.01	-4.64
Venezuela	12,049	6,439	9,209	11,946	13,737	0.08	14.99
EAST ASIA AND THE PACIFIC	**1,209,706**	**900,328**	**1,221,981**	**1,282,007**	**1,282,444**	**7.02**	**0.03**
North-East Asia	**909,690**	**637,902**	**908,367**	**931,421**	**928,189**	**5.08**	**-0.35**
China	96,142	76,475	101,883	117,490	144,601	0.79	23.08
Taiwan (Province of China)	105,139	68,224	106,636	98,238	92,855	0.51	-5.48
Hong Kong, China	119,449	91,632	115,449	111,415	109,677	0.60	-1.56
Japan	436,510	262,182	414,057	423,881	386,485	2.12	-8.82
Korea, Dem. People's Republic of	67	47	29	46	17		-63.04
Korea, Republic of	151,476	138,563	169,866	179,961	193,665	1.06	7.61
Macao, China	660	515	116	22	372		1,590.91
Mongolia	247	264	331	368	517		40.49
South-East Asia	**108,929**	**78,869**	**95,162**	**106,600**	**113,823**	**0.62**	**6.78**
Brunei Darussalam	548	343	528	438	503		14.84
Myanmar	273	178	126	223	256		14.80
Cambodia	420	405	464	527	773		46.68
Indonesia	14,195	11,410	11,430	11,363	12,080	0.07	6.31
Lao People's Democratic Republic	166	103	134	176	255		44.89
Malaysia	15,171	6,524	9,419	10,027	10,935	0.06	9.06
Philippines	39,317	31,925	36,379	42,560	48,985	0.27	15.10
Singapore	22,544	16,951	22,870	24,570	23,336	0.13	-5.02
Viet Nam	3,006	2,923	2,872	3,668	3,997	0.02	8.97
Thailand	13,289	8,107	10,940	13,048	12,703	0.07	-2.64
Australasia	**188,625**	**181,498**	**215,918**	**240,807**	**237,335**	**1.30**	**-1.44**
Australia	157,610	152,087	179,782	201,939	199,691	1.09	-1.11
New Zealand	31,015	29,411	36,136	38,868	37,644	0.21	-3.15
Melanesia	**1,462**	**1,321**	**1,589**	**1,848**	**1,701**	**0.01**	**-7.95**
Solomon Islands	12	20	22	24	34		41.67
Fiji	948	935	1,060	1,233	1,275	0.01	3.41
New Caledonia	333	243	266	304	186		-38.82
Vanuatu	44	34	57	99			
Papua New Guinea	125	89	184	188	206		9.57
Micronesia	**101**	**133**	**154**	**180**	**143**		**-20.56**
Kiribati	8	12	10	15	10		-33.33
Guam	35	31	34	53	44		-16.98
Nauru	16	6		4	2		-50.00
Northern Mariana Islands	10	19	18	16	13		-18.75
Micronesia (Federated States of)	18	46	83	53	52		-1.89
Marshall Islands	14	19	9	39	22		-43.59
Polynesia	**846**	**605**	**781**	**1,146**	**1,215**	**0.01**	**6.02**
American Samoa	28	34	16	22	29		31.82
Cook Islands	10	15	11	26	37		42.31
French Polynesia	730	486	726	1,067	1,108	0.01	3.84
Tonga	48	35	19	22	20		-9.09

CANADA

1. Arrivals of non-resident tourists at national borders, by country of residence

	2002	2003	2004	2005	2006	Market share 06	% Change 06-05
Tuvalu	17	5	7	4			
Wallis and Futuna Islands					5		
Samoa	13	30	2	5	16		220.00
Other East Asia and the Pacific	**53**		**10**	**5**	**38**		**660.00**
Other countries East Asia/Pacific					38		
Other countries of Oceania	53		10	5			
EUROPE	**2,095,148**	**1,872,693**	**2,202,397**	**2,397,323**	**2,359,997**	**12.92**	**-1.56**
Central/Eastern Europe	**82,934**	**76,405**	**86,205**	**95,150**	**104,153**	**0.57**	**9.46**
Azerbaijan	108	207	227	272	396		45.59
Armenia	308	258	217	461	346		-24.95
Bulgaria	2,094	1,907	2,028	2,457	2,875	0.02	17.01
Belarus	1,068	1,214	976	1,203	1,113	0.01	-7.48
Czech Republic	10,460	10,035	10,690	11,367	11,429	0.06	0.55
Estonia	817	963	965	1,167	1,167	0.01	
Georgia	178	92	116	152	221		45.39
Hungary	8,129	7,501	8,065	8,985	8,548	0.05	-4.86
Kazakhstan	651	652	835	1,021	1,460	0.01	43.00
Kyrgyzstan	160	134	140	182	242		32.97
Latvia	1,076	849	867	1,197	1,381	0.01	15.37
Lithuania	1,104	851	839	868	824		-5.07
Republic of Moldova	328	330	270	466	676		45.06
Poland	24,468	20,171	22,575	22,284	25,276	0.14	13.43
Romania	10,144	10,355	12,059	13,565	15,882	0.09	17.08
Russian Federation	12,586	12,526	15,238	18,643	20,155	0.11	8.11
Slovakia	4,105	3,667	4,315	4,165	4,326	0.02	3.87
Tajikistan	38	54	22	85	115		35.29
Turkmenistan	17	8	13	23	45		95.65
Ukraine	4,949	4,477	5,635	6,345	7,432	0.04	17.13
Uzbekistan	146	154	113	242	244		0.83
Northern Europe	**863,773**	**815,967**	**951,497**	**1,045,916**	**1,014,241**	**5.55**	**-3.03**
Denmark	21,231	22,223	24,307	26,259	27,439	0.15	4.49
Faeroe Islands	99	89	111	59	68		15.25
Finland	12,871	10,796	13,681	15,271	15,346	0.08	0.49
Iceland	2,143	2,444	2,921	3,263	4,300	0.02	31.78
Ireland	30,097	30,254	37,772	42,673	49,185	0.27	15.26
Norway	19,241	16,193	18,059	20,113	21,109	0.12	4.95
Sweden	28,432	25,876	29,888	32,099	30,495	0.17	-5.00
United Kingdom	749,659	708,092	824,758	906,179	866,299	4.74	-4.40
Southern Europe	**185,978**	**126,638**	**171,654**	**190,643**	**189,946**	**1.04**	**-0.37**
Albania	509	564	768	1,078	1,172	0.01	8.72
Andorra	215	212	203	275	198		-28.00
Bosnia and Herzegovina	1,475	1,334	1,861	1,700	1,644	0.01	-3.29
Croatia	3,516	2,609	3,302	3,884	3,393	0.02	-12.64
Gibraltar	54	95	88	224	127		-43.30
Greece	13,627	10,404	11,958	13,714	13,046	0.07	-4.87
Holy See	12	2	3				
Italy	97,313	57,314	82,476	90,585	85,288	0.47	-5.85
Malta	2,119	1,331	2,299	2,401	1,993	0.01	-16.99
Portugal	17,146	16,136	19,997	19,867	20,720	0.11	4.29
San Marino	15	18	28	24	20		-16.67
Slovenia	2,534	2,048	2,945	3,445	2,829	0.02	-17.88
Spain	42,195	29,907	40,270	47,252	52,970	0.29	12.10
TFYR of Macedonia	703	723	728	824	831		0.85
Serbia and Montenegro	4,545	3,941	4,728	5,370	5,715	0.03	6.42

CANADA

1. Arrivals of non-resident tourists at national borders, by country of residence

	2002	2003	2004	2005	2006	Market share 06	% Change 06-05
Western Europe	880,652	789,313	917,570	976,020	964,463	5.28	-1.18
Austria	29,824	25,007	30,279	31,912	32,287	0.18	1.18
Belgium	40,307	37,045	43,297	43,335	44,828	0.25	3.45
France	313,987	276,672	331,978	356,489	369,624	2.02	3.68
Germany	295,715	260,247	299,802	324,373	302,323	1.66	-6.80
Liechtenstein	383	348	377	351	475		35.33
Luxembourg	2,674	2,428	2,967	3,209	3,267	0.02	1.81
Monaco	1,002	816	824	999	1,034	0.01	3.50
Netherlands	107,769	104,283	116,890	118,805	118,998	0.65	0.16
Switzerland	88,991	82,467	91,156	96,547	91,627	0.50	-5.10
East Mediterranean Europe	81,811	64,367	75,471	89,594	87,074	0.48	-2.81
Cyprus	1,465	1,306	1,590	1,728	1,734	0.01	0.35
Israel	74,501	58,169	67,051	80,082	76,639	0.42	-4.30
Turkey	5,845	4,892	6,830	7,784	8,701	0.05	11.78
Other Europe		3			120		
Other countries of Europe		3			120		
MIDDLE EAST	42,506	40,257	47,637	52,131	59,270	0.32	13.69
Middle East	42,506	40,257	47,637	52,131	59,270	0.32	13.69
Bahrain	823	869	1,096	1,237	1,298	0.01	4.93
Iraq	317	193	220	352	496		40.91
Jordan	1,795	1,531	1,614	2,155	2,479	0.01	15.03
Kuwait	2,397	2,311	3,110	3,137	3,131	0.02	-0.19
Lebanon	7,509	6,582	7,087	7,309	9,606	0.05	31.43
Libyan Arab Jamahiriya	1,035	1,060	1,262	1,485	1,524	0.01	2.63
Oman	982	926	1,057	1,284	1,377	0.01	7.24
Qatar	1,276	1,407	1,703	2,078	2,583	0.01	24.30
Saudi Arabia	9,553	8,453	10,942	11,836	12,178	0.07	2.89
Syrian Arab Republic	1,516	1,243	1,406	1,586	1,428	0.01	-9.96
United Arab Emirates	8,479	8,964	10,635	11,511	14,301	0.08	24.24
Egypt	6,565	6,429	7,168	7,745	8,473	0.05	9.40
Yemen	259	289	337	416	396		-4.81
SOUTH ASIA	79,073	79,792	96,342	109,681	118,728	0.65	8.25
South Asia	79,073	79,792	96,342	109,681	118,728	0.65	8.25
Afghanistan	356	312	335	589	605		2.72
Bangladesh	2,812	2,668	2,923	3,214	3,580	0.02	11.39
Bhutan	102	67	76	107	90		-15.89
Sri Lanka	3,787	3,177	3,377	3,969	4,458	0.02	12.32
India	55,492	57,010	68,315	77,849	87,210	0.48	12.02
Iran, Islamic Republic of	7,165	8,152	10,459	10,380	6,654	0.04	-35.90
Maldives	85	80	98	76	75		-1.32
Nepal	586	564	678	649	915	0.01	40.99
Pakistan	8,688	7,756	10,067	12,848	15,141	0.08	17.85
Other countries of South Asia		6	14				

Source: World Tourism Organization (UNWTO)

CANADA

2. Arrivals of non-resident visitors at national borders, by country of residence

	2002	2003	2004	2005	2006	Market share 06	% Change 06-05
TOTAL	44,896,100	38,902,800	38,844,600	36,160,300	33,389,900	100.00	-7.66
AFRICA	62,300	60,500	68,100	71,900	83,200	0.25	15.72
Southern Africa	18,600	17,200	20,300	21,700	22,700	0.07	4.61
South Africa	18,600	17,200	20,300	21,700	22,700	0.07	4.61
Other Africa	43,700	43,300	47,800	50,200	60,500	0.18	20.52
Other countries of Africa	43,700	43,300	47,800	50,200	60,500	0.18	20.52
AMERICAS	41,293,500	35,870,500	35,065,600	32,141,100	29,395,800	88.04	-8.54
Caribbean	120,300	107,400	124,800	128,700	133,700	0.40	3.89
Bermuda	23,000	23,300	24,200	24,000	23,000	0.07	-4.17
Jamaica	18,700	16,100	21,300	20,800	23,600	0.07	13.46
Trinidad and Tobago	19,900	17,800	20,900	22,400	24,900	0.07	11.16
Other countries of the Caribbean	58,700	50,200	58,400	61,500	62,200	0.19	1.14
North America	41,057,400	35,668,200	34,819,500	31,865,300	29,104,000	87.16	-8.67
Greenland	300	200	400	300	300		
Mexico	165,100	144,100	177,300	194,300	213,900	0.64	10.09
Saint Pierre and Miquelon	13,800	14,500	15,700	15,700	17,100	0.05	8.92
United States	40,878,200	35,509,400	34,626,100	31,655,000	28,872,700	86.47	-8.79
South America	96,800	78,100	105,300	131,300	141,700	0.42	7.92
Argentina	11,400	9,700	12,100	14,100	15,600	0.05	10.64
Brazil	36,900	31,600	50,500	62,200	65,600	0.20	5.47
Colombia	9,600	7,800	8,800	11,400	14,400	0.04	26.32
Venezuela	12,200	6,600	9,600	12,200	13,900	0.04	13.93
Other countries of South America	26,700	22,400	24,300	31,400	32,200	0.10	2.55
Other Americas	19,000	16,800	16,000	15,800	16,400	0.05	3.80
Other countries of the Americas	19,000	16,800	16,000	15,800	16,400	0.05	3.80
EAST ASIA AND THE PACIFIC	1,258,200	935,000	1,287,400	1,331,600	1,324,700	3.97	-0.52
North-East Asia	946,500	663,600	963,000	968,200	958,100	2.87	-1.04
China (*)	99,500	77,800	105,200	120,700	148,400	0.44	22.95
Taiwan (Province of China)	106,600	69,300	108,600	100,600	94,900	0.28	-5.67
Hong Kong, China	122,800	94,000	121,000	113,800	111,900	0.34	-1.67
Japan	452,500	273,900	437,200	441,800	401,100	1.20	-9.21
Korea, Republic of	165,100	148,600	191,000	191,300	201,800	0.60	5.49
South-East Asia	108,900	77,800	94,800	105,300	111,500	0.33	5.89
Indonesia	15,100	12,000	11,800	11,800	12,400	0.04	5.08
Malaysia	15,800	6,700	9,600	10,300	11,400	0.03	10.68
Philippines	41,100	33,300	38,200	44,100	50,500	0.15	14.51
Singapore	23,200	17,500	23,900	25,700	24,300	0.07	-5.45
Thailand	13,700	8,300	11,300	13,400	12,900	0.04	-3.73
Australasia	195,100	186,900	222,600	249,700	245,700	0.74	-1.60
Australia	162,800	156,600	185,100	209,200	206,500	0.62	-1.29
New Zealand	32,300	30,300	37,500	40,500	39,200	0.12	-3.21
Other East Asia and the Pacific	7,700	6,700	7,000	8,400	9,400	0.03	11.90
Other countries of Asia	5,200	4,600	4,400	5,200	6,300	0.02	21.15
Other countries of Oceania	2,500	2,100	2,600	3,200	3,100	0.01	-3.13
EUROPE	2,162,500	1,919,700	2,282,000	2,455,900	2,412,700	7.23	-1.76
Central/Eastern Europe	84,600	77,800	88,700	97,600	109,400	0.33	12.09
Bulgaria (*)	12,800	12,900	14,900	17,200	20,000	0.06	16.28
Czech Republic/Slovakia	14,800	13,900	15,400	15,700	16,100	0.05	2.55

CANADA

2. Arrivals of non-resident visitors at national borders, by country of residence

		2002	2003	2004	2005	2006	Market share 06	% Change 06-05
Estonia	(*)	3,000	2,700	2,700	3,200	3,400	0.01	6.25
Hungary		8,400	7,600	8,400	9,200	11,600	0.03	26.09
Poland		24,900	20,400	23,000	22,800	25,600	0.08	12.28
Commonwealth Independent State		20,700	20,300	24,300	29,500	32,700	0.10	10.85
Northern Europe		**887,200**	**834,200**	**978,500**	**1,064,900**	**1,033,100**	**3.09**	**-2.99**
Denmark	(*)	22,300	23,200	25,600	27,300	28,400	0.09	4.03
Finland		13,200	11,000	14,100	15,800	15,700	0.05	-0.63
Iceland		2,200	2,500	3,000	3,400	4,300	0.01	26.47
Ireland		31,100	31,100	39,400	43,500	50,000	0.15	14.94
Norway		20,000	16,800	18,800	20,800	21,600	0.06	3.85
Sweden		29,400	26,400	30,800	32,700	31,200	0.09	-4.59
United Kingdom		769,000	723,200	846,800	921,400	881,900	2.64	-4.29
Southern Europe		**195,300**	**132,100**	**186,400**	**201,600**	**198,400**	**0.59**	**-1.59**
Greece		14,400	10,800	12,600	14,200	13,700	0.04	-3.52
Italy	(*)	104,800	62,200	96,100	100,900	95,100	0.28	-5.75
Portugal		17,500	16,400	20,500	20,100	21,000	0.06	4.48
Spain		45,600	31,900	43,400	51,000	56,900	0.17	11.57
Yugoslavia, Sfr (Former)		13,000	10,800	13,800	15,400	11,700	0.04	-24.03
Western Europe		**909,900**	**809,300**	**952,700**	**1,000,900**	**984,800**	**2.95**	**-1.61**
Austria		30,400	25,400	31,200	32,500	32,800	0.10	0.92
France	(*)	321,900	281,900	342,600	363,300	374,800	1.12	3.17
Germany		311,700	271,600	318,300	336,600	313,000	0.94	-7.01
Netherlands		110,800	106,200	120,000	122,200	121,800	0.36	-0.33
Switzerland	(*)	91,100	84,000	93,100	99,100	93,600	0.28	-5.55
Belgium / Luxembourg		44,000	40,200	47,500	47,200	48,800	0.15	3.39
East Mediterranean Europe		**83,300**	**64,900**	**75,700**	**90,900**	**87,000**	**0.26**	**-4.29**
Israel		77,300	59,900	68,600	82,900	78,100	0.23	-5.79
Turkey		6,000	5,000	7,100	8,000	8,900	0.03	11.25
Other Europe		**2,200**	**1,400**					
Other countries of Europe		2,200	1,400					
MIDDLE EAST		**44,400**	**43,000**	**52,700**	**56,400**	**58,700**	**0.18**	**4.08**
Middle East		**44,400**	**43,000**	**52,700**	**56,400**	**58,700**	**0.18**	**4.08**
All countries of Middle East		44,400	43,000	52,700	56,400	58,700	0.18	4.08
SOUTH ASIA		**75,200**	**74,100**	**88,800**	**103,400**	**114,800**	**0.34**	**11.03**
South Asia		**75,200**	**74,100**	**88,800**	**103,400**	**114,800**	**0.34**	**11.03**
All countries of South Asia		75,200	74,100	88,800	103,400	114,800	0.34	11.03

Source: World Tourism Organization (UNWTO)

CANADA

6. Overnight stays of non-resident tourists in all types of accommodation establishments, by country of residence

		2002	2003	2004	2005	2006	Market share 06	% Change 06-05
TOTAL		122,150,000	107,697,900	123,425,600	125,656,400	120,703,000	100.00	-3.94
AFRICA		1,179,100	1,281,900	1,401,300	1,653,100	1,722,700	1.43	4.21
Southern Africa		398,700	310,600	293,000	427,200	488,600	0.40	14.37
South Africa		398,700	310,600	293,000	427,200	488,600	0.40	14.37
Other Africa		780,400	971,300	1,108,300	1,225,900	1,234,100	1.02	0.67
Other countries of Africa		780,400	971,300	1,108,300	1,225,900	1,234,100	1.02	0.67
AMERICAS		70,744,900	62,294,400	67,984,500	64,785,100	63,985,100	53.01	-1.23
Caribbean		2,203,600	1,906,000	1,915,700	1,719,900	2,188,000	1.81	27.22
Bermuda		266,800	316,900	301,100	207,500	476,300	0.39	129.54
Jamaica		504,700	351,000	281,100	297,100	334,300	0.28	12.52
Trinidad and Tobago		604,300	392,300	371,500	440,900	512,200	0.42	16.17
Other countries of the Caribbean		827,800	845,800	962,000	774,400	865,200	0.72	11.73
North America		66,815,300	58,910,000	63,827,800	60,639,300	59,248,100	49.09	-2.29
Greenland		2,100	900	2,700	2,400	1,600		-33.33
Mexico		2,187,400	2,100,500	2,885,700	3,149,000	3,864,300	3.20	22.72
Saint Pierre and Miquelon		118,500	85,300	201,500	157,200	104,400	0.09	-33.59
United States		64,507,300	56,723,300	60,737,900	57,330,700	55,277,800	45.80	-3.58
South America		1,498,500	1,283,800	2,005,700	2,227,100	2,353,900	1.95	5.69
Argentina		253,400	110,900	152,400	237,400	255,600	0.21	7.67
Brazil		550,600	569,500	1,048,500	929,100	1,070,100	0.89	15.18
Colombia		151,000	127,100	246,800	339,600	344,100	0.29	1.33
Venezuela		153,300	123,100	120,800	168,800	200,300	0.17	18.66
Other countries of South America		390,200	353,200	437,200	552,200	483,800	0.40	-12.39
Other Americas		227,500	194,600	235,300	198,800	195,100	0.16	-1.86
Other countries of the Americas		227,500	194,600	235,300	198,800	195,100	0.16	-1.86
EAST ASIA AND THE PACIFIC		18,809,400	15,006,500	19,843,300	21,355,400	19,140,200	15.86	-10.37
North-East Asia		14,297,500	11,365,300	15,228,600	16,636,000	14,217,400	11.78	-14.54
China	(*)	2,472,200	2,328,600	3,113,700	3,722,800	3,639,100	3.01	-2.25
Taiwan (Province of China)		1,440,500	1,078,800	1,307,900	1,535,700	1,237,600	1.03	-19.41
Hong Kong, China		2,014,700	1,622,700	2,168,400	2,161,500	1,707,400	1.41	-21.01
Japan		4,883,900	2,994,300	4,741,700	4,749,800	3,893,200	3.23	-18.03
Korea, Republic of		3,486,200	3,340,900	3,896,900	4,466,200	3,740,100	3.10	-16.26
South-East Asia		1,945,500	1,313,900	1,636,400	1,676,200	2,173,700	1.80	29.68
Indonesia		226,900	179,600	179,000	175,700	183,600	0.15	4.50
Malaysia		430,600	52,400	154,100	181,800	113,100	0.09	-37.79
Philippines		666,700	686,900	745,200	875,400	1,355,700	1.12	54.87
Singapore		382,000	259,600	319,300	225,100	258,800	0.21	14.97
Thailand		239,300	135,400	238,800	218,200	262,500	0.22	20.30
Australasia		2,494,200	2,258,900	2,874,000	2,895,300	2,610,700	2.16	-9.83
Australia		2,051,500	1,764,900	2,446,500	2,446,600	2,079,600	1.72	-15.00
New Zealand		442,700	494,000	427,500	448,700	531,100	0.44	18.36
Other East Asia and the Pacific		72,200	68,400	104,300	147,900	138,400	0.11	-6.42
Other countries of Asia		51,300	50,600	82,300	121,200	107,100	0.09	-11.63
Other countries of Oceania		20,900	17,800	22,000	26,700	31,300	0.03	17.23
EUROPE		29,068,600	26,920,900	31,581,600	34,806,800	32,141,500	26.63	-7.66
Central/Eastern Europe		2,133,800	1,889,200	2,092,100	2,423,300	2,185,500	1.81	-9.81
Bulgaria	(*)	410,800	364,500	465,500	679,500	467,900	0.39	-31.14

CANADA

6. Overnight stays of non-resident tourists in all types of accommodation establishments, by country of residence

		2002	2003	2004	2005	2006	Market share 06	% Change 06-05
Czech Republic/Slovakia		282,900	355,900	317,100	355,400	256,700	0.21	-27.77
Estonia	(*)	42,600	48,800	40,200	54,500	55,600	0.05	2.02
Hungary		200,100	136,900	147,000	140,100	130,600	0.11	-6.78
Poland		669,700	553,000	575,200	596,600	565,400	0.47	-5.23
Commonwealth Independent State		527,700	430,100	547,100	597,200	709,300	0.59	18.77
Northern Europe		**10,758,300**	**10,221,800**	**11,807,600**	**13,681,200**	**12,149,300**	**10.07**	**-11.20**
Denmark	(*)	261,700	259,900	354,700	379,100	460,300	0.38	21.42
Finland		170,500	87,300	175,600	167,300	161,800	0.13	-3.29
Iceland		23,700	29,100	35,000	34,500	52,000	0.04	50.72
Ireland		402,900	444,100	408,300	509,800	587,000	0.49	15.14
Norway		239,400	188,600	230,600	235,100	241,400	0.20	2.68
Sweden		288,600	251,600	382,800	473,900	307,000	0.25	-35.22
United Kingdom		9,371,500	8,961,200	10,220,600	11,881,500	10,339,800	8.57	-12.98
Southern Europe		**2,641,700**	**1,905,900**	**2,817,700**	**2,627,300**	**2,590,000**	**2.15**	**-1.42**
Greece		225,800	211,300	192,900	195,100	188,400	0.16	-3.43
Italy	(*)	1,207,500	726,600	1,135,900	1,061,400	1,185,400	0.98	11.68
Portugal		336,600	310,600	465,300	331,800	318,700	0.26	-3.95
Spain		611,400	421,700	660,600	660,900	640,400	0.53	-3.10
Yugoslavia, Sfr (Former)		260,400	235,700	363,000	378,100	257,100	0.21	-32.00
Western Europe		**12,330,200**	**12,043,200**	**13,883,200**	**14,941,900**	**14,093,200**	**11.68**	**-5.68**
Austria		402,400	318,400	503,800	477,300	459,100	0.38	-3.81
France	(*)	4,143,900	4,180,500	4,891,100	5,835,900	5,555,500	4.60	-4.80
Germany		4,319,500	3,941,700	4,587,500	4,900,300	4,412,600	3.66	-9.95
Netherlands		1,577,500	1,499,100	1,829,600	1,580,300	1,655,900	1.37	4.78
Switzerland	(*)	1,379,000	1,605,200	1,504,800	1,684,000	1,493,900	1.24	-11.29
Belgium / Luxembourg		507,900	498,300	566,400	464,100	516,200	0.43	11.23
East Mediterranean Europe		**1,157,700**	**826,500**	**981,000**	**1,133,100**	**1,123,500**	**0.93**	**-0.85**
Israel		1,009,300	681,900	734,800	928,800	853,200	0.71	-8.14
Turkey		148,400	144,600	246,200	204,300	270,300	0.22	32.31
Other Europe		**46,900**	**34,300**					
Other countries of Europe		46,900	34,300					
MIDDLE EAST		**970,700**	**896,800**	**1,183,100**	**1,284,800**	**1,424,600**	**1.18**	**10.88**
Middle East		**970,700**	**896,800**	**1,183,100**	**1,284,800**	**1,424,600**	**1.18**	**10.88**
All countries of Middle East		970,700	896,800	1,183,100	1,284,800	1,424,600	1.18	10.88
SOUTH ASIA		**1,377,300**	**1,297,400**	**1,431,800**	**1,771,200**	**2,288,900**	**1.90**	**29.23**
South Asia		**1,377,300**	**1,297,400**	**1,431,800**	**1,771,200**	**2,288,900**	**1.90**	**29.23**
All countries of South Asia		1,377,300	1,297,400	1,431,800	1,771,200	2,288,900	1.90	29.23

Source: World Tourism Organization (UNWTO)

CAPE VERDE

3. Arrivals of non-resident tourists in hotels and similar establishments, by country of residence

	2002	2003	2004	2005	2006	Market share 06	% Change 06-05
TOTAL	125,852	150,048	157,052	197,844	241,742	100.00	22.19
AFRICA	10,003	5,225	10,034	9,432	4,659	1.93	-50.60
Southern Africa	10,003	5,225	10,034	9,432	4,659	1.93	-50.60
South Africa	10,003	5,225	10,034	9,432	4,659	1.93	-50.60
AMERICAS	1,665	1,740	1,472	2,102	5,949	2.46	183.02
North America	1,665	1,740	1,472	2,102	5,949	2.46	183.02
United States	1,665	1,740	1,472	2,102	5,949	2.46	183.02
EUROPE	105,790	134,749	136,304	173,318	207,964	86.03	19.99
Northern Europe	833	1,140	824	2,284	5,106	2.11	123.56
United Kingdom	833	1,140	824	2,284	5,106	2.11	123.56
Southern Europe	74,094	90,505	103,610	127,594	132,790	54.93	4.07
Italy	35,080	54,278	55,200	69,728	65,109	26.93	-6.62
Portugal	34,292	28,548	38,129	50,240	59,881	24.77	19.19
Spain	4,722	7,679	10,281	7,626	7,800	3.23	2.28
Western Europe	30,863	43,104	31,870	43,440	70,068	28.98	61.30
Austria	662	822	703	938	1,326	0.55	41.36
Belgium (*)	2,798	9,702	4,159	5,121	10,675	4.42	108.46
France	11,813	12,847	11,160	14,284	25,145	10.40	76.04
Germany	13,796	18,095	14,433	21,121	30,485	12.61	44.34
Switzerland	1,794	1,638	1,415	1,976	2,437	1.01	23.33
REGION NOT SPECIFIED	8,394	8,334	9,242	12,992	23,170	9.58	78.34
Not Specified	8,394	8,334	9,242	12,992	23,170	9.58	78.34
Other countries of the World	8,394	8,334	9,242	12,992	23,170	9.58	78.34

Source: World Tourism Organization (UNWTO)

CAPE VERDE

5. Overnight stays of non-resident tourists in hotels and similar establishments, by country of residence

		2002	2003	2004	2005	2006	Market share 06	% Change 06-05
TOTAL		623,733	819,726	786,771	850,297	1,261,497	100.00	48.36
AFRICA		51,991	31,922	11,110	10,794	6,196	0.49	-42.60
Southern Africa		51,991	31,922	11,110	10,794	6,196	0.49	-42.60
South Africa		51,991	31,922	11,110	10,794	6,196	0.49	-42.60
AMERICAS		5,313	5,015	4,693	7,087	16,474	1.31	132.45
North America		5,313	5,015	4,693	7,087	16,474	1.31	132.45
United States		5,313	5,015	4,693	7,087	16,474	1.31	132.45
EUROPE		541,387	752,756	737,221	787,761	1,150,159	91.17	46.00
Northern Europe		3,183	3,565	3,296	8,039	21,460	1.70	166.95
United Kingdom		3,183	3,565	3,296	8,039	21,460	1.70	166.95
Southern Europe		404,477	534,476	604,075	591,483	787,084	62.39	33.07
Italy		245,964	375,566	387,797	326,554	469,108	37.19	43.65
Portugal		142,279	122,800	184,571	235,788	284,194	22.53	20.53
Spain		16,234	36,110	31,707	29,141	33,782	2.68	15.93
Western Europe		133,727	214,715	129,850	188,239	341,615	27.08	81.48
Austria		3,176	3,360	2,177	3,507	5,288	0.42	50.78
Belgium	(*)	10,424	54,231	20,251	25,526	54,785	4.34	114.62
France		38,131	40,345	32,494	47,188	100,456	7.96	112.88
Germany		75,303	111,107	70,333	104,397	169,457	13.43	62.32
Switzerland		6,693	5,672	4,595	7,621	11,629	0.92	52.59
REGION NOT SPECIFIED		25,042	30,033	33,747	44,655	88,668	7.03	98.56
Not Specified		25,042	30,033	33,747	44,655	88,668	7.03	98.56
Other countries of the World		25,042	30,033	33,747	44,655	88,668	7.03	98.56

Source: World Tourism Organization (UNWTO)

CAYMAN ISLANDS

1. Arrivals of non-resident tourists at national borders, by country of residence

		2002	2003	2004	2005	2006	Market share 06	% Change 06-05
TOTAL	(*)	302,797	293,513	259,929	167,802	267,257	100.00	59.27
AFRICA		353	373	321	325	435	0.16	33.85
East Africa		46	33	26	27	35	0.01	29.63
British Indian Ocean Territory				1				
Burundi			1					
Comoros				1				
Ethiopia						1		
Eritrea				1				
Kenya		2	4	4	7	7		
Madagascar		2		1	3	2		-33.33
Malawi					2	2		
Mauritius		6	2	1	2	5		150.00
Reunion		5		1				
Rwanda		1	2					
Seychelles		2			1			
Somalia		1						
Zimbabwe		22	19	12	9	12		33.33
Uganda		1	3	1	1	1		
United Republic of Tanzania			1			2		
Zambia		4	1	3	2	3		50.00
Central Africa		3	9	21	6	15	0.01	150.00
Cameroon		1	4			1		
Central African Republic			5					
Chad		2		1				
Congo				1				
Gabon				4	4	5		25.00
Sao Tome and Principe				15	2	9		350.00
North Africa		2	1		2	2		
Morocco			1					
Tunisia		2			2	2		
Southern Africa		275	316	261	265	360	0.13	35.85
Botswana		3		3	7	8		14.29
Lesotho		2			1			
Namibia		1	1	1	1	2		100.00
South Africa		229	290	243	235	330	0.12	40.43
Swaziland		40	25	14	21	20	0.01	-4.76
West Africa		27	14	13	25	23	0.01	-8.00
Cape Verde		2						
Gambia		1						
Ghana		7	3	2	8	4		-50.00
Cote D'Ivoire			2	1	1	1		
Liberia						2		
Niger		2				1		
Nigeria		9	5	9	12	10		-16.67
Guinea-Bissau			1		1	2		100.00
Saint Helena		1						
Senegal			1			1		
Sierra Leone		4						
Togo		1	2	1	2	2		
Burkina Faso					1			
AMERICAS		281,796	272,381	242,012	152,735	247,420	92.58	61.99
Caribbean		18,754	21,679	21,330	20,000	11,122	4.16	-44.39

CAYMAN ISLANDS

1. Arrivals of non-resident tourists at national borders, by country of residence

	2002	2003	2004	2005	2006	Market share 06	% Change 06-05
Antigua and Barbuda	44	58	26	64	77	0.03	20.31
Bahamas	529	570	570	556	554	0.21	-0.36
Barbados	547	511	429	418	556	0.21	33.01
Bermuda	384	327	444	422	480	0.18	13.74
British Virgin Islands	64	59	48	63	76	0.03	20.63
Cuba	287	295	377	317	342	0.13	7.89
Dominica	13	12	9	11	22	0.01	100.00
Dominican Republic	173	92	117	122	199	0.07	63.11
Grenada	21	46	22	20	23	0.01	15.00
Guadeloupe	2	2	2		2		
Haiti	24	8	11	8	18	0.01	125.00
Jamaica	15,544	18,639	18,306	17,005	7,610	2.85	-55.25
Martinique	9	1		3	1		-66.67
Montserrat	15	11	13	11	4		-63.64
Netherlands Antilles	11	5	7	7	23	0.01	228.57
Puerto Rico	96	74	55	74	90	0.03	21.62
Saint Kitts and Nevis	42	34	25	35	33	0.01	-5.71
Anguilla	31	21	15	23	20	0.01	-13.04
Saint Lucia	97	77	64	64	98	0.04	53.13
Saint Maarten	11	7	10	4	14	0.01	250.00
Saint Vincent and the Grenadines	52	58	57	34	49	0.02	44.12
Trinidad and Tobago	612	672	581	554	674	0.25	21.66
Turks and Caicos Islands	112	74	108	128	89	0.03	-30.47
United States Virgin Islands	34	26	34	57	68	0.03	19.30
Central America	**2,523**	**2,599**	**2,026**	**2,159**	**2,199**	**0.82**	**1.85**
Belize	121	100	80	89	98	0.04	10.11
Costa Rica	232	313	296	325	192	0.07	-40.92
El Salvador	31	26	34	31	32	0.01	3.23
Guatemala	55	99	64	40	61	0.02	52.50
Honduras	1,732	1,737	1,255	1,399	1,455	0.54	4.00
Nicaragua	223	195	143	137	172	0.06	25.55
Panama	129	129	154	138	189	0.07	36.96
North America	**259,019**	**246,832**	**217,631**	**129,614**	**232,803**	**87.11**	**79.61**
Canada	13,569	14,125	12,116	10,480	14,910	5.58	42.27
Mexico	587	294	309	291	530	0.20	82.13
Saint Pierre and Miquelon	1						
United States	244,862	232,413	205,206	118,843	217,363	81.33	82.90
South America	**1,500**	**1,271**	**1,025**	**962**	**1,296**	**0.48**	**34.72**
Argentina	214	139	110	69	165	0.06	139.13
Bolivia	19	3	7	3	8		166.67
Brazil	365	296	222	229	290	0.11	26.64
Chile	60	66	53	51	63	0.02	23.53
Colombia	344	319	276	294	362	0.14	23.13
Ecuador	77	61	49	34	55	0.02	61.76
Falkland Islands (Malvinas)	4	3			2		
Guyana	100	116	115	117	136	0.05	16.24
Paraguay	19	5	1				
Peru	62	95	35	65	50	0.02	-23.08
Suriname	5	5	12	10	9		-10.00
Uruguay	31	16	9	6	13		116.67
Venezuela	200	147	136	84	143	0.05	70.24
EAST ASIA AND THE PACIFIC	**1,382**	**1,201**	**1,216**	**1,129**	**1,370**	**0.51**	**21.35**
North-East Asia	**403**	**331**	**359**	**269**	**351**	**0.13**	**30.48**
China	53	23	31	40	68	0.03	70.00

142

CAYMAN ISLANDS

1. Arrivals of non-resident tourists at national borders, by country of residence

	2002	2003	2004	2005	2006	Market share 06	% Change 06-05
Taiwan (Province of China)	7	1	9	5	14	0.01	180.00
Hong Kong, China	34	51	41	47	40	0.01	-14.89
Japan	279	231	263	169	211	0.08	24.85
Korea, Republic of	29	23	15	7	18	0.01	157.14
Macao, China	1	2		1			
South-East Asia	**288**	**135**	**159**	**208**	**252**	**0.09**	**21.15**
Brunei Darussalam					1		
Myanmar					2		
Cambodia					1		
Indonesia	49	25	21	29	33	0.01	13.79
Malaysia	12	10	19	7	30	0.01	328.57
Philippines	171	65	73	119	112	0.04	-5.88
Singapore	39	23	40	45	56	0.02	24.44
Viet Nam	2	5	1	2	1		-50.00
Thailand	15	7	5	6	16	0.01	166.67
Australasia	**674**	**730**	**683**	**630**	**729**	**0.27**	**15.71**
Australia	490	542	513	453	526	0.20	16.11
New Zealand	184	188	170	177	203	0.08	14.69
Melanesia	**13**	**1**	**13**	**17**	**28**	**0.01**	**64.71**
Solomon Islands					1		
Fiji	13	1	13	17	26	0.01	52.94
Papua New Guinea					1		
Micronesia	**1**			**2**	**5**		**150.00**
Cocos (Keeling) Islands	1			1			
Kiribati				1			
Guam					1		
Nauru					1		
Marshall Islands					3		
Polynesia	**3**	**4**	**2**	**3**	**5**		**66.67**
American Samoa				1	1		
Cook Islands	1	2	1	1			
Niue	1	1					
Tonga					1		
Tuvalu					1		
Wallis and Futuna Islands		1					
Samoa	1		1	1	2		100.00
EUROPE	**18,705**	**19,001**	**15,938**	**13,221**	**17,516**	**6.55**	**32.49**
Central/Eastern Europe	**245**	**228**	**196**	**194**	**302**	**0.11**	**55.67**
Bulgaria	18	7	10	6	9		50.00
Belarus				1	3		200.00
Czech Republic/Slovakia	31	27	63	24	50	0.02	108.33
Czech Republic	11	42					
Estonia	3			13	1		-92.31
Hungary	33	31	24	24	55	0.02	129.17
Latvia	3	4	5	7	7		
Lithuania	3	2		4	2		-50.00
Poland	35	39	20	30	45	0.02	50.00
Romania	33	11	17	29	31	0.01	6.90
Russian Federation	54	43	40	48	83	0.03	72.92
Slovakia	11	13					
Ukraine	10	9	17	8	16	0.01	100.00
Northern Europe	**14,345**	**14,673**	**12,626**	**10,383**	**13,269**	**4.96**	**27.80**
Denmark	144	153	104	108	125	0.05	15.74

CAYMAN ISLANDS

1. Arrivals of non-resident tourists at national borders, by country of residence

	2002	2003	2004	2005	2006	Market share 06	% Change 06-05
Finland	63	48	38	33	60	0.02	81.82
Iceland	3	17	5	5	18	0.01	260.00
Ireland	693	743	737	651	791	0.30	21.51
Norway	189	119	134	97	107	0.04	10.31
Sweden	255	221	163	149	171	0.06	14.77
United Kingdom	12,998	13,372	11,445	9,340	11,997	4.49	28.45
Southern Europe	**1,605**	**1,480**	**1,124**	**881**	**1,130**	**0.42**	**28.26**
Albania	1				1		
Andorra	155	158	130	79	101	0.04	27.85
Croatia	11	5	8	3	6		100.00
Gibraltar	6		3	4	7		75.00
Greece	57	57	50	9	37	0.01	311.11
Holy See		2	1	1	1		
Italy	976	842	657	478	606	0.23	26.78
Malta	7	2	6	13	7		-46.15
Portugal	103	99	57	78	94	0.04	20.51
San Marino		2	1		1		
Slovenia	3	8	4	4	9		125.00
Spain	284	304	206	210	256	0.10	21.90
Serbia and Montenegro	2	1	1	2	4		100.00
Western Europe	**2,395**	**2,540**	**1,939**	**1,712**	**2,709**	**1.01**	**58.24**
Austria	206	222	193	124	200	0.07	61.29
Belgium	70	78	85	61	118	0.04	93.44
France	450	530	384	305	529	0.20	73.44
Germany	778	750	583	579	902	0.34	55.79
Liechtenstein	1	5		2	3		50.00
Luxembourg	9	9	3	4	9		125.00
Monaco	7	4	2	7	8		14.29
Netherlands	354	468	327	281	414	0.15	47.33
Switzerland	520	474	362	349	526	0.20	50.72
East Mediterranean Europe	**115**	**80**	**53**	**51**	**106**	**0.04**	**107.84**
Cyprus	15	6	5	15	6		-60.00
Israel	69	55	26	24	74	0.03	208.33
Turkey	31	19	22	12	26	0.01	116.67
MIDDLE EAST	**100**	**65**	**72**	**24**	**53**	**0.02**	**120.83**
Middle East	**100**	**65**	**72**	**24**	**53**	**0.02**	**120.83**
Bahrain	8	2	6	1	3		200.00
Jordan	2	2	1		7		
Kuwait	1	5	5	2	3		50.00
Lebanon	7	3	5	3	3		
Libyan Arab Jamahiriya		1					
Oman	7	2					
Qatar		7			1		
Saudi Arabia	53	35	44	13	18	0.01	38.46
Syrian Arab Republic					1		
United Arab Emirates	9		1	1	4		300.00
Egypt	13	8	10	3	13		333.33
Yemen				1			
SOUTH ASIA	**238**	**274**	**176**	**97**	**158**	**0.06**	**62.89**
South Asia	**238**	**274**	**176**	**97**	**158**	**0.06**	**62.89**
Afghanistan	21	34	10				
Bangladesh		1	2		5		
Bhutan				1			

CAYMAN ISLANDS

1. Arrivals of non-resident tourists at national borders, by country of residence

	2002	2003	2004	2005	2006	Market share 06	% Change 06-05
Sri Lanka	5	4	6	8	8		
India	206	205	150	81	140	0.05	72.84
Iran, Islamic Republic of	1	1	1	1			
Maldives		3		1			
Nepal	1		1	4	1		-75.00
Pakistan	4	26	6	1	4		300.00
REGION NOT SPECIFIED	**223**	**218**	**194**	**271**	**305**	**0.11**	**12.55**
Not Specified	**223**	**218**	**194**	**271**	**305**	**0.11**	**12.55**
Other countries of the World	223	218	194	271	305	0.11	12.55

Source: World Tourism Organization (UNWTO)

CENTRAL AFRICAN REPUBLIC

1. Arrivals of non-resident tourists at national borders, by nationality

	2002	2003	2004	2005	2006	Market share 06	% Change 06-05
TOTAL (*)	**2,910**	**5,687**	**8,156**	**11,969**	**13,764**	**100.00**	**15.00**
AFRICA	**1,455**	**3,111**	**3,501**	**6,156**	**7,079**	**51.43**	**14.99**
East Africa	**9**	**45**	**51**	**169**	**194**	**1.41**	**14.79**
Rwanda	9	45	18	43	49	0.36	13.95
Other countries of East Africa			33	126	145	1.05	15.08
Central Africa	**929**	**1,472**	**2,023**	**2,832**	**3,257**	**23.66**	**15.01**
Cameroon	455	604	904	1,165	1,340	9.74	15.02
Chad	134	212	352	566	651	4.73	15.02
Congo	156	411	418	468	538	3.91	14.96
Democratic Republic of the Congo	69	103	142	248	285	2.07	14.92
Gabon	94	32	166	251	289	2.10	15.14
Other countries of Central Africa	21	110	41	134	154	1.12	14.93
North Africa	**30**	**147**	**218**	**225**	**259**	**1.88**	**15.11**
Sudan	11	58	72	44	51	0.37	15.91
Other countries of North Africa	19	89	146	181	208	1.51	14.92
Southern Africa	**88**	**112**	**147**	**196**	**225**	**1.63**	**14.80**
South Africa	39	45	73	108	124	0.90	14.81
Other countries of Southern Africa	49	67	74	88	101	0.73	14.77
West Africa	**399**	**1,335**	**1,062**	**1,925**	**2,214**	**16.09**	**15.01**
Benin	33	54	119	190	219	1.59	15.26
Cote D'Ivoire	97	182	127	280	322	2.34	15.00
Mali	33	37	65	106	122	0.89	15.09
Nigeria	43	72	107	182	209	1.52	14.84
Senegal	60	139	315	383	440	3.20	14.88
Togo	23	164	81	119	137	1.00	15.13
Other countries of West Africa	110	687	248	665	765	5.56	15.04
Other Africa				**809**	**930**	**6.76**	**14.96**
Other countries of Africa				809	930	6.76	14.96
AMERICAS	**176**	**374**	**449**	**639**	**735**	**5.34**	**15.02**
North America	**151**	**300**	**368**	**481**	**553**	**4.02**	**14.97**
Canada	34	180	104	104	120	0.87	15.38
United States	117	120	264	377	433	3.15	14.85
Other Americas	**25**	**74**	**81**	**158**	**182**	**1.32**	**15.19**
Other countries of the Americas	25	74	81	158	182	1.32	15.19
EAST ASIA AND THE PACIFIC	**170**	**288**	**317**	**373**	**429**	**3.12**	**15.01**
North-East Asia	**85**	**253**	**166**	**198**	**228**	**1.66**	**15.15**
China	31	141	134	150	173	1.26	15.33
Japan	54	112	32	48	55	0.40	14.58
Other East Asia and the Pacific	**85**	**35**	**151**	**175**	**201**	**1.46**	**14.86**
Other countries of Asia	85	35	151	175	201	1.46	14.86
EUROPE	**1,025**	**1,881**	**3,674**	**4,349**	**5,001**	**36.33**	**14.99**
Northern Europe	**13**	**50**	**42**	**42**	**48**	**0.35**	**14.29**
United Kingdom	13	50	42	42	48	0.35	14.29
Southern Europe	**84**	**130**	**383**	**475**	**546**	**3.97**	**14.95**
Italy	84	130	383	475	546	3.97	14.95
Western Europe	**832**	**1,311**	**2,864**	**3,351**	**3,854**	**28.00**	**15.01**
Belgium	89	153	196	219	252	1.83	15.07

CENTRAL AFRICAN REPUBLIC

1. Arrivals of non-resident tourists at national borders, by nationality

	2002	2003	2004	2005	2006	Market share 06	% Change 06-05
France	672	1,010	2,492	2,913	3,350	24.34	15.00
Germany	48	80	117	132	152	1.10	15.15
Switzerland	23	68	59	87	100	0.73	14.94
Other Europe	**96**	**390**	**385**	**481**	**553**	**4.02**	**14.97**
Other countries of Europe	96	390	385	481	553	4.02	14.97
MIDDLE EAST	**15**	**18**	**192**	**397**	**457**	**3.32**	**15.11**
Middle East	**15**	**18**	**192**	**397**	**457**	**3.32**	**15.11**
Lebanon	15	18	192	255	293	2.13	14.90
Other countries of Middle East				142	164	1.19	15.49
REGION NOT SPECIFIED	**69**	**15**	**23**	**55**	**63**	**0.46**	**14.55**
Not Specified	**69**	**15**	**23**	**55**	**63**	**0.46**	**14.55**
Other countries of the World	69	15	23	55	63	0.46	14.55

Source: World Tourism Organization (UNWTO)

CHAD

3. Arrivals of non-resident tourists in hotels and similar establishments, by nationality

	2002	2003	2004	2005	2006	Market share 06	% Change 06-05
TOTAL	32,334	20,974	25,899	29,356			
AFRICA	7,514	5,141	5,855	6,695			
East Africa	241	182	209	329			
All countries of East Africa	241	182	209	329			
Central Africa	3,773	3,004	3,397	3,559			
All countries of Central Africa	3,773	3,004	3,397	3,559			
North Africa	606	256	296	357			
All countries of North Africa	606	256	296	357			
West Africa	2,424	1,603	1,854	2,334			
All countries of West Africa	2,424	1,603	1,854	2,334			
Other Africa	470	96	99	116			
Other countries of Africa	470	96	99	116			
AMERICAS	6,485	4,368	5,609	5,976			
North America	6,125	4,250	5,375	5,628			
Canada	1,212	1,044	1,942	1,935			
United States	4,913	3,206	3,433	3,693			
Other Americas	360	118	234	348			
Other countries of the Americas	360	118	234	348			
EAST ASIA AND THE PACIFIC	1,000	297	398	550			
North-East Asia	273	146	195	270			
China	103	96	128	183			
Japan	98	34	45	45			
Korea, Republic of	72	16	22	42			
Other East Asia and the Pacific	727	151	203	280			
Other countries East Asia/Pacific	727	151	203	280			
EUROPE	15,225	10,029	12,690	14,805			
Northern Europe	561	296	378	430			
United Kingdom	497	270	336	363			
Scandinavia	64	26	42	67			
Southern Europe	328	166	202	246			
Italy	328	166	202	246			
Western Europe	12,179	8,803	11,145	13,090			
Belgium	352	164	219	241			
France	10,835	7,897	9,986	11,757			
Germany	469	405	508	547			
Netherlands	99	34	51	87			
Switzerland	424	303	381	458			
Other Europe	2,157	764	965	1,039			
Other countries of Europe	2,157	764	965	1,039			
MIDDLE EAST	2,110	1,139	1,347	1,330			
Middle East	2,110	1,139	1,347	1,330			
Lebanon	75	50	43	40			
Libyan Arab Jamahiriya	812	473	563	549			
Saudi Arabia	345	121	143	149			
Syrian Arab Republic	65	17	36	32			
Egypt	550	370	440	426			

CHAD

3. Arrivals of non-resident tourists in hotels and similar establishments, by nationality

	2002	2003	2004	2005	2006	Market share 06	% Change 06-05
Other countries of Middle East	263	108	122	134			

Source: World Tourism Organization (UNWTO)

CHAD

5. Overnight stays of non-resident tourists in hotels and similar establishments, by nationality

	2002	2003	2004	2005	2006	Market share 06	% Change 06-05
TOTAL	106,615	60,395	75,967	64,293			
AFRICA	23,798	15,241	17,787	15,875			
East Africa	844	562	637	779			
All countries of East Africa	844	562	637	779			
Central Africa	12,092	8,884	10,232	8,334			
All countries of Central Africa	12,092	8,884	10,232	8,334			
North Africa	1,636	757	874	712			
All countries of North Africa	1,636	757	874	712			
West Africa	7,696	4,733	5,681	5,768			
All countries of West Africa	7,696	4,733	5,681	5,768			
Other Africa	1,530	305	363	282			
Other countries of Africa	1,530	305	363	282			
AMERICAS	20,086	12,508	16,816	12,277			
North America	18,930	12,165	16,130	11,724			
Canada	3,648	2,974	5,716	4,090			
United States	15,282	9,191	10,414	7,634			
Other Americas	1,156	343	686	553			
Other countries of the Americas	1,156	343	686	553			
EAST ASIA AND THE PACIFIC	3,363	1,230	1,223	1,280			
North-East Asia	853	571	634	592			
China	347	385	401	418			
Japan	283	124	159	99			
Korea, Republic of	223	62	74	75			
Other East Asia and the Pacific	2,510	659	589	688			
Other countries East Asia/Pacific	2,510	659	589	688			
EUROPE	53,397	28,094	36,161	31,836			
Northern Europe	1,922	874	1,051	987			
United Kingdom	1,728	802	901	821			
Scandinavia	194	72	150	166			
Southern Europe	1,078	546	618	555			
Italy	1,078	546	618	555			
Western Europe	43,219	24,432	31,587	28,147			
Belgium	1,120	479	528	496			
France	38,700	21,707	28,514	24,968			
Germany	1,658	1,227	1,279	1,310			
Netherlands	322	123	183	219			
Switzerland	1,419	896	1,083	1,154			
Other Europe	7,178	2,242	2,905	2,147			
Other countries of Europe	7,178	2,242	2,905	2,147			
MIDDLE EAST	5,971	3,322	3,980	3,025			
Middle East	5,971	3,322	3,980	3,025			
Lebanon	244	166	140	88			
Libyan Arab Jamahiriya	2,260	1,188	1,659	1,209			
Saudi Arabia	996	369	482	374			
Syrian Arab Republic	160	53	112	66			

CHAD

5. **Overnight stays of non-resident tourists in hotels and similar establishments, by nationality**

	2002	2003	2004	2005	2006	Market share 06	% Change 06-05
Egypt	1,654	1,196	1,224	913			
Other countries of Middle East	657	350	363	375			

Source: World Tourism Organization (UNWTO)

CHILE

1. Arrivals of non-resident tourists at national borders, by nationality

	2002	2003	2004	2005	2006	Market share 06	% Change 06-05
TOTAL	1,412,315	1,613,523	1,785,024	2,027,082	2,252,952	100.00	11.14
AFRICA	2,476	2,872	3,653	3,544	4,150	0.18	17.10
East Africa	92	63	59	107	104		-2.80
Kenya	62	41	42	65	62		-4.62
Somalia	1		5		9		
Zimbabwe	29	22	12	42	33		-21.43
Central Africa	38	16	79	39	87		123.08
Angola	38	16	79	39	83		112.82
Democratic Republic of the Congo					4		
North Africa	108	171	303	119	257	0.01	115.97
Algeria	18	17	39	22	19		-13.64
Morocco	70	75	242	54	111		105.56
Tunisia	20	79	22	43	127	0.01	195.35
Southern Africa	1,897	2,305	2,730	2,815	3,063	0.14	8.81
South Africa	1,897	2,305	2,730	2,815	3,063	0.14	8.81
West Africa	42	52	40	118	196	0.01	66.10
Cape Verde	3	9	8	19	7		-63.16
Ghana	16	12	10	11	130	0.01	1,081.82
Nigeria	23	31	22	88	59		-32.95
Other Africa	299	265	442	346	443	0.02	28.03
Other countries of Africa	299	265	442	346	443	0.02	28.03
AMERICAS	1,119,232	1,242,956	1,360,342	1,553,381	1,754,599	77.88	12.95
Caribbean	3,857	4,576	5,030	4,533	5,313	0.24	17.21
Bahamas	49	57	449	137	73		-46.72
Barbados	296	407	110	108	133	0.01	23.15
Bermuda	15	15	11	95	63		-33.68
Cuba	1,440	1,519	1,669	1,846	1,908	0.08	3.36
Dominica	140	337	644	713	627	0.03	-12.06
Dominican Republic	1,417	1,445	995	971	1,390	0.06	43.15
Grenada	186	88	271	131	136	0.01	3.82
Haiti	59	106	63	141	167	0.01	18.44
Jamaica	81	322	275	114	298	0.01	161.40
Puerto Rico	25	110	227	63	56		-11.11
Saint Lucia	33	33	81	65	168	0.01	158.46
Saint Vincent and the Grenadines	9	14	41	21	110		423.81
Trinidad and Tobago	107	123	194	128	184	0.01	43.75
Central America	9,274	10,686	11,327	12,047	15,387	0.68	27.72
Belize	64	149	68	132	199	0.01	50.76
Costa Rica	2,962	3,141	3,351	3,533	3,936	0.17	11.41
El Salvador	1,228	1,411	1,967	1,735	2,391	0.11	37.81
Guatemala	1,489	1,670	1,631	2,076	2,337	0.10	12.57
Honduras	646	688	698	702	980	0.04	39.60
Nicaragua	580	912	663	794	1,873	0.08	135.89
Panama	2,305	2,715	2,949	3,075	3,671	0.16	19.38
North America	170,714	200,826	228,714	253,776	279,545	12.41	10.15
Canada	17,830	21,417	28,118	33,618	39,240	1.74	16.72
Mexico	22,316	32,088	34,275	36,325	40,781	1.81	12.27
United States	130,568	147,321	166,321	183,833	199,524	8.86	8.54
South America	934,990	1,026,315	1,114,617	1,281,942	1,453,659	64.52	13.40
Argentina	514,711	536,010	576,817	606,567	684,406	30.38	12.83

CHILE

1. Arrivals of non-resident tourists at national borders, by nationality

	2002	2003	2004	2005	2006	Market share 06	% Change 06-05
Bolivia	107,703	132,312	134,709	177,278	231,062	10.26	30.34
Brazil	79,198	100,341	119,271	167,291	179,348	7.96	7.21
Colombia	18,987	26,724	29,596	33,740	41,489	1.84	22.97
Ecuador	22,710	26,392	23,674	23,755	24,352	1.08	2.51
Guyana	37	412	23	30	24		-20.00
Paraguay	10,370	9,590	9,226	13,497	12,419	0.55	-7.99
Peru	154,842	163,718	186,088	221,384	237,457	10.54	7.26
Suriname	27	49	58	29	65		124.14
Uruguay	18,223	20,227	23,581	24,954	26,666	1.18	6.86
Venezuela	8,182	10,540	11,574	13,417	16,371	0.73	22.02
Other Americas	**397**	**553**	**654**	**1,083**	**695**	**0.03**	**-35.83**
Other countries of the Americas	397	553	654	1,083	695	0.03	-35.83
EAST ASIA AND THE PACIFIC	**40,786**	**54,476**	**69,883**	**74,927**	**83,683**	**3.71**	**11.69**
North-East Asia	**18,825**	**21,688**	**27,957**	**28,117**	**29,340**	**1.30**	**4.35**
China	705	2,857	6,356	6,397	7,707	0.34	20.48
Taiwan (Province of China)	3,137	1,059	190	1,185	372	0.02	-68.61
Japan	11,694	12,409	14,335	13,882	13,230	0.59	-4.70
Korea, Dem. People's Republic of	509	1,024	876	686	651	0.03	-5.10
Korea, Republic of	2,765	4,291	6,181	5,951	7,333	0.33	23.22
Mongolia	15	48	19	16	47		193.75
South-East Asia	**2,367**	**3,517**	**6,915**	**7,200**	**10,133**	**0.45**	**40.74**
Brunei Darussalam	14	4	38	7	8		14.29
Myanmar		102	225	338	333	0.01	-1.48
Cambodia	2		4	13	79		507.69
Indonesia	277	521	371	417	536	0.02	28.54
Lao People's Democratic Republic	2	5	51	14	386	0.02	2,657.14
Malaysia	312	453	467	368	657	0.03	78.53
Philippines	1,399	1,907	5,024	5,356	7,078	0.31	32.15
Singapore	187	269	407	368	476	0.02	29.35
Viet Nam	37	85	98	37	178	0.01	381.08
Thailand	137	171	230	282	402	0.02	42.55
Australasia	**19,241**	**28,564**	**33,162**	**38,100**	**42,407**	**1.88**	**11.30**
Australia	15,567	23,384	26,703	31,121	34,057	1.51	9.43
New Zealand	3,674	5,180	6,459	6,979	8,350	0.37	19.64
Polynesia		**8**	**155**	**173**	**222**	**0.01**	**28.32**
Tuvalu			140	143	89		-37.76
Samoa		8	15	30	133	0.01	343.33
Other East Asia and the Pacific	**353**	**699**	**1,694**	**1,337**	**1,581**	**0.07**	**18.25**
Other countries of Asia	118	461	1,100	792	707	0.03	-10.73
Other countries of Oceania	235	238	594	545	874	0.04	60.37
EUROPE	**245,494**	**309,008**	**344,774**	**384,886**	**401,775**	**17.83**	**4.39**
Central/Eastern Europe	**5,661**	**6,506**	**8,418**	**9,912**	**13,032**	**0.58**	**31.48**
Azerbaijan			2	17	41		141.18
Armenia	12			12	29		141.67
Bulgaria	116	216	303	476	427	0.02	-10.29
Belarus	1,702	619	61	516	365	0.02	-29.26
Czech Republic			277				
Estonia	105	66	143	393	169	0.01	-57.00
Georgia			96	109	106		-2.75
Hungary	505	642	538	652	879	0.04	34.82
Kazakhstan				27	28		3.70
Kyrgyzstan				23	134	0.01	482.61

CHILE

1. Arrivals of non-resident tourists at national borders, by nationality

	2002	2003	2004	2005	2006	Market share 06	% Change 06-05
Latvia	3	1	9	22	52		136.36
Lithuania	9	36	79	120	466	0.02	288.33
Republic of Moldova		4	10	12	5		-58.33
Poland	1,440	2,216	2,787	2,866	3,000	0.13	4.68
Romania	247	470	298	768	1,149	0.05	49.61
Russian Federation	166	976	3,014	2,391	3,469	0.15	45.09
Slovakia	1,107	999	554	398	676	0.03	69.85
Tajikistan		30	25	11	451	0.02	4,000.00
Turkmenistan					12		
Ukraine	248	231	222	1,082	1,564	0.07	44.55
Uzbekistan	1			17	10		-41.18
Northern Europe	**58,352**	**78,965**	**80,081**	**86,707**	**92,905**	**4.12**	**7.15**
Denmark	3,188	3,694	4,527	5,349	5,362	0.24	0.24
Finland	1,994	2,902	3,198	3,018	3,417	0.15	13.22
Iceland	168	215	236	419	503	0.02	20.05
Ireland	3,000	4,677	4,976	6,260	6,595	0.29	5.35
Norway	3,861	4,912	5,335	5,527	6,174	0.27	11.71
Sweden	8,872	11,581	11,523	13,113	12,342	0.55	-5.88
United Kingdom	37,269	50,984	50,286	53,021	58,512	2.60	10.36
Southern Europe	**57,788**	**69,821**	**84,036**	**94,016**	**98,659**	**4.38**	**4.94**
Albania	312	68	280	272	653	0.03	140.07
Andorra	49	53	78	127	115	0.01	-9.45
Bosnia and Herzegovina	4	11	24	20	22		10.00
Croatia	173	181	804	678	545	0.02	-19.62
Greece	1,199	1,254	1,511	1,426	1,621	0.07	13.67
Italy	18,111	21,506	25,986	26,060	27,615	1.23	5.97
Malta	73	48	101	107	103		-3.74
Portugal	2,215	2,770	3,344	4,085	4,914	0.22	20.29
San Marino	14	9	394	25	37		48.00
Serbia					457	0.02	
Slovenia	442	390	288	524	368	0.02	-29.77
Spain	34,655	42,841	50,472	60,078	62,201	2.76	3.53
TFYR of Macedonia					8		
Serbia and Montenegro	541	690	754	614			
Western Europe	**111,850**	**136,963**	**151,340**	**169,254**	**173,564**	**7.70**	**2.55**
Austria	4,563	5,642	6,639	7,359	8,169	0.36	11.01
Belgium	6,140	7,117	8,448	9,096	8,945	0.40	-1.66
France	38,241	42,644	48,098	53,492	55,357	2.46	3.49
Germany	41,598	54,402	58,857	68,225	65,139	2.89	-4.52
Liechtenstein	19	43	17	27	29		7.41
Luxembourg	178	203	309	341	385	0.02	12.90
Monaco	11	24	35	58	41		-29.31
Netherlands	10,282	12,544	12,243	13,997	17,409	0.77	24.38
Switzerland	10,818	14,344	16,694	16,659	18,090	0.80	8.59
East Mediterranean Europe	**11,240**	**15,512**	**18,086**	**19,657**	**20,197**	**0.90**	**2.75**
Cyprus	59	64	25	23	40		73.91
Israel	10,754	14,871	17,330	18,715	18,467	0.82	-1.33
Turkey	427	577	731	919	1,690	0.08	83.90
Other Europe	**603**	**1,241**	**2,813**	**5,340**	**3,418**	**0.15**	**-35.99**
Other countries of Europe	603	1,241	2,813	5,340	3,418	0.15	-35.99
MIDDLE EAST	**728**	**637**	**812**	**682**	**2,015**	**0.09**	**195.45**
Middle East	**728**	**637**	**812**	**682**	**2,015**	**0.09**	**195.45**
Bahrain	1	1	4	4	7		75.00

CHILE

1. Arrivals of non-resident tourists at national borders, by nationality

	2002	2003	2004	2005	2006	Market share 06	% Change 06-05
Iraq	15	6	16	16	91		468.75
Jordan	39	42	112	56	825	0.04	1,373.21
Kuwait	5	14	6	68	274	0.01	302.94
Lebanon	257	205	144	124	115	0.01	-7.26
Libyan Arab Jamahiriya	12	20	11	7	4		-42.86
Oman	1	6	3	3	56		1,766.67
Qatar	2	8		10	18		80.00
Saudi Arabia	8	20	7	20	55		175.00
Syrian Arab Republic	48	33	41	92	48		-47.83
United Arab Emirates	13	17	5	17	30		76.47
Egypt	99	97	52	105	88		-16.19
Yemen	148	10	34	14	62		342.86
Other countries of Middle East	80	158	377	146	342	0.02	134.25
SOUTH ASIA	**1,697**	**2,039**	**3,605**	**4,257**	**4,100**	**0.18**	**-3.69**
South Asia	**1,697**	**2,039**	**3,605**	**4,257**	**4,100**	**0.18**	**-3.69**
Afghanistan	8	9	58	20	30		50.00
Bangladesh	5	27	14	29	39		34.48
Bhutan	1	2	12	14	5		-64.29
Sri Lanka	25	33	63	123	114	0.01	-7.32
India	1,296	1,647	3,148	3,474	3,499	0.16	0.72
Iran, Islamic Republic of	58	74	69	209	98		-53.11
Maldives	5	10	2	28	22		-21.43
Nepal	26	17	30	30	37		23.33
Pakistan	273	220	209	330	256	0.01	-22.42
REGION NOT SPECIFIED	**1,902**	**1,535**	**1,955**	**5,405**	**2,630**	**0.12**	**-51.34**
Not Specified	**1,902**	**1,535**	**1,955**	**5,405**	**2,630**	**0.12**	**-51.34**
Other countries of the World	1,902	1,535	1,955	5,405	2,630	0.12	-51.34

Source: World Tourism Organization (UNWTO)

CHINA

2. Arrivals of non-resident visitors at national borders, by nationality

	2002	2003	2004	2005	2006	Market share 06	% Change 06-05
TOTAL	97,908,252	91,662,082	109,038,218	120,292,255	124,942,096	100.00	3.87
AFRICA	84,541	91,949	154,223	210,533	255,288	0.20	21.26
East Africa	20,112	17,360	29,649	41,787	51,933	0.04	24.28
Burundi	193	185	261	291	558		91.75
Comoros	105	94	99	177	195		10.17
Ethiopia	3,218	3,184	5,356	6,889	8,637	0.01	25.37
Kenya	1,235	1,363	2,730	5,037	7,006	0.01	39.09
Madagascar	1,863	1,125	2,095	2,515	2,946		17.14
Mauritius	8,813	5,873	9,578	11,796	13,128	0.01	11.29
Mozambique	427	378	585	643	854		32.81
Seychelles	1,066	917	940	1,142	998		-12.61
Somalia	153	142	229	281	311		10.68
Zimbabwe	606	663	1,736	3,566	3,665		2.78
Uganda	968	1,165	2,050	2,670	3,546		32.81
United Republic of Tanzania	831	1,334	2,579	4,660	7,275	0.01	56.12
Zambia	634	937	1,411	2,120	2,814		32.74
Central Africa	2,431	4,263	8,754	10,437	14,633	0.01	40.20
Cameroon	756	1,513	3,625	2,929	3,837		31.00
Central African Republic	51	58	134	150	217		44.67
Chad	39	56	81	138	289		109.42
Congo	1,282	2,383	4,392	6,706	9,544	0.01	42.32
Democratic Republic of the Congo	72	63	50	58	22		-62.07
Gabon	231	190	472	456	724		58.77
North Africa	9,827	9,509	20,877	28,017	36,966	0.03	31.94
Algeria	3,168	3,905	9,386	11,418	15,289	0.01	33.90
Morocco	3,529	2,694	5,459	7,287	9,008	0.01	23.62
Sudan	1,570	1,535	3,226	4,712	6,765	0.01	43.57
Tunisia	1,560	1,375	2,806	4,600	5,904		28.35
Southern Africa	19,842	19,244	35,554	53,359	57,610	0.05	7.97
Botswana	159	152	373	622	897		44.21
Lesotho	117	157	294	403	446		10.67
Namibia	493	230	335	437	583		33.41
South Africa	18,970	18,632	34,401	51,759	55,514	0.04	7.25
Swaziland	103	73	151	138	170		23.19
West Africa	27,027	37,136	52,338	67,656	81,126	0.06	19.91
Benin	520	622	1,255	2,073	2,916		40.67
Gambia	1,015	1,226	1,698	2,013	2,251		11.82
Ghana	2,022	2,730	7,724	13,169	16,981	0.01	28.95
Guinea	2,046	4,630	7,098	7,707	6,674	0.01	-13.40
Cote D'Ivoire	421	1,114	1,677	1,769	2,111		19.33
Mali	3,778	8,262	11,813	12,009	13,334	0.01	11.03
Niger	1,213	1,065	1,638	2,076	2,724		31.21
Nigeria	13,667	14,997	14,783	19,916	25,400	0.02	27.54
Senegal	567	886	2,350	3,732	5,062		35.64
Sierra Leone	879	569	614	722	860		19.11
Togo	899	1,035	1,688	2,470	2,813		13.89
Other Africa	5,302	4,437	7,051	9,277	13,020	0.01	40.35
Other countries of Africa	5,302	4,437	7,051	9,277	13,020	0.01	40.35
AMERICAS	1,509,574	1,132,937	1,789,500	2,145,758	2,405,829	1.93	12.12
Caribbean	10,009	7,963	10,270	12,030	14,188	0.01	17.94
Antigua and Barbuda	265	93	131	116	164		41.38

CHINA

2. Arrivals of non-resident visitors at national borders, by nationality

	2002	2003	2004	2005	2006	Market share 06	% Change 06-05
Bahamas	135	167	456	573	800		39.62
Cuba	1,437	2,191	2,778	3,120	3,188		2.18
Dominica	808	648	751	1,018	980		-3.73
Dominican Republic	4,367	2,867	2,915	3,357	4,160		23.92
Haiti	54	34	63	136	166		22.06
Jamaica	1,614	1,309	2,025	2,195	2,687		22.41
Netherlands Antilles	297	15	39	19	61		221.05
Puerto Rico	125	19	11	8	20		150.00
Trinidad and Tobago	907	620	1,101	1,488	1,962		31.85
Central America	**19,376**	**14,425**	**15,767**	**15,928**	**18,303**	**0.01**	**14.91**
Belize	5,173	4,857	5,508	5,023	4,965		-1.15
Costa Rica	2,438	1,615	2,453	2,933	3,346		14.08
El Salvador	455	325	469	751	1,141		51.93
Guatemala	662	423	915	1,237	1,572		27.08
Honduras	2,526	1,730	2,060	1,596	2,246		40.73
Panama	8,122	5,475	4,362	4,388	5,033		14.70
North America	**1,425,780**	**1,063,279**	**1,679,529**	**2,016,537**	**2,247,997**	**1.80**	**11.48**
Canada	291,329	230,326	348,046	429,784	499,651	0.40	16.26
Mexico	13,254	10,442	22,856	31,303	38,054	0.03	21.57
United States	1,121,197	822,511	1,308,627	1,555,450	1,710,292	1.37	9.95
South America	**53,198**	**45,201**	**74,044**	**100,472**	**124,391**	**0.10**	**23.81**
Argentina	5,158	4,723	9,149	12,501	14,630	0.01	17.03
Bolivia	2,189	1,662	1,990	1,977	2,199		11.23
Brazil	19,928	17,325	29,511	37,934	47,790	0.04	25.98
Chile	4,231	3,114	5,413	7,948	10,549	0.01	32.73
Colombia	4,341	4,132	6,794	12,211	15,354	0.01	25.74
Ecuador	1,914	1,336	2,477	3,232	4,369		35.18
Guyana	270	324	378	539	515		-4.45
Paraguay	788	680	884	908	875		-3.63
Peru	5,178	4,085	5,510	7,312	8,052	0.01	10.12
Suriname	1,618	1,265	2,307	2,230	2,320		4.04
Uruguay	1,226	768	1,367	1,568	1,720		9.69
Venezuela	6,357	5,787	8,264	12,112	16,018	0.01	32.25
Other Americas	**1,211**	**2,069**	**9,890**	**791**	**950**		**20.10**
Other countries of the Americas	1,211	2,069	9,890	791	950		20.10
EAST ASIA AND THE PACIFIC	**92,865,905**	**87,214,341**	**102,393,763**	**112,053,459**	**115,700,406**	**92.60**	**3.25**
North-East Asia	**90,050,997**	**84,954,908**	**98,950,648**	**107,740,220**	**111,142,976**	**88.96**	**3.16**
Taiwan (Province of China)	3,660,565	2,731,897	3,685,250	4,109,187	4,413,470	3.53	7.40
Hong Kong, China	61,879,427	58,770,063	66,538,862	70,193,786	73,909,666	59.16	5.29
Japan	2,925,553	2,254,800	3,334,255	3,389,976	3,745,881	3.00	10.50
Korea, Dem. People's Republic of	79,253	77,140	112,052	125,800	110,095	0.09	-12.48
Korea, Republic of	2,124,310	1,945,484	2,844,862	3,545,341	3,923,986	3.14	10.68
Macao, China	18,928,763	18,757,267	21,881,600	25,734,145	24,408,694	19.54	-5.15
Mongolia	453,126	418,257	553,767	641,985	631,184	0.51	-1.68
South-East Asia	**2,461,007**	**1,959,214**	**2,990,809**	**3,739,444**	**3,918,691**	**3.14**	**4.79**
Brunei Darussalam	4,671	3,148	5,414	5,353	6,007		12.22
Myanmar	44,396	44,360	54,332	232,861	86,791	0.07	-62.73
Cambodia	6,513	4,651	10,219	11,577	14,216	0.01	22.80
Indonesia	274,717	231,838	349,832	377,622	433,028	0.35	14.67
Lao People's Democratic Republic	2,715	3,440	8,966	15,132	10,366	0.01	-31.50
Malaysia	592,447	430,137	741,909	899,643	910,458	0.73	1.20
Philippines	508,572	457,725	549,390	654,000	704,167	0.56	7.67
Singapore	497,149	378,074	636,826	755,883	827,883	0.66	9.53

CHINA

2. Arrivals of non-resident visitors at national borders, by nationality

	2002	2003	2004	2005	2006	Market share 06	% Change 06-05
Viet Nam	143,499	130,412	169,742	201,106	333,819	0.27	65.99
Thailand	386,328	275,429	464,179	586,267	591,956	0.47	0.97
Australasia	**341,501**	**288,845**	**440,875**	**561,333**	**620,384**	**0.50**	**10.52**
Australia	291,303	245,417	376,308	482,968	538,068	0.43	11.41
New Zealand	50,198	43,428	64,567	78,365	82,316	0.07	5.04
Melanesia	**2,926**	**2,377**	**3,036**	**2,471**	**2,623**		**6.15**
Fiji	1,762	1,461	2,134	2,244	2,347		4.59
Vanuatu	1,164	916	902	227	276		21.59
Micronesia	**3,229**	**3,093**	**2,379**	**2,953**	**2,978**		**0.85**
Kiribati	3,229	3,093	2,379	2,953	2,978		0.85
Polynesia	**1,499**	**1,736**	**1,763**	**1,347**	**1,235**		**-8.31**
Tonga	1,499	1,736	1,763	1,347	1,235		-8.31
Other East Asia and the Pacific	**4,746**	**4,168**	**4,253**	**5,691**	**11,519**	**0.01**	**102.41**
Other countries of Asia	218	106	176	216	186		-13.89
Other countries of Oceania	4,528	4,062	4,077	5,475	11,333	0.01	107.00
EUROPE	**3,007,483**	**2,789,888**	**4,096,999**	**5,165,588**	**5,769,346**	**4.62**	**11.69**
Central/Eastern Europe	**1,503,268**	**1,628,640**	**2,180,578**	**2,695,875**	**3,016,053**	**2.41**	**11.88**
Azerbaijan	5,535	6,814	8,453	10,887	12,623	0.01	15.95
Armenia	1,698	2,445	2,596	3,041	3,698		21.60
Bulgaria	9,418	8,874	13,223	16,438	17,646	0.01	7.35
Belarus	3,273	2,631	3,496	4,731	6,522	0.01	37.86
Czech Republic	5,745	4,309	8,874	11,639	13,941	0.01	19.78
Georgia	1,520	1,651	2,451	3,384	4,096		21.04
Hungary	4,462	3,271	7,435	10,773	13,702	0.01	27.19
Kazakhstan	65,748	89,661	162,467	186,647	270,417	0.22	44.88
Kyrgyzstan	36,749	31,667	39,602	37,466	37,819	0.03	0.94
Latvia	2,494	2,540	3,723	4,476	5,522		23.37
Lithuania	2,753	2,705	3,430	4,844	5,459		12.70
Poland	23,341	19,048	30,551	45,409	52,698	0.04	16.05
Romania	13,374	13,385	16,391	20,983	27,110	0.02	29.20
Russian Federation	1,271,635	1,380,650	1,792,193	2,223,875	2,405,063	1.92	8.15
Slovakia	1,982	1,684	3,634	3,861	4,666		20.85
Tajikistan	4,081	7,838	11,379	13,671	16,067	0.01	17.53
Turkmenistan	2,362	2,283	5,056	5,205	5,287		1.58
Ukraine	34,509	37,835	48,293	64,516	80,992	0.06	25.54
Uzbekistan	12,589	9,349	17,331	24,029	32,725	0.03	36.19
Northern Europe	**521,141**	**432,506**	**666,439**	**820,426**	**921,708**	**0.74**	**12.35**
Denmark	36,812	32,024	55,987	72,459	83,400	0.07	15.10
Finland	33,621	26,385	45,188	59,388	69,024	0.06	16.23
Iceland	1,534	874	1,718	2,963	3,270		10.36
Ireland	14,221	12,666	22,385	30,607	34,773	0.03	13.61
Norway	29,175	22,188	35,839	45,127	49,058	0.04	8.71
Sweden	62,811	50,043	87,174	110,253	129,607	0.10	17.55
United Kingdom	342,967	288,326	418,148	499,629	552,576	0.44	10.60
Southern Europe	**209,986**	**157,536**	**269,869**	**400,046**	**440,257**	**0.35**	**10.05**
Albania	2,295	1,498	1,995	2,514	2,751		9.43
Croatia	9,576	9,712	12,463	17,180	18,544	0.01	7.94
Greece	19,560	15,595	22,260	31,697	34,339	0.03	8.34
Italy	91,711	65,834	122,377	176,989	195,330	0.16	10.36
Malta	1,003	665	1,125	1,409	1,707		21.15
Portugal	36,092	30,097	39,527	43,781	44,493	0.04	1.63
Spain	44,456	29,664	62,115	114,758	129,252	0.10	12.63

CHINA

2. Arrivals of non-resident visitors at national borders, by nationality

	2002	2003	2004	2005	2006	Market share 06	% Change 06-05
Serbia and Montenegro	5,293	4,471	8,007	11,718	13,841	0.01	18.12
Western Europe	**710,065**	**519,368**	**890,656**	**1,130,778**	**1,249,897**	**1.00**	**10.53**
Austria	35,540	24,626	43,803	53,832	61,498	0.05	14.24
Belgium	36,325	24,118	40,533	50,510	57,289	0.05	13.42
France	222,135	156,063	281,108	371,987	402,174	0.32	8.12
Germany	281,835	222,022	365,329	454,859	500,567	0.40	10.05
Liechtenstein	124	69	175	200	211		5.50
Luxembourg	1,238	721	1,463	1,979	2,257		14.05
Monaco	224	126	162	203	180		-11.33
Netherlands	100,405	67,921	117,359	145,823	167,846	0.13	15.10
Switzerland	32,239	23,702	40,724	51,385	57,875	0.05	12.63
East Mediterranean Europe	**56,936**	**47,388**	**80,410**	**107,209**	**127,395**	**0.10**	**18.83**
Cyprus	2,008	859	1,643	2,640	2,819		6.78
Israel	30,141	22,276	41,701	54,459	61,494	0.05	12.92
Turkey	24,787	24,253	37,066	50,110	63,082	0.05	25.89
Other Europe	**6,087**	**4,450**	**9,047**	**11,254**	**14,036**	**0.01**	**24.72**
Other countries of Europe	6,087	4,450	9,047	11,254	14,036	0.01	24.72
MIDDLE EAST	**52,122**	**46,856**	**84,376**	**110,966**	**136,429**	**0.11**	**22.95**
Middle East	**52,122**	**46,856**	**84,376**	**110,966**	**136,429**	**0.11**	**22.95**
Bahrain	897	607	1,082	1,718	1,877		9.25
Palestine	1,507	1,575	2,541	3,480	3,775		8.48
Iraq	2,140	968	3,793	7,283	9,348	0.01	28.35
Jordan	7,502	7,223	12,341	14,377	15,793	0.01	9.85
Kuwait	1,817	1,158	3,488	5,836	6,445	0.01	10.44
Lebanon	5,981	5,594	10,277	12,088	13,295	0.01	9.99
Libyan Arab Jamahiriya	3,851	3,205	4,330	5,377	7,169	0.01	33.33
Oman	363	320	769	1,141	1,566		37.25
Qatar	351	350	934	1,158	1,697		46.55
Saudi Arabia	5,394	4,022	7,239	10,379	13,086	0.01	26.08
Syrian Arab Republic	4,676	4,794	9,529	11,618	14,712	0.01	26.63
United Arab Emirates	1,059	917	1,702	1,764	2,663		50.96
Egypt	10,133	9,072	14,827	22,136	31,333	0.03	41.55
Yemen	6,451	7,051	11,524	12,611	13,670	0.01	8.40
SOUTH ASIA	**380,512**	**383,121**	**514,163**	**599,435**	**670,505**	**0.54**	**11.86**
South Asia	**380,512**	**383,121**	**514,163**	**599,435**	**670,505**	**0.54**	**11.86**
Afghanistan	1,417	3,410	6,308	8,550	10,645	0.01	24.50
Bangladesh	24,709	24,839	40,933	54,269	60,783	0.05	12.00
Bhutan	244	163	421	514	654		27.24
Sri Lanka	9,503	8,511	14,167	23,461	24,344	0.02	3.76
India	213,611	219,097	309,411	356,460	405,091	0.32	13.64
Iran, Islamic Republic of	22,270	23,674	33,930	42,526	52,471	0.04	23.39
Maldives	553	574	1,121	826	1,134		37.29
Nepal	25,146	26,852	29,080	29,016	28,754	0.02	-0.90
Pakistan	83,059	76,001	78,792	83,813	86,629	0.07	3.36
REGION NOT SPECIFIED	**8,115**	**2,990**	**5,194**	**6,516**	**4,293**		**-34.12**
Not Specified	**8,115**	**2,990**	**5,194**	**6,516**	**4,293**		**-34.12**
Other countries of the World	8,115	2,990	5,194	6,516	4,293		-34.12

Source: World Tourism Organization (UNWTO)

COLOMBIA

2. Arrivals of non-resident visitors at national borders, by nationality

		2002	2003	2004	2005	2006	Market share 06	% Change 06-05
TOTAL	(*)	566,761	624,909	790,940	933,243	1,053,348	100.00	12.87
AFRICA		976	897	935	1,380	1,695	0.16	22.83
East Africa		156	153	138	195	201	0.02	3.08
Burundi		1	1		1	1		
Ethiopia		8	15	7	17	25		47.06
Eritrea		17	2	1		4		
Kenya		70	70	51	51	76	0.01	49.02
Madagascar		6	9	3	6	7		16.67
Malawi		6	4	5		2		
Mauritius		6	2	7	4	5		25.00
Mozambique		8	5	8	23	19		-17.39
Reunion		3	1		1			
Rwanda		7	3	6	8	7		-12.50
Seychelles		2			2	1		-50.00
Somalia					1	1		
Zimbabwe				15	15	12		-20.00
Uganda		10	18	20	22	19		-13.64
United Republic of Tanzania		10	17	11	38	20		-47.37
Zambia		2	6	4	6	2		-66.67
Central Africa		75	61	80	167	153	0.01	-8.38
Angola		17	18	21	17	18		5.88
Cameroon		18	17	17	21	13		-38.10
Central African Republic		5	2	6	71	78	0.01	9.86
Chad		6	6	4	3	2		-33.33
Democratic Republic of the Congo		23	17	29	51	39		-23.53
Equatorial Guinea		2	1	1	1	2		100.00
Gabon		4		1	3	1		-66.67
Sao Tome and Principe				1				
North Africa		203	114	155	195	206	0.02	5.64
Algeria		51	27	34	39	57	0.01	46.15
Morocco		126	68	104	133	129	0.01	-3.01
Western Sahara		11	5					
Sudan		6	1	4	3	2		-33.33
Tunisia		9	13	13	20	18		-10.00
Southern Africa		374	377	388	565	877	0.08	55.22
Botswana		1		4	1	1		
Lesotho		1	1					
Namibia			1	1	2			
South Africa		371	375	381	561	874	0.08	55.79
Swaziland		1		2	1	2		100.00
West Africa		140	165	138	188	258	0.02	37.23
Cape Verde		3		5	4	2		-50.00
Benin		2	7	4	12	6		-50.00
Gambia		3		2	6	1		-83.33
Ghana		18	18	15	21	26		23.81
Guinea		5	6	10	7	15		114.29
Cote D'Ivoire		8	17	4	7	20		185.71
Liberia		7	5	1		4		
Mali		3	1	2		5		
Mauritania			1	1	1	1		
Niger		16	14	7	9	2		-77.78
Nigeria		43	73	65	106	142	0.01	33.96
Guinea-Bissau		1	1	2	3	1		-66.67

COLOMBIA

2. Arrivals of non-resident visitors at national borders, by nationality

	2002	2003	2004	2005	2006	Market share 06	% Change 06-05
Senegal	8	11	11	3	9		200.00
Sierra Leone	3	1	2	3	2		-33.33
Togo	16	3	4	1	14		1,300.00
Burkina Faso	4	7	3	5	8		60.00
Other Africa	**28**	**27**	**36**	**70**			
Other countries of Africa	28	27	36	70			
AMERICAS	**428,403**	**484,379**	**617,896**	**730,495**	**825,335**	**78.35**	**12.98**
Caribbean	**6,223**	**7,919**	**10,043**	**12,545**	**16,007**	**1.52**	**27.60**
Antigua and Barbuda	9	17	13	22	33		50.00
Bahamas	132	140	152	175	280	0.03	60.00
Barbados	56	66	79	89	295	0.03	231.46
Bermuda	5	6	15	24	37		54.17
British Virgin Islands		2		1	6		500.00
Cayman Islands	73	89	211	241	186	0.02	-22.82
Cuba	2,219	2,491	2,820	3,226	4,568	0.43	41.60
Dominica	60	61	59	87	136	0.01	56.32
Dominican Republic	2,408	2,627	3,051	4,711	5,995	0.57	27.26
Grenada	10	12	12	13	49		276.92
Guadeloupe	13	11	27	18			
Haiti	145	105	168	208	247	0.02	18.75
Jamaica	361	326	334	342	564	0.05	64.91
Martinique					1		
Montserrat	2	1	1	1	1		
Aruba	317	1,198	1,852	1,736	1,932	0.18	11.29
Curacao	48	308	539	727			
Puerto Rico	59	61	156	354	634	0.06	79.10
Saint Kitts and Nevis	8	11		10	35		250.00
Anguilla	4	2	2	5			
Saint Lucia	24	21	20	23	34		47.83
Saint Vincent and the Grenadines	8	7	4	13	33		153.85
Trinidad and Tobago	262	357	424	514	941	0.09	83.07
Other countries of the Caribbean			104	5			
Central America	**38,158**	**48,553**	**62,262**	**70,260**	**74,698**	**7.09**	**6.32**
Belize	54	76	78	88	110	0.01	25.00
Costa Rica	11,380	18,410	24,478	25,002	25,138	2.39	0.54
El Salvador	2,017	2,339	3,291	4,424	4,532	0.43	2.44
Guatemala	5,470	5,378	5,703	7,174	8,215	0.78	14.51
Honduras	1,977	2,744	2,973	3,134	3,650	0.35	16.46
Nicaragua	646	842	1,376	1,627	1,876	0.18	15.30
Panama	16,614	18,764	24,363	28,811	31,177	2.96	8.21
North America	**196,413**	**215,196**	**257,766**	**302,437**	**337,731**	**32.06**	**11.67**
Canada	15,944	16,292	20,147	24,471	27,115	2.57	10.80
Mexico	25,092	26,998	34,016	42,580	52,037	4.94	22.21
United States	155,377	171,906	203,603	235,386	258,579	24.55	9.85
South America	**187,609**	**212,711**	**287,825**	**345,253**	**396,899**	**37.68**	**14.96**
Argentina	13,667	16,028	23,059	34,025	40,254	3.82	18.31
Bolivia	2,806	3,258	4,771	5,827	4,667	0.44	-19.91
Brazil	14,040	16,938	21,910	27,209	31,712	3.01	16.55
Chile	9,782	9,858	13,289	19,091	23,765	2.26	24.48
Ecuador	55,701	64,431	91,682	95,816	100,222	9.51	4.60
French Guiana	3	7	10	22	14		-36.36
Guyana	42	70	95	83	117	0.01	40.96
Paraguay	592	702	884	1,023	1,077	0.10	5.28
Peru	23,216	25,732	36,654	44,490	47,706	4.53	7.23

COLOMBIA

2. Arrivals of non-resident visitors at national borders, by nationality

	2002	2003	2004	2005	2006	Market share 06	% Change 06-05
Suriname	30	24	46	123	234	0.02	90.24
Uruguay	1,949	2,096	2,902	3,870	5,535	0.53	43.02
Venezuela	65,781	73,567	92,523	113,674	141,596	13.44	24.56
EAST ASIA AND THE PACIFIC	**11,854**	**11,271**	**13,294**	**15,395**	**17,141**	**1.63**	**11.34**
North-East Asia	**8,145**	**7,648**	**9,075**	**10,228**	**11,270**	**1.07**	**10.19**
China	949	762	864	1,336	2,287	0.22	71.18
Taiwan (Province of China)	881	1,143	1,655	1,927	1,283	0.12	-33.42
Hong Kong, China	45	56	82	80	107	0.01	33.75
Japan	4,004	3,665	4,188	4,336	4,466	0.42	3.00
Korea, Dem. People's Republic of	369	128	2,232	2,307	747	0.07	-67.62
Korea, Republic of	1,896	1,886	52	239	2,378	0.23	894.98
Mongolia	1	8	2	3	2		-33.33
South-East Asia	**1,085**	**1,236**	**1,102**	**1,235**	**1,409**	**0.13**	**14.09**
Brunei Darussalam	4	11			3		
Myanmar	6	1			11		
Cambodia	5	1	5	3	5		66.67
Indonesia	232	457	309	288	209	0.02	-27.43
Lao People's Democratic Republic	6	1	2	1	18		1,700.00
Malaysia	94	95	84	172	131	0.01	-23.84
Philippines	577	484	475	564	783	0.07	38.83
Singapore	87	120	143	135	147	0.01	8.89
Viet Nam	15	31	18	17	7		-58.82
Thailand	59	35	66	55	95	0.01	72.73
Australasia	**2,207**	**2,353**	**3,046**	**3,834**	**4,410**	**0.42**	**15.02**
Australia	1,847	1,989	2,586	3,187	3,714	0.35	16.54
New Zealand	360	364	460	647	696	0.07	7.57
Melanesia	**5**	**5**	**6**	**12**	**23**		**91.67**
Solomon Islands	2			1	1		
Fiji	2	3	4	4	5		25.00
New Caledonia	1	2	1	5	14		180.00
Papua New Guinea			1	2	3		50.00
Micronesia	**2**		**8**	**8**	**6**		**-25.00**
Kiribati	1				3		
Guam	1						
Midway Islands			8	7	3		-57.14
Northern Mariana Islands				1			
Polynesia	**108**	**29**	**57**	**77**	**23**		**-70.13**
French Polynesia	9	4		4	8		100.00
Tokelau	1						
Tonga			2	3	2		-33.33
Wallis and Futuna Islands	98	24	54	69	13		-81.16
Samoa		1	1	1			
Other East Asia and the Pacific	**302**				**1**		
Other countries of Asia	302				1		
EUROPE	**117,500**	**125,073**	**155,657**	**182,822**	**204,298**	**19.40**	**11.75**
Central/Eastern Europe	**2,424**	**2,371**	**3,010**	**3,990**	**4,939**	**0.47**	**23.78**
Azerbaijan	1	12	6	4	10		150.00
Armenia	1	5	4	7	7		
Bulgaria	124	77	84	137	144	0.01	5.11
Belarus	14	15	20	33	27		-18.18
Czech Republic/Slovakia	34				229	0.02	

COLOMBIA

2. Arrivals of non-resident visitors at national borders, by nationality

	2002	2003	2004	2005	2006	Market share 06	% Change 06-05
Czech Republic	124	222	319	581	555	0.05	-4.48
Estonia	10	20	30	41	29		-29.27
Georgia	7	70	38	40	4		-90.00
Hungary	89	103	166	260	368	0.03	41.54
Kazakhstan	11	17	39	31	35		12.90
Kyrgyzstan			1	1	2		100.00
Latvia	4	9	24	44	36		-18.18
Lithuania	159	106	84	70	134	0.01	91.43
Republic of Moldova	3	9	4	6	19		216.67
Poland	409	363	452	556	722	0.07	29.86
Romania	187	166	200	294	510	0.05	73.47
Russian Federation	1,002	932	1,206	1,522	1,655	0.16	8.74
Slovakia	67	76	135	127	229	0.02	80.31
Turkmenistan	1	1	3	3	2		-33.33
Ukraine	171	166	187	225	208	0.02	-7.56
Uzbekistan	6	2	8	8	14		75.00
Northern Europe	**18,042**	**18,624**	**21,627**	**24,333**	**26,747**	**2.54**	**9.92**
Denmark	910	860	1,146	1,430	1,559	0.15	9.02
Finland	534	596	642	889	1,038	0.10	16.76
Iceland	41	483	173	118	94	0.01	-20.34
Ireland	366	318	459	465	525	0.05	12.90
Norway	1,247	1,137	1,517	1,724	2,011	0.19	16.65
Sweden	2,385	2,707	3,041	3,614	3,810	0.36	5.42
United Kingdom	12,559	12,522	14,645	16,089	17,707	1.68	10.06
Isle of Man		1	4	4	3		-25.00
Southern Europe	**48,174**	**49,176**	**65,301**	**79,556**	**92,358**	**8.77**	**16.09**
Albania	17	16	12	14	26		85.71
Andorra	37	52	48	48	54	0.01	12.50
Bosnia and Herzegovina	6	6	9	16	12		-25.00
Croatia	74	80	72	154	249	0.02	61.69
Gibraltar	1						
Greece	455	429	470	629	601	0.06	-4.45
Holy See	7	3	5	4	15		275.00
Italy	16,303	14,899	17,936	19,955	22,487	2.13	12.69
Malta	22	31	24	38	27		-28.95
Portugal	942	1,016	1,385	1,541	1,987	0.19	28.94
San Marino	2	11	2	6	6		
Serbia					23		
Slovenia	64	31	99	86	275	0.03	219.77
Spain	30,109	32,527	45,239	57,064	66,422	6.31	16.40
TFYR of Macedonia	16	6			151	0.01	
Serbia and Montenegro	119	69		1	23		2,200.00
Western Europe	**44,984**	**50,919**	**61,078**	**69,161**	**73,774**	**7.00**	**6.67**
Austria	1,271	1,441	1,560	1,928	2,067	0.20	7.21
Belgium	1,799	1,850	2,551	2,653	2,850	0.27	7.43
France	16,951	16,545	20,458	23,060	24,815	2.36	7.61
Germany	13,921	14,163	15,881	18,130	19,050	1.81	5.07
Liechtenstein	7	19	27	25	16		-36.00
Luxembourg	52	79	122	113	122	0.01	7.96
Monaco	5	2	7	10	3		-70.00
Netherlands	5,856	11,594	13,726	15,721	16,843	1.60	7.14
Switzerland	5,122	5,226	6,746	7,521	8,008	0.76	6.48
East Mediterranean Europe	**3,876**	**3,983**	**4,517**	**5,690**	**6,480**	**0.62**	**13.88**
Cyprus	48	56	24	59	45		-23.73
Israel	3,553	3,717	4,263	5,295	6,012	0.57	13.54

COLOMBIA

2. Arrivals of non-resident visitors at national borders, by nationality

	2002	2003	2004	2005	2006	Market share 06	% Change 06-05
Turkey	275	210	230	336	423	0.04	25.89
Other Europe			**124**	**92**			
Other countries of Europe			124	92			
MIDDLE EAST	**1,062**	**1,004**	**1,399**	**1,167**	**1,348**	**0.13**	**15.51**
Middle East	**1,062**	**1,004**	**1,399**	**1,167**	**1,348**	**0.13**	**15.51**
Bahrain	3	1	1	4	4		
Palestine	12	62	28	30	19		-36.67
Iraq	18	6	7	4	7		75.00
Jordan	67	50	80	62	61	0.01	-1.61
Kuwait	6	5	2	12	10		-16.67
Lebanon	785	742	1,040	874	1,005	0.10	14.99
Libyan Arab Jamahiriya	13	4	1	4	4		
Oman	3	2	4	7	7		
Qatar	6	2	2		4		
Saudi Arabia	28	14	31	19	38		100.00
Syrian Arab Republic	41	38	50	44	27		-38.64
United Arab Emirates	4	8	11	2	10		400.00
Egypt	74	69	134	101	152	0.01	50.50
Yemen	2	1	8	4			
SOUTH ASIA	**1,226**	**1,119**	**1,404**	**1,618**	**1,841**	**0.17**	**13.78**
South Asia	**1,226**	**1,119**	**1,404**	**1,618**	**1,841**	**0.17**	**13.78**
Afghanistan	1	2	6	9	6		-33.33
Bangladesh	10	17	10	19	22		15.79
Bhutan				1			
Sri Lanka	13	19	30	29	22		-24.14
India	960	917	1,161	1,348	1,549	0.15	14.91
Iran, Islamic Republic of	195	121	133	128	149	0.01	16.41
Maldives	1						
Nepal	13	12	10	15	12		-20.00
Pakistan	33	31	51	69	81	0.01	17.39
Other countries of South Asia			3				
REGION NOT SPECIFIED	**5,740**	**1,166**	**355**	**366**	**1,690**	**0.16**	**361.75**
Not Specified	**5,740**	**1,166**	**355**	**366**	**1,690**	**0.16**	**361.75**
Other countries of the World	5,740	1,166	355	366	1,690	0.16	361.75

Source: World Tourism Organization (UNWTO)

COMOROS

1. Arrivals of non-resident tourists at national borders, by nationality

		2002	2003	2004	2005	2006	Market share 06	% Change 06-05
TOTAL	(*)	18,936	14,229	17,603	19,551	17,060	100.00	-12.74
AFRICA		8,715	5,590	6,344	8,793	6,123	35.89	-30.37
East Africa		6,680	3,188	3,577	5,737	4,499	26.37	-21.58
Madagascar		789	269	656	1,315	838	4.91	-36.27
Mauritius		135	180	360	96	164	0.96	70.83
Reunion		2,164	1,670	1,429	2,835	1,585	9.29	-44.09
Zimbabwe			613	786	650	182	1.07	-72.00
Other countries of East Africa		3,592	456	346	841	1,730	10.14	105.71
Southern Africa		1,247	36	71	706	480	2.81	-32.01
South Africa		1,247	36	71	706	480	2.81	-32.01
Other Africa		788	2,366	2,696	2,350	1,144	6.71	-51.32
Other countries of Africa		788	2,366	2,696	2,350	1,144	6.71	-51.32
AMERICAS		60	26	162	83	358	2.10	331.33
Other Americas		60	26	162	83	358	2.10	331.33
All countries of the Americas		60	26	162	83	358	2.10	331.33
EAST ASIA AND THE PACIFIC		64	610	165	543	582	3.41	7.18
Other East Asia and the Pacific		64	610	165	543	582	3.41	7.18
All countries of Asia		13	609	114	201	382	2.24	90.05
All countries of Oceania		51	1	51	342	200	1.17	-41.52
EUROPE		9,490	8,003	10,562	9,625	9,470	55.51	-1.61
Northern Europe		172				240	1.41	
United Kingdom		172				240	1.41	
Western Europe		9,115	7,883	9,460	9,174	8,810	51.64	-3.97
France		9,076	7,883	9,460	9,133	8,615	50.50	-5.67
Germany		39			41	195	1.14	375.61
Other Europe		203	120	1,102	451	420	2.46	-6.87
Other countries of Europe		203	120	1,102	451	420	2.46	-6.87
REGION NOT SPECIFIED		607		370	507	527	3.09	3.94
Not Specified		607		370	507	527	3.09	3.94
Other countries of the World		607		370	507	527	3.09	3.94

Source: World Tourism Organization (UNWTO)

COOK ISLANDS

1. Arrivals of non-resident tourists at national borders, by country of residence

		2002	2003	2004	2005	2006	Market share 06	% Change 06-05
TOTAL	(*)	72,781	78,328	83,333	88,405	92,251	100.00	4.35
AMERICAS		11,505	11,390	8,445	6,463	7,677	8.32	18.78
North America		11,505	11,390	8,445	6,463	7,677	8.32	18.78
Canada		4,789	3,760	2,419	2,029	2,210	2.40	8.92
United States		6,716	7,630	6,026	4,434	5,467	5.93	23.30
EAST ASIA AND THE PACIFIC		41,277	45,008	53,962	63,319	65,972	71.51	4.19
Australasia		38,793	42,391	50,605	60,401	63,260	68.57	4.73
Australia		9,952	11,470	11,850	11,313	11,479	12.44	1.47
New Zealand		28,841	30,921	38,755	49,088	51,781	56.13	5.49
Polynesia		936	1,089	1,442	1,334	1,159	1.26	-13.12
French Polynesia		936	1,089	1,442	1,334	1,159	1.26	-13.12
Other East Asia and the Pacific		1,548	1,528	1,915	1,584	1,553	1.68	-1.96
All countries of Asia		503	581	552	546	549	0.60	0.55
Other countries of Oceania		1,045	947	1,363	1,038	1,004	1.09	-3.28
EUROPE		19,630	21,559	20,410	18,162	18,112	19.63	-0.28
Northern Europe		12,747	14,193	13,678	11,894	11,360	12.31	-4.49
Denmark		191	184	243	248	381	0.41	53.63
Finland		118	99	107	96	113	0.12	17.71
Norway		643	623	562	450	501	0.54	11.33
Sweden		1,183	906	643	573	939	1.02	63.87
United Kingdom		10,612	12,381	12,123	10,527	9,426	10.22	-10.46
Southern Europe		1,072	774	725	691	693	0.75	0.29
Italy		895	537	498	484	469	0.51	-3.10
Spain		177	237	227	207	224	0.24	8.21
Western Europe		5,034	4,811	4,724	4,206	4,357	4.72	3.59
Austria		344	394	519	363	360	0.39	-0.83
Belgium		196	91	83	82	59	0.06	-28.05
France		312	268	283	207	184	0.20	-11.11
Germany		3,298	3,192	3,048	2,693	2,902	3.15	7.76
Netherlands		113	59	81	85	156	0.17	83.53
Switzerland		771	807	710	776	696	0.75	-10.31
Other Europe		777	1,781	1,283	1,371	1,702	1.84	24.14
Other countries of Europe		777	1,781	1,283	1,371	1,702	1.84	24.14
REGION NOT SPECIFIED		369	371	516	461	490	0.53	6.29
Not Specified		369	371	516	461	490	0.53	6.29
Other countries of the World		369	371	516	461	490	0.53	6.29

Source: World Tourism Organization (UNWTO)

COSTA RICA

1. Arrivals of non-resident tourists at national borders, by nationality

	2002	2003	2004	2005	2006	Market share 06	% Change 06-05
TOTAL	1,113,359	1,238,692	1,452,926	1,679,051	1,725,261	100.00	2.75
AFRICA	900	1,048	1,194	1,164	1,204	0.07	3.44
Other Africa	900	1,048	1,194	1,164	1,204	0.07	3.44
All countries of Africa	900	1,048	1,194	1,164	1,204	0.07	3.44
AMERICAS	927,509	1,017,831	1,213,784	1,411,640	1,456,947	84.45	3.21
Caribbean	8,836	9,639	11,696	12,412	11,935	0.69	-3.84
Cuba	3,570	3,165	3,842	4,395	4,398	0.25	0.07
Dominican Republic	3,664	3,128	3,110	3,674	3,749	0.22	2.04
Jamaica	662	663	905	962	1,032	0.06	7.28
Puerto Rico		493	1,019	807	664	0.04	-17.72
Trinidad and Tobago	447	1,146	1,206	981	745	0.04	-24.06
Other countries of the Caribbean	493	1,044	1,614	1,593	1,347	0.08	-15.44
Central America	320,615	312,936	359,979	415,464	478,147	27.71	15.09
Belize		744	655	659	826	0.05	25.34
El Salvador	33,531	33,892	38,264	44,873	46,414	2.69	3.43
Guatemala	33,150	35,174	40,166	37,771	41,057	2.38	8.70
Honduras	23,705	23,004	25,540	27,719	32,550	1.89	17.43
Nicaragua	174,455	163,632	191,398	231,712	281,086	16.29	21.31
Panama	55,774	56,490	63,956	72,730	76,214	4.42	4.79
North America	509,253	611,520	754,982	895,370	875,959	50.77	-2.17
Canada	49,168	54,656	74,212	86,906	88,304	5.12	1.61
Mexico	37,870	46,113	47,130	50,330	56,419	3.27	12.10
United States	422,215	510,751	633,640	758,134	731,236	42.38	-3.55
South America	88,805	83,736	87,127	88,394	90,906	5.27	2.84
Argentina	12,123	13,804	14,887	15,622	16,805	0.97	7.57
Bolivia		1,759	2,227	2,366	2,461	0.14	4.02
Brazil	6,157	6,754	7,608	8,607	9,730	0.56	13.05
Chile	7,329	6,700	7,297	7,039	7,864	0.46	11.72
Colombia	35,220	26,645	26,786	27,130	27,706	1.61	2.12
Ecuador	6,064	5,471	5,168	4,825	4,446	0.26	-7.85
Paraguay		440	563	464	402	0.02	-13.36
Peru	7,482	6,430	6,969	6,319	5,900	0.34	-6.63
Uruguay		2,098	2,139	1,800	1,991	0.12	10.61
Venezuela	10,421	13,635	13,483	14,222	13,601	0.79	-4.37
Other countries of South America	4,009						
EAST ASIA AND THE PACIFIC	16,140	16,403	16,043	23,687	23,425	1.36	-1.11
North-East Asia	13,167	13,537	12,971	13,806	13,040	0.76	-5.55
China	4,937	2,249	1,517	1,203	1,545	0.09	28.43
Taiwan (Province of China)		2,934	3,315	3,309	3,314	0.19	0.15
Japan	5,813	5,883	5,695	6,056	5,478	0.32	-9.54
Korea, Republic of	2,417	2,471	2,444	3,238	2,703	0.16	-16.52
Australasia				6,586	6,627	0.38	0.62
Australia, New Zealand				6,586	6,627	0.38	0.62
Other East Asia and the Pacific	2,973	2,866	3,072	3,295	3,758	0.22	14.05
Other countries of Asia	2,973	2,866	3,072	3,295	3,758	0.22	14.05
EUROPE	164,263	198,242	215,072	241,751	243,100	14.09	0.56
Central/Eastern Europe	999						
Russian Federation	999						
Northern Europe	26,796	32,822	34,590	39,498	40,879	2.37	3.50

COSTA RICA

1. Arrivals of non-resident tourists at national borders, by nationality

	2002	2003	2004	2005	2006	Market share 06	% Change 06-05
Denmark	1,997	2,525	2,409	3,115	3,316	0.19	6.45
Finland	832	926	1,056	1,266	1,187	0.07	-6.24
Norway	1,744	1,812	1,910	2,253	2,583	0.15	14.65
Sweden	3,186	4,540	5,057	5,947	5,903	0.34	-0.74
United Kingdom	19,037	23,019	24,158	26,917	27,890	1.62	3.61
Southern Europe	**45,859**	**52,803**	**61,864**	**69,944**	**69,400**	**4.02**	**-0.78**
Italy	15,985	18,361	19,483	20,726	19,175	1.11	-7.48
Spain	29,874	34,442	42,381	49,218	50,225	2.91	2.05
Western Europe	**79,440**	**97,776**	**101,440**	**110,605**	**110,770**	**6.42**	**0.15**
Austria	3,311	3,957	4,660	5,212	5,107	0.30	-2.01
Belgium	4,182	5,504	5,650	5,602	5,977	0.35	6.69
France	18,309	23,606	23,467	24,365	24,392	1.41	0.11
Germany	23,848	29,151	34,154	38,523	37,847	2.19	-1.75
Netherlands	19,938	24,665	21,905	24,173	24,303	1.41	0.54
Switzerland	9,852	10,893	11,604	12,730	13,144	0.76	3.25
East Mediterranean Europe	**5,274**	**6,143**	**6,850**	**8,862**	**8,419**	**0.49**	**-5.00**
Israel	5,274	6,143	6,850	8,862	8,419	0.49	-5.00
Other Europe	**5,895**	**8,698**	**10,328**	**12,842**	**13,632**	**0.79**	**6.15**
Other countries of Europe	5,895	8,698	10,328	12,842	13,632	0.79	6.15
REGION NOT SPECIFIED	**4,547**	**5,168**	**6,833**	**809**	**585**	**0.03**	**-27.69**
Not Specified	**4,547**	**5,168**	**6,833**	**809**	**585**	**0.03**	**-27.69**
Other countries of the World	4,547	5,168	6,833	809	585	0.03	-27.69

Source: World Tourism Organization (UNWTO)

CROATIA

3. Arrivals of non-resident tourists in hotels and similar establishments, by country of residence

	2002	2003	2004	2005	2006	Market share 06	% Change 06-05
TOTAL	2,988,313	3,086,506	3,361,842	3,743,874	3,741,966	100.00	-0.05
AMERICAS	58,381	64,339	95,096	111,434	141,299	3.78	26.80
North America	58,381	64,339	95,096	111,434	141,299	3.78	26.80
Canada	12,913	14,150	16,459	18,343	18,705	0.50	1.97
United States	45,468	50,189	78,637	93,091	122,594	3.28	31.69
EAST ASIA AND THE PACIFIC	27,134	29,127	41,750	62,369	99,657	2.66	59.79
North-East Asia	14,250	13,740	20,220	29,889	60,549	1.62	102.58
Japan	14,250	13,740	20,220	29,889	60,549	1.62	102.58
Australasia	12,884	15,387	21,530	32,480	39,108	1.05	20.41
Australia	10,221	12,381	17,801	27,035	34,009	0.91	25.80
New Zealand	2,663	3,006	3,729	5,445	5,099	0.14	-6.35
EUROPE	2,883,283	2,967,356	3,193,870	3,531,370	3,452,638	92.27	-2.23
Central/Eastern Europe	666,202	574,810	558,560	575,866	581,845	15.55	1.04
Bulgaria	10,540	10,698	11,443	11,479	16,317	0.44	42.15
Belarus	1,819	1,303	2,051	1,704	1,781	0.05	4.52
Czech Republic	231,719	212,667	184,579	157,971	137,823	3.68	-12.75
Estonia	1,254	2,358	2,452	5,928	5,373	0.14	-9.36
Hungary	123,486	128,586	137,015	152,041	131,821	3.52	-13.30
Latvia	2,092	2,541	3,483	4,611	6,041	0.16	31.01
Lithuania	5,605	6,706	6,802	9,566	10,449	0.28	9.23
Poland	150,338	76,475	72,117	76,298	78,395	2.10	2.75
Romania	9,299	9,107	10,120	13,957	17,951	0.48	28.62
Russian Federation	49,004	48,506	57,078	68,775	93,232	2.49	35.56
Slovakia	75,358	69,160	64,066	63,288	68,337	1.83	7.98
Ukraine	5,688	6,703	7,354	10,248	14,325	0.38	39.78
Northern Europe	139,555	175,777	257,528	350,889	352,625	9.42	0.49
Denmark	9,335	13,097	17,210	26,457	26,543	0.71	0.33
Finland	5,375	6,131	8,558	11,377	11,411	0.30	0.30
Iceland	577	824	4,375	3,400	3,056	0.08	-10.12
Ireland	13,044	21,342	26,482	31,410	24,915	0.67	-20.68
Norway	7,656	10,882	19,286	36,029	38,179	1.02	5.97
Sweden	15,412	25,791	46,027	68,741	70,474	1.88	2.52
United Kingdom	88,156	97,710	135,590	173,475	178,047	4.76	2.64
Southern Europe	859,345	894,974	912,214	957,161	961,834	25.70	0.49
Bosnia and Herzegovina	82,714	75,788	73,960	75,386	75,725	2.02	0.45
Greece	2,308	3,144	3,481	4,389	5,461	0.15	24.42
Italy	459,543	488,930	500,138	504,043	487,335	13.02	-3.31
Portugal	4,984	6,428	10,618	14,276	21,592	0.58	51.25
Slovenia	280,668	284,357	273,432	283,520	275,884	7.37	-2.69
Spain	18,688	27,753	39,877	64,051	83,192	2.22	29.88
TFYR of Macedonia	10,440	8,574	10,708	11,496	12,645	0.34	9.99
Western Europe	1,116,794	1,223,360	1,360,665	1,540,937	1,463,624	39.11	-5.02
Austria	313,429	314,530	327,854	341,863	367,584	9.82	7.52
Belgium	32,508	36,096	40,206	46,352	45,524	1.22	-1.79
France	59,328	102,839	231,918	384,553	323,087	8.63	-15.98
Germany	635,617	680,066	653,875	638,769	589,192	15.75	-7.76
Luxembourg	948	1,536	1,468	1,947	1,618	0.04	-16.90
Netherlands	46,180	51,497	60,690	75,692	73,526	1.96	-2.86
Switzerland	28,784	36,796	44,654	51,761	63,093	1.69	21.89
East Mediterranean Europe	80,265	71,206	60,335	55,922	41,113	1.10	-26.48

169

CROATIA

3. Arrivals of non-resident tourists in hotels and similar establishments, by country of residence

	2002	2003	2004	2005	2006	Market share 06	% Change 06-05
Israel	75,831	66,833	55,514	49,974	32,429	0.87	-35.11
Turkey	4,434	4,373	4,821	5,948	8,684	0.23	46.00
Other Europe	**21,122**	**27,229**	**44,568**	**50,595**	**51,597**	**1.38**	**1.98**
Other countries of Europe	21,122	27,229	44,568	50,595	51,597	1.38	1.98
REGION NOT SPECIFIED	**19,515**	**25,684**	**31,126**	**38,701**	**48,372**	**1.29**	**24.99**
Not Specified	**19,515**	**25,684**	**31,126**	**38,701**	**48,372**	**1.29**	**24.99**
Other countries of the World	19,515	25,684	31,126	38,701	48,372	1.29	24.99

Source: World Tourism Organization (UNWTO)

CROATIA

4. Arrivals of non-resident tourists in all types of accommodation establishments, by country of residence

		2002	2003	2004	2005	2006	Market share 06	% Change 06-05
TOTAL	(*)	6,944,345	7,408,590	7,911,874	8,466,886	8,658,876	100.00	2.27
AMERICAS		74,938	84,470	119,485	140,031	182,916	2.11	30.63
North America		74,938	84,470	119,485	140,031	182,916	2.11	30.63
Canada		16,409	19,040	21,921	24,742	28,851	0.33	16.61
United States		58,529	65,430	97,564	115,289	154,065	1.78	33.63
EAST ASIA AND THE PACIFIC		36,068	43,173	58,370	83,273	132,824	1.53	59.50
North-East Asia		15,340	16,040	22,932	32,748	64,751	0.75	97.73
Japan		15,340	16,040	22,932	32,748	64,751	0.75	97.73
Australasia		20,728	27,133	35,438	50,525	68,073	0.79	34.73
Australia		15,602	20,258	28,138	40,825	57,550	0.66	40.97
New Zealand		5,126	6,875	7,300	9,700	10,523	0.12	8.48
EUROPE		6,806,518	7,244,346	7,692,506	8,192,055	8,281,634	95.64	1.09
Central/Eastern Europe		1,675,198	1,607,522	1,621,098	1,664,923	1,716,849	19.83	3.12
Bulgaria		13,072	17,386	14,211	14,384	20,720	0.24	44.05
Belarus		2,364	1,642	2,636	2,694	3,149	0.04	16.89
Czech Republic		697,902	699,473	663,794	615,535	593,276	6.85	-3.62
Estonia		2,330	4,496	4,542	8,935	9,621	0.11	7.68
Hungary		318,015	356,139	403,443	453,395	402,782	4.65	-11.16
Latvia		2,710	4,721	5,744	7,495	10,121	0.12	35.04
Lithuania		13,065	16,523	15,355	19,646	22,335	0.26	13.69
Poland		358,065	237,968	240,654	241,868	275,845	3.19	14.05
Romania		13,947	15,756	17,308	22,691	33,723	0.39	48.62
Russian Federation		55,479	56,972	67,696	80,335	108,672	1.26	35.27
Slovakia		191,176	187,955	176,294	184,891	217,986	2.52	17.90
Ukraine		7,073	8,491	9,421	13,054	18,619	0.22	42.63
Northern Europe		236,862	312,587	444,630	592,591	608,502	7.03	2.68
Denmark		29,697	42,298	59,830	83,220	78,877	0.91	-5.22
Finland		8,195	10,292	14,832	20,060	18,504	0.21	-7.76
Iceland		1,074	1,443	5,057	4,192	4,299	0.05	2.55
Ireland		18,727	29,027	36,123	43,631	38,063	0.44	-12.76
Norway		12,390	23,797	32,679	58,601	69,691	0.80	18.92
Sweden		34,619	53,211	87,750	127,387	130,291	1.50	2.28
United Kingdom		132,160	152,519	208,359	255,500	268,777	3.10	5.20
Southern Europe		2,207,786	2,398,058	2,408,140	2,478,878	2,568,229	29.66	3.60
Bosnia and Herzegovina		173,214	177,662	163,104	170,581	188,774	2.18	10.67
Greece		3,405	4,659	4,887	5,535	6,975	0.08	26.02
Italy		1,099,427	1,205,532	1,231,901	1,252,684	1,235,413	14.27	-1.38
Portugal		6,690	9,616	14,646	18,697	26,010	0.30	39.11
Slovenia		869,900	918,462	884,273	878,882	913,072	10.54	3.89
Spain		26,022	43,791	56,907	84,183	114,188	1.32	35.64
TFYR of Macedonia		15,928	14,893	16,568	18,821	20,907	0.24	11.08
Serbia and Montenegro		13,200	23,443	35,854	49,495	62,890	0.73	27.06
Western Europe		2,577,556	2,820,774	3,114,721	3,358,353	3,306,627	38.19	-1.54
Austria		690,366	708,506	740,960	742,498	790,083	9.12	6.41
Belgium		60,194	72,989	81,456	91,925	92,041	1.06	0.13
France		134,708	220,636	392,911	591,098	505,139	5.83	-14.54
Germany		1,481,659	1,551,844	1,580,244	1,572,090	1,544,801	17.84	-1.74
Luxembourg		1,882	4,433	3,374	3,182	2,970	0.03	-6.66
Netherlands		148,140	179,483	212,090	243,651	241,856	2.79	-0.74
Switzerland		60,607	82,883	103,686	113,909	129,737	1.50	13.90

CROATIA

4. Arrivals of non-resident tourists in all types of accommodation establishments, by country of residence

	2002	2003	2004	2005	2006	Market share 06	% Change 06-05
East Mediterranean Europe	86,312	80,904	71,262	68,755	55,064	0.64	-19.91
Israel	80,740	75,173	64,956	61,313	43,676	0.50	-28.77
Turkey	5,572	5,731	6,306	7,442	11,388	0.13	53.02
Other Europe	22,804	24,501	32,655	28,555	26,363	0.30	-7.68
Other countries of Europe	22,804	24,501	32,655	28,555	26,363	0.30	-7.68
REGION NOT SPECIFIED	26,821	36,601	41,513	51,527	61,502	0.71	19.36
Not Specified	26,821	36,601	41,513	51,527	61,502	0.71	19.36
Other countries of the World	26,821	36,601	41,513	51,527	61,502	0.71	19.36

Source: World Tourism Organization (UNWTO)

CROATIA

5. Overnight stays of non-resident tourists in hotels and similar establishments, by country of residence

	2002	2003	2004	2005	2006	Market share 06	% Change 06-05
TOTAL	16,905,241	16,829,558	17,072,286	18,415,158	17,807,231	100.00	-3.30
AMERICAS	151,344	166,065	238,697	263,828	334,274	1.88	26.70
North America	151,344	166,065	238,697	263,828	334,274	1.88	26.70
Canada	33,054	39,059	43,210	42,725	46,231	0.26	8.21
United States	118,290	127,006	195,487	221,103	288,043	1.62	30.28
EAST ASIA AND THE PACIFIC	52,629	60,674	81,730	114,176	173,888	0.98	52.30
North-East Asia	24,437	25,564	34,500	48,301	92,167	0.52	90.82
Japan	24,437	25,564	34,500	48,301	92,167	0.52	90.82
Australasia	28,192	35,110	47,230	65,875	81,721	0.46	24.05
Australia	22,632	28,152	39,328	54,828	71,007	0.40	29.51
New Zealand	5,560	6,958	7,902	11,047	10,714	0.06	-3.01
EUROPE	16,643,151	16,527,048	16,673,937	17,944,416	17,184,174	96.50	-4.24
Central/Eastern Europe	4,452,913	3,751,170	3,506,787	3,536,735	3,559,250	19.99	0.64
Bulgaria	26,238	27,227	26,151	23,423	40,101	0.23	71.20
Belarus	12,758	8,599	12,441	10,267	9,365	0.05	-8.79
Czech Republic	1,639,992	1,498,258	1,246,022	1,050,731	891,239	5.00	-15.18
Estonia	4,760	5,560	7,178	21,326	17,636	0.10	-17.30
Hungary	698,359	712,921	737,040	830,894	690,445	3.88	-16.90
Latvia	5,464	4,329	6,097	9,377	12,463	0.07	32.91
Lithuania	18,398	21,125	19,861	24,807	26,464	0.15	6.68
Poland	1,012,058	479,396	416,655	427,387	428,660	2.41	0.30
Romania	30,269	32,011	34,765	47,011	65,574	0.37	39.49
Russian Federation	456,292	451,585	531,336	618,467	832,283	4.67	34.57
Slovakia	509,564	459,999	420,360	410,346	445,878	2.50	8.66
Ukraine	38,761	50,160	48,881	62,699	99,142	0.56	58.12
Northern Europe	783,727	993,451	1,478,575	2,067,298	2,024,428	11.37	-2.07
Denmark	46,943	72,772	97,699	165,188	160,477	0.90	-2.85
Finland	21,287	24,859	40,590	48,655	49,565	0.28	1.87
Iceland	1,495	3,892	26,046	27,696	22,294	0.13	-19.50
Ireland	63,279	127,925	152,936	175,409	133,501	0.75	-23.89
Norway	26,999	45,340	102,681	206,739	212,116	1.19	2.60
Sweden	68,940	137,733	258,058	395,840	412,863	2.32	4.30
United Kingdom	554,784	580,930	800,565	1,047,771	1,033,612	5.80	-1.35
Southern Europe	3,952,168	4,043,748	3,999,416	4,167,665	3,904,552	21.93	-6.31
Bosnia and Herzegovina	277,408	260,493	243,522	242,694	242,820	1.36	0.05
Greece	6,342	8,323	8,723	11,127	13,305	0.07	19.57
Italy	1,999,182	2,100,587	2,098,383	2,187,036	2,013,671	11.31	-7.93
Portugal	9,793	12,781	19,357	27,044	38,908	0.22	43.87
Slovenia	1,578,057	1,572,282	1,513,400	1,548,156	1,394,199	7.83	-9.94
Spain	54,286	65,410	88,059	123,451	167,099	0.94	35.36
TFYR of Macedonia	27,100	23,872	27,972	28,157	34,550	0.19	22.70
Western Europe	7,200,433	7,517,766	7,428,206	7,895,325	7,472,358	41.96	-5.36
Austria	1,673,465	1,636,322	1,613,845	1,661,825	1,761,760	9.89	6.01
Belgium	211,851	220,563	216,381	238,837	221,243	1.24	-7.37
France	203,739	352,281	787,954	1,301,509	1,165,366	6.54	-10.46
Germany	4,680,003	4,802,922	4,264,911	4,050,301	3,655,175	20.53	-9.76
Luxembourg	3,742	8,142	5,692	9,559	6,698	0.04	-29.93
Netherlands	310,152	341,433	355,937	415,959	398,956	2.24	-4.09
Switzerland	117,481	156,103	183,486	217,335	263,160	1.48	21.08
East Mediterranean Europe	190,760	147,243	136,211	151,811	97,470	0.55	-35.80

CROATIA

5. Overnight stays of non-resident tourists in hotels and similar establishments, by country of residence

	2002	2003	2004	2005	2006	Market share 06	% Change 06-05
Israel	178,915	136,262	123,794	137,533	77,420	0.43	-43.71
Turkey	11,845	10,981	12,417	14,278	20,050	0.11	40.43
Other Europe	**63,150**	**73,670**	**124,742**	**125,582**	**126,116**	**0.71**	**0.43**
Other countries of Europe	63,150	73,670	124,742	125,582	126,116	0.71	0.43
REGION NOT SPECIFIED	**58,117**	**75,771**	**77,922**	**92,738**	**114,895**	**0.65**	**23.89**
Not Specified	**58,117**	**75,771**	**77,922**	**92,738**	**114,895**	**0.65**	**23.89**
Other countries of the World	58,117	75,771	77,922	92,738	114,895	0.65	23.89

Source: World Tourism Organization (UNWTO)

CROATIA

6. Overnight stays of non-resident tourists in all types of accommodation establishments, by country of residence

		2002	2003	2004	2005	2006	Market share 06	% Change 06-05
TOTAL	(*)	39,711,064	41,323,148	42,516,325	45,986,517	47,021,944	100.00	2.25
AMERICAS		204,528	231,448	317,405	358,583	465,270	0.99	29.75
North America		204,528	231,448	317,405	358,583	465,270	0.99	29.75
Canada		44,911	54,756	63,296	66,836	81,453	0.17	21.87
United States		159,617	176,692	254,109	291,747	383,817	0.82	31.56
EAST ASIA AND THE PACIFIC		75,368	96,648	125,594	171,167	262,842	0.56	53.56
North-East Asia		27,222	29,766	39,805	53,721	99,410	0.21	85.05
Japan		27,222	29,766	39,805	53,721	99,410	0.21	85.05
Australasia		48,146	66,882	85,789	117,446	163,432	0.35	39.16
Australia		36,818	50,599	69,174	95,022	139,113	0.30	46.40
New Zealand		11,328	16,283	16,615	22,424	24,319	0.05	8.45
EUROPE		39,343,538	40,881,870	41,958,426	45,314,004	46,127,387	98.10	1.79
Central/Eastern Europe		10,423,624	9,765,931	9,519,865	10,051,744	10,579,977	22.50	5.26
Bulgaria		36,001	51,263	37,759	36,132	55,604	0.12	53.89
Belarus		15,814	10,450	16,380	17,574	18,491	0.04	5.22
Czech Republic		4,560,486	4,554,400	4,172,787	4,051,780	3,921,345	8.34	-3.22
Estonia		7,172	9,689	12,001	29,414	30,409	0.06	3.38
Hungary		1,732,576	1,905,285	2,092,449	2,405,145	2,196,365	4.67	-8.68
Latvia		6,972	10,253	14,196	19,211	26,270	0.06	36.74
Lithuania		50,085	55,218	49,474	65,702	75,835	0.16	15.42
Poland		2,185,814	1,330,517	1,285,529	1,374,595	1,612,013	3.43	17.27
Romania		53,341	62,574	70,881	92,313	149,152	0.32	61.57
Russian Federation		503,822	510,098	605,285	695,201	936,639	1.99	34.73
Slovakia		1,223,480	1,204,963	1,100,947	1,183,499	1,428,346	3.04	20.69
Ukraine		48,061	61,221	62,177	81,178	129,508	0.28	59.54
Northern Europe		1,188,866	1,599,319	2,339,050	3,328,563	3,330,913	7.08	0.07
Denmark		195,774	302,064	434,202	624,648	573,473	1.22	-8.19
Finland		34,452	36,086	59,232	84,141	70,911	0.15	-15.72
Iceland		3,223	7,213	27,999	31,206	29,439	0.06	-5.66
Ireland		80,086	152,067	185,015	225,025	192,543	0.41	-14.43
Norway		48,519	109,908	160,256	324,955	379,064	0.81	16.65
Sweden		166,087	270,660	457,317	690,014	719,217	1.53	4.23
United Kingdom		660,725	721,321	1,015,029	1,348,574	1,366,266	2.91	1.31
Southern Europe		10,864,077	11,656,969	11,523,880	12,116,410	12,292,739	26.14	1.46
Bosnia and Herzegovina		787,299	848,368	755,006	829,161	948,397	2.02	14.38
Greece		8,833	12,392	12,994	15,575	17,983	0.04	15.46
Italy		4,883,496	5,323,234	5,374,998	5,698,791	5,474,456	11.64	-3.94
Portugal		14,307	19,598	27,605	38,173	51,165	0.11	34.03
Slovenia		4,993,371	5,207,786	5,032,470	5,099,116	5,245,881	11.16	2.88
Spain		72,240	101,176	123,753	169,701	230,384	0.49	35.76
TFYR of Macedonia		61,217	60,554	67,799	79,700	84,501	0.18	6.02
Serbia and Montenegro		43,314	83,861	129,255	186,193	239,972	0.51	28.88
Western Europe		16,599,336	17,623,483	18,325,325	19,569,514	19,731,860	41.96	0.83
Austria		3,543,456	3,585,371	3,638,005	3,756,535	4,069,302	8.65	8.33
Belgium		384,753	433,873	441,259	492,681	471,986	1.00	-4.20
France		418,172	688,715	1,241,729	1,920,288	1,707,718	3.63	-11.07
Germany		10,789,069	11,056,130	10,887,638	11,001,142	10,986,866	23.37	-0.13
Luxembourg		7,739	22,277	14,399	15,479	13,485	0.03	-12.88
Netherlands		1,204,240	1,496,973	1,690,241	1,910,080	1,938,295	4.12	1.48
Switzerland		251,907	340,144	412,054	473,309	544,208	1.16	14.98

CROATIA

6. Overnight stays of non-resident tourists in all types of accommodation establishments, by country of residence

	2002	2003	2004	2005	2006	Market share 06	% Change 06-05
East Mediterranean Europe	204,589	166,706	158,624	178,666	129,703	0.28	-27.40
Israel	188,467	150,882	140,489	158,155	100,676	0.21	-36.34
Turkey	16,122	15,824	18,135	20,511	29,027	0.06	41.52
Other Europe	63,046	69,462	91,682	69,107	62,195	0.13	-10.00
Other countries of Europe	63,046	69,462	91,682	69,107	62,195	0.13	-10.00
REGION NOT SPECIFIED	87,630	113,182	114,900	142,763	166,445	0.35	16.59
Not Specified	87,630	113,182	114,900	142,763	166,445	0.35	16.59
Other countries of the World	87,630	113,182	114,900	142,763	166,445	0.35	16.59

Source: World Tourism Organization (UNWTO)

CUBA

2. Arrivals of non-resident visitors at national borders, by country of residence

	2002	2003	2004	2005	2006	Market share 06	% Change 06-05
TOTAL	1,686,162	1,905,682	2,048,572	2,319,334	2,220,567	100.00	-4.26
AFRICA	5,641	6,679	5,868	6,619	6,636	0.30	0.26
East Africa	572	667	836	889	880	0.04	-1.01
All countries of East Africa	572	667	836	889	880	0.04	-1.01
Central Africa	1,033	1,215	1,042	957	1,133	0.05	18.39
Angola	588	474	568	545	626	0.03	14.86
Other countries of Central Africa	445	741	474	412	507	0.02	23.06
North Africa	1,616	1,345	1,341	1,468	1,328	0.06	-9.54
All countries of North Africa	1,616	1,345	1,341	1,468	1,328	0.06	-9.54
Southern Africa	972	1,218	1,172	1,398	1,651	0.07	18.10
All countries of Southern Africa	972	1,218	1,172	1,398	1,651	0.07	18.10
West Africa	1,448	2,234	1,477	1,907	1,644	0.07	-13.79
All countries of West Africa	1,448	2,234	1,477	1,907	1,644	0.07	-13.79
AMERICAS	787,729	916,818	1,025,756	1,215,857	1,149,135	51.75	-5.49
Caribbean	179,525	190,914	144,293	172,353	182,426	8.22	5.84
Antigua and Barbuda	92	105	126	631	470	0.02	-25.52
Bahamas	7,028	7,280	6,188	5,526	5,382	0.24	-2.61
Barbados	549	458	665	358	377	0.02	5.31
Bermuda	184	75	58	54	126	0.01	133.33
Cayman Islands	1,036	1,207	1,525	1,306	715	0.03	-45.25
Dominica	1,250	1,072	595	1,801	1,323	0.06	-26.54
Dominican Republic	5,322	5,872	3,255	4,576	4,807	0.22	5.05
Grenada	136	126	173	1,134	556	0.03	-50.97
Guadeloupe	49	22	32	20	26		30.00
Haiti	891	742	854	1,187	1,989	0.09	67.57
Jamaica	4,219	4,034	3,521	4,118	4,754	0.21	15.44
Martinique	83	61	49	57	42		-26.32
Puerto Rico	166	180	131	127	123	0.01	-3.15
Saint Lucia	271	291	186	937	1,578	0.07	68.41
Saint Vincent and the Grenadines	90	96	142	921	1,045	0.05	13.46
Trinidad and Tobago	658	1,042	1,351	709	650	0.03	-8.32
Other countries of the Caribbean	157,501	168,251	125,442	148,891	158,463	7.14	6.43
Central America	21,539	20,813	24,937	31,259	36,937	1.66	18.16
Belize	272	176	231	1,461	576	0.03	-60.57
Costa Rica	4,698	4,313	6,276	4,557	4,739	0.21	3.99
El Salvador	3,022	2,990	2,589	3,304	5,893	0.27	78.36
Guatemala	4,213	3,860	6,895	8,060	6,103	0.27	-24.28
Honduras	1,856	2,263	2,451	6,442	5,933	0.27	-7.90
Nicaragua	1,678	1,719	1,502	1,672	3,394	0.15	102.99
Panama	5,800	5,492	4,993	5,763	10,299	0.46	78.71
North America	513,704	625,756	692,983	728,777	739,057	33.28	1.41
Canada	348,468	452,438	563,371	602,377	604,263	27.21	0.31
Greenland	1	2	4	11	2		-81.82
Mexico	87,589	88,787	79,752	89,154	97,984	4.41	9.90
United States	77,646	84,529	49,856	37,233	36,808	1.66	-1.14
Other countries of North America				2			
South America	72,961	79,335	163,543	283,468	190,715	8.59	-32.72
Argentina	9,389	13,929	23,460	24,922	30,383	1.37	21.91
Bolivia	2,296	1,631	1,862	5,697	5,901	0.27	3.58
Brazil	7,067	8,802	9,216	15,836	11,024	0.50	-30.39
Chile	12,512	11,938	14,500	16,744	16,110	0.73	-3.79

CUBA

2. Arrivals of non-resident visitors at national borders, by country of residence

	2002	2003	2004	2005	2006	Market share 06	% Change 06-05
Colombia	15,802	13,122	13,408	16,175	16,053	0.72	-0.75
Ecuador	6,292	6,408	6,231	7,014	9,920	0.45	41.43
French Guiana	15	8	6	88	119	0.01	35.23
Guyana	393	458	281	2,312	2,392	0.11	3.46
Paraguay	428	557	532	832	2,724	0.12	227.40
Peru	5,655	5,704	6,072	6,225	6,436	0.29	3.39
Suriname	61	46	56	329	2,183	0.10	563.53
Uruguay	2,050	1,464	1,632	2,113	3,629	0.16	71.75
Venezuela	10,977	15,228	86,258	185,157	83,832	3.78	-54.72
Other countries of South America	24	40	29	24	9		-62.50
EAST ASIA AND THE PACIFIC	**27,354**	**32,463**	**33,861**	**41,858**	**43,819**	**1.97**	**4.68**
North-East Asia	**13,403**	**12,855**	**15,974**	**19,002**	**20,014**	**0.90**	**5.33**
China	4,366	4,811	7,007	8,700	9,276	0.42	6.62
Taiwan (Province of China)	228	367	304	354	418	0.02	18.08
Hong Kong, China	10	7	6	7	9		28.57
Japan	7,101	5,317	5,748	6,409	5,282	0.24	-17.58
Korea, Dem. People's Republic of	44	76	26	224	306	0.01	36.61
Korea, Republic of	1,482	2,121	2,674	2,242	3,317	0.15	47.95
Mongolia	36	63	46	54	79		46.30
Other countries of North-East Asia	136	93	163	1,012	1,327	0.06	31.13
South-East Asia	**10,223**	**14,981**	**11,910**	**16,125**	**16,475**	**0.74**	**2.17**
Myanmar	121						
Cambodia	2	1			23		
Indonesia	615	1,052	630	1,039	1,246	0.06	19.92
Lao People's Democratic Republic	22	21	11	8	24		200.00
Malaysia	271	260	269	337	367	0.02	8.90
Philippines	8,518	12,718	9,932	13,389	13,405	0.60	0.12
Singapore	110	128	113	130	157	0.01	20.77
Viet Nam	433	600	768	617	632	0.03	2.43
Thailand	118	165	176	239	455	0.02	90.38
Other countries of South-East Asia	13	36	11	366	166	0.01	-54.64
Australasia	**3,712**	**4,611**	**5,966**	**6,625**	**7,287**	**0.33**	**9.99**
Australia	2,747	3,587	4,701	5,316	5,996	0.27	12.79
New Zealand	965	1,024	1,265	1,309	1,291	0.06	-1.38
Melanesia	**6**	**6**	**10**	**13**	**17**		**30.77**
Fiji	2	4	2	1	8		700.00
New Caledonia	4	1	6	4	2		-50.00
Papua New Guinea		1	2	8	7		-12.50
Micronesia	**2**	**4**	**1**	**2**	**6**		**200.00**
All countries of Micronesia	2	4	1	2	6		200.00
Polynesia	**7**	**6**		**64**	**11**		**-82.81**
All countries of Polynesia	7	6		64	11		-82.81
Other East Asia and the Pacific	**1**			**27**	**9**		**-66.67**
Other countries of Oceania	1			27	9		-66.67
EUROPE	**859,129**	**942,052**	**976,727**	**1,047,669**	**1,013,273**	**45.63**	**-3.28**
Central/Eastern Europe	**27,015**	**37,402**	**47,926**	**61,207**	**71,048**	**3.20**	**16.08**
Bulgaria	807	1,727	1,076	1,859	2,187	0.10	17.64
Czech Republic	1,822	2,795	4,102	7,425	7,562	0.34	1.85
Estonia	176	246	604	503	648	0.03	28.83
Hungary	1,557	3,447	5,113	7,127	5,932	0.27	-16.77
Latvia	87	172	245	523	710	0.03	35.76

CUBA

2. Arrivals of non-resident visitors at national borders, by country of residence

	2002	2003	2004	2005	2006	Market share 06	% Change 06-05
Lithuania	293	469	564	1,047	1,015	0.05	-3.06
Poland	5,304	5,562	7,439	8,295	8,569	0.39	3.30
Romania	1,393	2,633	2,100	3,224	3,817	0.17	18.39
Russian Federation	10,653	12,610	17,457	20,711	27,861	1.25	34.52
Slovakia	688	1,203	1,860	2,617	3,766	0.17	43.91
Ukraine	3,695	5,662	6,558	6,706	7,378	0.33	10.02
Uzbekistan	21	27	38	42	46		9.52
Other countries Central/East Europ	519	849	770	1,128	1,557	0.07	38.03
Northern Europe	**127,017**	**148,768**	**193,574**	**238,114**	**252,259**	**11.36**	**5.94**
Denmark	4,509	6,327	7,975	9,163	9,296	0.42	1.45
Finland	2,903	3,560	4,070	5,349	5,930	0.27	10.86
Iceland	700	869	1,233	2,485	3,770	0.17	51.71
Ireland	5,080	5,783	6,476	7,492	6,911	0.31	-7.75
Norway	5,493	6,062	6,076	6,962	8,211	0.37	17.94
Sweden	4,581	5,277	6,535	7,184	7,026	0.32	-2.20
United Kingdom	103,741	120,866	161,189	199,399	211,075	9.51	5.86
Other countries of Northern Europe	10	24	20	80	40		-50.00
Southern Europe	**324,699**	**347,701**	**367,066**	**407,510**	**372,284**	**16.77**	**-8.64**
Albania	85	164	237	252	237	0.01	-5.95
Andorra	143	140	202	249	234	0.01	-6.02
Bosnia and Herzegovina	234	304	260	286	389	0.02	36.01
Croatia	1,468	1,747	1,579	2,402	2,527	0.11	5.20
Greece	5,878	6,420	9,074	6,462	6,089	0.27	-5.77
Italy	147,750	177,627	178,570	169,317	144,249	6.50	-14.81
Malta	97	94	97	112	117	0.01	4.46
Montenegro					6		
Portugal	27,117	28,469	25,608	28,780	27,304	1.23	-5.13
San Marino	207	189	209	193	147	0.01	-23.83
Slovenia	1,621	2,694	2,860	2,942	2,807	0.13	-4.59
Spain	138,609	127,666	146,236	194,103	185,531	8.36	-4.42
Serbia and Montenegro	6	80	191	251	471	0.02	87.65
Other countries Southern Europe	1,484	2,107	1,943	2,161	2,176	0.10	0.69
Western Europe	**374,461**	**400,850**	**360,121**	**329,761**	**308,759**	**13.90**	**-6.37**
Austria	16,673	18,739	17,403	16,222	15,384	0.69	-5.17
Belgium	21,211	24,318	22,007	20,813	18,886	0.85	-9.26
France	129,907	144,548	119,868	107,518	103,469	4.66	-3.77
Germany	152,662	157,721	143,644	124,527	114,292	5.15	-8.22
Liechtenstein	71	106	74	83	80		-3.61
Luxembourg	927	1,267	999	803	762	0.03	-5.11
Monaco	43	68	37	49	44		-10.20
Netherlands	27,437	29,453	32,983	37,828	35,880	1.62	-5.15
Switzerland	25,530	24,630	23,106	21,918	19,962	0.90	-8.92
East Mediterranean Europe	**5,937**	**7,331**	**8,040**	**11,077**	**8,923**	**0.40**	**-19.45**
Cyprus	209	320	304	407	408	0.02	0.25
Israel	2,913	3,727	3,920	5,389	3,232	0.15	-40.03
Turkey	2,815	3,284	3,816	5,281	5,283	0.24	0.04
MIDDLE EAST	**1,737**	**1,514**	**1,517**	**1,622**	**1,643**	**0.07**	**1.29**
Middle East	**1,737**	**1,514**	**1,517**	**1,622**	**1,643**	**0.07**	**1.29**
Bahrain	4	12	5	13	21		61.54
Palestine	52	62	73	85	72		-15.29
Iraq	64	60	38	81	87		7.41
Jordan	143	165	187	147	134	0.01	-8.84
Kuwait	12	38	24	25	37		48.00
Lebanon	105	162	209	311	462	0.02	48.55

CUBA

2. Arrivals of non-resident visitors at national borders, by country of residence

	2002	2003	2004	2005	2006	Market share 06	% Change 06-05
Libyan Arab Jamahiriya	286	304	222	118	81		-31.36
Oman	5	12	22	19	33		73.68
Qatar	29	45	2	43	36		-16.28
Saudi Arabia	21	19	19	51	40		-21.57
Syrian Arab Republic	259	177	407	347	219	0.01	-36.89
Egypt	702	369	243	310	320	0.01	3.23
Yemen	14	22	17	29	69		137.93
Other countries of Middle East	41	67	49	43	32		-25.58
SOUTH ASIA	**4,096**	**5,559**	**4,176**	**5,149**	**5,248**	**0.24**	**1.92**
South Asia	**4,096**	**5,559**	**4,176**	**5,149**	**5,248**	**0.24**	**1.92**
Afghanistan	16	12	11	20	25		25.00
Bangladesh	78	56	201	121	88		-27.27
Sri Lanka	221	356	394	228	407	0.02	78.51
India	2,995	4,174	2,717	3,783	3,437	0.15	-9.15
Iran, Islamic Republic of	482	595	513	562	705	0.03	25.44
Maldives	4	66	48	140	164	0.01	17.14
Pakistan	150	151	244	160	273	0.01	70.63
Other countries of South Asia	150	149	48	135	149	0.01	10.37
REGION NOT SPECIFIED	**476**	**597**	**667**	**560**	**813**	**0.04**	**45.18**
Not Specified	**476**	**597**	**667**	**560**	**813**	**0.04**	**45.18**
Other countries of the World	476	597	667	560	813	0.04	45.18

Source: World Tourism Organization (UNWTO)

CURACAO

1. Arrivals of non-resident tourists at national borders, by country of residence

		2002	2003	2004	2005	2006	Market share 06	% Change 06-05
TOTAL	(*)	**217,963**	**221,395**	**223,439**	**222,061**	**234,383**	**100.00**	**5.55**
AMERICAS		**141,006**	**125,794**	**128,873**	**123,353**	**126,521**	**53.98**	**2.57**
Caribbean		**45,319**	**42,282**	**40,149**	**33,384**	**33,514**	**14.30**	**0.39**
Barbados		568	490	421	546	489	0.21	-10.44
Dominican Republic		8,620	7,009	6,435	4,639	3,366	1.44	-27.44
Haiti		5,491	4,836	2,924	1,832	1,697	0.72	-7.37
Jamaica		8,396	7,119	7,473	7,816	7,829	3.34	0.17
Aruba		11,989	12,561	13,102	10,709	12,729	5.43	18.86
Puerto Rico		1,287	1,127	1,188	963	1,249	0.53	29.70
Trinidad and Tobago		6,833	6,895	6,246	4,889	4,309	1.84	-11.86
Other countries of the Caribbean		2,135	2,245	2,360	1,990	1,846	0.79	-7.24
North America		**40,903**	**43,805**	**47,206**	**50,792**	**54,850**	**23.40**	**7.99**
Canada		1,956	3,786	4,101	5,224	7,422	3.17	42.08
United States		38,947	40,019	43,105	45,568	47,428	20.24	4.08
South America		**54,784**	**39,707**	**41,518**	**39,177**	**38,157**	**16.28**	**-2.60**
Argentina		446	461	448	437	532	0.23	21.74
Brazil		1,043	749	1,029	1,460	1,967	0.84	34.73
Colombia		15,001	5,241	3,004	3,480	3,656	1.56	5.06
Ecuador		719	682	1,514	2,371	4,111	1.75	73.39
Guyana		1,091	1,059	796	737	613	0.26	-16.82
Peru					616	238	0.10	-61.36
Suriname		4,067	3,990	4,352	4,051	3,807	1.62	-6.02
Venezuela		30,389	25,099	27,639	24,259	21,446	9.15	-11.60
Other countries of South America		2,028	2,426	2,736	1,766	1,787	0.76	1.19
EUROPE		**70,390**	**91,384**	**89,752**	**94,957**	**104,232**	**44.47**	**9.77**
Northern Europe		**3,336**	**4,162**	**4,715**	**5,559**	**6,400**	**2.73**	**15.13**
Denmark		339	398	336	382	582	0.25	52.36
Finland					838	845	0.36	0.84
Norway		445	314	318	336	319	0.14	-5.06
Sweden		455	675	871	1,361	2,123	0.91	55.99
United Kingdom		2,097	2,775	3,190	2,642	2,531	1.08	-4.20
Southern Europe		**3,499**	**2,417**	**1,722**	**1,524**	**1,808**	**0.77**	**18.64**
Italy		987	1,025	772	654	711	0.30	8.72
Portugal		333	454	301	262	387	0.17	47.71
Spain		2,179	938	649	608	710	0.30	16.78
Western Europe		**60,561**	**81,593**	**80,301**	**85,259**	**93,266**	**39.79**	**9.39**
Austria		210	224	268	242	281	0.12	16.12
Belgium		1,266	1,626	2,102	2,435	2,810	1.20	15.40
Germany		3,160	2,975	3,471	4,073	4,229	1.80	3.83
Netherlands		55,256	75,999	73,798	77,879	85,246	36.37	9.46
Switzerland		669	769	662	630	700	0.30	11.11
Other Europe		**2,994**	**3,212**	**3,014**	**2,615**	**2,758**	**1.18**	**5.47**
Other countries of Europe		2,994	3,212	3,014	2,615	2,758	1.18	5.47
REGION NOT SPECIFIED		**6,567**	**4,217**	**4,814**	**3,751**	**3,630**	**1.55**	**-3.23**
Not Specified		**6,567**	**4,217**	**4,814**	**3,751**	**3,630**	**1.55**	**-3.23**
Other countries of the World		6,567	4,217	4,814	3,751	3,630	1.55	-3.23

Source: World Tourism Organization (UNWTO)

CURACAO

3. Arrivals of non-resident tourists in hotels and similar establishments, by country of residence

	2002	2003	2004	2005	2006	Market share 06	% Change 06-05
TOTAL	119,510	126,763	128,752	135,015	139,255	100.00	3.14
AMERICAS	85,883	85,539	89,410	91,660	92,926	66.73	1.38
Caribbean	24,074	25,701	24,537	22,062	21,783	15.64	-1.26
Barbados	468	419	339	492	440	0.32	-10.57
Dominican Republic	2,558	2,535	2,239	2,032	1,567	1.13	-22.88
Haiti	2,489	2,375	1,376	838	776	0.56	-7.40
Jamaica	6,321	5,784	6,357	6,474	6,247	4.49	-3.51
Aruba	5,868	6,563	6,792	6,009	7,051	5.06	17.34
Puerto Rico	939	911	976	771	979	0.70	26.98
Trinidad and Tobago	5,431	5,822	5,165	4,218	3,653	2.62	-13.39
Other countries of the Caribbean		1,292	1,293	1,228	1,070	0.77	-12.87
North America	31,572	35,740	39,211	42,806	45,283	32.52	5.79
Canada	1,408	3,132	3,362	4,398	6,451	4.63	46.68
United States	30,164	32,608	35,849	38,408	38,832	27.89	1.10
South America	30,237	24,098	25,662	26,792	25,860	18.57	-3.48
Argentina	303	364	319	323	405	0.29	25.39
Brazil	751	572	787	1,088	1,618	1.16	48.71
Colombia	7,069	2,529	1,161	1,645	1,647	1.18	0.12
Ecuador	484	500	1,331	2,208	3,883	2.79	75.86
Guyana	770	842	568	556	412	0.30	-25.90
Peru					140	0.10	
Suriname	1,448	1,696	1,939	1,767	1,478	1.06	-16.36
Venezuela	19,412	15,700	17,388	17,439	14,921	10.71	-14.44
Other countries of South America		1,895	2,169	1,766	1,356	0.97	-23.22
EUROPE	27,010	39,691	37,606	42,069	45,193	32.45	7.43
Northern Europe	1,856	2,526	2,899	3,169	4,427	3.18	39.70
Denmark	166	201	163	219	402	0.29	83.56
Finland					593	0.43	
Norway	159	153	155	247	211	0.15	-14.57
Sweden	267	415	579	1,093	1,716	1.23	57.00
United Kingdom	1,264	1,757	2,002	1,610	1,505	1.08	-6.52
Southern Europe	1,831	1,399	911	851	1,009	0.72	18.57
Italy	498	593	413	369	390	0.28	5.69
Portugal	191	285	116	144	191	0.14	32.64
Spain	1,142	521	382	338	428	0.31	26.63
Western Europe	23,323	34,069	32,261	36,126	38,432	27.60	6.38
Austria	133	146	164	163	193	0.14	18.40
Belgium	692	983	1,230	1,441	1,568	1.13	8.81
Germany	1,721	1,584	1,810	2,183	2,205	1.58	1.01
Netherlands	20,336	30,841	28,591	31,902	33,999	24.41	6.57
Switzerland	441	515	466	437	467	0.34	6.86
Other Europe		1,697	1,535	1,923	1,325	0.95	-31.10
Other countries of Europe		1,697	1,535	1,923	1,325	0.95	-31.10
REGION NOT SPECIFIED	6,617	1,533	1,736	1,286	1,136	0.82	-11.66
Not Specified	6,617	1,533	1,736	1,286	1,136	0.82	-11.66
Other countries of the World	6,617	1,533	1,736	1,286	1,136	0.82	-11.66

Source: World Tourism Organization (UNWTO)

CURACAO

6. Overnight stays of non-resident tourists in all types of accommodation establishments, by country of residence

	2002	2003	2004	2005	2006	Market share 06	% Change 06-05
TOTAL	1,814,997	1,919,036	1,919,656	1,957,758	2,155,853	100.00	10.12
AMERICAS	886,315	796,780	802,096	773,468	833,760	38.67	7.80
Caribbean	261,079	239,322	218,376	187,667	181,646	8.43	-3.21
Dominican Republic	87,581	72,442	68,043	52,436	36,299	1.68	-30.77
Haiti	42,304	40,753	24,019	14,922	16,780	0.78	12.45
Jamaica	38,680	32,452	30,671	33,860	35,022	1.62	3.43
Aruba	54,384	54,460	54,411	49,872	56,760	2.63	13.81
Puerto Rico	5,878	5,000	5,029	4,275	6,391	0.30	49.50
Trinidad and Tobago	16,795	16,636	17,134	15,993	14,647	0.68	-8.42
Other countries of the Caribbean	15,457	17,579	19,069	16,309	15,747	0.73	-3.45
North America	262,789	285,448	318,706	341,605	382,655	17.75	12.02
Canada	14,527	29,782	33,589	42,542	58,694	2.72	37.97
United States	248,262	255,666	285,117	299,063	323,961	15.03	8.33
South America	362,447	272,010	265,014	244,196	269,459	12.50	10.35
Argentina	2,714	2,651	2,493	2,819	3,051	0.14	8.23
Brazil	5,752	4,095	5,106	7,669	9,725	0.45	26.81
Colombia	156,394	92,366	65,628	67,411	74,988	3.48	11.24
Venezuela	145,170	121,315	135,342	110,463	120,237	5.58	8.85
Other countries of South America	52,417	51,583	56,445	55,834	61,458	2.85	10.07
EUROPE	861,610	1,090,004	1,079,342	1,155,893	1,291,824	59.92	11.76
Northern Europe	18,510	26,115	32,317	27,953	27,310	1.27	-2.30
United Kingdom	18,510	26,115	32,317	27,953	27,310	1.27	-2.30
Southern Europe	8,766	7,548	5,919	4,460	5,816	0.27	30.40
Italy	8,766	7,548	5,919	4,460	5,816	0.27	30.40
Western Europe	778,524	1,004,202	994,028	1,070,715	1,186,396	55.03	10.80
Austria	2,078	1,832	3,067	2,313	2,843	0.13	22.91
Belgium	13,060	16,024	22,374	26,068	32,123	1.49	23.23
Germany	35,398	33,169	41,634	50,179	51,087	2.37	1.81
Netherlands	721,817	946,203	920,886	986,528	1,093,471	50.72	10.84
Switzerland	6,171	6,974	6,067	5,627	6,872	0.32	22.13
Other Europe	55,810	52,139	47,078	52,765	72,302	3.35	37.03
Other countries of Europe	55,810	52,139	47,078	52,765	72,302	3.35	37.03
REGION NOT SPECIFIED	67,072	32,252	38,218	28,397	30,269	1.40	6.59
Not Specified	67,072	32,252	38,218	28,397	30,269	1.40	6.59
Other countries of the World	67,072	32,252	38,218	28,397	30,269	1.40	6.59

Source: World Tourism Organization (UNWTO)

CYPRUS

1. Arrivals of non-resident tourists at national borders, by country of residence

	2002	2003	2004	2005	2006	Market share 06	% Change 06-05
TOTAL	2,418,238	2,303,246	2,349,012	2,470,063	2,400,924	100.00	-2.80
AFRICA	6,890	6,752	4,936	7,097	6,641	0.28	-6.43
Southern Africa	5,548	5,460	4,053	5,816	4,882	0.20	-16.06
South Africa	5,548	5,460	4,053	5,816	4,882	0.20	-16.06
Other Africa	1,342	1,292	883	1,281	1,759	0.07	37.31
Other countries of Africa	1,342	1,292	883	1,281	1,759	0.07	37.31
AMERICAS	26,734	23,246	22,924	28,984	26,353	1.10	-9.08
North America	25,826	22,483	22,203	28,273	25,242	1.05	-10.72
Canada	5,260	4,386	4,007	6,222	5,194	0.22	-16.52
United States	20,566	18,097	18,196	22,051	20,048	0.84	-9.08
Other Americas	908	763	721	711	1,111	0.05	56.26
Other countries of the Americas	908	763	721	711	1,111	0.05	56.26
EAST ASIA AND THE PACIFIC	11,697	12,266	13,042	15,043	16,262	0.68	8.10
North-East Asia	1,440	1,746	1,668	1,578	1,557	0.06	-1.33
China	305	525	482	424	403	0.02	-4.95
Japan	375	558	545	540	518	0.02	-4.07
Korea, Republic of	146	25	12	51	49		-3.92
Other countries of North-East Asia	614	638	629	563	587	0.02	4.26
Australasia	8,570	8,691	9,894	11,509	12,726	0.53	10.57
Australia	8,252	7,881	9,295	10,761	12,061	0.50	12.08
New Zealand	318	810	599	748	665	0.03	-11.10
Other East Asia and the Pacific	1,687	1,829	1,480	1,956	1,979	0.08	1.18
Other countries of Asia	1,687	1,829	1,458	1,931	1,947	0.08	0.83
Other countries of Oceania			22	25	32		28.00
EUROPE	2,323,568	2,207,434	2,263,145	2,375,402	2,307,885	96.12	-2.84
Central/Eastern Europe	176,093	160,915	152,844	165,085	192,291	8.01	16.48
Bulgaria	2,619	3,446	2,486	3,408	3,765	0.16	10.48
Belarus	1,777	1,923	1,071	1,612	1,933	0.08	19.91
Czech Republic	13,826	13,082	18,740	14,580	18,764	0.78	28.70
Estonia	1,238	219	731	911	1,456	0.06	59.82
Georgia	462	107	209	122	316	0.01	159.02
Hungary	8,080	8,760	11,150	11,174	11,458	0.48	2.54
Latvia	573	491	846	2,754	3,074	0.13	11.62
Lithuania	1,564	356	787	1,501	2,792	0.12	86.01
Poland	19,520	11,764	16,962	14,904	13,707	0.57	-8.03
Romania	3,163	3,529	4,047	4,980	7,032	0.29	41.20
Russian Federation	108,821	105,050	83,818	97,600	114,763	4.78	17.59
Slovakia	3,941	3,721	4,968	5,241	5,055	0.21	-3.55
Ukraine	8,558	6,673	5,778	5,083	6,374	0.27	25.40
Other countries Central/East Europ	1,951	1,794	1,251	1,215	1,802	0.08	48.31
Northern Europe	1,629,363	1,609,959	1,574,255	1,640,030	1,613,549	67.21	-1.61
Denmark	31,805	28,517	30,281	29,547	30,802	1.28	4.25
Finland	45,443	28,865	31,676	29,290	30,333	1.26	3.56
Iceland	356	1,041	484	227	123	0.01	-45.81
Ireland	56,654	61,571	44,292	52,711	47,463	1.98	-9.96
Norway	57,706	56,098	50,706	48,281	50,664	2.11	4.94
Sweden	99,753	86,824	83,964	88,125	94,028	3.92	6.70
United Kingdom	1,337,646	1,347,043	1,332,852	1,391,849	1,360,136	56.65	-2.28
Southern Europe	116,442	132,042	166,587	162,566	157,077	6.54	-3.38

CYPRUS

1. Arrivals of non-resident tourists at national borders, by country of residence

	2002	2003	2004	2005	2006	Market share 06	% Change 06-05
Greece	93,225	110,226	133,407	130,156	126,768	5.28	-2.60
Italy	12,185	13,381	20,681	20,202	17,865	0.74	-11.57
Malta	1,219	1,606	2,077	1,998	2,581	0.11	29.18
Portugal	715	429	1,302	1,378	1,202	0.05	-12.77
Slovenia	1,017	477	625	1,029	1,273	0.05	23.71
Spain	2,913	2,828	5,402	4,948	4,218	0.18	-14.75
Serbia and Montenegro	5,168	3,095	3,093	2,855	3,170	0.13	11.03
Western Europe	**361,004**	**276,570**	**331,941**	**365,776**	**309,058**	**12.87**	**-15.51**
Austria	29,053	25,894	28,643	36,988	23,788	0.99	-35.69
Belgium	23,098	20,101	20,719	22,879	24,267	1.01	6.07
France	29,545	31,419	46,798	52,783	37,779	1.57	-28.43
Germany	173,718	129,034	161,574	182,689	152,808	6.36	-16.36
Luxembourg	1,111	495	681	657	869	0.04	32.27
Netherlands	39,788	32,008	32,234	29,493	28,210	1.17	-4.35
Switzerland	64,691	37,619	41,292	40,287	41,337	1.72	2.61
East Mediterranean Europe	**40,042**	**27,271**	**37,130**	**41,168**	**34,451**	**1.43**	**-16.32**
Israel	39,943	27,206	36,917	40,940	34,197	1.42	-16.47
Turkey	99	65	213	228	254	0.01	11.40
Other Europe	**624**	**677**	**388**	**777**	**1,459**	**0.06**	**87.77**
Other countries of Europe	624	677	388	777	1,459	0.06	87.77
MIDDLE EAST	**45,170**	**49,413**	**41,379**	**40,233**	**39,291**	**1.64**	**-2.34**
Middle East	**45,170**	**49,413**	**41,379**	**40,233**	**39,291**	**1.64**	**-2.34**
Bahrain	1,875	2,332	1,993	1,249	1,799	0.07	44.04
Iraq	143	282	157	172	261	0.01	51.74
Jordan	4,562	6,476	4,342	4,303	3,892	0.16	-9.55
Kuwait	2,792	2,844	1,826	1,531	1,612	0.07	5.29
Lebanon	15,203	16,993	14,575	13,762	11,442	0.48	-16.86
Libyan Arab Jamahiriya	377	489	350	469	364	0.02	-22.39
Saudi Arabia	4,919	4,915	3,953	3,852	3,874	0.16	0.57
Syrian Arab Republic	2,230	2,754	1,915	1,559	1,896	0.08	21.62
United Arab Emirates	5,634	5,979	6,294	6,627	8,154	0.34	23.04
Egypt	6,029	5,296	4,686	5,470	4,441	0.18	-18.81
Other countries of Middle East	1,406	1,053	1,288	1,239	1,556	0.06	25.59
SOUTH ASIA	**3,383**	**3,130**	**1,992**	**2,777**	**3,808**	**0.16**	**37.13**
South Asia	**3,383**	**3,130**	**1,992**	**2,777**	**3,808**	**0.16**	**37.13**
Iran, Islamic Republic of	1,492	1,558	536	1,205	2,213	0.09	83.65
Other countries of South Asia	1,891	1,572	1,456	1,572	1,595	0.07	1.46
REGION NOT SPECIFIED	**796**	**1,005**	**1,594**	**527**	**684**	**0.03**	**29.79**
Not Specified	**796**	**1,005**	**1,594**	**527**	**684**	**0.03**	**29.79**
Other countries of the World	796	1,005	1,594	527	684	0.03	29.79

Source: World Tourism Organization (UNWTO)

CYPRUS

3. Arrivals of non-resident tourists in hotels and similar establishments, by country of residence

	2002	2003	2004	2005	2006	Market share 06	% Change 06-05
TOTAL	2,034,398	1,817,936	1,725,070	1,750,168	1,761,316	100.00	0.64
AFRICA				929	921	0.05	-0.86
Southern Africa				929	921	0.05	-0.86
South Africa				929	921	0.05	-0.86
AMERICAS				11,615	16,779	0.95	44.46
North America				11,615	16,779	0.95	44.46
Canada				2,341	4,583	0.26	95.77
United States				9,274	12,196	0.69	31.51
EAST ASIA AND THE PACIFIC				5,870	5,948	0.34	1.33
North-East Asia				2,181	2,047	0.12	-6.14
China				679	790	0.04	16.35
Japan				1,502	1,257	0.07	-16.31
Australasia				3,689	3,901	0.22	5.75
Australia				3,689	3,901	0.22	5.75
EUROPE	1,866,583	1,655,991	1,563,561	1,625,452	1,629,923	92.54	0.28
Central/Eastern Europe	140,642	114,577	91,352	124,622	157,646	8.95	26.50
Bulgaria				1,976	2,573	0.15	30.21
Czech Republic				11,358	14,405	0.82	26.83
Estonia				1,759	2,231	0.13	26.83
Hungary				6,330	9,453	0.54	49.34
Latvia				714	1,158	0.07	62.18
Lithuania				730	1,245	0.07	70.55
Poland				9,597	12,794	0.73	33.31
Romania				3,220	6,730	0.38	109.01
Russian Federation	140,642	114,577	91,352	86,457	103,961	5.90	20.25
Slovakia				2,481	3,096	0.18	24.79
Northern Europe	1,298,962	1,221,091	1,062,308	1,068,400	1,088,551	61.80	1.89
Denmark	23,629	27,403	25,984	21,928	23,264	1.32	6.09
Finland	40,832	31,705	25,821	22,771	27,666	1.57	21.50
Iceland				3,338	2,155	0.12	-35.44
Ireland	28,764	21,947	17,571	20,742	16,932	0.96	-18.37
Norway	63,469	104,061	41,344	37,721	46,022	2.61	22.01
Sweden	102,990	104,675	75,718	76,243	83,110	4.72	9.01
United Kingdom	1,039,278	931,300	875,870	885,657	889,402	50.50	0.42
Southern Europe	74,174	69,151	95,946	97,257	91,910	5.22	-5.50
Greece	49,831	48,372	64,736	64,668	61,982	3.52	-4.15
Italy	21,299	16,703	24,026	22,756	20,918	1.19	-8.08
Malta				1,382	1,423	0.08	2.97
Portugal	975	1,697	2,041	2,166	1,991	0.11	-8.08
Slovenia				901	1,248	0.07	38.51
Spain	2,069	2,379	5,143	5,384	4,348	0.25	-19.24
Western Europe	352,805	251,172	313,955	335,173	291,816	16.57	-12.94
Austria	23,229	20,372	21,337	28,849	20,118	1.14	-30.26
Belgium	18,424	15,325	18,909	16,281	17,818	1.01	9.44
France	35,674	37,179	60,630	62,311	50,302	2.86	-19.27
Germany	178,932	120,345	149,074	167,212	143,655	8.16	-14.09
Luxembourg	1,616	445	442	791	1,577	0.09	99.37
Netherlands	34,404	24,016	25,693	24,835	26,381	1.50	6.23
Switzerland	60,526	33,490	37,870	34,894	31,965	1.81	-8.39

CYPRUS

3. Arrivals of non-resident tourists in hotels and similar establishments, by country of residence

	2002	2003	2004	2005	2006	Market share 06	% Change 06-05
REGION NOT SPECIFIED	167,815	161,945	161,509	106,302	107,745	6.12	1.36
Not Specified	167,815	161,945	161,509	106,302	107,745	6.12	1.36
Other countries of the World	167,815	161,945	161,509	106,302	107,745	6.12	1.36

Source: World Tourism Organization (UNWTO)

CYPRUS

4. Arrivals of non-resident tourists in all types of accommodation establishments, by country of residence

	2002	2003	2004	2005	2006	Market share 06	% Change 06-05
TOTAL	2,040,436	1,825,827	1,734,586	1,762,658	1,770,704	100.00	0.46
AFRICA				941	925	0.05	-1.70
Southern Africa				941	925	0.05	-1.70
South Africa				941	925	0.05	-1.70
AMERICAS				11,622	16,810	0.95	44.64
North America				11,622	16,810	0.95	44.64
Canada				2,342	4,584	0.26	95.73
United States				9,280	12,226	0.69	31.75
EAST ASIA AND THE PACIFIC				5,870	5,953	0.34	1.41
North-East Asia				2,181	2,047	0.12	-6.14
China				679	790	0.04	16.35
Japan				1,502	1,257	0.07	-16.31
Australasia				3,689	3,906	0.22	5.88
Australia				3,689	3,906	0.22	5.88
EUROPE	1,872,323	1,663,680	1,572,764	1,637,192	1,639,033	92.56	0.11
Central/Eastern Europe	140,725	114,703	91,490	124,778	157,735	8.91	26.41
Bulgaria				1,976	2,573	0.15	30.21
Czech Republic				11,371	14,444	0.82	27.02
Estonia				1,762	2,231	0.13	26.62
Hungary				6,343	9,453	0.53	49.03
Latvia				714	1,161	0.07	62.61
Lithuania				730	1,245	0.07	70.55
Poland				9,609	12,814	0.72	33.35
Romania				3,222	6,730	0.38	108.88
Russian Federation	140,725	114,703	91,490	86,568	103,987	5.87	20.12
Slovakia				2,483	3,097	0.17	24.73
Northern Europe	1,303,904	1,227,741	1,070,168	1,078,145	1,096,330	61.91	1.69
Denmark	23,632	27,412	25,984	21,937	23,323	1.32	6.32
Finland	40,832	31,705	25,824	22,779	27,682	1.56	21.52
Iceland				3,343	2,182	0.12	-34.73
Ireland	28,775	21,976	17,685	21,047	17,084	0.96	-18.83
Norway	63,476	104,061	41,364	37,753	46,034	2.60	21.93
Sweden	102,990	104,681	75,741	76,294	83,176	4.70	9.02
United Kingdom	1,044,199	937,906	883,570	894,992	896,849	50.65	0.21
Southern Europe	74,239	69,287	96,113	97,474	92,129	5.20	-5.48
Greece	49,892	48,438	64,834	64,753	62,086	3.51	-4.12
Italy	21,301	16,760	24,071	22,832	21,024	1.19	-7.92
Malta				1,382	1,423	0.08	2.97
Portugal	975	1,697	2,041	2,170	1,993	0.11	-8.16
Slovenia				901	1,248	0.07	38.51
Spain	2,071	2,392	5,167	5,436	4,355	0.25	-19.89
Western Europe	353,455	251,949	314,993	336,795	292,839	16.54	-13.05
Austria	23,239	20,399	21,391	28,956	20,174	1.14	-30.33
Belgium	18,435	15,382	19,005	16,397	17,881	1.01	9.05
France	35,713	37,361	60,999	62,725	50,532	2.85	-19.44
Germany	179,316	120,698	149,393	167,892	144,130	8.14	-14.15
Luxembourg	1,616	447	442	791	1,577	0.09	99.37
Netherlands	34,597	24,163	25,860	25,035	26,543	1.50	6.02
Switzerland	60,539	33,499	37,903	34,999	32,002	1.81	-8.56

CYPRUS

4. Arrivals of non-resident tourists in all types of accommodation establishments, by country of residence

	2002	2003	2004	2005	2006	Market share 06	% Change 06-05
REGION NOT SPECIFIED	168,113	162,147	161,822	107,033	107,983	6.10	0.89
Not Specified	168,113	162,147	161,822	107,033	107,983	6.10	0.89
Other countries of the World	168,113	162,147	161,822	107,033	107,983	6.10	0.89

Source: World Tourism Organization (UNWTO)

CYPRUS

5. Overnight stays of non-resident tourists in hotels and similar establishments, by country of residence

	2002	2003	2004	2005	2006	Market share 06	% Change 06-05
TOTAL	15,235,497	13,424,102	13,554,335	13,899,099	13,227,357	100.00	-4.83
AFRICA				4,342	3,470	0.03	-20.08
Southern Africa				4,342	3,470	0.03	-20.08
South Africa				4,342	3,470	0.03	-20.08
AMERICAS				45,980	63,881	0.48	38.93
North America				45,980	63,881	0.48	38.93
Canada				9,206	18,952	0.14	105.87
United States				36,774	44,929	0.34	22.18
EAST ASIA AND THE PACIFIC				22,461	19,601	0.15	-12.73
North-East Asia				8,069	5,732	0.04	-28.96
China				3,243	2,615	0.02	-19.36
Japan				4,826	3,117	0.02	-35.41
Australasia				14,392	13,869	0.10	-3.63
Australia				14,392	13,869	0.10	-3.63
EUROPE	14,433,734	12,739,212	12,789,872	13,371,361	12,714,879	96.13	-4.91
Central/Eastern Europe	1,060,091	863,640	685,071	976,502	1,141,394	8.63	16.89
Bulgaria				8,502	16,610	0.13	95.37
Czech Republic				90,759	92,763	0.70	2.21
Estonia				12,924	13,507	0.10	4.51
Hungary				41,565	47,428	0.36	14.11
Latvia				4,352	7,513	0.06	72.63
Lithuania				4,155	7,668	0.06	84.55
Poland				73,383	79,853	0.60	8.82
Romania				14,104	29,629	0.22	110.08
Russian Federation	1,060,091	863,640	685,071	709,113	826,960	6.25	16.62
Slovakia				17,645	19,463	0.15	10.30
Northern Europe	10,301,055	9,582,269	9,288,967	9,359,468	9,036,553	68.32	-3.45
Denmark	155,099	181,351	200,113	171,378	176,403	1.33	2.93
Finland	272,148	198,991	220,620	190,348	218,455	1.65	14.77
Iceland				22,372	15,598	0.12	-30.28
Ireland	232,277	182,024	142,163	156,892	131,561	0.99	-16.15
Norway	458,526	508,710	473,448	422,763	469,386	3.55	11.03
Sweden	709,201	646,213	667,792	674,531	731,206	5.53	8.40
United Kingdom	8,473,804	7,864,980	7,584,831	7,721,184	7,293,944	55.14	-5.53
Southern Europe	295,981	289,319	402,878	412,031	374,809	2.83	-9.03
Greece	175,638	178,508	235,667	230,404	217,302	1.64	-5.69
Italy	97,987	89,919	136,164	129,460	116,059	0.88	-10.35
Malta				7,384	7,433	0.06	0.66
Portugal	15,310	10,054	9,824	16,352	8,324	0.06	-49.09
Slovenia				6,157	7,300	0.06	18.56
Spain	7,046	10,838	21,223	22,274	18,391	0.14	-17.43
Western Europe	2,776,607	2,003,984	2,412,956	2,623,360	2,162,123	16.35	-17.58
Austria	184,494	176,643	173,704	235,126	158,357	1.20	-32.65
Belgium	148,081	120,342	141,917	125,961	132,608	1.00	5.28
France	187,757	183,544	302,417	326,710	256,426	1.94	-21.51
Germany	1,462,933	1,048,322	1,287,811	1,465,712	1,181,744	8.93	-19.37
Luxembourg	10,728	1,977	2,400	4,025	10,590	0.08	163.11
Netherlands	277,421	183,900	185,213	179,191	164,516	1.24	-8.19
Switzerland	505,193	289,256	319,494	286,635	257,882	1.95	-10.03

CYPRUS

5. Overnight stays of non-resident tourists in hotels and similar establishments, by country of residence

	2002	2003	2004	2005	2006	Market share 06	% Change 06-05
REGION NOT SPECIFIED	801,763	684,890	764,463	454,955	425,526	3.22	-6.47
Not Specified	801,763	684,890	764,463	454,955	425,526	3.22	-6.47
Other countries of the World	801,763	684,890	764,463	454,955	425,526	3.22	-6.47

Source: World Tourism Organization (UNWTO)

CYPRUS

6. Overnight stays of non-resident tourists in all types of accommodation establishments, by country of residence

	2002	2003	2004	2005	2006	Market share 06	% Change 06-05
TOTAL	15,289,044	13,490,132	13,636,517	14,006,282	13,310,257	100.00	-4.97
AFRICA				4,382	3,498	0.03	-20.17
Southern Africa				4,382	3,498	0.03	-20.17
South Africa				4,382	3,498	0.03	-20.17
AMERICAS				46,030	64,009	0.48	39.06
North America				46,030	64,009	0.48	39.06
Canada				9,208	18,954	0.14	105.84
United States				36,822	45,055	0.34	22.36
EAST ASIA AND THE PACIFIC				22,461	19,657	0.15	-12.48
North-East Asia				8,069	5,732	0.04	-28.96
China				3,243	2,615	0.02	-19.36
Japan				4,826	3,117	0.02	-35.41
Australasia				14,392	13,925	0.10	-3.24
Australia				14,392	13,925	0.10	-3.24
EUROPE	14,486,055	12,804,118	12,870,772	13,474,986	12,796,817	96.14	-5.03
Central/Eastern Europe	1,060,728	864,995	687,144	978,277	1,141,853	8.58	16.72
Bulgaria				8,502	16,610	0.12	95.37
Czech Republic				90,781	92,822	0.70	2.25
Estonia				12,927	13,507	0.10	4.49
Hungary				41,581	47,428	0.36	14.06
Latvia				4,352	7,518	0.06	72.75
Lithuania				4,155	7,668	0.06	84.55
Poland				73,400	79,885	0.60	8.84
Romania				14,124	29,629	0.22	109.78
Russian Federation	1,060,728	864,995	687,144	710,806	827,085	6.21	16.36
Slovakia				17,649	19,701	0.15	11.63
Northern Europe	10,346,302	9,641,731	9,363,551	9,451,180	9,111,194	68.45	-3.60
Denmark	155,102	181,392	200,113	171,417	176,542	1.33	2.99
Finland	272,148	198,991	220,623	190,432	218,504	1.64	14.74
Iceland				22,377	15,679	0.12	-29.93
Ireland	232,326	182,195	142,538	158,050	132,057	0.99	-16.45
Norway	458,724	508,710	473,498	422,834	469,408	3.53	11.01
Sweden	709,201	646,227	667,820	674,630	731,312	5.49	8.40
United Kingdom	8,518,801	7,924,216	7,658,959	7,811,440	7,367,692	55.35	-5.68
Southern Europe	296,519	289,690	403,577	413,829	375,584	2.82	-9.24
Greece	176,150	178,704	236,245	230,788	217,778	1.64	-5.64
Italy	98,001	90,037	136,245	129,644	116,349	0.87	-10.26
Malta				7,384	7,433	0.06	0.66
Portugal	15,310	10,054	9,824	16,356	8,326	0.06	-49.10
Slovenia				6,157	7,300	0.05	18.56
Spain	7,058	10,895	21,263	23,500	18,398	0.14	-21.71
Western Europe	2,782,506	2,007,702	2,416,500	2,631,700	2,168,186	16.29	-17.61
Austria	184,634	176,697	173,860	235,559	158,621	1.19	-32.66
Belgium	148,142	120,647	142,253	126,691	133,002	1.00	4.98
France	188,095	184,095	303,340	327,688	256,862	1.93	-21.61
Germany	1,466,103	1,050,067	1,288,889	1,469,546	1,185,322	8.91	-19.34
Luxembourg	10,728	1,979	2,400	4,025	10,590	0.08	163.11
Netherlands	279,398	184,880	186,024	180,636	165,763	1.25	-8.23
Switzerland	505,406	289,337	319,734	287,555	258,026	1.94	-10.27

CYPRUS

6. Overnight stays of non-resident tourists in all types of accommodation establishments, by country of residence

	2002	2003	2004	2005	2006	Market share 06	% Change 06-05
REGION NOT SPECIFIED	**802,989**	**686,014**	**765,745**	**458,423**	**426,276**	**3.20**	**-7.01**
Not Specified	**802,989**	**686,014**	**765,745**	**458,423**	**426,276**	**3.20**	**-7.01**
Other countries of the World	802,989	686,014	765,745	458,423	426,276	3.20	-7.01

Source: World Tourism Organization (UNWTO)

CZECH REPUBLIC

3. Arrivals of non-resident tourists in hotels and similar establishments, by nationality

	2002	2003	2004	2005	2006	Market share 06	% Change 06-05
TOTAL	4,314,111	4,484,989	5,346,485	5,685,757	5,780,674	100.00	1.67
AFRICA	11,316	12,704	13,999	17,258	17,336	0.30	0.45
Southern Africa				2,778	3,951	0.07	42.22
South Africa				2,778	3,951	0.07	42.22
Other Africa	11,316	12,704	13,999	14,480	13,385	0.23	-7.56
Other countries of Africa				14,480	13,385	0.23	-7.56
All countries of Africa	11,316	12,704	13,999				
AMERICAS	228,481	261,314	349,230	374,038	410,125	7.09	9.65
North America	209,257	237,808	316,543	338,641	368,201	6.37	8.73
Canada	16,732	22,188	33,387	40,071	44,106	0.76	10.07
Mexico	9,776	10,210	12,252	12,141	17,721	0.31	45.96
United States	182,749	205,410	270,904	286,429	306,374	5.30	6.96
South America				10,487	15,068	0.26	43.68
Brazil				10,487	15,068	0.26	43.68
Other Americas	19,224	23,506	32,687	24,910	26,856	0.46	7.81
Other countries of the Americas	19,224	23,506	32,687	24,910	26,856	0.46	7.81
EAST ASIA AND THE PACIFIC	231,488	233,058	326,114	398,218	470,080	8.13	18.05
North-East Asia	99,914	90,672	119,668	213,132	244,228	4.22	14.59
China				16,463	28,028	0.48	70.25
Japan	99,914	90,672	119,668	151,310	142,639	2.47	-5.73
Korea, Republic of				45,359	73,561	1.27	62.18
Australasia	20,615	24,243	32,360	35,229	43,379	0.75	23.13
Australia	18,800	20,393	27,393	30,742	37,998	0.66	23.60
New Zealand	1,815	3,850	4,967	4,487	5,381	0.09	19.92
Other East Asia and the Pacific	110,959	118,143	174,086	149,857	182,473	3.16	21.76
Other countries of Asia	110,959	118,143	174,086	147,438	180,379	3.12	22.34
Other countries of Oceania				2,419	2,094	0.04	-13.44
EUROPE	3,842,826	3,977,913	4,657,142	4,896,243	4,883,133	84.47	-0.27
Central/Eastern Europe	657,323	651,026	678,814	786,081	892,307	15.44	13.51
Bulgaria	11,549	17,330	11,438	12,212	12,007	0.21	-1.68
Estonia	7,006	6,074	6,979	10,752	12,790	0.22	18.95
Hungary	50,575	58,604	73,636	95,262	82,388	1.43	-13.51
Latvia	4,739	7,373	9,571	11,874	15,194	0.26	27.96
Lithuania	19,522	19,683	24,421	30,360	45,601	0.79	50.20
Poland	278,210	225,197	195,719	212,750	224,419	3.88	5.48
Romania	8,950	11,314	14,774	18,225	22,029	0.38	20.87
Russian Federation	96,710	110,297	144,959	166,462	215,854	3.73	29.67
Slovakia	180,062	195,154	197,317	199,720	218,274	3.78	9.29
Ukraine				28,464	43,751	0.76	53.71
Northern Europe	542,236	678,258	964,916	988,993	895,768	15.50	-9.43
Denmark	84,500	87,524	105,767	97,981	98,149	1.70	0.17
Finland	29,723	35,789	40,758	45,527	42,208	0.73	-7.29
Iceland	5,620	4,628	3,488	5,700	4,076	0.07	-28.49
Ireland	13,243	30,498	41,506	40,654	38,398	0.66	-5.55
Norway	38,244	49,571	61,935	83,976	85,609	1.48	1.94
Sweden	71,987	74,860	82,846	77,988	76,942	1.33	-1.34
United Kingdom	298,919	395,388	628,616	637,167	550,386	9.52	-13.62
Southern Europe	474,079	514,108	687,451	748,641	736,307	12.74	-1.65

CZECH REPUBLIC

3. Arrivals of non-resident tourists in hotels and similar establishments, by nationality

	2002	2003	2004	2005	2006	Market share 06	% Change 06-05
Croatia	24,630	29,622	37,155	41,024	40,048	0.69	-2.38
Greece	40,881	43,389	57,601	55,596	53,703	0.93	-3.40
Italy	244,167	268,129	364,035	384,475	382,027	6.61	-0.64
Malta				6,559	2,448	0.04	-62.68
Portugal	9,957	11,034	17,933	20,590	20,678	0.36	0.43
Slovenia	13,598	13,361	17,353	18,631	17,470	0.30	-6.23
Spain	140,846	148,573	193,374	217,675	213,046	3.69	-2.13
Serbia and Montenegro				4,091	6,887	0.12	68.35
Western Europe	**1,916,946**	**1,863,360**	**2,064,293**	**2,156,300**	**2,123,307**	**36.73**	**-1.53**
Austria	164,313	155,748	171,882	173,223	162,704	2.81	-6.07
Belgium	53,461	57,984	67,543	69,697	64,544	1.12	-7.39
France	186,906	179,822	231,403	238,925	221,830	3.84	-7.15
Germany	1,311,490	1,259,530	1,366,183	1,429,761	1,434,390	24.81	0.32
Liechtenstein				856	955	0.02	11.57
Luxembourg	2,052	3,228	3,105	3,907	3,619	0.06	-7.37
Netherlands	147,794	152,081	161,200	174,188	168,536	2.92	-3.24
Switzerland	50,930	54,967	62,977	65,743	66,729	1.15	1.50
East Mediterranean Europe	**125,460**	**99,104**	**93,920**	**86,580**	**97,174**	**1.68**	**12.24**
Cyprus	5,305	6,388	8,952	9,734	9,385	0.16	-3.59
Israel	104,097	68,532	61,516	52,055	56,204	0.97	7.97
Turkey	16,058	24,184	23,452	24,791	31,585	0.55	27.41
Other Europe	**126,782**	**172,057**	**167,748**	**129,648**	**138,270**	**2.39**	**6.65**
Other countries of Europe	126,782	172,057	167,748	129,648	138,270	2.39	6.65

Source: World Tourism Organization (UNWTO)

CZECH REPUBLIC

4. Arrivals of non-resident tourists in all types of accommodation establishments, by nationality

	2002	2003	2004	2005	2006	Market share 06	% Change 06-05
TOTAL	4,742,773	5,075,756	6,061,225	6,336,128	6,435,474	100.00	1.57
AFRICA	12,842	14,097	15,394	18,539	19,411	0.30	4.70
Southern Africa				2,984	4,353	0.07	45.88
South Africa				2,984	4,353	0.07	45.88
Other Africa	12,842	14,097	15,394	15,555	15,058	0.23	-3.20
Other countries of Africa				15,555	15,058	0.23	-3.20
All countries of Africa	12,842	14,097	15,394				
AMERICAS	238,767	282,239	380,056	400,840	435,280	6.76	8.59
North America	218,491	257,099	345,302	362,522	389,793	6.06	7.52
Canada	18,024	24,759	39,103	45,439	48,625	0.76	7.01
Mexico	10,110	11,029	13,611	13,442	19,142	0.30	42.40
United States	190,357	221,311	292,588	303,641	322,026	5.00	6.05
South America				11,652	16,513	0.26	41.72
Brazil				11,652	16,513	0.26	41.72
Other Americas	20,276	25,140	34,754	26,666	28,974	0.45	8.66
Other countries of the Americas	20,276	25,140	34,754	26,666	28,974	0.45	8.66
EAST ASIA AND THE PACIFIC	242,257	251,411	351,652	420,989	492,842	7.66	17.07
North-East Asia	100,567	93,110	122,613	218,636	250,421	3.89	14.54
China				17,806	29,710	0.46	66.85
Japan	100,567	93,110	122,613	153,980	145,804	2.27	-5.31
Korea, Republic of				46,850	74,907	1.16	59.89
Australasia	23,796	30,391	45,911	46,194	52,653	0.82	13.98
Australia	21,393	25,004	39,152	40,046	45,815	0.71	14.41
New Zealand	2,403	5,387	6,759	6,148	6,838	0.11	11.22
Other East Asia and the Pacific	117,894	127,910	183,128	156,159	189,768	2.95	21.52
Other countries of Asia	117,894	127,910	183,128	153,457	187,486	2.91	22.17
Other countries of Oceania				2,702	2,282	0.04	-15.54
EUROPE	4,248,907	4,528,009	5,314,123	5,495,760	5,487,941	85.28	-0.14
Central/Eastern Europe	806,904	814,281	852,408	944,207	1,059,085	16.46	12.17
Bulgaria	12,735	19,497	13,571	14,410	13,877	0.22	-3.70
Estonia	9,632	8,082	9,154	12,579	14,459	0.22	14.95
Hungary	59,334	72,289	88,169	108,957	94,806	1.47	-12.99
Latvia	5,716	8,331	10,844	12,627	15,914	0.25	26.03
Lithuania	21,615	24,377	29,402	35,285	51,165	0.80	45.00
Poland	349,374	291,344	253,916	261,576	273,659	4.25	4.62
Romania	9,849	12,943	16,399	20,039	24,155	0.38	20.54
Russian Federation	112,850	124,655	164,036	185,705	239,632	3.72	29.04
Slovakia	225,799	252,763	266,917	260,212	281,854	4.38	8.32
Ukraine				32,817	49,564	0.77	51.03
Northern Europe	568,095	728,079	1,026,252	1,042,121	941,549	14.63	-9.65
Denmark	95,955	105,273	127,671	117,738	115,336	1.79	-2.04
Finland	32,160	39,659	45,221	48,981	45,413	0.71	-7.28
Iceland	5,665	5,017	3,709	5,918	4,439	0.07	-24.99
Ireland	13,829	32,502	44,299	42,728	40,270	0.63	-5.75
Norway	39,850	52,783	65,975	86,360	88,222	1.37	2.16
Sweden	74,960	80,443	88,755	83,286	81,644	1.27	-1.97
United Kingdom	305,676	412,402	650,622	657,110	566,225	8.80	-13.83
Southern Europe	486,600	537,256	728,408	783,431	767,308	11.92	-2.06

CZECH REPUBLIC

4. Arrivals of non-resident tourists in all types of accommodation establishments, by nationality

	2002	2003	2004	2005	2006	Market share 06	% Change 06-05
Croatia	25,607	31,125	39,081	42,672	41,569	0.65	-2.58
Greece	41,505	44,558	58,604	56,853	54,869	0.85	-3.49
Italy	250,586	281,420	391,192	405,079	399,023	6.20	-1.50
Malta				7,680	2,920	0.05	-61.98
Portugal	10,605	12,079	19,066	21,958	22,144	0.34	0.85
Slovenia	15,005	14,743	19,355	20,414	18,897	0.29	-7.43
Spain	143,292	153,331	201,110	224,327	220,050	3.42	-1.91
Serbia and Montenegro				4,448	7,836	0.12	76.17
Western Europe	**2,123,576**	**2,163,492**	**2,430,800**	**2,500,285**	**2,468,638**	**38.36**	**-1.27**
Austria	173,766	165,283	183,871	184,235	175,911	2.73	-4.52
Belgium	58,240	66,071	77,477	80,811	74,694	1.16	-7.57
France	194,616	193,215	256,429	257,683	240,280	3.73	-6.75
Germany	1,451,325	1,439,124	1,569,369	1,606,947	1,617,431	25.13	0.65
Liechtenstein				982	1,140	0.02	16.09
Luxembourg	2,203	3,436	3,478	4,038	3,823	0.06	-5.32
Netherlands	190,369	238,564	273,757	295,856	284,499	4.42	-3.84
Switzerland	53,057	57,799	66,419	69,733	70,860	1.10	1.62
East Mediterranean Europe	**128,585**	**103,167**	**97,407**	**88,754**	**101,003**	**1.57**	**13.80**
Cyprus	5,501	7,082	9,230	9,876	9,570	0.15	-3.10
Israel	106,904	71,602	64,125	53,606	59,171	0.92	10.38
Turkey	16,180	24,483	24,052	25,272	32,262	0.50	27.66
Other Europe	**135,147**	**181,734**	**178,848**	**136,962**	**150,358**	**2.34**	**9.78**
Other countries of Europe	135,147	181,734	178,848	136,962	150,358	2.34	9.78

Source: World Tourism Organization (UNWTO)

CZECH REPUBLIC

5. Overnight stays of non-resident tourists in hotels and similar establishments, by nationality

	2002	2003	2004	2005	2006	Market share 06	% Change 06-05
TOTAL	13,326,843	13,688,095	15,880,594	16,607,497	17,035,170	100.00	2.58
AFRICA	46,961	46,367	48,421	58,148	64,118	0.38	10.27
Southern Africa				8,608	11,154	0.07	29.58
South Africa				8,608	11,154	0.07	29.58
Other Africa	46,961	46,367	48,421	49,540	52,964	0.31	6.91
Other countries of Africa				49,540	52,964	0.31	6.91
All countries of Africa	46,961	46,367	48,421				
AMERICAS	685,081	763,667	996,302	1,060,848	1,178,892	6.92	11.13
North America	629,706	697,185	906,216	964,346	1,067,265	6.27	10.67
Canada	54,667	65,873	91,684	108,863	118,845	0.70	9.17
Mexico	34,126	28,193	33,667	31,556	42,403	0.25	34.37
United States	540,913	603,119	780,865	823,927	906,017	5.32	9.96
South America				29,698	41,166	0.24	38.62
Brazil				29,698	41,166	0.24	38.62
Other Americas	55,375	66,482	90,086	66,804	70,461	0.41	5.47
Other countries of the Americas	55,375	66,482	90,086	66,804	70,461	0.41	5.47
EAST ASIA AND THE PACIFIC	529,817	571,874	731,954	856,962	978,180	5.74	14.15
North-East Asia	206,552	208,487	289,602	446,999	474,079	2.78	6.06
China				35,453	60,713	0.36	71.25
Japan	206,552	208,487	289,602	341,228	301,560	1.77	-11.63
Korea, Republic of				70,318	111,806	0.66	59.00
Australasia	45,965	60,651	85,136	92,115	111,995	0.66	21.58
Australia	41,460	50,979	70,096	80,277	97,933	0.57	21.99
New Zealand	4,505	9,672	15,040	11,838	14,062	0.08	18.79
Other East Asia and the Pacific	277,300	302,736	357,216	317,848	392,106	2.30	23.36
Other countries of Asia	277,300	302,736	357,216	310,075	386,739	2.27	24.72
Other countries of Oceania				7,773	5,367	0.03	-30.95
EUROPE	12,064,984	12,306,187	14,103,917	14,631,539	14,813,980	86.96	1.25
Central/Eastern Europe	1,816,328	1,847,826	1,984,919	2,312,805	2,718,892	15.96	17.56
Bulgaria	25,291	39,778	26,129	30,438	29,736	0.17	-2.31
Estonia	15,267	12,348	16,995	24,370	28,297	0.17	16.11
Hungary	125,449	136,344	166,154	223,301	179,264	1.05	-19.72
Latvia	9,504	16,731	19,907	22,168	27,194	0.16	22.67
Lithuania	37,775	35,685	42,811	53,377	74,567	0.44	39.70
Poland	624,313	455,999	385,065	421,878	456,946	2.68	8.31
Romania	20,689	27,890	37,318	47,273	60,975	0.36	28.98
Russian Federation	518,491	593,832	782,544	892,794	1,153,365	6.77	29.19
Slovakia	439,549	529,219	507,996	483,584	534,318	3.14	10.49
Ukraine				113,622	174,230	1.02	53.34
Northern Europe	1,554,302	1,956,408	2,736,746	2,789,401	2,517,448	14.78	-9.75
Denmark	271,260	276,760	327,704	311,539	318,401	1.87	2.20
Finland	94,202	118,569	127,648	140,996	129,268	0.76	-8.32
Iceland	20,646	16,984	12,450	15,712	13,221	0.08	-15.85
Ireland	36,447	85,985	121,047	113,924	108,069	0.63	-5.14
Norway	106,337	139,099	173,018	251,507	254,876	1.50	1.34
Sweden	201,012	211,126	225,506	209,704	205,224	1.20	-2.14
United Kingdom	824,398	1,107,885	1,749,373	1,746,019	1,488,389	8.74	-14.76
Southern Europe	1,403,328	1,532,653	2,062,524	2,221,559	2,175,135	12.77	-2.09

CZECH REPUBLIC

5. Overnight stays of non-resident tourists in hotels and similar establishments, by nationality

	2002	2003	2004	2005	2006	Market share 06	% Change 06-05
Croatia	78,625	93,516	116,339	125,558	117,552	0.69	-6.38
Greece	110,441	125,618	171,898	165,668	159,669	0.94	-3.62
Italy	716,317	777,932	1,078,700	1,108,969	1,100,699	6.46	-0.75
Malta				20,783	8,416	0.05	-59.51
Portugal	31,423	33,633	54,848	60,858	63,456	0.37	4.27
Slovenia	30,259	27,322	35,881	35,948	32,096	0.19	-10.72
Spain	436,263	474,632	604,858	690,490	675,435	3.96	-2.18
Serbia and Montenegro				13,285	17,812	0.10	34.08
Western Europe	**6,540,312**	**6,125,350**	**6,507,461**	**6,653,537**	**6,671,729**	**39.16**	**0.27**
Austria	344,492	324,219	353,833	353,221	331,088	1.94	-6.27
Belgium	145,963	161,372	189,343	191,979	174,898	1.03	-8.90
France	499,144	482,021	603,080	616,173	569,990	3.35	-7.50
Germany	4,915,371	4,506,301	4,659,109	4,753,089	4,874,551	28.61	2.56
Liechtenstein				1,682	2,250	0.01	33.77
Luxembourg	4,924	10,350	8,569	11,127	9,732	0.06	-12.54
Netherlands	497,673	494,908	521,426	558,492	543,176	3.19	-2.74
Switzerland	132,745	146,179	172,101	167,774	166,044	0.97	-1.03
East Mediterranean Europe	**380,004**	**332,751**	**322,044**	**292,568**	**328,236**	**1.93**	**12.19**
Cyprus	18,700	24,907	29,582	31,316	30,889	0.18	-1.36
Israel	317,064	242,635	227,236	189,753	200,695	1.18	5.77
Turkey	44,240	65,209	65,226	71,499	96,652	0.57	35.18
Other Europe	**370,710**	**511,199**	**490,223**	**361,669**	**402,540**	**2.36**	**11.30**
Other countries of Europe	370,710	511,199	490,223	361,669	402,540	2.36	11.30

Source: World Tourism Organization (UNWTO)

CZECH REPUBLIC

6. Overnight stays of non-resident tourists in all types of accommodation establishments, by nationality

	2002	2003	2004	2005	2006	Market share 06	% Change 06-05
TOTAL	15,569,156	16,510,618	18,980,462	19,595,035	20,090,349	100.00	2.53
AFRICA	57,284	57,217	59,815	67,633	72,719	0.36	7.52
Southern Africa				9,524	12,369	0.06	29.87
South Africa				9,524	12,369	0.06	29.87
Other Africa	57,284	57,217	59,815	58,109	60,350	0.30	3.86
Other countries of Africa				58,109	60,350	0.30	3.86
All countries of Africa	57,284	57,217	59,815				
AMERICAS	744,023	869,208	1,101,591	1,160,087	1,272,553	6.33	9.69
North America	682,078	796,444	1,005,329	1,055,190	1,150,965	5.73	9.08
Canada	60,948	75,062	107,590	122,732	132,686	0.66	8.11
Mexico	35,447	30,271	36,965	34,412	46,040	0.23	33.79
United States	585,683	691,111	860,774	898,046	972,239	4.84	8.26
South America				32,423	45,003	0.22	38.80
Brazil				32,423	45,003	0.22	38.80
Other Americas	61,945	72,764	96,262	72,474	76,585	0.38	5.67
Other countries of the Americas	61,945	72,764	96,262	72,474	76,585	0.38	5.67
EAST ASIA AND THE PACIFIC	629,830	679,302	831,414	964,772	1,101,219	5.48	14.14
North-East Asia	209,372	215,509	296,621	459,543	488,832	2.43	6.37
China				38,788	65,233	0.32	68.18
Japan	209,372	215,509	296,621	347,290	308,799	1.54	-11.08
Korea, Republic of				73,465	114,800	0.57	56.26
Australasia	53,710	74,317	111,664	115,738	133,770	0.67	15.58
Australia	47,945	61,196	92,668	100,305	116,297	0.58	15.94
New Zealand	5,765	13,121	18,996	15,433	17,473	0.09	13.22
Other East Asia and the Pacific	366,748	389,476	423,129	389,491	478,617	2.38	22.88
Other countries of Asia	366,748	389,476	423,129	381,075	472,791	2.35	24.07
Other countries of Oceania				8,416	5,826	0.03	-30.77
EUROPE	14,138,019	14,904,891	16,987,642	17,402,543	17,643,858	87.82	1.39
Central/Eastern Europe	2,412,560	2,486,772	2,649,749	2,971,238	3,453,512	17.19	16.23
Bulgaria	30,869	48,520	34,886	39,909	36,321	0.18	-8.99
Estonia	20,154	17,076	21,471	28,046	32,161	0.16	14.67
Hungary	152,439	181,870	208,169	260,715	212,133	1.06	-18.63
Latvia	13,174	18,576	23,295	24,354	29,674	0.15	21.84
Lithuania	42,100	44,277	51,727	62,187	85,475	0.43	37.45
Poland	854,572	655,365	542,320	556,565	609,872	3.04	9.58
Romania	23,747	34,593	42,343	52,607	66,760	0.33	26.90
Russian Federation	650,862	720,617	930,187	1,045,907	1,356,792	6.75	29.72
Slovakia	624,643	765,878	795,351	760,077	806,174	4.01	6.06
Ukraine				140,871	218,150	1.09	54.86
Northern Europe	1,635,472	2,126,632	2,920,904	2,935,654	2,649,912	13.19	-9.73
Denmark	306,698	333,877	394,872	368,890	371,128	1.85	0.61
Finland	104,839	134,585	141,855	151,144	138,180	0.69	-8.58
Iceland	20,789	18,326	13,132	16,565	14,262	0.07	-13.90
Ireland	37,772	92,025	129,434	119,959	112,694	0.56	-6.06
Norway	110,815	150,057	185,439	258,273	262,735	1.31	1.73
Sweden	209,055	230,366	241,923	223,494	218,920	1.09	-2.05
United Kingdom	845,504	1,167,396	1,814,249	1,797,329	1,531,993	7.63	-14.76
Southern Europe	1,446,273	1,600,974	2,177,746	2,326,897	2,259,392	11.25	-2.90

CZECH REPUBLIC

6. Overnight stays of non-resident tourists in all types of accommodation establishments, by nationality

	2002	2003	2004	2005	2006	Market share 06	% Change 06-05
Croatia	82,524	98,318	122,584	131,586	122,061	0.61	-7.24
Greece	113,180	130,839	176,895	170,410	163,383	0.81	-4.12
Italy	737,245	815,552	1,150,016	1,168,315	1,142,234	5.69	-2.23
Malta				25,358	11,988	0.06	-52.72
Portugal	33,890	36,732	58,497	65,154	68,115	0.34	4.54
Slovenia	34,295	30,982	41,523	41,810	36,463	0.18	-12.79
Spain	445,139	488,551	628,231	709,448	693,476	3.45	-2.25
Serbia and Montenegro				14,816	21,672	0.11	46.27
Western Europe	**7,813,101**	**7,756,955**	**8,334,559**	**8,468,978**	**8,480,395**	**42.21**	**0.13**
Austria	372,893	352,047	386,177	389,526	363,692	1.81	-6.63
Belgium	163,735	190,736	220,919	227,737	204,193	1.02	-10.34
France	523,251	520,018	666,379	660,786	612,873	3.05	-7.25
Germany	5,956,746	5,662,032	5,902,332	5,887,902	6,055,215	30.14	2.84
Liechtenstein				2,059	2,907	0.01	41.19
Luxembourg	5,264	10,863	9,606	11,548	10,278	0.05	-11.00
Netherlands	650,594	865,654	967,322	1,108,994	1,052,352	5.24	-5.11
Switzerland	140,618	155,605	181,824	180,426	178,885	0.89	-0.85
East Mediterranean Europe	**420,072**	**373,696**	**353,348**	**310,320**	**358,345**	**1.78**	**15.48**
Cyprus	20,478	28,407	31,211	31,919	31,941	0.16	0.07
Israel	354,798	278,900	255,063	204,919	227,553	1.13	11.05
Turkey	44,796	66,389	67,074	73,482	98,851	0.49	34.52
Other Europe	**410,541**	**559,862**	**551,336**	**389,456**	**442,302**	**2.20**	**13.57**
Other countries of Europe	410,541	559,862	551,336	389,456	442,302	2.20	13.57

Source: World Tourism Organization (UNWTO)

DEMOCRATIC REPUBLIC OF THE CONGO

1. Arrivals of non-resident tourists at national borders, by nationality

	2002	2003	2004	2005	2006	Market share 06	% Change 06-05
TOTAL (*)	28,179	35,141	36,238	61,007	55,148	100.00	-9.60
AFRICA	9,088	20,380	14,531	36,489	33,089	60.00	-9.32
Central Africa	489	672	668	1,909	2,425	4.40	27.03
Congo		121	109	437	1,453	2.63	232.49
Other countries of Central Africa		551	559	1,472	972	1.76	-33.97
All countries of Central Africa	489						
Other Africa	8,599	19,708	13,863	34,580	30,664	55.60	-11.32
Other countries of Africa	8,599	19,708	13,863	34,580	30,664	55.60	-11.32
AMERICAS	3,678	2,568	4,592	3,824	3,309	6.00	-13.47
Other Americas	3,678	2,568	4,592	3,824	3,309	6.00	-13.47
All countries of the Americas	3,678	2,568	4,592	3,824	3,309	6.00	-13.47
EAST ASIA AND THE PACIFIC	4,140	3,156	3,998	5,943	5,515	10.00	-7.20
Other East Asia and the Pacific	4,140	3,156	3,998	5,943	5,515	10.00	-7.20
All countries of Asia	3,710	3,018	3,865	5,654	5,239	9.50	-7.34
All countries of Oceania	430	138	133	289	276	0.50	-4.50
EUROPE	11,273	9,037	13,117	14,751	13,235	24.00	-10.28
Southern Europe	1,148	475	785	1,038	1,977	3.58	90.46
Italy	1,148	475	785	1,038	926	1.68	-10.79
Other countries Southern Europe					1,051	1.91	
Western Europe	5,500	4,733	8,431	8,984	8,591	15.58	-4.37
Belgium	2,985	2,337	4,446	4,788	4,368	7.92	-8.77
France	1,896	2,012	3,348	3,245	1,588	2.88	-51.06
Germany	619	384	637	951	926	1.68	-2.63
Other countries of Western Europe					1,709	3.10	
Other Europe	4,625	3,829	3,901	4,729	2,667	4.84	-43.60
Other countries of Europe	4,625	3,829	3,901	4,729	2,667	4.84	-43.60

Source: World Tourism Organization (UNWTO)

DENMARK

3. Arrivals of non-resident tourists in hotels and similar establishments, by country of residence

		2002	2003	2004	2005	2006	Market share 06	% Change 06-05
TOTAL	(*)	1,378,932	1,384,520	1,969,968	2,230,351	2,216,495	100.00	-0.62
AMERICAS		77,403	76,410	122,807	142,948	179,696	8.11	25.71
North America		71,361	71,345	113,890	130,279	150,817	6.80	15.76
Canada		7,220	6,620	6,020	10,572	12,835	0.58	21.41
United States		64,141	64,725	107,870	119,707	137,982	6.23	15.27
Other Americas		6,042	5,065	8,917	12,669	28,879	1.30	127.95
Other countries of the Americas		6,042	5,065	8,917	12,669	28,879	1.30	127.95
EAST ASIA AND THE PACIFIC		48,643	46,154	81,293	106,909	86,971	3.92	-18.65
North-East Asia		29,162	27,880	38,526	38,348	34,750	1.57	-9.38
Japan		29,162	27,880	38,526	38,348	34,750	1.57	-9.38
South-East Asia		19,481	18,274	42,767	68,561	52,221	2.36	-23.83
All countries of South-East Asia		19,481	18,274	42,767	68,561	52,221	2.36	-23.83
EUROPE		1,194,439	1,197,902	1,656,136	1,943,513	1,918,717	86.57	-1.28
Central/Eastern Europe		8,207	6,028	19,879	18,742	21,033	0.95	12.22
Poland		8,207	6,028	19,879	18,742	21,033	0.95	12.22
Northern Europe		864,461	880,799	1,176,074	1,243,749	1,227,865	55.40	-1.28
Finland		33,167	32,594	38,187	54,120	50,626	2.28	-6.46
Norway		290,043	307,956	378,815	404,884	416,757	18.80	2.93
Sweden		419,434	427,229	542,083	559,592	558,611	25.20	-0.18
United Kingdom		121,817	113,020	216,989	225,153	201,871	9.11	-10.34
Southern Europe		46,913	47,036	76,826	94,873	100,565	4.54	6.00
Italy		32,087	32,431	50,921	47,593	47,699	2.15	0.22
Spain		14,826	14,605	25,905	47,280	52,866	2.39	11.81
Western Europe		211,152	201,842	290,813	403,117	390,960	17.64	-3.02
Austria		3,905	3,311	5,959	11,144	8,940	0.40	-19.78
France		23,962	21,726	26,336	39,062	38,668	1.74	-1.01
Germany		126,841	123,602	160,186	231,499	208,905	9.43	-9.76
Netherlands		33,266	33,843	65,215	63,416	74,230	3.35	17.05
Switzerland		12,986	10,971	19,793	29,822	33,306	1.50	11.68
Belgium / Luxembourg		10,192	8,389	13,324	28,174	26,911	1.21	-4.48
Other Europe		63,706	62,197	92,544	183,032	178,294	8.04	-2.59
Other countries of Europe		63,706	62,197	92,544	183,032	178,294	8.04	-2.59
REGION NOT SPECIFIED		58,447	64,054	109,732	36,981	31,111	1.40	-15.87
Not Specified		58,447	64,054	109,732	36,981	31,111	1.40	-15.87
Other countries of the World		58,447	64,054	109,732	36,981	31,111	1.40	-15.87

Source: World Tourism Organization (UNWTO)

DENMARK

4. Arrivals of non-resident tourists in all types of accommodation establishments, by country of residence

		2002	2003	2004	2005	2006	Market share 06	% Change 06-05
TOTAL	(*)	3,435,563	3,473,808	4,421,442	4,698,668	4,716,257	100.00	0.37
AMERICAS		79,513	78,382	126,276	147,289	185,668	3.94	26.06
North America		73,236	73,103	116,861	133,854	154,936	3.29	15.75
Canada		7,654	7,089	6,397	10,962	13,291	0.28	21.25
United States		65,582	66,014	110,464	122,892	141,645	3.00	15.26
Other Americas		6,277	5,279	9,415	13,435	30,732	0.65	128.75
Other countries of the Americas		6,277	5,279	9,415	13,435	30,732	0.65	128.75
EAST ASIA AND THE PACIFIC		49,299	46,850	82,957	110,098	90,776	1.92	-17.55
North-East Asia		29,585	28,317	39,631	39,963	36,318	0.77	-9.12
Japan		29,585	28,317	39,631	39,963	36,318	0.77	-9.12
South-East Asia		19,714	18,533	43,326	70,135	54,458	1.15	-22.35
All countries of South-East Asia		19,714	18,533	43,326	70,135	54,458	1.15	-22.35
EUROPE		3,220,983	3,253,489	4,065,043	4,357,752	4,364,147	92.53	0.15
Central/Eastern Europe		12,846	9,958	29,356	30,492	37,222	0.79	22.07
Poland		12,846	9,958	29,356	30,492	37,222	0.79	22.07
Northern Europe		1,351,737	1,363,948	1,771,714	1,814,254	1,755,326	37.22	-3.25
Finland		37,783	37,359	49,575	65,414	61,736	1.31	-5.62
Norway		504,907	526,611	643,273	669,356	667,775	14.16	-0.24
Sweden		681,547	681,520	854,915	846,014	813,210	17.24	-3.88
United Kingdom		127,500	118,458	223,951	233,470	212,605	4.51	-8.94
Southern Europe		52,761	53,187	86,750	105,930	111,096	2.36	4.88
Italy		36,726	37,503	58,631	55,814	54,988	1.17	-1.48
Spain		16,035	15,684	28,119	50,116	56,108	1.19	11.96
Western Europe		1,733,692	1,757,845	2,072,364	2,206,163	2,258,869	47.90	2.39
Austria		5,175	4,703	8,094	13,376	11,399	0.24	-14.78
France		27,143	25,819	37,894	50,308	50,943	1.08	1.26
Germany		1,557,773	1,574,028	1,751,172	1,857,014	1,889,856	40.07	1.77
Netherlands		112,679	125,822	227,215	211,973	229,942	4.88	8.48
Switzerland		16,868	14,937	25,763	36,039	40,133	0.85	11.36
Belgium / Luxembourg		14,054	12,536	22,226	37,453	36,596	0.78	-2.29
Other Europe		69,947	68,551	104,859	200,913	201,634	4.28	0.36
Other countries of Europe		69,947	68,551	104,859	200,913	201,634	4.28	0.36
REGION NOT SPECIFIED		85,768	95,087	147,166	83,529	75,666	1.60	-9.41
Not Specified		85,768	95,087	147,166	83,529	75,666	1.60	-9.41
Other countries of the World		85,768	95,087	147,166	83,529	75,666	1.60	-9.41

Source: World Tourism Organization (UNWTO)

DENMARK

5. Overnight stays of non-resident tourists in hotels and similar establishments, by country of residence

		2002	2003	2004	2005	2006	Market share 06	% Change 06-05
TOTAL	(*)	4,734,635	4,729,569	4,984,255	5,014,913	4,954,783	100.00	-1.20
AMERICAS		365,045	360,257	390,947	427,769	535,645	10.81	25.22
North America		337,027	336,772	367,115	395,090	437,035	8.82	10.62
Canada		33,560	30,617	23,580	25,036	30,181	0.61	20.55
United States		303,467	306,155	343,535	370,054	406,854	8.21	9.94
Other Americas		28,018	23,485	23,832	32,679	98,610	1.99	201.75
Other countries of the Americas		28,018	23,485	23,832	32,679	98,610	1.99	201.75
EAST ASIA AND THE PACIFIC		189,176	179,169	198,077	267,201	226,085	4.56	-15.39
North-East Asia		99,458	95,034	97,228	100,010	89,455	1.81	-10.55
Japan		99,458	95,034	97,228	100,010	89,455	1.81	-10.55
South-East Asia		89,718	84,135	100,849	167,191	136,630	2.76	-18.28
All countries of South-East Asia		89,718	84,135	100,849	167,191	136,630	2.76	-18.28
EUROPE		3,897,966	3,879,870	4,036,366	4,215,274	4,102,735	82.80	-2.67
Central/Eastern Europe		37,611	27,439	24,542	37,790	42,477	0.86	12.40
Poland		37,611	27,439	24,542	37,790	42,477	0.86	12.40
Northern Europe		2,542,344	2,580,276	2,672,863	2,562,482	2,472,263	49.90	-3.52
Finland		96,314	94,669	100,953	108,959	104,423	2.11	-4.16
Norway		897,116	952,555	945,196	909,367	872,437	17.61	-4.06
Sweden		1,060,400	1,080,090	1,088,186	1,001,152	967,613	19.53	-3.35
United Kingdom		488,514	452,962	538,528	543,004	527,790	10.65	-2.80
Southern Europe		214,502	214,947	244,071	267,886	266,065	5.37	-0.68
Italy		144,733	146,221	162,233	158,639	158,451	3.20	-0.12
Spain		69,769	68,726	81,838	109,247	107,614	2.17	-1.49
Western Europe		831,919	792,052	819,523	889,196	874,665	17.65	-1.63
Austria		18,336	15,538	18,163	24,430	22,457	0.45	-8.08
France		94,482	85,666	88,539	100,706	105,170	2.12	4.43
Germany		470,611	458,300	476,753	501,142	461,960	9.32	-7.82
Netherlands		137,489	139,869	146,811	156,277	176,197	3.56	12.75
Switzerland		62,361	52,667	50,801	60,264	62,426	1.26	3.59
Belgium / Luxembourg		48,640	40,012	38,456	46,377	46,455	0.94	0.17
Other Europe		271,590	265,156	275,367	457,920	447,265	9.03	-2.33
Other countries of Europe		271,590	265,156	275,367	457,920	447,265	9.03	-2.33
REGION NOT SPECIFIED		282,448	310,273	358,865	104,669	90,318	1.82	-13.71
Not Specified		282,448	310,273	358,865	104,669	90,318	1.82	-13.71
Other countries of the World		282,448	310,273	358,865	104,669	90,318	1.82	-13.71

Source: World Tourism Organization (UNWTO)

DENMARK

6. Overnight stays of non-resident tourists in all types of accommodation establishments, by country of residence

	2002	2003	2004	2005	2006	Market share 06	% Change 06-05
TOTAL (*)	25,662,666	26,152,075	24,925,387	23,012,024	23,370,962	100.00	1.56
AMERICAS	384,150	378,243	406,394	447,013	554,047	2.37	23.94
North America	354,079	352,879	381,103	412,030	455,437	1.95	10.53
Canada	37,441	35,006	26,741	28,281	34,016	0.15	20.28
United States	316,638	317,873	354,362	383,749	421,421	1.80	9.82
Other Americas	30,071	25,364	25,291	34,983	98,610	0.42	181.88
Other countries of the Americas	30,071	25,364	25,291	34,983	98,610	0.42	181.88
EAST ASIA AND THE PACIFIC	194,875	185,193	203,891	278,840	238,695	1.02	-14.40
North-East Asia	103,026	98,654	100,927	105,420	94,686	0.41	-10.18
Japan	103,026	98,654	100,927	105,420	94,686	0.41	-10.18
South-East Asia	91,849	86,539	102,964	173,420	144,009	0.62	-16.96
All countries of South-East Asia	91,849	86,539	102,964	173,420	144,009	0.62	-16.96
EUROPE	24,549,075	24,981,908	23,625,146	21,926,472	22,232,708	95.13	1.40
Central/Eastern Europe	82,529	65,874	68,615	93,612	115,737	0.50	23.63
Poland	82,529	65,874	68,615	93,612	115,737	0.50	23.63
Northern Europe	5,760,744	5,817,821	5,879,053	5,493,133	5,257,574	22.50	-4.29
Finland	143,962	144,197	140,274	148,183	143,126	0.61	-3.41
Norway	2,572,510	2,673,442	2,629,338	2,469,966	2,396,029	10.25	-2.99
Sweden	2,499,720	2,493,529	2,518,825	2,273,225	2,120,846	9.07	-6.70
United Kingdom	544,552	506,653	590,616	601,759	597,573	2.56	-0.70
Southern Europe	275,046	279,603	307,951	338,750	331,226	1.42	-2.22
Italy	193,738	200,423	212,314	212,155	204,760	0.88	-3.49
Spain	81,308	79,180	95,637	126,595	126,466	0.54	-0.10
Western Europe	18,095,141	18,487,925	17,016,957	15,454,855	15,962,683	68.30	3.29
Austria	31,904	30,454	33,308	40,887	37,391	0.16	-8.55
France	127,503	129,169	129,046	139,213	146,839	0.63	5.48
Germany	16,718,819	16,967,211	15,427,519	13,906,248	14,347,502	61.39	3.17
Netherlands	1,030,420	1,188,884	1,267,409	1,188,366	1,243,037	5.32	4.60
Switzerland	103,477	94,386	88,091	98,427	104,738	0.45	6.41
Belgium / Luxembourg	83,018	77,821	71,584	81,714	83,176	0.36	1.79
Other Europe	335,615	330,685	352,570	546,122	565,488	2.42	3.55
Other countries of Europe	335,615	330,685	352,570	546,122	565,488	2.42	3.55
REGION NOT SPECIFIED	534,566	606,731	689,956	359,699	345,512	1.48	-3.94
Not Specified	534,566	606,731	689,956	359,699	345,512	1.48	-3.94
Other countries of the World	534,566	606,731	689,956	359,699	345,512	1.48	-3.94

Source: World Tourism Organization (UNWTO)

DOMINICA

1. Arrivals of non-resident tourists at national borders, by country of residence

	2002	2003	2004	2005	2006	Market share 06	% Change 06-05
TOTAL	69,193	73,190	80,087	79,257	84,041	100.00	6.04
AMERICAS	58,153	61,536	69,115	68,164	71,832	85.47	5.38
Caribbean	39,896	43,196	48,967	46,752	46,205	54.98	-1.17
Antigua and Barbuda	5,326	5,134	4,978	5,264	5,495	6.54	4.39
Bahamas	82	70	106	93	107	0.13	15.05
Barbados	2,387	2,167	2,429	2,298	2,963	3.53	28.94
Bermuda	40	36	47	51	51	0.06	
British Virgin Islands	1,292	1,054	1,091	1,244	1,722	2.05	38.42
Cayman Islands	11	17	15	20	11	0.01	-45.00
Cuba	165	96	104	222	242	0.29	9.01
Dominican Republic	588	798	485	1,065	160	0.19	-84.98
Grenada	415	433	366	433	596	0.71	37.64
Guadeloupe	11,112	11,757	13,515	12,342	12,977	15.44	5.15
Haiti	1,112	4,475	7,391	5,808	462	0.55	-92.05
Jamaica	466	481	472	507	607	0.72	19.72
Martinique	5,823	5,938	6,905	6,175	6,498	7.73	5.23
Montserrat	229	158	204	220	201	0.24	-8.64
Aruba	50	59	34	54	58	0.07	7.41
Bonaire	5	4	1	1	2		100.00
Curacao	112	92	83	96	82	0.10	-14.58
Puerto Rico	362	312	341	243	247	0.29	1.65
Saint Kitts and Nevis	834	664	617	601	726	0.86	20.80
Anguilla	208	135	128	107	142	0.17	32.71
Saint Lucia	2,201	2,352	2,471	2,290	2,973	3.54	29.83
Saint Maarten	2,103	1,861	1,987	2,126	2,558	3.04	20.32
Saint Vincent and the Grenadines	554	574	492	608	908	1.08	49.34
Trinidad and Tobago	1,463	1,550	1,510	1,527	2,224	2.65	45.65
Turks and Caicos Islands	14	12	7	4	14	0.02	250.00
United States Virgin Islands	2,919	2,948	3,152	3,345	4,157	4.95	24.28
Other countries of the Caribbean	23	19	36	8	22	0.03	175.00
Central America	69	124	72	73	91	0.11	24.66
Belize	20	29	18	22	24	0.03	9.09
Other countries of Central America	49	95	54	51	67	0.08	31.37
North America	17,546	17,630	19,342	20,496	24,602	29.27	20.03
Canada	2,039	1,968	1,724	1,977	2,552	3.04	29.08
Mexico	43	24	44	27	39	0.05	44.44
United States	15,464	15,638	17,574	18,492	22,011	26.19	19.03
South America	642	586	734	843	934	1.11	10.79
Argentina	14	17	20	18	30	0.04	66.67
Brazil	36	33	40	41	28	0.03	-31.71
Colombia	17	13	18	53	31	0.04	-41.51
French Guiana		5	2	5	6	0.01	20.00
Guyana	352	308	358	321	318	0.38	-0.93
Suriname	21	28	24	31	32	0.04	3.23
Venezuela	161	168	236	337	444	0.53	31.75
Other countries of South America	41	14	36	37	45	0.05	21.62
EAST ASIA AND THE PACIFIC	455	486	387	529	495	0.59	-6.43
North-East Asia	372	380	322	455	426	0.51	-6.37
China	165	182	149	307	266	0.32	-13.36
Taiwan (Province of China)	50	64	27	23	24	0.03	4.35
Japan	157	134	146	125	136	0.16	8.80
Australasia	83	106	65	74	69	0.08	-6.76

DOMINICA

1. Arrivals of non-resident tourists at national borders, by country of residence

	2002	2003	2004	2005	2006	Market share 06	% Change 06-05
Australia	83	106	65	74	69	0.08	-6.76
EUROPE	**10,131**	**10,772**	**10,208**	**10,258**	**11,303**	**13.45**	**10.19**
Northern Europe	**5,972**	**6,400**	**6,350**	**6,471**	**6,932**	**8.25**	**7.12**
Denmark	49	62	72	90	85	0.10	-5.56
Ireland	66	64	62	69	86	0.10	24.64
Norway	32	51	35	25	30	0.04	20.00
Sweden	173	189	166	170	228	0.27	34.12
United Kingdom	5,652	6,034	6,015	6,117	6,503	7.74	6.31
Southern Europe	**215**	**229**	**191**	**208**	**192**	**0.23**	**-7.69**
Greece	29	4	6	5	5	0.01	
Italy	131	177	117	144	101	0.12	-29.86
Portugal	13	7	7	8	9	0.01	12.50
Spain	42	41	61	51	77	0.09	50.98
Western Europe	**3,738**	**3,960**	**3,426**	**3,413**	**3,836**	**4.56**	**12.39**
Austria	106	100	168	85	97	0.12	14.12
Belgium	192	189	183	166	193	0.23	16.27
France	2,353	2,532	1,866	1,853	2,239	2.66	20.83
Germany	572	639	751	727	775	0.92	6.60
Netherlands	246	200	186	312	288	0.34	-7.69
Switzerland	269	300	272	270	244	0.29	-9.63
Other Europe	**206**	**183**	**241**	**166**	**343**	**0.41**	**106.63**
Other countries of Europe	206	183	241	166	343	0.41	106.63
REGION NOT SPECIFIED	**454**	**396**	**377**	**306**	**411**	**0.49**	**34.31**
Not Specified	**454**	**396**	**377**	**306**	**411**	**0.49**	**34.31**
Other countries of the World	454	396	377	306	411	0.49	34.31

Source: World Tourism Organization (UNWTO)

DOMINICAN REPUBLIC

1. Arrivals of non-resident tourists at national borders, by country of residence

		2002	2003	2004	2005	2006	Market share 06	% Change 06-05
TOTAL	(*)	2,793,209	3,282,138	3,450,180	3,690,692	3,965,055	100.00	7.43
AMERICAS		1,260,558	1,503,896	1,597,342	1,711,341	1,947,796	49.12	13.82
Caribbean		113,726	148,402	132,987	145,445	170,713	4.31	17.37
Bahamas		413	492	585	649	1,265	0.03	94.92
Cuba		3,724	3,004	3,047	3,394	4,830	0.12	42.31
Haiti		1,057	3,952	4,515	7,081	6,660	0.17	-5.95
Jamaica		1,639	1,339	874	1,305	1,713	0.04	31.26
Curacao		3,283	3,135	2,777	2,768	3,478	0.09	25.65
Puerto Rico		102,742	134,864	119,535	128,057	149,681	3.78	16.89
Trinidad and Tobago		846	859	966	1,105	1,604	0.04	45.16
Turks and Caicos Islands		22	757	688	1,086	1,482	0.04	36.46
Central America		14,724	13,874	11,015	14,024	18,623	0.47	32.79
Costa Rica		4,418	3,694	2,751	3,530	4,899	0.12	38.78
El Salvador		1,777	1,407	1,353	1,775	1,923	0.05	8.34
Guatemala		2,656	3,538	2,411	3,144	3,797	0.10	20.77
Honduras		580	1,004	771	1,497	1,356	0.03	-9.42
Nicaragua		640	486	500	498	953	0.02	91.37
Panama		4,653	3,745	3,229	3,580	5,695	0.14	59.08
North America		992,660	1,240,221	1,357,022	1,433,111	1,626,032	41.01	13.46
Canada		313,920	414,463	451,983	429,006	512,806	12.93	19.53
Mexico		19,611	13,129	13,275	17,171	21,000	0.53	22.30
United States		659,129	812,629	891,764	986,934	1,092,226	27.55	10.67
South America		131,337	91,574	88,452	108,260	119,158	3.01	10.07
Argentina		13,155	9,331	7,779	12,349	12,367	0.31	0.15
Bolivia		696	403	821	407	962	0.02	136.36
Brazil		3,689	4,797	4,543	6,741	9,033	0.23	34.00
Chile		17,387	16,663	17,337	18,187	19,253	0.49	5.86
Colombia		36,858	22,676	20,338	21,739	21,068	0.53	-3.09
Ecuador		4,800	3,843	3,558	5,563	9,807	0.25	76.29
Peru		12,457	8,520	8,273	9,081	8,598	0.22	-5.32
Uruguay		1,764	776	411	900	2,232	0.06	148.00
Venezuela		40,131	24,070	24,810	32,705	34,353	0.87	5.04
Other countries of South America		400	495	582	588	1,485	0.04	152.55
Other Americas		8,111	9,825	7,866	10,501	13,270	0.33	26.37
Other countries of the Americas		8,111	9,825	7,866	10,501	13,270	0.33	26.37
EAST ASIA AND THE PACIFIC		3,106	3,417	3,511	4,280	4,631	0.12	8.20
North-East Asia		2,535	2,793	2,756	2,968	3,148	0.08	6.06
China		336	255	249	199	262	0.01	31.66
Taiwan (Province of China)		502	268	345	541	481	0.01	-11.09
Japan		1,294	1,605	1,684	1,520	1,611	0.04	5.99
Korea, Republic of		403	665	478	708	794	0.02	12.15
Australasia		201	395	557	832	780	0.02	-6.25
Australia		201	395	557	832	780	0.02	-6.25
Other East Asia and the Pacific		370	229	198	480	703	0.02	46.46
Other countries of Asia		370	229	198	480	703	0.02	46.46
EUROPE		1,031,456	1,250,608	1,271,299	1,371,663	1,388,757	35.02	1.25
Central/Eastern Europe		7,283	4,809	9,437	17,380	23,568	0.59	35.60
Bulgaria		189	362	172	170	290	0.01	70.59
Hungary		525	353	899	509	341	0.01	-33.01
Poland		2,557	1,574	1,437	4,732	9,147	0.23	93.30

DOMINICAN REPUBLIC

1. Arrivals of non-resident tourists at national borders, by country of residence

	2002	2003	2004	2005	2006	Market share 06	% Change 06-05
Romania	265	10	22	158	154		-2.53
Russian Federation	3,747	2,510	6,898	11,521	12,935	0.33	12.27
Ukraine			9	290	701	0.02	141.72
Northern Europe	**159,643**	**178,762**	**210,296**	**242,815**	**251,355**	**6.34**	**3.52**
Denmark	915	504	461	732	1,232	0.03	68.31
Finland	3,449	1,144	4,216	6,568	3,653	0.09	-44.38
Ireland	1,815	1,977	123	3,917	1,001	0.03	-74.44
Norway	2,155	1,160	953	1,076	1,185	0.03	10.13
Sweden	6,488	3,502	8,002	8,825	4,956	0.12	-43.84
United Kingdom	144,821	170,475	196,541	221,697	239,328	6.04	7.95
Southern Europe	**268,861**	**369,435**	**378,235**	**420,068**	**440,057**	**11.10**	**4.76**
Greece	491	586	426	538	652	0.02	21.19
Italy	111,418	131,934	121,700	129,926	138,590	3.50	6.67
Portugal	22,854	34,037	29,208	34,780	28,592	0.72	-17.79
Spain	134,098	202,878	226,901	254,824	272,223	6.87	6.83
Western Europe	**591,070**	**694,408**	**671,207**	**687,057**	**668,874**	**16.87**	**-2.65**
Austria	9,819	10,066	10,471	13,101	8,942	0.23	-31.75
Belgium	35,671	51,024	41,198	43,371	45,315	1.14	4.48
France	239,311	313,098	296,164	303,720	299,168	7.55	-1.50
Germany	239,431	243,533	233,004	233,215	223,715	5.64	-4.07
Luxembourg	375	171	242	361	160		-55.68
Netherlands	29,531	35,333	51,273	59,469	60,352	1.52	1.48
Switzerland	36,932	41,183	38,855	33,820	31,222	0.79	-7.68
East Mediterranean Europe	**475**	**823**	**918**	**1,297**	**1,103**	**0.03**	**-14.96**
Israel	475	823	918	1,297	1,103	0.03	-14.96
Other Europe	**4,124**	**2,371**	**1,206**	**3,046**	**3,800**	**0.10**	**24.75**
Other countries of Europe	4,124	2,371	1,206	3,046	3,800	0.10	24.75
SOUTH ASIA	**75**	**236**	**249**	**337**	**279**	**0.01**	**-17.21**
South Asia	**75**	**236**	**249**	**337**	**279**	**0.01**	**-17.21**
India	75	236	249	337	279	0.01	-17.21
REGION NOT SPECIFIED	**498,014**	**523,981**	**577,779**	**603,071**	**623,592**	**15.73**	**3.40**
Not Specified	**498,014**	**523,981**	**577,779**	**603,071**	**623,592**	**15.73**	**3.40**
Other countries of the World	435	393	279	626	643	0.02	2.72
Nationals Residing Abroad	497,579	523,588	577,500	602,445	622,949	15.71	3.40

Source: World Tourism Organization (UNWTO)

ECUADOR

2. Arrivals of non-resident visitors at national borders, by nationality

	2002	2003	2004	2005	2006	Market share 06	% Change 06-05
TOTAL (*)	682,962	760,776	818,927	859,888	840,555	100.00	-2.25
AFRICA	2,107	1,720	2,191	1,919	1,240	0.15	-35.38
Other Africa	2,107	1,720	2,191	1,919	1,240	0.15	-35.38
All countries of Africa	2,107	1,720	2,191	1,919	1,240	0.15	-35.38
AMERICAS	549,927	617,088	662,019	690,743	642,075	76.39	-7.05
Caribbean	3,948	4,075	5,097	5,301	5,483	0.65	3.43
All countries of the Caribbean	3,948	4,075	5,097	5,301	5,483	0.65	3.43
Central America	11,048	10,976	12,079	12,010	10,858	1.29	-9.59
Costa Rica	2,955	2,753	3,244	2,986	2,723	0.32	-8.81
Panama	4,403	4,495	4,748	4,813	3,731	0.44	-22.48
Other countries of Central America	3,690	3,728	4,087	4,211	4,404	0.52	4.58
North America	172,025	182,664	208,169	235,314	231,201	27.51	-1.75
Canada	12,774	13,370	15,308	16,428	17,059	2.03	3.84
Mexico	8,669	9,443	10,747	12,047	9,065	1.08	-24.75
United States	150,582	159,851	182,114	206,839	205,077	24.40	-0.85
South America	362,900	419,359	436,668	438,116	394,531	46.94	-9.95
Argentina	14,265	15,395	15,354	16,720	16,666	1.98	-0.32
Bolivia	3,532	3,343	4,020	3,730	3,579	0.43	-4.05
Brazil	7,718	8,305	10,295	11,255	11,892	1.41	5.66
Chile	18,571	16,656	17,541	18,228	18,341	2.18	0.62
Colombia	197,080	205,353	179,434	177,700	179,487	21.35	1.01
Peru	106,777	153,520	191,303	191,048	145,410	17.30	-23.89
Uruguay	1,698	1,893	2,212	2,313	2,185	0.26	-5.53
Venezuela	12,460	14,084	15,544	16,276	16,178	1.92	-0.60
Other countries of South America	799	810	965	846	793	0.09	-6.26
Other Americas	6	14	6	2	2		
Other countries of the Americas	6	14	6	2	2		
EAST ASIA AND THE PACIFIC	17,493	17,831	21,195	20,222	19,488	2.32	-3.63
North-East Asia	4,098	3,979	4,690	4,271	4,002	0.48	-6.30
Japan	4,098	3,979	4,690	4,271	4,002	0.48	-6.30
Australasia	4,110	4,487	5,778	6,643	6,396	0.76	-3.72
Australia	3,249	3,637	4,654	5,549	5,206	0.62	-6.18
New Zealand	861	850	1,124	1,094	1,190	0.14	8.78
Other East Asia and the Pacific	9,285	9,365	10,727	9,308	9,090	1.08	-2.34
Other countries of Asia	9,192	9,264	10,643	9,224	9,044	1.08	-1.95
Other countries of Oceania	93	101	84	84	46	0.01	-45.24
EUROPE	113,435	124,137	133,495	146,537	144,682	17.21	-1.27
Northern Europe	17,844	19,554	20,867	22,822	22,008	2.62	-3.57
United Kingdom	17,844	19,554	20,867	22,822	22,008	2.62	-3.57
Southern Europe	26,881	30,506	38,413	44,234	47,940	5.70	8.38
Italy	9,938	10,395	11,744	12,278	11,438	1.36	-6.84
Spain	16,943	20,111	26,669	31,956	36,502	4.34	14.23
Western Europe	46,476	49,836	49,544	53,629	48,416	5.76	-9.72
France	12,671	13,490	13,336	15,363	14,181	1.69	-7.69
Germany	17,541	18,598	19,451	20,809	18,586	2.21	-10.68
Netherlands	9,106	10,158	8,766	9,115	7,875	0.94	-13.60
Switzerland	7,158	7,590	7,991	8,342	7,774	0.92	-6.81
East Mediterranean Europe	3,564	3,335	3,107	2,739	3,098	0.37	13.11

ECUADOR

2. Arrivals of non-resident visitors at national borders, by nationality

	2002	2003	2004	2005	2006	Market share 06	% Change 06-05
Israel	3,564	3,335	3,107	2,739	3,098	0.37	13.11
Other Europe	**18,670**	**20,906**	**21,564**	**23,113**	**23,220**	**2.76**	**0.46**
Other countries of Europe	18,670	20,906	21,564	23,113	23,220	2.76	0.46
REGION NOT SPECIFIED			**27**	**467**	**33,070**	**3.93**	**6,981.37**
Not Specified			**27**	**467**	**33,070**	**3.93**	**6,981.37**
Other countries of the World			27	467	33,070	3.93	6,981.37

Source: World Tourism Organization (UNWTO)

EGYPT

2. Arrivals of non-resident visitors at national borders, by nationality

		2002	2003	2004	2005	2006	Market share 06	% Change 06-05
TOTAL	(*)	5,191,678	6,044,160	8,103,609	8,607,807	9,082,777	100.00	5.52
AFRICA		161,497	183,035	244,662	263,847	301,866	3.32	14.41
East Africa		15,928	15,634	18,876	22,215	22,821	0.25	2.73
Burundi		119	182	308	300	582	0.01	94.00
Comoros		1,146	1,454	1,658	1,449	1,540	0.02	6.28
Ethiopia		3,496	3,435	3,762	4,115	4,269	0.05	3.74
Eritrea		1,634	1,729	2,117	3,002	3,270	0.04	8.93
Djibouti		762	806	903	1,135	1,236	0.01	8.90
Kenya		2,918	2,569	3,983	4,747	4,822	0.05	1.58
Malawi		99	139	179	217	236		8.76
Mauritius		371	536	594	643	699	0.01	8.71
Mozambique		187	171	235	209	285		36.36
Rwanda		105	228	322	386	467	0.01	20.98
Seychelles		42	47	78	79	129		63.29
Somalia		2,501	862	1,123	1,901	1,929	0.02	1.47
Zimbabwe		623	1,394	1,166	905			
Uganda		793	898	1,090	1,771	1,628	0.02	-8.07
United Republic of Tanzania		915	832	1,020	1,027	1,206	0.01	17.43
Zambia		217	352	338	329	523	0.01	58.97
Central Africa		1,611	2,242	2,911	3,160	5,123	0.06	62.12
Angola		175	307	351	408	1,010	0.01	147.55
Cameroon		375	591	717	814	1,201	0.01	47.54
Central African Republic		84	74					
Chad		477	514	754	821	1,391	0.02	69.43
Congo		336	572	827	771	910	0.01	18.03
Democratic Republic of the Congo		68	93	97	71	297		318.31
Gabon		96	82	165	275	314		14.18
Sao Tome and Principe			9					
North Africa		110,075	129,213	173,314	186,032	209,805	2.31	12.78
Algeria		14,764	17,918	20,809	20,682	26,321	0.29	27.27
Morocco		18,075	17,215	20,585	22,487	22,702	0.25	0.96
Sudan		55,587	70,021	102,585	113,777	127,422	1.40	11.99
Tunisia		21,649	24,059	29,335	29,086	33,360	0.37	14.69
Southern Africa		16,747	15,224	19,631	22,732	25,624	0.28	12.72
Lesotho		47	50	45	58	71		22.41
Namibia		92	117	169	196	228		16.33
South Africa		16,580	15,007	19,225	22,423	25,237	0.28	12.55
Swaziland		28	50	192	55	88		60.00
West Africa		16,387	20,063	28,530	28,697	35,800	0.39	24.75
Benin		98	170	380	303	321		5.94
Gambia		120	111	151	201	237		17.91
Ghana		1,682	2,398	3,593	4,448	3,977	0.04	-10.59
Guinea		849	579	685	1,088	1,380	0.02	26.84
Cote D'Ivoire		601	675	967	687	1,166	0.01	69.72
Liberia		168	180	207	262	303		15.65
Mali		483	499	586	601	581	0.01	-3.33
Mauritania		653	627	712	725	771	0.01	6.34
Niger		140	176	230	306	345		12.75
Nigeria		10,578	13,611	19,676	18,599	24,840	0.27	33.56
Guinea-Bissau		23	48		104	69		-33.65
Senegal		799	748	981	974	1,224	0.01	25.67
Sierra Leone		104	111	154	215	227		5.58
Togo		89	130	208	184	359		95.11

EGYPT

2. Arrivals of non-resident visitors at national borders, by nationality

	2002	2003	2004	2005	2006	Market share 06	% Change 06-05
Other Africa	749	659	1,400	1,011	2,693	0.03	166.37
Other countries of Africa	749	659	1,400	1,011	2,693	0.03	166.37
AMERICAS	171,458	187,828	257,418	297,675	340,530	3.75	14.40
Caribbean	983	1,215	1,780	2,196	2,668	0.03	21.49
Bahamas	9	23	45	44	74		68.18
Barbados	29	26	46	58	30		-48.28
Cuba	453	529	734	700	716	0.01	2.29
Dominica	215	288	461	762	1,035	0.01	35.83
Haiti	32	44	38	52	59		13.46
Jamaica	123	128	175	268	390		45.52
Trinidad and Tobago	122	177	281	312	364		16.67
Central America	1,301	2,043	2,409	3,884	3,730	0.04	-3.96
Costa Rica	227	238	438	604	637	0.01	5.46
El Salvador	122	152	240	315	257		-18.41
Guatemala	210	275	494	784	736	0.01	-6.12
Honduras	588	1,227	1,042	1,932	1,822	0.02	-5.69
Nicaragua	35	62	55	99	105		6.06
Panama	119	89	140	150	173		15.33
North America	155,991	168,570	228,374	259,931	299,079	3.29	15.06
Canada	32,128	36,056	48,259	52,152	58,948	0.65	13.03
Mexico	6,467	6,736	10,457	11,958	11,948	0.13	-0.08
United States	117,396	125,778	169,658	195,821	228,183	2.51	16.53
South America	12,804	15,564	24,458	31,171	34,610	0.38	11.03
Argentina	1,817	2,635	4,421	5,568	5,841	0.06	4.90
Bolivia	173	305	319	336	318		-5.36
Brazil	3,755	4,185	6,799	8,584	9,974	0.11	16.19
Chile	1,211	1,458	2,528	2,940	2,755	0.03	-6.29
Colombia	2,514	3,208	4,920	6,810	7,365	0.08	8.15
Ecuador	807	884	1,078	1,461	1,704	0.02	16.63
Guyana	8		49	40	61		52.50
Paraguay	79	105	119	123	123		
Peru	692	940	1,724	2,534	3,062	0.03	20.84
Suriname	52	54	57	73	61		-16.44
Uruguay	825	857	845	920	1,254	0.01	36.30
Venezuela	871	933	1,599	1,782	2,092	0.02	17.40
Other Americas	379	436	397	493	443		-10.14
Other countries of the Americas	379	436	397	493	443		-10.14
EAST ASIA AND THE PACIFIC	213,771	226,756	296,189	411,048	389,304	4.29	-5.29
North-East Asia	109,844	119,221	139,848	178,944	196,571	2.16	9.85
China	21,801	21,381	30,363	35,327	51,371	0.57	45.42
Taiwan (Province of China)	6,742	9,710					
Japan	54,043	60,860	70,597	74,446	87,939	0.97	18.12
Korea, Republic of	27,043	27,096	38,624	68,912	56,976	0.63	-17.32
Mongolia	215	174	264	259	285		10.04
South-East Asia	68,379	71,682	85,822	98,870	113,616	1.25	14.91
Cambodia	15	36	31	46	64		39.13
Indonesia	16,002	18,477	23,172	27,539	28,824	0.32	4.67
Malaysia	14,128	12,373	17,081	16,050	16,418	0.18	2.29
Philippines	31,463	32,456	31,945	39,537	50,440	0.56	27.58
Singapore	2,373	2,821	5,126	5,508	5,063	0.06	-8.08
Viet Nam	408	945	938	927			
Thailand	3,990	4,574	7,529	9,263	12,807	0.14	38.26

214

EGYPT

2. Arrivals of non-resident visitors at national borders, by nationality

	2002	2003	2004	2005	2006	Market share 06	% Change 06-05
Australasia	33,515	31,874	47,000	54,902	55,205	0.61	0.55
Australia	27,572	26,079	38,523	45,744	45,438	0.50	-0.67
New Zealand	5,943	5,795	8,477	9,158	9,767	0.11	6.65
Polynesia	13	57	22	39			
Samoa	13	57	22	39			
Other East Asia and the Pacific	2,020	3,922	23,497	78,293	23,912	0.26	-69.46
Other countries of Asia	2,020	3,922	23,497	78,293	23,912	0.26	-69.46
EUROPE	3,583,791	4,203,687	5,919,575	6,047,194	6,259,732	68.92	3.51
Central/Eastern Europe	578,244	792,412	1,242,524	1,228,453	1,477,389	16.27	20.26
Azerbaijan	1,135	1,199	2,744	1,970	1,571	0.02	-20.25
Armenia	714	977	1,650	1,519	1,871	0.02	23.17
Bulgaria	8,943	9,385	8,223	8,877	11,890	0.13	33.94
Czech Republic/Slovakia	64,416	96,840	198,286	176,357	164,217	1.81	-6.88
Estonia	5,256	8,734	18,849	24,559	26,748	0.29	8.91
Georgia	1,153	1,431	1,833	2,456	2,197	0.02	-10.55
Hungary	24,296	36,513	51,775	49,389	39,188	0.43	-20.65
Kazakhstan	2,793	3,055	4,453	6,567	8,537	0.09	30.00
Poland	72,468	120,158	145,414	153,729	197,469	2.17	28.45
Romania	13,628	15,695	22,761	24,250	24,418	0.27	0.69
Russian Federation	382,536	497,465	785,419	777,665	998,149	10.99	28.35
Uzbekistan	906	960	1,117	1,115	1,134	0.01	1.70
Northern Europe	489,828	517,562	801,718	1,173,594	1,264,969	13.93	7.79
Denmark	43,058	46,491	68,437	92,132	43,458	0.48	-52.83
Finland	16,165	27,524	39,936	47,807	31,150	0.34	-34.84
Iceland	283	358	650	882	830	0.01	-5.90
Ireland	18,696	11,129	13,849	20,893	28,447	0.31	36.16
Norway	18,216	25,126	42,989	51,529	35,494	0.39	-31.12
Sweden	35,864	49,686	88,965	122,401	91,829	1.01	-24.98
United Kingdom	357,546	357,248	546,892	837,950	1,033,761	11.38	23.37
Southern Europe	850,195	991,858	1,257,436	1,071,345	1,018,850	11.22	-4.90
Albania	1,021	1,900	2,275				
Croatia	3,549	4,637	6,596	6,366	6,803	0.07	6.86
Greece	31,544	34,797	44,822	43,139	36,598	0.40	-15.16
Italy	701,210	795,903	1,010,444	823,199	786,130	8.66	-4.50
Malta	1,395	1,652	1,909	1,821	1,580	0.02	-13.23
Portugal	7,642	18,883	23,470	16,337	10,113	0.11	-38.10
Slovenia	4,209	8,089	12,138	11,172	10,795	0.12	-3.37
Spain	92,052	102,113	155,782	147,344	148,002	1.63	0.45
Serbia and Montenegro	7,573	23,884		21,967	18,829	0.21	-14.29
Western Europe	1,401,929	1,434,642	2,072,386	2,108,199	1,967,262	21.66	-6.69
Austria	88,024	105,173	150,698	137,135	142,875	1.57	4.19
Belgium	78,293	94,634	136,906	154,414	148,624	1.64	-3.75
France	280,230	310,791	465,174	495,164	372,449	4.10	-24.78
Germany	730,323	693,445	993,178	979,631	966,386	10.64	-1.35
Luxembourg	2,769	3,291	4,779	4,993	4,497	0.05	-9.93
Monaco	60	157	261	228			
Netherlands	117,282	131,537	188,504	205,877	210,585	2.32	2.29
Switzerland	104,948	95,614	132,886	130,757	121,846	1.34	-6.81
East Mediterranean Europe	187,796	365,534	445,851	305,771	223,034	2.46	-27.06
Cyprus	17,331	10,931	16,658	10,852	8,589	0.09	-20.85
Israel	146,741	309,994	389,897	256,346	171,051	1.88	-33.27
Turkey	23,724	44,609	39,296	38,573	43,394	0.48	12.50

EGYPT

2. Arrivals of non-resident visitors at national borders, by nationality

	2002	2003	2004	2005	2006	Market share 06	% Change 06-05
Other Europe	75,799	101,679	99,660	159,832	308,228	3.39	92.84
Other countries of Europe	75,799	101,679	99,660	159,832	308,228	3.39	92.84
MIDDLE EAST	1,012,613	1,188,994	1,317,883	1,511,285	1,706,423	18.79	12.91
Middle East	1,012,613	1,188,994	1,317,883	1,511,285	1,706,423	18.79	12.91
Bahrain	12,117	15,425	14,883	14,851	16,836	0.19	13.37
Palestine	155,471	187,785	172,166	217,365	228,881	2.52	5.30
Iraq	9,976	7,205	19,975	44,324	60,565	0.67	36.64
Jordan	86,835	98,716	118,108	125,673	146,973	1.62	16.95
Kuwait	71,977	79,235	89,825	99,363	115,956	1.28	16.70
Lebanon	40,638	41,729	45,087	47,903	55,128	0.61	15.08
Libyan Arab Jamahiriya	225,159	305,393	344,490	376,378	443,197	4.88	17.75
Oman	10,624	12,184	11,950	14,327	16,773	0.18	17.07
Qatar	11,528	12,806	15,035	17,642	22,307	0.25	26.44
Saudi Arabia	248,837	269,120	309,606	361,108	388,280	4.27	7.52
Syrian Arab Republic	74,317	81,267	86,484	93,010	98,030	1.08	5.40
United Arab Emirates	28,777	31,984	31,790	34,958	42,580	0.47	21.80
Yemen	36,357	46,145	58,484	64,383	70,917	0.78	10.15
SOUTH ASIA	46,110	51,042	63,310	73,000	80,501	0.89	10.28
South Asia	46,110	51,042	63,310	73,000	80,501	0.89	10.28
Afghanistan	211	305	2,024	447	420		-6.04
Bangladesh	1,393	1,659	1,729	2,071	2,593	0.03	25.21
Sri Lanka	3,778	3,348	4,572	4,870	4,700	0.05	-3.49
India	31,834	34,941	45,313	54,141	61,301	0.67	13.22
Iran, Islamic Republic of	876	747	881	929	749	0.01	-19.38
Maldives	169	149		162	162		
Nepal	427	312	492	725	1,109	0.01	52.97
Pakistan	7,422	9,581	8,299	9,655	9,467	0.10	-1.95
REGION NOT SPECIFIED	2,438	2,818	4,572	3,758	4,421	0.05	17.64
Not Specified	2,438	2,818	4,572	3,758	4,421	0.05	17.64
Other countries of the World	2,438	2,818	4,572	3,758	4,421	0.05	17.64

Source: World Tourism Organization (UNWTO)

EGYPT

5. Overnight stays of non-resident tourists in hotels and similar establishments, by nationality

	2002	2003	2004	2005	2006	Market share 06	% Change 06-05
TOTAL	32,663,941	53,129,907	81,667,918	85,171,917	89,304,053	100.00	4.85
AFRICA	957,477	1,854,276	2,903,607	3,271,880	3,869,249	4.33	18.26
East Africa	76,687	136,850	192,885	220,264	247,882	0.28	12.54
Burundi	1,035	1,145	2,427	2,852	6,523	0.01	128.72
Comoros	5,656	18,849	24,584	22,031	25,909	0.03	17.60
Ethiopia	18,382	29,258	39,642	46,236	52,063	0.06	12.60
Eritrea	9,209	15,733	25,429	34,165	32,611	0.04	-4.55
Djibouti	5,134	12,332	13,490	15,220	16,766	0.02	10.16
Kenya	12,640	16,003	28,368	35,383	30,503	0.03	-13.79
Malawi	721	1,209	1,304	1,345	1,948		44.83
Mauritius	1,652	4,470	6,479	6,511	6,395	0.01	-1.78
Mozambique	984	1,343	1,655	1,547	2,889		86.75
Rwanda	819	2,753	2,264	3,869	4,144		7.11
Seychelles	217	688	997	1,230	1,692		37.56
Somalia	6,779	13,953	20,295	21,065	28,985	0.03	37.60
Zimbabwe	3,365	5,553	6,918	7,456	8,293	0.01	11.23
Uganda	3,828	6,101	7,569	8,850	12,218	0.01	38.06
United Republic of Tanzania	4,286	5,056	7,855	9,366	11,185	0.01	19.42
Zambia	1,980	2,404	3,609	3,138	5,758	0.01	83.49
Central Africa	11,044	22,174	43,677	42,023	80,140	0.09	90.71
Angola	1,790	3,175	5,888	4,482	9,037	0.01	101.63
Cameroon	2,235	4,258	8,543	7,949	15,694	0.02	97.43
Chad	4,073	7,749	14,485	14,116	32,449	0.04	129.87
Congo	2,434	6,055	12,041	12,518	18,775	0.02	49.98
Gabon	512	937	2,720	2,958	4,185		41.48
North Africa	748,174	1,532,429	2,390,728	2,704,532	3,142,739	3.52	16.20
Algeria	72,287	143,272	192,620	184,832	234,121	0.26	26.67
Morocco	113,224	167,524	236,839	228,823	256,391	0.29	12.05
Sudan	462,560	1,053,349	1,694,715	2,033,291	2,350,148	2.63	15.58
Tunisia	100,103	168,284	266,554	257,586	302,079	0.34	17.27
Southern Africa	62,346	77,216	132,674	150,697	174,802	0.20	16.00
Lesotho	260	215	736	1,156	429		-62.89
Namibia	960	1,567	3,517	2,309	3,602		56.00
South Africa	60,966	74,886	127,302	147,080	170,290	0.19	15.78
Swaziland	160	548	1,119	152	481		216.45
West Africa	54,354	76,221	132,616	140,874	204,798	0.23	45.38
Ghana	5,396	6,153	10,947	13,303	17,627	0.02	32.50
Guinea	3,456	4,436	7,516	8,087	14,276	0.02	76.53
Cote D'Ivoire	2,618	6,361	7,174	7,462	14,640	0.02	96.19
Liberia	1,065	2,796	3,123	2,465	4,429		79.68
Mali	2,472	3,997	6,795	4,294	7,059	0.01	64.39
Mauritania	2,512	4,542	10,438	9,598	10,333	0.01	7.66
Niger	1,087	2,376	1,596	3,910	5,397	0.01	38.03
Nigeria	29,801	37,010	67,204	76,989	104,322	0.12	35.50
Senegal	4,882	6,227	12,453	10,668	19,679	0.02	84.47
Sierra Leone	598	1,298	2,568	1,695	1,898		11.98
Togo	467	1,025	2,802	2,403	5,138	0.01	113.82
Other Africa	4,872	9,386	11,027	13,490	18,888	0.02	40.01
Other countries of Africa	4,872	9,386	11,027	13,490	18,888	0.02	40.01
AMERICAS	1,196,807	2,179,705	3,467,555	3,820,742	4,324,854	4.84	13.19
Caribbean	4,340	7,926	13,712	14,835	17,236	0.02	16.18

EGYPT

5. Overnight stays of non-resident tourists in hotels and similar establishments, by nationality

	2002	2003	2004	2005	2006	Market share 06	% Change 06-05
Bahamas	58	201	191	125	446		256.80
Barbados	177	238	296	696	323		-53.59
Cuba	1,210	3,096	5,750	4,548	4,682	0.01	2.95
Dominica	880	1,785	3,304	3,114	4,275		37.28
Haiti	137	260	254	525	608		15.81
Jamaica	646	562	1,041	1,677	1,529		-8.83
Trinidad and Tobago	1,232	1,784	2,876	4,150	5,373	0.01	29.47
Central America	**4,784**	**8,531**	**14,363**	**17,435**	**18,577**	**0.02**	**6.55**
Costa Rica	1,108	1,204	3,731	5,223	5,108	0.01	-2.20
El Salvador	673	939	1,961	1,854	2,350		26.75
Guatemala	933	2,081	4,282	3,737	4,371		16.97
Honduras	1,212	2,475	2,469	4,219	4,385		3.93
Nicaragua	274	544	616	855	609		-28.77
Panama	584	1,288	1,304	1,547	1,754		13.38
North America	**1,120,322**	**2,045,082**	**3,214,368**	**3,512,293**	**3,985,817**	**4.46**	**13.48**
Canada	215,733	407,337	662,433	732,531	822,967	0.92	12.35
Mexico	40,239	47,482	93,232	103,477	103,839	0.12	0.35
United States	864,350	1,590,263	2,458,703	2,676,285	3,059,011	3.43	14.30
South America	**66,661**	**116,274**	**222,090**	**272,848**	**299,854**	**0.34**	**9.90**
Argentina	9,224	20,594	42,163	51,383	55,345	0.06	7.71
Bolivia	1,098	4,027	3,685	3,943	3,732		-5.35
Brazil	18,973	29,145	58,586	71,045	88,517	0.10	24.59
Chile	6,479	11,961	25,842	26,799	27,757	0.03	3.57
Colombia	11,097	21,622	38,241	57,606	55,686	0.06	-3.33
Ecuador	4,241	7,202	11,168	13,406	15,685	0.02	17.00
Paraguay	116	941	1,122	1,333	893		-33.01
Peru	4,122	6,303	13,762	15,898	16,226	0.02	2.06
Suriname	722	1,225	731	864	701		-18.87
Uruguay	4,562	5,550	10,573	8,850	12,439	0.01	40.55
Venezuela	6,027	7,704	16,217	21,721	22,873	0.03	5.30
Other Americas	**700**	**1,892**	**3,022**	**3,331**	**3,370**		**1.17**
Other countries of the Americas	700	1,892	3,022	3,331	3,370		1.17
EAST ASIA AND THE PACIFIC	**989,082**	**1,462,108**	**2,489,566**	**2,669,229**	**2,968,323**	**3.32**	**11.21**
North-East Asia	**479,914**	**658,192**	**988,612**	**1,067,893**	**1,291,378**	**1.45**	**20.93**
China	112,593	139,988	232,051	264,026	363,056	0.41	37.51
Taiwan (Province of China)	35,136	48,213	81,066	83,158	78,667	0.09	-5.40
Japan	249,418	355,316	486,921	493,030	573,424	0.64	16.31
Korea, Republic of	80,668	113,021	184,967	225,002	272,249	0.30	21.00
Mongolia	2,099	1,654	3,607	2,677	3,982		48.75
South-East Asia	**263,518**	**456,458**	**757,039**	**799,449**	**909,656**	**1.02**	**13.79**
Cambodia	142	79	133	397	1,414		256.17
Indonesia	85,447	171,804	281,449	277,092	310,117	0.35	11.92
Malaysia	62,791	82,558	134,521	136,990	132,037	0.15	-3.62
Philippines	92,573	157,600	240,389	278,844	349,434	0.39	25.32
Singapore	10,969	22,716	50,615	51,456	49,066	0.05	-4.64
Thailand	11,596	21,701	49,932	54,670	67,588	0.08	23.63
Australasia	**238,959**	**327,893**	**654,594**	**722,683**	**707,700**	**0.79**	**-2.07**
Australia	201,428	274,004	550,567	619,947	599,213	0.67	-3.34
New Zealand	37,531	53,889	104,027	102,736	108,487	0.12	5.60
Polynesia	**19**	**57**	**20**	**39**	**79**		**102.56**

EGYPT

5. Overnight stays of non-resident tourists in hotels and similar establishments, by nationality

	2002	2003	2004	2005	2006	Market share 06	% Change 06-05
Samoa	19	57	20	39	79		102.56
Other East Asia and the Pacific	**6,672**	**19,508**	**89,301**	**79,165**	**59,510**	**0.07**	**-24.83**
Other countries of Asia	6,672	19,508	89,301	79,165	59,510	0.07	-24.83
EUROPE	**22,942,555**	**33,764,887**	**54,311,491**	**55,269,360**	**55,716,325**	**62.39**	**0.81**
Central/Eastern Europe	**3,134,573**	**6,596,396**	**11,074,847**	**11,258,452**	**13,810,374**	**15.46**	**22.67**
Azerbaijan	3,331	6,694	20,920	17,386	14,877	0.02	-14.43
Armenia	2,358	8,340	17,933	16,495	20,436	0.02	23.89
Bulgaria	18,403	30,809	46,669	41,897	66,044	0.07	57.63
Czech Republic/Slovakia	332,022	916,664	1,924,327	1,595,189	1,435,403	1.61	-10.02
Estonia	18,855	46,465	139,048	175,185	210,325	0.24	20.06
Georgia	6,014	7,490	12,139	15,636	15,961	0.02	2.08
Hungary	134,887	266,027	449,589	405,562	313,998	0.35	-22.58
Kazakhstan	6,658	23,799	59,025	59,025	88,372	0.10	49.72
Poland	371,051	1,147,142	1,442,053	1,446,176	1,704,746	1.91	17.88
Romania	40,767	88,182	177,820	168,136	175,844	0.20	4.58
Russian Federation	2,200,227	4,054,784	6,785,324	7,317,765	9,764,368	10.93	33.43
Northern Europe	**2,874,142**	**3,954,588**	**7,297,269**	**10,658,241**	**11,314,200**	**12.67**	**6.15**
Denmark	248,256	348,103	653,569	878,637	430,595	0.48	-50.99
Finland	80,889	170,952	386,743	400,973	258,470	0.29	-35.54
Iceland	1,403	5,365	4,484	9,577	9,274	0.01	-3.16
Ireland	71,163	72,193	128,539	196,936	289,489	0.32	47.00
Norway	94,164	182,931	415,700	518,259	341,791	0.38	-34.05
Sweden	235,797	381,571	854,107	1,157,870	878,982	0.98	-24.09
United Kingdom	2,142,470	2,793,473	4,854,127	7,495,989	9,105,599	10.20	21.47
Southern Europe	**5,725,619**	**8,609,742**	**11,548,951**	**9,430,036**	**8,048,297**	**9.01**	**-14.65**
Albania	3,094	14,726	20,700	18,809	41,618	0.05	121.27
Croatia	12,473	27,992	62,409	59,126	72,294	0.08	22.27
Greece	105,984	182,559	307,758	288,335	260,463	0.29	-9.67
Italy	4,693,327	6,442,011	8,547,755	6,582,930	5,971,142	6.69	-9.29
Malta	8,485	13,887	19,467	20,876	17,309	0.02	-17.09
Portugal	41,592	132,504	206,849	145,786	94,071	0.11	-35.47
Slovenia	18,576	50,806	113,728	95,382	93,821	0.11	-1.64
Spain	709,030	1,008,868	1,423,183	1,344,425	1,313,338	1.47	-2.31
Yugoslavia, Sfr (Former)	107,648	493,058					
Serbia and Montenegro	25,410	243,331		230,808	184,241	0.21	-20.18
Other countries Southern Europe			847,102	643,559			
Western Europe	**10,533,174**	**12,890,742**	**21,532,423**	**21,210,283**	**18,820,679**	**21.07**	**-11.27**
Austria	650,369	933,102	1,563,129	1,391,870	1,388,251	1.55	-0.26
Belgium	554,622	826,479	1,395,212	1,507,295	1,430,803	1.60	-5.07
France	2,069,751	2,763,301	4,380,786	4,577,583	3,302,927	3.70	-27.85
Germany	5,694,412	6,310,407	10,921,832	10,352,593	9,426,758	10.56	-8.94
Luxembourg	8,260	16,913	51,553	46,637	39,524	0.04	-15.25
Monaco	165	667	2,471	1,856	2,418		30.28
Netherlands	878,434	1,242,608	1,913,390	2,114,398	2,093,495	2.34	-0.99
Switzerland	677,161	797,265	1,304,050	1,218,051	1,136,503	1.27	-6.69
East Mediterranean Europe	**543,175**	**1,576,202**	**2,130,235**	**1,460,633**	**1,190,869**	**1.33**	**-18.47**
Cyprus	32,270	53,787	83,843	59,232	51,038	0.06	-13.83
Israel	416,207	1,307,079	1,781,840	1,133,583	804,860	0.90	-29.00
Turkey	94,698	215,336	264,552	267,818	334,971	0.38	25.07
Other Europe	**131,872**	**137,217**	**727,766**	**1,251,715**	**2,531,906**	**2.84**	**102.27**
Other countries of Europe	131,872	137,217	727,766	1,251,715	2,531,906	2.84	102.27

EGYPT

5. Overnight stays of non-resident tourists in hotels and similar establishments, by nationality

	2002	2003	2004	2005	2006	Market share 06	% Change 06-05
MIDDLE EAST	6,353,247	13,495,221	17,928,497	19,486,816	21,670,371	24.27	11.21
Middle East	6,353,247	13,495,221	17,928,497	19,486,816	21,670,371	24.27	11.21
Bahrain	90,023	215,886	263,088	257,296	278,684	0.31	8.31
Palestine	595,433	1,703,241	1,907,097	2,182,823	2,414,825	2.70	10.63
Iraq	36,211	65,333	252,772	608,245	839,992	0.94	38.10
Jordan	473,560	857,381	1,171,889	1,239,064	1,392,667	1.56	12.40
Kuwait	596,156	1,048,435	1,385,414	1,498,350	1,874,277	2.10	25.09
Lebanon	254,672	354,475	429,173	432,930	591,593	0.66	36.65
Libyan Arab Jamahiriya	1,133,536	3,566,009	4,401,213	4,537,073	4,828,285	5.41	6.42
Oman	82,561	170,548	225,888	264,655	325,967	0.37	23.17
Qatar	98,094	173,836	238,430	280,417	335,836	0.38	19.76
Saudi Arabia	2,001,536	3,532,114	5,014,559	5,353,870	5,635,454	6.31	5.26
Syrian Arab Republic	395,473	628,169	858,685	919,897	1,021,164	1.14	11.01
United Arab Emirates	252,036	455,256	572,401	576,010	695,861	0.78	20.81
Yemen	343,956	724,538	1,207,888	1,336,186	1,435,766	1.61	7.45
SOUTH ASIA	210,220	342,351	502,502	597,447	683,917	0.77	14.47
South Asia	210,220	342,351	502,502	597,447	683,917	0.77	14.47
Afghanistan	716	4,079	6,428	6,274	3,998		-36.28
Bangladesh	6,663	10,182	15,727	15,386	21,140	0.02	37.40
Sri Lanka	22,474	42,910	66,660	64,286	70,187	0.08	9.18
India	142,810	220,689	328,601	389,493	443,867	0.50	13.96
Iran, Islamic Republic of	5,153	6,910		10,620	10,241	0.01	-3.57
Maldives	3,659	3,007	8,369	11,370	21,240	0.02	86.81
Nepal	1,523	3,632		9,810	10,802	0.01	10.11
Pakistan	27,222	50,942	76,717	90,208	102,442	0.11	13.56
REGION NOT SPECIFIED	14,553	31,359	64,700	56,443	71,014	0.08	25.82
Not Specified	14,553	31,359	64,700	56,443	71,014	0.08	25.82
Other countries of the World	14,553	31,359	64,700	56,443	71,014	0.08	25.82

Source: World Tourism Organization (UNWTO)

EL SALVADOR

1. Arrivals of non-resident tourists at national borders, by nationality

	2002	2003	2004	2005	2006	Market share 06	% Change 06-05
TOTAL	798,243	719,963	811,527	969,372	1,138,378	100.00	17.43
AFRICA		368	499	537	674	0.06	25.51
Southern Africa		207	232	163	128	0.01	-21.47
South Africa		207	232	163	128	0.01	-21.47
Other Africa		161	267	374	546	0.05	45.99
Other countries of Africa		161	267	374	546	0.05	45.99
AMERICAS	732,738	681,953	775,117	934,002	1,103,716	96.96	18.17
Caribbean	12	1,251	1,709	1,760	2,214	0.19	25.80
Cuba		219	244	288	415	0.04	44.10
Dominican Republic		758	935	1,031	1,099	0.10	6.60
Haiti		54	57	68	39		-42.65
Jamaica		59	187	52	151	0.01	190.38
Trinidad and Tobago		49	94	64	145	0.01	126.56
Other countries of the Caribbean		112	192	257	365	0.03	42.02
All countries of the Caribbean	12						
Central America	563,230	485,788	535,314	679,970	836,739	73.50	23.06
Belize	1,894	1,809	2,275	2,490	2,254	0.20	-9.48
Costa Rica	22,784	22,248	24,691	29,174	29,542	2.60	1.26
Guatemala	316,859	276,327	274,049	329,319	462,736	40.65	40.51
Honduras	115,172	87,834	107,752	170,668	225,868	19.84	32.34
Nicaragua	100,198	90,779	118,929	139,653	107,483	9.44	-23.04
Panama	6,323	6,791	7,618	8,666	8,856	0.78	2.19
North America	169,011	178,503	221,426	233,835	241,919	21.25	3.46
Canada	10,112	10,631	12,431	13,823	18,836	1.65	36.27
Mexico	18,021	16,962	19,291	21,050	20,689	1.82	-1.71
United States	140,878	150,910	189,704	198,962	202,394	17.78	1.72
South America	485	16,411	16,668	18,437	22,844	2.01	23.90
Argentina		3,298	3,258	3,672	3,960	0.35	7.84
Bolivia		330	296	317	518	0.05	63.41
Brazil		1,448	1,737	2,384	2,849	0.25	19.51
Chile		2,293	2,242	2,197	2,261	0.20	2.91
Colombia		4,276	3,868	4,364	5,232	0.46	19.89
Ecuador		836	970	1,030	1,410	0.12	36.89
Paraguay		182	219	176	179	0.02	1.70
Peru		1,634	1,565	1,685	3,368	0.30	99.88
Uruguay		615	695	650	579	0.05	-10.92
Venezuela		1,407	1,570	1,817	2,369	0.21	30.38
Other countries of South America		92	248	145	119	0.01	-17.93
All countries of South America	485						
EAST ASIA AND THE PACIFIC	3,127	7,474	8,115	8,360	8,616	0.76	3.06
North-East Asia	3,127	5,326	5,370	5,368	5,013	0.44	-6.61
China	436	145	111	145	553	0.05	281.38
Taiwan (Province of China)		1,301	1,457	1,494	1,252	0.11	-16.20
Japan	2,691	2,088	1,945	1,711	1,933	0.17	12.97
Korea, Republic of		1,792	1,857	2,018	1,275	0.11	-36.82
Australasia		1,295	1,817	2,102	1,855	0.16	-11.75
Australia		1,272	1,680	1,930	1,710	0.15	-11.40
New Zealand		23	137	172	145	0.01	-15.70
Other East Asia and the Pacific		853	928	890	1,748	0.15	96.40
Other countries of Asia		751	811	727	1,623	0.14	123.25

EL SALVADOR

1. Arrivals of non-resident tourists at national borders, by nationality

	2002	2003	2004	2005	2006	Market share 06	% Change 06-05
Other countries of Oceania		102	117	163	125	0.01	-23.31
EUROPE	**22,272**	**30,144**	**27,785**	**26,451**	**25,357**	**2.23**	**-4.14**
Central/Eastern Europe		**76**	**133**	**238**	**311**	**0.03**	**30.67**
Czech Republic/Slovakia		32	67	137	114	0.01	-16.79
Poland		44	66	101	197	0.02	95.05
Northern Europe	**2,820**	**5,843**	**5,888**	**5,486**	**4,963**	**0.44**	**-9.53**
Denmark		639	529	475	436	0.04	-8.21
Finland		270	241	176	257	0.02	46.02
Iceland		21	20	40	43		7.50
Ireland		322	334	503	465	0.04	-7.55
Norway		397	523	439	373	0.03	-15.03
Sweden		1,246	1,510	1,566	1,374	0.12	-12.26
United Kingdom	2,820	2,948	2,731	2,287	2,015	0.18	-11.89
Southern Europe	**12,415**	**12,053**	**11,480**	**11,407**	**11,017**	**0.97**	**-3.42**
Greece		99	83	85	138	0.01	62.35
Italy	3,419	3,308	3,459	3,268	2,911	0.26	-10.92
Portugal		199	138	222	266	0.02	19.82
Spain	8,996	8,414	7,786	7,817	7,572	0.67	-3.13
Yugoslavia, Sfr (Former)		33	14	15	130	0.01	766.67
Western Europe	**6,130**	**10,650**	**8,863**	**7,694**	**7,502**	**0.66**	**-2.50**
Austria		444	412	398	372	0.03	-6.53
Belgium		792	763	681	845	0.07	24.08
France	3,382	2,635	1,401	683	744	0.07	8.93
Germany	2,748	4,359	4,038	3,882	3,552	0.31	-8.50
Netherlands		1,232	1,197	1,134	1,080	0.09	-4.76
Switzerland		1,188	1,052	916	909	0.08	-0.76
East Mediterranean Europe	**907**	**903**	**761**	**766**	**577**	**0.05**	**-24.67**
Israel	907	903	761	766	577	0.05	-24.67
Other Europe		**619**	**660**	**860**	**987**	**0.09**	**14.77**
Other countries of Europe		619	660	860	987	0.09	14.77
MIDDLE EAST		**24**	**11**	**22**	**15**		**-31.82**
Middle East		**24**	**11**	**22**	**15**		**-31.82**
Egypt		24	11	22	15		-31.82
REGION NOT SPECIFIED	**40,106**						
Not Specified	**40,106**						
Other countries of the World	40,106						

Source: World Tourism Organization (UNWTO)

EL SALVADOR

3. Arrivals of non-resident tourists in hotels and similar establishments, by nationality

		2002	2003	2004	2005	2006	Market share 06	% Change 06-05
TOTAL	(*)	484,804	436,028	426,052	576,778	698,964	100.00	21.18
AFRICA			216	262	320	414	0.06	29.38
Southern Africa				122	97	79	0.01	-18.56
South Africa				122	97	79	0.01	-18.56
Other Africa			216	140	223	335	0.05	50.22
Other countries of Africa				140	223	335	0.05	50.22
All countries of Africa			216					
AMERICAS		445,019	414,218	406,937	555,732	677,683	96.96	21.94
Caribbean		7	755	897	1,046	1,360	0.19	30.02
Cuba				128	171	255	0.04	49.12
Dominican Republic				491	613	675	0.10	10.11
Jamaica				98	31	93	0.01	200.00
Trinidad and Tobago				49	38	89	0.01	134.21
Other countries of the Caribbean				131	193	248	0.04	28.50
All countries of the Caribbean		7	755					
Central America		342,071	295,087	281,040	404,583	513,759	73.50	26.98
Belize		1,150	1,099	1,194	1,482	1,384	0.20	-6.61
Costa Rica		13,838	13,512	12,963	17,359	18,139	2.60	4.49
Guatemala		192,438	167,873	143,876	195,945	284,120	40.65	45.00
Honduras		69,950	53,345	56,570	101,547	138,683	19.84	36.57
Nicaragua		60,855	55,134	62,438	83,094	65,995	9.44	-20.58
Panama		3,840	4,124	3,999	5,156	5,438	0.78	5.47
North America		102,647	108,411	116,249	139,132	148,538	21.25	6.76
Canada		6,141	6,457	6,526	8,225	11,565	1.65	40.61
Mexico		10,946	10,301	10,128	12,525	12,703	1.82	1.42
United States		85,560	91,653	99,595	118,382	124,270	17.78	4.97
South America		294	9,965	5,387	6,866	9,166	1.31	33.50
Argentina				1,710	2,185	2,431	0.35	11.26
Colombia				2,031	2,597	3,212	0.46	23.68
Peru				822	1,003	2,068	0.30	106.18
Venezuela				824	1,081	1,455	0.21	34.60
All countries of South America		294	9,965					
Other Americas				3,364	4,105	4,860	0.70	18.39
Other countries of the Americas				3,364	4,105	4,860	0.70	18.39
EAST ASIA AND THE PACIFIC		1,900	4,513	4,259	4,972	5,289	0.76	6.38
North-East Asia		1,900	1,356	1,079	1,104	1,527	0.22	38.32
China		265	89	58	86	340	0.05	295.35
Japan		1,635	1,267	1,021	1,018	1,187	0.17	16.60
Australasia			819	954	1,250	1,139	0.16	-8.88
Australia			773	882	1,148	1,050	0.15	-8.54
New Zealand			46	72	102	89	0.01	-12.75
Other East Asia and the Pacific			2,338	2,226	2,618	2,623	0.38	0.19
Other countries of Asia			2,338	2,165	2,521	2,547	0.36	1.03
Other countries of Oceania				61	97	76	0.01	-21.65
EUROPE		13,527	17,040	14,588	15,741	15,569	2.23	-1.09
Northern Europe		1,713		1,609	1,660	1,523	0.22	-8.25
Ireland				175	299	286	0.04	-4.35
United Kingdom		1,713		1,434	1,361	1,237	0.18	-9.11

EL SALVADOR

3. Arrivals of non-resident tourists in hotels and similar establishments, by nationality

	2002	2003	2004	2005	2006	Market share 06	% Change 06-05
Southern Europe	**7,539**	**7,119**	**5,904**	**6,595**	**6,436**	**0.92**	**-2.41**
Italy	2,077	2,009	1,816	1,944	1,787	0.26	-8.08
Spain	5,462	5,110	4,088	4,651	4,649	0.67	-0.04
Western Europe	**3,724**	**4,246**	**3,484**	**3,391**	**3,301**	**0.47**	**-2.65**
France	2,055	1,600	736	406	457	0.07	12.56
Germany	1,669	2,646	2,120	2,310	2,181	0.31	-5.58
Netherlands			628	675	663	0.09	-1.78
East Mediterranean Europe	**551**	**549**	**400**	**456**	**354**	**0.05**	**-22.37**
Israel	551	549	400	456	354	0.05	-22.37
Other Europe		**5,126**	**3,191**	**3,639**	**3,955**	**0.57**	**8.68**
Other countries of Europe		5,126	3,191	3,639	3,955	0.57	8.68
MIDDLE EAST		**13**	**6**	**13**	**9**		**-30.77**
Middle East		13	6	13	9		-30.77
Egypt		13	6	13	9		-30.77
REGION NOT SPECIFIED	**24,358**	**28**					
Not Specified	24,358	28					
Other countries of the World	24,358	28					

Source: World Tourism Organization (UNWTO)

EL SALVADOR

5. Overnight stays of non-resident tourists in hotels and similar establishments, by nationality

		2002	2003	2004	2005	2006	Market share 06	% Change 06-05
TOTAL	(*)	3,802,388	3,429,512	4,057,635	5,816,232	8,310,159	100.00	42.88
AFRICA			1,696	2,495	3,222	4,920	0.06	52.70
Other Africa			1,696	2,495	3,222	4,920	0.06	52.70
All countries of Africa			1,696	2,495	3,222	4,920	0.06	52.70
AMERICAS		3,490,352	3,248,768	3,875,585	5,604,012	8,057,127	96.96	43.77
Caribbean		56	5,924	8,545	10,560	16,162	0.19	53.05
All countries of the Caribbean		56	5,924	8,545	10,560	16,162	0.19	53.05
Central America		2,682,912	2,314,408	2,676,570	4,079,820	6,108,195	73.50	49.72
Belize		9,024	8,616	11,375	14,940	16,454	0.20	10.13
Costa Rica		108,536	105,980	123,455	175,044	215,657	2.60	23.20
Guatemala		1,509,316	1,316,648	1,370,245	1,975,914	3,377,973	40.65	70.96
Honduras		548,624	418,392	538,760	1,024,008	1,648,836	19.84	61.02
Nicaragua		477,292	432,424	594,645	837,918	784,626	9.44	-6.36
Panama		30,120	32,348	38,090	51,996	64,649	0.78	24.33
North America		805,076	850,280	1,107,130	1,403,010	1,766,009	21.25	25.87
Canada		48,168	50,640	62,155	82,938	137,503	1.65	65.79
Mexico		85,848	80,792	96,455	126,300	151,030	1.82	19.58
United States		671,060	718,848	948,520	1,193,772	1,477,476	17.78	23.77
South America		2,308	78,156	83,340	110,622	166,761	2.01	50.75
All countries of South America		2,308	78,156	83,340	110,622	166,761	2.01	50.75
EAST ASIA AND THE PACIFIC		14,904	35,396	34,765	41,298	52,764	0.63	27.76
Other East Asia and the Pacific		14,904	35,396	34,765	41,298	52,764	0.63	27.76
All countries East Asia/Pacific		14,904	35,396	34,765	41,298	52,764	0.63	27.76
EUROPE		106,092	143,432	135,120	154,110	180,894	2.18	17.38
Southern Europe		42,844	40,076	38,930	46,902	55,276	0.67	17.85
Spain		42,844	40,076	38,930	46,902	55,276	0.67	17.85
Western Europe		13,092	20,756	20,190	23,292	25,930	0.31	11.33
Germany		13,092	20,756	20,190	23,292	25,930	0.31	11.33
Other Europe		50,156	82,600	76,000	83,916	99,688	1.20	18.79
Other countries of Europe		50,156	82,600	76,000	83,916	99,688	1.20	18.79
REGION NOT SPECIFIED		191,040	220	9,670	13,590	14,454	0.17	6.36
Not Specified		191,040	220	9,670	13,590	14,454	0.17	6.36
Other countries of the World		191,040	220	9,670	13,590	14,454	0.17	6.36

Source: World Tourism Organization (UNWTO)

ERITREA

2. Arrivals of non-resident visitors at national borders, by nationality

	2002	2003	2004	2005	2006	Market share 06	% Change 06-05
TOTAL	100,828	80,029	87,298	83,307	78,451	100.00	-5.83
AFRICA	8,185	3,147	4,503	3,182	3,645	4.65	14.55
East Africa	922	1,166	2,153	1,437	1,242	1.58	-13.57
Ethiopia	70	76	77	109	74	0.09	-32.11
Kenya	480	695	1,481	796	735	0.94	-7.66
Madagascar	10	4	2	1	5	0.01	400.00
Malawi	11	4	16	28	16	0.02	-42.86
Mauritius	3			1	3		200.00
Mozambique	4	21	28	16	20	0.03	25.00
Somalia	88	92	107	59	95	0.12	61.02
Zimbabwe	59	48	69	69	77	0.10	11.59
Uganda	102	117	196	169	74	0.09	-56.21
United Republic of Tanzania	60	59	106	138	77	0.10	-44.20
Zambia	35	50	71	51	66	0.08	29.41
North Africa	6,262	717	992	664	1,285	1.64	93.52
Sudan	6,262	717	992	664	1,285	1.64	93.52
Southern Africa	289	247	298	261	248	0.32	-4.98
Botswana	7	5	19	26	26	0.03	
Namibia	7	10	16	15	13	0.02	-13.33
South Africa	275	232	263	220	209	0.27	-5.00
Other Africa	712	1,017	1,060	820	870	1.11	6.10
Other countries of Africa	712	1,017	1,060	820	870	1.11	6.10
AMERICAS	2,094	2,321	2,559	2,263	1,474	1.88	-34.87
North America	2,024	2,112	2,342	1,968	1,257	1.60	-36.13
Canada	331	367	731	357	290	0.37	-18.77
United States	1,693	1,745	1,611	1,611	967	1.23	-39.98
Other Americas	70	209	217	295	217	0.28	-26.44
Other countries of the Americas	70	209	217	295	217	0.28	-26.44
EAST ASIA AND THE PACIFIC	1,700	1,953	2,484	2,267	2,275	2.90	0.35
North-East Asia	1,051	1,040	1,494	1,347	1,478	1.88	9.73
China	210	279	340	245	327	0.42	33.47
Japan	701	103	1,063	1,018	1,087	1.39	6.78
Korea, Republic of	140	658	91	84	64	0.08	-23.81
South-East Asia	133	117	182	191	140	0.18	-26.70
Indonesia	27	15	7	19	23	0.03	21.05
Malaysia	14	18	36	28	20	0.03	-28.57
Philippines	84	76	123	127	89	0.11	-29.92
Singapore	8	8	16	17	8	0.01	-52.94
Australasia	193	337	317	278	221	0.28	-20.50
Australia	141	237	260	239	173	0.22	-27.62
New Zealand	52	100	57	39	48	0.06	23.08
Other East Asia and the Pacific	323	459	491	451	436	0.56	-3.33
Other countries of Asia	323	459	491	451	436	0.56	-3.33
EUROPE	8,378	8,367	10,142	8,364	5,983	7.63	-28.47
Northern Europe	1,601	2,316	2,677	1,723	1,128	1.44	-34.53
United Kingdom	750	1,106	1,079	888	666	0.85	-25.00
Scandinavia	851	1,210	1,598	835	462	0.59	-44.67
Southern Europe	2,859	2,334	3,476	3,246	2,254	2.87	-30.56

ERITREA

2. Arrivals of non-resident visitors at national borders, by nationality

	2002	2003	2004	2005	2006	Market share 06	% Change 06-05
Italy	2,859	2,334	3,476	3,246	2,254	2.87	-30.56
Western Europe	**2,017**	**2,522**	**2,590**	**2,129**	**1,972**	**2.51**	**-7.37**
France	386	461	416	410	399	0.51	-2.68
Germany	1,015	1,252	1,005	1,045	1,022	1.30	-2.20
Netherlands			487	353	238	0.30	-32.58
Switzerland	243	187	299	237	222	0.28	-6.33
Benelux	373	622	77	84	69	0.09	-17.86
Other countries of Western Europe			306		22	0.03	
East Mediterranean Europe	**211**	**147**	**231**	**115**	**42**	**0.05**	**-63.48**
Israel	211	147	231	115	42	0.05	-63.48
Other Europe	**1,690**	**1,048**	**1,168**	**1,151**	**587**	**0.75**	**-49.00**
Other countries of Europe	1,690	1,048	1,168	1,151	587	0.75	-49.00
MIDDLE EAST	**3,565**	**2,857**	**4,196**	**3,862**	**3,241**	**4.13**	**-16.08**
Middle East	**3,565**	**2,857**	**4,196**	**3,862**	**3,241**	**4.13**	**-16.08**
Saudi Arabia	540	550	484	600	354	0.45	-41.00
Egypt	501	537	698	678	480	0.61	-29.20
Yemen	401	342	402	349	335	0.43	-4.01
Other countries of Middle East	2,123	1,428	2,612	2,235	2,072	2.64	-7.29
SOUTH ASIA	**2,549**	**2,580**	**2,420**	**2,985**	**2,895**	**3.69**	**-3.02**
South Asia	**2,549**	**2,580**	**2,420**	**2,985**	**2,895**	**3.69**	**-3.02**
India	2,549	2,580	2,420	2,985	2,895	3.69	-3.02
REGION NOT SPECIFIED	**74,357**	**58,804**	**60,994**	**60,384**	**58,938**	**75.13**	**-2.39**
Not Specified	**74,357**	**58,804**	**60,994**	**60,384**	**58,938**	**75.13**	**-2.39**
Nationals Residing Abroad	74,357	58,804	60,994	60,384	58,938	75.13	-2.39

Source: World Tourism Organization (UNWTO)

ESTONIA

3. Arrivals of non-resident tourists in hotels and similar establishments, by country of residence

	2002	2003	2004	2005	2006	Market share 06	% Change 06-05
TOTAL	936,737	1,008,631	1,300,070	1,358,089	1,329,688	100.00	-2.09
AMERICAS	15,117	12,574	20,114	20,837	20,193	1.52	-3.09
North America	15,117	12,574	20,114	20,837	20,193	1.52	-3.09
Canada	1,928	1,314	2,582	2,823	2,426	0.18	-14.06
United States	13,189	11,260	17,532	18,014	17,767	1.34	-1.37
EAST ASIA AND THE PACIFIC	6,820	6,389	7,105	7,726	7,766	0.58	0.52
North-East Asia	6,820	6,389	7,105	7,726	7,766	0.58	0.52
Japan	6,820	6,389	7,105	7,726	7,766	0.58	0.52
EUROPE	901,265	980,537	1,263,489	1,320,886	1,289,249	96.96	-2.40
Central/Eastern Europe	73,438	81,216	104,080	131,423	163,657	12.31	24.53
Czech Republic/Slovakia	1,382	2,246	4,034	5,390	4,740	0.36	-12.06
Hungary	1,046	1,049	1,878	2,807	2,827	0.21	0.71
Latvia	25,119	22,589	32,696	38,848	50,754	3.82	30.65
Lithuania	13,767	12,291	17,922	20,164	24,728	1.86	22.63
Poland	7,089	11,402	9,541	12,586	12,396	0.93	-1.51
Russian Federation	24,462	30,806	37,046	48,404	63,704	4.79	31.61
Other countries Central/East Europ	573	833	963	3,224	4,508	0.34	39.83
Northern Europe	733,523	785,093	992,947	992,882	943,116	70.93	-5.01
Denmark	11,427	12,590	13,242	14,732	15,183	1.14	3.06
Finland	615,117	656,977	820,994	773,259	719,819	54.13	-6.91
Norway	22,197	26,538	34,558	39,471	46,668	3.51	18.23
Sweden	55,998	60,483	85,165	103,443	101,265	7.62	-2.11
United Kingdom/Ireland	28,784	28,505	38,988	61,977	60,181	4.53	-2.90
Southern Europe	16,146	20,808	37,982	43,236	42,964	3.23	-0.63
Greece	632	1,057	1,236	1,574	1,599	0.12	1.59
Italy	8,289	11,428	22,627	23,796	23,503	1.77	-1.23
Slovenia	217	291	576	1,025	2,075	0.16	102.44
Spain,Portugal	7,008	8,032	13,543	16,841	15,787	1.19	-6.26
Western Europe	68,596	82,309	113,380	142,614	125,548	9.44	-11.97
Austria	2,787	2,792	5,169	8,611	8,915	0.67	3.53
France	5,919	6,993	12,923	14,168	14,209	1.07	0.29
Germany	49,150	59,942	78,153	99,083	80,348	6.04	-18.91
Switzerland	2,877	3,339	4,283	4,721	4,737	0.36	0.34
Benelux	7,863	9,243	12,852	16,031	17,339	1.30	8.16
Other Europe	9,562	11,111	15,100	10,731	13,964	1.05	30.13
Other countries of Europe	9,562	11,111	15,100	10,731	13,964	1.05	30.13
REGION NOT SPECIFIED	13,535	9,131	9,362	8,640	12,480	0.94	44.44
Not Specified	13,535	9,131	9,362	8,640	12,480	0.94	44.44
Other countries of the World	13,535	9,131	9,362	8,640	12,480	0.94	44.44

Source: World Tourism Organization (UNWTO)

ESTONIA

4. Arrivals of non-resident tourists in all types of accommodation establishments, by country of residence

	2002	2003	2004	2005	2006	Market share 06	% Change 06-05
TOTAL	1,003,383	1,112,746	1,374,414	1,453,418	1,427,583	100.00	-1.78
AFRICA		542	641	1,033	723	0.05	-30.01
Southern Africa				334	158	0.01	-52.69
South Africa				334	158	0.01	-52.69
Other Africa		542	641	699	565	0.04	-19.17
Other countries of Africa				699	565	0.04	-19.17
All countries of Africa		542	641				
AMERICAS	15,601	14,823	23,448	24,037	24,359	1.71	1.34
North America	15,601	14,328	22,392	22,760	22,787	1.60	0.12
Canada	2,111	1,567	2,981	3,254	2,931	0.21	-9.93
United States	13,490	12,761	19,411	19,506	19,856	1.39	1.79
South America				450	435	0.03	-3.33
Brazil				450	435	0.03	-3.33
Other Americas		495	1,056	827	1,137	0.08	37.48
Other countries of the Americas		495	1,056	827	1,137	0.08	37.48
EAST ASIA AND THE PACIFIC	6,587	10,663	13,456	15,130	17,663	1.24	16.74
North-East Asia	6,587	6,901	7,362	9,230	9,991	0.70	8.24
China				804	1,152	0.08	43.28
Japan	6,587	6,901	7,362	8,066	8,093	0.57	0.33
Korea, Republic of				360	746	0.05	107.22
Australasia		1,839	2,848	3,174	4,002	0.28	26.09
Australia		1,612	2,457	3,174	4,002	0.28	26.09
New Zealand		227	391				
Other East Asia and the Pacific		1,923	3,246	2,726	3,670	0.26	34.63
Other countries of Asia		1,725	2,980	2,121	2,649	0.19	24.89
Other countries of Oceania		198	266	605	1,021	0.07	68.76
EUROPE	967,167	1,080,977	1,333,979	1,411,062	1,382,143	96.82	-2.05
Central/Eastern Europe	93,209	105,644	129,071	156,996	190,550	13.35	21.37
Bulgaria				688	913	0.06	32.70
Czech Republic/Slovakia	1,531						
Czech Republic		2,111	4,433	5,046	4,696	0.33	-6.94
Hungary	1,280	1,489	2,267	3,464	3,322	0.23	-4.10
Latvia	33,511	29,230	40,956	51,558	65,559	4.59	27.16
Lithuania	16,425	14,320	20,555	24,703	29,889	2.09	20.99
Poland	8,052	13,018	11,301	14,194	14,240	1.00	0.32
Romania				800	708	0.05	-11.50
Russian Federation	31,754	37,320	42,348	53,427	67,201	4.71	25.78
Slovakia		513	564	1,255	830	0.06	-33.86
Ukraine				1,861	3,192	0.22	71.52
Other countries Central/East Europ	656	7,643	6,647				
Northern Europe	772,812	850,809	1,025,503	1,034,029	987,454	69.17	-4.50
Denmark	12,459	14,894	13,915	15,407	16,206	1.14	5.19
Finland	647,866	706,473	843,871	799,139	749,132	52.48	-6.26
Iceland		625	916	2,209	1,742	0.12	-21.14
Ireland		2,073	3,058	4,841	4,179	0.29	-13.67
Norway	22,875	29,842	35,798	41,273	48,863	3.42	18.39
Sweden	61,305	66,751	89,042	108,234	105,939	7.42	-2.12
United Kingdom		30,151	38,903	62,926	61,393	4.30	-2.44

ESTONIA

4. Arrivals of non-resident tourists in all types of accommodation establishments, by country of residence

	2002	2003	2004	2005	2006	Market share 06	% Change 06-05
United Kingdom/Ireland	28,307						
Southern Europe	**16,354**	**23,897**	**42,904**	**49,453**	**49,327**	**3.46**	**-0.25**
Albania				141	92	0.01	-34.75
Croatia				416	573	0.04	37.74
Greece	627	1,240	1,564	1,696	1,731	0.12	2.06
Italy	8,638	13,127	25,642	26,712	26,753	1.87	0.15
Malta				169	127	0.01	-24.85
Portugal		1,131	2,781	3,488	2,697	0.19	-22.68
Slovenia	249	478	740	1,298	2,206	0.15	69.95
Spain		7,921	12,177	15,533	15,148	1.06	-2.48
Spain,Portugal	6,840						
Western Europe	**73,191**	**94,759**	**126,167**	**159,108**	**141,502**	**9.91**	**-11.07**
Austria	2,955	3,487	5,757	9,368	9,559	0.67	2.04
Belgium		2,828	4,043	4,940	5,886	0.41	19.15
France	6,132	8,326	15,086	16,921	16,510	1.16	-2.43
Germany	52,794	68,151	85,643	109,346	90,073	6.31	-17.63
Luxembourg		350	454	561	584	0.04	4.10
Netherlands		7,826	10,490	12,714	13,688	0.96	7.66
Switzerland	3,017	3,791	4,694	5,258	5,202	0.36	-1.07
Benelux	8,293						
East Mediterranean Europe		**175**	**461**	**698**	**830**	**0.06**	**18.91**
Cyprus				223	251	0.02	12.56
Turkey		175	461	475	579	0.04	21.89
Other Europe	**11,601**	**5,693**	**9,873**	**10,778**	**12,480**	**0.87**	**15.79**
Other countries of Europe	11,601	5,693	9,873	10,778	12,480	0.87	15.79
REGION NOT SPECIFIED	**14,028**	**5,741**	**2,890**	**2,156**	**2,695**	**0.19**	**25.00**
Not Specified	**14,028**	**5,741**	**2,890**	**2,156**	**2,695**	**0.19**	**25.00**
Other countries of the World	14,028	5,741	2,890	2,156	2,695	0.19	25.00

Source: World Tourism Organization (UNWTO)

ESTONIA

5. Overnight stays of non-resident tourists in hotels and similar establishments, by country of residence

	2002	2003	2004	2005	2006	Market share 06	% Change 06-05
TOTAL	1,886,642	2,086,265	2,601,818	2,790,595	2,771,868	100.00	-0.67
AMERICAS	44,834	31,744	47,082	47,626	48,785	1.76	2.43
North America	44,834	31,744	47,082	47,626	48,785	1.76	2.43
Canada	5,666	3,913	6,448	7,322	6,140	0.22	-16.14
United States	39,168	27,831	40,634	40,304	42,645	1.54	5.81
EAST ASIA AND THE PACIFIC	14,776	11,635	13,668	14,624	14,668	0.53	0.30
North-East Asia	14,776	11,635	13,668	14,624	14,668	0.53	0.30
Japan	14,776	11,635	13,668	14,624	14,668	0.53	0.30
EUROPE	1,798,055	2,023,435	2,521,417	2,709,783	2,680,607	96.71	-1.08
Central/Eastern Europe	163,502	217,048	196,978	261,925	333,255	12.02	27.23
Czech Republic/Slovakia	4,329	4,623	6,518	10,009	9,376	0.34	-6.32
Hungary	3,248	3,567	3,928	7,005	6,673	0.24	-4.74
Latvia	45,296	39,264	48,396	56,884	75,402	2.72	32.55
Lithuania	27,177	21,137	28,184	32,856	40,891	1.48	24.46
Poland	14,719	71,128	19,587	23,146	24,286	0.88	4.93
Russian Federation	66,634	74,809	87,920	123,850	165,043	5.95	33.26
Other countries Central/East Europ	2,099	2,520	2,445	8,175	11,584	0.42	41.70
Northern Europe	1,403,254	1,574,180	1,998,753	2,045,278	1,971,137	71.11	-3.62
Denmark	28,669	23,925	27,002	30,878	31,624	1.14	2.42
Finland	1,118,167	1,298,582	1,621,533	1,531,646	1,436,243	51.81	-6.23
Norway	54,376	56,466	78,334	100,627	127,964	4.62	27.17
Sweden	116,500	123,443	176,384	224,594	223,381	8.06	-0.54
United Kingdom/Ireland	85,542	71,764	95,500	157,533	151,925	5.48	-3.56
Southern Europe	42,155	44,431	74,378	90,128	88,090	3.18	-2.26
Greece	2,356	2,621	2,582	4,030	3,972	0.14	-1.44
Italy	23,710	25,942	46,582	52,323	50,964	1.84	-2.60
Slovenia	667	1,083	1,000	2,215	3,200	0.12	44.47
Spain,Portugal	15,422	14,785	24,214	31,560	29,954	1.08	-5.09
Western Europe	160,765	160,263	218,379	288,185	257,554	9.29	-10.63
Austria	7,246	5,907	9,528	21,129	20,105	0.73	-4.85
France	15,438	14,121	25,269	29,175	29,677	1.07	1.72
Germany	109,520	112,404	147,925	194,489	160,416	5.79	-17.52
Switzerland	6,717	6,494	8,134	9,798	9,902	0.36	1.06
Benelux	21,844	21,337	27,523	33,594	37,454	1.35	11.49
Other Europe	28,379	27,513	32,929	24,267	30,571	1.10	25.98
Other countries of Europe	28,379	27,513	32,929	24,267	30,571	1.10	25.98
REGION NOT SPECIFIED	28,977	19,451	19,651	18,562	27,808	1.00	49.81
Not Specified	28,977	19,451	19,651	18,562	27,808	1.00	49.81
Other countries of the World	28,977	19,451	19,651	18,562	27,808	1.00	49.81

Source: World Tourism Organization (UNWTO)

ESTONIA

6. Overnight stays of non-resident tourists in all types of accommodation establishments, by country of residence

	2002	2003	2004	2005	2006	Market share 06	% Change 06-05
TOTAL	1,997,588	2,267,873	2,746,806	2,982,459	3,020,367	100.00	1.27
AFRICA		1,035	1,281	2,648	1,844	0.06	-30.36
Southern Africa				1,159	417	0.01	-64.02
South Africa				1,159	417	0.01	-64.02
Other Africa		1,035	1,281	1,489	1,427	0.05	-4.16
Other countries of Africa				1,489	1,427	0.05	-4.16
All countries of Africa		1,035	1,281				
AMERICAS	40,199	35,596	53,916	55,228	60,107	1.99	8.83
North America	40,199	34,508	51,737	52,701	57,023	1.89	8.20
Canada	5,519	4,254	7,245	8,352	7,563	0.25	-9.45
United States	34,680	30,254	44,492	44,349	49,460	1.64	11.52
South America				973	910	0.03	-6.47
Brazil				973	910	0.03	-6.47
Other Americas		1,088	2,179	1,554	2,174	0.07	39.90
Other countries of the Americas		1,088	2,179	1,554	2,174	0.07	39.90
EAST ASIA AND THE PACIFIC	12,015	20,550	25,991	29,591	39,309	1.30	32.84
North-East Asia	12,015	12,648	14,174	17,410	21,655	0.72	24.38
China				1,480	4,524	0.15	205.68
Japan	12,015	12,648	14,174	15,350	15,516	0.51	1.08
Korea, Republic of				580	1,615	0.05	178.45
Australasia		3,499	5,793	6,704	9,200	0.30	37.23
Australia		3,085	5,075	6,704	9,200	0.30	37.23
New Zealand		414	718				
Other East Asia and the Pacific		4,403	6,024	5,477	8,454	0.28	54.35
Other countries of Asia		3,967	5,510	4,289	6,286	0.21	46.56
Other countries of Oceania		436	514	1,188	2,168	0.07	82.49
EUROPE	1,918,203	2,199,573	2,658,858	2,889,863	2,913,599	96.47	0.82
Central/Eastern Europe	185,592	252,034	247,702	308,517	395,620	13.10	28.23
Bulgaria				1,851	3,365	0.11	81.79
Czech Republic/Slovakia	3,831						
Czech Republic		3,910	9,127	8,183	9,065	0.30	10.78
Hungary	3,543	3,877	4,844	8,063	8,842	0.29	9.66
Latvia	57,820	42,682	59,532	74,880	101,300	3.35	35.28
Lithuania	29,853	22,977	32,068	40,925	52,202	1.73	27.56
Poland	15,175	77,320	22,681	26,459	31,802	1.05	20.19
Romania				1,926	2,380	0.08	23.57
Russian Federation	72,996	81,321	101,546	138,508	176,862	5.86	27.69
Slovakia		1,115	1,128	3,230	2,320	0.08	-28.17
Ukraine				4,492	7,482	0.25	66.56
Other countries Central/East Europ	2,374	18,832	16,776				
Northern Europe	1,513,324	1,712,668	2,063,069	2,131,911	2,079,610	68.85	-2.45
Denmark	30,611	26,008	28,510	32,445	34,358	1.14	5.90
Finland	1,241,788	1,411,623	1,664,799	1,581,685	1,501,481	49.71	-5.07
Iceland		1,455	1,915	5,953	4,965	0.16	-16.60
Ireland		4,952	6,843	12,053	11,400	0.38	-5.42
Norway	47,454	61,381	81,288	105,432	134,741	4.46	27.80
Sweden	123,781	134,189	184,871	235,202	236,998	7.85	0.76
United Kingdom		73,060	94,843	159,141	155,667	5.15	-2.18

ESTONIA

6. Overnight stays of non-resident tourists in all types of accommodation establishments, by country of residence

	2002	2003	2004	2005	2006	Market share 06	% Change 06-05
United Kingdom/Ireland	69,690						
Southern Europe	**36,265**	**48,298**	**83,999**	**104,305**	**106,439**	**3.52**	**2.05**
Albania				374	238	0.01	-36.36
Croatia				1,152	1,670	0.06	44.97
Greece	1,902	2,849	3,149	4,669	4,347	0.14	-6.90
Italy	20,866	28,200	52,507	59,553	61,348	2.03	3.01
Malta				493	317	0.01	-35.70
Portugal		2,441	5,113	6,745	5,637	0.19	-16.43
Slovenia	630	1,177	1,352	2,685	3,520	0.12	31.10
Spain		13,631	21,878	28,634	29,362	0.97	2.54
Spain,Portugal	12,867						
Western Europe	**156,529**	**174,212**	**243,511**	**320,755**	**298,479**	**9.88**	**-6.94**
Austria	6,902	6,420	10,620	22,543	22,128	0.73	-1.84
Belgium		6,324	8,458	10,269	13,303	0.44	29.55
France	13,305	15,350	28,962	33,990	35,817	1.19	5.38
Germany	110,084	122,189	163,842	215,892	185,550	6.14	-14.05
Luxembourg		776	1,026	1,269	1,478	0.05	16.47
Netherlands		16,094	21,698	26,095	29,145	0.96	11.69
Switzerland	6,246	7,059	8,905	10,697	11,058	0.37	3.37
Benelux	19,992						
East Mediterranean Europe		**648**	**1,049**	**1,880**	**2,579**	**0.09**	**37.18**
Cyprus				782	668	0.02	-14.58
Turkey		648	1,049	1,098	1,911	0.06	74.04
Other Europe	**26,493**	**11,713**	**19,528**	**22,495**	**30,872**	**1.02**	**37.24**
Other countries of Europe	26,493	11,713	19,528	22,495	30,872	1.02	37.24
REGION NOT SPECIFIED	**27,171**	**11,119**	**6,760**	**5,129**	**5,508**	**0.18**	**7.39**
Not Specified	**27,171**	**11,119**	**6,760**	**5,129**	**5,508**	**0.18**	**7.39**
Other countries of the World	27,171	11,119	6,760	5,129	5,508	0.18	7.39

Source: World Tourism Organization (UNWTO)

ETHIOPIA

1. Arrivals of non-resident tourists at national borders, by nationality

	2002	2003	2004	2005	2006	Market share 06	% Change 06-05
TOTAL (*)	156,327	179,910	184,079	227,398	290,458	100.00	27.73
AFRICA	59,640	82,152	65,744	85,501	89,923	30.96	5.17
East Africa	30,173	28,780	21,844	13,456	13,340	4.59	-0.86
Djibouti	26,447	21,708	14,627	4,179	4,650	1.60	11.27
Kenya	3,726	7,072	7,217	9,277	8,690	2.99	-6.33
North Africa	3,091	3,769	3,787	5,343	6,233	2.15	16.66
Sudan	3,091	3,769	3,787	5,343	6,233	2.15	16.66
Other Africa	26,376	49,603	40,113	66,702	70,350	24.22	5.47
Other countries of Africa	26,376	49,603	40,113	66,702	70,350	24.22	5.47
AMERICAS	19,433	27,456	33,895	41,380	61,353	21.12	48.27
North America	18,867	26,930	33,281	40,678	50,959	17.54	25.27
Canada	3,895	4,434	5,169	8,396	7,349	2.53	-12.47
United States	14,972	22,496	28,112	32,282	43,610	15.01	35.09
Other Americas	566	526	614	702	10,394	3.58	1,380.63
Other countries of the Americas	566	526	614	702	10,394	3.58	1,380.63
EAST ASIA AND THE PACIFIC	7,916	7,645	9,825	12,188	20,058	6.91	64.57
North-East Asia	1,857	1,622	1,658	1,708	2,402	0.83	40.63
Japan	1,857	1,622	1,658	1,708	2,402	0.83	40.63
Other East Asia and the Pacific	6,059	6,023	8,167	10,480	17,656	6.08	68.47
Other countries of Asia	6,059	6,023	8,167	10,480	17,656	6.08	68.47
EUROPE	34,280	43,647	47,955	57,103	76,466	26.33	33.91
Central/Eastern Europe	801	430	682	654	969	0.33	48.17
Russian Federation	801	430	682	654	969	0.33	48.17
Northern Europe	6,123	8,978	10,627	11,254	16,076	5.53	42.85
United Kingdom	6,123	8,978	10,627	11,254	16,076	5.53	42.85
Southern Europe	4,297	6,348	7,696	7,983	8,386	2.89	5.05
Italy	4,297	6,348	7,696	7,983	8,386	2.89	5.05
Western Europe	12,350	16,317	15,838	18,979	21,382	7.36	12.66
France	4,270	5,482	4,501	5,899	6,649	2.29	12.71
Germany	4,499	5,719	6,256	6,731	7,428	2.56	10.36
Netherlands	2,544	3,044	3,227	4,387	4,659	1.60	6.20
Switzerland	1,037	2,072	1,854	1,962	2,646	0.91	34.86
Other Europe	10,709	11,574	13,112	18,233	29,653	10.21	62.63
Other countries of Europe	10,709	11,574	13,112	18,233	29,653	10.21	62.63
MIDDLE EAST	9,189	14,366	20,618	22,162	30,556	10.52	37.88
Middle East	9,189	14,366	20,618	22,162	30,556	10.52	37.88
Saudi Arabia	2,610	6,283	9,778	5,382	8,463	2.91	57.25
Yemen	2,651	2,651	2,975	3,102	4,724	1.63	52.29
Other countries of Middle East	3,928	5,432	7,865	13,678	17,369	5.98	26.98
SOUTH ASIA	3,778	3,602	4,641	7,125	7,975	2.75	11.93
South Asia	3,778	3,602	4,641	7,125	7,975	2.75	11.93
India	3,778	3,602	4,641	7,125	7,975	2.75	11.93
REGION NOT SPECIFIED	22,091	1,042	1,401	1,939	4,127	1.42	112.84
Not Specified	22,091	1,042	1,401	1,939	4,127	1.42	112.84
Other countries of the World	28	1,042	1,401	1,939	4,127	1.42	112.84

ETHIOPIA

1. Arrivals of non-resident tourists at national borders, by nationality

	2002	2003	2004	2005	2006	Market share 06	% Change 06-05
Nationals Residing Abroad	22,063						

Source: World Tourism Organization (UNWTO)

FIJI

1. Arrivals of non-resident tourists at national borders, by country of residence

		2002	2003	2004	2005	2006	Market share 06	% Change 06-05
TOTAL	(*)	397,859	430,800	502,765	549,911			
AMERICAS		68,617	69,313	77,605	85,536			
North America		68,617	69,313	77,605	85,536			
Canada		9,802	10,990	12,417	13,564			
United States		58,815	58,323	65,188	71,972			
EAST ASIA AND THE PACIFIC		261,690	288,321	351,819	383,691			
North-East Asia		34,296	32,714	34,004	38,724			
Taiwan (Province of China)		922	870	731	1,005			
Japan		26,382	23,464	24,173	27,380			
Korea, Republic of		6,992	8,380	9,100	10,339			
South-East Asia		316	268	311				
Malaysia		316	268	311				
Australasia		191,899	216,889	280,228	302,987			
Australia		123,606	141,873	176,310	184,996			
New Zealand		68,293	75,016	103,918	117,991			
Other East Asia and the Pacific		35,179	38,450	37,276	41,980			
Other countries of Asia		11,128	10,283	11,847	13,909			
Other countries East Asia/Pacific		24,051	28,167	25,429	28,071			
EUROPE		65,047	71,641	71,372	78,507			
Northern Europe		48,200	54,576	48,819	54,754			
Denmark		1,035	997					
Finland		333	287					
Norway		1,300	1,330					
Sweden		2,139	2,168					
United Kingdom		43,393	49,794	48,819	54,754			
Southern Europe		3,070	3,002					
Italy		2,457	2,348					
Spain		613	654					
Western Europe		12,845	12,905					
Austria		811	807					
Belgium		420	299					
France		1,901	2,493					
Germany		6,104	5,808					
Netherlands		1,561	1,557					
Switzerland		2,048	1,941					
Other Europe		932	1,158	22,553	23,753			
Other countries of Europe		932	1,158	22,553	23,753			
REGION NOT SPECIFIED		2,505	1,525	1,969	2,177			
Not Specified		2,505	1,525	1,969	2,177			
Other countries of the World		2,505	1,525	1,969	2,177			

Source: World Tourism Organization (UNWTO)

FIJI

5. Overnight stays of non-resident tourists in hotels and similar establishments, by country of residence

	2002	2003	2004	2005	2006	Market share 06	% Change 06-05
TOTAL	1,914,446	2,015,182	2,488,770	2,760,230	2,640,817	100.00	-4.33
AMERICAS	236,561	247,782	274,991	273,842	297,610	11.27	8.68
North America	236,561	247,782	274,991	273,842	297,610	11.27	8.68
Canada	34,673	34,369	31,419	31,340	38,062	1.44	21.45
United States	201,888	213,413	243,572	242,502	259,548	9.83	7.03
EAST ASIA AND THE PACIFIC	1,366,474	1,423,208	1,807,084	2,064,437	1,922,934	72.82	-6.85
North-East Asia	114,677	108,179	111,751	109,200	94,853	3.59	-13.14
Japan	114,677	108,179	111,751	109,200	94,853	3.59	-13.14
Australasia	1,201,864	1,263,703	1,638,632	1,894,530	1,761,623	66.71	-7.02
Australia	808,546	884,376	1,091,982	1,227,201	1,201,421	45.49	-2.10
New Zealand	393,318	379,327	546,650	667,329	560,202	21.21	-16.05
Other East Asia and the Pacific	49,933	51,326	56,701	60,707	66,458	2.52	9.47
Other countries of Oceania	49,933	51,326	56,701	60,707	66,458	2.52	9.47
EUROPE	224,664	254,038	305,565	302,013	294,039	11.13	-2.64
Northern Europe	134,392	158,702	203,984	199,195	199,043	7.54	-0.08
United Kingdom	134,392	158,702	203,984	199,195	199,043	7.54	-0.08
Other Europe	90,272	95,336	101,581	102,818	94,996	3.60	-7.61
Other countries of Europe	90,272	95,336	101,581	102,818	94,996	3.60	-7.61
REGION NOT SPECIFIED	86,747	90,154	101,130	119,938	126,234	4.78	5.25
Not Specified	86,747	90,154	101,130	119,938	126,234	4.78	5.25
Other countries of the World	86,747	90,154	101,130	119,938	126,234	4.78	5.25

Source: World Tourism Organization (UNWTO)

FINLAND

2. Arrivals of non-resident visitors at national borders, by country of residence

	2002	2003	2004	2005	2006	Market share 06	% Change 06-05
TOTAL (*)	4,687,000	4,527,000	4,854,000	5,038,000	5,345,000	100.00	6.09
AFRICA	7,000	9,000	6,000	12,000	13,000	0.24	8.33
Other Africa	7,000	9,000	6,000	12,000	13,000	0.24	8.33
All countries of Africa	7,000	9,000	6,000	12,000	13,000	0.24	8.33
AMERICAS	182,000	151,000	159,000	160,000	167,000	3.12	4.38
North America	159,000	134,000	141,000	142,000	142,000	2.66	
Canada	28,000	14,000	17,000	14,000	21,000	0.39	50.00
Mexico	1,000	1,000	5,000	2,000	2,000	0.04	
United States	130,000	119,000	119,000	126,000	119,000	2.23	-5.56
South America	23,000	17,000	18,000	18,000	25,000	0.47	38.89
All countries of South America	23,000	17,000	18,000	18,000	25,000	0.47	38.89
EAST ASIA AND THE PACIFIC	244,000	210,000	268,000	273,000	262,000	4.90	-4.03
North-East Asia	190,000	140,000	218,000	197,000	190,000	3.55	-3.55
China	72,000	54,000	71,000	75,000	69,000	1.29	-8.00
Taiwan (Province of China)	10,000	3,000	5,000	7,000	8,000	0.15	14.29
Hong Kong, China	7,000	2,000	7,000	3,000	3,000	0.06	
Japan	86,000	68,000	110,000	98,000	89,000	1.67	-9.18
Korea, Republic of	15,000	13,000	25,000	14,000	21,000	0.39	50.00
South-East Asia	6,000	5,000	4,000	2,000	7,000	0.13	250.00
Singapore	6,000	2,000	4,000	2,000	3,000	0.06	50.00
Thailand		3,000			4,000	0.07	
Australasia	21,000	21,000	24,000	18,000	32,000	0.60	77.78
Australia	19,000	19,000	22,000	16,000	30,000	0.56	87.50
New Zealand	2,000	2,000	2,000	2,000	2,000	0.04	
Other East Asia and the Pacific	27,000	44,000	22,000	56,000	33,000	0.62	-41.07
Other countries of Asia	27,000	44,000	22,000	56,000	33,000	0.62	-41.07
EUROPE	4,245,000	4,157,000	4,417,000	4,581,000	4,891,000	91.51	6.77
Central/Eastern Europe	1,979,000	1,942,000	2,144,000	2,278,000	2,404,000	44.98	5.53
Czech Republic	20,000	12,000	12,000	9,000	22,000	0.41	144.44
Estonia	303,000	228,000	383,000	457,000	503,000	9.41	10.07
Hungary	17,000	25,000	17,000	27,000	21,000	0.39	-22.22
Kazakhstan	6,000						
Latvia	47,000	31,000	31,000	34,000	33,000	0.62	-2.94
Lithuania	14,000	19,000	13,000	24,000	30,000	0.56	25.00
Poland	32,000	27,000	26,000	35,000	48,000	0.90	37.14
Romania			4,000	3,000	4,000	0.07	33.33
Russian Federation	1,530,000	1,589,000	1,647,000	1,684,000	1,737,000	32.50	3.15
Slovakia		2,000		2,000	3,000	0.06	50.00
Ukraine	10,000	9,000	11,000	3,000	3,000	0.06	
Northern Europe	1,331,000	1,323,000	1,324,000	1,322,000	1,404,000	26.27	6.20
Denmark	84,000	85,000	84,000	96,000	106,000	1.98	10.42
Iceland		2,000		4,000	4,000	0.07	
Ireland	22,000	20,000	13,000	9,000	11,000	0.21	22.22
Norway	186,000	175,000	182,000	197,000	187,000	3.50	-5.08
Sweden	763,000	779,000	794,000	783,000	779,000	14.57	-0.51
United Kingdom	276,000	262,000	251,000	233,000	317,000	5.93	36.05
Southern Europe	154,000	163,000	178,000	185,000	214,000	4.00	15.68
Greece	10,000	9,000	9,000	9,000	13,000	0.24	44.44
Italy	73,000	70,000	85,000	80,000	112,000	2.10	40.00

FINLAND

2. Arrivals of non-resident visitors at national borders, by country of residence

	2002	2003	2004	2005	2006	Market share 06	% Change 06-05
Portugal	12,000	12,000	12,000	6,000	7,000	0.13	16.67
Slovenia		2,000	3,000	2,000	3,000	0.06	50.00
Spain	59,000	70,000	69,000	88,000	79,000	1.48	-10.23
Western Europe	**741,000**	**692,000**	**724,000**	**711,000**	**798,000**	**14.93**	**12.24**
Austria	31,000	31,000	43,000	47,000	47,000	0.88	
Belgium	48,000	46,000	56,000	53,000	62,000	1.16	16.98
France	98,000	99,000	95,000	110,000	133,000	2.49	20.91
Germany	393,000	344,000	363,000	342,000	369,000	6.90	7.89
Luxembourg	5,000	6,000	4,000	2,000	2,000	0.04	
Netherlands	97,000	98,000	93,000	86,000	107,000	2.00	24.42
Switzerland	69,000	68,000	70,000	71,000	78,000	1.46	9.86
East Mediterranean Europe	**7,000**	**8,000**	**27,000**	**8,000**	**10,000**	**0.19**	**25.00**
Cyprus			6,000	1,000	1,000	0.02	
Israel	4,000	8,000	14,000	4,000	5,000	0.09	25.00
Turkey	3,000		7,000	3,000	4,000	0.07	33.33
Other Europe	**33,000**	**29,000**	**20,000**	**77,000**	**61,000**	**1.14**	**-20.78**
Other countries of Europe	33,000	29,000	20,000	77,000	61,000	1.14	-20.78
MIDDLE EAST	**4,000**			**4,000**	**4,000**	**0.07**	
Middle East	**4,000**			**4,000**	**4,000**	**0.07**	
All countries of Middle East	4,000			4,000	4,000	0.07	
SOUTH ASIA	**5,000**		**4,000**	**8,000**	**8,000**	**0.15**	
South Asia	**5,000**		**4,000**	**8,000**	**8,000**	**0.15**	
India			4,000	5,000	8,000	0.15	60.00
Other countries of South Asia	5,000			3,000			

Source: World Tourism Organization (UNWTO)

FINLAND

4. Arrivals of non-resident tourists in all types of accommodation establishments, by country of residence

		2002	2003	2004	2005	2006	Market share 06	% Change 06-05
TOTAL	(*)	2,042,540	2,047,444	2,083,487	2,080,194	2,325,330	100.00	11.78
AFRICA		3,646	3,370	3,185	4,123	5,147	0.22	24.84
East Africa		422	433	424	712	834	0.04	17.13
Burundi					4	23		475.00
Ethiopia		42	70	56	104	73		-29.81
Eritrea		5	3		12	4		-66.67
Djibouti						4		
Kenya		143	150	120	214	238	0.01	11.21
Malawi		5	4		6	3		-50.00
Mauritius		17	9		5	92		1,740.00
Mozambique		13	7	11	34	21		-38.24
Reunion						3		
Rwanda			31		9	24		166.67
Seychelles		16		6	7	7		
Somalia		70	28	15	59	53		-10.17
Zimbabwe		12	8	5	17	25		47.06
Uganda		30	9	5	22	27		22.73
United Republic of Tanzania		52	97	174	190	195	0.01	2.63
Zambia		17	17	32	29	42		44.83
Central Africa		62	84	38	80	100		25.00
Angola		21	11	7	5			
Cameroon		3	17	10	44	55		25.00
Central African Republic		4	3					
Chad					4			
Congo		34	45	21	18	33		83.33
Gabon			8		9	12		33.33
North Africa		992	636	661	798	1,057	0.05	32.46
Algeria		536	363	380	415	542	0.02	30.60
Morocco		345	150	164	217	302	0.01	39.17
Sudan		16	40	33	33	60		81.82
Tunisia		95	83	84	133	153	0.01	15.04
Southern Africa		1,694	1,635	1,509	1,893	2,440	0.10	28.90
Botswana		10			10	19		90.00
Namibia		34	24	27	138	186	0.01	34.78
South Africa		1,650	1,607	1,471	1,735	2,215	0.10	27.67
Swaziland			4	11	10	20		100.00
West Africa		476	582	553	640	716	0.03	11.88
Benin		14	10	13	14	10		-28.57
Gambia		15	6	15	9	7		-22.22
Ghana		35	32	30	26	35		34.62
Guinea		3	16		5	11		120.00
Cote D'Ivoire		5	19	21	90	32		-64.44
Liberia				4	4			
Mali		37	57		5	15		200.00
Mauritania			3	16	4	4		
Niger		32	36	105	74	89		20.27
Nigeria		55	124	145	130	187	0.01	43.85
Senegal		27	43	31	54	40		-25.93
Sierra Leone		244	223	173	207	271	0.01	30.92
Togo					5	7		40.00
Burkina Faso		9	13		13	8		-38.46
AMERICAS		108,446	102,034	111,245	105,992	110,530	4.75	4.28

240

FINLAND

4. Arrivals of non-resident tourists in all types of accommodation establishments, by country of residence

	2002	2003	2004	2005	2006	Market share 06	% Change 06-05
Caribbean	236	257	245	461	316	0.01	-31.45
Antigua and Barbuda	12		4				
Bahamas	5	14	22	153	129	0.01	-15.69
Barbados			3	6			
Bermuda	3	7	8	10	4		-60.00
Cayman Islands		6		5	3		-40.00
Cuba	128	140	83	156	71		-54.49
Dominican Republic	18	16	22	11	15		36.36
Guadeloupe	9	6					
Haiti	3			9	7		-22.22
Jamaica	22	23	5	42	36		-14.29
Netherlands Antilles	11	7	10	13	23		76.92
Puerto Rico	5	6	68	24	5		-79.17
Saint Kitts and Nevis	9	5					
Anguilla				3			
Saint Vincent and the Grenadines				3			
Trinidad and Tobago	11	27	20	11	4		-63.64
Turks and Caicos Islands				8	3		-62.50
United States Virgin Islands				7	16		128.57
Central America	171	232	123	114	218	0.01	91.23
Belize	17	11	6	20	46		130.00
Costa Rica	70	94	68	39	73		87.18
El Salvador	6		7	16	13		-18.75
Guatemala	39	83	7	9	32		255.56
Honduras	13				17		
Nicaragua	17	26	24	18	23		27.78
Panama	9	18	11	12	14		16.67
North America	102,232	96,559	105,902	99,854	102,839	4.42	2.99
Canada	10,488	12,199	10,988	10,888	12,172	0.52	11.79
Greenland	12	47	79	7	55		685.71
Mexico	1,460	1,491	1,351	1,905	1,874	0.08	-1.63
United States	90,272	82,822	93,484	87,054	88,738	3.82	1.93
South America	5,807	4,986	4,975	5,563	7,157	0.31	28.65
Argentina	905	1,077	948	628	775	0.03	23.41
Bolivia	67	92	65	42	55		30.95
Brazil	2,902	2,136	2,691	3,331	3,518	0.15	5.61
Chile	655	635	604	675	1,110	0.05	64.44
Colombia	155	123	152	200	261	0.01	30.50
Ecuador	48	24	26	34	69		102.94
Falkland Islands (Malvinas)					9		
Guyana	3	12					
Paraguay	7	3		7	5		-28.57
Peru	111	104	118	135	167	0.01	23.70
Suriname				3	4		33.33
Uruguay	693	715	258	337	966	0.04	186.65
Venezuela	261	65	113	171	218	0.01	27.49
EAST ASIA AND THE PACIFIC	157,635	146,652	167,808	158,128	188,447	8.10	19.17
North-East Asia	135,041	125,730	143,240	131,510	156,079	6.71	18.68
China	44,577	40,755	49,384	37,435	49,399	2.12	31.96
Taiwan (Province of China)	4,996	3,283	5,269	6,992	8,222	0.35	17.59
Hong Kong, China	1,899	2,169	2,154	2,461	3,087	0.13	25.44

FINLAND

4. Arrivals of non-resident tourists in all types of accommodation establishments, by country of residence

	2002	2003	2004	2005	2006	Market share 06	% Change 06-05
Japan	74,173	69,063	70,694	70,434	78,940	3.39	12.08
Korea, Dem. People's Republic of	461	178	299	602	716	0.03	18.94
Korea, Republic of	8,864	10,242	15,418	13,544	15,648	0.67	15.53
Macao, China	5		3	7	13		85.71
Mongolia	66	40	19	35	54		54.29
South-East Asia	**7,804**	**7,009**	**8,088**	**9,167**	**10,772**	**0.46**	**17.51**
Brunei Darussalam	5	4		11	29		163.64
Myanmar	18	46	13	132	188	0.01	42.42
Cambodia	5		6		3		
Indonesia	810	592	787	760	1,200	0.05	57.89
Lao People's Democratic Republic	7	7	9	7	40		471.43
Malaysia	528	589	669	845	1,201	0.05	42.13
Philippines	521	753	529	515	649	0.03	26.02
Singapore	1,721	2,033	2,283	2,361	2,670	0.11	13.09
Viet Nam	176	192	194	203	296	0.01	45.81
Thailand	4,013	2,793	3,598	4,333	4,496	0.19	3.76
Australasia	**14,469**	**13,657**	**16,362**	**17,367**	**21,405**	**0.92**	**23.25**
Australia	12,562	11,832	14,443	15,659	19,424	0.84	24.04
New Zealand	1,907	1,825	1,919	1,708	1,981	0.09	15.98
Melanesia	**20**	**24**	**4**	**2**	**75**		**3,650.00**
Solomon Islands		18			6		
Fiji	9		4				
Papua New Guinea	11	6		2	69		3,350.00
Micronesia	**7**	**3**	**3**	**8**	**23**		**187.50**
Guam	7	3	3	8	20		150.00
Micronesia (Federated States of)					3		
Polynesia	**294**	**229**	**111**	**74**	**93**		**25.68**
American Samoa	287	224	106	68	83		22.06
Cook Islands	7						
French Polynesia				3	4		33.33
Tokelau		5	5	3	6		100.00
EUROPE	**1,659,534**	**1,683,624**	**1,698,936**	**1,712,228**	**1,884,448**	**81.04**	**10.06**
Central/Eastern Europe	**325,967**	**310,367**	**312,794**	**358,429**	**465,768**	**20.03**	**29.95**
Azerbaijan	95	14	38	58	62		6.90
Armenia	129	76	52	103	156	0.01	51.46
Bulgaria	1,287	1,205	1,219	1,266	1,681	0.07	32.78
Belarus	491	481	296	565	686	0.03	21.42
Czech Republic	8,367	9,450	8,019	9,216	10,712	0.46	16.23
Estonia	51,796	54,577	60,359	68,037	81,597	3.51	19.93
Georgia	203	243	230	458	803	0.03	75.33
Hungary	7,527	7,417	8,936	9,144	11,379	0.49	24.44
Kazakhstan	180	202	232	642	499	0.02	-22.27
Kyrgyzstan	7	33		41	6		-85.37
Latvia	12,759	13,201	11,789	13,072	16,729	0.72	27.98
Lithuania	6,274	6,549	6,616	7,246	9,560	0.41	31.93
Republic of Moldova	16	56	64	43	111		158.14
Poland	17,016	16,395	19,123	19,636	23,083	0.99	17.55
Romania	1,770	2,077	2,570	2,823	4,181	0.18	48.10
Russian Federation	215,159	194,388	190,190	221,088	298,898	12.85	35.19
Slovakia	1,654	2,287	1,630	2,389	2,952	0.13	23.57
Tajikistan					9		
Turkmenistan	9	11					

FINLAND

4. Arrivals of non-resident tourists in all types of accommodation establishments, by country of residence

	2002	2003	2004	2005	2006	Market share 06	% Change 06-05
Ukraine	1,187	1,675	1,402	2,578	2,617	0.11	1.51
Uzbekistan	41	30	29	24	47		95.83
Northern Europe	**673,986**	**677,651**	**677,467**	**659,727**	**697,505**	**30.00**	**5.73**
Denmark	55,063	54,287	58,191	57,825	62,966	2.71	8.89
Faeroe Islands	68	169	80	66	71		7.58
Iceland	2,799	3,550	3,097	3,589	3,713	0.16	3.46
Ireland	9,628	9,250	9,810	9,361	10,849	0.47	15.90
Norway	110,291	101,478	98,025	93,722	98,654	4.24	5.26
Sweden	344,115	341,100	338,292	328,014	332,634	14.30	1.41
United Kingdom	152,022	167,817	169,972	167,150	188,618	8.11	12.84
Southern Europe	**137,001**	**142,818**	**149,942**	**140,959**	**164,952**	**7.09**	**17.02**
Albania	735	812	969	625	535	0.02	-14.40
Andorra	297	94	86	30	45		50.00
Bosnia and Herzegovina	247	192	137	108	167	0.01	54.63
Croatia	797	959	1,234	1,088	1,235	0.05	13.51
Greece	9,024	7,486	8,955	8,583	12,772	0.55	48.81
Holy See				3			
Italy	67,666	72,501	77,287	68,213	78,588	3.38	15.21
Malta	972	242	408	175	404	0.02	130.86
Portugal	5,405	6,158	5,986	5,585	6,920	0.30	23.90
San Marino	16	22	10	12	31		158.33
Slovenia	1,509	2,177	2,234	2,223	3,253	0.14	46.33
Spain	49,301	50,518	51,608	53,158	60,861	2.62	14.49
TFYR of Macedonia	60	109			141	0.01	
Serbia and Montenegro	972	1,548	1,028	1,156			
Western Europe	**514,578**	**545,788**	**550,275**	**544,852**	**546,178**	**23.49**	**0.24**
Austria	19,099	19,164	20,163	23,055	24,417	1.05	5.91
Belgium	21,103	23,249	23,982	22,622	26,392	1.13	16.67
France	73,536	81,065	87,451	85,326	90,778	3.90	6.39
Germany	247,143	256,049	263,160	268,642	263,502	11.33	-1.91
Liechtenstein	1,632	559	449	191	229	0.01	19.90
Luxembourg	1,164	1,072	1,377	1,479	1,551	0.07	4.87
Monaco	56	82	122	91	97		6.59
Netherlands	104,260	110,847	101,452	93,077	87,524	3.76	-5.97
Switzerland	46,585	53,701	52,119	50,369	51,688	2.22	2.62
East Mediterranean Europe	**8,002**	**7,000**	**8,458**	**8,261**	**10,045**	**0.43**	**21.60**
Cyprus	878	547	1,074	760	775	0.03	1.97
Israel	4,369	3,716	4,160	4,338	5,318	0.23	22.59
Turkey	2,755	2,737	3,224	3,163	3,952	0.17	24.94
MIDDLE EAST	**3,857**	**3,463**	**3,168**	**3,613**	**3,824**	**0.16**	**5.84**
Middle East	**3,857**	**3,463**	**3,168**	**3,613**	**3,824**	**0.16**	**5.84**
Bahrain	434	400	659	859	742	0.03	-13.62
Iraq	86	109	139	111	88		-20.72
Jordan	113	114	67	105	93		-11.43
Kuwait	476	226	88	105	351	0.02	234.29
Lebanon	229	349	499	132	147	0.01	11.36
Libyan Arab Jamahiriya	36	14	14	36	63		75.00
Oman	4			6	20		233.33
Qatar	91	12	14	20	52		160.00
Saudi Arabia	1,432	1,491	905	1,314	1,163	0.05	-11.49
Syrian Arab Republic	81	58	52	44	92		109.09
United Arab Emirates	168	92	218	299	350	0.02	17.06

FINLAND

4. Arrivals of non-resident tourists in all types of accommodation establishments, by country of residence

	2002	2003	2004	2005	2006	Market share 06	% Change 06-05
Egypt	707	585	513	582	658	0.03	13.06
Yemen		13			5		
SOUTH ASIA	**5,285**	**5,361**	**5,965**	**7,445**	**10,707**	**0.46**	**43.81**
South Asia	**5,285**	**5,361**	**5,965**	**7,445**	**10,707**	**0.46**	**43.81**
Afghanistan	864	674	321	684	791	0.03	15.64
Bangladesh	19	17	174	216	173	0.01	-19.91
Sri Lanka	64	59	102	50	48		-4.00
India	3,452	3,730	4,100	5,245	8,339	0.36	58.99
Iran, Islamic Republic of	685	627	976	926	887	0.04	-4.21
Nepal	19	29	55	61	109		78.69
Pakistan	182	225	237	263	360	0.02	36.88
REGION NOT SPECIFIED	**104,137**	**102,940**	**93,180**	**88,665**	**122,227**	**5.26**	**37.85**
Not Specified	**104,137**	**102,940**	**93,180**	**88,665**	**122,227**	**5.26**	**37.85**
Other countries of the World	104,137	102,940	93,180	88,665	122,227	5.26	37.85

Source: World Tourism Organization (UNWTO)

FINLAND

5. Overnight stays of non-resident tourists in hotels and similar establishments, by country of residence

		2002	2003	2004	2005	2006	Market share 06	% Change 06-05
TOTAL	(*)	3,720,579	3,757,653	3,758,073	3,886,679	4,353,595	100.00	12.01
AFRICA		9,004	8,919	9,969	13,339	14,569	0.33	9.22
East Africa		1,227	1,088	1,205	2,320	1,905	0.04	-17.89
British Indian Ocean Territory					2			
Burundi					3	27		800.00
Ethiopia		172	213	157	265	258	0.01	-2.64
Eritrea		20	6	3	22	15		-31.82
Djibouti						4		
Kenya		339	306	283	733	603	0.01	-17.74
Madagascar					57	4		-92.98
Malawi		20	8	3	30	10		-66.67
Mauritius		50	11	3	21	133		533.33
Mozambique		31	17	26	139	118		-15.11
Reunion		5				4		
Rwanda		3	41		38	44		15.79
Seychelles		23		10	6	8		33.33
Somalia		221	68	15	166	93		-43.98
Zimbabwe		30	11	5	52	46		-11.54
Uganda		60	6	40	64	71		10.94
United Republic of Tanzania		202	336	402	628	320	0.01	-49.04
Zambia		51	65	258	94	147		56.38
Central Africa		50	145	98	280	143		-48.93
Angola		13	18	24	23	3		-86.96
Cameroon		3	34	20	210	82		-60.95
Central African Republic		5	4	8	2	4		100.00
Chad					7			
Congo		29	75	37	23	51		121.74
Gabon			14	9	15	3		-80.00
North Africa		2,324	1,360	2,218	2,952	3,112	0.07	5.42
Algeria		1,275	688	1,407	1,601	1,732	0.04	8.18
Morocco		643	313	445	722	651	0.01	-9.83
Sudan		38	126	130	121	287	0.01	137.19
Tunisia		368	233	236	508	442	0.01	-12.99
Southern Africa		4,581	4,703	5,015	5,682	7,491	0.17	31.84
Botswana		8			38	30		-21.05
Namibia		89	55	80	410	486	0.01	18.54
South Africa		4,484	4,644	4,915	5,218	6,940	0.16	33.00
Swaziland			4	20	16	35		118.75
West Africa		822	1,623	1,433	2,105	1,898	0.04	-9.83
Benin		61	66	102	48	30		-37.50
Gambia		25	3	119	22	11		-50.00
Ghana		65	252	263	399	479	0.01	20.05
Guinea		3	4	3	37	42		13.51
Cote D'Ivoire		13	84	52	142	80		-43.66
Liberia		4		10	39	18		-53.85
Mali		51	117		20	70		250.00
Mauritania				35	17	21		23.53
Niger		50	79	229	184	237	0.01	28.80
Nigeria		142	503	271	332	426	0.01	28.31
Saint Helena					4	3		-25.00
Senegal		75	117	53	212	64		-69.81
Sierra Leone		311	364	291	603	385	0.01	-36.15

FINLAND

5. Overnight stays of non-resident tourists in hotels and similar establishments, by country of residence

	2002	2003	2004	2005	2006	Market share 06	% Change 06-05
Togo	3	6		18	10		-44.44
Burkina Faso	19	28	5	28	22		-21.43
Other Africa					**20**		
All countries of Africa					20		
AMERICAS	**243,624**	**237,161**	**251,547**	**254,252**	**254,050**	**5.84**	**-0.08**
Caribbean	**833**	**1,242**	**533**	**1,530**	**647**	**0.01**	**-57.71**
Antigua and Barbuda	48	6	19	2	11		450.00
Bahamas	7	20	31	249	169		-32.13
Barbados	7			31	3		-90.32
Bermuda		12	11	91	7		-92.31
Cayman Islands		13		9	21		133.33
Cuba	304	895	267	464	187		-59.70
Dominica				2			
Dominican Republic	60	39	67	26	28		7.69
Grenada				6			
Guadeloupe	9	4					
Haiti	7		4	18	18		
Jamaica	86	69	10	305	74		-75.74
Netherlands Antilles	47	16	21	25	45		80.00
Aruba		3	7				
Puerto Rico	8	17	67	90	23		-74.44
Saint Kitts and Nevis	27	6					
Anguilla		4	4	9			
Saint Vincent and the Grenadines	11			27			
Trinidad and Tobago	210	136	19	88	14		-84.09
Turks and Caicos Islands	2	2		31			
United States Virgin Islands			6	57	47		-17.54
Central America	**540**	**781**	**265**	**403**	**598**	**0.01**	**48.39**
Belize	48	41	21	89	196		120.22
Costa Rica	254	487	98	103	166		61.17
El Salvador	15		13	72	33		-54.17
Guatemala	90	156	13	39	69		76.92
Honduras	35			8	39		387.50
Nicaragua	77	74	105	48	63		31.25
Panama	21	23	15	44	32		-27.27
North America	**230,104**	**223,957**	**238,908**	**238,693**	**236,395**	**5.43**	**-0.96**
Canada	25,993	31,888	29,474	29,665	29,123	0.67	-1.83
Greenland	30	138	155	23	111		382.61
Mexico	3,137	3,866	3,201	4,575	4,255	0.10	-6.99
United States	200,944	188,065	206,078	204,430	202,906	4.66	-0.75
South America	**12,147**	**11,174**	**11,841**	**13,626**	**16,390**	**0.38**	**20.28**
Argentina	2,489	3,508	1,905	1,539	1,649	0.04	7.15
Bolivia	91	113	60	79	197		149.37
Brazil	6,751	5,336	6,996	8,675	8,684	0.20	0.10
Chile	1,390	1,407	1,840	1,620	2,337	0.05	44.26
Colombia	388	239	324	426	469	0.01	10.09
Ecuador	110	54	28	77	337	0.01	337.66
Guyana	15	83		14	3		-78.57
Paraguay	22	8		13	8		-38.46
Peru	192	173	241	357	332	0.01	-7.00
Suriname				30	14		-53.33
Uruguay	110	119	185	398	1,831	0.04	360.05

FINLAND

5. Overnight stays of non-resident tourists in hotels and similar establishments, by country of residence

	2002	2003	2004	2005	2006	Market share 06	% Change 06-05
Venezuela	589	134	262	398	529	0.01	32.91
Other Americas		7			20		
Other countries of the Americas		7			20		
EAST ASIA AND THE PACIFIC	**280,739**	**271,734**	**298,035**	**299,147**	**345,204**	**7.93**	**15.40**
North-East Asia	**238,502**	**229,997**	**251,860**	**246,692**	**282,523**	**6.49**	**14.52**
China	80,238	76,745	86,485	71,904	92,845	2.13	29.12
Taiwan (Province of China)	7,063	5,209	7,198	10,080	11,042	0.25	9.54
Hong Kong, China	2,984	3,382	3,473	4,346	6,715	0.15	54.51
Japan	132,447	126,595	129,669	136,040	145,210	3.34	6.74
Korea, Dem. People's Republic of	1,877	452	558	1,631	1,738	0.04	6.56
Korea, Republic of	13,724	17,478	24,418	22,599	24,880	0.57	10.09
Macao, China	6		11	15	24		60.00
Mongolia	163	136	48	77	69		-10.39
South-East Asia	**16,801**	**16,724**	**16,739**	**20,425**	**22,395**	**0.51**	**9.65**
Brunei Darussalam	24	13		42	148		252.38
Myanmar	84	80	21	391	310	0.01	-20.72
Cambodia	19		16		6		
Indonesia	2,179	1,896	1,768	2,156	3,315	0.08	53.76
Lao People's Democratic Republic	5	11	26	18	75		316.67
Malaysia	1,459	1,395	1,875	2,988	3,010	0.07	0.74
Philippines	1,483	2,398	1,286	981	1,524	0.04	55.35
Singapore	4,585	5,480	5,581	6,293	6,121	0.14	-2.73
Viet Nam	658	740	659	1,022	1,054	0.02	3.13
Thailand	6,305	4,711	5,507	6,534	6,832	0.16	4.56
Australasia	**24,871**	**24,563**	**28,957**	**31,682**	**39,801**	**0.91**	**25.63**
Australia	21,719	21,288	25,629	28,305	35,406	0.81	25.09
New Zealand	3,152	3,275	3,328	3,377	4,395	0.10	30.15
Melanesia	**33**	**51**	**5**	**9**	**146**		**1,522.22**
Solomon Islands		28			19		
Fiji	11				4		
New Caledonia	16				6		
Papua New Guinea	6	23			117		
All countries of Melanesia			5	9			
Micronesia	**14**	**11**	**8**	**28**	**38**		**35.71**
Guam	4	3	8	15	32		113.33
Nauru	10	8		13	3		-76.92
Micronesia (Federated States of)					3		
Polynesia	**518**	**388**	**466**	**311**	**301**	**0.01**	**-3.22**
American Samoa	509	374	459	300	283	0.01	-5.67
Cook Islands	5						
French Polynesia				8	5		-37.50
Tokelau	4	14	7	3	13		333.33
EUROPE	**2,977,271**	**3,037,811**	**3,011,341**	**3,109,190**	**3,460,910**	**79.50**	**11.31**
Central/Eastern Europe	**713,387**	**661,908**	**640,470**	**732,206**	**949,784**	**21.82**	**29.72**
Azerbaijan	205	17	92	85	180		111.76
Armenia	283	206	151	355	456	0.01	28.45
Bulgaria	2,705	3,046	2,934	3,641	4,423	0.10	21.48
Belarus	2,476	1,704	809	1,900	2,128	0.05	12.00
Czech Republic	19,954	20,593	17,646	20,471	22,913	0.53	11.93
Estonia	92,169	89,838	103,928	121,916	147,889	3.40	21.30

FINLAND

5. Overnight stays of non-resident tourists in hotels and similar establishments, by country of residence

	2002	2003	2004	2005	2006	Market share 06	% Change 06-05
Georgia	598	579	486	979	1,510	0.03	54.24
Hungary	20,058	17,514	19,950	21,996	28,771	0.66	30.80
Kazakhstan	823	903	1,611	2,863	1,532	0.04	-46.49
Kyrgyzstan	48	183	56	147	25		-82.99
Latvia	20,628	22,947	19,625	19,872	24,428	0.56	22.93
Lithuania	12,472	11,346	12,420	15,333	16,042	0.37	4.62
Republic of Moldova	42	143	62	152	381	0.01	150.66
Poland	37,375	32,907	36,427	44,537	65,324	1.50	46.67
Romania	4,614	4,704	4,079	5,965	9,736	0.22	63.22
Russian Federation	491,162	445,120	411,989	457,904	607,883	13.96	32.75
Slovakia	3,452	4,895	3,179	4,572	8,032	0.18	75.68
Tajikistan	7			3	52		1,633.33
Turkmenistan	14	14		9			
Ukraine	4,211	5,132	4,975	9,420	7,912	0.18	-16.01
Uzbekistan	91	117	51	86	167		94.19
Northern Europe	**1,115,875**	**1,136,373**	**1,111,677**	**1,100,492**	**1,177,420**	**27.04**	**6.99**
Denmark	93,930	90,558	95,652	92,443	100,789	2.32	9.03
Faeroe Islands	164	739	215	146	135		-7.53
Iceland	6,412	8,218	8,247	10,507	10,405	0.24	-0.97
Ireland	21,435	25,834	20,991	20,496	25,650	0.59	25.15
Norway	169,936	155,860	153,509	143,441	150,457	3.46	4.89
Sweden	463,962	470,392	461,128	450,344	452,864	10.40	0.56
United Kingdom	360,036	384,772	371,935	383,115	437,120	10.04	14.10
Southern Europe	**258,554**	**274,110**	**282,941**	**274,866**	**315,811**	**7.25**	**14.90**
Albania	2,266	2,431	2,602	1,883	1,316	0.03	-30.11
Andorra	524	205	239	30	80		166.67
Bosnia and Herzegovina	369	754	275	412	315	0.01	-23.54
Croatia	1,689	2,249	2,905	3,055	3,720	0.09	21.77
Greece	22,200	19,586	22,555	21,386	29,128	0.67	36.20
Holy See	4			3			
Italy	122,945	132,681	143,132	130,143	146,546	3.37	12.60
Malta	1,866	475	873	421	971	0.02	130.64
Portugal	11,357	14,256	11,741	11,586	15,057	0.35	29.96
San Marino	54	21	25	15	90		500.00
Slovenia	3,111	4,556	3,866	4,155	5,710	0.13	37.42
Spain	89,580	92,985	92,703	99,169	112,519	2.58	13.46
TFYR of Macedonia	121	379			359	0.01	
Serbia and Montenegro	2,468	3,532	2,025	2,608			
Western Europe	**871,440**	**950,630**	**956,349**	**980,918**	**991,013**	**22.76**	**1.03**
Austria	39,417	37,169	35,091	41,382	41,315	0.95	-0.16
Belgium	37,664	42,115	45,193	45,780	51,748	1.19	13.04
France	144,936	168,450	190,304	203,782	206,705	4.75	1.43
Germany	399,242	420,542	429,679	439,363	440,827	10.13	0.33
Liechtenstein	3,139	1,067	952	527	525	0.01	-0.38
Luxembourg	2,768	2,267	2,932	3,447	3,320	0.08	-3.68
Monaco	111	199	259	274	191		-30.29
Netherlands	163,559	182,432	164,406	164,682	160,640	3.69	-2.45
Switzerland	80,604	96,389	87,533	81,681	85,742	1.97	4.97
East Mediterranean Europe	**18,015**	**14,790**	**19,904**	**20,708**	**26,882**	**0.62**	**29.81**
Cyprus	1,567	1,251	2,016	2,025	2,616	0.06	29.19
Israel	9,388	7,504	9,841	9,471	13,919	0.32	46.96
Turkey	7,060	6,035	8,047	9,212	10,347	0.24	12.32
MIDDLE EAST	**12,383**	**11,254**	**8,537**	**12,500**	**12,224**	**0.28**	**-2.21**

FINLAND

5. Overnight stays of non-resident tourists in hotels and similar establishments, by country of residence

	2002	2003	2004	2005	2006	Market share 06	% Change 06-05
Middle East	**12,383**	**11,254**	**8,537**	**12,500**	**12,224**	**0.28**	**-2.21**
Bahrain	1,012	761	1,533	2,385	1,303	0.03	-45.37
Iraq	230	306	280	368	322	0.01	-12.50
Jordan	364	364	159	402	227	0.01	-43.53
Kuwait	796	460	361	357	1,677	0.04	369.75
Lebanon	550	623	851	393	485	0.01	23.41
Libyan Arab Jamahiriya	120	28	63	135	311	0.01	130.37
Oman	8	14	11	30	56		86.67
Qatar	203	43	27	54	78		44.44
Saudi Arabia	5,839	6,051	2,561	5,589	4,322	0.10	-22.67
Syrian Arab Republic	268	133	144	108	257	0.01	137.96
United Arab Emirates	784	291	604	796	695	0.02	-12.69
Egypt	2,209	2,164	1,943	1,877	2,472	0.06	31.70
Yemen		16		6	19		216.67
SOUTH ASIA	**18,616**	**18,841**	**24,338**	**35,322**	**44,978**	**1.03**	**27.34**
South Asia	**18,616**	**18,841**	**24,338**	**35,322**	**44,978**	**1.03**	**27.34**
Afghanistan	1,651	1,300	920	2,885	1,785	0.04	-38.13
Bangladesh	16	8	203	260	269	0.01	3.46
Bhutan				4			
Sri Lanka	800	1,291	871	167	99		-40.72
India	13,542	13,665	18,464	26,984	38,971	0.90	44.42
Iran, Islamic Republic of	1,866	1,814	3,190	4,139	2,631	0.06	-36.43
Maldives			9	4			
Nepal	43	72	53	106	278	0.01	162.26
Pakistan	698	691	628	773	945	0.02	22.25
REGION NOT SPECIFIED	**178,942**	**171,933**	**154,306**	**162,929**	**221,660**	**5.09**	**36.05**
Not Specified	**178,942**	**171,933**	**154,306**	**162,929**	**221,660**	**5.09**	**36.05**
Other countries of the World	178,942	171,933	154,306	162,929	221,660	5.09	36.05

Source: World Tourism Organization (UNWTO)

FINLAND

6. Overnight stays of non-resident tourists in all types of accommodation establishments, by country of residence

		2002	2003	2004	2005	2006	Market share 06	% Change 06-05
TOTAL	(*)	4,290,287	4,330,690	4,383,198	4,498,635	5,036,202	100.00	11.95
AFRICA		9,659	9,572	10,793	14,146	15,320	0.30	8.30
East Africa		1,335	1,190	1,404	2,449	2,025	0.04	-17.31
Burundi					7	39		457.14
Ethiopia		183	215	213	270	261	0.01	-3.33
Eritrea		20	6	3	22	15		-31.82
Djibouti						4		
Kenya		383	344	338	755	605	0.01	-19.87
Madagascar					57	4		-92.98
Malawi		20	8		30	10		-66.67
Mauritius		51	46	6	21	134		538.10
Mozambique		31	18	26	139	118		-15.11
Reunion		5				4		
Rwanda		3	41		39	44		12.82
Seychelles		24		10	10	8		-20.00
Somalia		252	72	21	214	100		-53.27
Zimbabwe		32	13	13	57	48		-15.79
Uganda		78	14	40	64	76		18.75
United Republic of Tanzania		202	348	472	669	407	0.01	-39.16
Zambia		51	65	262	95	148		55.79
Central Africa		114	174	275	507	351	0.01	-30.77
Angola		55	27	24	25	3		-88.00
Cameroon		3	40	22	240	145		-39.58
Central African Republic		5	5	8	9	5		-44.44
Congo		51	88	37	28	51		82.14
Democratic Republic of the Congo				175	190	134		-29.47
Gabon			14	9	15	13		-13.33
North Africa		2,511	1,590	2,264	3,020	3,177	0.06	5.20
Algeria		1,380	839	1,418	1,621	1,743	0.03	7.53
Morocco		709	352	467	760	682	0.01	-10.26
Sudan		38	126	131	121	299	0.01	147.11
Tunisia		384	273	248	518	453	0.01	-12.55
Southern Africa		4,747	4,840	5,302	5,932	7,721	0.15	30.16
Botswana		35			38	32		-15.79
Lesotho					4			
Namibia		94	55	160	419	486	0.01	15.99
South Africa		4,618	4,781	5,122	5,455	7,165	0.14	31.35
Swaziland			4	20	16	38		137.50
West Africa		952	1,778	1,548	2,238	2,046	0.04	-8.58
Benin		61	66	102	48	30		-37.50
Gambia		27	6	119	25	13		-48.00
Ghana		102	264	295	411	495	0.01	20.44
Guinea		3	53	3	37	43		16.22
Cote D'Ivoire		13	84	52	142	80		-43.66
Liberia		4		8	39	18		-53.85
Mali		51	117		20	70		250.00
Mauritania		3	3	37	17	22		29.41
Niger		54	81	229	184	237		28.80
Nigeria		151	545	348	389	524	0.01	34.70
Guinea-Bissau					7			
Saint Helena					4	3		-25.00
Senegal		85	121	57	246	71		-71.14

FINLAND

6. Overnight stays of non-resident tourists in all types of accommodation establishments, by country of residence

	2002	2003	2004	2005	2006	Market share 06	% Change 06-05
Sierra Leone	370	404	293	622	397	0.01	-36.17
Togo	5	6		19	13		-31.58
Burkina Faso	23	28	5	28	30		7.14
AMERICAS	**251,963**	**245,506**	**258,749**	**261,010**	**262,825**	**5.22**	**0.70**
Caribbean	**863**	**1,321**	**616**	**1,542**	**687**	**0.01**	**-55.45**
Antigua and Barbuda	48	6	19		11		
Bahamas	7	23	31	249	169		-32.13
Barbados	6		3	37	3		-91.89
Bermuda	4	13	52	91	7		-92.31
Cayman Islands		13		11	21		90.91
Cuba	332	961	267	469	214		-54.37
Dominica					2		
Dominican Republic	66	38	68	44	27		-38.64
Grenada				8			
Guadeloupe	9	6					
Haiti	7		4	18	18		
Jamaica	89	76	12	307	74		-75.90
Netherlands Antilles	47	16	21	24	46		91.67
Puerto Rico	8	17	71	99	22		-77.78
Saint Kitts and Nevis	27	6					
Anguilla		4		9			
Saint Lucia			8				
Trinidad and Tobago	211	140	52	88	12		-86.36
Turks and Caicos Islands	2	2		31	3		-90.32
United States Virgin Islands			8	57	58		1.75
Central America	**595**	**809**	**343**	**431**	**628**	**0.01**	**45.71**
Belize	48	41	21	89	198		122.47
Costa Rica	303	508	166	116	173		49.14
El Salvador	15		13	74	39		-47.30
Guatemala	91	162	17	47	77		63.83
Honduras	37			8	39		387.50
Nicaragua	77	74	107	48	69		43.75
Panama	24	24	19	49	33		-32.65
North America	**236,366**	**230,111**	**244,997**	**244,475**	**243,357**	**4.83**	**-0.46**
Canada	27,296	33,360	30,197	30,861	31,074	0.62	0.69
Greenland	30	4,190	333	23	111		382.61
Mexico	3,481	138	3,518	4,896	4,607	0.09	-5.90
United States	205,559	192,423	210,949	208,695	207,565	4.12	-0.54
South America	**14,139**	**13,265**	**12,793**	**14,562**	**18,153**	**0.36**	**24.66**
Argentina	2,582	3,589	2,022	1,636	1,752	0.03	7.09
Bolivia	196	204	99	93	200		115.05
Brazil	7,167	5,808	7,173	8,922	8,843	0.18	-0.89
Chile	1,533	1,475	1,956	1,684	2,435	0.05	44.60
Colombia	424	278	353	469	518	0.01	10.45
Ecuador	123	64	69	85	360	0.01	323.53
Falkland Islands (Malvinas)					12		
French Guiana					4		
Guyana	15	84		16	3		-81.25
Paraguay	22	8		13	8		-38.46
Peru	227	204	286	397	407	0.01	2.52
Suriname				30	14		-53.33
Uruguay	1,231	1,390	546	779	3,005	0.06	285.75
Venezuela	619	161	289	438	592	0.01	35.16

FINLAND

6. Overnight stays of non-resident tourists in all types of accommodation establishments, by country of residence

	2002	2003	2004	2005	2006	Market share 06	% Change 06-05
EAST ASIA AND THE PACIFIC	291,888	283,532	310,044	309,799	357,420	7.10	15.37
North-East Asia	244,265	236,715	257,912	252,245	289,041	5.74	14.59
China	80,929	77,368	87,444	72,579	94,198	1.87	29.79
Taiwan (Province of China)	7,301	5,392	7,446	10,332	11,520	0.23	11.50
Hong Kong, China	3,287	3,696	3,664	4,586	6,975	0.14	52.09
Japan	136,247	131,062	133,799	139,912	148,973	2.96	6.48
Korea, Dem. People's Republic of	1,885	457	175	1,631	1,746	0.03	7.05
Korea, Republic of	14,418	18,454	25,321	23,111	25,500	0.51	10.34
Macao, China	8		11	15	24		60.00
Mongolia	190	286	52	79	105		32.91
South-East Asia	17,566	17,368	17,234	20,905	23,077	0.46	10.39
Brunei Darussalam	24	13		45	148		228.89
Myanmar	96	86	29	390	310	0.01	-20.51
Cambodia	19		16		6		
Indonesia	2,226	1,919	1,788	2,197	3,371	0.07	53.44
Lao People's Democratic Republic	7	19	26	19	75		294.74
Malaysia	1,663	1,638	1,996	3,068	3,167	0.06	3.23
Philippines	1,536	2,419	1,297	1,049	1,557	0.03	48.43
Singapore	4,746	5,625	5,727	6,431	6,352	0.13	-1.23
Viet Nam	721	814	720	1,054	1,082	0.02	2.66
Thailand	6,528	4,835	5,635	6,652	7,009	0.14	5.37
Australasia	29,455	28,996	34,405	36,301	44,816	0.89	23.46
Australia	25,575	25,098	30,315	32,264	39,872	0.79	23.58
New Zealand	3,880	3,898	4,090	4,037	4,944	0.10	22.47
Melanesia	57	51	5	9	145		1,511.11
Solomon Islands		28			19		
Fiji	11			9	3		-66.67
New Caledonia	16				6		
Papua New Guinea	30	23			117		
All countries of Melanesia			5				
Micronesia	32	11	8	28	40		42.86
Guam	6	3	8	15	32		113.33
Nauru	26	8		13	8		-38.46
Polynesia	513	391	480	311	301	0.01	-3.22
American Samoa	509	377	459	300	283	0.01	-5.67
French Polynesia				8	5		-37.50
Tokelau	4	14	7	3	13		333.33
Tuvalu			14				
EUROPE	3,520,649	3,584,932	3,610,277	3,698,704	4,114,247	81.69	11.23
Central/Eastern Europe	787,270	732,837	726,921	839,875	1,100,156	21.84	30.99
Azerbaijan	221	23	108	122	192		57.38
Armenia	324	302	151	355	463	0.01	30.42
Bulgaria	2,862	3,141	3,085	3,795	4,581	0.09	20.71
Belarus	2,584	1,730	1,060	3,010	4,116	0.08	36.74
Czech Republic	23,049	23,784	20,798	23,774	26,573	0.53	11.77
Estonia	104,753	105,952	128,246	157,521	195,550	3.88	24.14
Georgia	655	707	728	1,214	1,567	0.03	29.08
Hungary	22,140	19,610	22,494	24,876	31,608	0.63	27.06
Kazakhstan	823	906	1,611	2,891	1,546	0.03	-46.52
Kyrgyzstan	50	183	56	147	25		-82.99
Latvia	25,438	27,885	24,997	27,909	35,799	0.71	28.27

FINLAND

6. Overnight stays of non-resident tourists in all types of accommodation establishments, by country of residence

	2002	2003	2004	2005	2006	Market share 06	% Change 06-05
Lithuania	14,070	13,797	15,007	17,405	19,348	0.38	11.16
Republic of Moldova	72	174	135	155	388	0.01	150.32
Poland	44,831	39,801	45,994	53,522	74,790	1.49	39.74
Romania	5,090	5,510	5,700	7,680	12,386	0.25	61.28
Russian Federation	531,556	478,433	447,210	499,307	673,120	13.37	34.81
Slovakia	4,154	5,478	4,022	5,841	9,241	0.18	58.21
Tajikistan	7		7	10	59		490.00
Turkmenistan	14	14		9			
Ukraine	4,486	5,284	5,449	10,242	8,631	0.17	-15.73
Uzbekistan	91	123	63	90	173		92.22
Northern Europe	**1,359,965**	**1,376,009**	**1,359,352**	**1,344,376**	**1,438,825**	**28.57**	**7.03**
Denmark	102,650	98,005	104,317	100,546	110,460	2.19	9.86
Faeroe Islands	210	749	229	157	154		-1.91
Iceland	6,740	8,945	8,523	11,213	10,611	0.21	-5.37
Ireland	22,383	26,803	22,121	21,820	27,217	0.54	24.73
Norway	235,756	215,098	205,087	191,533	206,241	4.10	7.68
Sweden	613,494	612,607	608,765	597,641	606,714	12.05	1.52
United Kingdom	378,732	413,802	410,310	421,466	477,428	9.48	13.28
Southern Europe	**286,347**	**303,102**	**315,219**	**303,867**	**348,516**	**6.92**	**14.69**
Albania	2,279	2,491	2,612	1,891	1,333	0.03	-29.51
Andorra	525	209	243	74	81		9.46
Bosnia and Herzegovina	650	1,448	284	434	343	0.01	-20.97
Croatia	1,880	959	3,005	3,150	3,755	0.07	19.21
Greece	23,614	20,474	24,008	22,330	30,126	0.60	34.91
Holy See	8			3			
Italy	139,158	150,962	162,101	146,311	163,540	3.25	11.78
Malta	1,881	503	895	499	1,011	0.02	102.61
Portugal	12,396	15,100	12,574	12,312	15,952	0.32	29.56
San Marino	56	35	31	25	102		308.00
Slovenia	3,902	5,343	4,599	4,900	6,821	0.14	39.20
Spain	97,376	101,641	102,668	109,114	125,069	2.48	14.62
TFYR of Macedonia	123	387			383	0.01	
Serbia and Montenegro	2,499	3,550	2,199	2,824			
Western Europe	**1,068,248**	**1,157,212**	**1,187,932**	**1,189,083**	**1,198,747**	**23.80**	**0.81**
Austria	47,837	45,757	44,570	49,516	49,700	0.99	0.37
Belgium	42,497	47,094	51,999	50,896	56,817	1.13	11.63
France	164,687	192,403	217,631	230,976	236,896	4.70	2.56
Germany	514,796	532,953	543,114	542,984	541,641	10.75	-0.25
Liechtenstein	3,179	1,140	1,009	728	534	0.01	-26.65
Luxembourg	3,156	2,527	3,307	4,061	3,768	0.07	-7.21
Monaco	116	199	269	282	191		-32.27
Netherlands	196,896	219,479	212,244	200,972	197,363	3.92	-1.80
Switzerland	95,084	115,660	113,789	108,668	111,837	2.22	2.92
East Mediterranean Europe	**18,819**	**15,772**	**20,853**	**21,503**	**28,003**	**0.56**	**30.23**
Cyprus	1,621	1,346	2,185	2,041	2,687	0.05	31.65
Israel	10,036	8,298	10,489	10,005	14,661	0.29	46.54
Turkey	7,162	6,128	8,179	9,457	10,655	0.21	12.67
MIDDLE EAST	**12,611**	**11,449**	**8,890**	**12,688**	**12,466**	**0.25**	**-1.75**
Middle East	**12,611**	**11,449**	**8,890**	**12,688**	**12,466**	**0.25**	**-1.75**
Bahrain	1,039	805	1,540	2,385	1,303	0.03	-45.37
Iraq	261	317	388	420	336	0.01	-20.00
Jordan	382	365	151	409	231		-43.52

FINLAND

6. Overnight stays of non-resident tourists in all types of accommodation establishments, by country of residence

	2002	2003	2004	2005	2006	Market share 06	% Change 06-05
Kuwait	803	460	375	357	1,680	0.03	370.59
Lebanon	551	643	913	417	535	0.01	28.30
Libyan Arab Jamahiriya	123	35	65	150	323	0.01	115.33
Oman	10	14	11	31	57		83.87
Qatar	203	51	27	54	78		44.44
Saudi Arabia	5,911	6,089	2,585	5,604	4,331	0.09	-22.72
Syrian Arab Republic	298	138	152	115	262	0.01	127.83
United Arab Emirates	786	291	660	800	707	0.01	-11.63
Egypt	2,244	2,225	2,023	1,940	2,623	0.05	35.21
Yemen		16		6			
SOUTH ASIA	**19,326**	**19,518**	**25,227**	**35,812**	**45,745**	**0.91**	**27.74**
South Asia	**19,326**	**19,518**	**25,227**	**35,812**	**45,745**	**0.91**	**27.74**
Afghanistan	1,848	1,372	920	2,891	1,832	0.04	-36.63
Bangladesh	36	28	205	276	279	0.01	1.09
Bhutan				4			
Sri Lanka	819	1,298	900	185	116		-37.30
India	13,911	14,021	19,009	27,250	39,516	0.78	45.01
Iran, Islamic Republic of	1,920	1,993	3,444	4,273	2,669	0.05	-37.54
Maldives			9	4			
Nepal	74	74	77	129	344	0.01	166.67
Pakistan	718	732	663	800	989	0.02	23.63
REGION NOT SPECIFIED	**184,191**	**176,181**	**159,218**	**166,476**	**228,179**	**4.53**	**37.06**
Not Specified	**184,191**	**176,181**	**159,218**	**166,476**	**228,179**	**4.53**	**37.06**
Other countries of the World	184,191	176,181	159,218	166,476	228,179	4.53	37.06

Source: World Tourism Organization (UNWTO)

FRANCE

1. Arrivals of non-resident tourists at national borders, by country of residence

	2002	2003	2004	2005	2006	Market share 06	% Change 06-05
TOTAL (*)	77,012,000	75,048,000	75,121,000	75,908,000	79,083,000	100.00	4.18
AFRICA	924,000	889,000	895,000	1,252,000	1,213,000	1.53	-3.12
North Africa	442,000			672,000	617,000	0.78	-8.18
All countries of North Africa	442,000			672,000	617,000	0.78	-8.18
Other Africa	482,000	889,000	895,000	580,000	596,000	0.75	2.76
Other countries of Africa	482,000			580,000	596,000	0.75	2.76
All countries of Africa		889,000	895,000				
AMERICAS	4,639,000	3,954,000	4,206,000	5,086,000	5,562,000	7.03	9.36
North America	3,733,000	3,009,000	3,207,000	4,129,000	4,560,000	5.77	10.44
Canada	636,000	562,000	586,000	712,000	990,000	1.25	39.04
Mexico	101,000			369,000	395,000	0.50	7.05
United States	2,996,000	2,447,000	2,621,000	3,048,000	3,175,000	4.01	4.17
Other Americas	906,000	945,000	999,000	957,000	1,002,000	1.27	4.70
Other countries of the Americas	906,000	945,000	999,000	957,000	1,002,000	1.27	4.70
EAST ASIA AND THE PACIFIC	2,080,000	1,890,000	2,058,000	3,192,000	3,338,000	4.22	4.57
North-East Asia	723,000	601,000	642,000	735,000	689,000	0.87	-6.26
Japan	723,000	601,000	642,000	735,000	689,000	0.87	-6.26
Australasia	493,000			824,000	754,000	0.95	-8.50
Australia, New Zealand (*)	493,000			824,000	754,000	0.95	-8.50
Other East Asia and the Pacific	864,000	1,289,000	1,416,000	1,633,000	1,895,000	2.40	16.04
Other countries East Asia/Pacific	864,000	1,289,000	1,416,000	1,633,000	1,895,000	2.40	16.04
EUROPE	69,078,000	68,072,000	67,711,000	66,029,000	68,590,000	86.73	3.88
Central/Eastern Europe	1,589,000			1,567,000	1,939,000	2.45	23.74
Czech Republic/Slovakia	389,000			383,000	491,000	0.62	28.20
Poland	593,000			312,000	427,000	0.54	36.86
Other countries Central/East Europ	607,000			872,000	1,021,000	1.29	17.09
Northern Europe	16,484,000	16,363,000	16,116,000	16,111,000	16,539,000	20.91	2.66
Denmark	776,000			719,000	740,000	0.94	2.92
Finland	113,000			184,000	176,000	0.22	-4.35
Norway	168,000			449,000	567,000	0.72	26.28
Sweden	469,000			589,000	659,000	0.83	11.88
United Kingdom/Ireland	14,958,000	14,845,000	14,648,000	14,170,000	14,397,000	18.20	1.60
Scandinavia		1,518,000	1,468,000				
Southern Europe	11,949,000	11,454,000	11,511,000	12,324,000	13,676,000	17.29	10.97
Greece	503,000	496,000	506,000	185,000	222,000	0.28	20.00
Italy	7,874,000	7,511,000	7,400,000	6,961,000	7,624,000	9.64	9.52
Portugal	607,000	586,000	596,000	781,000	862,000	1.09	10.37
Spain	2,965,000	2,861,000	3,009,000	4,397,000	4,968,000	6.28	12.99
Western Europe	38,975,000	38,610,000	38,397,000	35,575,000	36,007,000	45.53	1.21
Austria	452,000	461,000	432,000	559,000	571,000	0.72	2.15
Germany	14,346,000	14,047,000	13,728,000	13,689,000	13,079,000	16.54	-4.46
Netherlands	12,631,000	12,486,000	12,387,000	6,816,000	7,730,000	9.77	13.41
Switzerland	3,074,000	3,002,000	3,079,000	4,295,000	4,821,000	6.10	12.25
Belgium / Luxembourg	8,472,000	8,614,000	8,771,000	10,216,000	9,806,000	12.40	-4.01
East Mediterranean Europe	81,000			146,000	141,000	0.18	-3.42
Turkey	81,000			146,000	141,000	0.18	-3.42
Other Europe		1,645,000	1,687,000	306,000	288,000	0.36	-5.88

FRANCE

1. Arrivals of non-resident tourists at national borders, by country of residence

	2002	2003	2004	2005	2006	Market share 06	% Change 06-05
Other countries of Europe		1,645,000	1,687,000	306,000	288,000	0.36	-5.88
MIDDLE EAST	**249,000**	**210,000**	**237,000**	**349,000**	**380,000**	**0.48**	**8.88**
Middle East	**249,000**	**210,000**	**237,000**	**349,000**	**380,000**	**0.48**	**8.88**
All countries of Middle East	249,000	210,000	237,000	349,000	380,000	0.48	8.88
REGION NOT SPECIFIED	**42,000**	**33,000**	**14,000**				
Not Specified	**42,000**	**33,000**	**14,000**				
Other countries of the World	42,000	33,000	14,000				

Source: World Tourism Organization (UNWTO)

FRANCE

3. Arrivals of non-resident tourists in hotels and similar establishments, by country of residence

	2002	2003	2004	2005	2006	Market share 06	% Change 06-05
TOTAL (*)	36,093,096	32,520,140	33,987,944	34,805,571	32,303,960	100.00	-7.19
AFRICA	372,396	340,363	353,156	322,031	426,625	1.32	32.48
North Africa	193,434	164,997	168,626	143,594	191,326	0.59	33.24
All countries of North Africa	193,434	164,997	168,626	143,594	191,326	0.59	33.24
Other Africa	178,962	175,366	184,530	178,437	235,299	0.73	31.87
Other countries of Africa	178,962	175,366	184,530	178,437	235,299	0.73	31.87
AMERICAS	4,303,811	3,243,285	3,610,645	3,986,074	3,855,359	11.93	-3.28
North America	3,826,128	2,878,443	3,198,696	3,529,818	3,373,732	10.44	-4.42
Canada	308,388	275,988	303,206	370,401	375,143	1.16	1.28
United States	3,517,740	2,602,455	2,895,490	3,159,417	2,998,589	9.28	-5.09
Other Americas	477,683	364,842	411,949	456,256	481,627	1.49	5.56
Other countries of the Americas	477,683	364,842	411,949	456,256	481,627	1.49	5.56
EAST ASIA AND THE PACIFIC	2,519,053	2,194,057	2,589,638	2,923,409	2,893,874	8.96	-1.01
North-East Asia	1,521,790	1,253,753	1,398,020	1,459,097	1,353,623	4.19	-7.23
Japan	1,521,790	1,253,753	1,398,020	1,459,097	1,353,623	4.19	-7.23
Other East Asia and the Pacific	997,263	940,304	1,191,618	1,464,312	1,540,251	4.77	5.19
Other countries East Asia/Pacific	997,263	940,304	1,191,618	1,464,312	1,540,251	4.77	5.19
EUROPE	27,105,487	25,105,652	25,698,385	25,697,834	24,721,851	76.53	-3.80
Central/Eastern Europe	466,791	448,840	481,968	537,891	720,553	2.23	33.96
Czech Republic	28,864	27,329	44,879	44,570	99,218	0.31	122.61
Hungary	19,721	17,756	26,656	42,438	63,259	0.20	49.06
Poland	86,127	64,236	94,029	92,263	141,554	0.44	53.42
Russian Federation	313,342	325,985	301,435	339,305	401,129	1.24	18.22
Slovakia	18,737	13,534	14,969	19,315	15,393	0.05	-20.31
Northern Europe	9,917,815	9,108,667	9,272,960	9,248,232	8,305,255	25.71	-10.20
Denmark	238,245	248,007	222,088	236,859	225,424	0.70	-4.83
Finland	75,362	57,992	65,786	81,168	81,429	0.25	0.32
Iceland	15,211	10,811	10,769	14,579	16,853	0.05	15.60
Ireland	137,285	139,887	177,758	204,794	235,808	0.73	15.14
Norway	151,944	129,545	111,979	117,249	121,511	0.38	3.63
Sweden	231,059	235,267	216,514	224,520	212,628	0.66	-5.30
United Kingdom	9,068,709	8,287,158	8,468,066	8,369,063	7,411,602	22.94	-11.44
Southern Europe	5,866,642	5,524,555	5,754,972	5,906,064	5,875,635	18.19	-0.52
Greece	103,894	110,364	117,691	124,341	128,766	0.40	3.56
Italy	3,458,338	3,222,679	3,254,657	3,156,640	3,002,411	9.29	-4.89
Portugal	227,235	218,428	227,888	220,887	269,457	0.83	21.99
Spain	2,077,175	1,973,084	2,154,736	2,404,196	2,475,001	7.66	2.95
Western Europe	10,376,209	9,564,854	9,646,571	9,380,928	9,014,547	27.91	-3.91
Austria	181,492	175,648	156,809	166,218	173,566	0.54	4.42
Belgium	2,342,600	2,268,384	2,333,278	2,380,253	2,506,784	7.76	5.32
Germany	4,216,409	3,698,838	3,779,941	3,584,195	3,356,919	10.39	-6.34
Luxembourg	74,983	69,266	77,725	85,093	81,636	0.25	-4.06
Netherlands	2,192,136	1,998,657	2,007,278	1,931,094	1,748,182	5.41	-9.47
Switzerland	1,368,589	1,354,061	1,291,540	1,234,075	1,147,460	3.55	-7.02
East Mediterranean Europe	31,503	40,847	47,759	53,480	64,246	0.20	20.13
Turkey	31,503	40,847	47,759	53,480	64,246	0.20	20.13
Other Europe	446,527	417,889	494,155	571,239	741,615	2.30	29.83

FRANCE

3. Arrivals of non-resident tourists in hotels and similar establishments, by country of residence

	2002	2003	2004	2005	2006	Market share 06	% Change 06-05
Other countries of Europe	446,527	417,889	494,155	571,239	741,615	2.30	29.83
MIDDLE EAST	**418,635**	**393,570**	**408,880**	**417,879**	**406,251**	**1.26**	**-2.78**
Middle East	**418,635**	**393,570**	**408,880**	**417,879**	**406,251**	**1.26**	**-2.78**
All countries of Middle East	418,635	393,570	408,880	417,879	406,251	1.26	-2.78
REGION NOT SPECIFIED	**1,373,714**	**1,243,213**	**1,327,240**	**1,458,344**			
Not Specified	**1,373,714**	**1,243,213**	**1,327,240**	**1,458,344**			
Other countries of the World	1,373,714	1,243,213	1,327,240	1,458,344			

Source: World Tourism Organization (UNWTO)

FRANCE

5. Overnight stays of non-resident tourists in hotels and similar establishments, by country of residence

		2002	2003	2004	2005	2006	Market share 06	% Change 06-05
TOTAL	(*)	77,601,969	69,323,495	70,390,676	72,054,385	68,820,502	100.00	-4.49
AFRICA		949,470	901,406	885,306	845,428	969,970	1.41	14.73
North Africa		499,947	437,793	415,514	383,145	418,020	0.61	9.10
All countries of North Africa		499,947	437,793	415,514	383,145	418,020	0.61	9.10
Other Africa		449,523	463,613	469,792	462,283	551,950	0.80	19.40
Other countries of Africa		449,523	463,613	469,792	462,283	551,950	0.80	19.40
AMERICAS		10,401,643	7,711,369	8,223,547	9,235,041	8,852,363	12.86	-4.14
North America		9,106,096	6,744,435	7,182,014	8,090,511	7,700,554	11.19	-4.82
Canada		776,115	665,662	689,976	909,020	863,998	1.26	-4.95
United States		8,329,981	6,078,773	6,492,038	7,181,491	6,836,556	9.93	-4.80
Other Americas		1,295,547	966,934	1,041,533	1,144,530	1,151,809	1.67	0.64
Other countries of the Americas		1,295,547	966,934	1,041,533	1,144,530	1,151,809	1.67	0.64
EAST ASIA AND THE PACIFIC		5,291,783	4,665,934	5,275,340	6,058,304	6,050,333	8.79	-0.13
North-East Asia		3,161,737	2,651,001	2,830,990	3,057,734	2,912,198	4.23	-4.76
Japan		3,161,737	2,651,001	2,830,990	3,057,734	2,912,198	4.23	-4.76
Other East Asia and the Pacific		2,130,046	2,014,933	2,444,350	3,000,570	3,138,135	4.56	4.58
Other countries East Asia/Pacific		2,130,046	2,014,933	2,444,350	3,000,570	3,138,135	4.56	4.58
EUROPE		56,909,177	52,445,543	52,341,521	52,109,771	51,925,405	75.45	-0.35
Central/Eastern Europe		1,340,207	1,401,684	1,328,743	1,503,085	1,746,548	2.54	16.20
Czech Republic		67,531	58,179	98,601	110,061	220,376	0.32	100.23
Hungary		49,334	44,201	61,822	100,637	149,090	0.22	48.15
Poland		183,072	134,310	212,959	214,551	300,621	0.44	40.12
Russian Federation		958,991	1,115,358	913,140	1,013,693	1,042,582	1.51	2.85
Slovakia		81,279	49,636	42,221	64,143	33,879	0.05	-47.18
Northern Europe		20,341,768	18,750,057	18,487,281	18,119,983	17,066,789	24.80	-5.81
Denmark		578,095	633,577	507,447	535,021	488,139	0.71	-8.76
Finland		195,017	132,984	151,364	184,006	188,622	0.27	2.51
Iceland		36,266	25,873	25,303	39,873	37,824	0.05	-5.14
Ireland		446,527	444,667	503,631	564,041	613,937	0.89	8.85
Norway		351,751	319,739	261,079	287,592	274,871	0.40	-4.42
Sweden		563,428	641,767	522,526	566,244	499,670	0.73	-11.76
United Kingdom		18,170,684	16,551,450	16,515,931	15,943,206	14,963,726	21.74	-6.14
Southern Europe		12,821,300	11,862,370	12,180,293	12,561,363	13,137,164	19.09	4.58
Greece		306,764	315,952	333,495	335,342	335,149	0.49	-0.06
Italy		7,630,865	7,001,378	6,869,974	6,815,039	6,700,989	9.74	-1.67
Portugal		478,842	467,703	475,105	453,197	568,368	0.83	25.41
Spain		4,404,829	4,077,337	4,501,719	4,957,785	5,532,658	8.04	11.60
Western Europe		21,190,830	19,247,628	19,041,627	18,407,724	18,176,490	26.41	-1.26
Austria		427,740	453,898	388,993	368,421	387,844	0.56	5.27
Belgium		5,115,786	4,871,385	4,912,260	4,923,099	5,147,611	7.48	4.56
Germany		8,425,932	7,250,932	7,250,810	6,999,520	6,798,651	9.88	-2.87
Luxembourg		173,567	157,507	171,002	184,592	173,934	0.25	-5.77
Netherlands		4,182,441	3,737,379	3,772,372	3,515,655	3,299,976	4.80	-6.13
Switzerland		2,865,364	2,776,527	2,546,190	2,416,437	2,368,474	3.44	-1.98
East Mediterranean Europe		92,306	114,762	128,972	144,395	165,102	0.24	14.34
Turkey		92,306	114,762	128,972	144,395	165,102	0.24	14.34
Other Europe		1,122,766	1,069,042	1,174,605	1,373,221	1,633,312	2.37	18.94

FRANCE

5. Overnight stays of non-resident tourists in hotels and similar establishments, by country of residence

	2002	2003	2004	2005	2006	Market share 06	% Change 06-05
Other countries of Europe	1,122,766	1,069,042	1,174,605	1,373,221	1,633,312	2.37	18.94
MIDDLE EAST	**1,116,621**	**950,978**	**1,056,981**	**1,123,020**	**1,022,431**	**1.49**	**-8.96**
Middle East	**1,116,621**	**950,978**	**1,056,981**	**1,123,020**	**1,022,431**	**1.49**	**-8.96**
All countries of Middle East	1,116,621	950,978	1,056,981	1,123,020	1,022,431	1.49	-8.96
REGION NOT SPECIFIED	**2,933,275**	**2,648,265**	**2,607,981**	**2,682,821**			
Not Specified	**2,933,275**	**2,648,265**	**2,607,981**	**2,682,821**			
Other countries of the World	2,933,275	2,648,265	2,607,981	2,682,821			

Source: World Tourism Organization (UNWTO)

FRANCE

6. Overnight stays of non-resident tourists in all types of accommodation establishments, by country of residence

	2002	2003	2004	2005	2006	Market share 06	% Change 06-05
TOTAL (*)	588,430,000	567,006,000	561,294,000	491,139,000	496,951,000	100.00	1.18
AFRICA	15,085,000	14,638,000	14,277,000	15,996,000	14,741,000	2.97	-7.85
North Africa	7,392,000			8,822,000	7,397,000	1.49	-16.15
All countries of North Africa	7,392,000			8,822,000	7,397,000	1.49	-16.15
Other Africa	7,693,000	14,638,000	14,277,000	7,174,000	7,344,000	1.48	2.37
Other countries of Africa	7,693,000			7,174,000	7,344,000	1.48	2.37
All countries of Africa		14,638,000	14,277,000				
AMERICAS	49,746,000	42,125,000	43,900,000	41,008,000	44,092,000	8.87	7.52
North America	41,100,000	32,915,000	34,280,000	33,887,000	36,302,000	7.30	7.13
Canada	9,307,000	7,936,000	8,050,000	6,306,000	9,044,000	1.82	43.42
Mexico	961,000			2,966,000	2,911,000	0.59	-1.85
United States	30,832,000	24,979,000	26,230,000	24,615,000	24,347,000	4.90	-1.09
Other Americas	8,646,000	9,210,000	9,620,000	7,121,000	7,790,000	1.57	9.39
Other countries of the Americas	8,646,000	9,210,000	9,620,000	7,121,000	7,790,000	1.57	9.39
EAST ASIA AND THE PACIFIC	17,701,000	16,542,000	18,339,000	19,787,000	21,349,000	4.30	7.89
North-East Asia	4,414,000	3,813,000	3,985,000	4,392,000	3,962,000	0.80	-9.79
Japan	4,414,000	3,813,000	3,985,000	4,392,000	3,962,000	0.80	-9.79
Australasia	6,723,000			5,332,000	5,977,000	1.20	12.10
Australia, New Zealand (*)	6,723,000			5,332,000	5,977,000	1.20	12.10
Other East Asia and the Pacific	6,564,000	12,729,000	14,354,000	10,063,000	11,410,000	2.30	13.39
Other countries East Asia/Pacific	6,564,000	12,729,000	14,354,000	10,063,000	11,410,000	2.30	13.39
EUROPE	502,210,000	490,294,000	481,724,000	410,095,000	413,642,000	83.24	0.86
Central/Eastern Europe	14,340,000			12,336,000	13,207,000	2.66	7.06
Czech Republic/Slovakia	3,372,000			2,962,000	2,512,000	0.51	-15.19
Poland	3,230,000			2,426,000	3,315,000	0.67	36.64
Other countries Central/East Europ	7,738,000			6,948,000	7,380,000	1.49	6.22
Northern Europe	123,805,000	124,009,000	119,144,000	98,503,000	99,015,000	19.92	0.52
Denmark	7,880,000			5,435,000	5,324,000	1.07	-2.04
Finland	1,028,000			1,157,000	1,071,000	0.22	-7.43
Norway	1,169,000			2,760,000	3,324,000	0.67	20.43
Sweden	4,459,000			4,495,000	4,504,000	0.91	0.20
United Kingdom/Ireland	109,269,000	108,957,000	105,193,000	84,656,000	84,792,000	17.06	0.16
Scandinavia		15,052,000	13,951,000				
Southern Europe	82,777,000	78,107,000	78,226,000	68,334,000	70,422,000	14.17	3.06
Greece	5,477,000	5,268,000	5,319,000	2,035,000	1,836,000	0.37	-9.78
Italy	53,416,000	50,186,000	49,129,000	35,686,000	36,451,000	7.33	2.14
Portugal	3,726,000	3,534,000	3,564,000	7,623,000	6,878,000	1.38	-9.77
Spain	20,158,000	19,119,000	20,214,000	22,990,000	25,257,000	5.08	9.86
Western Europe	280,436,000	273,072,000	269,173,000	227,861,000	227,116,000	45.70	-0.33
Austria	4,167,000	4,429,000	4,088,000	4,138,000	4,248,000	0.85	2.66
Germany	109,634,000	105,848,000	102,474,000	91,733,000	84,450,000	16.99	-7.94
Netherlands	82,018,000	79,053,000	78,008,000	51,074,000	56,783,000	11.43	11.18
Switzerland	20,302,000	19,784,000	19,863,000	23,970,000	25,705,000	5.17	7.24
Belgium / Luxembourg	64,315,000	63,958,000	64,740,000	56,946,000	55,930,000	11.25	-1.78
East Mediterranean Europe	852,000			944,000	988,000	0.20	4.66
Turkey	852,000			944,000	988,000	0.20	4.66
Other Europe		15,106,000	15,181,000	2,117,000	2,894,000	0.58	36.70

FRANCE

6. Overnight stays of non-resident tourists in all types of accommodation establishments, by country of residence

	2002	2003	2004	2005	2006	Market share 06	% Change 06-05
Other countries of Europe		15,106,000	15,181,000	2,117,000	2,894,000	0.58	36.70
MIDDLE EAST	**2,531,000**	**2,246,000**	**2,372,000**	**4,253,000**	**3,127,000**	**0.63**	**-26.48**
Middle East	**2,531,000**	**2,246,000**	**2,372,000**	**4,253,000**	**3,127,000**	**0.63**	**-26.48**
All countries of Middle East	2,531,000	2,246,000	2,372,000	4,253,000	3,127,000	0.63	-26.48
REGION NOT SPECIFIED	**1,157,000**	**1,161,000**	**682,000**				
Not Specified	**1,157,000**	**1,161,000**	**682,000**				
Other countries of the World	1,157,000	1,161,000	682,000				

Source: World Tourism Organization (UNWTO)

FRENCH POLYNESIA

1. Arrivals of non-resident tourists at national borders, by country of residence

		2002	2003	2004	2005	2006	Market share 06	% Change 06-05
TOTAL	(*)	188,998	212,692	211,828	208,045	221,549	100.00	6.49
AFRICA		253	294	257	235	255	0.12	8.51
Other Africa		253	294	257	235	255	0.12	8.51
All countries of Africa		253	294	257	235	255	0.12	8.51
AMERICAS		72,468	89,454	86,032	80,067	88,991	40.17	11.15
Central America		68	86	126	92	111	0.05	20.65
All countries of Central America		68	86	126	92	111	0.05	20.65
North America		68,518	85,144	81,001	75,132	82,633	37.30	9.98
Canada		2,793	5,523	5,679	5,554	6,731	3.04	21.19
Mexico		1,523	1,853	1,737	1,252	1,444	0.65	15.34
United States		61,888	75,608	71,447	65,773	71,621	32.33	8.89
Hawaii (Usa)		2,314	2,160	2,138	2,553	2,837	1.28	11.12
South America		3,882	4,224	4,905	4,843	6,247	2.82	28.99
Argentina		680	710	1,103	1,142	1,569	0.71	37.39
Bolivia		41	27	13				
Brazil		1,257	1,292	1,727	1,705	2,298	1.04	34.78
Chile		1,452	1,661	1,546	1,566	1,819	0.82	16.16
Colombia		79	129	87				
Ecuador		32	40	59				
Paraguay		37	17	33				
Peru		94	152	128				
Uruguay		110	60	78				
Venezuela		94	135	129				
Other countries of South America		6	1	2	430	561	0.25	30.47
EAST ASIA AND THE PACIFIC		39,697	42,235	45,083	45,655	48,344	21.82	5.89
North-East Asia		24,222	23,505	24,475	22,987	22,642	10.22	-1.50
Taiwan (Province of China)		266	152	196	153	86	0.04	-43.79
Hong Kong, China		192	198	211	267	319	0.14	19.48
Japan		23,632	22,882	23,630	21,986	21,739	9.81	-1.12
Korea, Republic of		132	273	438	581	498	0.22	-14.29
South-East Asia		462	460	506	593	611	0.28	3.04
Indonesia		43	53	35	76	70	0.03	-7.89
Malaysia		66	53	53	78	83	0.04	6.41
Philippines		65	55	73	144	229	0.10	59.03
Singapore		241	172	244	210	167	0.08	-20.48
Thailand		47	127	101	85	62	0.03	-27.06
Australasia		10,628	13,612	15,408	17,196	19,963	9.01	16.09
Australia		5,346	7,506	7,687	9,609	11,426	5.16	18.91
New Zealand		5,282	6,106	7,721	7,587	8,537	3.85	12.52
Melanesia		3,308	3,797	3,577	3,685	3,880	1.75	5.29
Fiji		83	157	103	78	163	0.07	108.97
New Caledonia		3,225	3,640	3,474	3,607	3,717	1.68	3.05
Polynesia		281	341	493	602	804	0.36	33.55
Cook Islands		252	309	421	562	717	0.32	27.58
Tonga		22	16	17	20	24	0.01	20.00
Samoa	(*)	7	16	55	20	63	0.03	215.00
Other East Asia and the Pacific		796	520	624	592	444	0.20	-25.00
Other countries of Asia		230	173	227	213	48	0.02	-77.46
Other countries of Oceania		566	347	397	379	396	0.18	4.49

FRENCH POLYNESIA

1. Arrivals of non-resident tourists at national borders, by country of residence

	2002	2003	2004	2005	2006	Market share 06	% Change 06-05
EUROPE	76,100	80,182	79,944	81,643	82,580	37.27	1.15
Central/Eastern Europe	235	318	440	638	507	0.23	-20.53
Ussr (Former)	235	318	440	638	507	0.23	-20.53
Northern Europe	6,619	8,454	9,126	9,157	8,397	3.79	-8.30
Denmark	212	251	198	213	223	0.10	4.69
Finland	167	215	240	256	284	0.13	10.94
Norway	357	347	246	372	452	0.20	21.51
Sweden	484	437	392	384	348	0.16	-9.38
United Kingdom	5,399	7,204	8,050	7,932	7,090	3.20	-10.62
Southern Europe	11,752	12,604	14,089	15,559	19,380	8.75	24.56
Italy	8,853	9,213	10,278	10,970	13,697	6.18	24.86
Portugal	576	652	543	613	481	0.22	-21.53
Spain	2,323	2,739	3,268	3,976	5,202	2.35	30.84
Western Europe	55,899	57,310	54,487	54,205	52,248	23.58	-3.61
Austria	701	692	676	755	762	0.34	0.93
Belgium	1,158	1,057	1,136	1,030	1,145	0.52	11.17
France	46,602	48,177	45,069	45,264	42,397	19.14	-6.33
Germany	4,190	4,165	4,412	3,952	4,440	2.00	12.35
Luxembourg	163	161	156	199	146	0.07	-26.63
Netherlands	609	603	587	613	709	0.32	15.66
Switzerland	2,476	2,455	2,451	2,392	2,649	1.20	10.74
Other Europe	1,595	1,496	1,802	2,084	2,048	0.92	-1.73
Other countries of Europe	1,595	1,496	1,802	2,084	2,048	0.92	-1.73
MIDDLE EAST	182	163	172	165	226	0.10	36.97
Middle East	182	163	172	165	226	0.10	36.97
All countries of Middle East	182	163	172	165	226	0.10	36.97
SOUTH ASIA	46	62	75	69	116	0.05	68.12
South Asia	46	62	75	69	116	0.05	68.12
India	46	62	75	69	116	0.05	68.12
REGION NOT SPECIFIED	252	302	265	211	1,037	0.47	391.47
Not Specified	252	302	265	211	1,037	0.47	391.47
Other countries of the World	252	302	265	211	1,037	0.47	391.47

Source: World Tourism Organization (UNWTO)

FRENCH POLYNESIA

3. Arrivals of non-resident tourists in hotels and similar establishments, by country of residence

		2002	2003	2004	2005	2006	Market share 06	% Change 06-05
TOTAL	(*)	155,144	179,799	177,774	175,605	192,794	100.00	9.79
AFRICA		182	197	181	161	190	0.10	18.01
Other Africa		182	197	181	161	190	0.10	18.01
All countries of Africa		182	197	181	161	190	0.10	18.01
AMERICAS		68,489	85,882	81,860	75,944	84,740	43.95	11.58
Central America		1,565	1,907	1,824	1,319	1,525	0.79	15.62
All countries of Central America		1,565	1,907	1,824	1,319	1,525	0.79	15.62
North America		63,443	80,107	75,475	70,212	77,479	40.19	10.35
Canada		2,557	5,275	5,437	5,222	6,413	3.33	22.81
United States		59,478	73,483	68,786	63,481	69,205	35.90	9.02
Hawaii (Usa)		1,408	1,349	1,252	1,509	1,861	0.97	23.33
South America		3,481	3,868	4,561	4,413	5,736	2.98	29.98
All countries of South America		3,481	3,868	4,561	4,413	5,736	2.98	29.98
EAST ASIA AND THE PACIFIC		35,225	37,871	40,431	40,862	43,265	22.44	5.88
North-East Asia		23,834	23,207	24,161	22,729	22,407	11.62	-1.42
Taiwan (Province of China)		257	132	187	147	75	0.04	-48.98
Hong Kong, China		162	182	174	254	278	0.14	9.45
Japan		23,290	22,628	23,412	21,753	21,567	11.19	-0.86
Korea, Republic of		125	265	388	575	487	0.25	-15.30
South-East Asia		397	403	434	531	534	0.28	0.56
Indonesia		31	46	20	68	55	0.03	-19.12
Malaysia		53	38	45	64	69	0.04	7.81
Philippines		57	48	65	140	208	0.11	48.57
Singapore		220	167	220	194	154	0.08	-20.62
Thailand		36	104	84	65	48	0.02	-26.15
Australasia		9,106	12,177	13,826	15,537	18,174	9.43	16.97
Australia		4,817	6,931	7,124	8,983	10,792	5.60	20.14
New Zealand		4,289	5,246	6,702	6,554	7,382	3.83	12.63
Melanesia		1,303	1,623	1,439	1,557	1,697	0.88	8.99
Fiji		52	99	91	66	114	0.06	72.73
New Caledonia		1,251	1,524	1,348	1,491	1,583	0.82	6.17
Polynesia		85	94	150	156	239	0.12	53.21
Cook Islands		69	82	110	146	195	0.10	33.56
Tonga		11	7	14	6	10	0.01	66.67
Samoa		5	5	26	4	34	0.02	750.00
Other East Asia and the Pacific		500	367	421	352	214	0.11	-39.20
Other countries of Asia		185	139	170	155	41	0.02	-73.55
Other countries of Oceania		315	228	251	197	173	0.09	-12.18
EUROPE		50,857	55,390	54,847	58,219	63,522	32.95	9.11
Central/Eastern Europe		228	310	420	621	497	0.26	-19.97
Ussr (Former)		228	310	420	621	497	0.26	-19.97
Northern Europe		6,302	8,133	8,806	8,844	8,072	4.19	-8.73
Denmark		170	240	170	198	201	0.10	1.52
Finland		162	198	232	246	272	0.14	10.57
Norway		345	318	226	344	421	0.22	22.38
Sweden		456	414	359	348	327	0.17	-6.03
United Kingdom		5,169	6,963	7,819	7,708	6,851	3.55	-11.12

FRENCH POLYNESIA

3. Arrivals of non-resident tourists in hotels and similar establishments, by country of residence

	2002	2003	2004	2005	2006	Market share 06	% Change 06-05
Southern Europe	**11,396**	**12,225**	**13,735**	**15,209**	**19,068**	**9.89**	**25.37**
Italy	8,609	8,952	10,057	10,778	13,518	7.01	25.42
Portugal	548	628	520	588	470	0.24	-20.07
Spain	2,239	2,645	3,158	3,843	5,080	2.63	32.19
Western Europe	**31,424**	**33,302**	**30,171**	**31,555**	**33,935**	**17.60**	**7.54**
Austria	675	669	656	729	718	0.37	-1.51
Belgium	999	894	992	870	1,006	0.52	15.63
France	22,835	24,809	21,447	23,260	24,701	12.81	6.20
Germany	3,998	3,993	4,201	3,763	4,255	2.21	13.07
Luxembourg	130	145	138	174	130	0.07	-25.29
Netherlands	558	580	556	598	660	0.34	10.37
Switzerland	2,229	2,212	2,181	2,161	2,465	1.28	14.07
Other Europe	**1,507**	**1,420**	**1,715**	**1,990**	**1,950**	**1.01**	**-2.01**
Other countries of Europe	1,507	1,420	1,715	1,990	1,950	1.01	-2.01
MIDDLE EAST	**146**	**144**	**147**	**142**	**194**	**0.10**	**36.62**
Middle East	**146**	**144**	**147**	**142**	**194**	**0.10**	**36.62**
All countries of Middle East	146	144	147	142	194	0.10	36.62
SOUTH ASIA	**38**	**52**	**69**	**68**	**106**	**0.05**	**55.88**
South Asia	**38**	**52**	**69**	**68**	**106**	**0.05**	**55.88**
India	38	52	69	68	106	0.05	55.88
REGION NOT SPECIFIED	**207**	**263**	**239**	**209**	**777**	**0.40**	**271.77**
Not Specified	**207**	**263**	**239**	**209**	**777**	**0.40**	**271.77**
Other countries of the World	207	263	239	209	777	0.40	271.77

Source: World Tourism Organization (UNWTO)

FRENCH POLYNESIA

5. Overnight stays of non-resident tourists in hotels and similar establishments, by country of residence

		2002	2003	2004	2005	2006	Market share 06	% Change 06-05
TOTAL	(*)	1,666,156	1,948,952	1,916,607	1,897,174	2,093,260	100.00	10.34
AFRICA		3,399	3,922	3,414	2,251	4,258	0.20	89.16
Other Africa		3,399	3,922	3,414	2,251	4,258	0.20	89.16
All countries of Africa		3,399	3,922	3,414	2,251	4,258	0.20	89.16
AMERICAS		635,015	826,231	806,520	757,332	817,723	39.06	7.97
Central America		13,284	17,442	17,916	13,271	15,800	0.75	19.06
All countries of Central America		13,284	17,442	17,916	13,271	15,800	0.75	19.06
North America		586,779	769,621	739,338	696,013	740,554	35.38	6.40
Canada		29,363	62,949	66,790	64,469	74,605	3.56	15.72
United States		542,402	692,292	658,772	615,658	647,884	30.95	5.23
Hawaii (Usa)		15,014	14,380	13,776	15,886	18,065	0.86	13.72
South America		34,952	39,168	49,266	48,048	61,369	2.93	27.72
All countries of South America		34,952	39,168	49,266	48,048	61,369	2.93	27.72
EAST ASIA AND THE PACIFIC		289,096	314,003	330,327	332,186	349,258	16.68	5.14
North-East Asia		176,862	169,894	173,782	160,999	153,028	7.31	-4.95
Taiwan (Province of China)		4,430	1,948	2,127	1,711	961	0.05	-43.83
Hong Kong, China		1,557	1,785	1,576	2,164	2,225	0.11	2.82
Japan		169,990	164,203	167,110	153,445	146,837	7.01	-4.31
Korea, Republic of		885	1,958	2,969	3,679	3,005	0.14	-18.32
South-East Asia		9,822	8,263	6,990	13,868	27,557	1.32	98.71
Indonesia		729	1,634	449	1,205	908	0.04	-24.65
Malaysia		443	534	456	759	617	0.03	-18.71
Philippines		6,099	3,506	3,130	8,998	24,333	1.16	170.43
Singapore		2,184	1,578	1,939	1,714	1,241	0.06	-27.60
Thailand		367	1,011	1,016	1,192	458	0.02	-61.58
Australasia		82,938	115,448	128,206	138,291	148,689	7.10	7.52
Australia		45,958	71,384	74,386	86,248	94,918	4.53	10.05
New Zealand		36,980	44,064	53,820	52,043	53,771	2.57	3.32
Melanesia		13,689	16,664	14,683	14,541	16,298	0.78	12.08
Fiji		524	918	759	427	860	0.04	101.41
New Caledonia		13,165	15,746	13,924	14,114	15,438	0.74	9.38
Polynesia		564	772	1,215	992	1,735	0.08	74.90
Cook Islands		419	690	907	943	1,239	0.06	31.39
Tonga		90	56	80	32	51		59.38
Samoa		55	26	228	17	445	0.02	2,517.65
Other East Asia and the Pacific		5,221	2,962	5,451	3,495	1,951	0.09	-44.18
Other countries of Asia		2,177	1,071	2,007	1,721	472	0.02	-72.57
Other countries of Oceania		3,044	1,891	3,444	1,774	1,479	0.07	-16.63
EUROPE		734,470	800,079	770,954	800,922	907,809	43.37	13.35
Central/Eastern Europe		2,709	4,135	4,864	8,780			
Ussr (Former)		2,709	4,135	4,864	8,780			
Northern Europe		60,002	78,857	83,269	76,915	74,347	3.55	-3.34
Denmark		3,667	3,074	2,049	2,131	2,372	0.11	11.31
Finland		2,128	2,483	1,695	2,373	2,388	0.11	0.63
Norway		3,786	3,229	2,514	3,779	5,095	0.24	34.82
Sweden		4,623	5,988	4,687	3,676	3,788	0.18	3.05
United Kingdom		45,798	64,083	72,324	64,956	60,704	2.90	-6.55

FRENCH POLYNESIA

5. Overnight stays of non-resident tourists in hotels and similar establishments, by country of residence

	2002	2003	2004	2005	2006	Market share 06	% Change 06-05
Southern Europe	139,861	151,237	172,688	182,831	225,027	10.75	23.08
Italy	111,231	119,112	134,747	140,455	170,776	8.16	21.59
Portugal	5,867	5,356	5,610	5,955	5,269	0.25	-11.52
Spain	22,763	26,769	32,331	36,421	48,982	2.34	34.49
Western Europe	511,201	548,018	487,888	505,607	572,481	27.35	13.23
Austria	9,306	9,340	8,124	10,871	10,626	0.51	-2.25
Belgium	16,116	15,085	14,388	14,131	15,251	0.73	7.93
France	396,354	435,033	370,594	388,009	443,221	21.17	14.23
Germany	46,684	47,932	52,847	49,210	55,395	2.65	12.57
Luxembourg	2,299	2,171	1,898	2,321	1,754	0.08	-24.43
Netherlands	5,938	6,668	7,227	6,616	7,560	0.36	14.27
Switzerland	34,504	31,789	32,810	34,449	38,674	1.85	12.26
Other Europe	20,697	17,832	22,245	26,789	35,954	1.72	34.21
Other countries of Europe	20,697	17,832	22,245	26,789	35,954	1.72	34.21
MIDDLE EAST	1,714	1,845	1,833	1,621	2,220	0.11	36.95
Middle East	1,714	1,845	1,833	1,621	2,220	0.11	36.95
All countries of Middle East	1,714	1,845	1,833	1,621	2,220	0.11	36.95
SOUTH ASIA	344	444	1,122	707	1,543	0.07	118.25
South Asia	344	444	1,122	707	1,543	0.07	118.25
India	344	444	1,122	707	1,543	0.07	118.25
REGION NOT SPECIFIED	2,118	2,428	2,437	2,155	10,449	0.50	384.87
Not Specified	2,118	2,428	2,437	2,155	10,449	0.50	384.87
Other countries of the World	2,118	2,428	2,437	2,155	10,449	0.50	384.87

Source: World Tourism Organization (UNWTO)

FRENCH POLYNESIA

6. Overnight stays of non-resident tourists in all types of accommodation establishments, by country of residence

	2002	2003	2004	2005	2006	Market share 06	% Change 06-05
TOTAL	2,592,482	2,886,012	2,860,286	2,787,046	2,925,754	100.00	4.98
AFRICA	5,621	6,777	5,510	3,892	6,575	0.22	68.94
Other Africa	5,621	6,777	5,510	3,892	6,575	0.22	68.94
All countries of Africa	5,621	6,777	5,510	3,892	6,575	0.22	68.94
AMERICAS	702,034	884,466	877,094	827,402	890,247	30.43	7.60
Central America	13,854	18,078	18,752	13,705	16,863	0.58	23.04
All countries of Central America	13,854	18,078	18,752	13,705	16,863	0.58	23.04
North America	645,664	820,844	802,049	757,455	804,107	27.48	6.16
Canada	34,870	69,328	72,685	73,094	81,971	2.80	12.14
United States	583,332	725,867	702,755	653,885	30,728	1.05	-95.30
Hawaii (Usa)	27,462	25,649	26,609	30,476	691,408	23.63	2,168.70
South America	42,516	45,544	56,293	56,242	69,277	2.37	23.18
All countries of South America	42,516	45,544	56,293	56,242	69,277	2.37	23.18
EAST ASIA AND THE PACIFIC	376,531	393,601	415,901	410,187	431,183	14.74	5.12
North-East Asia	184,269	175,349	181,181	164,825	157,029	5.37	-4.73
Taiwan (Province of China)	4,603	2,272	2,536	1,870	1,140	0.04	-39.04
Hong Kong, China	2,091	2,119	2,077	2,359	3,490	0.12	47.94
Japan	176,564	168,838	173,137	156,833	149,256	5.10	-4.83
Korea, Republic of	1,011	2,120	3,431	3,763	3,143	0.11	-16.48
South-East Asia	11,681	9,827	9,184	15,829	32,126	1.10	102.96
Indonesia	1,122	1,879	807	1,550	1,259	0.04	-18.77
Malaysia	733	720	681	1,112	911	0.03	-18.08
Philippines	6,504	3,711	3,532	9,213	27,607	0.94	199.65
Singapore	2,510	1,707	2,516	2,001	1,461	0.05	-26.99
Thailand	812	1,810	1,648	1,953	888	0.03	-54.53
Australasia	110,457	140,749	153,767	164,498	174,424	5.96	6.03
Australia	56,402	82,900	84,773	96,942	105,261	3.60	8.58
New Zealand	54,055	57,849	68,994	67,556	69,163	2.36	2.38
Melanesia	55,424	58,109	58,045	51,758	54,058	1.85	4.44
Fiji	1,550	1,774	997	517	1,511	0.05	192.26
New Caledonia	53,874	56,335	57,048	51,241	52,547	1.80	2.55
Polynesia	3,674	3,346	5,901	5,796	7,645	0.26	31.90
Cook Islands	3,378	3,030	5,183	5,414	6,601	0.23	21.92
Tonga	235	145	208	234	193	0.01	-17.52
Samoa	61	171	510	148	851	0.03	475.00
Other East Asia and the Pacific	11,026	6,221	7,823	7,481	5,901	0.20	-21.12
Other countries of Asia	3,718	2,116	3,424	3,601	655	0.02	-81.81
Other countries of Oceania	7,308	4,105	4,399	3,880	5,246	0.18	35.21
EUROPE	1,501,350	1,594,162	1,554,950	1,540,030	1,574,869	53.83	2.26
Central/Eastern Europe	2,950	4,575	5,267	9,150			
Ussr (Former)	2,950	4,575	5,267	9,150			
Northern Europe	67,102	84,332	90,129	83,327	80,329	2.75	-3.60
Denmark	5,151	3,255	2,659	2,445	3,249	0.11	32.88
Finland	2,268	2,838	1,804	2,592	2,719	0.09	4.90
Norway	3,954	3,783	2,924	4,292	5,634	0.19	31.27
Sweden	5,322	6,605	5,967	4,605	4,259	0.15	-7.51
United Kingdom	50,407	67,851	76,775	69,393	64,468	2.20	-7.10

FRENCH POLYNESIA

6. Overnight stays of non-resident tourists in all types of accommodation establishments, by country of residence

	2002	2003	2004	2005	2006	Market share 06	% Change 06-05
Southern Europe	148,014	161,435	181,292	191,607	232,431	7.94	21.31
Italy	116,745	125,515	139,758	145,006	174,823	5.98	20.56
Portugal	6,530	6,519	6,504	6,506	5,621	0.19	-13.60
Spain	24,739	29,401	35,030	40,095	51,987	1.78	29.66
Western Europe	1,260,557	1,324,331	1,253,932	1,226,741	1,223,146	41.81	-0.29
Austria	9,826	9,843	8,585	11,328	11,742	0.40	3.65
Belgium	19,852	19,430	17,836	18,499	19,371	0.66	4.71
France	1,127,448	1,192,990	1,118,981	1,092,227	1,076,496	36.79	-1.44
Germany	52,138	52,686	58,044	54,289	60,770	2.08	11.94
Luxembourg	3,129	2,666	2,308	2,825	2,171	0.07	-23.15
Netherlands	7,131	7,286	8,348	6,893	8,479	0.29	23.01
Switzerland	41,033	39,430	39,830	40,680	44,117	1.51	8.45
Other Europe	22,727	19,489	24,330	29,205	38,963	1.33	33.41
Other countries of Europe	22,727	19,489	24,330	29,205	38,963	1.33	33.41
MIDDLE EAST	2,586	2,255	2,579	2,132	3,175	0.11	48.92
Middle East	2,586	2,255	2,579	2,132	3,175	0.11	48.92
All countries of Middle East	2,586	2,255	2,579	2,132	3,175	0.11	48.92
SOUTH ASIA	845	975	1,320	737	2,127	0.07	188.60
South Asia	845	975	1,320	737	2,127	0.07	188.60
India	845	975	1,320	737	2,127	0.07	188.60
REGION NOT SPECIFIED	3,515	3,776	2,932	2,666	17,578	0.60	559.34
Not Specified	3,515	3,776	2,932	2,666	17,578	0.60	559.34
Other countries of the World	3,515	3,776	2,932	2,666	17,578	0.60	559.34

Source: World Tourism Organization (UNWTO)

GAMBIA

1. Arrivals of non-resident tourists at national borders, by nationality

		2002	2003	2004	2005	2006	Market share 06	% Change 06-05
TOTAL	(*)	81,005	73,485	90,095	107,904	124,800	100.00	15.66
AFRICA		726	4,542	1,330	11,497	18,135	14.53	57.74
Other Africa		726	4,542	1,330	11,497	18,135	14.53	57.74
All countries of Africa		726	4,542	1,330	11,497	18,135	14.53	57.74
AMERICAS		1,075	643	3,248	1,387	2,189	1.75	57.82
North America		1,075	643	3,248	1,387	2,189	1.75	57.82
Canada		209	198	189	204	359	0.29	75.98
United States		866	445	3,059	1,183	1,830	1.47	54.69
EUROPE		77,155	63,625	81,955	86,181	91,194	73.07	5.82
Northern Europe		57,459	48,692	59,761	60,114	64,771	51.90	7.75
Denmark		2,260	2,616	1,997	3,146	3,604	2.89	14.56
Norway		711	999	5,513	1,028	1,186	0.95	15.37
Sweden		5,594	4,205	3,954	6,754	6,361	5.10	-5.82
United Kingdom		48,894	40,872	48,297	49,186	53,620	42.96	9.01
Southern Europe		210	200	230	232	325	0.26	40.09
Italy		210	200	230	232	325	0.26	40.09
Western Europe		19,486	14,733	21,964	25,835	26,098	20.91	1.02
Austria		257	153	275	400	445	0.36	11.25
Belgium		4,268	1,707	4,961	2,575	2,710	2.17	5.24
France		645	653	432	546	659	0.53	20.70
Germany		3,707	4,253	2,891	4,941	6,561	5.26	32.79
Netherlands		10,419	7,262	13,112	17,017	15,298	12.26	-10.10
Switzerland		190	705	293	356	425	0.34	19.38
REGION NOT SPECIFIED		2,049	4,675	3,562	8,839	13,282	10.64	50.27
Not Specified		2,049	4,675	3,562	8,839	13,282	10.64	50.27
Other countries of the World		2,049	4,675	3,562	8,839	13,282	10.64	50.27

Source: World Tourism Organization (UNWTO)

GEORGIA

2. Arrivals of non-resident visitors at national borders, by country of residence

	2002	2003	2004	2005	2006	Market share 06	% Change 06-05
TOTAL	298,469	313,442	368,312	560,021	983,114	100.00	75.55
AFRICA	586	306	788	431	777	0.08	80.28
East Africa	131	78	388	91	173	0.02	90.11
Ethiopia	15	13	15	10	15		50.00
Kenya	14	14	11	26	47		80.77
Madagascar	1	29	3	3	10		233.33
Malawi				4	7		75.00
Mozambique	5		5	14	43		207.14
Rwanda	71	4	4	9	11		22.22
Somalia	7	13	333	2	10		400.00
Zimbabwe	3	3	9	9	19		111.11
Uganda	11	2	6	11	7		-36.36
Zambia	4		2	3	4		33.33
Central Africa	16	36	43	50	90	0.01	80.00
Angola	2		15		5		
Cameroon	10	10	13	9	40		344.44
Central African Republic					12		
Chad				11	4		-63.64
Congo	2	26	14	30	29		-3.33
Gabon	2		1				
North Africa	28	15	52	48	65	0.01	35.42
Algeria	3	5	19	8	14		75.00
Morocco	13	8	23	13	17		30.77
Sudan	9		3	22	27		22.73
Tunisia	3	2	7	5	7		40.00
Southern Africa	234	115	224	176	296	0.03	68.18
Botswana				1			
Lesotho				1			
South Africa	234	115	224	172	272	0.03	58.14
Other countries of Southern Africa				2	24		1,100.00
West Africa	177	62	81	66	153	0.02	131.82
Cape Verde	46	2	2	6	2		-66.67
Benin	84		2	2	1		-50.00
Gambia	15		7	1			
Ghana	10	14	11	14	32		128.57
Guinea				1	7		600.00
Cote D'Ivoire				4	4		
Liberia	1		14	12	9		-25.00
Mauritania	11	25	21	6	7		16.67
Niger	4	7	5		9		
Nigeria	6	14	19	12	71	0.01	491.67
Senegal				1	3		200.00
Sierra Leone				6	7		16.67
Burkina Faso				1	1		
AMERICAS	8,156	8,731	11,209	14,842	19,417	1.98	30.82
Caribbean	32	93	35	46	102	0.01	121.74
Barbados				2			
Cuba	23	71	18	11	13		18.18
Dominica	5	13	8	1	4		300.00
Jamaica				9	20		122.22
Trinidad and Tobago	4	9	9	23	65	0.01	182.61
Central America	57	69	68	53	155	0.02	192.45

GEORGIA

2. Arrivals of non-resident visitors at national borders, by country of residence

	2002	2003	2004	2005	2006	Market share 06	% Change 06-05
Belize				1	3		200.00
Costa Rica	29	20	23	20	55	0.01	175.00
El Salvador	19	43	38	13	45		246.15
Guatemala	3			6	17		183.33
Honduras		1	2	5	12		140.00
Nicaragua	2			2	3		50.00
Panama	4	5	5	6	20		233.33
North America	**7,750**	**8,226**	**10,530**	**14,098**	**18,389**	**1.87**	**30.44**
Canada	596	719	867	1,104	1,663	0.17	50.63
Mexico	22	21	54	66	104	0.01	57.58
United States	7,132	7,486	9,609	12,928	16,622	1.69	28.57
South America	**317**	**343**	**576**	**645**	**771**	**0.08**	**19.53**
Argentina	56	34	88	68	174	0.02	155.88
Bolivia	16	19	12	16	29		81.25
Brazil	36	43	82	105	123	0.01	17.14
Chile	34	16	11	37	35		-5.41
Colombia	19	149	280	300	209	0.02	-30.33
Ecuador	19		6	3	22		633.33
Guyana	1		2	2	7		250.00
Paraguay	2						
Peru	19	48	67	73	95	0.01	30.14
Suriname	5		1		1		
Uruguay	59	14	11	13	54	0.01	315.38
Venezuela	51	20	16	28	22		-21.43
EAST ASIA AND THE PACIFIC	**6,865**	**6,756**	**4,952**	**3,244**	**13,732**	**1.40**	**323.30**
North-East Asia	**1,665**	**1,737**	**1,503**	**2,057**	**4,415**	**0.45**	**114.63**
China	791	955	730	747	2,083	0.21	178.85
Taiwan (Province of China)	36	1	29	5	88	0.01	1,660.00
Hong Kong, China				8	11		37.50
Japan	677	672	571	1,054	1,611	0.16	52.85
Korea, Dem. People's Republic of	161	76	170	5	21		320.00
Korea, Republic of		33	3	238	601	0.06	152.52
South-East Asia	**4,793**	**4,640**	**3,045**	**583**	**8,210**	**0.84**	**1,308.23**
Myanmar	117	164	15	1	142	0.01	*********
Cambodia			2	5	1		-80.00
Indonesia	164	114	117	57	190	0.02	233.33
Malaysia	34	33	52	96	87	0.01	-9.38
Philippines	4,464	4,210	2,767	253	7,584	0.77	2,897.63
Singapore	8	20	22	67	138	0.01	105.97
Viet Nam	2	15	14	21	27		28.57
Thailand	4	84	56	83	41		-50.60
Australasia	**407**	**379**	**401**	**601**	**1,103**	**0.11**	**83.53**
Australia	407	379	401	601	1,103	0.11	83.53
Melanesia				**2**	**1**		**-50.00**
Fiji				2	1		-50.00
Polynesia			**3**	**1**	**3**		**200.00**
Samoa			3	1	3		200.00
EUROPE	**275,332**	**288,648**	**342,596**	**533,129**	**935,747**	**95.18**	**75.52**
Central/Eastern Europe	**189,348**	**185,204**	**228,949**	**375,068**	**658,976**	**67.03**	**75.70**
Azerbaijan	52,115	42,790	63,663	153,467	244,444	24.86	59.28
Armenia	61,978	61,351	71,261	100,508	245,146	24.94	143.91

GEORGIA

2. Arrivals of non-resident visitors at national borders, by country of residence

	2002	2003	2004	2005	2006	Market share 06	% Change 06-05
Bulgaria	6,825	5,841	4,973	2,653	10,785	1.10	306.52
Belarus	952	1,129	1,160	1,236	1,562	0.16	26.38
Czech Republic	768	563	729	1,108	1,691	0.17	52.62
Estonia	221	191	266	552	1,582	0.16	186.59
Hungary	315	415	287	363	721	0.07	98.62
Kazakhstan	1,011	1,398	1,651	2,825	4,374	0.44	54.83
Kyrgyzstan	458	677	859	1,546	1,597	0.16	3.30
Latvia	656	576	789	753	2,226	0.23	195.62
Lithuania	568	936	787	925	1,612	0.16	74.27
Republic of Moldova	1,886	2,820	1,753	1,589	1,528	0.16	-3.84
Poland	1,117	1,242	1,637	1,553	3,856	0.39	148.29
Romania	2,335	1,209	783	786	1,490	0.15	89.57
Russian Federation	41,390	46,699	61,400	90,277	104,111	10.59	15.32
Slovakia	124	229	150	321	653	0.07	103.43
Tajikistan	83	126	136	267	263	0.03	-1.50
Turkmenistan	166	201	226	729	927	0.09	27.16
Ukraine	15,550	15,354	14,721	12,431	29,163	2.97	134.60
Uzbekistan	830	1,457	1,718	1,179	1,245	0.13	5.60
Northern Europe	**6,595**	**6,756**	**9,129**	**9,794**	**17,775**	**1.81**	**81.49**
Denmark	708	534	708	708	989	0.10	39.69
Faeroe Islands				6	12		100.00
Finland	221	218	318	354	639	0.06	80.51
Iceland	19	31	28	18	85	0.01	372.22
Ireland	448	665	531	592	950	0.10	60.47
Norway	287	244	422	496	891	0.09	79.64
Sweden	513	545	725	943	1,467	0.15	55.57
United Kingdom	4,399	4,519	6,397	6,677	12,742	1.30	90.83
Southern Europe	**7,001**	**7,882**	**8,415**	**11,633**	**22,587**	**2.30**	**94.16**
Albania	68	184	126	54	124	0.01	129.63
Andorra				2	4		100.00
Bosnia and Herzegovina	30	38	58	92	124	0.01	34.78
Croatia	327	416	321	225	622	0.06	176.44
Greece	4,130	4,646	4,148	7,098	13,135	1.34	85.05
Holy See				42	47		11.90
Italy	1,680	1,777	2,625	2,732	5,331	0.54	95.13
Malta	60	41	26	46	92	0.01	100.00
Portugal	106	73	224	161	244	0.02	51.55
San Marino				5	8		60.00
Slovenia	88	62	112	260	1,113	0.11	328.08
Spain	344	488	538	594	1,066	0.11	79.46
TFYR of Macedonia				127	219	0.02	72.44
Yugoslavia, Sfr (Former)				2	426	0.04	*********
Serbia and Montenegro	168	157	237	193	32		-83.42
Western Europe	**12,410**	**13,431**	**15,911**	**20,418**	**32,304**	**3.29**	**58.21**
Austria	797	853	923	2,259	2,085	0.21	-7.70
Belgium	441	497	737	978	1,372	0.14	40.29
France	2,249	2,574	3,489	3,996	6,577	0.67	64.59
Germany	6,423	6,533	7,208	8,840	14,884	1.51	68.37
Liechtenstein				7	14		100.00
Luxembourg	25	17	36	53	78	0.01	47.17
Monaco	2				4		
Netherlands	1,550	1,776	2,416	3,095	5,352	0.54	72.92
Switzerland	923	1,181	1,102	1,190	1,938	0.20	62.86
East Mediterranean Europe	**59,790**	**75,275**	**79,975**	**116,216**	**204,105**	**20.76**	**75.63**
Cyprus	54	55	108	102	207	0.02	102.94

GEORGIA

2. Arrivals of non-resident visitors at national borders, by country of residence

	2002	2003	2004	2005	2006	Market share 06	% Change 06-05
Israel	3,276	3,469	5,167	6,318	11,462	1.17	81.42
Turkey	56,460	71,751	74,700	109,796	192,436	19.57	75.27
Other Europe	**188**	**100**	**217**				
Other countries of Europe	188	100	217				
MIDDLE EAST	**1,250**	**1,835**	**1,563**	**973**	**2,105**	**0.21**	**116.34**
Middle East	**1,250**	**1,835**	**1,563**	**973**	**2,105**	**0.21**	**116.34**
Bahrain	4	2	2		2		
Iraq	55	33	53	55	54	0.01	-1.82
Jordan	52	35	66	94	105	0.01	11.70
Kuwait	4	2	2	2	174	0.02	8,600.00
Lebanon	103	242	225	175	316	0.03	80.57
Libyan Arab Jamahiriya	5			12			
Oman	1			2	5		150.00
Saudi Arabia	9	1	5	7	18		157.14
Syrian Arab Republic	847	1,222	956	522	1,116	0.11	113.79
United Arab Emirates	6	1	45	9	29		222.22
Egypt	163	297	201	92	283	0.03	207.61
Yemen	1		8	3	3		
SOUTH ASIA	**5,822**	**6,683**	**6,635**	**6,641**	**9,977**	**1.01**	**50.23**
South Asia	**5,822**	**6,683**	**6,635**	**6,641**	**9,977**	**1.01**	**50.23**
Afghanistan	4		11	8	34		325.00
Bangladesh	76	198	57	37	81	0.01	118.92
Sri Lanka	105	16	15	24	55	0.01	129.17
India	1,861	2,200	2,853	1,335	3,088	0.31	131.31
Iran, Islamic Republic of	3,479	3,984	3,490	5,033	6,409	0.65	27.34
Nepal	32	16	40	35	31		-11.43
Pakistan	265	269	169	169	279	0.03	65.09
REGION NOT SPECIFIED	**458**	**483**	**569**	**761**	**1,359**	**0.14**	**78.58**
Not Specified	**458**	**483**	**569**	**761**	**1,359**	**0.14**	**78.58**
Other countries of the World	458	483	569	761	1,359	0.14	78.58

Source: World Tourism Organization (UNWTO)

GEORGIA

3. Arrivals of non-resident tourists in hotels and similar establishments, by country of residence

	2002	2003	2004	2005	2006	Market share 06	% Change 06-05
TOTAL	29,369	38,891	60,805	63,201	82,208	100.00	30.07
AFRICA	125	132	4,467	274	429	0.52	56.57
Other Africa	125	132	4,467	274	429	0.52	56.57
All countries of Africa	125	132	4,467	274	429	0.52	56.57
AMERICAS	5,368	7,641	11,060	14,158	11,501	13.99	-18.77
North America	5,123	7,230	10,431	13,503	11,372	13.83	-15.78
Canada	148	304	371	394	660	0.80	67.51
Mexico	32	9	85	125	7	0.01	-94.40
United States	4,943	6,917	9,975	12,984	10,705	13.02	-17.55
South America	61	58	226	226	39	0.05	-82.74
Argentina	28	44	150	115	20	0.02	-82.61
Brazil	14	8	74	107	14	0.02	-86.92
Chile	8	2	2		4		
Uruguay	11	4		4	1		-75.00
Other Americas	184	353	403	429	90	0.11	-79.02
Other countries of the Americas	184	353	403	429	90	0.11	-79.02
EAST ASIA AND THE PACIFIC	1,189	3,090	2,700	1,817	2,344	2.85	29.00
North-East Asia	639	1,231	908	1,060	1,533	1.86	44.62
China	196	568	147	271	737	0.90	171.96
Japan	443	663	761	789	796	0.97	0.89
Australasia	67	1,349	427	234	393	0.48	67.95
Australia	67	1,349	427	234	393	0.48	67.95
Other East Asia and the Pacific	483	510	1,365	523	418	0.51	-20.08
Other countries of Asia	483	510	1,365	523	418	0.51	-20.08
EUROPE	22,287	26,850	41,109	45,900	65,699	79.92	43.14
Central/Eastern Europe	5,630	11,600	13,349	19,246	24,063	29.27	25.03
Azerbaijan	1,094	2,406	2,613	3,221			
Armenia	985	2,595	3,065	6,489			
Bulgaria	224	156	223	272			
Belarus	54	181	140	183			
Czech Republic	157	114	202	313			
Hungary	56	75	54	170			
Kazakhstan	29	55	107	485			
Kyrgyzstan	15	8	59	46			
Republic of Moldova	66	42	139	44			
Poland	82	130	1,087	403			
Romania	74	58	139	203			
Russian Federation	2,314	4,277	4,394	5,467			
Slovakia	15	52	31	194			
Tajikistan	14	15	31	156			
Turkmenistan	40	26	112	38			
Ukraine	356	1,319	772	1,411			
Uzbekistan	55	91	181	151			
All countries Central/East Europe					24,063	29.27	
Northern Europe	2,556	2,944	5,906	6,793	91	0.11	-98.66
Denmark	332	81	177	204			
Finland	114	38	236	66			
Iceland	17	65	48	76	37	0.05	-51.32

GEORGIA

3. Arrivals of non-resident tourists in hotels and similar establishments, by country of residence

	2002	2003	2004	2005	2006	Market share 06	% Change 06-05
Ireland	69	299	113	174			
Norway	60	67	214	339	54	0.07	-84.07
Sweden	84	90	249	214			
United Kingdom	1,880	2,304	4,869	5,720			
Southern Europe	**1,112**	**1,179**	**1,775**	**2,959**			
Greece	363	418	476	755			
Italy	379	469	932	1,365			
Portugal	192	79	52	75			
Spain	162	193	315	764			
Serbia and Montenegro	16	20					
Western Europe	**2,937**	**4,522**	**6,351**	**7,717**	**321**	**0.39**	**-95.84**
Austria	473	409	518	848			
Belgium	176	176	591	463			
France	525	1,065	1,162	1,554			
Germany	1,443	2,234	2,537	2,907			
Luxembourg	25	71	41	69			
Netherlands	99	155	875	1,245			
Switzerland	196	412	627	631	321	0.39	-49.13
East Mediterranean Europe	**7,427**	**5,638**	**11,243**	**7,707**	**10,400**	**12.65**	**34.94**
Israel	731	928	1,165	1,882	2,947	3.58	56.59
Turkey	6,696	4,710	10,078	5,825	7,453	9.07	27.95
Other Europe	**2,625**	**967**	**2,485**	**1,478**	**30,824**	**37.50**	**1,985.52**
Other countries of Europe	2,625	967	2,485	1,478	30,824	37.50	1,985.52
SOUTH ASIA	**400**	**1,178**	**1,469**	**1,052**	**1,853**	**2.25**	**76.14**
South Asia	**400**	**1,178**	**1,469**	**1,052**	**1,853**	**2.25**	**76.14**
India	149	913	1,238	420	1,276	1.55	203.81
Iran, Islamic Republic of	251	265	231	632	577	0.70	-8.70
REGION NOT SPECIFIED					**382**	**0.46**	
Not Specified					**382**	**0.46**	
Other countries of the World					382	0.46	

Source: World Tourism Organization (UNWTO)

GERMANY

3. Arrivals of non-resident tourists in hotels and similar establishments, by country of residence

	2002	2003	2004	2005	2006	Market share 06	% Change 06-05
TOTAL	16,092,817	16,357,037	17,982,621	19,171,249	21,057,208	100.00	9.84
AFRICA	127,547	128,191	130,634	129,330	151,983	0.72	17.52
Southern Africa	38,687	35,202	39,180	40,893	49,069	0.23	19.99
South Africa	38,687	35,202	39,180	40,893	49,069	0.23	19.99
Other Africa	88,860	92,989	91,454	88,437	102,914	0.49	16.37
Other countries of Africa	88,860	92,989	91,454	88,437	102,914	0.49	16.37
AMERICAS	2,047,711	1,940,721	2,212,529	2,254,406	2,614,111	12.41	15.96
North America	1,903,628	1,801,298	2,058,151	2,086,640	2,325,978	11.05	11.47
Canada	157,740	152,092	172,341	181,274	211,052	1.00	16.43
Mexico	42,671	40,678	42,199	46,691	98,737	0.47	111.47
United States	1,703,217	1,608,528	1,843,611	1,858,675	2,016,189	9.57	8.47
South America	65,875	65,025	76,768	85,442	141,962	0.67	66.15
Brazil	65,875	65,025	76,768	85,442	141,962	0.67	66.15
Other Americas	78,208	74,398	77,610	82,324	146,171	0.69	77.56
Other countries of the Americas	78,208	74,398	77,610	82,324	146,171	0.69	77.56
EAST ASIA AND THE PACIFIC	1,598,178	1,484,957	1,794,362	1,867,721	2,023,918	9.61	8.36
North-East Asia	1,132,631	1,028,928	1,245,289	1,302,458	1,375,185	6.53	5.58
China (*)	258,791	257,185	372,873	403,272	424,832	2.02	5.35
Taiwan (Province of China)	49,753	63,403	77,781	79,185	86,765	0.41	9.57
Japan	732,911	616,149	685,871	702,867	730,206	3.47	3.89
Korea, Republic of	91,176	92,191	108,764	117,134	133,382	0.63	13.87
Australasia	132,978	133,610	163,309	177,186	215,192	1.02	21.45
Australia, New Zealand	132,978	133,610	163,309	177,186	215,192	1.02	21.45
Other East Asia and the Pacific	332,569	322,419	385,764	388,077	433,541	2.06	11.72
Other countries East Asia/Pacific	332,569	322,419	385,764	388,077	433,541	2.06	11.72
EUROPE	11,666,360	12,104,419	13,074,637	14,097,349	15,379,091	73.03	9.09
Central/Eastern Europe	936,040	991,261	1,063,396	1,145,089	1,261,129	5.99	10.13
Czech Republic	181,197	195,773	209,784	225,045	224,402	1.07	-0.29
Hungary	136,023	142,297	154,492	157,785	166,194	0.79	5.33
Poland	278,550	290,675	323,243	351,493	425,070	2.02	20.93
Russian Federation	248,350	258,194	274,571	299,457	342,243	1.63	14.29
Baltic countries	91,920	104,322	101,306	111,309	103,220	0.49	-7.27
Northern Europe	3,329,633	3,341,703	3,596,880	3,796,733	4,164,995	19.78	9.70
Denmark	607,410	618,742	652,566	741,458	803,542	3.82	8.37
Finland	153,271	163,860	187,286	190,542	202,114	0.96	6.07
Iceland	19,316	20,241	22,422	25,119	39,862	0.19	58.69
Ireland	60,511	61,731	70,856	86,965	117,495	0.56	35.11
Norway	247,144	233,010	240,459	260,819	281,566	1.34	7.95
Sweden	698,975	712,816	751,228	763,143	803,923	3.82	5.34
United Kingdom	1,543,006	1,531,303	1,672,063	1,728,687	1,916,493	9.10	10.86
Southern Europe	1,554,198	1,642,118	1,818,094	1,996,776	2,180,026	10.35	9.18
Greece	101,796	111,378	129,633	138,914	151,752	0.72	9.24
Italy	972,077	1,028,589	1,088,070	1,174,996	1,250,331	5.94	6.41
Portugal	68,699	74,977	84,794	88,603	127,923	0.61	44.38
Spain	411,626	427,174	515,597	594,263	650,020	3.09	9.38
Western Europe	5,317,659	5,568,439	6,000,815	6,496,295	6,974,932	33.12	7.37
Austria	768,406	799,553	857,027	923,708	989,574	4.70	7.13

GERMANY

3. Arrivals of non-resident tourists in hotels and similar establishments, by country of residence

	2002	2003	2004	2005	2006	Market share 06	% Change 06-05
Belgium	620,500	658,002	707,246	762,851	837,928	3.98	9.84
France	765,990	802,071	888,779	926,117	1,009,837	4.80	9.04
Luxembourg	102,423	113,295	122,376	131,143	149,292	0.71	13.84
Netherlands	1,983,019	2,034,892	2,126,097	2,322,597	2,479,199	11.77	6.74
Switzerland	1,077,321	1,160,626	1,299,290	1,429,879	1,509,102	7.17	5.54
East Mediterranean Europe	**221,134**	**237,151**	**246,412**	**265,051**	**282,587**	**1.34**	**6.62**
Israel	108,797	108,974	105,433	110,611	125,079	0.59	13.08
Turkey	112,337	128,177	140,979	154,440	157,508	0.75	1.99
Other Europe	**307,696**	**323,747**	**349,040**	**397,405**	**515,422**	**2.45**	**29.70**
Other countries of Europe	307,696	323,747	349,040	397,405	515,422	2.45	29.70
MIDDLE EAST	**125,152**	**135,086**	**152,837**	**177,564**	**195,137**	**0.93**	**9.90**
Middle East	**125,152**	**135,086**	**152,837**	**177,564**	**195,137**	**0.93**	**9.90**
All countries of Middle East	125,152	135,086	152,837	177,564	195,137	0.93	9.90
REGION NOT SPECIFIED	**527,869**	**563,663**	**617,622**	**644,879**	**692,968**	**3.29**	**7.46**
Not Specified	**527,869**	**563,663**	**617,622**	**644,879**	**692,968**	**3.29**	**7.46**
Other countries of the World	527,869	563,663	617,622	644,879	692,968	3.29	7.46

Source: World Tourism Organization (UNWTO)

GERMANY

4. Arrivals of non-resident tourists in all types of accommodation establishments, by country of residence

		2002	2003	2004	2005	2006	Market share 06	% Change 06-05
TOTAL		17,969,396	18,399,093	20,136,979	21,500,067	23,569,145	100.00	9.62
AFRICA		143,714	143,156	146,454	144,391	167,005	0.71	15.66
Southern Africa		42,509	38,574	43,308	44,990	53,510	0.23	18.94
South Africa		42,509	38,574	43,308	44,990	53,510	0.23	18.94
Other Africa		101,205	104,582	103,146	99,401	113,495	0.48	14.18
Other countries of Africa		101,205	104,582	103,146	99,401	113,495	0.48	14.18
AMERICAS		2,150,961	2,048,770	2,337,209	2,397,527	2,782,911	11.81	16.07
North America		1,988,494	1,893,163	2,163,951	2,206,344	2,461,694	10.44	11.57
Canada		172,232	169,329	190,439	203,187	235,523	1.00	15.91
Mexico		47,987	45,699	47,886	53,332	107,607	0.46	101.77
United States		1,768,275	1,678,135	1,925,626	1,949,825	2,118,564	8.99	8.65
South America		72,184	70,499	83,184	93,836	156,196	0.66	66.46
Brazil		72,184	70,499	83,184	93,836	156,196	0.66	66.46
Other Americas		90,283	85,108	90,074	97,347	165,021	0.70	69.52
Other countries of the Americas		90,283	85,108	90,074	97,347	165,021	0.70	69.52
EAST ASIA AND THE PACIFIC		1,715,992	1,605,064	1,931,265	2,000,752	2,176,143	9.23	8.77
North-East Asia		1,199,959	1,097,726	1,316,677	1,371,010	1,448,840	6.15	5.68
China	(*)	270,459	268,057	387,375	418,235	441,495	1.87	5.56
Taiwan (Province of China)		55,803	68,733	83,205	84,891	93,455	0.40	10.09
Japan		762,471	646,778	715,209	730,232	759,899	3.22	4.06
Korea, Republic of		111,226	114,158	130,888	137,652	153,991	0.65	11.87
Australasia		166,068	168,213	206,733	220,328	272,988	1.16	23.90
Australia, New Zealand		166,068	168,213	206,733	220,328	272,988	1.16	23.90
Other East Asia and the Pacific		349,965	339,125	407,855	409,414	454,315	1.93	10.97
Other countries East Asia/Pacific		349,965	339,125	407,855	409,414	454,315	1.93	10.97
EUROPE		13,288,813	13,877,895	14,918,028	16,099,891	17,504,005	74.27	8.72
Central/Eastern Europe		1,056,098	1,105,104	1,180,078	1,268,889	1,389,464	5.90	9.50
Czech Republic		200,903	216,286	232,286	248,674	250,555	1.06	0.76
Hungary		153,502	159,146	172,047	175,953	182,185	0.77	3.54
Poland		321,948	330,501	368,832	396,985	474,979	2.02	19.65
Russian Federation		270,138	276,781	292,840	319,026	363,169	1.54	13.84
Baltic countries		109,607	122,390	114,073	128,251	118,576	0.50	-7.54
Northern Europe		3,682,271	3,716,859	3,973,198	4,229,848	4,664,758	19.79	10.28
Denmark		733,991	758,736	785,494	885,696	960,057	4.07	8.40
Finland		180,114	193,053	214,682	222,688	230,596	0.98	3.55
Iceland		20,694	22,288	24,172	28,388	43,432	0.18	52.99
Ireland		69,156	69,429	79,602	98,196	132,008	0.56	34.43
Norway		272,727	259,957	265,918	289,143	314,735	1.34	8.85
Sweden		761,083	778,246	815,387	827,788	877,261	3.72	5.98
United Kingdom		1,644,506	1,635,150	1,787,943	1,877,949	2,106,669	8.94	12.18
Southern Europe		1,680,202	1,786,113	1,974,922	2,183,976	2,365,661	10.04	8.32
Greece		105,900	116,061	134,609	145,120	158,620	0.67	9.30
Italy		1,052,110	1,122,622	1,188,712	1,291,134	1,358,051	5.76	5.18
Portugal		74,237	79,774	90,210	94,254	135,952	0.58	44.24
Spain		447,955	467,656	561,391	653,468	713,038	3.03	9.12
Western Europe		6,292,688	6,658,416	7,140,584	7,697,675	8,220,409	34.88	6.79
Austria		821,182	865,977	920,358	995,313	1,066,289	4.52	7.13

GERMANY

4. Arrivals of non-resident tourists in all types of accommodation establishments, by country of residence

	2002	2003	2004	2005	2006	Market share 06	% Change 06-05
Belgium	688,054	731,312	786,512	849,812	929,212	3.94	9.34
France	850,786	899,646	996,348	1,040,483	1,128,644	4.79	8.47
Luxembourg	113,548	125,740	137,063	144,928	164,093	0.70	13.22
Netherlands	2,657,211	2,765,182	2,883,669	3,105,694	3,274,954	13.90	5.45
Switzerland	1,161,907	1,270,559	1,416,634	1,561,445	1,657,217	7.03	6.13
East Mediterranean Europe	**231,964**	**251,054**	**260,856**	**281,470**	**299,272**	**1.27**	**6.32**
Israel	114,058	115,802	111,916	118,018	134,367	0.57	13.85
Turkey	117,906	135,252	148,940	163,452	164,905	0.70	0.89
Other Europe	**345,590**	**360,349**	**388,390**	**438,033**	**564,441**	**2.39**	**28.86**
Other countries of Europe	345,590	360,349	388,390	438,033	564,441	2.39	28.86
MIDDLE EAST	**128,054**	**142,732**	**160,110**	**185,497**	**202,369**	**0.86**	**9.10**
Middle East	**128,054**	**142,732**	**160,110**	**185,497**	**202,369**	**0.86**	**9.10**
All countries of Middle East	128,054	142,732	160,110	185,497	202,369	0.86	9.10
REGION NOT SPECIFIED	**541,862**	**581,476**	**643,913**	**672,009**	**736,712**	**3.13**	**9.63**
Not Specified	**541,862**	**581,476**	**643,913**	**672,009**	**736,712**	**3.13**	**9.63**
Other countries of the World	541,862	581,476	643,913	672,009	736,712	3.13	9.63

Source: World Tourism Organization (UNWTO)

GERMANY

5. Overnight stays of non-resident tourists in hotels and similar establishments, by country of residence

	2002	2003	2004	2005	2006	Market share 06	% Change 06-05
TOTAL	34,553,098	35,172,320	38,490,701	40,838,704	44,920,506	100.00	9.99
AFRICA	332,085	358,208	363,161	353,708	424,111	0.94	19.90
Southern Africa	94,198	99,376	107,703	107,503	130,147	0.29	21.06
South Africa	94,198	99,376	107,703	107,503	130,147	0.29	21.06
Other Africa	237,887	258,832	255,458	246,205	293,964	0.65	19.40
Other countries of Africa	237,887	258,832	255,458	246,205	293,964	0.65	19.40
AMERICAS	4,599,093	4,329,808	4,944,634	5,088,815	5,844,549	13.01	14.85
North America	4,236,253	3,981,945	4,547,435	4,655,419	5,062,827	11.27	8.75
Canada	338,199	328,775	361,555	381,379	436,201	0.97	14.37
Mexico	106,291	102,084	103,800	120,562	272,538	0.61	126.06
United States	3,791,763	3,551,086	4,082,080	4,153,478	4,354,088	9.69	4.83
South America	173,751	168,867	202,366	220,223	389,317	0.87	76.78
Brazil	173,751	168,867	202,366	220,223	389,317	0.87	76.78
Other Americas	189,089	178,996	194,833	213,173	392,405	0.87	84.08
Other countries of the Americas	189,089	178,996	194,833	213,173	392,405	0.87	84.08
EAST ASIA AND THE PACIFIC	3,111,782	3,013,218	3,645,478	3,801,999	4,187,181	9.32	10.13
North-East Asia	2,074,766	1,961,827	2,373,874	2,471,096	2,650,126	5.90	7.24
China (*)	533,523	542,835	754,421	805,701	873,436	1.94	8.41
Taiwan (Province of China)	118,259	130,246	164,243	156,344	179,846	0.40	15.03
Japan	1,235,034	1,099,432	1,215,214	1,244,198	1,311,780	2.92	5.43
Korea, Republic of	187,950	189,314	239,996	264,853	285,064	0.63	7.63
Australasia	283,907	279,447	333,177	361,827	469,091	1.04	29.65
Australia, New Zealand	283,907	279,447	333,177	361,827	469,091	1.04	29.65
Other East Asia and the Pacific	753,109	771,944	938,427	969,076	1,067,964	2.38	10.20
Other countries East Asia/Pacific	753,109	771,944	938,427	969,076	1,067,964	2.38	10.20
EUROPE	25,071,161	25,988,393	27,886,623	29,794,517	32,557,959	72.48	9.28
Central/Eastern Europe	2,254,739	2,357,164	2,494,092	2,606,227	2,830,598	6.30	8.61
Czech Republic	436,270	454,933	473,632	489,016	482,291	1.07	-1.38
Hungary	303,256	321,329	348,324	346,198	362,769	0.81	4.79
Poland	640,469	652,313	731,214	768,029	935,016	2.08	21.74
Russian Federation	652,526	676,702	719,636	758,961	857,751	1.91	13.02
Baltic countries	222,218	251,887	221,286	244,023	192,771	0.43	-21.00
Northern Europe	6,402,229	6,422,845	6,923,530	7,316,867	8,184,094	18.22	11.85
Denmark	1,126,532	1,182,535	1,258,238	1,421,036	1,577,118	3.51	10.98
Finland	301,712	314,856	351,572	360,705	384,087	0.86	6.48
Iceland	41,274	42,994	50,089	53,231	96,359	0.21	81.02
Ireland	145,361	142,111	164,850	197,833	262,248	0.58	32.56
Norway	418,781	396,106	429,981	460,303	506,583	1.13	10.05
Sweden	1,150,431	1,184,087	1,250,037	1,277,456	1,369,741	3.05	7.22
United Kingdom	3,218,138	3,160,156	3,418,763	3,546,303	3,987,958	8.88	12.45
Southern Europe	3,317,745	3,474,136	3,852,620	4,250,861	4,633,339	10.31	9.00
Greece	273,868	282,450	333,264	355,438	382,108	0.85	7.50
Italy	1,991,247	2,104,067	2,231,026	2,399,298	2,576,867	5.74	7.40
Portugal	170,468	175,718	196,898	200,412	284,471	0.63	41.94
Spain	882,162	911,901	1,091,432	1,295,713	1,389,893	3.09	7.27
Western Europe	11,824,829	12,390,544	13,187,073	14,079,072	15,036,329	33.47	6.80
Austria	1,555,566	1,602,873	1,717,395	1,847,474	1,953,996	4.35	5.77

GERMANY

5. Overnight stays of non-resident tourists in hotels and similar establishments, by country of residence

	2002	2003	2004	2005	2006	Market share 06	% Change 06-05
Belgium	1,452,549	1,575,676	1,677,769	1,791,584	1,952,511	4.35	8.98
France	1,448,654	1,514,471	1,665,116	1,723,678	1,883,650	4.19	9.28
Luxembourg	247,015	268,654	290,143	307,024	344,884	0.77	12.33
Netherlands	5,024,891	5,146,288	5,284,359	5,601,033	5,914,285	13.17	5.59
Switzerland	2,096,154	2,282,582	2,552,291	2,808,279	2,987,003	6.65	6.36
East Mediterranean Europe	**533,395**	**567,600**	**597,390**	**636,158**	**691,940**	**1.54**	**8.77**
Israel	264,729	261,004	261,454	284,597	331,939	0.74	16.63
Turkey	268,666	306,596	335,936	351,561	360,001	0.80	2.40
Other Europe	**738,224**	**776,104**	**831,918**	**905,332**	**1,181,659**	**2.63**	**30.52**
Other countries of Europe	738,224	776,104	831,918	905,332	1,181,659	2.63	30.52
MIDDLE EAST	**382,667**	**409,750**	**470,323**	**594,068**	**612,529**	**1.36**	**3.11**
Middle East	**382,667**	**409,750**	**470,323**	**594,068**	**612,529**	**1.36**	**3.11**
All countries of Middle East	382,667	409,750	470,323	594,068	612,529	1.36	3.11
REGION NOT SPECIFIED	**1,056,310**	**1,072,943**	**1,180,482**	**1,205,597**	**1,294,177**	**2.88**	**7.35**
Not Specified	**1,056,310**	**1,072,943**	**1,180,482**	**1,205,597**	**1,294,177**	**2.88**	**7.35**
Other countries of the World	1,056,310	1,072,943	1,180,482	1,205,597	1,294,177	2.88	7.35

Source: World Tourism Organization (UNWTO)

GERMANY

6. Overnight stays of non-resident tourists in all types of accommodation establishments, by country of residence

	2002	2003	2004	2005	2006	Market share 06	% Change 06-05
TOTAL	40,654,517	41,745,569	45,373,852	48,246,436	52,947,373	100.00	9.74
AFRICA	390,687	414,927	423,742	413,610	486,421	0.92	17.60
Southern Africa	108,104	110,763	120,454	123,791	145,116	0.27	17.23
South Africa	108,104	110,763	120,454	123,791	145,116	0.27	17.23
Other Africa	282,583	304,164	303,288	289,819	341,305	0.64	17.76
Other countries of Africa	282,583	304,164	303,288	289,819	341,305	0.64	17.76
AMERICAS	4,891,199	4,635,771	5,305,727	5,505,402	6,329,960	11.96	14.98
North America	4,470,847	4,239,470	4,832,700	5,000,785	5,449,402	10.29	8.97
Canada	374,665	373,434	409,132	440,695	501,286	0.95	13.75
Mexico	119,709	114,318	102,183	137,115	295,727	0.56	115.68
United States	3,976,473	3,751,718	4,321,385	4,422,975	4,652,389	8.79	5.19
South America	196,316	184,456	221,108	244,692	426,484	0.81	74.29
Brazil	196,316	184,456	221,108	244,692	426,484	0.81	74.29
Other Americas	224,036	211,845	251,919	259,925	454,074	0.86	74.69
Other countries of the Americas	224,036	211,845	251,919	259,925	454,074	0.86	74.69
EAST ASIA AND THE PACIFIC	3,376,208	3,297,986	3,970,559	4,148,214	4,584,406	8.66	10.52
North-East Asia	2,221,923	2,114,837	2,530,558	2,638,730	2,826,083	5.34	7.10
China (*)	572,903	578,012	789,429	853,449	924,673	1.75	8.35
Taiwan (Province of China)	128,866	139,363	174,224	167,188	193,059	0.36	15.47
Japan	1,298,516	1,171,636	1,286,058	1,312,456	1,382,668	2.61	5.35
Korea, Republic of	221,638	225,826	280,847	305,637	325,683	0.62	6.56
Australasia	348,592	349,138	424,311	464,093	607,298	1.15	30.86
Australia, New Zealand	348,592	349,138	424,311	464,093	607,298	1.15	30.86
Other East Asia and the Pacific	805,693	834,011	1,015,690	1,045,391	1,151,025	2.17	10.10
Other countries East Asia/Pacific	805,693	834,011	1,015,690	1,045,391	1,151,025	2.17	10.10
EUROPE	30,478,054	31,812,286	33,899,288	36,227,694	39,390,360	74.40	8.73
Central/Eastern Europe	2,801,352	2,853,370	3,007,332	3,118,896	3,351,098	6.33	7.45
Czech Republic	512,711	529,972	550,949	577,457	571,899	1.08	-0.96
Hungary	370,546	384,711	415,692	413,237	427,251	0.81	3.39
Poland	839,855	837,957	952,862	975,934	1,156,982	2.19	18.55
Russian Federation	776,831	779,287	822,932	862,592	964,888	1.82	11.86
Baltic countries	301,409	321,443	264,897	289,676	230,078	0.43	-20.57
Northern Europe	7,265,443	7,340,958	7,861,875	8,388,279	9,440,888	17.83	12.55
Denmark	1,433,712	1,519,593	1,582,548	1,773,335	1,956,103	3.69	10.31
Finland	355,632	373,749	407,207	426,536	447,951	0.85	5.02
Iceland	44,849	48,359	54,671	63,153	105,881	0.20	67.66
Ireland	170,855	162,740	190,414	228,794	302,911	0.57	32.39
Norway	472,571	451,643	484,871	522,744	575,253	1.09	10.04
Sweden	1,267,071	1,307,825	1,374,284	1,402,910	1,521,611	2.87	8.46
United Kingdom	3,520,753	3,477,049	3,767,880	3,970,807	4,531,178	8.56	14.11
Southern Europe	3,646,844	3,849,122	4,259,238	4,742,350	5,152,904	9.73	8.66
Greece	291,505	301,787	353,283	378,237	410,752	0.78	8.60
Italy	2,182,632	2,326,512	2,476,530	2,681,855	2,853,427	5.39	6.40
Portugal	189,675	195,916	213,314	222,007	318,936	0.60	43.66
Spain	983,032	1,024,907	1,216,111	1,460,251	1,569,789	2.96	7.50
Western Europe	15,303,444	16,225,017	17,119,457	18,212,817	19,322,019	36.49	6.09
Austria	1,711,127	1,778,717	1,899,613	2,053,432	2,193,167	4.14	6.80

GERMANY

6. Overnight stays of non-resident tourists in all types of accommodation establishments, by country of residence

	2002	2003	2004	2005	2006	Market share 06	% Change 06-05
Belgium	1,681,713	1,833,558	1,941,318	2,079,083	2,254,192	4.26	8.42
France	1,690,147	1,788,048	1,964,765	2,047,255	2,223,960	4.20	8.63
Luxembourg	311,442	342,815	366,346	381,150	420,353	0.79	10.29
Netherlands	7,534,861	7,858,861	8,021,092	8,428,199	8,778,442	16.58	4.16
Switzerland	2,374,154	2,623,018	2,926,323	3,223,698	3,451,905	6.52	7.08
East Mediterranean Europe	**582,568**	**632,547**	**663,842**	**705,591**	**766,404**	**1.45**	**8.62**
Israel	289,579	296,556	296,619	317,058	373,525	0.71	17.81
Turkey	292,989	335,991	367,223	388,533	392,879	0.74	1.12
Other Europe	**878,403**	**911,272**	**987,544**	**1,059,761**	**1,357,047**	**2.56**	**28.05**
Other countries of Europe	878,403	911,272	987,544	1,059,761	1,357,047	2.56	28.05
MIDDLE EAST	**399,336**	**441,635**	**512,287**	**648,997**	**666,143**	**1.26**	**2.64**
Middle East	**399,336**	**441,635**	**512,287**	**648,997**	**666,143**	**1.26**	**2.64**
All countries of Middle East	399,336	441,635	512,287	648,997	666,143	1.26	2.64
REGION NOT SPECIFIED	**1,119,033**	**1,142,964**	**1,262,249**	**1,302,519**	**1,490,083**	**2.81**	**14.40**
Not Specified	**1,119,033**	**1,142,964**	**1,262,249**	**1,302,519**	**1,490,083**	**2.81**	**14.40**
Other countries of the World	1,119,033	1,142,964	1,262,249	1,302,519	1,490,083	2.81	14.40

Source: World Tourism Organization (UNWTO)

GHANA

1. Arrivals of non-resident tourists at national borders, by nationality

	2002	2003	2004	2005	2006	Market share 06	% Change 06-05
TOTAL	482,637	530,827	583,819	428,533			
AFRICA	164,210	180,609	198,638	172,913			
West Africa	144,112	158,501	174,326	147,333			
Benin	4,165	4,581	5,039	6,197			
Cote D'Ivoire	23,204	25,521	28,069	25,155			
Liberia	12,656	13,920	15,310	14,472			
Mali	7,860	8,645	9,508	2,046			
Niger	7,860	8,645	9,508	2,048			
Nigeria	66,244	72,857	80,131	74,983			
Togo	14,444	15,886	17,472	11,888			
Burkina Faso	7,679	8,446	9,289	10,544			
Other Africa	20,098	22,108	24,312	25,580			
Other countries of Africa	20,098	22,108	24,312	25,580			
AMERICAS	40,534	44,581	49,031	62,572			
North America	38,319	42,145	46,352	59,426			
Canada	6,485	7,132	7,844	8,951			
United States	31,834	35,013	38,508	50,475			
Other Americas	2,215	2,436	2,679	3,146			
Other countries of the Americas	2,215	2,436	2,679	3,146			
EAST ASIA AND THE PACIFIC	23,214	25,532	28,081	16,812			
North-East Asia	8,448	9,292	10,220	7,436			
China	5,430	5,972	6,569	5,572			
Japan	3,018	3,320	3,651	1,864			
Other East Asia and the Pacific	14,766	16,240	17,861	9,376			
Other countries East Asia/Pacific	14,766	16,240	17,861	9,376			
EUROPE	119,642	131,587	144,724	100,509			
Northern Europe	48,229	53,044	58,339	45,498			
United Kingdom	41,787	45,959	50,547	36,747			
Scandinavia	6,442	7,085	7,792	8,751			
Southern Europe	5,860	6,445	7,089	6,716			
Italy	5,860	6,445	7,089	6,716			
Western Europe	59,410	65,341	71,865	43,384			
Belgium	2,423	2,665	2,931	3,147			
France	17,440	19,181	21,096	10,089			
Germany	23,286	25,611	28,168	14,094			
Netherlands	11,684	12,850	14,133	13,663			
Switzerland	4,577	5,034	5,537	2,391			
Other Europe	6,143	6,757	7,431	4,911			
Other countries of Europe	6,143	6,757	7,431	4,911			
MIDDLE EAST	3,661	4,026	4,428	10,632			
Middle East	3,661	4,026	4,428	10,632			
All countries of Middle East	3,661	4,026	4,428	10,632			
REGION NOT SPECIFIED	131,376	144,492	158,917	65,095			
Not Specified	131,376	144,492	158,917	65,095			
Other countries of the World				5,274			
Nationals Residing Abroad	131,376	144,492	158,917	59,821			

Source: World Tourism Organization (UNWTO)

GREECE

1. Arrivals of non-resident tourists at national borders, by nationality

		2002	2003	2004	2005	2006	Market share 06	% Change 06-05
TOTAL	(*)	14,179,999	13,969,393	13,312,629	14,765,463	16,039,216	100.00	8.63
AFRICA		22,265	19,184	23,073	22,961	30,296	0.19	31.95
Southern Africa		12,204	10,714	12,476	13,912	17,798	0.11	27.93
South Africa		12,204	10,714	12,476	13,912	17,798	0.11	27.93
Other Africa		10,061	8,470	10,597	9,049	12,498	0.08	38.11
Other countries of Africa		10,061	8,470	10,597	9,049	12,498	0.08	38.11
AMERICAS		217,369	219,391	236,274	416,746	513,402	3.20	23.19
North America		207,386	208,822	221,726	394,221	482,034	3.01	22.28
Canada		56,194	55,801	54,166	80,984	113,402	0.71	40.03
Mexico		4,438	4,270	6,162	7,397	10,008	0.06	35.30
United States		146,754	148,751	161,398	305,840	358,624	2.24	17.26
South America		4,268	4,737	5,877	14,222	19,264	0.12	35.45
Argentina		1,460	2,112	2,197	5,462	7,997	0.05	46.41
Brazil		2,808	2,625	3,680	8,760	11,267	0.07	28.62
Other Americas		5,715	5,832	8,671	8,303	12,104	0.08	45.78
Other countries of the Americas		5,715	5,832	8,671	8,303	12,104	0.08	45.78
EAST ASIA AND THE PACIFIC		242,040	212,791	226,973	253,686	315,691	1.97	24.44
North-East Asia		69,719	55,917	55,838	45,609	50,525	0.32	10.78
Japan		69,719	55,917	55,838	45,609	50,525	0.32	10.78
Australasia		55,160	49,607	59,763	78,849	97,087	0.61	23.13
Australia		55,160	49,607	59,763	78,849	97,087	0.61	23.13
Other East Asia and the Pacific		117,161	107,267	111,372	129,228	168,079	1.05	30.06
Other countries of Asia		108,510	98,884	102,690	118,573	155,555	0.97	31.19
Other countries of Oceania		8,651	8,383	8,682	10,655	12,524	0.08	17.54
EUROPE		13,630,328	13,459,272	12,766,224	13,996,356	15,104,338	94.17	7.92
Central/Eastern Europe		1,399,214	1,401,893	1,016,534	1,550,651	1,857,895	11.58	19.81
Bulgaria		470,232	459,554	440,263	599,872	677,368	4.22	12.92
Czech Republic		139,982	158,129	41,535	240,694	264,362	1.65	9.83
Estonia		14,145	2,253	1,242	2,010	3,058	0.02	52.14
Hungary		144,509	176,113	88,393	104,125	107,959	0.67	3.68
Latvia		4,196	4,255	2,194	8,100	9,194	0.06	13.51
Lithuania		6,975	7,017	2,150	6,474	13,021	0.08	101.13
Poland		235,704	183,648	69,317	166,086	198,412	1.24	19.46
Romania		118,885	142,012	148,853	225,570	285,049	1.78	26.37
Russian Federation		135,978	144,685	142,346	182,334	261,253	1.63	43.28
Slovakia		79,862	83,442	36,272	15,386	38,219	0.24	148.40
Ukraine	(*)	48,746	40,785	43,969				
Northern Europe		4,054,437	4,099,148	3,936,155	3,753,693	3,899,458	24.31	3.88
Denmark		342,966	294,076	282,340	288,858	325,472	2.03	12.68
Finland		147,322	143,592	148,197	150,198	166,361	1.04	10.76
Ireland		58,634	69,961	69,509	69,027	70,251	0.44	1.77
Norway		181,383	230,232	232,222	210,847	293,204	1.83	39.06
Sweden		465,772	352,905	334,150	316,042	428,334	2.67	35.53
United Kingdom		2,858,360	3,008,382	2,869,737	2,718,721	2,615,836	16.31	-3.78
Southern Europe		2,733,133	2,813,461	2,836,506	3,019,007	3,685,098	22.98	22.06
Albania		1,255,738	1,118,558	1,193,936	1,478,197	1,591,688	9.92	7.68
Italy		805,008	865,730	898,208	1,128,506	1,187,598	7.40	5.24
Malta					1,057	7,898	0.05	647.21

GREECE

1. Arrivals of non-resident tourists at national borders, by nationality

		2002	2003	2004	2005	2006	Market share 06	% Change 06-05
Portugal		18,927	9,244	25,703	11,013	12,697	0.08	15.29
Slovenia					41,010	47,492	0.30	15.81
Spain		153,039	134,441	135,082	151,140	202,230	1.26	33.80
TFYR of Macedonia	(*)	309,607	443,319	411,103		350,043	2.18	
Serbia and Montenegro		190,814	242,169	172,474	208,084	285,452	1.78	37.18
Western Europe		**5,007,988**	**4,712,400**	**4,467,015**	**4,673,783**	**4,965,201**	**30.96**	**6.24**
Austria		461,672	443,595	440,391	464,470	492,921	3.07	6.13
Belgium					371,790	400,219	2.50	7.65
France		735,568	714,821	621,407	676,658	712,131	4.44	5.24
Germany		2,510,849	2,267,063	2,189,222	2,241,942	2,267,961	14.14	1.16
Luxembourg					29,276	29,460	0.18	0.63
Netherlands		721,413	635,882	611,990	666,287	782,154	4.88	17.39
Switzerland		220,476	266,246	229,448	223,360	280,355	1.75	25.52
Belgium / Luxembourg		358,010	384,793	374,557				
East Mediterranean Europe		**393,818**	**386,348**	**442,250**	**482,234**	**516,157**	**3.22**	**7.03**
Cyprus		139,080	150,358	146,405	168,415	196,128	1.22	16.46
Israel		115,720	92,454	94,029	132,511	139,254	0.87	5.09
Turkey		139,018	143,536	201,816	181,308	180,775	1.13	-0.29
Other Europe		**41,738**	**46,022**	**67,764**	**516,988**	**180,529**	**1.13**	**-65.08**
Other countries of Europe		41,738	46,022	67,764	516,988	180,529	1.13	-65.08
MIDDLE EAST		**63,745**	**54,836**	**55,257**	**72,057**	**75,315**	**0.47**	**4.52**
Middle East		**63,745**	**54,836**	**55,257**	**72,057**	**75,315**	**0.47**	**4.52**
Lebanon	(*)	24,344	21,628	20,900	28,096	25,308	0.16	-9.92
Egypt	(*)	30,535	25,008	26,092	31,725	37,069	0.23	16.84
Other countries of Middle East		8,866	8,200	8,265	12,236	12,938	0.08	5.74
SOUTH ASIA		**4,252**	**3,919**	**4,828**	**3,657**	**174**		**-95.24**
South Asia		**4,252**	**3,919**	**4,828**	**3,657**	**174**		**-95.24**
Iran, Islamic Republic of		4,252	3,919	4,828	3,657	174		-95.24

Source: World Tourism Organization (UNWTO)

GREECE

3. Arrivals of non-resident tourists in hotels and similar establishments, by country of residence

	2002	2003	2004	2005	2006	Market share 06	% Change 06-05
TOTAL	6,654,333	6,574,470	6,313,228	7,142,860	7,547,667	100.00	5.67
AFRICA	30,582	31,529	30,852	26,462	33,928	0.45	28.21
Southern Africa				2,402	1,545	0.02	-35.68
South Africa				2,402	1,545	0.02	-35.68
Other Africa	30,582	31,529	30,852	24,060	32,383	0.43	34.59
Other countries of Africa				24,060	32,383	0.43	34.59
All countries of Africa	30,582	31,529	30,852				
AMERICAS	481,432	423,107	479,614	724,861	843,046	11.17	16.30
North America	437,922	386,217	434,346	680,681	783,865	10.39	15.16
Canada	73,966	68,827	61,877	100,681	103,291	1.37	2.59
United States	363,956	317,390	372,469	580,000	680,574	9.02	17.34
South America				14,511	24,426	0.32	68.33
Brazil				14,511	24,426	0.32	68.33
Other Americas	43,510	36,890	45,268	29,669	34,755	0.46	17.14
Other countries of the Americas	43,510	36,890	45,268	29,669	34,755	0.46	17.14
EAST ASIA AND THE PACIFIC	525,783	496,828	481,641	388,566	449,440	5.95	15.67
North-East Asia	106,450	94,315	96,073	117,708	141,459	1.87	20.18
China				26,669	40,461	0.54	51.72
Japan	106,450	94,315	96,073	91,039	100,998	1.34	10.94
Australasia				105,820	114,883	1.52	8.56
Australia				105,820	114,883	1.52	8.56
Other East Asia and the Pacific	419,333	402,513	385,568	165,038	193,098	2.56	17.00
Other countries of Asia	336,750	318,927	312,939	161,110	187,619	2.49	16.45
Other countries of Oceania				3,928	5,479	0.07	39.49
All countries of Oceania	82,583	83,586	72,629				
EUROPE	5,587,080	5,565,529	5,291,390	6,000,943	6,220,198	82.41	3.65
Central/Eastern Europe	209,906	197,414	202,827	462,069	585,632	7.76	26.74
Czech Republic	52,372	63,164	69,610	82,949	96,745	1.28	16.63
Estonia				6,560	7,967	0.11	21.45
Hungary	28,389	33,021	33,359	44,284	51,573	0.68	16.46
Latvia				4,139	6,053	0.08	46.24
Lithuania				5,830	11,345	0.15	94.60
Poland	108,184	79,213	75,175	108,578	132,702	1.76	22.22
Russian Federation				166,746	229,010	3.03	37.34
Slovakia	20,961	22,016	24,683	32,231	32,213	0.43	-0.06
Ukraine				10,752	18,024	0.24	67.63
Northern Europe	1,620,725	1,586,917	1,558,721	1,608,437	1,612,266	21.36	0.24
Denmark	125,095	117,316	113,549	109,737	130,172	1.72	18.62
Finland	82,873	88,343	96,256	89,108	93,221	1.24	4.62
Iceland				4,795	4,122	0.05	-14.04
Ireland	27,468	33,231	37,029	35,407	39,379	0.52	11.22
Norway	145,243	139,406	140,666	132,483	144,717	1.92	9.23
Sweden	214,646	190,695	183,705	173,911	194,531	2.58	11.86
United Kingdom	1,025,400	1,017,926	987,516	1,062,996	1,006,124	13.33	-5.35
Southern Europe	630,064	637,257	657,186	811,670	862,034	11.42	6.20
Italy	468,355	488,649	548,283	616,301	631,389	8.37	2.45
Malta				2,139	5,080	0.07	137.49

GREECE

3. Arrivals of non-resident tourists in hotels and similar establishments, by country of residence

	2002	2003	2004	2005	2006	Market share 06	% Change 06-05
Portugal	19,919	17,846	13,382	22,732	22,576	0.30	-0.69
Slovenia				22,504	27,999	0.37	24.42
Spain	141,790	130,762	95,521	147,994	174,990	2.32	18.24
Western Europe	**2,665,926**	**2,651,329**	**2,389,971**	**2,594,690**	**2,579,345**	**34.17**	**-0.59**
Austria	195,082	204,006	209,754	192,384	203,720	2.70	5.89
Belgium	199,268	219,307	192,954	215,678	221,034	2.93	2.48
France	609,982	637,668	497,392	607,468	577,691	7.65	-4.90
Germany	1,224,232	1,172,757	1,101,739	1,150,160	1,095,795	14.52	-4.73
Luxembourg				11,296	13,082	0.17	15.81
Netherlands	288,011	275,554	251,215	284,619	329,579	4.37	15.80
Switzerland	149,351	142,037	136,917	133,085	138,444	1.83	4.03
East Mediterranean Europe	**38,042**	**44,214**	**45,550**	**210,572**	**211,350**	**2.80**	**0.37**
Cyprus				156,277	145,679	1.93	-6.78
Turkey	38,042	44,214	45,550	54,295	65,671	0.87	20.95
Other Europe	**422,417**	**448,398**	**437,135**	**313,505**	**369,571**	**4.90**	**17.88**
Other countries of Europe	422,417	448,398	437,135	313,505	369,571	4.90	17.88
REGION NOT SPECIFIED	**29,456**	**57,477**	**29,731**	**2,028**	**1,055**	**0.01**	**-47.98**
Not Specified	**29,456**	**57,477**	**29,731**	**2,028**	**1,055**	**0.01**	**-47.98**
Other countries of the World	29,456	57,477	29,731	2,028	1,055	0.01	-47.98

Source: World Tourism Organization (UNWTO)

GREECE

4. Arrivals of non-resident tourists in all types of accommodation establishments, by country of residence

	2002	2003	2004	2005	2006	Market share 06	% Change 06-05
TOTAL	6,843,179	6,767,976	6,461,062	7,348,706	7,748,208	100.00	5.44
AFRICA	30,874	31,796	30,973	26,626	34,060	0.44	27.92
Southern Africa				2,429	1,583	0.02	-34.83
South Africa				2,429	1,583	0.02	-34.83
Other Africa	30,874	31,796	30,973	24,197	32,477	0.42	34.22
Other countries of Africa				24,197	32,477	0.42	34.22
All countries of Africa	30,874	31,796	30,973				
AMERICAS	483,501	424,722	480,865	726,828	844,516	10.90	16.19
North America	439,656	387,534	435,401	682,325	785,196	10.13	15.08
Canada	74,589	69,283	62,258	101,230	103,810	1.34	2.55
United States	365,067	318,251	373,143	581,095	681,386	8.79	17.26
South America				14,601	24,464	0.32	67.55
Brazil				14,601	24,464	0.32	67.55
Other Americas	43,845	37,188	45,464	29,902	34,856	0.45	16.57
Other countries of the Americas	43,845	37,188	45,464	29,902	34,856	0.45	16.57
EAST ASIA AND THE PACIFIC	528,876	499,777	484,064	391,631	453,035	5.85	15.68
North-East Asia	106,593	94,443	96,208	117,911	141,536	1.83	20.04
China				26,699	40,489	0.52	51.65
Japan	106,593	94,443	96,208	91,212	101,047	1.30	10.78
Australasia				107,869	117,294	1.51	8.74
Australia				107,869	117,294	1.51	8.74
Other East Asia and the Pacific	422,283	405,334	387,856	165,851	194,205	2.51	17.10
Other countries of Asia	337,419	319,565	313,472	161,571	188,049	2.43	16.39
Other countries of Oceania				4,280	6,156	0.08	43.83
All countries of Oceania	84,864	85,769	74,384				
EUROPE	5,770,048	5,753,982	5,435,400	6,201,587	6,415,540	82.80	3.45
Central/Eastern Europe	218,121	203,925	208,133	471,324	596,089	7.69	26.47
Czech Republic	54,777	65,332	70,930	85,005	99,387	1.28	16.92
Estonia				6,657	8,019	0.10	20.46
Hungary	30,079	34,302	34,557	46,538	54,041	0.70	16.12
Latvia				4,238	6,161	0.08	45.38
Lithuania				5,928	11,448	0.15	93.12
Poland	111,895	81,938	77,582	112,364	137,247	1.77	22.14
Russian Federation				166,989	229,087	2.96	37.19
Slovakia	21,370	22,353	25,064	32,793	32,636	0.42	-0.48
Ukraine				10,812	18,063	0.23	67.06
Northern Europe	1,629,719	1,595,272	1,566,164	1,617,375	1,619,306	20.90	0.12
Denmark	127,490	119,417	115,261	112,401	132,261	1.71	17.67
Finland	83,086	88,593	96,529	89,544	93,444	1.21	4.36
Iceland				4,816	4,124	0.05	-14.37
Ireland	27,829	33,913	37,304	35,740	39,663	0.51	10.98
Norway	145,767	139,628	140,851	133,501	144,854	1.87	8.50
Sweden	215,065	191,103	184,184	174,576	194,941	2.52	11.67
United Kingdom	1,030,482	1,022,618	992,035	1,066,797	1,010,019	13.04	-5.32
Southern Europe	658,120	666,242	677,513	852,636	901,371	11.63	5.72
Italy	494,417	515,766	567,219	653,608	666,697	8.60	2.00
Malta				2,168	5,081	0.07	134.36

GREECE

4. Arrivals of non-resident tourists in all types of accommodation establishments, by country of residence

	2002	2003	2004	2005	2006	Market share 06	% Change 06-05
Portugal	20,294	18,048	13,524	22,952	22,788	0.29	-0.71
Slovenia				23,924	30,013	0.39	25.45
Spain	143,409	132,428	96,770	149,984	176,792	2.28	17.87
Western Europe	**2,795,844**	**2,787,234**	**2,493,963**	**2,730,910**	**2,713,160**	**35.02**	**-0.65**
Austria	206,164	215,944	218,967	203,561	215,200	2.78	5.72
Belgium	203,340	223,353	195,914	219,701	224,769	2.90	2.31
France	645,020	677,143	520,589	646,486	613,813	7.92	-5.05
Germany	1,278,649	1,225,978	1,146,156	1,204,580	1,146,719	14.80	-4.80
Luxembourg				11,346	13,105	0.17	15.50
Netherlands	307,782	296,302	269,894	305,310	354,115	4.57	15.99
Switzerland	154,889	148,514	142,443	139,926	145,439	1.88	3.94
East Mediterranean Europe	**38,229**	**44,409**	**45,679**	**211,272**	**211,747**	**2.73**	**0.22**
Cyprus				156,634	145,944	1.88	-6.82
Turkey	38,229	44,409	45,679	54,638	65,803	0.85	20.43
Other Europe	**430,015**	**456,900**	**443,948**	**318,070**	**373,867**	**4.83**	**17.54**
Other countries of Europe	430,015	456,900	443,948	318,070	373,867	4.83	17.54
REGION NOT SPECIFIED	**29,880**	**57,699**	**29,760**	**2,034**	**1,057**	**0.01**	**-48.03**
Not Specified	**29,880**	**57,699**	**29,760**	**2,034**	**1,057**	**0.01**	**-48.03**
Other countries of the World	29,880	57,699	29,760	2,034	1,057	0.01	-48.03

Source: World Tourism Organization (UNWTO)

GREECE

5. Overnight stays of non-resident tourists in hotels and similar establishments, by country of residence

	2002	2003	2004	2005	2006	Market share 06	% Change 06-05
TOTAL	40,349,621	39,759,557	38,309,783	40,074,798	42,458,767	100.00	5.95
AFRICA	91,615	99,021	104,932	79,727	101,407	0.24	27.19
Southern Africa				7,316	5,366	0.01	-26.65
South Africa				7,316	5,366	0.01	-26.65
Other Africa	91,615	99,021	104,932	72,411	96,041	0.23	32.63
Other countries of Africa				72,411	96,041	0.23	32.63
All countries of Africa	91,615	99,021	104,932				
AMERICAS	1,121,377	1,063,263	1,252,259	1,607,363	1,873,069	4.41	16.53
North America	1,009,459	965,565	1,115,362	1,488,521	1,722,020	4.06	15.69
Canada	172,993	181,897	180,149	240,122	248,828	0.59	3.63
United States	836,466	783,668	935,213	1,248,399	1,473,192	3.47	18.01
South America				44,589	64,308	0.15	44.22
Brazil				44,589	64,308	0.15	44.22
Other Americas	111,918	97,698	136,897	74,253	86,741	0.20	16.82
Other countries of the Americas	111,918	97,698	136,897	74,253	86,741	0.20	16.82
EAST ASIA AND THE PACIFIC	1,405,688	1,337,652	1,315,348	940,782	1,031,948	2.43	9.69
North-East Asia	191,212	175,512	212,094	209,835	256,139	0.60	22.07
China				53,096	80,776	0.19	52.13
Japan	191,212	175,512	212,094	156,739	175,363	0.41	11.88
Australasia				256,897	287,795	0.68	12.03
Australia				256,897	287,795	0.68	12.03
Other East Asia and the Pacific	1,214,476	1,162,140	1,103,254	474,050	488,014	1.15	2.95
Other countries of Asia	1,028,751	935,691	914,702	465,380	474,928	1.12	2.05
Other countries of Oceania				8,670	13,086	0.03	50.93
All countries of Oceania	185,725	226,449	188,552				
EUROPE	37,644,757	37,094,564	35,550,119	37,442,866	39,448,496	92.91	5.36
Central/Eastern Europe	1,453,247	1,457,657	1,520,250	3,147,302	4,264,029	10.04	35.48
Czech Republic	428,183	525,841	593,061	684,803	799,977	1.88	16.82
Estonia				34,270	45,291	0.11	32.16
Hungary	169,341	198,075	201,432	272,485	335,009	0.79	22.95
Latvia				19,156	33,935	0.08	77.15
Lithuania				31,139	65,583	0.15	110.61
Poland	705,485	558,938	524,806	707,877	849,687	2.00	20.03
Russian Federation				1,107,415	1,759,194	4.14	58.86
Slovakia	150,238	174,803	200,951	235,758	270,724	0.64	14.83
Ukraine				54,399	104,629	0.25	92.34
Northern Europe	12,543,826	12,100,879	11,672,993	11,432,255	11,390,847	26.83	-0.36
Denmark	844,473	779,740	751,124	709,826	860,758	2.03	21.26
Finland	587,315	613,199	676,490	619,536	645,497	1.52	4.19
Iceland				29,204	18,755	0.04	-35.78
Ireland	182,830	245,166	267,236	225,579	243,315	0.57	7.86
Norway	1,137,948	1,128,478	1,162,849	1,051,885	1,123,098	2.65	6.77
Sweden	1,514,625	1,341,138	1,301,040	1,162,058	1,310,034	3.09	12.73
United Kingdom	8,276,635	7,993,158	7,514,254	7,634,167	7,189,390	16.93	-5.83
Southern Europe	2,727,174	2,787,568	2,941,700	3,506,147	3,769,522	8.88	7.51
Italy	2,332,751	2,439,688	2,623,686	2,914,474	3,113,610	7.33	6.83
Malta				9,363	24,872	0.06	165.64

GREECE

5. Overnight stays of non-resident tourists in hotels and similar establishments, by country of residence

	2002	2003	2004	2005	2006	Market share 06	% Change 06-05
Portugal	60,229	51,380	65,366	109,472	69,358	0.16	-36.64
Slovenia				135,003	156,243	0.37	15.73
Spain	334,194	296,500	252,648	337,835	405,439	0.95	20.01
Western Europe	**19,035,104**	**18,786,695**	**17,357,821**	**17,638,169**	**18,091,916**	**42.61**	**2.57**
Austria	1,628,720	1,651,881	1,681,903	1,460,367	1,618,590	3.81	10.83
Belgium	1,467,084	1,560,174	1,386,037	1,417,256	1,533,015	3.61	8.17
France	2,424,763	2,645,860	2,262,547	2,687,697	2,571,489	6.06	-4.32
Germany	10,573,793	10,089,727	9,233,860	9,114,835	8,946,469	21.07	-1.85
Luxembourg				74,816	99,468	0.23	32.95
Netherlands	1,919,782	1,866,440	1,803,155	2,024,577	2,427,813	5.72	19.92
Switzerland	1,020,962	972,613	990,319	858,621	895,072	2.11	4.25
East Mediterranean Europe	**85,626**	**93,631**	**93,821**	**590,670**	**575,640**	**1.36**	**-2.54**
Cyprus				472,092	441,473	1.04	-6.49
Turkey	85,626	93,631	93,821	118,578	134,167	0.32	13.15
Other Europe	**1,799,780**	**1,868,134**	**1,963,534**	**1,128,323**	**1,356,542**	**3.19**	**20.23**
Other countries of Europe	1,799,780	1,868,134	1,963,534	1,128,323	1,356,542	3.19	20.23
REGION NOT SPECIFIED	**86,184**	**165,057**	**87,125**	**4,060**	**3,847**	**0.01**	**-5.25**
Not Specified	**86,184**	**165,057**	**87,125**	**4,060**	**3,847**	**0.01**	**-5.25**
Other countries of the World	86,184	165,057	87,125	4,060	3,847	0.01	-5.25

Source: World Tourism Organization (UNWTO)

GREECE

6. Overnight stays of non-resident tourists in all types of accommodation establishments, by country of residence

	2002	2003	2004	2005	2006	Market share 06	% Change 06-05
TOTAL	40,952,769	40,407,463	38,796,196	40,734,354	43,055,381	100.00	5.70
AFRICA	92,673	99,906	105,354	80,135	101,854	0.24	27.10
Southern Africa				7,418	5,523	0.01	-25.55
South Africa				7,418	5,523	0.01	-25.55
Other Africa	92,673	99,906	105,354	72,717	96,331	0.22	32.47
Other countries of Africa				72,717	96,331	0.22	32.47
All countries of Africa	92,673	99,906	105,354				
AMERICAS	1,127,975	1,068,011	1,255,494	1,611,536	1,876,421	4.36	16.44
North America	1,014,768	969,044	1,117,928	1,491,949	1,725,030	4.01	15.62
Canada	175,082	183,385	181,152	241,305	249,816	0.58	3.53
United States	839,686	785,659	936,776	1,250,644	1,475,214	3.43	17.96
South America				44,779	64,387	0.15	43.79
Brazil				44,779	64,387	0.15	43.79
Other Americas	113,207	98,967	137,566	74,808	87,004	0.20	16.30
Other countries of the Americas	113,207	98,967	137,566	74,808	87,004	0.20	16.30
EAST ASIA AND THE PACIFIC	1,413,748	1,345,012	1,320,791	947,380	1,039,157	2.41	9.69
North-East Asia	191,592	175,800	212,365	210,137	256,246	0.60	21.94
China				53,147	80,809	0.19	52.05
Japan	191,592	175,800	212,365	156,990	175,437	0.41	11.75
Australasia				261,294	292,720	0.68	12.03
Australia				261,294	292,720	0.68	12.03
Other East Asia and the Pacific	1,222,156	1,169,212	1,108,426	475,949	490,191	1.14	2.99
Other countries of Asia	1,030,491	936,999	915,789	466,341	475,612	1.10	1.99
Other countries of Oceania				9,608	14,579	0.03	51.74
All countries of Oceania	191,665	232,213	192,637				
EUROPE	38,230,116	37,728,784	36,027,300	38,091,232	40,034,100	92.98	5.10
Central/Eastern Europe	1,481,049	1,475,787	1,536,797	3,176,491	4,290,109	9.96	35.06
Czech Republic	436,390	531,758	596,775	689,636	805,848	1.87	16.85
Estonia				34,482	45,393	0.11	31.64
Hungary	175,185	201,847	205,631	279,374	341,690	0.79	22.31
Latvia				19,302	34,068	0.08	76.50
Lithuania				31,265	65,758	0.15	110.32
Poland	718,088	566,342	531,547	718,981	861,842	2.00	19.87
Russian Federation				1,109,127	1,759,361	4.09	58.63
Slovakia	151,386	175,840	202,844	239,721	271,442	0.63	13.23
Ukraine				54,603	104,707	0.24	91.76
Northern Europe	12,588,084	12,132,542	11,701,891	11,478,784	11,417,641	26.52	-0.53
Denmark	861,369	791,221	758,958	725,952	872,004	2.03	20.12
Finland	587,855	613,840	677,226	621,603	646,219	1.50	3.96
Iceland				29,276	18,759	0.04	-35.92
Ireland	183,865	246,565	268,254	226,541	244,181	0.57	7.79
Norway	1,139,271	1,128,987	1,163,437	1,062,403	1,123,322	2.61	5.73
Sweden	1,516,205	1,342,467	1,302,704	1,165,471	1,311,783	3.05	12.55
United Kingdom	8,299,519	8,009,462	7,531,312	7,647,538	7,201,373	16.73	-5.83
Southern Europe	2,811,833	2,875,510	2,997,228	3,619,450	3,872,607	8.99	6.99
Italy	2,413,019	2,523,360	2,676,296	3,020,081	3,208,883	7.45	6.25
Malta				9,422	24,876	0.06	164.02

GREECE

6. Overnight stays of non-resident tourists in all types of accommodation establishments, by country of residence

	2002	2003	2004	2005	2006	Market share 06	% Change 06-05
Portugal	60,888	51,888	65,781	109,986	69,879	0.16	-36.47
Slovenia				138,400	160,505	0.37	15.97
Spain	337,926	300,262	255,151	341,561	408,464	0.95	19.59
Western Europe	**19,432,875**	**19,245,917**	**17,695,103**	**18,063,054**	**18,492,598**	**42.95**	**2.38**
Austria	1,671,354	1,696,203	1,716,289	1,507,950	1,665,573	3.87	10.45
Belgium	1,478,826	1,571,301	1,394,075	1,428,808	1,542,828	3.58	7.98
France	2,504,148	2,766,510	2,308,198	2,772,072	2,644,434	6.14	-4.60
Germany	10,758,055	10,289,315	9,407,589	9,309,365	9,122,766	21.19	-2.00
Luxembourg				74,955	99,523	0.23	32.78
Netherlands	1,985,373	1,932,057	1,862,091	2,091,326	2,503,353	5.81	19.70
Switzerland	1,035,119	990,531	1,006,861	878,578	914,121	2.12	4.05
East Mediterranean Europe	**85,931**	**93,977**	**94,218**	**592,869**	**576,717**	**1.34**	**-2.72**
Cyprus				473,059	442,172	1.03	-6.53
Turkey	85,931	93,977	94,218	119,810	134,545	0.31	12.30
Other Europe	**1,830,344**	**1,905,051**	**2,002,063**	**1,160,584**	**1,384,428**	**3.22**	**19.29**
Other countries of Europe	1,830,344	1,905,051	2,002,063	1,160,584	1,384,428	3.22	19.29
REGION NOT SPECIFIED	**88,257**	**165,750**	**87,257**	**4,071**	**3,849**	**0.01**	**-5.45**
Not Specified	**88,257**	**165,750**	**87,257**	**4,071**	**3,849**	**0.01**	**-5.45**
Other countries of the World	88,257	165,750	87,257	4,071	3,849	0.01	-5.45

Source: World Tourism Organization (UNWTO)

GRENADA

1. Arrivals of non-resident tourists at national borders, by nationality

	2002	2003	2004	2005	2006	Market share 06	% Change 06-05
TOTAL	132,416	142,355	133,865	98,548	118,654	100.00	20.40
AFRICA	494	522	562	325	461	0.39	41.85
East Africa	53	66	89	51	61	0.05	19.61
Ethiopia		1		1			
Kenya	14	22	45	21	26	0.02	23.81
Mauritius		2		4			
Zimbabwe	29	22	17	9	6	0.01	-33.33
Uganda	4	5	1	5	12	0.01	140.00
Zambia	6	14	26	11	17	0.01	54.55
Central Africa	4	1	2	2	1		-50.00
Cameroon	4		1	1	1		
Democratic Republic of the Congo		1	1	1			
North Africa	2	5	34		5		
Algeria		4	1				
Morocco	2	1	32		5		
Sudan			1				
Southern Africa	259	233	260	108	198	0.17	83.33
Botswana	79	53	56	38	65	0.05	71.05
South Africa	180	180	204	70	133	0.11	90.00
West Africa	136	166	157	146	166	0.14	13.70
Ghana	11	7	6	13	21	0.02	61.54
Liberia	1	4	6				
Mali			3				
Nigeria	124	154	142	132	142	0.12	7.58
Senegal		1		1	3		200.00
Other Africa	40	51	20	18	30	0.03	66.67
Other countries of Africa	40	51	20	18	30	0.03	66.67
AMERICAS	76,572	80,126	77,126	58,629	65,292	55.03	11.36
Caribbean	32,790	36,509	38,870	25,813	28,729	24.21	11.30
Antigua and Barbuda	746	746	1,068	485	499	0.42	2.89
Bahamas	137	141	155	82	98	0.08	19.51
Barbados	6,354	6,040	6,624	4,569	4,797	4.04	4.99
Cayman Islands	67	95	60	29	29	0.02	
Cuba	214	177	177	211	226	0.19	7.11
Dominica	513	636	668	529	572	0.48	8.13
Dominican Republic	39	55	27	20	32	0.03	60.00
Guadeloupe	69	71	151	41	50	0.04	21.95
Haiti	17	28	20	18	9	0.01	-50.00
Jamaica	1,076	1,365	1,499	1,133	1,160	0.98	2.38
Montserrat	91	157	115	73	33	0.03	-54.79
Saint Kitts and Nevis	409	293	423	223	293	0.25	31.39
Anguilla	88	97	146	46	61	0.05	32.61
Saint Lucia	2,046	2,367	2,306	2,202	2,016	1.70	-8.45
Saint Maarten	138	141	189	130	140	0.12	7.69
Saint Vincent and the Grenadines	2,208	2,836	3,010	2,181	2,639	2.22	21.00
Trinidad and Tobago	17,217	19,959	20,228	13,055	15,522	13.08	18.90
Other countries of the Caribbean	1,361	1,305	2,004	786	553	0.47	-29.64
Central America	137	128	132	197	113	0.10	-42.64
Belize	70	64	44	33	46	0.04	39.39
Costa Rica	20	26	42	15	10	0.01	-33.33
Honduras	12	4	13	9	3		-66.67

GRENADA

1. Arrivals of non-resident tourists at national borders, by nationality

	2002	2003	2004	2005	2006	Market share 06	% Change 06-05
Nicaragua	4	10	11	11	5		-54.55
Panama	31	24	22	19	39	0.03	105.26
Other countries of Central America				110	10	0.01	-90.91
North America	**41,300**	**40,892**	**35,532**	**29,617**	**33,538**	**28.27**	**13.24**
Canada	4,684	5,599	5,309	4,341	6,335	5.34	45.93
Mexico	112	102	96	95	76	0.06	-20.00
United States	36,504	35,191	30,127	25,181	27,127	22.86	7.73
South America	**2,345**	**2,597**	**2,592**	**3,002**	**2,912**	**2.45**	**-3.00**
Argentina	187	36	49	30	52	0.04	73.33
Bolivia	16	19	16	18	12	0.01	-33.33
Brazil	124	80	81	77	132	0.11	71.43
Chile	13	23	15	22	16	0.01	-27.27
Colombia	54	127	102	29	77	0.06	165.52
Ecuador	13	9	8	2	1		-50.00
Guyana	1,340	1,489	1,674	2,164	1,781	1.50	-17.70
Paraguay	1	3	5		2		
Peru	13	7	14	9	32	0.03	255.56
Suriname	76	72	52	57	73	0.06	28.07
Uruguay	15	7	7	3	5		66.67
Venezuela	493	725	569	586	726	0.61	23.89
Other countries of South America				5	3		-40.00
EAST ASIA AND THE PACIFIC	**980**	**1,062**	**722**	**1,054**	**1,515**	**1.28**	**43.74**
North-East Asia	**131**	**194**	**157**	**84**	**87**	**0.07**	**3.57**
Japan	131	194	157	84	87	0.07	3.57
Australasia	**325**	**421**	**270**	**160**	**237**	**0.20**	**48.13**
Australia	220	378	220	115	199	0.17	73.04
New Zealand	105	43	50	45	38	0.03	-15.56
Melanesia	**1**	**1**	**1**	**2**	**1**		**-50.00**
Fiji	1	1	1	2	1		-50.00
Other East Asia and the Pacific	**523**	**446**	**294**	**808**	**1,190**	**1.00**	**47.28**
Other countries of Asia	523	446	294	808	1,190	1.00	47.28
EUROPE	**38,976**	**43,167**	**36,222**	**22,423**	**32,556**	**27.44**	**45.19**
Central/Eastern Europe	**235**	**253**	**269**	**181**	**401**	**0.34**	**121.55**
Bulgaria	4	4	3	2	4		100.00
Czech Republic/Slovakia	36	77	41	25	59	0.05	136.00
Hungary	23	11	32	6	39	0.03	550.00
Poland	41	68	66	52	62	0.05	19.23
Romania	9	13	24	12	22	0.02	83.33
Ussr (Former)	122	80	103	79	215	0.18	172.15
Other countries Central/East Europ				5			
Northern Europe	**31,275**	**34,654**	**29,378**	**16,425**	**26,006**	**21.92**	**58.33**
Denmark	199	301	197	150	295	0.25	96.67
Finland	66	69	78	69	69	0.06	
Ireland	395	341	258	202	152	0.13	-24.75
Norway	354	253	187	160	125	0.11	-21.88
Sweden	501	404	426	239	323	0.27	35.15
United Kingdom	29,760	33,286	28,232	15,605	25,042	21.11	60.47
Southern Europe	**972**	**1,011**	**1,023**	**726**	**815**	**0.69**	**12.26**
Albania	1	1	3	1			
Greece	27	30	28	24	18	0.02	-25.00
Italy	779	778	746	545	603	0.51	10.64

GRENADA

1. Arrivals of non-resident tourists at national borders, by nationality

	2002	2003	2004	2005	2006	Market share 06	% Change 06-05
Malta	9	8	4	2	5		150.00
Portugal	13	33	26	11	32	0.03	190.91
Spain	138	152	215	137	156	0.13	13.87
Yugoslavia, Sfr (Former)					1		
Serbia and Montenegro	5	9	1	6			
Western Europe	**6,452**	**7,169**	**5,495**	**5,035**	**5,295**	**4.46**	**5.16**
Austria	702	719	613	520	576	0.49	10.77
Belgium	222	159	107	97	99	0.08	2.06
France	1,134	1,336	1,048	812	959	0.81	18.10
Germany	2,981	3,533	2,701	2,809	2,597	2.19	-7.55
Liechtenstein	1	1					
Luxembourg	11	9	19	10	5		-50.00
Netherlands	696	675	478	394	519	0.44	31.73
Switzerland	705	737	529	393	540	0.46	37.40
East Mediterranean Europe	**32**	**28**	**5**	**42**	**22**	**0.02**	**-47.62**
Cyprus	9	3	1	1			
Israel	17	24		39	19	0.02	-51.28
Turkey	6	1	4	2	3		50.00
Other Europe	**10**	**52**	**52**	**14**	**17**	**0.01**	**21.43**
Other countries of Europe	10	52	52	14	17	0.01	21.43
MIDDLE EAST	**115**	**109**	**132**	**121**	**110**	**0.09**	**-9.09**
Middle East	**115**	**109**	**132**	**121**	**110**	**0.09**	**-9.09**
Jordan	3	3	10	9	3		-66.67
Lebanon	62	56	59	38	38	0.03	
Saudi Arabia	4	4	2	3	4		33.33
Syrian Arab Republic	20	33	34	57	53	0.04	-7.02
Egypt	2	3	5	6	2		-66.67
Other countries of Middle East	24	10	22	8	10	0.01	25.00
REGION NOT SPECIFIED	**15,279**	**17,369**	**19,101**	**15,996**	**18,720**	**15.78**	**17.03**
Not Specified	**15,279**	**17,369**	**19,101**	**15,996**	**18,720**	**15.78**	**17.03**
Other countries of the World	443	654	25	89	320	0.27	259.55
Nationals Residing Abroad	14,836	16,715	19,076	15,907	18,400	15.51	15.67

Source: World Tourism Organization (UNWTO)

GRENADA

3. Arrivals of non-resident tourists in hotels and similar establishments, by nationality

	2002	2003	2004	2005	2006	Market share 06	% Change 06-05
TOTAL	62,921	71,548	71,732	35,737	53,827	100.00	50.62
AMERICAS	36,514	40,110	42,837	23,405	31,462	58.45	34.42
Caribbean	17,432	19,781	19,634	12,004	15,732	29.23	31.06
All countries of the Caribbean	17,432	19,781	19,634	12,004	15,732	29.23	31.06
North America	18,810	19,923	22,884	11,090	15,692	29.15	41.50
Canada	2,027	2,915	2,972	1,511	3,082	5.73	103.97
United States	16,783	17,008	19,912	9,579	12,610	23.43	31.64
South America	272	406	319	311	38	0.07	-87.78
Venezuela	272	406	319	311	38	0.07	-87.78
EUROPE	24,577	29,242	26,351	10,810	20,181	37.49	86.69
Northern Europe	20,072	23,766	20,609	7,109	16,058	29.83	125.88
Sweden	274	252	327	120	202	0.38	68.33
United Kingdom	19,798	23,514	20,282	6,989	15,856	29.46	126.87
Southern Europe	380	484	572	306	372	0.69	21.57
Italy	380	484	572	306	372	0.69	21.57
Western Europe	2,443	3,111	3,260	2,406	2,486	4.62	3.33
France	420	419	614	328	384	0.71	17.07
Germany	1,714	2,334	2,223	1,901	1,774	3.30	-6.68
Switzerland	309	358	423	177	328	0.61	85.31
Other Europe	1,682	1,881	1,910	989	1,265	2.35	27.91
Other countries of Europe	1,682	1,881	1,910	989	1,265	2.35	27.91
REGION NOT SPECIFIED	1,830	2,196	2,544	1,522	2,184	4.06	43.50
Not Specified	1,830	2,196	2,544	1,522	2,184	4.06	43.50
Other countries of the World	1,223	1,366	1,700	897	1,503	2.79	67.56
Nationals Residing Abroad	607	830	844	625	681	1.27	8.96

Source: World Tourism Organization (UNWTO)

GRENADA

4. Arrivals of non-resident tourists in all types of accommodation establishments, by nationality

	2002	2003	2004	2005	2006	Market share 06	% Change 06-05
TOTAL	132,416	142,355	133,865	98,548	118,654	100.00	20.40
AMERICAS	75,957	79,911	76,069	58,175	64,456	54.32	10.80
Caribbean	34,276	38,396	40,064	28,067	30,927	26.06	10.19
All countries of the Caribbean	34,276	38,396	40,064	28,067	30,927	26.06	10.19
North America	41,188	40,790	35,436	29,522	33,462	28.20	13.35
Canada	4,684	5,599	5,309	4,341	6,335	5.34	45.93
United States	36,504	35,191	30,127	25,181	27,127	22.86	7.73
South America	493	725	569	586	67	0.06	-88.57
Venezuela	493	725	569	586	67	0.06	-88.57
EUROPE	38,968	43,143	36,177	22,384	32,531	27.42	45.33
Northern Europe	30,261	33,690	28,658	15,844	25,365	21.38	60.09
Sweden	501	404	426	239	323	0.27	35.15
United Kingdom	29,760	33,286	28,232	15,605	25,042	21.11	60.47
Southern Europe	779	778	746	545	603	0.51	10.64
Italy	779	778	746	545	603	0.51	10.64
Western Europe	4,820	5,606	4,278	4,014	4,096	3.45	2.04
France	1,134	1,336	1,048	812	959	0.81	18.10
Germany	2,981	3,533	2,701	2,809	2,597	2.19	-7.55
Switzerland	705	737	529	393	540	0.46	37.40
Other Europe	3,108	3,069	2,495	1,981	2,467	2.08	24.53
Other countries of Europe	3,108	3,069	2,495	1,981	2,467	2.08	24.53
REGION NOT SPECIFIED	17,491	19,301	21,619	17,989	21,667	18.26	20.45
Not Specified	17,491	19,301	21,619	17,989	21,667	18.26	20.45
Other countries of the World	2,648	2,586	2,543	2,082	3,267	2.75	56.92
Nationals Residing Abroad	14,843	16,715	19,076	15,907	18,400	15.51	15.67

Source: World Tourism Organization (UNWTO)

GUADELOUPE

3. Arrivals of non-resident tourists in hotels and similar establishments, by country of residence

		2002	2003	2004	2005	2006	Market share 06	% Change 06-05
TOTAL	(*)		438,819	455,981	371,985			
EUROPE			386,737	406,204	369,800			
Northern Europe					1,600			
United Kingdom					1,600			
Southern Europe					7,413			
Italy					6,083			
Spain,Portugal					1,330			
Western Europe			386,737	406,204	349,568			
France			386,737	406,204	343,755			
Germany					2,118			
Belgium / Luxembourg					3,695			
Other Europe					11,219			
Other countries of Europe					11,219			
REGION NOT SPECIFIED			52,082	49,777	2,185			
Not Specified			52,082	49,777	2,185			
Other countries of the World			52,082	49,777	2,185			

Source: World Tourism Organization (UNWTO)

GUAM

1. Arrivals of non-resident tourists at national borders, by country of residence

	2002	2003	2004	2005	2006	Market share 06	% Change 06-05
TOTAL	1,058,704	909,506	1,159,881	1,227,587	1,211,674	100.00	-1.30
AMERICAS	42,975	41,160	46,754	46,362	44,811	3.70	-3.35
North America	42,975	41,160	46,754	46,362	44,811	3.70	-3.35
Canada	1,454		595	503	585	0.05	16.30
United States	41,521	41,160	46,159	45,859	44,226	3.65	-3.56
EAST ASIA AND THE PACIFIC	984,373	808,623	1,068,997	1,133,807	1,134,264	93.61	0.04
North-East Asia	944,434	770,226	1,026,257	1,093,324	1,093,689	90.26	0.03
China	1,236		914	840	1,124	0.09	33.81
Taiwan (Province of China)	19,500	18,673	24,157	23,386	16,729	1.38	-28.47
Hong Kong, China	8,444	4,620	5,156	4,518	6,123	0.51	35.52
Japan	786,947	659,593	906,106	955,245	952,687	78.63	-0.27
Korea, Republic of	128,307	87,340	89,924	109,335	117,026	9.66	7.03
South-East Asia	6,810	6,470	7,378	7,242	8,378	0.69	15.69
Philippines	6,530	6,470	7,066	7,051	8,144	0.67	15.50
Viet Nam	51		42	21	34		61.90
Thailand	229		270	170	200	0.02	17.65
Australasia	1,788		2,913	2,546	2,328	0.19	-8.56
Australia	1,788		2,913	2,546	2,328	0.19	-8.56
Micronesia	30,668	31,927	32,449	30,695	29,869	2.47	-2.69
Nauru	10		14	5	9		80.00
Northern Mariana Islands	19,080		19,419	18,042	17,813	1.47	-1.27
Micronesia (Federated States of)	8,388		8,598	8,394	8,027	0.66	-4.37
Marshall Islands			824	958	986	0.08	2.92
Palau	3,190		3,594	3,296	3,034	0.25	-7.95
All countries of Micronesia		31,927					
Other East Asia and the Pacific	673						
Other countries East Asia/Pacific	673						
EUROPE	1,436		1,511	1,750	1,382	0.11	-21.03
Other Europe	1,436		1,511	1,750	1,382	0.11	-21.03
All countries of Europe	1,436		1,511	1,750	1,382	0.11	-21.03
REGION NOT SPECIFIED	29,920	59,723	42,619	45,668	31,217	2.58	-31.64
Not Specified	29,920	59,723	42,619	45,668	31,217	2.58	-31.64
Other countries of the World	29,920	59,723	42,619	45,668	31,217	2.58	-31.64

Source: World Tourism Organization (UNWTO)

GUATEMALA

1. Arrivals of non-resident tourists at national borders, by nationality

	2002	2003	2004	2005	2006	Market share 06	% Change 06-05
TOTAL	884,190	880,223	1,181,526	1,315,646	1,502,069	100.00	14.17
AMERICAS	712,261	703,841	1,006,614	1,148,318	1,325,209	88.23	15.40
Caribbean	4,761	4,553	5,918	7,824	6,881	0.46	-12.05
Cuba	1,856	1,765	2,831	4,218	2,657	0.18	-37.01
Dominican Republic	2,080	2,026	2,048	2,698	2,809	0.19	4.11
Other countries of the Caribbean	825	762	1,039	908	1,415	0.09	55.84
Central America	381,481	354,090	602,573	708,377	814,550	54.23	14.99
Belize	17,434	13,296	13,604	13,112	26,340	1.75	100.88
Costa Rica	28,918	29,529	31,979	34,693	35,842	2.39	3.31
El Salvador	228,018	209,745	411,277	497,430	582,676	38.79	17.14
Honduras	75,355	64,242	93,975	106,473	122,428	8.15	14.99
Nicaragua	24,607	29,815	42,876	46,936	36,478	2.43	-22.28
Panama	7,149	7,463	8,862	9,733	10,786	0.72	10.82
North America	288,890	307,027	355,138	384,599	450,471	29.99	17.13
Canada	23,945	27,048	20,510	24,820	32,268	2.15	30.01
Mexico	65,331	70,732	67,502	72,908	79,731	5.31	9.36
United States	199,614	209,247	267,126	286,871	338,472	22.53	17.99
South America	37,129	38,171	42,985	47,518	53,307	3.55	12.18
Argentina	7,667	8,334	8,457	8,952	9,353	0.62	4.48
Brazil	3,732	3,905	4,509	5,485	8,203	0.55	49.55
Chile	3,672	3,721	4,674	5,059	5,831	0.39	15.26
Colombia	12,469	12,387	10,751	13,211	14,330	0.95	8.47
Ecuador	1,979	1,970	2,948	2,963	3,170	0.21	6.99
Peru	3,053	3,165	3,281	3,522	3,952	0.26	12.21
Venezuela	2,299	2,481	5,466	5,077	5,210	0.35	2.62
Other countries of South America	2,258	2,208	2,899	3,249	3,258	0.22	0.28
EAST ASIA AND THE PACIFIC	24,370	21,999	23,167	24,921	26,802	1.78	7.55
North-East Asia	19,069	16,265	16,953	17,838	17,129	1.14	-3.97
China	6,355	4,530	3,059	3,455	299	0.02	-91.35
Japan	6,085	5,104	6,235	4,834	6,446	0.43	33.35
Korea, Republic of	6,629	6,631	7,659	9,549	10,384	0.69	8.74
Australasia	4,410	4,662	4,783	5,547	4,526	0.30	-18.41
Australia	4,410	4,662	4,783	5,547	4,526	0.30	-18.41
Other East Asia and the Pacific	891	1,072	1,431	1,536	5,147	0.34	235.09
Other countries East Asia/Pacific	891	1,072	1,431	1,536	5,147	0.34	235.09
EUROPE	144,846	150,920	149,871	139,996	147,227	9.80	5.17
Central/Eastern Europe	1,768	1,289	2,897	3,120	4,024	0.27	28.97
Azerbaijan	32	14	30	2	12		500.00
Armenia	12		26	11	32		190.91
Bulgaria	143	47	64	53	221	0.01	316.98
Belarus	9	72	5	16	57		256.25
Czech Republic	373	362	687	927	868	0.06	-6.36
Estonia	5	9	24	55	124	0.01	125.45
Hungary	312	155	264	365	288	0.02	-21.10
Latvia	4	42	2	5			
Lithuania	8	12	26	46	99	0.01	115.22
Republic of Moldova	10		4	7	62		785.71
Poland	490	385	716	759	1,049	0.07	38.21
Romania	101	27	102	170	211	0.01	24.12
Russian Federation	166	135	692	450	676	0.05	50.22

GUATEMALA

1. Arrivals of non-resident tourists at national borders, by nationality

	2002	2003	2004	2005	2006	Market share 06	% Change 06-05
Slovakia	68	14	96	166	183	0.01	10.24
Ukraine	35	15	159	74	135	0.01	82.43
Uzbekistan				14	7		-50.00
Northern Europe	**24,878**	**24,370**	**27,263**	**28,421**	**34,588**	**2.30**	**21.70**
Denmark	2,310	2,386	2,721	2,989	3,584	0.24	19.91
Finland	871	1,146	934	908	1,000	0.07	10.13
Iceland	79	38	73	131	131	0.01	
Ireland	1,582	1,588	1,379	1,397	1,547	0.10	10.74
Norway	1,936	2,146	2,874	2,658	2,918	0.19	9.78
Sweden	2,049	2,290	3,327	3,535	4,221	0.28	19.41
United Kingdom	16,051	14,776	15,955	16,803	21,187	1.41	26.09
Southern Europe	**42,293**	**43,138**	**42,028**	**39,391**	**39,600**	**2.64**	**0.53**
Albania	9	189	19	7	13		85.71
Andorra	43	6	69	38	69		81.58
Bosnia and Herzegovina	59	6	11	10	14		40.00
Croatia	55	8	47	104	73		-29.81
Gibraltar	16	75	2	34	1		-97.06
Greece	230	327	424	483	530	0.04	9.73
Holy See	34	17	11	4	1		-75.00
Italy	17,310	17,272	17,708	16,467	14,960	1.00	-9.15
Malta	32	23	74	84	71		-15.48
Portugal	265	263	579	713	842	0.06	18.09
San Marino	23	44	29	7	7		
Slovenia	92	39	191	226	192	0.01	-15.04
Spain	24,125	24,869	22,824	21,182	22,794	1.52	7.61
TFYR of Macedonia			5	1	33		3,200.00
Serbia and Montenegro			35	31			
Western Europe	**71,496**	**77,460**	**72,061**	**62,492**	**62,858**	**4.18**	**0.59**
Austria	2,600	2,437	2,679	2,643	2,637	0.18	-0.23
Belgium	6,556	6,300	5,712	4,901	4,888	0.33	-0.27
France	16,119	18,433	20,793	19,219	18,351	1.22	-4.52
Germany	23,559	27,734	21,786	18,258	18,178	1.21	-0.44
Liechtenstein	180	38	98	15	14		-6.67
Luxembourg	200	84	168	107	69		-35.51
Monaco	25		12	16	8		-50.00
Netherlands	14,871	14,938	15,080	12,061	13,633	0.91	13.03
Switzerland	7,386	7,496	5,733	5,272	5,080	0.34	-3.64
East Mediterranean Europe	**4,404**	**4,661**	**5,621**	**6,571**	**5,976**	**0.40**	**-9.05**
Cyprus					29		
Israel	4,351	4,628	5,549	6,339	5,690	0.38	-10.24
Turkey	53	33	72	232	257	0.02	10.78
Other Europe	**7**	**2**	**1**	**1**	**181**	**0.01**	*********
Other countries of Europe	7	2	1	1	181	0.01	*********
MIDDLE EAST	**590**	**603**	**365**	**1,182**	**446**	**0.03**	**-62.27**
Middle East	**590**	**603**	**365**	**1,182**	**446**	**0.03**	**-62.27**
All countries of Middle East	590	603	365	1,182	446	0.03	-62.27
REGION NOT SPECIFIED	**2,123**	**2,860**	**1,509**	**1,229**	**2,385**	**0.16**	**94.06**
Not Specified	**2,123**	**2,860**	**1,509**	**1,229**	**2,385**	**0.16**	**94.06**
Other countries of the World	2,123	2,860	1,509	1,229	2,385	0.16	94.06

Source: World Tourism Organization (UNWTO)

GUINEA

1. Arrivals of non-resident tourists at national borders, by nationality

	2002	2003	2004	2005	2006	Market share 06	% Change 06-05
TOTAL (*)	42,507	43,966	44,622	45,330	46,096	100.00	1.69
AFRICA	21,868	15,771	13,330	15,427	18,118	39.30	17.44
East Africa		352		276	351	0.76	27.17
Burundi		52		46	27	0.06	-41.30
Comoros		20		33	24	0.05	-27.27
Ethiopia		59		33	20	0.04	-39.39
Kenya		33		79	51	0.11	-35.44
Madagascar		22			14	0.03	
Malawi				23	2		-91.30
Mauritius					10	0.02	
Mozambique		51			8	0.02	
Rwanda		68		34	53	0.11	55.88
Seychelles					2		
Somalia					9	0.02	
Zimbabwe		24		16	6	0.01	-62.50
Uganda		12			14	0.03	
United Republic of Tanzania		11		12	9	0.02	-25.00
Zambia					102	0.22	
Central Africa		612		580	604	1.31	4.14
Angola		22		19	15	0.03	-21.05
Cameroon		251		236	265	0.57	12.29
Central African Republic		24		20	20	0.04	
Chad		31		38	30	0.07	-21.05
Congo		152		192	202	0.44	5.21
Democratic Republic of the Congo		74			8	0.02	
Gabon		58		75	64	0.14	-14.67
North Africa		556		685	842	1.83	22.92
Algeria		31		91	60	0.13	-34.07
Morocco		415		386	467	1.01	20.98
Sudan		13		18	16	0.03	-11.11
Tunisia		97		190	299	0.65	57.37
Southern Africa		186		203	345	0.75	69.95
South Africa		163		203	345	0.75	69.95
Swaziland		23					
West Africa		14,065		13,683	15,976	34.66	16.76
Cape Verde		61		38	57	0.12	50.00
Benin		271		386	334	0.72	-13.47
Gambia		530		541	372	0.81	-31.24
Ghana		423		489	959	2.08	96.11
Cote D'Ivoire		2,078		2,453	1,261	2.74	-48.59
Liberia		528		434	621	1.35	43.09
Mali		1,598		1,295	818	1.77	-36.83
Mauritania		229		303	249	0.54	-17.82
Niger		262		132	168	0.36	27.27
Nigeria		571		807	5,247	11.38	550.19
Guinea-Bissau		170		229	237	0.51	3.49
Senegal		3,634		4,523	3,406	7.39	-24.70
Sierra Leone		3,135		1,328	1,620	3.51	21.99
Togo		271		364	329	0.71	-9.62
Burkina Faso		304		361	298	0.65	-17.45
Other Africa	21,868		13,330				
All countries of Africa	21,868		13,330				

GUINEA

1. Arrivals of non-resident tourists at national borders, by nationality

	2002	2003	2004	2005	2006	Market share 06	% Change 06-05
AMERICAS	3,430	3,546	4,378	4,589	1,883	4.08	-58.97
Caribbean		64		16	174	0.38	987.50
Cuba		40			90	0.20	
Dominica					5	0.01	
Haiti		12		16	19	0.04	18.75
Jamaica					6	0.01	
Saba					1		
Puerto Rico					13	0.03	
Trinidad and Tobago		12			40	0.09	
Central America					2		
Honduras					2		
North America		3,420		4,412	1,403	3.04	-68.20
Canada		897		1,135	1,023	2.22	-9.87
Mexico		28		40			
United States		2,495		3,237	380	0.82	-88.26
South America		62		119	304	0.66	155.46
Argentina					14	0.03	
Bolivia					1		
Brazil		40		78	106	0.23	35.90
Chile				12	4	0.01	-66.67
Colombia		11		29	128	0.28	341.38
Peru					13	0.03	
Suriname					4	0.01	
Uruguay					1		
Venezuela		11			33	0.07	
Other Americas	3,430		4,378	42			
Other countries of the Americas				42			
All countries of the Americas	3,430		4,378				
EAST ASIA AND THE PACIFIC	2,447	1,940	2,454	2,607	2,997	6.50	14.96
North-East Asia		1,580		2,218	2,352	5.10	6.04
China		1,041		1,575	1,696	3.68	7.68
Taiwan (Province of China)					24	0.05	
Japan		307		404	357	0.77	-11.63
Korea, Dem. People's Republic of		232		239	275	0.60	15.06
South-East Asia		148		165	294	0.64	78.18
Cambodia					48	0.10	
Indonesia					48	0.10	
Lao People's Democratic Republic					2		
Malaysia		85		83	42	0.09	-49.40
Philippines		33		45	83	0.18	84.44
Singapore		16			7	0.02	
Viet Nam		14		37	57	0.12	54.05
Thailand					7	0.02	
Australasia		212		224	341	0.74	52.23
Australia		191		224	318	0.69	41.96
New Zealand		21			23	0.05	
Melanesia					10	0.02	
Fiji					10	0.02	
Other East Asia and the Pacific	2,447		2,454				
All countries of Asia	2,447		2,454				
	11,646	15,162	15,500	15,312	14,622	31.72	-4.51

GUINEA

1. Arrivals of non-resident tourists at national borders, by nationality

	2002	2003	2004	2005	2006	Market share 06	% Change 06-05
EUROPE							
Central/Eastern Europe		1,033		1,470	1,627	3.53	10.68
Azerbaijan					1		
Armenia				18	16	0.03	-11.11
Bulgaria		23		39	21	0.05	-46.15
Belarus		32		47	102	0.22	117.02
Czech Republic		27		35			
Georgia				13	5	0.01	-61.54
Hungary		29			20	0.04	
Lithuania					21	0.05	
Poland		15		37	39	0.08	5.41
Romania		44		41	58	0.13	41.46
Russian Federation		661		919	1,013	2.20	10.23
Slovakia		12		12	8	0.02	-33.33
Turkmenistan				64	21	0.05	-67.19
Ukraine		190		245	302	0.66	23.27
Northern Europe		1,022		1,043	1,151	2.50	10.35
Denmark		60		47	62	0.13	31.91
Finland		34		28	46	0.10	64.29
Iceland					3	0.01	
Ireland		56		25	53	0.11	112.00
Norway		74		90	2		-97.78
Sweden		170		224	183	0.40	-18.30
United Kingdom		628		629	802	1.74	27.50
Southern Europe		1,082		1,238	795	1.72	-35.78
Albania					1		
Croatia		18			7	0.02	
Greece		66		52	75	0.16	44.23
Italy		631		767	631	1.37	-17.73
Portugal		94		98	81	0.18	-17.35
Spain		250		294			
Serbia and Montenegro		23		27			
Western Europe		11,947		11,351	10,753	23.33	-5.27
Austria		46		22	29	0.06	31.82
Belgium		905		1,126	970	2.10	-13.85
France		9,378		7,984	7,376	16.00	-7.62
Germany		841		1,029	1,114	2.42	8.26
Luxembourg				22	14	0.03	-36.36
Netherlands		448		697	887	1.92	27.26
Switzerland		329		471	363	0.79	-22.93
East Mediterranean Europe		78		210	296	0.64	40.95
Israel		20		38	71	0.15	86.84
Turkey		58		172	225	0.49	30.81
Other Europe	11,646		15,500				
All countries of Europe	11,646		15,500				
MIDDLE EAST	1,705	1,042	566	653	941	2.04	44.10
Middle East	1,705	1,042	566	653	941	2.04	44.10
Iraq					1		
Jordan		21		17	20	0.04	17.65
Kuwait					1		
Lebanon		631		397	619	1.34	55.92
Libyan Arab Jamahiriya		17		19	33	0.07	73.68

GUINEA

1. Arrivals of non-resident tourists at national borders, by nationality

	2002	2003	2004	2005	2006	Market share 06	% Change 06-05
Saudi Arabia		49		60	61	0.13	1.67
Syrian Arab Republic		17		29	16	0.03	-44.83
Egypt		307		131	189	0.41	44.27
Yemen					1		
All countries of Middle East	1,705		566				
SOUTH ASIA	**794**	**732**	**985**	**1,334**	**863**	**1.87**	**-35.31**
South Asia	**794**	**732**	**985**	**1,334**	**863**	**1.87**	**-35.31**
Bangladesh		34		12	12	0.03	
Sri Lanka				11	20	0.04	81.82
India		548		950	473	1.03	-50.21
Iran, Islamic Republic of		24		52	67	0.15	28.85
Nepal					1		
Pakistan		126		309	290	0.63	-6.15
All countries of South Asia	794		985				
REGION NOT SPECIFIED	**617**	**5,773**	**7,409**	**5,408**	**6,672**	**14.47**	**23.37**
Not Specified	**617**	**5,773**	**7,409**	**5,408**	**6,672**	**14.47**	**23.37**
Other countries of the World		190	2,581	194	3,164	6.86	1,530.93
Nationals Residing Abroad	617	5,583	4,828	5,214	3,508	7.61	-32.72

Source: World Tourism Organization (UNWTO)

GUINEA

1. Arrivals of non-resident tourists at national borders, by country of residence

	2002	2003	2004	2005	2006	Market share 06	% Change 06-05
TOTAL (*)		43,966	42,041	45,334	46,096	100.00	1.68
AFRICA		19,227	17,915	17,008	6,562	14.24	-61.42
East Africa		349	240	297	66	0.14	-77.78
Burundi		38	25	32	21	0.05	-34.38
Comoros		16	18	29	20	0.04	-31.03
Ethiopia		65	25	47	20	0.04	-57.45
Eritrea		2	3				
Djibouti		1	3	2	1		-50.00
Kenya		43	7	85			
Madagascar		16	16	12			
Malawi		1		23			
Mauritius		12	6	3			
Mozambique		53	10	2			
Reunion		6					
Rwanda		35	22	15			
Seychelles		3					
Somalia		2	4	3			
Zimbabwe		33	24	20			
Uganda		6	63	8			
United Republic of Tanzania		12	5	7			
Zambia		5	9	9	4	0.01	-55.56
Central Africa		648	601	629	655	1.42	4.13
Angola		48	32	34	28	0.06	-17.65
Cameroon		201	228	208	244	0.53	17.31
Central African Republic		19		9	16	0.03	77.78
Chad		28	25	36	34	0.07	-5.56
Congo		90	184	160	147	0.32	-8.13
Democratic Republic of the Congo		93	3		9	0.02	
Equatorial Guinea		1		1			
Gabon		167	129	181	177	0.38	-2.21
Sao Tome and Principe		1					
North Africa		694	766	836	504	1.09	-39.71
Algeria		21	36	86	49	0.11	-43.02
Morocco		570	579	533	361	0.78	-32.27
Sudan		7	10	16			
Tunisia		96	141	201	94	0.20	-53.23
Southern Africa		198	201	228	1		-99.56
Botswana		1	17	2			
Namibia		2	8	14			
South Africa		174	167	207	1		-99.52
Swaziland		21	9	5			
West Africa		17,338	15,638	15,015	5,219	11.32	-65.24
Cape Verde		54	40	33	56	0.12	69.70
Benin		242	247	348	291	0.63	-16.38
Gambia		657	521	649	1,158	2.51	78.43
Ghana		521	518	582	1,054	2.29	81.10
Cote D'Ivoire		4,504	3,397	3,434	160	0.35	-95.34
Liberia		367	329	257	738	1.60	187.16
Mali		1,659	1,287	1,382	215	0.47	-84.44
Mauritania		185	233	212	1		-99.53
Niger		238	103	119	16	0.03	-86.55
Nigeria		512	549	716	175	0.38	-75.56
Guinea-Bissau		152	102	200			

GUINEA

1. Arrivals of non-resident tourists at national borders, by country of residence

	2002	2003	2004	2005	2006	Market share 06	% Change 06-05
Saint Helena			6	2			
Senegal		4,358	4,993	5,536	888	1.93	-83.96
Sierra Leone		3,345	2,714	848	228	0.49	-73.11
Togo		256	343	386			
Burkina Faso		288	256	311	239	0.52	-23.15
Other Africa			**469**	**3**	**117**	**0.25**	**3,800.00**
Other countries of Africa			469	3	117	0.25	3,800.00
AMERICAS		**4,064**	**4,377**	**5,336**	**2,260**	**4.90**	**-57.65**
Caribbean		**62**	**60**	**48**	**98**	**0.21**	**104.17**
Antigua and Barbuda			1				
Bahamas		2	3		1		
Barbados			3				
Cuba		43	18	9	90	0.20	900.00
Dominica		2			3	0.01	
Dominican Republic		3			3	0.01	
Grenada			2				
Guadeloupe		1	1	4			
Haiti		8	14	10			
Jamaica		2		1	1		
Saba			2	18			
Martinique		1	6				
Puerto Rico			5	6			
Trinidad and Tobago			5				
Central America		**1**	**10**	**4**			
Costa Rica				1			
Honduras		1	4	3			
Nicaragua			2				
Panama			4				
North America		**3,927**	**4,106**	**5,109**	**1,926**	**4.18**	**-62.30**
Canada		914	969	1,144	1,125	2.44	-1.66
Mexico		26	16	40			
United States		2,987	3,121	3,925	801	1.74	-79.59
South America		**74**	**172**	**126**	**236**	**0.51**	**87.30**
Argentina		4	17	10	8	0.02	-20.00
Bolivia		6	3	1	1		
Brazil		35	95	60	101	0.22	68.33
Chile		3	7	12	4	0.01	-66.67
Colombia		5	29	28	121	0.26	332.14
Ecuador			1	1			
Guyana		1	3	1			
Paraguay		1	1				
Peru		6	7	3			
Suriname			4	1			
Uruguay		4	5	5	1		-80.00
Venezuela		9		4			
Other Americas			**29**	**49**			
Other countries of the Americas			29	49			
EAST ASIA AND THE PACIFIC		**1,833**	**2,160**	**2,545**	**2,002**	**4.34**	**-21.34**
North-East Asia		**1,482**	**1,784**	**2,152**	**1,681**	**3.65**	**-21.89**
China		1,002	1,515	1,562	1,681	3.65	7.62
Taiwan (Province of China)		5	11	6			
Hong Kong, China		4					

GUINEA

1. Arrivals of non-resident tourists at national borders, by country of residence

	2002	2003	2004	2005	2006	Market share 06	% Change 06-05
Japan		274	8	374			
Korea, Dem. People's Republic of		192	224	210			
Korea, Republic of		5					
Macao, China			26				
South-East Asia		**149**	**185**	**170**			
Brunei Darussalam			7	1			
Cambodia		4	16	2			
Indonesia		2	8	4			
Lao People's Democratic Republic			13	3			
Malaysia		79	80	71			
Philippines		23	22	43			
Singapore		20	8	9			
Viet Nam		14	21	34			
Thailand		7	10	3			
Australasia		**198**	**183**	**213**	**307**	**0.67**	**44.13**
Australia		183	180	210	307	0.67	46.19
New Zealand		15	3	3			
Melanesia		**3**	**3**	**7**	**14**	**0.03**	**100.00**
Fiji		1		5	14	0.03	180.00
New Caledonia		1					
Vanuatu		1	3	2			
Micronesia			**5**	**3**			
Kosrae State			5	3			
Polynesia		**1**					
Niue		1					
EUROPE		**17,114**	**15,564**	**18,007**	**13,717**	**29.76**	**-23.82**
Central/Eastern Europe		**1,048**	**1,319**	**1,503**	**108**	**0.23**	**-92.81**
Azerbaijan		2			1		
Armenia			1	17	16	0.03	-5.88
Bulgaria		21	24	40	20	0.04	-50.00
Belarus		12	13	13	40	0.09	207.69
Czech Republic/Slovakia		10	16	10			
Czech Republic		16	6	35			
Estonia		8	1	2	5	0.01	150.00
Georgia		4	11	10	6	0.01	-40.00
Hungary		31	23	11	20	0.04	81.82
Kyrgyzstan			73				
Latvia		3					
Lithuania		2	9	1			
Republic of Moldova		3					
Poland		16	18	36			
Romania		32	41	43			
Russian Federation		686	735	985			
Slovakia		12	2	10			
Tajikistan		2	9	1			
Turkmenistan		3	105	52			
Ukraine		180	232	237			
Ussr (Former)		4					
Uzbekistan		1					
Northern Europe		**980**	**686**	**988**	**169**	**0.37**	**-82.89**
Denmark		58	59	51			
Finland		30	31	22	42	0.09	90.91
Iceland		3	10	11			

GUINEA

1. Arrivals of non-resident tourists at national borders, by country of residence

	2002	2003	2004	2005	2006	Market share 06	% Change 06-05
Ireland		46	61	24	44	0.10	83.33
Norway		75	53	76			
Sweden		163	150	195			
United Kingdom		605	322	608	83	0.18	-86.35
Isle of Man				1			
Southern Europe		**1,316**	**1,310**	**1,530**	**107**	**0.23**	**-93.01**
Albania		5	3	2	1		-50.00
Andorra		1	2	1			
Bosnia and Herzegovina			2				
Croatia		17	9	6	5	0.01	-16.67
Greece		51	46	43	101	0.22	134.88
Italy		736	785	848			
Malta		5		1			
Portugal		107	86	110			
Slovenia		2					
Spain		370	368	494			
Serbia and Montenegro		22	9	25			
Western Europe		**13,700**	**12,156**	**13,785**	**13,173**	**28.58**	**-4.44**
Austria		44	9	21	24	0.05	14.29
Belgium		1,067	973	1,353	1,349	2.93	-0.30
France		10,654	9,168	9,783	10,519	22.82	7.52
Germany		879	920	1,160	1,281	2.78	10.43
Luxembourg		14	11	32			
Monaco			4	2			
Netherlands		512	521	748			
Switzerland		530	550	686			
East Mediterranean Europe		**69**	**86**	**201**	**160**	**0.35**	**-20.40**
Cyprus				1			
Israel		19	45	38	160	0.35	321.05
Turkey		50	41	162			
Other Europe		**1**	**7**				
Other countries of Europe		1	7				
MIDDLE EAST		**938**	**1,040**	**628**	**755**	**1.64**	**20.22**
Middle East		**938**	**1,040**	**628**	**755**	**1.64**	**20.22**
Bahrain			1				
Palestine		3	2	2	9	0.02	350.00
Iraq			1				
Jordan		18	325	16			
Kuwait		5	14	9			
Lebanon		454	2	293	194	0.42	-33.79
Libyan Arab Jamahiriya		21	505	23	300	0.65	1,204.35
Qatar		1	3	1			
Saudi Arabia		107	43	87	252	0.55	189.66
Syrian Arab Republic		11	2	28			
United Arab Emirates		4	17	16			
Egypt		311	124	153			
Yemen		3	1				
SOUTH ASIA		**641**	**985**	**1,251**	**20,800**	**45.12**	**1,562.67**
South Asia		**641**	**985**	**1,251**	**20,800**	**45.12**	**1,562.67**
Afghanistan				2	1		-50.00
Bangladesh		30	49	10	12	0.03	20.00
Sri Lanka		2	3	9	18	0.04	100.00

GUINEA

1. Arrivals of non-resident tourists at national borders, by country of residence

	2002	2003	2004	2005	2006	Market share 06	% Change 06-05
India		463	677	900	20,769	45.06	2,207.67
Iran, Islamic Republic of		25	37	46			
Maldives				1			
Nepal		8	15	1			
Pakistan		113	204	282			
REGION NOT SPECIFIED		**149**		**559**			
Not Specified		**149**		**559**			
Nationals Residing Abroad		149		559			

Source: World Tourism Organization (UNWTO)

GUINEA

3. Arrivals of non-resident tourists in hotels and similar establishments, by country of residence

		2002	2003	2004	2005	2006	Market share 06	% Change 06-05
TOTAL	(*)		15,953	13,942	14,988	18,549	100.00	23.76
AFRICA			6,161	6,194	6,620	2,545	13.72	-61.56
East Africa			185	120	150	22	0.12	-85.33
Burundi			13	10	12	9	0.05	-25.00
Comoros			4			2	0.01	
Ethiopia			32	12	20	11	0.06	-45.00
Eritrea			2	1				
Djibouti					1			
Kenya			21	1	54			
Madagascar			13	11	6			
Malawi					22			
Mauritius			5	4	2			
Mozambique			41	2				
Rwanda			14	8	2			
Somalia			1	1	1			
Zimbabwe			27	20	18			
Uganda			4	40	5			
United Republic of Tanzania			4	5	3			
Zambia			4	5	4			
Central Africa			260	197	200	217	1.17	8.50
Angola			9	8	3	10	0.05	233.33
Cameroon			109	88	76	83	0.45	9.21
Central African Republic			8		7	6	0.03	-14.29
Chad			14	13	16	12	0.06	-25.00
Congo			45	65	64	56	0.30	-12.50
Democratic Republic of the Congo			31	1		4	0.02	
Equatorial Guinea			1					
Gabon			42	22	34	46	0.25	35.29
Sao Tome and Principe			1					
North Africa			270	295	328	147	0.79	-55.18
Algeria			9	11	41	20	0.11	-51.22
Morocco			204	212	161	98	0.53	-39.13
Sudan			4	6	7			
Tunisia			53	66	119	29	0.16	-75.63
Southern Africa			101	125	145	1	0.01	-99.31
Botswana			1	15	2			
Namibia			2	6	13			
South Africa			92	100	127	1	0.01	-99.21
Swaziland			6	4	3			
West Africa			5,345	5,351	5,797	2,061	11.11	-64.45
Cape Verde			33	24	16	33	0.18	106.25
Benin			123	125	192	148	0.80	-22.92
Gambia			152	115	133	360	1.94	170.68
Ghana			260	239	354	549	2.96	55.08
Cote D'Ivoire			1,002	887	1,096	50	0.27	-95.44
Liberia			73	53	102	274	1.48	168.63
Mali			472	487	564	78	0.42	-86.17
Mauritania			63	124	75	1	0.01	-98.67
Niger			135	58	82	7	0.04	-91.46
Nigeria			195	231	288	89	0.48	-69.10
Guinea-Bissau			59	35	112			
Saint Helena				1	2			

GUINEA

3. Arrivals of non-resident tourists in hotels and similar establishments, by country of residence

	2002	2003	2004	2005	2006	Market share 06	% Change 06-05
Senegal		1,554	1,759	2,148	236	1.27	-89.01
Sierra Leone		897	861	229	94	0.51	-58.95
Togo		158	186	194			
Burkina Faso		169	166	210	142	0.77	-32.38
Other Africa			**106**		**97**	**0.52**	
Other countries of Africa			106		97	0.52	
AMERICAS		**1,378**	**1,335**	**1,513**	**803**	**4.33**	**-46.93**
Caribbean		**9**	**19**	**14**	**47**	**0.25**	**235.71**
Antigua and Barbuda			1				
Barbados			2				
Cuba		6	2	1	47	0.25	4,600.00
Grenada			2				
Guadeloupe				3			
Haiti		1	7	5			
Jamaica		2					
Saba			2	1			
Martinique			2				
Puerto Rico				4			
Trinidad and Tobago			1				
Central America		**1**	**2**	**2**			
Honduras		1	1	2			
Nicaragua			1				
North America		**1,335**	**1,238**	**1,438**	**630**	**3.40**	**-56.19**
Canada		367	412	494	436	2.35	-11.74
Mexico		4	4	15			
United States		964	822	929	194	1.05	-79.12
South America		**33**	**61**	**47**	**126**	**0.68**	**168.09**
Argentina		1	7	5	2	0.01	-60.00
Bolivia		3	1				
Brazil		8	35	25	68	0.37	172.00
Chile		2	2	4	1	0.01	-75.00
Colombia		2	9	10	55	0.30	450.00
Guyana		1	1	1			
Peru		5	3				
Suriname				1			
Uruguay		2	3				
Venezuela		9		1			
Other Americas			**15**	**12**			
Other countries of the Americas			15	12			
EAST ASIA AND THE PACIFIC		**522**	**451**	**733**	**678**	**3.66**	**-7.50**
North-East Asia		**366**	**311**	**576**	**548**	**2.95**	**-4.86**
China		136	244	292	536	2.89	83.56
Taiwan (Province of China)		4	3	6	12	0.06	100.00
Hong Kong, China		3					
Japan		183	3	210			
Korea, Dem. People's Republic of		39	56	68			
Korea, Republic of		1					
Macao, China			5				
South-East Asia		**82**	**82**	**75**			
Brunei Darussalam			3				

GUINEA

3. Arrivals of non-resident tourists in hotels and similar establishments, by country of residence

	2002	2003	2004	2005	2006	Market share 06	% Change 06-05
Cambodia		1	9				
Indonesia			1	1			
Lao People's Democratic Republic			9	1			
Malaysia		50	35	40			
Philippines		8	8	9			
Singapore		16	6	6			
Viet Nam		3	5	17			
Thailand		4	6	1			
Australasia		**74**	**58**	**78**	**124**	**0.67**	**58.97**
Australia		66	56	77	124	0.67	61.04
New Zealand		8	2	1			
Melanesia				**4**	**6**	**0.03**	**50.00**
Fiji				2	6	0.03	200.00
Vanuatu				2			
EUROPE		**7,332**	**5,283**	**5,352**	**4,422**	**23.84**	**-17.38**
Central/Eastern Europe		**322**	**465**	**339**	**60**	**0.32**	**-82.30**
Armenia				2	4	0.02	100.00
Bulgaria		9	7	7	15	0.08	114.29
Belarus		3	3	5	13	0.07	160.00
Czech Republic/Slovakia		3	4	1			
Czech Republic		5	1	9	10	0.05	11.11
Estonia		3		1	5	0.03	400.00
Georgia		1	2	6	3	0.02	-50.00
Hungary		22	8	4	10	0.05	150.00
Kyrgyzstan			47				
Latvia		3					
Lithuania		1	2				
Poland		11	8	17			
Romania		18	20	17			
Russian Federation		177	243	209			
Slovakia		6	2	5			
Tajikistan		2	4				
Turkmenistan		1	29	5			
Ukraine		56	85	51			
Ussr (Former)		1					
Northern Europe		**463**	**273**	**445**	**94**	**0.51**	**-78.88**
Denmark		27	20	19	16	0.09	-15.79
Finland		20	20	13	28	0.15	115.38
Iceland			4	6			
Ireland		17	16	6	16	0.09	166.67
Norway		35	22	31			
Sweden		39	51	72			
United Kingdom		325	140	297	34	0.18	-88.55
Isle of Man				1			
Southern Europe		**503**	**448**	**582**	**38**	**0.20**	**-93.47**
Albania		3	1				
Andorra			1				
Bosnia and Herzegovina			2				
Croatia		8	6	1	1	0.01	
Greece		24	20	23	37	0.20	60.87
Italy		251	260	332			
Malta		5		1			

GUINEA

3. Arrivals of non-resident tourists in hotels and similar establishments, by country of residence

	2002	2003	2004	2005	2006	Market share 06	% Change 06-05
Portugal		40	25	32			
Slovenia		1					
Spain		164	130	181			
Serbia and Montenegro		7	3	12			
Western Europe		**6,006**	**4,044**	**3,929**	**4,150**	**22.37**	**5.62**
Austria		21	7	4	15	0.08	275.00
Belgium		402	278	463	445	2.40	-3.89
France		4,939	3,136	2,639	3,210	17.31	21.64
Germany		292	279	367	480	2.59	30.79
Luxembourg		11	5	15			
Monaco			1				
Netherlands		124	155	218			
Switzerland		217	183	223			
East Mediterranean Europe		**38**	**51**	**57**	**80**	**0.43**	**40.35**
Cyprus				1			
Israel		7	27	18	80	0.43	344.44
Turkey		31	24	38			
Other Europe			**2**				
Other countries of Europe			2				
MIDDLE EAST		**347**	**404**	**251**	**409**	**2.20**	**62.95**
Middle East		**347**	**404**	**251**	**409**	**2.20**	**62.95**
Palestine		2	2	1	3	0.02	200.00
Jordan		13	182	8			
Kuwait		2	4	3			
Lebanon		95	2	97	194	1.05	100.00
Libyan Arab Jamahiriya		6	133	8	202	1.09	2,425.00
Qatar			3	1			
Saudi Arabia		20	13	26	10	0.05	-61.54
Syrian Arab Republic		2		10			
United Arab Emirates		4	6	7			
Egypt		203	59	90			
SOUTH ASIA		**183**	**275**	**369**	**9,692**	**52.25**	**2,526.56**
South Asia		**183**	**275**	**369**	**9,692**	**52.25**	**2,526.56**
Afghanistan				1			
Bangladesh		25	7	5	7	0.04	40.00
Sri Lanka		2	2	5	7	0.04	40.00
India		117	218	291	9,678	52.18	3,225.77
Iran, Islamic Republic of		8	9	16			
Nepal		5	12	1			
Pakistan		26	27	50			
REGION NOT SPECIFIED		**30**		**150**			
Not Specified		**30**		**150**			
Nationals Residing Abroad		30		150			

Source: World Tourism Organization (UNWTO)

GUINEA-BISSAU

1. Arrivals of non-resident tourists at national borders, by nationality

	2002	2003	2004	2005	2006	Market share 06	% Change 06-05
TOTAL (*)				4,978	11,617	100.00	133.37
AFRICA				1,224	2,705	23.28	121.00
East Africa				124	215	1.85	73.39
Burundi					60	0.52	
Kenya				15	7	0.06	-53.33
Mozambique				70	60	0.52	-14.29
Zimbabwe					5	0.04	
Uganda				39	81	0.70	107.69
Zambia					2	0.02	
Central Africa				143	183	1.58	27.97
Angola				14	45	0.39	221.43
Cameroon				80	23	0.20	-71.25
Central African Republic					2	0.02	
Chad					1	0.01	
Congo				49	39	0.34	-20.41
Equatorial Guinea					36	0.31	
Gabon					3	0.03	
Sao Tome and Principe					34	0.29	
North Africa					45	0.39	
Algeria					9	0.08	
Morocco					32	0.28	
Tunisia					4	0.03	
Southern Africa					23	0.20	
South Africa					23	0.20	
West Africa				957	2,239	19.27	133.96
Cape Verde				159	401	3.45	152.20
Benin				14	56	0.48	300.00
Gambia				60	27	0.23	-55.00
Ghana					22	0.19	
Guinea				34	73	0.63	114.71
Cote D'Ivoire				28	140	1.21	400.00
Liberia				15	25	0.22	66.67
Mali				252	103	0.89	-59.13
Mauritania				30	67	0.58	123.33
Nigeria				68	249	2.14	266.18
Senegal				235	921	7.93	291.91
Sierra Leone				25	8	0.07	-68.00
Togo				26	63	0.54	142.31
Burkina Faso				11	84	0.72	663.64
AMERICAS				451	1,992	17.15	341.69
Caribbean				29	329	2.83	1,034.48
Cuba				29	329	2.83	1,034.48
Central America					302	2.60	
Nicaragua					302	2.60	
North America				135	512	4.41	279.26
Canada				19	124	1.07	552.63
Mexico				59	68	0.59	15.25
United States				57	320	2.75	461.40
South America				287	849	7.31	195.82
Argentina				15	104	0.90	593.33
Bolivia					101	0.87	

GUINEA-BISSAU

1. Arrivals of non-resident tourists at national borders, by nationality

	2002	2003	2004	2005	2006	Market share 06	% Change 06-05
Brazil				176	195	1.68	10.80
Colombia				55	213	1.83	287.27
Paraguay					77	0.66	
Peru				27	58	0.50	114.81
Venezuela				14	101	0.87	621.43
EAST ASIA AND THE PACIFIC				102	1,601	13.78	1,469.61
North-East Asia				82	1,494	12.86	1,721.95
China				46	659	5.67	1,332.61
Japan					312	2.69	
Korea, Republic of				36	523	4.50	1,352.78
South-East Asia					107	0.92	
Philippines					107	0.92	
Australasia				20			
Australia				20			
EUROPE				3,123	5,063	43.58	62.12
Central/Eastern Europe				133	322	2.77	142.11
Bulgaria				10			
Czech Republic				50	32	0.28	-36.00
Poland					100	0.86	
Romania				58	101	0.87	74.14
Russian Federation				15	35	0.30	133.33
Ukraine					54	0.46	
Northern Europe				92	403	3.47	338.04
Denmark				30	110	0.95	266.67
Finland				40			
Ireland					52	0.45	
Norway					104	0.90	
Sweden				22	44	0.38	100.00
United Kingdom					93	0.80	
Southern Europe				2,138	3,201	27.55	49.72
Greece					28	0.24	
Italy				213	343	2.95	61.03
Portugal				1,552	2,599	22.37	67.46
Spain				324	231	1.99	-28.70
Serbia and Montenegro				49			
Western Europe				760	1,133	9.75	49.08
Austria				1	39	0.34	3,800.00
Belgium				30	65	0.56	116.67
France				599	834	7.18	39.23
Germany				65	76	0.65	16.92
Luxembourg					51	0.44	
Netherlands				41	68	0.59	65.85
Switzerland				24			
East Mediterranean Europe					4	0.03	
Israel					1	0.01	
Turkey					3	0.03	
MIDDLE EAST				12	94	0.81	683.33
Middle East				12	94	0.81	683.33
Palestine					20	0.17	
Iraq					2	0.02	

GUINEA-BISSAU

1. Arrivals of non-resident tourists at national borders, by nationality

	2002	2003	2004	2005	2006	Market share 06	% Change 06-05
Libyan Arab Jamahiriya				12	68	0.59	466.67
Egypt					4	0.03	
SOUTH ASIA				**66**	**162**	**1.39**	**145.45**
South Asia				**66**	**162**	**1.39**	**145.45**
India				66	131	1.13	98.48
Pakistan					31	0.27	

Source: World Tourism Organization (UNWTO)

GUYANA

1. Arrivals of non-resident tourists at national borders, by country of residence

		2002	2003	2004	2005	2006	Market share 06	% Change 06-05
TOTAL	(*)	104,341	100,911	121,989	116,596	113,474	100.00	-2.68
AMERICAS		94,620	91,022	111,078	105,468	102,627	90.44	-2.69
Caribbean		28,211	24,779	28,091	26,810	28,437	25.06	6.07
All countries of the Caribbean		28,211	24,779	28,091	26,810	28,437	25.06	6.07
North America		64,248	63,769	80,847	75,947	71,773	63.25	-5.50
Canada		14,190	14,144	15,900	15,876	14,580	12.85	-8.16
United States		50,058	49,625	64,947	60,071	57,193	50.40	-4.79
Other Americas		2,161	2,474	2,140	2,711	2,417	2.13	-10.84
Other countries of the Americas		2,161	2,474	2,140	2,711	2,417	2.13	-10.84
EUROPE		8,190	8,136	9,056	8,704	8,390	7.39	-3.61
Other Europe		8,190	8,136	9,056	8,704	8,390	7.39	-3.61
All countries of Europe		8,190	8,136	9,056	8,704	8,390	7.39	-3.61
REGION NOT SPECIFIED		1,531	1,753	1,855	2,424	2,457	2.17	1.36
Not Specified		1,531	1,753	1,855	2,424	2,457	2.17	1.36
Other countries of the World		1,531	1,753	1,855	2,424	2,457	2.17	1.36

Source: World Tourism Organization (UNWTO)

HAITI

1. Arrivals of non-resident tourists at national borders, by country of residence

	2002	2003	2004	2005	2006	Market share 06	% Change 06-05
TOTAL	140,112	136,031	96,439	112,267			
AMERICAS	126,683	125,214	90,615	103,595			
Caribbean	15,364	14,679	7,514	13,339			
Dominican Republic	7,807	6,586	3,648	5,543			
Jamaica	3,124	4,548	2,091	3,649			
Other countries of the Caribbean	4,433	3,545	1,775	4,147			
North America	107,354	106,220	81,146	87,400			
Canada	15,013	11,354	8,014	9,986			
Mexico	485	351	237	367			
United States	91,856	94,515	72,895	77,047			
Other Americas	3,965	4,315	1,955	2,856			
Other countries of the Americas	3,965	4,315	1,955	2,856			
EUROPE	11,312	7,659	4,246	6,720			
Western Europe	5,567	3,754	1,831	3,349			
France	5,567	3,754	1,831	3,349			
Other Europe	5,745	3,905	2,415	3,371			
Other countries of Europe	5,745	3,905	2,415	3,371			
REGION NOT SPECIFIED	2,117	3,158	1,578	1,952			
Not Specified	2,117	3,158	1,578	1,952			
Other countries of the World	2,117	3,158	1,578	1,952			

Source: World Tourism Organization (UNWTO)

HONDURAS

1. Arrivals of non-resident tourists at national borders, by nationality

	2002	2003	2004	2005	2006	Market share 06	% Change 06-05
TOTAL	549,500	610,535	640,981	673,035	738,667	100.00	9.75
AFRICA	297	206	251	231	330	0.04	42.86
East Africa	16	22	23	18	26		44.44
Ethiopia	7	4	4	3	4		33.33
Kenya	8	14	15	13	19		46.15
Zimbabwe	1	4	4	2	3		50.00
Central Africa	19	7	7	14	19		35.71
Cameroon	8	5	5	8	11		37.50
Congo			1	3	4		33.33
Democratic Republic of the Congo	11	1					
Gabon		1	1	3	4		33.33
North Africa	21	9	9	10	13		30.00
Algeria	7	1	1	1	1		
Morocco	8	7	7	8	11		37.50
Tunisia	6	1	1	1	1		
Southern Africa	178	137	152	163	233	0.03	42.94
South Africa	178	137	152	163	233	0.03	42.94
West Africa	51	17	20	20	28		40.00
Ghana	8	1	1	5	7		40.00
Cote D'Ivoire			3	1	1		
Mauritania	4						
Nigeria	36	16	16	12	17		41.67
Togo	3		2	3			50.00
Other Africa	12	14	40	6	11		83.33
Other countries of Africa	12	14	40	6	11		83.33
AMERICAS	493,330	557,262	584,831	610,179	666,017	90.16	9.15
Caribbean	4,030	4,035	4,214	5,314	6,162	0.83	15.96
Antigua and Barbuda	2	2	2	2	2		
Bahamas	35	37	39	66	79	0.01	19.70
Barbados	35	15	16	23	28		21.74
Bermuda	1	1	1	2	2		
Cayman Islands	1,613	1,205	1,272	2,225	2,672	0.36	20.09
Cuba	899	1,065	1,097	1,169	1,294	0.18	10.69
Dominica	18	11	12	11	13		18.18
Dominican Republic	961	1,019	1,076	1,157	1,280	0.17	10.63
Haiti	116	185	195	217	261	0.04	20.28
Jamaica	199	187	200	243	292	0.04	20.16
Puerto Rico	38	90	99	99	119	0.02	20.20
Saint Vincent and the Grenadines	11	8	8	8	10		25.00
Trinidad and Tobago	60	54	58	74	89	0.01	20.27
Other countries of the Caribbean	42	156	139	18	21		16.67
Central America	318,617	353,110	370,694	360,770	377,867	51.16	4.74
Belize	1,636	1,770	1,894	2,717	3,170	0.43	16.67
Costa Rica	17,845	19,621	20,740	20,855	23,902	3.24	14.61
El Salvador	110,931	130,547	137,084	159,546	158,198	21.42	-0.84
Guatemala	86,068	99,894	104,725	92,612	106,063	14.36	14.52
Nicaragua	96,532	94,174	98,735	76,646	76,874	10.41	0.30
Panama	5,605	7,104	7,516	8,394	9,660	1.31	15.08
North America	157,745	185,427	194,408	225,815	260,861	35.32	15.52
Canada	8,844	10,324	10,803	11,002	12,442	1.68	13.09
Mexico	10,948	13,149	13,913	17,212	20,417	2.76	18.62

HONDURAS

1. Arrivals of non-resident tourists at national borders, by nationality

	2002	2003	2004	2005	2006	Market share 06	% Change 06-05
United States	137,953	161,954	169,692	197,601	228,002	30.87	15.39
South America	**12,938**	**14,690**	**15,515**	**18,280**	**21,127**	**2.86**	**15.57**
Argentina	2,525	2,831	3,000	3,365	3,809	0.52	13.19
Bolivia	455	557	594	750	872	0.12	16.27
Brazil	1,215	1,506	1,580	1,916	2,229	0.30	16.34
Chile	1,458	1,828	1,915	2,134	2,345	0.32	9.89
Colombia	3,134	3,521	3,723	4,410	5,160	0.70	17.01
Ecuador	1,242	1,026	1,079	1,320	1,593	0.22	20.68
French Guiana	31	12	13	14	16		14.29
Guyana	11	33	36	27	31		14.81
Paraguay	108	181	189	213	248	0.03	16.43
Peru	1,193	1,260	1,343	1,483	1,743	0.24	17.53
Suriname	15	7	4	3	3		
Uruguay	422	468	494	577	671	0.09	16.29
Venezuela	1,129	1,460	1,541	2,068	2,406	0.33	16.34
Other countries of South America			4		1		
EAST ASIA AND THE PACIFIC	**6,727**	**7,115**	**7,542**	**8,437**	**11,069**	**1.50**	**31.20**
North-East Asia	**5,062**	**5,145**	**5,236**	**5,780**	**7,577**	**1.03**	**31.09**
China	892	1,055	1,120	1,330	2,313	0.31	73.91
Taiwan (Province of China)		69	63		129	0.02	
Hong Kong, China	256	200	9	17	31		82.35
Japan	2,235	1,928	2,026	2,282	2,569	0.35	12.58
Korea, Dem. People's Republic of	48	789	1,129	113	407	0.06	260.18
Korea, Republic of	1,631	1,104	889	2,038	2,128	0.29	4.42
South-East Asia	**308**	**392**	**419**	**425**	**580**	**0.08**	**36.47**
Indonesia	19	51	56	39	72	0.01	84.62
Malaysia	24	54	59	52	95	0.01	82.69
Philippines	236	276	293	318	384	0.05	20.75
Thailand	29	11	11	16	29		81.25
Australasia	**1,305**	**1,421**	**1,530**	**1,879**	**2,263**	**0.31**	**20.44**
Australia	1,002	1,136	1,222	1,553	1,830	0.25	17.84
New Zealand	303	285	308	326	433	0.06	32.82
Other East Asia and the Pacific	**52**	**157**	**357**	**353**	**649**	**0.09**	**83.85**
Other countries of Asia	52	157	357	353	649	0.09	83.85
EUROPE	**48,681**	**45,152**	**47,504**	**53,482**	**60,324**	**8.17**	**12.79**
Central/Eastern Europe	**770**	**1,061**	**1,116**	**891**	**912**	**0.12**	**2.36**
Bulgaria	89	264	276	211	216	0.03	2.37
Czech Republic/Slovakia	134	184	199	192	197	0.03	2.60
Hungary	72	45	47	51	52	0.01	1.96
Poland	237	231	237	210	215	0.03	2.38
Romania	81	57	60	48	49	0.01	2.08
Russian Federation	113	215	226	125	128	0.02	2.40
Ukraine	44	65	71	54	55	0.01	1.85
Northern Europe	**9,232**	**9,709**	**10,333**	**11,617**	**12,850**	**1.74**	**10.61**
Denmark	1,113	1,042	1,110	1,249	1,281	0.17	2.56
Finland	318	372	402	451	463	0.06	2.66
Iceland	37	58	61	40	41	0.01	2.50
Ireland	504	485	517	551	565	0.08	2.54
Norway	599	724	787	821	842	0.11	2.56
Sweden	1,199	1,454	1,573	1,627	1,669	0.23	2.58
United Kingdom	5,462	5,574	5,883	6,878	7,989	1.08	16.15
Southern Europe	**19,139**	**17,717**	**18,434**	**20,880**	**23,930**	**3.24**	**14.61**

HONDURAS

1. Arrivals of non-resident tourists at national borders, by nationality

	2002	2003	2004	2005	2006	Market share 06	% Change 06-05
Andorra	13	6	6	24	25		4.17
Croatia	26	24	24	7	7		
Greece	110	133	136	118	121	0.02	2.54
Holy See	2	1	1	3	3		
Italy	11,684	10,020	10,376	11,975	13,762	1.86	14.92
Malta	12	7	7	15	15		
Portugal	249	179	190	202	207	0.03	2.48
Spain	7,029	7,335	7,694	8,536	9,790	1.33	14.69
Serbia and Montenegro	14	12					
Western Europe	**18,669**	**15,784**	**16,678**	**18,933**	**21,440**	**2.90**	**13.24**
Austria	683	471	499	585	600	0.08	2.56
Belgium	1,503	1,108	1,176	1,370	1,405	0.19	2.55
France	4,498	3,298	3,478	3,903	4,479	0.61	14.76
Germany	6,018	5,945	6,293	7,010	7,988	1.08	13.95
Luxembourg	21	12	12	8	8		
Netherlands	3,964	3,136	3,294	3,845	4,438	0.60	15.42
Switzerland	1,982	1,814	1,926	2,212	2,522	0.34	14.01
East Mediterranean Europe	**871**	**881**	**923**	**1,151**	**1,180**	**0.16**	**2.52**
Cyprus	72	4	4	7	7		
Israel	761	839	878	1,105	1,133	0.15	2.53
Turkey	38	38	41	39	40	0.01	2.56
Other Europe			**20**	**10**	**12**		**20.00**
Other countries of Europe			20	10	12		20.00
MIDDLE EAST	**96**	**102**	**109**	**90**	**135**	**0.02**	**50.00**
Middle East	**96**	**102**	**109**	**90**	**135**	**0.02**	**50.00**
Palestine	27	36	40	18	27		50.00
Iraq	4			2	3		50.00
Jordan	27	19	20	32	48	0.01	50.00
Kuwait	3	5	5	4	6		50.00
Lebanon	4	10	11	8	12		50.00
Libyan Arab Jamahiriya	1	1	1	1	2		100.00
Saudi Arabia	9			2	2		
Syrian Arab Republic		4	4				
Egypt	21	27	28	23	35		52.17
SOUTH ASIA	**209**	**260**	**278**	**321**	**396**	**0.05**	**23.36**
South Asia	**209**	**260**	**278**	**321**	**396**	**0.05**	**23.36**
Bangladesh	7	6	6	5	6		20.00
Sri Lanka	2	13	14	14	17		21.43
India	163	207	221	278	343	0.05	23.38
Iran, Islamic Republic of	19	11	11	7	9		28.57
Pakistan	18	23	26	17	21		23.53
REGION NOT SPECIFIED	**160**	**438**	**466**	**295**	**396**	**0.05**	**34.24**
Not Specified	**160**	**438**	**466**	**295**	**396**	**0.05**	**34.24**
Other countries of the World	160	438	466	295	396	0.05	34.24

Source: World Tourism Organization (UNWTO)

HONG KONG, CHINA

1. Arrivals of non-resident tourists at national borders, by country of residence

	2002	2003	2004	2005	2006	Market share 06	% Change 06-05
TOTAL	10,688,700	9,676,300	13,655,100	14,773,200	15,821,400	100.00	7.10
AFRICA	63,600	68,100	91,100	116,600	123,400	0.78	5.83
Southern Africa	20,700	18,600	30,800	36,600	37,300	0.24	1.91
South Africa	20,700	18,600	30,800	36,600	37,300	0.24	1.91
Other Africa	42,900	49,500	60,300	80,000	86,100	0.54	7.63
Other countries of Africa	42,900	49,500	60,300	80,000	86,100	0.54	7.63
AMERICAS	1,094,900	713,400	1,091,600	1,196,700	1,229,500	7.77	2.74
North America	1,032,600	674,300	1,037,000	1,113,900	1,133,000	7.16	1.71
Canada	211,500	141,800	211,200	236,000	254,700	1.61	7.92
United States	821,100	532,500	825,800	877,900	878,300	5.55	0.05
Other Americas	62,300	39,100	54,600	82,800	96,500	0.61	16.55
Other countries of the Americas	62,300	39,100	54,600	82,800	96,500	0.61	16.55
EAST ASIA AND THE PACIFIC	8,486,600	8,154,000	11,368,600	12,124,500	12,989,900	82.10	7.14
North-East Asia	6,822,600	7,044,200	9,596,600	10,033,000	10,665,800	67.41	6.31
China	4,757,300	5,692,500	7,793,900	8,029,700	8,434,300	53.31	5.04
Taiwan (Province of China)	558,300	407,100	546,800	619,900	676,800	4.28	9.18
Japan	1,001,900	563,300	746,500	810,900	874,100	5.52	7.79
Korea, Republic of	303,400	225,200	322,300	379,300	457,600	2.89	20.64
Macao, China	201,700	156,100	187,100	193,200	223,000	1.41	15.42
South-East Asia	1,251,600	808,800	1,318,200	1,529,400	1,735,100	10.97	13.45
Indonesia	184,500	133,200	190,900	206,800	255,200	1.61	23.40
Malaysia	242,600	148,000	244,300	284,800	327,400	2.07	14.96
Philippines	267,600	178,700	257,400	301,100	361,100	2.28	19.93
Singapore	328,200	184,200	352,200	428,300	444,000	2.81	3.67
Thailand	197,800	140,100	237,000	276,700	295,700	1.87	6.87
Other countries of South-East Asia	30,900	24,600	36,400	31,700	51,700	0.33	63.09
Australasia	323,400	231,800	381,200	491,200	525,900	3.32	7.06
Australia	274,900	196,900	325,800	422,200	451,300	2.85	6.89
New Zealand	48,500	34,900	55,400	69,000	74,600	0.47	8.12
Other East Asia and the Pacific	89,000	69,200	72,600	70,900	63,100	0.40	-11.00
Other countries of Asia	85,700	67,000	70,800	67,600	59,100	0.37	-12.57
Other countries of Oceania	3,300	2,200	1,800	3,300	4,000	0.03	21.21
EUROPE	855,000	588,000	888,700	1,083,900	1,198,700	7.58	10.59
Northern Europe	388,500	276,800	401,100	460,600	512,700	3.24	11.31
United Kingdom	330,700	235,100	345,200	387,700	431,000	2.72	11.17
Scandinavia	57,800	41,700	55,900	72,900	81,700	0.52	12.07
Southern Europe	75,800	54,500	90,400	114,100	124,100	0.78	8.76
Italy	49,600	33,000	54,300	67,800	73,600	0.47	8.55
Spain,Portugal	26,200	21,500	36,100	46,300	50,500	0.32	9.07
Western Europe	342,700	222,900	346,300	430,500	461,400	2.92	7.18
Austria	13,200	8,000	11,200	15,400	15,900	0.10	3.25
Belgium	14,700	10,800	15,000	20,000	21,700	0.14	8.50
France	101,900	64,800	108,000	136,200	147,500	0.93	8.30
Germany	135,200	88,100	131,500	157,500	162,800	1.03	3.37
Netherlands	49,900	33,700	54,500	67,900	79,300	0.50	16.79
Switzerland	27,800	17,500	26,100	33,500	34,200	0.22	2.09
Other Europe	48,000	33,800	50,900	78,700	100,500	0.64	27.70
Other countries of Europe	48,000	33,800	50,900	78,700	100,500	0.64	27.70

HONG KONG, CHINA

1. Arrivals of non-resident tourists at national borders, by country of residence

	2002	2003	2004	2005	2006	Market share 06	% Change 06-05
MIDDLE EAST	**57,200**	**39,100**	**55,600**	**71,000**	**88,100**	**0.56**	**24.08**
Middle East	**57,200**	**39,100**	**55,600**	**71,000**	**88,100**	**0.56**	**24.08**
All countries of Middle East	57,200	39,100	55,600	71,000	88,100	0.56	24.08
SOUTH ASIA	**131,400**	**113,700**	**159,500**	**180,500**	**191,800**	**1.21**	**6.26**
South Asia	**131,400**	**113,700**	**159,500**	**180,500**	**191,800**	**1.21**	**6.26**
India	131,400	113,700	159,500	180,500	191,800	1.21	6.26

Source: World Tourism Organization (UNWTO)

HONG KONG, CHINA

2. Arrivals of non-resident visitors at national borders, by country of residence

	2002	2003	2004	2005	2006	Market share 06	% Change 06-05
TOTAL	16,566,382	15,536,839	21,810,630	23,359,417	25,251,124	100.00	8.10
AFRICA	91,670	98,862	146,130	206,487	218,315	0.86	5.73
East Africa	22,738	18,607	29,576	47,179	53,563	0.21	13.53
Burundi		14	5	24	24		
Comoros	6	6	8	75	74		-1.33
Ethiopia	469	391	602	1,639	1,461	0.01	-10.86
Eritrea	89	8	2	23	31		34.78
Djibouti		57	10	78	68		-12.82
Kenya	1,662	2,361	3,854	6,927	5,512	0.02	-20.43
Madagascar	570	822	1,638	2,462	2,732	0.01	10.97
Malawi	85	82	50	352	462		31.25
Mauritius	14,287	8,307	14,263	18,657	21,076	0.08	12.97
Mozambique	255	222	265	562	666		18.51
Rwanda	25	10	41	226	223		-1.33
Seychelles	435	246	186	397	414		4.28
Somalia	17	26	43	72	60		-16.67
Zimbabwe	733	712	767	974	1,260		29.36
Uganda	1,594	1,728	2,157	3,452	4,280	0.02	23.99
United Republic of Tanzania	1,915	2,684	4,363	8,646	11,908	0.05	37.73
Zambia	596	931	1,322	2,613	3,312	0.01	26.75
Central Africa	3,071	5,049	6,951	6,702	4,765	0.02	-28.90
Angola	108	490	745	481	446		-7.28
Cameroon	1,977	2,820	4,199	1,378	1,197		-13.13
Central African Republic	3	4	1	87	74		-14.94
Chad	3		5	150	266		77.33
Congo	878	1,294	1,733	1,738	698		-59.84
Democratic Republic of the Congo	69	314	236	2,612	1,656	0.01	-36.60
Equatorial Guinea	6	2	1	27	66		144.44
Gabon	26	125	31	198	303		53.03
Sao Tome and Principe	1			31	59		90.32
North Africa	10,258	8,913	13,125	16,137	21,413	0.08	32.70
Algeria	5,669	5,096	8,509	9,020	12,002	0.05	33.06
Morocco	3,247	2,704	3,436	4,751	6,442	0.03	35.59
Sudan	20		1	83	101		21.69
Tunisia	1,322	1,113	1,179	2,283	2,868	0.01	25.62
Southern Africa	31,005	29,529	54,696	78,983	79,011	0.31	0.04
Botswana	143	125	194	740	1,187		60.41
Lesotho	12	21	1	182	277		52.20
Namibia	40	46	96	267	376		40.82
South Africa	30,793	29,278	54,371	77,520	76,820	0.30	-0.90
Swaziland	17	59	34	274	351		28.10
West Africa	24,598	36,764	41,782	57,486	59,563	0.24	3.61
Cape Verde	185	165	139	544	546		0.37
Benin	630	668	617	1,743	2,302	0.01	32.07
Gambia	1,322	1,416	1,155	2,216	2,511	0.01	13.31
Ghana	2,772	3,770	9,072	15,106	18,126	0.07	19.99
Guinea	3,031	6,076	7,193	8,302	7,348	0.03	-11.49
Cote D'Ivoire	333	1,198	949	898	580		-35.41
Liberia	43	27	21	225	282		25.33
Mali	5,961	11,169	12,721	13,212	11,323	0.04	-14.30
Mauritania	150	125	48	387	433		11.89
Niger	596	1,053	1,338	2,438	2,774	0.01	13.78
Nigeria	7,086	7,423	4,897	5,754	6,385	0.03	10.97

HONG KONG, CHINA

2. Arrivals of non-resident visitors at national borders, by country of residence

	2002	2003	2004	2005	2006	Market share 06	% Change 06-05
Guinea-Bissau	61	36	61	428	588		37.38
Senegal	1,368	1,546	1,389	2,166	1,960	0.01	-9.51
Sierra Leone	31	35	47	180	242		34.44
Togo	791	1,613	1,824	2,511	2,152	0.01	-14.30
Burkina Faso	238	444	311	1,376	2,011	0.01	46.15
AMERICAS	**1,346,840**	**925,907**	**1,399,572**	**1,565,350**	**1,630,637**	**6.46**	**4.17**
Caribbean	**5,812**	**3,864**	**3,569**	**7,489**	**8,454**	**0.03**	**12.89**
Antigua and Barbuda	13	7	2	109	130		19.27
Bahamas	86	92	121	455	581		27.69
Barbados	60	30	79	184	201		9.24
Cuba	106	138	158	278	294		5.76
Dominica	331	198	96	524	574		9.54
Dominican Republic	3,054	1,950	1,257	2,368	2,565	0.01	8.32
Grenada	7	2	3	21	31		47.62
Haiti		6	2	95	113		18.95
Jamaica	1,261	1,042	1,244	1,984	2,356	0.01	18.75
Saint Kitts and Nevis		1	5	59	53		-10.17
Saint Lucia	7	8	1	55	33		-40.00
Saint Vincent and the Grenadines				26	30		15.38
Trinidad and Tobago	887	390	601	1,331	1,493	0.01	12.17
Central America	**11,375**	**8,228**	**7,430**	**12,149**	**15,038**	**0.06**	**23.78**
Belize	4,264	3,366	1,908	3,702	4,125	0.02	11.43
Costa Rica	1,873	1,381	1,702	2,618	3,403	0.01	29.98
El Salvador	125	139	96	439	664		51.25
Guatemala	629	357	468	1,172	1,704	0.01	45.39
Honduras	1,404	888	637	1,125	1,600	0.01	42.22
Nicaragua	5	4	3	124	81		-34.68
Panama	3,075	2,093	2,616	2,969	3,461	0.01	16.57
North America	**1,284,842**	**881,773**	**1,345,429**	**1,478,162**	**1,524,791**	**6.04**	**3.15**
Canada	264,967	186,809	273,925	308,842	335,697	1.33	8.70
Mexico	19,031	11,173	19,808	26,231	30,069	0.12	14.63
United States (*)	1,000,844	683,791	1,051,696	1,143,089	1,159,025	4.59	1.39
South America	**44,811**	**32,042**	**43,144**	**67,550**	**82,354**	**0.33**	**21.92**
Argentina	3,522	2,765	4,576	7,530	8,743	0.03	16.11
Bolivia	1,461	1,143	944	1,408	1,595	0.01	13.28
Brazil	15,654	11,776	17,743	23,906	30,078	0.12	25.82
Chile	4,593	2,701	3,716	6,166	7,779	0.03	26.16
Colombia	4,569	3,572	5,280	10,233	12,766	0.05	24.75
Ecuador	1,590	981	1,023	2,114	2,858	0.01	35.19
French Guiana		5			15		
Guyana	208	144	149	417	449		7.67
Paraguay	784	543	578	857	915		6.77
Peru	4,047	2,877	2,986	4,567	4,867	0.02	6.57
Suriname	1,463	783	1,262	2,127	2,236	0.01	5.12
Uruguay	754	282	379	967	1,075		11.17
Venezuela	6,166	4,470	4,508	7,258	8,978	0.04	23.70
EAST ASIA AND THE PACIFIC	**13,654,656**	**13,410,004**	**18,705,602**	**19,706,889**	**21,330,293**	**84.47**	**8.24**
North-East Asia	**11,651,065**	**12,015,660**	**16,489,497**	**17,049,300**	**18,388,861**	**72.82**	**7.86**
China	6,825,199	8,467,211	12,245,862	12,541,400	13,591,342	53.82	8.37
Taiwan (Province of China)	2,428,776	1,852,378	2,074,795	2,130,565	2,177,232	8.62	2.19
Japan	1,395,020	867,160	1,126,250	1,210,848	1,311,111	5.19	8.28
Korea, Dem. People's Republic of	18		4	45	79		75.56
Korea, Republic of	457,438	368,176	539,190	642,480	718,758	2.85	11.87

HONG KONG, CHINA

2. Arrivals of non-resident visitors at national borders, by country of residence

	2002	2003	2004	2005	2006	Market share 06	% Change 06-05
Macao, China	534,590	443,622	484,038	510,031	577,792	2.29	13.29
Mongolia	10,024	17,113	19,358	13,931	12,547	0.05	-9.93
South-East Asia	**1,593,395**	**1,088,057**	**1,732,858**	**2,037,372**	**2,273,748**	**9.00**	**11.60**
Brunei Darussalam	5,108	3,212	4,448	5,079	5,688	0.02	11.99
Myanmar	2,685	1,932	3,403	4,483	5,580	0.02	24.47
Cambodia	4,009	3,671	5,395	6,833	8,948	0.04	30.95
Indonesia	223,590	165,101	232,311	260,487	323,987	1.28	24.38
Lao People's Democratic Republic	205	179	218	730	1,128		54.52
Malaysia	318,854	208,686	339,709	392,047	445,993	1.77	13.76
Philippines	329,604	234,260	336,673	391,049	454,036	1.80	16.11
Timor-Leste		32	13	196	290		47.96
Singapore	426,166	265,729	463,920	573,330	588,474	2.33	2.64
Viet Nam	23,838	19,857	29,858	22,726	44,092	0.17	94.02
Thailand	259,336	185,398	316,910	380,412	395,532	1.57	3.97
Australasia	**405,181**	**302,744**	**480,682**	**615,099**	**661,730**	**2.62**	**7.58**
Australia	343,294	254,254	408,940	525,577	563,933	2.23	7.30
New Zealand (*)	61,887	48,490	71,742	89,522	97,797	0.39	9.24
Melanesia	**1,660**	**1,219**	**1,330**	**2,692**	**3,273**	**0.01**	**21.58**
Solomon Islands	53	42	59	126	153		21.43
Fiji	1,412	1,037	1,137	2,050	2,275	0.01	10.98
Vanuatu	46	21	11	199	235		18.09
Papua New Guinea	149	119	123	317	610		92.43
Micronesia	**2,641**	**1,778**	**906**	**1,541**	**1,700**	**0.01**	**10.32**
Kiribati	331	202	59	53	213		301.89
Nauru	2,115	1,461	796	1,140	1,057		-7.28
Micronesia (Federated States of)	11	2	2	148	135		-8.78
Marshall Islands	184	113	49	200	295		47.50
Polynesia	**706**	**529**	**290**	**747**	**929**		**24.36**
Tonga	555	486	224	504	673		33.53
Tuvalu	87	19	23	105	156		48.57
Samoa	64	24	43	138	100		-27.54
Other East Asia and the Pacific	**8**	**17**	**39**	**138**	**52**		**-62.32**
Other countries of Oceania	8	17	39	138	52		-62.32
EUROPE	**1,135,044**	**822,146**	**1,201,751**	**1,471,602**	**1,634,925**	**6.47**	**11.10**
Central/Eastern Europe	**34,579**	**26,777**	**41,557**	**64,492**	**85,802**	**0.34**	**33.04**
Azerbaijan	23	27	13	138	277		100.72
Armenia	45	59	30	153	222		45.10
Bulgaria	563	418	600	1,726	3,146	0.01	82.27
Belarus	130	126	97	403	626		55.33
Czech Republic	4,112	2,937	5,296	6,638	7,441	0.03	12.10
Estonia	853	425	513	1,248	1,827	0.01	46.39
Georgia	26	44	32	196	251		28.06
Hungary	3,053	2,408	2,652	4,435	5,937	0.02	33.87
Kazakhstan	125	148	346	1,178	2,549	0.01	116.38
Kyrgyzstan	9	4		98	214		118.37
Latvia	282	223	289	731	1,091		49.25
Lithuania	677	614	654	1,181	1,605	0.01	35.90
Republic of Moldova	19	15	2	98	161		64.29
Poland	8,236	6,310	10,072	15,929	18,900	0.07	18.65
Romania	1,251	1,436	1,520	3,235	5,132	0.02	58.64
Russian Federation	12,852	9,764	16,740	22,198	29,137	0.12	31.26
Slovakia	945	668	956	1,795	2,402	0.01	33.82
Tajikistan	1	1		33	38		15.15

HONG KONG, CHINA

2. Arrivals of non-resident visitors at national borders, by country of residence

	2002	2003	2004	2005	2006	Market share 06	% Change 06-05
Turkmenistan		6		27	31		14.81
Ukraine	1,013	964	1,593	2,587	4,080	0.02	57.71
Uzbekistan	364	180	145	433	731		68.82
Other countries Central/East Europ			7	32	4		-87.50
Northern Europe	**468,515**	**347,117**	**497,312**	**579,840**	**648,690**	**2.57**	**11.87**
Denmark	17,155	14,248	18,395	23,920	26,201	0.10	9.54
Finland	13,033	8,700	9,054	14,235	17,427	0.07	22.42
Iceland	378	285	357	1,102	1,181		7.17
Ireland	14,996	11,282	16,573	23,551	28,542	0.11	21.19
Norway	13,576	9,556	11,039	14,856	16,068	0.06	8.16
Sweden	29,412	21,728	30,607	37,575	42,776	0.17	13.84
United Kingdom	379,965	281,318	411,287	464,601	516,495	2.05	11.17
Southern Europe	**122,556**	**97,989**	**146,633**	**184,749**	**201,931**	**0.80**	**9.30**
Albania	51	31	31	69	101		46.38
Andorra	3	5	25	110	101		-8.18
Bosnia and Herzegovina	55	16					
Croatia	1,761	1,189	1,115	1,974	2,747	0.01	39.16
Greece	6,248	3,806	5,887	8,600	9,667	0.04	12.41
Holy See				6	5		-16.67
Italy	71,969	50,756	79,016	97,926	108,374	0.43	10.67
Malta	427	240	286	793	936		18.03
Portugal	10,793	20,114	22,814	22,922	19,217	0.08	-16.16
San Marino	6	13	11	91	119		30.77
Slovenia	744	493	670	1,447	2,146	0.01	48.31
Spain	29,974	20,803	36,404	49,304	56,649	0.22	14.90
TFYR of Macedonia	110	80	76	355	398		12.11
Serbia and Montenegro	415	443	298	1,152	1,471	0.01	27.69
Western Europe	**457,019**	**308,169**	**456,254**	**567,276**	**609,746**	**2.41**	**7.49**
Austria	16,303	10,219	14,234	19,443	20,446	0.08	5.16
Belgium	20,062	15,215	19,931	26,245	28,672	0.11	9.25
France (*)	146,714	95,844	148,131	185,601	200,820	0.80	8.20
Germany	172,654	116,966	169,661	204,625	213,837	0.85	4.50
Liechtenstein	41	38	9	187	206		10.16
Luxembourg	820	389	405	1,213	1,369	0.01	12.86
Monaco	49	66	21	111	103		-7.21
Netherlands	67,073	47,756	72,248	89,067	102,231	0.40	14.78
Switzerland	33,303	21,676	31,614	40,784	42,062	0.17	3.13
East Mediterranean Europe	**52,375**	**42,094**	**59,995**	**75,245**	**88,756**	**0.35**	**17.96**
Cyprus	1,219	791	910	1,630	1,995	0.01	22.39
Israel	33,661	24,530	37,652	46,785	50,914	0.20	8.83
Turkey	17,495	16,773	21,433	26,830	35,847	0.14	33.61
MIDDLE EAST	**35,378**	**24,816**	**31,392**	**45,951**	**61,659**	**0.24**	**34.18**
Middle East	**35,378**	**24,816**	**31,392**	**45,951**	**61,659**	**0.24**	**34.18**
Bahrain	1,647	877	1,016	2,158	2,566	0.01	18.91
Iraq	27	4	3	69	94		36.23
Jordan	5,783	4,776	5,365	7,017	8,411	0.03	19.87
Kuwait	1,397	718	1,156	2,004	3,127	0.01	56.04
Lebanon	1,088	645	587	1,303	1,518	0.01	16.50
Libyan Arab Jamahiriya	15	1		46	45		-2.17
Oman	482	255	192	581	1,020		75.56
Qatar	233	71	97	387	1,325	0.01	242.38
Saudi Arabia	6,676	4,063	6,214	9,348	13,549	0.05	44.94
Syrian Arab Republic	641	257	164	459	665		44.88
United Arab Emirates	7,705	4,982	6,664	8,056	10,461	0.04	29.85

HONG KONG, CHINA

2. Arrivals of non-resident visitors at national borders, by country of residence

	2002	2003	2004	2005	2006	Market share 06	% Change 06-05
Egypt	5,973	4,568	6,097	9,616	13,192	0.05	37.19
Yemen	3,711	3,599	3,837	4,907	5,686	0.02	15.88
SOUTH ASIA	**302,794**	**255,104**	**326,183**	**363,080**	**375,205**	**1.49**	**3.34**
South Asia	**302,794**	**255,104**	**326,183**	**363,080**	**375,205**	**1.49**	**3.34**
Afghanistan	14	14	7	54	67		24.07
Bangladesh	33,032	29,929	46,487	59,635	55,769	0.22	-6.48
Bhutan	727	172	177	369	557		50.95
Sri Lanka	12,691	11,343	16,142	15,240	8,350	0.03	-45.21
India	193,705	178,130	244,364	273,487	294,079	1.16	7.53
Iran, Islamic Republic of	818	518	553	1,244	1,645	0.01	32.23
Maldives	205	134	166	210	227		8.10
Nepal	6,187	6,366	7,582	5,299	5,458	0.02	3.00
Pakistan	55,415	28,498	10,705	7,542	9,053	0.04	20.03
REGION NOT SPECIFIED				**58**	**90**		**55.17**
Not Specified				**58**	**90**		**55.17**
Other countries of the World				58	90		55.17

Source: World Tourism Organization (UNWTO)

HUNGARY

2. Arrivals of non-resident visitors at national borders, by nationality

	2002	2003	2004	2005	2006	Market share 06	% Change 06-05
TOTAL (*)	31,739,243	31,412,483	36,635,132	38,554,561	40,962,830	100.00	6.25
AFRICA	11,026	14,300	15,833	13,502	16,675	0.04	23.50
East Africa	933	1,925	1,346	1,303	2,143	0.01	64.47
Burundi	8	24	26	41	12		-70.73
Comoros		5	6	7			
Ethiopia	157	58	170	94	159		69.15
Djibouti	6	5	11	5	3		-40.00
Kenya	233	273	384	242	318		31.40
Madagascar	20	24	45	80	36		-55.00
Malawi	7	12	13	17	13		-23.53
Mauritius	106	127	155	194	236		21.65
Mozambique	23	11	36	27	26		-3.70
Reunion	8		21	62	15		-75.81
Rwanda	43	1,154	54	161	932		478.88
Seychelles	38	32	37	36	37		2.78
Somalia	11	11	29	18	26		44.44
Zimbabwe	87	58	148	94	99		5.32
Uganda	45	40	55	92	81		-11.96
United Republic of Tanzania	117	60	102	67	87		29.85
Zambia	24	31	54	66	63		-4.55
Central Africa	911	648	939	622	752		20.90
Angola	367	153	227	205	187		-8.78
Cameroon	180	117	184	165	274		66.06
Central African Republic	14	26	148	42	60		42.86
Chad	13	26	21	25	35		40.00
Congo	272	307	328	165	166		0.61
Equatorial Guinea	47						
Gabon	16	16	24	19	25		31.58
Sao Tome and Principe	2	3	7	1	5		400.00
North Africa	3,166	3,050	4,726	4,021	4,071	0.01	1.24
Algeria	1,118	867	1,045	748	784		4.81
Morocco	669	705	1,033	869	1,100		26.58
Sudan	104	76	204	133	126		-5.26
Tunisia	1,275	1,402	2,444	2,271	2,061	0.01	-9.25
Southern Africa	4,220	6,792	5,759	5,224	6,311	0.02	20.81
Botswana	4	10	14	4	6		50.00
Lesotho	6	5	2	2	11		450.00
Namibia	46	52	73	49	66		34.69
South Africa	4,137	6,713	5,656	5,156	6,219	0.02	20.62
Swaziland	27	12	14	13	9		-30.77
West Africa	1,796	1,885	3,063	2,332	3,398	0.01	45.71
Benin	74	26	26	18	29		61.11
Gambia	28	10	25	13	23		76.92
Ghana	145	151	301	218	204		-6.42
Guinea	47	92	126	77	136		76.62
Cote D'Ivoire	114	88	104	74	103		39.19
Liberia	37	10	25	25	14		-44.00
Mali	79	21	765	44	127		188.64
Mauritania	36	42	51	62	127		104.84
Niger	93	303	89	132	227		71.97
Nigeria	1,002	970	1,319	1,430	1,618		13.15
Guinea-Bissau	9		1	7	20		185.71
Senegal	41	90	108	96	670		597.92

HUNGARY

2. Arrivals of non-resident visitors at national borders, by nationality

	2002	2003	2004	2005	2006	Market share 06	% Change 06-05
Sierra Leone	20	32	56	39	37		-5.13
Togo	41	27	38	65	34		-47.69
Burkina Faso	30	23	29	32	29		-9.38
AMERICAS	**427,547**	**385,191**	**515,112**	**490,440**	**521,151**	**1.27**	**6.26**
Caribbean	**1,537**	**1,039**	**1,534**	**1,380**	**1,827**		**32.39**
Antigua and Barbuda	5	18	6	8	4		-50.00
Bahamas	33	25	35	15	19		26.67
Barbados	68	18	28	44	23		-47.73
Bermuda	11	3	31	5	3		-40.00
Cuba	540	417	687	653	743		13.78
Dominica	235	141	305	217	223		2.76
Grenada	11	16	20	16	11		-31.25
Haiti	33	91	56	65	85		30.77
Jamaica	503	219	199	165	490		196.97
Netherlands Antilles	20	18	8	17	106		523.53
Saint Kitts and Nevis	3	2	16	12	9		-25.00
Saint Lucia	9	3	23	8	3		-62.50
Saint Vincent and the Grenadines	7	3	11	8	6		-25.00
Trinidad and Tobago	59	65	109	147	102		-30.61
Central America	**1,236**	**1,293**	**2,049**	**2,818**	**1,830**		**-35.06**
Belize	21	18	7	8	8		
Costa Rica	277	254	447	444	471		6.08
El Salvador	89	112	236	224	242		8.04
Guatemala	418	381	718	396	425		7.32
Honduras	100	125	152	133	124		-6.77
Nicaragua	96	214	175	1,079	317		-70.62
Panama	235	189	314	534	243		-54.49
North America	**407,298**	**367,339**	**485,218**	**459,901**	**487,412**	**1.19**	**5.98**
Canada	60,633	54,219	83,226	78,413	85,118	0.21	8.55
Mexico	11,738	9,575	12,558	12,506	14,139	0.03	13.06
United States	334,927	303,545	389,434	368,982	388,155	0.95	5.20
South America	**17,476**	**15,520**	**26,311**	**26,341**	**30,082**	**0.07**	**14.20**
Argentina	3,797	2,823	4,775	5,832	5,729	0.01	-1.77
Bolivia	253	1,218	3,593	507	315		-37.87
Brazil	6,671	5,928	9,707	13,625	17,359	0.04	27.41
Chile	2,081	1,380	2,092	1,945	2,029		4.32
Colombia	1,381	872	1,389	1,127	1,022		-9.32
Ecuador	766	1,335	1,828	541	553		2.22
Falkland Islands (Malvinas)	37	6	1	165	4		-97.58
Guyana	9	32	36	27	29		7.41
Paraguay	199	88	145	132	160		21.21
Peru	614	669	996	749	849		13.35
Suriname	12	27	16	28	31		10.71
Uruguay	476	355	411	370	451		21.89
Venezuela	1,180	787	1,322	1,293	1,551		19.95
EAST ASIA AND THE PACIFIC	**183,789**	**167,361**	**247,520**	**272,207**	**290,992**	**0.71**	**6.90**
North-East Asia	**138,377**	**131,184**	**181,059**	**199,187**	**206,485**	**0.50**	**3.66**
China	12,152	12,080	25,255	30,891	33,243	0.08	7.61
Taiwan (Province of China)	3,048	4,346	10,220	8,527	9,129	0.02	7.06
Hong Kong, China	3,237	3,963	7,941	5,875	6,424	0.02	9.34
Japan	87,148	78,983	95,393	108,338	99,653	0.24	-8.02
Korea, Dem. People's Republic of	125	115	217	405	599		47.90
Korea, Republic of	31,413	30,575	40,742	43,790	56,116	0.14	28.15

HUNGARY

2. Arrivals of non-resident visitors at national borders, by nationality

	2002	2003	2004	2005	2006	Market share 06	% Change 06-05
Mongolia	1,254	1,122	1,291	1,361	1,321		-2.94
South-East Asia	**16,428**	**14,693**	**23,502**	**18,699**	**18,876**	**0.05**	**0.95**
Brunei Darussalam	3	7	18	32	31		-3.13
Myanmar	692	19	107	60	74		23.33
Cambodia	338	52	622	43	58		34.88
Indonesia	2,303	2,035	3,007	2,046	2,149	0.01	5.03
Lao People's Democratic Republic	51	145	21	32	53		65.63
Malaysia	3,061	2,762	4,497	5,444	4,321	0.01	-20.63
Philippines	1,614	1,160	1,755	1,248	1,503		20.43
Singapore	2,417	2,211	2,953	2,728	2,834	0.01	3.89
Viet Nam	2,901	3,436	4,519	3,738	3,846	0.01	2.89
Thailand	3,048	2,866	6,003	3,328	4,007	0.01	20.40
Australasia	**28,902**	**21,452**	**42,853**	**54,245**	**65,578**	**0.16**	**20.89**
Australia	24,194	16,566	35,319	46,807	58,456	0.14	24.89
New Zealand	4,708	4,886	7,534	7,438	7,122	0.02	-4.25
Melanesia	**64**	**14**	**94**	**47**	**28**		**-40.43**
Solomon Islands	3	1	1		1		
Fiji	19	11	24	30	18		-40.00
New Caledonia	31	1	54	14	6		-57.14
Vanuatu	2		2	1			
Papua New Guinea	9	1	13	2	3		50.00
Micronesia	**14**	**12**	**8**	**11**	**2**		**-81.82**
Kiribati	9	4	8	5	1		-80.00
Nauru	5	8		6	1		-83.33
Polynesia	**4**	**6**	**4**	**18**	**23**		**27.78**
Tonga	2	4	4	10	20		100.00
Tuvalu	2	2		8	3		-62.50
EUROPE	**31,081,931**	**30,817,730**	**35,781,644**	**37,744,758**	**40,100,380**	**97.89**	**6.24**
Central/Eastern Europe	**14,789,177**	**15,300,705**	**18,721,181**	**20,499,888**	**22,103,448**	**53.96**	**7.82**
Azerbaijan	491	497	656	791	741		-6.32
Armenia	918	790	971	867	788		-9.11
Bulgaria	772,036	771,377	989,574	1,018,885	985,746	2.41	-3.25
Belarus	12,891	13,571	17,282	18,790	24,279	0.06	29.21
Czech Republic	512,833	658,793	855,596	845,260	978,083	2.39	15.71
Estonia	13,500	12,719	13,277	15,549	15,058	0.04	-3.16
Kazakhstan	4,271	5,448	3,393	1,882	2,126	0.01	12.96
Kyrgyzstan	430	392	455	325	27		-91.69
Latvia	18,300	17,584	19,870	30,669	34,885	0.09	13.75
Lithuania	41,725	35,897	41,246	57,124	67,605	0.17	18.35
Republic of Moldova	65,570	73,835	124,823	88,278	90,476	0.22	2.49
Poland	905,789	768,315	1,007,216	1,176,292	1,303,201	3.18	10.79
Romania	5,660,088	5,975,837	7,434,795	7,445,185	8,650,871	21.12	16.19
Russian Federation	88,039	90,850	99,927	90,953	108,148	0.26	18.91
Slovakia	4,050,526	4,424,643	5,548,385	7,322,448	7,967,608	19.45	8.81
Ukraine	2,641,770	2,450,157	2,563,715	2,386,590	1,873,806	4.57	-21.49
Northern Europe	**523,226**	**538,362**	**759,970**	**866,316**	**834,641**	**2.04**	**-3.66**
Denmark	58,423	66,527	92,027	96,983	96,733	0.24	-0.26
Finland	66,969	59,232	83,358	76,110	81,107	0.20	6.57
Iceland	3,912	3,670	3,454	3,318	2,618	0.01	-21.10
Ireland	26,938	30,788	49,246	52,854	51,982	0.13	-1.65
Norway	37,333	38,038	49,804	65,107	67,575	0.16	3.79
Sweden	122,736	132,171	163,545	166,913	173,921	0.42	4.20
United Kingdom	206,915	207,936	318,536	405,031	360,705	0.88	-10.94

HUNGARY

2. Arrivals of non-resident visitors at national borders, by nationality

	2002	2003	2004	2005	2006	Market share 06	% Change 06-05
Southern Europe	7,375,425	6,264,455	6,645,598	6,252,786	6,494,811	15.86	3.87
Albania	2,282	2,478	31,854	8,812	2,969	0.01	-66.31
Andorra	117	44	215	87	56		-35.63
Bosnia and Herzegovina	131,320	99,481	87,525	71,472	80,274	0.20	12.32
Croatia	2,114,916	1,539,812	1,280,140	1,195,369	1,306,733	3.19	9.32
Gibraltar	11		12		1		
Greece	68,064	74,194	121,295	123,191	123,872	0.30	0.55
Holy See	53	42	43	70	46		-34.29
Italy	417,627	465,707	631,605	689,192	702,239	1.71	1.89
Malta	1,883	2,251	2,753	2,418	1,728		-28.54
Portugal	18,162	17,448	26,613	37,551	42,519	0.10	13.23
San Marino	298	177	203	273	206		-24.54
Slovenia	598,116	611,774	688,289	728,863	730,821	1.78	0.27
Spain	80,695	83,839	125,192	139,475	151,680	0.37	8.75
TFYR of Macedonia	29,743	20,074	31,880	27,014	36,448	0.09	34.92
Serbia and Montenegro	3,912,138	3,347,134	3,617,979	3,228,999	3,315,219	8.09	2.67
Western Europe	8,149,793	8,481,969	9,351,793	9,884,359	10,428,996	25.46	5.51
Austria	4,735,086	4,870,479	5,236,789	5,599,891	6,088,178	14.86	8.72
Belgium	72,695	84,997	122,265	137,408	148,968	0.36	8.41
France	233,389	249,383	331,522	374,584	368,183	0.90	-1.71
Germany	2,738,617	2,875,177	3,136,165	3,198,643	3,222,211	7.87	0.74
Liechtenstein	482	845	1,311	1,137	2,156	0.01	89.62
Luxembourg	3,194	3,478	9,322	8,567	9,982	0.02	16.52
Monaco	93	213	236	202	185		-8.42
Netherlands	239,216	239,819	295,596	324,828	339,192	0.83	4.42
Switzerland	127,021	157,578	218,587	239,099	249,941	0.61	4.53
East Mediterranean Europe	244,310	232,239	303,102	241,409	238,484	0.58	-1.21
Cyprus	10,882	9,535	15,400	10,078	11,570	0.03	14.80
Israel	89,933	104,478	137,966	99,179	94,786	0.23	-4.43
Turkey	143,495	118,226	149,736	132,152	132,128	0.32	-0.02
MIDDLE EAST	8,775	8,478	26,037	9,538	9,477	0.02	-0.64
Middle East	8,775	8,478	26,037	9,538	9,477	0.02	-0.64
Bahrain	82	33	88	48	44		-8.33
Palestine	71	55	188	118	137		16.10
Iraq	254	222	936	355	330		-7.04
Jordan	766	786	991	885	865		-2.26
Kuwait	596	835	395	366	499		36.34
Lebanon	791	830	5,264	1,251	1,421		13.59
Libyan Arab Jamahiriya	868	928	2,826	770	582		-24.42
Oman	78	78	65	82	99		20.73
Qatar	156	252	113	144	109		-24.31
Saudi Arabia	386	377	990	472	435		-7.84
Syrian Arab Republic	1,122	1,070	3,847	1,811	1,710		-5.58
United Arab Emirates	722	639	546	447	597		33.56
Egypt	2,736	2,223	9,589	2,598	2,472	0.01	-4.85
Yemen	147	150	199	191	177		-7.33
SOUTH ASIA	9,899	10,858	15,641	15,179	15,500	0.04	2.11
South Asia	9,899	10,858	15,641	15,179	15,500	0.04	2.11
Afghanistan	296	82	244	661	206		-68.84
Bangladesh	116	89	271	154	148		-3.90
Bhutan	4	8	26	18	9		-50.00
Sri Lanka	172	346	262	195	252		29.23
India	4,695	4,331	6,523	6,417	6,903	0.02	7.57

HUNGARY

2. Arrivals of non-resident visitors at national borders, by nationality

	2002	2003	2004	2005	2006	Market share 06	% Change 06-05
Iran, Islamic Republic of	4,142	5,383	7,014	6,594	6,767	0.02	2.62
Maldives	13	7	12	3	13		333.33
Nepal	78	74	242	178	236		32.58
Pakistan	383	538	1,047	959	966		0.73
REGION NOT SPECIFIED	**16,276**	**8,565**	**33,345**	**8,937**	**8,655**	**0.02**	**-3.16**
Not Specified	**16,276**	**8,565**	**33,345**	**8,937**	**8,655**	**0.02**	**-3.16**
Other countries of the World	16,276	8,565	33,345	8,937	8,655	0.02	-3.16

Source: World Tourism Organization (UNWTO)

HUNGARY

3. Arrivals of non-resident tourists in hotels and similar establishments, by nationality

	2002	2003	2004	2005	2006	Market share 06	% Change 06-05
TOTAL	2,658,735	2,598,861	2,950,930	3,140,248	3,009,203	100.00	-4.17
AFRICA	5,551	5,312	11,989	10,025	7,365	0.24	-26.53
Other Africa	5,551	5,312	11,989	10,025	7,365	0.24	-26.53
All countries of Africa	5,551	5,312	11,989	10,025	7,365	0.24	-26.53
AMERICAS	165,121	167,937	195,475	211,480	234,820	7.80	11.04
North America	144,423	146,977	172,221	188,125	211,145	7.02	12.24
Canada	13,639	12,705	16,125	17,499	21,241	0.71	21.38
United States	130,784	134,272	156,096	170,626	189,904	6.31	11.30
Other Americas	20,698	20,960	23,254	23,355	23,675	0.79	1.37
Other countries of the Americas	20,698	20,960	23,254	23,355	23,675	0.79	1.37
EAST ASIA AND THE PACIFIC	80,836	74,766	101,864	128,668	118,536	3.94	-7.87
North-East Asia	70,715	64,860	87,896	111,416	101,291	3.37	-9.09
Japan	70,715	64,860	87,896	111,416	101,291	3.37	-9.09
Australasia	10,121	9,906	13,968	17,252	17,245	0.57	-0.04
Australia	10,121	9,906	13,968	17,252	17,245	0.57	-0.04
EUROPE	2,342,760	2,287,370	2,553,355	2,547,218	2,543,725	84.53	-0.14
Central/Eastern Europe	328,000	320,128	332,352	370,809	430,955	14.32	16.22
Bulgaria	12,534	11,964	13,695	16,559	16,327	0.54	-1.40
Czech Republic	40,078	44,146	49,092	51,561	57,643	1.92	11.80
Poland	74,378	57,209	62,918	71,102	71,550	2.38	0.63
Romania	83,821	81,480	92,248	105,574	131,719	4.38	24.76
Russian Federation	43,566	49,747	44,569	45,297	55,829	1.86	23.25
Slovakia	24,888	24,740	27,128	31,239	33,777	1.12	8.12
Ukraine	48,735	50,842	42,702	49,477	64,110	2.13	29.58
Northern Europe	272,491	275,092	362,605	453,189	419,505	13.94	-7.43
Denmark	27,133	28,299	29,963	30,800	31,711	1.05	2.96
Finland	39,603	37,813	42,492	40,756	37,769	1.26	-7.33
Norway	19,753	20,920	23,602	28,318	31,896	1.06	12.64
Sweden	47,207	51,996	53,692	59,542	57,224	1.90	-3.89
United Kingdom	138,795	136,064	212,856	293,773	260,905	8.67	-11.19
Southern Europe	406,541	410,690	465,727	463,845	421,400	14.00	-9.15
Croatia	29,297	31,133	35,462	29,343	26,211	0.87	-10.67
Greece	26,728	29,762	34,013	35,490	38,370	1.28	8.11
Italy	167,080	176,306	220,201	215,911	186,256	6.19	-13.73
Slovenia	17,726	19,188	18,172	17,227	15,401	0.51	-10.60
Spain	88,013	91,617	117,573	129,322	128,979	4.29	-0.27
Serbia and Montenegro	77,697	62,684	40,306	36,552	26,183	0.87	-28.37
Western Europe	1,147,636	1,103,562	1,168,062	1,167,118	1,049,108	34.86	-10.11
Austria	221,188	217,295	221,246	218,741	222,690	7.40	1.81
Belgium	33,194	34,395	42,859	42,620	39,163	1.30	-8.11
France	105,161	110,704	137,707	132,446	121,884	4.05	-7.97
Germany	664,287	623,636	635,894	648,800	553,990	18.41	-14.61
Netherlands	73,580	67,388	69,263	69,497	63,882	2.12	-8.08
Switzerland	50,226	50,144	61,093	55,014	47,499	1.58	-13.66
East Mediterranean Europe	80,136	80,432	95,143	76,028	67,105	2.23	-11.74
Israel	66,793	61,822	77,829	56,432	46,520	1.55	-17.56
Turkey	13,343	18,610	17,314	19,596	20,585	0.68	5.05
Other Europe	107,956	97,466	129,466	16,229	155,652	5.17	859.10

HUNGARY

3. Arrivals of non-resident tourists in hotels and similar establishments, by nationality

	2002	2003	2004	2005	2006	Market share 06	% Change 06-05
Other countries of Europe	107,956	97,466	129,466	16,229	155,652	5.17	859.10
REGION NOT SPECIFIED	64,467	63,476	88,247	242,857	104,757	3.48	-56.86
Not Specified	64,467	63,476	88,247	242,857	104,757	3.48	-56.86
Other countries of the World	64,467	63,476	88,247	242,857	104,757	3.48	-56.86

Source: World Tourism Organization (UNWTO)

HUNGARY

4. Arrivals of non-resident tourists in all types of accommodation establishments, by nationality

		2002	2003	2004	2005	2006	Market share 06	% Change 06-05
TOTAL	(*)	3,013,116	2,948,224	3,269,868	3,446,362	3,309,753	100.00	-3.96
AFRICA		5,739	5,756	12,379	10,310	7,557	0.23	-26.70
Other Africa		5,739	5,756	12,379	10,310	7,557	0.23	-26.70
All countries of Africa		5,739	5,756	12,379	10,310	7,557	0.23	-26.70
AMERICAS		169,967	173,862	202,180	218,304	244,890	7.40	12.18
North America		148,454	152,016	177,497	193,525	218,919	6.61	13.12
Canada		14,581	13,821	17,377	18,882	23,013	0.70	21.88
United States		133,873	138,195	160,120	174,643	195,906	5.92	12.18
Other Americas		21,513	21,846	24,683	24,779	25,971	0.78	4.81
Other countries of the Americas		21,513	21,846	24,683	24,779	25,971	0.78	4.81
EAST ASIA AND THE PACIFIC		82,781	77,189	104,805	132,564	122,687	3.71	-7.45
North-East Asia		71,331	65,578	88,545	112,127	102,168	3.09	-8.88
Japan		71,331	65,578	88,545	112,127	102,168	3.09	-8.88
Australasia		11,450	11,611	16,260	20,437	20,519	0.62	0.40
Australia		11,450	11,611	16,260	20,437	20,519	0.62	0.40
EUROPE		2,688,940	2,626,677	2,860,588	2,985,842	2,827,586	85.43	-5.30
Central/Eastern Europe		400,930	387,523	389,803	433,100	500,856	15.13	15.64
Bulgaria		13,337	13,184	14,711	17,294	17,326	0.52	0.19
Czech Republic		51,137	55,779	58,994	61,019	68,766	2.08	12.70
Poland		112,442	86,896	90,710	97,826	100,008	3.02	2.23
Romania		89,569	88,913	97,462	113,261	138,925	4.20	22.66
Russian Federation		48,050	53,616	46,484	48,500	59,746	1.81	23.19
Slovakia		34,199	35,520	36,482	42,352	47,334	1.43	11.76
Ukraine		52,196	53,615	44,960	52,848	68,751	2.08	30.09
Northern Europe		302,569	310,703	398,091	487,424	453,637	13.71	-6.93
Denmark		47,638	51,237	52,752	50,190	47,241	1.43	-5.88
Finland		41,596	40,352	44,710	42,925	40,056	1.21	-6.68
Norway		20,460	21,919	24,520	29,338	33,228	1.00	13.26
Sweden		50,212	55,528	56,881	62,571	60,113	1.82	-3.93
United Kingdom		142,663	141,667	219,228	302,400	272,999	8.25	-9.72
Southern Europe		420,428	428,682	483,264	481,654	441,825	13.35	-8.27
Croatia		30,261	33,227	36,684	31,653	28,688	0.87	-9.37
Greece		27,012	30,049	34,502	35,932	39,017	1.18	8.59
Italy		173,877	185,455	229,811	223,893	195,205	5.90	-12.81
Slovenia		18,977	20,568	19,512	18,562	17,014	0.51	-8.34
Spain		90,001	93,947	120,462	131,926	132,798	4.01	0.66
Serbia and Montenegro		80,300	65,436	42,293	39,688	29,103	0.88	-26.67
Western Europe		1,371,161	1,312,852	1,356,137	1,338,078	1,200,248	36.26	-10.30
Austria		247,029	245,448	245,121	242,390	245,831	7.43	1.42
Belgium		39,703	41,387	49,265	48,580	44,830	1.35	-7.72
France		113,136	119,951	149,742	143,159	132,446	4.00	-7.48
Germany		810,059	748,232	744,400	745,672	636,671	19.24	-14.62
Netherlands		106,690	102,743	102,310	99,459	89,079	2.69	-10.44
Switzerland		54,544	55,091	65,299	58,818	51,391	1.55	-12.63
East Mediterranean Europe		80,566	80,985	95,892	76,643	67,842	2.05	-11.48
Israel		67,031	62,162	78,270	56,794	46,864	1.42	-17.48
Turkey		13,535	18,823	17,622	19,849	20,978	0.63	5.69
Other Europe		113,286	105,932	137,401	168,943	163,178	4.93	-3.41

HUNGARY

4. Arrivals of non-resident tourists in all types of accommodation establishments, by nationality

	2002	2003	2004	2005	2006	Market share 06	% Change 06-05
Other countries of Europe	113,286	105,932	137,401	168,943	163,178	4.93	-3.41
REGION NOT SPECIFIED	**65,689**	**64,740**	**89,916**	**99,342**	**107,033**	**3.23**	**7.74**
Not Specified	**65,689**	**64,740**	**89,916**	**99,342**	**107,033**	**3.23**	**7.74**
Other countries of the World	65,689	64,740	89,916	99,342	107,033	3.23	7.74

Source: World Tourism Organization (UNWTO)

HUNGARY

5. Overnight stays of non-resident tourists in hotels and similar establishments, by nationality

	2002	2003	2004	2005	2006	Market share 06	% Change 06-05
TOTAL	8,260,020	8,046,366	8,728,682	9,126,522	8,524,182	100.00	-6.60
AFRICA	18,744	20,032	32,230	30,560	25,504	0.30	-16.54
Other Africa	18,744	20,032	32,230	30,560	25,504	0.30	-16.54
All countries of Africa	18,744	20,032	32,230	30,560	25,504	0.30	-16.54
AMERICAS	493,791	508,616	564,315	610,367	647,326	7.59	6.06
North America	436,676	449,036	500,983	549,020	584,998	6.86	6.55
Canada	45,667	43,002	49,395	51,325	58,914	0.69	14.79
United States	391,009	406,034	451,588	497,695	526,084	6.17	5.70
Other Americas	57,115	59,580	63,332	61,347	62,328	0.73	1.60
Other countries of the Americas	57,115	59,580	63,332	61,347	62,328	0.73	1.60
EAST ASIA AND THE PACIFIC	178,769	174,965	234,761	298,292	255,625	3.00	-14.30
North-East Asia	151,443	146,410	195,635	253,561	209,888	2.46	-17.22
Japan	151,443	146,410	195,635	253,561	209,888	2.46	-17.22
Australasia	27,326	28,555	39,126	44,731	45,737	0.54	2.25
Australia	27,326	28,555	39,126	44,731	45,737	0.54	2.25
EUROPE	7,404,226	7,174,481	7,708,974	7,980,543	7,356,864	86.31	-7.81
Central/Eastern Europe	813,040	793,583	795,254	874,336	997,833	11.71	14.12
Bulgaria	24,654	23,014	32,181	29,962	30,467	0.36	1.69
Czech Republic	110,176	120,803	124,937	139,669	157,807	1.85	12.99
Poland	207,746	139,983	145,408	168,478	178,149	2.09	5.74
Romania	161,792	170,134	172,740	187,666	216,717	2.54	15.48
Russian Federation	143,882	164,989	154,254	159,131	208,433	2.45	30.98
Slovakia	60,360	56,746	61,846	72,258	71,128	0.83	-1.56
Ukraine	104,430	117,914	103,888	117,172	135,132	1.59	15.33
Northern Europe	802,741	810,654	1,052,775	1,301,681	1,187,062	13.93	-8.81
Denmark	96,728	102,239	107,157	107,901	103,657	1.22	-3.93
Finland	126,945	120,001	136,708	132,450	118,006	1.38	-10.91
Norway	61,680	64,188	73,953	89,343	99,971	1.17	11.90
Sweden	137,011	153,361	162,939	172,344	164,968	1.94	-4.28
United Kingdom	380,377	370,865	572,018	799,643	700,460	8.22	-12.40
Southern Europe	996,876	1,019,337	1,172,376	1,184,003	1,068,327	12.53	-9.77
Croatia	58,139	58,580	69,655	62,143	54,785	0.64	-11.84
Greece	69,277	77,808	82,817	87,414	94,987	1.11	8.66
Italy	435,408	461,930	581,948	575,903	497,814	5.84	-13.56
Slovenia	35,258	37,035	34,762	31,899	30,382	0.36	-4.76
Spain	235,381	244,480	310,687	341,015	331,109	3.88	-2.90
Serbia and Montenegro	163,413	139,504	92,507	85,629	59,250	0.70	-30.81
Western Europe	4,250,767	4,012,643	4,042,228	3,977,444	3,506,110	41.13	-11.85
Austria	606,023	575,610	592,407	583,869	594,608	6.98	1.84
Belgium	92,446	96,531	118,229	116,153	108,157	1.27	-6.88
France	247,677	269,993	331,897	321,576	298,124	3.50	-7.29
Germany	2,904,686	2,688,141	2,591,532	2,568,588	2,175,010	25.52	-15.32
Netherlands	219,552	197,900	198,092	194,760	167,126	1.96	-14.19
Switzerland	180,383	184,468	210,071	192,498	163,085	1.91	-15.28
East Mediterranean Europe	246,659	262,169	302,008	233,266	207,518	2.43	-11.04
Israel	210,041	210,998	255,479	181,429	154,697	1.81	-14.73
Turkey	36,618	51,171	46,529	51,837	52,821	0.62	1.90
Other Europe	294,143	276,095	344,333	409,813	390,014	4.58	-4.83

HUNGARY

5. Overnight stays of non-resident tourists in hotels and similar establishments, by nationality

	2002	2003	2004	2005	2006	Market share 06	% Change 06-05
Other countries of Europe	294,143	276,095	344,333	409,813	390,014	4.58	-4.83
REGION NOT SPECIFIED	**164,490**	**168,272**	**188,402**	**206,760**	**238,863**	**2.80**	**15.53**
Not Specified	**164,490**	**168,272**	**188,402**	**206,760**	**238,863**	**2.80**	**15.53**
Other countries of the World	164,490	168,272	188,402	206,760	238,863	2.80	15.53

Source: World Tourism Organization (UNWTO)

HUNGARY

6. Overnight stays of non-resident tourists in all types of accommodation establishments, by nationality

	2002	2003	2004	2005	2006	Market share 06	% Change 06-05
TOTAL (*)	10,360,959	10,040,338	10,508,109	10,778,899	10,045,891	100.00	-6.80
AFRICA	19,492	20,723	33,847	31,917	26,059	0.26	-18.35
Other Africa	19,492	20,723	33,847	31,917	26,059	0.26	-18.35
All countries of Africa	19,492	20,723	33,847	31,917	26,059	0.26	-18.35
AMERICAS	506,221	522,770	580,181	626,591	670,541	6.67	7.01
North America	447,344	461,285	513,809	561,582	603,955	6.01	7.55
Canada	47,900	45,402	52,298	54,432	63,142	0.63	16.00
United States	399,444	415,883	461,511	507,150	540,813	5.38	6.64
Other Americas	58,877	61,485	66,372	65,009	66,586	0.66	2.43
Other countries of the Americas	58,877	61,485	66,372	65,009	66,586	0.66	2.43
EAST ASIA AND THE PACIFIC	183,278	179,785	241,120	306,856	263,916	2.63	-13.99
North-East Asia	152,947	147,734	197,153	255,105	211,587	2.11	-17.06
Japan	152,947	147,734	197,153	255,105	211,587	2.11	-17.06
Australasia	30,331	32,051	43,967	51,751	52,329	0.52	1.12
Australia	30,331	32,051	43,967	51,751	52,329	0.52	1.12
EUROPE	9,485,101	9,145,810	9,458,986	9,602,150	8,840,467	88.00	-7.93
Central/Eastern Europe	1,106,301	1,050,346	978,586	1,085,768	1,238,881	12.33	14.10
Bulgaria	26,817	24,778	34,058	31,249	33,303	0.33	6.57
Czech Republic	143,687	155,381	152,944	166,930	191,520	1.91	14.73
Poland	370,719	246,366	240,722	256,391	276,310	2.75	7.77
Romania	179,241	210,005	188,748	221,417	245,554	2.44	10.90
Russian Federation	178,128	198,629	164,382	182,252	238,702	2.38	30.97
Slovakia	89,699	87,080	86,421	99,556	103,745	1.03	4.21
Ukraine	118,010	128,107	111,311	127,973	149,747	1.49	17.01
Northern Europe	992,536	1,039,404	1,276,225	1,499,150	1,355,678	13.49	-9.57
Denmark	256,605	292,627	292,640	262,807	222,871	2.22	-15.20
Finland	131,620	126,391	142,028	137,508	123,589	1.23	-10.12
Norway	64,105	67,286	76,938	92,882	104,385	1.04	12.38
Sweden	148,801	167,037	175,925	183,746	175,132	1.74	-4.69
United Kingdom	391,405	386,063	588,694	822,207	729,701	7.26	-11.25
Southern Europe	1,029,391	1,060,956	1,214,849	1,229,072	1,118,388	11.13	-9.01
Croatia	60,637	65,654	73,255	67,844	59,771	0.59	-11.90
Greece	69,944	78,774	84,800	88,897	97,019	0.97	9.14
Italy	450,403	480,372	602,368	594,850	519,365	5.17	-12.69
Slovenia	39,009	40,614	37,694	35,159	33,848	0.34	-3.73
Spain	239,584	249,874	318,775	347,396	341,783	3.40	-1.62
Serbia and Montenegro	169,814	145,668	97,957	94,926	66,602	0.66	-29.84
Western Europe	5,799,166	5,434,736	5,316,574	5,126,781	4,511,237	44.91	-12.01
Austria	743,086	718,685	721,128	709,184	712,905	7.10	0.52
Belgium	129,751	138,505	152,276	148,895	140,384	1.40	-5.72
France	266,988	290,278	359,423	346,370	322,971	3.21	-6.76
Germany	4,019,608	3,648,117	3,439,627	3,317,406	2,815,305	28.02	-15.14
Netherlands	440,594	434,272	416,215	395,903	341,199	3.40	-13.82
Switzerland	199,139	204,879	227,905	209,023	178,473	1.78	-14.62
East Mediterranean Europe	248,110	263,936	305,090	235,503	209,851	2.09	-10.89
Israel	210,721	212,179	257,291	182,474	155,692	1.55	-14.68
Turkey	37,389	51,757	47,799	53,029	54,159	0.54	2.13
Other Europe	309,597	296,432	367,662	425,876	406,432	4.05	-4.57

HUNGARY

6. Overnight stays of non-resident tourists in all types of accommodation establishments, by nationality

	2002	2003	2004	2005	2006	Market share 06	% Change 06-05
Other countries of Europe	309,597	296,432	367,662	425,876	406,432	4.05	-4.57
REGION NOT SPECIFIED	**166,867**	**171,250**	**193,975**	**211,385**	**244,908**	**2.44**	**15.86**
Not Specified	**166,867**	**171,250**	**193,975**	**211,385**	**244,908**	**2.44**	**15.86**
Other countries of the World	166,867	171,250	193,975	211,385	244,908	2.44	15.86

Source: World Tourism Organization (UNWTO)

ICELAND

3. Arrivals of non-resident tourists in hotels and similar establishments, by nationality

	2002	2003	2004	2005	2006	Market share 06	% Change 06-05
TOTAL	513,075	569,194	614,923	643,376	714,298	100.00	11.02
AFRICA				894	1,271	0.18	42.17
Other Africa				894	1,271	0.18	42.17
All countries of Africa				894	1,271	0.18	42.17
AMERICAS	60,015	62,478	64,189	71,377	74,349	10.41	4.16
North America	60,015	62,478	64,189	70,212	73,117	10.24	4.14
Canada	4,357	5,459	5,144	4,473	5,902	0.83	31.95
United States	55,658	57,019	59,045	65,739	67,215	9.41	2.25
Other Americas				1,165	1,232	0.17	5.75
Other countries of the Americas				1,165	1,232	0.17	5.75
EAST ASIA AND THE PACIFIC	6,219	8,131	9,398	25,989	28,904	4.05	11.22
North-East Asia	6,219	8,131	9,398	18,386	18,951	2.65	3.07
China				5,519	7,208	1.01	30.60
Japan	6,219	8,131	9,398	12,867	11,743	1.64	-8.74
Australasia				2,969	3,728	0.52	25.56
Australia				2,969	3,728	0.52	25.56
Other East Asia and the Pacific				4,634	6,225	0.87	34.33
Other countries of Asia				4,634	6,225	0.87	34.33
EUROPE	415,968	455,784	502,877	509,221	553,839	77.54	8.76
Northern Europe	153,771	167,377	184,748	191,790	214,644	30.05	11.92
Denmark	30,025	31,158	36,801	40,590	46,759	6.55	15.20
Finland	7,076	6,176	7,603	9,049	9,122	1.28	0.81
Ireland	2,045	2,369	2,757	2,800	3,604	0.50	28.71
Norway	23,632	26,640	28,064	27,549	30,672	4.29	11.34
Sweden	26,392	28,315	30,456	33,748	31,096	4.35	-7.86
United Kingdom	64,601	72,719	79,067	78,054	93,391	13.07	19.65
Southern Europe	42,666	51,762	55,985	58,574	64,724	9.06	10.50
Italy	31,425	36,948	37,073	36,823	37,777	5.29	2.59
Spain	11,241	14,814	18,912	21,751	26,947	3.77	23.89
Western Europe	207,575	223,082	237,318	236,332	244,128	34.18	3.30
Austria	7,196	7,894	9,292	9,750	9,276	1.30	-4.86
Belgium	5,386	5,042	6,509	6,472	6,444	0.90	-0.43
France	56,364	58,208	60,489	56,757	58,970	8.26	3.90
Germany	96,446	105,510	109,621	112,056	113,913	15.95	1.66
Netherlands	24,985	27,726	27,490	30,443	35,131	4.92	15.40
Switzerland	17,198	18,702	23,917	20,854	20,394	2.86	-2.21
Other Europe	11,956	13,563	24,826	22,525	30,343	4.25	34.71
Other countries of Europe	11,956	13,563	24,826	22,525	30,343	4.25	34.71
REGION NOT SPECIFIED	30,873	42,801	38,459	35,895	55,935	7.83	55.83
Not Specified	30,873	42,801	38,459	35,895	55,935	7.83	55.83
Other countries of the World	30,873	42,801	38,459	35,895	55,935	7.83	55.83

Source: World Tourism Organization (UNWTO)

ICELAND

4. Arrivals of non-resident tourists in all types of accommodation establishments, by nationality

	2002	2003	2004	2005	2006	Market share 06	% Change 06-05
TOTAL	704,633	771,323	836,230	871,401	970,821	100.00	11.41
AFRICA				1,104	1,508	0.16	36.59
Other Africa				1,104	1,508	0.16	36.59
All countries of Africa				1,104	1,508	0.16	36.59
AMERICAS	69,342	72,174	74,857	84,839	86,650	8.93	2.13
North America	69,342	72,174	74,857	83,400	85,123	8.77	2.07
Canada	5,813	7,086	6,855	6,501	8,016	0.83	23.30
United States	63,529	65,088	68,002	76,899	77,107	7.94	0.27
Other Americas				1,439	1,527	0.16	6.12
Other countries of the Americas				1,439	1,527	0.16	6.12
EAST ASIA AND THE PACIFIC	7,048	9,013	10,520	29,723	32,943	3.39	10.83
North-East Asia	7,048	9,013	10,520	19,698	20,425	2.10	3.69
China				5,843	7,721	0.80	32.14
Japan	7,048	9,013	10,520	13,855	12,704	1.31	-8.31
Australasia				4,490	5,410	0.56	20.49
Australia				4,490	5,410	0.56	20.49
Other East Asia and the Pacific				5,535	7,108	0.73	28.42
Other countries of Asia				5,535	7,108	0.73	28.42
EUROPE	593,315	642,762	706,580	714,982	785,148	80.87	9.81
Northern Europe	192,197	208,869	233,281	242,606	266,670	27.47	9.92
Denmark	40,126	41,588	49,242	53,917	60,074	6.19	11.42
Finland	8,613	7,536	9,624	11,149	10,876	1.12	-2.45
Ireland	2,826	3,178	3,917	4,514	4,847	0.50	7.38
Norway	28,701	32,589	34,230	33,030	35,750	3.68	8.23
Sweden	32,285	34,357	37,779	41,680	38,736	3.99	-7.06
United Kingdom	79,646	89,621	98,489	98,316	116,387	11.99	18.38
Southern Europe	58,271	70,487	76,628	78,908	94,359	9.72	19.58
Italy	41,385	48,324	49,425	48,361	53,007	5.46	9.61
Spain	16,886	22,163	27,203	30,547	41,352	4.26	35.37
Western Europe	323,658	342,889	363,411	361,169	382,663	39.42	5.95
Austria	12,048	13,243	15,770	16,111	15,828	1.63	-1.76
Belgium	9,044	8,974	11,049	12,159	11,850	1.22	-2.54
France	88,279	90,536	94,817	88,972	97,068	10.00	9.10
Germany	149,202	159,712	164,304	167,228	174,701	18.00	4.47
Netherlands	38,943	41,855	42,117	44,990	52,177	5.37	15.97
Switzerland	26,142	28,569	35,354	31,709	31,039	3.20	-2.11
Other Europe	19,189	20,517	33,260	32,299	41,456	4.27	28.35
Other countries of Europe	19,189	20,517	33,260	32,299	41,456	4.27	28.35
REGION NOT SPECIFIED	34,928	47,374	44,273	40,753	64,572	6.65	58.45
Not Specified	34,928	47,374	44,273	40,753	64,572	6.65	58.45
Other countries of the World	34,928	47,374	44,273	40,753	64,572	6.65	58.45

Source: World Tourism Organization (UNWTO)

ICELAND

5. Overnight stays of non-resident tourists in hotels and similar establishments, by nationality

	2002	2003	2004	2005	2006	Market share 06	% Change 06-05
TOTAL	970,256	1,070,066	1,145,809	1,208,030	1,340,822	100.00	10.99
AFRICA				2,069	2,628	0.20	27.02
Other Africa				2,069	2,628	0.20	27.02
All countries of Africa				2,069	2,628	0.20	27.02
AMERICAS	128,203	127,489	133,451	150,189	154,348	11.51	2.77
North America	128,203	127,489	133,451	148,073	151,709	11.31	2.46
Canada	10,438	13,346	11,500	9,264	12,201	0.91	31.70
United States	117,765	114,143	121,951	138,809	139,508	10.40	0.50
Other Americas				2,116	2,639	0.20	24.72
Other countries of the Americas				2,116	2,639	0.20	24.72
EAST ASIA AND THE PACIFIC	11,782	15,374	16,906	49,765	54,702	4.08	9.92
North-East Asia	11,782	15,374	16,906	34,724	35,333	2.64	1.75
China				11,022	13,863	1.03	25.78
Japan	11,782	15,374	16,906	23,702	21,470	1.60	-9.42
Australasia				5,711	7,188	0.54	25.86
Australia				5,711	7,188	0.54	25.86
Other East Asia and the Pacific				9,330	12,181	0.91	30.56
Other countries of Asia				9,330	12,181	0.91	30.56
EUROPE	775,693	847,911	924,918	944,731	1,029,649	76.79	8.99
Northern Europe	362,034	388,853	419,537	438,877	481,296	35.90	9.67
Denmark	61,560	63,701	72,529	80,825	90,514	6.75	11.99
Finland	19,772	18,754	19,749	24,784	24,673	1.84	-0.45
Ireland	4,386	5,934	6,921	6,448	7,702	0.57	19.45
Norway	58,629	64,320	68,090	67,040	71,537	5.34	6.71
Sweden	66,539	68,764	75,451	85,845	76,520	5.71	-10.86
United Kingdom	151,148	167,380	176,797	173,935	210,350	15.69	20.94
Southern Europe	56,991	68,858	73,905	79,247	86,256	6.43	8.84
Italy	40,978	47,683	48,156	48,912	49,237	3.67	0.66
Spain	16,013	21,175	25,749	30,335	37,019	2.76	22.03
Western Europe	331,472	362,178	381,423	380,293	392,089	29.24	3.10
Austria	11,233	11,383	13,303	13,594	13,176	0.98	-3.07
Belgium	9,507	8,487	11,169	11,099	10,370	0.77	-6.57
France	77,481	81,784	84,412	81,890	82,660	6.16	0.94
Germany	163,721	180,289	189,519	191,535	193,318	14.42	0.93
Netherlands	42,226	48,461	44,421	49,355	56,875	4.24	15.24
Switzerland	27,304	31,774	38,599	32,820	35,690	2.66	8.74
Other Europe	25,196	28,022	50,053	46,314	70,008	5.22	51.16
Other countries of Europe	25,196	28,022	50,053	46,314	70,008	5.22	51.16
REGION NOT SPECIFIED	54,578	79,292	70,534	61,276	99,495	7.42	62.37
Not Specified	54,578	79,292	70,534	61,276	99,495	7.42	62.37
Other countries of the World	54,578	79,292	70,534	61,276	99,495	7.42	62.37

Source: World Tourism Organization (UNWTO)

ICELAND

6. Overnight stays of non-resident tourists in all types of accommodation establishments, by nationality

	2002	2003	2004	2005	2006	Market share 06	% Change 06-05
TOTAL	1,256,518	1,376,788	1,478,848	1,550,183	1,719,140	100.00	10.90
AFRICA				2,403	2,990	0.17	24.43
Other Africa				2,403	2,990	0.17	24.43
All countries of Africa				2,403	2,990	0.17	24.43
AMERICAS	143,739	143,468	150,682	171,670	173,352	10.08	0.98
North America	143,739	143,468	150,682	169,115	170,089	9.89	0.58
Canada	12,653	15,782	14,113	12,309	15,329	0.89	24.53
United States	131,086	127,686	136,569	156,806	154,760	9.00	-1.30
Other Americas				2,555	3,263	0.19	27.71
Other countries of the Americas				2,555	3,263	0.19	27.71
EAST ASIA AND THE PACIFIC	13,072	16,746	18,639	55,528	61,053	3.55	9.95
North-East Asia	13,072	16,746	18,639	36,773	37,777	2.20	2.73
China				11,506	14,646	0.85	27.29
Japan	13,072	16,746	18,639	25,267	23,131	1.35	-8.45
Australasia				8,035	9,877	0.57	22.92
Australia				8,035	9,877	0.57	22.92
Other East Asia and the Pacific				10,720	13,399	0.78	24.99
Other countries of Asia				10,720	13,399	0.78	24.99
EUROPE	1,038,506	1,130,206	1,230,128	1,252,668	1,370,096	79.70	9.37
Northern Europe	422,764	456,325	498,413	519,622	565,639	32.90	8.86
Denmark	77,188	81,102	92,068	101,947	112,640	6.55	10.49
Finland	22,024	20,937	22,885	27,909	27,404	1.59	-1.81
Ireland	5,383	7,047	8,752	8,900	9,427	0.55	5.92
Norway	66,894	73,613	78,520	75,812	80,773	4.70	6.54
Sweden	75,901	78,549	86,934	98,414	88,805	5.17	-9.76
United Kingdom	175,374	195,077	209,254	206,640	246,590	14.34	19.33
Southern Europe	78,539	94,816	102,938	107,591	125,576	7.30	16.72
Italy	54,202	63,007	65,094	64,785	69,353	4.03	7.05
Spain	24,337	31,809	37,844	42,806	56,223	3.27	31.34
Western Europe	501,580	540,166	566,191	563,918	592,736	34.48	5.11
Austria	18,236	19,473	22,827	23,097	22,368	1.30	-3.16
Belgium	14,500	13,904	17,665	18,917	17,742	1.03	-6.21
France	122,090	127,889	131,787	127,517	132,808	7.73	4.15
Germany	243,497	262,218	271,919	274,234	286,728	16.68	4.56
Netherlands	63,211	70,568	66,691	71,772	82,525	4.80	14.98
Switzerland	40,046	46,114	55,302	48,381	50,565	2.94	4.51
Other Europe	35,623	38,899	62,586	61,537	86,145	5.01	39.99
Other countries of Europe	35,623	38,899	62,586	61,537	86,145	5.01	39.99
REGION NOT SPECIFIED	61,201	86,368	79,399	67,914	111,649	6.49	64.40
Not Specified	61,201	86,368	79,399	67,914	111,649	6.49	64.40
Other countries of the World	61,201	86,368	79,399	67,914	111,649	6.49	64.40

Source: World Tourism Organization (UNWTO)

INDIA

1. Arrivals of non-resident tourists at national borders, by nationality

	2002	2003	2004	2005	2006	Market share 06	% Change 06-05
TOTAL (*)	2,384,364	2,726,214	3,457,477	3,918,610	4,447,167	100.00	13.49
AFRICA	80,317	89,201	111,711	130,753	137,285	3.09	5.00
East Africa	47,377	50,209	57,639	63,375	66,367	1.49	4.72
Burundi	24	17	69	83	199		139.76
Comoros	71	65	56	192	113		-41.15
Ethiopia	2,535	2,301	2,661	3,248	3,140	0.07	-3.33
Eritrea		336	344	265	356	0.01	34.34
Djibouti					340	0.01	
Kenya	17,275	16,563	17,538	19,816	20,313	0.46	2.51
Madagascar	78	100	106	274	283	0.01	3.28
Malawi	202	252	306	355	520	0.01	46.48
Mauritius	14,425	16,308	19,823	19,760	20,607	0.46	4.29
Mozambique	667	810	1,044	1,293	1,331	0.03	2.94
Reunion	10	23	10	58	86		48.28
Rwanda	152	138	130	127	363	0.01	185.83
Seychelles	687	1,030	1,383	1,402	1,425	0.03	1.64
Somalia	207	346	357	508	439	0.01	-13.58
Zimbabwe	639	622	851	1,030	1,133	0.03	10.00
Uganda	1,492	1,400	1,540	1,923	1,696	0.04	-11.80
United Republic of Tanzania	7,459	8,515	9,953	11,193	11,954	0.27	6.80
Zambia	1,126	1,383	1,468	1,848	2,069	0.05	11.96
Other countries of East Africa	328						
Central Africa	1,220	1,204	1,212	3,250	3,471	0.08	6.80
Angola	254	454	474	559	385	0.01	-31.13
Cameroon	53	69	81	151	217		43.71
Central African Republic	434	207	198	1,656	1,861	0.04	12.38
Chad	264	179	121	362	348	0.01	-3.87
Congo	143	203	244	369	447	0.01	21.14
Democratic Republic of the Congo			2	7			
Equatorial Guinea	11	12	42	24	29		20.83
Gabon	35	35	23	73	153		109.59
Sao Tome and Principe	26	45	27	49	31		-36.73
North Africa	3,459	4,044	6,222	6,647	7,646	0.17	15.03
Algeria	451	514	795	778	1,174	0.03	50.90
Morocco	509	882	1,144	1,304	1,225	0.03	-6.06
Sudan	1,899	2,025	2,487	3,660	4,355	0.10	18.99
Tunisia	600	623	1,796	905	892	0.02	-1.44
Southern Africa	18,920	24,906	33,460	41,309	43,940	0.99	6.37
Botswana	216	359	421	656	490	0.01	-25.30
Lesotho	123	218	192	272	279	0.01	2.57
Namibia	1	2	112		248	0.01	
South Africa	18,238	23,873	32,148	39,229	41,954	0.94	6.95
Swaziland	342	454	587	1,152	969	0.02	-15.89
West Africa	9,341	8,838	13,178	16,172	15,000	0.34	-7.25
Cape Verde	5	9	7	22	32		45.45
Benin			148	589	24		-95.93
Gambia	172	215	111	398	307	0.01	-22.86
Ghana	708	759	925	1,039	1,237	0.03	19.06
Guinea	144		171	158	159		0.63
Cote D'Ivoire	246		243	489	397	0.01	-18.81
Liberia	58	133	123	172	164		-4.65
Mali	54	57	2,541	114	162		42.11
Mauritania	447	315	364	429	1,095	0.02	155.24

INDIA

1. Arrivals of non-resident tourists at national borders, by nationality

	2002	2003	2004	2005	2006	Market share 06	% Change 06-05
Niger	771	689	1,178	1,188	529	0.01	-55.47
Nigeria	5,997	5,713	6,659	10,049	9,348	0.21	-6.98
Guinea-Bissau	23	26	25	89	98		10.11
Senegal	399	394	391	552	694	0.02	25.72
Sierra Leone	150	122	118	565	509	0.01	-9.91
Togo		103			163		
Burkina Faso	16		34	29	81		179.31
Other countries of West Africa	151	303	140	290	1		-99.66
Other Africa					**861**	**0.02**	
Other countries of Africa					861	0.02	
AMERICAS	**459,462**	**540,128**	**690,169**	**804,394**	**912,051**	**20.51**	**13.38**
Caribbean	**3,750**	**4,168**	**3,733**	**8,191**	**6,025**	**0.14**	**-26.44**
Antigua and Barbuda	7	6	3	19	17		-10.53
Bahamas	75	31	36	93	105		12.90
Barbados	131	163	201	203	269	0.01	32.51
Cuba	156	160	179	202	234	0.01	15.84
Dominican Republic	102	191	265	836	347	0.01	-58.49
Grenada	2,006	1,938	1,233	3,865	2,319	0.05	-40.00
Guadeloupe	4	3	7	23	11		-52.17
Haiti	38	52	101	144	95		-34.03
Jamaica	275	285	340	374	514	0.01	37.43
Martinique	175	194	145	352	189		-46.31
Netherlands Antilles			89	465			
Saint Lucia	48	30	38	56	153		173.21
Trinidad and Tobago	635	753	1,095	1,559	1,508	0.03	-3.27
Other countries of the Caribbean	98	362	1		264	0.01	
Central America	**1,505**	**2,402**	**2,908**	**3,749**	**2,933**	**0.07**	**-21.77**
Belize	246	355	388	815	624	0.01	-23.44
Costa Rica	278	379	389	528	444	0.01	-15.91
El Salvador	404	946	1,078	1,396	575	0.01	-58.81
Guatemala	131	122	390	177	263	0.01	48.59
Honduras	42	81	80	123	225	0.01	82.93
Nicaragua	40	55	91	107	80		-25.23
Panama	364	464	492	603	722	0.02	19.73
North America	**444,885**	**522,037**	**666,574**	**774,206**	**879,808**	**19.78**	**13.64**
Canada	93,598	107,671	135,884	157,643	176,567	3.97	12.00
Mexico	3,105	3,563	4,570	5,398	6,502	0.15	20.45
United States	348,182	410,803	526,120	611,165	696,739	15.67	14.00
South America	**9,312**	**11,521**	**16,954**	**18,248**	**23,285**	**0.52**	**27.60**
Argentina	1,359	1,805	2,799	3,313	4,493	0.10	35.62
Bolivia	42	44	154	52	175		236.54
Brazil	3,622	4,528	7,397	7,005	9,148	0.21	30.59
Chile	829	1,035	1,636	1,637	1,812	0.04	10.69
Colombia	1,019	1,364	1,725	1,995	2,535	0.06	27.07
Ecuador	165	232	226	318	415	0.01	30.50
Guyana	316	367	359	440	413	0.01	-6.14
Paraguay	162	212	161	161	305	0.01	89.44
Peru	345	463	639	662	815	0.02	23.11
Suriname	317	344	614	738	750	0.02	1.63
Uruguay	487	360	336	398	688	0.02	72.86
Venezuela	649	767	908	1,529	1,518	0.03	-0.72
Other countries of South America					218		
Other Americas	**10**						

INDIA

1. Arrivals of non-resident tourists at national borders, by nationality

	2002	2003	2004	2005	2006	Market share 06	% Change 06-05
Other countries of the Americas	10						
EAST ASIA AND THE PACIFIC	**327,976**	**393,281**	**511,681**	**584,753**	**702,147**	**15.79**	**20.08**
North-East Asia	**115,424**	**150,506**	**201,627**	**223,567**	**282,985**	**6.36**	**26.58**
China	15,422	21,152	34,100	44,897	62,330	1.40	38.83
Taiwan (Province of China)	7,785	12,685	18,179	18,894	26,503	0.60	40.27
Hong Kong, China	581	1,070	1,965	1,908	1,466	0.03	-23.17
Japan	59,709	77,996	96,851	103,082	119,292	2.68	15.73
Korea, Dem. People's Republic of	2,178	1,398	1,479	3,690	1,513	0.03	-59.00
Korea, Republic of	29,374	35,584	47,835	49,895	70,407	1.58	41.11
Macao, China	47	20	73	104	78		-25.00
Mongolia	321	595	1,143	1,043	1,395	0.03	33.75
Other countries of North-East Asia	7	6	2	54	1		-98.15
South-East Asia	**149,291**	**168,926**	**209,110**	**241,408**	**281,726**	**6.33**	**16.70**
Brunei Darussalam	205	278	498	604	538	0.01	-10.93
Myanmar	3,037	3,609	4,932	5,652	7,734	0.17	36.84
Cambodia	329	549	640	578	804	0.02	39.10
Indonesia	8,694	9,078	11,408	12,640	16,990	0.38	34.41
Lao People's Democratic Republic	125	181		215	164		-23.72
Malaysia	63,748	70,750	84,390	96,276	107,286	2.41	11.44
Philippines	7,647	8,091	10,492	11,422	15,644	0.35	36.96
Singapore	44,306	48,368	60,710	68,666	82,574	1.86	20.25
Viet Nam	1,551	2,268	2,598	3,377	3,369	0.08	-0.24
Thailand	19,649	25,754	33,442	41,978	46,623	1.05	11.07
Australasia	**61,554**	**72,013**	**98,370**	**116,721**	**133,360**	**3.00**	**14.26**
Australia	50,743	58,730	81,608	96,258	109,867	2.47	14.14
New Zealand	10,811	13,283	16,762	20,463	23,493	0.53	14.81
Melanesia	**1,561**	**1,553**	**2,329**	**2,735**	**2,707**	**0.06**	**-1.02**
Solomon Islands		34	27	28	58		107.14
Fiji	1,499	1,519	2,003	2,326	2,412	0.05	3.70
Papua New Guinea	62		299	381	237	0.01	-37.80
Micronesia	**14**		**20**	**28**	**239**	**0.01**	**753.57**
Kiribati	9		7	14	74		428.57
Nauru	5		13	14	165		1,078.57
Polynesia	**64**		**202**	**250**	**989**	**0.02**	**295.60**
Niue	9		15	68	52		-23.53
Tonga			140	41	16		-60.98
Tuvalu	47		41	117	483	0.01	312.82
Samoa	8		6	24	438	0.01	1,725.00
Other East Asia and the Pacific	**68**	**283**	**23**	**44**	**141**		**220.45**
Other countries East Asia/Pacific	68	283	23	44	141		220.45
EUROPE	**796,613**	**942,061**	**1,257,239**	**1,434,983**	**1,662,362**	**37.38**	**15.85**
Central/Eastern Europe	**39,167**	**54,418**	**80,547**	**99,505**	**119,107**	**2.68**	**19.70**
Azerbaijan	265	418	456	617	755	0.02	22.37
Armenia	123	242	264	327	371	0.01	13.46
Bulgaria	1,124	1,300	1,304	1,706	2,087	0.05	22.33
Belarus	331			621	1,077	0.02	73.43
Czech Republic/Slovakia	2,561	3,466	4,114	4,783			
Czech Republic					5,760	0.13	
Estonia	333	478	593	892	2,234	0.05	150.45
Georgia	238	360	438	479	659	0.01	37.58
Hungary	1,557	1,997	3,527	3,704	4,262	0.10	15.06

INDIA

1. Arrivals of non-resident tourists at national borders, by nationality

	2002	2003	2004	2005	2006	Market share 06	% Change 06-05
Kazakhstan	1,763	2,332	2,468	3,376	3,883	0.09	15.02
Kyrgyzstan	533	548	568	553	543	0.01	-1.81
Latvia	286	375	605	1,059	1,409	0.03	33.05
Lithuania	269	445	720	926	1,331	0.03	43.74
Republic of Moldova	58	66	245	138	227	0.01	64.49
Poland	4,468	6,336	8,445	10,983	14,808	0.33	34.83
Romania	1,144	1,495	1,938	2,368	3,102	0.07	31.00
Russian Federation	18,643	28,246	47,077	56,446	62,203	1.40	10.20
Slovakia				35	1,118	0.03	3,094.29
Tajikistan	394	370	447	961	899	0.02	-6.45
Turkmenistan	188	257	454	550	1,193	0.03	116.91
Ukraine	3,448	4,043	5,103	6,769	8,479	0.19	25.26
Uzbekistan	1,432	1,644	1,749	2,149	2,170	0.05	0.98
Other countries Central/East Europ	9		32	63	537	0.01	752.38
Northern Europe	**434,571**	**484,002**	**630,354**	**738,097**	**846,351**	**19.03**	**14.67**
Denmark	10,230	11,327	15,805	20,170	21,592	0.49	7.05
Finland	7,673	8,001	12,525	16,258	22,860	0.51	40.61
Iceland	120	176	245	414	755	0.02	82.37
Ireland	5,793	7,083	8,996	10,052	14,936	0.34	48.59
Norway	7,475	8,400	10,631	11,194	14,216	0.32	27.00
Sweden	15,330	18,098	26,154	28,799	36,013	0.81	25.05
United Kingdom	387,846	430,917	555,998	651,210	734,240	16.51	12.75
Other countries of Northern Europe	104				1,739	0.04	
Southern Europe	**69,135**	**91,380**	**126,165**	**132,909**	**156,942**	**3.53**	**18.08**
Albania	57	72	112	242	228	0.01	-5.79
Andorra	24	26	42	39	100		156.41
Croatia	730	892	1,338	1,308	2,202	0.05	68.35
Greece	3,207	3,455	4,468	4,793	5,146	0.12	7.36
Holy See			25	7			
Italy	37,136	46,908	65,561	67,642	79,978	1.80	18.24
Malta	412	511	535	1,542	1,284	0.03	-16.73
Portugal	7,262	8,158	10,648	11,457	13,108	0.29	14.41
Slovenia					1,129	0.03	
Spain	19,567	30,551	42,895	45,247	53,520	1.20	18.28
Serbia and Montenegro	731	807	541	632			
Other countries Southern Europe	9				247	0.01	
Western Europe	**224,538**	**274,200**	**373,657**	**413,053**	**486,180**	**10.93**	**17.70**
Austria	13,801	16,903	21,093	27,187	28,045	0.63	3.16
Belgium	13,945	17,309	24,007	25,596	29,156	0.66	13.91
France	78,194	97,654	131,824	152,258	175,345	3.94	15.16
Germany	64,891	76,868	116,679	120,243	156,808	3.53	30.41
Luxembourg	432	438	583	703	769	0.02	9.39
Netherlands	31,669	40,565	51,211	52,755	58,611	1.32	11.10
Switzerland	21,606	24,463	28,260	34,311	37,446	0.84	9.14
East Mediterranean Europe	**29,202**	**38,061**	**46,516**	**51,419**	**53,782**	**1.21**	**4.60**
Cyprus	345	376	425	647	826	0.02	27.67
Israel	25,503	32,157	39,083	42,866	42,735	0.96	-0.31
Turkey	3,354	5,528	7,008	7,906	10,221	0.23	29.28
MIDDLE EAST	**66,051**	**68,917**	**80,073**	**86,450**	**98,439**	**2.21**	**13.87**
Middle East	**66,051**	**68,917**	**80,073**	**86,450**	**98,439**	**2.21**	**13.87**
Bahrain	3,754	4,182	4,414	4,923	4,793	0.11	-2.64
Palestine	354		672	314	832	0.02	164.97
Iraq	767	726	1,153	1,968	2,432	0.05	23.58
Jordan	1,768	1,686	2,400	3,333	3,933	0.09	18.00

INDIA

1. Arrivals of non-resident tourists at national borders, by nationality

	2002	2003	2004	2005	2006	Market share 06	% Change 06-05
Kuwait	1,838	2,361	2,965	3,103	3,773	0.08	21.59
Lebanon	1,211	2,081	2,257	2,208	2,496	0.06	13.04
Libyan Arab Jamahiriya				510	594	0.01	16.47
Oman	13,256	12,352	14,927	14,979	17,849	0.40	19.16
Qatar	1,215	1,434	1,788	2,176	2,392	0.05	9.93
Saudi Arabia	8,663	9,961	11,929	12,444	14,006	0.31	12.55
Syrian Arab Republic	1,452	1,661	2,289	2,385	2,645	0.06	10.90
United Arab Emirates	22,027	21,374	22,668	24,560	27,593	0.62	12.35
Egypt	2,688	3,382	3,781	4,048	5,528	0.12	36.56
Yemen	6,770	7,717	8,830	9,499	9,573	0.22	0.78
Other countries of Middle East	288						
SOUTH ASIA	**630,653**	**666,889**	**790,698**	**841,969**	**908,916**	**20.44**	**7.95**
South Asia	**630,653**	**666,889**	**790,698**	**841,969**	**908,916**	**20.44**	**7.95**
Afghanistan	6,012	10,079	12,705	14,025	18,799	0.42	34.04
Bangladesh	435,867	454,611	477,446	456,371	484,401	10.89	6.14
Bhutan	4,123	4,082	7,054	6,934	8,502	0.19	22.61
Sri Lanka	108,008	109,098	128,711	136,400	154,813	3.48	13.50
Iran, Islamic Republic of	11,815	17,539	24,733	28,691	29,771	0.67	3.76
Maldives	18,826	18,345	21,099	33,915	37,652	0.85	11.02
Nepal	43,056	42,771	51,534	77,024	91,552	2.06	18.86
Pakistan	2,946	10,364	67,416	88,609	83,426	1.88	-5.85
REGION NOT SPECIFIED	**23,292**	**25,737**	**15,906**	**35,308**	**25,967**	**0.58**	**-26.46**
Not Specified	**23,292**	**25,737**	**15,906**	**35,308**	**25,967**	**0.58**	**-26.46**
Other countries of the World	23,292	25,737	15,906	35,308	25,967	0.58	-26.46

Source: World Tourism Organization (UNWTO)

INDONESIA

1. Arrivals of non-resident tourists at national borders, by nationality

	2002	2003	2004	2005	2006	Market share 06	% Change 06-05
TOTAL	5,033,400	4,467,021	5,321,165	5,002,101	4,871,351	100.00	-2.61
AFRICA	25,410	19,965	25,069	51,673	27,899	0.57	-46.01
Southern Africa				23,327	11,632	0.24	-50.14
South Africa				23,327	11,632	0.24	-50.14
Other Africa	25,410	19,965	25,069	28,346	16,267	0.33	-42.61
Other countries of Africa				28,346	16,267	0.33	-42.61
All countries of Africa	25,410	19,965	25,069				
AMERICAS	244,133	191,271	224,856	283,082	196,038	4.02	-30.75
Central America	9,389	5,182	7,013	33,927	10,889	0.22	-67.90
All countries of Central America	9,389	5,182	7,013	33,927	10,889	0.22	-67.90
North America	220,824	176,040	203,430	215,799	172,229	3.54	-20.19
Canada	45,350	34,405	40,803	46,567	43,077	0.88	-7.49
United States	175,474	141,635	162,627	169,232	129,152	2.65	-23.68
South America	13,920	10,049	14,413	33,356	12,920	0.27	-61.27
All countries of South America	13,920	10,049	14,413	33,356	12,920	0.27	-61.27
EAST ASIA AND THE PACIFIC	3,730,743	3,487,224	4,182,183	3,534,447	3,696,800	75.89	4.59
North-East Asia	1,313,182	1,083,800	1,370,104	1,202,618	1,212,202	24.88	0.80
China	19,840	31,497	39,936	128,681	182,341	3.74	41.70
Taiwan (Province of China)	384,062	345,398	368,680	230,235	226,611	4.65	-1.57
Hong Kong, China	11,518	13,278	62,089	69,339	72,033	1.48	3.89
Japan	679,607	502,997	652,854	511,007	432,989	8.89	-15.27
Korea, Republic of	218,155	190,630	246,545	263,356	298,228	6.12	13.24
South-East Asia	1,954,213	2,026,193	2,294,766	1,896,846	2,199,764	45.16	15.97
Brunei Darussalam	14,957	10,680	13,819	15,454	11,154	0.23	-27.82
Myanmar				2,714	20,538	0.42	656.74
Cambodia				2,419			
Lao People's Democratic Republic				2,261			
Malaysia	397,983	407,958	482,059	564,321	699,124	14.35	23.89
Philippines	61,711	54,549	66,679	100,176	187,711	3.85	87.38
Singapore	1,288,496	1,415,565	1,619,572	1,066,461	1,164,082	23.90	9.15
Viet Nam				9,745	17,154	0.35	76.03
Thailand	43,486	33,762	49,333	73,936	66,864	1.37	-9.57
Other countries of South-East Asia	147,580	103,679	63,304	59,359	33,137	0.68	-44.18
Australasia	432,314	343,517	483,590	406,820	239,713	4.92	-41.08
Australia	384,667	310,742	444,040	356,287	208,205	4.27	-41.56
New Zealand	47,647	32,775	39,550	50,533	31,508	0.65	-37.65
Other East Asia and the Pacific	31,034	33,714	33,723	28,163	45,121	0.93	60.21
Other countries of Asia	30,001	32,640	32,973	26,335	35,331	0.73	34.16
Other countries of Oceania	1,033	1,074	750	1,828	9,790	0.20	435.56
EUROPE	934,140	681,402	789,838	955,917	782,060	16.05	-18.19
Central/Eastern Europe	25,027	24,377	33,339	52,607	78,825	1.62	49.84
Ussr (Former)	12,643	13,930	19,139	47,212	43,167	0.89	-8.57
Other countries Central/East Europ	12,384	10,447	14,200	5,395	35,658	0.73	560.95
Northern Europe	260,027	184,349	196,889	321,576	194,033	3.98	-39.66
Denmark	25,190	18,894	19,234	18,972	12,382	0.25	-34.74
Finland	10,094	7,992	8,766	17,662	9,397	0.19	-46.80
Norway	17,288	11,897	13,338	22,943	14,121	0.29	-38.45
Sweden	34,323	24,205	26,973	47,484	20,478	0.42	-56.87

INDONESIA

1. Arrivals of non-resident tourists at national borders, by nationality

	2002	2003	2004	2005	2006	Market share 06	% Change 06-05
United Kingdom	173,132	121,361	128,578	214,515	137,655	2.83	-35.83
Southern Europe	**118,925**	**70,329**	**88,275**	**86,667**	**80,620**	**1.65**	**-6.98**
Italy	70,608	39,750	50,567	44,058	40,992	0.84	-6.96
Portugal				9,527			
Spain				33,082			
Spain,Portugal	48,317	30,579	37,708		39,628	0.81	
Western Europe	**489,966**	**380,949**	**441,027**	**457,251**	**379,241**	**7.79**	**-17.06**
Austria	18,597	14,643	22,773	15,880	16,692	0.34	5.11
Belgium	26,874	23,975	26,535	23,554	21,869	0.45	-7.15
France	113,434	81,314	97,225	120,122	108,697	2.23	-9.51
Germany	166,501	131,012	152,063	144,983	106,916	2.19	-26.26
Netherlands	125,855	103,866	107,919	105,954	93,147	1.91	-12.09
Switzerland	38,705	26,139	34,512	46,758	31,920	0.66	-31.73
Other Europe	**40,195**	**21,398**	**30,308**	**37,816**	**49,341**	**1.01**	**30.48**
Other countries of Europe	40,195	21,398	30,308	37,816	49,341	1.01	30.48
MIDDLE EAST	**40,676**	**34,189**	**37,506**	**68,440**	**51,479**	**1.06**	**-24.78**
Middle East	**40,676**	**34,189**	**37,506**	**68,440**	**51,479**	**1.06**	**-24.78**
Bahrain	504	419	593	964	213		-77.90
Kuwait				2,097	3,717	0.08	77.25
Qatar				623	1,440	0.03	131.14
Saudi Arabia	38,500	32,167	35,277	45,537	27,821	0.57	-38.90
United Arab Emirates				2,498	2,442	0.05	-2.24
Egypt	1,672	1,603	1,636	4,325	2,493	0.05	-42.36
Yemen				2,956	4,995	0.10	68.98
Other countries of Middle East				9,440	8,358	0.17	-11.46
SOUTH ASIA	**58,298**	**52,970**	**61,713**	**108,542**	**117,075**	**2.40**	**7.86**
South Asia	**58,298**	**52,970**	**61,713**	**108,542**	**117,075**	**2.40**	**7.86**
Bangladesh	4,312	7,557	6,731	23,332	7,407	0.15	-68.25
Sri Lanka	6,052	5,283	5,927	7,366	8,309	0.17	12.80
India	39,314	32,823	41,582	58,359	94,258	1.93	61.51
Pakistan	8,620	7,307	7,473	19,485	7,101	0.15	-63.56

Source: World Tourism Organization (UNWTO)

INDONESIA

1. Arrivals of non-resident tourists at national borders, by country of residence

	2002	2003	2004	2005	2006	Market share 06	% Change 06-05
TOTAL	5,033,400	4,467,021	5,321,165	5,002,101	4,871,351	100.00	-2.61
AFRICA	36,503	30,244	35,507	27,450	22,655	0.47	-17.47
Southern Africa				12,374	7,526	0.15	-39.18
South Africa				12,374	7,526	0.15	-39.18
Other Africa	36,503	30,244	35,507	15,076	15,129	0.31	0.35
Other countries of Africa				15,076	15,129	0.31	0.35
All countries of Africa	36,503	30,244	35,507				
AMERICAS	222,052	175,546	209,779	209,511	184,525	3.79	-11.93
Central America	11,697	7,688	10,087	8,314	8,775	0.18	5.54
All countries of Central America	11,697	7,688	10,087	8,314	8,775	0.18	5.54
North America	193,672	155,380	184,265	186,742	160,881	3.30	-13.85
Canada	32,690	25,104	30,997	28,806	29,918	0.61	3.86
United States	160,982	130,276	153,268	157,936	130,963	2.69	-17.08
South America	16,683	12,478	15,427	14,455	14,869	0.31	2.86
All countries of South America	16,683	12,478	15,427	14,455	14,869	0.31	2.86
EAST ASIA AND THE PACIFIC	3,877,195	3,575,842	4,265,551	3,837,107	3,795,481	77.91	-1.08
North-East Asia	1,346,340	1,159,704	1,358,987	1,203,919	1,176,742	24.16	-2.26
China	36,685	40,870	50,856	112,164	147,245	3.02	31.28
Taiwan (Province of China)	400,334	381,877	384,226	247,037	236,384	4.85	-4.31
Hong Kong, China	78,018	72,128	79,777	74,868	78,386	1.61	4.70
Japan	620,722	463,088	615,720	517,879	419,213	8.61	-19.05
Korea, Republic of	210,581	201,741	228,408	251,971	295,514	6.07	17.28
South-East Asia	2,112,343	2,083,320	2,431,154	2,174,006	2,328,345	47.80	7.10
Brunei Darussalam	15,310	11,408	14,146	16,234	8,965	0.18	-44.78
Malaysia	475,163	466,811	622,541	591,358	769,988	15.81	30.21
Philippines	84,060	76,665	76,742	78,402	74,982	1.54	-4.36
Singapore	1,447,315	1,469,282	1,644,717	1,417,803	1,401,804	28.78	-1.13
Viet Nam				9,729	9,229	0.19	-5.14
Thailand	50,589	42,585	55,024	44,897	42,155	0.87	-6.11
Other countries of South-East Asia	39,906	16,569	17,984	15,583	21,222	0.44	36.19
Australasia	375,918	289,608	432,492	420,115	251,238	5.16	-40.20
Australia	346,245	268,538	406,389	391,862	226,981	4.66	-42.08
New Zealand	29,673	21,070	26,103	28,253	24,257	0.50	-14.14
Other East Asia and the Pacific	42,594	43,210	42,918	39,067	39,156	0.80	0.23
Other countries of Asia	39,906	41,086	40,977	37,228	37,074	0.76	-0.41
Other countries of Oceania	2,688	2,124	1,941	1,839	2,082	0.04	13.21
EUROPE	808,067	605,904	720,706	798,408	730,398	14.99	-8.52
Central/Eastern Europe	21,530	26,584	34,518	27,235	45,727	0.94	67.90
Ussr (Former)	14,155	14,413	18,770	17,138	34,116	0.70	99.07
Other countries Central/East Europ	7,375	12,171	15,748	10,097	11,611	0.24	14.99
Northern Europe	238,486	158,891	179,314	232,537	169,370	3.48	-27.16
Denmark	19,773	16,172	18,289	19,306	12,937	0.27	-32.99
Finland	8,564	6,708	6,936	7,377	8,653	0.18	17.30
Norway	19,301	15,010	15,226	16,819	15,956	0.33	-5.13
Sweden	30,771	22,085	25,285	25,137	21,412	0.44	-14.82
United Kingdom	160,077	98,916	113,578	163,898	110,412	2.27	-32.63
Southern Europe	112,225	61,436	80,719	70,126	82,859	1.70	18.16
Italy	56,857	33,467	42,504	38,118	35,859	0.74	-5.93

INDONESIA

1. Arrivals of non-resident tourists at national borders, by country of residence

	2002	2003	2004	2005	2006	Market share 06	% Change 06-05
Spain,Portugal	55,368	27,969	38,215	32,008	47,000	0.96	46.84
Western Europe	**421,925**	**339,165**	**401,214**	**445,583**	**388,380**	**7.97**	**-12.84**
Austria	18,874	14,220	24,235	19,365	18,759	0.39	-3.13
Belgium	24,079	22,730	26,254	15,084	26,652	0.55	76.69
France	96,844	75,945	91,710	109,567	98,853	2.03	-9.78
Germany	142,649	113,895	134,625	156,414	106,629	2.19	-31.83
Netherlands	110,631	91,446	92,152	114,687	110,272	2.26	-3.85
Switzerland	28,848	20,929	32,238	30,466	27,215	0.56	-10.67
Other Europe	**13,901**	**19,828**	**24,941**	**22,927**	**44,062**	**0.90**	**92.18**
Other countries of Europe	13,901	19,828	24,941	22,927	44,062	0.90	92.18
MIDDLE EAST	**37,987**	**31,371**	**35,783**	**60,601**	**55,033**	**1.13**	**-9.19**
Middle East	**37,987**	**31,371**	**35,783**	**60,601**	**55,033**	**1.13**	**-9.19**
Bahrain	854	479	666	553	531	0.01	-3.98
Kuwait				3,369	2,977	0.06	-11.64
Saudi Arabia	35,500	29,423	33,121	45,917	39,789	0.82	-13.35
Egypt	1,633	1,469	1,996	1,981	2,897	0.06	46.24
Other countries of Middle East				8,781	8,839	0.18	0.66
SOUTH ASIA	**51,596**	**48,114**	**53,839**	**69,024**	**83,259**	**1.71**	**20.62**
South Asia	**51,596**	**48,114**	**53,839**	**69,024**	**83,259**	**1.71**	**20.62**
Bangladesh	4,948	7,698	6,293	9,712	9,662	0.20	-0.51
Sri Lanka	5,289	4,579	5,073	11,071	11,845	0.24	6.99
India	35,063	29,895	36,169	36,679	54,346	1.12	48.17
Pakistan	6,296	5,942	6,304	11,562	7,406	0.15	-35.95

Source: World Tourism Organization (UNWTO)

INDONESIA

3. Arrivals of non-resident tourists in hotels and similar establishments, by country of residence

	2002	2003	2004	2005	2006	Market share 06	% Change 06-05
TOTAL	3,947,445	3,379,748	4,248,015	3,882,635	3,621,000	100.00	-6.74
AFRICA	25,925	19,318	25,830	21,917	13,541	0.37	-38.22
Other Africa	25,925	19,318	25,830	21,917	13,541	0.37	-38.22
All countries of Africa	25,925	19,318	25,830	21,917	13,541	0.37	-38.22
AMERICAS	171,235	128,513	164,177	163,228	137,121	3.79	-15.99
Central America	10,800	6,943	9,424	7,626	8,133	0.22	6.65
All countries of Central America	10,800	6,943	9,424	7,626	8,133	0.22	6.65
North America	145,599	110,939	141,053	142,786	117,341	3.24	-17.82
Canada	25,231	18,496	24,407	22,901	21,390	0.59	-6.60
United States	120,368	92,443	116,646	119,885	95,951	2.65	-19.96
South America	14,836	10,631	13,700	12,816	11,647	0.32	-9.12
All countries of South America	14,836	10,631	13,700	12,816	11,647	0.32	-9.12
EAST ASIA AND THE PACIFIC	3,008,333	2,707,488	3,399,632	2,952,704	2,804,614	77.45	-5.02
North-East Asia	1,104,967	900,691	1,132,948	1,019,638	975,900	26.95	-4.29
China	27,682	31,559	41,826	84,895	110,208	3.04	29.82
Taiwan (Province of China)	321,330	296,075	311,965	211,487	205,732	5.68	-2.72
Hong Kong, China	59,704	53,797	62,060	58,625	57,965	1.60	-1.13
Japan	537,106	370,870	535,648	462,384	370,310	10.23	-19.91
Korea, Republic of	159,145	148,390	181,449	202,247	231,685	6.40	14.56
South-East Asia	1,549,474	1,532,981	1,845,964	1,520,223	1,628,002	44.96	7.09
Brunei Darussalam	11,912	8,074	10,938	10,917	4,699	0.13	-56.96
Malaysia	378,954	377,123	522,921	471,065	587,318	16.22	24.68
Philippines	52,717	45,321	48,289	49,043	45,612	1.26	-7.00
Singapore	1,054,980	1,060,090	1,206,551	934,370	940,013	25.96	0.60
Thailand	41,053	33,209	44,672	35,809	31,935	0.88	-10.82
Other countries of South-East Asia	9,858	9,164	12,593	19,019	18,425	0.51	-3.12
Australasia	322,557	241,971	387,909	373,535	175,823	4.86	-52.93
Australia	297,341	224,355	364,928	350,529	158,674	4.38	-54.73
New Zealand	25,216	17,616	22,981	23,006	17,149	0.47	-25.46
Other East Asia and the Pacific	31,335	31,845	32,811	39,308	24,889	0.69	-36.68
Other countries of Asia	29,308	30,256	31,430	37,901	23,308	0.64	-38.50
Other countries of Oceania	2,027	1,589	1,381	1,407	1,581	0.04	12.37
EUROPE	681,998	476,426	598,346	665,633	581,941	16.07	-12.57
Central/Eastern Europe	24,149	22,251	29,931	23,722	38,159	1.05	60.86
Ussr (Former)	12,117	12,229	16,702	14,851	30,285	0.84	103.93
Other countries Central/East Europ	12,032	10,022	13,229	8,871	7,874	0.22	-11.24
Northern Europe	191,965	125,268	147,158	192,247	134,989	3.73	-29.78
Denmark	15,708	13,610	15,674	16,985	9,399	0.26	-44.66
Finland	6,366	4,860	5,238	5,671	5,470	0.15	-3.54
Norway	15,236	12,969	13,274	14,852	14,028	0.39	-5.55
Sweden	24,200	18,393	22,046	22,093	17,017	0.47	-22.98
United Kingdom	130,455	75,436	90,926	132,646	89,075	2.46	-32.85
Southern Europe	100,420	51,086	68,998	60,840	67,135	1.85	10.35
Italy	48,856	26,555	34,907	31,342	27,429	0.76	-12.48
Spain,Portugal	51,564	24,531	34,091	29,498	39,706	1.10	34.61
Western Europe	337,038	260,293	329,628	368,263	307,399	8.49	-16.53
Austria	15,551	11,633	21,000	16,416	14,887	0.41	-9.31

INDONESIA

3. Arrivals of non-resident tourists in hotels and similar establishments, by country of residence

	2002	2003	2004	2005	2006	Market share 06	% Change 06-05
Belgium	19,595	18,102	22,307	13,500	21,207	0.59	57.09
France	78,483	58,489	75,272	90,101	79,868	2.21	-11.36
Germany	116,745	90,645	113,746	133,537	86,505	2.39	-35.22
Netherlands	82,019	64,645	69,788	88,038	82,511	2.28	-6.28
Switzerland	24,645	16,779	27,515	26,671	22,421	0.62	-15.93
Other Europe	**28,426**	**17,528**	**22,631**	**20,561**	**34,259**	**0.95**	**66.62**
Other countries of Europe	28,426	17,528	22,631	20,561	34,259	0.95	66.62
MIDDLE EAST	**26,188**	**18,865**	**25,086**	**32,965**	**32,628**	**0.90**	**-1.02**
Middle East	**26,188**	**18,865**	**25,086**	**32,965**	**32,628**	**0.90**	**-1.02**
Bahrain	691	321	517	425	375	0.01	-11.76
Saudi Arabia	24,324	17,519	23,019	31,098	25,551	0.71	-17.84
Egypt	1,173	1,025	1,550	1,442	2,083	0.06	44.45
Other countries of Middle East					4,619	0.13	
SOUTH ASIA	**33,766**	**29,138**	**34,944**	**46,188**	**51,155**	**1.41**	**10.75**
South Asia	**33,766**	**29,138**	**34,944**	**46,188**	**51,155**	**1.41**	**10.75**
Bangladesh	3,651	6,378	5,110	6,823	6,840	0.19	0.25
Sri Lanka	3,687	2,932	3,496	7,622	6,666	0.18	-12.54
India	20,811	16,252	22,319	24,226	34,067	0.94	40.62
Pakistan	5,617	3,576	4,019	7,517	3,582	0.10	-52.35

Source: World Tourism Organization (UNWTO)

IRELAND

1. Arrivals of non-resident tourists at national borders, by country of residence

		2002	2003	2004	2005	2006	Market share 06	% Change 06-05
TOTAL		6,477,000	6,764,000	6,953,000	7,334,000	8,001,000	100.00	9.09
AFRICA		29,000	32,000	42,000	39,000	48,000	0.60	23.08
Other Africa		29,000	32,000	42,000	39,000	48,000	0.60	23.08
All countries of Africa		29,000	32,000	42,000	39,000	48,000	0.60	23.08
AMERICAS		860,000	913,000	975,000	956,000	1,058,000	13.22	10.67
North America		844,000	893,000	956,000	937,000	1,034,000	12.92	10.35
Canada		85,000	84,000	89,000	83,000	89,000	1.11	7.23
United States		759,000	809,000	867,000	854,000	945,000	11.81	10.66
Other Americas		16,000	20,000	19,000	19,000	24,000	0.30	26.32
Other countries of the Americas		16,000	20,000	19,000	19,000	24,000	0.30	26.32
EAST ASIA AND THE PACIFIC		201,000	196,000	259,000	226,000	237,000	2.96	4.87
North-East Asia		22,000	22,000	31,000	19,000	19,000	0.24	
Japan		22,000	22,000	31,000	19,000	19,000	0.24	
Australasia		115,000	112,000	149,000	137,000	139,000	1.74	1.46
Australia		96,000	92,000	125,000	111,000	115,000	1.44	3.60
New Zealand		19,000	20,000	24,000	26,000	24,000	0.30	-7.69
Other East Asia and the Pacific		64,000	62,000	79,000	70,000	79,000	0.99	12.86
Other countries East Asia/Pacific		64,000	62,000	79,000	70,000	79,000	0.99	12.86
EUROPE		5,387,000	5,623,000	5,677,000	6,113,000	6,658,000	83.21	8.92
Central/Eastern Europe		13,000	17,000	39,000	125,000	230,000	2.87	84.00
Poland		13,000	17,000	39,000	125,000	230,000	2.87	84.00
Northern Europe		4,117,000	4,263,000	4,221,000	4,210,000	4,406,000	55.07	4.66
Denmark		24,000	27,000					
Finland		17,000	23,000					
Iceland		8,000	3,000					
Norway		16,000	20,000					
Sweden		43,000	51,000					
United Kingdom	(*)	4,009,000	4,139,000	4,095,000	4,210,000	4,406,000	55.07	4.66
Scandinavia				126,000				
Southern Europe		286,000	309,000	343,000	361,000	446,000	5.57	23.55
Greece	(*)	8,000						
Italy		157,000	176,000	186,000	190,000	248,000	3.10	30.53
Portugal		8,000						
Spain		113,000	133,000	157,000	171,000	198,000	2.47	15.79
Western Europe		920,000	916,000	911,000	1,007,000	1,079,000	13.49	7.15
Austria		26,000						
Belgium		96,000	85,000	92,000	84,000	95,000	1.19	13.10
France		298,000	321,000	297,000	310,000	360,000	4.50	16.13
Germany		288,000	302,000	298,000	402,000	417,000	5.21	3.73
Luxembourg		8,000	11,000	8,000				
Netherlands		162,000	146,000	151,000	157,000	155,000	1.94	-1.27
Switzerland		42,000	51,000	65,000	54,000	52,000	0.65	-3.70
Other Europe		51,000	118,000	163,000	410,000	497,000	6.21	21.22
Other countries of Europe		51,000	118,000	163,000	410,000	497,000	6.21	21.22

Source: World Tourism Organization (UNWTO)

IRELAND

6. Overnight stays of non-resident tourists in all types of accommodation establishments, by country of residence

		2002	2003	2004	2005	2006	Market share 06	% Change 06-05
TOTAL	(*)	46,979,000	47,611,000	47,377,000	50,676,000	56,343,000	100.00	11.18
AMERICAS		8,053,000	8,868,000	8,862,000	8,836,000	9,210,000	16.35	4.23
North America		8,053,000	8,868,000	8,862,000	8,836,000	9,210,000	16.35	4.23
Canada		904,000	1,188,000	701,000	896,000	888,000	1.58	-0.89
United States		7,149,000	7,680,000	8,161,000	7,940,000	8,322,000	14.77	4.81
EAST ASIA AND THE PACIFIC		1,693,000	1,685,000	1,835,000	1,118,000	1,084,000	1.92	-3.04
Australasia		1,693,000	1,685,000	1,835,000	1,118,000	1,084,000	1.92	-3.04
Australia					1,118,000	1,084,000	1.92	-3.04
Australia, New Zealand		1,693,000	1,685,000	1,835,000				
EUROPE		35,282,000	34,859,000	34,119,000	38,087,000	43,334,000	76.91	13.78
Northern Europe		21,011,000	19,609,000	18,446,000	17,460,000	18,316,000	32.51	4.90
United Kingdom	(*)	19,924,000	18,464,000	17,573,000	17,460,000	18,316,000	32.51	4.90
Scandinavia	(*)	1,087,000	1,145,000	873,000				
Southern Europe		2,058,000	2,288,000	2,119,000	3,747,000	5,164,000	9.17	37.82
Italy		2,058,000	2,288,000	2,119,000	1,794,000	2,596,000	4.61	44.70
Spain					1,953,000	2,568,000	4.56	31.49
Western Europe		8,677,000	9,025,000	8,505,000	8,820,000	10,186,000	18.08	15.49
Belgium					591,000	748,000	1.33	26.57
France		3,354,000	3,303,000	3,351,000	3,256,000	4,149,000	7.36	27.43
Germany		3,025,000	3,224,000	2,942,000	3,614,000	3,786,000	6.72	4.76
Netherlands		1,185,000	1,101,000	942,000	928,000	1,075,000	1.91	15.84
Switzerland		451,000	663,000	682,000	431,000	428,000	0.76	-0.70
Belgium / Luxembourg		662,000	734,000	588,000				
Other Europe		3,536,000	3,937,000	5,049,000	8,060,000	9,668,000	17.16	19.95
Other countries of Europe		3,536,000	3,937,000	5,049,000	8,060,000	9,668,000	17.16	19.95
REGION NOT SPECIFIED		1,951,000	2,199,000	2,561,000	2,635,000	2,715,000	4.82	3.04
Not Specified		1,951,000	2,199,000	2,561,000	2,635,000	2,715,000	4.82	3.04
Other countries of the World		1,951,000	2,199,000	2,561,000	2,635,000	2,715,000	4.82	3.04

Source: World Tourism Organization (UNWTO)

ISRAEL

1. Arrivals of non-resident tourists at national borders, by country of residence

		2002	2003	2004	2005	2006	Market share 06	% Change 06-05
TOTAL	(*)	861,859	1,063,381	1,505,606	1,902,787	1,825,207	100.00	-4.08
AFRICA		29,323	29,547	40,122	41,450	54,337	2.98	31.09
East Africa		2,516	1,926	3,226	5,705	6,265	0.34	9.82
Burundi		23	11	18	21	18		-14.29
Comoros		1	1	5		2		
Ethiopia		814	115	712	1,785	1,161	0.06	-34.96
Eritrea					3	11		266.67
Kenya		858	866	776	763	1,000	0.05	31.06
Madagascar		26	25	40	36	42		16.67
Malawi		35	56	163	47	22		-53.19
Mauritius		14	15	115	185	112	0.01	-39.46
Mozambique		15	21	14	43	58		34.88
Reunion			1					
Rwanda		44	76	80	58	93	0.01	60.34
Seychelles		13	8	12	18	13		-27.78
Somalia		4	3	9	15	22		46.67
Zimbabwe		339	418	807	2,016	2,948	0.16	46.23
Uganda		124	178	243	286	377	0.02	31.82
United Republic of Tanzania		132	106	172	367	300	0.02	-18.26
Zambia		74	26	60	62	86		38.71
Central Africa		650	584	901	1,240	906	0.05	-26.94
Angola		214	208	374	602	338	0.02	-43.85
Cameroon		130	158	181	257	261	0.01	1.56
Central African Republic		10	21	24	29	25		-13.79
Chad		9	2	16	12	7		-41.67
Congo		225	152	235	270	264	0.01	-2.22
Equatorial Guinea		1		51	38	2		-94.74
Gabon		61	43	20	32	9		-71.88
North Africa		2,927	4,147	4,892	4,996	3,679	0.20	-26.36
Algeria		13	21	7	20	13		-35.00
Morocco		2,158	2,841	3,355	3,275	2,512	0.14	-23.30
Sudan		6	18	24	16	1		-93.75
Tunisia		750	1,267	1,506	1,685	1,153	0.06	-31.57
Southern Africa		9,245	9,897	12,862	16,656	16,853	0.92	1.18
Botswana		36	17	71	38	37		-2.63
Lesotho		7	6	7	22	21		-4.55
Namibia				41	39	20		-48.72
South Africa		9,054	9,776	12,609	16,457	16,603	0.91	0.89
Swaziland		148	98	134	100	172	0.01	72.00
West Africa		13,946	12,944	18,226	12,835	26,584	1.46	107.12
Cape Verde				9	49	31		-36.73
Benin		17	15	41	70	23		-67.14
Gambia		21	3	8	9	12		33.33
Ghana		365	441	534	575	614	0.03	6.78
Guinea		30	29	11	55	125	0.01	127.27
Cote D'Ivoire		183	391	437	619	658	0.04	6.30
Liberia		46	18	38	27	28		3.70
Mali		19	14	14	9	22		144.44
Mauritania		76	56					
Niger		74	5	143	43	95	0.01	120.93
Nigeria		12,931	11,820	16,814	10,726	24,608	1.35	129.42
Guinea-Bissau			4					
Saint Helena		1		1				

ISRAEL

1. Arrivals of non-resident tourists at national borders, by country of residence

	2002	2003	2004	2005	2006	Market share 06	% Change 06-05
Senegal	53	48	79	467	129	0.01	-72.38
Sierra Leone	19	17	20	32	19		-40.63
Togo	54	46	30	101	127	0.01	25.74
Burkina Faso	57	37	47	53	93	0.01	75.47
Other Africa	**39**	**49**	**15**	**18**	**50**		**177.78**
Other countries of Africa	39	49	15	18	50		177.78
AMERICAS	**260,912**	**347,622**	**486,508**	**602,578**	**606,771**	**33.24**	**0.70**
Caribbean	**643**	**860**	**1,448**	**2,310**	**1,509**	**0.08**	**-34.68**
Antigua and Barbuda	1	4	8	15	4		-73.33
Bahamas	10	6	32	136	102	0.01	-25.00
Barbados	49	56	71	67	62		-7.46
Bermuda	20	11	9	20	44		120.00
Cayman Islands				1	3		200.00
Cuba	109	140	205	226	137	0.01	-39.38
Dominica	14	25	20	61	40		-34.43
Dominican Republic	168	334	638	1,294	474	0.03	-63.37
Grenada	9	5	1	3	11		266.67
Haiti	37	57	71	81	79		-2.47
Jamaica	108	104	197	196	309	0.02	57.65
Martinique	1		1	3	1		-66.67
Montserrat				1			
Netherlands Antilles		1			1		
Puerto Rico	6	1	12	3	2		-33.33
Saint Kitts and Nevis	1	3	2	5	7		40.00
Saint Lucia	4	4	7	8	7		-12.50
Saint Vincent and the Grenadines	2	2	1	4	9		125.00
Trinidad and Tobago	103	106	172	185	217	0.01	17.30
Turks and Caicos Islands	1	1					
United States Virgin Islands			1	1			
Central America	**2,016**	**3,255**	**4,857**	**7,018**	**4,124**	**0.23**	**-41.24**
Belize	14	14	19	20	14		-30.00
Costa Rica	452	680	949	1,310	927	0.05	-29.24
El Salvador	372	706	619	1,319	806	0.04	-38.89
Guatemala	437	805	1,195	1,837	805	0.04	-56.18
Honduras	253	202	480	580	323	0.02	-44.31
Nicaragua	46	225	171	331	276	0.02	-16.62
Panama	442	623	1,424	1,616	946	0.05	-41.46
All countries of Central America				5	27		440.00
North America	**235,416**	**311,415**	**437,369**	**532,290**	**558,698**	**30.61**	**4.96**
Canada	25,116	31,268	43,573	50,784	51,409	2.82	1.23
Mexico	4,240	8,230	14,668	23,987	13,318	0.73	-44.48
United States	206,060	271,917	379,128	457,519	493,971	27.06	7.97
South America	**22,837**	**32,092**	**42,834**	**60,960**	**42,440**	**2.33**	**-30.38**
Argentina	7,307	9,957	11,734	14,777	11,815	0.65	-20.04
Bolivia	357	486	644	564	341	0.02	-39.54
Brazil	5,401	7,761	11,415	19,764	15,489	0.85	-21.63
Chile	1,501	2,425	3,644	5,135	2,793	0.15	-45.61
Colombia	3,204	4,110	6,298	8,920	5,070	0.28	-43.16
Ecuador	899	1,382	1,886	2,918	1,691	0.09	-42.05
Falkland Islands (Malvinas)	1	1		3			
Guyana	28	26	19	31	41		32.26
Paraguay	219	307	414	457	223	0.01	-51.20
Peru	783	855	1,277	1,874	1,054	0.06	-43.76
Suriname	16	11	13	33	18		-45.45

ISRAEL

1. Arrivals of non-resident tourists at national borders, by country of residence

	2002	2003	2004	2005	2006	Market share 06	% Change 06-05
Uruguay	1,980	2,705	2,994	3,235	1,975	0.11	-38.95
Venezuela	1,141	2,066	2,492	3,248	1,924	0.11	-40.76
Other countries of South America			4	1	6		500.00
EAST ASIA AND THE PACIFIC	**35,885**	**42,384**	**65,953**	**87,572**	**94,407**	**5.17**	**7.81**
North-East Asia	**16,129**	**18,066**	**30,361**	**41,647**	**52,176**	**2.86**	**25.28**
China	2,605	1,935	2,960	4,046	10,818	0.59	167.38
Taiwan (Province of China)	798	1,053	1,913	2,224	3,007	0.16	35.21
Hong Kong, China	112	235	495	997	744	0.04	-25.38
Japan	4,123	4,764	6,203	8,329	9,424	0.52	13.15
Korea, Republic of	8,237	9,743	18,502	25,886	28,024	1.54	8.26
Macao, China	8	8	17		28		
Mongolia	246	328	271	165	131	0.01	-20.61
South-East Asia	**9,788**	**12,457**	**17,999**	**23,182**	**20,774**	**1.14**	**-10.39**
Brunei Darussalam	1		1				
Myanmar	204	286	278	202	102	0.01	-49.50
Cambodia	26	6	13	9	5		-44.44
Indonesia	1,102	2,734	5,608	8,412	7,325	0.40	-12.92
Lao People's Democratic Republic	11	4	7	4	7		75.00
Malaysia	87	100	649	1,451	1,248	0.07	-13.99
Philippines	5,066	4,618	4,256	5,614	4,525	0.25	-19.40
Timor-Leste				5	1		-80.00
Singapore	1,735	2,774	5,764	5,773	5,246	0.29	-9.13
Viet Nam	54	104	159	232	404	0.02	74.14
Thailand	1,502	1,831	1,264	1,480	1,911	0.10	29.12
Australasia	**9,436**	**11,335**	**17,003**	**22,147**	**20,687**	**1.13**	**-6.59**
Australia	8,164	9,874	14,871	19,710	18,184	1.00	-7.74
New Zealand	1,272	1,461	2,132	2,437	2,503	0.14	2.71
Melanesia	**83**	**114**	**164**	**202**	**181**	**0.01**	**-10.40**
Solomon Islands	4	6	8	14	3		-78.57
Fiji	58	94	122	149	148	0.01	-0.67
New Caledonia	1						
Vanuatu	2	4	6	7	6		-14.29
Papua New Guinea	18	10	28	32	24		-25.00
Micronesia	**16**	**12**	**36**	**28**	**11**		**-60.71**
Kiribati	13	2	25	22			
Guam			1				
Micronesia (Federated States of)		7	9	6			
Palau	3	3	1		11		
Polynesia	**14**	**4**	**24**	**21**	**15**		**-28.57**
American Samoa		2	1				
Cook Islands	4				3		
Tonga	10		9	11	2		-81.82
Tuvalu			5	10	1		-90.00
Samoa		2	9		9		
Other East Asia and the Pacific	**419**	**396**	**366**	**345**	**563**	**0.03**	**63.19**
Other countries of Asia	406	385	350	274	550	0.03	100.73
Other countries of Oceania	13	11	16	71	13		-81.69
EUROPE	**484,353**	**598,231**	**857,133**	**1,107,142**	**1,015,624**	**55.64**	**-8.27**
Central/Eastern Europe	**96,816**	**102,722**	**141,739**	**185,583**	**218,311**	**11.96**	**17.64**
Azerbaijan	1,621	1,646	1,863	1,860	1,837	0.10	-1.24
Armenia	213	252	298	399	376	0.02	-5.76

ISRAEL

1. Arrivals of non-resident tourists at national borders, by country of residence

	2002	2003	2004	2005	2006	Market share 06	% Change 06-05
Bulgaria	2,467	2,112	2,711	3,098	3,459	0.19	11.65
Belarus	4,029	4,196	4,519	5,640	5,874	0.32	4.15
Czech Republic	3,248	3,100	5,455	9,978	14,361	0.79	43.93
Estonia	493	495	777	1,146	1,167	0.06	1.83
Georgia	1,944	1,904	2,125	2,700	3,166	0.17	17.26
Hungary	5,050	5,161	6,868	8,720	7,590	0.42	-12.96
Kazakhstan	1,469	1,504	1,817	2,149	2,594	0.14	20.71
Kyrgyzstan	266	262	269	267	284	0.02	6.37
Latvia	1,672	1,583	2,160	309	4,252	0.23	1,276.05
Lithuania	1,339	1,283	1,910	2,369	3,341	0.18	41.03
Republic of Moldova	1,491	1,621	1,940	2,382	2,257	0.12	-5.25
Poland	5,301	6,138	10,287	26,786	42,071	2.30	57.06
Romania	5,925	6,695	7,853	9,610	11,354	0.62	18.15
Russian Federation	25,431	32,343	49,061	64,584	73,579	4.03	13.93
Slovakia	1,873	1,797	6,912	7,059	4,956	0.27	-29.79
Tajikistan	39	42	82	63	94	0.01	49.21
Turkmenistan	89	63	81	72	58		-19.44
Ukraine	18,394	19,252	24,207	28,275	30,638	1.68	8.36
Ussr (Former)	11,454	8,973	6,641	3,427			
Uzbekistan	3,008	2,288	2,258	2,140	2,108	0.12	-1.50
Other countries Central/East Europ		12	1,645	2,550	2,895	0.16	13.53
Northern Europe	**120,374**	**131,048**	**185,447**	**211,002**	**211,436**	**11.58**	**0.21**
Denmark	6,050	6,920	8,657	11,807	10,530	0.58	-10.82
Finland	3,588	4,114	6,530	7,609	7,843	0.43	3.08
Iceland	113	114	218	285	244	0.01	-14.39
Ireland	2,525	2,786	4,247	7,042	5,660	0.31	-19.63
Norway	4,113	4,332	6,719	9,179	9,237	0.51	0.63
Sweden	6,719	8,586	12,595	18,334	16,769	0.92	-8.54
United Kingdom	97,266	104,196	146,481	156,746	161,153	8.83	2.81
Southern Europe	**34,790**	**52,854**	**79,657**	**152,968**	**114,769**	**6.29**	**-24.97**
Albania	103	117	199	148	224	0.01	51.35
Andorra	11	11	67	71	34		-52.11
Bosnia and Herzegovina	159	140	196	346	434	0.02	25.43
Croatia	991	1,001	1,433	2,367	2,932	0.16	23.87
Greece	4,801	6,146	9,983	15,045	16,731	0.92	11.21
Holy See	152	159	189	235	252	0.01	7.23
Italy	16,864	26,016	41,991	72,875	58,111	3.18	-20.26
Malta	112	187	257	569	375	0.02	-34.09
Portugal	1,252	1,482	3,241	7,991	3,413	0.19	-57.29
San Marino	31	17	36	92	43		-53.26
Slovenia	416	496	649	1,327	1,341	0.07	1.06
Spain	8,584	15,886	21,395	51,867	30,651	1.68	-40.90
TFYR of Macedonia	116	97	1	1	158	0.01	*********
Serbia and Montenegro	1,198	1,099	20	34	70		105.88
Western Europe	**216,578**	**294,000**	**430,636**	**531,315**	**447,794**	**24.53**	**-15.72**
Austria	7,581	8,272	11,116	13,263	15,290	0.84	15.28
Belgium	15,352	17,780	22,763	25,522	24,490	1.34	-4.04
France	117,894	174,353	257,484	311,438	252,151	13.81	-19.04
Germany	38,813	49,034	75,895	105,224	89,595	4.91	-14.85
Liechtenstein	11	15	31	43	51		18.60
Luxembourg	186	242	344	362	403	0.02	11.33
Monaco	12	11	25	36	14		-61.11
Netherlands	22,820	27,303	40,380	49,807	42,981	2.35	-13.70
Switzerland	13,909	16,990	22,598	25,620	22,819	1.25	-10.93
East Mediterranean Europe	**15,795**	**17,607**	**19,654**	**23,273**	**23,314**	**1.28**	**0.18**

ISRAEL

1. Arrivals of non-resident tourists at national borders, by country of residence

	2002	2003	2004	2005	2006	Market share 06	% Change 06-05
Cyprus	3,840	4,539	5,870	7,574	7,683	0.42	1.44
Turkey	11,955	13,068	13,784	15,699	15,631	0.86	-0.43
Other Europe				3,001			
Other countries of Europe				3,001			
MIDDLE EAST	**28,356**	**23,159**	**28,561**	**29,946**	**20,613**	**1.13**	**-31.17**
Middle East	**28,356**	**23,159**	**28,561**	**29,946**	**20,613**	**1.13**	**-31.17**
Bahrain	4	8	6	16	2		-87.50
Iraq	42	41	56	82	55		-32.93
Jordan	24,491	18,372	22,927	23,143	15,125	0.83	-34.65
Kuwait	9	25	44	55	12		-78.18
Lebanon	338	272	255	287	311	0.02	8.36
Libyan Arab Jamahiriya	3	108	76	91	6		-93.41
Oman	5	3	7	15	1		-93.33
Qatar	33	88	101	140	24		-82.86
Saudi Arabia	85	657	850	910	65		-92.86
Syrian Arab Republic	87	69	67	80	75		-6.25
United Arab Emirates	92	658	1,013	773	81		-89.52
Egypt	3,148	2,791	3,130	4,309	4,834	0.26	12.18
Yemen	19	67	29	45	22		-51.11
SOUTH ASIA	**10,745**	**10,172**	**15,155**	**22,911**	**23,219**	**1.27**	**1.34**
South Asia	**10,745**	**10,172**	**15,155**	**22,911**	**23,219**	**1.27**	**1.34**
Afghanistan	14	15	8	10	6		-40.00
Bangladesh	77	36	25	49	27		-44.90
Bhutan	2	2	5	6	5		-16.67
Sri Lanka	643	663	1,114	2,420	2,124	0.12	-12.23
India	9,330	8,431	12,743	19,018	20,233	1.11	6.39
Iran, Islamic Republic of	463	777	1,000	931	566	0.03	-39.21
Maldives	12	28	16	19	3		-84.21
Nepal	160	179	212	398	220	0.01	-44.72
Pakistan	44	41	32	60	35		-41.67
REGION NOT SPECIFIED	**12,285**	**12,266**	**12,174**	**11,188**	**10,236**	**0.56**	**-8.51**
Not Specified	**12,285**	**12,266**	**12,174**	**11,188**	**10,236**	**0.56**	**-8.51**
Other countries of the World	12,285	12,266	12,174	11,188	10,236	0.56	-8.51

Source: World Tourism Organization (UNWTO)

ISRAEL

2. Arrivals of non-resident visitors at national borders, by country of residence

		2002	2003	2004	2005	2006	Market share 06	% Change 06-05
TOTAL	(*)	862,114		1,505,808	1,916,116	1,833,689	100.00	-4.30
AFRICA		29,340		40,122	41,453	54,287	2.96	30.96
East Africa		2,518		3,226	5,705	6,265	0.34	9.82
Burundi		23		18	21	18		-14.29
Comoros		1		5		2		
Ethiopia		814		712	1,785	1,161	0.06	-34.96
Eritrea		1			3	11		266.67
Kenya		858		776	763	1,000	0.05	31.06
Madagascar		26		40	36	42		16.67
Malawi		35		163	47	22		-53.19
Mauritius		14		115	185	112	0.01	-39.46
Mozambique		15		14	43	58		34.88
Rwanda		44		80	58	93	0.01	60.34
Seychelles		13		12	18	13		-27.78
Somalia		4		9	15	22		46.67
Zimbabwe		340		807	2,016	2,948	0.16	46.23
Uganda		124		243	286	377	0.02	31.82
United Republic of Tanzania		132		172	367	300	0.02	-18.26
Zambia		74		60	62	86		38.71
Central Africa		652		901	1,240	906	0.05	-26.94
Angola		214		374	602	338	0.02	-43.85
Cameroon		130		181	257	261	0.01	1.56
Central African Republic		10		24	29	25		-13.79
Chad		9		16	12	7		-41.67
Congo		225		235	270	264	0.01	-2.22
Democratic Republic of the Congo		2						
Equatorial Guinea		1		51	38	2		-94.74
Gabon		61		20	32	9		-71.88
North Africa		2,928		4,892	4,996	3,679	0.20	-26.36
Algeria		13		7	20	13		-35.00
Morocco		2,159		3,355	3,275	2,512	0.14	-23.30
Sudan		6		24	16	1		-93.75
Tunisia		750		1,506	1,685	1,153	0.06	-31.57
Southern Africa		9,281		12,862	16,656	16,853	0.92	1.18
Botswana		36		71	38	37		-2.63
Lesotho		7		7	22	21		-4.55
Namibia		36		41	39	20		-48.72
South Africa		9,054		12,609	16,457	16,603	0.91	0.89
Swaziland		148		134	100	172	0.01	72.00
West Africa		13,952		18,226	12,835	26,584	1.45	107.12
Cape Verde		6		9	49	31		-36.73
Benin		17		41	70	23		-67.14
Gambia		21		8	9	12		33.33
Ghana		365		534	575	614	0.03	6.78
Guinea		30		11	55	125	0.01	127.27
Cote D'Ivoire		183		437	619	658	0.04	6.30
Liberia		46		38	27	28		3.70
Mali		19		14	9	22		144.44
Mauritania		76						
Niger		74		143	43	95	0.01	120.93
Nigeria		12,931		16,814	10,726	24,608	1.34	129.42
Saint Helena		1		1				
Senegal		53		79	467	129	0.01	-72.38

ISRAEL

2. Arrivals of non-resident visitors at national borders, by country of residence

	2002	2003	2004	2005	2006	Market share 06	% Change 06-05
Sierra Leone	19		20	32	19		-40.63
Togo	54		30	101	127	0.01	25.74
Burkina Faso	57		47	53	93	0.01	75.47
Other Africa	**9**		**15**	**21**			
Other countries of Africa	9		15	21			
AMERICAS	**261,047**		**486,508**	**602,776**	**606,889**	**33.10**	**0.68**
Caribbean	**643**		**1,448**	**2,309**	**1,508**	**0.08**	**-34.69**
Antigua and Barbuda	1		8	15	4		-73.33
Bahamas	10		32	136	102	0.01	-25.00
Barbados	49		71	67	62		-7.46
Bermuda	20		9	20	44		120.00
Cayman Islands				1	3		200.00
Cuba	109		205	226	137	0.01	-39.38
Dominica	14		20	61	40		-34.43
Dominican Republic	168		638	1,294	474	0.03	-63.37
Grenada	9		1	3	11		266.67
Haiti	37		71	81	79		-2.47
Jamaica	108		197	196	309	0.02	57.65
Martinique	1		1	3	1		-66.67
Puerto Rico	6		12	3	2		-33.33
Saint Kitts and Nevis	1		2	5	7		40.00
Saint Lucia	4		7	8	7		-12.50
Saint Vincent and the Grenadines	2		1	4	9		125.00
Trinidad and Tobago	103		172	185	217	0.01	17.30
Turks and Caicos Islands	1						
United States Virgin Islands			1	1			
Central America	**2,016**		**4,857**	**7,013**	**4,097**	**0.22**	**-41.58**
Belize	14		19	20	14		-30.00
Costa Rica	452		949	1,310	927	0.05	-29.24
El Salvador	372		619	1,319	806	0.04	-38.89
Guatemala	437		1,195	1,837	805	0.04	-56.18
Honduras	253		480	580	323	0.02	-44.31
Nicaragua	46		171	331	276	0.02	-16.62
Panama	442		1,424	1,616	946	0.05	-41.46
North America	**235,551**		**437,369**	**532,427**	**558,771**	**30.47**	**4.95**
Canada	25,116		43,573	50,812	51,425	2.80	1.21
Mexico	4,240		14,668	23,991	13,320	0.73	-44.48
United States	206,195		379,128	457,624	494,026	26.94	7.95
South America	**22,837**		**42,830**	**61,014**	**42,467**	**2.32**	**-30.40**
Argentina	7,307		11,734	14,829	11,846	0.65	-20.12
Bolivia	357		644	564	341	0.02	-39.54
Brazil	5,401		11,415	19,767	15,491	0.84	-21.63
Chile	1,501		3,644	5,135	2,793	0.15	-45.61
Colombia	3,204		6,298	8,920	5,070	0.28	-43.16
Ecuador	899		1,886	2,918	1,691	0.09	-42.05
Falkland Islands (Malvinas)	1			3			
Guyana	28		19	31	41		32.26
Paraguay	219		414	457	223	0.01	-51.20
Peru	783		1,277	1,874	1,054	0.06	-43.76
Suriname	16		13	33	18		-45.45
Uruguay	1,980		2,994	3,235	1,975	0.11	-38.95
Venezuela	1,141		2,492	3,248	1,924	0.10	-40.76
Other Americas			**4**	**13**	**46**		**253.85**

ISRAEL

2. Arrivals of non-resident visitors at national borders, by country of residence

	2002	2003	2004	2005	2006	Market share 06	% Change 06-05
Other countries of the Americas			4	13	46		253.85
EAST ASIA AND THE PACIFIC	**35,884**		**65,953**	**87,683**	**94,586**	**5.16**	**7.87**
North-East Asia	**16,129**		**30,361**	**41,647**	**52,176**	**2.85**	**25.28**
China	2,605		2,960	4,046	10,818	0.59	167.38
Taiwan (Province of China)	798		1,913	2,224	3,007	0.16	35.21
Hong Kong, China	112		495	997	744	0.04	-25.38
Japan	4,123		6,203	8,329	9,424	0.51	13.15
Korea, Republic of	8,237		18,502	25,886	28,024	1.53	8.26
Macao, China	8		17		28		
Mongolia	246		271	165	131	0.01	-20.61
South-East Asia	**9,789**		**17,999**	**23,182**	**20,774**	**1.13**	**-10.39**
Brunei Darussalam	1		1				
Myanmar	204		278	202	102	0.01	-49.50
Cambodia	26		13	9	5		-44.44
Indonesia	1,102		5,608	8,412	7,325	0.40	-12.92
Lao People's Democratic Republic	11		7	4	7		75.00
Malaysia	87		649	1,451	1,248	0.07	-13.99
Philippines	5,066		4,256	5,614	4,525	0.25	-19.40
Timor-Leste	1			5	1		-80.00
Singapore	1,735		5,764	5,773	5,246	0.29	-9.13
Viet Nam	54		159	232	404	0.02	74.14
Thailand	1,502		1,264	1,480	1,911	0.10	29.12
Australasia	**9,436**		**17,003**	**22,207**	**20,747**	**1.13**	**-6.57**
Australia	8,164		14,871	19,769	18,242	0.99	-7.72
New Zealand	1,272		2,132	2,438	2,505	0.14	2.75
Melanesia	**83**		**164**	**202**	**181**	**0.01**	**-10.40**
Solomon Islands	4		8	14	3		-78.57
Fiji	58		122	149	148	0.01	-0.67
New Caledonia	1						
Vanuatu	2		6	7	6		-14.29
Papua New Guinea	18		28	32	24		-25.00
Micronesia	**16**		**36**	**28**	**11**		**-60.71**
Kiribati	13		25	22			
Guam			1				
Micronesia (Federated States of)			9	6			
Palau	3		1		11		
Polynesia	**14**		**24**	**21**	**15**		**-28.57**
American Samoa			1				
Cook Islands					3		
Tonga	10		9	11	2		-81.82
Tuvalu	4		5	10	1		-90.00
Samoa			9		9		
Other East Asia and the Pacific	**417**		**366**	**396**	**682**	**0.04**	**72.22**
Other countries of Asia	397		350	325	669	0.04	105.85
Other countries of Oceania	20		16	71	13		-81.69
EUROPE	**484,356**		**857,335**	**1,120,010**	**1,023,923**	**55.84**	**-8.58**
Central/Eastern Europe	**96,816**		**141,739**	**193,048**	**224,148**	**12.22**	**16.11**
Azerbaijan	1,621		1,863	1,860	1,837	0.10	-1.24
Armenia	213		298	399	376	0.02	-5.76
Bulgaria	2,467		2,711	3,098	3,483	0.19	12.43
Belarus	4,029		4,519	5,708	5,874	0.32	2.91

ISRAEL

2. Arrivals of non-resident visitors at national borders, by country of residence

	2002	2003	2004	2005	2006	Market share 06	% Change 06-05
Czech Republic	3,248		5,455	10,021	14,371	0.78	43.41
Estonia	493		777	1,146	1,167	0.06	1.83
Georgia	1,944		2,125	2,700	3,166	0.17	17.26
Hungary	5,050		6,868	8,735	7,611	0.42	-12.87
Kazakhstan	1,469		1,817	2,149	2,594	0.14	20.71
Kyrgyzstan	266		269	267	284	0.02	6.37
Latvia	1,672		2,160	309	4,252	0.23	1,276.05
Lithuania	1,339		1,910	2,369	3,341	0.18	41.03
Republic of Moldova	1,491		1,940	2,382	2,257	0.12	-5.25
Poland	5,301		10,287	26,895	42,180	2.30	56.83
Romania	5,925		7,853	9,610	11,354	0.62	18.15
Russian Federation	25,431		49,061	71,134	78,687	4.29	10.62
Slovakia	1,873		6,912	7,099	4,961	0.27	-30.12
Tajikistan	39		82	63	94	0.01	49.21
Turkmenistan	89		81	72	58		-19.44
Ukraine	18,394		24,207	28,275	30,638	1.67	8.36
Ussr (Former)	11,454		6,641	4,067			
Uzbekistan	3,008		2,258	2,140	2,108	0.11	-1.50
Other countries Central/East Europ			1,645	2,550	3,455	0.19	35.49
Northern Europe	**120,375**		**185,646**	**212,297**	**212,841**	**11.61**	**0.26**
Denmark	6,050		8,657	11,811	10,533	0.57	-10.82
Finland	3,588		6,530	7,621	7,852	0.43	3.03
Iceland	113		218	285	244	0.01	-14.39
Ireland	2,525		4,247	7,264	5,757	0.31	-20.75
Norway	4,113		6,719	9,191	9,244	0.50	0.58
Sweden	6,719		12,596	18,353	16,787	0.92	-8.53
United Kingdom	97,267		146,679	157,772	162,424	8.86	2.95
Southern Europe	**34,792**		**79,659**	**153,652**	**114,936**	**6.27**	**-25.20**
Albania	103		199	148	224	0.01	51.35
Andorra	11		67	71	34		-52.11
Bosnia and Herzegovina	159		196	346	434	0.02	25.43
Croatia	991		1,433	2,367	2,932	0.16	23.87
Greece	4,802		9,985	15,698	16,887	0.92	7.57
Holy See	152		189	235	252	0.01	7.23
Italy	16,864		41,991	72,890	58,119	3.17	-20.26
Malta	112		257	569	375	0.02	-34.09
Portugal	1,252		3,241	7,991	3,413	0.19	-57.29
San Marino	31		36	92	43		-53.26
Slovenia	416		649	1,327	1,341	0.07	1.06
Spain	8,584		21,395	51,883	30,654	1.67	-40.92
TFYR of Macedonia	116		1	1	158	0.01	*********
Serbia and Montenegro	1,199		20	34	70		105.88
Western Europe	**216,578**		**430,637**	**532,691**	**448,154**	**24.44**	**-15.87**
Austria	7,581		11,117	13,284	15,314	0.84	15.28
Belgium	15,352		22,763	25,528	24,492	1.34	-4.06
France	117,894		257,484	311,458	252,189	13.75	-19.03
Germany	38,813		75,895	106,466	89,825	4.90	-15.63
Liechtenstein	11		31	43	51		18.60
Luxembourg	186		344	362	403	0.02	11.33
Monaco	12		25	36	14		-61.11
Netherlands	22,820		40,380	49,868	43,041	2.35	-13.69
Switzerland	13,909		22,598	25,646	22,825	1.24	-11.00
East Mediterranean Europe	**15,795**		**19,654**	**25,271**	**23,844**	**1.30**	**-5.65**
Cyprus	3,840		5,870	9,572	8,213	0.45	-14.20
Turkey	11,955		13,784	15,699	15,631	0.85	-0.43

ISRAEL

2. Arrivals of non-resident visitors at national borders, by country of residence

	2002	2003	2004	2005	2006	Market share 06	% Change 06-05
Other Europe				3,051			
Other countries of Europe				3,051			
MIDDLE EAST	**28,356**		**28,561**	**30,028**	**20,613**	**1.12**	**-31.35**
Middle East	**28,356**		**28,561**	**30,028**	**20,613**	**1.12**	**-31.35**
Bahrain	4		6	16	2		-87.50
Iraq	42		56	82	55		-32.93
Jordan	24,491		22,927	23,143	15,125	0.82	-34.65
Kuwait	9		44	55	12		-78.18
Lebanon	338		255	287	311	0.02	8.36
Libyan Arab Jamahiriya	3		76	91	6		-93.41
Oman	5		7	15	1		-93.33
Qatar	33		101	140	24		-82.86
Saudi Arabia	85		850	910	65		-92.86
Syrian Arab Republic	87		67	80	75		-6.25
United Arab Emirates	92		1,013	773	81		-89.52
Egypt	3,148		3,130	4,391	4,834	0.26	10.09
Yemen	19		29	45	22		-51.11
SOUTH ASIA	**10,745**		**15,155**	**22,949**	**23,243**	**1.27**	**1.28**
South Asia	**10,745**		**15,155**	**22,949**	**23,243**	**1.27**	**1.28**
Afghanistan	14		8	10	6		-40.00
Bangladesh	77		25	49	27		-44.90
Bhutan	2		5	6	5		-16.67
Sri Lanka	643		1,114	2,420	2,124	0.12	-12.23
India	9,330		12,743	19,056	20,257	1.10	6.30
Iran, Islamic Republic of	463		1,000	931	566	0.03	-39.21
Maldives	12		16	19	3		-84.21
Nepal	160		212	398	220	0.01	-44.72
Pakistan	44		32	60	35		-41.67
REGION NOT SPECIFIED	**12,386**		**12,174**	**11,217**	**10,148**	**0.55**	**-9.53**
Not Specified	**12,386**		**12,174**	**11,217**	**10,148**	**0.55**	**-9.53**
Other countries of the World	12,386		12,174	11,217	10,148	0.55	-9.53

Source: World Tourism Organization (UNWTO)

ISRAEL

3. Arrivals of non-resident tourists in hotels and similar establishments, by country of residence

		2002	2003	2004	2005	2006	Market share 06	% Change 06-05
TOTAL	(*)	694,100	899,700	1,373,700	2,004,700	2,131,300	100.00	6.32
AMERICAS		248,500	357,100	568,400	816,800	811,200	38.06	-0.69
North America		232,500	333,700	529,100	748,100	755,300	35.44	0.96
All countries of North America		232,500	333,700	529,100	748,100	755,300	35.44	0.96
South America		16,000	23,400	39,300	68,700	55,900	2.62	-18.63
All countries of South America	(*)	16,000	23,400	39,300	68,700	55,900	2.62	-18.63
EUROPE		290,900	376,500	540,900	837,800	863,700	40.52	3.09
Other Europe		290,900	376,500	540,900	837,800	863,700	40.52	3.09
All countries of Europe		290,900	376,500	540,900	837,800	863,700	40.52	3.09
REGION NOT SPECIFIED		154,700	166,100	264,400	350,100	456,400	21.41	30.36
Not Specified		154,700	166,100	264,400	350,100	456,400	21.41	30.36
Other countries of the World		154,700	166,100	264,400	350,100	456,400	21.41	30.36

Source: World Tourism Organization (UNWTO)

ISRAEL

5. Overnight stays of non-resident tourists in hotels and similar establishments, by country of residence

		2002	2003	2004	2005	2006	Market share 06	% Change 06-05
TOTAL	(*)	2,629,200	3,285,000	4,770,700	6,783,300	6,853,800	100.00	1.04
AMERICAS		839,800	1,183,100	1,760,900	2,538,800	2,537,100	37.02	-0.07
North America		788,700	1,109,600	1,640,000	2,331,300	2,359,200	34.42	1.20
All countries of North America		788,700	1,109,600	1,640,000	2,331,300	2,359,200	34.42	1.20
South America		51,100	73,500	120,900	207,500	177,900	2.60	-14.27
All countries of South America	(*)	51,100	73,500	120,900	207,500	177,900	2.60	-14.27
EUROPE		1,320,400	1,589,300	2,230,800	3,194,800	3,117,100	45.48	-2.43
Other Europe		1,320,400	1,589,300	2,230,800	3,194,800	3,117,100	45.48	-2.43
All countries of Europe		1,320,400	1,589,300	2,230,800	3,194,800	3,117,100	45.48	-2.43
REGION NOT SPECIFIED		469,000	512,600	779,000	1,049,700	1,199,600	17.50	14.28
Not Specified		469,000	512,600	779,000	1,049,700	1,199,600	17.50	14.28
Other countries of the World		469,000	512,600	779,000	1,049,700	1,199,600	17.50	14.28

Source: World Tourism Organization (UNWTO)

ITALY

1. Arrivals of non-resident tourists at national borders, by nationality

	2002	2003	2004	2005	2006	Market share 06	% Change 06-05
TOTAL (*)	39,798,969	39,604,118	37,070,775	36,512,500	41,057,834	100.00	12.45
AFRICA	179,251	122,472	205,617	250,705	253,863	0.62	1.26
East Africa	3,917	3,243	24,228	24,596	20,678	0.05	-15.93
All countries of East Africa	3,917	3,243	24,228	24,596	20,678	0.05	-15.93
Central Africa	1,231	1,030	10,032	5,884	8,838	0.02	50.20
All countries of Central Africa	1,231	1,030	10,032	5,884	8,838	0.02	50.20
North Africa	116,464	74,318	83,321	118,056	107,263	0.26	-9.14
Algeria	14,468	9,999	11,195	28,926	14,233	0.03	-50.80
Morocco	36,487	26,413	49,434	46,567	46,194	0.11	-0.80
Tunisia	65,507	37,903	21,920	38,058	43,245	0.11	13.63
Other countries of North Africa	2	3	772	4,505	3,591	0.01	-20.29
Southern Africa	29,974	23,962	59,518	62,616	75,454	0.18	20.50
South Africa	29,431	23,743	57,487	60,823	74,761	0.18	22.92
Other countries of Southern Africa	543	219	2,031	1,793	693		-61.35
West Africa	27,665	19,919	28,518	39,553	41,630	0.10	5.25
All countries of West Africa	27,665	19,919	28,518	39,553	41,630	0.10	5.25
AMERICAS	2,064,520	1,680,228	2,988,244	3,250,284	3,579,393	8.72	10.13
Caribbean	6,557	6,534	22,814	16,413	20,668	0.05	25.92
All countries of the Caribbean	6,557	6,534	22,814	16,413	20,668	0.05	25.92
Central America	3,950	4,596	21,518	15,780	18,212	0.04	15.41
Panama	1,307	632	4,031	1,257	3,476	0.01	176.53
Other countries of Central America	2,643	3,964	17,487	14,523	14,736	0.04	1.47
North America	1,827,608	1,470,404	2,584,734	2,826,668	3,118,197	7.59	10.31
Canada	247,806	182,283	330,098	394,488	436,501	1.06	10.65
Mexico	81,422	73,289	79,172	105,378	93,576	0.23	-11.20
United States	1,498,380	1,214,832	2,174,794	2,326,802	2,588,120	6.30	11.23
Other countries of North America			670				
South America	226,405	198,694	359,178	391,423	422,316	1.03	7.89
Argentina	55,037	64,518	82,856	104,734	98,192	0.24	-6.25
Brazil	114,348	86,246	128,722	181,762	219,059	0.53	20.52
Chile	14,235	14,059	26,501	38,767	34,443	0.08	-11.15
Suriname			807	757	215		-71.60
Venezuela	18,007	11,023	50,711	27,756	28,702	0.07	3.41
Other countries of South America	24,778	22,848	69,581	37,647	41,705	0.10	10.78
EAST ASIA AND THE PACIFIC	1,382,734	1,074,563	1,088,281	1,111,603	1,188,781	2.90	6.94
North-East Asia	1,139,881	860,606	522,993	493,477	555,797	1.35	12.63
China	162,315	125,695	95,554	95,471	117,446	0.29	23.02
Taiwan (Province of China)	7,869	5,664	10,352	14,756	19,434	0.05	31.70
Hong Kong, China	12,304	8,566	13,830	23,009	17,964	0.04	-21.93
Japan	849,967	611,536	308,901	281,278	323,451	0.79	14.99
Korea, Republic of	107,421	109,142	77,713	78,027	77,502	0.19	-0.67
Other countries of North-East Asia	5	3	16,643	936			
South-East Asia	54,617	30,787	85,556	95,168	89,655	0.22	-5.79
Indonesia	5,185	3,301	11,043	18,600	13,135	0.03	-29.38
Malaysia	6,940	3,999	11,324	7,128	9,896	0.02	38.83
Thailand	11,908	9,698	20,991	30,262	23,436	0.06	-22.56
Other countries of South-East Asia	30,584	13,789	42,198	39,178	43,188	0.11	10.24
Australasia	188,232	182,716	473,287	518,896	539,557	1.31	3.98

ITALY

1. Arrivals of non-resident tourists at national borders, by nationality

	2002	2003	2004	2005	2006	Market share 06	% Change 06-05
Australia	163,823	163,537	405,829	468,555	478,522	1.17	2.13
New Zealand	24,409	19,179	67,458	50,341	61,035	0.15	21.24
Melanesia	**4**	**453**	**340**	**155**	**1,253**		**708.39**
All countries of Melanesia	4	453	340	155	1,253		708.39
Micronesia		**1**	**332**				
All countries of Micronesia		1	332				
Polynesia			**5,773**	**3,907**	**2,519**	**0.01**	**-35.53**
Samoa					999		
Other countries of Polynesia					1,520		
All countries of Polynesia			5,773	3,907			
EUROPE	**36,001,041**	**36,583,819**	**32,521,819**	**31,571,338**	**35,594,161**	**86.69**	**12.74**
Central/Eastern Europe	**1,902,596**	**1,966,576**	**2,379,038**	**3,087,275**	**4,224,081**	**10.29**	**36.82**
Hungary	435,983	413,918	469,243	639,327	945,037	2.30	47.82
Poland	515,498	426,312	485,337	734,545	1,020,702	2.49	38.96
Romania	155,785	185,319	366,053	530,616	642,613	1.57	21.11
Russian Federation	174,710	268,698	140,570	175,460	212,143	0.52	20.91
Other countries Central/East Europ	620,620	672,329	917,835	1,007,327	1,403,586	3.42	39.34
Northern Europe	**3,611,177**	**3,952,987**	**4,886,599**	**5,202,519**	**5,839,011**	**14.22**	**12.23**
Denmark	330,354	377,886	363,794	396,112	418,413	1.02	5.63
Finland	106,156	114,118	195,934	180,166	224,810	0.55	24.78
Ireland	180,412	189,393	268,769	261,104	372,454	0.91	42.65
Norway	103,644	136,496	178,224	179,715	237,107	0.58	31.94
Sweden	262,337	272,617	379,349	360,923	408,792	1.00	13.26
United Kingdom	2,624,903	2,853,558	3,470,941	3,810,856	4,160,863	10.13	9.18
Other countries of Northern Europe	3,371	8,919	29,588	13,643	16,572	0.04	21.47
Southern Europe	**2,535,168**	**2,633,901**	**2,076,271**	**2,472,964**	**3,078,803**	**7.50**	**24.50**
Croatia	268,167	233,368	154,408	89,045	148,296	0.36	66.54
Greece	688,930	826,218	324,515	292,832	334,780	0.82	14.32
Portugal	127,241	127,187	141,851	137,053	192,591	0.47	40.52
Slovenia	158,984	125,918	90,970	147,011	92,497	0.23	-37.08
Spain	1,187,514	1,220,510	1,226,494	1,650,991	2,090,999	5.09	26.65
Serbia and Montenegro	26,826	25,163	32,883	44,892	68,935	0.17	53.56
Other countries Southern Europe	77,506	75,537	105,150	111,140	150,705	0.37	35.60
Western Europe	**27,761,493**	**27,783,639**	**22,991,605**	**20,600,526**	**22,160,461**	**53.97**	**7.57**
Austria	4,780,176	5,433,588	3,075,899	2,390,367	2,610,440	6.36	9.21
Belgium	919,782	864,327	909,542	915,703	935,102	2.28	2.12
France	5,431,090	5,140,594	4,201,504	3,890,193	4,889,428	11.91	25.69
Germany	11,800,324	11,536,345	10,292,544	9,257,866	8,982,845	21.88	-2.97
Luxembourg	30,325	43,219	132,282	75,766	112,065	0.27	47.91
Netherlands	1,529,383	1,491,204	1,552,315	1,390,013	1,384,276	3.37	-0.41
Switzerland	3,149,373	3,140,760	2,774,647	2,622,048	3,194,159	7.78	21.82
Other countries of Western Europe	121,040	133,602	52,872	58,570	52,146	0.13	-10.97
East Mediterranean Europe	**187,448**	**241,126**	**168,542**	**201,099**	**265,089**	**0.65**	**31.82**
Israel	62,481	75,819	94,348	86,196	82,331	0.20	-4.48
Turkey	124,967	165,307	74,194	114,903	182,758	0.45	59.05
Other Europe	**3,159**	**5,590**	**19,764**	**6,955**	**26,716**	**0.07**	**284.13**
Other countries of Europe	3,159	5,590	19,764	6,955	26,716	0.07	284.13
MIDDLE EAST	**82,093**	**76,035**	**129,760**	**212,716**	**246,956**	**0.60**	**16.10**
Middle East	**82,093**	**76,035**	**129,760**	**212,716**	**246,956**	**0.60**	**16.10**
Kuwait	1,944	1,645	7,592	10,052	10,884	0.03	8.28
Libyan Arab Jamahiriya	7,236	5,168	9,834	28,015	32,999	0.08	17.79

ITALY

1. Arrivals of non-resident tourists at national borders, by nationality

	2002	2003	2004	2005	2006	Market share 06	% Change 06-05
Saudi Arabia	18,039	8,397	14,652	19,086	27,199	0.07	42.51
Egypt	29,236	28,105	29,292	59,651	51,045	0.12	-14.43
Other countries of Middle East	25,638	32,720	68,390	95,912	124,829	0.30	30.15
SOUTH ASIA	**89,329**	**67,001**	**135,290**	**115,193**	**189,745**	**0.46**	**64.72**
South Asia	**89,329**	**67,001**	**135,290**	**115,193**	**189,745**	**0.46**	**64.72**
India	65,839	48,807	77,134	59,056	116,951	0.28	98.03
Iran, Islamic Republic of	6,107	4,635	32,461	24,828	28,027	0.07	12.88
Other countries of South Asia	17,383	13,559	25,695	31,309	44,767	0.11	42.98
REGION NOT SPECIFIED	**1**		**1,764**	**661**	**4,935**	**0.01**	**646.60**
Not Specified	**1**		**1,764**	**661**	**4,935**	**0.01**	**646.60**
Other countries of the World	1		1,764	661	4,935	0.01	646.60

Source: World Tourism Organization (UNWTO)

ITALY

2. Arrivals of non-resident visitors at national borders, by nationality

		2002	2003	2004	2005	2006	Market share 06	% Change 06-05
TOTAL	(*)	63,561,320	63,026,059	58,479,841	59,229,523	66,352,961	100.00	12.03
AFRICA		215,222	133,876	307,268	413,366	377,774	0.57	-8.61
East Africa		4,718	3,243	34,070	43,172	27,837	0.04	-35.52
All countries of East Africa		4,718	3,243	34,070	43,172	27,837	0.04	-35.52
Central Africa		1,751	1,030	10,252	8,634	9,248	0.01	7.11
All countries of Central Africa		1,751	1,030	10,252	8,634	9,248	0.01	7.11
North Africa		145,880	85,373	118,273	196,963	173,140	0.26	-12.10
Algeria		14,469	9,999	17,995	51,692	27,186	0.04	-47.41
Morocco		38,390	27,673	56,720	64,284	60,168	0.09	-6.40
Tunisia		93,019	47,698	41,749	75,725	81,525	0.12	7.66
Other countries of North Africa		2	3	1,809	5,262	4,261	0.01	-19.02
Southern Africa		30,002	24,157	68,327	65,944	78,126	0.12	18.47
South Africa		29,458	23,937	66,296	64,151	77,062	0.12	20.13
Other countries of Southern Africa		544	220	2,031	1,793	1,064		-40.66
West Africa		32,871	20,073	76,346	98,653	89,423	0.13	-9.36
All countries of West Africa		32,871	20,073	76,346	98,653	89,423	0.13	-9.36
AMERICAS		2,117,923	1,721,889	3,577,035	3,886,975	4,243,422	6.40	9.17
Caribbean		6,853	6,535	29,467	17,319	23,697	0.04	36.83
All countries of the Caribbean		6,853	6,535	29,467	17,319	23,697	0.04	36.83
Central America		3,951	4,596	30,956	21,831	24,281	0.04	11.22
Panama		1,307	632	4,490	3,611	3,975	0.01	10.08
Other countries of Central America		2,644	3,964	26,466	18,220	20,306	0.03	11.45
North America		1,871,133	1,504,373	3,038,607	3,300,441	3,625,188	5.46	9.84
Canada		253,256	186,626	409,856	511,557	557,796	0.84	9.04
Mexico		86,613	73,655	81,723	107,898	96,356	0.15	-10.70
United States		1,531,264	1,244,092	2,546,358	2,680,986	2,971,036	4.48	10.82
Other countries of North America				670				
South America		235,986	206,385	478,005	547,384	570,256	0.86	4.18
Argentina		59,109	67,979	104,242	152,174	131,636	0.20	-13.50
Brazil		118,858	89,444	175,658	241,221	295,749	0.45	22.60
Chile		14,240	14,060	28,054	41,913	38,526	0.06	-8.08
Suriname				807	757	215		-71.60
Venezuela		18,996	11,026	70,237	45,091	43,104	0.06	-4.41
Other countries of South America		24,783	23,876	99,007	66,228	61,026	0.09	-7.85
EAST ASIA AND THE PACIFIC		1,428,335	1,090,849	1,227,670	1,207,181	1,283,524	1.93	6.32
North-East Asia		1,178,061	871,478	594,955	542,730	607,388	0.92	11.91
China		162,318	125,696	105,047	100,607	124,781	0.19	24.03
Taiwan (Province of China)		7,869	5,874	12,704	19,046	20,858	0.03	9.51
Hong Kong, China		12,658	8,762	15,615	23,875	18,482	0.03	-22.59
Japan		887,786	622,001	359,404	315,550	363,388	0.55	15.16
Korea, Republic of		107,421	109,142	85,034	79,700	78,760	0.12	-1.18
Other countries of North-East Asia		9	3	17,151	3,952	1,119		-71.69
South-East Asia		55,040	31,687	94,379	113,393	101,922	0.15	-10.12
Indonesia		5,185	3,302	11,925	18,824	13,499	0.02	-28.29
Malaysia		6,940	3,999	11,636	8,547	11,162	0.02	30.60
Thailand		12,049	9,823	23,880	36,778	25,477	0.04	-30.73
Other countries of South-East Asia		30,866	14,563	46,938	49,244	51,784	0.08	5.16
Australasia		195,218	187,230	531,891	545,723	563,021	0.85	3.17

ITALY

2. Arrivals of non-resident visitors at national borders, by nationality

	2002	2003	2004	2005	2006	Market share 06	% Change 06-05
Australia	168,952	167,394	457,791	493,415	498,100	0.75	0.95
New Zealand	26,266	19,836	74,100	52,308	64,921	0.10	24.11
Melanesia	**4**	**453**	**340**	**155**	**3,265**		**2,006.45**
All countries of Melanesia	4	453	340	155	3,265		2,006.45
Micronesia	**12**	**1**	**332**		**102**		
All countries of Micronesia	12	1	332		102		
Polynesia			**5,773**	**5,180**	**7,826**	**0.01**	**51.08**
Samoa					999		
Other countries of Polynesia					6,827	0.01	
All countries of Polynesia			5,773	5,180			
EUROPE	**59,616,111**	**59,924,509**	**52,861,556**	**53,020,380**	**59,700,683**	**89.97**	**12.60**
Central/Eastern Europe	**2,236,508**	**2,185,614**	**2,779,870**	**3,604,088**	**5,004,981**	**7.54**	**38.87**
Hungary	499,480	470,693	508,699	727,857	1,083,645	1.63	48.88
Poland	609,538	452,860	539,534	817,705	1,144,719	1.73	39.99
Romania	208,004	226,069	467,668	673,942	858,154	1.29	27.33
Russian Federation	175,938	269,802	149,587	187,760	256,186	0.39	36.44
Other countries Central/East Europ	743,548	766,190	1,114,382	1,196,824	1,662,277	2.51	38.89
Northern Europe	**3,752,480**	**4,106,819**	**5,369,586**	**5,749,467**	**6,353,523**	**9.58**	**10.51**
Denmark	347,261	394,295	412,781	459,075	480,888	0.72	4.75
Finland	107,721	116,029	225,697	195,727	245,399	0.37	25.38
Ireland	184,158	196,032	303,482	284,297	413,445	0.62	45.43
Norway	105,787	138,485	187,563	196,515	252,955	0.38	28.72
Sweden	270,369	286,732	429,197	409,311	466,202	0.70	13.90
United Kingdom	2,733,811	2,966,239	3,781,278	4,186,865	4,473,477	6.74	6.85
Other countries of Northern Europe	3,373	9,007	29,588	17,677	21,157	0.03	19.69
Southern Europe	**10,370,204**	**9,480,442**	**6,449,898**	**6,541,480**	**7,338,038**	**11.06**	**12.18**
Croatia	3,016,344	2,326,734	767,580	567,598	888,696	1.34	56.57
Greece	855,578	983,329	534,687	486,259	515,985	0.78	6.11
Portugal	146,600	145,456	164,672	158,423	230,812	0.35	45.69
Slovenia	4,927,941	4,564,071	3,276,459	3,083,339	2,909,398	4.38	-5.64
Spain	1,265,694	1,324,321	1,447,185	1,956,876	2,463,351	3.71	25.88
Serbia and Montenegro	29,225	26,002	52,051	77,094	89,133	0.13	15.62
Other countries Southern Europe	128,822	110,529	207,264	211,891	240,663	0.36	13.58
Western Europe	**43,045,708**	**43,890,325**	**37,991,975**	**36,832,742**	**40,631,598**	**61.24**	**10.31**
Austria	6,890,158	7,826,921	5,450,339	5,876,487	6,211,684	9.36	5.70
Belgium	1,008,854	914,589	1,033,796	1,095,192	1,185,090	1.79	8.21
France	8,950,388	8,644,079	8,159,853	8,382,663	10,262,027	15.47	22.42
Germany	14,400,925	13,772,914	11,876,402	10,978,777	10,741,804	16.19	-2.16
Luxembourg	33,605	45,823	140,018	97,447	225,013	0.34	130.91
Netherlands	1,671,956	1,654,957	1,744,957	1,607,986	1,590,187	2.40	-1.11
Switzerland	9,759,976	10,594,762	9,365,521	8,604,012	10,185,354	15.35	18.38
Other countries of Western Europe	329,846	436,280	221,089	190,178	230,439	0.35	21.17
East Mediterranean Europe	**207,477**	**254,893**	**236,144**	**277,335**	**337,664**	**0.51**	**21.75**
Israel	66,651	79,471	145,887	124,275	111,924	0.17	-9.94
Turkey	140,826	175,422	90,257	153,060	225,740	0.34	47.48
Other Europe	**3,734**	**6,416**	**34,083**	**15,268**	**34,879**	**0.05**	**128.45**
Other countries of Europe	3,734	6,416	34,083	15,268	34,879	0.05	128.45
MIDDLE EAST	**88,995**	**82,955**	**239,165**	**375,865**	**373,103**	**0.56**	**-0.73**
Middle East	**88,995**	**82,955**	**239,165**	**375,865**	**373,103**	**0.56**	**-0.73**
Kuwait	1,944	1,646	13,593	16,008	13,573	0.02	-15.21
Libyan Arab Jamahiriya	7,412	6,286	19,013	40,236	47,745	0.07	18.66

ITALY

2. Arrivals of non-resident visitors at national borders, by nationality

	2002	2003	2004	2005	2006	Market share 06	% Change 06-05
Saudi Arabia	18,337	9,126	18,204	24,724	35,973	0.05	45.50
Egypt	31,912	30,624	54,445	122,168	87,051	0.13	-28.74
Other countries of Middle East	29,390	35,273	133,910	172,729	188,761	0.28	9.28
SOUTH ASIA	**94,733**	**71,981**	**265,383**	**322,235**	**363,377**	**0.55**	**12.77**
South Asia	**94,733**	**71,981**	**265,383**	**322,235**	**363,377**	**0.55**	**12.77**
India	70,774	53,119	177,502	237,315	258,195	0.39	8.80
Iran, Islamic Republic of	6,108	4,853	50,361	45,832	55,232	0.08	20.51
Other countries of South Asia	17,851	14,009	37,520	39,088	49,950	0.08	27.79
REGION NOT SPECIFIED	**1**		**1,764**	**3,521**	**11,078**	**0.02**	**214.63**
Not Specified	**1**		**1,764**	**3,521**	**11,078**	**0.02**	**214.63**
Other countries of the World	1		1,764	3,521	11,078	0.02	214.63

Source: World Tourism Organization (UNWTO)

ITALY

3. Arrivals of non-resident tourists in hotels and similar establishments, by nationality

		2002	2003	2004	2005	2006	Market share 06	% Change 06-05
TOTAL	(*)	29,339,827	28,174,361	29,916,163	30,943,456	33,512,760	100.00	8.30
AFRICA		245,797	250,445	236,758	246,027	235,049	0.70	-4.46
Southern Africa		38,161	43,403	52,300	60,347	62,670	0.19	3.85
South Africa		38,161	43,403	52,300	60,347	62,670	0.19	3.85
Other Africa		207,636	207,042	184,458	185,680	172,379	0.51	-7.16
Other countries of Africa		207,636	207,042	184,458	185,680	172,379	0.51	-7.16
AMERICAS		4,353,803	4,042,332	4,836,540	5,176,340	5,774,615	17.23	11.56
North America		3,753,513	3,511,324	4,291,341	4,589,515	5,119,935	15.28	11.56
Canada		344,635	334,521	390,742	473,012	530,453	1.58	12.14
Mexico		194,363	173,807	170,446	167,097	170,836	0.51	2.24
United States		3,214,515	3,002,996	3,730,153	3,949,406	4,418,646	13.18	11.88
South America		600,290	531,008	545,199	586,825	654,680	1.95	11.56
Argentina		114,798	117,456	118,110	119,044	129,742	0.39	8.99
Brazil		209,850	175,650	204,381	239,511	287,503	0.86	20.04
Venezuela		39,382	28,653	32,213	42,093	41,961	0.13	-0.31
Other countries of South America		236,260	209,249	190,495	186,177	195,474	0.58	4.99
EAST ASIA AND THE PACIFIC		3,314,008	2,995,336	3,477,151	3,483,371	3,684,046	10.99	5.76
North-East Asia		2,508,227	2,233,333	2,574,552	2,612,948	2,771,181	8.27	6.06
China		521,226	467,345	713,586	707,106	794,541	2.37	12.37
Japan		1,773,942	1,560,950	1,614,928	1,617,388	1,602,025	4.78	-0.95
Korea, Republic of		213,059	205,038	246,038	288,454	374,615	1.12	29.87
Australasia		407,753	392,277	515,255	552,621	587,852	1.75	6.38
Australia		350,840	336,634	443,696	474,137	509,199	1.52	7.39
New Zealand		56,913	55,643	71,559	78,484	78,653	0.23	0.22
Other East Asia and the Pacific		398,028	369,726	387,344	317,802	325,013	0.97	2.27
Other countries of Asia		398,028	369,726	387,344	317,802	325,013	0.97	2.27
EUROPE		20,753,679	20,233,060	20,647,700	21,381,802	23,031,489	68.72	7.72
Central/Eastern Europe		1,046,781	1,080,668	1,159,467	1,437,474	1,767,208	5.27	22.94
Czech Republic		152,487	164,365	183,883	202,179	223,684	0.67	10.64
Estonia					19,501	19,737	0.06	1.21
Hungary		178,009	182,403	187,389	213,929	232,823	0.69	8.83
Latvia					9,852	17,344	0.05	76.05
Lithuania					30,562	54,405	0.16	78.02
Poland		338,312	330,084	315,993	415,371	467,632	1.40	12.58
Russian Federation		344,933	363,357	432,714	496,325	694,425	2.07	39.91
Slovakia		33,040	40,459	39,488	49,755	57,158	0.17	14.88
Northern Europe		3,356,738	3,483,115	3,807,867	4,143,581	4,294,166	12.81	3.63
Denmark		210,002	206,819	237,092	266,467	305,940	0.91	14.81
Finland		109,921	119,554	130,273	159,714	173,573	0.52	8.68
Iceland		15,904	16,681	19,460	21,170	23,858	0.07	12.70
Ireland		204,738	208,389	243,306	278,814	342,862	1.02	22.97
Norway		151,966	168,807	204,425	247,830	277,597	0.83	12.01
Sweden		325,262	314,872	374,519	377,020	394,056	1.18	4.52
United Kingdom		2,338,945	2,447,993	2,598,792	2,792,566	2,776,280	8.28	-0.58
Southern Europe		1,721,284	1,717,021	2,003,164	2,163,546	2,453,172	7.32	13.39
Croatia		121,976	124,267	125,796	128,483	145,534	0.43	13.27
Greece		265,776	243,712	272,088	279,023	345,374	1.03	23.78
Malta					22,829	40,641	0.12	78.02
Portugal		149,387	139,276	148,762	153,943	169,282	0.51	9.96

ITALY

3. Arrivals of non-resident tourists in hotels and similar establishments, by nationality

	2002	2003	2004	2005	2006	Market share 06	% Change 06-05
Slovenia	106,420	102,440	114,885	115,288	127,777	0.38	10.83
Spain	1,077,725	1,107,326	1,341,633	1,463,980	1,624,564	4.85	10.97
Western Europe	**12,859,371**	**12,370,623**	**12,520,708**	**12,499,485**	**13,192,438**	**39.37**	**5.54**
Austria	1,346,012	1,252,722	1,287,585	1,261,656	1,346,623	4.02	6.73
Belgium	663,637	658,522	669,110	659,287	712,139	2.12	8.02
France	2,331,204	2,365,785	2,465,437	2,443,936	2,609,991	7.79	6.79
Germany	6,535,425	6,131,991	6,092,496	6,055,755	6,366,837	19.00	5.14
Luxembourg	42,099	42,810	45,356	47,719	49,330	0.15	3.38
Netherlands	716,762	695,007	721,101	747,488	799,647	2.39	6.98
Switzerland	1,224,232	1,223,786	1,239,623	1,283,644	1,307,871	3.90	1.89
East Mediterranean Europe	**371,184**	**346,434**	**333,599**	**338,227**	**370,127**	**1.10**	**9.43**
Cyprus				9,040	13,690	0.04	51.44
Israel	278,107	242,812	209,729	194,190	196,098	0.59	0.98
Turkey	93,077	103,622	123,870	134,997	160,339	0.48	18.77
Other Europe	**1,398,321**	**1,235,199**	**822,895**	**799,489**	**954,378**	**2.85**	**19.37**
Other countries of Europe	1,398,321	1,235,199	822,895	799,489	954,378	2.85	19.37
MIDDLE EAST	**151,202**	**145,316**	**155,211**	**142,095**	**153,428**	**0.46**	**7.98**
Middle East	**151,202**	**145,316**	**155,211**	**142,095**	**153,428**	**0.46**	**7.98**
Egypt	29,617	28,939	26,517	28,351	34,541	0.10	21.83
Other countries of Middle East	121,585	116,377	128,694	113,744	118,887	0.35	4.52
SOUTH ASIA				**90,267**	**126,666**	**0.38**	**40.32**
South Asia				**90,267**	**126,666**	**0.38**	**40.32**
India				90,267	126,666	0.38	40.32
REGION NOT SPECIFIED	**521,338**	**507,872**	**562,803**	**423,554**	**507,467**	**1.51**	**19.81**
Not Specified	**521,338**	**507,872**	**562,803**	**423,554**	**507,467**	**1.51**	**19.81**
Other countries of the World	521,338	507,872	562,803	423,554	507,467	1.51	19.81

Source: World Tourism Organization (UNWTO)

ITALY

4. Arrivals of non-resident tourists in all types of accommodation establishments, by nationality

	2002	2003	2004	2005	2006	Market share 06	% Change 06-05
TOTAL	36,355,046	35,006,124	36,715,739	38,126,691	41,193,827	100.00	8.04
AFRICA	268,438	276,566	265,808	275,237	265,458	0.64	-3.55
Southern Africa	43,352	50,079	62,101	68,179	71,409	0.17	4.74
South Africa	43,352	50,079	62,101	68,179	71,409	0.17	4.74
Other Africa	225,086	226,487	203,707	207,058	194,049	0.47	-6.28
Other countries of Africa	225,086	226,487	203,707	207,058	194,049	0.47	-6.28
AMERICAS	4,731,739	4,460,589	5,318,441	5,724,257	6,380,061	15.49	11.46
North America	4,074,029	3,869,864	4,711,867	5,069,667	5,649,726	13.71	11.44
Canada	392,799	389,321	451,422	549,092	612,886	1.49	11.62
Mexico	211,096	191,194	187,496	185,931	192,133	0.47	3.34
United States	3,470,134	3,289,349	4,072,949	4,334,644	4,844,707	11.76	11.77
South America	657,710	590,725	606,574	654,590	730,335	1.77	11.57
Argentina	128,780	131,243	132,942	134,353	147,148	0.36	9.52
Brazil	227,390	194,026	224,960	263,990	315,415	0.77	19.48
Venezuela	42,117	31,986	35,237	45,567	45,813	0.11	0.54
Other countries of South America	259,423	233,470	213,435	210,680	221,959	0.54	5.35
EAST ASIA AND THE PACIFIC	3,490,388	3,191,155	3,680,727	3,693,226	3,919,908	9.52	6.14
North-East Asia	2,571,064	2,301,413	2,641,833	2,684,795	2,862,450	6.95	6.62
China	531,449	480,225	727,647	724,444	816,940	1.98	12.77
Japan	1,815,520	1,603,479	1,656,214	1,657,688	1,648,220	4.00	-0.57
Korea, Republic of	224,095	217,709	257,972	302,663	397,290	0.96	31.26
Australasia	501,885	496,877	626,596	668,638	707,846	1.72	5.86
Australia	428,007	418,772	533,252	567,578	605,300	1.47	6.65
New Zealand	73,878	78,105	93,344	101,060	102,546	0.25	1.47
Other East Asia and the Pacific	417,439	392,865	412,298	339,793	349,612	0.85	2.89
Other countries of Asia	417,439	392,865	412,298	339,793	349,612	0.85	2.89
EUROPE	27,125,873	26,356,270	26,667,322	27,692,293	29,738,884	72.19	7.39
Central/Eastern Europe	1,520,241	1,511,079	1,595,713	1,912,512	2,289,685	5.56	19.72
Czech Republic	323,732	327,174	344,706	371,923	404,709	0.98	8.82
Estonia				22,488	23,280	0.06	3.52
Hungary	283,818	295,265	302,364	331,981	357,466	0.87	7.68
Latvia				11,147	20,239	0.05	81.56
Lithuania				33,691	61,404	0.15	82.26
Poland	473,032	429,470	416,486	534,523	599,443	1.46	12.15
Russian Federation	360,373	381,340	453,064	518,828	720,758	1.75	38.92
Slovakia	79,286	77,830	79,093	87,931	102,386	0.25	16.44
Northern Europe	3,993,353	4,165,388	4,506,349	4,958,280	5,141,201	12.48	3.69
Denmark	394,226	387,175	426,008	488,252	537,366	1.30	10.06
Finland	131,028	139,224	150,799	183,421	197,312	0.48	7.57
Iceland	18,034	18,867	21,922	24,812	28,080	0.07	13.17
Ireland	236,681	245,437	281,336	330,116	405,204	0.98	22.75
Norway	185,939	203,029	241,839	289,890	323,275	0.78	11.52
Sweden	401,773	389,880	451,314	456,881	473,760	1.15	3.69
United Kingdom	2,625,672	2,781,776	2,933,131	3,184,908	3,176,204	7.71	-0.27
Southern Europe	1,916,568	1,938,619	2,232,161	2,403,575	2,718,292	6.60	13.09
Croatia	137,079	140,598	143,006	145,576	163,055	0.40	12.01
Greece	279,187	260,339	287,459	295,626	361,336	0.88	22.23
Malta				26,019	45,705	0.11	75.66

ITALY

4. Arrivals of non-resident tourists in all types of accommodation establishments, by nationality

	2002	2003	2004	2005	2006	Market share 06	% Change 06-05
Portugal	166,670	158,689	168,221	175,994	190,791	0.46	8.41
Slovenia	135,257	136,644	150,273	154,123	169,080	0.41	9.70
Spain	1,198,375	1,242,349	1,483,202	1,606,237	1,788,325	4.34	11.34
Western Europe	**17,615,765**	**16,962,979**	**16,994,177**	**17,085,885**	**18,049,900**	**43.82**	**5.64**
Austria	1,810,603	1,718,364	1,731,915	1,697,571	1,803,623	4.38	6.25
Belgium	815,030	811,911	814,680	833,335	899,784	2.18	7.97
France	2,746,459	2,826,718	2,915,678	2,936,714	3,134,361	7.61	6.73
Germany	9,332,069	8,693,108	8,586,149	8,504,489	8,961,197	21.75	5.37
Luxembourg	48,095	49,402	52,156	56,907	57,776	0.14	1.53
Netherlands	1,352,650	1,329,544	1,342,951	1,444,923	1,536,493	3.73	6.34
Switzerland	1,510,859	1,533,932	1,550,648	1,611,946	1,656,666	4.02	2.77
East Mediterranean Europe	**395,083**	**370,636**	**358,311**	**367,285**	**402,794**	**0.98**	**9.67**
Cyprus				9,789	14,448	0.04	47.59
Israel	296,788	262,160	229,768	215,316	219,462	0.53	1.93
Turkey	98,295	108,476	128,543	142,180	168,884	0.41	18.78
Other Europe	**1,684,863**	**1,407,569**	**980,611**	**964,756**	**1,137,012**	**2.76**	**17.85**
Other countries of Europe	1,684,863	1,407,569	980,611	964,756	1,137,012	2.76	17.85
MIDDLE EAST	**157,488**	**152,103**	**162,766**	**149,510**	**164,490**	**0.40**	**10.02**
Middle East	**157,488**	**152,103**	**162,766**	**149,510**	**164,490**	**0.40**	**10.02**
Egypt	30,922	30,384	28,004	29,996	37,563	0.09	25.23
Other countries of Middle East	126,566	121,719	134,762	119,514	126,927	0.31	6.20
SOUTH ASIA				**94,166**	**132,953**	**0.32**	**41.19**
South Asia				**94,166**	**132,953**	**0.32**	**41.19**
India				94,166	132,953	0.32	41.19
REGION NOT SPECIFIED	**581,120**	**569,441**	**620,675**	**498,002**	**592,073**	**1.44**	**18.89**
Not Specified	**581,120**	**569,441**	**620,675**	**498,002**	**592,073**	**1.44**	**18.89**
Other countries of the World	581,120	569,441	620,675	498,002	592,073	1.44	18.89

Source: World Tourism Organization (UNWTO)

ITALY

5. Overnight stays of non-resident tourists in hotels and similar establishments, by nationality

		2002	2003	2004	2005	2006	Market share 06	% Change 06-05
TOTAL	(*)	97,837,167	93,934,636	97,174,844	102,311,911	107,858,735	100.00	5.42
AFRICA		777,974	782,505	777,302	796,492	751,591	0.70	-5.64
Southern Africa		116,298	119,932	147,884	177,937	176,323	0.16	-0.91
South Africa		116,298	119,932	147,884	177,937	176,323	0.16	-0.91
Other Africa		661,676	662,573	629,418	618,555	575,268	0.53	-7.00
Other countries of Africa		661,676	662,573	629,418	618,555	575,268	0.53	-7.00
AMERICAS		10,667,829	9,901,361	11,926,104	13,048,455	13,960,770	12.94	6.99
North America		9,062,502	8,472,579	10,483,941	11,467,015	12,290,752	11.40	7.18
Canada		870,077	819,774	995,135	1,244,139	1,389,443	1.29	11.68
Mexico		437,326	384,912	397,878	413,920	411,445	0.38	-0.60
United States		7,755,099	7,267,893	9,090,928	9,808,956	10,489,864	9.73	6.94
South America		1,605,327	1,428,782	1,442,163	1,581,440	1,670,018	1.55	5.60
Argentina		342,831	340,370	341,402	344,967	339,483	0.31	-1.59
Brazil		546,869	468,941	521,087	634,590	720,640	0.67	13.56
Venezuela		114,797	84,207	93,481	117,163	120,274	0.11	2.66
Other countries of South America		600,830	535,264	486,193	484,720	489,621	0.45	1.01
EAST ASIA AND THE PACIFIC		6,736,301	6,225,806	7,101,950	6,973,629	7,240,403	6.71	3.83
North-East Asia		4,904,440	4,461,861	4,976,349	4,833,295	4,987,926	4.62	3.20
China		937,290	860,382	1,220,916	1,128,318	1,233,958	1.14	9.36
Japan		3,557,188	3,221,901	3,310,153	3,195,830	3,038,778	2.82	-4.91
Korea, Republic of		409,962	379,578	445,280	509,147	715,190	0.66	40.47
Australasia		982,901	937,706	1,271,715	1,392,315	1,476,754	1.37	6.06
Australia		841,932	802,943	1,091,124	1,191,674	1,257,043	1.17	5.49
New Zealand		140,969	134,763	180,591	200,641	219,711	0.20	9.50
Other East Asia and the Pacific		848,960	826,239	853,886	748,019	775,723	0.72	3.70
Other countries of Asia		848,960	826,239	853,886	748,019	775,723	0.72	3.70
EUROPE		77,722,014	75,154,939	75,380,294	79,475,841	83,709,708	77.61	5.33
Central/Eastern Europe		3,871,938	3,914,996	4,188,204	5,197,789	6,204,372	5.75	19.37
Czech Republic		677,277	722,006	797,775	857,516	950,885	0.88	10.89
Estonia					62,409	59,261	0.05	-5.04
Hungary		604,517	620,688	636,108	735,702	773,333	0.72	5.11
Latvia					29,351	57,679	0.05	96.51
Lithuania					76,557	126,437	0.12	65.15
Poland		1,221,036	1,080,467	1,094,566	1,433,835	1,595,106	1.48	11.25
Russian Federation		1,203,580	1,282,170	1,488,531	1,780,621	2,376,835	2.20	33.48
Slovakia		165,528	209,665	171,224	221,798	264,836	0.25	19.40
Northern Europe		12,546,927	12,846,497	13,778,983	15,652,824	16,034,338	14.87	2.44
Denmark		746,472	725,229	835,402	1,003,517	1,164,164	1.08	16.01
Finland		415,860	467,107	477,489	614,642	634,974	0.59	3.31
Iceland		65,307	70,214	80,497	84,122	99,733	0.09	18.56
Ireland		768,080	807,451	892,254	1,137,494	1,353,188	1.25	18.96
Norway		489,940	551,615	647,017	834,546	932,756	0.86	11.77
Sweden		1,134,064	1,097,404	1,246,319	1,315,704	1,339,940	1.24	1.84
United Kingdom		8,927,204	9,127,477	9,600,005	10,662,799	10,509,583	9.74	-1.44
Southern Europe		4,309,477	4,224,001	4,957,507	5,718,684	6,277,237	5.82	9.77
Croatia		447,951	435,880	429,018	443,038	469,210	0.44	5.91
Greece		655,813	588,886	672,399	740,722	875,090	0.81	18.14
Malta					85,051	134,895	0.13	58.60

ITALY

5. Overnight stays of non-resident tourists in hotels and similar establishments, by nationality

	2002	2003	2004	2005	2006	Market share 06	% Change 06-05
Portugal	417,814	384,094	413,548	436,921	490,124	0.45	12.18
Slovenia	342,157	328,251	343,993	362,899	371,609	0.34	2.40
Spain	2,445,742	2,486,890	3,098,549	3,650,053	3,936,309	3.65	7.84
Western Europe	**51,866,063**	**49,323,866**	**48,746,342**	**49,194,506**	**51,033,224**	**47.31**	**3.74**
Austria	5,030,249	4,577,743	4,614,437	4,606,809	4,810,415	4.46	4.42
Belgium	2,646,169	2,587,877	2,540,584	2,627,135	2,826,259	2.62	7.58
France	6,738,219	7,014,445	7,072,781	7,213,648	7,486,430	6.94	3.78
Germany	30,094,125	27,792,975	27,253,386	27,058,931	27,997,167	25.96	3.47
Luxembourg	214,936	215,502	222,575	226,155	235,462	0.22	4.12
Netherlands	2,435,692	2,408,372	2,397,675	2,654,763	2,767,527	2.57	4.25
Switzerland	4,706,673	4,726,952	4,644,904	4,807,065	4,909,964	4.55	2.14
East Mediterranean Europe	**946,585**	**909,676**	**891,677**	**929,108**	**1,004,656**	**0.93**	**8.13**
Cyprus				22,785	39,139	0.04	71.78
Israel	680,984	611,734	554,241	521,685	536,612	0.50	2.86
Turkey	265,601	297,942	337,436	384,638	428,905	0.40	11.51
Other Europe	**4,181,024**	**3,935,903**	**2,817,581**	**2,782,930**	**3,155,881**	**2.93**	**13.40**
Other countries of Europe	4,181,024	3,935,903	2,817,581	2,782,930	3,155,881	2.93	13.40
MIDDLE EAST	**472,650**	**457,795**	**477,977**	**521,690**	**547,002**	**0.51**	**4.85**
Middle East	**472,650**	**457,795**	**477,977**	**521,690**	**547,002**	**0.51**	**4.85**
Egypt	98,491	100,852	96,086	109,134	126,142	0.12	15.58
Other countries of Middle East	374,159	356,943	381,891	412,556	420,860	0.39	2.01
SOUTH ASIA				**222,606**	**276,404**	**0.26**	**24.17**
South Asia				**222,606**	**276,404**	**0.26**	**24.17**
India				222,606	276,404	0.26	24.17
REGION NOT SPECIFIED	**1,460,399**	**1,412,230**	**1,511,217**	**1,273,198**	**1,372,857**	**1.27**	**7.83**
Not Specified	**1,460,399**	**1,412,230**	**1,511,217**	**1,273,198**	**1,372,857**	**1.27**	**7.83**
Other countries of the World	1,460,399	1,412,230	1,511,217	1,273,198	1,372,857	1.27	7.83

Source: World Tourism Organization (UNWTO)

ITALY

6. Overnight stays of non-resident tourists in all types of accommodation establishments, by nationality

	2002	2003	2004	2005	2006	Market share 06	% Change 06-05
TOTAL	145,559,930	139,653,425	141,169,236	148,501,052	156,861,341	100.00	5.63
AFRICA	991,479	1,043,179	1,041,128	1,076,795	1,053,777	0.67	-2.14
Southern Africa	139,906	143,307	179,957	210,694	210,295	0.13	-0.19
South Africa	139,906	143,307	179,957	210,694	210,295	0.13	-0.19
Other Africa	851,573	899,872	861,171	866,101	843,482	0.54	-2.61
Other countries of Africa	851,573	899,872	861,171	866,101	843,482	0.54	-2.61
AMERICAS	12,217,093	11,708,021	13,935,406	15,348,032	16,320,268	10.40	6.33
North America	10,344,315	9,975,273	12,159,666	13,396,182	14,266,146	9.09	6.49
Canada	1,038,961	1,014,222	1,211,549	1,557,272	1,708,176	1.09	9.69
Mexico	490,891	438,489	449,125	472,139	479,135	0.31	1.48
United States	8,814,463	8,522,562	10,498,992	11,366,771	12,078,835	7.70	6.26
South America	1,872,778	1,732,748	1,775,740	1,951,850	2,054,122	1.31	5.24
Argentina	404,894	418,652	427,147	426,457	419,175	0.27	-1.71
Brazil	627,421	562,106	633,122	776,372	867,651	0.55	11.76
Venezuela	125,881	99,936	109,309	134,480	139,951	0.09	4.07
Other countries of South America	714,582	652,054	606,162	614,541	627,345	0.40	2.08
EAST ASIA AND THE PACIFIC	7,342,791	6,881,556	7,792,898	7,747,634	8,128,744	5.18	4.92
North-East Asia	5,115,531	4,691,891	5,212,954	5,096,256	5,342,186	3.41	4.83
China	991,533	920,375	1,290,942	1,219,151	1,325,467	0.84	8.72
Japan	3,680,211	3,357,816	3,442,861	3,325,128	3,198,038	2.04	-3.82
Korea, Republic of	443,787	413,700	479,151	551,977	818,681	0.52	48.32
Australasia	1,267,730	1,238,177	1,595,664	1,770,428	1,865,890	1.19	5.39
Australia	1,074,014	1,037,104	1,352,856	1,488,957	1,570,348	1.00	5.47
New Zealand	193,716	201,073	242,808	281,471	295,542	0.19	5.00
Other East Asia and the Pacific	959,530	951,488	984,280	880,950	920,668	0.59	4.51
Other countries of Asia	959,530	951,488	984,280	880,950	920,668	0.59	4.51
EUROPE	122,694,105	117,765,762	116,038,033	121,740,503	128,562,214	81.96	5.60
Central/Eastern Europe	7,265,228	6,950,747	7,206,116	8,406,311	9,709,868	6.19	15.51
Czech Republic	1,928,608	1,911,548	1,923,849	1,991,646	2,171,142	1.38	9.01
Estonia				78,876	72,228	0.05	-8.43
Hungary	1,272,561	1,369,519	1,396,755	1,517,082	1,579,201	1.01	4.09
Latvia				35,826	69,899	0.04	95.11
Lithuania				91,201	155,740	0.10	70.77
Poland	2,218,431	1,739,441	1,772,883	2,239,811	2,485,889	1.58	10.99
Russian Federation	1,329,702	1,425,615	1,635,710	1,943,064	2,555,305	1.63	31.51
Slovakia	515,926	504,624	476,919	508,805	620,464	0.40	21.95
Northern Europe	16,939,145	17,406,387	18,241,026	20,809,567	21,403,272	13.64	2.85
Denmark	2,256,095	2,152,018	2,355,494	2,804,034	3,028,064	1.93	7.99
Finland	548,099	576,741	579,055	731,976	758,234	0.48	3.59
Iceland	78,789	84,279	97,829	102,851	118,110	0.08	14.84
Ireland	941,822	1,023,524	1,094,809	1,426,626	1,714,027	1.09	20.15
Norway	741,975	798,400	897,748	1,091,636	1,224,791	0.78	12.20
Sweden	1,676,414	1,626,242	1,743,808	1,823,154	1,827,900	1.17	0.26
United Kingdom	10,695,951	11,145,183	11,472,283	12,829,290	12,732,146	8.12	-0.76
Southern Europe	5,278,894	5,296,222	5,986,868	6,796,110	7,409,137	4.72	9.02
Croatia	592,116	596,657	572,391	576,430	590,363	0.38	2.42
Greece	771,175	709,164	782,444	855,484	983,339	0.63	14.95
Malta				105,739	165,573	0.11	56.59

ITALY

6. Overnight stays of non-resident tourists in all types of accommodation establishments, by nationality

	2002	2003	2004	2005	2006	Market share 06	% Change 06-05
Portugal	500,884	471,012	511,070	542,504	587,757	0.37	8.34
Slovenia	500,571	538,194	528,640	565,111	601,531	0.38	6.44
Spain	2,914,148	2,981,195	3,592,323	4,150,842	4,480,574	2.86	7.94
Western Europe	**86,215,408**	**81,881,803**	**79,655,931**	**80,633,822**	**84,390,742**	**53.80**	**4.66**
Austria	8,296,115	7,747,951	7,562,650	7,509,287	7,750,180	4.94	3.21
Belgium	3,694,801	3,623,186	3,479,354	3,733,645	3,986,334	2.54	6.77
France	8,779,738	9,175,360	9,097,018	9,380,687	9,816,174	6.26	4.64
Germany	50,809,661	46,503,480	45,186,374	44,440,599	46,401,151	29.58	4.41
Luxembourg	260,636	262,250	268,593	274,641	283,989	0.18	3.40
Netherlands	7,547,469	7,594,986	7,264,030	8,264,105	8,922,123	5.69	7.96
Switzerland	6,826,988	6,974,590	6,797,912	7,030,858	7,230,791	4.61	2.84
East Mediterranean Europe	**1,064,296**	**1,033,842**	**1,020,029**	**1,078,061**	**1,160,081**	**0.74**	**7.61**
Cyprus				25,714	41,425	0.03	61.10
Israel	768,255	709,957	656,806	627,226	646,795	0.41	3.12
Turkey	296,041	323,885	363,223	425,121	471,861	0.30	10.99
Other Europe	**5,931,134**	**5,196,761**	**3,928,063**	**4,016,632**	**4,489,114**	**2.86**	**11.76**
Other countries of Europe	5,931,134	5,196,761	3,928,063	4,016,632	4,489,114	2.86	11.76
MIDDLE EAST	**527,391**	**516,841**	**540,191**	**586,688**	**651,949**	**0.42**	**11.12**
Middle East	**527,391**	**516,841**	**540,191**	**586,688**	**651,949**	**0.42**	**11.12**
Egypt	113,062	113,538	110,470	125,441	154,378	0.10	23.07
Other countries of Middle East	414,329	403,303	429,721	461,247	497,571	0.32	7.88
SOUTH ASIA				**238,070**	**303,731**	**0.19**	**27.58**
South Asia				**238,070**	**303,731**	**0.19**	**27.58**
India				238,070	303,731	0.19	27.58
REGION NOT SPECIFIED	**1,787,071**	**1,738,066**	**1,821,580**	**1,763,330**	**1,840,658**	**1.17**	**4.39**
Not Specified	**1,787,071**	**1,738,066**	**1,821,580**	**1,763,330**	**1,840,658**	**1.17**	**4.39**
Other countries of the World	1,787,071	1,738,066	1,821,580	1,763,330	1,840,658	1.17	4.39

Source: World Tourism Organization (UNWTO)

JAMAICA

1. Arrivals of non-resident tourists at national borders, by country of residence

	2002	2003	2004	2005	2006	Market share 06	% Change 06-05
TOTAL (*)	1,266,366	1,350,285	1,414,786	1,478,663	1,678,905	100.00	13.54
AFRICA	1,131	1,084	1,139	889	1,032	0.06	16.09
Other Africa	1,131	1,084	1,139	889	1,032	0.06	16.09
All countries of Africa	1,131	1,084	1,139	889	1,032	0.06	16.09
AMERICAS	1,076,044	1,119,679	1,161,840	1,233,846	1,411,339	84.06	14.39
Caribbean	41,138	43,829	47,953	46,748	51,823	3.09	10.86
Antigua and Barbuda	1,842	1,986	2,003	1,946	2,397	0.14	23.18
Bahamas	3,950	2,946	3,237	2,801	3,606	0.21	28.74
Barbados	4,778	5,428	5,741	5,320	6,078	0.36	14.25
Bermuda	2,104	2,442	2,446	2,751	3,107	0.19	12.94
British Virgin Islands	497	620	878	872	1,018	0.06	16.74
Cayman Islands	11,036	11,966	15,036	15,822	16,901	1.01	6.82
Cuba	719	628	381	521	217	0.01	-58.35
Dominica	399	403	323	425	497	0.03	16.94
Dominican Republic	984	875	1,210	1,128	1,051	0.06	-6.83
Grenada	612	680	633	799	575	0.03	-28.04
Guadeloupe	69	72	145	78	85	0.01	8.97
Haiti	802	677	472	164	122	0.01	-25.61
Montserrat	78	130	98	98	152	0.01	55.10
Aruba	424	534	482	419	431	0.03	2.86
Curacao	1,016	1,422	1,226	1,069	1,083	0.06	1.31
Saint Kitts and Nevis	744	822	882	847	982	0.06	15.94
Saint Lucia	1,722	1,920	2,097	1,389	1,423	0.08	2.45
Saint Maarten	528	732	819	665	780	0.05	17.29
Saint Vincent and the Grenadines	645	651	650	595	742	0.04	24.71
Trinidad and Tobago	6,605	7,308	7,263	7,520	8,382	0.50	11.46
Turks and Caicos Islands	1,062	1,021	1,125	977	1,527	0.09	56.29
Other countries of the Caribbean	522	566	806	542	667	0.04	23.06
Central America	3,213	3,202	2,941	2,631	3,160	0.19	20.11
Belize	646	936	487	520	641	0.04	23.27
Costa Rica	655	550	619	579	639	0.04	10.36
El Salvador	186	135	202	98	116	0.01	18.37
Guatemala	418	380	348	269	344	0.02	27.88
Honduras	165	167	225	163	152	0.01	-6.75
Nicaragua	67	47	64	63	62		-1.59
Panama	1,076	987	996	939	1,206	0.07	28.43
North America	1,025,052	1,066,856	1,105,517	1,178,167	1,348,062	80.29	14.42
Canada	97,413	95,265	105,623	116,862	153,569	9.15	31.41
Mexico	2,010	1,892	2,273	1,665	2,167	0.13	30.15
United States (*)	925,629	969,699	997,621	1,059,640	1,192,326	71.02	12.52
South America	6,641	5,792	5,429	6,300	8,294	0.49	31.65
Argentina	442	601	495	613	993	0.06	61.99
Bolivia	49	65	44	50	52		4.00
Brazil	847	735	956	982	1,471	0.09	49.80
Chile	611	405	420	391	516	0.03	31.97
Colombia	882	767	281	475	891	0.05	87.58
Ecuador	151	88	114	319	239	0.01	-25.08
Guyana	1,740	1,650	1,771	1,826	2,082	0.12	14.02
Paraguay	71	40	17	14	19		35.71
Peru	351	338	267	296	497	0.03	67.91
Suriname	180	277	335	342	438	0.03	28.07
Uruguay	90	54	91	56	102	0.01	82.14

JAMAICA

1. Arrivals of non-resident tourists at national borders, by country of residence

	2002	2003	2004	2005	2006	Market share 06	% Change 06-05
Venezuela	1,197	761	637	927	992	0.06	7.01
Other countries of South America	30	11	1	9	2		-77.78
EAST ASIA AND THE PACIFIC	**8,292**	**9,051**	**7,971**	**8,129**	**8,240**	**0.49**	**1.37**
North-East Asia	**5,491**	**5,031**	**5,227**	**5,309**	**4,978**	**0.30**	**-6.23**
China	542	585	532	750	976	0.06	30.13
Taiwan (Province of China)	66	85	52	73	69		-5.48
Japan	4,664	4,182	4,430	4,304	3,755	0.22	-12.76
Korea, Republic of	219	179	213	182	178	0.01	-2.20
South-East Asia	**817**	**1,181**	**653**	**725**	**722**	**0.04**	**-0.41**
Philippines	727	1,090	556	614	627	0.04	2.12
Singapore	90	91	97	111	95	0.01	-14.41
Australasia	**1,760**	**2,536**	**1,756**	**1,823**	**2,126**	**0.13**	**16.62**
Australia	1,463	2,080	1,488	1,556	1,817	0.11	16.77
New Zealand	297	456	268	267	309	0.02	15.73
Other East Asia and the Pacific	**224**	**303**	**335**	**272**	**414**	**0.02**	**52.21**
Other countries of Asia	224	303	335	272	414	0.02	52.21
EUROPE	**179,902**	**219,406**	**242,904**	**234,952**	**257,224**	**15.32**	**9.48**
Central/Eastern Europe	**2,239**	**2,559**	**2,263**	**2,847**	**2,573**	**0.15**	**-9.62**
Czech Republic/Slovakia	343	369	349	372	577	0.03	55.11
Hungary	225	205	249	324	247	0.01	-23.77
Poland	612	852	682	818	655	0.04	-19.93
Russian Federation	1,059	1,133	983	1,333	1,094	0.07	-17.93
Northern Europe	**128,669**	**152,348**	**164,477**	**155,258**	**181,764**	**10.83**	**17.07**
Denmark	536	370	704	595	1,191	0.07	100.17
Finland	371	456	379	311	320	0.02	2.89
Norway	818	801	650	690	739	0.04	7.10
Sweden	1,085	1,007	1,138	1,179	1,085	0.06	-7.97
United Kingdom	125,859	149,714	161,606	152,483	178,429	10.63	17.02
Southern Europe	**22,038**	**32,079**	**36,326**	**33,383**	**28,632**	**1.71**	**-14.23**
Greece	267	278	249	274	221	0.01	-19.34
Italy	14,237	24,303	24,915	24,424	17,564	1.05	-28.09
Portugal	919	456	823	1,871	3,420	0.20	82.79
Spain	6,615	7,042	10,339	6,814	7,427	0.44	9.00
Western Europe	**25,061**	**30,423**	**37,234**	**40,700**	**41,187**	**2.45**	**1.20**
Austria	1,819	2,138	2,990	2,998	3,142	0.19	4.80
Belgium	1,231	2,354	4,174	4,450	4,774	0.28	7.28
France	2,651	2,597	3,122	3,648	3,124	0.19	-14.36
Germany	14,554	16,290	18,090	19,860	19,668	1.17	-0.97
Luxembourg	105	116	203	202	282	0.02	39.60
Netherlands	2,596	3,990	4,180	6,190	7,355	0.44	18.82
Switzerland	2,105	2,938	4,475	3,352	2,842	0.17	-15.21
East Mediterranean Europe	**813**	**906**	**979**	**1,073**	**1,150**	**0.07**	**7.18**
Israel	710	781	825	948	983	0.06	3.69
Turkey	103	125	154	125	167	0.01	33.60
Other Europe	**1,082**	**1,091**	**1,625**	**1,691**	**1,918**	**0.11**	**13.42**
Other countries of Europe	1,082	1,091	1,625	1,691	1,918	0.11	13.42
MIDDLE EAST	**392**	**363**	**350**	**347**	**394**	**0.02**	**13.54**
Middle East	**392**	**363**	**350**	**347**	**394**	**0.02**	**13.54**
Saudi Arabia	56	40	30	19	26		36.84

JAMAICA

1. Arrivals of non-resident tourists at national borders, by country of residence

	2002	2003	2004	2005	2006	Market share 06	% Change 06-05
Other countries of Middle East	336	323	320	328	368	0.02	12.20
SOUTH ASIA	**530**	**643**	**554**	**464**	**600**	**0.04**	**29.31**
South Asia	**530**	**643**	**554**	**464**	**600**	**0.04**	**29.31**
India, Pakistan	530	643	554	464	600	0.04	29.31
REGION NOT SPECIFIED	**75**	**59**	**28**	**36**	**76**		**111.11**
Not Specified	**75**	**59**	**28**	**36**	**76**		**111.11**
Other countries of the World	75	59	28	36	76		111.11

Source: World Tourism Organization (UNWTO)

JAMAICA

6. Overnight stays of non-resident tourists in all types of accommodation establishments, by country of residence

		2002	2003	2004	2005	2006	Market share 06	% Change 06-05
TOTAL	(*)	12,037,787	12,843,703	13,134,253	13,607,597	15,465,405	100.00	13.65
AMERICAS		9,000,970	9,292,650	9,470,028	10,138,677	11,448,804	74.03	12.92
Caribbean		438,051	390,001	395,979	350,933	409,989	2.65	16.83
All countries of the Caribbean		438,051	390,001	395,979	350,933	409,989	2.65	16.83
North America		8,446,938	8,801,377	8,988,107	9,693,972	10,944,362	70.77	12.90
Canada, United States		8,446,938	8,801,377	8,988,107	9,693,972	10,944,362	70.77	12.90
Other Americas		115,981	101,272	85,942	93,772	94,453	0.61	0.73
Other countries of the Americas	(*)	115,981	101,272	85,942	93,772	94,453	0.61	0.73
EUROPE		2,886,751	3,450,220	3,536,656	3,337,672	3,841,933	24.84	15.11
Other Europe		2,886,751	3,450,220	3,536,656	3,337,672	3,841,933	24.84	15.11
All countries of Europe	(*)	2,886,751	3,450,220	3,536,656	3,337,672	3,841,933	24.84	15.11
REGION NOT SPECIFIED		150,066	100,833	127,569	131,248	174,668	1.13	33.08
Not Specified		150,066	100,833	127,569	131,248	174,668	1.13	33.08
Other countries of the World		150,066	100,833	127,569	131,248	174,668	1.13	33.08

Source: World Tourism Organization (UNWTO)

JAPAN

2. Arrivals of non-resident visitors at national borders, by nationality

	2002	2003	2004	2005	2006	Market share 06	% Change 06-05
TOTAL (*)	5,238,963	5,211,725	6,137,905	6,727,926	7,334,077	100.00	9.01
AFRICA	16,698	16,434	16,946	20,583	18,678	0.25	-9.26
Southern Africa	4,750	4,595	5,107	5,953	5,777	0.08	-2.96
South Africa	4,750	4,595	5,107	5,953	5,777	0.08	-2.96
West Africa	2,756	2,373	2,122	2,107	1,946	0.03	-7.64
Ghana	905	932	829	821	886	0.01	7.92
Nigeria	1,851	1,441	1,293	1,286	1,060	0.01	-17.57
Other Africa	9,192	9,466	9,717	12,523	10,955	0.15	-12.52
Other countries of Africa	9,192	9,466	9,717	12,523	10,955	0.15	-12.52
AMERICAS	927,598	824,345	951,074	1,032,140	1,035,300	14.12	0.31
Central America	489	305	356				
El Salvador	489	305	356				
North America	887,141	792,973	918,333	990,668	994,539	13.56	0.39
Canada	131,542	126,065	142,091	150,012	157,438	2.15	4.95
Mexico	23,699	11,087	16,489	18,623	20,374	0.28	9.40
United States	731,900	655,821	759,753	822,033	816,727	11.14	-0.65
South America	31,750	24,874	26,172	33,229	32,798	0.45	-1.30
Argentina	3,786	4,058	3,336	3,793	4,046	0.06	6.67
Bolivia	623	608	671	935	629	0.01	-32.73
Brazil	14,513	11,520	13,061	17,201	18,135	0.25	5.43
Chile	2,351	1,825	2,113	2,383	2,409	0.03	1.09
Colombia	3,365	2,598	2,547	2,764	2,641	0.04	-4.45
Ecuador	2,260	406	556	840	629	0.01	-25.12
Peru	3,179	2,902	2,575	3,280	2,565	0.03	-21.80
Venezuela	1,673	957	1,313	2,033	1,744	0.02	-14.22
Other Americas	8,218	6,193	6,213	8,243	7,963	0.11	-3.40
Other countries of the Americas	8,218	6,193	6,213	8,243	7,963	0.11	-3.40
EAST ASIA AND THE PACIFIC	3,528,489	3,625,013	4,337,788	4,761,395	5,362,608	73.12	12.63
North-East Asia	2,899,307	2,960,292	3,591,259	3,980,866	4,598,917	62.71	15.53
China	452,420	448,782	616,009	652,820	811,675	11.07	24.33
Taiwan (Province of China)	877,709	785,379	1,080,590	1,274,612	1,309,121	17.85	2.71
Hong Kong, China	290,624	260,214	300,246	298,810	352,265	4.80	17.89
Korea, Republic of	1,271,835	1,459,333	1,588,472	1,747,171	2,117,325	28.87	21.19
Mongolia	6,719	6,584	5,942	7,453	8,531	0.12	14.46
South-East Asia	419,873	448,705	503,562	521,622	516,862	7.05	-0.91
Brunei Darussalam	724	651	653	762	818	0.01	7.35
Myanmar	3,018	2,945	3,301	3,639	3,942	0.05	8.33
Cambodia	1,461	1,664	1,890	2,423	2,174	0.03	-10.28
Indonesia	55,668	64,637	55,259	58,974	59,911	0.82	1.59
Lao People's Democratic Republic	1,200	1,843	1,505	1,542	1,649	0.02	6.94
Malaysia	64,346	65,369	72,445	78,173	85,627	1.17	9.54
Philippines	129,914	137,584	154,588	139,572	95,530	1.30	-31.56
Singapore	76,688	76,896	90,001	94,161	115,870	1.58	23.06
Viet Nam	14,158	17,094	19,056	22,138	25,637	0.35	15.81
Thailand	72,696	80,022	104,864	120,238	125,704	1.71	4.55
Australasia	197,658	203,723	228,955	241,160	227,433	3.10	-5.69
Australia	164,896	172,134	194,276	206,179	195,094	2.66	-5.38
New Zealand	32,762	31,589	34,679	34,981	32,339	0.44	-7.55
Other East Asia and the Pacific	11,651	12,293	14,012	17,747	19,396	0.26	9.29

JAPAN

2. Arrivals of non-resident visitors at national borders, by nationality

	2002	2003	2004	2005	2006	Market share 06	% Change 06-05
Other countries of Asia	8,520	9,022	11,090	14,013	16,082	0.22	14.76
Other countries of Oceania	3,131	3,271	2,922	3,734	3,314	0.05	-11.25
EUROPE	**688,250**	**665,187**	**744,142**	**817,092**	**817,670**	**11.15**	**0.07**
Central/Eastern Europe	**65,962**	**73,444**	**87,124**	**96,189**	**89,491**	**1.22**	**-6.96**
Bulgaria	1,553	1,490	1,850	2,301	2,186	0.03	-5.00
Czech Republic	4,265	4,723	4,917	5,832	4,784	0.07	-17.97
Hungary	4,394	3,855	4,397	4,405	4,269	0.06	-3.09
Poland	5,070	5,245	6,117	6,910	7,694	0.10	11.35
Romania	7,166	7,315	7,196	6,787	4,099	0.06	-39.61
Russian Federation	37,963	44,512	56,554	63,609	60,654	0.83	-4.65
Slovakia	1,875	1,958	1,891	1,766	1,790	0.02	1.36
Ukraine	3,676	4,346	4,202	4,579	4,015	0.05	-12.32
Northern Europe	**285,786**	**258,803**	**279,924**	**292,317**	**291,112**	**3.97**	**-0.41**
Denmark	10,924	10,567	11,054	12,382	12,992	0.18	4.93
Finland	9,391	10,414	11,793	12,895	15,242	0.21	18.20
Iceland	550	560	694				
Ireland	17,771	10,689	11,480	13,712	12,623	0.17	-7.94
Norway	6,906	7,322	8,097	8,696	8,480	0.12	-2.48
Sweden	20,973	18,708	21,102	23,097	25,299	0.34	9.53
United Kingdom	219,271	200,543	215,704	221,535	216,476	2.95	-2.28
Southern Europe	**66,805**	**64,825**	**74,167**	**86,969**	**91,590**	**1.25**	**5.31**
Croatia	1,664	1,143	1,077	1,598	1,386	0.02	-13.27
Greece	3,479	3,029	3,356	4,278	4,866	0.07	13.74
Italy	36,396	35,826	38,923	44,691	46,407	0.63	3.84
Portugal	9,246	9,327	11,440	10,673	12,246	0.17	14.74
Spain	15,344	14,772	18,619	25,729	26,685	0.36	3.72
Serbia and Montenegro	676	728	752				
Western Europe	**244,677**	**242,546**	**275,746**	**309,469**	**312,218**	**4.26**	**0.89**
Austria	10,150	10,011	11,559	12,319	12,853	0.18	4.33
Belgium	11,596	10,925	12,020	14,162	13,131	0.18	-7.28
France	87,034	85,179	95,894	110,822	117,785	1.61	6.28
Germany	93,936	93,571	106,297	118,429	115,337	1.57	-2.61
Luxembourg	402	402	448				
Netherlands	24,050	25,127	29,434	30,507	30,592	0.42	0.28
Switzerland	17,509	17,331	20,094	23,230	22,520	0.31	-3.06
East Mediterranean Europe	**16,755**	**16,692**	**17,617**	**18,301**	**19,709**	**0.27**	**7.69**
Israel	10,620	10,039	10,932	11,334	11,586	0.16	2.22
Turkey	6,135	6,653	6,685	6,967	8,123	0.11	16.59
Other Europe	**8,265**	**8,877**	**9,564**	**13,847**	**13,550**	**0.18**	**-2.14**
Other countries of Europe	8,265	8,877	9,564	13,847	13,550	0.18	-2.14
MIDDLE EAST	**3,394**	**3,166**	**3,285**	**3,072**	**3,218**	**0.04**	**4.75**
Middle East	**3,394**	**3,166**	**3,285**	**3,072**	**3,218**	**0.04**	**4.75**
Lebanon	739	585	711				
Egypt	2,655	2,581	2,574	3,072	3,218	0.04	4.75
SOUTH ASIA	**72,580**	**76,217**	**83,856**	**92,676**	**95,555**	**1.30**	**3.11**
South Asia	**72,580**	**76,217**	**83,856**	**92,676**	**95,555**	**1.30**	**3.11**
Bangladesh	5,072	5,862	6,896	6,884	6,487	0.09	-5.77
Sri Lanka	8,684	8,784	9,341	10,697	10,218	0.14	-4.48
India	45,394	47,520	53,000	58,572	62,505	0.85	6.71
Iran, Islamic Republic of	4,142	4,666	4,222	4,623	3,624	0.05	-21.61
Nepal	3,689	4,004	4,503	5,349	5,676	0.08	6.11

JAPAN

2. Arrivals of non-resident visitors at national borders, by nationality

	2002	2003	2004	2005	2006	Market share 06	% Change 06-05
Pakistan	5,599	5,381	5,894	6,551	7,045	0.10	7.54
REGION NOT SPECIFIED	**1,954**	**1,363**	**814**	**968**	**1,048**	**0.01**	**8.26**
Not Specified	**1,954**	**1,363**	**814**	**968**	**1,048**	**0.01**	**8.26**
Other countries of the World	1,954	1,363	814	968	1,048	0.01	8.26

Source: World Tourism Organization (UNWTO)

JORDAN

1. Arrivals of non-resident tourists at national borders, by nationality

	2002	2003	2004	2005	2006	Market share 06	% Change 06-05
TOTAL	2,384,472	2,353,087	2,852,803	2,986,589	3,225,409	100.00	8.00
AFRICA	19,582	17,537	19,938	30,234	50,670	1.57	67.59
East Africa	1,709	1,508	1,232	1,686	3,256	0.10	93.12
Ethiopia	311	331	342	445	890	0.03	100.00
Eritrea	305	412	260	117			
Djibouti	142	59	101	14	43		207.14
Kenya	421	192	210	338	535	0.02	58.28
Mauritius	19	13	23	19			
Somalia	511	501	296	753	1,788	0.06	137.45
Central Africa	101	68	40	47			
Chad	101	68	40	47			
North Africa	14,448	13,301	14,052	21,438	36,994	1.15	72.56
Algeria	2,416	2,581	2,388	4,859	11,109	0.34	128.63
Morocco	2,682	2,243	2,555	4,618	5,382	0.17	16.54
Sudan	7,145	6,008	6,753	8,908	14,955	0.46	67.88
Tunisia	2,205	2,469	2,356	3,053	5,548	0.17	81.72
Southern Africa	1,925	1,796	3,744	3,993	5,862	0.18	46.81
South Africa	1,925	1,796	3,744	3,993	5,862	0.18	46.81
West Africa	471	351	355	987	368	0.01	-62.72
Mauritania	177	173	164	161	368	0.01	128.57
Nigeria	243	146	152	163			
Senegal	51	32	39	663			
Other Africa	928	513	515	2,083	4,190	0.13	101.15
Other countries of Africa	928	513	515	2,083	4,190	0.13	101.15
AMERICAS	51,908	64,545	93,477	111,975	163,918	5.08	46.39
North America	49,737	61,591	89,200	106,698	155,943	4.83	46.15
Canada	8,030	9,049	12,513	13,234	21,683	0.67	63.84
Mexico	309	496	632	1,219	1,717	0.05	40.85
United States	41,398	52,046	76,055	92,245	132,543	4.11	43.69
South America	1,453	2,020	2,712	3,797	4,844	0.15	27.57
Argentina	220	350	403	533	800	0.02	50.09
Brazil	614	866	1,200	1,686	2,169	0.07	28.65
Chile	233	283	532	843	698	0.02	-17.20
Colombia	111	283	254	200	401	0.01	100.50
Venezuela	275	238	323	535	776	0.02	45.05
Other Americas	718	934	1,565	1,480	3,131	0.10	111.55
Other countries of the Americas	718	934	1,565	1,480	3,131	0.10	111.55
EAST ASIA AND THE PACIFIC	43,251	43,883	60,121	64,191	82,943	2.57	29.21
North-East Asia	13,000	15,446	19,625	18,703	25,079	0.78	34.09
China	4,945	3,828	5,419	5,106	5,385	0.17	5.46
Taiwan (Province of China)	279	372	613	540	1,303	0.04	141.30
Hong Kong, China	209	444	446	207	160		-22.71
Japan	4,419	5,287	6,296	6,677	10,255	0.32	53.59
Korea, Dem. People's Republic of	76	138	65		7		
Korea, Republic of	3,072	5,377	6,786	6,173	7,969	0.25	29.09
South-East Asia	23,375	21,174	25,090	33,794	39,744	1.23	17.61
Brunei Darussalam	181	129	200	148			
Indonesia	11,883	11,980	14,554	18,083	25,712	0.80	42.19
Malaysia	2,228	1,421	2,006	2,794	3,700	0.11	32.43

JORDAN

1. Arrivals of non-resident tourists at national borders, by nationality

	2002	2003	2004	2005	2006	Market share 06	% Change 06-05
Philippines	7,090	6,213	6,652	9,683	8,296	0.26	-14.32
Singapore	1,013	421	898	968	691	0.02	-28.62
Viet Nam	383	77	42	45	209	0.01	364.44
Thailand	597	933	738	2,073	1,136	0.04	-45.20
Australasia	**6,755**	**7,088**	**9,967**	**11,428**	**17,598**	**0.55**	**53.99**
Australia	5,472	5,849	9,841	9,476	14,434	0.45	52.32
New Zealand	1,283	1,239	126	1,952	3,164	0.10	62.09
Melanesia	**23**	**7**	**2,126**	**247**	**172**	**0.01**	**-30.36**
Fiji	23	7	2,126	247	172	0.01	-30.36
Other East Asia and the Pacific	**98**	**168**	**3,313**	**19**	**350**	**0.01**	**1,742.11**
Other countries of Asia	98	168	3,313	19	350	0.01	1,742.11
EUROPE	**313,467**	**314,858**	**374,428**	**391,846**	**424,583**	**13.16**	**8.35**
Central/Eastern Europe	**13,523**	**29,418**	**38,103**	**30,698**	**27,366**	**0.85**	**-10.85**
Bulgaria	798	970	916	1,053	1,113	0.03	5.70
Belarus	123	177	179	80			
Czech Republic	741	743	1,420	1,904	2,141	0.07	12.45
Hungary	2,863	14,979	16,807	3,492	851	0.03	-75.63
Poland	1,078	1,149	2,163	3,214			
Romania	1,588	1,733	1,535	1,468	1,123	0.03	-23.50
Russian Federation	4,001	6,925	9,624	12,858	19,564	0.61	52.15
Slovakia	384	648	1,260	3,254			
Ukraine	1,004	1,190	1,884	2,443	2,574	0.08	5.36
Other countries Central/East Europ	943	904	2,315	932			
Northern Europe	**34,073**	**36,485**	**50,284**	**53,107**	**69,827**	**2.16**	**31.48**
Denmark	2,338	2,708	2,846	2,950	3,506	0.11	18.85
Finland	759	705	998	797	1,030	0.03	29.23
Iceland	38	90	106	26	124		376.92
Ireland	1,382	1,454	1,819	2,043	2,199	0.07	7.64
Norway	1,324	1,746	1,426	1,817	2,025	0.06	11.45
Sweden	3,848	4,490	4,720	5,198	6,648	0.21	27.90
United Kingdom	24,384	25,292	38,369	40,276	54,295	1.68	34.81
Southern Europe	**21,202**	**19,842**	**30,117**	**44,600**	**42,982**	**1.33**	**-3.63**
Bosnia and Herzegovina	2,115	1,166	923	1,797	1,229	0.04	-31.61
Croatia	224	269	398	546	484	0.02	-11.36
Greece	1,649	1,811	2,083	2,335	4,000	0.12	71.31
Holy See		149	84	97			
Italy	7,326	7,268	11,605	13,933	17,507	0.54	25.65
Malta	78	86	149	158	200	0.01	26.58
Portugal	314	379	308	604	763	0.02	26.32
Slovenia	181	270	1,092	2,193	506	0.02	-76.93
Spain	4,975	5,912	10,940	20,465	17,734	0.55	-13.34
TFYR of Macedonia	2,921	1,526	1,512				
Serbia and Montenegro	1,224	943	975	604	559	0.02	-7.45
Other countries Southern Europe	195	63	48	1,868			
Western Europe	**44,636**	**40,453**	**52,746**	**59,843**	**83,309**	**2.58**	**39.21**
Austria	2,513	2,056	3,361	3,783	4,779	0.15	26.33
Belgium	2,310	2,009	2,729	2,935	3,782	0.12	28.86
France	15,784	12,984	16,359	20,458	29,369	0.91	43.56
Germany	16,517	14,675	19,839	21,179	30,456	0.94	43.80
Luxembourg	43	47	64	83	116		39.76
Netherlands	4,543	5,808	6,505	7,573	9,521	0.30	25.72
Switzerland	2,926	2,874	3,889	3,832	5,286	0.16	37.94
	199,626	187,511	202,792	199,897	185,544	5.75	-7.18

JORDAN

1. Arrivals of non-resident tourists at national borders, by nationality

	2002	2003	2004	2005	2006	Market share 06	% Change 06-05
East Mediterranean Europe							
Cyprus	758	902	894	1,017	1,280	0.04	25.86
Israel	108,259	105,807	121,506	124,540	153,076	4.75	22.91
Turkey	90,609	80,802	80,392	74,340	31,188	0.97	-58.05
Other Europe	**407**	**1,149**	**386**	**3,701**	**15,555**	**0.48**	**320.29**
Other countries of Europe	407	1,149	386	3,701	15,555	0.48	320.29
MIDDLE EAST	**1,497,960**	**1,464,910**	**1,780,755**	**1,828,735**	**1,879,541**	**58.27**	**2.78**
Middle East	**1,497,960**	**1,464,910**	**1,780,755**	**1,828,735**	**1,879,541**	**58.27**	**2.78**
Bahrain	35,572	32,252	33,785	38,708	20,478	0.63	-47.10
Palestine	22,421	23,887	29,867	47,540	96,702	3.00	103.41
Iraq	189,457	190,208	35,993	324,869	469,620	14.56	44.56
Kuwait	53,374	34,078	283,767	71,566	39,078	1.21	-45.40
Lebanon	47,117	41,472	43,467	60,560	73,890	2.29	22.01
Libyan Arab Jamahiriya	10,574	10,000	11,948	11,649	31,306	0.97	168.74
Oman	6,344	6,401	6,448	8,362	14,156	0.44	69.29
Qatar	4,075	4,204	4,729	8,979	13,953	0.43	55.40
Saudi Arabia	321,922	305,587	347,498	388,311	469,998	14.57	21.04
Syrian Arab Republic	660,422	653,433	792,410	695,364	499,230	15.48	-28.21
United Arab Emirates	8,812	7,930	9,135	10,852	17,998	0.56	65.85
Egypt	121,722	140,883	167,536	147,810	100,797	3.13	-31.81
Yemen	16,077	14,553	14,132	14,165	32,335	1.00	128.27
Other countries of Middle East	71	22	40				
SOUTH ASIA	**36,421**	**27,034**	**37,885**	**42,947**	**41,884**	**1.30**	**-2.48**
South Asia	**36,421**	**27,034**	**37,885**	**42,947**	**41,884**	**1.30**	**-2.48**
Afghanistan	201	258	231	205	346	0.01	68.78
Bangladesh	1,560	1,258	1,750	2,370	4,374	0.14	84.56
Sri Lanka	9,891	8,179	8,431	9,505	5,017	0.16	-47.22
India	16,932	12,141	17,801	19,605	19,103	0.59	-2.56
Iran, Islamic Republic of	1,383	1,270	1,546	1,627	1,665	0.05	2.34
Nepal	228	260	1,035	700	1,173	0.04	67.57
Pakistan	6,223	3,666	7,069	8,935	10,206	0.32	14.22
Other countries of South Asia	3	2	22				
REGION NOT SPECIFIED	**421,883**	**420,320**	**486,199**	**516,661**	**581,870**	**18.04**	**12.62**
Not Specified	**421,883**	**420,320**	**486,199**	**516,661**	**581,870**	**18.04**	**12.62**
Other countries of the World (*)	8,295	7,357	6,516	4,746	4,890	0.15	3.03
Nationals Residing Abroad	413,588	412,963	479,683	511,915	576,980	17.89	12.71

Source: World Tourism Organization (UNWTO)

JORDAN

2. Arrivals of non-resident visitors at national borders, by nationality

	2002	2003	2004	2005	2006	Market share 06	% Change 06-05
TOTAL	4,677,017	4,599,706	5,586,657	5,817,370	6,573,357	100.00	13.00
AFRICA	42,441	38,356	42,303	64,285	71,641	1.09	11.44
East Africa	3,044	2,670	2,124	3,122	4,419	0.07	41.54
Ethiopia	439	466	483	627	1,126	0.02	79.59
Eritrea	430	581	367	165			
Djibouti	338	141	241	34	61		79.41
Kenya	594	271	296	477	677	0.01	41.93
Mauritius	27	19	33	27			
Somalia	1,216	1,192	704	1,792	2,555	0.04	42.58
Central Africa	142	96	56	66			
Chad	142	96	56	66			
North Africa	34,396	31,671	33,457	51,042	53,973	0.82	5.74
Algeria	5,751	6,146	5,686	11,568	15,870	0.24	37.19
Morocco	6,385	5,342	6,083	10,996	7,689	0.12	-30.07
Sudan	17,011	14,304	16,079	21,209	22,488	0.34	6.03
Tunisia	5,249	5,879	5,609	7,269	7,926	0.12	9.04
Southern Africa	2,715	2,534	5,281	5,632	7,420	0.11	31.75
South Africa	2,715	2,534	5,281	5,632	7,420	0.11	31.75
West Africa	835	662	659	1,549	526	0.01	-66.04
Mauritania	420	411	390	384	526	0.01	36.98
Nigeria	343	206	215	229			
Senegal	72	45	54	936			
Other Africa	1,309	723	726	2,874	5,303	0.08	84.52
Other countries of Africa	1,309	723	726	2,874	5,303	0.08	84.52
AMERICAS	73,213	91,037	131,844	157,934	199,209	3.03	26.13
North America	70,151	86,870	125,812	150,491	189,303	2.88	25.79
Canada	11,326	12,763	17,649	18,666	26,901	0.41	44.12
Mexico	436	699	892	1,719	2,133	0.03	24.08
United States	58,389	73,408	107,271	130,106	160,269	2.44	23.18
South America	2,049	2,849	3,826	5,355	6,017	0.09	12.36
Argentina	310	493	569	752	994	0.02	32.18
Brazil	865	1,222	1,693	2,379	2,694	0.04	13.24
Chile	329	399	750	1,188	867	0.01	-27.02
Colombia	157	399	359	282	498	0.01	76.60
Venezuela	388	336	455	754	964	0.01	27.85
Other Americas	1,013	1,318	2,206	2,088	3,889	0.06	86.25
Other countries of the Americas	1,013	1,318	2,206	2,088	3,889	0.06	86.25
EAST ASIA AND THE PACIFIC	61,004	61,891	84,798	90,574	112,541	1.71	24.25
North-East Asia	18,336	21,785	27,681	26,378	32,298	0.49	22.44
China	6,975	5,399	7,643	7,202	7,990	0.12	10.94
Taiwan (Province of China)	394	525	865	761	1,933	0.03	154.01
Hong Kong, China	295	626	629	291			
Japan	6,232	7,457	8,881	9,418	10,551	0.16	12.03
Korea, Dem. People's Republic of	107	194	92				
Korea, Republic of	4,333	7,584	9,571	8,706	11,824	0.18	35.81
South-East Asia	32,713	29,682	35,107	47,676	58,411	0.89	22.52
Indonesia	16,760	16,897	20,528	25,505	38,148	0.58	49.57
Malaysia	3,142	2,004	2,829	3,941	4,933	0.08	25.17
Philippines	10,000	8,763	9,383	13,658	12,309	0.19	-9.88

JORDAN

2. Arrivals of non-resident visitors at national borders, by nationality

	2002	2003	2004	2005	2006	Market share 06	% Change 06-05
Singapore	1,429	593	1,266	1,365	1,025	0.02	-24.91
Viet Nam	540	109	59	63	310		392.06
Thailand	842	1,316	1,042	2,924	1,686	0.03	-42.34
Other countries of South-East Asia				220			
Australasia	**9,528**	**9,996**	**16,879**	**16,119**	**20,810**	**0.32**	**29.10**
Australia	7,718	8,249	13,880	13,366	17,412	0.26	30.27
New Zealand	1,810	1,747	2,999	2,753	3,398	0.05	23.43
Melanesia	**33**	**9**	**177**	**349**	**254**		**-27.22**
Fiji	33	9	177	349	254		-27.22
Other East Asia and the Pacific	**394**	**419**	**4,954**	**52**	**768**	**0.01**	**1,376.92**
Other countries of Asia	394	419	4,954	52	768	0.01	1,376.92
EUROPE	**442,128**	**444,088**	**528,112**	**552,674**	**643,219**	**9.79**	**16.38**
Central/Eastern Europe	**19,075**	**41,495**	**53,744**	**43,297**	**44,145**	**0.67**	**1.96**
Bulgaria	1,126	1,368	1,292	1,485	1,579	0.02	6.33
Belarus	174	250	253	113			
Czech Republic	1,045	1,084	2,003	2,685	3,037	0.05	13.11
Hungary	4,038	21,126	23,706	4,925	1,207	0.02	-75.49
Poland	1,521	1,621	3,051	4,533	6,415	0.10	41.52
Romania	2,240	2,444	2,165	2,070	1,592	0.02	-23.09
Russian Federation	5,643	9,768	13,574	18,136	25,309	0.39	39.55
Slovakia	542	914	1,778	4,589	1,355	0.02	-70.47
Ukraine	1,416	1,679	2,657	3,446	3,651	0.06	5.95
Other countries Central/East Europ	1,330	1,241	3,265	1,315			
Northern Europe	**48,059**	**51,457**	**70,924**	**74,905**	**90,339**	**1.37**	**20.60**
Denmark	3,298	3,819	4,014	4,160	4,973	0.08	19.54
Finland	1,071	994	1,407	1,124	1,462	0.02	30.07
Iceland	54	126	150	37	176		375.68
Ireland	1,949	2,050	2,566	2,882	3,120	0.05	8.26
Norway	1,867	2,463	2,011	2,563	2,563	0.04	
Sweden	5,428	6,333	6,658	7,332	9,835	0.15	34.14
United Kingdom	34,392	35,672	54,118	56,807	68,210	1.04	20.07
Southern Europe	**29,904**	**27,987**	**42,480**	**62,907**	**48,053**	**0.73**	**-23.61**
Bosnia and Herzegovina	2,983	1,644	1,302	2,534	1,743	0.03	-31.22
Croatia	316	380	561	770	687	0.01	-10.78
Greece	2,325	2,555	2,939	3,294	4,120	0.06	25.08
Holy See	122	210	119	137	156		13.87
Italy	10,332	10,251	16,368	19,652	19,561	0.30	-0.46
Malta	110	121	210	223	283		26.91
Portugal	442	535	435	852	1,082	0.02	27.00
Slovenia	255	381	1,540	3,093	717	0.01	-76.82
Spain	7,017	8,339	15,431	28,865	19,704	0.30	-31.74
Serbia and Montenegro	1,727	1,331	1,376	852			
Other countries Southern Europe	4,275	2,240	2,199	2,635			
Western Europe	**62,957**	**57,055**	**74,396**	**84,404**	**97,192**	**1.48**	**15.15**
Austria	3,544	2,899	4,741	5,335	5,020	0.08	-5.90
Belgium	3,258	2,834	3,849	4,140	5,305	0.08	28.14
France	22,263	18,314	23,074	28,855	32,097	0.49	11.24
Germany	23,296	20,698	27,982	29,872	35,663	0.54	19.39
Luxembourg	61	66	90	117	164		40.17
Netherlands	6,408	8,191	9,175	10,681	12,113	0.18	13.41
Switzerland	4,127	4,053	5,485	5,404	6,830	0.10	26.39
East Mediterranean Europe	**281,559**	**264,472**	**286,024**	**281,942**	**348,559**	**5.30**	**23.63**

JORDAN

2. Arrivals of non-resident visitors at national borders, by nationality

	2002	2003	2004	2005	2006	Market share 06	% Change 06-05
Cyprus	1,069	1,272	1,261	1,434	1,816	0.03	26.64
Israel	152,692	149,234	171,376	175,656	203,019	3.09	15.58
Turkey	127,798	113,966	113,387	104,852	143,724	2.19	37.07
Other Europe	**574**	**1,622**	**544**	**5,219**	**14,931**	**0.23**	**186.09**
Other countries of Europe	574	1,622	544	5,219	14,931	0.23	186.09
MIDDLE EAST	**3,566,572**	**3,487,886**	**4,239,895**	**4,354,129**	**4,881,060**	**74.26**	**12.10**
Middle East	**3,566,572**	**3,487,886**	**4,239,895**	**4,354,129**	**4,881,060**	**74.26**	**12.10**
Bahrain	84,695	76,791	80,441	92,162	80,942	1.23	-12.17
Palestine	53,383	56,874	71,113	113,190	111,923	1.70	-1.12
Iraq	451,089	452,877	675,637	773,498	494,337	7.52	-36.09
Kuwait	127,081	81,139	85,696	170,395	141,074	2.15	-17.21
Lebanon	112,183	98,743	103,493	144,190	186,591	2.84	29.41
Libyan Arab Jamahiriya	25,345	23,862	28,542	27,735	31,751	0.48	14.48
Oman	15,104	15,240	15,353	19,910	19,313	0.29	-3.00
Qatar	9,703	10,008	11,260	21,379	21,303	0.32	-0.36
Saudi Arabia	766,480	727,589	827,376	924,550	1,189,867	18.10	28.70
Syrian Arab Republic	1,572,432	1,555,793	1,886,691	1,655,629	2,106,457	32.05	27.23
United Arab Emirates	20,982	18,881	21,749	25,837	27,775	0.42	7.50
Egypt	289,815	335,437	398,896	351,928	432,603	6.58	22.92
Yemen	38,280	34,652	33,648	33,726	37,124	0.56	10.08
SOUTH ASIA	**51,372**	**38,130**	**53,434**	**60,598**	**61,590**	**0.94**	**1.64**
South Asia	**51,372**	**38,130**	**53,434**	**60,598**	**61,590**	**0.94**	**1.64**
Afghanistan	284	364	325	289	513	0.01	77.51
Bangladesh	2,201	1,774	2,468	3,342	6,490	0.10	94.20
Sri Lanka	13,951	11,536	11,892	13,406	7,444	0.11	-44.47
India	23,882	17,125	25,108	27,651	28,640	0.44	3.58
Iran, Islamic Republic of	1,951	1,792	2,181	2,294	2,162	0.03	-5.75
Nepal	322	366	1,460	987	1,740	0.03	76.29
Pakistan	8,777	5,170	9,970	12,603	14,601	0.22	15.85
Other countries of South Asia	4	3	30	26			
REGION NOT SPECIFIED	**440,287**	**438,318**	**506,271**	**537,176**	**604,097**	**9.19**	**12.46**
Not Specified	**440,287**	**438,318**	**506,271**	**537,176**	**604,097**	**9.19**	**12.46**
Other countries of the World	11,699	10,377	9,190	6,694	6,190	0.09	-7.53
Nationals Residing Abroad	428,588	427,941	497,081	530,482	597,907	9.10	12.71

Source: World Tourism Organization (UNWTO)

KAZAKHSTAN

2. Arrivals of non-resident visitors at national borders, by country of residence

	2002	2003	2004	2005	2006	Market share 06	% Change 06-05
TOTAL	3,677,921	3,236,788	4,291,040	4,364,949	4,706,742	100.00	7.83
AFRICA	1,159	1,064	1,506	1,703	5,023	0.11	194.95
East Africa	416	302	691	200	357	0.01	78.50
Ethiopia	27	28	14	8	14		75.00
Kenya	14	24	28	47	35		-25.53
Madagascar		1	15	4	2		-50.00
Zimbabwe	18	186	20	106	121		14.15
Uganda	338	25	606	15	175		1,066.67
United Republic of Tanzania	7	29	2	6	5		-16.67
Zambia	12	9	6	14	5		-64.29
Central Africa	8	2	15	14	27		92.86
Angola	8	2	7	6	17		183.33
Chad			5	3	1		-66.67
Congo			3	5	9		80.00
North Africa	230	274	134	238	2,559	0.05	975.21
Algeria	96	83		88	102		15.91
Morocco	39	129	69	79	94		18.99
Sudan	52	35	26	27	40		48.15
Tunisia	43	27	39	44	2,323	0.05	5,179.55
Southern Africa	376	352	473	1,077	1,194	0.03	10.86
South Africa	376	352	473	1,077	1,194	0.03	10.86
West Africa	129	134	193	174	886	0.02	409.20
Ghana	12	13	14	15	27		80.00
Cote D'Ivoire	1	1	3	4	6		50.00
Liberia	3	3	1	2	10		400.00
Mali	7	6	4	3	6		100.00
Mauritania	8	5	3	5	3		-40.00
Niger	1		20	5	14		180.00
Nigeria	79	90	135	126	618	0.01	390.48
Guinea-Bissau	3	2	4	4			
Senegal	13	11	3	6	7		16.67
Burkina Faso	2	3	6	4	195		4,775.00
AMERICAS	24,699	23,203	32,345	30,768	31,978	0.68	3.93
Caribbean	208	158	8,519	200	288	0.01	44.00
Barbados	1			2	1		-50.00
Cuba	99	88	146	147	197		34.01
Dominica	1		8				
Jamaica	91	43	364	8	24		200.00
Anguilla	8	10		5	1		-80.00
Saint Lucia	1		7,983	2	19		850.00
Trinidad and Tobago	7	17	18	36	46		27.78
Central America	52	7	41	31	31		
Costa Rica	8		2	7			
El Salvador	6		11	6	5		-16.67
Guatemala	7	3	10		4		
Honduras	14	1	4	4	8		100.00
Panama	17	3	14	14	14		
North America	23,952	22,590	23,298	29,876	30,737	0.65	2.88
Canada	3,641	3,646	3,724	4,440	4,597	0.10	3.54
Mexico	112	98	61	90	63		-30.00
United States	20,199	18,846	19,513	25,346	26,077	0.55	2.88

KAZAKHSTAN

2. Arrivals of non-resident visitors at national borders, by country of residence

	2002	2003	2004	2005	2006	Market share 06	% Change 06-05
South America	487	448	487	661	922	0.02	39.49
Argentina	89	118	152	208	208		
Brazil	103	103	153	183	264	0.01	44.26
Chile	42	30	19	22	52		136.36
Colombia	180	115	77	122	167		36.89
Ecuador	12	10	7	37	56		51.35
Peru	19	27	19	37	45		21.62
Uruguay	1	2	5	4	6		50.00
Venezuela	41	43	55	48	124		158.33
EAST ASIA AND THE PACIFIC	**65,929**	**72,359**	**96,660**	**113,842**	**152,929**	**3.25**	**34.33**
North-East Asia	**62,326**	**68,834**	**93,080**	**108,561**	**144,945**	**3.08**	**33.51**
China	48,306	55,482	76,806	85,696	117,279	2.49	36.85
Taiwan (Province of China)	129	251	295	1,487	179		-87.96
Hong Kong, China	2	13		8	6		-25.00
Japan	2,550	3,071	2,681	3,171	4,222	0.09	33.14
Korea, Dem. People's Republic of	2,198	102	109	80	132		65.00
Korea, Republic of	5,999	6,871	9,311	10,412	13,450	0.29	29.18
Macao, China					1		
Mongolia	3,142	3,044	3,878	7,707	9,676	0.21	25.55
South-East Asia	**1,820**	**1,764**	**1,670**	**2,828**	**5,096**	**0.11**	**80.20**
Myanmar				2	6		200.00
Cambodia	4	1	14	11	31		181.82
Indonesia	118	87	132	211	328	0.01	55.45
Lao People's Democratic Republic		7			4		
Malaysia	293	375	301	647	1,235	0.03	90.88
Philippines	908	636	584	999	2,112	0.04	111.41
Singapore	167	316	429	578	700	0.01	21.11
Viet Nam	72	65	51	88	114		29.55
Thailand	258	277	159	292	566	0.01	93.84
Australasia	**1,778**	**1,761**	**1,909**	**2,453**	**2,886**	**0.06**	**17.65**
Australia	1,346	1,465	1,614	2,040	2,385	0.05	16.91
New Zealand	432	296	295	413	501	0.01	21.31
Melanesia	**3**				**2**		
Papua New Guinea	3				2		
Polynesia	**2**		**1**				
Samoa	2		1				
EUROPE	**3,569,412**	**3,114,377**	**4,125,909**	**4,194,081**	**4,486,983**	**95.33**	**6.98**
Central/Eastern Europe	**3,450,027**	**2,980,660**	**3,964,759**	**3,993,456**	**4,239,881**	**90.08**	**6.17**
Azerbaijan	19,958	24,677	37,179	67,030	49,417	1.05	-26.28
Armenia	896	9,630	4,684	5,765	7,220	0.15	25.24
Bulgaria	599	902	664	1,081	1,322	0.03	22.29
Belarus	2,283	6,956	41,341	15,916	16,438	0.35	3.28
Czech Republic	749	782	1,234	1,330	1,686	0.04	26.77
Estonia	332	205	336	487	536	0.01	10.06
Georgia	1,669	2,651	5,375	5,278	6,865	0.15	30.07
Hungary	1,897	1,494	1,502	2,261	2,965	0.06	31.14
Kyrgyzstan	1,962,465	1,381,963	1,091,923	851,568	1,018,524	21.64	19.61
Latvia	502	905	1,398	1,687	1,771	0.04	4.98
Lithuania	595	1,264	2,639	4,122	4,641	0.10	12.59
Republic of Moldova	2,030	6,266	3,781	4,022	7,708	0.16	91.65
Poland	1,861	2,525	3,551	4,491	5,669	0.12	26.23
Romania	909	1,050	1,428	1,580	2,606	0.06	64.94

KAZAKHSTAN

2. Arrivals of non-resident visitors at national borders, by country of residence

	2002	2003	2004	2005	2006	Market share 06	% Change 06-05
Russian Federation	163,784	604,930	1,628,823	1,405,543	1,385,964	29.45	-1.39
Slovakia	368	422	335	588	702	0.01	19.39
Tajikistan	95,051	202,734	260,487	286,042	301,971	6.42	5.57
Turkmenistan	6,378	15,210	19,327	12,686	16,221	0.34	27.87
Ukraine	6,593	27,644	91,590	55,578	54,776	1.16	-1.44
Uzbekistan	1,181,108	688,450	767,162	1,266,401	1,352,879	28.74	6.83
Northern Europe	**23,836**	**20,541**	**20,062**	**24,197**	**28,273**	**0.60**	**16.85**
Denmark	785	819	648	920	1,018	0.02	10.65
Finland	691	827	704	982	1,269	0.03	29.23
Iceland	44	22	22	47	50		6.38
Ireland	766	694	757	878	1,124	0.02	28.02
Norway	400	426	570	723	839	0.02	16.04
Sweden	783	797	831	988	1,118	0.02	13.16
United Kingdom	20,367	16,956	16,530	19,659	22,855	0.49	16.26
Southern Europe	**9,063**	**9,441**	**9,916**	**12,620**	**14,332**	**0.30**	**13.57**
Albania	42	43	114	90	86		-4.44
Bosnia and Herzegovina	57	54	82	122	171		40.16
Croatia	656	570	468	500	684	0.01	36.80
Greece	765	703	742	1,364	1,234	0.03	-9.53
Italy	5,492	6,586	6,996	8,462	9,640	0.20	13.92
Malta	31	19	29	24	37		54.17
Portugal	284	273	349	359	454	0.01	26.46
Slovenia	251	256	247	389	423	0.01	8.74
Spain	728	937	889	1,307	1,603	0.03	22.65
Serbia and Montenegro	757						
Other countries Southern Europe				3			
Western Europe	**59,286**	**69,128**	**85,638**	**100,970**	**111,184**	**2.36**	**10.12**
Austria	1,223	1,477	1,433	1,964	2,422	0.05	23.32
Belgium	962	902	1,050	1,399	1,523	0.03	8.86
France	3,249	3,962	3,834	4,712	5,893	0.13	25.06
Germany	47,994	56,383	72,529	84,534	92,429	1.96	9.34
Liechtenstein	4	3	14	3	8		166.67
Luxembourg	35	36	76	67	98		46.27
Monaco	1	1	206	135	1		-99.26
Netherlands	4,760	5,276	5,375	6,576	6,978	0.15	6.11
Switzerland	1,058	1,088	1,121	1,580	1,832	0.04	15.95
East Mediterranean Europe	**27,200**	**34,607**	**45,534**	**62,838**	**93,313**	**1.98**	**48.50**
Cyprus	36	158	43	67	77		14.93
Israel	2,493	3,120	3,427	4,737	5,166	0.11	9.06
Turkey	24,671	31,329	42,064	58,034	88,070	1.87	51.76
MIDDLE EAST	**3,330**	**2,917**	**1,984**	**2,276**	**3,212**	**0.07**	**41.12**
Middle East	**3,330**	**2,917**	**1,984**	**2,276**	**3,212**	**0.07**	**41.12**
Bahrain	7	40	2	26	22		-15.38
Palestine	186	90	46	83	57		-31.33
Iraq	32	17	39	40	66		65.00
Jordan	514	329	191	342	405	0.01	18.42
Kuwait	60	37	34	15	67		346.67
Lebanon	727	588	284	461	476	0.01	3.25
Libyan Arab Jamahiriya	63	48			77		
Oman	16	11	32	54	67		24.07
Qatar	29	67	29	25	30		20.00
Saudi Arabia	378	468	348	237	310	0.01	30.80
Syrian Arab Republic	308	227	304	321	358	0.01	11.53
United Arab Emirates	422	620	356	280	612	0.01	118.57

KAZAKHSTAN

2. Arrivals of non-resident visitors at national borders, by country of residence

	2002	2003	2004	2005	2006	Market share 06	% Change 06-05
Egypt	417	365	306	381	651	0.01	70.87
Yemen	171	10	13	11	14		27.27
SOUTH ASIA	**12,437**	**17,733**	**20,849**	**19,036**	**21,811**	**0.46**	**14.58**
South Asia	**12,437**	**17,733**	**20,849**	**19,036**	**21,811**	**0.46**	**14.58**
Afghanistan	464	652	886	1,071	2,237	0.05	108.87
Bangladesh	68	120	19	47	108		129.79
Bhutan			4	3	4		33.33
Sri Lanka	142	63	78	66	66		
India	4,217	4,809	5,868	6,160	7,197	0.15	16.83
Iran, Islamic Republic of	6,245	10,273	11,331	9,659	9,474	0.20	-1.92
Nepal	56	70	61	86	102		18.60
Pakistan	1,245	1,746	2,602	1,944	2,623	0.06	34.93
REGION NOT SPECIFIED	**955**	**5,135**	**11,787**	**3,243**	**4,806**	**0.10**	**48.20**
Not Specified	**955**	**5,135**	**11,787**	**3,243**	**4,806**	**0.10**	**48.20**
Other countries of the World	955	5,135	11,787	3,243	4,806	0.10	48.20

Source: World Tourism Organization (UNWTO)

KENYA

2. Arrivals of non-resident visitors at national borders, by country of residence

		2002	2003	2004	2005	2006	Market share 06	% Change 06-05
TOTAL	(*)	1,001,297	1,146,099					
AFRICA		272,429	311,819					
East Africa		191,876	219,625					
Uganda		70,218	80,373					
United Republic of Tanzania		112,435	128,695					
Zambia		9,223	10,557					
Other Africa		80,553	92,194					
Other countries of Africa		80,553	92,194					
AMERICAS		85,083	97,389					
North America		84,359	96,560					
Canada		18,704	21,410					
Mexico		56	64					
United States		65,599	75,086					
South America		174	199					
Brazil		174	199					
Other Americas		550	630					
Other countries of the Americas		550	630					
EAST ASIA AND THE PACIFIC		44,278	50,681					
North-East Asia		15,421	17,651					
Japan		15,421	17,651					
Australasia		8,339	9,545					
Australia		4,575	5,237					
New Zealand		3,764	4,308					
Other East Asia and the Pacific		20,518	23,485					
Other countries of Asia		20,518	23,485					
EUROPE		575,197	658,384					
Northern Europe		211,155	241,691					
Denmark		9,151	10,474					
Finland		6,863	7,855					
Ireland		3,648	4,176					
Norway		1,969	2,254					
Sweden		34,591	39,593					
United Kingdom		154,933	177,339					
Southern Europe		65,896	75,431					
Greece		1,476	1,689					
Italy		53,662	61,428					
Portugal		565	647					
Spain		10,193	11,667					
Western Europe		289,287	331,122					
Austria		20,054	22,954					
Belgium		6,486	7,424					
France		48,101	55,057					
Germany		157,394	180,156					
Netherlands		17,926	20,518					
Switzerland		39,326	45,013					
East Mediterranean Europe		7,383	8,451					
Israel		7,383	8,451					
Other Europe		1,476	1,689					

KENYA

2. Arrivals of non-resident visitors at national borders, by country of residence

	2002	2003	2004	2005	2006	Market share 06	% Change 06-05
Other countries of Europe	1,476	1,689					
SOUTH ASIA	**24,007**	**27,479**					
South Asia	**24,007**	**27,479**					
India	24,007	27,479					
REGION NOT SPECIFIED	**303**	**347**					
Not Specified	**303**	**347**					
Other countries of the World	303	347					

Source: World Tourism Organization (UNWTO)

KENYA

5. Overnight stays of non-resident tourists in hotels and similar establishments, by country of residence

		2002	2003	2004	2005	2006	Market share 06	% Change 06-05
TOTAL	(*)	2,766,000	1,889,900					
AFRICA		191,500	162,700					
East Africa		53,600	56,600					
Uganda		26,900	26,200					
United Republic of Tanzania		26,700	30,400					
North Africa		12,700	16,500					
All countries of North Africa		12,700	16,500					
Southern Africa		42,700	34,400					
All countries of Southern Africa		42,700	34,400					
West Africa		25,100	15,400					
All countries of West Africa		25,100	15,400					
Other Africa		57,400	39,800					
Other countries of Africa		57,400	39,800					
AMERICAS		194,500	144,700					
North America		172,200	127,200					
Canada		22,400	17,600					
United States		149,800	109,600					
Other Americas		22,300	17,500					
Other countries of the Americas		22,300	17,500					
EAST ASIA AND THE PACIFIC		83,400	121,200					
North-East Asia		44,200	26,200					
Japan		44,200	26,200					
Australasia		21,900	76,800					
Australia, New Zealand		21,900	76,800					
Other East Asia and the Pacific		17,300	18,200					
Other countries of Asia		17,300	18,200					
EUROPE		2,208,900	1,387,600					
Northern Europe		647,700	369,900					
United Kingdom		591,400	324,300					
Scandinavia		56,300	45,600					
Southern Europe		211,900	144,000					
Italy		211,900	144,000					
Western Europe		1,104,400	660,200					
France		164,800	113,900					
Germany		721,300	420,400					
Switzerland		218,300	125,900					
Other Europe		244,900	213,500					
Other countries of Europe		244,900	213,500					
MIDDLE EAST		37,700	20,300					
Middle East		37,700	20,300					
All countries of Middle East		37,700	20,300					
SOUTH ASIA		25,000	29,200					
South Asia		25,000	29,200					
India		25,000	29,200					

KENYA

5. Overnight stays of non-resident tourists in hotels and similar establishments, by country of residence

	2002	2003	2004	2005	2006	Market share 06	% Change 06-05
REGION NOT SPECIFIED	**25,000**	**24,200**					
Not Specified	**25,000**	**24,200**					
Other countries of the World	25,000	24,200					

Source: World Tourism Organization (UNWTO)

KIRIBATI

1. Arrivals of non-resident tourists at national borders, by nationality

		2002	2003	2004	2005	2006	Market share 06	% Change 06-05
TOTAL	(*)	4,935	4,905	3,616	3,037	4,406	100.00	45.08
AMERICAS		1,112	786	123	300	760	17.25	153.33
North America		1,112	786	123	300	760	17.25	153.33
Canada						27	0.61	
United States		1,112	786	123	300	733	16.64	144.33
EAST ASIA AND THE PACIFIC		2,722	2,875	2,463	2,185	2,744	62.28	25.58
North-East Asia		494	228	181	229	167	3.79	-27.07
Japan		494	228	181	229	167	3.79	-27.07
Australasia		1,114	1,084	1,073	1,011	1,046	23.74	3.46
Australia		802	745	757	765	821	18.63	7.32
New Zealand		312	339	316	246	225	5.11	-8.54
Melanesia		563	831	566	574			
Solomon Islands		95	266	65	136			
Fiji		468	565	501	438			
Micronesia		288	533	361	196			
Nauru		138	293	128	148			
Marshall Islands		150	240	233	48			
Polynesia		34	39	110	60			
Tuvalu		34	39	110	60			
Other East Asia and the Pacific		229	160	172	115	1,531	34.75	1,231.30
Other countries of Asia						96	2.18	
Other countries of Oceania		229	160	172	115	1,435	32.57	1,147.83
EUROPE		504	388	387	133	232	5.27	74.44
Northern Europe		213	146	129	80	125	2.84	56.25
United Kingdom		213	146	129	80	125	2.84	56.25
Southern Europe						4	0.09	
Italy						4	0.09	
Western Europe		291	242	258	53	103	2.34	94.34
France						43	0.98	
Germany		291	242	258	53	60	1.36	13.21
REGION NOT SPECIFIED		597	856	643	419	670	15.21	59.90
Not Specified		597	856	643	419	670	15.21	59.90
Other countries of the World		597	856	643	419	670	15.21	59.90

Source: World Tourism Organization (UNWTO)

KOREA, REPUBLIC OF

2. Arrivals of non-resident visitors at national borders, by nationality

	2002	2003	2004	2005	2006	Market share 06	% Change 06-05
TOTAL (*)	5,347,468	4,753,604	5,818,138	6,022,752	6,155,046	100.00	2.20
AFRICA	16,322	14,834	14,649	14,464	16,071	0.26	11.11
East Africa	1,247	1,246	1,381	1,458	1,839	0.03	26.13
Burundi	13	5	12	10	20		100.00
Ethiopia	315	326	268	332	481	0.01	44.88
Eritrea	19	7	40	9	11		22.22
Kenya	321	354	436	515	567	0.01	10.10
Madagascar	47	24	19	38	41		7.89
Malawi	13	10	20	16	15		-6.25
Mozambique	42	14	43	22	26		18.18
Rwanda	20	21	16	24	39		62.50
Somalia	7	11	10	9	9		
Zimbabwe	108	68	80	120	154		28.33
Uganda	96	118	106	140	204		45.71
United Republic of Tanzania	184	255	256	172	220		27.91
Zambia	62	33	75	51	52		1.96
Central Africa	421	392	398	519	658	0.01	26.78
Angola	83	130	135	157	286		82.17
Cameroon	156	94	123	143	155		8.39
Chad	17	10	14	18	16		-11.11
Congo	117	119	87	111	127		14.41
Gabon	48	39	39	90	74		-17.78
North Africa	1,523	1,492	1,860	1,910	2,278	0.04	19.27
Algeria	289	373	309	302	455	0.01	50.66
Morocco	613	573	717	602	582	0.01	-3.32
Sudan	327	378	566	664	723	0.01	8.89
Tunisia	294	168	268	342	518	0.01	51.46
Southern Africa	5,254	4,305	4,460	4,621	4,873	0.08	5.45
Botswana	25	18	16	16	26		62.50
Lesotho	12	9	26	13	27		107.69
Namibia	42	26	25	23	19		-17.39
South Africa	5,153	4,183	4,325	4,534	4,756	0.08	4.90
Swaziland	22	69	68	35	45		28.57
West Africa	7,514	7,106	6,201	5,516	5,886	0.10	6.71
Cape Verde	64	67	59	53	45		-15.09
Benin	190	125	118	101	121		19.80
Gambia	15	30	22	14	10		-28.57
Ghana	1,575	1,794	1,871	1,787	2,081	0.03	16.45
Guinea	146	146	100	98	76		-22.45
Liberia	56	30	61	64	115		79.69
Mali	75	57	76	45	58		28.89
Mauritania	43	24	15	12	7		-41.67
Niger	10	12	17	8	21		162.50
Nigeria	4,733	4,611	3,653	3,167	3,110	0.05	-1.80
Senegal	496	138	120	109	175		60.55
Sierra Leone	27	31	30	32	27		-15.63
Togo	84	41	59	26	40		53.85
Other Africa	363	293	349	440	537	0.01	22.05
Other countries of Africa	363	293	349	440	537	0.01	22.05
AMERICAS	556,440	505,067	610,562	640,050	673,118	10.94	5.17
Caribbean	1,080	821	777	823	1,549	0.03	88.21

KOREA, REPUBLIC OF

2. Arrivals of non-resident visitors at national borders, by nationality

	2002	2003	2004	2005	2006	Market share 06	% Change 06-05
Antigua and Barbuda	20	13	11	19	12		-36.84
Bahamas	48	42	38	30	59		96.67
Barbados	45	40	47	25	46		84.00
Cuba	182	260	115	224	474	0.01	111.61
Dominica	54	17	14	28	222		692.86
Dominican Republic	294	198	173	216	362	0.01	67.59
Haiti	38	23	21	23	39		69.57
Jamaica	150	123	165	141	168		19.15
Puerto Rico	101	15	11	1	4		300.00
Saint Vincent and the Grenadines	10	6	22	11	13		18.18
Trinidad and Tobago	138	84	160	105	150		42.86
Central America	**3,728**	**1,415**	**1,581**	**1,689**	**2,266**	**0.04**	**34.16**
Belize	150	79	65	66	69		4.55
Costa Rica	2,053	256	307	394	378	0.01	-4.06
El Salvador	316	273	342	446	838	0.01	87.89
Guatemala	401	215	282	290	310	0.01	6.90
Honduras	253	201	163	171	260		52.05
Nicaragua	58	49	72	55	65		18.18
Panama	497	342	350	267	346	0.01	29.59
North America	**534,738**	**491,674**	**594,050**	**622,739**	**654,017**	**10.63**	**5.02**
Canada	67,041	66,189	77,597	86,399	92,791	1.51	7.40
Mexico	8,335	3,776	5,283	5,711	5,522	0.09	-3.31
United States	459,362	421,709	511,170	530,629	555,704	9.03	4.73
South America	**16,614**	**10,893**	**13,811**	**14,486**	**14,980**	**0.24**	**3.41**
Argentina	1,390	1,185	1,390	1,707	1,619	0.03	-5.16
Bolivia	418	192	261	209	267		27.75
Brazil	7,278	4,811	5,849	6,324	6,694	0.11	5.85
Chile	1,796	1,391	2,274	1,912	1,703	0.03	-10.93
Colombia	1,641	1,150	1,351	1,600	1,484	0.02	-7.25
Ecuador	781	279	397	437	423	0.01	-3.20
Guyana	25	26	38	13	26		100.00
Paraguay	488	195	381	292	225		-22.95
Peru	1,269	955	1,012	1,087	1,562	0.03	43.70
Suriname	30	21	34	32	36		12.50
Uruguay	602	237	175	115	122		6.09
Venezuela	896	451	649	758	819	0.01	8.05
Other Americas	**280**	**264**	**343**	**313**	**306**		**-2.24**
Other countries of the Americas	280	264	343	313	306		-2.24
EAST ASIA AND THE PACIFIC	**3,829,548**	**3,334,633**	**4,252,976**	**4,441,757**	**4,557,030**	**74.04**	**2.60**
North-East Asia	**3,185,090**	**2,680,823**	**3,549,031**	**3,691,207**	**3,746,078**	**60.86**	**1.49**
China	539,466	513,236	627,264	709,836	893,986	14.52	25.94
Taiwan (Province of China)	136,921	194,681	304,908	351,421	338,162	5.49	-3.77
Hong Kong, China	179,299	156,373	155,058	166,204	142,786	2.32	-14.09
Japan	2,320,837	1,802,171	2,443,070	2,439,809	2,338,921	38.00	-4.14
Mongolia	8,567	14,362	18,731	23,937	32,223	0.52	34.62
South-East Asia	**575,687**	**585,634**	**622,249**	**657,962**	**709,158**	**11.52**	**7.78**
Brunei Darussalam	554	525	625	810	807	0.01	-0.37
Myanmar	33,559	30,483	29,289	33,704	40,758	0.66	20.93
Cambodia	936	1,682	1,885	2,047	3,590	0.06	75.38
Indonesia	65,093	62,733	61,506	62,282	62,869	1.02	0.94
Malaysia	82,720	90,643	93,982	96,583	89,854	1.46	-6.97
Philippines	215,848	216,647	213,434	222,622	248,262	4.03	11.52
Singapore	79,403	76,433	85,202	81,751	88,386	1.44	8.12

KOREA, REPUBLIC OF

2. Arrivals of non-resident visitors at national borders, by nationality

	2002	2003	2004	2005	2006	Market share 06	% Change 06-05
Viet Nam	23,574	28,244	33,738	45,439	46,077	0.75	1.40
Thailand	74,000	78,244	102,588	112,724	128,555	2.09	14.04
Australasia	**63,114**	**62,491**	**73,883**	**79,882**	**85,830**	**1.39**	**7.45**
Australia	49,759	48,613	57,834	63,464	68,328	1.11	7.66
New Zealand	13,355	13,878	16,049	16,418	17,502	0.28	6.60
Melanesia	**589**	**537**	**1,426**	**1,858**	**2,205**	**0.04**	**18.68**
Solomon Islands	32			119			
Fiji	387	537	1,296	1,528	2,205	0.04	44.31
Vanuatu	21		18	35			
Papua New Guinea	149		112	176			
Micronesia	**1,759**	**1,590**	**1,852**	**2,624**	**2,434**	**0.04**	**-7.24**
Kiribati	1,622	1,526	1,681	2,491	2,350	0.04	-5.66
Micronesia (Federated States of)	51		33	45			
Marshall Islands	33	24	61	42	48		14.29
Palau	53	40	77	46	36		-21.74
Polynesia	**1,403**	**843**	**599**	**730**	**750**	**0.01**	**2.74**
Tonga	133	233	176	88	239		171.59
Tuvalu	1,192	557	288	496	421	0.01	-15.12
Samoa	78	53	135	146	90		-38.36
Other East Asia and the Pacific	**1,906**	**2,715**	**3,936**	**7,494**	**10,575**	**0.17**	**41.11**
Other countries of Asia	1,798	2,442	3,612	7,388	10,278	0.17	39.12
Other countries of Oceania	108	273	324	106	297		180.19
EUROPE	**536,261**	**514,403**	**531,257**	**540,694**	**571,612**	**9.29**	**5.72**
Central/Eastern Europe	**234,082**	**242,994**	**227,893**	**211,709**	**226,342**	**3.68**	**6.91**
Azerbaijan	119	61	140	118	203		72.03
Bulgaria	8,794	10,107	10,417	10,138	10,499	0.17	3.56
Belarus	575	710	739	793	739	0.01	-6.81
Czech Republic	1,320	1,605	2,014	2,464	3,375	0.05	36.97
Estonia	489	458	445	484	500	0.01	3.31
Georgia	365	162	483	400	324	0.01	-19.00
Hungary	2,139	1,625	1,328	1,621	1,713	0.03	5.68
Kazakhstan	3,655	5,073	4,651	3,542	4,106	0.07	15.92
Kyrgyzstan	1,607	1,371	1,924	1,337	2,931	0.05	119.22
Latvia	3,461	3,633	3,578	3,808	3,434	0.06	-9.82
Lithuania	1,052	931	973	1,026	1,117	0.02	8.87
Republic of Moldova	244	191	292	165	197		19.39
Poland	11,082	10,113	8,671	9,497	10,174	0.17	7.13
Romania	5,623	6,262	6,635	6,652	8,098	0.13	21.74
Russian Federation	165,341	168,051	156,890	143,850	144,611	2.35	0.53
Tajikistan	185	88	156	177	232		31.07
Ukraine	17,743	20,145	17,913	16,523	19,296	0.31	16.78
Uzbekistan	10,288	12,408	10,644	9,114	14,793	0.24	62.31
Northern Europe	**100,234**	**89,393**	**98,039**	**107,466**	**113,601**	**1.85**	**5.71**
Denmark	8,024	6,567	7,388	7,989	8,409	0.14	5.26
Finland	3,870	3,725	4,042	4,372	4,745	0.08	8.53
Iceland	235	190	217	210	231		10.00
Ireland	6,590	3,979	4,600	4,941	4,833	0.08	-2.19
Norway	7,050	6,641	6,930	7,274	8,119	0.13	11.62
Sweden	7,769	7,688	8,881	10,097	11,867	0.19	17.53
United Kingdom	66,696	60,603	65,981	72,583	75,397	1.22	3.88
Southern Europe	**48,892**	**40,331**	**41,610**	**43,357**	**48,115**	**0.78**	**10.97**
Albania	77	83	105	164	89		-45.73

KOREA, REPUBLIC OF

2. Arrivals of non-resident visitors at national borders, by nationality

	2002	2003	2004	2005	2006	Market share 06	% Change 06-05
Bosnia and Herzegovina	22	11	34	37	45		21.62
Croatia	7,105	6,824	6,081	6,317	7,785	0.13	23.24
Greece	9,068	9,260	9,014	7,833	7,746	0.13	-1.11
Italy	14,981	12,732	14,724	15,713	18,797	0.31	19.63
Malta	117	56	99	101	166		64.36
Portugal	7,114	3,639	4,115	5,121	3,818	0.06	-25.44
Slovenia	2,247	849	753	679	647	0.01	-4.71
Spain	6,662	5,167	6,166	6,789	7,133	0.12	5.07
Serbia and Montenegro	1,499	1,710	519	603	1,889	0.03	213.27
Western Europe	**133,967**	**126,028**	**145,416**	**157,566**	**164,016**	**2.66**	**4.09**
Austria	4,338	4,316	4,541	5,489	6,113	0.10	11.37
Belgium	5,370	5,348	5,613	6,392	6,186	0.10	-3.22
France	41,207	35,540	41,229	44,440	47,111	0.77	6.01
Germany	59,698	58,805	68,850	74,962	76,407	1.24	1.93
Liechtenstein	22	21	42	31	27		-12.90
Luxembourg	340	239	224	339	330	0.01	-2.65
Monaco	10		9	8			
Netherlands	16,288	15,469	18,167	18,248	19,285	0.31	5.68
Switzerland	6,694	6,290	6,741	7,657	8,557	0.14	11.75
East Mediterranean Europe	**17,008**	**14,422**	**15,777**	**16,805**	**16,565**	**0.27**	**-1.43**
Cyprus	185	161	121	169	185		9.47
Israel	6,498	6,274	7,011	7,660	7,411	0.12	-3.25
Turkey	10,325	7,987	8,645	8,976	8,969	0.15	-0.08
Other Europe	**2,078**	**1,235**	**2,522**	**3,791**	**2,973**	**0.05**	**-21.58**
Other countries of Europe	2,078	1,235	2,522	3,791	2,973	0.05	-21.58
MIDDLE EAST	**10,715**	**8,045**	**11,155**	**13,050**	**15,000**	**0.24**	**14.94**
Middle East	**10,715**	**8,045**	**11,155**	**13,050**	**15,000**	**0.24**	**14.94**
Bahrain	256	104	139	168	132		-21.43
Palestine	111	62	100	145	118		-18.62
Iraq	247	362	732	1,346	1,750	0.03	30.01
Jordan	1,573	1,657	2,437	2,323	1,998	0.03	-13.99
Kuwait	627	257	462	583	581	0.01	-0.34
Lebanon	689	428	648	727	680	0.01	-6.46
Libyan Arab Jamahiriya	592	429	624	1,078	1,606	0.03	48.98
Oman	202	176	224	389	259		-33.42
Qatar	549	145	263	279	347	0.01	24.37
Saudi Arabia	1,266	753	1,024	1,377	1,488	0.02	8.06
Syrian Arab Republic	978	729	1,055	982	1,401	0.02	42.67
United Arab Emirates	433	221	463	613	794	0.01	29.53
Egypt	2,663	2,446	2,633	2,623	3,413	0.06	30.12
Yemen	438	254	339	397	397	0.01	
Other countries of Middle East	91	22	12	20	36		80.00
SOUTH ASIA	**81,648**	**86,000**	**95,398**	**92,189**	**95,430**	**1.55**	**3.52**
South Asia	**81,648**	**86,000**	**95,398**	**92,189**	**95,430**	**1.55**	**3.52**
Afghanistan	245	379	427	367	305		-16.89
Bangladesh	6,479	10,912	9,799	5,742	6,948	0.11	21.00
Bhutan	103	68	69	63	70		11.11
Sri Lanka	3,624	5,317	6,756	10,463	8,336	0.14	-20.33
India	52,725	50,215	56,966	58,560	62,531	1.02	6.78
Iran, Islamic Republic of	7,743	7,328	7,202	6,389	6,579	0.11	2.97
Maldives	594	434	382	310	351	0.01	13.23
Nepal	2,048	3,045	3,020	2,143	2,750	0.04	28.32
Pakistan	8,087	8,302	10,777	8,152	7,560	0.12	-7.26

KOREA, REPUBLIC OF

2. Arrivals of non-resident visitors at national borders, by nationality

	2002	2003	2004	2005	2006	Market share 06	% Change 06-05
REGION NOT SPECIFIED	316,534	290,622	302,141	280,548	226,785	3.68	-19.16
Not Specified	316,534	290,622	302,141	280,548	226,785	3.68	-19.16
Other countries of the World	1,705	3,104	2,246	84	83		-1.19
Nationals Residing Abroad	314,829	287,518	299,895	280,464	226,702	3.68	-19.17

Source: World Tourism Organization (UNWTO)

KUWAIT

2. Arrivals of non-resident visitors at national borders, by nationality

	2002	2003	2004	2005	2006	Market share 06	% Change 06-05
TOTAL	2,315,568	2,602,300	3,056,093				
AFRICA	24,407	26,167	29,144				
East Africa	4,168	4,779	5,079				
Burundi	8	11	10				
Comoros	25	17	22				
Ethiopia	600	652	930				
Eritrea	530	770	840				
Djibouti	23	23	38				
Kenya	377	625	794				
Madagascar	2	3	3				
Malawi	12	8	12				
Mauritius	64	45	80				
Mozambique	14	17	18				
Rwanda	6	12	4				
Seychelles	21	26	23				
Somalia	2,269	2,132	1,792				
Zimbabwe	77	214	324				
Uganda	35	70	50				
United Republic of Tanzania	98	141	130				
Zambia	7	13	9				
Central Africa	318	706	398				
Angola	5	7	6				
Cameroon	57	47	77				
Central African Republic	8	8	5				
Chad	237	627	276				
Congo	5	12	15				
Democratic Republic of the Congo	2	2	2				
Gabon	4	3	17				
North Africa	16,157	15,578	17,361				
Algeria	561	685	708				
Morocco	10,348	8,867	8,873				
Sudan	2,323	3,235	4,759				
Tunisia	2,925	2,791	3,021				
Southern Africa	1,609	2,407	3,268				
Botswana	1	1	1				
Lesotho			3				
Namibia	2	2	11				
South Africa	1,606	2,399	3,252				
Swaziland		5	1				
West Africa	2,155	2,697	3,038				
Cape Verde	1		1				
Benin	93	110	126				
Gambia	45	40	81				
Ghana	280	574	773				
Guinea	46	121	115				
Cote D'Ivoire	30	38	54				
Liberia	241	283	319				
Mali	71	82	81				
Mauritania	160	161	250				
Niger	58	159	102				
Nigeria	647	677	706				
Guinea-Bissau	2	3	13				
Saint Helena			4				

KUWAIT

2. Arrivals of non-resident visitors at national borders, by nationality

	2002	2003	2004	2005	2006	Market share 06	% Change 06-05
Senegal	389	358	299				
Sierra Leone	43	35	37				
Togo	15	20	25				
Burkina Faso	34	36	52				
AMERICAS	**50,267**	**103,447**	**115,260**				
Caribbean	**563**	**998**	**953**				
Bahamas		1	5				
Barbados	7	7	5				
Bermuda	4		4				
Cuba	24	44	43				
Dominican Republic	408	799	681				
Grenada	28	24	30				
Guadeloupe		1					
Haiti	12	20	76				
Jamaica	17	21	39				
Martinique	1		2				
Aruba		2	2				
Curacao		1	1				
Puerto Rico		1					
Saint Kitts and Nevis	2	2					
Anguilla		2					
Saint Lucia	7	5	3				
Saint Vincent and the Grenadines	5	6					
Trinidad and Tobago	48	62	62				
Central America	**216**	**279**	**289**				
Belize	154	167	155				
Costa Rica	7	20	12				
El Salvador	34	40	24				
Guatemala	6	15	43				
Honduras	5	18	35				
Nicaragua	2	7	6				
Panama	8	12	14				
North America	**48,000**	**100,620**	**112,272**				
Canada	12,718	14,551	19,399				
Mexico	63	81	112				
United States	35,219	85,988	92,761				
South America	**1,488**	**1,550**	**1,746**				
Argentina	384	150	175				
Bolivia	115	282	152				
Brazil	437	581	648				
Chile	43	45	65				
Colombia	133	141	264				
Ecuador	14	26	28				
Falkland Islands (Malvinas)			1				
French Guiana	2		1				
Guyana	18	14	1				
Paraguay	5	4	7				
Peru	7	16	34				
Suriname	10	23	15				
Uruguay	36	18	7				
Venezuela	284	250	348				
EAST ASIA AND THE PACIFIC	**117,923**	**124,868**	**158,006**				
North-East Asia	**12,471**	**11,075**	**23,109**				

KUWAIT

2. Arrivals of non-resident visitors at national borders, by nationality

	2002	2003	2004	2005	2006	Market share 06	% Change 06-05
China	3,879	2,819	6,558				
Taiwan (Province of China)	166	120	129				
Hong Kong, China	22	14	49				
Japan	4,432	3,982	8,826				
Korea, Dem. People's Republic of	693	542	885				
Korea, Republic of	3,256	3,560	6,569				
Macao, China		1	1				
Mongolia	23	37	92				
South-East Asia	**100,222**	**106,574**	**123,975**				
Brunei Darussalam	8	10	7				
Myanmar	42	52	42				
Cambodia	19	17	17				
Indonesia	35,990	39,969	43,647				
Lao People's Democratic Republic	1	2	3				
Malaysia	914	820	1,308				
Philippines	56,335	60,264	73,656				
Timor-Leste			22				
Singapore	904	750	939				
Viet Nam	51	42	60				
Thailand	5,958	4,648	4,274				
Australasia	**5,109**	**7,092**	**10,247**				
Australia	4,286	5,767	8,049				
New Zealand	823	1,325	2,198				
Melanesia	**103**	**106**	**651**				
Fiji	103	106	651				
Micronesia	**17**	**18**	**14**				
Kiribati	13	13	3				
Marshall Islands	4	3	3				
Palau		2	8				
Polynesia	**1**	**3**	**10**				
Cook Islands		1					
Tonga	1	2	9				
Samoa			1				
EUROPE	**80,650**	**94,168**	**125,509**				
Central/Eastern Europe	**10,705**	**12,135**	**15,935**				
Azerbaijan	193	148	176				
Armenia	150	227	349				
Bulgaria	2,506	3,474	6,016				
Belarus	46	44	69				
Czech Republic/Slovakia	38	17	21				
Czech Republic	974	931	909				
Estonia	10	75	41				
Georgia	62	83	100				
Hungary	663	613	704				
Kazakhstan	68	88	98				
Kyrgyzstan	36	12	40				
Latvia	54	75	58				
Lithuania	38	56	114				
Republic of Moldova	6	40	151				
Poland	1,061	1,264	1,584				
Romania	2,322	2,160	2,209				
Russian Federation	1,356	1,431	1,463				
Slovakia	405	409	433				

KUWAIT

2. Arrivals of non-resident visitors at national borders, by nationality

	2002	2003	2004	2005	2006	Market share 06	% Change 06-05
Tajikistan	18	46	71				
Turkmenistan	4	6	7				
Ukraine	437	741	943				
Uzbekistan	73	96	270				
Other countries Central/East Europ	185	99	109				
Northern Europe	**38,285**	**46,935**	**60,265**				
Denmark	1,620	2,788	3,513				
Finland	448	420	576				
Iceland	66	78	48				
Ireland	1,279	1,590	1,856				
Norway	598	957	1,059				
Sweden	1,072	1,439	2,565				
United Kingdom	33,202	39,663	50,648				
Southern Europe	**8,425**	**9,385**	**11,824**				
Albania	59	117	151				
Andorra		5	1				
Bosnia and Herzegovina	829	795	950				
Croatia	224	290	269				
Greece	1,485	1,492	1,488				
Holy See	19	18	22				
Italy	3,641	3,734	5,374				
Malta	80	92	127				
Portugal	229	316	309				
San Marino	3		3				
Slovenia	54	71	120				
Spain	1,062	1,443	1,681				
TFYR of Macedonia	117	294	408				
Serbia and Montenegro	623	718	921				
Western Europe	**18,667**	**18,918**	**26,811**				
Austria	1,022	951	1,268				
Belgium	1,039	1,064	1,231				
France	6,375	6,369	9,058				
Germany	6,403	6,208	9,157				
Liechtenstein	4	2	8				
Luxembourg	86	68	93				
Monaco		1	6				
Netherlands	2,557	2,999	4,469				
Switzerland	1,181	1,256	1,521				
East Mediterranean Europe	**4,568**	**6,795**	**10,674**				
Cyprus	267	193	261				
Turkey	4,301	6,602	10,413				
MIDDLE EAST	**1,391,296**	**1,505,733**	**1,769,220**				
Middle East	**1,391,296**	**1,505,733**	**1,769,220**				
Bahrain	74,979	77,512	84,934				
Palestine	5,473	5,489	5,935				
Iraq	4,690	15,793	36,539				
Jordan	37,706	42,140	50,938				
Lebanon	61,687	63,735	74,629				
Libyan Arab Jamahiriya	381	248	311				
Oman	11,554	11,880	12,424				
Qatar	19,564	18,385	23,065				
Saudi Arabia	725,025	777,831	896,102				
Syrian Arab Republic	176,375	185,946	234,726				
United Arab Emirates	13,588	13,173	16,783				

KUWAIT

2. Arrivals of non-resident visitors at national borders, by nationality

	2002	2003	2004	2005	2006	Market share 06	% Change 06-05
Egypt	256,867	289,401	327,460				
Yemen	3,407	4,200	5,374				
SOUTH ASIA	**648,075**	**745,679**	**855,730**				
South Asia	**648,075**	**745,679**	**855,730**				
Afghanistan	8,492	6,776	7,334				
Bangladesh	75,423	90,327	111,060				
Bhutan	19	16	70				
Sri Lanka	62,586	63,269	62,676				
India	314,054	363,724	413,109				
Iran, Islamic Republic of	99,066	100,474	121,642				
Maldives	28	48	72				
Nepal	4,183	9,990	16,639				
Pakistan	84,224	111,055	123,128				
REGION NOT SPECIFIED	**2,950**	**2,238**	**3,224**				
Not Specified	**2,950**	**2,238**	**3,224**				
Other countries of the World	2,950	2,238	3,224				

Source: World Tourism Organization (UNWTO)

KYRGYZSTAN

1. Arrivals of non-resident tourists at national borders, by country of residence

	2002	2003	2004	2005	2006	Market share 06	% Change 06-05
TOTAL (*)	139,589	341,990	398,078	315,290	765,850	100.00	142.90
AMERICAS	11,936	12,744	12,266	13,023	14,140	1.85	8.58
North America	11,936	12,744	12,266	13,023	14,140	1.85	8.58
Canada	1,053	1,077	1,155	1,296	1,368	0.18	5.56
United States	10,883	11,667	11,111	11,727	12,772	1.67	8.91
EAST ASIA AND THE PACIFIC	11,333	14,005	16,766	22,099	26,288	3.43	18.96
North-East Asia	10,620	12,972	15,975	21,033	25,026	3.27	18.98
China	7,495	8,268	11,822	15,747	18,681	2.44	18.63
Japan	1,436	2,004	1,026	1,436	1,678	0.22	16.85
Korea, Republic of	1,689	2,700	3,127	3,850	4,667	0.61	21.22
South-East Asia	196			106			
Malaysia	196			106			
Australasia	517	1,033	791	960	1,262	0.16	31.46
Australia	517	616	621	732	1,084	0.14	48.09
New Zealand		417	170	228	178	0.02	-21.93
EUROPE	88,148	269,575	356,982	273,696	715,435	93.42	161.40
Central/Eastern Europe	59,951	242,383	326,381	241,517	681,498	88.99	182.17
Azerbaijan		400	621	492	403	0.05	-18.09
Armenia		274	294	266	405	0.05	52.26
Belarus		336	444	394	910	0.12	130.96
Czech Republic	207			414	395	0.05	-4.59
Georgia		342	478	345	292	0.04	-15.36
Hungary	116			106	127	0.02	19.81
Kazakhstan		160,335	236,712	150,904	479,119	62.56	217.50
Lithuania	150			161	150	0.02	-6.83
Republic of Moldova		103	201	189	216	0.03	14.29
Poland	346	351	444	393	464	0.06	18.07
Russian Federation		36,071	36,540	32,001	83,438	10.89	160.74
Tajikistan		6,289	8,190	4,565	16,588	2.17	263.37
Turkmenistan		457	724	757	830	0.11	9.64
Ukraine		1,272	1,078	1,154	3,070	0.40	166.03
Uzbekistan		36,153	40,655	49,376	95,091	12.42	92.59
Commonwealth Independent State	59,132						
Northern Europe	5,395	4,720	3,577	4,554	4,873	0.64	7.00
Denmark	864	951	260	355	248	0.03	-30.14
Finland	208			168	233	0.03	38.69
Ireland	119			264	293	0.04	10.98
Norway	989	676	423	355	286	0.04	-19.44
Sweden	257	350	396	438	548	0.07	25.11
United Kingdom	2,958	2,743	2,498	2,974	3,265	0.43	9.78
Southern Europe	2,303	1,641	1,638	2,744	2,996	0.39	9.18
Italy	734	704	740	946	965	0.13	2.01
Spain	1,569	937	898	1,798	2,031	0.27	12.96
Western Europe	14,125	13,774	15,525	14,945	15,240	1.99	1.97
Austria	465	350	579	439	529	0.07	20.50
Belgium	252	254	425	448	581	0.08	29.69
France	4,462	2,028	2,611	2,641	2,651	0.35	0.38
Germany	6,820	8,553	9,724	9,128	9,148	1.19	0.22
Netherlands	1,102	1,647	1,074	1,029	1,110	0.14	7.87
Switzerland	1,024	942	1,112	1,260	1,221	0.16	-3.10

KYRGYZSTAN

1. Arrivals of non-resident tourists at national borders, by country of residence

	2002	2003	2004	2005	2006	Market share 06	% Change 06-05
East Mediterranean Europe	6,374	7,057	9,861	9,936	10,828	1.41	8.98
Israel	510	659	829	574	847	0.11	47.56
Turkey	5,864	6,398	9,032	9,362	9,981	1.30	6.61
MIDDLE EAST	45			80	134	0.02	67.50
Middle East	45			80	134	0.02	67.50
Saudi Arabia	45			80	134	0.02	67.50
SOUTH ASIA	3,400	5,395	5,864	6,364	5,142	0.67	-19.20
South Asia	3,400	5,395	5,864	6,364	5,142	0.67	-19.20
Afghanistan	191	235	430	384	362	0.05	-5.73
India	1,590	3,171	2,080	1,211	1,030	0.13	-14.95
Iran, Islamic Republic of	1,112	1,292	2,166	1,796	2,640	0.34	46.99
Pakistan	507	697	1,188	2,973	1,110	0.14	-62.66
REGION NOT SPECIFIED	24,727	40,271	6,200	28	4,711	0.62	*********
Not Specified	24,727	40,271	6,200	28	4,711	0.62	*********
Other countries of the World	24,727	40,271	6,200	28	4,711	0.62	*********

Source: World Tourism Organization (UNWTO)

LAO PEOPLE'S DEMOCRATIC REPUBLIC

2. Arrivals of non-resident visitors at national borders, by nationality

	2002	2003	2004	2005	2006	Market share 06	% Change 06-05
TOTAL	735,662	636,361	894,806	1,095,315	1,215,107	100.00	10.94
AMERICAS	46,704	39,453	47,153	60,061	60,883	5.01	1.37
North America	44,794	38,139	46,229	58,874	59,248	4.88	0.64
Canada	9,060	8,006	9,048	11,447	12,419	1.02	8.49
United States	35,734	30,133	37,181	47,427	46,829	3.85	-1.26
Other Americas	1,910	1,314	924	1,187	1,635	0.13	37.74
Other countries of the Americas	1,910	1,314	924	1,187	1,635	0.13	37.74
EAST ASIA AND THE PACIFIC	575,268	495,253	728,262	897,177	1,006,564	82.84	12.19
North-East Asia	50,334	47,756	62,596	75,739	86,595	7.13	14.33
China	21,724	21,232	33,019	39,210	50,317	4.14	28.33
Taiwan (Province of China)	3,918	3,316	2,160	4,739	2,168	0.18	-54.25
Japan	19,801	17,766	20,319	22,601	23,147	1.90	2.42
Korea, Republic of	4,891	5,442	7,098	9,189	10,963	0.90	19.31
South-East Asia	508,783	432,720	638,747	794,044	891,808	73.39	12.31
Brunei Darussalam	582	357	385	385	302	0.02	-21.56
Myanmar	1,365	744	939	1,632	1,126	0.09	-31.00
Cambodia	2,620	2,702	3,871	5,179	3,888	0.32	-24.93
Indonesia	1,903	1,443	1,770	2,784	2,415	0.20	-13.25
Malaysia	3,543	3,072	4,563	6,609	6,846	0.56	3.59
Philippines	2,549	2,618	3,317	5,247	6,433	0.53	22.60
Singapore	2,454	2,442	3,409	3,868	4,511	0.37	16.62
Viet Nam	71,001	41,594	130,816	165,151	190,442	15.67	15.31
Thailand	422,766	377,748	489,677	603,189	675,845	55.62	12.05
Australasia	14,882	13,674	18,170	24,101	25,588	2.11	6.17
Australia	12,611	11,697	15,149	20,323	22,021	1.81	8.36
New Zealand	2,271	1,977	3,021	3,778	3,567	0.29	-5.58
Other East Asia and the Pacific	1,269	1,103	8,749	3,293	2,573	0.21	-21.86
Other countries East Asia/Pacific	1,269	1,103	8,749	3,293	2,573	0.21	-21.86
EUROPE	107,439	97,314	116,180	134,472	143,716	11.83	6.87
Central/Eastern Europe	1,371	1,031	1,315	1,672	1,799	0.15	7.60
Russian Federation	1,371	1,031	1,315	1,672	1,799	0.15	7.60
Northern Europe	32,783	31,833	38,075	42,959	46,815	3.85	8.98
Denmark	3,345	2,414	2,563	2,852	3,658	0.30	28.26
Finland	1,072	982	1,293	1,494	2,110	0.17	41.23
Norway	2,110	1,652	1,823	2,176	2,721	0.22	25.05
Sweden	4,507	4,244	4,994	6,460	6,642	0.55	2.82
United Kingdom	21,749	22,541	27,402	29,977	31,684	2.61	5.69
Southern Europe	5,456	4,313	6,444	7,863	9,550	0.79	21.45
Greece	489	179	324	271	538	0.04	98.52
Italy	3,517	3,241	4,103	5,032	5,884	0.48	16.93
Spain	1,450	893	2,017	2,560	3,128	0.26	22.19
Western Europe	55,662	51,286	58,397	71,052	72,094	5.93	1.47
Austria	890	938	1,394	1,687	2,041	0.17	20.98
Belgium	4,111	3,762	3,921	4,256	4,345	0.36	2.09
France	26,748	23,958	27,806	35,371	32,453	2.67	-8.25
Germany	12,777	12,146	14,009	16,752	18,004	1.48	7.47
Netherlands	6,656	6,638	6,957	7,796	9,294	0.76	19.21
Switzerland	4,480	3,844	4,310	5,190	5,957	0.49	14.78
East Mediterranean Europe	5,515	3,354	4,088	3,146	4,781	0.39	51.97

LAO PEOPLE'S DEMOCRATIC REPUBLIC

2. Arrivals of non-resident visitors at national borders, by nationality

	2002	2003	2004	2005	2006	Market share 06	% Change 06-05
Israel	5,515	3,354	4,088	3,146	4,781	0.39	51.97
Other Europe	**6,652**	**5,497**	**7,861**	**7,780**	**8,677**	**0.71**	**11.53**
Other countries of Europe	6,652	5,497	7,861	7,780	8,677	0.71	11.53
SOUTH ASIA	**3,763**	**2,932**	**1,845**	**2,096**	**2,100**	**0.17**	**0.19**
South Asia	**3,763**	**2,932**	**1,845**	**2,096**	**2,100**	**0.17**	**0.19**
Bangladesh	669	792					
Sri Lanka	278	187					
India	2,319	1,590	1,845	2,096	2,100	0.17	0.19
Nepal	171	90					
Pakistan	251	211					
Other countries of South Asia	75	62					
REGION NOT SPECIFIED	**2,488**	**1,409**	**1,366**	**1,509**	**1,844**	**0.15**	**22.20**
Not Specified	**2,488**	**1,409**	**1,366**	**1,509**	**1,844**	**0.15**	**22.20**
Other countries of the World	2,488	1,409	1,366	1,509	1,844	0.15	22.20

Source: World Tourism Organization (UNWTO)

LATVIA

2. Arrivals of non-resident visitors at national borders, by country of residence

		2002	2003	2004	2005	2006	Market share 06	% Change 06-05
TOTAL	(*)	2,273,539	2,469,888	3,033,405	3,774,422	4,644,636	100.00	23.06
AFRICA		198	161	754	224	1,460	0.03	551.79
East Africa		3	1	7				
Zimbabwe			1					
All countries of East Africa		3		7				
Central Africa		7	7	262				
Angola			3					
Central African Republic			1					
Congo			2	165				
Other countries of Central Africa		7	1	97				
North Africa		2	10	108	224	667	0.01	197.77
Morocco			4	107	224	667	0.01	197.77
All countries of North Africa		2	6	1				
Southern Africa		170	133	371		267	0.01	
South Africa		170	133	371		267	0.01	
West Africa		16	10	6		526	0.01	
Benin			7					
Gambia			1			117		
Liberia			1					
Niger						409	0.01	
Other countries of West Africa		16	1	6				
AMERICAS		23,590	22,263	32,027	22,441	20,438	0.44	-8.93
Caribbean		83	45	358	109	433	0.01	297.25
Barbados			14					
Cuba			30	353	109			
Dominican Republic			1					
Jamaica						433	0.01	
Other countries of the Caribbean		83		5				
Central America		83		148				
All countries of Central America		83		148				
North America		22,447	21,395	30,846	19,798	18,681	0.40	-5.64
Canada		2,808	2,206	4,354	3,043	4,079	0.09	34.05
Mexico		32	54	667	376	433	0.01	15.16
United States		19,607	19,135	25,825	16,379	14,169	0.31	-13.49
South America		977	823	675	2,534	1,324	0.03	-47.75
Argentina		50	70		702			
Brazil		725	411	128	1,268	1,163	0.03	-8.28
Chile		83	208	496	224			
Colombia			6					
Ecuador				7				
Peru			14	44	170			
Suriname			4					
Uruguay						161		
Venezuela		15	6		170			
Other countries of South America		104	104					
EAST ASIA AND THE PACIFIC		17,571	16,833	12,932	8,088	18,703	0.40	131.24
North-East Asia		6,660	7,083	3,277	2,585	8,883	0.19	243.64
China		260	450		686	1,568	0.03	128.57
Taiwan (Province of China)		165	219	88	129			

LATVIA

2. Arrivals of non-resident visitors at national borders, by country of residence

	2002	2003	2004	2005	2006	Market share 06	% Change 06-05
Hong Kong, China	109	345		108			
Japan	5,719	5,652	2,510	1,662	6,475	0.14	289.59
Korea, Dem. People's Republic of	13	174	176		190		
Korea, Republic of	392	219	503				
Mongolia	2	24			650	0.01	
South-East Asia	**8,430**	**6,381**	**5,567**	**596**	**3,129**	**0.07**	**425.00**
Indonesia		1	1,939				
Malaysia	16	6	165	212	267	0.01	25.94
Philippines	8,091	6,122	2,847	298	1,862	0.04	524.83
Singapore	211	199	165		217		
Viet Nam	109	27			190		
Thailand	3	26	451	86	593	0.01	589.53
Australasia	**2,481**	**3,369**	**4,088**	**4,907**	**6,691**	**0.14**	**36.36**
Australia	2,146	3,245	3,459	4,157	4,682	0.10	12.63
New Zealand	335	124	629	750	2,009	0.04	167.87
EUROPE	**2,217,608**	**2,428,531**	**2,985,157**	**3,739,348**	**4,601,125**	**99.06**	**23.05**
Central/Eastern Europe	**1,730,721**	**1,811,834**	**2,262,804**	**2,875,886**	**3,529,011**	**75.98**	**22.71**
Azerbaijan	76	229	189	188	2,541	0.05	1,251.60
Armenia	120	86	109	529			
Bulgaria	490	1,243	2,050	4,639	421	0.01	-90.92
Belarus	53,746	50,696	48,643	42,234	78,873	1.70	86.75
Czech Republic	20,771	19,667	19,496	27,624	31,037	0.67	12.36
Estonia	600,233	645,235	839,411	970,620	1,101,607	23.72	13.50
Georgia	302	379	564	674	1,324	0.03	96.44
Hungary	12,382	12,821	16,476	14,492	13,840	0.30	-4.50
Kazakhstan	24,430	18,576	14,121	15,883	19,321	0.42	21.65
Kyrgyzstan	9,876	5		265	670	0.01	152.83
Lithuania	711,416	753,676	912,412	1,328,156	1,762,095	37.94	32.67
Republic of Moldova	81	123	858	1,539	1,665	0.04	8.19
Poland	91,495	94,358	169,273	202,134	209,845	4.52	3.81
Romania	2,744	761	1,319	4,698	866	0.02	-81.57
Russian Federation	174,154	190,691	206,353	224,629	271,862	5.85	21.03
Slovakia	11,545	5,780	12,670	13,864	7,112	0.15	-48.70
Tajikistan	20	23		170			
Turkmenistan	5	13					
Ukraine	16,132	17,224	18,227	22,128	23,464	0.51	6.04
Uzbekistan	703	248	633	1,420	2,468	0.05	73.80
Northern Europe	**281,777**	**311,080**	**324,020**	**446,304**	**654,991**	**14.10**	**46.76**
Denmark	18,250	24,017	27,634	42,247	52,392	1.13	24.01
Finland	171,558	165,328	149,610	141,325	249,443	5.37	76.50
Iceland	1,088	692	2,776	2,435	3,080	0.07	26.49
Ireland	2,858	4,325	4,047	11,242	23,526	0.51	109.27
Norway	14,005	16,069	33,293	26,284	54,272	1.17	106.48
Sweden	53,746	77,710	69,583	145,978	186,515	4.02	27.77
United Kingdom	20,272	22,939	37,077	76,793	85,763	1.85	11.68
Southern Europe	**39,028**	**42,852**	**83,208**	**67,171**	**75,794**	**1.63**	**12.84**
Albania	28	13		170			
Andorra	26	92		464			
Bosnia and Herzegovina	32	126					
Croatia	699	835	1,384	2,309	977	0.02	-57.69
Greece	1,284	1,813	811	3,787	3,683	0.08	-2.75
Italy	27,698	29,946	62,584	42,304	40,119	0.86	-5.16
Malta	1,410	574	429	844	2,225	0.05	163.63
Portugal	661	1,232	2,597	2,794	6,622	0.14	137.01

LATVIA

2. Arrivals of non-resident visitors at national borders, by country of residence

	2002	2003	2004	2005	2006	Market share 06	% Change 06-05
Slovenia	4,168	2,959	1,855	3,513	5,339	0.11	51.98
Spain	2,995	5,237	13,391	10,986	16,639	0.36	51.46
TFYR of Macedonia	27	25	138				
Serbia and Montenegro			19		190		
Western Europe	**157,209**	**255,784**	**307,460**	**345,659**	**329,282**	**7.09**	**-4.74**
Austria	8,092	11,636	21,692	31,624	18,860	0.41	-40.36
Belgium	5,232	4,822	9,164	9,496	12,437	0.27	30.97
France	9,236	17,993	28,621	29,566	31,490	0.68	6.51
Germany	118,727	191,858	202,640	234,905	233,407	5.03	-0.64
Liechtenstein	4	120	176	170			
Luxembourg	544	438	1,259	1,268	1,018	0.02	-19.72
Monaco	4	21					
Netherlands	10,063	23,321	34,438	27,849	22,063	0.48	-20.78
Switzerland	5,307	5,575	9,470	10,781	10,007	0.22	-7.18
East Mediterranean Europe	**8,873**	**6,981**	**7,665**	**4,328**	**12,047**	**0.26**	**178.35**
Cyprus	2,244	502	1,699	69	419	0.01	507.25
Israel	3,363	5,465	4,943	3,198	5,445	0.12	70.26
Turkey	3,266	1,014	1,023	1,061	6,183	0.13	482.75
MIDDLE EAST	**167**	**151**	**2**	**280**	**588**	**0.01**	**110.00**
Middle East	**167**	**151**	**2**	**280**	**588**	**0.01**	**110.00**
Bahrain		14					
Iraq	5						
Jordan		10			181		
Kuwait	2						
Lebanon	17	24					
Libyan Arab Jamahiriya	3						
Qatar		4		110			
Saudi Arabia		21					
Syrian Arab Republic		6					
United Arab Emirates	39	17					
Egypt	91	55		170	407	0.01	139.41
Other countries of Middle East	10		2				
SOUTH ASIA	**1,290**	**1,259**	**861**	**1,616**	**1,450**	**0.03**	**-10.27**
South Asia	**1,290**	**1,259**	**861**	**1,616**	**1,450**	**0.03**	**-10.27**
Afghanistan	223	76					
Bangladesh	3	2		515			
Sri Lanka	8	2		57			
India	959	1,059	861	832	1,450	0.03	74.28
Iran, Islamic Republic of	14	14		212			
Nepal		2					
Pakistan	83	104					
REGION NOT SPECIFIED	**13,115**	**690**	**1,672**	**2,425**	**872**	**0.02**	**-64.04**
Not Specified	**13,115**	**690**	**1,672**	**2,425**	**872**	**0.02**	**-64.04**
Other countries of the World	13,115	690	1,672	2,425	872	0.02	-64.04

Source: World Tourism Organization (UNWTO)

LATVIA

4. Arrivals of non-resident tourists in all types of accommodation establishments, by country of residence

	2002	2003	2004	2005	2006	Market share 06	% Change 06-05
TOTAL	360,927	414,924	545,366	730,146	816,297	100.00	11.80
AFRICA	87	151	83	71	137	0.02	92.96
East Africa	3	1	6	6	6		
Kenya	1	1	3	2	6		200.00
Zimbabwe	2		2	4			
United Republic of Tanzania			1				
Central Africa	7	7	12	6	10		66.67
Angola	5	3	10	3			
Cameroon	1	1	2	3			
Central African Republic		1			7		
Congo	1	2			3		
North Africa	2		22	13	31		138.46
Algeria			7	6	2		-66.67
Morocco	2		3	3	25		733.33
Tunisia			12	4	4		
Southern Africa	68	133	23	40	74	0.01	85.00
Namibia				9	4		-55.56
South Africa	68	133	23	31	66	0.01	112.90
Swaziland					4		
West Africa	7	10	20	6	16		166.67
Benin	1	7					
Gambia		1	1				
Liberia		1		2			
Mauritania		1			1		
Niger			10				
Nigeria	5		9		8		
Senegal	1			1	2		100.00
Sierra Leone				3	5		66.67
AMERICAS	15,014	14,128	21,091	20,423	22,517	2.76	10.25
Caribbean	4	28	5	27	19		-29.63
Cuba	4	27	4	24	3		-87.50
Dominican Republic		1		1	13		1,200.00
Jamaica			1	2	3		50.00
Central America	10		7	16	20		25.00
Belize			7	5	4		-20.00
Costa Rica	5			2	7		250.00
Guatemala	4						
Panama	1			9	9		
North America	14,816	13,840	20,695	19,917	21,832	2.67	9.61
Canada	1,979	1,383	2,316	2,279	3,092	0.38	35.67
Greenland			2				
Mexico	32	43	132	261	200	0.02	-23.37
United States	12,805	12,414	18,245	17,377	18,540	2.27	6.69
South America	184	260	384	463	646	0.08	39.52
Argentina	50	59	98	186	250	0.03	34.41
Bolivia			5	23	30		30.43
Brazil	38	115	170	168	151	0.02	-10.12
Chile	77	69	81	48	192	0.02	300.00
Colombia	2	6	10	28	4		-85.71

LATVIA

4. Arrivals of non-resident tourists in all types of accommodation establishments, by country of residence

	2002	2003	2004	2005	2006	Market share 06	% Change 06-05
Ecuador	1		7		8		
Peru	1	5	1		3		
Uruguay					5		
Venezuela	15	6	12	10	3		-70.00
EAST ASIA AND THE PACIFIC	**7,611**	**7,603**	**9,511**	**9,941**	**10,131**	**1.24**	**1.91**
North-East Asia	**6,273**	**6,123**	**6,762**	**6,645**	**6,392**	**0.78**	**-3.81**
China	244	203	389	359	457	0.06	27.30
Taiwan (Province of China)	131	3	232	113	75	0.01	-33.63
Hong Kong, China	79	70	286	291	134	0.02	-53.95
Japan	5,719	5,652	5,677	5,732	5,249	0.64	-8.43
Korea, Dem. People's Republic of	13	79	56	10	35		250.00
Korea, Republic of	85	92	116	138	434	0.05	214.49
Mongolia	2	24	6	2	8		300.00
South-East Asia	**106**	**182**	**296**	**337**	**359**	**0.04**	**6.53**
Indonesia		1	8	5	13		160.00
Lao People's Democratic Republic			1	6	6		
Malaysia	3	6	10	117	51	0.01	-56.41
Philippines	60	127	107	114	127	0.02	11.40
Singapore	4	9	35	54	41	0.01	-24.07
Viet Nam	36	27	48	16	6		-62.50
Thailand	3	12	87	25	115	0.01	360.00
Australasia	**1,232**	**1,298**	**2,453**	**2,959**	**3,380**	**0.41**	**14.23**
Australia	1,145	1,234	2,294	2,630	3,094	0.38	17.64
New Zealand	87	64	159	329	286	0.04	-13.07
EUROPE	**332,107**	**386,070**	**500,979**	**680,362**	**757,385**	**92.78**	**11.32**
Central/Eastern Europe	**130,932**	**144,005**	**185,533**	**223,758**	**263,267**	**32.25**	**17.66**
Azerbaijan	71	229	163	132	250	0.03	89.39
Armenia	48	85	48	42	97	0.01	130.95
Bulgaria	474	411	944	1,129	986	0.12	-12.67
Belarus	8,364	8,470	10,140	10,766	9,584	1.17	-10.98
Czech Republic	4,012	4,702	7,132	8,525	8,162	1.00	-4.26
Estonia	35,187	39,298	50,883	64,103	82,074	10.05	28.03
Georgia	128	164	167	213	425	0.05	99.53
Hungary	1,056	1,180	1,867	2,057	2,591	0.32	25.96
Kazakhstan	163	384	185	175	230	0.03	31.43
Kyrgyzstan	31	5	10	29			
Lithuania	28,382	30,830	45,193	62,279	72,790	8.92	16.88
Republic of Moldova	81	123	118	292	373	0.05	27.74
Poland	11,735	14,759	17,514	23,732	23,030	2.82	-2.96
Romania	314	761	514	762	1,376	0.17	80.58
Russian Federation	36,403	37,238	43,545	40,488	50,040	6.13	23.59
Slovakia	812	856	1,183	1,588	2,550	0.31	60.58
Tajikistan	20	23	9	8	1		-87.50
Turkmenistan	5	13	17	4	1		-75.00
Ukraine	3,570	4,279	5,162	6,066	8,074	0.99	33.10
Uzbekistan	76	195	739	1,368	633	0.08	-53.73
Northern Europe	**115,274**	**131,474**	**153,472**	**233,248**	**282,915**	**34.66**	**21.29**
Denmark	10,211	11,288	14,326	15,325	14,739	1.81	-3.82
Finland	55,702	61,507	65,321	90,845	88,533	10.85	-2.54
Iceland	178	258	486	439	467	0.06	6.38
Ireland	1,275	1,667	2,560	4,354	9,581	1.17	120.05
Norway	11,516	13,119	15,573	20,894	43,687	5.35	109.09

LATVIA

4. Arrivals of non-resident tourists in all types of accommodation establishments, by country of residence

	2002	2003	2004	2005	2006	Market share 06	% Change 06-05
Sweden	20,735	22,725	26,116	45,021	52,115	6.38	15.76
United Kingdom	15,657	20,910	29,090	56,370	73,793	9.04	30.91
Southern Europe	**12,376**	**18,418**	**28,234**	**40,715**	**41,407**	**5.07**	**1.70**
Albania	28	13	12	23	36		56.52
Andorra	26	92	34	60	24		-60.00
Bosnia and Herzegovina	32	117	17	22	29		31.82
Croatia	201	212	189	236	289	0.04	22.46
Gibraltar			10	1			
Greece	529	1,005	1,241	1,291	1,477	0.18	14.41
Italy	7,676	11,191	17,472	25,394	25,551	3.13	0.62
Malta	131	69	120	93	135	0.02	45.16
Portugal	661	1,040	1,631	2,416	1,887	0.23	-21.90
San Marino					2		
Slovenia	463	459	681	1,213	1,277	0.16	5.28
Spain	2,602	4,195	6,764	9,966	10,606	1.30	6.42
TFYR of Macedonia	27	25	44		14		
Serbia and Montenegro			19		80	0.01	
Western Europe	**69,791**	**87,206**	**128,719**	**178,106**	**164,742**	**20.18**	**-7.50**
Austria	3,893	4,192	7,494	11,581	10,609	1.30	-8.39
Belgium	2,359	2,766	4,908	6,206	6,252	0.77	0.74
France	5,498	7,104	10,992	14,399	15,884	1.95	10.31
Germany	48,544	62,649	87,757	123,981	108,716	13.32	-12.31
Liechtenstein	4	5	5	43	77	0.01	79.07
Luxembourg	405	421	629	1,045	788	0.10	-24.59
Monaco	4	21	6	49	13		-73.47
Netherlands	4,949	6,492	12,012	15,663	16,140	1.98	3.05
Switzerland	4,135	3,556	4,916	5,139	6,263	0.77	21.87
East Mediterranean Europe	**3,734**	**4,967**	**5,021**	**4,535**	**5,054**	**0.62**	**11.44**
Cyprus	338	294	370	1,033	688	0.08	-33.40
Israel	2,915	3,948	4,012	2,662	2,966	0.36	11.42
Turkey	481	725	639	840	1,400	0.17	66.67
MIDDLE EAST	**158**	**131**	**196**	**524**	**233**	**0.03**	**-55.53**
Middle East	**158**	**131**	**196**	**524**	**233**	**0.03**	**-55.53**
Bahrain		14	8		1		
Iraq	5		9	5			
Jordan		4		211			
Kuwait	2		1		7		
Lebanon	17	14	2	8	92	0.01	1,050.00
Libyan Arab Jamahiriya	3		1	3	2		-33.33
Qatar				2			
Saudi Arabia		21	13	4	1		-75.00
Syrian Arab Republic	1	6	4	4	1		-75.00
United Arab Emirates	39	17	51	26	41	0.01	57.69
Egypt	91	55	107	261	88	0.01	-66.28
SOUTH ASIA	**403**	**294**	**308**	**570**	**620**	**0.08**	**8.77**
South Asia	**403**	**294**	**308**	**570**	**620**	**0.08**	**8.77**
Afghanistan	223	76	63	102	190	0.02	86.27
Bangladesh	3	2	2	15	16		6.67
Sri Lanka	8	2	5	5	7		40.00
India	151	171	208	420	358	0.04	-14.76
Iran, Islamic Republic of	14	14	13	13	24		84.62
Nepal		2	2	10	8		-20.00

LATVIA

4. Arrivals of non-resident tourists in all types of accommodation establishments, by country of residence

	2002	2003	2004	2005	2006	Market share 06	% Change 06-05
Pakistan	4	27	15	5	17		240.00
REGION NOT SPECIFIED	**5,547**	**6,547**	**13,198**	**18,255**	**25,274**	**3.10**	**38.45**
Not Specified	**5,547**	**6,547**	**13,198**	**18,255**	**25,274**	**3.10**	**38.45**
Other countries of the World	5,547	6,547	13,198	18,255	25,274	3.10	38.45

Source: World Tourism Organization (UNWTO)

LATVIA

6. Overnight stays of non-resident tourists in all types of accommodation establishments, by country of residence

	2002	2003	2004	2005	2006	Market share 06	% Change 06-05
TOTAL	871,430	982,542	1,200,569	1,612,671	1,872,393	100.00	16.11
AFRICA	262	550	326	157	369	0.02	135.03
East Africa	9	8	24	14	25		78.57
Kenya	3	8	17	7	25		257.14
Zimbabwe	6		6	7			
United Republic of Tanzania			1				
Central Africa	23	15	141	22	24		9.09
Angola	12	3	21	5			
Cameroon	8	1	120	17			
Central African Republic		2			21		
Congo	3	9			3		
North Africa	2		76	25	49		96.00
Algeria			17	12	2		-83.33
Morocco	2		16	9	31		244.44
Tunisia			43	4	16		300.00
Southern Africa	213	515	47	88	252	0.01	186.36
Namibia				12	12		
South Africa	213	515	47	76	230	0.01	202.63
Swaziland					10		
West Africa	15	12	38	8	19		137.50
Benin	3	7					
Gambia		3	2				
Liberia		1		2			
Mauritania		1			1		
Niger			19				
Nigeria	11	17			9		
Senegal	1			1	3		200.00
Sierra Leone				5	6		20.00
AMERICAS	45,442	42,598	57,170	53,730	69,329	3.70	29.03
Caribbean	6	57	13	65	30		-53.85
Cuba	6	56	7	57	4		-92.98
Dominican Republic		1		2	20		900.00
Jamaica			6	6	6		
Central America	16		17	28	176	0.01	528.57
Belize			17	10	22		120.00
Costa Rica	7			2	119	0.01	5,850.00
Guatemala	8						
Panama	1			16	35		118.75
North America	44,886	41,866	56,234	52,565	66,933	3.57	27.33
Canada	6,363	4,570	6,264	6,516	9,499	0.51	45.78
Greenland			6				
Mexico	116	181	353	659	395	0.02	-40.06
United States	38,407	37,115	49,611	45,390	57,039	3.05	25.66
South America	534	675	906	1,072	2,190	0.12	104.29
Argentina	144	153	234	480	638	0.03	32.92
Bolivia			7	37	167	0.01	351.35
Brazil	89	337	421	348	408	0.02	17.24
Chile	266	157	168	135	920	0.05	581.48
Colombia	2	9	29	47	9		-80.85

LATVIA

6. Overnight stays of non-resident tourists in all types of accommodation establishments, by country of residence

	2002	2003	2004	2005	2006	Market share 06	% Change 06-05
Ecuador	6		19		21		
Peru	1	10	1		8		
Uruguay					15		
Venezuela	26	9	27	25	4		-84.00
EAST ASIA AND THE PACIFIC	**14,560**	**16,725**	**18,060**	**21,384**	**23,086**	**1.23**	**7.96**
North-East Asia	**10,945**	**12,254**	**11,241**	**11,315**	**12,609**	**0.67**	**11.44**
China	543	586	828	792	1,272	0.07	60.61
Taiwan (Province of China)	254	32	298	181	170	0.01	-6.08
Hong Kong, China	172	153	541	543	208	0.01	-61.69
Japan	9,805	10,561	9,031	9,514	9,960	0.53	4.69
Korea, Dem. People's Republic of	17	189	306	25	68		172.00
Korea, Republic of	144	462	223	257	857	0.05	233.46
Mongolia	10	271	14	3	74		2,366.67
South-East Asia	**206**	**425**	**532**	**656**	**822**	**0.04**	**25.30**
Indonesia		2	8	8	40		400.00
Lao People's Democratic Republic			2	6	15		150.00
Malaysia	7	11	29	172	99	0.01	-42.44
Philippines	99	271	150	182	348	0.02	91.21
Singapore	4	18	92	200	129	0.01	-35.50
Viet Nam	88	95	65	23	19		-17.39
Thailand	8	28	186	65	172	0.01	164.62
Australasia	**3,409**	**4,046**	**6,287**	**9,413**	**9,655**	**0.52**	**2.57**
Australia	3,249	3,908	5,910	8,220	8,930	0.48	8.64
New Zealand	160	138	377	1,193	725	0.04	-39.23
EUROPE	**797,374**	**904,945**	**1,092,746**	**1,489,500**	**1,719,008**	**91.81**	**15.41**
Central/Eastern Europe	**353,807**	**367,604**	**424,089**	**536,345**	**603,008**	**32.21**	**12.43**
Azerbaijan	246	534	439	419	594	0.03	41.77
Armenia	119	267	205	137	709	0.04	417.52
Bulgaria	1,307	1,013	3,891	7,571	1,995	0.11	-73.65
Belarus	96,507	93,998	94,086	98,477	53,135	2.84	-46.04
Czech Republic	7,381	8,909	11,444	12,762	15,746	0.84	23.38
Estonia	54,746	60,336	74,683	98,308	134,994	7.21	37.32
Georgia	399	416	433	651	1,100	0.06	68.97
Hungary	2,162	2,496	3,519	4,131	5,178	0.28	25.34
Kazakhstan	815	1,345	733	440	660	0.04	50.00
Kyrgyzstan	97	15	56	73	114	0.01	56.16
Lithuania	47,806	49,401	72,319	104,224	135,311	7.23	29.83
Republic of Moldova	242	298	300	873	1,212	0.06	38.83
Poland	22,353	23,069	30,492	52,366	46,544	2.49	-11.12
Romania	936	1,650	1,340	1,848	3,639	0.19	96.92
Russian Federation	106,310	109,929	112,706	116,459	151,113	8.07	29.76
Slovakia	2,500	2,017	2,741	3,692	6,411	0.34	73.65
Tajikistan	49	99	48	29	3		-89.66
Turkmenistan	13	56	61	14	1		-92.86
Ukraine	9,478	10,988	12,314	26,740	38,243	2.04	43.02
Uzbekistan	341	768	2,279	7,131	6,306	0.34	-11.57
Northern Europe	**241,835**	**285,297**	**317,926**	**485,074**	**646,858**	**34.55**	**33.35**
Denmark	22,153	25,007	28,369	30,428	31,668	1.69	4.08
Finland	107,553	120,683	125,404	177,892	187,603	10.02	5.46
Iceland	676	717	985	864	1,076	0.06	24.54
Ireland	3,037	4,400	5,510	9,662	21,566	1.15	123.20
Norway	25,548	28,795	34,355	44,301	121,402	6.48	174.04

LATVIA

6. Overnight stays of non-resident tourists in all types of accommodation establishments, by country of residence

	2002	2003	2004	2005	2006	Market share 06	% Change 06-05
Sweden	43,598	51,766	53,740	90,250	111,334	5.95	23.36
United Kingdom	39,270	53,929	69,563	131,677	172,209	9.20	30.78
Southern Europe	**28,172**	**41,277**	**58,463**	**84,477**	**95,309**	**5.09**	**12.82**
Albania	43	42	48	39	82		110.26
Andorra	63	216	65	86	45		-47.67
Bosnia and Herzegovina	132	133	46	61	151	0.01	147.54
Croatia	457	766	600	578	1,696	0.09	193.43
Gibraltar			20	2			
Greece	1,658	2,667	2,831	2,989	3,599	0.19	20.41
Italy	17,022	24,906	35,753	52,846	58,176	3.11	10.09
Malta	286	186	247	505	432	0.02	-14.46
Portugal	1,566	2,091	3,542	4,627	5,448	0.29	17.74
San Marino					3		
Slovenia	1,062	1,143	1,298	2,490	2,900	0.15	16.47
Spain	5,762	8,829	13,882	20,254	22,548	1.20	11.33
TFYR of Macedonia	121	298	73		51		
Serbia and Montenegro			58		178	0.01	
Western Europe	**153,032**	**184,123**	**266,397**	**369,492**	**355,918**	**19.01**	**-3.67**
Austria	7,636	8,624	15,228	27,039	20,823	1.11	-22.99
Belgium	6,358	7,399	10,667	13,155	13,859	0.74	5.35
France	13,240	15,364	22,509	29,990	34,299	1.83	14.37
Germany	102,942	129,062	181,273	255,557	238,061	12.71	-6.85
Liechtenstein	7	11	5	54	84		55.56
Luxembourg	1,110	853	1,397	2,626	1,699	0.09	-35.30
Monaco	10	60	12	74	18		-75.68
Netherlands	11,574	14,485	24,949	29,672	31,100	1.66	4.81
Switzerland	10,155	8,265	10,357	11,325	15,975	0.85	41.06
East Mediterranean Europe	**20,528**	**26,644**	**25,871**	**14,112**	**17,915**	**0.96**	**26.95**
Cyprus	1,038	960	1,069	2,312	1,890	0.10	-18.25
Israel	18,045	23,609	23,210	9,179	11,895	0.64	29.59
Turkey	1,445	2,075	1,592	2,621	4,130	0.22	57.57
MIDDLE EAST	**556**	**793**	**420**	**1,283**	**397**	**0.02**	**-69.06**
Middle East	**556**	**793**	**420**	**1,283**	**397**	**0.02**	**-69.06**
Bahrain		32	24		2		
Iraq	5		45	35			
Jordan		21		408			
Kuwait	2		1		10		
Lebanon	180	198	8	41	92		124.39
Libyan Arab Jamahiriya	6		6	9	2		-77.78
Qatar				2			
Saudi Arabia		76	24	6	1		-83.33
Syrian Arab Republic	1	11	6	8	4		-50.00
United Arab Emirates	112	58	100	63	78		23.81
Egypt	250	397	206	711	208	0.01	-70.75
SOUTH ASIA	**1,134**	**742**	**1,131**	**1,201**	**1,904**	**0.10**	**58.53**
South Asia	**1,134**	**742**	**1,131**	**1,201**	**1,904**	**0.10**	**58.53**
Afghanistan	731	198	158	245	727	0.04	196.73
Bangladesh	7	2	3	24	275	0.01	1,045.83
Sri Lanka	22	7	25	18	20		11.11
India	345	438	847	779	769	0.04	-1.28
Iran, Islamic Republic of	21	19	53	34	50		47.06
Nepal		2	14	94	33		-64.89

LATVIA

6. Overnight stays of non-resident tourists in all types of accommodation establishments, by country of residence

	2002	2003	2004	2005	2006	Market share 06	% Change 06-05
Pakistan	8	76	31	7	30		328.57
REGION NOT SPECIFIED	**12,102**	**16,189**	**30,716**	**45,416**	**58,300**	**3.11**	**28.37**
Not Specified	**12,102**	**16,189**	**30,716**	**45,416**	**58,300**	**3.11**	**28.37**
Other countries of the World	12,102	16,189	30,716	45,416	58,300	3.11	28.37

Source: World Tourism Organization (UNWTO)

LEBANON

1. Arrivals of non-resident tourists at national borders, by nationality

	2002	2003	2004	2005	2006	Market share 06	% Change 06-05
TOTAL (*)	956,464	1,015,793	1,278,469	1,139,524	1,062,625	100.00	-6.75
AFRICA	37,240	39,453	45,095	31,073	39,021	3.67	25.58
East Africa	11,109	14,234	10,156	5,119	12,977	1.22	153.51
Burundi	28	8	20	4	5		25.00
Comoros	28	12	5	8	5		-37.50
Ethiopia	8,976	12,169	8,082	3,459	11,230	1.06	224.66
Eritrea	856	907	1,019	781	591	0.06	-24.33
Djibouti	104	63	42	14	15		7.14
Kenya	250	273	388	234	322	0.03	37.61
Madagascar	92	137	120	129	195	0.02	51.16
Malawi	6	7	18	36	51		41.67
Mauritius	88	90	69	74	52		-29.73
Mozambique	39	85	11	19	75	0.01	294.74
Rwanda	24	10	19	9	15		66.67
Seychelles	19	9	31	18	18		
Somalia	149	125	112	158	217	0.02	37.34
Zimbabwe	357	252	75	60	43		-28.33
Uganda	13	12	12	24	25		4.17
United Republic of Tanzania	47	55	94	56	74	0.01	32.14
Zambia	33	20	39	36	44		22.22
Central Africa	987	880	907	1,143	1,209	0.11	5.77
Angola	76	58	57	140	62	0.01	-55.71
Cameroon	151	118	119	144	133	0.01	-7.64
Central African Republic	96	66	58	50	85	0.01	70.00
Chad	101	47	74	14	18		28.57
Congo	195	216	225	189	186	0.02	-1.59
Equatorial Guinea	25	8	15	40	15		-62.50
Gabon	326	350	359	565	710	0.07	25.66
Other countries of Central Africa	17	17		1			
North Africa	16,376	15,823	23,542	13,792	14,550	1.37	5.50
Algeria	3,925	3,419	5,194	2,988	3,247	0.31	8.67
Morocco	4,165	4,044	4,692	3,859	4,584	0.43	18.79
Sudan	3,322	3,242	3,945	2,799	2,888	0.27	3.18
Tunisia	4,964	5,118	9,711	4,146	3,831	0.36	-7.60
Southern Africa	896	953	1,352	1,278	1,339	0.13	4.77
Namibia	13	9	12	8	7		-12.50
South Africa	883	944	1,340	1,270	1,332	0.13	4.88
West Africa	7,872	7,563	9,138	9,741	8,946	0.84	-8.16
Cape Verde	16	18	3	1	7		600.00
Benin	349	300	340	315	328	0.03	4.13
Gambia	106	225	219	193	142	0.01	-26.42
Ghana	1,196	1,136	2,133	3,028	2,405	0.23	-20.57
Guinea	449	406	446	378	427	0.04	12.96
Cote D'Ivoire	744	828	1,029	1,011	1,099	0.10	8.70
Liberia	128	91	111	189	150	0.01	-20.63
Mali	137	74	103	100	96	0.01	-4.00
Mauritania	210	137	205	137	165	0.02	20.44
Niger	215	181	148	117	94	0.01	-19.66
Nigeria	1,980	1,621	1,772	1,592	1,594	0.15	0.13
Guinea-Bissau	33	104	43	40	87	0.01	117.50
Senegal	1,259	1,286	1,478	1,399	1,148	0.11	-17.94
Sierra Leone	515	708	695	809	771	0.07	-4.70
Togo	205	126	114	132	143	0.01	8.33

LEBANON

1. Arrivals of non-resident tourists at national borders, by nationality

	2002	2003	2004	2005	2006	Market share 06	% Change 06-05
Burkina Faso	330	322	299	300	290	0.03	-3.33
AMERICAS	**108,329**	**120,239**	**152,175**	**136,904**	**130,117**	**12.24**	**-4.96**
Caribbean	**494**	**612**	**711**	**646**	**464**	**0.04**	**-28.17**
Antigua and Barbuda	3	25	19	18	24		33.33
Bahamas	8	2		2	2		
Barbados	28	16	16	11	7		-36.36
Cuba	188	243	230	278	144	0.01	-48.20
Dominica	49	40					
Dominican Republic	30	78	241	173	120	0.01	-30.64
Grenada	12	15	18	13	6		-53.85
Haiti	49	33	45	26	22		-15.38
Jamaica	40	54	64	46	30		-34.78
Puerto Rico	3	2		1	1		
Saint Lucia	2	3	3	2	1		-50.00
Saint Vincent and the Grenadines	12	15	17	10	6		-40.00
Trinidad and Tobago	70	86	58	66	101	0.01	53.03
Central America	**615**	**697**	**850**	**690**	**653**	**0.06**	**-5.36**
Belize	186	231	209	165	158	0.01	-4.24
Costa Rica	91	75	126	80	56	0.01	-30.00
El Salvador	11	14	51	12	15		25.00
Guatemala	47	30	52	50	29		-42.00
Honduras	40	24	31	47	38		-19.15
Nicaragua	18	54	67	29	17		-41.38
Panama	222	269	314	307	340	0.03	10.75
North America	**93,545**	**104,815**	**133,273**	**119,007**	**114,066**	**10.73**	**-4.15**
Canada	39,685	43,136	52,425	48,453	48,324	4.55	-0.27
Mexico	1,289	1,629	2,021	2,193	1,606	0.15	-26.77
United States	52,571	60,050	78,827	68,361	64,136	6.04	-6.18
South America	**13,675**	**14,115**	**17,341**	**16,561**	**14,934**	**1.41**	**-9.82**
Argentina	756	910	1,156	1,018	775	0.07	-23.87
Bolivia	81	59	86	81	69	0.01	-14.81
Brazil	6,112	6,200	8,031	7,432	6,789	0.64	-8.65
Chile	389	467	624	681	394	0.04	-42.14
Colombia	1,057	1,117	1,236	1,197	1,174	0.11	-1.92
Ecuador	182	237	271	179	154	0.01	-13.97
Paraguay	445	416	420	401	419	0.04	4.49
Peru	71	114	105	146	116	0.01	-20.55
Suriname	29	47	59	40	34		-15.00
Uruguay	61	81	90	83	120	0.01	44.58
Venezuela	4,492	4,467	5,263	5,303	4,890	0.46	-7.79
EAST ASIA AND THE PACIFIC	**60,543**	**65,581**	**92,285**	**87,813**	**74,461**	**7.01**	**-15.21**
North-East Asia	**7,091**	**6,381**	**8,471**	**9,531**	**8,125**	**0.76**	**-14.75**
China	1,463	950	1,559	1,642	1,734	0.16	5.60
Taiwan (Province of China)	67	163	205	368	254	0.02	-30.98
Hong Kong, China	20	61	55	30	33		10.00
Japan	3,944	3,046	4,753	5,475	3,594	0.34	-34.36
Korea, Dem. People's Republic of	550	491	625	553	207	0.02	-62.57
Korea, Republic of	1,037	1,196	1,248	1,409	2,300	0.22	63.24
Mongolia	10	474	26	54	3		-94.44
South-East Asia	**22,267**	**26,361**	**36,475**	**38,458**	**33,485**	**3.15**	**-12.93**
Brunei Darussalam	16	8	11	6	11		83.33
Myanmar	2,000	10	34	24	48		100.00

LEBANON

1. Arrivals of non-resident tourists at national borders, by nationality

	2002	2003	2004	2005	2006	Market share 06	% Change 06-05
Cambodia	21	30	31	24	16		-33.33
Indonesia	5,605	6,466	8,263	5,401	5,264	0.50	-2.54
Lao People's Democratic Republic	121	3					
Malaysia	1,061	1,122	1,889	1,418	1,512	0.14	6.63
Philippines	12,768	18,069	25,296	30,655	26,104	2.46	-14.85
Singapore	191	259	480	541	286	0.03	-47.13
Viet Nam	168	76	100	79	55	0.01	-30.38
Thailand	316	318	371	310	189	0.02	-39.03
Australasia	**31,149**	**32,818**	**47,297**	**39,797**	**32,821**	**3.09**	**-17.53**
Australia	30,122	31,854	45,915	38,577	31,929	3.00	-17.23
New Zealand	1,027	964	1,382	1,220	892	0.08	-26.89
Melanesia	**36**	**21**	**42**	**27**	**30**		**11.11**
Fiji	33	21	42	27	30		11.11
New Caledonia	3						
EUROPE	**250,817**	**267,077**	**337,337**	**316,561**	**269,263**	**25.34**	**-14.94**
Central/Eastern Europe	**26,513**	**27,369**	**30,539**	**31,224**	**27,853**	**2.62**	**-10.80**
Azerbaijan	56	169	105	83	78	0.01	-6.02
Armenia	1,237	1,395	212	1,396	1,159	0.11	-16.98
Bulgaria	1,523	1,410	1,569	1,210	1,096	0.10	-9.42
Belarus	1,410	1,431	1,518	1,623	1,506	0.14	-7.21
Czech Republic	1,821	1,591	1,726	1,653	1,200	0.11	-27.40
Estonia	49	94	173	136	209	0.02	53.68
Georgia	87	160	275	257	181	0.02	-29.57
Hungary	1,123	926	1,438	1,314	1,069	0.10	-18.65
Kazakhstan	164	239	313	256	299	0.03	16.80
Kyrgyzstan	25	23	43	58	47		-18.97
Latvia	73	120	272	256	228	0.02	-10.94
Lithuania	269	180	258	323	247	0.02	-23.53
Republic of Moldova	896	769	980	780	925	0.09	18.59
Poland	3,172	2,684	3,598	3,932	3,003	0.28	-23.63
Romania	2,209	2,285	2,134	1,928	2,123	0.20	10.11
Russian Federation	6,762	7,881	8,994	9,157	8,065	0.76	-11.93
Slovakia	569	554	616	620	415	0.04	-33.06
Tajikistan	17	15	21	24	34		41.67
Turkmenistan	9	15	60	36	36		
Ukraine	4,925	5,262	6,140	6,048	5,808	0.55	-3.97
Uzbekistan	56	94	94	131	125	0.01	-4.58
Other countries Central/East Europ	61	72		3			
Northern Europe	**56,440**	**59,245**	**75,508**	**74,524**	**65,606**	**6.17**	**-11.97**
Denmark	9,321	10,479	13,487	13,367	12,155	1.14	-9.07
Finland	1,033	1,126	1,369	1,392	1,303	0.12	-6.39
Iceland	66	132	201	109	99	0.01	-9.17
Ireland	1,766	2,000	2,417	2,237	2,034	0.19	-9.07
Norway	2,269	2,752	3,284	3,567	2,792	0.26	-21.73
Sweden	13,407	14,732	20,218	18,314	17,331	1.63	-5.37
United Kingdom	28,578	28,024	34,532	35,538	29,892	2.81	-15.89
Southern Europe	**24,744**	**26,886**	**33,902**	**31,398**	**27,955**	**2.63**	**-10.97**
Albania	80	72	90	50	60	0.01	20.00
Andorra	3		3	1	2		100.00
Bosnia and Herzegovina	108	160	153	114	154	0.01	35.09
Croatia	342	395	593	344	412	0.04	19.77
Greece	4,837	5,628	7,397	6,424	5,755	0.54	-10.41
Holy See	97	88	79	43	34		-20.93
Italy	12,332	13,119	15,567	14,104	13,290	1.25	-5.77

LEBANON

1. Arrivals of non-resident tourists at national borders, by nationality

	2002	2003	2004	2005	2006	Market share 06	% Change 06-05
Malta	184	202	194	198	151	0.01	-23.74
Portugal	439	468	581	598	629	0.06	5.18
San Marino	645	5	6	6	8		33.33
Slovenia	151	124	181	178	183	0.02	2.81
Spain	4,701	5,646	7,868	8,442	6,324	0.60	-25.09
TFYR of Macedonia	824	964	1,165	857	841	0.08	-1.87
Serbia and Montenegro	1	15	25	39	112	0.01	187.18
Western Europe	**131,133**	**138,746**	**175,412**	**161,842**	**129,519**	**12.19**	**-19.97**
Austria	3,376	3,216	4,406	4,022	3,014	0.28	-25.06
Belgium	7,090	7,136	9,048	8,342	7,230	0.68	-13.33
France	70,872	76,409	94,347	80,480	66,764	6.28	-17.04
Germany	36,287	37,942	48,370	51,948	39,314	3.70	-24.32
Liechtenstein	14	7	10	7	5		-28.57
Luxembourg	183	212	200	221	156	0.01	-29.41
Monaco	21	28	29	11	8		-27.27
Netherlands	6,594	6,839	9,071	8,567	6,387	0.60	-25.45
Switzerland	6,693	6,957	9,931	8,239	6,641	0.62	-19.40
Other countries of Western Europe	3			5			
East Mediterranean Europe	**11,987**	**14,831**	**21,976**	**17,573**	**18,330**	**1.72**	**4.31**
Cyprus	5,566	8,032	12,347	8,955	7,920	0.75	-11.56
Turkey	6,421	6,799	9,629	8,618	10,410	0.98	20.79
MIDDLE EAST	**403,000**	**421,148**	**520,230**	**436,549**	**433,323**	**40.78**	**-0.74**
Middle East	**403,000**	**421,148**	**520,230**	**436,549**	**433,323**	**40.78**	**-0.74**
Bahrain	20,947	25,002	27,184	17,624	10,012	0.94	-43.19
Iraq	13,467	7,863	17,159	20,677	60,414	5.69	192.18
Jordan	81,705	87,798	92,840	135,227	144,166	13.57	6.61
Kuwait	69,516	55,959	79,830	64,193	50,108	4.72	-21.94
Libyan Arab Jamahiriya	3,623	3,451	4,297	3,519	2,626	0.25	-25.38
Oman	4,371	4,424	5,392	3,742	3,072	0.29	-17.90
Qatar	7,986	10,728	14,819	12,064	11,666	1.10	-3.30
Saudi Arabia	144,569	162,230	200,899	124,687	93,570	8.81	-24.96
United Arab Emirates	14,127	20,261	26,837	17,044	16,051	1.51	-5.83
Egypt	38,571	39,022	46,056	34,271	38,678	3.64	12.86
Yemen	4,118	4,410	4,917	3,500	2,960	0.28	-15.43
Other countries of Middle East				1			
SOUTH ASIA	**95,647**	**102,035**	**128,120**	**129,315**	**115,243**	**10.85**	**-10.88**
South Asia	**95,647**	**102,035**	**128,120**	**129,315**	**115,243**	**10.85**	**-10.88**
Afghanistan	406	295	311	311	198	0.02	-36.33
Bangladesh	2,443	2,283	1,512	1,499	3,504	0.33	133.76
Bhutan	1	2			4		
Sri Lanka	16,718	17,124	22,089	20,436	11,429	1.08	-44.07
India	8,565	9,603	11,240	11,111	10,079	0.95	-9.29
Iran, Islamic Republic of	65,318	70,400	89,770	92,863	86,385	8.13	-6.98
Maldives	1	1	28	1	2		100.00
Nepal	287	312	285	910	1,306	0.12	43.52
Pakistan	1,908	2,015	2,885	2,184	2,336	0.22	6.96
REGION NOT SPECIFIED	**888**	**260**	**3,227**	**1,309**	**1,197**	**0.11**	**-8.56**
Not Specified	**888**	**260**	**3,227**	**1,309**	**1,197**	**0.11**	**-8.56**
Other countries of the World	888	260	3,227	1,309	1,197	0.11	-8.56

Source: World Tourism Organization (UNWTO)

LESOTHO

2. Arrivals of non-resident visitors at national borders, by country of residence

	2002	2003	2004	2005	2006	Market share 06	% Change 06-05
TOTAL	287,280	329,301	303,530	303,578	356,913	100.00	17.57
AFRICA	278,662	302,924	290,295	289,342	329,838	92.41	14.00
East Africa	1,937	4,570	2,634	2,781	6,690	1.87	140.56
Kenya	144	231	169	173	300	0.08	73.41
Malawi					535	0.15	
Mauritius					128	0.04	
Mozambique	168	298	204	211	310	0.09	46.92
Zimbabwe	1,384	3,590	1,963	2,088	3,899	1.09	86.73
Uganda					262	0.07	
United Republic of Tanzania					404	0.11	
Zambia	241	451	298	309	852	0.24	175.73
Southern Africa	275,693	292,699	285,451	284,009	321,867	90.18	13.33
Botswana	1,272	3,970	1,973	2,129	1,903	0.53	-10.62
South Africa	273,365	286,349	282,070	280,399	318,458	89.23	13.57
Swaziland	1,056	2,380	1,408	1,481	1,506	0.42	1.69
West Africa					229	0.06	
Ghana					65	0.02	
Nigeria					164	0.05	
Other Africa	1,032	5,655	2,210	2,552	1,052	0.29	-58.78
Other countries of Africa	1,032	5,655	2,210	2,552	1,052	0.29	-58.78
AMERICAS	861	2,842	1,375	1,490	3,412	0.96	128.99
North America	730	2,588	1,210	1,319	3,287	0.92	149.20
Canada	203	392	255	265	1,409	0.39	431.70
United States	527	2,196	955	1,054	1,878	0.53	78.18
Other Americas	131	254	165	171	125	0.04	-26.90
Other countries of the Americas	131	254	165	171	125	0.04	-26.90
EAST ASIA AND THE PACIFIC	2,011	4,009	2,551	2,657	3,456	0.97	30.07
North-East Asia					1,521	0.43	
China					1,222	0.34	
Taiwan (Province of China)					299	0.08	
Australasia	575	389	540	523	702	0.20	34.23
Australia	575	389	540	523	702	0.20	34.23
Other East Asia and the Pacific	1,436	3,620	2,011	2,134	1,233	0.35	-42.22
Other countries of Asia					1,233	0.35	
All countries of Asia	1,436	3,620	2,011	2,134			
EUROPE	5,746	12,569	7,568	7,930	19,641	5.50	147.68
Northern Europe	2,588	2,424	2,598	2,556	5,644	1.58	120.81
Denmark					173	0.05	
Ireland	492	198	428	406	242	0.07	-40.39
Sweden	188	221	200	200	292	0.08	46.00
United Kingdom	1,908	2,005	1,970	1,950	4,937	1.38	153.18
Southern Europe					273	0.08	
Italy					273	0.08	
Western Europe	2,781	2,878	1,687	1,775	11,125	3.12	526.76
France					965	0.27	
Germany	1,256	2,878	1,687	1,775	5,901	1.65	232.45
Netherlands	1,525				4,259	1.19	
Other Europe	377	7,267	3,283	3,599	2,599	0.73	-27.79

LESOTHO

2. Arrivals of non-resident visitors at national borders, by country of residence

	2002	2003	2004	2005	2006	Market share 06	% Change 06-05
Other countries of Europe	377	7,267	3,283	3,599	2,599	0.73	-27.79
MIDDLE EAST					**117**	**0.03**	
Middle East					117	0.03	
All countries of Middle East					117	0.03	
SOUTH ASIA					**318**	**0.09**	
South Asia					318	0.09	
India					318	0.09	
REGION NOT SPECIFIED		6,957	1,741	2,159	131	0.04	-93.93
Not Specified		6,957	1,741	2,159	131	0.04	-93.93
Other countries of the World		6,957	1,741	2,159	131	0.04	-93.93

Source: World Tourism Organization (UNWTO)

LIBYAN ARAB JAMAHIRIYA

2. Arrivals of non-resident visitors at national borders, by nationality

	2002	2003	2004	2005	2006	Market share 06	% Change 06-05
TOTAL (*)	857,952	957,896	999,343				
AFRICA	438,881	457,721	482,704				
East Africa	445	378	446				
Comoros	22	23	25				
Ethiopia	141	150	155				
Eritrea	7	7	15				
Djibouti	36	37	44				
Kenya	16	2	12				
Malawi	16	9	13				
Mauritius	88	93	98				
Rwanda	24	10	18				
Somalia	17	17	21				
Uganda	56	29	34				
United Republic of Tanzania	22	1	11				
Central Africa	550	523	594				
Cameroon	10	8	11				
Chad	520	498	568				
Democratic Republic of the Congo	20	17	15				
North Africa	435,401	454,476	479,032				
Algeria	70,416	71,657	73,459				
Morocco	19,076	19,120	20,803				
Western Sahara	462	471	564				
Sudan	16,302	16,897	17,335				
Tunisia	329,145	346,331	366,871				
Southern Africa	71	73	87				
South Africa	71	73	87				
West Africa	2,296	2,149	2,399				
Benin	86	80	98				
Gambia	26	30	43				
Ghana	100	71	88				
Guinea	156	142	157				
Cote D'Ivoire	38	27	35				
Mali	284	195	213				
Mauritania	1,028	1,159	1,179				
Niger	196	121	176				
Nigeria	154	140	166				
Senegal	82	99	135				
Sierra Leone	20	11	19				
Togo	32	19	23				
Burkina Faso	94	55	67				
Other Africa	118	122	146				
Other countries of Africa	118	122	146				
AMERICAS	1,943	1,926	2,201				
Caribbean	19	16	19				
Cuba	18	15	19				
Jamaica	1	1					
Central America	10	7	10				
Costa Rica	4	2	3				
Nicaragua	6	5	7				
North America	1,724	1,756	1,968				
Canada	1,504	1,541	1,684				

LIBYAN ARAB JAMAHIRIYA

2. Arrivals of non-resident visitors at national borders, by nationality

	2002	2003	2004	2005	2006	Market share 06	% Change 06-05
Mexico	40	33	49				
United States	180	182	235				
South America	**134**	**103**	**144**				
Argentina	44	35	49				
Bolivia	4	2	5				
Brazil	48	37	54				
Colombia	14	11	13				
Peru	6	4	7				
Venezuela	18	14	16				
Other Americas	**56**	**44**	**60**				
Other countries of the Americas	56	44	60				
EAST ASIA AND THE PACIFIC	**6,611**	**6,601**	**6,942**				
North-East Asia	**2,407**	**2,568**	**2,919**				
China	552	644	853				
Taiwan (Province of China)	80	91	75				
Japan	601	578	684				
Korea, Republic of	1,174	1,255	1,307				
South-East Asia	**3,954**	**3,835**	**3,808**				
Indonesia	140	125	135				
Malaysia	192	210	247				
Philippines	2,268	2,287	2,356				
Singapore	4	3	4				
Viet Nam	378	198	24				
Thailand	972	1,012	1,042				
Australasia	**250**	**198**	**215**				
Australia	198	156	166				
New Zealand	52	42	49				
EUROPE	**36,418**	**42,056**	**45,657**				
Central/Eastern Europe	**3,754**	**3,969**	**4,405**				
Azerbaijan	10	7	8				
Bulgaria	932	894	910				
Czech Republic	146	201	263				
Georgia	4	3	6				
Hungary	176	183	210				
Poland	726	701	776				
Romania	680	589	689				
Russian Federation	408	591	629				
Slovakia	112	85	129				
Ukraine	560	715	785				
Northern Europe	**6,098**	**7,073**	**7,411**				
Denmark	202	191	253				
Finland	130	157	169				
Ireland	644	743	792				
Norway	94	86	96				
Sweden	244	254	298				
United Kingdom	4,784	5,642	5,803				
Southern Europe	**14,702**	**14,170**	**15,469**				
Albania	8	18	21				
Bosnia and Herzegovina	8	24	40				
Croatia	662	521	601				
Greece	274	174	213				

LIBYAN ARAB JAMAHIRIYA

2. Arrivals of non-resident visitors at national borders, by nationality

	2002	2003	2004	2005	2006	Market share 06	% Change 06-05
Italy	8,266	7,289	7,982				
Malta	3,496	3,243	3,587				
Portugal	72	44	65				
Slovenia	24	15	30				
Spain	638	1,389	1,452				
Serbia and Montenegro	1,254	1,453	1,478				
Western Europe	**10,334**	**15,734**	**17,104**				
Austria	1,014	1,415	1,526				
Belgium	438	501	558				
France	4,022	6,514	6,951				
Germany	3,442	6,190	6,759				
Netherlands	610	425	567				
Switzerland	808	689	743				
East Mediterranean Europe	**1,526**	**1,106**	**1,259**				
Cyprus	320	85	117				
Turkey	1,206	1,021	1,142				
Other Europe	**4**	**4**	**9**				
Other countries of Europe	4	4	9				
MIDDLE EAST	**369,774**	**445,561**	**458,124**				
Middle East	**369,774**	**445,561**	**458,124**				
Bahrain	17	17	20				
Palestine	771	778	801				
Iraq	6,110	5,668	5,940				
Jordan	2,021	2,141	2,267				
Kuwait	83	84	89				
Lebanon	367	371	350				
Oman	13	13	16				
Qatar	17	17	22				
Saudi Arabia	223	225	198				
Syrian Arab Republic	5,680	6,742	6,878				
United Arab Emirates	60	60	77				
Egypt	354,189	429,220	441,230				
Yemen	223	225	236				
SOUTH ASIA	**4,325**	**4,031**	**3,704**				
South Asia	**4,325**	**4,031**	**3,704**				
Afghanistan	15	16	15				
Bangladesh	1,016	665	605				
Sri Lanka	128	87	99				
India	1,958	2,045	2,089				
Iran, Islamic Republic of	522	658	286				
Maldives	12	7	9				
Nepal	2	5	4				
Pakistan	672	548	597				
REGION NOT SPECIFIED			**11**				
Not Specified			**11**				
Other countries of the World			11				

Source: World Tourism Organization (UNWTO)

LIECHTENSTEIN

3. Arrivals of non-resident tourists in hotels and similar establishments, by country of residence

	2002	2003	2004	2005	2006	Market share 06	% Change 06-05
TOTAL	48,727	49,002	48,501	49,767	54,856	100.00	10.23
AFRICA	223	214	198	170	189	0.34	11.18
Southern Africa	87	99	100	66	98	0.18	48.48
South Africa	87	99	100	66	98	0.18	48.48
Other Africa	136	115	98	104	91	0.17	-12.50
Other countries of Africa	136	115	98	104	91	0.17	-12.50
AMERICAS	2,852	2,414	2,739	2,888	2,999	5.47	3.84
North America	2,483	2,119	2,309	2,561	2,596	4.73	1.37
Canada	230	260	271	240	299	0.55	24.58
Mexico				48	44	0.08	-8.33
United States	2,253	1,859	2,038	2,271	2,253	4.11	-0.79
Other countries of North America				2			
South America				137	152	0.28	10.95
Brazil				137	152	0.28	10.95
Other Americas	369	295	430	190	251	0.46	32.11
Other countries of the Americas	369	295	430	190	251	0.46	32.11
EAST ASIA AND THE PACIFIC	1,662	1,634	1,728	1,635	1,740	3.17	6.42
North-East Asia	802	741	737	843	914	1.67	8.42
China				156	210	0.38	34.62
Taiwan (Province of China)				75	67	0.12	-10.67
Hong Kong, China				21	18	0.03	-14.29
Japan	697	629	640	484	502	0.92	3.72
Korea, Republic of	105	112	97	107	117	0.21	9.35
Australasia	19	47	37	279	317	0.58	13.62
Australia				212	277	0.50	30.66
New Zealand	19	47	37	67	40	0.07	-40.30
Other East Asia and the Pacific	841	846	954	513	509	0.93	-0.78
Other countries of Asia	671	674	707	510	509	0.93	-0.20
Other countries of Oceania	170	172	247	3			
EUROPE	43,990	44,740	43,836	44,944	49,818	90.82	10.84
Central/Eastern Europe	1,034	1,101	881	1,866	2,081	3.79	11.52
Bulgaria				87	100	0.18	14.94
Czech Republic	365	473	344	459	420	0.77	-8.50
Estonia				24	35	0.06	45.83
Hungary	216	245	197	329	396	0.72	20.36
Latvia				21	35	0.06	66.67
Lithuania				22	29	0.05	31.82
Poland	271	238	255	264	325	0.59	23.11
Romania				150	144	0.26	-4.00
Russian Federation				304	474	0.86	55.92
Slovakia	182	145	85	206	123	0.22	-40.29
Northern Europe	3,077	3,664	3,385	3,466	4,205	7.67	21.32
Denmark	285	219	374	477	654	1.19	37.11
Finland	159	207	191	166	188	0.34	13.25
Iceland	13	43	17	34	46	0.08	35.29
Ireland	144	119	243	78	115	0.21	47.44
Norway	305	337	315	295	328	0.60	11.19
Sweden	365	359	351	365	536	0.98	46.85

LIECHTENSTEIN

3. Arrivals of non-resident tourists in hotels and similar establishments, by country of residence

	2002	2003	2004	2005	2006	Market share 06	% Change 06-05
United Kingdom	1,806	2,380	1,894	2,051	2,338	4.26	13.99
Southern Europe	**3,050**	**3,394**	**2,974**	**2,852**	**3,347**	**6.10**	**17.36**
Croatia				56	101	0.18	80.36
Greece	192	245	210	199	292	0.53	46.73
Italy	1,887	2,107	1,778	1,803	2,040	3.72	13.14
Malta				22	6	0.01	-72.73
Portugal	176	221	207	206	197	0.36	-4.37
Slovenia				125	152	0.28	21.60
Spain	569	571	517	441	559	1.02	26.76
Yugoslavia, Sfr (Former)	226	250	262				
Western Europe	**35,929**	**35,512**	**35,568**	**36,288**	**39,853**	**72.65**	**9.82**
Austria	2,286	2,256	2,400	2,348	2,774	5.06	18.14
Belgium	654	676	772	833	754	1.37	-9.48
France	1,345	1,379	1,201	1,504	1,580	2.88	5.05
Germany	17,140	15,630	15,772	16,069	18,389	33.52	14.44
Luxembourg	331	381	466	493	534	0.97	8.32
Netherlands	1,159	1,174	1,197	1,283	1,166	2.13	-9.12
Switzerland	13,014	14,016	13,760	13,758	14,656	26.72	6.53
East Mediterranean Europe	**181**	**238**	**207**	**376**	**96**	**0.18**	**-74.47**
Cyprus				19	6	0.01	-68.42
Israel	142	167	132	161			
Turkey	39	71	75	196	90	0.16	-54.08
Other Europe	**719**	**831**	**821**	**96**	**236**	**0.43**	**145.83**
Other countries of Europe	719	831	821	96	236	0.43	145.83
SOUTH ASIA				**47**	**59**	**0.11**	**25.53**
South Asia				**47**	**59**	**0.11**	**25.53**
India				47	59	0.11	25.53
REGION NOT SPECIFIED				**83**	**51**	**0.09**	**-38.55**
Not Specified				**83**	**51**	**0.09**	**-38.55**
Other countries of the World				83	51	0.09	-38.55

Source: World Tourism Organization (UNWTO)

LIECHTENSTEIN

5. Overnight stays of non-resident tourists in hotels and similar establishments, by country of residence

	2002	2003	2004	2005	2006	Market share 06	% Change 06-05
TOTAL	105,862	104,551	101,140	108,371	115,442	100.00	6.52
AFRICA	629	576	552	496	527	0.46	6.25
Southern Africa	200	226	231	141	223	0.19	58.16
South Africa	200	226	231	141	223	0.19	58.16
Other Africa	429	350	321	355	304	0.26	-14.37
Other countries of Africa	429	350	321	355	304	0.26	-14.37
AMERICAS	5,725	5,257	5,865	6,166	6,385	5.53	3.55
North America	4,838	4,446	4,616	5,437	5,452	4.72	0.28
Canada	345	430	565	418	565	0.49	35.17
Mexico				123	110	0.10	-10.57
United States	4,493	4,016	4,051	4,891	4,777	4.14	-2.33
Other countries of North America				5			
South America				320	382	0.33	19.38
Brazil				320	382	0.33	19.38
Other Americas	887	811	1,249	409	551	0.48	34.72
Other countries of the Americas	887	811	1,249	409	551	0.48	34.72
EAST ASIA AND THE PACIFIC	4,665	4,852	5,016	4,539	4,997	4.33	10.09
North-East Asia	1,959	1,910	2,146	2,558	3,024	2.62	18.22
China				588	1,141	0.99	94.05
Taiwan (Province of China)				249	199	0.17	-20.08
Hong Kong, China				42	42	0.04	
Japan	1,681	1,406	1,815	1,248	1,206	1.04	-3.37
Korea, Republic of	278	504	331	431	436	0.38	1.16
Australasia	29	94	56	485	586	0.51	20.82
Australia				342	517	0.45	51.17
New Zealand	29	94	56	143	69	0.06	-51.75
Other East Asia and the Pacific	2,677	2,848	2,814	1,496	1,387	1.20	-7.29
Other countries of Asia	2,395	2,613	2,462	1,488	1,387	1.20	-6.79
Other countries of Oceania	282	235	352	8			
EUROPE	94,843	93,866	89,707	96,893	103,342	89.52	6.66
Central/Eastern Europe	1,839	2,052	1,365	4,050	3,671	3.18	-9.36
Bulgaria				225	169	0.15	-24.89
Czech Republic	737	958	518	900	636	0.55	-29.33
Estonia				47	40	0.03	-14.89
Hungary	347	372	293	541	601	0.52	11.09
Latvia				27	58	0.05	114.81
Lithuania				34	38	0.03	11.76
Poland	461	494	438	490	615	0.53	25.51
Romania				278	335	0.29	20.50
Russian Federation				624	930	0.81	49.04
Slovakia	294	228	116	884	249	0.22	-71.83
Northern Europe	6,031	7,287	6,164	6,372	7,888	6.83	23.79
Denmark	525	348	560	713	965	0.84	35.34
Finland	346	372	322	293	289	0.25	-1.37
Iceland	22	66	21	49	74	0.06	51.02
Ireland	330	270	452	156	236	0.20	51.28
Norway	441	631	417	404	455	0.39	12.62
Sweden	672	611	606	642	1,066	0.92	66.04

LIECHTENSTEIN

5. Overnight stays of non-resident tourists in hotels and similar establishments, by country of residence

	2002	2003	2004	2005	2006	Market share 06	% Change 06-05
United Kingdom	3,695	4,989	3,786	4,115	4,803	4.16	16.72
Southern Europe	**5,303**	**6,462**	**5,373**	**5,123**	**5,597**	**4.85**	**9.25**
Croatia				137	141	0.12	2.92
Greece	644	774	600	461	722	0.63	56.62
Italy	2,804	3,594	3,007	2,993	3,229	2.80	7.89
Malta				66	16	0.01	-75.76
Portugal	424	670	401	400	364	0.32	-9.00
Slovenia				304	225	0.19	-25.99
Spain	823	900	845	762	900	0.78	18.11
Yugoslavia, Sfr (Former)	608	524	520				
Western Europe	**79,541**	**75,230**	**74,499**	**80,336**	**85,548**	**74.10**	**6.49**
Austria	3,939	4,228	4,034	4,534	5,252	4.55	15.84
Belgium	1,471	1,577	1,634	2,818	2,204	1.91	-21.79
France	2,475	2,931	1,946	3,314	3,411	2.95	2.93
Germany	39,316	33,550	34,339	36,238	40,436	35.03	11.58
Luxembourg	1,243	1,738	1,789	1,802	2,064	1.79	14.54
Netherlands	2,821	2,650	2,806	3,188	2,491	2.16	-21.86
Switzerland	28,276	28,556	27,951	28,442	29,690	25.72	4.39
East Mediterranean Europe	**400**	**504**	**436**	**888**	**222**	**0.19**	**-75.00**
Cyprus				31	16	0.01	-48.39
Israel	321	275	278	412			
Turkey	79	229	158	445	206	0.18	-53.71
Other Europe	**1,729**	**2,331**	**1,870**	**124**	**416**	**0.36**	**235.48**
Other countries of Europe	1,729	2,331	1,870	124	416	0.36	235.48
SOUTH ASIA				**172**	**132**	**0.11**	**-23.26**
South Asia				**172**	**132**	**0.11**	**-23.26**
India				172	132	0.11	-23.26
REGION NOT SPECIFIED				**105**	**59**	**0.05**	**-43.81**
Not Specified				**105**	**59**	**0.05**	**-43.81**
Other countries of the World				105	59	0.05	-43.81

Source: World Tourism Organization (UNWTO)

LITHUANIA

3. Arrivals of non-resident tourists in hotels and similar establishments, by country of residence

		2002	2003	2004	2005	2006	Market share 06	% Change 06-05
TOTAL	(*)	334,861	368,933	516,431	603,249	669,594	100.00	11.00
AFRICA		262	380	513	1,141	1,347	0.20	18.05
Other Africa		262	380	513	1,141	1,347	0.20	18.05
All countries of Africa		262	380	513	1,141	1,347	0.20	18.05
AMERICAS		14,626	15,099	21,469	22,426	24,050	3.59	7.24
North America		13,950	14,358	20,517	20,585	21,755	3.25	5.68
Canada		1,218	1,054	1,817	1,570	1,768	0.26	12.61
United States		12,732	13,304	18,700	19,015	19,987	2.98	5.11
Other Americas		676	741	952	1,841	2,295	0.34	24.66
Other countries of the Americas		676	741	952	1,841	2,295	0.34	24.66
EAST ASIA AND THE PACIFIC		9,348	10,518	14,906	14,242	15,160	2.26	6.45
North-East Asia		6,677	8,213	10,175	9,738	9,846	1.47	1.11
China		957	532	1,172	947	1,165	0.17	23.02
Japan		5,720	7,681	9,003	8,791	8,681	1.30	-1.25
Other East Asia and the Pacific		2,671	2,305	4,731	4,504	5,314	0.79	17.98
Other countries of Asia		2,074	1,350	2,448	2,381	2,552	0.38	7.18
All countries of Oceania		597	955	2,283	2,123	2,762	0.41	30.10
EUROPE		301,412	336,735	466,455	546,143	608,305	90.85	11.38
Central/Eastern Europe		147,249	149,896	195,526	221,973	258,994	38.68	16.68
Bulgaria		460	430	740	1,023	1,036	0.15	1.27
Belarus		16,294	14,293	13,983	20,439	26,689	3.99	30.58
Czech Republic		3,371	4,334	6,493	6,387	7,291	1.09	14.15
Estonia		12,020	15,357	20,164	23,230	28,094	4.20	20.94
Hungary		880	1,606	2,198	2,454	2,553	0.38	4.03
Latvia		21,208	23,252	30,184	36,824	48,727	7.28	32.32
Poland		43,428	45,519	75,189	84,029	89,308	13.34	6.28
Romania		274	340	445	703	1,114	0.17	58.46
Russian Federation		40,736	34,798	35,968	37,688	43,361	6.48	15.05
Slovakia		906	635	1,160	1,676	2,019	0.30	20.47
Ukraine		4,801	3,574	4,471	5,537	5,943	0.89	7.33
Other countries Central/East Europ		2,871	5,758	4,531	1,983	2,859	0.43	44.18
Northern Europe		62,500	74,472	95,398	115,463	135,031	20.17	16.95
Denmark		9,655	10,208	15,891	14,877	15,305	2.29	2.88
Finland		17,872	20,332	26,064	31,343	33,546	5.01	7.03
Iceland		471	526	881	1,150	1,571	0.23	36.61
Ireland		1,290	1,682	2,494	2,767	4,013	0.60	45.03
Norway		7,756	8,630	11,135	13,855	18,959	2.83	36.84
Sweden		13,052	13,945	16,784	19,363	22,709	3.39	17.28
United Kingdom		12,404	19,149	22,149	32,108	38,928	5.81	21.24
Southern Europe		10,570	17,335	34,348	40,404	41,723	6.23	3.26
Greece		511	808	1,106	1,812	1,722	0.26	-4.97
Italy		7,021	11,051	22,357	25,583	25,910	3.87	1.28
Portugal		613	1,080	2,058	2,176	2,418	0.36	11.12
Spain		2,425	4,396	8,827	10,833	11,673	1.74	7.75
Western Europe		77,632	90,044	135,897	163,578	163,122	24.36	-0.28
Austria		2,892	3,054	6,460	7,576	9,827	1.47	29.71
Belgium		2,703	3,155	4,783	5,455	5,048	0.75	-7.46
France		6,230	7,857	15,322	17,793	18,829	2.81	5.82

LITHUANIA

3. Arrivals of non-resident tourists in hotels and similar establishments, by country of residence

	2002	2003	2004	2005	2006	Market share 06	% Change 06-05
Germany	59,058	67,707	97,014	120,522	116,052	17.33	-3.71
Luxembourg	206	382	428	525	573	0.09	9.14
Netherlands	4,118	5,399	8,251	8,246	8,952	1.34	8.56
Switzerland	2,425	2,490	3,639	3,461	3,841	0.57	10.98
East Mediterranean Europe	**3,461**	**4,988**	**5,286**	**4,725**	**9,435**	**1.41**	**99.68**
Israel	2,814	4,453	4,365	3,972	7,643	1.14	92.42
Turkey	647	535	921	753	1,792	0.27	137.98
REGION NOT SPECIFIED	**9,213**	**6,201**	**13,088**	**19,297**	**20,732**	**3.10**	**7.44**
Not Specified	**9,213**	**6,201**	**13,088**	**19,297**	**20,732**	**3.10**	**7.44**
Other countries of the World	9,213	6,201	13,088	19,297	20,732	3.10	7.44

Source: World Tourism Organization (UNWTO)

LITHUANIA

4. Arrivals of non-resident tourists in all types of accommodation establishments, by country of residence

	2002	2003	2004	2005	2006	Market share 06	% Change 06-05
TOTAL	393,126	438,299	590,043	681,487	756,855	100.00	11.06
AFRICA	271	400	525	1,159	1,360	0.18	17.34
Other Africa	271	400	525	1,159	1,360	0.18	17.34
All countries of Africa	271	400	525	1,159	1,360	0.18	17.34
AMERICAS	15,673	16,324	22,385	23,626	25,955	3.43	9.86
North America	15,335	15,649	21,700	22,731	24,296	3.21	6.88
Canada	1,331	1,247	1,990	1,717	1,960	0.26	14.15
United States	13,598	14,267	19,419	19,980	21,652	2.86	8.37
Other countries of North America	406	135	291	1,034	684	0.09	-33.85
South America	338	675	685	895	1,659	0.22	85.36
Brazil				321	1,046	0.14	225.86
Other countries of South America				574	613	0.08	6.79
All countries of South America	338	675	685				
EAST ASIA AND THE PACIFIC	9,808	11,003	15,472	15,032	16,260	2.15	8.17
North-East Asia	6,792	8,382	10,355	10,302	10,414	1.38	1.09
China	971	594	1,186	983	1,197	0.16	21.77
Japan	5,821	7,788	9,169	8,936	8,833	1.17	-1.15
Korea, Republic of				383	384	0.05	0.26
Australasia			2,594	2,496	3,185	0.42	27.60
Australia			2,594	2,496	3,185	0.42	27.60
Other East Asia and the Pacific	3,016	2,621	2,523	2,234	2,661	0.35	19.11
Other countries of Asia	2,217	1,385	2,523	2,234	2,661	0.35	19.11
All countries of Oceania	799	1,236					
EUROPE	357,990	400,338	538,078	623,045	694,241	91.73	11.43
Central/Eastern Europe	189,304	194,767	240,620	270,360	315,449	41.68	16.68
Bulgaria	470	445	766	1,079	1,096	0.14	1.58
Belarus	23,926	21,810	22,039	29,977	37,517	4.96	25.15
Czech Republic	4,088	5,603	7,834	7,481	8,579	1.13	14.68
Estonia	14,629	19,067	23,456	27,834	32,212	4.26	15.73
Hungary	1,033	1,730	2,462	2,851	2,844	0.38	-0.25
Latvia	25,881	28,114	35,769	43,660	56,299	7.44	28.95
Poland	59,797	59,564	85,457	94,881	102,539	13.55	8.07
Romania	295	362	462	772	1,184	0.16	53.37
Russian Federation	48,831	50,290	49,240	50,829	59,743	7.89	17.54
Slovakia	975	704	1,329	1,878	2,291	0.30	21.99
Ukraine	5,598	4,277	5,463	6,742	8,148	1.08	20.85
Other countries Central/East Europ	3,781	2,801	6,343	2,376	2,997	0.40	26.14
Northern Europe	65,569	77,692	99,158	119,963	139,256	18.40	16.08
Denmark	10,312	10,855	16,438	15,337	15,817	2.09	3.13
Finland	18,756	21,300	27,303	32,996	34,898	4.61	5.76
Iceland	557	533	901	1,170	1,599	0.21	36.67
Ireland	1,364	1,732	2,586	3,001	4,182	0.55	39.35
Norway	7,982	8,884	11,492	14,385	19,424	2.57	35.03
Sweden	13,863	14,618	17,687	20,133	23,410	3.09	16.28
United Kingdom	12,735	19,770	22,751	32,941	39,926	5.28	21.20
Southern Europe	11,062	18,087	35,844	42,699	44,814	5.92	4.95
Greece	527	828	1,121	1,860	1,756	0.23	-5.59
Italy	7,319	11,548	23,475	26,518	27,071	3.58	2.09

LITHUANIA

4. Arrivals of non-resident tourists in all types of accommodation establishments, by country of residence

	2002	2003	2004	2005	2006	Market share 06	% Change 06-05
Malta				120	195	0.03	62.50
Portugal	639	1,111	2,092	2,226	2,491	0.33	11.90
Slovenia				798	1,246	0.16	56.14
Spain	2,577	4,600	9,156	11,177	12,055	1.59	7.86
Western Europe	**86,866**	**103,164**	**156,132**	**184,095**	**183,707**	**24.27**	**-0.21**
Austria	3,011	3,199	6,776	7,844	10,058	1.33	28.23
Belgium	2,849	3,320	5,012	5,799	5,496	0.73	-5.23
France	6,643	8,532	16,803	19,292	20,214	2.67	4.78
Germany	66,937	79,182	113,974	137,317	132,540	17.51	-3.48
Luxembourg	359	395	434	571	623	0.08	9.11
Netherlands	4,515	5,969	9,324	9,623	10,840	1.43	12.65
Switzerland	2,552	2,567	3,809	3,649	3,936	0.52	7.87
East Mediterranean Europe	**5,189**	**6,628**	**6,324**	**5,928**	**11,015**	**1.46**	**85.81**
Cyprus				478	751	0.10	57.11
Israel	4,524	6,017	5,351	4,673	8,367	1.11	79.05
Turkey	665	611	973	777	1,897	0.25	144.14
REGION NOT SPECIFIED	**9,384**	**10,234**	**13,583**	**18,625**	**19,039**	**2.52**	**2.22**
Not Specified	**9,384**	**10,234**	**13,583**	**18,625**	**19,039**	**2.52**	**2.22**
Other countries of the World	9,384	10,234	13,583	18,625	19,039	2.52	2.22

Source: World Tourism Organization (UNWTO)

LITHUANIA

5. Overnight stays of non-resident tourists in hotels and similar establishments, by country of residence

	2002	2003	2004	2005	2006	Market share 06	% Change 06-05
TOTAL (*)	707,655	746,946	1,113,096	1,298,719	1,417,143	100.00	9.12
AFRICA	1,041	1,000	1,986	2,653	2,893	0.20	9.05
Other Africa	1,041	1,000	1,986	2,653	2,893	0.20	9.05
All countries of Africa	1,041	1,000	1,986	2,653	2,893	0.20	9.05
AMERICAS	39,161	36,547	55,154	59,356	57,708	4.07	-2.78
North America	37,530	34,659	52,898	54,957	51,628	3.64	-6.06
Canada	3,244	2,777	4,544	4,624	4,070	0.29	-11.98
United States	34,286	31,882	48,354	50,333	47,558	3.36	-5.51
Other Americas	1,631	1,888	2,256	4,399	6,080	0.43	38.21
Other countries of the Americas	1,631	1,888	2,256	4,399	6,080	0.43	38.21
EAST ASIA AND THE PACIFIC	19,128	19,537	28,057	29,641	29,843	2.11	0.68
North-East Asia	13,223	14,600	18,218	18,548	17,997	1.27	-2.97
China	2,741	1,164	2,595	2,123	2,642	0.19	24.45
Japan	10,482	13,436	15,623	16,425	15,355	1.08	-6.51
Other East Asia and the Pacific	5,905	4,937	9,839	11,093	11,846	0.84	6.79
Other countries of Asia	4,228	2,967	5,055	5,627	6,002	0.42	6.66
All countries of Oceania	1,677	1,970	4,784	5,466	5,844	0.41	6.92
EUROPE	627,613	671,925	997,244	1,167,301	1,234,460	87.11	5.75
Central/Eastern Europe	296,921	290,702	422,112	471,734	504,353	35.59	6.91
Bulgaria	1,373	1,171	2,074	3,247	2,592	0.18	-20.17
Belarus	28,919	27,190	28,702	38,839	46,951	3.31	20.89
Czech Republic	6,376	7,787	13,728	13,064	13,002	0.92	-0.47
Estonia	22,144	26,904	33,211	37,863	48,059	3.39	26.93
Hungary	1,937	3,606	4,459	5,534	5,448	0.38	-1.55
Latvia	37,880	37,745	49,851	59,854	74,792	5.28	24.96
Poland	88,185	87,113	145,645	165,225	184,488	13.02	11.66
Romania	1,100	963	1,328	1,856	2,805	0.20	51.13
Russian Federation	74,794	73,912	98,546	100,566	113,117	7.98	12.48
Slovakia	2,068	1,259	2,509	3,507	13,099	0.92	273.51
Ukraine	26,139	17,937	31,593	36,785			
Other countries Central/East Europ	6,006	5,115	10,466	5,394			
Northern Europe	136,151	158,749	212,489	251,843	278,314	19.64	10.51
Denmark	21,185	21,851	36,041	31,390	28,364	2.00	-9.64
Finland	32,438	39,856	47,445	59,124	63,519	4.48	7.43
Iceland	1,173	1,352	2,098	3,274	4,134	0.29	26.27
Ireland	3,270	3,924	5,660	6,548	10,333	0.73	57.80
Norway	18,618	19,001	25,015	36,024	43,174	3.05	19.85
Sweden	26,321	28,175	33,434	36,782	42,385	2.99	15.23
United Kingdom	33,146	44,590	62,796	78,701	86,405	6.10	9.79
Southern Europe	26,660	34,816	70,046	89,966	101,340	7.15	12.64
Greece	1,610	2,266	3,165	5,476	4,245	0.30	-22.48
Italy	17,664	21,933	43,274	54,464	56,150	3.96	3.10
Portugal	1,491	2,024	4,408	5,178	5,728	0.40	10.62
Spain	5,895	8,593	19,199	24,848	35,217	2.49	41.73
Western Europe	159,258	172,549	273,702	333,382	317,249	22.39	-4.84
Austria	6,040	6,053	16,357	13,665	17,251	1.22	26.24
Belgium	6,449	6,430	13,999	12,101	12,496	0.88	3.26
France	13,845	17,215	31,424	36,301	38,844	2.74	7.01

LITHUANIA

5. Overnight stays of non-resident tourists in hotels and similar establishments, by country of residence

	2002	2003	2004	2005	2006	Market share 06	% Change 06-05
Germany	117,257	125,403	187,256	243,097	221,806	15.65	-8.76
Luxembourg	464	665	735	1,046	1,077	0.08	2.96
Netherlands	10,188	11,979	16,857	20,080	18,239	1.29	-9.17
Switzerland	5,015	4,804	7,074	7,092	7,536	0.53	6.26
East Mediterranean Europe	**8,623**	**15,109**	**18,895**	**20,376**	**33,204**	**2.34**	**62.96**
Israel	6,417	13,745	16,706	18,408	20,716	1.46	12.54
Turkey	2,206	1,364	2,189	1,968	12,488	0.88	534.55
REGION NOT SPECIFIED	**20,712**	**17,937**	**30,655**	**39,768**	**92,239**	**6.51**	**131.94**
Not Specified	**20,712**	**17,937**	**30,655**	**39,768**	**92,239**	**6.51**	**131.94**
Other countries of the World	20,712	17,937	30,655	39,768	92,239	6.51	131.94

Source: World Tourism Organization (UNWTO)

LITHUANIA

6. Overnight stays of non-resident tourists in all types of accommodation establishments, by country of residence

	2002	2003	2004	2005	2006	Market share 06	% Change 06-05
TOTAL	1,144,557	1,170,369	1,526,282	1,762,498	1,906,408	100.00	8.17
AFRICA	1,064	1,062	2,069	2,691	2,918	0.15	8.44
Other Africa	1,064	1,062	2,069	2,691	2,918	0.15	8.44
All countries of Africa	1,064	1,062	2,069	2,691	2,918	0.15	8.44
AMERICAS	44,069	40,481	58,446	66,367	61,839	3.24	-6.82
North America	43,093	38,670	56,810	63,777	57,723	3.03	-9.49
Canada	3,612	3,219	4,970	5,026	4,534	0.24	-9.79
United States	38,584	35,118	51,090	56,600	51,093	2.68	-9.73
Other countries of North America	897	333	750	2,151	2,096	0.11	-2.56
South America	976	1,811	1,636	2,590	4,116	0.22	58.92
Brazil				1,015	2,591	0.14	155.27
Other countries of South America				1,575	1,525	0.08	-3.17
All countries of South America	976	1,811	1,636				
EAST ASIA AND THE PACIFIC	19,972	20,779	29,434	32,254	35,374	1.86	9.67
North-East Asia	13,472	14,849	18,543	19,983	19,337	1.01	-3.23
China	2,791	1,180	2,613	2,175	2,776	0.15	27.63
Japan	10,681	13,669	15,930	16,725	15,631	0.82	-6.54
Korea, Republic of				1,083	930	0.05	-14.13
Australasia			5,434	6,327	6,649	0.35	5.09
Australia			5,434	6,327	6,649	0.35	5.09
Other East Asia and the Pacific	6,500	5,930	5,457	5,944	9,388	0.49	57.94
Other countries of Asia	4,346	3,091	5,457	5,944	9,388	0.49	57.94
All countries of Oceania	2,154	2,839					
EUROPE	1,062,092	1,079,464	1,405,039	1,624,758	1,768,052	92.74	8.82
Central/Eastern Europe	629,517	615,579	700,569	763,855	851,197	44.65	11.43
Bulgaria	1,409	1,198	2,167	3,462	2,662	0.14	-23.11
Belarus	180,053	174,828	183,310	196,998	197,638	10.37	0.32
Czech Republic	7,668	9,857	15,948	15,514	16,315	0.86	5.16
Estonia	28,292	33,472	39,091	47,137	56,267	2.95	19.37
Hungary	2,222	3,821	4,876	6,131	5,918	0.31	-3.47
Latvia	47,892	48,616	60,153	73,340	91,113	4.78	24.23
Poland	219,108	189,103	209,676	226,142	245,831	12.89	8.71
Romania	1,355	999	1,374	2,074	3,413	0.18	64.56
Russian Federation	103,721	108,277	134,746	143,116	165,685	8.69	15.77
Slovakia	2,241	1,404	2,765	3,796	13,583	0.71	257.82
Ukraine	28,319	18,654	33,837	39,696	44,328	2.33	11.67
Other countries Central/East Europ	7,237	25,350	12,626	6,449	8,444	0.44	30.94
Northern Europe	145,612	166,720	220,590	264,560	288,986	15.16	9.23
Denmark	23,803	24,088	37,381	32,507	29,630	1.55	-8.85
Finland	34,483	41,477	49,364	61,636	66,061	3.47	7.18
Iceland	1,464	1,366	2,134	3,321	4,188	0.22	26.11
Ireland	3,401	4,020	5,838	6,981	10,708	0.56	53.39
Norway	19,579	19,531	25,805	40,440	44,949	2.36	11.15
Sweden	28,517	29,674	35,493	38,826	44,062	2.31	13.49
United Kingdom	34,365	46,564	64,575	80,849	89,388	4.69	10.56
Southern Europe	28,098	36,600	72,759	95,272	110,636	5.80	16.13
Greece	1,659	2,316	3,189	5,716	4,304	0.23	-24.70
Italy	18,515	22,957	45,158	56,401	58,916	3.09	4.46

LITHUANIA

6. Overnight stays of non-resident tourists in all types of accommodation establishments, by country of residence

	2002	2003	2004	2005	2006	Market share 06	% Change 06-05
Malta				304	426	0.02	40.13
Portugal	1,536	2,103	4,453	5,296	5,876	0.31	10.95
Slovenia				2,096	5,143	0.27	145.37
Spain	6,388	9,224	19,959	25,459	35,971	1.89	41.29
Western Europe	**220,586**	**246,900**	**380,135**	**467,559**	**470,199**	**24.66**	**0.56**
Austria	6,326	6,298	16,863	14,060	17,685	0.93	25.78
Belgium	6,763	6,732	14,379	12,868	13,444	0.71	4.48
France	15,202	18,760	34,607	39,438	41,869	2.20	6.16
Germany	174,816	196,121	285,958	366,638	365,661	19.18	-0.27
Luxembourg	921	706	745	1,131	1,168	0.06	3.27
Netherlands	11,183	13,332	20,153	26,009	22,648	1.19	-12.92
Switzerland	5,375	4,951	7,430	7,415	7,724	0.41	4.17
East Mediterranean Europe	**38,279**	**13,665**	**30,986**	**33,512**	**47,034**	**2.47**	**40.35**
Cyprus				2,437	2,097	0.11	-13.95
Israel	36,041	12,143	28,723	29,075	31,620	1.66	8.75
Turkey	2,238	1,522	2,263	2,000	13,317	0.70	565.85
REGION NOT SPECIFIED	**17,360**	**28,583**	**31,294**	**36,428**	**38,225**	**2.01**	**4.93**
Not Specified	**17,360**	**28,583**	**31,294**	**36,428**	**38,225**	**2.01**	**4.93**
Other countries of the World	17,360	28,583	31,294	36,428	38,225	2.01	4.93

Source: World Tourism Organization (UNWTO)

LUXEMBOURG

3. Arrivals of non-resident tourists in hotels and similar establishments, by country of residence

		2002	2003	2004	2005	2006	Market share 06	% Change 06-05
TOTAL	(*)	598,683	581,450	613,244	666,862	673,366	100.00	0.98
AMERICAS		28,587	25,623	26,872	28,897	30,633	4.55	6.01
North America		21,769	19,001	20,427	21,266	21,642	3.21	1.77
United States		21,769	19,001	20,427	21,266	21,642	3.21	1.77
Other Americas		6,818	6,622	6,445	7,631	8,991	1.34	17.82
Other countries of the Americas		6,818	6,622	6,445	7,631	8,991	1.34	17.82
EUROPE		533,121	523,711	550,298	602,120	604,599	89.79	0.41
Central/Eastern Europe		5,562	7,109	9,272	15,487	14,898	2.21	-3.80
Bulgaria					1,009	1,226	0.18	21.51
Czech Republic		1,402	1,654	1,924	2,853	2,493	0.37	-12.62
Estonia		233	373	493	814	620	0.09	-23.83
Hungary		1,549	1,758	1,928	2,101	2,135	0.32	1.62
Latvia		3	149	538	729	607	0.09	-16.74
Lithuania		437	458	868	1,192	1,187	0.18	-0.42
Poland		1,616	2,071	2,664	4,075	4,105	0.61	0.74
Romania					1,663	1,653	0.25	-0.60
Slovakia		322	646	857	1,051	872	0.13	-17.03
Northern Europe		63,028	58,254	64,703	68,751	70,660	10.49	2.78
Denmark		4,911	5,405	5,129	5,697	5,807	0.86	1.93
Finland		2,622	2,660	2,840	3,410	3,202	0.48	-6.10
Ireland		2,635	2,896	3,425	3,195	3,257	0.48	1.94
Sweden		6,460	6,516	6,702	7,658	7,584	1.13	-0.97
United Kingdom		46,400	40,777	46,607	48,791	50,810	7.55	4.14
Southern Europe		42,632	40,009	40,957	49,910	50,525	7.50	1.23
Greece		2,672	2,899	2,994	3,810	3,265	0.48	-14.30
Italy		21,014	18,749	19,447	21,531	21,482	3.19	-0.23
Malta		274	269	456	705	588	0.09	-16.60
Portugal		5,508	5,638	5,259	5,887	6,288	0.93	6.81
Slovenia		481	673	715	1,076	915	0.14	-14.96
Spain		12,683	11,781	12,086	16,901	17,987	2.67	6.43
Western Europe		406,694	402,041	417,415	451,610	450,932	66.97	-0.15
Austria		4,600	4,627	4,080	4,711	5,393	0.80	14.48
Belgium		146,857	141,200	147,821	154,050	149,952	22.27	-2.66
France		67,697	68,732	75,305	89,090	95,158	14.13	6.81
Germany		86,405	90,726	89,580	97,789	98,864	14.68	1.10
Netherlands		86,238	83,157	86,940	92,236	86,156	12.79	-6.59
Switzerland		14,897	13,599	13,689	13,734	15,409	2.29	12.20
East Mediterranean Europe		301	256	593	669	617	0.09	-7.77
Cyprus		301	256	593	669	617	0.09	-7.77
Other Europe		14,904	16,042	17,358	15,693	16,967	2.52	8.12
Other countries of Europe		14,904	16,042	17,358	15,693	16,967	2.52	8.12
REGION NOT SPECIFIED		36,975	32,116	36,074	35,845	38,134	5.66	6.39
Not Specified		36,975	32,116	36,074	35,845	38,134	5.66	6.39
Other countries of the World		36,975	32,116	36,074	35,845	38,134	5.66	6.39

Source: World Tourism Organization (UNWTO)

LUXEMBOURG

4. Arrivals of non-resident tourists in all types of accommodation establishments, by country of residence

		2002	2003	2004	2005	2006	Market share 06	% Change 06-05
TOTAL	(*)	884,674	867,048	877,712	912,798	908,171	100.00	-0.51
AMERICAS		33,136	28,562	29,777	32,249	34,516	3.80	7.03
North America		24,356	20,587	22,056	23,115	23,781	2.62	2.88
United States		24,356	20,587	22,056	23,115	23,781	2.62	2.88
Other Americas		8,780	7,975	7,721	9,134	10,735	1.18	17.53
Other countries of the Americas		8,780	7,975	7,721	9,134	10,735	1.18	17.53
EUROPE		809,403	801,138	806,575	840,259	831,114	91.52	-1.09
Central/Eastern Europe		9,304	9,370	11,236	17,952	17,768	1.96	-1.02
Bulgaria					1,043	1,356	0.15	30.01
Czech Republic		1,815	2,180	2,424	3,360	2,909	0.32	-13.42
Estonia		291	405	523	861	671	0.07	-22.07
Hungary		1,741	1,992	2,192	2,402	2,398	0.26	-0.17
Latvia		3	164	569	739	628	0.07	-15.02
Lithuania		524	532	889	1,226	1,250	0.14	1.96
Poland		4,459	3,346	3,649	5,272	5,803	0.64	10.07
Romania					1,815	1,812	0.20	-0.17
Slovakia		471	751	990	1,234	941	0.10	-23.74
Northern Europe		82,028	72,935	80,067	83,798	85,047	9.36	1.49
Denmark		8,460	8,596	8,122	8,990	8,397	0.92	-6.60
Finland		3,452	3,643	3,801	4,238	4,178	0.46	-1.42
Ireland		3,421	3,495	4,169	3,658	3,891	0.43	6.37
Sweden		7,542	7,378	7,679	8,468	8,384	0.92	-0.99
United Kingdom		59,153	49,823	56,296	58,444	60,197	6.63	3.00
Southern Europe		49,646	45,380	45,966	55,270	55,504	6.11	0.42
Greece		2,748	2,947	3,154	3,913	3,429	0.38	-12.37
Italy		23,181	20,481	21,137	23,347	22,920	2.52	-1.83
Malta		290	297	473	750	596	0.07	-20.53
Portugal		6,256	6,403	5,945	6,499	6,866	0.76	5.65
Slovenia		671	798	843	1,415	1,126	0.12	-20.42
Spain		16,500	14,454	14,414	19,346	20,567	2.26	6.31
Western Europe		650,894	655,609	649,356	665,616	653,842	72.00	-1.77
Austria		5,165	5,472	4,593	5,379	5,974	0.66	11.06
Belgium		187,563	185,627	186,274	190,902	185,784	20.46	-2.68
France		75,125	76,842	83,694	97,732	104,481	11.50	6.91
Germany		112,889	117,352	114,985	124,002	123,207	13.57	-0.64
Netherlands		253,676	255,140	244,552	232,421	217,347	23.93	-6.49
Switzerland		16,476	15,176	15,258	15,180	17,049	1.88	12.31
East Mediterranean Europe		328	268	626	675	625	0.07	-7.41
Cyprus		328	268	626	675	625	0.07	-7.41
Other Europe		17,203	17,576	19,324	16,948	18,328	2.02	8.14
Other countries of Europe		17,203	17,576	19,324	16,948	18,328	2.02	8.14
REGION NOT SPECIFIED		42,135	37,348	41,360	40,290	42,541	4.68	5.59
Not Specified		42,135	37,348	41,360	40,290	42,541	4.68	5.59
Other countries of the World		42,135	37,348	41,360	40,290	42,541	4.68	5.59

Source: World Tourism Organization (UNWTO)

LUXEMBOURG

5. Overnight stays of non-resident tourists in hotels and similar establishments, by country of residence

		2002	2003	2004	2005	2006	Market share 06	% Change 06-05
TOTAL	(*)	1,166,769	1,143,831	1,194,689	1,274,898	1,284,174	100.00	0.73
AMERICAS		69,178	61,314	62,291	65,144	70,797	5.51	8.68
North America		52,609	46,236	47,512	47,585	49,541	3.86	4.11
United States		52,609	46,236	47,512	47,585	49,541	3.86	4.11
Other Americas		16,569	15,078	14,779	17,559	21,256	1.66	21.05
Other countries of the Americas		16,569	15,078	14,779	17,559	21,256	1.66	21.05
EUROPE		1,029,528	1,029,617	1,070,517	1,145,252	1,144,832	89.15	-0.04
Central/Eastern Europe		16,266	19,894	25,882	42,415	40,635	3.16	-4.20
Bulgaria					2,838	3,717	0.29	30.97
Czech Republic		4,425	4,491	4,978	6,770	6,561	0.51	-3.09
Estonia		731	1,369	1,832	2,038	1,625	0.13	-20.26
Hungary		4,413	5,133	5,303	5,663	5,681	0.44	0.32
Latvia		3	559	2,074	1,847	1,576	0.12	-14.67
Lithuania		1,372	1,236	2,189	3,456	3,308	0.26	-4.28
Poland		4,345	5,180	6,894	12,251	11,725	0.91	-4.29
Romania					4,485	4,018	0.31	-10.41
Slovakia		977	1,926	2,612	3,067	2,424	0.19	-20.97
Northern Europe		128,698	115,548	126,356	131,128	136,407	10.62	4.03
Denmark		8,597	9,849	9,011	10,187	10,243	0.80	0.55
Finland		4,968	5,274	5,546	7,108	6,460	0.50	-9.12
Ireland		6,825	6,562	7,306	6,368	7,773	0.61	22.06
Sweden		11,501	12,232	12,436	14,177	14,255	1.11	0.55
United Kingdom		96,807	81,631	92,057	93,288	97,676	7.61	4.70
Southern Europe		83,249	82,689	82,629	99,599	97,071	7.56	-2.54
Greece		5,683	6,410	6,872	8,465	7,605	0.59	-10.16
Italy		39,876	36,935	37,460	43,878	42,732	3.33	-2.61
Malta		1,386	1,055	2,177	2,837	3,028	0.24	6.73
Portugal		11,989	14,782	11,965	13,812	12,938	1.01	-6.33
Slovenia		1,745	1,939	1,593	2,134	2,185	0.17	2.39
Spain		22,570	21,568	22,562	28,473	28,583	2.23	0.39
Western Europe		767,497	774,867	794,528	837,421	834,307	64.97	-0.37
Austria		10,052	9,135	8,597	9,941	13,039	1.02	31.16
Belgium		276,020	273,919	280,528	287,219	278,851	21.71	-2.91
France		119,258	127,260	131,263	146,116	158,405	12.34	8.41
Germany		158,123	163,710	166,171	180,437	179,183	13.95	-0.69
Netherlands		177,663	178,379	183,835	188,449	176,542	13.75	-6.32
Switzerland		26,381	22,464	24,134	25,259	28,287	2.20	11.99
East Mediterranean Europe		1,005	702	1,116	1,638	1,653	0.13	0.92
Cyprus		1,005	702	1,116	1,638	1,653	0.13	0.92
Other Europe		32,813	35,917	40,006	33,051	34,759	2.71	5.17
Other countries of Europe		32,813	35,917	40,006	33,051	34,759	2.71	5.17
REGION NOT SPECIFIED		68,063	52,900	61,881	64,502	68,545	5.34	6.27
Not Specified		68,063	52,900	61,881	64,502	68,545	5.34	6.27
Other countries of the World		68,063	52,900	61,881	64,502	68,545	5.34	6.27

Source: World Tourism Organization (UNWTO)

LUXEMBOURG

6. Overnight stays of non-resident tourists in all types of accommodation establishments, by country of residence

	2002	2003	2004	2005	2006	Market share 06	% Change 06-05
TOTAL	2,469,360	2,541,362	2,514,115	2,465,479	2,414,243	100.00	-2.08
AMERICAS	78,410	66,561	69,247	72,366	78,352	3.25	8.27
North America	58,141	48,996	51,901	52,422	54,346	2.25	3.67
United States	58,141	48,996	51,901	52,422	54,346	2.25	3.67
Other Americas	20,269	17,565	17,346	19,944	24,006	0.99	20.37
Other countries of the Americas	20,269	17,565	17,346	19,944	24,006	0.99	20.37
EUROPE	2,311,173	2,409,371	2,372,343	2,319,130	2,259,114	93.57	-2.59
Central/Eastern Europe	24,632	27,423	33,199	52,135	50,030	2.07	-4.04
Bulgaria				2,984	4,014	0.17	34.52
Czech Republic	5,243	6,442	6,730	8,945	7,260	0.30	-18.84
Estonia	799	1,463	1,891	2,164	1,755	0.07	-18.90
Hungary	4,937	5,846	5,914	6,471	6,697	0.28	3.49
Latvia	3	612	2,208	1,858	1,689	0.07	-9.10
Lithuania	1,560	1,408	2,228	3,570	3,612	0.15	1.18
Poland	10,295	9,260	11,138	17,314	17,825	0.74	2.95
Romania				4,847	4,554	0.19	-6.04
Slovakia	1,795	2,392	3,090	3,982	2,624	0.11	-34.10
Northern Europe	184,928	156,959	174,559	172,916	176,381	7.31	2.00
Denmark	18,760	18,956	18,443	19,560	17,640	0.73	-9.82
Finland	6,373	7,031	7,566	8,870	9,111	0.38	2.72
Ireland	8,864	7,930	9,452	7,555	9,526	0.39	26.09
Sweden	13,910	14,082	15,396	16,120	16,299	0.68	1.11
United Kingdom	137,021	108,960	123,702	120,811	123,805	5.13	2.48
Southern Europe	96,836	93,938	94,993	109,944	108,479	4.49	-1.33
Greece	5,970	6,628	7,251	8,661	7,969	0.33	-7.99
Italy	43,694	40,015	40,898	47,194	46,159	1.91	-2.19
Malta	1,408	1,133	2,295	3,016	3,089	0.13	2.42
Portugal	15,159	17,291	15,934	15,615	15,852	0.66	1.52
Slovenia	2,186	2,187	2,290	2,885	2,543	0.11	-11.85
Spain	28,419	26,684	26,325	32,573	32,867	1.36	0.90
Western Europe	1,963,385	2,087,985	2,021,789	1,945,601	1,883,684	78.02	-3.18
Austria	11,433	11,189	10,263	11,614	14,488	0.60	24.75
Belgium	510,555	512,621	491,379	480,530	470,768	19.50	-2.03
France	148,217	164,188	167,746	175,498	189,731	7.86	8.11
Germany	228,696	248,337	246,940	258,323	252,159	10.44	-2.39
Netherlands	1,035,028	1,125,291	1,078,014	991,150	924,954	38.31	-6.68
Switzerland	29,456	26,359	27,447	28,486	31,584	1.31	10.88
East Mediterranean Europe	1,104	760	1,376	1,664	1,689	0.07	1.50
Cyprus	1,104	760	1,376	1,664	1,689	0.07	1.50
Other Europe	40,288	42,306	46,427	36,870	38,851	1.61	5.37
Other countries of Europe	40,288	42,306	46,427	36,870	38,851	1.61	5.37
REGION NOT SPECIFIED	79,777	65,430	72,525	73,983	76,777	3.18	3.78
Not Specified	79,777	65,430	72,525	73,983	76,777	3.18	3.78
Other countries of the World	79,777	65,430	72,525	73,983	76,777	3.18	3.78

Source: World Tourism Organization (UNWTO)

MACAO, CHINA

2. Arrivals of non-resident visitors at national borders, by nationality

		2002	2003	2004	2005	2006	Market share 06	% Change 06-05
TOTAL	(*)	11,530,841	11,887,876	16,672,556	18,711,187	21,998,122	100.00	17.57
AFRICA		4,439	4,668	6,042	8,082	13,693	0.06	69.43
East Africa		886	857	1,074	1,190	1,387	0.01	16.55
Burundi		9	4	5	8	12	*	50.00
Ethiopia		15	18	29	43	57		32.56
Kenya		56	64	53	102	79		-22.55
Madagascar		68	45	148	134	171		27.61
Malawi		6	2	5	15	6		-60.00
Mauritius		263	174	265	271	277		2.21
Mozambique		127	151	170	196	349		78.06
Rwanda		3	4	3	5	11		120.00
Seychelles		188	273	148	224	196		-12.50
Somalia		5	16	6	1			
Zimbabwe		74	48	153	85	78		-8.24
Uganda		25	19	37	30	57		90.00
United Republic of Tanzania		40	30	46	61	74		21.31
Zambia		7	9	6	15	20		33.33
Central Africa		120	248	363	717	1,821	0.01	153.97
Angola		38	114	150	244	462		89.34
Cameroon		39	58	144	289	436		50.87
Congo		10	25	40	99	402		306.06
Democratic Republic of the Congo					7	423		5,942.86
Equatorial Guinea		22	40	4	2	15		650.00
Gabon		1	1	11	30	6		-80.00
Sao Tome and Principe		10	10	14	46	77		67.39
North Africa		257	156	353	456	554		21.49
Algeria		37	34	42	64	90		40.63
Morocco		106	52	109	117	203		73.50
Sudan		65	55	149	154	182		18.18
Tunisia		49	15	53	121	79		-34.71
Southern Africa		1,923	1,866	2,424	3,260	3,841	0.02	17.82
Botswana		1	1	8	7	39		457.14
Lesotho		2		5	6	16		166.67
Namibia		2	1	4	11	21		90.91
South Africa		1,913	1,862	2,399	3,231	3,762	0.02	16.43
Swaziland		5	2	8	5	3		-40.00
West Africa		1,221	1,530	1,683	2,318	5,834	0.03	151.68
Cape Verde		183	203	211	195	389		99.49
Benin		6	7	7	27	32		18.52
Gambia		34	25	26	45	100		122.22
Ghana		23	51	114	338	622		84.02
Guinea		16	13	16	74	335		352.70
Cote D'Ivoire		15	11	23	90	302		235.56
Liberia		30	17	23	54	79		46.30
Mali		45	66	48	133	2,070	0.01	1,456.39
Mauritania		20	14	4	2	28		1,300.00
Niger		9	8	12	20	91		355.00
Nigeria		671	864	829	850	825		-2.94
Guinea-Bissau		44	85	92	94	202		114.89
Saint Helena		1		10	15	12		-20.00
Senegal		17	36	106	272	542		99.26
Sierra Leone		84	63	66	34	68		100.00
Togo		16	24	19	39	111		184.62

MACAO, CHINA

2. Arrivals of non-resident visitors at national borders, by nationality

	2002	2003	2004	2005	2006	Market share 06	% Change 06-05
Burkina Faso	7	43	77	36	26		-27.78
Other Africa	**32**	**11**	**145**	**141**	**256**		**81.56**
Other countries of Africa	32	11	145	141	256		81.56
AMERICAS	**128,219**	**95,502**	**147,953**	**182,830**	**218,277**	**0.99**	**19.39**
Caribbean	**711**	**403**	**401**	**392**	**586**		**49.49**
Antigua and Barbuda	24	13	12	3	8		166.67
Bahamas	23	30	21	23	21		-8.70
Barbados	12	7	17	11	13		18.18
Bermuda	1	2	5	1			
Cayman Islands	3	5	10	9	2		-77.78
Cuba	71	24	26	47	120		155.32
Dominican Republic	320	128	63	37	51		37.84
Guadeloupe	1		1		2		
Haiti	2	2	3	5	8		60.00
Jamaica	88	124	96	70	86		22.86
Martinique	2	3	7	3	2		-33.33
Netherlands Antilles		1	2		2		
Aruba	3	2	1		1		
Curacao	1	1			1		
Puerto Rico			2				
Saint Lucia	2	3	11	8	3		-62.50
Saint Vincent and the Grenadines	3	2	2	3	4		33.33
Trinidad and Tobago	155	56	122	172	262		52.33
Central America	**1,924**	**1,305**	**1,614**	**1,835**	**2,195**	**0.01**	**19.62**
Belize	572	439	400	543	655		20.63
Costa Rica	452	339	420	521	677		29.94
El Salvador	29	19	27	23	80		247.83
Guatemala	123	62	113	125	151		20.80
Honduras	300	90	113	93	127		36.56
Nicaragua	12	8	16	10	7		-30.00
Panama	436	348	525	520	498		-4.23
North America	**119,723**	**89,693**	**139,496**	**170,701**	**204,511**	**0.93**	**19.81**
Canada	31,152	24,842	37,937	46,541	55,242	0.25	18.70
Mexico	1,923	942	1,783	2,063	2,801	0.01	35.77
United States	86,648	63,909	99,776	122,097	146,468	0.67	19.96
South America	**5,861**	**4,101**	**6,442**	**9,902**	**10,985**	**0.05**	**10.94**
Argentina	336	263	456	785	765		-2.55
Bolivia	231	75	155	196	210		7.14
Brazil	2,657	1,968	3,300	5,038	6,506	0.03	29.14
Chile	383	221	392	478	699		46.23
Colombia	465	283	449	1,077	1,205	0.01	11.88
Ecuador	223	126	196	378	349		-7.67
Falkland Islands (Malvinas)	3	1		4	1		-75.00
French Guiana		1	1		1		
Guyana	27	9	10	29	38		31.03
Paraguay	37	29	38	46	39		-15.22
Peru	647	480	669	716	898		25.42
Suriname	128	59	82	107	92		-14.02
Uruguay	73	36	53	60	62		3.33
Venezuela	651	550	641	988	120		-87.85
EAST ASIA AND THE PACIFIC	**11,249,556**	**11,673,256**	**16,361,807**	**18,321,056**	**21,525,911**	**97.85**	**17.49**
North-East Asia	**11,029,879**	**11,487,853**	**16,056,173**	**17,851,890**	**20,746,404**	**94.31**	**16.21**

MACAO, CHINA

2. Arrivals of non-resident visitors at national borders, by nationality

	2002	2003	2004	2005	2006	Market share 06	% Change 06-05
China	4,183,725	5,681,102	9,518,336	10,462,787	11,985,655	54.48	14.56
Taiwan (Province of China)	1,557,611	1,045,755	1,313,288	1,482,287	1,437,752	6.54	-3.00
Hong Kong, China	5,070,850	4,621,203	5,027,090	5,611,145	6,935,586	31.53	23.60
Japan	164,429	97,051	130,423	169,487	220,642	1.00	30.18
Korea, Dem. People's Republic of	1,511	1,219	1,491	1,712	1,155	0.01	-32.54
Korea, Republic of	50,657	40,092	63,456	120,876	162,834	0.74	34.71
Mongolia	1,096	1,431	2,089	3,596	2,780	0.01	-22.69
South-East Asia	**175,910**	**149,904**	**250,830**	**397,258**	**694,961**	**3.16**	**74.94**
Brunei Darussalam	122	125	237	435	662		52.18
Myanmar	1,167	810	1,586	2,223	3,448	0.02	55.11
Cambodia	990	905	2,096	2,400	2,944	0.01	22.67
Indonesia	20,035	18,130	30,063	46,316	68,398	0.31	47.68
Lao People's Democratic Republic	68	28	113	258	334		29.46
Malaysia	33,153	26,086	48,810	98,527	202,938	0.92	105.97
Philippines	55,343	51,101	68,563	94,400	176,940	0.80	87.44
Timor-Leste	9	94	80	127	266		109.45
Singapore	32,424	26,821	45,910	82,338	126,377	0.57	53.49
Viet Nam	6,537	6,337	10,454	12,115	22,913	0.10	89.13
Thailand	26,062	19,467	42,918	58,119	89,741	0.41	54.41
Australasia	**42,559**	**34,603**	**53,728**	**70,997**	**83,802**	**0.38**	**18.04**
Australia	36,282	29,607	46,427	61,851	73,115	0.33	18.21
New Zealand	6,277	4,996	7,301	9,146	10,687	0.05	16.85
Melanesia	**205**	**192**	**359**	**379**	**448**		**18.21**
Solomon Islands	2	10	29	31	62		100.00
Fiji	130	149	283	304	290		-4.61
New Caledonia	2	2	1				
Vanuatu	13	8	29	19	39		105.26
Papua New Guinea	58	23	17	25	57		128.00
Micronesia	**757**	**595**	**617**	**447**	**185**		**-58.61**
Nauru	702	536	563	405	157		-61.23
Marshall Islands	55	59	54	42	28		-33.33
Polynesia	**246**	**109**	**100**	**85**	**111**		**30.59**
Tonga	229	93	89	70	109		55.71
Samoa	17	16	11	15	2		-86.67
EUROPE	**127,614**	**94,078**	**128,887**	**161,204**	**188,189**	**0.86**	**16.74**
Central/Eastern Europe	**5,674**	**4,329**	**6,941**	**9,682**	**11,700**	**0.05**	**20.84**
Bulgaria	47	78	185	351	578		64.67
Czech Republic/Slovakia	501	498	1,007	1,004	1,013		0.90
Hungary	601	411	568	787	799		1.52
Poland	1,340	774	1,393	2,448	3,388	0.02	38.40
Romania	216	210	528	832	1,429	0.01	71.75
Ussr (Former)	2,969	2,358	3,260	4,260	4,493	0.02	5.47
Northern Europe	**59,258**	**45,503**	**54,723**	**62,818**	**73,132**	**0.33**	**16.42**
Denmark	1,568	1,409	1,840	2,611	2,924	0.01	11.99
Finland	1,765	954	1,089	2,196	3,010	0.01	37.07
Iceland	140	55	69	117	143		22.22
Ireland	1,877	1,361	2,089	2,576	3,134	0.01	21.66
Norway	1,096	797	1,046	1,269	1,358	0.01	7.01
Sweden	2,857	2,093	3,178	3,843	4,766	0.02	24.02
United Kingdom	49,955	38,834	45,412	50,206	57,797	0.26	15.12
Southern Europe	**18,920**	**12,620**	**18,606**	**23,657**	**28,233**	**0.13**	**19.34**
Albania	7	11	22	16	29		81.25

MACAO, CHINA

2. Arrivals of non-resident visitors at national borders, by nationality

	2002	2003	2004	2005	2006	Market share 06	% Change 06-05
Andorra	1	4	48	20	16		-20.00
Greece	339	211	310	489	816		66.87
Holy See		2		5	1		-80.00
Italy	4,847	3,249	4,603	6,782	8,703	0.04	28.32
Malta	84	45	84	85	66		-22.35
Portugal	11,170	7,666	10,260	11,961	13,216	0.06	10.49
San Marino		3	3	2			
Spain	2,429	1,380	3,184	4,157	5,255	0.02	26.41
Yugoslavia, Sfr (Former)	43	49	92	140	131		-6.43
Western Europe	**41,434**	**29,593**	**46,064**	**61,625**	**70,221**	**0.32**	**13.95**
Austria	1,660	1,035	1,894	2,763	3,149	0.01	13.97
Belgium	1,660	1,451	2,096	3,060	3,447	0.02	12.65
France	16,809	11,925	19,484	25,991	28,909	0.13	11.23
Germany	12,694	9,479	13,618	18,108	20,805	0.09	14.89
Liechtenstein	3	8	22	24	29		20.83
Luxembourg	128	69	95	109	117		7.34
Monaco	19	18	18	10	17		70.00
Netherlands	5,292	3,761	5,855	7,508	9,381	0.04	24.95
Switzerland	3,169	1,847	2,982	4,052	4,367	0.02	7.77
East Mediterranean Europe	**2,328**	**2,033**	**2,553**	**3,422**	**4,903**	**0.02**	**43.28**
Cyprus	45	41	40	66	77		16.67
Israel	1,638	1,427	1,635	2,313	3,284	0.01	41.98
Turkey	645	565	878	1,043	1,542	0.01	47.84
MIDDLE EAST	**943**	**1,171**	**1,905**	**2,679**	**3,747**	**0.02**	**39.87**
Middle East	**943**	**1,171**	**1,905**	**2,679**	**3,747**	**0.02**	**39.87**
Bahrain	23	18	14	37	61		64.86
Iraq	32	17	20	40	72		80.00
Jordan	188	173	171	174	190		9.20
Kuwait	79	54	62	152	152		
Lebanon	132	251	617	946	1,254	0.01	32.56
Libyan Arab Jamahiriya	4	7	29	64	115		79.69
Oman	5	10	7	83	91		9.64
Qatar	15	22	17	41	97		136.59
Saudi Arabia	113	126	197	330	613		85.76
Syrian Arab Republic	85	259	475	366	326		-10.93
Egypt	156	150	202	327	574		75.54
Yemen	67	60	32	41	86		109.76
Other countries of Middle East	44	24	62	78	116		48.72
SOUTH ASIA	**17,719**	**17,324**	**23,771**	**32,335**	**42,604**	**0.19**	**31.76**
South Asia	**17,719**	**17,324**	**23,771**	**32,335**	**42,604**	**0.19**	**31.76**
Afghanistan	13	7	26	27	26		-3.70
Bangladesh	1,398	1,048	2,102	3,039	3,482	0.02	14.58
Bhutan	85	50	62	62	95		53.23
Sri Lanka	707	567	856	941	751		-20.19
India	10,460	9,847	13,816	21,065	29,160	0.13	38.43
Iran, Islamic Republic of	351	529	1,044	807	540		-33.09
Maldives	66	10	30	13	24		84.62
Nepal	2,168	2,655	3,923	4,552	6,452	0.03	41.74
Pakistan	2,471	2,611	1,912	1,829	2,074	0.01	13.40
REGION NOT SPECIFIED	**2,351**	**1,877**	**2,191**	**3,001**	**5,701**	**0.03**	**89.97**
Not Specified	**2,351**	**1,877**	**2,191**	**3,001**	**5,701**	**0.03**	**89.97**
Other countries of the World	2,351	1,877	2,191	3,001	5,701	0.03	89.97

Source: World Tourism Organization (UNWTO)

MACAO, CHINA

2. Arrivals of non-resident visitors at national borders, by country of residence

	2002	2003	2004	2005	2006	Market share 06	% Change 06-05
TOTAL	11,530,841	11,887,876	16,672,556	18,711,187	21,998,122	100.00	17.57
AFRICA	4,125	4,308	5,549	7,935	13,469	0.06	69.74
Other Africa	4,125	4,308	5,549	7,935	13,469	0.06	69.74
All countries of Africa	4,125	4,308	5,549	7,935	13,469	0.06	69.74
AMERICAS	115,383	86,674	143,513	182,768	219,610	1.00	20.16
North America	107,079	80,653	134,426	170,400	204,511	0.93	20.02
Canada	28,552	23,202	37,782	46,447	55,242	0.25	18.94
Mexico	1,623	809	1,554	2,064	2,801	0.01	35.71
United States	76,904	56,642	95,090	121,889	146,468	0.67	20.17
South America	2,485	1,899	3,496	5,033	6,497	0.03	29.09
Brazil	2,485	1,899	3,496	5,033	6,497	0.03	29.09
Other Americas	5,819	4,122	5,591	7,335	8,602	0.04	17.27
Other countries of the Americas	5,819	4,122	5,591	7,335	8,602	0.04	17.27
EAST ASIA AND THE PACIFIC	11,280,134	11,693,497	16,371,823	18,325,116	21,529,964	97.87	17.49
North-East Asia	11,070,558	11,514,601	16,059,121	17,855,497	20,750,935	94.33	16.22
China	4,240,446	5,742,036	9,529,739	10,462,966	11,985,617	54.48	14.55
Taiwan (Province of China)	1,532,929	1,022,830	1,286,949	1,482,483	1,437,824	6.54	-3.01
Hong Kong, China	5,101,437	4,623,162	5,051,059	5,614,892	6,940,656	31.55	23.61
Japan	142,588	85,613	122,184	169,115	220,190	1.00	30.20
Korea, Dem. People's Republic of	1,528	1,237	1,536	1,709	1,158	0.01	-32.24
Korea, Republic of	50,447	38,281	65,631	120,739	162,709	0.74	34.76
Other countries of North-East Asia	1,183	1,442	2,023	3,593	2,781	0.01	-22.60
South-East Asia	171,176	147,829	262,706	397,939	694,807	3.16	74.60
Indonesia	19,423	17,705	32,939	46,154	68,114	0.31	47.58
Malaysia	31,323	24,555	48,391	98,450	202,821	0.92	106.01
Philippines	54,739	52,162	76,878	93,878	176,246	0.80	87.74
Singapore	30,940	25,767	45,760	82,298	126,291	0.57	53.46
Thailand	24,625	18,096	41,841	57,876	89,448	0.41	54.55
Other countries of South-East Asia	10,126	9,544	16,897	19,283	31,887	0.14	65.36
Australasia	36,517	29,743	48,760	70,740	83,457	0.38	17.98
Australia	31,028	25,385	42,059	61,646	72,810	0.33	18.11
New Zealand	5,489	4,358	6,701	9,094	10,647	0.05	17.08
Other East Asia and the Pacific	1,883	1,324	1,236	940	765		-18.62
Other countries of Oceania	1,883	1,324	1,236	940	765		-18.62
EUROPE	111,526	83,592	123,402	160,142	187,530	0.85	17.10
Central/Eastern Europe					4,481	0.02	
Russian Federation					4,481	0.02	
Northern Europe	44,692	36,737	48,745	55,764	64,984	0.30	16.53
Ireland	1,651	1,208	2,064	2,565	3,126	0.01	21.87
Sweden	2,524	1,701	2,672	3,836	4,752	0.02	23.88
United Kingdom	40,517	33,828	44,009	49,363	57,106	0.26	15.69
Southern Europe	16,494	11,043	17,063	22,761	27,074	0.12	18.95
Italy	4,327	3,240	4,536	6,771	8,692	0.04	28.37
Portugal	10,057	6,576	9,560	11,843	13,125	0.06	10.82
Spain	2,110	1,227	2,967	4,147	5,257	0.02	26.77
Western Europe	36,029	25,372	42,001	58,347	66,497	0.30	13.97
Austria	1,452	941	1,704	2,754	3,139	0.01	13.98
France	16,304	11,676	20,308	25,986	28,872	0.13	11.11

MACAO, CHINA

2. Arrivals of non-resident visitors at national borders, by country of residence

	2002	2003	2004	2005	2006	Market share 06	% Change 06-05
Germany	10,721	7,643	11,881	18,082	20,769	0.09	14.86
Netherlands	4,781	3,554	5,344	7,494	9,375	0.04	25.10
Switzerland	2,771	1,558	2,764	4,031	4,342	0.02	7.72
Other Europe	**14,311**	**10,440**	**15,593**	**23,270**	**24,494**	**0.11**	**5.26**
Other countries of Europe	14,311	10,440	15,593	23,270	24,494	0.11	5.26
MIDDLE EAST	**1,105**	**1,334**	**2,041**	**2,666**	**3,735**	**0.02**	**40.10**
Middle East	**1,105**	**1,334**	**2,041**	**2,666**	**3,735**	**0.02**	**40.10**
All countries of Middle East	1,105	1,334	2,041	2,666	3,735	0.02	40.10
SOUTH ASIA	**16,832**	**16,763**	**24,240**	**30,015**	**40,281**	**0.18**	**34.20**
South Asia	**16,832**	**16,763**	**24,240**	**30,015**	**40,281**	**0.18**	**34.20**
Bangladesh	1,564	1,604	2,455	2,977	3,432	0.02	15.28
India	10,574	9,820	15,278	20,846	28,903	0.13	38.65
Nepal	2,248	2,749	4,146	4,437	5,972	0.03	34.60
Pakistan	2,446	2,590	2,361	1,755	1,974	0.01	12.48
REGION NOT SPECIFIED	**1,736**	**1,708**	**1,988**	**2,545**	**3,533**	**0.02**	**38.82**
Not Specified	**1,736**	**1,708**	**1,988**	**2,545**	**3,533**	**0.02**	**38.82**
Other countries of the World	1,736	1,708	1,988	2,545	3,533	0.02	38.82

Source: World Tourism Organization (UNWTO)

MACAO, CHINA

3. Arrivals of non-resident tourists in hotels and similar establishments, by country of residence

	2002	2003	2004	2005	2006	Market share 06	% Change 06-05
TOTAL	2,996,079	2,870,465	3,789,860	3,903,397	4,428,783	100.00	13.46
AMERICAS	16,900	15,000	28,143	34,655	52,303	1.18	50.92
North America	16,900	15,000	28,143	34,655	52,303	1.18	50.92
Canada	3,970	3,813	5,451	6,716	11,999	0.27	78.66
United States	12,930	11,187	22,692	27,939	40,304	0.91	44.26
EAST ASIA AND THE PACIFIC	2,947,196	2,823,542	3,714,710	3,801,379	4,278,447	96.61	12.55
North-East Asia	2,919,454	2,797,618	3,665,045	3,717,641	4,120,602	93.04	10.84
China	1,451,250	1,431,294	2,190,736	2,369,738	2,627,460	59.33	10.88
Taiwan (Province of China)	166,332	111,410	120,330	133,284	133,238	3.01	-0.03
Hong Kong, China	1,249,155	1,218,648	1,301,881	1,127,220	1,235,601	27.90	9.61
Japan	39,718	25,230	37,876	59,963	86,010	1.94	43.44
Korea, Republic of	12,999	11,036	14,222	27,436	38,293	0.86	39.57
South-East Asia	22,181	20,637	39,503	69,441	139,521	3.15	100.92
Indonesia	3,121	4,402	4,533	8,302	12,651	0.29	52.38
Malaysia	4,871	3,971	9,409	17,715	34,736	0.78	96.08
Philippines	3,434	2,265	4,856	6,835	22,131	0.50	223.79
Singapore	6,193	6,339	10,283	21,053	38,772	0.88	84.16
Thailand	4,562	3,660	10,422	15,536	31,231	0.71	101.02
Australasia	5,561	5,287	10,162	14,297	18,324	0.41	28.17
Australia	4,489	4,234	8,822	12,696	16,200	0.37	27.60
New Zealand	1,072	1,053	1,340	1,601	2,124	0.05	32.67
EUROPE	20,310	19,843	28,282	33,907	44,669	1.01	31.74
Northern Europe	6,958	8,725	7,887	8,259	9,890	0.22	19.75
United Kingdom	6,958	8,725	7,887	8,259	9,890	0.22	19.75
Southern Europe	3,705	2,952	4,685	6,310	7,938	0.18	25.80
Italy	1,048	708	1,038	1,946	2,486	0.06	27.75
Portugal	2,657	2,244	3,647	4,364	5,452	0.12	24.93
Western Europe	4,971	3,629	5,576	8,107	10,232	0.23	26.21
France	2,579	1,765	3,048	4,575	5,670	0.13	23.93
Germany	2,392	1,864	2,528	3,532	4,562	0.10	29.16
Other Europe	4,676	4,537	10,134	11,231	16,609	0.38	47.89
Other countries of Europe	4,676	4,537	10,134	11,231	16,609	0.38	47.89
SOUTH ASIA	1,892	2,068	3,934	6,761	11,737	0.27	73.60
South Asia	1,892	2,068	3,934	6,761	11,737	0.27	73.60
India	1,892	2,068	3,934	6,761	11,737	0.27	73.60
REGION NOT SPECIFIED	9,781	10,012	14,791	26,695	41,627	0.94	55.94
Not Specified	9,781	10,012	14,791	26,695	41,627	0.94	55.94
Other countries of the World	9,781	10,012	14,791	26,695	41,627	0.94	55.94

Source: World Tourism Organization (UNWTO)

MACAO, CHINA

5. Overnight stays of non-resident tourists in hotels and similar establishments, by country of residence

	2002	2003	2004	2005	2006	Market share 06	% Change 06-05
TOTAL	3,656,239	3,456,057	4,426,091	4,563,044	5,128,274	100.00	12.39
AMERICAS	33,536	36,662	55,357	61,890	94,207	1.84	52.22
North America	33,536	36,662	55,357	61,890	94,207	1.84	52.22
Canada	10,976	15,182	12,435	12,042	25,675	0.50	113.21
United States	22,560	21,480	42,922	49,848	68,532	1.34	37.48
EAST ASIA AND THE PACIFIC	3,563,783	3,359,285	4,293,507	4,385,070	4,873,787	95.04	11.15
North-East Asia	3,515,708	3,292,564	4,204,492	4,256,404	4,640,609	90.49	9.03
China	1,726,084	1,655,341	2,466,222	2,638,927	2,845,243	55.48	7.82
Taiwan (Province of China)	201,253	133,004	157,015	167,882	169,924	3.31	1.22
Hong Kong, China	1,513,772	1,449,451	1,504,642	1,322,798	1,459,362	28.46	10.32
Japan	54,443	38,706	55,939	87,893	117,138	2.28	33.27
Korea, Republic of	20,156	16,062	20,674	38,904	48,942	0.95	25.80
South-East Asia	37,284	55,446	71,225	103,720	200,639	3.91	93.44
Indonesia	3,915	5,730	7,127	13,825	19,730	0.38	42.71
Malaysia	7,585	6,787	14,716	25,462	48,671	0.95	91.15
Philippines	4,654	3,428	8,105	9,886	33,445	0.65	238.31
Singapore	13,206	31,312	24,445	30,841	54,373	1.06	76.30
Thailand	7,924	8,189	16,832	23,706	44,420	0.87	87.38
Australasia	10,791	11,275	17,790	24,946	32,539	0.63	30.44
Australia	8,903	8,492	15,287	22,243	28,659	0.56	28.85
New Zealand	1,888	2,783	2,503	2,703	3,880	0.08	43.54
EUROPE	41,501	39,001	50,807	64,754	78,398	1.53	21.07
Northern Europe	11,312	13,610	14,273	15,968	18,245	0.36	14.26
United Kingdom	11,312	13,610	14,273	15,968	18,245	0.36	14.26
Southern Europe	10,854	8,822	11,019	14,613	18,795	0.37	28.62
Italy	2,346	1,967	1,912	3,955	5,716	0.11	44.53
Portugal	8,508	6,855	9,107	10,658	13,079	0.26	22.72
Western Europe	11,495	9,115	10,825	15,399	17,501	0.34	13.65
France	7,422	5,666	6,452	9,036	9,682	0.19	7.15
Germany	4,073	3,449	4,373	6,363	7,819	0.15	22.88
Other Europe	7,840	7,454	14,690	18,774	23,857	0.47	27.07
Other countries of Europe	7,840	7,454	14,690	18,774	23,857	0.47	27.07
SOUTH ASIA	2,528	3,065	5,368	9,936	17,655	0.34	77.69
South Asia	2,528	3,065	5,368	9,936	17,655	0.34	77.69
India	2,528	3,065	5,368	9,936	17,655	0.34	77.69
REGION NOT SPECIFIED	14,891	18,044	21,052	41,394	64,227	1.25	55.16
Not Specified	14,891	18,044	21,052	41,394	64,227	1.25	55.16
Other countries of the World	14,891	18,044	21,052	41,394	64,227	1.25	55.16

Source: World Tourism Organization (UNWTO)

MADAGASCAR

1. Arrivals of non-resident tourists at national borders, by nationality

	2002	2003	2004	2005	2006	Market share 06	% Change 06-05
TOTAL	61,674	139,230	228,785	277,422	311,730	100.00	12.37
AFRICA	6,218	21,725	39,302	52,277	58,520	18.77	11.94
East Africa	6,218	16,707	32,667	41,965	47,264	15.16	12.63
Comoros			125	201	226	0.07	12.44
Kenya			55	78	87	0.03	11.54
Mauritius	3,134	6,961	9,609	9,825	11,253	3.61	14.53
Reunion	3,084	9,746	22,878	31,861	35,698	11.45	12.04
Southern Africa		2,785	3,203	5,860	6,416	2.06	9.49
South Africa		2,785	3,203	5,860	6,416	2.06	9.49
Other Africa		2,233	3,432	4,452	4,840	1.55	8.72
Other countries of Africa		2,233	3,432	4,452	4,840	1.55	8.72
AMERICAS	1,880	4,177	9,180	13,853	15,587	5.00	12.52
North America	1,880	4,177	9,151	13,808	15,587	5.00	12.88
Canada, United States	1,880	4,177	9,151	13,808	15,587	5.00	12.88
Other Americas			29	45			
Other countries of the Americas			29	45			
EAST ASIA AND THE PACIFIC	617	4,872	3,432	6,404	7,206	2.31	12.52
North-East Asia	617	1,392	3,432	5,952	6,697	2.15	12.52
Japan	617	1,392	3,432	5,952	6,697	2.15	12.52
Other East Asia and the Pacific		3,480		452	509	0.16	12.61
Other countries of Asia		3,480		452	509	0.16	12.61
EUROPE	43,172	99,271	175,727	202,530	228,452	73.29	12.80
Northern Europe	2,467	5,152	6,884	6,969	7,861	2.52	12.80
United Kingdom	2,467	5,152	6,864	6,732	7,594	2.44	12.80
Scandinavia			20	237	267	0.09	12.66
Southern Europe	3,084	6,265	17,159	23,027	25,974	8.33	12.80
Italy	3,084	6,265	17,159	22,657	25,556	8.20	12.80
Spain				370	418	0.13	12.97
Western Europe	37,621	87,854	151,684	172,083	193,565	62.09	12.48
France	32,070	79,361	129,263	145,192	163,180	52.35	12.39
Germany	3,084	4,873	9,609	12,025	13,526	4.34	12.48
Switzerland	2,467	3,620	4,576	4,987	5,610	1.80	12.49
Benelux			8,236	9,879	11,249	3.61	13.87
Other Europe				451	1,052	0.34	133.26
Other countries of Europe				451	1,052	0.34	133.26
REGION NOT SPECIFIED	9,787	9,185	1,144	2,358	1,965	0.63	-16.67
Not Specified	9,787	9,185	1,144	2,358	1,965	0.63	-16.67
Other countries of the World	9,787	9,185	1,144	2,358	1,965	0.63	-16.67

Source: World Tourism Organization (UNWTO)

MADAGASCAR

5. Overnight stays of non-resident tourists in hotels and similar establishments, by nationality

		2002	2003	2004	2005	2006	Market share 06	% Change 06-05
TOTAL	(*)	555,066	2,088,210	3,536,098	5,221,156	5,299,474	100.00	1.50
AFRICA		55,962	325,785	374,844	485,523	493,298	9.31	1.60
East Africa		55,962	250,605	206,679	299,203	303,490	5.73	1.43
Comoros				1,598	6,231	6,320	0.12	1.43
Kenya				550	1,170	1,062	0.02	-9.23
Mauritius		28,206	104,415	67,263	68,775	69,760	1.32	1.43
Reunion		27,756	146,190	137,268	223,027	226,348	4.27	1.49
Southern Africa			41,775	48,045	52,740	53,585	1.01	1.60
South Africa			41,775	48,045	52,740	53,585	1.01	1.60
Other Africa			33,405	120,120	133,580	136,223	2.57	1.98
Other countries of Africa			33,405	120,120	133,580	136,223	2.57	1.98
AMERICAS		16,920	62,655	183,890	277,510	281,160	5.31	1.32
North America		16,920	62,655	183,020	276,160	279,137	5.27	1.08
Canada, United States		16,920	62,655	183,020	276,160	279,137	5.27	1.08
Other Americas				870	1,350	2,023	0.04	49.85
Other countries of the Americas				870	1,350	2,023	0.04	49.85
EAST ASIA AND THE PACIFIC		5,556	73,080	102,960	219,530	223,304	4.21	1.72
North-East Asia		5,556	20,880	102,960	208,230	211,124	3.98	1.39
Japan		5,556	20,880	102,960	208,230	211,124	3.98	1.39
Other East Asia and the Pacific			52,200		11,300	12,180	0.23	7.79
Other countries of Asia			52,200		11,300	12,180	0.23	7.79
EUROPE		388,548	1,489,065	2,857,244	4,210,297	4,273,290	80.64	1.50
Northern Europe		22,203	77,280	103,320	124,496	125,862	2.37	1.10
United Kingdom		22,203	77,280	102,960	121,178	122,817	2.32	1.35
Scandinavia				360	3,318	3,045	0.06	-8.23
Southern Europe		27,756	93,975	240,226	180,886	183,724	3.47	1.57
Italy		27,756	93,975	240,226	178,296	181,087	3.42	1.57
Spain					2,590	2,637	0.05	1.81
Western Europe		338,589	1,317,810	2,513,698	3,900,856	3,959,585	74.72	1.51
France		288,630	1,190,415	2,304,589	3,629,800	3,683,500	69.51	1.48
Germany		27,756	73,095	86,481	132,275	133,982	2.53	1.29
Switzerland		22,203	54,300	32,032	49,870	51,767	0.98	3.80
Benelux				90,596	88,911	90,336	1.70	1.60
Other Europe					4,059	4,119	0.08	1.48
Other countries of Europe					4,059	4,119	0.08	1.48
REGION NOT SPECIFIED		88,080	137,625	17,160	28,296	28,422	0.54	0.45
Not Specified		88,080	137,625	17,160	28,296	28,422	0.54	0.45
Other countries of the World		88,080	137,625	17,160	28,296	28,422	0.54	0.45

Source: World Tourism Organization (UNWTO)

MALAWI

1. Arrivals of non-resident tourists at national borders, by country of residence

		2002	2003	2004	2005	2006	Market share 06	% Change 06-05
TOTAL	(*)	382,647	424,000	427,360	437,718			
AFRICA		299,973	320,360	335,651	336,856			
East Africa		247,923	265,570	275,737	282,299			
Mozambique		83,064	92,200	104,698	95,019			
Zimbabwe		54,075	63,910	57,518	60,807			
Zambia		39,677	50,540	45,817	43,855			
Other countries of East Africa		71,107	58,920	67,704	82,618			
Southern Africa		42,655	49,200	54,230	48,155			
All countries of Southern Africa		42,655	49,200	54,230	48,155			
Other Africa		9,395	5,590	5,684	6,402			
Other countries of Africa		9,395	5,590	5,684	6,402			
AMERICAS		15,251	18,070	20,828	18,725			
North America		14,885	17,210	19,431	17,278			
Canada, United States		14,885	17,210	19,431	17,278			
Other Americas		366	860	1,397	1,447			
Other countries of the Americas		366	860	1,397	1,447			
EAST ASIA AND THE PACIFIC		5,542	9,940	11,313	8,698			
Other East Asia and the Pacific		5,542	9,940	11,313	8,698			
All countries of Asia		5,542	9,940	11,313	8,698			
EUROPE		55,222	67,500	48,929	60,437			
Northern Europe		20,693	31,220	17,030	28,157			
United Kingdom/Ireland		20,693	31,220	17,030	28,157			
Other Europe		34,529	36,280	31,899	32,280			
Other countries of Europe		34,529	36,280	31,899	32,280			
SOUTH ASIA		1,659	3,620	6,815	9,549			
South Asia		1,659	3,620	6,815	9,549			
All countries of South Asia		1,659	3,620	6,815	9,549			
REGION NOT SPECIFIED		5,000	4,510	3,824	3,453			
Not Specified		5,000	4,510	3,824	3,453			
Other countries of the World		5,000	4,510	3,824	3,453			

Source: World Tourism Organization (UNWTO)

MALAWI

6. Overnight stays of non-resident tourists in all types of accommodation establishments, by country of residence

		2002	2003	2004	2005	2006	Market share 06	% Change 06-05
TOTAL	(*)	2,892,726	3,258,728	3,617,187				
AFRICA		2,276,085	2,668,424	2,961,950				
East Africa		1,880,505	2,204,650	2,447,161				
Mozambique		631,286	740,097	821,508				
Zimbabwe		410,970	481,812	534,811				
Zambia		297,836	349,175	387,584				
Other countries of East Africa		540,413	633,566	703,258				
Southern Africa		355,338	416,591	462,416				
All countries of Southern Africa		355,338	416,591	462,416				
Other Africa		40,242	47,183	52,373				
Other countries of Africa		40,242	47,183	52,373				
AMERICAS		113,126						
North America		113,126						
Canada, United States		113,126						
EUROPE		423,396	496,376	550,977				
Northern Europe		157,267	184,372	204,653				
United Kingdom/Ireland		157,267	184,372	204,653				
Other Europe		266,129	312,004	346,324				
Other countries of Europe		266,129	312,004	346,324				
REGION NOT SPECIFIED		80,119	93,928	104,260				
Not Specified		80,119	93,928	104,260				
Other countries of the World		80,119	93,928	104,260				

Source: World Tourism Organization (UNWTO)

473

MALAYSIA

1. Arrivals of non-resident tourists at national borders, by country of residence

	2002	2003	2004	2005	2006	Market share 06	% Change 06-05
TOTAL (*)	13,292,010	10,576,915	15,703,406	16,431,055	17,546,863	100.00	6.79
AFRICA	148,102	133,762	136,587	128,208	157,342	0.90	22.72
East Africa	60,275	53,558	55,579	57,069	70,661	0.40	23.82
Mauritius	7,814	5,300	5,360	5,601	6,500	0.04	16.05
Other countries of East Africa	52,461	48,258	50,219	51,468	64,161	0.37	24.66
Central Africa	11,627	12,641	16,967	11,886	13,138	0.07	10.53
All countries of Central Africa	11,627	12,641	16,967	11,886	13,138	0.07	10.53
North Africa	17,332	13,355	12,835	13,943	18,242	0.10	30.83
All countries of North Africa	17,332	13,355	12,835	13,943	18,242	0.10	30.83
Southern Africa	47,699	43,863	40,928	34,718	40,021	0.23	15.27
South Africa	13,720	12,577	16,511	16,381	20,174	0.11	23.15
Other countries of Southern Africa	33,979	31,286	24,417	18,337	19,847	0.11	8.23
West Africa	11,169	10,345	10,278	10,592	15,280	0.09	44.26
All countries of West Africa	11,169	10,345	10,278	10,592	15,280	0.09	44.26
AMERICAS	283,216	270,157	271,901	274,915	312,478	1.78	13.66
Caribbean	52,193	50,969	37,982	36,072	37,727	0.22	4.59
All countries of the Caribbean	52,193	50,969	37,982	36,072	37,727	0.22	4.59
Central America	17,771	15,724	10,823	10,932	11,708	0.07	7.10
All countries of Central America	17,771	15,724	10,823	10,932	11,708	0.07	7.10
North America	166,349	161,410	181,517	186,445	213,111	1.21	14.30
Canada	34,996	26,978	32,822	31,167	34,730	0.20	11.43
Mexico	2,284	1,491	1,773	1,944	2,588	0.01	33.13
United States	127,920	131,071	145,094	151,354	174,336	0.99	15.18
Other countries of North America	1,149	1,870	1,828	1,980	1,457	0.01	-26.41
South America	46,903	42,054	41,579	41,466	49,932	0.28	20.42
Argentina	1,211	2,030	2,919	4,565	4,388	0.03	-3.88
Brazil	2,560	2,184	1,924	2,235	2,995	0.02	34.00
Venezuela	6,636	7,748	10,362	9,664	10,468	0.06	8.32
Other countries of South America	36,496	30,092	26,374	25,002	32,081	0.18	28.31
EAST ASIA AND THE PACIFIC	11,456,003	9,073,882	13,983,381	14,685,975	15,475,553	88.20	5.38
North-East Asia	1,314,707	832,632	1,226,125	1,107,919	1,263,360	7.20	14.03
China	557,647	350,597	550,241	352,089	439,294	2.50	24.77
Taiwan (Province of China)	209,706	137,419	190,083	172,456	181,829	1.04	5.44
Hong Kong, China	116,409	72,027	80,326	77,528	89,577	0.51	15.54
Japan	354,563	213,527	301,429	340,027	354,213	2.02	4.17
Korea, Dem. People's Republic of		10,789	10,536	4,689	4,940	0.03	5.35
Korea, Republic of	64,301	46,246	91,270	158,177	189,464	1.08	19.78
Macao, China		2,027	2,240	2,953	4,043	0.02	36.91
Other countries of North-East Asia	12,081						
South-East Asia	9,887,122	8,042,189	12,491,030	13,238,898	13,856,726	78.97	4.67
Brunei Darussalam	256,952	215,634	453,664	486,344	784,446	4.47	61.29
Myanmar	6,962	7,112	10,418	10,847	13,030	0.07	20.13
Cambodia		8,725	10,951	9,957	14,694	0.08	47.57
Indonesia	769,128	621,651	789,925	962,957	1,217,024	6.94	26.38
Lao People's Democratic Republic	1,808	2,372	1,427	1,944	4,371	0.02	124.85
Philippines	107,527	90,430	143,799	178,961	211,123	1.20	17.97
Singapore	7,547,761	5,922,306	9,520,306	9,634,506	9,656,251	55.03	0.23
Viet Nam	21,158	21,663	42,088	52,543	63,866	0.36	21.55
Thailand	1,166,937	1,152,296	1,518,452	1,900,839	1,891,921	10.78	-0.47

MALAYSIA

1. Arrivals of non-resident tourists at national borders, by country of residence

	2002	2003	2004	2005	2006	Market share 06	% Change 06-05
Other countries of South-East Asia	8,889						
Australasia	**218,951**	**163,489**	**227,908**	**299,192**	**311,890**	**1.78**	**4.24**
Australia	193,794	144,507	204,053	265,346	277,125	1.58	4.44
New Zealand	25,157	18,982	23,855	33,846	34,765	0.20	2.72
Other East Asia and the Pacific	**35,223**	**35,572**	**38,318**	**39,966**	**43,577**	**0.25**	**9.04**
Other countries of Oceania	35,223	35,572	38,318	39,966	43,577	0.25	9.04
EUROPE	**636,972**	**456,351**	**540,306**	**618,188**	**673,118**	**3.84**	**8.89**
Central/Eastern Europe	**77,395**	**68,294**	**30,328**	**27,479**	**34,379**	**0.20**	**25.11**
Czech Republic				2,063	2,890	0.02	40.09
Poland				10,369	11,282	0.06	8.81
Other countries Central/East Europ	72,328	63,059	23,701	6,661	7,262	0.04	9.02
Commonwealth Independent State	5,067	5,235	6,627	8,386	12,945	0.07	54.36
Northern Europe	**324,203**	**193,909**	**276,646**	**323,234**	**349,195**	**1.99**	**8.03**
Denmark	17,297	13,434	11,884	11,681	12,773	0.07	9.35
Finland	12,908	11,041	11,308	13,172	19,918	0.11	51.21
Ireland	11,182	9,391	11,557	13,742	14,170	0.08	3.11
Norway	11,589	7,856	9,437	9,823	11,290	0.06	14.93
Sweden	29,044	23,560	25,960	32,408	36,280	0.21	11.95
United Kingdom	239,294	125,569	204,409	240,030	252,035	1.44	5.00
Other countries of Northern Europe	2,889	3,058	2,091	2,378	2,729	0.02	14.76
Southern Europe	**74,824**	**64,316**	**78,562**	**79,588**	**79,000**	**0.45**	**-0.74**
Italy	16,805	12,872	20,036	21,561	26,248	0.15	21.74
Portugal		6,221	24,388	25,107	23,422	0.13	-6.71
Spain	34,477	29,432	19,229	17,064	15,179	0.09	-11.05
Other countries Southern Europe	23,542	15,791	14,909	15,856	14,151	0.08	-10.75
Western Europe	**154,808**	**124,641**	**148,643**	**181,214**	**202,890**	**1.16**	**11.96**
Austria	7,543	6,599	8,643	11,121	11,550	0.07	3.86
Belgium	7,812	6,387	7,449	9,387	8,686	0.05	-7.47
France	27,434	23,845	32,562	40,473	49,378	0.28	22.00
Germany	54,645	41,145	53,783	59,344	66,171	0.38	11.50
Luxembourg	579	492	578	595	558		-6.22
Netherlands	39,303	28,822	28,112	40,493	46,065	0.26	13.76
Switzerland	15,614	14,475	15,584	17,700	18,326	0.10	3.54
Other countries of Western Europe	1,878	2,876	1,932	2,101	2,156	0.01	2.62
East Mediterranean Europe	**5,742**	**5,191**	**6,127**	**6,673**	**7,654**	**0.04**	**14.70**
Turkey	5,742	5,191	6,127	6,673	7,654	0.04	14.70
MIDDLE EAST	**126,239**	**78,324**	**124,331**	**145,448**	**173,750**	**0.99**	**19.46**
Middle East	**126,239**	**78,324**	**124,331**	**145,448**	**173,750**	**0.99**	**19.46**
Jordan	3,611	2,143	2,029	2,086	2,657	0.02	27.37
Kuwait	10,470	3,599	12,063	11,506	13,369	0.08	16.19
Lebanon	5,336	7,787	9,838	8,522	6,885	0.04	-19.21
Oman	8,634	5,703	7,983	9,228	11,905	0.07	29.01
Saudi Arabia	45,007	20,077	39,432	53,682	67,679	0.39	26.07
Syrian Arab Republic	21,109	16,776	8,367	5,613	5,772	0.03	2.83
United Arab Emirates	14,124	6,047	21,161	29,606	35,118	0.20	18.62
Egypt		3,299	4,408	4,888	5,682	0.03	16.24
Other countries of Middle East	17,948	12,893	19,050	20,317	24,683	0.14	21.49
SOUTH ASIA	**244,351**	**209,120**	**248,673**	**321,246**	**390,189**	**2.22**	**21.46**
South Asia	**244,351**	**209,120**	**248,673**	**321,246**	**390,189**	**2.22**	**21.46**
Bangladesh	17,450	21,005	21,230	29,540	27,580	0.16	-6.64

MALAYSIA

1. Arrivals of non-resident tourists at national borders, by country of residence

	2002	2003	2004	2005	2006	Market share 06	% Change 06-05
Sri Lanka	12,882	13,268	16,746	17,001	20,200	0.12	18.82
India	183,360	145,153	172,966	225,789	279,046	1.59	23.59
Iran, Islamic Republic of	9,414	10,412	11,236	12,309	18,753	0.11	52.35
Nepal		6,003	8,588	10,611	11,465	0.07	8.05
Pakistan	11,723	9,484	13,835	20,882	26,708	0.15	27.90
Other countries of South Asia	9,522	3,795	4,072	5,114	6,437	0.04	25.87
REGION NOT SPECIFIED	**397,127**	**355,319**	**398,227**	**257,075**	**364,433**	**2.08**	**41.76**
Not Specified	**397,127**	**355,319**	**398,227**	**257,075**	**364,433**	**2.08**	**41.76**
Other countries of the World	397,127	355,319	398,227	257,075	364,433	2.08	41.76

Source: World Tourism Organization (UNWTO)

MALAYSIA

3. Arrivals of non-resident tourists in hotels and similar establishments, by country of residence

	2002	2003	2004	2005	2006	Market share 06	% Change 06-05
TOTAL	15,615,497	13,239,227	20,009,306	21,448,190			
AFRICA	104,526	103,847	247,033	244,513			
Southern Africa	70,635	65,441	122,002	122,458			
South Africa	70,635	65,441	122,002	122,458			
Other Africa	33,891	38,406	125,031	122,055			
Other countries of Africa	33,891	38,406	125,031	122,055			
AMERICAS	574,832	480,022	721,751	783,300			
North America	497,890	420,687	551,288	662,216			
Canada	101,826	80,029	144,183	150,681			
United States	396,064	340,658	407,105	511,535			
Other Americas	76,942	59,335	170,463	121,084			
Other countries of the Americas	76,942	59,335	170,463	121,084			
EAST ASIA AND THE PACIFIC	10,180,318	8,668,586	12,012,694	12,333,736			
North-East Asia	4,513,080	3,268,111	5,079,503	5,046,637			
China	1,421,768	1,007,679	1,713,093	1,598,550			
Taiwan (Province of China)	713,402	479,765	1,005,641	889,659			
Hong Kong, China	739,686	576,062	802,243	863,221			
Japan	1,432,142	1,059,415	1,192,217	1,248,421			
Korea, Republic of	206,082	145,190	366,309	446,786			
South-East Asia	4,469,553	4,398,609	5,292,672	5,232,506			
Brunei Darussalam	247,137	231,530	263,445	265,339			
Indonesia	735,788	811,353	1,064,160	1,107,510			
Philippines	166,429	189,329	278,781	289,205			
Singapore	2,956,297	2,692,035	2,893,195	2,671,245			
Viet Nam	34,147	75,587	269,819	405,950			
Thailand	329,755	398,775	523,272	493,257			
Australasia	971,191	754,994	1,130,313	1,412,372			
Australia	844,400	660,302	1,008,152	1,253,950			
New Zealand	126,791	94,692	122,161	158,422			
Other East Asia and the Pacific	226,494	246,872	510,206	642,221			
Other countries of Asia	226,494	246,872	510,206	642,221			
EUROPE	3,186,049	2,701,960	3,937,121	4,223,480			
Central/Eastern Europe	44,161	48,415	137,039	116,282			
Commonwealth Independent State	44,161	48,415	137,039	116,282			
Northern Europe	1,659,536	1,449,465	1,892,266	1,912,716			
Denmark	60,355	47,500	83,117	93,494			
Finland	44,663	29,847	65,229	68,363			
Ireland	42,885	26,996	82,272	87,210			
Norway	39,502	49,569	76,494	76,645			
Sweden	108,659	92,239	226,500	230,494			
United Kingdom	1,363,472	1,203,314	1,358,654	1,356,510			
Southern Europe	131,234	116,188	244,024	250,969			
Italy	105,679	84,551	170,671	182,559			
Spain	25,555	31,637	73,353	68,410			
Western Europe	1,091,462	885,577	1,275,877	1,426,728			
Austria	104,601	84,262	78,458	99,453			
Belgium	62,890	37,977	58,852	73,802			

MALAYSIA

3. Arrivals of non-resident tourists in hotels and similar establishments, by country of residence

	2002	2003	2004	2005	2006	Market share 06	% Change 06-05
France	139,051	106,976	247,155	264,684			
Germany	357,656	303,290	382,890	392,364			
Luxembourg	8,380	8,640	36,007	36,916			
Netherlands	297,036	253,443	298,525	353,728			
Switzerland	121,848	90,989	173,990	205,781			
Other Europe	**259,656**	**202,315**	**387,915**	**516,785**			
Other countries of Europe	259,656	202,315	387,915	516,785			
MIDDLE EAST	**825,684**	**554,881**	**1,435,713**	**1,991,052**			
Middle East	**825,684**	**554,881**	**1,435,713**	**1,991,052**			
All countries of Middle East	825,684	554,881	1,435,713	1,991,052			
SOUTH ASIA	**448,417**	**518,427**	**969,831**	**1,070,829**			
South Asia	**448,417**	**518,427**	**969,831**	**1,070,829**			
Bangladesh	47,344	46,624	95,906	126,746			
Sri Lanka	23,463	33,809	50,042	68,455			
India	324,818	356,378	706,646	715,008			
Pakistan	52,792	81,616	117,237	160,620			
REGION NOT SPECIFIED	**295,671**	**211,504**	**685,163**	**801,280**			
Not Specified	**295,671**	**211,504**	**685,163**	**801,280**			
Other countries of the World	295,671	211,504	685,163	801,280			

Source: World Tourism Organization (UNWTO)

MALDIVES

1. Arrivals of non-resident tourists at national borders, by nationality

		2002	2003	2004	2005	2006	Market share 06	% Change 06-05
TOTAL	(*)	484,680	563,593	616,716	395,320	601,923	100.00	52.26
AFRICA		3,002	3,984	5,325	3,460	4,169	0.69	20.49
East Africa		418	442	846	443	238	0.04	-46.28
Comoros			1					
Ethiopia		20	4	2	16			
Eritrea		9	38	13	6	17		183.33
Djibouti				24	7	5		-28.57
Kenya		120	79	4	87	5		-94.25
Madagascar		7	4	5		5		
Malawi		10		1	7	30		328.57
Mauritius		18	48	234	91	49	0.01	-46.15
Mozambique		10	9	14	11	5		-54.55
Seychelles		125	146	397	155	53	0.01	-65.81
Somalia		5	10	3	1	1		
Zimbabwe		53	57	40	22	34	0.01	54.55
Uganda		6	23	71	9	12		33.33
United Republic of Tanzania		27	16	18	25	18		-28.00
Zambia		8	7	20	6	4		-33.33
Central Africa		13	24	28	21	20		-4.76
Angola		1	9	5	3	3		
Cameroon		7	10	12	14	15		7.14
Chad				2				
Congo		5	5	9	4	2		-50.00
North Africa		517	386	232	353	526	0.09	49.01
Algeria		200	70	85	66	115	0.02	74.24
Morocco		218	186	11	147	267	0.04	81.63
Sudan		19	57	41	43	37	0.01	-13.95
Tunisia		80	73	95	97	107	0.02	10.31
Southern Africa		1,934	2,954	3,895	2,415	3,008	0.50	24.55
Botswana		7	3	2				
Lesotho		3	2	4		2		
Namibia		9	17	24	16	5		-68.75
South Africa		1,914	2,929	3,846	2,392	2,973	0.49	24.29
Swaziland		1	3	19	7	28		300.00
West Africa		101	139	306	198	208	0.03	5.05
Cape Verde		1	1	1		1		
Gambia		1	1	6	4	3		-25.00
Ghana		5	15	2	13	21		61.54
Guinea				3				
Cote D'Ivoire		8	28	97	11	11		
Liberia		16	17	1	7	19		171.43
Mali		4	3	36	1			
Mauritania		26	27	125	103	87	0.01	-15.53
Nigeria		19	26	22	37	38	0.01	2.70
Senegal		4	18	9	11	5		-54.55
Sierra Leone		17	2	2	5	14		180.00
Togo			1		1	2		100.00
Burkina Faso				2	5	7		40.00
Other Africa		19	39	18	30	169	0.03	463.33
Other countries of Africa		19	39	18	30	169	0.03	463.33
AMERICAS		7,487	7,660	9,385	7,238	10,813	1.80	49.39
Caribbean		66	86	65	80	98	0.02	22.50

MALDIVES

1. Arrivals of non-resident tourists at national borders, by nationality

	2002	2003	2004	2005	2006	Market share 06	% Change 06-05
Antigua and Barbuda			8				
Bahamas	6	4	2	6	2		-66.67
Barbados	2	3	3	3	2		-33.33
Cuba	28	39	21	20	39	0.01	95.00
Dominica	10	10	8	4	7		75.00
Grenada		1	2	8			
Haiti	1	2		4			
Jamaica	9	8	5	9	15		66.67
Saint Lucia	1	1		2	2		
Trinidad and Tobago	9	18	16	24	31	0.01	29.17
Central America	**47**	**33**	**70**	**53**	**58**	**0.01**	**9.43**
Belize	27	6	13	11	4		-63.64
Costa Rica	10	7	10	9	12		33.33
El Salvador	4	8	5	5	9		80.00
Guatemala	3	7	21	25	26		4.00
Honduras	1	1	14		3		
Nicaragua	1	4	1	2	1		-50.00
Panama	1		6	1	3		200.00
North America	**6,706**	**6,783**	**8,310**	**6,406**	**9,641**	**1.60**	**50.50**
Canada	1,569	1,649	2,069	1,426	2,196	0.36	54.00
Mexico	107	129	242	147	295	0.05	100.68
United States	5,030	5,005	5,999	4,833	7,150	1.19	47.94
South America	**665**	**756**	**933**	**696**	**1,010**	**0.17**	**45.11**
Argentina	93	113	148	78	116	0.02	48.72
Bolivia	6	3	25	2	17		750.00
Brazil	381	447	533	429	564	0.09	31.47
Chile	34	32	49	20	45	0.01	125.00
Colombia	59	62	50	54	97	0.02	79.63
Ecuador	14	7	11	9	24		166.67
Paraguay	7		1	2	4		100.00
Peru	21	43	65	39	66	0.01	69.23
Suriname	1		2		1		
Uruguay	8	11	4	36	14		-61.11
Venezuela	41	38	45	27	62	0.01	129.63
Other Americas	**3**	**2**	**7**	**3**	**6**		**100.00**
Other countries of the Americas	3	2	7	3	6		100.00
EAST ASIA AND THE PACIFIC	**77,289**	**83,640**	**99,735**	**55,985**	**102,277**	**16.99**	**82.69**
North-East Asia	**63,803**	**65,542**	**79,974**	**42,150**	**83,402**	**13.86**	**97.87**
China	12,092	15,021	20,599	11,609	26,396	4.39	127.38
Taiwan (Province of China)	17		1,842	685	1,281	0.21	87.01
Hong Kong, China	291		917	38	28		-26.32
Japan	43,705	42,081	46,939	23,269	39,528	6.57	69.87
Korea, Republic of	7,696	8,417	9,672	6,543	16,157	2.68	146.94
Mongolia	2	23	5	6	12		100.00
South-East Asia	**7,709**	**11,048**	**10,463**	**7,970**	**10,895**	**1.81**	**36.70**
Brunei Darussalam	26	87	9	2	36	0.01	1,700.00
Myanmar	21	59	52	71	51	0.01	-28.17
Cambodia	3	4	3	19	31	0.01	63.16
Indonesia	460	566	622	520	625	0.10	20.19
Lao People's Democratic Republic	1	2	1	6	10		66.67
Malaysia	2,240	2,251	2,908	2,366	2,915	0.48	23.20
Philippines	405	376	499	565	666	0.11	17.88
Singapore	2,520	4,653	3,016	3,258	4,255	0.71	30.60

MALDIVES

1. Arrivals of non-resident tourists at national borders, by nationality

	2002	2003	2004	2005	2006	Market share 06	% Change 06-05
Viet Nam	31	41	64	49	55	0.01	12.24
Thailand	2,002	3,009	3,289	1,114	2,251	0.37	102.06
Australasia	**5,696**	**6,864**	**9,209**	**5,784**	**7,898**	**1.31**	**36.55**
Australia	5,063	6,110	8,216	5,087	6,892	1.14	35.48
New Zealand	633	754	993	697	1,006	0.17	44.33
Melanesia	**9**	**11**	**13**	**16**	**9**		**-43.75**
Fiji	5	11	10	15	9		-40.00
Vanuatu			3	1			
Norfolk Island	4						
Micronesia	**6**	**4**	**2**	**5**	**1**		**-80.00**
Kiribati	3	2		4			
Micronesia (Federated States of)				1			
Marshall Islands	3	2	2		1		
Polynesia	**2**	**7**	**5**	**6**	**1**		**-83.33**
Tonga		2			1		
Samoa	2	5	5	6			
Other East Asia and the Pacific	**64**	**164**	**69**	**54**	**71**	**0.01**	**31.48**
Other countries of Asia			7	1	1		
Other countries of Oceania	64	164	62	53	70	0.01	32.08
EUROPE	**373,428**	**443,093**	**475,707**	**306,856**	**457,535**	**76.01**	**49.10**
Central/Eastern Europe	**14,259**	**21,935**	**30,601**	**21,144**	**35,445**	**5.89**	**67.64**
Azerbaijan	23	39	33	28	69	0.01	146.43
Armenia	13	12	18	27	32	0.01	18.52
Bulgaria	190	342	332	232	451	0.07	94.40
Czech Republic	1,493	1,936	2,433	1,433	2,295	0.38	60.15
Estonia	80	83	107	111	314	0.05	182.88
Georgia	26	111	17	13	49	0.01	276.92
Hungary	1,589	2,543	3,568	1,124	2,661	0.44	136.74
Kazakhstan	99	362	318	265	595	0.10	124.53
Kyrgyzstan	3	23	20	13	23		76.92
Latvia	147	172	254	146	585	0.10	300.68
Lithuania	144	164	148	140	275	0.05	96.43
Republic of Moldova	39	70	104	64	130	0.02	103.13
Poland	1,116	982	1,366	1,019	1,844	0.31	80.96
Romania	256	363	470	306	661	0.11	116.01
Russian Federation	7,550	12,108	18,075	14,582	21,955	3.65	50.56
Slovakia	707	1,552	1,936	501	944	0.16	88.42
Tajikistan	1		1	12	19		58.33
Turkmenistan	37	37	14	14	25		78.57
Ukraine	720	995	1,316	1,060	2,427	0.40	128.96
Uzbekistan	26	41	71	54	91	0.02	68.52
Northern Europe	**85,560**	**100,310**	**122,108**	**92,680**	**116,123**	**19.29**	**25.29**
Denmark	938	1,073	1,256	1,095	1,499	0.25	36.89
Finland	388	614	788	357	518	0.09	45.10
Iceland	33	23	58	53	50	0.01	-5.66
Ireland	1,303	1,684	2,202	1,452	2,648	0.44	82.37
Norway	772	987	1,331	1,141	1,613	0.27	41.37
Sweden	1,749	1,940	2,482	1,318	1,800	0.30	36.57
United Kingdom	80,377	93,989	113,991	87,264	107,995	17.94	23.76
Southern Europe	**126,647**	**153,503**	**146,688**	**78,607**	**134,274**	**22.31**	**70.82**
Albania	29	44	54	38	63	0.01	65.79
Andorra	18	6	30	1	18		1,700.00

MALDIVES

1. Arrivals of non-resident tourists at national borders, by nationality

	2002	2003	2004	2005	2006	Market share 06	% Change 06-05
Bosnia and Herzegovina	78	96	107	78	100	0.02	28.21
Croatia	316	304	365	291	458	0.08	57.39
Greece	2,446	2,287	2,949	1,703	3,584	0.60	110.45
Italy	114,955	140,304	131,044	70,115	118,758	19.73	69.38
Malta	157	99	213	63	87	0.01	38.10
Portugal	2,785	3,379	3,608	2,238	3,655	0.61	63.32
Slovenia	703	661	755	569	796	0.13	39.89
Spain	5,160	6,323	7,561	3,510	6,678	1.11	90.26
TFYR of Macedonia					69	0.01	
Serbia and Montenegro			2	1	8		700.00
Western Europe	**144,363**	**163,356**	**171,805**	**112,257**	**167,471**	**27.82**	**49.19**
Austria	10,480	12,391	13,059	9,358	14,100	2.34	50.67
Belgium	2,606	2,795	3,085	1,595	3,990	0.66	150.16
France	31,228	41,055	46,156	21,640	43,627	7.25	101.60
Germany	63,212	70,762	72,967	55,782	70,830	11.77	26.98
Liechtenstein	91	88	130	79	143	0.02	81.01
Luxembourg	344	404	458	307	430	0.07	40.07
Monaco	33	27	59	24	50	0.01	108.33
Netherlands	4,662	5,047	6,639	4,151	8,050	1.34	93.93
Switzerland	31,707	30,787	29,252	19,321	26,251	4.36	35.87
East Mediterranean Europe	**1,986**	**3,233**	**3,545**	**1,507**	**3,074**	**0.51**	**103.98**
Cyprus	274	243	188	71	184	0.03	159.15
Israel	391	548	747	567	846	0.14	49.21
Turkey	1,321	2,442	2,610	869	2,044	0.34	135.21
Other Europe	**613**	**756**	**960**	**661**	**1,148**	**0.19**	**73.68**
Other countries of Europe	613	756	960	661	1,148	0.19	73.68
MIDDLE EAST	**2,941**	**3,636**	**4,517**	**2,404**	**4,372**	**0.73**	**81.86**
Middle East	**2,941**	**3,636**	**4,517**	**2,404**	**4,372**	**0.73**	**81.86**
Bahrain	80	101	132	112	227	0.04	102.68
Palestine	18	27	46	18	36	0.01	100.00
Iraq	22	23	32	47	45	0.01	-4.26
Jordan	202	204	347	237	245	0.04	3.38
Kuwait	492	533	573	290	668	0.11	130.34
Lebanon	314	342	438	238	402	0.07	68.91
Libyan Arab Jamahiriya	33	60	36	41	46	0.01	12.20
Oman	63	115	118	56	86	0.01	53.57
Qatar	75	87	68	75	172	0.03	129.33
Saudi Arabia	975	1,296	1,872	691	1,530	0.25	121.42
Syrian Arab Republic	74	105	86	66	76	0.01	15.15
United Arab Emirates	348	360	406	230	492	0.08	113.91
Egypt	221	358	337	291	321	0.05	10.31
Yemen	24	25	26	12	26		116.67
SOUTH ASIA	**20,533**	**21,580**	**22,047**	**19,377**	**22,757**	**3.78**	**17.44**
South Asia	**20,533**	**21,580**	**22,047**	**19,377**	**22,757**	**3.78**	**17.44**
Afghanistan	5	7	12	16	20		25.00
Bangladesh	241	313	667	643	1,050	0.17	63.30
Bhutan	24	41	42	34	22		-35.29
Sri Lanka	6,909	7,296	8,351	7,165	7,954	1.32	11.01
India	11,377	11,502	10,999	10,260	12,071	2.01	17.65
Iran, Islamic Republic of	556	345	212	141	294	0.05	108.51
Nepal	92	134	235	178	227	0.04	27.53
Pakistan	1,329	1,942	1,529	940	1,119	0.19	19.04

Source: World Tourism Organization (UNWTO)

MALI

3. Arrivals of non-resident tourists in hotels and similar establishments, by nationality

	2002	2003	2004	2005	2006	Market share 06	% Change 06-05
TOTAL	95,851	110,365	112,654	142,814	152,660	100.00	6.89
AFRICA	21,165	27,816	29,256	35,985	38,892	25.48	8.08
West Africa	18,125	19,000	21,993	23,972	18,902	12.38	-21.15
All countries of West Africa	18,125	19,000	21,993	23,972	18,902	12.38	-21.15
Other Africa	3,040	8,816	7,263	12,013	19,990	13.09	66.40
Other countries of Africa	3,040	8,816	7,263	12,013	19,990	13.09	66.40
AMERICAS	9,232	9,393	12,494	13,287	18,507	12.12	39.29
North America	9,232	9,393	12,494	13,287	18,507	12.12	39.29
Canada	3,217	3,280	3,543	3,646	4,285	2.81	17.53
United States	6,015	6,113	8,951	9,641	14,222	9.32	47.52
EAST ASIA AND THE PACIFIC	1,189	1,200	3,117	2,090	1,636	1.07	-21.72
North-East Asia	1,189	1,200	3,117	2,090	1,636	1.07	-21.72
Japan	1,189	1,200	3,117	2,090	1,636	1.07	-21.72
EUROPE	55,763	62,744	64,252	80,968	86,443	56.62	6.76
Central/Eastern Europe	1,572	728	1,842	2,410	1,435	0.94	-40.46
Ussr (Former)	681	728	1,842	524	539	0.35	2.86
Other countries Central/East Europ	891			1,886	896	0.59	-52.49
Northern Europe	4,071	4,480	1,360	7,126	7,021	4.60	-1.47
United Kingdom	1,395	1,752	560	5,180	5,006	3.28	-3.36
Scandinavia	2,676	2,728	800	1,946	2,015	1.32	3.55
Southern Europe	14,235	16,262	10,409	14,135	16,402	10.74	16.04
Italy	10,676	11,570	6,087	7,066	8,615	5.64	21.92
Spain	3,559	4,692	4,322	7,069	7,787	5.10	10.16
Western Europe	35,885	41,274	50,641	57,297	61,585	40.34	7.48
Austria	201	636	1,167	2,175	977	0.64	-55.08
France	22,325	27,047	37,971	37,851	42,661	27.95	12.71
Germany	3,103	3,200	3,676	5,885	6,623	4.34	12.54
Switzerland	1,285	1,345	1,236	2,384	2,066	1.35	-13.34
Benelux	8,971	9,046	6,591	9,002	9,258	6.06	2.84
MIDDLE EAST	2,567	2,712	1,524	1,064	1,128	0.74	6.02
Middle East	2,567	2,712	1,524	1,064	1,128	0.74	6.02
All countries of Middle East	2,567	2,712	1,524	1,064	1,128	0.74	6.02
REGION NOT SPECIFIED	5,935	6,500	2,011	9,420	6,054	3.97	-35.73
Not Specified	5,935	6,500	2,011	9,420	6,054	3.97	-35.73
Other countries of the World	5,935	6,500	2,011	9,420	6,054	3.97	-35.73

Source: World Tourism Organization (UNWTO)

MALI

5. Overnight stays of non-resident tourists in hotels and similar establishments, by nationality

	2002	2003	2004	2005	2006	Market share 06	% Change 06-05
TOTAL	193,167	228,663	291,447	310,202	321,549	100.00	3.66
AFRICA	58,178	74,291	81,352	103,149	82,762	25.74	-19.76
West Africa	52,360	43,830	60,658	75,701	51,594	16.05	-31.85
All countries of West Africa	52,360	43,830	60,658	75,701	51,594	16.05	-31.85
Other Africa	5,818	30,461	20,694	27,448	31,168	9.69	13.55
Other countries of Africa	5,818	30,461	20,694	27,448	31,168	9.69	13.55
AMERICAS	13,575	22,213	73,152	36,722	57,662	17.93	57.02
North America	13,575	22,213	73,152	36,722	57,662	17.93	57.02
Canada	5,430	8,094	9,376	9,675	10,278	3.20	6.23
United States	8,145	14,119	63,776	27,047	47,384	14.74	75.19
EAST ASIA AND THE PACIFIC	1,645	2,421	5,052	3,294	2,382	0.74	-27.69
North-East Asia	1,645	2,421	5,052	3,294	2,382	0.74	-27.69
Japan	1,645	2,421	5,052	3,294	2,382	0.74	-27.69
EUROPE	108,600	114,300	112,158	147,278	156,727	48.74	6.42
Central/Eastern Europe	2,715	2,650	6,996	4,803	2,735	0.85	-43.06
Ussr (Former)	1,005	1,580	3,258	855	1,034	0.32	20.94
Other countries Central/East Europ	1,710	1,070	3,738	3,948	1,701	0.53	-56.91
Northern Europe	6,516	7,767	3,188	14,256	17,582	5.47	23.33
United Kingdom	2,477	2,480	1,030	8,891	11,118	3.46	25.05
Scandinavia	4,039	5,287	2,158	5,365	6,464	2.01	20.48
Southern Europe	20,634	23,912	16,901	20,620	27,521	8.56	33.47
Italy	12,380	15,525	10,519	10,209	14,761	4.59	44.59
Spain	8,254	8,387	6,382	10,411	12,760	3.97	22.56
Western Europe	78,735	79,971	85,073	107,599	108,889	33.86	1.20
Austria	362	1,048	1,690	3,812	1,873	0.58	-50.87
France	56,000	54,335	63,776	71,953	74,278	23.10	3.23
Germany	5,604	6,406	5,990	10,082	12,353	3.84	22.53
Switzerland	1,810	2,736	2,823	6,286	4,573	1.42	-27.25
Benelux	14,959	15,446	10,794	15,466	15,812	4.92	2.24
MIDDLE EAST	3,412	4,322	2,605	2,342	2,787	0.87	19.00
Middle East	3,412	4,322	2,605	2,342	2,787	0.87	19.00
All countries of Middle East	3,412	4,322	2,605	2,342	2,787	0.87	19.00
REGION NOT SPECIFIED	7,757	11,116	17,128	17,417	19,229	5.98	10.40
Not Specified	7,757	11,116	17,128	17,417	19,229	5.98	10.40
Other countries of the World	7,757	11,116	17,128	17,417	19,229	5.98	10.40

Source: World Tourism Organization (UNWTO)

MALTA

1. Arrivals of non-resident tourists at national borders, by nationality

		2002	2003	2004	2005	2006	Market share 06	% Change 06-05
TOTAL	(*)	1,133,814	1,126,601	1,156,028	1,170,610	1,124,233	100.00	-3.96
AFRICA		9,086						
East Africa		460						
Burundi		4						
Ethiopia		6						
Djibouti		32						
Kenya		124						
Madagascar		6						
Malawi		6						
Mauritius		35						
Mozambique		4						
Rwanda		2						
Seychelles		26						
Somalia		10						
Zimbabwe		73						
Uganda		52						
United Republic of Tanzania		44						
Zambia		36						
Central Africa		66						
Angola		12						
Cameroon		28						
Congo		20						
Equatorial Guinea		4						
Gabon		2						
North Africa		7,047						
Algeria		791						
Morocco		1,210						
Sudan		86						
Tunisia		4,960						
Southern Africa		1,004						
Botswana		4						
Namibia		8						
South Africa		988						
Swaziland		4						
West Africa		509						
Cape Verde		4						
Benin		8						
Gambia		24						
Ghana		100						
Guinea		4						
Cote D'Ivoire		36						
Liberia		4						
Mali		6						
Mauritania		38						
Nigeria		227						
Senegal		18						
Sierra Leone		32						
Togo		8						
AMERICAS		27,005	20,657	18,720	18,136	16,970	1.51	-6.43
North America		26,738	20,657	18,720	18,136	16,970	1.51	-6.43
Canada		6,658						
United States		20,080	20,657	18,720	18,136	16,970	1.51	-6.43

MALTA

1. Arrivals of non-resident tourists at national borders, by nationality

	2002	2003	2004	2005	2006	Market share 06	% Change 06-05
South America	267						
Argentina	267						
EAST ASIA AND THE PACIFIC	25,020						
North-East Asia	14,327						
China	1,446						
Japan	12,881						
Australasia	10,693						
Australia	9,542						
New Zealand	1,151						
EUROPE	1,039,904	939,793	982,623	989,283	939,798	83.59	-5.00
Central/Eastern Europe	54,542	21,096	19,697	16,647	21,770	1.94	30.77
Azerbaijan	64						
Armenia	180						
Bulgaria	2,113						
Czech Republic	5,816						
Estonia	211						
Georgia	112						
Hungary	8,245						
Kazakhstan	200						
Latvia	272						
Lithuania	367						
Republic of Moldova	186						
Poland	6,856						
Romania	1,421						
Russian Federation	22,919	21,096	19,697	16,647	21,770	1.94	30.77
Slovakia	1,820						
Tajikistan	3						
Ukraine	3,617						
Uzbekistan	140						
Northern Europe	509,377	507,267	521,734	546,907	494,417	43.98	-9.60
Denmark	17,427	17,747	20,039	22,665	23,947	2.13	5.66
Faeroe Islands	50						
Finland	4,306	6,113	6,759				
Iceland	419						
Ireland	21,316						
Norway	9,786	11,825	16,351	15,515	15,167	1.35	-2.24
Sweden	11,738	12,017	25,705	26,112	23,964	2.13	-8.23
United Kingdom	444,335	459,565	452,880	482,615	431,339	38.37	-10.62
Southern Europe	131,901	94,175	102,169	92,406	112,548	10.01	21.80
Albania	355						
Andorra	64						
Bosnia and Herzegovina	270						
Croatia	1,061						
Greece	6,982						
Italy	100,875	94,175	102,169	92,406	112,548	10.01	21.80
Portugal	3,964						
San Marino	78						
Slovenia	2,473						
Spain	12,883						
TFYR of Macedonia	323						
Serbia and Montenegro	2,573						
Western Europe	336,512	317,255	339,023	333,323	311,063	27.67	-6.68

MALTA

1. Arrivals of non-resident tourists at national borders, by nationality

	2002	2003	2004	2005	2006	Market share 06	% Change 06-05
Austria	24,448	28,416	24,030	26,393	23,540	2.09	-10.81
Belgium	24,018	23,724	31,434	28,730	29,077	2.59	1.21
France	80,101	76,384	87,129	82,607	73,400	6.53	-11.15
Germany	142,106	125,811	135,138	138,217	125,810	11.19	-8.98
Liechtenstein	74						
Luxembourg	977						
Monaco	18						
Netherlands	44,395	40,810	38,446	37,102	37,833	3.37	1.97
Switzerland	20,375	22,110	22,846	20,274	21,403	1.90	5.57
East Mediterranean Europe	**7,572**						
Cyprus	2,524						
Israel	1,310						
Turkey	3,738						
MIDDLE EAST	**25,484**	**20,218**	**12,831**	**10,662**	**9,198**	**0.82**	**-13.73**
Middle East	**25,484**	**20,218**	**12,831**	**10,662**	**9,198**	**0.82**	**-13.73**
Lebanon	329						
Libyan Arab Jamahiriya	22,783	20,218	12,831	10,662	9,198	0.82	-13.73
Oman	8						
Qatar	4						
Saudi Arabia	116						
Syrian Arab Republic	260						
United Arab Emirates	52						
Egypt	1,932						
SOUTH ASIA	**1,549**						
South Asia	**1,549**						
Afghanistan	9						
Bangladesh	55						
India	1,048						
Iran, Islamic Republic of	138						
Maldives	42						
Nepal	6						
Pakistan	251						
REGION NOT SPECIFIED	**5,766**	**145,933**	**141,854**	**152,529**	**158,267**	**14.08**	**3.76**
Not Specified	**5,766**	**145,933**	**141,854**	**152,529**	**158,267**	**14.08**	**3.76**
Other countries of the World	5,766	145,933	141,854	152,529	158,267	14.08	3.76

Source: World Tourism Organization (UNWTO)

MALTA

3. Arrivals of non-resident tourists in hotels and similar establishments, by nationality

	2002	2003	2004	2005	2006	Market share 06	% Change 06-05
TOTAL (*)	796,508	862,893	903,767	905,917	867,978	100.00	-4.19
AMERICAS	15,899	10,232	13,413	12,045	11,741	1.35	-2.52
North America	15,899	10,232	13,413	12,045	11,741	1.35	-2.52
Canada	2,944						
United States	12,955	10,232	13,413	12,045	11,741	1.35	-2.52
EUROPE	692,068	733,930	768,456	770,839	729,523	84.05	-5.36
Central/Eastern Europe		13,360	14,273	13,132	16,723	1.93	27.35
Russian Federation		13,360	14,273	13,132	16,723	1.93	27.35
Northern Europe	368,747	407,056	411,469	422,785	383,173	44.15	-9.37
Denmark	15,480	8,385	8,657	9,462	12,594	1.45	33.10
Ireland	16,750						
Norway	6,896	9,249	14,457	12,450	13,187	1.52	5.92
Sweden	7,136	8,389	21,758	21,163	20,068	2.31	-5.17
United Kingdom	322,485	381,033	366,597	379,710	337,324	38.86	-11.16
Southern Europe	72,703	59,880	66,691	61,420	76,724	8.84	24.92
Italy	59,354	59,880	66,691	61,420	76,724	8.84	24.92
Portugal	3,357						
Spain	9,992						
Western Europe	247,215	253,634	276,023	273,502	252,903	29.14	-7.53
Austria	15,395	19,373	18,168	20,130	16,408	1.89	-18.49
Belgium	19,574	23,577	28,109	25,734	25,936	2.99	0.78
France	62,256	60,044	70,507	66,506	61,148	7.04	-8.06
Germany	102,219	100,573	109,036	114,798	101,799	11.73	-11.32
Netherlands	32,942	32,762	32,124	30,974	31,616	3.64	2.07
Switzerland	14,829	17,305	18,079	15,360	15,996	1.84	4.14
East Mediterranean Europe	3,403						
Israel	970						
Turkey	2,433						
MIDDLE EAST	11,168	13,678	9,427	7,894	6,590	0.76	-16.52
Middle East	11,168	13,678	9,427	7,894	6,590	0.76	-16.52
Libyan Arab Jamahiriya	11,168	13,678	9,427	7,894	6,590	0.76	-16.52
REGION NOT SPECIFIED	77,373	105,053	112,471	115,139	120,124	13.84	4.33
Not Specified	77,373	105,053	112,471	115,139	120,124	13.84	4.33
Other countries of the World	77,373	105,053	112,471	115,139	120,124	13.84	4.33

Source: World Tourism Organization (UNWTO)

MALTA

4. Arrivals of non-resident tourists in all types of accommodation establishments, by nationality

		2002	2003	2004	2005	2006	Market share 06	% Change 06-05
TOTAL	(*)	1,133,814	1,089,089	1,127,407	1,150,769	1,104,269	100.00	-4.04
AMERICAS		26,738	13,896	17,001	16,820	16,321	1.48	-2.97
North America		26,738	13,896	17,001	16,820	16,321	1.48	-2.97
Canada		6,658						
United States		20,080	13,896	17,001	16,820	16,321	1.48	-2.97
EAST ASIA AND THE PACIFIC		10,693						
Australasia		10,693						
Australia		9,542						
New Zealand		1,151						
EUROPE		931,134	922,203	951,317	972,976	921,875	83.48	-5.25
Central/Eastern Europe			16,601	19,242	16,461	21,770	1.97	32.25
Russian Federation			16,601	19,242	16,461	21,770	1.97	32.25
Northern Europe		494,816	513,267	513,973	546,224	494,055	44.74	-9.55
Denmark		17,427	19,909	20,039	22,665	23,946	2.17	5.65
Ireland		21,316						
Norway			11,027	16,309	15,479	15,167	1.37	-2.02
Sweden		11,738	10,433	25,628	26,112	23,930	2.17	-8.36
United Kingdom		444,335	471,898	451,997	481,968	431,012	39.03	-10.57
Southern Europe		100,875	78,366	80,991	78,392	96,055	8.70	22.53
Italy		100,875	78,366	80,991	78,392	96,055	8.70	22.53
Western Europe		335,443	313,969	337,111	331,899	309,995	28.07	-6.60
Austria		24,448	24,423	23,928	26,242	23,362	2.12	-10.97
Belgium		24,018	26,268	31,245	28,730	29,001	2.63	0.94
France		80,101	77,029	86,061	81,779	73,069	6.62	-10.65
Germany		142,106	124,773	134,758	138,127	125,594	11.37	-9.07
Netherlands		44,395	39,807	38,341	36,747	37,565	3.40	2.23
Switzerland		20,375	21,669	22,778	20,274	21,404	1.94	5.57
MIDDLE EAST		22,783	17,455	12,831	10,662	9,198	0.83	-13.73
Middle East		22,783	17,455	12,831	10,662	9,198	0.83	-13.73
Libyan Arab Jamahiriya		22,783	17,455	12,831	10,662	9,198	0.83	-13.73
REGION NOT SPECIFIED		142,466	135,535	146,258	150,311	156,875	14.21	4.37
Not Specified		142,466	135,535	146,258	150,311	156,875	14.21	4.37
Other countries of the World		142,466	135,535	146,258	150,311	156,875	14.21	4.37

Source: World Tourism Organization (UNWTO)

MALTA

5. Overnight stays of non-resident tourists in hotels and similar establishments, by nationality

		2002	2003	2004	2005	2006	Market share 06	% Change 06-05
TOTAL	(*)	7,020,619	7,711,720	7,724,811	7,602,598	7,377,050	100.00	-2.97
AFRICA		22,436						
North Africa		22,436						
Tunisia		22,436						
AMERICAS		127,275	71,091	99,486	86,829	92,027	1.25	5.99
North America		127,275	71,091	99,486	86,829	92,027	1.25	5.99
Canada		25,417						
United States		101,858	71,091	99,486	86,829	92,027	1.25	5.99
EAST ASIA AND THE PACIFIC		88,299						
North-East Asia		63,512						
Japan		63,512						
Australasia		24,787						
Australia		24,787						
EUROPE		6,585,137	6,725,938	6,668,596	6,565,452	6,293,670	85.31	-4.14
Central/Eastern Europe		319,468	139,072	148,747	139,772	185,285	2.51	32.56
Czech Republic		28,031						
Hungary		47,317						
Poland		29,118						
Russian Federation			139,072	148,747	139,772	185,285	2.51	32.56
Other countries Central/East Europ		215,002						
Northern Europe		3,720,930	4,160,919	3,966,685	3,905,002	3,585,646	48.61	-8.18
Denmark		117,415	66,315	67,084	72,261	99,752	1.35	38.04
Finland		25,778						
Ireland		165,422						
Norway		66,249	81,034	121,465	108,934	114,361	1.55	4.98
Sweden		60,451	67,511	166,952	169,869	160,683	2.18	-5.41
United Kingdom		3,285,615	3,946,059	3,611,184	3,553,938	3,210,850	43.52	-9.65
Southern Europe		516,645	408,465	411,441	406,535	517,399	7.01	27.27
Greece		24,535						
Italy		409,092	408,465	411,441	406,535	517,399	7.01	27.27
Portugal		20,493						
Spain		62,525						
Western Europe		2,007,461	2,017,482	2,141,723	2,114,143	2,005,340	27.18	-5.15
Austria		106,463	141,050	132,408	145,520	114,114	1.55	-21.58
Belgium		167,384	196,461	215,188	195,784	200,815	2.72	2.57
France		445,511	425,103	486,581	477,980	467,117	6.33	-2.27
Germany		900,404	846,340	896,971	917,294	846,932	11.48	-7.67
Netherlands		272,462	278,173	274,732	246,628	248,143	3.36	0.61
Switzerland		115,237	130,355	135,843	130,937	128,219	1.74	-2.08
East Mediterranean Europe		20,633						
Israel		5,999						
Turkey		14,634						
MIDDLE EAST		79,348	82,640	59,776	63,120	51,332	0.70	-18.68
Middle East		79,348	82,640	59,776	63,120	51,332	0.70	-18.68
Libyan Arab Jamahiriya		79,348	82,640	59,776	63,120	51,332	0.70	-18.68
REGION NOT SPECIFIED		118,124	832,051	896,953	887,197	940,021	12.74	5.95
		118,124	832,051	896,953	887,197	940,021	12.74	5.95

MALTA

5. Overnight stays of non-resident tourists in hotels and similar establishments, by nationality

	2002	2003	2004	2005	2006	Market share 06	% Change 06-05
Not Specified							
Other countries of the World	118,124	832,051	896,953	887,197	940,021	12.74	5.95

Source: World Tourism Organization (UNWTO)

MALTA

6. Overnight stays of non-resident tourists in all types of accommodation establishments, by nationality

		2002	2003	2004	2005	2006	Market share 06	% Change 06-05
TOTAL	(*)	10,599,206	11,115,203	10,973,396	10,933,169	10,502,988	100.00	-3.93
AMERICAS		274,690	172,611	168,217	143,584	159,543	1.52	11.11
North America		274,690	172,611	168,217	143,584	159,543	1.52	11.11
Canada		79,279						
United States		195,411	172,611	168,217	143,584	159,543	1.52	11.11
EAST ASIA AND THE PACIFIC		154,269						
Australasia		154,269						
Australia		154,269						
EUROPE		8,715,429	9,177,861	8,894,199	9,011,911	8,614,769	82.02	-4.41
Central/Eastern Europe			201,463	259,691	196,311	329,273	3.14	67.73
Russian Federation			201,463	259,691	196,311	329,273	3.14	67.73
Northern Europe		5,049,974	5,568,920	5,139,991	5,353,688	4,815,087	45.84	-10.06
Denmark		130,173	170,311	166,142	188,682	203,759	1.94	7.99
Ireland		204,650						
Norway			110,720	141,979	149,327	147,379	1.40	-1.30
Sweden		115,072	123,021	220,946	227,624	222,881	2.12	-2.08
United Kingdom		4,600,079	5,164,868	4,610,924	4,788,055	4,241,068	40.38	-11.42
Southern Europe		739,117	627,109	574,993	601,710	747,091	7.11	24.16
Italy		739,117	627,109	574,993	601,710	747,091	7.11	24.16
Western Europe		2,926,338	2,780,369	2,919,524	2,860,202	2,723,318	25.93	-4.79
Austria		188,663	198,408	195,366	198,907	180,796	1.72	-9.11
Belgium		211,708	224,381	245,508	228,501	242,102	2.31	5.95
France		629,473	624,119	669,375	672,102	621,359	5.92	-7.55
Germany		1,323,534	1,182,857	1,243,800	1,234,389	1,164,706	11.09	-5.65
Netherlands		379,662	357,293	335,869	311,150	312,053	2.97	0.29
Switzerland		193,298	193,311	229,606	215,153	202,302	1.93	-5.97
MIDDLE EAST		177,002	144,391	132,174	102,760	82,999	0.79	-19.23
Middle East		177,002	144,391	132,174	102,760	82,999	0.79	-19.23
Libyan Arab Jamahiriya		177,002	144,391	132,174	102,760	82,999	0.79	-19.23
REGION NOT SPECIFIED		1,277,816	1,620,340	1,778,806	1,674,914	1,645,677	15.67	-1.75
Not Specified		1,277,816	1,620,340	1,778,806	1,674,914	1,645,677	15.67	-1.75
Other countries of the World		1,277,816	1,620,340	1,778,806	1,674,914	1,645,677	15.67	-1.75

Source: World Tourism Organization (UNWTO)

MARSHALL ISLANDS

1. Arrivals of non-resident tourists at national borders, by nationality

	2002	2003	2004	2005	2006	Market share 06	% Change 06-05
TOTAL (*)	6,002	7,195	9,007	9,173	5,780	100.00	-36.99
AMERICAS	2,127	2,281	3,388	2,554	1,849	31.99	-27.60
North America	2,124	2,273	3,335	2,526	1,844	31.90	-27.00
Canada	59	80	132	110	76	1.31	-30.91
United States	2,065	2,193	3,203	2,416	1,768	30.59	-26.82
Other Americas	3	8	53	28	5	0.09	-82.14
Other countries of the Americas	3	8	53	28	5	0.09	-82.14
EAST ASIA AND THE PACIFIC	3,569	4,518	5,037	6,048	3,604	62.35	-40.41
North-East Asia	1,654	1,431	1,604	2,264	1,379	23.86	-39.09
China	189	96	102	142	69	1.19	-51.41
Taiwan (Province of China)	402	224	352	476	255	4.41	-46.43
Japan	892	1,024	1,058	1,565	957	16.56	-38.85
Korea, Republic of	171	87	92	81	98	1.70	20.99
South-East Asia	258	258	582	532	259	4.48	-51.32
Philippines	258	258	582	532	259	4.48	-51.32
Australasia	325	350	400	578	332	5.74	-42.56
Australia	191	208	265	420	246	4.26	-41.43
New Zealand	134	142	135	158	86	1.49	-45.57
Melanesia	103	136	111	148	98	1.70	-33.78
Fiji	103	136	111	148	98	1.70	-33.78
Micronesia	689	1,159	1,217	1,638	989	17.11	-39.62
Kiribati	269	582	481	490	315	5.45	-35.71
Guam					48	0.83	
Nauru	130	153	126	397	177	3.06	-55.42
Micronesia (Federated States of)	245	353	543	664	405	7.01	-39.01
Palau	45	71	67	87	44	0.76	-49.43
Polynesia	17	27	11	18	8	0.14	-55.56
Tuvalu	17	27	11	18	8	0.14	-55.56
Other East Asia and the Pacific	523	1,157	1,112	870	539	9.33	-38.05
Other countries of Asia	414	1,039	978	650	464	8.03	-28.62
Other countries of Oceania	109	118	134	220	75	1.30	-65.91
EUROPE	261	325	501	404	284	4.91	-29.70
Northern Europe	133	167	101	126	127	2.20	0.79
United Kingdom	133	167	101	126	127	2.20	0.79
Western Europe	34	36	66	28	49	0.85	75.00
Germany	34	36	66	28	49	0.85	75.00
Other Europe	94	122	334	250	108	1.87	-56.80
Other countries of Europe	94	122	334	250	108	1.87	-56.80
REGION NOT SPECIFIED	45	71	81	167	43	0.74	-74.25
Not Specified	45	71	81	167	43	0.74	-74.25
Other countries of the World	45	71	81	167	43	0.74	-74.25

Source: World Tourism Organization (UNWTO)

MARSHALL ISLANDS

1. Arrivals of non-resident tourists at national borders, by country of residence

		2002	2003	2004	2005	2006	Market share 06	% Change 06-05
TOTAL	(*)	6,002	7,195	9,007	9,173	5,780	100.00	-36.99
AMERICAS		2,156	2,189	2,099	1,721	1,472	25.47	-14.47
North America		2,154	2,185	2,097	1,705	1,464	25.33	-14.13
Canada		26	40	36	55	56	0.97	1.82
United States		2,128	2,145	2,061	1,650	1,408	24.36	-14.67
Other Americas		2	4	2	16	8	0.14	-50.00
Other countries of the Americas		2	4	2	16	8	0.14	-50.00
EAST ASIA AND THE PACIFIC		3,397	4,422	4,466	5,577	3,850	66.61	-30.97
North-East Asia		1,446	1,286	1,466	1,892	1,272	22.01	-32.77
China		159	57	87	113	58	1.00	-48.67
Taiwan (Province of China)		347	209	321	448	228	3.94	-49.11
Japan		828	961	984	1,282	907	15.69	-29.25
Korea, Republic of		112	59	74	49	79	1.37	61.22
South-East Asia		239	245	192	199	204	3.53	2.51
Philippines		239	245	192	199	204	3.53	2.51
Australasia		263	279	277	440	293	5.07	-33.41
Australia		144	171	150	322	205	3.55	-36.34
New Zealand		119	108	127	118	88	1.52	-25.42
Melanesia		159	213	176	216	127	2.20	-41.20
Fiji		159	213	176	216	127	2.20	-41.20
Micronesia		711	1,180	1,174	1,606	1,302	22.53	-18.93
Kiribati		270	571	484	493	308	5.33	-37.53
Guam						359	6.21	
Nauru		130	155	130	405	172	2.98	-57.53
Micronesia (Federated States of)		279	397	499	621	416	7.20	-33.01
Palau		32	57	61	87	47	0.81	-45.98
Polynesia		7	18	4	12	9	0.16	-25.00
Tuvalu		7	18	4	12	9	0.16	-25.00
Other East Asia and the Pacific		572	1,201	1,177	1,212	643	11.12	-46.95
Other countries of Asia		377	962	862	601	486	8.41	-19.13
Other countries of Oceania		195	239	315	611	157	2.72	-74.30
EUROPE		147	196	160	160	180	3.11	12.50
Northern Europe		72	85	42	50	80	1.38	60.00
United Kingdom		72	85	42	50	80	1.38	60.00
Western Europe		20	26	47	19	24	0.42	26.32
Germany		20	26	47	19	24	0.42	26.32
Other Europe		55	85	71	91	76	1.31	-16.48
Other countries of Europe		55	85	71	91	76	1.31	-16.48
REGION NOT SPECIFIED		302	388	2,282	1,715	278	4.81	-83.79
Not Specified		302	388	2,282	1,715	278	4.81	-83.79
Other countries of the World		302	388	2,282	1,715	278	4.81	-83.79

Source: World Tourism Organization (UNWTO)

MARSHALL ISLANDS

6. Overnight stays of non-resident tourists in all types of accommodation establishments, by country of residence

	2002	2003	2004	2005	2006	Market share 06	% Change 06-05
TOTAL	**36,558**	**40,399**	**37,547**	**41,271**	**36,581**	**100.00**	**-11.36**
AMERICAS	**14,428**	**16,200**	**13,968**	**13,002**	**13,677**	**37.39**	**5.19**
North America	**14,428**	**16,178**	**13,960**	**12,769**	**13,625**	**37.25**	**6.70**
Canada	251	593	567	687	1,457	3.98	112.08
United States	14,177	15,585	13,393	12,082	12,168	33.26	0.71
Other Americas		**22**	**8**	**233**	**52**	**0.14**	**-77.68**
Other countries of the Americas		22	8	233	52	0.14	-77.68
EAST ASIA AND THE PACIFIC	**19,825**	**21,452**	**19,339**	**25,824**	**20,308**	**55.52**	**-21.36**
North-East Asia	**9,628**	**5,890**	**6,228**	**7,074**	**5,395**	**14.75**	**-23.73**
China	3,118	902	585	218	179	0.49	-17.89
Taiwan (Province of China)	2,145	1,063	1,315	2,029	927	2.53	-54.31
Japan	3,903	3,652	4,004	4,614	3,851	10.53	-16.54
Korea, Republic of	462	273	324	213	438	1.20	105.63
South-East Asia	**1,422**	**1,734**	**818**	**1,538**	**1,625**	**4.44**	**5.66**
Philippines	1,422	1,734	818	1,538	1,625	4.44	5.66
Australasia	**2,415**	**2,690**	**2,610**	**4,948**	**3,441**	**9.41**	**-30.46**
Australia	1,634	1,625	1,184	3,483	2,827	7.73	-18.83
New Zealand	781	1,065	1,426	1,465	614	1.68	-58.09
Melanesia	**1,376**	**2,050**	**1,299**	**1,868**	**1,028**	**2.81**	**-44.97**
Fiji	1,376	2,050	1,299	1,868	1,028	2.81	-44.97
Micronesia	**2,799**	**6,357**	**5,567**	**6,254**	**7,106**	**19.43**	**13.62**
Kiribati	1,018	2,720	2,148	1,402	2,230	6.10	59.06
Guam					1,801	4.92	
Nauru	524	1,525	1,057	2,078	1,005	2.75	-51.64
Micronesia (Federated States of)	1,132	1,822	2,126	2,423	1,865	5.10	-23.03
Palau	125	290	236	351	205	0.56	-41.60
Polynesia	**96**	**328**	**36**	**331**	**28**	**0.08**	**-91.54**
Tuvalu	96	328	36	331	28	0.08	-91.54
Other East Asia and the Pacific	**2,089**	**2,403**	**2,781**	**3,811**	**1,685**	**4.61**	**-55.79**
Other countries of Asia	968	766	646	971	956	2.61	-1.54
Other countries of Oceania	1,121	1,637	2,135	2,840	729	1.99	-74.33
EUROPE	**1,347**	**1,328**	**1,244**	**920**	**1,661**	**4.54**	**80.54**
Northern Europe	**806**	**726**	**498**	**367**	**610**	**1.67**	**66.21**
United Kingdom	806	726	498	367	610	1.67	66.21
Western Europe	**248**	**151**	**284**	**148**	**250**	**0.68**	**68.92**
Germany	248	151	284	148	250	0.68	68.92
Other Europe	**293**	**451**	**462**	**405**	**801**	**2.19**	**97.78**
Other countries of Europe	293	451	462	405	801	2.19	97.78
REGION NOT SPECIFIED	**958**	**1,419**	**2,996**	**1,525**	**935**	**2.56**	**-38.69**
Not Specified	**958**	**1,419**	**2,996**	**1,525**	**935**	**2.56**	**-38.69**
Other countries of the World	958	1,419	2,996	1,525	935	2.56	-38.69

Source: World Tourism Organization (UNWTO)

MARTINIQUE

1. Arrivals of non-resident tourists at national borders, by country of residence

	2002	2003	2004	2005	2006	Market share 06	% Change 06-05
TOTAL (*)	446,689	453,159	470,890	484,127	503,475	100.00	4.00
AMERICAS	70,378	71,559	73,011	81,247	79,335	15.76	-2.35
Caribbean	47,129	53,495	51,091	55,341	53,724	10.67	-2.92
Barbados	3,475	1,976	2,399	3,004	2,425	0.48	-19.27
Dominica	3,363	3,033	1,694	3,712	3,103	0.62	-16.41
Guadeloupe	31,713	40,668	40,644	37,030	38,645	7.68	4.36
Saint Lucia	5,168	5,842	4,603	9,079	7,153	1.42	-21.21
Other countries of the Caribbean	3,410	1,976	1,751	2,516	2,398	0.48	-4.69
North America	8,712	5,141	6,476	9,553	10,011	1.99	4.79
Canada	4,474	2,584	3,008	4,569	4,772	0.95	4.44
United States	4,238	2,557	3,468	4,984	5,239	1.04	5.12
South America	14,537	12,923	15,444	16,353	15,600	3.10	-4.60
French Guiana	11,247	10,619	13,407	11,582	12,963	2.57	11.92
Venezuela	3,290	2,304	2,037	4,771	2,637	0.52	-44.73
EUROPE	371,978	379,922	396,138	399,083	422,453	83.91	5.86
Northern Europe	3,206	3,802	3,448	4,745	3,324	0.66	-29.95
United Kingdom/Ireland	2,158	1,945	2,220	2,778	1,920	0.38	-30.89
Scandinavia	1,048	1,857	1,228	1,967	1,404	0.28	-28.62
Southern Europe	4,111	2,788	2,661	4,506	4,813	0.96	6.81
Italy	4,111	2,788	2,661	4,506	4,813	0.96	6.81
Western Europe	363,066	371,287	387,484	387,988	412,407	81.91	6.29
France	349,212	357,726	373,678	369,705	395,512	78.56	6.98
Germany	1,588	2,767	3,251	3,998	2,786	0.55	-30.32
Switzerland	5,728	2,963	3,857	5,574	4,156	0.83	-25.44
Benelux	6,538	7,831	6,698	8,711	9,953	1.98	14.26
Other Europe	1,595	2,045	2,545	1,844	1,909	0.38	3.52
Other countries of Europe	1,595	2,045	2,545	1,844	1,909	0.38	3.52
REGION NOT SPECIFIED	4,333	1,678	1,741	3,797	1,687	0.34	-55.57
Not Specified	4,333	1,678	1,741	3,797	1,687	0.34	-55.57
Other countries of the World	4,333	1,678	1,741	3,797	1,687	0.34	-55.57

Source: World Tourism Organization (UNWTO)

MARTINIQUE

3. Arrivals of non-resident tourists in hotels and similar establishments, by nationality

	2002	2003	2004	2005	2006	Market share 06	% Change 06-05
TOTAL	197,529	186,547	191,601	215,679	204,174	100.00	-5.33
AMERICAS	28,738	22,788	26,866	23,827	19,677	9.64	-17.42
Caribbean	23,882	20,138	23,814	19,603	14,356	7.03	-26.77
All countries of the Caribbean	23,882	20,138	23,814	19,603	14,356	7.03	-26.77
North America	4,856	2,650	3,052	4,224	5,321	2.61	25.97
Canada	2,280	1,301	1,361	1,961	2,483	1.22	26.62
United States	2,576	1,349	1,691	2,263	2,838	1.39	25.41
EUROPE	166,653	162,944	164,157	190,296	183,676	89.96	-3.48
Western Europe	153,210	150,746	153,148	174,746	170,407	83.46	-2.48
France	153,210	150,746	153,148	174,746	170,407	83.46	-2.48
Other Europe	13,443	12,198	11,009	15,550	13,269	6.50	-14.67
Other countries of Europe	13,443	12,198	11,009	15,550	13,269	6.50	-14.67
REGION NOT SPECIFIED	2,138	815	578	1,556	821	0.40	-47.24
Not Specified	2,138	815	578	1,556	821	0.40	-47.24
Other countries of the World	2,138	815	578	1,556	821	0.40	-47.24

Source: World Tourism Organization (UNWTO)

MARTINIQUE

4. Arrivals of non-resident tourists in all types of accommodation establishments, by nationality

	2002	2003	2004	2005	2006	Market share 06	% Change 06-05
TOTAL	446,688	453,162	470,890	484,127	503,475	100.00	4.00
AMERICAS	70,378	71,560	73,010	81,247	79,334	15.76	-2.35
Caribbean	61,666	66,418	66,534	71,694	69,323	13.77	-3.31
All countries of the Caribbean	61,666	66,418	66,534	71,694	69,323	13.77	-3.31
North America	8,712	5,142	6,476	9,553	10,011	1.99	4.79
Canada	4,474	2,584	3,008	4,569	4,772	0.95	4.44
United States	4,238	2,558	3,468	4,984	5,239	1.04	5.12
EUROPE	371,977	379,924	396,139	399,083	422,454	83.91	5.86
Western Europe	349,212	357,726	373,678	369,705	395,512	78.56	6.98
France	349,212	357,726	373,678	369,705	395,512	78.56	6.98
Other Europe	22,765	22,198	22,461	29,378	26,942	5.35	-8.29
Other countries of Europe	22,765	22,198	22,461	29,378	26,942	5.35	-8.29
REGION NOT SPECIFIED	4,333	1,678	1,741	3,797	1,687	0.34	-55.57
Not Specified	4,333	1,678	1,741	3,797	1,687	0.34	-55.57
Other countries of the World	4,333	1,678	1,741	3,797	1,687	0.34	-55.57

Source: World Tourism Organization (UNWTO)

MARTINIQUE

5. Overnight stays of non-resident tourists in hotels and similar establishments, by country of residence

	2002	2003	2004	2005	2006	Market share 06	% Change 06-05
TOTAL	1,991,313	1,693,378	1,705,263	1,923,949	1,707,290	100.00	-11.26
AMERICAS	197,522	215,410	213,811	188,496	164,545	9.64	-12.71
Caribbean	157,350	198,843	195,142	136,973	120,061	7.03	-12.35
All countries of the Caribbean	157,350	198,843	195,142	136,973	120,061	7.03	-12.35
North America	40,172	16,567	18,669	51,523	44,484	2.61	-13.66
Canada	21,850	10,114	10,580	30,062	23,723	1.39	-21.09
United States	18,322	6,453	8,089	21,461	20,761	1.22	-3.26
EUROPE	1,776,015	1,472,678	1,487,700	1,724,949	1,535,876	89.96	-10.96
Western Europe	1,663,288	1,407,028	1,428,449	1,606,674	1,424,924	83.46	-11.31
France	1,663,288	1,407,028	1,428,449	1,606,674	1,424,924	83.46	-11.31
Other Europe	112,727	65,650	59,251	118,275	110,952	6.50	-6.19
Other countries of Europe	112,727	65,650	59,251	118,275	110,952	6.50	-6.19
REGION NOT SPECIFIED	17,776	5,290	3,752	10,504	6,869	0.40	-34.61
Not Specified	17,776	5,290	3,752	10,504	6,869	0.40	-34.61
Other countries of the World	17,776	5,290	3,752	10,504	6,869	0.40	-34.61

Source: World Tourism Organization (UNWTO)

MARTINIQUE

6. Overnight stays of non-resident tourists in all types of accommodation establishments, by nationality

	2002	2003	2004	2005	2006	Market share 06	% Change 06-05
TOTAL	6,022,276	6,135,774	6,769,657	6,496,220	6,965,105	100.00	7.22
AMERICAS	640,173	780,515	662,848	941,953	863,017	12.39	-8.38
Caribbean	542,623	720,487	594,517	762,675	735,670	10.56	-3.54
All countries of the Caribbean	542,623	720,487	594,517	762,675	735,670	10.56	-3.54
North America	97,550	60,028	68,331	179,278	127,347	1.83	-28.97
Canada	57,329	36,647	32,333	106,668	62,928	0.90	-41.01
United States	40,221	23,381	35,998	72,610	64,419	0.92	-11.28
EUROPE	5,333,802	5,336,093	6,071,913	5,515,247	6,086,746	87.39	10.36
Western Europe	5,079,663	5,098,216	5,833,900	5,175,055	5,751,772	82.58	11.14
France	5,079,663	5,098,216	5,833,900	5,175,055	5,751,772	82.58	11.14
Other Europe	254,139	237,877	238,013	340,192	334,974	4.81	-1.53
Other countries of Europe	254,139	237,877	238,013	340,192	334,974	4.81	-1.53
REGION NOT SPECIFIED	48,301	19,166	34,896	39,020	15,342	0.22	-60.68
Not Specified	48,301	19,166	34,896	39,020	15,342	0.22	-60.68
Other countries of the World	48,301	19,166	34,896	39,020	15,342	0.22	-60.68

Source: World Tourism Organization (UNWTO)

MAURITIUS

1. Arrivals of non-resident tourists at national borders, by country of residence

	2002	2003	2004	2005	2006	Market share 06	% Change 06-05
TOTAL	681,648	702,018	718,861	761,063	788,276	100.00	3.58
AFRICA	172,351	173,996	175,295	184,821	189,026	23.98	2.28
East Africa	126,443	123,814	118,737	122,837	114,231	14.49	-7.01
Burundi	51	60	62	47	57	0.01	21.28
Comoros	945	1,437	949	1,166	819	0.10	-29.76
Ethiopia	49	142	83	69	125	0.02	81.16
Eritrea	14	8	15	14	26		85.71
Djibouti	16	49	32	36	76	0.01	111.11
Kenya	1,507	1,510	1,506	1,358	1,694	0.21	24.74
Madagascar	9,417	11,044	8,256	7,397	7,239	0.92	-2.14
Malawi	121	181	163	132	141	0.02	6.82
Mozambique	440	394	336	275	271	0.03	-1.45
Reunion	96,375	95,679	96,510	99,036	89,127	11.31	-10.01
Rwanda	40	92	47	41	59	0.01	43.90
Seychelles	13,468	9,869	7,456	10,084	12,023	1.53	19.23
Somalia	8	3		3	3		
Zimbabwe	3,185	2,343	2,345	2,419	1,587	0.20	-34.39
Uganda	176	205	160	138	183	0.02	32.61
United Republic of Tanzania	277	342	422	317	361	0.05	13.88
Zambia	354	456	395	305	440	0.06	44.26
Central Africa	301	438	552	470	463	0.06	-1.49
Angola	129	119	230	139	118	0.01	-15.11
Cameroon	51	110	52	119	137	0.02	15.13
Central African Republic	5	10	3	3	3		
Chad	4	8	3	12	11		-8.33
Congo	56	92	175	101	128	0.02	26.73
Democratic Republic of the Congo	9	12	21	14	20		42.86
Equatorial Guinea	2	3		1	1		
Gabon	43	83	64	76	44	0.01	-42.11
Sao Tome and Principe	2	1	4	5	1		-80.00
North Africa	352	607	476	558	654	0.08	17.20
Algeria	48	196	86	95	114	0.01	20.00
Morocco	157	149	183	191	224	0.03	17.28
Sudan	34	81	63	92	75	0.01	-18.48
Tunisia	113	181	144	180	241	0.03	33.89
Southern Africa	43,708	46,960	53,924	59,475	71,975	9.13	21.02
Botswana	463	445	449	375	407	0.05	8.53
Lesotho	94	97	106	69	78	0.01	13.04
Namibia	366	550	578	506	541	0.07	6.92
South Africa	42,685	45,756	52,609	58,446	70,796	8.98	21.13
Swaziland	100	112	182	79	153	0.02	93.67
West Africa	685	1,220	752	749	925	0.12	23.50
Cape Verde	15	24	26	18	21		16.67
Benin	14	56	34	50	36		-28.00
Gambia	52	50	26	18	26		44.44
Ghana	70	178	106	104	189	0.02	81.73
Guinea	99	148	55	54	14		-74.07
Cote D'Ivoire	111	134	72	88	116	0.01	31.82
Liberia	2	2		2	8		300.00
Mali	25	90	41	24	31		29.17
Mauritania	7	19	12	12	10		-16.67
Niger	3	13	9	6	9		50.00
Nigeria	123	231	221	180	233	0.03	29.44

MAURITIUS

1. Arrivals of non-resident tourists at national borders, by country of residence

	2002	2003	2004	2005	2006	Market share 06	% Change 06-05
Guinea-Bissau	1	1	2	2			
Senegal	121	183	105	111	161	0.02	45.05
Sierra Leone	12	18	10	8	13		62.50
Togo	16	27	14	26	25		-3.85
Burkina Faso	14	46	19	46	33		-28.26
Other Africa	**862**	**957**	**854**	**732**	**778**	**0.10**	**6.28**
Other countries of Africa	862	957	854	732	778	0.10	6.28
AMERICAS	**7,451**	**8,106**	**8,380**	**8,791**	**9,759**	**1.24**	**11.01**
Caribbean	**131**	**110**	**130**	**222**	**93**	**0.01**	**-58.11**
Antigua and Barbuda	4	2	3	3			
Bahamas	9	6	1	12	11		-8.33
Barbados	11	8	12	18	5		-72.22
Bermuda		1	3	10	3		-70.00
Cuba	7	20	4	28	14		-50.00
Dominica			1	7			
Dominican Republic	2	1	11	11	4		-63.64
Grenada	2	1	4	8	6		-25.00
Guadeloupe	33	9	12	21	3		-85.71
Haiti	4	11	5	10	3		-70.00
Jamaica	8	6	29	50	16		-68.00
Martinique	37	31	23	10	9		-10.00
Anguilla		1		1	1		
Trinidad and Tobago	14	13	22	33	17		-48.48
Turks and Caicos Islands					1		
Central America	**23**	**31**	**17**	**33**	**34**		**3.03**
Belize	3		1	3	2		-33.33
Costa Rica	11	11	5	3	5		66.67
El Salvador	3	13	6	18	21		16.67
Guatemala	1	4	2	2	2		
Honduras	2	1	1	6	1		-83.33
Nicaragua	3	2	2	1	3		200.00
North America	**5,988**	**6,424**	**6,702**	**7,087**	**7,588**	**0.96**	**7.07**
Canada	1,842	1,845	2,341	2,119	2,298	0.29	8.45
Greenland		1	1				
Mexico	30	73	55	78	70	0.01	-10.26
United States	4,116	4,505	4,305	4,890	5,220	0.66	6.75
South America	**1,297**	**1,518**	**1,510**	**1,416**	**2,024**	**0.26**	**42.94**
Argentina	191	264	453	394	489	0.06	24.11
Bolivia	2	3	1	1	5		400.00
Brazil	505	482	623	707	1,172	0.15	65.77
Chile	337	469	254	122	110	0.01	-9.84
Colombia	25	25	22	28	25		-10.71
Ecuador	5	5	11	6	16		166.67
Guyana	13	14	15	29	12		-58.62
Paraguay	13	3	3	5	3		-40.00
Peru	132	149	84	79	132	0.02	67.09
Suriname	7	22	14	17	12		-29.41
Uruguay	58	76	19	11	18		63.64
Venezuela	9	6	11	17	30		76.47
Other Americas	**12**	**23**	**21**	**33**	**20**		**-39.39**
Other countries of the Americas	12	23	21	33	20		-39.39
EAST ASIA AND THE PACIFIC	**24,694**	**21,934**	**27,026**	**28,924**	**34,103**	**4.33**	**17.91**

MAURITIUS

1. Arrivals of non-resident tourists at national borders, by country of residence

	2002	2003	2004	2005	2006	Market share 06	% Change 06-05
North-East Asia	**8,908**	**7,046**	**9,068**	**9,051**	**9,276**	**1.18**	**2.49**
China	4,248	3,738	5,291	5,526	4,875	0.62	-11.78
Taiwan (Province of China)	1,159	790	871	1,108	1,701	0.22	53.52
Hong Kong, China	1,201	676	836	508	519	0.07	2.17
Japan	1,958	1,572	1,724	1,638	1,695	0.22	3.48
Korea, Republic of	333	259	335	257	478	0.06	85.99
Macao, China	6	8	9	12	6		-50.00
Mongolia	3	3	2	2	2		
South-East Asia	**6,735**	**5,074**	**5,865**	**5,387**	**7,095**	**0.90**	**31.71**
Brunei Darussalam	12	8	6	7	6		-14.29
Myanmar	4	5	4	13	23		76.92
Cambodia	1	3	7	16	7		-56.25
Indonesia	285	295	445	706	1,109	0.14	57.08
Lao People's Democratic Republic			2	2	7		250.00
Malaysia	1,944	1,586	2,006	1,582	2,472	0.31	56.26
Philippines	670	562	685	845	981	0.12	16.09
Singapore	3,114	2,102	2,329	1,789	1,862	0.24	4.08
Viet Nam	175	133	132	233	356	0.05	52.79
Thailand	530	380	249	194	272	0.03	40.21
Australasia	**8,930**	**9,674**	**11,998**	**14,263**	**17,636**	**2.24**	**23.65**
Australia	8,387	9,103	11,373	13,486	16,660	2.11	23.54
New Zealand	543	571	625	777	976	0.12	25.61
Melanesia	**100**	**72**	**65**	**112**	**61**	**0.01**	**-45.54**
Solomon Islands		1	4	20			
Fiji	35	19	21	32	18		-43.75
New Caledonia	63	49	34	42	40	0.01	-4.76
Vanuatu	2	2		12	1		-91.67
Papua New Guinea		1	6	6	2		-66.67
Micronesia		**1**	**5**	**34**	**9**		**-73.53**
Kiribati			5	25	8		-68.00
Nauru		1		8	1		-87.50
Micronesia (Federated States of)				1			
Polynesia	**19**	**53**	**13**	**12**	**14**		**16.67**
American Samoa	6	42	1	6	8		33.33
French Polynesia	13	11	12	6	6		
Other East Asia and the Pacific	**2**	**14**	**12**	**65**	**12**		**-81.54**
Other countries of Asia	2	2		3			
Other countries of Oceania		12	12	62	12		-80.65
EUROPE	**451,791**	**465,620**	**477,347**	**503,037**	**510,872**	**64.81**	**1.56**
Central/Eastern Europe	**8,051**	**8,795**	**10,506**	**14,000**	**17,960**	**2.28**	**28.29**
Azerbaijan	8	10	11	20	17		-15.00
Armenia	5	14	18	18	22		22.22
Bulgaria	131	201	240	313	319	0.04	1.92
Belarus	32	40	46	83	107	0.01	28.92
Czech Republic	1,469	1,359	1,846	1,927	2,609	0.33	35.39
Estonia	123	181	208	198	251	0.03	26.77
Georgia	4	4	13	17	11		-35.29
Hungary	980	932	907	2,393	3,735	0.47	56.08
Kazakhstan	23	82	62	78	291	0.04	273.08
Latvia	165	86	102	213	190	0.02	-10.80
Lithuania	78	119	118	102	187	0.02	83.33
Republic of Moldova	2	6	5	3	24		700.00

MAURITIUS

1. Arrivals of non-resident tourists at national borders, by country of residence

	2002	2003	2004	2005	2006	Market share 06	% Change 06-05
Poland	1,499	1,329	1,504	1,862	2,258	0.29	21.27
Romania	156	419	451	456	620	0.08	35.96
Russian Federation	2,172	2,908	3,209	4,000	5,081	0.64	27.03
Slovakia	563	457	1,017	1,271	1,026	0.13	-19.28
Tajikistan					6		
Turkmenistan				2	1		-50.00
Ukraine	510	506	596	912	1,031	0.13	13.05
Ussr (Former)	82	116	118	100	127	0.02	27.00
Uzbekistan	11	9	11	10	12		20.00
Other countries Central/East Europ	38	17	24	22	35		59.09
Northern Europe	**94,573**	**105,899**	**108,403**	**111,638**	**123,253**	**15.64**	**10.40**
Denmark	1,521	1,836	2,239	2,570	3,599	0.46	40.04
Faeroe Islands	1	1	7				
Finland	1,948	1,914	2,353	2,430	2,927	0.37	20.45
Iceland	39	26	24	72	95	0.01	31.94
Ireland	3,032	3,414	3,492	3,964	5,075	0.64	28.03
Norway	2,718	2,641	3,027	2,971	2,850	0.36	-4.07
Sweden	4,647	4,857	4,609	4,224	6,374	0.81	50.90
United Kingdom	80,667	91,210	92,652	95,407	102,333	12.98	7.26
Southern Europe	**49,422**	**53,004**	**53,928**	**58,476**	**86,502**	**10.97**	**47.93**
Albania	4	8	14	20	40	0.01	100.00
Andorra	21	34	32	31	24		-22.58
Bosnia and Herzegovina	6	13	8	30	29		-3.33
Croatia	74	99	102	137	167	0.02	21.90
Gibraltar		6	5	1			
Greece	1,180	1,910	1,864	2,328	2,382	0.30	2.32
Italy	38,263	39,774	41,277	43,458	69,407	8.80	59.71
Malta	47	81	97	108	120	0.02	11.11
Portugal	1,733	1,616	1,599	1,851	2,055	0.26	11.02
San Marino	18	18	16	13	22		69.23
Slovenia	185	250	349	683	1,062	0.13	55.49
Spain	7,770	9,081	8,475	9,682	11,012	1.40	13.74
TFYR of Macedonia	9	4	19	3	8		166.67
Serbia and Montenegro	112	110	71	131	174	0.02	32.82
Western Europe	**298,968**	**296,561**	**303,360**	**317,664**	**281,651**	**35.73**	**-11.34**
Austria	8,782	8,893	10,304	10,440	10,483	1.33	0.41
Belgium	10,579	10,170	8,524	8,973	9,216	1.17	2.71
France	202,869	200,229	210,411	220,421	182,295	23.13	-17.30
Germany	53,762	53,970	52,277	55,983	57,251	7.26	2.26
Liechtenstein	27	37	36	36	30		-16.67
Luxembourg	726	758	692	765	592	0.08	-22.61
Monaco	227	172	139	162	98	0.01	-39.51
Netherlands	4,625	4,403	4,867	5,111	5,525	0.70	8.10
Switzerland	17,371	17,929	16,110	15,773	16,161	2.05	2.46
East Mediterranean Europe	**777**	**1,358**	**1,148**	**1,256**	**1,506**	**0.19**	**19.90**
Cyprus	101	439	412	504	525	0.07	4.17
Israel	286	235	295	321	393	0.05	22.43
Turkey	390	684	441	431	588	0.07	36.43
Other Europe		**3**	**2**	**3**			
Other countries of Europe		3	2	3			
MIDDLE EAST	**2,287**	**4,800**	**3,883**	**3,737**	**4,715**	**0.60**	**26.17**
Middle East	**2,287**	**4,800**	**3,883**	**3,737**	**4,715**	**0.60**	**26.17**
Bahrain	40	113	99	72	112	0.01	55.56

MAURITIUS

1. Arrivals of non-resident tourists at national borders, by country of residence

	2002	2003	2004	2005	2006	Market share 06	% Change 06-05
Palestine	4	9	5	8	14		75.00
Iraq	5	3	6	8	11		37.50
Jordan	47	76	70	92	138	0.02	50.00
Kuwait	130	319	348	359	325	0.04	-9.47
Lebanon	77	274	291	283	358	0.05	26.50
Libyan Arab Jamahiriya	20	38	70	54	47	0.01	-12.96
Oman	36	101	65	54	61	0.01	12.96
Qatar	32	55	39	44	68	0.01	54.55
Saudi Arabia	365	709	842	1,046	1,219	0.15	16.54
Syrian Arab Republic	59	145	49	36	56	0.01	55.56
United Arab Emirates	1,192	2,559	1,715	1,344	1,896	0.24	41.07
Egypt	270	390	279	332	385	0.05	15.96
Yemen	10	9	5	5	25		400.00
SOUTH ASIA	**22,869**	**27,277**	**26,558**	**31,087**	**39,070**	**4.96**	**25.68**
South Asia	**22,869**	**27,277**	**26,558**	**31,087**	**39,070**	**4.96**	**25.68**
Bangladesh	117	122	135	235	238	0.03	1.28
Bhutan	1	4	5	2	3		50.00
Sri Lanka	1,185	812	796	298	353	0.04	18.46
India	20,898	25,367	24,716	29,755	37,498	4.76	26.02
Iran, Islamic Republic of	47	68	81	75	109	0.01	45.33
Maldives	15	29	17	31	16		-48.39
Nepal	22	45	72	76	94	0.01	23.68
Pakistan	584	830	736	615	759	0.10	23.41
REGION NOT SPECIFIED	**205**	**285**	**372**	**666**	**731**	**0.09**	**9.76**
Not Specified	**205**	**285**	**372**	**666**	**731**	**0.09**	**9.76**
Other countries of the World	205	285	372	666	731	0.09	9.76

Source: World Tourism Organization (UNWTO)

MAURITIUS

5. Overnight stays of non-resident tourists in hotels and similar establishments, by country of residence

	2002	2003	2004	2005	2006	Market share 06	% Change 06-05
TOTAL	6,768,870	6,952,313	7,118,603	7,498,251	7,760,679	100.00	3.50
AFRICA	1,351,988	1,446,983	1,517,745	1,567,206	1,588,741	20.47	1.37
East Africa	930,497	1,013,685	1,044,287	1,052,729	969,040	12.49	-7.95
Comoros	11,026	15,971	12,270	12,434	10,991	0.14	-11.61
Kenya	8,784	11,347	11,069	12,258	13,875	0.18	13.19
Madagascar	81,758	128,437	83,961	73,964	84,400	1.09	14.11
Reunion	675,483	738,968	832,879	828,889	730,678	9.42	-11.85
Seychelles	113,942	92,493	75,277	93,951	108,603	1.40	15.60
Zimbabwe	39,504	26,469	28,831	31,233	20,493	0.26	-34.39
Southern Africa	376,588	379,561	425,680	467,603	565,627	7.29	20.96
South Africa	376,588	379,561	425,680	467,603	565,627	7.29	20.96
Other Africa	44,903	53,737	47,778	46,874	54,074	0.70	15.36
Other countries of Africa	44,903	53,737	47,778	46,874	54,074	0.70	15.36
AMERICAS	83,650	83,594	84,742	87,003	94,735	1.22	8.89
North America	68,326	66,063	72,123	71,119	77,756	1.00	9.33
Canada	29,848	27,268	33,084	29,821	32,929	0.42	10.42
United States	38,478	38,795	39,039	41,298	44,827	0.58	8.55
Other Americas	15,324	17,531	12,619	15,884	16,979	0.22	6.89
Other countries of the Americas	15,324	17,531	12,619	15,884	16,979	0.22	6.89
EAST ASIA AND THE PACIFIC	290,767	273,016	295,525	311,766	356,164	4.59	14.24
North-East Asia	68,924	60,175	68,067	79,939	81,271	1.05	1.67
China	46,813	44,106	50,202	64,707	67,643	0.87	4.54
Hong Kong, China	10,941	6,767	7,984	4,694	3,739	0.05	-20.35
Japan	11,170	9,302	9,881	10,538	9,889	0.13	-6.16
South-East Asia	37,541	27,129	32,254	23,974	33,032	0.43	37.78
Malaysia	17,138	12,258	16,160	11,868	18,866	0.24	58.97
Singapore	20,403	14,871	16,094	12,106	14,166	0.18	17.02
Australasia	98,869	100,332	111,546	115,851	126,859	1.63	9.50
Australia	98,869	100,332	111,546	115,851	126,859	1.63	9.50
Other East Asia and the Pacific	85,433	85,380	83,658	92,002	115,002	1.48	25.00
Other countries of Asia	79,944	79,386	78,389	83,001	105,478	1.36	27.08
Other countries of Oceania	5,489	5,994	5,269	9,001	9,524	0.12	5.81
EUROPE	4,786,630	4,858,369	4,947,904	5,226,722	5,374,469	69.25	2.83
Northern Europe	1,023,085	1,090,213	1,097,844	1,115,797	1,217,049	15.68	9.07
Sweden	45,368	47,100	43,963	45,612	64,926	0.84	42.34
United Kingdom	977,717	1,043,113	1,053,881	1,070,185	1,152,123	14.85	7.66
Southern Europe	384,938	411,350	423,497	464,884	695,824	8.97	49.68
Italy	329,809	346,865	362,758	397,160	619,089	7.98	55.88
Spain	55,129	64,485	60,739	67,724	76,735	0.99	13.31
Western Europe	3,156,636	3,119,525	3,164,154	3,332,133	3,078,847	39.67	-7.60
Austria	96,686	96,299	108,429	111,840	114,757	1.48	2.61
Belgium	124,586	121,687	105,445	117,210	120,987	1.56	3.22
France	2,020,850	1,996,305	2,101,125	2,208,575	1,931,005	24.88	-12.57
Germany	651,913	636,435	608,031	655,283	655,738	8.45	0.07
Netherlands	52,091	48,417	52,009	53,743	56,219	0.72	4.61
Switzerland	210,510	220,382	189,115	185,482	200,141	2.58	7.90
Other Europe	221,971	237,281	262,409	313,908	382,749	4.93	21.93

MAURITIUS

5. Overnight stays of non-resident tourists in hotels and similar establishments, by country of residence

	2002	2003	2004	2005	2006	Market share 06	% Change 06-05
Other countries of Europe	221,971	237,281	262,409	313,908	382,749	4.93	21.93
SOUTH ASIA	**253,340**	**287,741**	**265,174**	**295,698**	**336,048**	**4.33**	**13.65**
South Asia	**253,340**	**287,741**	**265,174**	**295,698**	**336,048**	**4.33**	**13.65**
India	253,340	287,741	265,174	295,698	336,048	4.33	13.65
REGION NOT SPECIFIED	**2,495**	**2,610**	**7,513**	**9,856**	**10,522**	**0.14**	**6.76**
Not Specified	**2,495**	**2,610**	**7,513**	**9,856**	**10,522**	**0.14**	**6.76**
Other countries of the World	2,495	2,610	7,513	9,856	10,522	0.14	6.76

Source: World Tourism Organization (UNWTO)

MEXICO

1. Arrivals of non-resident tourists at national borders, by nationality

		2002	2003	2004	2005	2006	Market share 06	% Change 06-05
TOTAL	(*)				21,914,917	21,352,605	100.00	-2.57
AMERICAS					19,045,615	18,711,456	87.63	-1.75
Central America					62,381	59,855	0.28	-4.05
Costa Rica					26,293	28,411	0.13	8.06
Guatemala					36,088	31,444	0.15	-12.87
North America					18,580,900	18,295,551	85.68	-1.54
Canada					675,216	785,428	3.68	16.32
United States	(*)				17,905,684	17,510,123	82.00	-2.21
South America					257,747	231,679	1.09	-10.11
Argentina					78,096	84,583	0.40	8.31
Brazil					78,026	31,890	0.15	-59.13
Chile					35,543	41,230	0.19	16.00
Colombia					33,863	35,954	0.17	6.17
Venezuela					32,219	38,022	0.18	18.01
Other Americas					144,587	124,371	0.58	-13.98
Other countries of the Americas					144,587	124,371	0.58	-13.98
EAST ASIA AND THE PACIFIC					91,595	99,726	0.47	8.88
North-East Asia					91,595	99,726	0.47	8.88
Japan					65,376	68,984	0.32	5.52
Korea, Republic of					26,219	30,742	0.14	17.25
EUROPE					1,149,162	1,310,318	6.14	14.02
Northern Europe					231,421	260,121	1.22	12.40
United Kingdom					231,421	260,121	1.22	12.40
Southern Europe					374,291	455,891	2.14	21.80
Italy					149,176	163,284	0.76	9.46
Portugal					21,399	31,151	0.15	45.57
Spain					203,716	261,456	1.22	28.34
Western Europe					402,543	434,579	2.04	7.96
Belgium					25,027	28,006	0.13	11.90
France					160,119	173,183	0.81	8.16
Germany					129,871	135,031	0.63	3.97
Netherlands					61,813	70,200	0.33	13.57
Switzerland					25,713	28,159	0.13	9.51
Other Europe					140,907	159,727	0.75	13.36
Other countries of Europe					140,907	159,727	0.75	13.36
REGION NOT SPECIFIED					1,628,545	1,231,105	5.77	-24.40
Not Specified					1,628,545	1,231,105	5.77	-24.40
Other countries of the World					1,628,545	1,231,105	5.77	-24.40

Source: World Tourism Organization (UNWTO)

MEXICO

1. Arrivals of non-resident tourists at national borders, by country of residence

		2002	2003	2004	2005	2006	Market share 06	% Change 06-05
TOTAL	(*)	19,666,677	18,665,384	20,617,746	21,914,917	21,352,605	100.00	-2.57
AMERICAS		19,133,397	18,155,315	19,705,636	20,691,415	20,094,345	94.11	-2.89
North America		18,861,872	17,858,021	19,705,636	20,691,415	20,094,345	94.11	-2.89
Canada		360,854	292,222	335,954	366,141	435,658	2.04	18.99
United States		18,501,018	17,565,799	19,369,682	20,325,274	19,658,687	92.07	-3.28
Other Americas		271,525	297,294					
Other countries of the Americas		271,525	297,294					
EUROPE		479,174	443,366					
Other Europe		479,174	443,366					
All countries of Europe		479,174	443,366					
REGION NOT SPECIFIED		54,106	66,703	912,110	1,223,502	1,258,260	5.89	2.84
Not Specified		54,106	66,703	912,110	1,223,502	1,258,260	5.89	2.84
Other countries of the World		54,106	66,703	912,110	1,223,502	1,258,260	5.89	2.84

Source: World Tourism Organization (UNWTO)

MICRONESIA (FEDERATED STATES OF)

1. Arrivals of non-resident tourists at national borders, by country of residence

		2002	2003	2004	2005	2006	Market share 06	% Change 06-05
TOTAL	(*)	19,056	18,211	19,260	18,958	19,136	100.00	0.94
AMERICAS		8,439	7,671	7,744	7,955	8,256	43.14	3.78
North America		8,439	7,671	7,744	7,955	8,256	43.14	3.78
Canada		222	214	212	245	203	1.06	-17.14
United States		8,217	7,457	7,532	7,710	8,053	42.08	4.45
EAST ASIA AND THE PACIFIC		9,044	8,884	9,982	8,895	8,361	43.69	-6.00
North-East Asia		4,058	3,903	3,822	3,354	3,071	16.05	-8.44
Japan		4,058	3,903	3,822	3,354	3,071	16.05	-8.44
South-East Asia		1,096	1,026	1,341	1,388	1,347	7.04	-2.95
Philippines		1,096	1,026	1,341	1,388	1,347	7.04	-2.95
Australasia		741	803	1,243	1,226	1,260	6.58	2.77
Australia		572	652	1,004	1,064	1,077	5.63	1.22
New Zealand		169	151	239	162	183	0.96	12.96
Other East Asia and the Pacific		3,149	3,152	3,576	2,927	2,683	14.02	-8.34
Other countries of Asia		1,711	1,801	2,184	1,743	1,525	7.97	-12.51
Other countries of Oceania		1,438	1,351	1,392	1,184	1,158	6.05	-2.20
EUROPE		1,483	1,568	1,408	2,019	2,398	12.53	18.77
Other Europe		1,483	1,568	1,408	2,019	2,398	12.53	18.77
All countries of Europe		1,483	1,568	1,408	2,019	2,398	12.53	18.77
REGION NOT SPECIFIED		90	88	126	89	121	0.63	35.96
Not Specified		90	88	126	89	121	0.63	35.96
Other countries of the World		90	88	126	89	121	0.63	35.96

Source: World Tourism Organization (UNWTO)

MONACO

3. Arrivals of non-resident tourists in hotels and similar establishments, by nationality

	2002	2003	2004	2005	2006	Market share 06	% Change 06-05
TOTAL	262,520	234,638	250,159	285,675	313,070	100.00	9.59
AFRICA	2,440	2,228	2,230	2,601	2,826	0.90	8.65
Other Africa	2,440	2,228	2,230	2,601	2,826	0.90	8.65
All countries of Africa	2,440	2,228	2,230	2,601	2,826	0.90	8.65
AMERICAS	32,499	23,660	25,132	28,626	34,071	10.88	19.02
North America	29,576	21,025	23,018	26,089	31,259	9.98	19.82
Canada	3,127	2,462	2,384	3,198	3,686	1.18	15.26
Mexico	1,019	776	773	715	801	0.26	12.03
United States	25,430	17,787	19,861	22,176	26,772	8.55	20.73
South America	1,520	1,635	1,352	1,606	1,801	0.58	12.14
Argentina	409	624	548	578	608	0.19	5.19
Brazil	1,111	1,011	804	1,028	1,193	0.38	16.05
Other Americas	1,403	1,000	762	931	1,011	0.32	8.59
Other countries of the Americas	1,403	1,000	762	931	1,011	0.32	8.59
EAST ASIA AND THE PACIFIC	12,143	9,781	12,653	11,746	10,632	3.40	-9.48
North-East Asia	9,950	7,681	10,303	9,140	7,988	2.55	-12.60
China	1,698	1,306	1,419	1,466	1,618	0.52	10.37
Japan	8,252	6,375	8,884	7,674	6,370	2.03	-16.99
Australasia	2,193	2,100	2,350	2,606	2,644	0.84	1.46
Australia	2,193	2,100	2,350	2,606	2,644	0.84	1.46
EUROPE	205,062	186,972	190,326	214,131	239,872	76.62	12.02
Central/Eastern Europe	3,748	3,047	4,478	6,591	7,234	2.31	9.76
Russian Federation	3,748	3,047	4,478	6,591	7,234	2.31	9.76
Northern Europe	43,857	37,243	41,408	45,135	51,350	16.40	13.77
Denmark	1,532	1,822	1,980	1,970	2,004	0.64	1.73
Norway	1,594	1,064	1,330	1,391	1,889	0.60	35.80
Sweden	2,660	1,775	1,951	2,203	2,463	0.79	11.80
United Kingdom	38,071	32,582	36,147	39,571	44,994	14.37	13.70
Southern Europe	68,541	65,795	65,864	70,096	73,036	23.33	4.19
Italy	60,822	58,797	57,708	62,781	64,287	20.53	2.40
Portugal	1,272	888	1,270	1,023	1,129	0.36	10.36
Spain	6,447	6,110	6,886	6,292	7,620	2.43	21.11
Western Europe	76,659	70,733	66,433	79,646	91,880	29.35	15.36
Austria	2,198	2,687	1,953	2,166	2,391	0.76	10.39
Belgium	4,525	3,906	3,891	4,710	5,235	1.67	11.15
France	41,392	40,643	40,158	47,441	57,660	18.42	21.54
Germany	14,983	12,455	9,479	12,465	12,593	4.02	1.03
Netherlands	5,319	4,486	4,203	4,999	5,340	1.71	6.82
Switzerland	8,242	6,556	6,749	7,865	8,661	2.77	10.12
East Mediterranean Europe	1,439	1,104	1,359	929	1,125	0.36	21.10
Israel	1,439	1,104	1,359	929	1,125	0.36	21.10
Other Europe	10,818	9,050	10,784	11,734	15,247	4.87	29.94
Other countries of Europe	10,818	9,050	10,784	11,734	15,247	4.87	29.94
MIDDLE EAST	4,024	3,320	3,367	3,190	3,694	1.18	15.80
Middle East	4,024	3,320	3,367	3,190	3,694	1.18	15.80
All countries of Middle East	4,024	3,320	3,367	3,190	3,694	1.18	15.80
REGION NOT SPECIFIED	6,352	8,677	16,451	25,381	21,975	7.02	-13.42

MONACO

3. Arrivals of non-resident tourists in hotels and similar establishments, by nationality

	2002	2003	2004	2005	2006	Market share 06	% Change 06-05
Not Specified	6,352	8,677	16,451	25,381	21,975	7.02	-13.42
Other countries of the World	6,352	8,677	16,451	25,381	21,975	7.02	-13.42

Source: World Tourism Organization (UNWTO)

MONACO

5. Overnight stays of non-resident tourists in hotels and similar establishments, by nationality

	2002	2003	2004	2005	2006	Market share 06	% Change 06-05
TOTAL	764,712	674,312	695,265	802,714	915,646	100.00	14.07
AFRICA	9,061	9,493	9,631	12,465	10,606	1.16	-14.91
Other Africa	9,061	9,493	9,631	12,465	10,606	1.16	-14.91
All countries of Africa	9,061	9,493	9,631	12,465	10,606	1.16	-14.91
AMERICAS	110,511	78,536	79,966	92,036	118,476	12.94	28.73
North America	99,122	68,049	71,266	80,923	103,575	11.31	27.99
Canada	12,021	9,724	9,915	15,233	15,097	1.65	-0.89
Mexico	2,656	2,553	2,230	2,279	2,603	0.28	14.22
United States	84,445	55,772	59,121	63,411	85,875	9.38	35.43
South America	4,976	7,274	5,786	7,216	7,476	0.82	3.60
Argentina	1,244	2,891	2,762	3,538	3,703	0.40	4.66
Brazil	3,732	4,383	3,024	3,678	3,773	0.41	2.58
Other Americas	6,413	3,213	2,914	3,897	7,425	0.81	90.53
Other countries of the Americas	6,413	3,213	2,914	3,897	7,425	0.81	90.53
EAST ASIA AND THE PACIFIC	32,709	26,837	38,908	34,130	34,355	3.75	0.66
North-East Asia	26,151	20,395	32,391	26,216	26,255	2.87	0.15
China	4,313	3,109	3,243	4,871	5,491	0.60	12.73
Japan	21,838	17,286	29,148	21,345	20,764	2.27	-2.72
Australasia	6,558	6,442	6,517	7,914	8,100	0.88	2.35
Australia	6,558	6,442	6,517	7,914	8,100	0.88	2.35
EUROPE	571,572	518,284	493,361	560,018	665,632	72.70	18.86
Central/Eastern Europe	17,658	15,744	19,539	28,804	35,717	3.90	24.00
Russian Federation	17,658	15,744	19,539	28,804	35,717	3.90	24.00
Northern Europe	130,696	108,061	108,743	119,354	140,150	15.31	17.42
Denmark	5,783	6,115	5,793	6,782	7,414	0.81	9.32
Norway	5,950	3,267	3,527	4,355	7,108	0.78	63.21
Sweden	9,214	5,810	5,526	8,371	7,952	0.87	-5.01
United Kingdom	109,749	92,869	93,897	99,846	117,676	12.85	17.86
Southern Europe	174,651	165,765	157,347	167,496	179,990	19.66	7.46
Italy	149,398	142,266	133,930	145,022	153,926	16.81	6.14
Portugal	5,813	4,793	5,204	5,222	4,874	0.53	-6.66
Spain	19,440	18,706	18,213	17,252	21,190	2.31	22.83
Western Europe	205,319	193,141	169,560	201,347	249,086	27.20	23.71
Austria	9,255	11,238	7,400	9,184	10,450	1.14	13.78
Belgium	14,220	13,156	12,605	14,608	18,148	1.98	24.23
France	97,673	94,866	88,740	103,665	133,679	14.60	28.95
Germany	38,806	34,459	26,957	34,526	37,074	4.05	7.38
Netherlands	17,567	14,297	12,218	15,459	18,955	2.07	22.61
Switzerland	27,798	25,125	21,640	23,905	30,780	3.36	28.76
East Mediterranean Europe	6,270	4,571	5,730	3,897	4,809	0.53	23.40
Israel	6,270	4,571	5,730	3,897	4,809	0.53	23.40
Other Europe	36,978	31,002	32,442	39,120	55,880	6.10	42.84
Other countries of Europe	36,978	31,002	32,442	39,120	55,880	6.10	42.84
MIDDLE EAST	21,120	14,809	15,962	16,509	22,982	2.51	39.21
Middle East	21,120	14,809	15,962	16,509	22,982	2.51	39.21
All countries of Middle East	21,120	14,809	15,962	16,509	22,982	2.51	39.21

MONACO

5. Overnight stays of non-resident tourists in hotels and similar establishments, by nationality

	2002	2003	2004	2005	2006	Market share 06	% Change 06-05
REGION NOT SPECIFIED	19,739	26,353	57,437	87,556	63,595	6.95	-27.37
Not Specified	19,739	26,353	57,437	87,556	63,595	6.95	-27.37
Other countries of the World	19,739	26,353	57,437	87,556	63,595	6.95	-27.37

Source: World Tourism Organization (UNWTO)

MONGOLIA

1. Arrivals of non-resident tourists at national borders, by nationality

	2002	2003	2004	2005	2006	Market share 06	% Change 06-05
TOTAL	228,719	201,153	300,537	337,790	385,989	100.00	14.27
AFRICA	143	209	263	297	502	0.13	69.02
East Africa	18	40	26	27	69	0.02	155.56
Burundi	1	4	2		1		
Ethiopia	3	5	4	8	5		-37.50
Eritrea					3		
Djibouti					1		
Kenya	5	8	5	2	7		250.00
Madagascar		2	3	1			
Malawi			3	3	3		
Mauritius		2		1			
Mozambique					8		
Reunion			2		13		
Rwanda					3		
Somalia	3				7		
Zimbabwe	1	2	2	7	3		-57.14
Uganda	2	7	5	2	12		500.00
United Republic of Tanzania	3	5		3	3		
Zambia		5					
Central Africa	26	37	31	25	57	0.01	128.00
Angola	6		7	1	12		1,100.00
Cameroon	11	6	11	6	15		150.00
Central African Republic					5		
Chad		1					
Congo	9	12	13	18	9		-50.00
Equatorial Guinea		4			16		
Gabon		14					
North Africa	8	8	15	24	42	0.01	75.00
Algeria	4	1	6	6	32	0.01	433.33
Morocco	1	3	7	12	3		-75.00
Sudan	2	3	2	4	1		-75.00
Tunisia	1	1		2	6		200.00
Southern Africa	78	82	145	167	253	0.07	51.50
Botswana		2	1		1		
Lesotho		2					
Namibia		6	2		1		
South Africa	78	72	142	167	224	0.06	34.13
Swaziland					27	0.01	
West Africa	13	42	46	54	81	0.02	50.00
Benin		6	1				
Gambia		2		2			
Ghana	6	5	1		17		
Guinea			2	4	16		300.00
Cote D'Ivoire					1		
Liberia	3	3			2		
Mali				1	1		
Mauritania	2	2			3		
Niger	2	11	40	45	27	0.01	-40.00
Nigeria					2		
Guinea-Bissau		3		2			
Senegal		1			1		
Sierra Leone		1	1		9		
Togo		7					

MONGOLIA

1. Arrivals of non-resident tourists at national borders, by nationality

	2002	2003	2004	2005	2006	Market share 06	% Change 06-05
Burkina Faso		1	1		2		
AMERICAS	**7,973**	**6,863**	**12,198**	**12,913**	**14,433**	**3.74**	**11.77**
Caribbean	18	41	51	58	55	0.01	-5.17
Antigua and Barbuda			1		1		
Bahamas					3		
Barbados	1				3		
Bermuda					1		
Cuba	14	37	45	55	28	0.01	-49.09
Dominica					2		
Dominican Republic		1	3		2		
Haiti					2		
Jamaica	1		2	3	7		133.33
Montserrat					1		
Aruba					2		
Puerto Rico					1		
Trinidad and Tobago	2	3			2		
Central America	11	30	14	19	30	0.01	57.89
Belize					1		
Costa Rica	5	5		6	2		-66.67
El Salvador	1	17			4		
Guatemala		3	3		6		
Honduras	3	1	4	8	4		-50.00
Nicaragua	2	4	1		1		
Panama			6	5	12		140.00
North America	7,807	6,701	11,819	12,504	13,977	3.62	11.78
Canada	1,057	1,149	2,332	2,300	2,528	0.65	9.91
Mexico	25	19	56	51	72	0.02	41.18
United States	6,725	5,533	9,431	10,153	11,377	2.95	12.06
South America	137	91	314	332	371	0.10	11.75
Argentina	30	18	52	49	81	0.02	65.31
Bolivia	1	1		2	2		
Brazil	45	37	98	178	168	0.04	-5.62
Chile	19	14	97	33	39	0.01	18.18
Colombia	23	9	15	27	27	0.01	
Ecuador	4	2	2	6	5		-16.67
Falkland Islands (Malvinas)					4		
French Guiana					1		
Guyana	6		1	7			
Paraguay	1	1		2	1		-50.00
Peru	6	4	16	20	25	0.01	25.00
Suriname	1						
Uruguay			6		7		
Venezuela	1	5	27	8	11		37.50
EAST ASIA AND THE PACIFIC	**122,106**	**120,691**	**188,250**	**223,411**	**245,760**	**63.67**	**10.00**
North-East Asia	**117,978**	**116,465**	**181,443**	**216,213**	**238,159**	**61.70**	**10.15**
China	89,041	90,337	139,283	170,345	178,941	46.36	5.05
Taiwan (Province of China)	589	438	1,277	1,145	1,238	0.32	8.12
Hong Kong, China	366	380	757	653	628	0.16	-3.83
Japan	13,262	7,717	13,092	12,952	16,707	4.33	28.99
Korea, Dem. People's Republic of	239	420	407	313	700	0.18	123.64
Korea, Republic of	14,474	17,166	26,602	30,787	39,930	10.34	29.70
Macao, China	7	7	25	18	15		-16.67
South-East Asia	**1,724**	**1,511**	**2,404**	**2,774**	**2,690**	**0.70**	**-3.03**

MONGOLIA

1. Arrivals of non-resident tourists at national borders, by nationality

	2002	2003	2004	2005	2006	Market share 06	% Change 06-05
Brunei Darussalam		3	5				
Myanmar	8	5	9	10	5		-50.00
Cambodia	14	12	2	21	51	0.01	142.86
Indonesia	88	236	117	179	165	0.04	-7.82
Lao People's Democratic Republic	20	19	11	28	18		-35.71
Malaysia	363	266	516	755	677	0.18	-10.33
Philippines	239	219	412	394	357	0.09	-9.39
Singapore	729	386	778	947	796	0.21	-15.95
Viet Nam	135	189	318	233	284	0.07	21.89
Thailand	128	176	236	207	337	0.09	62.80
Australasia	**2,387**	**2,694**	**4,382**	**4,406**	**4,732**	**1.23**	**7.40**
Australia	1,754	2,244	3,461	3,454	4,053	1.05	17.34
New Zealand	633	450	921	952	679	0.18	-28.68
Melanesia	**11**	**16**	**13**	**16**	**76**	**0.02**	**375.00**
Solomon Islands			1		1		
Fiji	7	14	12	16	70	0.02	337.50
New Caledonia					1		
Vanuatu	2	2			3		
Papua New Guinea	2				1		
Micronesia		**2**			**48**	**0.01**	
Kiribati		1			46	0.01	
Guam		1					
Nauru					1		
Micronesia (Federated States of)					1		
Polynesia	**6**	**3**	**8**	**2**	**55**	**0.01**	**2,650.00**
American Samoa					3		
Tonga	4	2	6		51	0.01	
Samoa	2	1	2	2	1		-50.00
EUROPE	**97,674**	**72,345**	**98,592**	**100,123**	**124,002**	**32.13**	**23.85**
Central/Eastern Europe	**74,881**	**55,980**	**61,436**	**65,305**	**88,044**	**22.81**	**34.82**
Azerbaijan	57	55	36	48	180	0.05	275.00
Armenia	102	99	56	61	113	0.03	85.25
Bulgaria	87	71	163	54	131	0.03	142.59
Belarus	185	139	285	155	206	0.05	32.90
Czech Republic	519	419	719	716	612	0.16	-14.53
Estonia	19	21	15	27	37	0.01	37.04
Georgia	9	4	7	10	155	0.04	1,450.00
Hungary	119	128	251	243	274	0.07	12.76
Kazakhstan	1,820	1,782	3,101	3,728	4,185	1.08	12.26
Kyrgyzstan	229	236	303	311	681	0.18	118.97
Latvia	26	33	51	27	40	0.01	48.15
Lithuania	13	6	8	15	35	0.01	133.33
Republic of Moldova	124	90	82	81	70	0.02	-13.58
Poland	731	205	902	613	825	0.21	34.58
Romania	19	30	38	40	33	0.01	-17.50
Russian Federation	69,778	51,438	53,917	57,926	79,163	20.51	36.66
Slovakia	57	76	164	95	147	0.04	54.74
Tajikistan	47	30	74	74	82	0.02	10.81
Turkmenistan		61	91	69	4		-94.20
Ukraine	879	994	1,069	902	900	0.23	-0.22
Uzbekistan	61	63	104	110	171	0.04	55.45
Northern Europe	**6,874**	**5,081**	**10,196**	**9,801**	**10,458**	**2.71**	**6.70**
Denmark	763	436	981	712	962	0.25	35.11

MONGOLIA

1. Arrivals of non-resident tourists at national borders, by nationality

	2002	2003	2004	2005	2006	Market share 06	% Change 06-05
Finland	480	264	603	635	654	0.17	2.99
Iceland		20	14	33	28	0.01	-15.15
Ireland	206	220	717	610	760	0.20	24.59
Norway	674	296	853	679	652	0.17	-3.98
Sweden	1,277	991	2,063	1,926	1,509	0.39	-21.65
United Kingdom	3,474	2,854	4,965	5,206	5,893	1.53	13.20
Southern Europe	**1,540**	**1,052**	**4,261**	**3,715**	**3,909**	**1.01**	**5.22**
Albania		4	1	2	8		300.00
Andorra		2		6	2		-66.67
Bosnia and Herzegovina	5	3	2	55	5		-90.91
Croatia	22	13	36	32	17		-46.88
Greece	87	153	911	749	161	0.04	-78.50
Holy See	1		2		2		
Italy	987	565	1,918	1,921	2,526	0.65	31.49
Malta			1		3		
Portugal	51	28	267	100	139	0.04	39.00
Slovenia	9	19	129	86	122	0.03	41.86
Spain	290	220	937	756	868	0.22	14.81
TFYR of Macedonia		43	1	3	5		66.67
Yugoslavia, Sfr (Former)					42	0.01	
Serbia and Montenegro	88	2	56	5	9		80.00
Western Europe	**13,559**	**9,786**	**21,779**	**20,377**	**20,386**	**5.28**	**0.04**
Austria	664	319	1,017	738	1,201	0.31	62.74
Belgium	708	405	1,060	788	1,009	0.26	28.05
France	2,845	2,744	5,545	5,822	5,237	1.36	-10.05
Germany	6,780	4,973	8,769	8,168	8,576	2.22	5.00
Liechtenstein	1		1	2	8		300.00
Luxembourg	19	10	16	43	46	0.01	6.98
Netherlands	1,679	697	3,140	2,576	2,556	0.66	-0.78
Switzerland	863	638	2,231	2,240	1,753	0.45	-21.74
East Mediterranean Europe	**820**	**446**	**920**	**925**	**1,205**	**0.31**	**30.27**
Cyprus		1	1	2	12		500.00
Israel	478	231	573	471	602	0.16	27.81
Turkey	342	214	346	452	591	0.15	30.75
MIDDLE EAST	**155**	**229**	**249**	**232**	**159**	**0.04**	**-31.47**
Middle East	**155**	**229**	**249**	**232**	**159**	**0.04**	**-31.47**
Bahrain		3	3		4		
Palestine					1		
Iraq	3	29	4	5	3		-40.00
Jordan	7	2	5	7	6		-14.29
Kuwait	69	64	74	74	59	0.02	-20.27
Lebanon	8	6	8	7	4		-42.86
Libyan Arab Jamahiriya		1	2				
Oman	2	1					
Qatar		8	11	10	9		-10.00
Saudi Arabia	13	12	43	16	13		-18.75
Syrian Arab Republic	39	93	55	89	26	0.01	-70.79
United Arab Emirates	3	3	29	7	10		42.86
Egypt	11	2	11	13	11		-15.38
Yemen		5	4	4	13		225.00
SOUTH ASIA	**655**	**803**	**966**	**792**	**1,129**	**0.29**	**42.55**
South Asia	**655**	**803**	**966**	**792**	**1,129**	**0.29**	**42.55**
Afghanistan		5	2		7		

518

MONGOLIA

1. Arrivals of non-resident tourists at national borders, by nationality

	2002	2003	2004	2005	2006	Market share 06	% Change 06-05
Bangladesh	44	53	54	47	106	0.03	125.53
Bhutan	4	38	9	9	20	0.01	122.22
Sri Lanka	43	55	51	84	104	0.03	23.81
India	340	402	556	417	656	0.17	57.31
Iran, Islamic Republic of	43	12	19	31	64	0.02	106.45
Maldives		25	4		7		
Nepal	77	72	100	85	10		-88.24
Pakistan	104	141	171	119	98	0.03	-17.65
Other countries of South Asia					57	0.01	
REGION NOT SPECIFIED	**13**	**13**	**19**	**22**	**4**		**-81.82**
Not Specified	**13**	**13**	**19**	**22**	**4**		**-81.82**
Other countries of the World	13	13	19	22	4		-81.82

Source: World Tourism Organization (UNWTO)

MONGOLIA

2. Arrivals of non-resident visitors at national borders, by nationality

	2002	2003	2004	2005	2006	Market share 06	% Change 06-05
TOTAL	235,165	204,845	305,115	344,635	389,666	100.00	13.07
AFRICA	143	209	268	314	507	0.13	61.46
East Africa	18	39	26	34	71	0.02	108.82
Burundi	1	4	2		1		
Ethiopia	3	5	4	10	5		-50.00
Eritrea					3		
Djibouti					1		
Kenya	5	8	5	4	7		75.00
Madagascar		1	3	2			
Malawi			3		3		
Mauritius		2		1			
Mozambique					8		
Reunion			2		14		
Rwanda					3		
Somalia	3				7		
Zimbabwe	1	2	2	9	3		-66.67
Uganda	2	7	5	4	13		225.00
United Republic of Tanzania	3	5		4	3		-25.00
Zambia		5					
Central Africa	26	37	32	26	59	0.02	126.92
Angola	6		7	1	12		1,100.00
Cameroon	11	6	11	6	16		166.67
Central African Republic					5		
Chad		1					
Congo	9	12	14	19	10		-47.37
Equatorial Guinea		4			16		
Gabon		14					
North Africa	8	8	15	24	42	0.01	75.00
Algeria	4	1	6	6	32	0.01	433.33
Morocco	1	3	7	12	3		-75.00
Sudan	2	3	2	4	1		-75.00
Tunisia	1	1		2	6		200.00
Southern Africa	78	83	148	167	254	0.07	52.10
Botswana		2	1		1		
Lesotho		1					
Namibia		6	2		1		
South Africa	78	74	145	167	224	0.06	34.13
Swaziland					28	0.01	
West Africa	13	42	47	63	81	0.02	28.57
Benin		6	1				
Gambia		2		2			
Ghana	6	5	1		17		
Guinea			2	6	16		166.67
Cote D'Ivoire					1		
Liberia	3	3			2		
Mali				1	1		
Mauritania	2	2	1	2	3		50.00
Niger	2	11	40	50	27	0.01	-46.00
Nigeria					2		
Guinea-Bissau		3		2			
Senegal		1			1		
Sierra Leone		1	1		9		
Togo		7					

MONGOLIA

2. Arrivals of non-resident visitors at national borders, by nationality

	2002	2003	2004	2005	2006	Market share 06	% Change 06-05
Burkina Faso		1	1		2		
AMERICAS	**8,115**	**6,900**	**12,326**	**13,023**	**14,664**	**3.76**	**12.60**
Caribbean	**18**	**41**	**51**	**58**	**55**	**0.01**	**-5.17**
Antigua and Barbuda			1		1		
Bahamas					3		
Barbados	1				3		
Bermuda					1		
Cuba	14	37	45	55	28	0.01	-49.09
Dominica					2		
Dominican Republic		1	3		2		
Haiti					2		
Jamaica	1		2	3	7		133.33
Montserrat					1		
Aruba					2		
Puerto Rico					1		
Trinidad and Tobago	2	3			2		
Central America	**11**	**30**	**14**	**19**	**31**	**0.01**	**63.16**
Belize					1		
Costa Rica	5	5		6	2		-66.67
El Salvador	1	17			5		
Guatemala		3	3		6		
Honduras	3	1	4	8	4		-50.00
Nicaragua	2	4	1		1		
Panama			6	5	12		140.00
North America	**7,949**	**6,738**	**11,945**	**12,605**	**14,199**	**3.64**	**12.65**
Canada	1,062	1,149	2,340	2,320	2,564	0.66	10.52
Mexico	27	19	56	51	72	0.02	41.18
United States	6,860	5,570	9,549	10,234	11,563	2.97	12.99
South America	**137**	**91**	**316**	**341**	**379**	**0.10**	**11.14**
Argentina	30	18	53	51	81	0.02	58.82
Bolivia	1	1			2		
Brazil	45	37	99	182	174	0.04	-4.40
Chile	19	14	97	38	39	0.01	2.63
Colombia	23	9	15	27	27	0.01	
Ecuador	4	2	2	6	5		-16.67
Falkland Islands (Malvinas)					4		
French Guiana					3		
Guyana	6		1	7			
Paraguay	1	1		2	1		-50.00
Peru	6	4	16	20	25	0.01	25.00
Suriname	1						
Uruguay			6		7		
Venezuela	1	5	27	8	11		37.50
EAST ASIA AND THE PACIFIC	**126,238**	**122,378**	**190,746**	**227,949**	**247,644**	**63.55**	**8.64**
North-East Asia	**122,103**	**118,142**	**183,911**	**220,399**	**239,979**	**61.59**	**8.88**
China	92,657	91,934	141,473	171,444	180,209	46.25	5.11
Taiwan (Province of China)	589	439	1,286	1,235	1,246	0.32	0.89
Hong Kong, China	366	380	762	712	633	0.16	-11.10
Japan	13,708	7,757	13,196	13,230	16,909	4.34	27.81
Korea, Dem. People's Republic of	240	420	415	402	701	0.18	74.38
Korea, Republic of	14,536	17,205	26,754	33,350	40,266	10.33	20.74
Macao, China	7	7	25	26	15		-42.31
South-East Asia	**1,724**	**1,517**	**2,416**	**3,070**	**2,721**	**0.70**	**-11.37**

MONGOLIA

2. Arrivals of non-resident visitors at national borders, by nationality

	2002	2003	2004	2005	2006	Market share 06	% Change 06-05
Brunei Darussalam		3	5				
Myanmar	8	5	9	10	5		-50.00
Cambodia	14	12	2	21	52	0.01	147.62
Indonesia	88	238	118	302	165	0.04	-45.36
Lao People's Democratic Republic	20	19	11	35	18		-48.57
Malaysia	363	267	518	807	692	0.18	-14.25
Philippines	239	221	413	409	358	0.09	-12.47
Singapore	729	386	778	1,013	804	0.21	-20.63
Viet Nam	135	190	325	251	290	0.07	15.54
Thailand	128	176	237	222	337	0.09	51.80
Australasia	**2,394**	**2,698**	**4,398**	**4,480**	**4,765**	**1.22**	**6.36**
Australia	1,761	2,247	3,473	3,465	4,074	1.05	17.58
New Zealand	633	451	925	1,015	691	0.18	-31.92
Melanesia	**11**	**16**	**13**		**76**	**0.02**	
Solomon Islands			1		1		
Fiji	7	14	12		70	0.02	
New Caledonia					1		
Vanuatu	2	2			3		
Papua New Guinea	2				1		
Micronesia		**2**			**48**	**0.01**	
Kiribati		1			46	0.01	
Guam		1					
Nauru					1		
Micronesia (Federated States of)					1		
Polynesia	**6**	**3**	**8**		**55**	**0.01**	
American Samoa					3		
Tonga	4	2	6		51	0.01	
Samoa	2	1	2		1		
EUROPE	**99,838**	**74,308**	**100,512**	**102,243**	**125,533**	**32.22**	**22.78**
Central/Eastern Europe	**76,648**	**57,885**	**63,174**	**70,724**	**89,353**	**22.93**	**26.34**
Azerbaijan	57	55	37	85	181	0.05	112.94
Armenia	102	99	56	87	114	0.03	31.03
Bulgaria	89	71	164	66	131	0.03	98.48
Belarus	185	139	289	167	207	0.05	23.95
Czech Republic	520	424	723	802	633	0.16	-21.07
Estonia	19	21	15	41	37	0.01	-9.76
Georgia	9	4	7	26	157	0.04	503.85
Hungary	119	128	261	275	279	0.07	1.45
Kazakhstan	1,976	1,785	3,144	4,226	4,205	1.08	-0.50
Kyrgyzstan	229	238	308	356	685	0.18	92.42
Latvia	29	33	51	35	40	0.01	14.29
Lithuania	13	6	8	31	35	0.01	12.90
Republic of Moldova	124	90	83	97	72	0.02	-25.77
Poland	731	205	905	721	829	0.21	14.98
Romania	19	30	38	52	34	0.01	-34.62
Russian Federation	71,368	53,330	55,563	62,151	80,403	20.63	29.37
Slovakia	57	76	164	105	147	0.04	40.00
Tajikistan	47	30	74	81	83	0.02	2.47
Turkmenistan		61	102	74	4		-94.59
Ukraine	894	997	1,078	1,119	905	0.23	-19.12
Uzbekistan	61	63	104	127	172	0.04	35.43
Northern Europe	**7,049**	**5,093**	**10,262**	**10,003**	**10,517**	**2.70**	**5.14**
Denmark	763	438	1,003	742	963	0.25	29.78

MONGOLIA

2. Arrivals of non-resident visitors at national borders, by nationality

	2002	2003	2004	2005	2006	Market share 06	% Change 06-05
Finland	480	264	604	654	655	0.17	0.15
Iceland		20	15	52	28	0.01	-46.15
Ireland	206	221	718	612	760	0.20	24.18
Norway	674	298	864	718	655	0.17	-8.77
Sweden	1,388	993	2,071	1,969	1,513	0.39	-23.16
United Kingdom	3,538	2,859	4,987	5,256	5,943	1.53	13.07
Southern Europe	**1,539**	**1,054**	**4,268**	**3,841**	**3,927**	**1.01**	**2.24**
Albania		4	1	2	8		300.00
Andorra		2		6	2		-66.67
Bosnia and Herzegovina	5	3	2	55	5		-90.91
Croatia	22	13	37	32	18		-43.75
Greece	87	153	912	764	161	0.04	-78.93
Holy See			2	2	2		
Italy	987	566	1,919	1,924	2,539	0.65	31.96
Malta		1	4	3		-25.00	
Portugal	51	28	269	109	139	0.04	27.52
Slovenia	9	19	129	86	122	0.03	41.86
Spain	290	221	939	849	872	0.22	2.71
TFYR of Macedonia		3	1	3	5		66.67
Yugoslavia, Sfr (Former)					42	0.01	
Serbia and Montenegro	88	42	56	5	9		80.00
Western Europe	**13,754**	**9,825**	**21,876**	**16,728**	**20,515**	**5.26**	**22.64**
Austria	665	321	1,022		1,212	0.31	
Belgium	708	405	1,066		1,013	0.26	
France	2,891	2,751	5,567	5,843	5,254	1.35	-10.08
Germany	6,856	4,999	8,826	8,204	8,652	2.22	5.46
Liechtenstein	1		1		8		
Luxembourg	19	10	17		46	0.01	
Netherlands	1,739	697	3,144	2,681	2,565	0.66	-4.33
Switzerland	875	642	2,233		1,765	0.45	
East Mediterranean Europe	**848**	**451**	**932**	**947**	**1,221**	**0.31**	**28.93**
Cyprus		1	1	4	12		200.00
Israel	478	232	577	478	608	0.16	27.20
Turkey	370	218	354	465	601	0.15	29.25
MIDDLE EAST	**155**	**229**	**250**	**256**	**164**	**0.04**	**-35.94**
Middle East	**155**	**229**	**250**	**256**	**164**	**0.04**	**-35.94**
Bahrain		3	3		4		
Palestine					1		
Iraq	3	29	5	8	3		-62.50
Jordan	7	2	5	7	6		-14.29
Kuwait	69	64	74	81	59	0.02	-27.16
Lebanon	8	6	8	9	4		-55.56
Libyan Arab Jamahiriya		1	2				
Oman	2	1					
Qatar		8	11	10	14		40.00
Saudi Arabia	13	12	43	21	13		-38.10
Syrian Arab Republic	39	93	55	96	26	0.01	-72.92
United Arab Emirates	3	3	29	7	10		42.86
Egypt	11	2	11	13	11		-15.38
Yemen		5	4	4	13		225.00
SOUTH ASIA	**662**	**806**	**980**	**828**	**1,150**	**0.30**	**38.89**
South Asia	**662**	**806**	**980**	**828**	**1,150**	**0.30**	**38.89**
Afghanistan		5	2		7		

MONGOLIA

2. Arrivals of non-resident visitors at national borders, by nationality

	2002	2003	2004	2005	2006	Market share 06	% Change 06-05
Bangladesh	44	53	61	52	106	0.03	103.85
Bhutan	4	38	9	12	20	0.01	66.67
Sri Lanka	43	57	52	87	105	0.03	20.69
India	347	403	557	420	672	0.17	60.00
Iran, Islamic Republic of	43	12	19	32	64	0.02	100.00
Maldives		25	4		7		
Nepal	77	72	101	97	10		-89.69
Pakistan	104	141	175	128	102	0.03	-20.31
Other countries of South Asia					57	0.01	
REGION NOT SPECIFIED	**14**	**15**	**33**	**22**	**4**		**-81.82**
Not Specified	**14**	**15**	**33**	**22**	**4**		**-81.82**
Other countries of the World	14	15	33	22	4		-81.82

Source: World Tourism Organization (UNWTO)

MONTENEGRO

4. Arrivals of non-resident tourists in all types of accommodation establishments, by nationality

	2002	2003	2004	2005	2006	Market share 06	% Change 06-05
TOTAL	136,160	141,787	188,060	272,005	377,798	100.00	38.89
AMERICAS	3,006	2,657	3,354	4,302	7,324	1.94	70.25
North America	3,006	2,657	3,354	4,302	7,324	1.94	70.25
Canada	617	501	590	870	1,342	0.36	54.25
United States	2,389	2,156	2,764	3,432	5,982	1.58	74.30
EAST ASIA AND THE PACIFIC	441	427	682	973	1,488	0.39	52.93
North-East Asia	196	177	257	381	585	0.15	53.54
Japan	196	177	257	381	585	0.15	53.54
Australasia	245	250	425	592	903	0.24	52.53
Australia	245	250	425	592	903	0.24	52.53
EUROPE	129,491	135,329	180,286	259,596	359,937	95.27	38.65
Central/Eastern Europe	51,824	47,561	57,295	84,720	120,323	31.85	42.02
Bulgaria	935	4,612	1,953	1,571	2,324	0.62	47.93
Czech Republic	19,763	16,842	24,356	23,517	28,674	7.59	21.93
Hungary	1,957	3,917	4,425	6,243	8,766	2.32	40.41
Poland	3,977	1,898	2,394	3,040	6,383	1.69	109.97
Romania	747	1,097	1,190	896	1,390	0.37	55.13
Russian Federation	11,742	10,115	16,270	41,011	61,092	16.17	48.96
Slovakia	12,703	9,080	6,707	8,442	11,694	3.10	38.52
Northern Europe	5,060	6,008	13,298	18,434	25,971	6.87	40.89
Denmark	411	457	399	630	1,221	0.32	93.81
Finland	177	249	169	1,192	2,390	0.63	100.50
Norway	1,770	1,816	2,152	3,801	5,119	1.35	34.68
Sweden	1,029	889	5,116	4,994	4,157	1.10	-16.76
United Kingdom	1,673	2,597	5,462	7,817	13,084	3.46	67.38
Southern Europe	46,190	54,816	73,535	108,318	144,169	38.16	33.10
Albania		5,068	8,853	13,234	25,925	6.86	95.90
Bosnia and Herzegovina	25,887	29,559	32,706	46,838	55,553	14.70	18.61
Croatia	4,352	3,952	5,368	7,543	11,636	3.08	54.26
Greece	561	714	665	669	1,277	0.34	90.88
Italy	3,633	3,295	5,642	11,435	17,702	4.69	54.81
Slovenia	6,491	6,813	10,114	13,659	17,607	4.66	28.90
TFYR of Macedonia	5,266	5,415	10,187	14,940	14,469	3.83	-3.15
Western Europe	18,188	21,731	30,558	38,420	54,391	14.40	41.57
Austria	1,393	1,509	2,062	3,193	5,023	1.33	57.31
Belgium	1,179	1,479	2,970	1,179	5,655	1.50	379.64
France	1,370	1,510	2,047	11,300	17,702	4.69	56.65
Germany	11,789	14,328	19,873	18,352	20,252	5.36	10.35
Luxembourg	47	157	101	99	201	0.05	103.03
Netherlands	1,229	1,687	1,852	2,477	3,235	0.86	30.60
Switzerland	1,181	1,061	1,653	1,820	2,323	0.61	27.64
Other Europe	8,229	5,213	5,600	9,704	15,083	3.99	55.43
Other countries of Europe	8,229	5,213	5,600	9,704	15,083	3.99	55.43
REGION NOT SPECIFIED	3,222	3,374	3,738	7,134	9,049	2.40	26.84
Not Specified	3,222	3,374	3,738	7,134	9,049	2.40	26.84
Other countries of the World	3,222	3,374	3,738	7,134	9,049	2.40	26.84

Source: World Tourism Organization (UNWTO)

MONTENEGRO

6. Overnight stays of non-resident tourists in all types of accommodation establishments, by nationality

	2002	2003	2004	2005	2006	Market share 06	% Change 06-05
TOTAL	911,909	915,738	1,223,847	1,583,510	2,196,061	100.00	38.68
AMERICAS	9,878	9,095	12,915	13,474	23,249	1.06	72.55
North America	9,878	9,095	12,915	13,474	23,249	1.06	72.55
Canada	2,574	2,224	2,708	3,592	5,570	0.25	55.07
United States	7,304	6,871	10,207	9,882	17,679	0.81	78.90
EAST ASIA AND THE PACIFIC	1,563	1,141	1,953	2,833	3,948	0.18	39.36
North-East Asia	822	363	613	929	1,389	0.06	49.52
Japan	822	363	613	929	1,389	0.06	49.52
Australasia	741	778	1,340	1,904	2,559	0.12	34.40
Australia	741	778	1,340	1,904	2,559	0.12	34.40
EUROPE	886,255	897,460	1,195,128	1,545,291	2,145,527	97.70	38.84
Central/Eastern Europe	416,087	355,899	447,627	586,356	862,796	39.29	47.15
Bulgaria	3,760	13,622	6,182	4,173	6,735	0.31	61.39
Czech Republic	152,387	133,230	211,430	206,418	222,169	10.12	7.63
Hungary	11,715	24,574	26,641	36,437	46,565	2.12	27.80
Poland	35,647	13,428	15,940	17,633	34,608	1.58	96.27
Romania	4,526	6,430	6,025	4,599	8,005	0.36	74.06
Russian Federation	105,146	90,529	128,507	253,178	455,502	20.74	79.91
Slovakia	102,906	74,086	52,902	63,918	89,212	4.06	39.57
Northern Europe	39,995	50,622	108,622	133,796	168,318	7.66	25.80
Denmark	1,671	2,009	1,377	2,874	5,006	0.23	74.18
Finland	538	757	453	6,093	14,698	0.67	141.23
Norway	28,295	29,808	32,787	45,011	46,395	2.11	3.07
Sweden	4,425	3,810	37,933	31,236	23,211	1.06	-25.69
United Kingdom	5,066	14,238	36,072	48,582	79,008	3.60	62.63
Southern Europe	260,073	286,759	365,554	536,358	703,645	32.04	31.19
Albania		16,430	26,806	40,091	99,621	4.54	148.49
Bosnia and Herzegovina	149,709	174,273	190,066	267,875	336,618	15.33	25.66
Croatia	28,237	15,775	21,388	30,278	48,810	2.22	61.21
Greece	1,303	1,849	1,785	2,302	3,263	0.15	41.75
Italy	14,136	10,573	19,961	49,210	64,477	2.94	31.02
Slovenia	32,193	33,312	53,506	57,697	76,325	3.48	32.29
TFYR of Macedonia	34,495	34,547	52,042	88,905	74,531	3.39	-16.17
Western Europe	141,152	179,642	246,922	247,188	340,184	15.49	37.62
Austria	5,658	6,686	8,028	12,505	18,536	0.84	48.23
Belgium	10,316	9,862	14,601	6,953	39,196	1.78	463.73
France	5,613	5,430	8,273	64,354	103,828	4.73	61.34
Germany	103,258	135,178	188,439	133,903	142,538	6.49	6.45
Luxembourg	134	488	438	261	745	0.03	185.44
Netherlands	9,212	15,890	19,708	20,701	25,661	1.17	23.96
Switzerland	6,961	6,108	7,435	8,511	9,680	0.44	13.74
Other Europe	28,948	24,538	26,403	41,593	70,584	3.21	69.70
Other countries of Europe	28,948	24,538	26,403	41,593	70,584	3.21	69.70
REGION NOT SPECIFIED	14,213	8,042	13,851	21,912	23,337	1.06	6.50
Not Specified	14,213	8,042	13,851	21,912	23,337	1.06	6.50
Other countries of the World	14,213	8,042	13,851	21,912	23,337	1.06	6.50

Source: World Tourism Organization (UNWTO)

MONTSERRAT

1. Arrivals of non-resident tourists at national borders, by country of residence

	2002	2003	2004	2005	2006	Market share 06	% Change 06-05
TOTAL	9,836	8,390	10,138	9,690	7,991	100.00	-17.53
AMERICAS	7,014	5,932	6,822	6,448	5,427	67.91	-15.83
Caribbean	4,666	4,073	4,385	3,987	2,868	35.89	-28.07
All countries of the Caribbean	4,666	4,073	4,385	3,987	2,868	35.89	-28.07
North America	2,325	1,838	2,418	2,438	2,546	31.86	4.43
Canada	375	297	334	404	393	4.92	-2.72
United States	1,950	1,541	2,084	2,034	2,153	26.94	5.85
Other Americas	23	21	19	23	13	0.16	-43.48
Other countries of the Americas	23	21	19	23	13	0.16	-43.48
EUROPE	2,759	2,414	3,197	3,196	2,501	31.30	-21.75
Northern Europe	2,581	2,269	3,021	2,968	2,321	29.05	-21.80
United Kingdom	2,581	2,269	3,021	2,968	2,321	29.05	-21.80
Other Europe	178	145	176	228	180	2.25	-21.05
Other countries of Europe	178	145	176	228	180	2.25	-21.05
REGION NOT SPECIFIED	63	44	119	46	63	0.79	36.96
Not Specified	63	44	119	46	63	0.79	36.96
Other countries of the World	63	44	119	46	63	0.79	36.96

Source: World Tourism Organization (UNWTO)

MONTSERRAT

2. Arrivals of non-resident visitors at national borders, by country of residence

	2002	2003	2004	2005	2006	Market share 06	% Change 06-05
TOTAL	14,995	13,565	15,221	13,085	9,500	100.00	-27.40
AMERICAS	10,424	8,947	9,364	8,390	6,482	68.23	-22.74
Caribbean	6,871	5,838	5,802	5,202	3,665	38.58	-29.55
All countries of the Caribbean	6,871	5,838	5,802	5,202	3,665	38.58	-29.55
North America	3,518	3,078	3,539	3,157	2,796	29.43	-11.43
Canada	628	505	537	575	467	4.92	-18.78
United States	2,890	2,573	3,002	2,582	2,329	24.52	-9.80
Other Americas	35	31	23	31	21	0.22	-32.26
Other countries of the Americas	35	31	23	31	21	0.22	-32.26
EUROPE	4,477	4,545	5,695	4,629	2,941	30.96	-36.47
Northern Europe	4,111	4,199	5,353	4,230	2,695	28.37	-36.29
United Kingdom	4,111	4,199	5,353	4,230	2,695	28.37	-36.29
Other Europe	366	346	342	399	246	2.59	-38.35
Other countries of Europe	366	346	342	399	246	2.59	-38.35
REGION NOT SPECIFIED	94	73	162	66	77	0.81	16.67
Not Specified	94	73	162	66	77	0.81	16.67
Other countries of the World	94	73	162	66	77	0.81	16.67

Source: World Tourism Organization (UNWTO)

MOROCCO

1. Arrivals of non-resident tourists at national borders, by nationality

	2002	2003	2004	2005	2006	Market share 06	% Change 06-05
TOTAL	4,453,259	4,761,271	5,476,712	5,843,360	6,558,269	100.00	12.23
AFRICA	91,698	103,194	123,070	143,855	165,307	2.52	14.91
East Africa	1,854	1,837	1,725	1,758	2,467	0.04	40.33
Burundi	37	42	39	99	92		-7.07
Comoros	397	410	276	165	188		13.94
Ethiopia	149	155	156	151	211		39.74
Eritrea	24	25	47	40	58		45.00
Djibouti	96	170	228	223	227		1.79
Kenya	471	346	329	356	489	0.01	37.36
Madagascar	71	71	91	219	260		18.72
Malawi	33	15	7	33	71		115.15
Mauritius	145	152	188	186	343	0.01	84.41
Mozambique	16	30	22	36	32		-11.11
Rwanda	126	101	78	67	59		-11.94
Seychelles	6	6	5	12	40		233.33
Somalia	61	58	60	23	102		343.48
Zimbabwe	117	105	60	52	70		34.62
Uganda	36	67	72	27	91		237.04
United Republic of Tanzania	57	37	39	48	72		50.00
Zambia	12	47	28	21	62		195.24
Central Africa	3,675	3,802	4,750	6,114	8,722	0.13	42.66
Angola	245	315	484	204	474	0.01	132.35
Cameroon	598	696	791	1,125	1,581	0.02	40.53
Central African Republic	129	140	156	230	243		5.65
Chad	208	175	193	172	299		73.84
Congo	1,427	1,346	1,747	2,288	2,679	0.04	17.09
Democratic Republic of the Congo	7	32	2	3	219		7,200.00
Equatorial Guinea	85	82	111	137	249		81.75
Gabon	976	1,016	1,266	1,955	2,978	0.05	52.33
North Africa	48,346	48,578	54,622	64,103	72,580	1.11	13.22
Algeria	22,527	23,095	29,744	37,298	43,691	0.67	17.14
Sudan	807	838	974	1,096	1,446	0.02	31.93
Tunisia	25,012	24,645	23,904	25,709	27,443	0.42	6.74
Southern Africa	2,344	1,996	2,326	3,161	4,815	0.07	52.33
Botswana	32	11	18	20	22		10.00
Lesotho	6		6	3	11		266.67
Namibia	31	31	65	36	23		-36.11
South Africa	2,236	1,950	2,233	3,093	4,472	0.07	44.58
Swaziland	39	4	4	9	287		3,088.89
West Africa	35,479	46,981	59,647	68,719	76,723	1.17	11.65
Cape Verde	87	80	81	66	135		104.55
Benin	216	236	332	364	753	0.01	106.87
Gambia	199	179	252	185	356	0.01	92.43
Ghana	250	297	510	312	430	0.01	37.82
Guinea	7,270	8,907	11,218	10,175	8,954	0.14	-12.00
Cote D'Ivoire	3,240	3,314	4,121	5,982	7,606	0.12	27.15
Liberia	67	74	154	249	216		-13.25
Mali	3,522	4,507	4,679	5,603	6,865	0.10	22.52
Mauritania	8,017	15,913	18,895	20,889	23,902	0.36	14.42
Niger	1,479	1,366	1,496	2,161	2,868	0.04	32.72
Nigeria	569	491	614	585	1,074	0.02	83.59
Guinea-Bissau	63	51	43	89	178		100.00
Senegal	9,670	10,674	16,208	20,922	21,122	0.32	0.96

MOROCCO

1. Arrivals of non-resident tourists at national borders, by nationality

	2002	2003	2004	2005	2006	Market share 06	% Change 06-05
Sierra Leone	167	158	223	220	183		-16.82
Togo	140	154	188	192	660	0.01	243.75
Burkina Faso	523	580	633	725	1,421	0.02	96.00
AMERICAS	**119,229**	**107,877**	**127,974**	**140,194**	**173,258**	**2.64**	**23.58**
Caribbean	**465**	**366**	**423**	**569**	**3,545**	**0.05**	**523.02**
Bahamas	2	5	3	12	42		250.00
Barbados	10	5	13	3	404	0.01	*********
Bermuda	11	3		22	7		-68.18
Cuba	77	108	109	90	174		93.33
Dominica	126	98	128	234	103		-55.98
Haiti	47	54	48	73	382	0.01	423.29
Jamaica	55	40	46	41	206		402.44
Puerto Rico	12	32	21	59	480	0.01	713.56
Trinidad and Tobago	125	21	55	35	1,747	0.03	4,891.43
Central America	**541**	**626**	**537**	**486**	**888**	**0.01**	**82.72**
Belize	10	3	5	5	4		-20.00
Costa Rica	155	207	148	132	162		22.73
El Salvador	49	103	79	76	143		88.16
Guatemala	140	118	123	118	198		67.80
Honduras	100	111	93	57	117		105.26
Nicaragua	40	55	45	46	222		382.61
Panama	47	29	44	52	42		-19.23
North America	**105,035**	**95,766**	**112,246**	**124,392**	**143,808**	**2.19**	**15.61**
Canada	28,503	27,606	31,321	36,825	44,493	0.68	20.82
Mexico	3,687	3,715	4,036	4,587	5,669	0.09	23.59
United States	72,845	64,445	76,889	82,980	93,646	1.43	12.85
South America	**13,177**	**11,065**	**14,757**	**14,740**	**24,815**	**0.38**	**68.35**
Argentina	2,697	3,433	5,001	4,403	7,000	0.11	58.98
Bolivia	113	78	79	59	139		135.59
Brazil	6,335	3,650	5,035	5,287	7,929	0.12	49.97
Chile	1,592	1,390	1,607	1,957	2,284	0.03	16.71
Colombia	505	533	546	615	844	0.01	37.24
Ecuador	163	150	189	220	305		38.64
Guyana	37	12	8	8	4		-50.00
Paraguay	19	46	28	20	51		155.00
Peru	442	522	824	859	844	0.01	-1.75
Suriname	9	3	2	3	93		3,000.00
Uruguay	276	342	431	326	4,193	0.06	1,186.20
Venezuela	989	906	1,007	983	1,129	0.02	14.85
Other Americas	**11**	**54**	**11**	**7**	**202**		**2,785.71**
Other countries of the Americas	11	54	11	7	202		2,785.71
EAST ASIA AND THE PACIFIC	**44,242**	**41,651**	**48,874**	**51,745**	**65,234**	**0.99**	**26.07**
North-East Asia	**23,078**	**22,194**	**25,093**	**28,009**	**34,004**	**0.52**	**21.40**
China	2,986	2,579	2,747	3,513	4,028	0.06	14.66
Taiwan (Province of China)	601	535	569	604	707	0.01	17.05
Hong Kong, China	28	26	39	164	849	0.01	417.68
Japan	14,262	13,982	15,723	17,044	18,255	0.28	7.11
Korea, Dem. People's Republic of	259	224	13	4			
Korea, Republic of	4,942	4,848	6,002	6,680	10,165	0.15	52.17
South-East Asia	**6,285**	**7,022**	**8,165**	**8,777**	**10,308**	**0.16**	**17.44**
Brunei Darussalam	11	47	22	48	29		-39.58
Myanmar	20	18	62	35	81		131.43

MOROCCO

1. Arrivals of non-resident tourists at national borders, by nationality

	2002	2003	2004	2005	2006	Market share 06	% Change 06-05
Cambodia	16	21	48	22	9		-59.09
Indonesia	956	1,241	1,319	1,270	1,710	0.03	34.65
Malaysia	1,431	1,194	1,462	1,246	2,117	0.03	69.90
Philippines	2,669	3,068	3,485	3,452	4,100	0.06	18.77
Singapore	561	800	794	784	890	0.01	13.52
Viet Nam	69	70	273	785	208		-73.50
Thailand	552	563	700	1,135	1,164	0.02	2.56
Australasia	**14,879**	**12,433**	**15,615**	**14,957**	**20,910**	**0.32**	**39.80**
Australia	12,164	10,047	12,544	12,327	17,732	0.27	43.85
New Zealand	2,715	2,386	3,071	2,630	3,178	0.05	20.84
Micronesia		**2**	**1**	**2**	**12**		**500.00**
Kiribati		2	1	2	12		500.00
EUROPE	**1,868,540**	**1,880,177**	**2,309,477**	**2,607,239**	**3,024,876**	**46.12**	**16.02**
Central/Eastern Europe	**27,278**	**32,213**	**43,399**	**41,513**	**57,645**	**0.88**	**38.86**
Azerbaijan	20	20	69	14	86		514.29
Armenia	13	26	17	39	125		220.51
Bulgaria	936	1,525	1,522	1,810	1,674	0.03	-7.51
Belarus	150	104	178	149	228		53.02
Czech Republic	3,292	5,031	4,048	3,566	3,902	0.06	9.42
Estonia	203	135	310	1,560	1,354	0.02	-13.21
Hungary	2,275	4,982	8,385	5,957	5,896	0.09	-1.02
Kazakhstan	87	73	114	89	169		89.89
Lithuania	235	906	400	669	1,310	0.02	95.81
Poland	6,972	5,457	8,913	10,632	20,571	0.31	93.48
Romania	2,174	2,773	3,437	3,773	4,541	0.07	20.36
Russian Federation	8,234	8,039	11,318	8,670	11,975	0.18	38.12
Slovakia	1,253	1,133	1,513	1,476	1,920	0.03	30.08
Ukraine	1,413	1,988	3,136	3,062	3,739	0.06	22.11
Uzbekistan	21	21	39	47	155		229.79
Northern Europe	**213,161**	**216,554**	**235,040**	**266,063**	**341,937**	**5.21**	**28.52**
Denmark	11,185	15,593	15,143	12,115	11,559	0.18	-4.59
Finland	9,197	9,661	10,012	9,290	8,631	0.13	-7.09
Iceland	233	330	664	668	648	0.01	-2.99
Ireland	14,263	15,166	18,112	13,202	18,706	0.29	41.69
Norway	12,057	17,651	13,988	10,585	9,552	0.15	-9.76
Sweden	19,650	24,094	26,723	26,638	27,305	0.42	2.50
United Kingdom	146,576	134,059	150,398	193,565	265,536	4.05	37.18
Southern Europe	**363,414**	**374,962**	**477,526**	**536,301**	**665,710**	**10.15**	**24.13**
Albania	57	45	71	94	84		-10.64
Andorra	143	129	157	215	513	0.01	138.60
Bosnia and Herzegovina	156	144	118	167	287		71.86
Croatia	654	599	477	1,047	1,346	0.02	28.56
Greece	5,212	5,337	5,809	6,663	7,432	0.11	11.54
Italy	112,518	100,001	112,807	120,955	140,923	2.15	16.51
Malta	378	282	505	453	581	0.01	28.26
Portugal	42,022	36,389	38,951	36,980	43,876	0.67	18.65
San Marino	31	27	9	63	48		-23.81
Slovenia	522	532	989	1,188	1,650	0.03	38.89
Spain	201,258	231,156	317,119	367,811	467,956	7.14	27.23
TFYR of Macedonia	109	68	69	72	420	0.01	483.33
Serbia and Montenegro	354	253	445	593	594	0.01	0.17
Western Europe	**1,259,230**	**1,248,186**	**1,544,114**	**1,750,244**	**1,936,686**	**29.53**	**10.65**
Austria	15,928	12,798	13,561	14,634	13,930	0.21	-4.81

MOROCCO

1. Arrivals of non-resident tourists at national borders, by nationality

	2002	2003	2004	2005	2006	Market share 06	% Change 06-05
Belgium	83,966	80,062	105,821	125,890	149,531	2.28	18.78
France	877,465	916,147	1,167,088	1,337,204	1,481,610	22.59	10.80
Germany	172,860	129,391	141,210	144,200	151,396	2.31	4.99
Liechtenstein	56	37	44	58	70		20.69
Luxembourg	1,596	1,000	1,326	1,548	1,934	0.03	24.94
Monaco	88	92	116	112	113		0.89
Netherlands	65,085	66,486	73,190	80,090	92,201	1.41	15.12
Switzerland	42,186	42,173	41,758	46,508	45,901	0.70	-1.31
East Mediterranean Europe	**5,457**	**8,262**	**9,398**	**13,118**	**22,898**	**0.35**	**74.55**
Cyprus	202	150	204	195	392	0.01	101.03
Israel	102	100	1,294	762	7,932	0.12	940.94
Turkey	5,153	8,012	7,900	12,161	14,574	0.22	19.84
MIDDLE EAST	**85,996**	**78,639**	**84,298**	**91,029**	**105,632**	**1.61**	**16.04**
Middle East	**85,996**	**78,639**	**84,298**	**91,029**	**105,632**	**1.61**	**16.04**
Bahrain	2,624	2,779	2,762	1,872	2,211	0.03	18.11
Palestine	971	950	937	1,103	1,077	0.02	-2.36
Iraq	1,351	821	1,092	1,469	1,548	0.02	5.38
Jordan	3,796	3,829	4,284	3,366	4,045	0.06	20.17
Kuwait	4,632	4,276	4,945	4,749	6,079	0.09	28.01
Lebanon	4,223	3,754	4,324	4,656	6,987	0.11	50.06
Libyan Arab Jamahiriya	11,723	9,572	9,426	9,653	12,128	0.18	25.64
Oman	2,084	2,174	1,946	1,720	2,399	0.04	39.48
Qatar	1,231	1,388	1,482	1,857	3,184	0.05	71.46
Saudi Arabia	32,305	28,921	31,478	36,406	36,983	0.56	1.58
Syrian Arab Republic	3,708	3,688	4,352	4,783	4,351	0.07	-9.03
United Arab Emirates	6,298	5,908	6,435	6,773	9,232	0.14	36.31
Egypt	10,209	9,648	9,890	11,553	14,246	0.22	23.31
Yemen	841	931	945	1,069	1,162	0.02	8.70
SOUTH ASIA	**6,053**	**5,383**	**6,486**	**7,723**	**8,795**	**0.13**	**13.88**
South Asia	**6,053**	**5,383**	**6,486**	**7,723**	**8,795**	**0.13**	**13.88**
Afghanistan	74	77	41	72	102		41.67
Bangladesh	264	149	244	215	197		-8.37
Sri Lanka	215	163	217	260	353	0.01	35.77
India	3,450	3,145	3,798	4,577	4,950	0.08	8.15
Iran, Islamic Republic of	576	790	822	951	1,344	0.02	41.32
Maldives	53	19	35	92	22		-76.09
Nepal	68	56	73	76	103		35.53
Pakistan	1,353	984	1,256	1,480	1,724	0.03	16.49
REGION NOT SPECIFIED	**2,237,501**	**2,544,350**	**2,776,533**	**2,801,575**	**3,015,167**	**45.98**	**7.62**
Not Specified	**2,237,501**	**2,544,350**	**2,776,533**	**2,801,575**	**3,015,167**	**45.98**	**7.62**
Other countries of the World	6,508	6,954	7,401	13,750	28,795	0.44	109.42
Nationals Residing Abroad	2,230,993	2,537,396	2,769,132	2,787,825	2,986,372	45.54	7.12

Source: World Tourism Organization (UNWTO)

MOROCCO

3. Arrivals of non-resident tourists in hotels and similar establishments, by nationality

		2002	2003	2004	2005	2006	Market share 06	% Change 06-05
TOTAL	(*)	2,632,507	2,446,496	2,874,226	3,469,706	3,814,708	100.00	9.94
AFRICA		55,774	64,477	65,520	72,527	80,991	2.12	11.67
North Africa		23,077	25,207	31,046	35,397	40,236	1.05	13.67
Algeria		10,099	11,521	17,781	21,116	24,812	0.65	17.50
Tunisia		12,978	13,686	13,265	14,281	15,424	0.40	8.00
West Africa		4,447	4,722	4,537	3,689	6,742	0.18	82.76
Mauritania		4,447	4,722	4,537	3,689	6,742	0.18	82.76
Other Africa		28,250	34,548	29,937	33,441	34,013	0.89	1.71
Other countries of Africa		28,250	34,548	29,937	33,441	34,013	0.89	1.71
AMERICAS		97,304	74,268	82,539	99,481	121,317	3.18	21.95
North America		97,304	74,268	82,539	99,481	121,317	3.18	21.95
Canada		16,330	16,145	17,635	22,051	24,923	0.65	13.02
United States		80,974	58,123	64,904	77,430	96,394	2.53	24.49
EAST ASIA AND THE PACIFIC		38,723	36,417	41,622	52,727	54,398	1.43	3.17
North-East Asia		38,723	36,417	41,622	52,727	54,398	1.43	3.17
Japan		38,723	36,417	41,622	52,727	54,398	1.43	3.17
EUROPE		2,202,994	2,038,916	2,383,194	2,870,106	3,129,308	82.03	9.03
Central/Eastern Europe		2,552	4,522	5,238	20,969	37,154	0.97	77.19
Commonwealth Independent State		2,552	4,522	5,238	20,969	37,154	0.97	77.19
Northern Europe		159,808	148,732	175,427	232,683	298,840	7.83	28.43
Denmark		5,584	6,224	6,818	7,314	7,929	0.21	8.41
Finland		6,273	6,366	6,224	6,232	6,490	0.17	4.14
Norway		5,393	6,766	5,517	5,065	5,168	0.14	2.03
Sweden		12,899	16,969	19,406	19,985	20,606	0.54	3.11
United Kingdom		129,659	112,407	137,462	194,087	258,647	6.78	33.26
Southern Europe		407,294	357,095	447,834	550,499	630,826	16.54	14.59
Italy		197,718	153,681	176,478	204,330	226,365	5.93	10.78
Portugal		39,920	30,789	26,693	31,796	37,239	0.98	17.12
Spain		169,656	172,625	244,663	314,373	367,222	9.63	16.81
Western Europe		1,633,340	1,528,567	1,754,695	2,065,955	2,162,488	56.69	4.67
Austria		17,926	18,555	18,839	17,234	19,166	0.50	11.21
Belgium		77,446	69,580	88,937	112,859	126,020	3.30	11.66
France		1,202,764	1,206,656	1,399,557	1,635,549	1,680,744	44.06	2.76
Germany		234,322	149,131	158,161	187,935	211,605	5.55	12.59
Netherlands		53,622	46,376	51,971	70,238	83,217	2.18	18.48
Switzerland		47,260	38,269	37,230	42,140	41,736	1.09	-0.96
MIDDLE EAST		81,658	74,432	82,662	91,907	107,570	2.82	17.04
Middle East		81,658	74,432	82,662	91,907	107,570	2.82	17.04
Libyan Arab Jamahiriya		7,788	5,877	5,852	5,943	7,466	0.20	25.63
Saudi Arabia		34,696	28,931	33,643	35,746	37,940	0.99	6.14
Syrian Arab Republic		2,674	2,359	2,758	3,408	2,991	0.08	-12.24
United Arab Emirates		5,473	5,571	6,442	6,799	12,181	0.32	79.16
Egypt		7,527	8,176	7,704	8,604	10,017	0.26	16.42
Other countries of Middle East		23,500	23,518	26,263	31,407	36,975	0.97	17.73
REGION NOT SPECIFIED		156,054	157,986	218,689	282,958	321,124	8.42	13.49
Not Specified		156,054	157,986	218,689	282,958	321,124	8.42	13.49
Other countries of the World		142,284	143,400	205,591	263,678	304,477	7.98	15.47

MOROCCO

3. Arrivals of non-resident tourists in hotels and similar establishments, by nationality

	2002	2003	2004	2005	2006	Market share 06	% Change 06-05
Nationals Residing Abroad	13,770	14,586	13,098	19,280	16,647	0.44	-13.66

Source: World Tourism Organization (UNWTO)

MOROCCO

5. Overnight stays of non-resident tourists in hotels and similar establishments, by nationality

		2002	2003	2004	2005	2006	Market share 06	% Change 06-05
TOTAL	(*)	8,865,997	8,515,293	10,307,268	12,259,489	13,345,867	100.00	8.86
AFRICA		161,465	172,589	193,527	195,873	225,224	1.69	14.98
North Africa		66,662	72,360	93,579	101,641	119,386	0.89	17.46
Algeria		29,445	33,478	54,997	59,556	76,665	0.57	28.73
Tunisia		37,217	38,882	38,582	42,085	42,721	0.32	1.51
West Africa		16,068	21,929	17,159	9,327	20,995	0.16	125.10
Mauritania		16,068	21,929	17,159	9,327	20,995	0.16	125.10
Other Africa		78,735	78,300	82,789	84,905	84,843	0.64	-0.07
Other countries of Africa		78,735	78,300	82,789	84,905	84,843	0.64	-0.07
AMERICAS		227,848	176,626	200,334	242,561	278,691	2.09	14.90
North America		227,848	176,626	200,334	242,561	278,691	2.09	14.90
Canada		42,780	43,293	46,609	57,927	62,122	0.47	7.24
United States		185,068	133,333	153,725	184,634	216,569	1.62	17.30
EAST ASIA AND THE PACIFIC		64,729	61,275	70,596	84,436	84,802	0.64	0.43
North-East Asia		64,729	61,275	70,596	84,436	84,802	0.64	0.43
Japan		64,729	61,275	70,596	84,436	84,802	0.64	0.43
EUROPE		7,652,392	7,353,335	8,867,906	10,662,398	11,604,385	86.95	8.83
Central/Eastern Europe		9,915	26,839	32,766	94,587	147,803	1.11	56.26
Commonwealth Independent State		9,915	26,839	32,766	94,587	147,803	1.11	56.26
Northern Europe		664,584	685,945	802,550	1,082,732	1,430,308	10.72	32.10
Denmark		31,482	34,278	36,137	39,044	37,667	0.28	-3.53
Finland		44,791	49,967	45,914	43,747	44,321	0.33	1.31
Norway		26,864	38,340	27,961	21,080	24,337	0.18	15.45
Sweden		76,166	112,706	125,153	117,957	121,760	0.91	3.22
United Kingdom		485,281	450,654	567,385	860,904	1,202,223	9.01	39.65
Southern Europe		1,000,023	885,349	1,149,489	1,356,919	1,549,360	11.61	14.18
Italy		551,389	439,014	519,290	568,695	633,102	4.74	11.33
Portugal		104,047	91,840	70,718	88,862	99,416	0.74	11.88
Spain		344,587	354,495	559,481	699,362	816,842	6.12	16.80
Western Europe		5,977,870	5,755,202	6,883,101	8,128,160	8,476,914	63.52	4.29
Austria		42,454	40,432	48,790	41,161	47,942	0.36	16.47
Belgium		386,412	356,957	498,876	624,088	688,878	5.16	10.38
France		4,152,369	4,329,870	5,240,184	6,231,344	6,405,761	48.00	2.80
Germany		1,089,132	761,604	823,916	904,777	985,685	7.39	8.94
Netherlands		152,236	136,800	140,202	181,167	208,963	1.57	15.34
Switzerland		155,267	129,539	131,133	145,623	139,685	1.05	-4.08
MIDDLE EAST		312,003	284,207	317,299	349,023	359,448	2.69	2.99
Middle East		312,003	284,207	317,299	349,023	359,448	2.69	2.99
Libyan Arab Jamahiriya		22,753	17,284	14,765	16,494	19,002	0.14	15.21
Saudi Arabia		156,404	131,269	155,768	158,516	147,125	1.10	-7.19
Syrian Arab Republic		8,518	8,556	10,446	13,012	9,350	0.07	-28.14
United Arab Emirates		15,735	15,945	16,213	16,761	29,820	0.22	77.91
Egypt		27,396	27,528	26,041	31,850	32,637	0.24	2.47
Other countries of Middle East		81,197	83,625	94,066	112,390	121,514	0.91	8.12
REGION NOT SPECIFIED		447,560	467,261	657,606	725,198	793,317	5.94	9.39
Not Specified		447,560	467,261	657,606	725,198	793,317	5.94	9.39

MOROCCO

5. Overnight stays of non-resident tourists in hotels and similar establishments, by nationality

	2002	2003	2004	2005	2006	Market share 06	% Change 06-05
Other countries of the World	421,493	442,066	633,650	691,168	765,954	5.74	10.82
Nationals Residing Abroad	26,067	25,195	23,956	34,030	27,363	0.21	-19.59

Source: World Tourism Organization (UNWTO)

MOZAMBIQUE

2. Arrivals of non-resident visitors at national borders, by country of residence

	2002	2003	2004	2005	2006	Market share 06	% Change 06-05
TOTAL	942,885	726,099	711,060	954,433	1,095,000	100.00	14.73
AFRICA	848,259	591,647	623,240	851,999	977,468	89.27	14.73
East Africa	463,440	236,203	140,829	189,030	216,892	19.81	14.74
Malawi	224,274	121,267	74,933	100,580	115,405	10.54	14.74
Zimbabwe	233,496	114,936	65,896	88,450	101,487	9.27	14.74
Zambia	5,670						
Southern Africa	374,238	355,444	245,877	330,033	378,679	34.58	14.74
South Africa	336,657	335,426	228,104	306,177	351,307	32.08	14.74
Swaziland	37,581	20,018	17,773	23,856	27,372	2.50	14.74
Other Africa	10,581		236,534	332,936	381,897	34.88	14.71
Other countries of Africa	10,581		236,534	332,936	381,897	34.88	14.71
AMERICAS	10,401	5,035	5,647	12,399	14,226	1.30	14.74
North America	6,627	5,035	5,647	7,878	9,039	0.83	14.74
United States	6,627	5,035	5,647	7,878	9,039	0.83	14.74
Other Americas	3,774			4,521	5,187	0.47	14.73
Other countries of the Americas	3,774			4,521	5,187	0.47	14.73
EAST ASIA AND THE PACIFIC	5,721			8,036	9,220	0.84	14.73
Other East Asia and the Pacific	5,721			8,036	9,220	0.84	14.73
All countries of Asia	5,721			8,036	9,220	0.84	14.73
EUROPE	53,691	42,698	56,508	47,999	55,074	5.03	14.74
Northern Europe	13,638	5,798	6,700	8,993	10,319	0.94	14.74
United Kingdom	13,638	5,798	6,700	8,993	10,319	0.94	14.74
Southern Europe	19,089	25,392	11,898	15,970	18,324	1.67	14.74
Portugal	19,089	25,392	11,898	15,970	18,324	1.67	14.74
Other Europe	20,964	11,508	37,910	23,036	26,431	2.41	14.74
Other countries of Europe	20,964	11,508	37,910	23,036	26,431	2.41	14.74
REGION NOT SPECIFIED	24,813	86,719	25,665	34,000	39,012	3.56	14.74
Not Specified	24,813	86,719	25,665	34,000	39,012	3.56	14.74
Other countries of the World	24,813	86,719	25,665	34,000	39,012	3.56	14.74

Source: World Tourism Organization (UNWTO)

MYANMAR

1. Arrivals of non-resident tourists at national borders, by nationality

		2002	2003	2004	2005	2006	Market share 06	% Change 06-05
TOTAL	(*)	217,212	205,610	241,938	232,218	263,514	100.00	13.48
AFRICA		430	390	395	488	502	0.19	2.87
Other Africa		430	390	395	488	502	0.19	2.87
All countries of Africa		430	390	395	488	502	0.19	2.87
AMERICAS		17,824	16,426	20,451	20,701	22,880	8.68	10.53
North America		16,953	15,775	19,260	19,509	21,350	8.10	9.44
Canada		2,476	2,519	2,828	2,911	3,298	1.25	13.29
United States		14,477	13,256	16,432	16,598	18,052	6.85	8.76
Other Americas		871	651	1,191	1,192	1,530	0.58	28.36
Other countries of the Americas		871	651	1,191	1,192	1,530	0.58	28.36
EAST ASIA AND THE PACIFIC		124,280	115,614	141,683	129,922	148,282	56.27	14.13
North-East Asia		70,492	64,074	72,035	70,307	81,089	30.77	15.34
China		17,732	15,564	17,890	19,596	24,893	9.45	27.03
Taiwan (Province of China)		22,849	19,645	20,424	17,600	15,827	6.01	-10.07
Hong Kong, China		1,277	1,667	3,020	2,593	3,159	1.20	21.83
Japan		20,744	18,799	20,296	19,584	18,945	7.19	-3.26
Korea, Republic of		7,890	8,399	10,405	10,934	18,265	6.93	67.05
South-East Asia		40,778	42,590	56,505	46,731	50,940	19.33	9.01
Malaysia		12,532	10,003	12,478	9,858	9,588	3.64	-2.74
Singapore		11,310	10,373	11,292	9,674	10,952	4.16	13.21
Thailand		16,936	22,214	32,735	27,199	30,400	11.54	11.77
Australasia		5,912	5,721	7,076	7,264	7,512	2.85	3.41
Australia		5,194	4,950	6,069	6,342	6,583	2.50	3.80
New Zealand		718	771	1,007	922	929	0.35	0.76
Other East Asia and the Pacific		7,098	3,229	6,067	5,620	8,741	3.32	55.53
Other countries of Asia		7,098	3,229	6,067	5,602	8,720	3.31	55.66
Other countries of Oceania					18	21	0.01	16.67
EUROPE		65,477	60,364	65,411	67,933	80,791	30.66	18.93
Central/Eastern Europe		2,077	2,203	2,510	3,402	4,024	1.53	18.28
Russian Federation		556	551	760	1,032	1,432	0.54	38.76
Other countries Central/East Europ		1,521	1,652	1,750	2,370	2,592	0.98	9.37
Northern Europe		8,620	7,848	7,720	8,126	7,465	2.83	-8.13
United Kingdom		8,620	7,848	7,720	8,126	7,465	2.83	-8.13
Southern Europe		11,764	8,300	12,058	12,030	18,543	7.04	54.14
Italy		7,908	6,129	7,924	7,083	10,774	4.09	52.11
Spain		3,856	2,171	4,134	4,947	7,769	2.95	57.04
Western Europe		37,735	37,639	37,966	38,941	44,664	16.95	14.70
Austria		3,616	4,756	4,168	3,156	3,637	1.38	15.24
Belgium		2,364	2,159	2,340	2,859	2,790	1.06	-2.41
France		14,108	13,125	13,372	15,295	15,498	5.88	1.33
Germany		12,952	13,341	14,112	13,689	18,003	6.83	31.51
Switzerland		4,695	4,258	3,974	3,942	4,736	1.80	20.14
Other Europe		5,281	4,374	5,157	5,434	6,095	2.31	12.16
Other countries of Europe		5,281	4,374	5,157	5,434	6,095	2.31	12.16
MIDDLE EAST		2,022	1,148	1,831	1,920	2,177	0.83	13.39
Middle East		2,022	1,148	1,831	1,920	2,177	0.83	13.39
All countries of Middle East		2,022	1,148	1,831	1,920	2,177	0.83	13.39

MYANMAR

1. Arrivals of non-resident tourists at national borders, by nationality

	2002	2003	2004	2005	2006	Market share 06	% Change 06-05
SOUTH ASIA	7,179	11,668	12,167	11,254	8,882	3.37	-21.08
South Asia	7,179	11,668	12,167	11,254	8,882	3.37	-21.08
Bangladesh	1,488	1,999	1,705	1,506	1,342	0.51	-10.89
India	5,691	6,291	8,357	7,679	7,540	2.86	-1.81
Pakistan		742	846	749			
Other countries of South Asia		2,636	1,259	1,320			

Source: World Tourism Organization (UNWTO)

MYANMAR

5. Overnight stays of non-resident tourists in hotels and similar establishments, by nationality

	2002	2003	2004	2005	2006	Market share 06	% Change 06-05
TOTAL	1,520,505	1,415,624	1,678,832	1,625,526	1,844,598	100.00	13.48
AFRICA	3,010	2,730	2,765	3,416	3,514	0.19	2.87
Other Africa	3,010	2,730	2,765	3,416	3,514	0.19	2.87
All countries of Africa	3,010	2,730	2,765	3,416	3,514	0.19	2.87
AMERICAS	124,768	114,982	143,157	144,907	160,160	8.68	10.53
North America	118,671	110,425	134,820	136,563	149,450	8.10	9.44
Canada	17,332	17,633	19,796	20,377	23,086	1.25	13.29
United States	101,339	92,792	115,024	116,186	126,364	6.85	8.76
Other Americas	6,097	4,557	8,337	8,344	10,710	0.58	28.36
Other countries of the Americas	6,097	4,557	8,337	8,344	10,710	0.58	28.36
EAST ASIA AND THE PACIFIC	869,960	809,298	991,781	923,937	1,037,974	56.27	12.34
North-East Asia	493,444	448,518	504,245	492,149	567,623	30.77	15.34
China	124,124	108,948	125,230	137,172	174,251	9.45	27.03
Taiwan (Province of China)	159,943	137,515	142,968	123,200	110,789	6.01	-10.07
Hong Kong, China	8,939	11,669	21,140	18,151	22,113	1.20	21.83
Japan	145,208	131,593	142,072	137,088	132,615	7.19	-3.26
Korea, Republic of	55,230	58,793	72,835	76,538	127,855	6.93	67.05
South-East Asia	285,446	298,130	395,535	327,117	356,580	19.33	9.01
Malaysia	87,724	70,021	87,346	69,006	67,116	3.64	-2.74
Singapore	79,170	72,611	79,044	67,718	76,664	4.16	13.21
Thailand	118,552	155,498	229,145	190,393	212,800	11.54	11.77
Australasia	41,384	40,047	49,532	50,848	52,584	2.85	3.41
Australia	36,358	34,650	42,483	44,394	46,081	2.50	3.80
New Zealand	5,026	5,397	7,049	6,454	6,503	0.35	0.76
Other East Asia and the Pacific	49,686	22,603	42,469	53,823	61,187	3.32	13.68
Other countries of Asia	49,686	22,603	42,469	53,823	61,187	3.32	13.68
EUROPE	458,360	422,548	457,878	475,531	565,537	30.66	18.93
Central/Eastern Europe	14,560	15,421	17,570	23,814	28,168	1.53	18.28
Russian Federation	3,892	3,857	5,320	7,224	10,024	0.54	38.76
Other countries Central/East Europ	10,668	11,564	12,250	16,590	18,144	0.98	9.37
Northern Europe	60,340	54,936	54,040	56,882	52,255	2.83	-8.13
United Kingdom	60,340	54,936	54,040	56,882	52,255	2.83	-8.13
Southern Europe	82,348	58,100	84,407	84,210	129,801	7.04	54.14
Italy	55,356	42,903	55,468	49,581	75,418	4.09	52.11
Spain	26,992	15,197	28,939	34,629	54,383	2.95	57.04
Western Europe	264,145	263,473	265,762	272,587	312,648	16.95	14.70
Austria	25,312	33,292	29,176	22,092	25,459	1.38	15.24
Belgium	16,548	15,113	16,380	20,013	19,530	1.06	-2.41
France	98,756	91,875	93,604	107,065	108,486	5.88	1.33
Germany	90,664	93,387	98,784	95,823	126,021	6.83	31.51
Switzerland	32,865	29,806	27,818	27,594	33,152	1.80	20.14
Other Europe	36,967	30,618	36,099	38,038	42,665	2.31	12.16
Other countries of Europe	36,967	30,618	36,099	38,038	42,665	2.31	12.16
MIDDLE EAST	14,154	8,036	12,817	13,440	15,239	0.83	13.39
Middle East	14,154	8,036	12,817	13,440	15,239	0.83	13.39
All countries of Middle East	14,154	8,036	12,817	13,440	15,239	0.83	13.39

MYANMAR

5. Overnight stays of non-resident tourists in hotels and similar establishments, by nationality

	2002	2003	2004	2005	2006	Market share 06	% Change 06-05
SOUTH ASIA	**50,253**	**58,030**	**70,434**	**64,295**	**62,174**	**3.37**	**-3.30**
South Asia	**50,253**	**58,030**	**70,434**	**64,295**	**62,174**	**3.37**	**-3.30**
Bangladesh	10,416	13,993	11,935	10,542	9,394	0.51	-10.89
India	39,837	44,037	58,499	53,753	52,780	2.86	-1.81

Source: World Tourism Organization (UNWTO)

NAMIBIA

1. Arrivals of non-resident tourists at national borders, by country of residence

	2002	2003	2004	2005	2006	Market share 06	% Change 06-05
TOTAL	757,201	695,221		777,890	833,345	100.00	7.13
AFRICA	591,612	525,885		601,737	628,588	75.43	4.46
East Africa	32,737	51,429		58,547	75,825	9.10	29.51
Zimbabwe	19,145	17,795		22,765	30,622	3.67	34.51
Zambia	13,592	33,634		35,782	45,203	5.42	26.33
Central Africa	278,816	222,752		281,365	278,058	33.37	-1.18
Angola	278,816	222,752		281,365	278,058	33.37	-1.18
Southern Africa	273,222	244,688		253,282	264,604	31.75	4.47
Botswana	29,328	22,679		22,333	24,719	2.97	10.68
South Africa	243,894	222,009		230,949	239,885	28.79	3.87
Other Africa	6,837	7,016		8,543	10,101	1.21	18.24
Other countries of Africa	6,837	7,016		8,543	10,101	1.21	18.24
AMERICAS	9,625	11,775		14,685	16,324	1.96	11.16
North America	9,625	11,775		14,685	16,324	1.96	11.16
United States	9,625	11,775		14,685	16,324	1.96	11.16
EAST ASIA AND THE PACIFIC	3,430	4,280		4,607	4,644	0.56	0.80
Australasia	3,430	4,280		4,607	4,644	0.56	0.80
Australia	3,430	4,280		4,607	4,644	0.56	0.80
EUROPE	140,781	141,834		146,362	166,974	20.04	14.08
Northern Europe	25,272	24,607		27,305	32,041	3.84	17.34
United Kingdom	19,560	19,291		20,978	24,736	2.97	17.91
Scandinavia	5,712	5,316		6,327	7,305	0.88	15.46
Southern Europe	16,714	16,792		14,802	17,753	2.13	19.94
Italy	9,059	8,809		8,557	9,406	1.13	9.92
Portugal	3,244	3,535		2,753	3,880	0.47	40.94
Spain	4,411	4,448		3,492	4,467	0.54	27.92
Western Europe	94,786	95,717		99,514	110,360	13.24	10.90
Austria	4,983	5,023		5,160	5,277	0.63	2.27
Belgium	3,444	4,197		3,240	3,752	0.45	15.80
France	9,194	9,364		9,959	12,000	1.44	20.49
Germany	61,236	58,036		61,222	68,214	8.19	11.42
Netherlands	9,654	11,778		11,570	12,196	1.46	5.41
Switzerland	6,275	7,319		8,363	8,921	1.07	6.67
Other Europe	4,009	4,718		4,741	6,820	0.82	43.85
Other countries of Europe	4,009	4,718		4,741	6,820	0.82	43.85
REGION NOT SPECIFIED	11,753	11,447		10,499	16,815	2.02	60.16
Not Specified	11,753	11,447		10,499	16,815	2.02	60.16
Other countries of the World	11,753	11,447		10,499	16,815	2.02	60.16

Source: World Tourism Organization (UNWTO)

NAMIBIA

2. Arrivals of non-resident visitors at national borders, by country of residence

	2002	2003	2004	2005	2006	Market share 06	% Change 06-05
TOTAL	947,778			973,168	1,031,677	100.00	6.01
AFRICA	745,709			770,866	801,745	77.71	4.01
East Africa	49,172			108,913	148,878	14.43	36.69
Zimbabwe	22,796			26,979	33,310	3.23	23.47
Zambia	26,376			81,934	115,568	11.20	41.05
Central Africa	330,764			337,317	311,323	30.18	-7.71
Angola	330,764			337,317	311,323	30.18	-7.71
Southern Africa	354,499			312,375	327,912	31.78	4.97
Botswana	39,784			30,075	32,541	3.15	8.20
South Africa	314,715			282,300	295,371	28.63	4.63
Other Africa	11,274			12,261	13,632	1.32	11.18
Other countries of Africa	11,274			12,261	13,632	1.32	11.18
AMERICAS	12,050			14,685	18,823	1.82	28.18
North America	12,050			14,685	18,823	1.82	28.18
United States				14,685	18,823	1.82	28.18
All countries of North America	12,050						
EAST ASIA AND THE PACIFIC				4,607	5,264	0.51	14.26
Australasia				4,607	5,264	0.51	14.26
Australia				4,607	5,264	0.51	14.26
EUROPE	169,689			165,391	185,727	18.00	12.30
Northern Europe	31,041			32,190	37,524	3.64	16.57
United Kingdom	23,945			24,990	29,491	2.86	18.01
Scandinavia	7,096			7,200	8,033	0.78	11.57
Southern Europe	10,161			17,428	19,965	1.94	14.56
Italy	10,161			9,107	9,969	0.97	9.47
Portugal				4,094	4,978	0.48	21.59
Spain				4,227	5,018	0.49	18.71
Western Europe	84,202			109,877	120,339	11.66	9.52
Austria				5,628	5,645	0.55	0.30
Belgium				3,583	4,106	0.40	14.60
France	10,716			10,683	13,054	1.27	22.19
Germany	73,486			68,390	74,552	7.23	9.01
Netherlands				12,830	13,490	1.31	5.14
Switzerland				8,763	9,492	0.92	8.32
Other Europe	44,285			5,896	7,899	0.77	33.97
Other countries of Europe	44,285			5,896	7,899	0.77	33.97
REGION NOT SPECIFIED	20,330			17,619	20,118	1.95	14.18
Not Specified	20,330			17,619	20,118	1.95	14.18
Other countries of the World	20,330			17,619	20,118	1.95	14.18

Source: World Tourism Organization (UNWTO)

NEPAL

1. Arrivals of non-resident tourists at national borders, by nationality

	2002	2003	2004	2005	2006	Market share 06	% Change 06-05
TOTAL	275,468	338,132	385,297	375,398	383,926	100.00	2.27
AFRICA	1,132	1,612	1,161	1,302	1,125	0.29	-13.59
Other Africa	1,132	1,612	1,161	1,302	1,125	0.29	-13.59
All countries of Africa	1,132	1,612	1,161	1,302	1,125	0.29	-13.59
AMERICAS	24,058	25,254	29,878	26,412	29,330	7.64	11.05
North America	22,255	23,887	26,523	23,984	25,589	6.67	6.69
Canada	3,747	4,154	4,825	4,314	4,733	1.23	9.71
Mexico	990	895	1,018	1,131	1,023	0.27	-9.55
United States	17,518	18,838	20,680	18,539	19,833	5.17	6.98
South America	610	866	1,877	1,526	2,399	0.62	57.21
Argentina	233	227	484	669	1,158	0.30	73.09
Brazil	377	639	1,393	857	1,241	0.32	44.81
Other Americas	1,193	501	1,478	902	1,342	0.35	48.78
Other countries of the Americas	1,193	501	1,478	902	1,342	0.35	48.78
EAST ASIA AND THE PACIFIC	65,697	91,314	96,236	91,207	94,282	24.56	3.37
North-East Asia	40,736	48,174	48,384	49,930	51,959	13.53	4.06
China	8,715	7,562	13,326	21,170	16,800	4.38	-20.64
Japan	23,223	27,412	24,231	18,460	22,242	5.79	20.49
Korea, Republic of	8,798	13,200	10,827	10,300	12,917	3.36	25.41
South-East Asia	10,191	23,783	26,088	22,803	22,454	5.85	-1.53
Indonesia	514	824	668	687	770	0.20	12.08
Malaysia	2,777	8,197	7,266	5,269	4,414	1.15	-16.23
Philippines	388	468	342	264	698	0.18	164.39
Singapore	1,818	3,165	3,164	3,075	2,828	0.74	-8.03
Thailand	4,694	11,129	14,648	13,508	13,744	3.58	1.75
Australasia	8,404	9,583	10,904	8,266	9,746	2.54	17.90
Australia	7,159	7,916	9,671	7,035	8,231	2.14	17.00
New Zealand	1,245	1,667	1,233	1,231	1,515	0.39	23.07
Other East Asia and the Pacific	6,366	9,774	10,860	10,208	10,123	2.64	-0.83
Other countries of Asia	6,350	9,749	10,817	10,157	10,106	2.63	-0.50
Other countries of Oceania	16	25	43	51	17		-66.67
EUROPE	99,474	112,346	131,857	112,482	113,155	29.47	0.60
Central/Eastern Europe	5,276	6,451	7,661	8,263	10,613	2.76	28.44
Czech Republic	929	989	848	721	1,098	0.29	52.29
Hungary	338	356	810	911	797	0.21	-12.51
Poland	1,117	1,817	1,615	1,948	2,572	0.67	32.03
Russian Federation	1,563	1,989	2,376	2,668	3,841	1.00	43.97
Other countries Central/East Europ	1,329	1,300	2,012	2,015	2,305	0.60	14.39
Northern Europe	26,504	28,812	31,423	30,590	29,395	7.66	-3.91
Denmark	2,040	2,178	2,633	1,807	1,956	0.51	8.25
Finland	714	813	676	768	842	0.22	9.64
Ireland	874	1,112	849	686	1,290	0.34	88.05
Norway	1,043	1,365	1,503	1,303	1,422	0.37	9.13
Sweden	826	1,243	1,095	875	1,177	0.31	34.51
United Kingdom	21,007	22,101	24,667	25,151	22,708	5.91	-9.71
Southern Europe	13,819	16,901	25,005	18,771	19,017	4.95	1.31
Greece (*)	495	393	862	988	904	0.24	-8.50
Italy	8,057	8,243	12,376	8,892	7,736	2.01	-13.00

544

NEPAL

1. Arrivals of non-resident tourists at national borders, by nationality

	2002	2003	2004	2005	2006	Market share 06	% Change 06-05
Spain	5,267	8,265	11,767	8,891	10,377	2.70	16.71
Western Europe	**46,795**	**48,027**	**57,913**	**46,726**	**46,660**	**12.15**	**-0.14**
Austria	3,140	3,025	4,341	2,506	3,474	0.90	38.63
Belgium	2,847	2,582	3,661	3,538	3,224	0.84	-8.88
France	13,376	15,865	18,938	14,128	14,835	3.86	5.00
Germany	15,774	14,866	16,025	14,444	14,361	3.74	-0.57
Netherlands	8,306	8,443	11,160	8,947	7,207	1.88	-19.45
Switzerland	3,352	3,246	3,788	3,163	3,559	0.93	12.52
East Mediterranean Europe	**6,286**	**10,733**	**7,691**	**6,173**	**5,264**	**1.37**	**-14.73**
Israel	6,286	10,733	7,691	6,173	5,264	1.37	-14.73
Other Europe	**794**	**1,422**	**2,164**	**1,959**	**2,206**	**0.57**	**12.61**
Other countries of Europe	794	1,422	2,164	1,959	2,206	0.57	12.61
SOUTH ASIA	**85,107**	**107,606**	**125,407**	**141,219**	**142,029**	**36.99**	**0.57**
South Asia	**85,107**	**107,606**	**125,407**	**141,219**	**142,029**	**36.99**	**0.57**
Bangladesh	5,507	5,031	14,607	20,201	16,474	4.29	-18.45
Bhutan	1,426	1,307	2,057	3,498	2,135	0.56	-38.97
Sri Lanka	9,805	13,930	16,124	18,770	27,413	7.14	46.05
India	66,777	86,363	90,326	96,434	93,722	24.41	-2.81
Iran, Islamic Republic of	121	49	117	254	243	0.06	-4.33
Maldives	230	165	156	309	181	0.05	-41.42
Pakistan	1,241	761	2,020	1,753	1,861	0.48	6.16
REGION NOT SPECIFIED			**758**	**2,776**	**4,005**	**1.04**	**44.27**
Not Specified			**758**	**2,776**	**4,005**	**1.04**	**44.27**
Other countries of the World			758	2,776	4,005	1.04	44.27

Source: World Tourism Organization (UNWTO)

NEPAL

1. Arrivals of non-resident tourists at national borders, by country of residence

	2002	2003	2004	2005	2006	Market share 06	% Change 06-05
TOTAL	275,468	338,132	385,297	375,398	383,926	100.00	2.27
AFRICA	1,117	1,501	1,346	1,285	1,571	0.41	22.26
Other Africa	1,117	1,501	1,346	1,285	1,571	0.41	22.26
All countries of Africa	1,117	1,501	1,346	1,285	1,571	0.41	22.26
AMERICAS	25,110	25,156	29,791	26,385	27,991	7.29	6.09
North America	21,403	23,751	26,404	23,769	24,414	6.36	2.71
Canada	3,366	3,984	4,783	4,168	4,379	1.14	5.06
Mexico	961	896	1,037	1,125	996	0.26	-11.47
United States	17,076	18,871	20,584	18,476	19,039	4.96	3.05
South America	518	902	1,899	1,627	2,336	0.61	43.58
Argentina	137	280	595	827	1,170	0.30	41.48
Brazil	381	622	1,304	800	1,166	0.30	45.75
Other Americas	3,189	503	1,488	989	1,241	0.32	25.48
Other countries of the Americas	3,189	503	1,488	989	1,241	0.32	25.48
EAST ASIA AND THE PACIFIC	67,985	91,582	96,565	92,733	95,407	24.85	2.88
North-East Asia	41,712	48,277	48,706	50,737	51,615	13.44	1.73
China	8,026	5,677	12,733	21,092	15,777	4.11	-25.20
Hong Kong, China	2,113	1,564	1,123	1,285	1,761	0.46	37.04
Japan	22,941	27,267	24,196	18,239	21,664	5.64	18.78
Korea, Republic of	8,632	13,769	10,654	10,121	12,413	3.23	22.65
South-East Asia	11,134	24,094	26,151	23,394	23,430	6.10	0.15
Indonesia	544	557	659	680	827	0.22	21.62
Malaysia	2,762	8,191	7,214	5,371	4,245	1.11	-20.96
Philippines	469	505	393	500	727	0.19	45.40
Singapore	2,193	3,449	3,205	3,229	3,299	0.86	2.17
Thailand	5,166	11,392	14,680	13,614	14,332	3.73	5.27
Australasia	8,335	9,519	11,049	8,269	9,551	2.49	15.50
Australia	7,179	7,916	9,839	7,093	8,204	2.14	15.66
New Zealand	1,156	1,603	1,210	1,176	1,347	0.35	14.54
Other East Asia and the Pacific	6,804	9,692	10,659	10,333	10,811	2.82	4.63
Other countries of Asia	6,781	9,663	10,599	10,278	10,793	2.81	5.01
Other countries of Oceania	23	29	60	55	18		-67.27
EUROPE	97,026	111,822	131,999	112,341	108,166	28.17	-3.72
Central/Eastern Europe	5,082	6,418	7,770	8,513	10,096	2.63	18.60
Czech Republic	893	1,016	836	711	1,041	0.27	46.41
Hungary	350	362	821	901	731	0.19	-18.87
Poland	1,104	1,780	1,609	1,944	2,501	0.65	28.65
Russian Federation	1,531	1,958	2,447	2,695	3,712	0.97	37.74
Other countries Central/East Europ	1,204	1,302	2,057	2,262	2,111	0.55	-6.68
Northern Europe	24,911	28,113	31,317	30,051	27,113	7.06	-9.78
Denmark	1,913	2,165	2,614	1,770	1,714	0.45	-3.16
Finland	676	790	664	552	705	0.18	27.72
Ireland	839	987	813	657	1,150	0.30	75.04
Norway	1,036	1,388	1,513	1,273	1,300	0.34	2.12
Sweden	768	1,233	1,069	849	1,064	0.28	25.32
United Kingdom	19,679	21,550	24,644	24,950	21,180	5.52	-15.11
Southern Europe	13,805	16,838	24,799	18,679	18,564	4.84	-0.62
Greece (*)	506	391	886	998	856	0.22	-14.23

NEPAL

1. Arrivals of non-resident tourists at national borders, by country of residence

	2002	2003	2004	2005	2006	Market share 06	% Change 06-05
Italy	8,002	8,201	12,121	8,785	7,472	1.95	-14.95
Spain	5,297	8,246	11,792	8,896	10,236	2.67	15.06
Western Europe	**46,192**	**48,165**	**58,264**	**47,202**	**45,136**	**11.76**	**-4.38**
Austria	3,080	3,199	4,649	3,007	3,606	0.94	19.92
Belgium	2,825	2,581	3,652	3,548	3,181	0.83	-10.34
France	13,135	15,730	18,992	14,108	14,293	3.72	1.31
Germany	15,570	14,875	16,031	14,345	13,686	3.56	-4.59
Netherlands	8,049	8,339	11,064	8,890	6,848	1.78	-22.97
Switzerland	3,533	3,441	3,876	3,304	3,522	0.92	6.60
East Mediterranean Europe	**6,266**	**10,921**	**7,690**	**6,002**	**5,094**	**1.33**	**-15.13**
Israel	6,266	10,921	7,690	6,002	5,094	1.33	-15.13
Other Europe	**770**	**1,367**	**2,159**	**1,894**	**2,163**	**0.56**	**14.20**
Other countries of Europe	770	1,367	2,159	1,894	2,163	0.56	14.20
SOUTH ASIA	**84,230**	**108,071**	**124,804**	**139,288**	**137,059**	**35.70**	**-1.60**
South Asia	**84,230**	**108,071**	**124,804**	**139,288**	**137,059**	**35.70**	**-1.60**
Bangladesh	5,756	5,215	14,640	19,206	16,623	4.33	-13.45
Bhutan	1,418	1,295	2,045	3,461	2,095	0.55	-39.47
Sri Lanka	9,756	13,960	16,045	18,686	27,382	7.13	46.54
India	65,743	86,578	89,861	95,685	88,857	23.14	-7.14
Iran, Islamic Republic of	105	97	111	241	221	0.06	-8.30
Maldives	221	163	150	281	179	0.05	-36.30
Pakistan	1,231	763	1,952	1,728	1,702	0.44	-1.50
REGION NOT SPECIFIED			**792**	**3,366**	**13,732**	**3.58**	**307.96**
Not Specified			**792**	**3,366**	**13,732**	**3.58**	**307.96**
Other countries of the World			792	3,366	13,732	3.58	307.96

Source: World Tourism Organization (UNWTO)

NETHERLANDS

3. Arrivals of non-resident tourists in hotels and similar establishments, by country of residence

	2002	2003	2004	2005	2006	Market share 06	% Change 06-05
TOTAL (*)	7,432,900	6,930,400	7,601,300	8,080,600	8,567,200	100.00	6.02
AFRICA	171,700	129,400	116,100	95,500	90,800	1.06	-4.92
Other Africa	171,700	129,400	116,100	95,500	90,800	1.06	-4.92
All countries of Africa	171,700	129,400	116,100	95,500	90,800	1.06	-4.92
AMERICAS	1,091,600	988,200	1,124,800	1,217,100	1,317,100	15.37	8.22
North America	974,500	903,500	1,014,200	1,092,900	1,174,300	13.71	7.45
Canada	95,600	87,300	114,700	125,700	133,200	1.55	5.97
United States	878,900	816,200	899,500	967,200	1,041,100	12.15	7.64
Other Americas	117,100	84,700	110,600	124,200	142,800	1.67	14.98
Other countries of the Americas	117,100	84,700	110,600	124,200	142,800	1.67	14.98
EAST ASIA AND THE PACIFIC	641,300	543,800	665,400	649,000	617,300	7.21	-4.88
North-East Asia	198,500	146,100	269,900	289,000	275,800	3.22	-4.57
China			81,700	96,300	95,300	1.11	-1.04
Taiwan (Province of China)	13,400	9,200	12,700	13,800	15,100	0.18	9.42
Japan	185,100	136,900	163,800	156,900	141,700	1.65	-9.69
Korea, Republic of			11,700	22,000	23,700	0.28	7.73
South-East Asia	12,800	10,900	25,200	15,600	12,300	0.14	-21.15
Indonesia	12,800	10,900	25,200	15,600	12,300	0.14	-21.15
Australasia	83,000	64,100	97,600	88,400	107,500	1.25	21.61
Australia	70,400	55,200	80,900	75,400	92,100	1.08	22.15
New Zealand	12,600	8,900	16,700	13,000	15,400	0.18	18.46
Other East Asia and the Pacific	347,000	322,700	272,700	256,000	221,700	2.59	-13.40
Other countries of Asia	328,300	303,200	257,400	243,000	212,400	2.48	-12.59
Other countries of Oceania	18,700	19,500	15,300	13,000	9,300	0.11	-28.46
EUROPE	5,528,300	5,269,000	5,670,900	6,084,800	6,505,000	75.93	6.91
Central/Eastern Europe	135,100	133,200	166,100	211,000	236,100	2.76	11.90
Czech Republic	23,100	20,800	26,900	26,400	31,700	0.37	20.08
Hungary	17,100	15,200	21,300	22,900	28,000	0.33	22.27
Poland	41,100	41,800	51,600	60,300	73,400	0.86	21.72
Russian Federation	45,300	48,600	57,800	93,800	94,400	1.10	0.64
Slovakia	8,500	6,800	8,500	7,600	8,600	0.10	13.16
Northern Europe	2,136,800	1,935,800	2,107,400	2,225,800	2,314,600	27.02	3.99
Denmark	85,100	93,800	108,100	127,500	148,100	1.73	16.16
Finland	41,700	40,500	44,100	45,900	47,300	0.55	3.05
Iceland	4,400	5,000	4,900	7,000	8,000	0.09	14.29
Ireland	91,600	86,700	88,900	104,000	105,000	1.23	0.96
Norway	66,600	62,300	77,100	78,100	85,100	0.99	8.96
Sweden	103,800	92,800	105,200	101,100	101,800	1.19	0.69
United Kingdom	1,743,600	1,554,700	1,679,100	1,762,200	1,819,300	21.24	3.24
Southern Europe	583,700	576,000	662,800	707,300	808,200	9.43	14.27
Greece	28,100	26,200	34,800	35,700	39,800	0.46	11.48
Italy	277,100	276,900	317,900	328,100	351,500	4.10	7.13
Portugal	36,600	33,400	38,500	45,300	47,800	0.56	5.52
Spain	241,900	239,500	271,600	298,200	369,100	4.31	23.78
Western Europe	2,335,300	2,297,500	2,396,300	2,559,100	2,767,700	32.31	8.15
Austria	56,500	50,400	52,800	58,900	62,100	0.72	5.43
Belgium	441,200	465,000	486,900	573,500	611,400	7.14	6.61

NETHERLANDS

3. Arrivals of non-resident tourists in hotels and similar establishments, by country of residence

	2002	2003	2004	2005	2006	Market share 06	% Change 06-05
France	448,800	389,900	442,900	467,500	515,400	6.02	10.25
Germany	1,247,000	1,259,800	1,266,500	1,309,100	1,403,500	16.38	7.21
Luxembourg	34,900	32,200	30,000	28,600	30,400	0.35	6.29
Switzerland	106,900	100,200	117,200	121,500	144,900	1.69	19.26
East Mediterranean Europe	**98,500**	**87,200**	**86,700**	**88,100**	**94,700**	**1.11**	**7.49**
Israel	78,800	64,900	55,700	58,900	58,300	0.68	-1.02
Turkey	19,700	22,300	31,000	29,200	36,400	0.42	24.66
Other Europe	**238,900**	**239,300**	**251,600**	**293,500**	**283,700**	**3.31**	**-3.34**
Other countries of Europe	238,900	239,300	251,600	293,500	283,700	3.31	-3.34
SOUTH ASIA			**24,100**	**34,200**	**37,000**	**0.43**	**8.19**
South Asia			**24,100**	**34,200**	**37,000**	**0.43**	**8.19**
India			24,100	34,200	37,000	0.43	8.19

Source: World Tourism Organization (UNWTO)

NETHERLANDS

4. Arrivals of non-resident tourists in all types of accommodation establishments, by country of residence

	2002	2003	2004	2005	2006	Market share 06	% Change 06-05
TOTAL	9,595,300	9,180,600	9,646,500	10,011,900	10,738,700	100.00	7.26
AFRICA	172,800	130,600	117,300	101,100	92,700	0.86	-8.31
Other Africa	172,800	130,600	117,300	101,100	92,700	0.86	-8.31
All countries of Africa	172,800	130,600	117,300	101,100	92,700	0.86	-8.31
AMERICAS	1,099,700	996,100	1,131,500	1,222,200	1,325,000	12.34	8.41
Other Americas	1,099,700	996,100	1,131,500	1,222,200	1,325,000	12.34	8.41
All countries of the Americas	1,099,700	996,100	1,131,500	1,222,200	1,325,000	12.34	8.41
EAST ASIA AND THE PACIFIC	731,200	622,100	753,700	748,700	722,600	6.73	-3.49
Other East Asia and the Pacific	731,200	622,100	753,700	748,700	722,600	6.73	-3.49
All countries of Asia	624,400	530,600	635,600	643,500	602,000	5.61	-6.45
All countries of Oceania	106,800	91,500	118,100	105,200	120,600	1.12	14.64
EUROPE	7,591,600	7,431,800	7,644,000	7,939,900	8,598,400	80.07	8.29
Northern Europe	2,065,400	1,867,800	1,997,900	2,110,900	2,197,200	20.46	4.09
Denmark	102,600	116,000	126,400	147,700	170,800	1.59	15.64
Sweden	111,600	105,800	111,700	110,600	113,700	1.06	2.80
United Kingdom	1,851,200	1,646,000	1,759,800	1,852,600	1,912,700	17.81	3.24
Southern Europe	621,500	613,600	666,400	696,400	789,100	7.35	13.31
Italy	345,700	338,900	368,600	374,100	397,500	3.70	6.26
Spain	275,800	274,700	297,800	322,300	391,600	3.65	21.50
Western Europe	4,097,900	4,162,200	4,111,800	4,155,100	4,583,600	42.68	10.31
Belgium	704,800	779,300	811,300	917,400	990,600	9.22	7.98
France	511,200	465,200	510,400	526,700	607,600	5.66	15.36
Germany	2,754,500	2,803,000	2,649,000	2,569,600	2,812,400	26.19	9.45
Switzerland	127,400	114,700	141,100	141,400	173,000	1.61	22.35
Other Europe	806,800	788,200	867,900	977,500	1,028,500	9.58	5.22
Other countries of Europe	806,800	788,200	867,900	977,500	1,028,500	9.58	5.22

Source: World Tourism Organization (UNWTO)

NETHERLANDS

5. Overnight stays of non-resident tourists in hotels and similar establishments, by country of residence

		2002	2003	2004	2005	2006	Market share 06	% Change 06-05
TOTAL	(*)	14,921,500	13,798,400	14,616,400	15,143,100	15,976,200	100.00	5.50
AFRICA		358,300	268,400	230,100	180,900	173,400	1.09	-4.15
Other Africa		358,300	268,400	230,100	180,900	173,400	1.09	-4.15
All countries of Africa		358,300	268,400	230,100	180,900	173,400	1.09	-4.15
AMERICAS		2,127,700	1,892,900	2,081,700	2,126,900	2,341,900	14.66	10.11
North America		1,895,300	1,713,400	1,859,900	1,904,200	2,068,200	12.95	8.61
Canada		195,700	173,900	213,800	232,000	255,900	1.60	10.30
United States		1,699,600	1,539,500	1,646,100	1,672,200	1,812,300	11.34	8.38
Other Americas		232,400	179,500	221,800	222,700	273,700	1.71	22.90
Other countries of the Americas		232,400	179,500	221,800	222,700	273,700	1.71	22.90
EAST ASIA AND THE PACIFIC		1,168,200	1,000,400	1,157,900	1,102,700	1,090,500	6.83	-1.11
North-East Asia		364,300	274,300	458,100	490,400	472,800	2.96	-3.59
China				131,800	150,100	150,300	0.94	0.13
Taiwan (Province of China)		23,800	16,600	23,300	25,400	26,000	0.16	2.36
Japan		340,500	257,700	279,000	270,700	250,800	1.57	-7.35
Korea, Republic of				24,000	44,200	45,700	0.29	3.39
South-East Asia		28,000	24,300	45,100	30,600	24,200	0.15	-20.92
Indonesia		28,000	24,300	45,100	30,600	24,200	0.15	-20.92
Australasia		157,700	129,900	188,500	168,700	215,100	1.35	27.50
Australia		135,100	112,700	157,500	144,700	183,800	1.15	27.02
New Zealand		22,600	17,200	31,000	24,000	31,300	0.20	30.42
Other East Asia and the Pacific		618,200	571,900	466,200	413,000	378,400	2.37	-8.38
Other countries of Asia		581,800	540,200	437,700	389,700	361,300	2.26	-7.29
Other countries of Oceania		36,400	31,700	28,500	23,300	17,100	0.11	-26.61
EUROPE		11,267,300	10,636,700	11,083,300	11,659,200	12,289,600	76.92	5.41
Central/Eastern Europe		306,300	279,000	332,800	412,200	426,500	2.67	3.47
Czech Republic		52,500	43,400	54,900	48,600	57,200	0.36	17.70
Hungary		35,900	32,300	44,200	44,300	53,200	0.33	20.09
Poland		99,800	89,700	105,200	126,100	133,000	0.83	5.47
Russian Federation		98,700	100,100	112,200	179,100	167,400	1.05	-6.53
Slovakia		19,400	13,500	16,300	14,100	15,700	0.10	11.35
Northern Europe		4,274,200	3,733,100	3,985,300	4,056,400	4,210,200	26.35	3.79
Denmark		166,700	178,100	216,400	241,900	281,500	1.76	16.37
Finland		81,900	74,700	84,700	84,700	85,500	0.54	0.94
Iceland		9,600	10,900	10,000	12,700	15,300	0.10	20.47
Ireland		197,000	173,900	179,800	199,400	200,900	1.26	0.75
Norway		130,800	118,600	144,800	146,800	159,000	1.00	8.31
Sweden		199,000	178,600	189,600	178,300	186,300	1.17	4.49
United Kingdom		3,489,200	2,998,300	3,160,000	3,192,600	3,281,700	20.54	2.79
Southern Europe		1,231,900	1,218,100	1,393,200	1,443,100	1,634,800	10.23	13.28
Greece		61,500	56,100	74,600	71,600	79,900	0.50	11.59
Italy		591,400	589,200	673,100	678,100	706,000	4.42	4.11
Portugal		77,800	66,800	80,400	87,100	92,000	0.58	5.63
Spain		501,200	506,000	565,100	606,300	756,900	4.74	24.84
Western Europe		4,755,400	4,735,800	4,692,100	4,998,200	5,243,000	32.82	4.90
Austria		112,300	102,400	105,000	115,500	124,100	0.78	7.45
Belgium		767,100	819,600	820,500	956,700	1,013,600	6.34	5.95

NETHERLANDS

5. Overnight stays of non-resident tourists in hotels and similar establishments, by country of residence

	2002	2003	2004	2005	2006	Market share 06	% Change 06-05
France	793,200	698,600	773,800	811,000	890,900	5.58	9.85
Germany	2,802,200	2,843,700	2,706,600	2,834,500	2,882,600	18.04	1.70
Luxembourg	66,800	71,900	64,000	53,900	61,200	0.38	13.54
Switzerland	213,800	199,600	222,200	226,600	270,600	1.69	19.42
East Mediterranean Europe	**227,100**	**190,300**	**184,900**	**180,400**	**184,100**	**1.15**	**2.05**
Israel	186,500	144,300	123,700	123,700	119,500	0.75	-3.40
Turkey	40,600	46,000	61,200	56,700	64,600	0.40	13.93
Other Europe	**472,400**	**480,400**	**495,000**	**568,900**	**591,000**	**3.70**	**3.88**
Other countries of Europe	472,400	480,400	495,000	568,900	591,000	3.70	3.88
SOUTH ASIA			**63,400**	**73,400**	**80,800**	**0.51**	**10.08**
South Asia			**63,400**	**73,400**	**80,800**	**0.51**	**10.08**
India			63,400	73,400	80,800	0.51	10.08

Source: World Tourism Organization (UNWTO)

NETHERLANDS

6. Overnight stays of non-resident tourists in all types of accommodation establishments, by country of residence

		2002	2003	2004	2005	2006	Market share 06	% Change 06-05
TOTAL	(*)	26,367,700	25,341,400	25,384,500	25,209,900	26,886,700	100.00	6.65
AFRICA		367,900	273,800	235,600	226,900	183,100	0.68	-19.30
Other Africa		367,900	273,800	235,600	226,900	183,100	0.68	-19.30
All countries of Africa		367,900	273,800	235,600	226,900	183,100	0.68	-19.30
AMERICAS		2,167,500	1,937,000	2,119,500	2,150,000	2,378,600	8.85	10.63
Other Americas		2,167,500	1,937,000	2,119,500	2,150,000	2,378,600	8.85	10.63
All countries of the Americas		2,167,500	1,937,000	2,119,500	2,150,000	2,378,600	8.85	10.63
EAST ASIA AND THE PACIFIC		1,405,300	1,206,900	1,379,900	1,330,600	1,332,900	4.96	0.17
Other East Asia and the Pacific		1,405,300	1,206,900	1,379,900	1,330,600	1,332,900	4.96	0.17
All countries of Asia		1,196,600	1,017,300	1,146,700	1,124,500	1,089,200	4.05	-3.14
All countries of Oceania		208,700	189,600	233,200	206,100	243,700	0.91	18.24
EUROPE		22,427,000	21,923,700	21,649,500	21,502,400	22,992,100	85.51	6.93
Northern Europe		4,464,900	3,974,500	4,059,000	4,162,800	4,348,800	16.17	4.47
Denmark		226,100	265,500	286,500	304,500	373,000	1.39	22.50
Sweden		222,600	224,600	210,400	195,400	230,900	0.86	18.17
United Kingdom		4,016,200	3,484,400	3,562,100	3,662,900	3,744,900	13.93	2.24
Southern Europe		1,382,400	1,416,100	1,526,500	1,548,700	1,696,400	6.31	9.54
Italy		775,400	786,200	851,500	838,400	856,200	3.18	2.12
Spain		607,000	629,900	675,000	710,300	840,200	3.12	18.29
Western Europe		14,708,600	14,706,800	14,145,700	13,756,000	14,792,300	55.02	7.53
Belgium		1,941,400	2,137,000	2,186,700	2,392,300	2,541,800	9.45	6.25
France		997,900	954,900	1,015,700	1,016,500	1,229,900	4.57	20.99
Germany		11,481,500	11,350,300	10,612,100	10,043,500	10,630,000	39.54	5.84
Switzerland		287,800	264,600	331,200	303,700	390,600	1.45	28.61
Other Europe		1,871,100	1,826,300	1,918,300	2,034,900	2,154,600	8.01	5.88
Other countries of Europe		1,871,100	1,826,300	1,918,300	2,034,900	2,154,600	8.01	5.88

Source: World Tourism Organization (UNWTO)

NEW CALEDONIA

1. Arrivals of non-resident tourists at national borders, by nationality

	2002	2003	2004	2005	2006	Market share 06	% Change 06-05
TOTAL	103,933	101,983	99,515	100,651	100,491	100.00	-0.16
AFRICA	137	132	201	124	177	0.18	42.74
Other Africa	137	132	201	124	177	0.18	42.74
All countries of Africa	137	132	201	124	177	0.18	42.74
AMERICAS	2,304	2,008	1,860	1,834	1,883	1.87	2.67
North America	2,114	1,735	1,632	1,605	1,740	1.73	8.41
Canada	741	541	708	737	919	0.91	24.69
United States	1,373	1,194	924	868	821	0.82	-5.41
South America	17	12	28	46	29	0.03	-36.96
Argentina	17	12	28	46	29	0.03	-36.96
Other Americas	173	261	200	183	114	0.11	-37.70
Other countries of the Americas	173	261	200	183	114	0.11	-37.70
EAST ASIA AND THE PACIFIC	52,906	52,125	53,537	54,868	52,166	51.91	-4.92
North-East Asia	27,439	28,768	29,355	31,902	30,139	29.99	-5.53
Taiwan (Province of China)	24	10	25	15			
Hong Kong, China	1	10	3	6	127	0.13	2,016.67
Japan	27,234	28,560	29,098	31,412	29,685	29.54	-5.50
Korea, Republic of	180	188	229	469	327	0.33	-30.28
Australasia	22,364	20,499	20,882	19,921	18,939	18.85	-4.93
Australia	16,683	14,667	14,839	14,074	12,527	12.47	-10.99
New Zealand	5,681	5,832	6,043	5,847	6,412	6.38	9.66
Melanesia	1,567	1,614	1,850	1,576	1,581	1.57	0.32
Vanuatu	1,567	1,614	1,850	1,576	1,581	1.57	0.32
Other East Asia and the Pacific	1,536	1,244	1,450	1,469	1,507	1.50	2.59
Other countries of Asia	1,017	842	928	924	948	0.94	2.60
Other countries of Oceania	519	402	522	545	559	0.56	2.57
EUROPE	48,527	47,616	43,795	43,795	46,263	46.04	5.64
Northern Europe	1,501	1,204	1,161	1,167	1,351	1.34	15.77
United Kingdom	1,501	1,204	1,161	1,167	1,351	1.34	15.77
Southern Europe	563	538	540	427	501	0.50	17.33
Italy	563	538	540	427	501	0.50	17.33
Western Europe	45,189	44,433	40,789	41,032	43,045	42.83	4.91
France	44,481	43,384	40,008	40,220	42,322	42.12	5.23
Germany	320	545	406	438	422	0.42	-3.65
Switzerland	388	504	375	374	301	0.30	-19.52
Other Europe	1,274	1,441	1,305	1,169	1,366	1.36	16.85
Other countries of Europe	1,274	1,441	1,305	1,169	1,366	1.36	16.85
REGION NOT SPECIFIED	59	102	122	30	2		-93.33
Not Specified	59	102	122	30	2		-93.33
Other countries of the World	59	102	122	30	2		-93.33

Source: World Tourism Organization (UNWTO)

NEW CALEDONIA

1. Arrivals of non-resident tourists at national borders, by country of residence

		2002	2003	2004	2005	2006	Market share 06	% Change 06-05
TOTAL	(*)	103,933	101,983	99,515	100,651	100,491	100.00	-0.16
AFRICA		520	489	615	637	705	0.70	10.68
East Africa		363	343	460	504	533	0.53	5.75
Reunion		363	343	460	504	533	0.53	5.75
Other Africa		157	146	155	133	172	0.17	29.32
Other countries of Africa		157	146	155	133	172	0.17	29.32
AMERICAS		2,141	1,753	1,676	1,785	1,854	1.84	3.87
Caribbean		226	152	178	156	187	0.19	19.87
All countries of the Caribbean	(*)	226	152	178	156	187	0.19	19.87
North America		1,724	1,381	1,326	1,416	1,543	1.54	8.97
Canada		522	387	555	609	728	0.72	19.54
United States		1,202	994	771	807	815	0.81	0.99
South America		20	15	25	44	19	0.02	-56.82
Argentina		20	15	25	44	19	0.02	-56.82
Other Americas		171	205	147	169	105	0.10	-37.87
Other countries of the Americas		171	205	147	169	105	0.10	-37.87
EAST ASIA AND THE PACIFIC		67,998	65,382	65,892	67,753	66,074	65.75	-2.48
North-East Asia		27,354	28,644	29,446	32,019	30,258	30.11	-5.50
Taiwan (Province of China)		42	8	24	124	136	0.14	9.68
Hong Kong, China		59	57	53	85	50	0.05	-41.18
Japan		27,202	28,490	29,229	31,486	29,833	29.69	-5.25
Korea, Republic of		51	89	140	324	239	0.24	-26.23
Australasia		25,151	21,987	22,580	22,390	21,705	21.60	-3.06
Australia		19,216	15,957	16,212	16,062	14,775	14.70	-8.01
New Zealand		5,935	6,030	6,368	6,328	6,930	6.90	9.51
Melanesia		2,538	2,373	2,518	2,267	2,363	2.35	4.23
Vanuatu		2,538	2,373	2,518	2,267	2,363	2.35	4.23
Polynesia		11,265	11,009	9,751	9,406	9,924	9.88	5.51
French Polynesia		3,706	3,866	3,750	4,227	4,114	4.09	-2.67
Wallis and Futuna Islands		7,559	7,143	6,001	5,179	5,810	5.78	12.18
Other East Asia and the Pacific		1,690	1,369	1,597	1,671	1,824	1.82	9.16
Other countries of Asia		1,081	851	969	944	1,101	1.10	16.63
Other countries of Oceania		609	518	628	727	723	0.72	-0.55
EUROPE		32,683	32,492	29,992	30,268	31,850	31.69	5.23
Northern Europe		551	473	409	468	573	0.57	22.44
United Kingdom		551	473	409	468	573	0.57	22.44
Southern Europe		461	486	491	359	422	0.42	17.55
Italy		461	486	491	359	422	0.42	17.55
Western Europe		30,677	30,398	28,069	28,469	29,735	29.59	4.45
France		29,964	29,440	27,358	27,727	29,030	28.89	4.70
Germany		318	453	314	339	359	0.36	5.90
Switzerland		395	505	397	403	346	0.34	-14.14
Other Europe		994	1,135	1,023	972	1,120	1.11	15.23
Other countries of Europe		994	1,135	1,023	972	1,120	1.11	15.23
REGION NOT SPECIFIED		591	1,867	1,340	208	8	0.01	-96.15
Not Specified		591	1,867	1,340	208	8	0.01	-96.15

NEW CALEDONIA

3. Arrivals of non-resident tourists in hotels and similar establishments, by country of residence

		2002	2003	2004	2005	2006	Market share 06	% Change 06-05
TOTAL	(*)	81,530	74,957	79,041	77,286	85,309	100.00	10.38
EAST ASIA AND THE PACIFIC		58,808	52,792	54,989	53,247	56,623	66.37	6.34
North-East Asia		34,381	31,334	32,635	35,160	35,614	41.75	1.29
Japan		34,381	31,334	32,635	35,160	35,614	41.75	1.29
Australasia		24,427	21,458	22,354	18,087	21,009	24.63	16.16
Australia		20,367	17,101	17,640	14,180	15,662	18.36	10.45
New Zealand		4,060	4,357	4,714	3,907	5,347	6.27	36.86
EUROPE		16,826	16,700	17,980	18,058	20,701	24.27	14.64
Western Europe		16,826	16,700	17,980	18,058	20,701	24.27	14.64
France		16,826	16,700	17,980	18,058	20,701	24.27	14.64
REGION NOT SPECIFIED		5,896	5,465	6,072	5,981	7,985	9.36	33.51
Not Specified		5,896	5,465	6,072	5,981	7,985	9.36	33.51
Other countries of the World		5,896	5,465	6,072	5,981	7,985	9.36	33.51

Source: World Tourism Organization (UNWTO)

NEW CALEDONIA

5. Overnight stays of non-resident tourists in hotels and similar establishments, by country of residence

		2002	2003	2004	2005	2006	Market share 06	% Change 06-05
TOTAL	(*)	**351,765**	**343,490**	**369,085**	**350,379**	**379,146**	**100.00**	**8.21**
EAST ASIA AND THE PACIFIC		**223,328**	**199,026**	**204,570**	**189,151**	**179,735**	**47.41**	**-4.98**
North-East Asia		**109,490**	**99,072**	**100,856**	**104,522**	**97,990**	**25.84**	**-6.25**
Japan		109,490	99,072	100,856	104,522	97,990	25.84	-6.25
Australasia		**113,838**	**99,954**	**103,714**	**84,629**	**81,745**	**21.56**	**-3.41**
Australia		93,744	79,590	79,914	65,518	57,591	15.19	-12.10
New Zealand		20,094	20,364	23,800	19,111	24,154	6.37	26.39
EUROPE		**100,296**	**117,642**	**130,623**	**129,863**	**157,957**	**41.66**	**21.63**
Western Europe		**100,296**	**117,642**	**130,623**	**129,863**	**157,957**	**41.66**	**21.63**
France		100,296	117,642	130,623	129,863	157,957	41.66	21.63
REGION NOT SPECIFIED		**28,141**	**26,822**	**33,892**	**31,365**	**41,454**	**10.93**	**32.17**
Not Specified		**28,141**	**26,822**	**33,892**	**31,365**	**41,454**	**10.93**	**32.17**
Other countries of the World		28,141	26,822	33,892	31,365	41,454	10.93	32.17

Source: World Tourism Organization (UNWTO)

NEW ZEALAND

2. Arrivals of non-resident visitors at national borders, by country of residence

	2002	2003	2004	2005	2006	Market share 06	% Change 06-05
TOTAL (*)	2,045,064	2,104,420	2,334,153	2,365,529	2,408,888	100.00	1.83
AFRICA	20,679	19,395	18,673	19,709	20,643	0.86	4.74
East Africa	3,970	2,876	2,081	1,950	1,809	0.08	-7.23
Ethiopia	55	47	46		26		
Eritrea	35						
Kenya	267	243	300	316	299	0.01	-5.38
Madagascar	13						
Malawi	51	49	57	71	92		29.58
Mauritius	152	176	150	204	243	0.01	19.12
Mozambique	56						
Reunion	161	173	116	132	186	0.01	40.91
Rwanda	18						
Seychelles		35	21	25	48		92.00
Somalia	36						
Zimbabwe	2,808	1,789	1,053	834	594	0.02	-28.78
Uganda	55						
United Republic of Tanzania	91	204	174	212	116		-45.28
Zambia	172	160	164	156	205	0.01	31.41
Central Africa	104	81	16	139	68		-51.08
Angola	53	81	16	139	68		-51.08
Chad	18						
Congo	18						
Democratic Republic of the Congo	15						
North Africa	137	31	20	46	22		-52.17
Algeria	69						
Western Sahara	14						
Sudan	36						
Tunisia	18	31	20	46	22		-52.17
Southern Africa	16,185	16,190	16,275	17,377	18,498	0.77	6.45
Botswana	219	246	196	183	153	0.01	-16.39
Lesotho	13	34	21				
Namibia	110	92	133	122	61		-50.00
South Africa	15,790	15,818	15,925	17,072	18,284	0.76	7.10
Swaziland	53						
West Africa	283	217	281	197	246	0.01	24.87
Ghana	66						
Cote D'Ivoire	33						
Mali	33						
Nigeria	118	217	281	136	220	0.01	61.76
Saint Helena	15						
Senegal				61	26		-57.38
Sierra Leone	18						
AMERICAS	261,273	266,245	275,699	275,616	294,450	12.22	6.83
Caribbean	1,349	908	775	828	992	0.04	19.81
Antigua and Barbuda	73						
Bahamas	84	122	60	70	85		21.43
Barbados	78						
Bermuda	304	289	298	356	385	0.02	8.15
British Virgin Islands	55						
Cayman Islands	183	289	206	188	269	0.01	43.09
Cuba	74						
Dominican Republic	70	19		50	45		-10.00

NEW ZEALAND

2. Arrivals of non-resident visitors at national borders, by country of residence

	2002	2003	2004	2005	2006	Market share 06	% Change 06-05
Guadeloupe	13						
Haiti	17						
Jamaica	86	90	107	92	39		-57.61
Netherlands Antilles	20						
Puerto Rico	142						
Saint Lucia	33						
Saint Vincent and the Grenadines	13						
Trinidad and Tobago	72	99	104	72	169	0.01	134.72
Turks and Caicos Islands	17						
United States Virgin Islands	15						
Central America	**352**	**206**	**326**	**311**	**292**	**0.01**	**-6.11**
Costa Rica	73	69	125	126	70		-44.44
Guatemala	138	100	144	142	110		-22.54
Honduras	53						
Nicaragua	17						
Panama	71	37	57	43	112		160.47
North America	**248,013**	**254,284**	**261,708**	**259,331**	**274,319**	**11.39**	**5.78**
Canada	39,669	39,940	40,602	42,182	45,955	1.91	8.94
Greenland	20	23			22		
Mexico	3,035	2,697	2,761	2,642	2,713	0.11	2.69
United States	205,289	211,624	218,345	214,507	225,629	9.37	5.18
South America	**11,559**	**10,847**	**12,870**	**15,146**	**18,803**	**0.78**	**24.14**
Argentina	2,603	2,252	2,756	3,161	4,053	0.17	28.22
Bolivia	66	43	83	66	68		3.03
Brazil	5,735	5,325	5,949	7,365	8,901	0.37	20.86
Chile	1,438	1,765	2,359	2,872	4,015	0.17	39.80
Colombia	510	442	529	466	447	0.02	-4.08
Ecuador	131	83	147	161	129	0.01	-19.88
Falkland Islands (Malvinas)	63	104	129	69	94		36.23
Paraguay	126	129	80	63	61		-3.17
Peru	273	228	239	349	335	0.01	-4.01
Uruguay	312	317	402	368	410	0.02	11.41
Venezuela	302	159	197	206	290	0.01	40.78
Other Americas			**20**		**44**		
Other countries of the Americas			20		44		
EAST ASIA AND THE PACIFIC	**1,240,381**	**1,271,657**	**1,468,307**	**1,484,424**	**1,512,292**	**62.78**	**1.88**
North-East Asia	**427,742**	**381,169**	**417,048**	**409,872**	**405,231**	**16.82**	**-1.13**
China	76,534	65,989	84,368	87,850	105,716	4.39	20.34
Taiwan (Province of China)	38,358	25,008	26,706	28,455	27,825	1.16	-2.21
Hong Kong, China	28,873	26,347	26,706	26,289	23,570	0.98	-10.34
Japan	173,567	150,851	165,023	154,925	136,401	5.66	-11.96
Korea, Dem. People's Republic of	17	19			17		
Korea, Republic of	109,936	112,658	113,908	112,005	111,361	4.62	-0.57
Macao, China	331	297	337	348	341	0.01	-2.01
Mongolia	126						
South-East Asia	**97,349**	**91,077**	**93,975**	**89,162**	**83,529**	**3.47**	**-6.32**
Brunei Darussalam	882	1,228	1,114	966	1,054	0.04	9.11
Myanmar	95	159	192	207	199	0.01	-3.86
Cambodia	441	359	458	420	444	0.02	5.71
Indonesia	8,248	8,557	8,005	7,213	6,929	0.29	-3.94
Lao People's Democratic Republic	103	135	164	208	87		-58.17
Malaysia	22,195	23,002	24,181	23,671	19,990	0.83	-15.55
Philippines	5,150	4,825	5,079	6,028	7,059	0.29	17.10

NEW ZEALAND

2. Arrivals of non-resident visitors at national borders, by country of residence

	2002	2003	2004	2005	2006	Market share 06	% Change 06-05
Timor-Leste	206						
Singapore	34,019	32,603	32,920	29,735	28,168	1.17	-5.27
Viet Nam	1,178	1,458	1,378	1,592	1,567	0.07	-1.57
Thailand	24,832	18,751	20,484	19,122	18,032	0.75	-5.70
Australasia	**632,470**	**702,162**	**855,933**	**874,738**	**903,504**	**37.51**	**3.29**
Australia	632,470	702,162	855,933	874,738	903,504	37.51	3.29
Melanesia	**29,475**	**29,897**	**31,775**	**36,052**	**39,004**	**1.62**	**8.19**
Solomon Islands	408	408	508	515	588	0.02	14.17
Fiji	15,633	15,999	16,848	20,509	22,580	0.94	10.10
New Caledonia	8,584	9,254	10,130	10,613	11,244	0.47	5.95
Vanuatu	1,586	1,433	1,468	1,419	1,724	0.07	21.49
Norfolk Island	1,125	947	1,139	1,363	1,072	0.04	-21.35
Papua New Guinea	2,139	1,856	1,682	1,633	1,796	0.07	9.98
Micronesia	**1,158**	**935**	**486**	**697**	**702**	**0.03**	**0.72**
Kiribati	660	576	226	321	326	0.01	1.56
Guam	199	154	172	190	199	0.01	4.74
Nauru	136	91		71	112		57.75
Northern Mariana Islands	35						
Micronesia (Federated States of)	70						
Marshall Islands	37	114	88	115	65		-43.48
Palau	21						
Polynesia	**52,187**	**54,162**	**55,346**	**57,901**	**61,307**	**2.55**	**5.88**
American Samoa	1,463	1,599	2,023	1,839	2,313	0.10	25.77
Cook Islands	7,972	8,163	8,880	10,274	10,457	0.43	1.78
French Polynesia	17,046	17,436	17,507	17,503	17,290	0.72	-1.22
Niue	892	1,097	1,197	1,328	1,771	0.07	33.36
Pitcairn	36						
Tokelau	176	195	206	266	155	0.01	-41.73
Tonga	9,854	10,131	10,655	10,047	11,775	0.49	17.20
Tuvalu	719	594	192	275	269	0.01	-2.18
Wallis and Futuna Islands	152						
Samoa	13,877	14,947	14,686	16,369	17,277	0.72	5.55
Other East Asia and the Pacific		**12,255**	**13,744**	**16,002**	**19,015**	**0.79**	**18.83**
Other countries of Asia		240	187	211	165	0.01	-21.80
Other countries of Oceania		12,015	13,557	15,791	18,850	0.78	19.37
EUROPE	**423,200**	**460,938**	**488,674**	**521,267**	**515,716**	**21.41**	**-1.06**
Central/Eastern Europe	**9,258**	**10,682**	**10,754**	**11,731**	**13,581**	**0.56**	**15.77**
Azerbaijan	36		62	124	83		-33.06
Bulgaria	140	134	83	185	198	0.01	7.03
Belarus	33	53	47	68	74		8.82
Czech Republic	2,116	3,498	3,077	3,163	3,436	0.14	8.63
Estonia	139	42	106	253	429	0.02	69.57
Georgia	17		54	22	46		109.09
Hungary	1,188	1,228	1,053	929	1,178	0.05	26.80
Kazakhstan	45	127	85	183	122	0.01	-33.33
Kyrgyzstan	35	18	25		18		
Latvia	74						
Lithuania	49	65	107	197	248	0.01	25.89
Poland	1,413	1,456	1,499	1,742	1,949	0.08	11.88
Romania	412	281	255	282	343	0.01	21.63
Russian Federation	1,648	1,852	2,263	2,502	2,922	0.12	16.79
Slovakia	422	349	303	452	576	0.02	27.43
Ukraine	1,491	1,579	1,735	1,629	1,959	0.08	20.26

NEW ZEALAND

2. Arrivals of non-resident visitors at national borders, by country of residence

	2002	2003	2004	2005	2006	Market share 06	% Change 06-05
Northern Europe	277,157	308,140	329,996	357,311	344,124	14.29	-3.69
Denmark	8,001	8,752	9,264	9,510	10,522	0.44	10.64
Faeroe Islands	57						
Finland	2,091	2,107	2,428	2,842	3,008	0.12	5.84
Iceland	138	200	296	268	277	0.01	3.36
Ireland	13,489	15,282	17,620	21,431	19,583	0.81	-8.62
Norway	4,086	4,352	3,987	3,925	3,896	0.16	-0.74
Sweden	12,309	12,628	12,701	12,520	12,026	0.50	-3.95
United Kingdom	236,986	264,819	283,700	306,815	294,812	12.24	-3.91
Southern Europe	15,874	15,617	16,297	17,563	18,859	0.78	7.38
Albania	20						
Andorra	105	54	66	85	22		-74.12
Bosnia and Herzegovina	58	51	46	21	22		4.76
Croatia	294	354	284	196	184	0.01	-6.12
Gibraltar	31						
Greece	469	517	497	703	632	0.03	-10.10
Holy See	16						
Italy	8,379	7,487	7,228	7,472	8,010	0.33	7.20
Malta	139	137	250	183	325	0.01	77.60
Portugal	617	806	1,004	1,070	913	0.04	-14.67
Slovenia	478	710	470	620	505	0.02	-18.55
Spain	5,030	5,247	6,223	6,952	8,064	0.33	16.00
TFYR of Macedonia	30	41	42	72	69		-4.17
Serbia and Montenegro	208	213	187	189	113		-40.21
Western Europe	112,775	119,108	123,793	126,362	131,476	5.46	4.05
Austria	4,824	5,171	6,118	6,411	6,217	0.26	-3.03
Belgium	3,962	3,953	4,489	4,451	4,652	0.19	4.52
France	13,239	14,800	15,992	16,977	18,663	0.77	9.93
Germany	48,951	52,534	55,736	57,549	59,353	2.46	3.13
Liechtenstein	83	22	67	54	48		-11.11
Luxembourg	324	357	407	387	368	0.02	-4.91
Monaco	122	108	113	141	163	0.01	15.60
Netherlands	26,037	26,388	25,841	26,122	27,476	1.14	5.18
Switzerland	15,233	15,775	15,030	14,270	14,536	0.60	1.86
East Mediterranean Europe	8,136	7,110	7,529	7,965	7,151	0.30	-10.22
Cyprus	191	197	235	284	435	0.02	53.17
Israel	7,481	6,454	6,728	6,894	5,887	0.24	-14.61
Turkey	464	459	566	787	829	0.03	5.34
Other Europe		281	305	335	525	0.02	56.72
Other countries of Europe		281	305	335	525	0.02	56.72
MIDDLE EAST	5,922	7,048	8,122	8,871	9,607	0.40	8.30
Middle East	5,922	7,048	8,122	8,871	9,607	0.40	8.30
Bahrain	291	300	335	352	293	0.01	-16.76
Iraq	117						
Jordan	139	140	191	113	56		-50.44
Kuwait	181	314	366	387	348	0.01	-10.08
Lebanon	15	75		72	114		58.33
Libyan Arab Jamahiriya	39		20		46		
Oman	463	510	519	500	632	0.03	26.40
Qatar	191	254	264	352	584	0.02	65.91
Saudi Arabia	1,503	1,723	1,835	2,349	2,843	0.12	21.03
Syrian Arab Republic	52	54	58	100			
United Arab Emirates	2,574	3,305	4,258	4,331	4,351	0.18	0.46

NEW ZEALAND

2. Arrivals of non-resident visitors at national borders, by country of residence

	2002	2003	2004	2005	2006	Market share 06	% Change 06-05
Egypt	323	373	276	315	340	0.01	7.94
Yemen	34						
SOUTH ASIA	**19,410**	**17,028**	**17,830**	**19,833**	**22,507**	**0.93**	**13.48**
South Asia	**19,410**	**17,028**	**17,830**	**19,833**	**22,507**	**0.93**	**13.48**
Bangladesh	534	623	451	255	273	0.01	7.06
Bhutan		19			44		
Sri Lanka	884	945	1,137	1,136	1,272	0.05	11.97
India	17,270	14,790	15,694	17,761	20,265	0.84	14.10
Iran, Islamic Republic of	160	323	251	282	282	0.01	
Maldives	70						
Nepal	152						
Pakistan	340	328	297	399	371	0.02	-7.02
REGION NOT SPECIFIED	**74,199**	**62,109**	**56,848**	**35,809**	**33,673**	**1.40**	**-5.96**
Not Specified	**74,199**	**62,109**	**56,848**	**35,809**	**33,673**	**1.40**	**-5.96**
Other countries of the World	59,025	62,109	56,848	35,809	33,673	1.40	-5.96
Nationals Residing Abroad	15,174						

Source: World Tourism Organization (UNWTO)

NICARAGUA

1. Arrivals of non-resident tourists at national borders, by nationality

		2002	2003	2004	2005	2006	Market share 06	% Change 06-05
TOTAL	(*)	471,622	525,775	614,782	712,444	773,398	100.00	8.56
AFRICA		287	378	515	621			
East Africa		39	47	126	184			
Burundi					2			
Ethiopia		12	13	66	107			
Kenya		5	9	9	38			
Madagascar			1	12	2			
Malawi		1	2	1	1			
Mauritius		9		1	2			
Mozambique		1	6	5	3			
Rwanda		1	1	5	2			
Zimbabwe		3	5	6	6			
Uganda		5	6	7	10			
United Republic of Tanzania		2	2	9	4			
Zambia			2	5	7			
Central Africa		16	9	16	10			
Angola		6	2	7	5			
Cameroon		6	5	4				
Central African Republic			1		4			
Congo		4	1	5	1			
North Africa		24	35	38	41			
Algeria		7	5	10	2			
Morocco		10	30	26	37			
Tunisia		7		2	2			
Southern Africa		98	109	134	204			
South Africa		98	109	134	204			
West Africa		34	26	29	21			
Cape Verde			2		3			
Benin		3						
Gambia		4						
Ghana		5	3	4	7			
Guinea		5	2	1	1			
Mali		5	2	2	1			
Mauritania		1	2	2				
Nigeria		6	7	12	6			
Saint Helena		1						
Senegal		1	7	4	2			
Sierra Leone		2	1	2	1			
Burkina Faso		1		2				
Other Africa		76	152	172	161			
Other countries of Africa		76	152	172	161			
AMERICAS		417,226	464,176	552,846	619,305	660,405	85.39	6.64
Caribbean		2,306	2,363	2,468	2,341			
Antigua and Barbuda		1	3	4	3			
Bahamas		17	39	18	33			
Barbados		8	20	12	21			
Bermuda			3	30	1			
Cayman Islands		92	72	90	67			
Cuba		1,114	1,179	1,230	1,175			
Dominica		3	9	7	9			
Dominican Republic		773	667	663	628			

NICARAGUA

1. Arrivals of non-resident tourists at national borders, by nationality

	2002	2003	2004	2005	2006	Market share 06	% Change 06-05
Grenada	8	15	7	6			
Haiti	68	54	62	52			
Jamaica	113	161	154	167			
Netherlands Antilles			1				
Puerto Rico	62	83	89	124			
Anguilla	1						
Saint Lucia	3	6	2	5			
Saint Vincent and the Grenadines	8	7	38	9			
Trinidad and Tobago	35	45	61	41			
Central America	**287,245**	**310,239**	**377,674**	**424,326**	**445,139**	**57.56**	**4.90**
Belize	274	289	428	410	477	0.06	16.34
Costa Rica	57,824	76,659	99,674	108,598	92,308	11.94	-15.00
El Salvador	69,691	73,806	88,103	100,574	113,793	14.71	13.14
Guatemala	36,964	40,132	48,990	58,019	67,510	8.73	16.36
Honduras	111,947	107,365	126,916	139,134	150,146	19.41	7.91
Panama	10,545	11,988	13,563	17,591	20,905	2.70	18.84
North America	**115,536**	**139,137**	**157,782**	**176,949**	**204,265**	**26.41**	**15.44**
Canada	9,800	13,124	15,586	18,068	22,200	2.87	22.87
Mexico	7,873	117,156	10,331	11,550	13,126	1.70	13.65
United States	97,863	8,857	131,865	147,331	168,939	21.84	14.67
South America	**12,139**	**12,437**	**14,922**	**15,689**	**11,001**	**1.42**	**-29.88**
Argentina	2,247	2,672	2,735	2,886	3,144	0.41	8.94
Bolivia	516	591	1,769	1,844			
Brazil	1,171	1,311	1,430	1,880			
Chile	1,431	1,407	1,394	1,486	1,506	0.19	1.35
Colombia	2,715	2,269	2,692	2,866	2,949	0.38	2.90
Ecuador	838	767	853	876			
Guyana	20	33	53	38			
Paraguay	117	117	151	140			
Peru	1,194	1,001	1,120	1,035	994	0.13	-3.96
Suriname	4	16	10	1			
Uruguay	381	437	485	506			
Venezuela	1,505	1,816	2,230	2,131	2,408	0.31	13.00
EAST ASIA AND THE PACIFIC	**8,732**	**10,674**	**8,326**	**11,235**			
North-East Asia	**4,920**	**5,865**	**5,252**	**5,571**			
China	716	1,418	438	522			
Taiwan (Province of China)	1,118	905	1,184	1,213			
Hong Kong, China	9	85	3	13			
Japan	1,799	1,908	1,837	1,806			
Korea, Republic of	1,278	1,547	1,783	2,016			
Mongolia		2	7	1			
South-East Asia	**2,478**	**2,929**	**951**	**3,089**			
Myanmar	126	42		14			
Indonesia	115	713	41	959			
Lao People's Democratic Republic	23	1	1				
Malaysia	32	35	24	34			
Philippines	2,115	2,074	797	2,034			
Singapore	31	33	36	31			
Viet Nam	3	7	7	7			
Thailand	33	24	45	10			
Australasia	**1,325**	**1,868**	**2,121**	**2,573**			
Australia	1,046	1,573	1,740	2,160			
New Zealand	279	295	381	413			

NICARAGUA

1. Arrivals of non-resident tourists at national borders, by nationality

	2002	2003	2004	2005	2006	Market share 06	% Change 06-05
Melanesia			1	1			
Fiji			1	1			
Micronesia		5	1				
Kiribati		5	1				
Polynesia	9	7		1			
Tonga	3	1		1			
Tuvalu	6	6					
EUROPE	44,730	49,147	52,564	58,964	55,026	7.11	-6.68
Central/Eastern Europe	1,972	1,593	1,965	2,018			
Armenia	1	1		3			
Bulgaria	71	256	80	233			
Belarus		3	1	7			
Czech Republic/Slovakia	156	252	343	327			
Estonia	26	23	6	25			
Georgia	41	3	2	50			
Hungary	25	91	73	174			
Latvia	75	4	12	35			
Lithuania	74	24	45	32			
Poland	304	276	315	339			
Romania	72	62	77	134			
Russian Federation	628	404	534	409			
Ukraine	486	188	477	240			
Ussr (Former)	13	6		10			
Northern Europe	9,849	11,947	11,860	17,430	17,168	2.22	-1.50
Denmark	1,142	1,395	1,612	1,708			
Finland	434	465	543	497			
Iceland	25	47	45	54			
Ireland	413	566	566	719			
Norway	897	995	1,055	1,163			
Sweden	1,765	1,879	2,017	2,400	2,662	0.34	10.92
United Kingdom	5,173	6,600	6,022	10,889	14,506	1.88	33.22
Southern Europe	13,584	14,004	15,032	14,598	14,363	1.86	-1.61
Albania	2	2	1	8			
Andorra	5	7	2	5			
Croatia	95	63	16	48			
Greece	268	222	102	159			
Italy	4,098	4,363	4,632	4,377	4,481	0.58	2.38
Malta	6	2	3	3			
Portugal	144	206	226	268			
San Marino	24	10	7				
Slovenia	44	88	81	109			
Spain	8,884	9,039	9,954	9,612	9,882	1.28	2.81
Serbia and Montenegro	14	2	8	9			
Western Europe	18,427	20,522	22,398	23,731	23,495	3.04	-0.99
Austria	793	576	807	1,006			
Belgium	1,236	1,326	1,377	1,320			
France	3,519	3,886	4,126	4,358	4,681	0.61	7.41
Germany	6,500	6,886	8,549	9,554	10,887	1.41	13.95
Liechtenstein		7	13	4			
Luxembourg	22	53	54	35			
Netherlands	4,236	5,417	4,817	4,819	5,090	0.66	5.62
Switzerland	2,121	2,371	2,655	2,635	2,837	0.37	7.67
East Mediterranean Europe	898	1,081	1,309	1,187			

NICARAGUA

1. Arrivals of non-resident tourists at national borders, by nationality

	2002	2003	2004	2005	2006	Market share 06	% Change 06-05
Cyprus	9	3	9	15			
Israel	855	971	1,171	1,052			
Turkey	34	107	129	120			
MIDDLE EAST	**64**	**89**	**76**	**82**			
Middle East	**64**	**89**	**76**	**82**			
Bahrain				4			
Palestine	6	13	16	10			
Jordan	21	15	16	13			
Kuwait	1			2			
Lebanon	2	11	8	2			
Libyan Arab Jamahiriya	28	36	22	44			
Qatar	1						
Saudi Arabia	1	2		4			
United Arab Emirates	1	10	14				
Egypt	3	2		3			
SOUTH ASIA	**549**	**1,254**	**437**	**1,522**			
South Asia	**549**	**1,254**	**437**	**1,522**			
Bangladesh	53	35	96	82			
Sri Lanka	11	2	6	6			
India	423	1,153	304	1,347			
Iran, Islamic Republic of	27	6	10	13			
Maldives	3	1	11	4			
Nepal	1	8	3	21			
Pakistan	31	49	7	49			
REGION NOT SPECIFIED	**34**	**57**	**18**	**20,715**	**57,967**	**7.50**	**179.83**
Not Specified	**34**	**57**	**18**	**20,715**	**57,967**	**7.50**	**179.83**
Other countries of the World	34	57	18	85	35,274	4.56	*********
Nationals Residing Abroad				20,630	22,693	2.93	10.00

Source: World Tourism Organization (UNWTO)

NIGER

1. Arrivals of non-resident tourists at national borders, by nationality

	2002	2003	2004	2005	2006	Market share 06	% Change 06-05
TOTAL	39,337	55,344	57,004	59,920	60,332	100.00	0.69
AFRICA	26,198	37,344	38,000	35,952	36,199	60.00	0.69
Other Africa	26,198	37,344	38,000	35,952	36,199	60.00	0.69
All countries of Africa	26,198	37,344	38,000	35,952	36,199	60.00	0.69
AMERICAS	1,574	2,000	2,500	4,194	4,223	7.00	0.69
North America	1,574	2,000	2,500	4,194	4,223	7.00	0.69
United States	1,574	2,000	2,500	4,194	4,223	7.00	0.69
EAST ASIA AND THE PACIFIC	983	1,400	1,500	2,996	3,017	5.00	0.70
Other East Asia and the Pacific	983	1,400	1,500	2,996	3,017	5.00	0.70
All countries of Asia	983	1,400	1,500	2,996	3,017	5.00	0.70
EUROPE	10,110	14,344	14,500	16,778	16,893	28.00	0.69
Southern Europe	300	400	500	1,000	1,005	1.67	0.50
Italy	300	400	500	1,000	1,005	1.67	0.50
Western Europe	9,810	13,800	14,000	15,778	15,888	26.33	0.70
France	8,037	11,000	12,000	13,344	13,448	22.29	0.78
Germany	965	1,500	1,000	1,256	1,260	2.09	0.32
Benelux	808	1,300	1,000	1,178	1,180	1.96	0.17
Other Europe		144					
Other countries of Europe		144					
REGION NOT SPECIFIED	472	256	504				
Not Specified	472	256	504				
Other countries of the World	472	256	504				

Source: World Tourism Organization (UNWTO)

NIGERIA

2. Arrivals of non-resident visitors at national borders, by nationality

	2002	2003	2004	2005	2006	Market share 06	% Change 06-05
TOTAL	2,045,543	2,253,115	2,646,411	2,778,365	3,055,800	100.00	9.99
AFRICA	1,450,814	1,554,308	1,825,312	1,916,246	2,107,870	68.98	10.00
East Africa	61,483	72,244	83,888	88,079	96,886	3.17	10.00
Ethiopia	25,604	30,085	35,350	37,117	40,828	1.34	10.00
Kenya	13,965	16,409	18,281	19,195	21,114	0.69	10.00
Mozambique	6,866	8,068	9,480	9,954	10,949	0.36	10.00
Rwanda	85	100	118	123	138		12.20
Somalia	180	212	249	261	287	0.01	9.96
Zimbabwe	7,234	8,500	9,988	10,487	11,535	0.38	9.99
Uganda	1,222	1,436	1,687	1,771	1,948	0.06	9.99
United Republic of Tanzania	5,559	6,532	7,675	8,058	8,863	0.29	9.99
Zambia	768	902	1,060	1,113	1,224	0.04	9.97
Central Africa	161,580	189,857	223,083	234,234	257,657	8.43	10.00
Angola	4,215	4,953	5,820	6,111	6,722	0.22	10.00
Cameroon	73,885	86,815	102,008	107,108	117,818	3.86	10.00
Central African Republic	5,053	5,937	6,976	7,324	8,056	0.26	9.99
Chad	58,688	68,958	81,026	85,077	93,584	3.06	10.00
Congo	5,336	6,270	7,367	7,735	8,508	0.28	9.99
Democratic Republic of the Congo	5,302	6,230	7,320	7,686	8,455	0.28	10.01
Equatorial Guinea	349	410	482	506	557	0.02	10.08
Gabon	8,560	10,058	11,818	12,408	13,649	0.45	10.00
Sao Tome and Principe	192	226	266	279	308	0.01	10.39
North Africa	126,230	148,321	174,277	182,989	201,288	6.59	10.00
Algeria	25,232	29,648	34,836	36,577	40,235	1.32	10.00
Morocco	39,748	46,704	54,877	57,620	63,382	2.07	10.00
Sudan	43,490	51,101	60,044	63,046	69,350	2.27	10.00
Tunisia	17,760	20,868	24,520	25,746	28,321	0.93	10.00
Southern Africa	26,657	31,322	36,802	38,639	42,503	1.39	10.00
Botswana	4,471	5,253	6,172	6,480	7,128	0.23	10.00
Lesotho	4,330	5,088	5,978	6,276	6,904	0.23	10.01
Namibia	11,527	13,544	15,914	16,709	18,380	0.60	10.00
South Africa	6,329	7,437	8,738	9,174	10,091	0.33	10.00
West Africa	1,074,864	1,112,564	1,307,262	1,372,305	1,509,536	49.40	10.00
Cape Verde	181	213	250	262	288	0.01	9.92
Benin	271,248	318,716	374,491	393,215	432,537	14.15	10.00
Gambia	12,430	14,605	17,161	18,019	19,820	0.65	10.00
Ghana	142,270	16,767	19,701	20,686	22,755	0.74	10.00
Guinea	13,517	15,882	18,661	19,594	21,553	0.71	10.00
Cote D'Ivoire	34,952	41,069	48,256	50,668	55,735	1.82	10.00
Liberia	74,088	87,053	102,287	107,401	118,141	3.87	10.00
Mali	25,514	29,979	35,225	36,986	40,685	1.33	10.00
Mauritania	585	687	807	847	932	0.03	10.04
Niger	428,141	503,066	591,103	620,658	642,724	21.03	3.56
Senegal	15,082	17,721	20,822	21,548	63,703	2.08	195.63
Sierra Leone	11,412	13,409	15,756	16,543	18,197	0.60	10.00
Togo	23,479	27,588	32,416	34,036	37,440	1.23	10.00
Burkina Faso	21,965	25,809	30,326	31,842	35,026	1.15	10.00
AMERICAS	80,412	94,486	111,020	116,563	129,219	4.23	10.86
Caribbean	9,961	11,705	13,753	14,437	15,881	0.52	10.00
Barbados	1,261	1,482	1,741	1,828	2,011	0.07	10.01
Cuba	1,436	1,687	1,982	2,080	2,288	0.07	10.00
Dominican Republic	403	474	557	584	642	0.02	9.93

NIGERIA

2. Arrivals of non-resident visitors at national borders, by nationality

	2002	2003	2004	2005	2006	Market share 06	% Change 06-05
Haiti	176	207	243	255	281	0.01	10.20
Jamaica	3,185	3,742	4,397	4,616	5,078	0.17	10.01
Trinidad and Tobago	3,500	4,113	4,833	5,074	5,581	0.18	9.99
Central America	**392**	**461**	**542**	**568**	**625**	**0.02**	**10.04**
Costa Rica	222	261	307	322	354	0.01	9.94
Nicaragua	170	200	235	246	271	0.01	10.16
North America	**48,500**	**56,987**	**66,960**	**70,307**	**77,338**	**2.53**	**10.00**
Canada	7,142	8,392	9,861	10,354	11,389	0.37	10.00
Mexico	28,797	33,836	39,757	41,744	25,918	0.85	-37.91
United States	12,561	14,759	17,342	18,209	40,031	1.31	119.84
South America	**21,559**	**25,333**	**29,765**	**31,251**	**35,375**	**1.16**	**13.20**
Argentina	4,552	5,349	6,285	6,599	7,009	0.23	6.21
Bolivia	261	307	360	378	666	0.02	76.19
Brazil	7,492	8,803	10,344	10,861	13,348	0.44	22.90
Chile	4,029	4,734	5,562	5,840	6,424	0.21	10.00
Colombia	3,342	3,927	4,614	4,844	5,328	0.17	9.99
Guyana	254	298	350	367	350	0.01	-4.63
Paraguay	536	630	740	777	909	0.03	16.99
Peru	672	790	928	974	840	0.03	-13.76
Venezuela	421	495	582	611	501	0.02	-18.00
EAST ASIA AND THE PACIFIC	**110,832**	**130,228**	**153,020**	**160,666**	**177,001**	**5.79**	**10.17**
North-East Asia	**60,486**	**71,071**	**83,509**	**87,683**	**96,719**	**3.17**	**10.31**
China	22,964	26,983	31,705	33,290	38,254	1.25	14.91
Taiwan (Province of China)	15,602	18,332	21,540	22,617	24,879	0.81	10.00
Hong Kong, China	11,548	13,569	15,944	16,741	18,415	0.60	10.00
Japan	8,574	10,074	11,837	12,428	13,671	0.45	10.00
Korea, Republic of	1,798	2,113	2,483	2,607	1,500	0.05	-42.46
South-East Asia	**47,811**	**56,178**	**66,010**	**69,308**	**76,239**	**2.49**	**10.00**
Myanmar	54	63	74	77	85		10.39
Indonesia	11,748	13,804	16,220	17,031	18,734	0.61	10.00
Malaysia	12,078	14,192	16,676	17,509	19,260	0.63	10.00
Philippines	9,942	11,682	13,726	14,412	15,853	0.52	10.00
Singapore	8,058	9,468	11,125	11,681	12,849	0.42	10.00
Thailand	5,931	6,969	8,189	8,598	9,458	0.31	10.00
Australasia	**2,535**	**2,979**	**3,501**	**3,675**	**4,043**	**0.13**	**10.01**
Australia	1,696	1,993	2,342	2,459	2,705	0.09	10.00
New Zealand	839	986	1,159	1,216	1,338	0.04	10.03
EUROPE	**317,317**	**372,846**	**438,093**	**459,985**	**506,000**	**16.56**	**10.00**
Central/Eastern Europe	**61,576**	**72,351**	**85,013**	**89,260**	**98,186**	**3.21**	**10.00**
Bulgaria	9,748	11,454	13,458	14,130	15,543	0.51	10.00
Czech Republic/Slovakia	7,887	9,267	10,889	11,433	12,576	0.41	10.00
Hungary	11,757	13,814	16,232	17,043	18,747	0.61	10.00
Poland	8,830	10,375	12,191	12,800	14,080	0.46	10.00
Romania	15,071	17,708	20,807	21,847	24,032	0.79	10.00
Ussr (Former)	8,283	9,733	11,436	12,007	13,208	0.43	10.00
Northern Europe	**74,295**	**87,297**	**102,574**	**107,700**	**118,486**	**3.88**	**10.01**
Denmark	11,271	13,243	15,561	16,339	17,973	0.59	10.00
Finland	12,581	14,783	17,370	18,238	20,062	0.66	10.00
Ireland	7,066	8,303	9,756	10,243	11,283	0.37	10.15
Norway	8,738	10,267	12,064	12,667	13,934	0.46	10.00
Sweden	7,992	9,391	11,034	11,585	12,743	0.42	10.00

NIGERIA

2. Arrivals of non-resident visitors at national borders, by nationality

	2002	2003	2004	2005	2006	Market share 06	% Change 06-05
United Kingdom	26,647	31,310	36,789	38,628	42,491	1.39	10.00
Southern Europe	**67,393**	**79,186**	**93,043**	**97,693**	**107,462**	**3.52**	**10.00**
Greece	1,402	1,647	1,935	2,031	2,234	0.07	10.00
Italy	45,248	53,166	62,470	65,593	72,152	2.36	10.00
Portugal	5,490	6,451	7,580	7,959	8,755	0.29	10.00
Spain	14,371	16,886	19,841	20,833	22,916	0.75	10.00
Yugoslavia, Sfr (Former)	882	1,036	1,217	1,277	1,405	0.05	10.02
Western Europe	**96,898**	**113,855**	**133,779**	**140,465**	**154,512**	**5.06**	**10.00**
Austria	2,928	3,440	4,042	4,244	4,668	0.15	9.99
Belgium	4,712	5,537	6,506	6,831	7,514	0.25	10.00
France	42,680	50,149	58,925	61,871	68,058	2.23	10.00
Germany	41,630	48,915	57,475	60,348	66,383	2.17	10.00
Luxembourg	765	899	1,056	1,108	1,219	0.04	10.02
Netherlands	3,701	4,349	5,110	5,365	5,902	0.19	10.01
Switzerland	482	566	665	698	768	0.03	10.03
East Mediterranean Europe	**17,155**	**20,157**	**23,684**	**24,867**	**27,354**	**0.90**	**10.00**
Cyprus	1,961	2,304	2,707	2,842	3,126	0.10	9.99
Israel	10,421	12,245	14,388	15,107	16,618	0.54	10.00
Turkey	4,773	5,608	6,589	6,918	7,610	0.25	10.00
MIDDLE EAST	**34,560**	**40,608**	**47,714**	**50,095**	**55,104**	**1.80**	**10.00**
Middle East	**34,560**	**40,608**	**47,714**	**50,095**	**55,104**	**1.80**	**10.00**
Iraq	2,621	3,080	3,619	3,799	4,179	0.14	10.00
Jordan	1,327	1,559	1,832	1,923	2,115	0.07	9.98
Kuwait	505	593	697	731	804	0.03	9.99
Lebanon	13,120	15,416	18,114	19,019	20,921	0.68	10.00
Libyan Arab Jamahiriya	3,304	3,882	4,561	4,789	5,268	0.17	10.00
Saudi Arabia	1,312	1,542	1,812	1,902	2,092	0.07	9.99
Syrian Arab Republic	624	733	861	904	994	0.03	9.96
Egypt	11,235	13,201	15,511	16,286	17,915	0.59	10.00
Yemen	512	602	707	742	816	0.03	9.97
SOUTH ASIA	**44,701**	**52,523**	**61,714**	**64,796**	**72,000**	**2.36**	**11.12**
South Asia	**44,701**	**52,523**	**61,714**	**64,796**	**72,000**	**2.36**	**11.12**
Afghanistan	259	304	357	374	435	0.01	16.31
Bangladesh	304	357	419	439	483	0.02	10.02
Sri Lanka	631	741	871	914	1,205	0.04	31.84
India	17,899	21,031	24,711	25,946	28,741	0.94	10.77
Iran, Islamic Republic of	6,467	7,599	8,929	9,375	10,513	0.34	12.14
Nepal	32	38	45	47	52		10.64
Pakistan	19,109	22,453	26,382	27,701	30,571	1.00	10.36
REGION NOT SPECIFIED	**6,907**	**8,116**	**9,538**	**10,014**	**8,606**	**0.28**	**-14.06**
Not Specified	**6,907**	**8,116**	**9,538**	**10,014**	**8,606**	**0.28**	**-14.06**
Other countries of the World	6,907	8,116	9,538	10,014	8,606	0.28	-14.06

Source: World Tourism Organization (UNWTO)

NIUE

1. Arrivals of non-resident tourists at national borders, by country of residence

		2002	2003	2004	2005	2006	Market share 06	% Change 06-05
TOTAL	(*)	2,084	2,706	2,550	2,793	3,008	100.00	7.70
AMERICAS		252	178	138	181	161	5.35	-11.05
North America		252	178	138	181	161	5.35	-11.05
Canada		31	25	31	45	32	1.06	-28.89
United States		221	153	107	136	129	4.29	-5.15
EAST ASIA AND THE PACIFIC		1,387	2,247	2,217	2,272	2,588	86.04	13.91
North-East Asia		9	18	11	8	6	0.20	-25.00
Japan		9	18	11	8	6	0.20	-25.00
Australasia		1,106	1,719	1,836	1,833	2,373	78.89	29.46
Australia		180	325	221	304	343	11.40	12.83
New Zealand		926	1,394	1,615	1,529	2,030	67.49	32.77
Other East Asia and the Pacific		272	510	370	431	209	6.95	-51.51
Other countries of Asia		17	20	21	36	41	1.36	13.89
Other countries of Oceania		255	490	349	395	168	5.59	-57.47
EUROPE		275	235	168	295	237	7.88	-19.66
Northern Europe		93	82	53	99	84	2.79	-15.15
United Kingdom		93	82	53	99	84	2.79	-15.15
Western Europe		72	80	61	68	62	2.06	-8.82
France		30	17	30	37	15	0.50	-59.46
Germany		42	63	31	31	47	1.56	51.61
Other Europe		110	73	54	128	91	3.03	-28.91
Other countries of Europe		110	73	54	128	91	3.03	-28.91
REGION NOT SPECIFIED		170	46	27	45	22	0.73	-51.11
Not Specified		170	46	27	45	22	0.73	-51.11
Other countries of the World		170	46	27	45	22	0.73	-51.11

Source: World Tourism Organization (UNWTO)

NORTHERN MARIANA ISLANDS

2. Arrivals of non-resident visitors at national borders, by nationality

	2002	2003	2004	2005	2006	Market share 06	% Change 06-05
TOTAL	475,547	459,458	535,873	506,846	435,494	100.00	-14.08
AMERICAS	36,451	34,670	37,334	37,989	32,582	7.48	-14.23
North America	36,451	34,670	37,334	37,989	32,582	7.48	-14.23
Canada	593	206	298	323	290	0.07	-10.22
United States	35,858	34,464	37,036	37,666	32,292	7.42	-14.27
EAST ASIA AND THE PACIFIC	437,322	422,811	494,826	465,360	398,952	91.61	-14.27
North-East Asia	432,173	415,912	486,815	460,005	392,238	90.07	-14.73
China	10,470	15,213	32,463	32,920	37,994	8.72	15.41
Taiwan (Province of China)	1,228	711	1,031	2,587	314	0.07	-87.86
Hong Kong, China	3,416	2,271	2,227	2,807	1,259	0.29	-55.15
Japan	326,735	328,075	382,792	351,739	269,780	61.95	-23.30
Korea, Republic of	90,324	69,642	68,302	69,952	82,891	19.03	18.50
South-East Asia	3,024	4,688	5,645	3,273	4,385	1.01	33.97
Philippines	2,906	4,570	5,369	3,168	4,320	0.99	36.36
Thailand	118	118	276	105	65	0.01	-38.10
Australasia	316	372	426	451	406	0.09	-9.98
Australia	316	372	426	451	406	0.09	-9.98
Micronesia	1,809	1,839	1,940	1,631	1,923	0.44	17.90
Micronesia (Federated States of)	1,061	1,100	1,057	1,039	1,178	0.27	13.38
Palau	748	739	883	592	745	0.17	25.84
EUROPE	598	439	666	1,300	2,324	0.53	78.77
Central/Eastern Europe					1,675	0.38	
Ussr (Former)					1,675	0.38	
Other Europe	598	439	666	1,300	649	0.15	-50.08
Other countries of Europe					649	0.15	
All countries of Europe	598	439	666	1,300			
REGION NOT SPECIFIED	1,176	1,538	3,047	2,197	1,636	0.38	-25.53
Not Specified	1,176	1,538	3,047	2,197	1,636	0.38	-25.53
Other countries of the World	1,176	1,538	3,047	2,197	1,636	0.38	-25.53

Source: World Tourism Organization (UNWTO)

NORWAY

1. Arrivals of non-resident tourists at national borders, by nationality

	2002	2003	2004	2005	2006	Market share 06	% Change 06-05
TOTAL (*)	3,111,000	3,269,000	3,628,000	3,824,000	3,945,000	100.00	3.16
AMERICAS	126,000	144,000	176,000	146,000	163,000	4.13	11.64
North America	126,000	144,000	176,000	146,000	163,000	4.13	11.64
United States	126,000	144,000	176,000	146,000	163,000	4.13	11.64
EAST ASIA AND THE PACIFIC	35,000	35,000	35,000	41,000	37,000	0.94	-9.76
North-East Asia	35,000	35,000	35,000	41,000	37,000	0.94	-9.76
Japan	35,000	35,000	35,000	41,000	37,000	0.94	-9.76
EUROPE	2,865,000	3,009,000	3,307,000	3,508,000	3,591,000	91.03	2.37
Central/Eastern Europe		20,000	28,000	31,000	42,000	1.06	35.48
Russian Federation		20,000	28,000	31,000	42,000	1.06	35.48
Northern Europe	1,878,000	1,873,000	2,015,000	2,106,000	2,141,000	54.27	1.66
Denmark	554,000	570,000	590,000	569,000	523,000	13.26	-8.08
Finland	215,000	191,000	214,000	264,000	249,000	6.31	-5.68
Sweden	860,000	858,000	916,000	955,000	1,003,000	25.42	5.03
United Kingdom	249,000	254,000	295,000	318,000	366,000	9.28	15.09
Southern Europe	76,000	100,000	127,000	119,000	125,000	3.17	5.04
Italy	44,000	57,000	68,000	62,000	62,000	1.57	
Spain	32,000	43,000	59,000	57,000	63,000	1.60	10.53
Western Europe	798,000	897,000	943,000	1,003,000	978,000	24.79	-2.49
Austria	22,000	22,000	27,000	25,000	22,000	0.56	-12.00
Belgium	28,000	35,000	38,000	41,000	41,000	1.04	
France	83,000	94,000	111,000	114,000	117,000	2.97	2.63
Germany	507,000	576,000	586,000	607,000	587,000	14.88	-3.29
Netherlands	120,000	132,000	142,000	170,000	166,000	4.21	-2.35
Switzerland	38,000	38,000	39,000	46,000	45,000	1.14	-2.17
Other Europe	113,000	119,000	194,000	249,000	305,000	7.73	22.49
Other countries of Europe	113,000	119,000	194,000	249,000	305,000	7.73	22.49
REGION NOT SPECIFIED	85,000	81,000	110,000	129,000	154,000	3.90	19.38
Not Specified	85,000	81,000	110,000	129,000	154,000	3.90	19.38
Other countries of the World	85,000	81,000	110,000	129,000	154,000	3.90	19.38

Source: World Tourism Organization (UNWTO)

NORWAY

5. Overnight stays of non-resident tourists in hotels and similar establishments, by nationality

	2002	2003	2004	2005	2006	Market share 06	% Change 06-05
TOTAL (*)	4,705,537	4,374,657	4,596,218	4,761,074	4,914,019	100.00	3.21
AFRICA	13,867	13,181	13,782	29,869	26,571	0.54	-11.04
Southern Africa				6,201	5,461	0.11	-11.93
South Africa				6,201	5,461	0.11	-11.93
Other Africa	13,867	13,181	13,782	23,668	21,110	0.43	-10.81
Other countries of Africa				23,668	21,110	0.43	-10.81
All countries of Africa	13,867	13,181	13,782				
AMERICAS	386,755	326,508	352,735	357,701	365,421	7.44	2.16
North America	373,589	315,405	339,830	338,157	340,074	6.92	0.57
Canada	14,724	14,575	15,817	18,444	18,175	0.37	-1.46
Mexico	2,638	2,749	3,060	3,373	4,945	0.10	46.61
United States	356,227	298,081	320,953	316,340	316,954	6.45	0.19
South America				19,544	25,347	0.52	29.69
Brazil				5,287	10,310	0.21	95.01
Other countries of South America				14,257	15,037	0.31	5.47
Other Americas	13,166	11,103	12,905				
Other countries of the Americas	13,166	11,103	12,905				
EAST ASIA AND THE PACIFIC	297,561	234,066	293,375	382,389	414,330	8.43	8.35
North-East Asia	147,048	112,559	123,364	205,753	222,562	4.53	8.17
China				54,039	66,736	1.36	23.50
Japan	147,048	112,559	123,364	124,710	122,132	2.49	-2.07
Korea, Republic of				27,004	33,694	0.69	24.77
Australasia	19,967	17,016	21,078	25,942	32,683	0.67	25.98
Australia	18,045	14,527	18,830	25,942	32,683	0.67	25.98
New Zealand	1,922	2,489	2,248				
Other East Asia and the Pacific	130,546	104,491	148,933	150,694	159,085	3.24	5.57
Other countries of Asia	130,546	104,491	148,933	135,953	145,361	2.96	6.92
Other countries of Oceania				14,741	13,724	0.28	-6.90
EUROPE	3,827,537	3,613,793	3,739,138	3,991,115	4,107,697	83.59	2.92
Central/Eastern Europe	40,681	44,511	49,893	146,325	237,067	4.82	62.01
Czech Republic	11,139	11,756	11,501	14,540	12,956	0.26	-10.89
Estonia				6,450	13,373	0.27	107.33
Hungary	6,024	7,649	7,875	8,734	8,728	0.18	-0.07
Latvia				4,256	7,563	0.15	77.70
Lithuania				5,370	8,441	0.17	57.19
Poland	20,507	21,904	26,566	41,327	87,094	1.77	110.74
Russian Federation				59,384	89,929	1.83	51.44
Slovakia	3,011	3,202	3,951	3,533	3,914	0.08	10.78
Ukraine				2,731	5,069	0.10	85.61
Northern Europe	1,920,697	1,688,138	1,803,513	1,841,189	1,860,713	37.87	1.06
Denmark	736,430	617,141	640,198	619,111	587,565	11.96	-5.10
Finland	69,899	60,315	60,602	62,168	67,295	1.37	8.25
Iceland	11,811	11,658	12,664	13,673	14,909	0.30	9.04
Ireland	7,934	7,435	9,211	12,631	12,635	0.26	0.03
Sweden	549,930	475,234	503,087	531,157	526,764	10.72	-0.83
United Kingdom	544,693	516,355	577,751	602,449	651,545	13.26	8.15
Southern Europe	333,158	350,888	351,097	367,351	438,944	8.93	19.49

NORWAY

5. Overnight stays of non-resident tourists in hotels and similar establishments, by nationality

	2002	2003	2004	2005	2006	Market share 06	% Change 06-05
Greece	12,884	14,265	13,775	14,769	15,741	0.32	6.58
Italy	130,396	142,275	146,398	141,938	163,982	3.34	15.53
Malta				509	710	0.01	39.49
Portugal	14,075	13,872	13,632	10,504	12,953	0.26	23.31
Slovenia				2,117	2,395	0.05	13.13
Spain	175,803	180,476	177,292	197,514	243,163	4.95	23.11
Western Europe	**1,396,009**	**1,396,725**	**1,370,245**	**1,445,178**	**1,374,290**	**27.97**	**-4.91**
Austria	24,497	25,296	27,126	25,789	31,434	0.64	21.89
Belgium	26,762	31,908	30,945	33,463	35,389	0.72	5.76
France	229,600	220,013	216,437	210,224	205,741	4.19	-2.13
Germany	767,787	773,724	738,372	810,092	746,031	15.18	-7.91
Liechtenstein				3,928	1,482	0.03	-62.27
Luxembourg	2,456	2,634	2,601	2,734	2,080	0.04	-23.92
Netherlands	280,081	283,355	291,182	296,252	285,178	5.80	-3.74
Switzerland	64,826	59,795	63,582	62,696	66,955	1.36	6.79
East Mediterranean Europe	**3,899**	**3,361**	**5,614**	**6,275**	**6,897**	**0.14**	**9.91**
Cyprus				742	1,277	0.03	72.10
Turkey	3,899	3,361	5,614	5,533	5,620	0.11	1.57
Other Europe	**133,093**	**130,170**	**158,776**	**184,797**	**189,786**	**3.86**	**2.70**
Other countries of Europe	133,093	130,170	158,776	184,797	189,786	3.86	2.70
REGION NOT SPECIFIED	**179,817**	**187,109**	**197,188**				
Not Specified	**179,817**	**187,109**	**197,188**				
Other countries of the World	179,817	187,109	197,188				

Source: World Tourism Organization (UNWTO)

NORWAY

6. Overnight stays of non-resident tourists in all types of accommodation establishments, by nationality

	2002	2003	2004	2005	2006	Market share 06	% Change 06-05
TOTAL				7,650,752	7,944,486	100.00	3.84
AFRICA				35,719	30,772	0.39	-13.85
Southern Africa				7,489	6,052	0.08	-19.19
South Africa				7,489	6,052	0.08	-19.19
Other Africa				28,230	24,720	0.31	-12.43
Other countries of Africa				28,230	24,720	0.31	-12.43
AMERICAS				377,849	390,917	4.92	3.46
North America				355,960	362,847	4.57	1.93
Canada				22,045	21,736	0.27	-1.40
Mexico				4,994	6,023	0.08	20.60
United States				328,921	335,088	4.22	1.87
South America				21,889	28,070	0.35	28.24
Brazil				6,411	11,690	0.15	82.34
Other countries of South America				15,478	16,380	0.21	5.83
EAST ASIA AND THE PACIFIC				407,803	443,646	5.58	8.79
North-East Asia				213,685	231,029	2.91	8.12
China				55,464	68,774	0.87	24.00
Japan				129,448	126,823	1.60	-2.03
Korea, Republic of				28,773	35,432	0.45	23.14
Australasia				33,498	42,769	0.54	27.68
Australia				33,498	42,769	0.54	27.68
Other East Asia and the Pacific				160,620	169,848	2.14	5.75
Other countries of Asia				143,967	154,052	1.94	7.01
Other countries of Oceania				16,653	15,796	0.20	-5.15
EUROPE				6,829,381	7,079,151	89.11	3.66
Central/Eastern Europe				311,730	489,201	6.16	56.93
Czech Republic				55,732	60,085	0.76	7.81
Estonia				22,132	38,030	0.48	71.83
Hungary				13,874	13,294	0.17	-4.18
Latvia				16,323	27,528	0.35	68.65
Lithuania				19,332	32,504	0.41	68.14
Poland				105,361	199,204	2.51	89.07
Russian Federation				66,993	103,383	1.30	54.32
Slovakia				7,965	8,892	0.11	11.64
Ukraine				4,018	6,281	0.08	56.32
Northern Europe				2,813,517	2,827,708	35.59	0.50
Denmark				1,065,423	1,017,941	12.81	-4.46
Finland				137,138	146,548	1.84	6.86
Iceland				17,897	21,346	0.27	19.27
Ireland				16,463	17,769	0.22	7.93
Sweden				871,881	867,354	10.92	-0.52
United Kingdom				704,715	756,750	9.53	7.38
Southern Europe				454,138	537,109	6.76	18.27
Greece				15,856	16,917	0.21	6.69
Italy				195,507	219,888	2.77	12.47
Malta				667	1,134	0.01	70.01
Portugal				13,463	16,186	0.20	20.23
Slovenia				3,869	5,244	0.07	35.54

NORWAY

6. Overnight stays of non-resident tourists in all types of accommodation establishments, by nationality

	2002	2003	2004	2005	2006	Market share 06	% Change 06-05
Spain				224,776	277,740	3.50	23.56
Western Europe				**3,036,935**	**3,006,537**	**37.84**	**-1.00**
Austria				60,390	65,600	0.83	8.63
Belgium				61,013	65,095	0.82	6.69
France				283,928	286,993	3.61	1.08
Germany				1,745,501	1,672,301	21.05	-4.19
Liechtenstein				4,693	2,970	0.04	-36.71
Luxembourg				4,297	21,621	0.27	403.16
Netherlands				765,287	769,103	9.68	0.50
Switzerland				111,826	122,854	1.55	9.86
East Mediterranean Europe				**7,177**	**7,975**	**0.10**	**11.12**
Cyprus				918	1,616	0.02	76.03
Turkey				6,259	6,359	0.08	1.60
Other Europe				**205,884**	**210,621**	**2.65**	**2.30**
Other countries of Europe				205,884	210,621	2.65	2.30

Source: World Tourism Organization (UNWTO)

OMAN

3. Arrivals of non-resident tourists in hotels and similar establishments, by nationality

	2002	2003	2004	2005	2006	Market share 06	% Change 06-05
TOTAL	643,326	629,525	908,466	989,390	1,306,128	100.00	32.01
AFRICA	17,277	19,035	28,266	14,598	15,161	1.16	3.86
East Africa	5,590	6,202	7,828	2,725	441	0.03	-83.82
United Republic of Tanzania	5,590	6,202	7,828	2,725	441	0.03	-83.82
North Africa	4,781	6,287	12,738	9,227	5,954	0.46	-35.47
Morocco	1,572	1,892	6,836	5,106	1,403	0.11	-72.52
Sudan	2,315	2,639	3,596	2,497	3,018	0.23	20.87
Tunisia	894	1,756	2,306	1,624	1,533	0.12	-5.60
Southern Africa	4,187	3,246	4,200	897	3,594	0.28	300.67
South Africa	4,187	3,246	4,200	897	3,594	0.28	300.67
Other Africa	2,719	3,300	3,500	1,749	5,172	0.40	195.71
Other countries of Africa	2,719	3,300	3,500	1,749	5,172	0.40	195.71
AMERICAS	36,022	36,356	40,154	17,938	47,639	3.65	165.58
North America	33,066	29,866	35,841	15,540	42,814	3.28	175.51
Canada	7,074	5,246	8,931	3,476	9,039	0.69	160.04
United States	25,992	24,620	26,910	12,064	33,775	2.59	179.97
South America	1,297	390	611	159	786	0.06	394.34
Brazil	1,297	390	611	159	786	0.06	394.34
Other Americas	1,659	6,100	3,702	2,239	4,039	0.31	80.39
Other countries of the Americas	1,659	6,100	3,702	2,239	4,039	0.31	80.39
EAST ASIA AND THE PACIFIC	66,416	51,026	54,971	56,245	82,616	6.33	46.89
North-East Asia	14,300	10,923	10,946	14,997	14,279	1.09	-4.79
China	4,178	4,351	3,667	6,870	7,594	0.58	10.54
Japan	10,122	6,572	7,279	8,127	6,685	0.51	-17.74
South-East Asia	8,547	5,609	5,986	5,727	5,932	0.45	3.58
Philippines	8,547	5,609	5,986	5,727	5,932	0.45	3.58
Australasia	8,153	7,926	9,893	5,864	15,667	1.20	167.17
Australia	6,046	6,379	7,177	4,953	13,307	1.02	168.67
New Zealand	2,107	1,547	2,716	911	2,360	0.18	159.06
Other East Asia and the Pacific	35,416	26,568	28,146	29,657	46,738	3.58	57.60
Other countries of Asia	23,976	20,903	22,849	19,022	34,349	2.63	80.58
Other countries of Oceania	11,440	5,665	5,297	10,635	12,389	0.95	16.49
EUROPE	197,015	163,855	280,727	403,962	577,546	44.22	42.97
Central/Eastern Europe				2,613	8,484	0.65	224.68
Czech Republic				175	606	0.05	246.29
Russian Federation				2,438	7,878	0.60	223.13
Northern Europe	83,741	64,359	99,486	163,185	290,107	22.21	77.78
Denmark	2,275	1,766	3,045	3,798	4,127	0.32	8.66
Finland				514	1,197	0.09	132.88
Ireland				940	2,943	0.23	213.09
Norway				1,687	1,795	0.14	6.40
Sweden	1,992	2,061	3,554	21,049	60,560	4.64	187.71
United Kingdom	79,474	60,532	92,887	135,197	219,485	16.80	62.34
Southern Europe	10,858	10,597	13,401	15,701	17,697	1.35	12.71
Italy	9,233	8,901	10,218	12,587	14,749	1.13	17.18
Portugal				531	533	0.04	0.38
Spain	1,625	1,696	3,183	2,583	2,415	0.18	-6.50

OMAN

3. Arrivals of non-resident tourists in hotels and similar establishments, by nationality

	2002	2003	2004	2005	2006	Market share 06	% Change 06-05
Western Europe	80,933	67,862	138,085	193,882	235,713	18.05	21.58
Austria	5,147	3,139	7,850	13,368	17,025	1.30	27.36
Belgium				3,035	4,590	0.35	51.24
France	15,263	14,803	23,495	26,621	36,669	2.81	37.74
Germany	38,457	31,133	78,129	112,276	125,285	9.59	11.59
Netherlands	9,510	9,052	11,408	12,084	13,849	1.06	14.61
Switzerland	12,556	9,735	17,203	26,498	38,295	2.93	44.52
Other Europe	21,483	21,037	29,755	28,581	25,545	1.96	-10.62
Other countries of Europe	21,483	21,037	29,755	28,581	25,545	1.96	-10.62
MIDDLE EAST	192,817	204,586	249,285	240,506	230,777	17.67	-4.05
Middle East	192,817	204,586	249,285	240,506	230,777	17.67	-4.05
Bahrain	26,121	29,881	26,536	37,586	37,360	2.86	-0.60
Jordan	8,277	9,167	11,953	11,132	8,256	0.63	-25.84
Kuwait	10,903	11,218	15,564	12,775	14,574	1.12	14.08
Lebanon	6,561	5,437	9,481	8,053	10,346	0.79	28.47
Qatar	7,585	8,697	12,998	11,608	9,976	0.76	-14.06
Saudi Arabia	24,068	22,163	31,066	33,256	25,597	1.96	-23.03
Syrian Arab Republic	4,806	5,206	7,081	4,917	4,806	0.37	-2.26
United Arab Emirates	77,966	87,407	103,317	94,902	95,334	7.30	0.46
Egypt	19,295	16,886	20,276	16,775	14,867	1.14	-11.37
Other countries of Middle East	7,235	8,524	11,013	9,502	9,661	0.74	1.67
SOUTH ASIA	85,238	101,971	130,565	140,832	133,180	10.20	-5.43
South Asia	85,238	101,971	130,565	140,832	133,180	10.20	-5.43
Sri Lanka	3,037	4,032	3,969	3,445	3,195	0.24	-7.26
India	72,090	83,065	106,456	116,375	110,841	8.49	-4.76
Iran, Islamic Republic of	2,355	2,857	3,634	2,269	3,151	0.24	38.87
Pakistan	7,756	12,017	16,506	18,743	15,993	1.22	-14.67
REGION NOT SPECIFIED	48,541	52,696	124,498	115,309	219,209	16.78	90.11
Not Specified	48,541	52,696	124,498	115,309	219,209	16.78	90.11
Other countries of the World	48,541	52,696	124,498	115,309	219,209	16.78	90.11

Source: World Tourism Organization (UNWTO)

OMAN

5. Overnight stays of non-resident tourists in hotels and similar establishments, by nationality

	2002	2003	2004	2005	2006	Market share 06	% Change 06-05
TOTAL	738,959	777,154	995,032	1,392,220	1,705,337	100.00	22.49
AFRICA	20,770	23,740	32,449	22,827	22,473	1.32	-1.55
East Africa	5,058	6,803	8,285	4,628	629	0.04	-86.41
United Republic of Tanzania	5,058	6,803	8,285	4,628	629	0.04	-86.41
North Africa	6,684	8,255	13,990	9,264	8,799	0.52	-5.02
Morocco	2,216	2,984	6,546	3,217	2,223	0.13	-30.90
Sudan	3,078	3,399	4,566	3,890	4,360	0.26	12.08
Tunisia	1,390	1,872	2,878	2,157	2,216	0.13	2.74
Southern Africa	4,537	4,433	5,280	3,824	4,820	0.28	26.05
South Africa	4,537	4,433	5,280	3,824	4,820	0.28	26.05
Other Africa	4,491	4,249	4,894	5,111	8,225	0.48	60.93
Other countries of Africa	4,491	4,249	4,894	5,111	8,225	0.48	60.93
AMERICAS	44,188	48,157	48,879	52,350	67,772	3.97	29.46
North America	40,795	40,485	43,812	46,387	60,961	3.57	31.42
Canada	9,612	7,560	12,600	11,275	13,165	0.77	16.76
United States	31,183	32,925	31,212	35,112	47,796	2.80	36.12
South America	1,041	481	699	524	997	0.06	90.27
Brazil	1,041	481	699	524	997	0.06	90.27
Other Americas	2,352	7,191	4,368	5,439	5,814	0.34	6.89
Other countries of the Americas	2,352	7,191	4,368	5,439	5,814	0.34	6.89
EAST ASIA AND THE PACIFIC	79,123	70,623	80,485	94,968	107,616	6.31	13.32
North-East Asia	13,895	15,691	16,645	20,570	20,748	1.22	0.87
China	4,644	6,856	5,649	9,028	9,888	0.58	9.53
Japan	9,251	8,835	10,996	11,542	10,860	0.64	-5.91
South-East Asia	8,538	8,330	8,556	9,502	9,050	0.53	-4.76
Philippines	8,538	8,330	8,556	9,502	9,050	0.53	-4.76
Australasia	12,066	12,527	17,440	18,033	20,428	1.20	13.28
Australia	9,873	9,822	14,352	15,212	17,475	1.02	14.88
New Zealand	2,193	2,705	3,088	2,821	2,953	0.17	4.68
Other East Asia and the Pacific	44,624	34,075	37,844	46,863	57,390	3.37	22.46
Other countries of Asia	28,292	28,216	33,507	25,505	40,540	2.38	58.95
Other countries of Oceania	16,332	5,859	4,337	21,358	16,850	0.99	-21.11
EUROPE	223,052	183,806	290,984	392,757	679,781	39.86	73.08
Central/Eastern Europe				4,834	11,726	0.69	142.57
Russian Federation				4,834	11,726	0.69	142.57
Northern Europe	93,111	72,624	106,415	153,659	323,069	18.94	110.25
Denmark	3,670	2,101	5,721	4,003	5,806	0.34	45.04
Sweden	2,836	2,279	4,115	16,860	62,090	3.64	268.27
United Kingdom	86,605	68,244	96,579	132,796	255,173	14.96	92.15
Southern Europe	15,278	18,256	16,077	15,973	21,718	1.27	35.97
Italy	13,463	16,530	12,240	12,851	18,646	1.09	45.09
Spain	1,815	1,726	3,837	3,122	3,072	0.18	-1.60
Western Europe	85,001	68,816	134,270	185,735	278,506	16.33	49.95
Austria	6,544	2,920	7,587	11,884	19,303	1.13	62.43
Belgium				3,343	5,278	0.31	57.88

OMAN

5. Overnight stays of non-resident tourists in hotels and similar establishments, by nationality

	2002	2003	2004	2005	2006	Market share 06	% Change 06-05
France	17,541	14,741	23,566	24,569	43,498	2.55	77.04
Germany	38,332	32,626	72,567	105,905	149,334	8.76	41.01
Netherlands	10,442	10,881	13,962	12,979	17,660	1.04	36.07
Switzerland	12,142	7,648	16,588	27,055	43,433	2.55	60.54
Other Europe	**29,662**	**24,110**	**34,222**	**32,556**	**44,762**	**2.62**	**37.49**
Other countries of Europe	29,662	24,110	34,222	32,556	44,762	2.62	37.49
MIDDLE EAST	**210,613**	**242,074**	**265,499**	**258,170**	**286,980**	**16.83**	**11.16**
Middle East	**210,613**	**242,074**	**265,499**	**258,170**	**286,980**	**16.83**	**11.16**
Bahrain	27,008	31,121	30,935	39,686	41,936	2.46	5.67
Jordan	10,381	14,350	15,890	16,587	13,151	0.77	-20.72
Kuwait	12,266	14,054	15,083	14,980	18,968	1.11	26.62
Lebanon	8,781	11,206	13,319	13,002	14,959	0.88	15.05
Qatar	8,651	9,562	11,876	12,443	13,471	0.79	8.26
Saudi Arabia	24,511	26,262	28,708	32,666	31,264	1.83	-4.29
Syrian Arab Republic	5,999	9,107	10,286	8,846	9,016	0.53	1.92
United Arab Emirates	75,910	88,217	98,616	84,209	106,613	6.25	26.61
Egypt	28,258	24,135	28,471	25,549	22,768	1.34	-10.88
Other countries of Middle East	8,848	14,060	12,315	10,202	14,834	0.87	45.40
SOUTH ASIA	**111,865**	**138,160**	**160,317**	**170,788**	**177,245**	**10.39**	**3.78**
South Asia	**111,865**	**138,160**	**160,317**	**170,788**	**177,245**	**10.39**	**3.78**
Sri Lanka	3,886	4,725	4,199	4,453	4,538	0.27	1.91
India	96,330	113,993	133,101	141,558	146,687	8.60	3.62
Iran, Islamic Republic of	2,817	4,360	4,285	3,360	5,699	0.33	69.61
Pakistan	8,832	15,082	18,732	21,417	20,321	1.19	-5.12
REGION NOT SPECIFIED	**49,348**	**70,594**	**116,419**	**400,360**	**363,470**	**21.31**	**-9.21**
Not Specified	**49,348**	**70,594**	**116,419**	**400,360**	**363,470**	**21.31**	**-9.21**
Other countries of the World	49,348	70,594	116,419	400,360	363,470	21.31	-9.21

Source: World Tourism Organization (UNWTO)

PAKISTAN

1. Arrivals of non-resident tourists at national borders, by nationality

	2002	2003	2004	2005	2006	Market share 06	% Change 06-05
TOTAL	498,059	500,918	647,993	798,260	898,389	100.00	12.54
AFRICA	11,620	11,721	12,521	14,691	18,970	2.11	29.13
East Africa	2,977	2,927	3,881	4,064	8,431	0.94	107.46
Burundi					49	0.01	
Comoros					12		
Ethiopia					356	0.04	
Eritrea	18	7	34	66	74	0.01	12.12
Djibouti					75	0.01	
Kenya	1,597	1,296	1,199	1,656	1,948	0.22	17.63
Madagascar					91	0.01	
Malawi					219	0.02	
Mauritius	72	331	710	919	1,062	0.12	15.56
Mozambique					539	0.06	
Reunion					70	0.01	
Rwanda					18		
Somalia	418	439	579	627	636	0.07	1.44
Zimbabwe					169	0.02	
Uganda	136	110	166	191	162	0.02	-15.18
United Republic of Tanzania	709	688	1,080	513	2,815	0.31	448.73
Zambia	27	56	113	92	136	0.02	47.83
Central Africa	8	23	34	45	168	0.02	273.33
Angola					33		
Cameroon	8	23	34	45	36		-20.00
Chad					35		
Congo					35		
Gabon					29		
North Africa	1,468	1,058	1,480	1,967	2,549	0.28	29.59
Algeria	200	76	35	85	131	0.01	54.12
Morocco	148	157	214	566	619	0.07	9.36
Sudan	889	680	1,090	1,104	1,378	0.15	24.82
Tunisia	231	145	141	212	421	0.05	98.58
Southern Africa	3,668	3,186	3,138	5,067	5,971	0.66	17.84
Botswana					49	0.01	
Lesotho					86	0.01	
Namibia					121	0.01	
South Africa	3,667	3,179	3,020	4,864	5,628	0.63	15.71
Swaziland	1	7	118	203	87	0.01	-57.14
West Africa	2,140	3,139	2,656	1,544	1,851	0.21	19.88
Benin					5		
Gambia					41		
Ghana	67	140	109	133	127	0.01	-4.51
Guinea					34		
Liberia					14		
Mali	38	35	18	23	43		86.96
Mauritania					32		
Niger					27		
Nigeria	1,830	2,728	2,277	1,259	1,312	0.15	4.21
Senegal	205	236	252	129	119	0.01	-7.75
Sierra Leone					63	0.01	
Togo					9		
Burkina Faso					25		
Other Africa	1,359	1,388	1,332	2,004			
Other countries of Africa	1,359	1,388	1,332	2,004			

PAKISTAN

1. Arrivals of non-resident tourists at national borders, by nationality

	2002	2003	2004	2005	2006	Market share 06	% Change 06-05
AMERICAS	87,884	85,910	103,104	146,548	160,713	17.89	9.67
Caribbean	13	19	5	369	414	0.05	12.20
Cuba	13	19	5	369	102	0.01	-72.36
Dominica					26		
Haiti					5		
Jamaica					69	0.01	
Anguilla					2		
Trinidad and Tobago					210	0.02	
Central America					638	0.07	
El Salvador					17		
Honduras					33		
Panama					588	0.07	
North America	87,233	85,508	102,423	144,714	157,216	17.50	8.64
Canada	18,150	12,991	15,014	22,953	30,833	3.43	34.33
Mexico	53	77	97	204	215	0.02	5.39
United States	69,030	72,440	87,312	121,557	126,168	14.04	3.79
South America	544	303	534	888	2,445	0.27	175.34
Argentina	213	123	153	226	291	0.03	28.76
Bolivia					42		
Brazil	201	107	195	336	387	0.04	15.18
Chile	52	24	58	122	1,318	0.15	980.33
Colombia	35	24	83	91	127	0.01	39.56
Ecuador					43		
Guyana					24		
Paraguay					12		
Peru	43	25	45	102	84	0.01	-17.65
Suriname					22		
Uruguay				11	17		54.55
Venezuela					78	0.01	
Other Americas	94	80	142	577			
Other countries of the Americas	94	80	142	577			
EAST ASIA AND THE PACIFIC	43,920	43,521	59,503	83,607	99,063	11.03	18.49
North-East Asia	24,392	24,175	35,796	50,585	58,585	6.52	15.81
China	8,896	10,324	17,176	29,601	37,137	4.13	25.46
Taiwan (Province of China)	183	373	611	1,001	1,116	0.12	11.49
Hong Kong, China	1,180	225	162	82	46	0.01	-43.90
Japan	9,975	9,361	13,440	14,136	14,343	1.60	1.46
Korea, Dem. People's Republic of					164	0.02	
Korea, Republic of	4,158	3,892	4,407	5,765	5,633	0.63	-2.29
Macao, China					74	0.01	
Mongolia					72	0.01	
South-East Asia	12,449	12,175	14,936	22,066	27,432	3.05	24.32
Brunei Darussalam					111	0.01	
Myanmar	335	468	704	528	847	0.09	60.42
Cambodia	1	74	121	193	147	0.02	-23.83
Indonesia	1,692	1,223	1,780	2,039	2,558	0.28	25.45
Lao People's Democratic Republic					44		
Malaysia	4,095	3,848	4,138	8,172	10,250	1.14	25.43
Philippines	2,079	1,703	2,526	2,990	4,000	0.45	33.78
Timor-Leste					19		
Singapore	1,772	2,348	2,840	3,811	5,389	0.60	41.41
Viet Nam	48	36	56	121	184	0.02	52.07

PAKISTAN

1. Arrivals of non-resident tourists at national borders, by nationality

	2002	2003	2004	2005	2006	Market share 06	% Change 06-05
Thailand	2,363	2,400	2,486	3,562	3,883	0.43	9.01
Other countries of South-East Asia	64	75	285	650			
Australasia	**7,079**	**7,171**	**8,771**	**10,956**	**12,948**	**1.44**	**18.18**
Australia	5,740	6,134	7,298	9,632	11,438	1.27	18.75
New Zealand	1,339	1,037	1,473	1,324	1,510	0.17	14.05
Melanesia					**98**	**0.01**	
Fiji					92	0.01	
Papua New Guinea					6		
EUROPE	**215,280**	**192,854**	**280,877**	**356,804**	**393,919**	**43.85**	**10.40**
Central/Eastern Europe	**3,863**	**3,965**	**5,450**	**8,671**	**11,025**	**1.23**	**27.15**
Azerbaijan	318	371	480	642	434	0.05	-32.40
Armenia					46	0.01	
Bulgaria	69	69	94	207	335	0.04	61.84
Belarus					234	0.03	
Czech Republic	199	242	404	652	643	0.07	-1.38
Estonia					59	0.01	
Georgia					111	0.01	
Hungary	116	149	201	404	396	0.04	-1.98
Kazakhstan	414	525	644	751	787	0.09	4.79
Kyrgyzstan	80	96	64	242	386	0.04	59.50
Latvia					84	0.01	
Lithuania					65	0.01	
Poland	370	411	636	947	1,170	0.13	23.55
Romania	174	297	294	366	461	0.05	25.96
Russian Federation	1,080	1,020	1,523	2,556	2,368	0.26	-7.36
Slovakia					139	0.02	
Tajikistan	167	266	259	299	227	0.03	-24.08
Turkmenistan					152	0.02	
Ukraine	595	318	491	1,155	1,865	0.21	61.47
Uzbekistan	281	201	360	450	1,063	0.12	136.22
Northern Europe	**167,437**	**147,293**	**219,515**	**278,035**	**305,488**	**34.00**	**9.87**
Denmark	4,846	4,280	6,458	7,880	7,937	0.88	0.72
Finland	346	32	785	997	963	0.11	-3.41
Iceland					53	0.01	
Ireland	927	1,333	1,871	2,418	2,679	0.30	10.79
Norway	7,075	7,343	10,545	13,461	13,841	1.54	2.82
Sweden	2,902	3,181	3,555	4,648	4,872	0.54	4.82
United Kingdom	151,341	131,124	196,301	248,631	275,143	30.63	10.66
Southern Europe	**5,464**	**5,456**	**8,748**	**9,416**	**10,277**	**1.14**	**9.14**
Albania	13	152	134	119	93	0.01	-21.85
Andorra					4		
Bosnia and Herzegovina					167	0.02	
Croatia					196	0.02	
Greece	525	461	660	706	727	0.08	2.97
Italy	3,036	3,089	5,060	4,759	4,813	0.54	1.13
Malta	28	48	370	65	63	0.01	-3.08
Portugal	444	381	543	787	993	0.11	26.18
Slovenia					110	0.01	
Spain	1,344	1,286	1,924	2,980	2,925	0.33	-1.85
Serbia and Montenegro	74	39	57		186	0.02	
Western Europe	**34,561**	**32,775**	**43,400**	**53,758**	**59,843**	**6.66**	**11.32**
Austria	1,667	1,092	2,223	2,355	2,634	0.29	11.85
Belgium	1,694	1,916	2,150	3,039	3,614	0.40	18.92

PAKISTAN

1. Arrivals of non-resident tourists at national borders, by nationality

	2002	2003	2004	2005	2006	Market share 06	% Change 06-05
France	6,892	5,657	8,119	10,062	11,783	1.31	17.10
Germany	12,243	13,658	18,959	24,726	27,286	3.04	10.35
Luxembourg					70	0.01	
Monaco					16		
Netherlands	9,751	9,112	9,938	10,670	11,251	1.25	5.45
Switzerland	2,314	1,340	2,011	2,906	3,189	0.35	9.74
East Mediterranean Europe	**3,024**	**2,543**	**3,197**	**5,411**	**7,286**	**0.81**	**34.65**
Cyprus	247	93	99	140	220	0.02	57.14
Turkey	2,777	2,450	3,098	5,271	7,066	0.79	34.05
Other Europe	**931**	**822**	**567**	**1,513**			
Other countries of Europe	931	822	567	1,513			
MIDDLE EAST	**22,329**	**19,593**	**28,365**	**31,920**	**37,661**	**4.19**	**17.99**
Middle East	**22,329**	**19,593**	**28,365**	**31,920**	**37,661**	**4.19**	**17.99**
Bahrain	915	1,275	7,380	1,941	2,405	0.27	23.91
Palestine	254	187	221	347	398	0.04	14.70
Iraq	254	99	190	242	314	0.03	29.75
Jordan	1,002	1,035	1,478	2,034	2,589	0.29	27.29
Kuwait	1,008	516	687	536	674	0.08	25.75
Lebanon	318	481	697	1,058	1,357	0.15	28.26
Libyan Arab Jamahiriya	330	162	280	380	578	0.06	52.11
Oman	4,702	4,689	4,918	7,835	8,480	0.94	8.23
Qatar	1,971	938	772	974	1,056	0.12	8.42
Saudi Arabia	4,220	4,565	5,265	8,050	9,093	1.01	12.96
Syrian Arab Republic	482	366	454	706	1,534	0.17	117.28
United Arab Emirates	4,563	3,810	3,936	4,564	5,381	0.60	17.90
Egypt	1,589	1,070	1,541	2,444	2,997	0.33	22.63
Yemen	719	400	546	809	805	0.09	-0.49
Other countries of Middle East	2						
SOUTH ASIA	**116,449**	**146,655**	**160,345**	**158,549**	**182,144**	**20.27**	**14.88**
South Asia	**116,449**	**146,655**	**160,345**	**158,549**	**182,144**	**20.27**	**14.88**
Afghanistan	98,498	119,936	117,559	77,639	84,956	9.46	9.42
Bangladesh	5,581	7,630	8,904	5,981	8,308	0.92	38.91
Bhutan					111	0.01	
Sri Lanka	1,960	2,645	3,708	4,114	4,842	0.54	17.70
India	2,618	7,096	19,658	59,560	70,174	7.81	17.82
Iran, Islamic Republic of	6,394	8,119	8,156	9,107	11,365	1.27	24.79
Maldives	248	176	427	378	422	0.05	11.64
Nepal	1,139	1,029	1,760	1,663	1,966	0.22	18.22
Other countries of South Asia	11	24	173	107			
REGION NOT SPECIFIED	**577**	**664**	**3,278**	**6,141**	**5,919**	**0.66**	**-3.62**
Not Specified	**577**	**664**	**3,278**	**6,141**	**5,919**	**0.66**	**-3.62**
Other countries of the World	577	664	3,278	6,141	5,919	0.66	-3.62

Source: World Tourism Organization (UNWTO)

PALAU

1. Arrivals of non-resident tourists at national borders, by country of residence

		2002	2003	2004	2005	2006	Market share 06	% Change 06-05
TOTAL	(*)	58,560	68,296	94,894	86,126	86,375	100.00	0.29
AMERICAS		4,774	4,511	6,507	5,910	7,019	8.13	18.76
North America		4,774	4,511	6,507	5,910	7,019	8.13	18.76
United States		4,774	4,511	6,507	5,910	7,019	8.13	18.76
EAST ASIA AND THE PACIFIC		51,504	61,400	84,449	75,503	75,542	87.46	0.05
North-East Asia		41,473	51,399	70,194	65,949	68,787	79.64	4.30
China		873	724	1,060	1,079	807	0.93	-25.21
Taiwan (Province of China)		15,819	28,088	38,739	34,494	28,659	33.18	-16.92
Hong Kong, China		536	443	409	1,392	279	0.32	-79.96
Japan		23,748	21,691	24,181	26,700	27,167	31.45	1.75
Korea, Republic of		497	453	5,805	2,284	11,875	13.75	419.92
South-East Asia		3,497	3,679	7,544	3,431	3,304	3.83	-3.70
Philippines		3,410	3,625	3,699	3,431	3,304	3.83	-3.70
Singapore		87	54	3,845				
Australasia		403	527	1,486	863	641	0.74	-25.72
Australia		403	527	1,486	863	641	0.74	-25.72
Micronesia		6,131	5,795	5,225	5,260	2,810	3.25	-46.58
Guam		3,729	3,688	2,780	3,023	1,525	1.77	-49.55
Northern Mariana Islands		1,335	1,010	1,220	993	355	0.41	-64.25
Micronesia (Federated States of)		1,067	1,097	1,225	1,244	930	1.08	-25.24
EUROPE		834	818	1,837	2,390	2,493	2.89	4.31
Northern Europe		250	117					
United Kingdom		250	117					
Southern Europe		97	123					
Italy		97	123					
Western Europe		487	578	524	627	558	0.65	-11.00
France		77	47					
Germany		256	414	524	627	558	0.65	-11.00
Switzerland		154	117					
Other Europe				1,313	1,763	1,935	2.24	9.76
Other countries of Europe				1,313	1,763	1,935	2.24	9.76
REGION NOT SPECIFIED		1,448	1,567	2,101	2,323	1,321	1.53	-43.13
Not Specified		1,448	1,567	2,101	2,323	1,321	1.53	-43.13
Other countries of the World		1,448	1,567	2,101	2,323	1,321	1.53	-43.13

Source: World Tourism Organization (UNWTO)

PALESTINE

3. Arrivals of non-resident tourists in hotels and similar establishments, by nationality

	2002	2003	2004	2005	2006	Market share 06	% Change 06-05
TOTAL	33,424	36,722	56,011	88,360	122,616	100.00	38.77
AFRICA	1,209	604	641	971	1,643	1.34	69.21
Other Africa	1,209	604	641	971	1,643	1.34	69.21
All countries of Africa	1,209	604	641	971	1,643	1.34	69.21
AMERICAS	6,480	6,407	10,649	13,735	18,728	15.27	36.35
North America	5,952	6,104	9,832	13,048	12,230	9.97	-6.27
Canada, United States	5,952	6,104	9,832	13,048	12,230	9.97	-6.27
Other Americas	528	303	817	687	6,498	5.30	845.85
Other countries of the Americas	528	303	817	687	6,498	5.30	845.85
EAST ASIA AND THE PACIFIC	6,487	4,872	8,399	16,490	16,595	13.53	0.64
Australasia	656	293	309	380	1,429	1.17	276.05
Australia, New Zealand	656	293	309	380	1,429	1.17	276.05
Other East Asia and the Pacific	5,831	4,579	8,090	16,110	15,166	12.37	-5.86
All countries of Asia	5,831	4,579	8,090	16,110	15,166	12.37	-5.86
EUROPE	18,352	23,701	35,210	55,324	83,178	67.84	50.35
East Mediterranean Europe	3,924	9,328	12,951	17,635	21,620	17.63	22.60
Israel	3,924	9,328	12,951	17,635	21,620	17.63	22.60
Other Europe	14,428	14,373	22,259	37,689	61,558	50.20	63.33
Other countries of Europe	14,428	14,373	22,259	37,689	61,558	50.20	63.33
MIDDLE EAST	896	1,138	1,112	1,840	2,472	2.02	34.35
Middle East	896	1,138	1,112	1,840	2,472	2.02	34.35
All countries of Middle East	896	1,138	1,112	1,840	2,472	2.02	34.35

Source: World Tourism Organization (UNWTO)

PALESTINE

5. Overnight stays of non-resident tourists in hotels and similar establishments, by nationality

	2002	2003	2004	2005	2006	Market share 06	% Change 06-05
TOTAL	103,266	112,807	164,375	251,357	331,294	100.00	31.80
AFRICA	2,868	1,560	1,374	2,077	3,342	1.01	60.91
Other Africa	2,868	1,560	1,374	2,077	3,342	1.01	60.91
All countries of Africa	2,868	1,560	1,374	2,077	3,342	1.01	60.91
AMERICAS	24,983	25,452	35,181	50,981	58,717	17.72	15.17
North America	23,807	24,645	33,603	48,943	42,382	12.79	-13.41
Canada, United States	23,807	24,645	33,603	48,943	42,382	12.79	-13.41
Other Americas	1,176	807	1,578	2,038	16,335	4.93	701.52
Other countries of the Americas	1,176	807	1,578	2,038	16,335	4.93	701.52
EAST ASIA AND THE PACIFIC	18,216	14,303	26,906	50,127	50,021	15.10	-0.21
Australasia	2,148	845	665	948	2,600	0.78	174.26
Australia, New Zealand	2,148	845	665	948	2,600	0.78	174.26
Other East Asia and the Pacific	16,068	13,458	26,241	49,179	47,421	14.31	-3.57
All countries of Asia	16,068	13,458	26,241	49,179	47,421	14.31	-3.57
EUROPE	54,936	69,416	99,054	144,942	213,003	64.29	46.96
East Mediterranean Europe	7,292	16,754	23,319	30,400	44,602	13.46	46.72
Israel	7,292	16,754	23,319	30,400	44,602	13.46	46.72
Other Europe	47,644	52,662	75,735	114,542	168,401	50.83	47.02
Other countries of Europe	47,644	52,662	75,735	114,542	168,401	50.83	47.02
MIDDLE EAST	2,263	2,076	1,860	3,230	6,211	1.87	92.29
Middle East	2,263	2,076	1,860	3,230	6,211	1.87	92.29
All countries of Middle East	2,263	2,076	1,860	3,230	6,211	1.87	92.29

Source: World Tourism Organization (UNWTO)

PANAMA

2. Arrivals of non-resident visitors at national borders, by country of residence

		2002	2003	2004	2005	2006	Market share 06	% Change 06-05
TOTAL	(*)	426,154	468,686	498,415	576,050	703,745	100.00	22.17
AFRICA		334	354	335	390	477	0.07	22.31
Southern Africa		103	126	134	175	213	0.03	21.71
South Africa		103	126	134	175	213	0.03	21.71
Other Africa		231	228	201	215	264	0.04	22.79
Other countries of Africa		231	228	201	215	264	0.04	22.79
AMERICAS		375,518	410,957	438,872	507,185	619,526	88.03	22.15
Caribbean		28,534	27,846	29,311	33,865	41,488	5.90	22.51
Bahamas		408	407	451	532	651	0.09	22.37
Barbados		240	317	357	396	492	0.07	24.24
Bermuda		70	90	60	55	96	0.01	74.55
Cuba		2,712	2,443	2,555	2,828	3,460	0.49	22.35
Dominican Republic		7,505	6,110	5,923	7,396	9,049	1.29	22.35
Haiti		3,973	4,114	4,479	4,939	6,008	0.85	21.64
Jamaica		4,669	4,576	4,629	5,593	6,890	0.98	23.19
Curacao		239	494	693	1,030	1,268	0.18	23.11
Puerto Rico		7,254	7,526	8,129	8,625	10,585	1.50	22.72
Other countries of the Caribbean		1,464	1,769	2,035	2,471	2,989	0.42	20.96
Central America		45,997	51,618	53,906	62,482	76,587	10.88	22.57
Belize		782	684	685	759	958	0.14	26.22
Costa Rica		19,480	20,378	21,459	25,455	31,248	4.44	22.76
El Salvador		5,543	7,624	8,031	9,279	11,545	1.64	24.42
Guatemala		11,760	12,121	12,400	14,349	17,361	2.47	20.99
Honduras		3,592	5,470	6,027	6,584	8,143	1.16	23.68
Nicaragua		4,840	5,341	5,304	6,056	7,332	1.04	21.07
North America		146,643	166,960	181,507	209,287	254,993	36.23	21.84
Canada		14,926	14,297	16,911	19,660	29,392	4.18	49.50
Mexico		20,078	23,765	24,532	29,280	34,507	4.90	17.85
United States		111,627	128,897	140,062	160,288	191,094	27.15	19.22
Other countries of North America		12	1	2	59			
South America		154,344	164,533	174,148	201,551	246,458	35.02	22.28
Argentina		6,736	8,950	10,108	11,629	14,230	2.02	22.37
Bolivia		2,149	2,361	2,581	3,030	3,708	0.53	22.38
Brazil		6,273	7,698	8,256	9,701	11,844	1.68	22.09
Chile		6,253	6,946	7,406	8,150	9,985	1.42	22.52
Colombia		84,555	90,697	93,510	108,628	129,418	18.39	19.14
Ecuador		21,928	20,252	22,391	25,903	35,024	4.98	35.21
Paraguay		411	645	671	818	1,004	0.14	22.74
Peru		10,337	10,514	11,058	12,592	15,416	2.19	22.43
Uruguay		1,133	1,358	1,379	1,625	1,999	0.28	23.02
Venezuela		14,109	14,607	16,249	18,892	23,113	3.28	22.34
Other countries of South America		460	505	539	583	717	0.10	22.98
EAST ASIA AND THE PACIFIC		11,864	13,968	13,919	16,095	20,241	2.88	25.76
North-East Asia		4,092	4,544	4,502	5,178	5,689	0.81	9.87
Taiwan (Province of China)		1,120	1,439	1,352	1,443	1,452	0.21	0.62
Japan		2,972	3,105	3,150	3,735	4,237	0.60	13.44
Australasia		631	1,063	1,137	1,327	1,612	0.23	21.48
Australia		501	842	915	1,073	1,304	0.19	21.53
New Zealand		130	221	222	254	308	0.04	21.26
Other East Asia and the Pacific		7,141	8,361	8,280	9,590	12,940	1.84	34.93

PANAMA

2. Arrivals of non-resident visitors at national borders, by country of residence

	2002	2003	2004	2005	2006	Market share 06	% Change 06-05
Other countries of Asia	7,089	8,332	8,246	9,555	12,897	1.83	34.98
Other countries of Oceania	52	29	34	35	43	0.01	22.86
EUROPE	**38,417**	**43,355**	**45,254**	**52,339**	**63,451**	**9.02**	**21.23**
Northern Europe	**3,924**	**4,197**	**4,820**	**5,828**	**7,064**	**1.00**	**21.21**
United Kingdom	3,924	4,197	4,820	5,828	7,064	1.00	21.21
Southern Europe	**16,207**	**14,740**	**15,337**	**18,080**	**23,615**	**3.36**	**30.61**
Greece	547	599	570	625	764	0.11	22.24
Italy	6,756	4,945	5,198	6,617	10,584	1.50	59.95
Spain	8,904	9,196	9,569	10,838	12,267	1.74	13.19
Western Europe	**9,816**	**14,542**	**14,990**	**16,365**	**20,937**	**2.98**	**27.94**
France	3,046	6,766	6,881	7,289	9,396	1.34	28.91
Germany	3,494	4,091	4,222	4,745	6,275	0.89	32.24
Netherlands	1,756	1,782	1,888	1,994	2,427	0.34	21.72
Switzerland	1,520	1,903	1,999	2,337	2,839	0.40	21.48
East Mediterranean Europe	**1,986**	**2,140**	**2,202**	**2,561**	**2,792**	**0.40**	**9.02**
Israel	1,986	2,140	2,202	2,561	2,792	0.40	9.02
Other Europe	**6,484**	**7,736**	**7,905**	**9,505**	**9,043**	**1.28**	**-4.86**
Other countries of Europe	6,484	7,736	7,905	9,505	9,043	1.28	-4.86
MIDDLE EAST	**21**	**52**	**35**	**41**	**50**	**0.01**	**21.95**
Middle East	**21**	**52**	**35**	**41**	**50**	**0.01**	**21.95**
Egypt	21	52	35	41	50	0.01	21.95

Source: World Tourism Organization (UNWTO)

PAPUA NEW GUINEA

1. Arrivals of non-resident tourists at national borders, by country of residence

	2002	2003	2004	2005	2006	Market share 06	% Change 06-05
TOTAL	53,761	56,282	59,013	69,251	77,731	100.00	12.25
AFRICA	271	193	241	353	500	0.64	41.64
Other Africa	271	193	241	353	500	0.64	41.64
All countries of Africa	271	193	241	353	500	0.64	41.64
AMERICAS	6,990	5,215	5,440	6,491	7,348	9.45	13.20
North America	6,901	5,143	5,334	6,369	7,202	9.27	13.08
Canada	848	577	586	660	978	1.26	48.18
United States	6,053	4,566	4,748	5,709	6,224	8.01	9.02
Other Americas	89	72	106	122	146	0.19	19.67
Other countries of the Americas	89	72	106	122	146	0.19	19.67
EAST ASIA AND THE PACIFIC	39,316	45,999	47,963	57,516	63,383	81.54	10.20
North-East Asia	5,930	5,369	4,548	6,668	6,304	8.11	-5.46
China	858	883	1,074	1,267	2,338	3.01	84.53
Hong Kong, China	505	111					
Japan	3,804	3,893	3,474	5,401	3,966	5.10	-26.57
Korea, Republic of	763	482					
South-East Asia	2,094	5,164	4,763	5,787	6,936	8.92	19.85
Malaysia	140	1,856	2,106	2,443	3,155	4.06	29.14
Philippines	416	2,790	2,657	3,344	3,781	4.86	13.07
Singapore	1,538	518					
Australasia	29,001	32,053	34,148	39,048	43,522	55.99	11.46
Australia	26,650	30,118	32,290	36,662	40,654	52.30	10.89
New Zealand	2,351	1,935	1,858	2,386	2,868	3.69	20.20
Other East Asia and the Pacific	2,291	3,413	4,504	6,013	6,621	8.52	10.11
Other countries of Asia	865	1,277	2,530	3,495	4,422	5.69	26.52
Other countries of Oceania	1,426	2,136	1,974	2,518	2,199	2.83	-12.67
EUROPE	4,733	4,218	4,739	4,155	5,498	7.07	32.32
Northern Europe	1,805	1,469	1,581	1,476	1,781	2.29	20.66
United Kingdom	1,805	1,469	1,581	1,476	1,781	2.29	20.66
Western Europe	1,048	1,105	1,336	814	1,116	1.44	37.10
France	246	220	164	217	298	0.38	37.33
Germany	802	885	1,172	597	818	1.05	37.02
Other Europe	1,880	1,644	1,822	1,865	2,601	3.35	39.46
Other countries of Europe	1,880	1,644	1,822	1,865	2,601	3.35	39.46
SOUTH ASIA	2,451	657	630	736	1,002	1.29	36.14
South Asia	2,451	657	630	736	1,002	1.29	36.14
India			630	736	1,002	1.29	36.14
All countries of South Asia	2,451	657					

Source: World Tourism Organization (UNWTO)

PARAGUAY

1. Arrivals of non-resident tourists at national borders, by nationality

		2002	2003	2004	2005	2006	Market share 06	% Change 06-05
TOTAL	(*)	250,423	268,175	309,287	340,845	388,465	100.00	13.97
AFRICA		161	185	211	253	358	0.09	41.50
East Africa				15	29	16		-44.83
Ethiopia				5	8	2		-75.00
Kenya				4	10	4		-60.00
Mozambique				2	8	5		-37.50
Rwanda				1	1			
Zimbabwe				1	2	1		-50.00
United Republic of Tanzania				1				
Zambia				1		4		
Central Africa				30	20	30	0.01	50.00
Angola				2	4	15		275.00
Cameroon				8	13	9		-30.77
Congo				20	3	6		100.00
North Africa				15	16	17		6.25
Algeria				2	3	9		200.00
Morocco				13	13	8		-38.46
Southern Africa				129	134	247	0.06	84.33
South Africa				129	134	247	0.06	84.33
West Africa				20	20	28	0.01	40.00
Ghana				5	9	10		11.11
Mauritania				1		2		
Nigeria				9	7	9		28.57
Senegal				4	1	7		600.00
Sierra Leone				1	3			
Other Africa		161	185	2	34	20	0.01	-41.18
All countries of Africa		161	185	2	34	20	0.01	-41.18
AMERICAS		231,727	248,364	284,325	311,628	349,105	89.87	12.03
Caribbean		435	419	511	618	761	0.20	23.14
Bahamas				2	4	2		-50.00
Barbados				2	2	3		50.00
Cuba				347	439	495	0.13	12.76
Dominican Republic				87	104	165	0.04	58.65
Haiti				8	33	15		-54.55
Jamaica				42	19	37	0.01	94.74
Puerto Rico				10	8	11		37.50
Saint Lucia				1	3	6		100.00
Trinidad and Tobago				12	6	19		216.67
All countries of the Caribbean		435	419			8		
Central America		660	636	837	994	1,158	0.30	16.50
Belize				5	9	4		-55.56
Costa Rica				313	364	359	0.09	-1.37
El Salvador				103	120	135	0.03	12.50
Guatemala				127	126	205	0.05	62.70
Honduras				57	88	89	0.02	1.14
Nicaragua				56	74	92	0.02	24.32
Panama				176	213	274	0.07	28.64
All countries of Central America		660	636					
North America		10,963	11,181	14,540	16,210	16,388	4.22	1.10
Canada		1,062	1,019	1,391	1,787	1,711	0.44	-4.25
Mexico		889	952	1,137	1,379	1,415	0.36	2.61

PARAGUAY

1. Arrivals of non-resident tourists at national borders, by nationality

	2002	2003	2004	2005	2006	Market share 06	% Change 06-05
United States	9,012	9,210	12,012	13,044	13,262	3.41	1.67
South America	**219,669**	**236,128**	**268,437**	**293,806**	**330,798**	**85.16**	**12.59**
Argentina	160,758	177,741	197,563	209,130	194,532	50.08	-6.98
Bolivia	3,119	2,177	2,825	3,418	4,850	1.25	41.90
Brazil	43,134	40,651	48,985	56,036	98,480	25.35	75.74
Chile	4,694	6,262	7,282	9,941	14,238	3.67	43.23
Colombia	815	849	1,446	2,108	2,801	0.72	32.87
Ecuador	304	512	496	635	1,109	0.29	74.65
Guyana			7	4	2		-50.00
Peru	1,559	1,749	2,348	2,422	3,526	0.91	45.58
Uruguay	4,939	5,775	6,692	9,287	10,295	2.65	10.85
Venezuela	345	408	793	822	963	0.25	17.15
Other countries of South America	2	4		3	2		-33.33
EAST ASIA AND THE PACIFIC	**4,620**	**4,251**	**4,718**	**5,466**	**8,058**	**2.07**	**47.42**
North-East Asia	**2,038**	**1,946**	**4,296**	**5,119**	**7,484**	**1.93**	**46.20**
China			550	598	413	0.11	-30.94
Taiwan (Province of China)					297	0.08	
Japan	2,038	1,946	2,287	2,836	3,364	0.87	18.62
Korea, Republic of			1,459	1,685	3,410	0.88	102.37
South-East Asia			**90**	**77**	**176**	**0.05**	**128.57**
Indonesia			6	11	33	0.01	200.00
Malaysia			23	14	69	0.02	392.86
Philippines			25	23	39	0.01	69.57
Singapore			28	17	3		-82.35
Viet Nam			2	5	4		-20.00
Thailand			6	7	28	0.01	300.00
Australasia			**331**	**255**	**354**	**0.09**	**38.82**
Australia			267	169	206	0.05	21.89
New Zealand			64	86	148	0.04	72.09
Other East Asia and the Pacific	**2,582**	**2,305**	**1**	**15**	**44**	**0.01**	**193.33**
Other countries of Asia	2,390	2,147		14	41	0.01	192.86
Other countries of Oceania	192	158	1	1	3		200.00
EUROPE	**13,915**	**15,375**	**19,788**	**23,201**	**30,531**	**7.86**	**31.59**
Central/Eastern Europe			**423**	**576**	**838**	**0.22**	**45.49**
Bulgaria			6	2	12		500.00
Czech Republic			67	66	133	0.03	101.52
Estonia			4	5	13		160.00
Hungary			62	53	69	0.02	30.19
Latvia			2	9	1		-88.89
Poland			62	101	207	0.05	104.95
Romania			13	60	25	0.01	-58.33
Russian Federation			139	193	225	0.06	16.58
Slovakia			6	1	85	0.02	8,400.00
Ukraine			62	86	68	0.02	-20.93
Northern Europe			**2,158**	**2,273**	**4,063**	**1.05**	**78.75**
Denmark			146	150	811	0.21	440.67
Finland			52	67	129	0.03	92.54
Iceland			11	18	21	0.01	16.67
Ireland			88	149	358	0.09	140.27
Norway			137	214	311	0.08	45.33
Sweden			223	282	356	0.09	26.24
United Kingdom			1,501	1,393	2,077	0.53	49.10

PARAGUAY

1. Arrivals of non-resident tourists at national borders, by nationality

	2002	2003	2004	2005	2006	Market share 06	% Change 06-05
Southern Europe	**4,028**	**4,665**	**6,129**	**7,503**	**9,168**	**2.36**	**22.19**
Albania			1	3	3		
Bosnia and Herzegovina			23	4	4		
Croatia			11	8	21	0.01	162.50
Greece			105	232	523	0.13	125.43
Italy	1,360	1,565	2,149	2,490	2,980	0.77	19.68
Portugal			203	280	331	0.09	18.21
Serbia					6		
Slovenia			18	26			
Spain	2,668	3,100	3,618	4,460	5,300	1.36	18.83
Serbia and Montenegro			1				
Western Europe	**6,015**	**6,436**	**10,603**	**12,417**	**15,684**	**4.04**	**26.31**
Austria			398	465	571	0.15	22.80
Belgium			362	424	613	0.16	44.58
France	1,510	1,610	2,002	2,341	2,936	0.76	25.42
Germany	4,505	4,826	6,336	7,622	9,324	2.40	22.33
Luxembourg			5	11	20	0.01	81.82
Netherlands			441	425	649	0.17	52.71
Switzerland			1,059	1,129	1,571	0.40	39.15
East Mediterranean Europe			**467**	**406**	**652**	**0.17**	**60.59**
Israel			411	399	572	0.15	43.36
Turkey			56	7	80	0.02	1,042.86
Other Europe	**3,872**	**4,274**	**8**	**26**	**126**	**0.03**	**384.62**
Other countries of Europe	3,872	4,274	8	26	126	0.03	384.62
MIDDLE EAST			**96**	**97**	**184**	**0.05**	**89.69**
Middle East			**96**	**97**	**184**	**0.05**	**89.69**
Iraq			2	2	1		-50.00
Jordan			6	3	26	0.01	766.67
Lebanon			67	76	133	0.03	75.00
Libyan Arab Jamahiriya			1		3		
Syrian Arab Republic			8	3	5		66.67
Egypt			12	13	16		23.08
SOUTH ASIA			**148**	**200**	**229**	**0.06**	**14.50**
South Asia			**148**	**200**	**229**	**0.06**	**14.50**
Bangladesh			5	4	5		25.00
Sri Lanka			6	5	11		120.00
India			122	157	187	0.05	19.11
Iran, Islamic Republic of			5	6	8		33.33
Nepal			1	16	2		-87.50
Pakistan			9	12	16		33.33
REGION NOT SPECIFIED			**1**				
Not Specified			**1**				
Other countries of the World			1				

Source: World Tourism Organization (UNWTO)

PERU

1. Arrivals of non-resident tourists at national borders, by nationality

		2002	2003	2004	2005	2006	Market share 06	% Change 06-05
TOTAL	(*)	997,628	1,069,517	1,276,639	1,486,502	1,634,745	100.00	9.97
AFRICA		1,889	2,127	2,703	3,347	3,025	0.19	-9.62
Southern Africa		1,301	1,560	1,789	2,117	2,248	0.14	6.19
South Africa		1,301	1,560	1,789	2,117	2,248	0.14	6.19
Other Africa		588	567	914	1,230	777	0.05	-36.83
Other countries of Africa		588	567	914	1,230	777	0.05	-36.83
AMERICAS		713,555	762,290	928,818	1,066,044	1,190,018	72.80	11.63
Caribbean		2,628	2,204	2,528	3,663	4,369	0.27	19.27
Cuba		1,122	963	1,010	1,422	1,831	0.11	28.76
Dominican Republic		1,294	1,054	1,190	1,883	2,132	0.13	13.22
Jamaica		122	78	116	115	154	0.01	33.91
Trinidad and Tobago		90	109	212	243	252	0.02	3.70
Central America		12,516	12,881	16,082	20,354	20,484	1.25	0.64
Costa Rica		3,166	3,187	4,679	5,386	4,804	0.29	-10.81
El Salvador		1,475	1,384	1,651	1,825	2,117	0.13	16.00
Guatemala		1,494	1,645	1,866	2,189	2,091	0.13	-4.48
Honduras		808	879	810	996	1,038	0.06	4.22
Nicaragua		630	681	824	861	859	0.05	-0.23
Panama		2,519	2,748	3,908	7,252	7,986	0.49	10.12
Other countries of Central America		2,424	2,357	2,344	1,845	1,589	0.10	-13.88
North America		225,745	239,554	292,910	355,135	365,492	22.36	2.92
Canada		21,066	21,846	25,610	33,933	40,007	2.45	17.90
Mexico		14,445	16,908	23,510	27,961	28,168	1.72	0.74
United States		190,234	200,800	243,790	293,241	297,317	18.19	1.39
South America		472,666	507,651	617,298	686,892	799,673	48.92	16.42
Argentina		35,928	38,039	46,035	56,232	63,543	3.89	13.00
Bolivia		59,495	59,337	65,906	71,718	84,068	5.14	17.22
Brazil		24,524	28,211	33,327	43,291	44,092	2.70	1.85
Chile		239,132	249,040	301,024	338,629	415,106	25.39	22.58
Colombia		32,449	33,782	39,026	48,365	53,639	3.28	10.90
Ecuador		61,910	81,411	110,294	100,808	111,239	6.80	10.35
Paraguay		1,227	1,584	1,479	1,749	1,838	0.11	5.09
Uruguay		3,070	3,209	3,722	4,989	5,166	0.32	3.55
Venezuela		14,840	12,939	16,357	20,995	20,868	1.28	-0.60
Other countries of South America		91	99	128	116	114	0.01	-1.72
EAST ASIA AND THE PACIFIC		44,454	49,918	61,781	73,618	81,627	4.99	10.88
North-East Asia		27,200	30,985	39,375	46,418	51,441	3.15	10.82
China		4,042	4,316	4,968	5,279	7,839	0.48	48.49
Taiwan (Province of China)		1,237	1,235	1,220	1,476	1,742	0.11	18.02
Japan		17,114	20,299	27,326	32,553	33,925	2.08	4.21
Korea, Dem. People's Republic of		195	106	100	434	255	0.02	-41.24
Korea, Republic of		4,612	5,029	5,761	6,676	7,680	0.47	15.04
South-East Asia		1,977	1,032	1,187	1,358	1,851	0.11	36.30
Malaysia		179	211	278	338	503	0.03	48.82
Philippines		1,581	669	644	717	1,076	0.07	50.07
Thailand		217	152	265	303	272	0.02	-10.23
Australasia		13,475	16,366	19,319	23,716	26,211	1.60	10.52
Australia		11,206	13,834	16,424	20,225	22,081	1.35	9.18
New Zealand		2,269	2,532	2,895	3,491	4,130	0.25	18.30
Other East Asia and the Pacific		1,802	1,535	1,900	2,126	2,124	0.13	-0.09

PERU

1. Arrivals of non-resident tourists at national borders, by nationality

	2002	2003	2004	2005	2006	Market share 06	% Change 06-05
Other countries of Asia	1,743	1,446	1,835	2,068	2,061	0.13	-0.34
Other countries of Oceania	59	89	65	58	63		8.62
EUROPE	**236,157**	**252,435**	**281,039**	**340,095**	**353,533**	**21.63**	**3.95**
Central/Eastern Europe	**6,043**	**6,812**	**7,890**	**10,698**	**12,988**	**0.79**	**21.41**
Czech Republic	1,395	1,917	1,959	2,539	2,999	0.18	18.12
Hungary	844	1,011	1,069	1,422	1,284	0.08	-9.70
Poland	2,124	1,971	2,441	3,666	4,639	0.28	26.54
Romania	229	300	215	349	500	0.03	43.27
Russian Federation	1,299	1,429	2,019	2,480	3,000	0.18	20.97
Slovakia	152	184	187	242	566	0.03	133.88
Northern Europe	**57,002**	**66,041**	**68,461**	**82,002**	**86,462**	**5.29**	**5.44**
Denmark	2,604	2,607	2,879	3,951	4,727	0.29	19.64
Finland	1,306	1,607	1,640	2,072	2,181	0.13	5.26
Ireland	3,278	4,245	4,994	6,563	7,267	0.44	10.73
Norway	3,202	3,524	3,637	3,846	4,652	0.28	20.96
Sweden	4,932	5,648	5,915	6,858	7,759	0.47	13.14
United Kingdom	41,680	48,410	49,396	58,712	59,876	3.66	1.98
Southern Europe	**54,511**	**54,162**	**70,590**	**90,403**	**92,879**	**5.68**	**2.74**
Greece	1,021	1,281	1,372	1,717	1,478	0.09	-13.92
Italy	21,867	21,679	24,296	27,258	26,755	1.64	-1.85
Portugal	1,223	1,139	1,686	2,382	2,176	0.13	-8.65
Spain	30,178	29,853	43,023	58,785	62,289	3.81	5.96
Yugoslavia, Sfr (Former)	222	210	213	261	181	0.01	-30.65
Western Europe	**108,197**	**114,622**	**122,174**	**143,075**	**144,662**	**8.85**	**1.11**
Austria	3,931	4,111	4,570	5,853	6,066	0.37	3.64
Belgium	7,505	7,126	8,230	8,867	8,867	0.54	
France	36,826	39,736	43,848	52,050	53,518	3.27	2.82
Germany	31,163	33,123	34,846	42,565	42,663	2.61	0.23
Luxembourg	251	256	358	349	371	0.02	6.30
Netherlands	16,641	17,594	16,290	17,346	17,681	1.08	1.93
Switzerland	11,880	12,676	14,032	16,045	15,496	0.95	-3.42
East Mediterranean Europe	**8,094**	**8,420**	**8,879**	**9,757**	**11,203**	**0.69**	**14.82**
Israel	7,877	8,145	8,458	9,334	10,612	0.65	13.69
Turkey	217	275	421	423	591	0.04	39.72
Other Europe	**2,310**	**2,378**	**3,045**	**4,160**	**5,339**	**0.33**	**28.34**
Other countries of Europe	2,310	2,378	3,045	4,160	5,339	0.33	28.34
MIDDLE EAST	**119**	**117**	**140**	**204**	**156**	**0.01**	**-23.53**
Middle East	**119**	**117**	**140**	**204**	**156**	**0.01**	**-23.53**
Jordan	19	28	45	67	33		-50.75
Lebanon	31	38	26	64	42		-34.38
Egypt	69	51	69	73	81		10.96
SOUTH ASIA	**1,320**	**1,294**	**1,237**	**1,825**	**1,931**	**0.12**	**5.81**
South Asia	**1,320**	**1,294**	**1,237**	**1,825**	**1,931**	**0.12**	**5.81**
India	841	956	984	1,355	1,462	0.09	7.90
Iran, Islamic Republic of	57	40	34	36	50		38.89
Pakistan	422	298	219	434	419	0.03	-3.46
REGION NOT SPECIFIED	**134**	**1,336**	**921**	**1,369**	**4,455**	**0.27**	**225.42**
Not Specified	**134**	**1,336**	**921**	**1,369**	**4,455**	**0.27**	**225.42**
Other countries of the World	134	1,336	921	1,369	4,455	0.27	225.42

Source: World Tourism Organization (UNWTO)

PERU

3. Arrivals of non-resident tourists in hotels and similar establishments, by nationality

		2002	2003	2004	2005	2006	Market share 06	% Change 06-05
TOTAL	(*)	1,434,327	2,050,515	2,376,481	2,708,887	2,793,000	100.00	3.11
AMERICAS		644,558	877,562	1,049,233	1,186,911	1,243,597	44.53	4.78
North America		390,120	526,516	650,199	758,287	747,900	26.78	-1.37
Canada		39,392	59,742	73,324	93,982	100,241	3.59	6.66
Mexico		25,758	38,057	51,329	53,651	58,217	2.08	8.51
United States		324,970	428,717	525,546	610,654	589,442	21.10	-3.47
South America		254,438	351,046	399,034	428,624	495,697	17.75	15.65
Argentina		42,865	70,404	81,077	84,224	95,047	3.40	12.85
Bolivia		19,015	23,495	26,017	29,727	31,870	1.14	7.21
Brazil		35,178	53,886	65,979	86,000	87,585	3.14	1.84
Chile		63,240	74,793	84,206	87,852	120,692	4.32	37.38
Colombia		38,954	54,336	58,205	59,244	71,255	2.55	20.27
Ecuador		35,783	55,406	61,925	58,947	61,102	2.19	3.66
Venezuela		19,403	18,726	21,625	22,630	28,146	1.01	24.37
EAST ASIA AND THE PACIFIC		48,509	78,586	104,215	111,464	123,010	4.40	10.36
North-East Asia		48,509	78,586	104,215	111,464	123,010	4.40	10.36
Japan		48,509	78,586	104,215	111,464	123,010	4.40	10.36
EUROPE		324,238	489,689	539,307	629,778	649,699	23.26	3.16
Southern Europe		130,159	171,288	210,826	254,522	278,524	9.97	9.43
Italy		59,860	76,324	87,841	96,168	96,189	3.44	0.02
Spain		70,299	94,964	122,985	158,354	182,335	6.53	15.14
Western Europe		194,079	318,401	328,481	375,256	371,175	13.29	-1.09
France		110,666	190,144	193,404	229,316	221,008	7.91	-3.62
Germany		83,413	128,257	135,077	145,940	150,167	5.38	2.90
REGION NOT SPECIFIED		417,022	604,678	683,726	780,734	776,694	27.81	-0.52
Not Specified		417,022	604,678	683,726	780,734	776,694	27.81	-0.52
Other countries of the World		417,022	604,678	683,726	780,734	776,694	27.81	-0.52

Source: World Tourism Organization (UNWTO)

PERU

5. Overnight stays of non-resident tourists in hotels and similar establishments, by nationality

		2002	2003	2004	2005	2006	Market share 06	% Change 06-05
TOTAL	(*)	2,801,944	3,870,161	4,494,980	5,023,933	5,367,090	100.00	6.83
AMERICAS		1,311,027	1,806,451	2,172,314	2,397,107	2,645,091	49.28	10.35
North America		765,807	1,034,217	1,270,411	1,460,031	1,531,694	28.54	4.91
Canada		75,384	113,635	141,818	177,075	202,012	3.76	14.08
Mexico		57,566	89,059	118,574	123,018	130,629	2.43	6.19
United States		632,857	831,523	1,010,019	1,159,938	1,199,053	22.34	3.37
South America		545,220	772,234	901,903	937,076	1,113,397	20.74	18.82
Argentina		95,551	178,127	203,109	185,693	221,053	4.12	19.04
Bolivia		35,718	44,271	52,842	60,361	62,030	1.16	2.77
Brazil		80,365	118,568	148,442	189,301	199,213	3.71	5.24
Chile		125,840	150,873	176,030	180,971	245,970	4.58	35.92
Colombia		96,983	131,987	144,218	147,844	176,984	3.30	19.71
Ecuador		69,994	102,097	121,780	113,081	134,405	2.50	18.86
Venezuela		40,769	46,311	55,482	59,825	73,742	1.37	23.26
EAST ASIA AND THE PACIFIC		85,793	133,081	165,863	171,264	191,690	3.57	11.93
North-East Asia		85,793	133,081	165,863	171,264	191,690	3.57	11.93
Japan		85,793	133,081	165,863	171,264	191,690	3.57	11.93
EUROPE		603,448	832,591	924,918	1,066,701	1,117,067	20.81	4.72
Southern Europe		250,856	312,810	378,113	458,060	511,646	9.53	11.70
Italy		110,721	136,241	153,036	170,433	170,360	3.17	-0.04
Spain		140,135	176,569	225,077	287,627	341,286	6.36	18.66
Western Europe		352,592	519,781	546,805	608,641	605,421	11.28	-0.53
France		197,114	295,175	312,842	356,177	348,107	6.49	-2.27
Germany		155,478	224,606	233,963	252,464	257,314	4.79	1.92
REGION NOT SPECIFIED		801,676	1,098,038	1,231,885	1,388,861	1,413,242	26.33	1.76
Not Specified		801,676	1,098,038	1,231,885	1,388,861	1,413,242	26.33	1.76
Other countries of the World		801,676	1,098,038	1,231,885	1,388,861	1,413,242	26.33	1.76

Source: World Tourism Organization (UNWTO)

PHILIPPINES

1. Arrivals of non-resident tourists at national borders, by country of residence

	2002	2003	2004	2005	2006	Market share 06	% Change 06-05
TOTAL	1,932,677	1,907,226	2,291,352	2,623,084	2,843,345	100.00	8.40
AFRICA	1,465	1,442	1,700	2,294	2,246	0.08	-2.09
Southern Africa	1,193	1,139	1,406	1,799	1,759	0.06	-2.22
South Africa	1,193	1,139	1,406	1,799	1,759	0.06	-2.22
West Africa	272	303	294	495	487	0.02	-1.62
Nigeria	272	303	294	495	487	0.02	-1.62
AMERICAS	453,667	444,264	545,867	604,793	651,705	22.92	7.76
North America	451,201	442,390	543,621	602,250	648,929	22.82	7.75
Canada	54,563	53,601	64,537	72,853	80,507	2.83	10.51
Mexico	1,315	910	993	904	1,067	0.04	18.03
United States	395,323	387,879	478,091	528,493	567,355	19.95	7.35
South America	2,466	1,874	2,246	2,543	2,776	0.10	9.16
Argentina	432	448	408	460	502	0.02	9.13
Brazil	1,256	876	1,150	1,284	1,408	0.05	9.66
Colombia	395	245	296	351	401	0.01	14.25
Peru	182	171	204	251	254	0.01	1.20
Venezuela	201	134	188	197	211	0.01	7.11
EAST ASIA AND THE PACIFIC	1,154,439	1,128,540	1,359,256	1,565,359	1,690,939	59.47	8.02
North-East Asia	917,126	891,295	1,078,053	1,242,518	1,338,777	47.08	7.75
China	27,803	32,039	39,581	107,456	133,585	4.70	24.32
Taiwan (Province of China)	103,024	92,740	115,182	122,946	114,955	4.04	-6.50
Hong Kong, China	155,964	139,753	162,381	107,195	96,296	3.39	-10.17
Japan	341,867	322,896	382,307	415,456	421,808	14.83	1.53
Korea, Republic of	288,468	303,867	378,602	489,465	572,133	20.12	16.89
South-East Asia	133,790	131,136	149,017	179,386	202,886	7.14	13.10
Brunei Darussalam	2,136	2,070	2,151	2,579	2,947	0.10	14.27
Myanmar	1,982	2,149	2,408	5,127	4,427	0.16	-13.65
Cambodia	1,054	1,040	1,214	1,619	1,613	0.06	-0.37
Indonesia	15,352	17,051	19,801	20,055	22,646	0.80	12.92
Lao People's Democratic Republic	475	502	480	700	733	0.03	4.71
Malaysia	31,735	31,161	34,170	43,059	53,279	1.87	23.73
Singapore	57,662	51,257	60,253	69,435	81,114	2.85	16.82
Viet Nam	4,577	5,507	6,475	9,878	9,686	0.34	-1.94
Thailand	18,817	20,399	22,065	26,934	26,441	0.93	-1.83
Australasia	77,304	76,010	96,950	105,263	110,740	3.89	5.20
Australia	70,735	69,846	89,175	96,465	101,313	3.56	5.03
New Zealand	6,569	6,164	7,775	8,798	9,427	0.33	7.15
Melanesia	1,185	867	904	939	1,069	0.04	13.84
Papua New Guinea	1,185	867	904	939	1,069	0.04	13.84
Micronesia	25,034	29,232	34,332	37,253	37,467	1.32	0.57
Guam	25,013	29,220	34,326	37,249	37,445	1.32	0.53
Nauru	21	12	6	4	22		450.00
EUROPE	183,910	177,338	212,305	246,449	264,353	9.30	7.26
Central/Eastern Europe	4,166	3,617	4,304	11,428	14,042	0.49	22.87
Poland	604	549	734	1,175	1,476	0.05	25.62
Russian Federation					3,566	0.13	
Other countries Central/East Europ					9,000	0.32	
Commonwealth Independent State	3,562	3,068	3,570	10,253			
Northern Europe	72,740	71,014	86,557	98,502	106,088	3.73	7.70

PHILIPPINES

1. Arrivals of non-resident tourists at national borders, by country of residence

	2002	2003	2004	2005	2006	Market share 06	% Change 06-05
Denmark	7,164	6,584	8,154	9,712	9,610	0.34	-1.05
Finland	1,597	1,528	1,878	2,053	2,298	0.08	11.93
Ireland	1,864	1,977	2,836	3,568	4,032	0.14	13.00
Norway	7,025	6,886	8,810	10,162	10,893	0.38	7.19
Sweden	6,612	6,592	8,109	10,005	10,765	0.38	7.60
United Kingdom	48,478	47,447	56,770	63,002	68,490	2.41	8.71
Southern Europe	**17,081**	**15,499**	**19,017**	**21,889**	**23,097**	**0.81**	**5.52**
Greece	1,031	944	1,091	1,311	1,486	0.05	13.35
Italy	8,483	7,711	9,691	10,904	11,599	0.41	6.37
Portugal	636	568	649	772	709	0.02	-8.16
Spain	6,349	6,026	7,494	8,737	9,060	0.32	3.70
Yugoslavia, Sfr (Former)	582	250					
Serbia and Montenegro			92	165	243	0.01	47.27
Western Europe	**87,861**	**85,488**	**100,337**	**112,109**	**117,167**	**4.12**	**4.51**
Austria	6,281	6,264	7,973	9,318	9,156	0.32	-1.74
Belgium	5,512	5,371	6,352	7,142	7,507	0.26	5.11
France	12,498	11,549	13,804	14,315	15,492	0.54	8.22
Germany	39,103	38,684	45,092	50,411	51,402	1.81	1.97
Luxembourg	307	262	323	372	372	0.01	
Netherlands	12,015	11,441	12,960	15,367	17,128	0.60	11.46
Switzerland	12,145	11,917	13,833	15,184	16,110	0.57	6.10
East Mediterranean Europe	**2,062**	**1,720**	**2,090**	**2,521**	**3,959**	**0.14**	**57.04**
Israel	2,062	1,720	2,090	2,521	3,959	0.14	57.04
MIDDLE EAST	**18,500**	**16,736**	**20,683**	**24,532**	**27,544**	**0.97**	**12.28**
Middle East	**18,500**	**16,736**	**20,683**	**24,532**	**27,544**	**0.97**	**12.28**
Bahrain	1,358	1,379	1,774	2,067	2,246	0.08	8.66
Jordan	292	185	310	351	431	0.02	22.79
Kuwait	1,469	1,449	2,084	2,339	2,632	0.09	12.53
Saudi Arabia	11,341	9,842	11,627	14,141	15,017	0.53	6.19
United Arab Emirates	3,460	3,305	4,198	5,070	6,414	0.23	26.51
Egypt	580	576	690	564	804	0.03	42.55
SOUTH ASIA	**20,822**	**21,543**	**24,997**	**28,485**	**31,975**	**1.12**	**12.25**
South Asia	**20,822**	**21,543**	**24,997**	**28,485**	**31,975**	**1.12**	**12.25**
Bangladesh	1,457	1,546	1,561	1,797	1,766	0.06	-1.73
Sri Lanka	1,341	1,424	1,543	2,307	3,567	0.13	54.62
India	14,826	15,644	18,221	21,034	22,703	0.80	7.93
Iran, Islamic Republic of	633	604	1,074	1,022	1,328	0.05	29.94
Nepal	974	897	1,044	1,055	1,014	0.04	-3.89
Pakistan	1,591	1,428	1,554	1,270	1,597	0.06	25.75
REGION NOT SPECIFIED	**99,874**	**117,363**	**126,544**	**151,172**	**174,583**	**6.14**	**15.49**
Not Specified	**99,874**	**117,363**	**126,544**	**151,172**	**174,583**	**6.14**	**15.49**
Other countries of the World	16,120	17,039	22,802	25,777	28,218	0.99	9.47
Nationals Residing Abroad (*)	83,754	100,324	103,742	125,395	146,365	5.15	16.72

Source: World Tourism Organization (UNWTO)

PHILIPPINES

3. Arrivals of non-resident tourists in hotels and similar establishments, by country of residence

	2002	2003	2004	2005	2006	Market share 06	% Change 06-05
TOTAL (*)	758,474	741,886	832,202	954,706	1,012,874	100.00	6.09
AFRICA	476	472	522	723	715	0.07	-1.11
Southern Africa	410	399	453	593	578	0.06	-2.53
South Africa	410	399	453	593	578	0.06	-2.53
West Africa	66	73	69	130	137	0.01	5.38
Nigeria	66	73	69	130	137	0.01	5.38
AMERICAS	95,318	97,010	103,437	118,928	154,125	15.22	29.60
North America	94,358	96,246	102,624	117,865	153,153	15.12	29.94
Canada	17,196	16,505	16,930	19,332	25,895	2.56	33.95
Mexico	776	376	449	385	421	0.04	9.35
United States	76,386	79,365	85,245	98,148	126,837	12.52	29.23
South America	960	764	813	1,063	972	0.10	-8.56
Argentina	119	122	132	197	163	0.02	-17.26
Brazil	548	439	470	587	538	0.05	-8.35
Colombia	133	62	75	97	126	0.01	29.90
Peru	110	85	82	128	63	0.01	-50.78
Venezuela	50	56	54	54	82	0.01	51.85
EAST ASIA AND THE PACIFIC	563,220	541,948	619,562	704,943	718,272	70.91	1.89
North-East Asia	462,113	442,129	507,959	580,385	574,793	56.75	-0.96
China	4,232	5,249	5,777	37,186	47,297	4.67	27.19
Taiwan (Province of China)	55,108	39,312	46,435	49,164	45,842	4.53	-6.76
Hong Kong, China	77,777	69,395	75,531	50,048	42,555	4.20	-14.97
Japan	163,230	151,213	171,788	186,220	173,956	17.17	-6.59
Korea, Republic of	161,766	176,960	208,428	257,767	265,143	26.18	2.86
South-East Asia	64,334	63,102	70,269	78,429	83,819	8.28	6.87
Brunei Darussalam	1,011	1,062	1,085	1,154	1,210	0.12	4.85
Myanmar	229	172	210	459	327	0.03	-28.76
Cambodia	265	317	363	466	496	0.05	6.44
Indonesia	5,383	6,619	7,141	7,153	7,799	0.77	9.03
Lao People's Democratic Republic	121	174	136	208	206	0.02	-0.96
Malaysia	13,366	13,037	14,442	16,939	18,913	1.87	11.65
Singapore	34,072	30,646	34,904	37,677	41,864	4.13	11.11
Viet Nam	1,066	1,275	1,571	2,302	2,098	0.21	-8.86
Thailand	8,821	9,800	10,417	12,071	10,906	1.08	-9.65
Australasia	31,461	30,745	33,749	37,518	45,121	4.45	20.26
Australia	28,430	27,851	30,623	33,863	41,263	4.07	21.85
New Zealand	3,031	2,894	3,126	3,655	3,858	0.38	5.55
Melanesia	643	368	371	341	344	0.03	0.88
Papua New Guinea	643	368	371	341	344	0.03	0.88
Micronesia	4,669	5,604	7,214	8,270	14,195	1.40	71.64
Guam	4,653	5,597	7,210	8,269	14,181	1.40	71.50
Nauru	16	7	4	1	14		1,300.00
EUROPE	68,624	66,715	70,287	81,892	84,975	8.39	3.76
Central/Eastern Europe	964	1,105	1,082	2,189	2,736	0.27	24.99
Poland	124	132	151	329	268	0.03	-18.54
Ussr (Former)					1,058	0.10	
Commonwealth Independent State	840	973	931	1,860	1,410	0.14	-24.19
Northern Europe	24,989	24,096	25,855	31,104	35,569	3.51	14.36

PHILIPPINES

3. Arrivals of non-resident tourists in hotels and similar establishments, by country of residence

	2002	2003	2004	2005	2006	Market share 06	% Change 06-05
Denmark	1,955	1,886	2,127	2,568	2,452	0.24	-4.52
Finland	659	717	791	825	789	0.08	-4.36
Ireland	712	786	880	1,309	1,309	0.13	
Norway	2,153	2,250	2,362	2,932	3,554	0.35	21.21
Sweden	1,889	1,922	2,051	2,604	3,216	0.32	23.50
United Kingdom	17,621	16,535	17,644	20,866	24,249	2.39	16.21
Southern Europe	**6,097**	**5,680**	**5,969**	**7,085**	**7,854**	**0.78**	**10.85**
Greece	315	314	305	415	468	0.05	12.77
Italy	3,190	2,998	3,182	3,519	3,923	0.39	11.48
Portugal	244	208	228	260	212	0.02	-18.46
Spain	2,274	2,089	2,216	2,836	3,146	0.31	10.93
Yugoslavia, Sfr (Former)	74	71	38	55	105	0.01	90.91
Western Europe	**35,654**	**35,012**	**36,377**	**40,386**	**36,857**	**3.64**	**-8.74**
Austria	2,766	2,865	2,905	3,169	2,759	0.27	-12.94
Belgium	2,877	2,797	2,829	3,219	2,723	0.27	-15.41
France	4,611	4,339	4,556	4,551	4,727	0.47	3.87
Germany	15,565	14,822	15,363	17,093	15,729	1.55	-7.98
Luxembourg	160	129	53	66	149	0.01	125.76
Netherlands	4,659	4,620	4,890	5,908	5,819	0.57	-1.51
Switzerland	5,016	5,440	5,781	6,380	4,951	0.49	-22.40
East Mediterranean Europe	**920**	**822**	**1,004**	**1,128**	**1,959**	**0.19**	**73.67**
Israel	920	822	1,004	1,128	1,959	0.19	73.67
MIDDLE EAST	**8,611**	**7,911**	**8,902**	**10,424**	**11,247**	**1.11**	**7.90**
Middle East	**8,611**	**7,911**	**8,902**	**10,424**	**11,247**	**1.11**	**7.90**
Bahrain	670	745	851	972	1,197	0.12	23.15
Jordan	114	83	118	150	189	0.02	26.00
Kuwait	664	629	815	962	1,092	0.11	13.51
Saudi Arabia	5,219	4,387	4,902	5,744	5,764	0.57	0.35
United Arab Emirates	1,749	1,883	2,008	2,429	2,783	0.27	14.57
Egypt	195	184	208	167	222	0.02	32.93
SOUTH ASIA	**4,748**	**4,951**	**5,372**	**6,862**	**6,908**	**0.68**	**0.67**
South Asia	**4,748**	**4,951**	**5,372**	**6,862**	**6,908**	**0.68**	**0.67**
Bangladesh	312	264	257	399	389	0.04	-2.51
Sri Lanka	411	438	469	579	591	0.06	2.07
India	3,128	3,450	3,901	4,851	4,815	0.48	-0.74
Iran, Islamic Republic of	159	161	171	284	396	0.04	39.44
Nepal	217	220	185	273	306	0.03	12.09
Pakistan	521	418	389	476	411	0.04	-13.66
REGION NOT SPECIFIED	**17,477**	**22,879**	**24,120**	**30,934**	**36,632**	**3.62**	**18.42**
Not Specified	**17,477**	**22,879**	**24,120**	**30,934**	**36,632**	**3.62**	**18.42**
Other countries of the World	5,627	6,010	8,145	9,261	9,171	0.91	-0.97
Nationals Residing Abroad (*)	11,850	16,869	15,975	21,673	27,461	2.71	26.71

Source: World Tourism Organization (UNWTO)

PHILIPPINES

4. Arrivals of non-resident tourists in all types of accommodation establishments, by country of residence

	2002	2003	2004	2005	2006	Market share 06	% Change 06-05
TOTAL (*)	1,904,891	1,880,067	2,260,235	2,586,367	2,807,234	100.00	8.54
AFRICA	1,416	1,406	1,681	2,229	2,218	0.08	-0.49
Southern Africa	1,146	1,106	1,389	1,739	1,732	0.06	-0.40
South Africa	1,146	1,106	1,389	1,739	1,732	0.06	-0.40
West Africa	270	300	292	490	486	0.02	-0.82
Nigeria	270	300	292	490	486	0.02	-0.82
AMERICAS	451,614	443,636	544,913	603,741	650,430	23.17	7.73
North America	449,249	441,775	542,677	601,206	647,680	23.07	7.73
Canada	54,314	53,546	64,425	72,783	80,313	2.86	10.35
Mexico	1,300	909	982	890	1,057	0.04	18.76
United States	393,635	387,320	477,270	527,533	566,310	20.17	7.35
South America	2,365	1,861	2,236	2,535	2,750	0.10	8.48
Argentina	431	448	408	458	500	0.02	9.17
Brazil	1,163	870	1,147	1,284	1,408	0.05	9.66
Colombia	391	239	295	349	396	0.01	13.47
Peru	180	170	201	251	235	0.01	-6.37
Venezuela	200	134	185	193	211	0.01	9.33
EAST ASIA AND THE PACIFIC	1,138,437	1,110,910	1,338,498	1,543,462	1,669,040	59.45	8.14
North-East Asia	907,924	882,280	1,068,307	1,232,656	1,329,313	47.35	7.84
China	23,247	26,471	32,846	100,516	126,558	4.51	25.91
Taiwan (Province of China)	102,548	91,931	114,753	122,567	114,564	4.08	-6.53
Hong Kong, China	155,583	139,315	162,370	107,185	96,281	3.43	-10.17
Japan	340,806	322,644	381,206	415,048	421,451	15.01	1.54
Korea, Republic of	285,740	301,919	377,132	487,340	570,459	20.32	17.06
South-East Asia	127,987	123,392	139,179	167,915	190,915	6.80	13.70
Brunei Darussalam	2,136	2,053	2,084	2,564	2,920	0.10	13.88
Myanmar	867	854	923	1,730	1,311	0.05	-24.22
Cambodia	1,054	1,030	1,185	1,619	1,613	0.06	-0.37
Indonesia	12,513	14,278	15,676	16,868	19,331	0.69	14.60
Lao People's Democratic Republic	475	502	451	698	733	0.03	5.01
Malaysia	31,287	30,248	32,702	42,157	52,116	1.86	23.62
Singapore	57,343	51,014	59,978	69,238	80,988	2.88	16.97
Viet Nam	3,822	4,002	4,821	7,010	6,340	0.23	-9.56
Thailand	18,490	19,411	21,359	26,031	25,563	0.91	-1.80
Australasia	76,307	75,144	95,777	104,699	110,277	3.93	5.33
Australia	69,784	69,019	88,062	95,923	100,889	3.59	5.18
New Zealand	6,523	6,125	7,715	8,776	9,388	0.33	6.97
Melanesia	1,185	862	903	939	1,068	0.04	13.74
Papua New Guinea	1,185	862	903	939	1,068	0.04	13.74
Micronesia	25,034	29,232	34,332	37,253	37,467	1.33	0.57
Guam	25,013	29,220	34,326	37,249	37,445	1.33	0.53
Nauru	21	12	6	4	22		450.00
EUROPE	178,022	172,612	207,254	237,659	256,214	9.13	7.81
Central/Eastern Europe	2,654	2,601	3,065	5,224	7,776	0.28	48.85
Poland	388	380	570	921	1,104	0.04	19.87
Ussr (Former)					2,349	0.08	
Commonwealth Independent State	2,266	2,221	2,495	4,303	4,323	0.15	0.46
Northern Europe	69,965	68,434	83,771	97,136	105,372	3.75	8.48

PHILIPPINES

4. Arrivals of non-resident tourists in all types of accommodation establishments, by country of residence

	2002	2003	2004	2005	2006	Market share 06	% Change 06-05
Denmark	7,103	6,544	8,056	9,626	9,562	0.34	-0.66
Finland	1,588	1,523	1,873	2,047	2,291	0.08	11.92
Ireland	1,805	1,914	2,800	3,548	4,016	0.14	13.19
Norway	6,966	6,845	8,790	10,128	10,847	0.39	7.10
Sweden	6,565	6,571	8,100	9,978	10,735	0.38	7.59
United Kingdom	45,938	45,037	54,152	61,809	67,921	2.42	9.89
Southern Europe	**16,604**	**15,166**	**18,782**	**21,634**	**22,854**	**0.81**	**5.64**
Greece	878	762	953	1,187	1,344	0.05	13.23
Italy	8,465	7,663	9,623	10,845	11,569	0.41	6.68
Portugal	619	552	645	766	701	0.02	-8.49
Spain	6,301	6,011	7,472	8,698	9,040	0.32	3.93
Yugoslavia, Sfr (Former)	341	178	89	138	200	0.01	44.93
Western Europe	**86,739**	**84,692**	**99,546**	**111,144**	**116,256**	**4.14**	**4.60**
Austria	6,236	6,233	7,915	9,267	9,129	0.33	-1.49
Belgium	5,461	5,340	6,340	7,135	7,493	0.27	5.02
France	12,456	11,491	13,777	14,270	15,398	0.55	7.90
Germany	38,395	38,092	44,505	49,681	50,881	1.81	2.42
Luxembourg	307	262	323	370	372	0.01	0.54
Netherlands	11,770	11,374	12,865	15,271	16,928	0.60	10.85
Switzerland	12,114	11,900	13,821	15,150	16,055	0.57	5.97
East Mediterranean Europe	**2,060**	**1,719**	**2,090**	**2,521**	**3,956**	**0.14**	**56.92**
Israel	2,060	1,719	2,090	2,521	3,956	0.14	56.92
MIDDLE EAST	**18,487**	**16,692**	**20,634**	**24,497**	**27,451**	**0.98**	**12.06**
Middle East	**18,487**	**16,692**	**20,634**	**24,497**	**27,451**	**0.98**	**12.06**
Bahrain	1,358	1,379	1,774	2,067	2,246	0.08	8.66
Jordan	292	184	310	350	431	0.02	23.14
Kuwait	1,469	1,449	2,074	2,338	2,632	0.09	12.57
Saudi Arabia	11,340	9,841	11,626	14,140	15,015	0.53	6.19
United Arab Emirates	3,460	3,305	4,198	5,070	6,414	0.23	26.51
Egypt	568	534	652	532	713	0.03	34.02
SOUTH ASIA	**18,019**	**18,370**	**22,255**	**25,228**	**28,341**	**1.01**	**12.34**
South Asia	**18,019**	**18,370**	**22,255**	**25,228**	**28,341**	**1.01**	**12.34**
Bangladesh	1,166	1,259	1,318	1,466	1,569	0.06	7.03
Sri Lanka	1,205	1,327	1,460	1,583	2,103	0.07	32.85
India	12,636	13,148	16,056	18,892	20,779	0.74	9.99
Iran, Islamic Republic of	563	520	918	993	1,327	0.05	33.64
Nepal	958	883	1,033	1,048	1,007	0.04	-3.91
Pakistan	1,491	1,233	1,470	1,246	1,556	0.06	24.88
REGION NOT SPECIFIED	**98,896**	**116,441**	**125,000**	**149,551**	**173,540**	**6.18**	**16.04**
Not Specified	**98,896**	**116,441**	**125,000**	**149,551**	**173,540**	**6.18**	**16.04**
Other countries of the World	15,142	16,117	21,258	24,156	27,175	0.97	12.50
Nationals Residing Abroad (*)	83,754	100,324	103,742	125,395	146,365	5.21	16.72

Source: World Tourism Organization (UNWTO)

POLAND

2. Arrivals of non-resident visitors at national borders, by nationality

	2002	2003	2004	2005	2006	Market share 06	% Change 06-05
TOTAL	50,734,623	52,129,778	61,917,759	64,606,085	65,114,865	100.00	0.79
AFRICA	8,699	9,538	11,114	13,217	14,914	0.02	12.84
East Africa	1,158	1,104	1,214	1,375	1,724		25.38
British Indian Ocean Territory	3	2					
Burundi	14	10	16	19	17		-10.53
Comoros	2	2	5	2	3		50.00
Ethiopia	53	57	58	60	91		51.67
Eritrea	14	24	20	30	15		-50.00
Djibouti	3	5	7		1		
Kenya	299	366	438	472	518		9.75
Madagascar	59	63	46	81	58		-28.40
Malawi	9	2	15	6	14		133.33
Mauritius	97	102	152	177	274		54.80
Mozambique	129	147	93	127	145		14.17
Reunion	8	5	11	18	7		-61.11
Rwanda	22	31	28	23	28		21.74
Seychelles	11	9	11	7	26		271.43
Somalia	8		21	8	21		162.50
Zimbabwe	118	98	118	139	183		31.65
Uganda	155	34	43	48	98		104.17
United Republic of Tanzania	109	117	84	106	168		58.49
Zambia	45	30	48	52	57		9.62
Central Africa	716	819	885	917	1,027		12.00
Angola	172	222	179	159	222		39.62
Cameroon	227	272	304	361	407		12.74
Central African Republic	10	12	5	6	6		
Chad	12	12	8	12	6		-50.00
Congo	240	228	347	317	342		7.89
Democratic Republic of the Congo	44	54	25	29			
Equatorial Guinea		2	1	4	1		-75.00
Gabon	10	15	12	23	43		86.96
Sao Tome and Principe	1	2	4	6			
North Africa	2,741	3,248	3,540	4,232	4,753	0.01	12.31
Algeria	854	1,117	1,234	1,325	1,326		0.08
Morocco	837	790	973	1,258	1,472		17.01
Western Sahara	2	1	1				
Sudan	79	89	79	91	97		6.59
Tunisia	969	1,251	1,253	1,558	1,858		19.26
Southern Africa	2,499	2,733	3,429	4,391	4,515	0.01	2.82
Botswana	11	11	10	17	10		-41.18
Lesotho	2	1	6		9		
Namibia	28	33	33	50	54		8.00
South Africa	2,454	2,680	3,374	4,320	4,439	0.01	2.75
Swaziland	4	8	6	4	3		-25.00
West Africa	1,585	1,634	2,046	2,302	2,895		25.76
Cape Verde	52	22	41	51	47		-7.84
Benin	45	51	45	57	62		8.77
Gambia	20	25	26	34	51		50.00
Ghana	180	230	273	279	345		23.66
Guinea	30	81	92	70	71		1.43
Cote D'Ivoire	75	76	54	114	77		-32.46
Liberia	26	26	18	6	18		200.00
Mali	53	60	61	58	75		29.31

POLAND

2. Arrivals of non-resident visitors at national borders, by nationality

	2002	2003	2004	2005	2006	Market share 06	% Change 06-05
Mauritania	18	17	10	17	14		-17.65
Niger	24	5	15	16	17		6.25
Nigeria	839	790	1,041	1,300	1,700		30.77
Guinea-Bissau	8	6	9	8	25		212.50
Saint Helena			1	1	1		
Senegal	109	119	171	141	185		31.21
Sierra Leone	30	32	52	44	51		15.91
Togo	55	60	86	65	83		27.69
Burkina Faso	21	34	51	41	73		78.05
AMERICAS	**272,329**	**294,313**	**345,181**	**439,417**	**466,299**	**0.72**	**6.12**
Caribbean	**1,156**	**1,289**	**1,036**	**1,629**	**1,463**		**-10.19**
Antigua and Barbuda	4	7	2	3	1		-66.67
Bahamas	36	8	4	10	24		140.00
Barbados	23	31	18	21	21		
Bermuda	21	23	5	12	6		-50.00
Cayman Islands	3	6	2	2	6		200.00
Cuba	712	658	647	846	790		-6.62
Dominica	16	41	20	14	15		7.14
Dominican Republic	76	97	70	278	143		-48.56
Grenada	4	2	16	10	12		20.00
Guadeloupe	1			2			
Haiti	12	7	13	24	60		150.00
Jamaica	59	95	114	189	212		12.17
Martinique		1					
Montserrat	2						
Netherlands Antilles	2	87	6	13	2		-84.62
Aruba		2					
Puerto Rico	33	1	1	13	9		-30.77
Saint Kitts and Nevis	3	1		1	1		
Anguilla		1	1				
Saint Lucia	27	100	10	5	5		
Saint Vincent and the Grenadines	18	2	3	12	9		-25.00
Trinidad and Tobago	72	119	100	166	140		-15.66
Turks and Caicos Islands	31		3	6	2		-66.67
United States Virgin Islands	1		1	2	5		150.00
Central America	**987**	**1,153**	**1,106**	**1,424**	**1,680**		**17.98**
Belize	2	8	6	18	12		-33.33
Costa Rica	414	368	420	447	504		12.75
El Salvador	68	66	73	149	227		52.35
Guatemala	132	145	151	263	388		47.53
Honduras	50	147	82	116	153		31.90
Nicaragua	238	190	170	149	141		-5.37
Panama	83	229	204	282	255		-9.57
North America	**258,485**	**279,012**	**327,904**	**413,872**	**438,018**	**0.67**	**5.83**
Canada	17,756	20,848	38,431	62,790	72,349	0.11	15.22
Greenland	1		1				
Mexico	5,286	7,962	8,714	11,363	12,178	0.02	7.17
United States	235,442	250,202	280,758	339,719	353,491	0.54	4.05
South America	**11,701**	**12,859**	**15,135**	**22,492**	**25,138**	**0.04**	**11.76**
Argentina	1,957	2,337	2,642	3,443	3,941	0.01	14.46
Bolivia	372	475	482	818	687		-16.01
Brazil	5,021	5,068	6,296	11,367	12,906	0.02	13.54
Chile	1,501	1,874	2,035	2,331	2,410		3.39
Colombia	681	730	875	1,034	1,459		41.10

POLAND

2. Arrivals of non-resident visitors at national borders, by nationality

	2002	2003	2004	2005	2006	Market share 06	% Change 06-05
Ecuador	680	758	795	693	569		-17.89
Falkland Islands (Malvinas)		1	2				
French Guiana	8	6	1	2	3		50.00
Guyana	16	21	23	19	13		-31.58
Paraguay	24	48	37	104	116		11.54
Peru	636	629	664	874	991		13.39
Suriname	11	42	19	23	20		-13.04
Uruguay	274	356	527	510	516		1.18
Venezuela	520	514	737	1,274	1,507		18.29
EAST ASIA AND THE PACIFIC	**87,430**	**88,693**	**123,114**	**163,414**	**193,899**	**0.30**	**18.66**
North-East Asia	**60,722**	**61,069**	**80,607**	**101,840**	**123,290**	**0.19**	**21.06**
China	6,445	5,077	7,660	11,345	15,133	0.02	33.39
Taiwan (Province of China)	3,842	2,250	3,898	4,596	4,926	0.01	7.18
Hong Kong, China	552	1,087	1,648	2,800	2,980		6.43
Japan	25,900	27,686	32,490	39,457	40,926	0.06	3.72
Korea, Dem. People's Republic of	319	458	331	256	172		-32.81
Korea, Republic of	19,052	22,033	31,300	39,402	53,202	0.08	35.02
Macao, China	21	47	41	34	14		-58.82
Mongolia	4,591	2,431	3,239	3,950	5,937	0.01	50.30
South-East Asia	**10,723**	**11,730**	**15,550**	**19,204**	**20,853**	**0.03**	**8.59**
Brunei Darussalam	6	13	8	37	36		-2.70
Myanmar	94	68	12	35	28		-20.00
Cambodia	9	16	17	30	55		83.33
Indonesia	867	1,157	1,381	1,133	1,162		2.56
Lao People's Democratic Republic	29	42	35	60	91		51.67
Malaysia	1,875	2,059	2,517	3,150	3,459	0.01	9.81
Philippines	1,452	1,365	1,439	1,840	2,071		12.55
Singapore	1,797	1,765	2,277	2,836	3,142		10.79
Viet Nam	3,528	3,986	5,971	8,007	8,880	0.01	10.90
Thailand	1,066	1,259	1,893	2,076	1,929		-7.08
Australasia	**15,864**	**15,451**	**26,914**	**42,325**	**49,712**	**0.08**	**17.45**
Australia	12,917	13,019	22,131	35,387	41,904	0.06	18.42
New Zealand	2,947	2,432	4,783	6,938	7,808	0.01	12.54
Melanesia	**35**	**411**	**19**	**19**	**26**		**36.84**
Solomon Islands					1		
Fiji	13	17	9	4	18		350.00
New Caledonia	17	388	3	1	1		
Vanuatu	4	1		5			
Norfolk Island		4					
Papua New Guinea	1	1	7	9	6		-33.33
Micronesia	**26**	**12**	**13**	**9**	**6**		**-33.33**
Christmas Island (Australia)	1						
Cocos (Keeling) Islands	4	3	3	8	4		-50.00
Kiribati	15	5	5	1	1		
Guam			2				
Nauru	6	2	3		1		
Palau		2					
Polynesia	**60**	**20**	**11**	**17**	**12**		**-29.41**
American Samoa		1		1	2		100.00
French Polynesia	7	6		3	2		-33.33
Niue	2			1	2		100.00
Pitcairn			2	1	1		
Tokelau		6	2	1	1		

POLAND

2. Arrivals of non-resident visitors at national borders, by nationality

	2002	2003	2004	2005	2006	Market share 06	% Change 06-05
Tonga	6	6	4	3	1		-66.67
Tuvalu	5	1	1	1			
Samoa	40		2	6	3		-50.00
EUROPE	**50,315,365**	**51,691,151**	**61,385,787**	**63,926,773**	**64,366,590**	**98.85**	**0.69**
Central/Eastern Europe	**24,720,972**	**24,300,596**	**25,143,967**	**24,114,672**	**24,400,713**	**37.47**	**1.19**
Azerbaijan	2,281	2,728	3,730	3,529	3,422	0.01	-3.03
Armenia	2,750	2,692	4,324	5,391	5,786	0.01	7.33
Bulgaria	57,244	55,235	53,454	61,194	65,616	0.10	7.23
Belarus	4,241,711	3,830,074	3,522,795	3,650,801	3,911,768	6.01	7.15
Czech Republic	8,313,159	8,826,943	9,285,762	7,855,432	7,101,529	10.91	-9.60
Estonia	186,125	194,442	165,646	156,098	185,566	0.28	18.88
Georgia	1,938	2,127	2,645	3,316	3,693	0.01	11.37
Hungary	138,544	169,931	214,059	248,698	268,061	0.41	7.79
Kazakhstan	50,565	48,578	48,885	45,074	42,148	0.06	-6.49
Kyrgyzstan	4,033	6,232	6,736	5,150	5,169	0.01	0.37
Latvia	400,605	421,767	391,688	344,996	409,685	0.63	18.75
Lithuania	1,397,746	1,365,823	1,336,031	1,344,205	1,459,386	2.24	8.57
Republic of Moldova	43,611	46,537	47,370	53,148	54,622	0.08	2.77
Romania	54,359	64,106	66,440	78,198	94,951	0.15	21.42
Russian Federation	1,843,844	1,534,054	1,420,438	1,598,840	1,722,214	2.64	7.72
Slovakia	2,126,032	2,896,310	4,047,745	3,378,091	3,421,869	5.26	1.30
Tajikistan	392	474	449	477	426		-10.69
Turkmenistan	221	162	148	215	237		10.23
Ukraine	5,853,478	4,829,789	4,523,010	5,278,924	5,641,930	8.66	6.88
Uzbekistan	2,334	2,592	2,612	2,895	2,635		-8.98
Northern Europe	**649,797**	**705,253**	**762,202**	**865,215**	**1,068,036**	**1.64**	**23.44**
Denmark	123,060	148,600	118,219	112,408	134,413	0.21	19.58
Faeroe Islands	2	6	3		1		
Finland	50,534	55,935	72,168	68,103	76,695	0.12	12.62
Iceland	1,937	2,874	5,334	5,034	6,368	0.01	26.50
Ireland	17,169	20,499	26,893	39,715	69,298	0.11	74.49
Norway	64,491	68,696	78,744	81,168	101,868	0.16	25.50
Sweden	191,092	197,997	213,765	213,717	224,010	0.34	4.82
United Kingdom	201,512	210,646	247,076	345,070	455,383	0.70	31.97
Southern Europe	**333,766**	**378,443**	**398,802**	**453,696**	**512,474**	**0.79**	**12.96**
Albania	939	1,014	1,188	1,428	1,513		5.95
Andorra	226	61	43	95	61		-35.79
Bosnia and Herzegovina	2,779	2,261	2,433	2,427	2,538		4.57
Croatia	29,020	31,494	28,737	35,250	35,604	0.05	1.00
Gibraltar				2			
Greece	27,746	27,094	25,187	28,819	30,551	0.05	6.01
Holy See	207	151	124	87	62		-28.74
Italy	185,126	215,204	221,648	247,024	276,176	0.42	11.80
Malta	794	933	1,264	1,886	1,158		-38.60
Portugal	16,550	19,060	26,888	27,305	36,652	0.06	34.23
San Marino	60	133	64	63	99		57.14
Slovenia	17,530	20,117	21,803	22,437	22,628	0.03	0.85
Spain	40,503	48,561	57,055	72,559	88,946	0.14	22.58
TFYR of Macedonia	4,041	3,451	3,116	3,686	3,742	0.01	1.52
Serbia and Montenegro	8,245	8,909	9,252	10,628	12,744	0.02	19.91
Western Europe	**24,539,779**	**26,233,378**	**34,996,549**	**38,390,565**	**38,277,735**	**58.78**	**-0.29**
Austria	247,761	265,682	288,340	282,197	303,962	0.47	7.71
Belgium	92,621	65,230	74,509	71,889	91,432	0.14	27.18
France	201,543	179,815	194,781	219,561	229,919	0.35	4.72

POLAND

2. Arrivals of non-resident visitors at national borders, by nationality

	2002	2003	2004	2005	2006	Market share 06	% Change 06-05
Germany	23,654,699	25,456,531	34,122,107	37,436,338	37,192,093	57.12	-0.65
Liechtenstein	317	201	145	174	160		-8.05
Luxembourg	2,156	2,612	4,407	3,289	3,014		-8.36
Monaco	50	53	39	40	48		20.00
Netherlands	302,882	224,991	263,423	334,702	409,909	0.63	22.47
Switzerland	37,750	38,263	48,798	42,375	47,198	0.07	11.38
East Mediterranean Europe	**71,051**	**73,481**	**84,267**	**102,625**	**107,632**	**0.17**	**4.88**
Cyprus	1,602	2,301	1,675	2,395	2,107		-12.03
Israel	48,611	48,422	54,731	65,849	66,260	0.10	0.62
Turkey	20,838	22,758	27,861	34,381	39,265	0.06	14.21
MIDDLE EAST	**6,277**	**6,065**	**6,471**	**7,636**	**8,265**	**0.01**	**8.24**
Middle East	**6,277**	**6,065**	**6,471**	**7,636**	**8,265**	**0.01**	**8.24**
Bahrain	58	74	34	48	51		6.25
Iraq	267	192	480	719	884		22.95
Jordan	593	510	619	673	702		4.31
Kuwait	483	533	431	470	553		17.66
Lebanon	1,083	1,020	1,094	1,545	1,380		-10.68
Libyan Arab Jamahiriya	1,012	921	810	768	768		
Oman	23	21	22	27	33		22.22
Qatar	100	56	63	55	88		60.00
Saudi Arabia	330	376	405	437	432		-1.14
Syrian Arab Republic	728	634	762	866	904		4.39
United Arab Emirates	98	148	133	144	177		22.92
Egypt	1,318	1,456	1,492	1,797	2,171		20.81
Yemen	184	124	126	87	122		40.23
SOUTH ASIA	**8,875**	**9,483**	**11,710**	**13,219**	**15,246**	**0.02**	**15.33**
South Asia	**8,875**	**9,483**	**11,710**	**13,219**	**15,246**	**0.02**	**15.33**
Afghanistan	442	366	301	338	464		37.28
Bangladesh	179	132	209	299	550		83.95
Bhutan	3	4	10	7	10		42.86
Sri Lanka	236	226	331	496	526		6.05
India	5,259	6,092	7,875	8,702	9,893	0.02	13.69
Iran, Islamic Republic of	1,500	1,393	1,540	1,578	1,721		9.06
Maldives	2	1	1	3	8		166.67
Nepal	135	97	133	185	335		81.08
Pakistan	1,119	1,172	1,310	1,611	1,739		7.95
REGION NOT SPECIFIED	**35,648**	**30,535**	**34,382**	**42,409**	**49,652**	**0.08**	**17.08**
Not Specified	**35,648**	**30,535**	**34,382**	**42,409**	**49,652**	**0.08**	**17.08**
Other countries of the World	35,648	30,535	34,382	42,409	49,652	0.08	17.08

Source: World Tourism Organization (UNWTO)

POLAND

3. Arrivals of non-resident tourists in hotels and similar establishments, by country of residence

	2002	2003	2004	2005	2006	Market share 06	% Change 06-05
TOTAL	2,535,642	2,700,717	3,385,121	3,723,176	3,737,865	100.00	0.39
AFRICA	4,579	5,205	4,459	4,942	6,134	0.16	24.12
East Africa	215	851	466	354	536	0.01	51.41
British Indian Ocean Territory	1			5	7		40.00
Burundi	4	6	10	47	63		34.04
Ethiopia	41	42	68	43	52		20.93
Eritrea	4	275	168	3	9		200.00
Djibouti	14	1	1				
Kenya	50	102	84	105	172		63.81
Madagascar	5	221	1	2	4		100.00
Malawi		50		3			
Mauritius	13	13	10	7	42		500.00
Mozambique	6	8	11	19	10		-47.37
Reunion	2			15	11		-26.67
Rwanda	7	4	13	1	36		3,500.00
Seychelles		11	7	6	8		33.33
Somalia	12	20	22	26	31		19.23
Zimbabwe	10	20	17	33	28		-15.15
Uganda	8	13	10	15	10		-33.33
United Republic of Tanzania	34	50	24	19	27		42.11
Zambia	4	15	20	5	26		420.00
Central Africa	1,832	370	258	335	879	0.02	162.39
Angola	1,259	130	101	161	453	0.01	181.37
Cameroon	112	82	19	28	295	0.01	953.57
Central African Republic	6	40	8	17	7		-58.82
Chad	44			22	8		-63.64
Congo	37	102	115	104	96		-7.69
Democratic Republic of the Congo	369	5	2	1	6		500.00
Equatorial Guinea		9	11		3		
Gabon	3	1	1	2	6		200.00
Sao Tome and Principe	2	1	1		5		
North Africa	908	2,257	1,581	1,438	2,006	0.05	39.50
Algeria	280	1,579	865	696	707	0.02	1.58
Morocco	257	161	294	365	764	0.02	109.32
Western Sahara	2	1	1	45	66		46.67
Sudan	19	80	28	34	22		-35.29
Tunisia	350	436	393	298	447	0.01	50.00
Southern Africa	557	762	1,295	1,357	1,335	0.04	-1.62
Botswana	3	6	12	58	50		-13.79
Lesotho			12	75	5		-93.33
Namibia	1	2	3	6	7		16.67
South Africa	534	746	1,267	1,214	1,204	0.03	-0.82
Swaziland	19	8	1	4	69		1,625.00
West Africa	1,067	965	859	1,458	1,378	0.04	-5.49
Cape Verde		1					
Benin	125	140	157	213	21		-90.14
Gambia		165	17	506	473	0.01	-6.52
Ghana	19	33	17	29	44		51.72
Guinea	6	3	50	21	33		57.14
Cote D'Ivoire	29	17	12	66	59		-10.61
Liberia	1	4		3	2		-33.33
Mali	27	24	22	19	30		57.89

POLAND

3. Arrivals of non-resident tourists in hotels and similar establishments, by country of residence

	2002	2003	2004	2005	2006	Market share 06	% Change 06-05
Mauritania	9	6	4	5	9		80.00
Niger	17	9	54	94	45		-52.13
Nigeria	736	398	306	394	512	0.01	29.95
Guinea-Bissau		13	12	2	9		350.00
Saint Helena		2	9	1	4		300.00
Senegal	41	38	72	38	35		-7.89
Sierra Leone	52	100	103	56	66		17.86
Togo		8	14	6	13		116.67
Burkina Faso	5	4	10	5	23		360.00
AMERICAS	**174,009**	**164,574**	**220,445**	**229,840**	**236,537**	**6.33**	**2.91**
Caribbean	**3,839**	**882**	**831**	**787**	**1,203**	**0.03**	**52.86**
Antigua and Barbuda	75	133	122	82	176		114.63
Bahamas	29	89	120	22	32		45.45
Barbados	14	26	32	23	76		230.43
British Virgin Islands		2		2	7		250.00
Cayman Islands			91	2	4		100.00
Cuba	102	353	290	352	353	0.01	0.28
Dominica	4		3	10	20		100.00
Dominican Republic	13	10	14	11	75		581.82
Grenada	26	90	15	38	17		-55.26
Guadeloupe		1	4				
Haiti	5	7		3	35		1,066.67
Jamaica	317	14	27	26	90		246.15
Martinique		1			122		
Montserrat	4		1	4			
Netherlands Antilles		17	17	81	11		-86.42
Aruba			1	1	9		800.00
Puerto Rico	53	45	37	21	52		147.62
Anguilla	37	43	22	51	3		-94.12
Trinidad and Tobago	2	28	8	34	57		67.65
Turks and Caicos Islands	5	4	15	1	32		3,100.00
United States Virgin Islands	3,153	19	12	23	32		39.13
Central America	**786**	**268**	**380**	**568**	**485**	**0.01**	**-14.61**
Belize	17	1	3	200	14		-93.00
Costa Rica	68	99	186	242	259	0.01	7.02
El Salvador	15	27	31	35	61		74.29
Guatemala	17	39	15	22	67		204.55
Honduras	628	61	31	28	43		53.57
Nicaragua	6	22	20	26	17		-34.62
Panama	35	19	94	15	24		60.00
North America	**164,681**	**158,654**	**211,910**	**218,245**	**224,819**	**6.01**	**3.01**
Canada	14,005	12,238	17,364	20,022	19,882	0.53	-0.70
Greenland	1		3	4	30		650.00
Mexico	1,852	2,554	3,110	3,492	4,309	0.12	23.40
Saint Pierre and Miquelon					2		
United States	148,823	143,862	191,433	194,727	200,596	5.37	3.01
South America	**4,703**	**4,770**	**7,324**	**10,240**	**10,030**	**0.27**	**-2.05**
Argentina	612	909	1,211	2,097	1,623	0.04	-22.60
Bolivia	72	81	89	107	99		-7.48
Brazil	2,990	2,464	4,414	6,320	6,769	0.18	7.10
Chile	625	577	771	645	501	0.01	-22.33
Colombia	73	168	175	205	253	0.01	23.41
Ecuador	39	147	115	73	74		1.37

POLAND

3. Arrivals of non-resident tourists in hotels and similar establishments, by country of residence

	2002	2003	2004	2005	2006	Market share 06	% Change 06-05
Falkland Islands (Malvinas)	47		15	1	1		
Guyana	1	10	5	5	7		40.00
Paraguay	23	5	23	17	23		35.29
Peru	79	96	225	128	181		41.41
Suriname	16	34	5	32	9		-71.88
Uruguay	44	127	146	384	169		-55.99
Venezuela	82	152	130	226	321	0.01	42.04
EAST ASIA AND THE PACIFIC	**56,393**	**59,435**	**90,359**	**104,078**	**108,967**	**2.92**	**4.70**
North-East Asia	**47,048**	**48,252**	**72,038**	**83,739**	**85,973**	**2.30**	**2.67**
China	4,231	3,598	8,790	12,726	14,187	0.38	11.48
Taiwan (Province of China)	1,908	1,139	1,982	2,211	797	0.02	-63.95
Hong Kong, China	990	893	1,125	1,207	786	0.02	-34.88
Japan	26,825	29,414	38,516	42,925	37,880	1.01	-11.75
Korea, Dem. People's Republic of	3,684	757	1,365	867	3,452	0.09	298.15
Korea, Republic of	9,174	12,173	19,821	23,186	28,359	0.76	22.31
Macao, China	1	9	93	257	12		-95.33
Mongolia	235	269	346	360	500	0.01	38.89
South-East Asia	**2,825**	**3,580**	**5,032**	**5,212**	**6,477**	**0.17**	**24.27**
Brunei Darussalam			12	2	75		3,650.00
Myanmar	13	14	21	10	21		110.00
Cambodia				167	27		-83.83
Indonesia	403	733	537	335	607	0.02	81.19
Lao People's Democratic Republic	7	10	5	7	6		-14.29
Malaysia	373	485	943	786	954	0.03	21.37
Philippines	585	527	585	766	1,010	0.03	31.85
Timor-Leste	5		7	22	8		-63.64
Singapore	749	630	932	878	936	0.03	6.61
Viet Nam	359	705	750	1,165	1,607	0.04	37.94
Thailand	331	476	1,240	1,074	1,226	0.03	14.15
Australasia	**6,293**	**7,467**	**11,612**	**14,609**	**16,167**	**0.43**	**10.66**
Australia	5,697	6,633	10,203	13,025	14,508	0.39	11.39
New Zealand	596	834	1,409	1,584	1,659	0.04	4.73
Melanesia	**37**	**24**	**39**	**58**	**46**		**-20.69**
Solomon Islands	8	16	12		4		
Fiji	2	2	6	3			
New Caledonia	25	5	5	10	37		270.00
Papua New Guinea	2	1	16	45	5		-88.89
Micronesia	**25**	**16**	**1,550**	**26**	**34**		**30.77**
Christmas Island (Australia)	2	14	3				
Cocos (Keeling) Islands			2	1			
Kiribati	8		1,507	15	9		-40.00
Guam			38		7		
Nauru	15	2		10	18		80.00
Polynesia	**165**	**96**	**88**	**434**	**270**	**0.01**	**-37.79**
American Samoa	53	29	70	92	162		76.09
French Polynesia	13	6	2	67	51		-23.88
Niue	1	5	4		1		
Pitcairn				3	2		-33.33
Tokelau	17	8	10	15	5		-66.67
Tonga	1	3	2	202			
Tuvalu	13	2		1			
Wallis and Futuna Islands		1			28		

POLAND

3. Arrivals of non-resident tourists in hotels and similar establishments, by country of residence

	2002	2003	2004	2005	2006	Market share 06	% Change 06-05
Samoa	67	42		54	21		-61.11
EUROPE	**2,237,073**	**2,418,844**	**2,995,509**	**3,317,251**	**3,319,752**	**88.81**	**0.08**
Central/Eastern Europe	**406,538**	**451,488**	**565,581**	**624,631**	**705,105**	**18.86**	**12.88**
Azerbaijan	245	381	588	506	391	0.01	-22.73
Armenia	512	741	1,159	1,056	906	0.02	-14.20
Bulgaria	4,355	5,658	6,088	5,595	4,920	0.13	-12.06
Belarus	60,872	60,410	73,205	79,276	84,392	2.26	6.45
Czech Republic	32,176	37,077	49,908	52,925	59,905	1.60	13.19
Estonia	14,053	16,229	25,325	36,598	45,876	1.23	25.35
Georgia	230	421	812	891	788	0.02	-11.56
Hungary	16,115	23,477	34,299	40,136	36,839	0.99	-8.21
Kazakhstan	822	2,036	2,884	2,294	2,503	0.07	9.11
Kyrgyzstan	63	75	145	72	74		2.78
Latvia	7,427	13,036	19,452	24,468	30,103	0.81	23.03
Lithuania	36,186	44,562	59,869	61,129	72,126	1.93	17.99
Republic of Moldova	1,688	2,122	3,975	3,182	2,966	0.08	-6.79
Romania	5,596	7,725	8,850	10,307	11,935	0.32	15.80
Russian Federation	130,172	140,657	152,137	176,065	206,371	5.52	17.21
Slovakia	11,803	14,406	18,723	22,326	21,618	0.58	-3.17
Tajikistan	72	64	91	53	37		-30.19
Turkmenistan	3	16	30	14	16		14.29
Ukraine	84,013	82,052	107,882	107,425	123,050	3.29	14.55
Uzbekistan	135	343	159	313	289	0.01	-7.67
Northern Europe	**355,640**	**399,671**	**504,539**	**591,287**	**682,670**	**18.26**	**15.45**
Denmark	65,196	76,306	89,358	93,533	91,802	2.46	-1.85
Faeroe Islands	3	12	52		38		
Finland	25,465	29,103	36,130	37,339	42,653	1.14	14.23
Iceland	582	879	1,989	3,321	3,501	0.09	5.42
Ireland	6,414	8,956	17,413	24,481	39,303	1.05	60.54
Norway	43,779	57,685	64,520	70,412	78,898	2.11	12.05
Svalbard and Jan Mayen Islands	1	1	2				
Sweden	71,315	74,436	89,609	100,689	108,403	2.90	7.66
United Kingdom	142,885	152,293	205,466	261,512	318,072	8.51	21.63
Southern Europe	**190,127**	**219,865**	**279,875**	**339,292**	**346,681**	**9.27**	**2.18**
Albania	779	868	1,052	906	858	0.02	-5.30
Andorra	15	229	49	88	383	0.01	335.23
Bosnia and Herzegovina	316	531	567	371	480	0.01	29.38
Croatia	3,472	4,998	5,646	5,560	6,053	0.16	8.87
Gibraltar			4		18		
Greece	6,165	7,357	7,821	12,035	9,248	0.25	-23.16
Holy See	6	10	6	2	662	0.02	*********
Italy	114,447	136,370	169,319	196,425	201,860	5.40	2.77
Malta	340	777	1,096	1,330	521	0.01	-60.83
Portugal	9,739	8,467	11,918	15,272	14,787	0.40	-3.18
San Marino	34	139	49	52	61		17.31
Slovenia	5,365	4,779	6,779	7,651	6,936	0.19	-9.35
Spain	46,630	52,284	71,606	96,220	102,563	2.74	6.59
TFYR of Macedonia	422	453	450	243	287	0.01	18.11
Serbia and Montenegro	2,397	2,603	3,513	3,137	1,964	0.05	-37.39
Western Europe	**1,183,876**	**1,246,658**	**1,515,347**	**1,627,157**	**1,447,184**	**38.72**	**-11.06**
Austria	43,685	45,183	52,890	54,853	52,894	1.42	-3.57
Belgium	36,624	36,783	47,585	51,307	50,814	1.36	-0.96
France	113,197	128,586	156,946	178,455	169,045	4.52	-5.27

POLAND

3. Arrivals of non-resident tourists in hotels and similar establishments, by country of residence

	2002	2003	2004	2005	2006	Market share 06	% Change 06-05
Germany	889,234	928,360	1,124,479	1,208,511	1,045,930	27.98	-13.45
Liechtenstein	82	180	250	194	126		-35.05
Luxembourg	3,973	5,657	5,370	4,927	3,174	0.08	-35.58
Monaco	57	79	79	84	354	0.01	321.43
Netherlands	70,512	75,173	97,957	101,642	98,865	2.64	-2.73
Switzerland	26,512	26,657	29,791	27,184	25,982	0.70	-4.42
East Mediterranean Europe	**100,892**	**101,162**	**130,167**	**134,884**	**138,112**	**3.69**	**2.39**
Cyprus	457	1,148	1,494	1,780	1,592	0.04	-10.56
Israel	97,014	93,940	120,568	123,396	126,425	3.38	2.45
Turkey	3,421	6,074	8,105	9,708	10,095	0.27	3.99
MIDDLE EAST	**2,193**	**3,391**	**3,999**	**3,342**	**5,390**	**0.14**	**61.28**
Middle East	**2,193**	**3,391**	**3,999**	**3,342**	**5,390**	**0.14**	**61.28**
Bahrain	118	156	190	56	47		-16.07
Iraq	164	86	299	308	2,011	0.05	552.92
Jordan	109	278	253	162	211	0.01	30.25
Kuwait	217	250	205	254	432	0.01	70.08
Lebanon	212	234	189	483	240	0.01	-50.31
Libyan Arab Jamahiriya	151	422	227	231	221	0.01	-4.33
Oman	53	79	107	44	145		229.55
Qatar	24	106	64	34	52		52.94
Saudi Arabia	193	498	286	339	466	0.01	37.46
Syrian Arab Republic	327	170	171	126	119		-5.56
United Arab Emirates	55	71	132	180	329	0.01	82.78
Egypt	340	980	1,731	1,047	1,030	0.03	-1.62
Yemen	230	61	145	78	87		11.54
SOUTH ASIA	**5,732**	**4,387**	**8,187**	**7,949**	**6,696**	**0.18**	**-15.76**
South Asia	**5,732**	**4,387**	**8,187**	**7,949**	**6,696**	**0.18**	**-15.76**
Afghanistan	250	318	424	717	328	0.01	-54.25
Bangladesh	695	42	329	190	459	0.01	141.58
Bhutan	2,383	365	2,384	810	14		-98.27
Sri Lanka	41	51	60	41	147		258.54
India	1,657	2,631	3,514	4,138	4,733	0.13	14.38
Iran, Islamic Republic of	456	686	1,179	1,497	382	0.01	-74.48
Nepal	76	83	59	45	205	0.01	355.56
Pakistan	174	211	238	511	428	0.01	-16.24
REGION NOT SPECIFIED	**55,663**	**44,881**	**62,163**	**55,774**	**54,389**	**1.46**	**-2.48**
Not Specified	**55,663**	**44,881**	**62,163**	**55,774**	**54,389**	**1.46**	**-2.48**
Other countries of the World	55,663	44,881	62,163	55,774	54,389	1.46	-2.48

Source: World Tourism Organization (UNWTO)

POLAND

4. Arrivals of non-resident tourists in all types of accommodation establishments, by country of residence

	2002	2003	2004	2005	2006	Market share 06	% Change 06-05
TOTAL	3,145,439	3,331,870	3,934,064	4,310,401	4,313,578	100.00	0.07
AFRICA	5,051	6,009	5,483	5,637	6,969	0.16	23.63
East Africa	271	992	624	440	607	0.01	37.95
British Indian Ocean Territory	1		1	5	8		60.00
Burundi	5	6	10	52	63		21.15
Ethiopia	49	53	70	74	55		-25.68
Eritrea	5	277	168	4	9		125.00
Djibouti	14	1	1				
Kenya	58	127	138	123	188		52.85
Madagascar	5	227	1	4	4		
Malawi		50		11			
Mauritius	21	16	13	7	48		585.71
Mozambique	6	12	64	20	11		-45.00
Reunion	2			15	11		-26.67
Rwanda	7	12	13	4	38		850.00
Seychelles		12	7	6	18		200.00
Somalia	36	33	45	33	32		-3.03
Zimbabwe	11	26	18	37	33		-10.81
Uganda	8	69	27	17	12		-29.41
United Republic of Tanzania	35	56	26	23	32		39.13
Zambia	8	15	22	5	45		800.00
Central Africa	1,851	450	291	492	914	0.02	85.77
Angola	1,262	143	109	163	459	0.01	181.60
Cameroon	118	100	33	36	314	0.01	772.22
Central African Republic	6	41	8	17	7		-58.82
Chad	44			22	9		-59.09
Congo	45	131	120	117	102		-12.82
Democratic Republic of the Congo	369	5	2	1	6		500.00
Equatorial Guinea	2	28	17	134	3		-97.76
Gabon	3	1	1	2	9		350.00
Sao Tome and Principe	2	1	1		5		
North Africa	1,117	2,559	1,977	1,576	2,154	0.05	36.68
Algeria	346	1,693	1,139	755	766	0.02	1.46
Morocco	315	179	350	385	778	0.02	102.08
Western Sahara	2	1	1	45	66		46.67
Sudan	20	92	34	38	25		-34.21
Tunisia	434	594	453	353	519	0.01	47.03
Southern Africa	624	901	1,601	1,543	1,620	0.04	4.99
Botswana	3	6	12	58	51		-12.07
Lesotho			12	75	5		-93.33
Namibia	2	2	5	6	8		33.33
South Africa	600	883	1,571	1,313	1,450	0.03	10.43
Swaziland	19	10	1	91	106		16.48
West Africa	1,188	1,107	990	1,586	1,674	0.04	5.55
Cape Verde		1					
Benin	125	142	161	244	54		-77.87
Gambia	6	179	18	524	480	0.01	-8.40
Ghana	20	38	28	36	50		38.89
Guinea	7	4	56	23	33		43.48
Cote D'Ivoire	34	19	14	66	157		137.88
Liberia	1	4		3	3		
Mali	51	26	23	23	30		30.43

POLAND

4. Arrivals of non-resident tourists in all types of accommodation establishments, by country of residence

	2002	2003	2004	2005	2006	Market share 06	% Change 06-05
Mauritania	9	9	4	6	9		50.00
Niger	19	15	57	94	47		-50.00
Nigeria	809	455	361	452	655	0.02	44.91
Guinea-Bissau		13	12	2	9		350.00
Saint Helena		2	9	1	4		300.00
Senegal	49	48	86	39	38		-2.56
Sierra Leone	53	139	106	57	68		19.30
Togo		9	45	6	13		116.67
Burkina Faso	5	4	10	10	24		140.00
AMERICAS	**189,177**	**182,309**	**232,723**	**242,264**	**250,413**	**5.81**	**3.36**
Caribbean	**3,902**	**915**	**855**	**824**	**1,234**	**0.03**	**49.76**
Antigua and Barbuda	75	137	122	82	176		114.63
Bahamas	31	89	120	22	36		63.64
Barbados	14	26	32	29	77		165.52
British Virgin Islands		2	1	2	7		250.00
Cayman Islands	16		91	4	5		25.00
Cuba	113	376	300	367	358	0.01	-2.45
Dominica	4		9	10	20		100.00
Dominican Republic	15	11	15	11	78		609.09
Grenada	31	90	15	38	20		-47.37
Guadeloupe		1	4		2		
Haiti	5	7		3	35		1,066.67
Jamaica	331	16	32	28	95		239.29
Martinique		1		1	123		*********
Montserrat	5		1	4			
Netherlands Antilles		17	17	81	11		-86.42
Aruba	5		1	1	10		900.00
Puerto Rico	57	46	37	27	54		100.00
Anguilla	37	43	23	51	3		-94.12
Trinidad and Tobago	3	29	8	37	60		62.16
Turks and Caicos Islands	5	4	15	3	32		966.67
United States Virgin Islands	3,155	20	12	23	32		39.13
Central America	**840**	**664**	**394**	**597**	**545**	**0.01**	**-8.71**
Belize	43	360	3	200	28		-86.00
Costa Rica	92	112	194	257	285	0.01	10.89
El Salvador	15	28	31	36	64		77.78
Guatemala	21	49	18	28	80		185.71
Honduras	628	70	33	29	44		51.72
Nicaragua	6	25	20	30	18		-40.00
Panama	35	20	95	17	26		52.94
North America	**179,150**	**175,129**	**223,263**	**229,535**	**237,455**	**5.50**	**3.45**
Canada	16,050	14,674	19,662	22,051	22,376	0.52	1.47
Greenland	1		3	4	30		650.00
Mexico	2,163	2,977	3,548	3,784	4,895	0.11	29.36
Saint Pierre and Miquelon		47			2		
United States	160,936	157,431	200,050	203,696	210,152	4.87	3.17
South America	**5,285**	**5,601**	**8,211**	**11,308**	**11,179**	**0.26**	**-1.14**
Argentina	727	1,074	1,382	2,236	1,751	0.04	-21.69
Bolivia	100	112	184	129	148		14.73
Brazil	3,159	2,800	4,733	6,935	7,364	0.17	6.19
Chile	669	666	841	697	589	0.01	-15.49
Colombia	186	228	199	224	332	0.01	48.21
Ecuador	82	183	150	196	94		-52.04

POLAND

4. Arrivals of non-resident tourists in all types of accommodation establishments, by country of residence

	2002	2003	2004	2005	2006	Market share 06	% Change 06-05
Falkland Islands (Malvinas)	54		15	1	7		600.00
Guyana	1	12	5	8	18		125.00
Paraguay	24	5	23	17	27		58.82
Peru	117	140	323	164	287	0.01	75.00
Suriname	16	36	5	35	9		-74.29
Uruguay	54	181	162	425	180		-57.65
Venezuela	96	164	189	241	373	0.01	54.77
EAST ASIA AND THE PACIFIC	**64,206**	**66,951**	**98,239**	**110,944**	**117,857**	**2.73**	**6.23**
North-East Asia	**50,711**	**51,603**	**75,492**	**87,137**	**89,868**	**2.08**	**3.13**
China	4,976	4,122	9,397	13,379	15,072	0.35	12.65
Taiwan (Province of China)	2,005	1,160	2,089	2,247	878	0.02	-60.93
Hong Kong, China	999	927	1,144	1,229	879	0.02	-28.48
Japan	28,907	31,497	40,404	44,631	39,746	0.92	-10.95
Korea, Dem. People's Republic of	3,880	908	1,487	897	3,534	0.08	293.98
Korea, Republic of	9,455	12,563	20,385	23,928	29,091	0.67	21.58
Macao, China	1	9	95	257	12		-95.33
Mongolia	488	417	491	569	656	0.02	15.29
South-East Asia	**3,344**	**4,178**	**5,597**	**5,758**	**7,366**	**0.17**	**27.93**
Brunei Darussalam	19		14	2	77		3,750.00
Myanmar	13	14	22	11	21		90.91
Cambodia			7	167	29		-82.63
Indonesia	414	754	694	351	664	0.02	89.17
Lao People's Democratic Republic	14	15	6	7	15		114.29
Malaysia	420	567	1,025	872	1,037	0.02	18.92
Philippines	681	608	629	811	1,496	0.03	84.46
Timor-Leste	6	1	9	22	8		-63.64
Singapore	815	716	997	950	1,026	0.02	8.00
Viet Nam	585	982	905	1,449	1,711	0.04	18.08
Thailand	377	521	1,289	1,116	1,282	0.03	14.87
Australasia	**9,888**	**10,952**	**15,429**	**17,486**	**20,252**	**0.47**	**15.82**
Australia	8,796	9,356	13,243	15,271	17,856	0.41	16.93
New Zealand	1,092	1,596	2,186	2,215	2,396	0.06	8.17
Melanesia	**37**	**32**	**39**	**69**	**56**		**-18.84**
Solomon Islands	8	16	12	1	4		300.00
Fiji	2	6	6	13	1		-92.31
New Caledonia	25	9	5	10	42		320.00
Papua New Guinea	2	1	16	45	9		-80.00
Micronesia	**39**	**16**	**1,588**	**26**	**41**		**57.69**
Christmas Island (Australia)	2	14	3		2		
Cocos (Keeling) Islands			2	1			
Kiribati	8		1,545	15	9		-40.00
Guam					7		
Nauru	29	2	38	10	23		130.00
Polynesia	**187**	**170**	**94**	**468**	**274**	**0.01**	**-41.45**
American Samoa	53	29	70	92	162		76.09
French Polynesia	14	41	2	98	52		-46.94
Niue	1	5	4	3	4		33.33
Pitcairn				3	2		-33.33
Tokelau	17	8	10	15	5		-66.67
Tonga	1	3	4	202			
Tuvalu	18	2	4	1			
Wallis and Futuna Islands	16	40			28		

POLAND

4. Arrivals of non-resident tourists in all types of accommodation establishments, by country of residence

	2002	2003	2004	2005	2006	Market share 06	% Change 06-05
Samoa	67	42		54	21		-61.11
EUROPE	**2,818,036**	**3,022,645**	**3,521,865**	**3,882,651**	**3,870,392**	**89.73**	**-0.32**
Central/Eastern Europe	**662,382**	**680,373**	**709,456**	**774,861**	**856,882**	**19.86**	**10.59**
Azerbaijan	333	611	631	547	491	0.01	-10.24
Armenia	1,104	987	1,326	1,198	1,024	0.02	-14.52
Bulgaria	6,658	7,527	7,286	6,826	6,286	0.15	-7.91
Belarus	110,555	102,980	90,485	95,697	100,850	2.34	5.38
Czech Republic	44,763	50,313	60,764	65,974	72,789	1.69	10.33
Estonia	22,063	23,248	28,976	40,268	49,677	1.15	23.37
Georgia	326	643	980	1,055	978	0.02	-7.30
Hungary	26,206	36,847	50,016	56,450	50,052	1.16	-11.33
Kazakhstan	1,527	2,385	3,324	2,759	3,116	0.07	12.94
Kyrgyzstan	78	137	269	96	199		107.29
Latvia	11,593	18,790	25,468	31,620	36,702	0.85	16.07
Lithuania	54,220	62,718	74,096	76,000	88,740	2.06	16.76
Republic of Moldova	4,473	5,659	5,230	4,191	3,827	0.09	-8.69
Romania	9,690	11,564	10,860	12,626	14,669	0.34	16.18
Russian Federation	163,391	170,786	170,491	197,456	226,694	5.26	14.81
Slovakia	18,415	21,729	25,450	30,718	30,973	0.72	0.83
Tajikistan	86	75	99	57	50		-12.28
Turkmenistan	11	16	30	17	59		247.06
Ukraine	186,709	162,945	153,463	150,964	169,384	3.93	12.20
Uzbekistan	181	413	212	342	322	0.01	-5.85
Northern Europe	**403,289**	**446,363**	**545,291**	**633,318**	**731,415**	**16.96**	**15.49**
Denmark	74,386	89,030	98,106	101,597	98,668	2.29	-2.88
Faeroe Islands	4	14	52		39		
Finland	29,376	33,265	40,668	41,514	47,190	1.09	13.67
Iceland	709	975	2,081	3,458	3,623	0.08	4.77
Ireland	8,053	10,758	19,113	26,156	42,372	0.98	62.00
Norway	48,437	60,680	66,818	73,512	85,552	1.98	16.38
Svalbard and Jan Mayen Islands	1	3	2				
Sweden	84,543	87,088	101,099	112,606	119,673	2.77	6.28
United Kingdom	157,780	164,550	217,352	274,475	334,298	7.75	21.80
Southern Europe	**211,088**	**243,789**	**305,634**	**365,820**	**374,385**	**8.68**	**2.34**
Albania	794	930	1,100	952	906	0.02	-4.83
Andorra	15	231	54	117	390	0.01	233.33
Bosnia and Herzegovina	415	654	654	403	596	0.01	47.89
Croatia	4,555	6,274	6,765	6,826	6,984	0.16	2.31
Gibraltar			7	6	19		216.67
Greece	6,745	7,879	8,182	12,607	10,237	0.24	-18.80
Holy See	170	10	8	2	664	0.02	*********
Italy	126,774	150,392	184,632	211,675	217,221	5.04	2.62
Malta	398	805	1,171	1,448	582	0.01	-59.81
Portugal	10,498	9,329	12,900	16,491	15,988	0.37	-3.05
San Marino	36	140	51	62	114		83.87
Slovenia	6,407	5,853	7,714	8,905	8,288	0.19	-6.93
Spain	50,909	57,746	78,086	102,575	109,722	2.54	6.97
TFYR of Macedonia	684	566	531	286	362	0.01	26.57
Serbia and Montenegro	2,688	2,980	3,779	3,465	2,312	0.05	-33.28
Western Europe	**1,436,772**	**1,548,029**	**1,828,698**	**1,971,111**	**1,766,542**	**40.95**	**-10.38**
Austria	47,615	52,119	57,568	59,898	59,182	1.37	-1.20
Belgium	42,933	43,767	54,466	59,185	57,668	1.34	-2.56
France	132,568	152,873	182,049	206,685	193,699	4.49	-6.28

POLAND

4. Arrivals of non-resident tourists in all types of accommodation establishments, by country of residence

	2002	2003	2004	2005	2006	Market share 06	% Change 06-05
Germany	1,089,917	1,166,907	1,378,878	1,487,163	1,305,798	30.27	-12.20
Liechtenstein	97	195	254	211	144		-31.75
Luxembourg	4,198	5,965	5,670	5,130	3,398	0.08	-33.76
Monaco	59	83	81	93	366	0.01	293.55
Netherlands	91,044	96,721	117,434	123,138	117,785	2.73	-4.35
Switzerland	28,341	29,399	32,298	29,608	28,502	0.66	-3.74
East Mediterranean Europe	**104,505**	**104,091**	**132,786**	**137,541**	**141,168**	**3.27**	**2.64**
Cyprus	506	1,225	1,531	1,887	1,665	0.04	-11.76
Israel	99,995	96,081	122,816	125,529	128,642	2.98	2.48
Turkey	4,004	6,785	8,439	10,125	10,861	0.25	7.27
MIDDLE EAST	**2,621**	**3,780**	**4,403**	**3,648**	**5,742**	**0.13**	**57.40**
Middle East	**2,621**	**3,780**	**4,403**	**3,648**	**5,742**	**0.13**	**57.40**
Bahrain	125	156	192	56	47		-16.07
Iraq	265	112	377	353	2,087	0.05	491.22
Jordan	113	295	282	170	222	0.01	30.59
Kuwait	239	275	238	272	461	0.01	69.49
Lebanon	259	287	218	509	262	0.01	-48.53
Libyan Arab Jamahiriya	179	466	247	250	261	0.01	4.40
Oman	55	79	107	44	145		229.55
Qatar	24	110	79	38	52		36.84
Saudi Arabia	221	550	310	364	491	0.01	34.89
Syrian Arab Republic	352	210	199	151	149		-1.32
United Arab Emirates	75	86	133	226	330	0.01	46.02
Egypt	416	1,068	1,811	1,129	1,144	0.03	1.33
Yemen	298	86	210	86	91		5.81
SOUTH ASIA	**6,238**	**4,843**	**8,659**	**8,293**	**7,093**	**0.16**	**-14.47**
South Asia	**6,238**	**4,843**	**8,659**	**8,293**	**7,093**	**0.16**	**-14.47**
Afghanistan	303	402	438	718	331	0.01	-53.90
Bangladesh	720	43	364	209	492	0.01	135.41
Bhutan	2,383	365	2,384	810	26		-96.79
Sri Lanka	42	65	72	54	150		177.78
India	1,939	2,857	3,764	4,305	4,933	0.11	14.59
Iran, Islamic Republic of	545	752	1,266	1,573	410	0.01	-73.94
Nepal	87	92	101	71	240	0.01	238.03
Pakistan	219	267	270	553	511	0.01	-7.59
REGION NOT SPECIFIED	**60,110**	**45,333**	**62,692**	**56,964**	**55,112**	**1.28**	**-3.25**
Not Specified	**60,110**	**45,333**	**62,692**	**56,964**	**55,112**	**1.28**	**-3.25**
Other countries of the World	60,110	45,333	62,692	56,964	55,112	1.28	-3.25

Source: World Tourism Organization (UNWTO)

POLAND

5. Overnight stays of non-resident tourists in hotels and similar establishments, by country of residence

	2002	2003	2004	2005	2006	Market share 06	% Change 06-05
TOTAL	4,999,289	5,450,416	6,876,141	7,868,754	7,910,690	100.00	0.53
AFRICA	9,414	15,132	11,578	13,750	23,003	0.29	67.29
East Africa	568	1,413	1,021	1,110	1,998	0.03	80.00
British Indian Ocean Territory	2			9	13		44.44
Burundi	7	15	12	93	209		124.73
Ethiopia	62	101	130	113	151		33.63
Eritrea	16	276	168	3	9		200.00
Djibouti	42	3	2				
Kenya	121	323	181	568	1,149	0.01	102.29
Madagascar	19	237	3	7	4		-42.86
Malawi		50		6			
Mauritius	111	26	27	11	111		909.09
Mozambique	6	38	28	59	26		-55.93
Reunion	7			17	11		-35.29
Rwanda	10	15	30	1	82		8,100.00
Seychelles		40	50	39	14		-64.10
Somalia	41	32	48	53	56		5.66
Zimbabwe	14	52	35	65	55		-15.38
Uganda	29	38	22	20	24		20.00
United Republic of Tanzania	75	148	242	37	55		48.65
Zambia	6	19	43	9	29		222.22
Central Africa	2,563	883	784	738	1,492	0.02	102.17
Angola	1,620	407	201	390	828	0.01	112.31
Cameroon	200	169	42	60	425	0.01	608.33
Central African Republic	8	70	8	46	9		-80.43
Chad	57			22	8		-63.64
Congo	75	217	505	210	187		-10.95
Democratic Republic of the Congo	598	9	5	7	10		42.86
Equatorial Guinea		9	19		4		
Gabon	3	1	3	3	14		366.67
Sao Tome and Principe	2	1	1		7		
North Africa	2,292	8,531	4,416	3,985	9,883	0.12	148.01
Algeria	1,156	6,417	2,543	2,185	2,637	0.03	20.69
Morocco	473	409	810	761	1,681	0.02	120.89
Western Sahara	4	1	1	69	113		63.77
Sudan	68	216	64	94	29		-69.15
Tunisia	591	1,488	998	876	5,423	0.07	519.06
Southern Africa	1,777	1,884	3,187	3,203	3,225	0.04	0.69
Botswana	6	8	26	66	87		31.82
Lesotho			27	131	13		-90.08
Namibia	1	4	4	18	17		-5.56
South Africa	1,731	1,844	3,128	2,982	3,021	0.04	1.31
Swaziland	39	28	2	6	87		1,350.00
West Africa	2,214	2,421	2,170	4,714	6,405	0.08	35.87
Cape Verde		1					
Benin	319	317	341	587	33		-94.38
Gambia		322	25	2,414	3,615	0.05	49.75
Ghana	320	97	54	54	226		318.52
Guinea	13	9	108	47	323		587.23
Cote D'Ivoire	48	55	26	123	102		-17.07
Liberia	3	10		9	26		188.89
Mali	77	42	31	34	111		226.47

POLAND

5. Overnight stays of non-resident tourists in hotels and similar establishments, by country of residence

	2002	2003	2004	2005	2006	Market share 06	% Change 06-05
Mauritania	12	26	4	7	24		242.86
Niger	20	14	97	173	78		-54.91
Nigeria	1,177	1,111	1,087	1,033	1,533	0.02	48.40
Guinea-Bissau		13	33	25	26		4.00
Saint Helena		3	16	1	8		700.00
Senegal	113	132	95	64	80		25.00
Sierra Leone	100	207	219	111	113		1.80
Togo		48	21	22	18		-18.18
Burkina Faso	12	14	13	10	89		790.00
AMERICAS	**388,458**	**360,395**	**468,862**	**501,983**	**510,655**	**6.46**	**1.73**
Caribbean	**8,123**	**2,221**	**1,671**	**1,989**	**2,891**	**0.04**	**45.35**
Antigua and Barbuda	162	250	220	351	587	0.01	67.24
Bahamas	86	265	288	105	51		-51.43
Barbados	43	42	59	54	141		161.11
British Virgin Islands		16		2	27		1,250.00
Cayman Islands			95	2	4		100.00
Cuba	234	920	561	937	1,074	0.01	14.62
Dominica	5		10	10	73		630.00
Dominican Republic	32	25	19	28	148		428.57
Grenada	33	202	20	74	50		-32.43
Guadeloupe		1	4				
Haiti	11	8		4	38		850.00
Jamaica	670	34	56	34	176		417.65
Martinique		6			122		
Montserrat	4		1	4			
Netherlands Antilles		35	63	81	14		-82.72
Aruba			1	2	12		500.00
Puerto Rico	141	245	150	52	156		200.00
Anguilla	41	92	67	116	3		-97.41
Trinidad and Tobago	42	38	19	95	137		44.21
Turks and Caicos Islands	9	20	18	2	39		1,850.00
United States Virgin Islands	6,610	22	20	36	39		8.33
Central America	**1,704**	**552**	**570**	**908**	**990**	**0.01**	**9.03**
Belize	23	3	3	211	28		-86.73
Costa Rica	184	198	255	479	370		-22.76
El Salvador	24	42	61	76	91		19.74
Guatemala	32	75	60	32	129		303.13
Honduras	1,360	148	51	48	263		447.92
Nicaragua	10	47	38	33	47		42.42
Panama	71	39	102	29	62		113.79
North America	**367,700**	**346,450**	**451,035**	**476,536**	**485,399**	**6.14**	**1.86**
Canada	32,499	33,053	39,130	45,139	44,493	0.56	-1.43
Greenland	2		3	11	31		181.82
Mexico	3,934	6,272	6,403	10,048	13,909	0.18	38.43
Saint Pierre and Miquelon					2		
United States	331,265	307,125	405,499	421,338	426,964	5.40	1.34
South America	**10,931**	**11,172**	**15,586**	**22,550**	**21,375**	**0.27**	**-5.21**
Argentina	1,517	2,304	2,664	4,416	3,801	0.05	-13.93
Bolivia	127	128	156	179	184		2.79
Brazil	6,587	5,650	9,402	14,099	13,799	0.17	-2.13
Chile	1,643	1,032	1,332	1,432	1,157	0.01	-19.20
Colombia	154	807	406	679	584	0.01	-13.99
Ecuador	100	255	273	127	147		15.75

POLAND

5. Overnight stays of non-resident tourists in hotels and similar establishments, by country of residence

	2002	2003	2004	2005	2006	Market share 06	% Change 06-05
Falkland Islands (Malvinas)	115		22	3	5		66.67
Guyana	1	21	8	10	25		150.00
Paraguay	74	9	37	93	44		-52.69
Peru	160	179	641	282	467	0.01	65.60
Suriname	36	62	18	88	28		-68.18
Uruguay	180	262	316	661	376		-43.12
Venezuela	237	463	311	481	758	0.01	57.59
EAST ASIA AND THE PACIFIC	**109,834**	**111,681**	**178,575**	**206,671**	**233,011**	**2.95**	**12.74**
North-East Asia	**91,014**	**87,583**	**140,215**	**164,381**	**181,465**	**2.29**	**10.39**
China	9,740	8,297	19,724	27,711	30,318	0.38	9.41
Taiwan (Province of China)	2,651	2,935	3,911	4,168	1,912	0.02	-54.13
Hong Kong, China	1,616	1,573	1,738	2,883	1,658	0.02	-42.49
Japan	55,866	57,085	84,828	98,259	83,168	1.05	-15.36
Korea, Dem. People's Republic of	8,090	1,545	2,136	1,971	4,847	0.06	145.92
Korea, Republic of	12,665	15,638	26,378	28,430	58,677	0.74	106.39
Macao, China	1	9	108	308	39		-87.34
Mongolia	385	501	1,392	651	846	0.01	29.95
South-East Asia	**5,893**	**8,011**	**11,093**	**11,107**	**17,515**	**0.22**	**57.69**
Brunei Darussalam			21	4	192		4,700.00
Myanmar	28	30	50	21	54		157.14
Cambodia				184	85		-53.80
Indonesia	790	1,324	1,550	896	1,185	0.01	32.25
Lao People's Democratic Republic	9	24	5	10	9		-10.00
Malaysia	899	1,118	1,818	1,810	2,246	0.03	24.09
Philippines	1,445	1,400	1,837	2,437	4,623	0.06	89.70
Timor-Leste	6		11	40	8		-80.00
Singapore	1,460	1,410	1,800	1,568	2,252	0.03	43.62
Viet Nam	568	1,620	2,010	2,352	4,171	0.05	77.34
Thailand	688	1,085	1,991	1,785	2,690	0.03	50.70
Australasia	**12,503**	**15,674**	**24,815**	**30,310**	**32,817**	**0.41**	**8.27**
Australia	11,244	13,766	21,527	27,049	29,054	0.37	7.41
New Zealand	1,259	1,908	3,288	3,261	3,763	0.05	15.39
Melanesia	**71**	**46**	**175**	**152**	**108**		**-28.95**
Solomon Islands	17	36	72		5		
Fiji	8	2	9	5			
New Caledonia	40	5	11	58	98		68.97
Papua New Guinea	6	3	83	89	5		-94.38
Micronesia	**35**	**27**	**2,120**	**65**	**73**		**12.31**
Christmas Island (Australia)	4	24	19				
Cocos (Keeling) Islands			6	1			
Kiribati	11		1,836	46	33		-28.26
Guam				7	9		28.57
Nauru	20	3	259	11	31		181.82
Polynesia	**318**	**340**	**157**	**656**	**1,033**	**0.01**	**57.47**
American Samoa	94	86	125	146	777	0.01	432.19
French Polynesia	14	7	4	77	170		120.78
Niue	3	9	5		1		
Pitcairn				13	6		-53.85
Tokelau	23	15	20	47	18		-61.70
Tonga	2	6	3	310			
Tuvalu	13	4		1			
Wallis and Futuna Islands		1			32		

POLAND

5. Overnight stays of non-resident tourists in hotels and similar establishments, by country of residence

	2002	2003	2004	2005	2006	Market share 06	% Change 06-05
Samoa	169	212		62	29		-53.23
EUROPE	**4,370,601**	**4,858,858**	**6,066,025**	**7,004,210**	**7,003,646**	**88.53**	**-0.01**
Central/Eastern Europe	**665,404**	**748,279**	**920,755**	**1,021,996**	**1,101,719**	**13.93**	**7.80**
Azerbaijan	844	1,241	1,493	1,320	1,020	0.01	-22.73
Armenia	1,391	1,832	2,185	2,342	2,164	0.03	-7.60
Bulgaria	8,115	10,726	12,258	11,816	12,992	0.16	9.95
Belarus	89,589	90,516	112,655	120,461	126,654	1.60	5.14
Czech Republic	56,340	64,746	86,726	91,240	102,512	1.30	12.35
Estonia	16,317	20,568	30,845	45,451	55,271	0.70	21.61
Georgia	695	1,041	2,184	2,179	1,875	0.02	-13.95
Hungary	32,506	48,120	65,414	76,837	69,622	0.88	-9.39
Kazakhstan	1,957	4,185	5,947	5,967	7,515	0.09	25.94
Kyrgyzstan	210	281	432	202	234		15.84
Latvia	11,568	20,246	24,261	30,560	37,157	0.47	21.59
Lithuania	53,820	64,264	80,838	83,724	97,415	1.23	16.35
Republic of Moldova	4,505	4,288	7,140	5,993	7,796	0.10	30.09
Romania	11,715	14,206	19,015	30,468	27,426	0.35	-9.98
Russian Federation	205,638	227,845	244,158	280,681	295,697	3.74	5.35
Slovakia	20,531	23,174	31,194	40,537	39,870	0.50	-1.65
Tajikistan	248	93	183	192	114		-40.63
Turkmenistan	8	50	65	66	41		-37.88
Ukraine	148,960	149,898	193,231	190,942	215,575	2.73	12.90
Uzbekistan	447	959	531	1,018	769	0.01	-24.46
Northern Europe	**754,796**	**831,942**	**1,058,503**	**1,305,732**	**1,504,276**	**19.02**	**15.21**
Denmark	158,164	171,679	204,284	220,325	218,833	2.77	-0.68
Faeroe Islands	9	20	276		77		
Finland	52,346	62,766	73,086	74,905	88,536	1.12	18.20
Iceland	1,276	2,270	5,138	7,055	7,223	0.09	2.38
Ireland	13,987	19,536	37,004	56,993	89,043	1.13	56.23
Norway	85,329	116,136	136,617	158,052	177,108	2.24	12.06
Svalbard and Jan Mayen Islands	1	3	2				
Sweden	134,295	140,291	171,725	202,550	210,288	2.66	3.82
United Kingdom	309,389	319,241	430,371	585,852	713,168	9.02	21.73
Southern Europe	**378,552**	**455,162**	**579,713**	**722,701**	**716,869**	**9.06**	**-0.81**
Albania	1,289	2,203	2,507	1,932	1,818	0.02	-5.90
Andorra	28	793	82	181	691	0.01	281.77
Bosnia and Herzegovina	762	1,083	1,397	1,779	1,026	0.01	-42.33
Croatia	6,236	9,464	10,941	12,919	13,993	0.18	8.31
Gibraltar			28		23		
Greece	12,202	16,582	17,843	28,535	22,402	0.28	-21.49
Holy See	10	11	14	2	800	0.01	*********
Italy	234,989	281,551	345,154	411,383	418,607	5.29	1.76
Malta	821	2,248	5,109	5,366	1,868	0.02	-65.19
Portugal	19,848	22,214	24,700	35,686	32,553	0.41	-8.78
San Marino	93	241	97	106	119		12.26
Slovenia	9,600	9,154	14,150	14,740	12,125	0.15	-17.74
Spain	87,825	103,769	149,431	202,117	205,834	2.60	1.84
TFYR of Macedonia	958	800	1,106	582	686	0.01	17.87
Serbia and Montenegro	3,891	5,049	7,154	7,373	4,324	0.05	-41.35
Western Europe	**2,398,337**	**2,629,849**	**3,262,651**	**3,692,729**	**3,421,915**	**43.26**	**-7.33**
Austria	75,762	81,461	95,851	100,344	99,755	1.26	-0.59
Belgium	69,048	71,333	91,314	105,113	99,078	1.25	-5.74
France	211,959	243,327	296,817	344,678	334,136	4.22	-3.06

POLAND

5. Overnight stays of non-resident tourists in hotels and similar establishments, by country of residence

	2002	2003	2004	2005	2006	Market share 06	% Change 06-05
Germany	1,856,800	2,037,396	2,533,222	2,881,699	2,641,073	33.39	-8.35
Liechtenstein	159	434	445	465	258		-44.52
Luxembourg	6,585	9,705	7,645	7,944	4,929	0.06	-37.95
Monaco	146	230	182	231	629	0.01	172.29
Netherlands	128,642	137,753	180,503	197,271	190,024	2.40	-3.67
Switzerland	49,236	48,210	56,672	54,984	52,033	0.66	-5.37
East Mediterranean Europe	**173,512**	**193,626**	**244,403**	**261,052**	**258,867**	**3.27**	**-0.84**
Cyprus	1,162	2,407	3,727	4,277	3,566	0.05	-16.62
Israel	164,554	177,857	220,778	235,860	233,820	2.96	-0.86
Turkey	7,796	13,362	19,898	20,915	21,481	0.27	2.71
MIDDLE EAST	**5,202**	**7,805**	**9,099**	**9,102**	**14,285**	**0.18**	**56.94**
Middle East	**5,202**	**7,805**	**9,099**	**9,102**	**14,285**	**0.18**	**56.94**
Bahrain	355	479	595	186	139		-25.27
Iraq	277	141	816	723	5,255	0.07	626.83
Jordan	249	542	627	407	474	0.01	16.46
Kuwait	570	575	525	618	1,123	0.01	81.72
Lebanon	519	634	357	1,155	510	0.01	-55.84
Libyan Arab Jamahiriya	337	837	570	490	719	0.01	46.73
Oman	152	221	289	118	163		38.14
Qatar	36	139	176	171	321		87.72
Saudi Arabia	463	784	812	1,123	1,160	0.01	3.29
Syrian Arab Republic	445	344	383	247	233		-5.67
United Arab Emirates	156	136	210	631	727	0.01	15.21
Egypt	1,239	2,864	3,490	2,870	3,295	0.04	14.81
Yemen	404	109	249	363	166		-54.27
SOUTH ASIA	**12,808**	**12,003**	**21,460**	**23,312**	**24,025**	**0.30**	**3.06**
South Asia	**12,808**	**12,003**	**21,460**	**23,312**	**24,025**	**0.30**	**3.06**
Afghanistan	488	954	906	3,851	998	0.01	-74.08
Bangladesh	1,077	120	2,053	449	2,787	0.04	520.71
Bhutan	3,525	599	2,756	2,337	23		-99.02
Sri Lanka	129	89	155	91	274		201.10
India	5,333	7,733	11,395	11,897	17,454	0.22	46.71
Iran, Islamic Republic of	1,366	1,691	3,301	3,172	955	0.01	-69.89
Nepal	395	119	282	78	539	0.01	591.03
Pakistan	495	698	612	1,437	995	0.01	-30.76
REGION NOT SPECIFIED	**102,972**	**84,542**	**120,542**	**109,726**	**102,065**	**1.29**	**-6.98**
Not Specified	**102,972**	**84,542**	**120,542**	**109,726**	**102,065**	**1.29**	**-6.98**
Other countries of the World	102,972	84,542	120,542	109,726	102,065	1.29	-6.98

Source: World Tourism Organization (UNWTO)

POLAND

6. Overnight stays of non-resident tourists in all types of accommodation establishments, by country of residence

	2002	2003	2004	2005	2006	Market share 06	% Change 06-05
TOTAL	7,085,019	7,828,230	9,312,939	10,542,368	10,555,119	100.00	0.12
AFRICA	11,506	18,410	16,471	15,967	25,028	0.24	56.75
East Africa	679	1,770	1,822	1,475	2,243	0.02	52.07
British Indian Ocean Territory	2		2	12	17		41.67
Burundi	8	15	12	128	209		63.28
Ethiopia	79	117	133	146	174		19.18
Eritrea	17	278	168	6	9		50.00
Djibouti	42	3	2				
Kenya	140	364	483	765	1,270	0.01	66.01
Madagascar	19	243	3	11	4		-63.64
Malawi		50		21			
Mauritius	133	30	35	11	120		990.91
Mozambique	6	43	178	60	27		-55.00
Reunion	7			17	11		-35.29
Rwanda	10	25	30	4	86		2,050.00
Seychelles		48	50	39	44		12.82
Somalia	68	215	346	63	57		-9.52
Zimbabwe	17	64	37	117	63		-46.15
Uganda	29	97	53	24	32		33.33
United Republic of Tanzania	76	159	245	42	70		66.67
Zambia	26	19	45	9	50		455.56
Central Africa	2,698	1,513	929	1,391	1,568	0.01	12.72
Angola	1,625	463	216	394	840	0.01	113.20
Cameroon	238	249	93	78	470		502.56
Central African Republic	8	71	8	46	9		-80.43
Chad	57			22	10		-54.55
Congo	165	691	556	344	199		-42.15
Democratic Republic of the Congo	598	9	5	7	10		42.86
Equatorial Guinea	2	28	47	497	4		-99.20
Gabon	3	1	3	3	19		533.33
Sao Tome and Principe	2	1	1		7		
North Africa	3,433	9,134	6,620	4,378	10,259	0.10	134.33
Algeria	1,298	6,619	4,307	2,289	2,846	0.03	24.33
Morocco	777	437	1,042	814	1,699	0.02	108.72
Western Sahara	4	1	1	69	113		63.77
Sudan	69	244	75	109	33		-69.72
Tunisia	1,285	1,833	1,195	1,097	5,568	0.05	407.57
Southern Africa	1,933	2,243	4,469	3,631	3,856	0.04	6.20
Botswana	6	8	26	66	90		36.36
Lesotho			27	131	13		-90.08
Namibia	4	4	14	18	20		11.11
South Africa	1,884	2,200	4,400	3,197	3,539	0.03	10.70
Swaziland	39	31	2	219	194		-11.42
West Africa	2,763	3,750	2,631	5,092	7,102	0.07	39.47
Cape Verde		1					
Benin	319	320	354	685	85		-87.59
Gambia	16	369	26	2,467	3,635	0.03	47.34
Ghana	322	130	83	79	242		206.33
Guinea	17	11	160	50	323		546.00
Cote D'Ivoire	64	57	28	123	316		156.91
Liberia	3	10		9	29		222.22
Mali	101	44	35	39	111		184.62

POLAND

6. Overnight stays of non-resident tourists in all types of accommodation establishments, by country of residence

	2002	2003	2004	2005	2006	Market share 06	% Change 06-05
Mauritania	12	31	4	8	24		200.00
Niger	22	65	101	173	80		-53.76
Nigeria	1,638	1,924	1,267	1,192	1,911	0.02	60.32
Guinea-Bissau		13	33	25	26		4.00
Saint Helena		3	16	1	8		700.00
Senegal	135	159	116	69	87		26.09
Sierra Leone	102	550	224	113	117		3.54
Togo		49	171	22	18		-18.18
Burkina Faso	12	14	13	37	90		143.24
AMERICAS	**442,423**	**418,809**	**512,092**	**551,123**	**561,933**	**5.32**	**1.96**
Caribbean	**8,299**	**2,304**	**1,752**	**2,052**	**2,990**	**0.03**	**45.71**
Antigua and Barbuda	162	266	220	351	587	0.01	67.24
Bahamas	93	265	288	105	65		-38.10
Barbados	43	42	59	60	144		140.00
British Virgin Islands		16	1	2	27		1,250.00
Cayman Islands	33		95	4	7		75.00
Cuba	246	971	597	957	1,103	0.01	15.26
Dominica	5		22	10	73		630.00
Dominican Republic	34	26	45	28	153		446.43
Grenada	55	202	20	74	55		-25.68
Guadeloupe		1	4		4		
Haiti	11	8		4	38		850.00
Jamaica	708	37	61	45	190		322.22
Martinique		6		1	125		*********
Montserrat	6		1	4			
Netherlands Antilles		35	63	81	14		-82.72
Aruba	40		1	2	15		650.00
Puerto Rico	145	249	150	64	165		157.81
Anguilla	41	92	68	116	3		-97.41
Trinidad and Tobago	56	40	19	98	144		46.94
Turks and Caicos Islands	9	20	18	10	39		290.00
United States Virgin Islands	6,612	28	20	36	39		8.33
Central America	**1,772**	**2,773**	**600**	**957**	**1,174**	**0.01**	**22.68**
Belize	51	2,160	3	211	52		-75.36
Costa Rica	218	222	271	509	498		-2.16
El Salvador	24	43	61	78	96		23.08
Guatemala	38	90	68	42	147		250.00
Honduras	1,360	165	55	49	264		438.78
Nicaragua	10	53	38	37	48		29.73
Panama	71	40	104	31	69		122.58
North America	**419,576**	**400,408**	**491,873**	**521,593**	**533,051**	**5.05**	**2.20**
Canada	37,999	39,931	46,408	51,228	52,366	0.50	2.22
Greenland	2		3	11	31		181.82
Mexico	4,613	7,186	7,500	10,736	15,610	0.15	45.40
Saint Pierre and Miquelon		141			2		
United States	376,962	353,150	437,962	459,618	465,042	4.41	1.18
South America	**12,776**	**13,324**	**17,867**	**26,521**	**24,718**	**0.23**	**-6.80**
Argentina	1,868	2,707	3,119	4,870	4,062	0.04	-16.59
Bolivia	175	193	295	210	259		23.33
Brazil	7,383	6,555	10,312	17,039	15,618	0.15	-8.34
Chile	1,720	1,201	1,509	1,525	1,350	0.01	-11.48
Colombia	532	1,122	464	737	996	0.01	35.14
Ecuador	150	319	388	269	202		-24.91

POLAND

6. Overnight stays of non-resident tourists in all types of accommodation establishments, by country of residence

	2002	2003	2004	2005	2006	Market share 06	% Change 06-05
Falkland Islands (Malvinas)	124		22	3	35		1,066.67
Guyana	1	33	8	15	62		313.33
Paraguay	75	9	37	93	62		-33.33
Peru	235	270	807	376	746	0.01	98.40
Suriname	36	72	18	94	28		-70.21
Uruguay	205	344	334	786	391		-50.25
Venezuela	272	499	554	504	907	0.01	79.96
EAST ASIA AND THE PACIFIC	**129,087**	**127,470**	**196,792**	**224,017**	**263,799**	**2.50**	**17.76**
North-East Asia	**100,065**	**94,525**	**148,491**	**172,569**	**193,366**	**1.83**	**12.05**
China	11,650	9,440	21,623	30,027	34,704	0.33	15.58
Taiwan (Province of China)	2,756	2,988	4,608	4,262	2,228	0.02	-47.72
Hong Kong, China	1,636	1,628	1,779	2,921	1,906	0.02	-34.75
Japan	61,290	61,198	88,642	102,135	87,667	0.83	-14.17
Korea, Dem. People's Republic of	8,647	1,942	2,491	2,039	5,039	0.05	147.13
Korea, Republic of	13,179	16,389	27,553	29,893	60,465	0.57	102.27
Macao, China	1	9	115	308	39		-87.34
Mongolia	906	931	1,680	984	1,318	0.01	33.94
South-East Asia	**8,219**	**9,698**	**12,760**	**14,032**	**27,930**	**0.26**	**99.05**
Brunei Darussalam	19		23	4	198		4,850.00
Myanmar	28	30	51	27	54		100.00
Cambodia			8	184	91		-50.54
Indonesia	876	1,389	1,973	939	1,499	0.01	59.64
Lao People's Democratic Republic	180	147	19	10	32		220.00
Malaysia	1,137	1,261	1,978	1,944	2,407	0.02	23.82
Philippines	1,807	1,522	1,904	2,531	13,855	0.13	447.41
Timor-Leste	8	6	16	40	8		-80.00
Singapore	1,569	1,600	1,927	1,693	2,469	0.02	45.84
Viet Nam	1,598	2,546	2,775	4,698	4,493	0.04	-4.36
Thailand	997	1,197	2,086	1,962	2,824	0.03	43.93
Australasia	**20,288**	**22,601**	**32,844**	**36,322**	**41,252**	**0.39**	**13.57**
Australia	17,850	19,332	27,859	31,918	36,113	0.34	13.14
New Zealand	2,438	3,269	4,985	4,404	5,139	0.05	16.69
Melanesia	**71**	**185**	**175**	**163**	**127**		**-22.09**
Solomon Islands	17	36	72	1	5		400.00
Fiji	8	137	9	15	1		-93.33
New Caledonia	40	9	11	58	112		93.10
Papua New Guinea	6	3	83	89	9		-89.89
Micronesia	**49**	**27**	**2,357**	**65**	**81**		**24.62**
Christmas Island (Australia)	4	24	19		3		
Cocos (Keeling) Islands			6	1			
Kiribati	11		2,073	46	33		-28.26
Guam				7	9		28.57
Nauru	34	3	259	11	36		227.27
Polynesia	**395**	**434**	**165**	**866**	**1,043**	**0.01**	**20.44**
American Samoa	94	86	125	146	777	0.01	432.19
French Polynesia	15	42	4	282	171		-39.36
Niue	3	9	5	5	10		100.00
Pitcairn				13	6		-53.85
Tokelau	23	15	20	47	18		-61.70
Tonga	2	6	7	310			
Tuvalu	18	4	4	1			
Wallis and Futuna Islands	71	60			32		

POLAND

6. Overnight stays of non-resident tourists in all types of accommodation establishments, by country of residence

	2002	2003	2004	2005	2006	Market share 06	% Change 06-05
Samoa	169	212		62	29		-53.23
EUROPE	**6,368,093**	**7,154,760**	**8,430,938**	**9,603,063**	**9,558,927**	**90.56**	**-0.46**
Central/Eastern Europe	**1,166,151**	**1,258,839**	**1,278,251**	**1,417,496**	**1,510,456**	**14.31**	**6.56**
Azerbaijan	1,130	2,052	1,598	1,419	1,375	0.01	-3.10
Armenia	4,078	2,489	2,703	2,830	2,601	0.02	-8.09
Bulgaria	14,401	14,767	15,835	15,387	19,574	0.19	27.21
Belarus	178,761	186,181	152,920	163,257	170,910	1.62	4.69
Czech Republic	85,424	95,988	110,598	120,163	132,722	1.26	10.45
Estonia	25,306	28,957	35,996	50,633	60,555	0.57	19.60
Georgia	905	2,095	3,388	3,006	2,630	0.02	-12.51
Hungary	54,816	80,258	100,495	114,861	100,635	0.95	-12.39
Kazakhstan	3,243	5,063	7,047	7,336	8,634	0.08	17.69
Kyrgyzstan	257	425	775	277	407		46.93
Latvia	17,795	30,357	34,723	40,880	46,997	0.45	14.96
Lithuania	86,836	94,933	110,804	112,350	128,201	1.21	14.11
Republic of Moldova	13,486	11,240	10,151	8,631	10,268	0.10	18.97
Romania	22,252	23,172	24,657	38,420	38,044	0.36	-0.98
Russian Federation	266,867	290,297	290,345	342,914	348,472	3.30	1.62
Slovakia	34,451	38,432	44,127	57,145	64,471	0.61	12.82
Tajikistan	288	132	248	209	157		-24.88
Turkmenistan	30	50	65	75	424		465.33
Ukraine	355,301	350,801	331,095	336,630	372,533	3.53	10.67
Uzbekistan	524	1,150	681	1,073	846	0.01	-21.16
Northern Europe	**893,725**	**962,272**	**1,183,030**	**1,429,149**	**1,646,133**	**15.60**	**15.18**
Denmark	188,265	208,023	233,537	246,764	241,700	2.29	-2.05
Faeroe Islands	14	26	276		82		
Finland	59,992	70,273	81,766	82,256	98,565	0.93	19.83
Iceland	1,655	2,455	5,464	7,306	7,508	0.07	2.76
Ireland	17,395	23,646	40,519	61,074	96,312	0.91	57.70
Norway	96,818	124,470	144,717	168,034	197,390	1.87	17.47
Svalbard and Jan Mayen Islands	1	11	2				
Sweden	179,298	181,872	213,141	243,174	248,231	2.35	2.08
United Kingdom	350,287	351,496	463,608	620,541	756,345	7.17	21.88
Southern Europe	**432,580**	**514,641**	**641,645**	**785,746**	**787,996**	**7.47**	**0.29**
Albania	1,350	2,352	2,663	2,007	1,913	0.02	-4.68
Andorra	28	799	88	212	771	0.01	263.68
Bosnia and Herzegovina	1,023	1,724	1,755	1,888	1,777	0.02	-5.88
Croatia	8,623	13,384	14,364	16,511	17,105	0.16	3.60
Gibraltar			31	12	26		116.67
Greece	14,573	18,512	19,078	30,749	26,837	0.25	-12.72
Holy See	269	11	20	2	806	0.01	*********
Italy	266,083	315,567	381,198	446,298	455,281	4.31	2.01
Malta	1,006	2,318	5,334	5,958	2,010	0.02	-66.26
Portugal	22,252	24,572	27,491	39,040	36,643	0.35	-6.14
San Marino	95	253	99	126	344		173.02
Slovenia	12,049	11,645	16,153	17,187	15,262	0.14	-11.20
Spain	97,959	115,759	164,139	216,175	222,094	2.10	2.74
TFYR of Macedonia	2,390	1,234	1,268	745	820	0.01	10.07
Serbia and Montenegro	4,880	6,511	7,964	8,836	6,307	0.06	-28.62
Western Europe	**3,689,163**	**4,212,369**	**5,073,823**	**5,701,691**	**5,342,274**	**50.61**	**-6.30**
Austria	85,462	98,593	107,612	113,913	113,605	1.08	-0.27
Belgium	85,412	88,619	109,632	125,656	117,552	1.11	-6.45
France	261,958	307,437	363,028	416,405	401,185	3.80	-3.66

POLAND

6. Overnight stays of non-resident tourists in all types of accommodation establishments, by country of residence

	2002	2003	2004	2005	2006	Market share 06	% Change 06-05
Germany	3,016,245	3,460,318	4,190,223	4,724,771	4,406,104	41.74	-6.74
Liechtenstein	187	515	455	499	390		-21.84
Luxembourg	7,292	10,330	8,439	8,461	5,647	0.05	-33.26
Monaco	149	245	184	253	647	0.01	155.73
Netherlands	179,055	192,233	231,265	251,316	239,281	2.27	-4.79
Switzerland	53,403	54,079	62,985	60,417	57,863	0.55	-4.23
East Mediterranean Europe	**186,474**	**206,639**	**254,189**	**268,981**	**272,068**	**2.58**	**1.15**
Cyprus	1,289	2,743	3,861	4,648	3,764	0.04	-19.02
Israel	175,641	188,686	229,549	242,559	243,838	2.31	0.53
Turkey	9,544	15,210	20,779	21,774	24,466	0.23	12.36
MIDDLE EAST	**8,159**	**9,571**	**11,655**	**10,682**	**15,744**	**0.15**	**47.39**
Middle East	**8,159**	**9,571**	**11,655**	**10,682**	**15,744**	**0.15**	**47.39**
Bahrain	376	479	603	186	139		-25.27
Iraq	453	304	1,593	786	5,751	0.05	631.68
Jordan	267	618	699	422	527		24.88
Kuwait	714	800	920	778	1,276	0.01	64.01
Lebanon	810	1,017	429	1,281	555	0.01	-56.67
Libyan Arab Jamahiriya	426	954	612	549	864	0.01	57.38
Oman	154	221	289	118	163		38.14
Qatar	36	153	355	203	321		58.13
Saudi Arabia	542	1,015	876	1,401	1,255	0.01	-10.42
Syrian Arab Republic	497	488	486	320	285		-10.94
United Arab Emirates	495	175	212	1,153	728	0.01	-36.86
Egypt	1,713	3,192	3,903	3,109	3,702	0.04	19.07
Yemen	1,676	155	678	376	178		-52.66
SOUTH ASIA	**14,307**	**13,477**	**23,061**	**24,513**	**25,598**	**0.24**	**4.43**
South Asia	**14,307**	**13,477**	**23,061**	**24,513**	**25,598**	**0.24**	**4.43**
Afghanistan	576	1,131	939	3,852	1,007	0.01	-73.86
Bangladesh	1,133	122	2,296	487	2,843	0.03	483.78
Bhutan	3,525	599	2,756	2,337	96		-95.89
Sri Lanka	130	115	190	144	283		96.53
India	5,995	8,315	12,173	12,373	18,067	0.17	46.02
Iran, Islamic Republic of	1,896	2,043	3,624	3,521	1,022	0.01	-70.97
Nepal	413	151	372	121	727	0.01	500.83
Pakistan	639	1,001	711	1,678	1,553	0.01	-7.45
REGION NOT SPECIFIED	**111,444**	**85,733**	**121,930**	**113,003**	**104,090**	**0.99**	**-7.89**
Not Specified	**111,444**	**85,733**	**121,930**	**113,003**	**104,090**	**0.99**	**-7.89**
Other countries of the World	111,444	85,733	121,930	113,003	104,090	0.99	-7.89

Source: World Tourism Organization (UNWTO)

PORTUGAL

1. Arrivals of non-resident tourists at national borders, by nationality

	2002	2003	2004	2005	2006	Market share 06	% Change 06-05
TOTAL (*)	11,644,231	11,707,228	10,639,000	10,612,000	11,282,000	100.00	6.31
AMERICAS	434,694	441,210	303,000	321,000	401,000	3.55	24.92
North America	329,080	332,236	175,000	172,000	211,000	1.87	22.67
Canada	99,155	102,025	59,000	53,000	57,000	0.51	7.55
United States	229,925	230,211	116,000	119,000	154,000	1.37	29.41
South America	105,614	108,974	128,000	149,000	190,000	1.68	27.52
Brazil	105,614	108,974	128,000	149,000	190,000	1.68	27.52
EAST ASIA AND THE PACIFIC	46,292	43,282	46,000	41,000	34,000	0.30	-17.07
North-East Asia	46,292	43,282	46,000	41,000	34,000	0.30	-17.07
Japan	46,292	43,282	46,000	41,000	34,000	0.30	-17.07
EUROPE	10,901,171	10,944,742	7,344,000	7,316,000	7,981,000	70.74	9.09
Northern Europe	2,362,125	2,393,802	2,388,000	2,502,000	2,688,000	23.83	7.43
Denmark	127,958	130,596	70,000	102,000	103,000	0.91	0.98
Finland	73,246	78,856	57,000	69,000	67,000	0.59	-2.90
Ireland	137,273	145,207	169,000	239,000	258,000	2.29	7.95
Norway	45,193	46,231	77,000	61,000	71,000	0.63	16.39
Sweden	136,685	134,437	111,000	100,000	106,000	0.94	6.00
United Kingdom	1,841,770	1,858,475	1,904,000	1,931,000	2,083,000	18.46	7.87
Southern Europe	5,991,771	5,997,709	2,535,000	2,405,000	2,612,000	23.15	8.61
Greece			39,000	13,000	12,000	0.11	-7.69
Italy	290,766	288,736	346,000	338,000	382,000	3.39	13.02
Spain	5,701,005	5,708,973	2,150,000	2,054,000	2,218,000	19.66	7.98
Western Europe	2,547,275	2,553,231	2,421,000	2,409,000	2,681,000	23.76	11.29
Austria	56,642	57,756	52,000	45,000	63,000	0.56	40.00
Belgium	243,690	255,098	128,000	136,000	203,000	1.80	49.26
France	823,761	823,646	862,000	830,000	848,000	7.52	2.17
Germany	814,286	807,786	846,000	861,000	952,000	8.44	10.57
Luxembourg	33,455	35,933	15,000	17,000	22,000	0.20	29.41
Netherlands	476,609	475,594	423,000	437,000	493,000	4.37	12.81
Switzerland	98,832	97,418	95,000	83,000	100,000	0.89	20.48
REGION NOT SPECIFIED	262,074	277,994	2,946,000	2,934,000	2,866,000	25.40	-2.32
Not Specified	262,074	277,994	2,946,000	2,934,000	2,866,000	25.40	-2.32
Other countries of the World	262,074	277,994	858,000	841,000	926,000	8.21	10.11
Nationals Residing Abroad			2,088,000	2,093,000	1,940,000	17.20	-7.31

Source: World Tourism Organization (UNWTO)

PORTUGAL

1. Arrivals of non-resident tourists at national borders, by country of residence

		2002	2003	2004	2005	2006	Market share 06	% Change 06-05
TOTAL	(*)	11,644,231	11,707,228	10,639,000	10,612,000	11,282,000	100.00	6.31
AMERICAS		463,847	480,544	367,000	413,000	499,000	4.42	20.82
North America		351,751	362,298	235,000	254,000	295,000	2.61	16.14
Canada		105,552	109,717	84,000	83,000	91,000	0.81	9.64
United States		246,199	252,581	151,000	171,000	204,000	1.81	19.30
South America		112,096	118,246	132,000	159,000	204,000	1.81	28.30
Brazil		112,096	118,246	132,000	159,000	204,000	1.81	28.30
EAST ASIA AND THE PACIFIC		43,964	40,055	43,000	37,000	32,000	0.28	-13.51
North-East Asia		43,964	40,055	43,000	37,000	32,000	0.28	-13.51
Japan		43,964	40,055	43,000	37,000	32,000	0.28	-13.51
EUROPE		10,849,103	10,887,861	9,343,000	9,271,000	9,831,000	87.14	6.04
Northern Europe		2,370,314	2,398,240	2,551,000	2,673,000	2,867,000	25.41	7.26
Denmark		121,574	126,287	70,000	105,000	105,000	0.93	
Finland		74,671	78,686	55,000	68,000	64,000	0.57	-5.88
Ireland		138,397	142,964	174,000	245,000	267,000	2.37	8.98
Norway		45,619	46,571	78,000	60,000	71,000	0.63	18.33
Sweden		131,876	129,733	122,000	107,000	106,000	0.94	-0.93
United Kingdom		1,858,177	1,873,999	2,052,000	2,088,000	2,254,000	19.98	7.95
Southern Europe		5,802,760	5,809,030	2,898,000	2,722,000	2,891,000	25.62	6.21
Greece		39,265	43,933	34,000	11,000	11,000	0.10	
Italy		367,185	333,809	350,000	341,000	384,000	3.40	12.61
Spain		5,396,310	5,431,288	2,514,000	2,370,000	2,496,000	22.12	5.32
Western Europe		2,676,029	2,680,591	3,894,000	3,876,000	4,073,000	36.10	5.08
Austria		58,073	61,539	54,000	49,000	66,000	0.59	34.69
Belgium		262,253	271,078	184,000	182,000	254,000	2.25	39.56
France		844,905	843,762	1,598,000	1,561,000	1,501,000	13.30	-3.84
Germany		851,596	848,339	1,047,000	1,075,000	1,191,000	10.56	10.79
Luxembourg		37,497	39,219	129,000	113,000	129,000	1.14	14.16
Netherlands		482,613	479,271	470,000	478,000	515,000	4.56	7.74
Switzerland		139,092	137,383	412,000	418,000	417,000	3.70	-0.24
REGION NOT SPECIFIED		287,317	298,768	886,000	891,000	920,000	8.15	3.25
Not Specified		287,317	298,768	886,000	891,000	920,000	8.15	3.25
Other countries of the World		287,317	298,768	886,000	891,000	920,000	8.15	3.25

Source: World Tourism Organization (UNWTO)

PORTUGAL

2. Arrivals of non-resident visitors at national borders, by nationality

	2002	2003	2004	2005	2006	Market share 06	% Change 06-05
TOTAL (*)	27,193,920	27,532,354	21,165,000	21,172,000	22,588,000	100.00	6.69
AMERICAS	485,292	508,010	304,000	323,000	401,000	1.78	24.15
North America	367,066	387,527	175,000	173,000	211,000	0.93	21.97
Canada	103,205	108,458	59,000	53,000	57,000	0.25	7.55
United States	263,861	279,069	116,000	120,000	154,000	0.68	28.33
South America	118,226	120,483	129,000	150,000	190,000	0.84	26.67
Brazil	118,226	120,483	129,000	150,000	190,000	0.84	26.67
EAST ASIA AND THE PACIFIC	48,176	45,460	46,000	41,000	34,000	0.15	-17.07
North-East Asia	48,176	45,460	46,000	41,000	34,000	0.15	-17.07
Japan	48,176	45,460	46,000	41,000	34,000	0.15	-17.07
EUROPE	26,285,125	26,580,675	17,348,000	16,812,000	18,705,000	82.81	11.26
Northern Europe	2,501,179	2,639,861	2,441,000	2,503,000	2,757,000	12.21	10.15
Denmark	129,296	132,163	74,000	102,000	103,000	0.46	0.98
Finland	75,888	81,285	57,000	69,000	67,000	0.30	-2.90
Ireland	138,042	146,897	169,000	239,000	258,000	1.14	7.95
Norway	46,042	48,179	77,000	61,000	71,000	0.31	16.39
Sweden	138,924	137,024	111,000	100,000	106,000	0.47	6.00
United Kingdom	1,972,987	2,094,313	1,953,000	1,932,000	2,152,000	9.53	11.39
Southern Europe	21,047,471	21,167,866	12,391,000	11,846,000	13,197,000	58.42	11.40
Greece	20,351	22,061	48,000	13,000	12,000	0.05	-7.69
Italy	321,259	320,497	347,000	338,000	382,000	1.69	13.02
Spain	20,705,861	20,825,308	11,996,000	11,495,000	12,803,000	56.68	11.38
Western Europe	2,736,475	2,772,948	2,516,000	2,463,000	2,751,000	12.18	11.69
Austria	59,287	61,050	52,000	45,000	63,000	0.28	40.00
Belgium	251,021	264,595	128,000	136,000	203,000	0.90	49.26
France	866,747	866,921	890,000	857,000	876,000	3.88	2.22
Germany	905,970	917,095	885,000	888,000	983,000	4.35	10.70
Luxembourg	34,253	38,051	15,000	17,000	22,000	0.10	29.41
Netherlands	507,553	512,121	450,000	437,000	504,000	2.23	15.33
Switzerland	111,644	113,115	96,000	83,000	100,000	0.44	20.48
REGION NOT SPECIFIED	375,327	398,209	3,467,000	3,996,000	3,448,000	15.26	-13.71
Not Specified	375,327	398,209	3,467,000	3,996,000	3,448,000	15.26	-13.71
Other countries of the World	375,327	398,209	990,000	1,081,000	1,119,000	4.95	3.52
Nationals Residing Abroad			2,477,000	2,915,000	2,329,000	10.31	-20.10

Source: World Tourism Organization (UNWTO)

PORTUGAL

2. Arrivals of non-resident visitors at national borders, by country of residence

	2002	2003	2004	2005	2006	Market share 06	% Change 06-05
TOTAL (*)	27,193,920	27,532,354	21,165,000	21,172,000	22,588,000	100.00	6.69
AMERICAS	511,029	546,289	367,000	413,000	499,000	2.21	20.82
North America	389,213	417,355	235,000	254,000	295,000	1.31	16.14
Canada	109,403	116,475	84,000	83,000	91,000	0.40	9.64
United States	279,810	300,880	151,000	171,000	204,000	0.90	19.30
South America	121,816	128,934	132,000	159,000	204,000	0.90	28.30
Brazil	121,816	128,934	132,000	159,000	204,000	0.90	28.30
EAST ASIA AND THE PACIFIC	44,877	41,430	43,000	37,000	32,000	0.14	-13.51
North-East Asia	44,877	41,430	43,000	37,000	32,000	0.14	-13.51
Japan	44,877	41,430	43,000	37,000	32,000	0.14	-13.51
EUROPE	26,288,255	26,571,956	19,853,000	19,823,000	21,127,000	93.53	6.58
Northern Europe	2,502,803	2,635,031	2,582,000	2,692,000	2,888,000	12.79	7.28
Denmark	122,742	127,676	74,000	105,000	105,000	0.46	
Finland	77,375	81,301	55,000	68,000	64,000	0.28	-5.88
Ireland	139,024	144,395	174,000	245,000	267,000	1.18	8.98
Norway	46,577	48,494	78,000	60,000	71,000	0.31	18.33
Sweden	133,632	131,891	122,000	107,000	106,000	0.47	-0.93
United Kingdom	1,983,453	2,101,274	2,079,000	2,107,000	2,275,000	10.07	7.97
Southern Europe	20,965,713	21,074,571	13,317,000	13,207,000	14,128,000	62.55	6.97
Greece	39,927	44,790	42,000	11,000	11,000	0.05	
Italy	396,377	364,220	351,000	341,000	384,000	1.70	12.61
Spain	20,529,409	20,665,561	12,924,000	12,855,000	13,733,000	60.80	6.83
Western Europe	2,819,739	2,862,354	3,954,000	3,924,000	4,111,000	18.20	4.77
Austria	60,322	64,486	54,000	49,000	66,000	0.29	34.69
Belgium	269,918	279,403	184,000	182,000	254,000	1.12	39.56
France	886,355	886,310	1,620,000	1,587,000	1,524,000	6.75	-3.97
Germany	908,067	929,334	1,065,000	1,091,000	1,202,000	5.32	10.17
Luxembourg	38,344	41,289	129,000	113,000	129,000	0.57	14.16
Netherlands	511,974	514,434	489,000	484,000	519,000	2.30	7.23
Switzerland	144,759	147,098	413,000	418,000	417,000	1.85	-0.24
REGION NOT SPECIFIED	349,759	372,679	902,000	899,000	930,000	4.12	3.45
Not Specified	349,759	372,679	902,000	899,000	930,000	4.12	3.45
Other countries of the World	349,759	372,679	902,000	899,000	930,000	4.12	3.45

Source: World Tourism Organization (UNWTO)

PORTUGAL

3. Arrivals of non-resident tourists in hotels and similar establishments, by country of residence

		2002	2003	2004	2005	2006	Market share 06	% Change 06-05
TOTAL	(*)	5,060,401	4,905,740	5,200,608	5,354,611	6,510,534	100.00	21.59
AFRICA		42,674	43,058	45,615	46,752	61,822	0.95	32.23
Southern Africa				9,826	10,460			
South Africa				9,826	10,460			
Other Africa		42,674	43,058	35,789	36,292	61,822	0.95	70.35
Other countries of Africa				35,789	36,292			
All countries of Africa		42,674	43,058			61,822	0.95	
AMERICAS		490,455	439,584	469,772	502,320	597,284	9.17	18.91
North America		315,634	275,448	284,349	290,436	338,608	5.20	16.59
Canada		70,811	60,124	64,925	64,527	80,532	1.24	24.80
United States		244,823	215,324	219,424	225,909	258,076	3.96	14.24
South America		174,821	164,136	144,648	167,434	203,132	3.12	21.32
Brazil				144,648	167,434	203,132	3.12	21.32
All countries of South America		174,821	164,136					
Other Americas				40,775	44,450	55,544	0.85	24.96
Other countries of the Americas				40,775	44,450	55,544	0.85	24.96
EAST ASIA AND THE PACIFIC		166,426	148,018	205,135	195,568	199,431	3.06	1.98
North-East Asia		96,346	79,599	141,137	125,791	79,312	1.22	-36.95
China				15,861	16,818			
Japan		96,346	79,599	117,161	98,456	79,312	1.22	-19.44
Korea, Republic of				8,115	10,517			
Australasia		24,207	21,672	23,997	24,644	26,925	0.41	9.26
Australia		20,346	18,343	23,997	24,644	26,925	0.41	9.26
New Zealand		3,861	3,329					
Other East Asia and the Pacific		45,873	46,747	40,001	45,133	93,194	1.43	106.49
Other countries of Asia		45,873	46,747	35,749	38,784	81,918	1.26	111.22
Other countries of Oceania				4,252	6,349	11,276	0.17	77.60
EUROPE		4,360,846	4,275,080	4,480,086	4,609,971	5,651,997	86.81	22.60
Central/Eastern Europe		33,507	33,200	62,839	70,019	105,994	1.63	51.38
Hungary		9,358	11,331	12,959	16,891	21,575	0.33	27.73
Poland		24,149	21,869	20,329	27,613	46,444	0.71	68.20
Ussr (Former)				29,551	25,515	37,975	0.58	48.83
Northern Europe		1,451,100	1,444,178	1,494,962	1,555,510	1,864,621	28.64	19.87
Denmark		60,084	64,015	71,699	85,778	105,708	1.62	23.23
Finland		53,532	55,191	59,520	60,907	68,058	1.05	11.74
Iceland		5,477	6,075	6,334	6,244			
Ireland		109,952	132,724	121,648	124,231	172,170	2.64	38.59
Norway		66,599	68,506	75,096	70,380	80,227	1.23	13.99
Sweden		117,600	97,226	112,734	104,762	115,532	1.77	10.28
United Kingdom		1,037,856	1,020,441	1,047,931	1,103,208	1,322,926	20.32	19.92
Southern Europe		1,161,050	1,152,198	1,313,292	1,384,825	1,698,784	26.09	22.67
Greece		15,646	15,608	31,981	15,647	16,780	0.26	7.24
Italy		322,732	295,722	300,414	292,565	390,554	6.00	33.49
Spain		822,672	840,868	980,897	1,076,613	1,291,450	19.84	19.95
Western Europe		1,645,296	1,570,024	1,542,630	1,535,183	1,886,296	28.97	22.87
Austria		51,412	49,332	62,107	50,817	76,442	1.17	50.43
Belgium		111,200	107,985	107,265	115,447	141,143	2.17	22.26

PORTUGAL

3. Arrivals of non-resident tourists in hotels and similar establishments, by country of residence

	2002	2003	2004	2005	2006	Market share 06	% Change 06-05
France	429,079	438,431	406,134	392,402	455,340	6.99	16.04
Germany	683,490	628,456	619,487	630,442	772,239	11.86	22.49
Luxembourg	7,728	7,904	7,799	8,980	11,321	0.17	26.07
Netherlands	274,505	253,900	245,544	253,592	327,328	5.03	29.08
Switzerland	87,882	84,016	94,294	83,503	102,483	1.57	22.73
East Mediterranean Europe	**4,465**	**6,092**	**6,105**	**7,341**			
Turkey	4,465	6,092	6,105	7,341			
Other Europe	**65,428**	**69,388**	**60,258**	**57,093**	**96,302**	**1.48**	**68.68**
Other countries of Europe	65,428	69,388	60,258	57,093	96,302	1.48	68.68

Source: World Tourism Organization (UNWTO)

PORTUGAL

4. Arrivals of non-resident tourists in all types of accommodation establishments, by country of residence

	2002	2003	2004	2005	2006	Market share 06	% Change 06-05
TOTAL (*)	5,559,905	6,383,055	5,654,081	5,769,293	6,976,978	100.00	20.93
AFRICA	45,210	44,889	48,259	48,328	63,766	0.91	31.94
Southern Africa			10,292	10,835			
South Africa			10,292	10,835			
Other Africa	45,210	44,889	37,967	37,493	63,766	0.91	70.07
Other countries of Africa			37,967	37,493			
All countries of Africa	45,210	44,889			63,766	0.91	
AMERICAS	507,229	456,005	486,603	518,384	615,053	8.82	18.65
North America	325,831	284,259	293,387	297,845	345,789	4.96	16.10
Canada	75,905	64,760	69,602	68,150	83,872	1.20	23.07
United States	249,926	219,499	223,785	229,695	261,917	3.75	14.03
South America	181,398	171,746	150,492	174,650	211,789	3.04	21.26
Brazil			150,492	174,650	211,789	3.04	21.26
All countries of South America	181,398	171,746					
Other Americas			42,724	45,889	57,475	0.82	25.25
Other countries of the Americas			42,724	45,889	57,475	0.82	25.25
EAST ASIA AND THE PACIFIC	180,488	161,474	217,657	205,028	209,409	3.00	2.14
North-East Asia	97,841	81,300	143,620	127,391	80,667	1.16	-36.68
China			16,120	16,971			
Japan	97,841	81,300	119,223	99,686	80,667	1.16	-19.08
Korea, Republic of			8,277	10,734			
Australasia	35,391	31,902	30,432	29,846	31,967	0.46	7.11
Australia	28,307	25,613	30,432	29,846	31,967	0.46	7.11
New Zealand	7,084	6,289					
Other East Asia and the Pacific	47,256	48,272	43,605	47,791	96,775	1.39	102.50
Other countries of Asia	47,247	48,266	36,778	39,435	83,290	1.19	111.21
Other countries of Oceania	9	6	6,827	8,356	13,485	0.19	61.38
EUROPE	4,826,978	5,720,687	4,901,562	4,997,553	6,088,750	87.27	21.83
Central/Eastern Europe	38,975	38,024	68,223	76,106	113,233	1.62	48.78
Hungary	10,685	12,533	14,331	18,230	22,692	0.33	24.48
Poland	28,290	25,491	23,557	32,006	51,674	0.74	61.45
Ussr (Former)			30,335	25,870	38,867	0.56	50.24
Northern Europe	1,492,966	1,489,971	1,548,040	1,598,834	1,911,165	27.39	19.53
Denmark	64,925	69,288	77,050	89,993	110,132	1.58	22.38
Finland	55,019	56,764	61,173	62,645	69,480	1.00	10.91
Iceland	5,504	6,118	6,371	6,283			
Ireland	112,117	135,558	124,573	126,756	175,222	2.51	38.24
Norway	68,133	70,360	76,647	71,606	81,440	1.17	13.73
Sweden	119,303	99,043	117,834	106,486	117,557	1.68	10.40
United Kingdom	1,067,965	1,052,840	1,084,392	1,135,065	1,357,334	19.45	19.58
Southern Europe	1,274,355	1,268,131	1,426,735	1,499,591	1,838,619	26.35	22.61
Greece	16,723	16,093	33,294	16,119	17,310	0.25	7.39
Italy	349,957	320,463	326,552	315,226	416,905	5.98	32.26
Spain	907,675	931,575	1,066,889	1,168,246	1,404,404	20.13	20.21
Western Europe	1,941,370	2,839,096	1,780,544	1,750,785	2,121,352	30.41	21.17
Austria	56,781	54,067	66,971	54,986	80,803	1.16	46.95
Belgium	131,856	1,127,573	124,122	129,653	158,005	2.26	21.87

PORTUGAL

4. Arrivals of non-resident tourists in all types of accommodation establishments, by country of residence

	2002	2003	2004	2005	2006	Market share 06	% Change 06-05
France	564,081	556,707	510,097	490,603	561,701	8.05	14.49
Germany	756,267	692,801	678,813	679,570	825,556	11.83	21.48
Luxembourg	8,628	8,920	8,350	9,458	11,815	0.17	24.92
Netherlands	329,986	308,510	289,716	296,951	374,224	5.36	26.02
Switzerland	93,771	90,518	102,475	89,564	109,248	1.57	21.98
East Mediterranean Europe	**4,527**	**6,171**	**6,362**	**7,415**			
Turkey	4,527	6,171	6,362	7,415			
Other Europe	**74,785**	**79,294**	**71,658**	**64,822**	**104,381**	**1.50**	**61.03**
Other countries of Europe	74,785	79,294	71,658	64,822	104,381	1.50	61.03

Source: World Tourism Organization (UNWTO)

PORTUGAL

5. Overnight stays of non-resident tourists in hotels and similar establishments, by country of residence

		2002	2003	2004	2005	2006	Market share 06	% Change 06-05
TOTAL	(*)	23,562,694	23,214,698	23,001,993	23,872,884	25,216,460	100.00	5.63
AFRICA		178,648	157,224	159,662	169,455	198,599	0.79	17.20
Southern Africa				35,526	39,032			
South Africa				35,526	39,032			
Other Africa		178,648	157,224	124,136	130,423	198,599	0.79	52.27
Other countries of Africa				124,136	130,423			
All countries of Africa		178,648	157,224			198,599	0.79	
AMERICAS		1,361,957	1,256,221	1,293,723	1,371,504	1,506,835	5.98	9.87
North America		928,581	856,431	848,071	842,638	914,541	3.63	8.53
Canada		303,105	295,195	271,854	263,812	290,853	1.15	10.25
United States		625,476	561,236	576,217	578,826	623,688	2.47	7.75
South America		433,376	399,790	336,379	411,175	461,807	1.83	12.31
Brazil				336,379	411,175	461,807	1.83	12.31
All countries of South America		433,376	399,790					
Other Americas				109,273	117,691	130,487	0.52	10.87
Other countries of the Americas				109,273	117,691	130,487	0.52	10.87
EAST ASIA AND THE PACIFIC		350,836	322,733	430,914	410,703	425,686	1.69	3.65
North-East Asia		169,785	143,574	255,298	224,684	142,854	0.57	-36.42
China				33,965	35,663			
Japan		169,785	143,574	208,294	170,206	142,854	0.57	-16.07
Korea, Republic of				13,039	18,815			
Australasia		63,018	57,782	66,373	64,701	66,917	0.27	3.42
Australia		53,044	49,147	66,373	64,701	66,917	0.27	3.42
New Zealand		9,974	8,635					
Other East Asia and the Pacific		118,033	121,377	109,243	121,318	215,915	0.86	77.97
Other countries of Asia		117,887	121,024	97,785	103,209	189,479	0.75	83.59
Other countries of Oceania		146	353	11,458	18,109	26,436	0.10	45.98
EUROPE		21,671,253	21,478,520	21,117,694	21,921,222	23,085,340	91.55	5.31
Central/Eastern Europe		137,249	137,817	287,094	265,093	387,720	1.54	46.26
Hungary		35,299	41,483	46,236	55,567	68,322	0.27	22.95
Poland		101,950	96,334	78,691	97,037	167,483	0.66	72.60
Ussr (Former)				162,167	112,489	151,915	0.60	35.05
Northern Europe		10,153,473	10,246,452	9,887,227	10,178,928	10,014,727	39.72	-1.61
Denmark		312,062	312,598	352,562	468,670	490,015	1.94	4.55
Finland		346,498	364,692	388,452	393,740	371,547	1.47	-5.64
Iceland		53,197	58,423	54,726	55,945			
Ireland		971,365	1,117,667	947,901	899,550	967,287	3.84	7.53
Norway		387,442	429,517	433,971	391,748	375,262	1.49	-4.21
Sweden		676,660	578,376	629,197	591,090	553,055	2.19	-6.43
United Kingdom		7,406,249	7,385,179	7,080,418	7,378,185	7,257,561	28.78	-1.63
Southern Europe		2,893,079	2,925,797	3,208,632	3,495,508	4,197,229	16.64	20.07
Greece		44,922	49,365	77,802	46,140	49,041	0.19	6.29
Italy		779,743	722,236	737,868	723,353	953,332	3.78	31.79
Spain		2,068,414	2,154,196	2,392,962	2,726,015	3,194,856	12.67	17.20
Western Europe		8,190,090	7,865,927	7,485,662	7,752,352	8,156,017	32.34	5.21
Austria		227,816	224,305	277,017	219,805	324,968	1.29	47.84
Belgium		528,793	538,687	481,942	509,422	556,438	2.21	9.23

PORTUGAL

5. Overnight stays of non-resident tourists in hotels and similar establishments, by country of residence

	2002	2003	2004	2005	2006	Market share 06	% Change 06-05
France	1,156,272	1,201,904	1,093,163	1,111,643	1,241,117	4.92	11.65
Germany	4,104,649	3,899,433	3,771,828	3,898,469	3,862,780	15.32	-0.92
Luxembourg	37,555	37,334	37,404	43,969	48,836	0.19	11.07
Netherlands	1,825,183	1,667,028	1,495,960	1,679,343	1,795,330	7.12	6.91
Switzerland	309,822	297,236	328,348	289,701	326,548	1.29	12.72
East Mediterranean Europe	**13,741**	**18,318**	**18,240**	**21,089**			
Turkey	13,741	18,318	18,240	21,089			
Other Europe	**283,621**	**284,209**	**230,839**	**208,252**	**329,647**	**1.31**	**58.29**
Other countries of Europe	283,621	284,209	230,839	208,252	329,647	1.31	58.29

Source: World Tourism Organization (UNWTO)

PORTUGAL

6. Overnight stays of non-resident tourists in all types of accommodation establishments, by country of residence

		2002	2003	2004	2005	2006	Market share 06	% Change 06-05
TOTAL	(*)	25,118,740	24,869,946	24,617,451	25,387,817	26,842,277	100.00	5.73
AFRICA		187,405	164,912	168,758	174,279	204,975	0.76	17.61
Southern Africa				36,583	39,887			
South Africa				36,583	39,887			
Other Africa		187,405	164,912	132,175	134,392	204,975	0.76	52.52
Other countries of Africa				132,175	134,392			
All countries of Africa		187,405	164,912			204,975	0.76	
AMERICAS		1,404,935	1,300,074	1,339,538	1,414,262	1,550,482	5.78	9.63
North America		953,374	878,266	871,283	861,856	932,347	3.47	8.18
Canada		315,754	306,271	283,811	273,396	298,862	1.11	9.31
United States		637,620	571,995	587,472	588,460	633,485	2.36	7.65
South America		451,561	421,808	353,611	431,257	483,529	1.80	12.12
Brazil				353,611	431,257	483,529	1.80	12.12
All countries of South America		451,561	421,808					
Other Americas				114,644	121,149	134,606	0.50	11.11
Other countries of the Americas				114,644	121,149	134,606	0.50	11.11
EAST ASIA AND THE PACIFIC		389,303	357,771	464,052	433,588	449,942	1.68	3.77
North-East Asia		172,780	147,137	261,132	228,281	145,829	0.54	-36.12
China				34,478	35,951			
Japan		172,780	147,137	213,306	173,038	145,829	0.54	-15.72
Korea, Republic of				13,348	19,292			
Australasia		93,655	84,487	83,632	77,544	79,618	0.30	2.67
Australia		73,187	66,921	83,632	77,544	79,618	0.30	2.67
New Zealand		20,468	17,566					
Other East Asia and the Pacific		122,868	126,147	119,288	127,763	224,495	0.84	75.71
Other countries of Asia		122,696	125,765	101,300	104,455	192,265	0.72	84.06
Other countries of Oceania		172	382	17,988	23,308	32,230	0.12	38.28
EUROPE		23,137,097	23,047,189	22,645,103	23,365,688	24,636,878	91.78	5.44
Central/Eastern Europe		150,293	148,546	302,424	278,480	404,439	1.51	45.23
Hungary		38,454	44,185	49,349	58,380	71,547	0.27	22.55
Poland		111,839	104,361	87,380	106,507	170,156	0.63	59.76
Ussr (Former)				165,695	113,593	162,736	0.61	43.26
Northern Europe		10,365,011	10,496,918	10,165,689	10,453,708	10,314,058	38.42	-1.34
Denmark		328,834	330,875	370,398	483,705	508,045	1.89	5.03
Finland		353,464	373,940	397,910	406,992	383,846	1.43	-5.69
Iceland		53,234	58,516	54,814	56,027			
Ireland		977,946	1,126,214	959,758	910,889	979,981	3.65	7.59
Norway		397,935	441,101	444,788	403,859	387,781	1.44	-3.98
Sweden		684,214	587,719	649,151	599,435	564,045	2.10	-5.90
United Kingdom		7,569,384	7,578,553	7,288,870	7,592,801	7,490,360	27.91	-1.35
Southern Europe		3,185,670	3,247,253	3,516,845	3,817,062	4,571,670	17.03	19.77
Greece		47,413	50,795	81,142	47,660	50,474	0.19	5.90
Italy		838,270	779,429	796,843	777,076	1,015,696	3.78	30.71
Spain		2,299,987	2,417,029	2,638,860	2,992,326	3,505,500	13.06	17.15
Western Europe		9,115,265	8,830,217	8,381,275	8,570,073	9,000,040	33.53	5.02
Austria		240,668	235,725	289,445	230,184	335,150	1.25	45.60
Belgium		598,433	609,253	544,118	567,586	617,793	2.30	8.85

PORTUGAL

6. Overnight stays of non-resident tourists in all types of accommodation establishments, by country of residence

	2002	2003	2004	2005	2006	Market share 06	% Change 06-05
France	1,522,652	1,552,585	1,407,731	1,410,496	1,562,185	5.82	10.75
Germany	4,343,082	4,147,372	4,016,705	4,104,940	4,069,391	15.16	-0.87
Luxembourg	40,070	40,253	39,384	45,649	50,761	0.19	11.20
Netherlands	2,044,648	1,929,895	1,732,676	1,905,614	2,019,129	7.52	5.96
Switzerland	325,712	315,134	351,216	305,604	345,631	1.29	13.10
East Mediterranean Europe	**13,876**	**18,502**	**19,022**	**21,295**			
Turkey	13,876	18,502	19,022	21,295			
Other Europe	**306,982**	**305,753**	**259,848**	**225,070**	**346,671**	**1.29**	**54.03**
Other countries of Europe	306,982	305,753	259,848	225,070	346,671	1.29	54.03

Source: World Tourism Organization (UNWTO)

PUERTO RICO

1. Arrivals of non-resident tourists at national borders, by country of residence

		2002	2003	2004	2005	2006	Market share 06	% Change 06-05
TOTAL	(*)	3,087,100	3,238,300	3,541,000	3,685,900	3,722,000	100.00	0.98
AMERICAS		2,230,400	2,470,500	2,754,400	2,847,400	2,929,900	78.72	2.90
Caribbean		17,500	16,200	18,700	18,800	19,200	0.52	2.13
United States Virgin Islands		17,500	16,200	18,700	18,800	19,200	0.52	2.13
North America		2,212,900	2,454,300	2,735,700	2,828,600	2,910,700	78.20	2.90
United States		2,212,900	2,454,300	2,735,700	2,828,600	2,910,700	78.20	2.90
REGION NOT SPECIFIED		856,700	767,800	786,600	838,500	792,100	21.28	-5.53
Not Specified		856,700	767,800	786,600	838,500	792,100	21.28	-5.53
Other countries of the World		856,700	767,800	786,600	838,500	792,100	21.28	-5.53

Source: World Tourism Organization (UNWTO)

PUERTO RICO

3. Arrivals of non-resident tourists in hotels and similar establishments, by country of residence

		2002	2003	2004	2005	2006	Market share 06	% Change 06-05
TOTAL	(*)	1,203,832	1,304,610	1,371,003	1,440,008	1,497,126	100.00	3.97
AFRICA		1,393	669	452	321	410	0.03	27.73
Other Africa		1,393	669	452	321	410	0.03	27.73
All countries of Africa		1,393	669	452	321	410	0.03	27.73
AMERICAS		1,123,499	1,219,366	1,295,431	1,359,514	1,410,520	94.22	3.75
Caribbean		42,232	40,769	49,254	53,471	51,573	3.44	-3.55
Cuba		124	231	239	231	293	0.02	26.84
Dominican Republic		6,490	7,631	7,759	9,833	7,670	0.51	-22.00
United States Virgin Islands		5,601	5,580	6,274	6,765	6,447	0.43	-4.70
Other countries of the Caribbean	(*)	30,017	27,327	34,982	36,642	37,163	2.48	1.42
Central America		4,552	4,350	3,969	4,199	4,465	0.30	6.33
Belize		70	146	117	120	144	0.01	20.00
Costa Rica		1,079	1,326	1,297	1,259	1,261	0.08	0.16
El Salvador		214	183	176	243	262	0.02	7.82
Guatemala		323	361	351	401	434	0.03	8.23
Honduras		121	99	135	115	137	0.01	19.13
Nicaragua		89	113	130	145	160	0.01	10.34
Panama		774	755	784	1,008	1,007	0.07	-0.10
Other countries of Central America		1,882	1,367	979	908	1,060	0.07	16.74
North America		1,057,743	1,156,300	1,227,439	1,284,815	1,339,280	89.46	4.24
Canada		12,530	12,238	18,783	21,220	17,639	1.18	-16.88
Mexico		12,049	12,113	9,940	12,529	11,319	0.76	-9.66
United States		1,033,164	1,131,949	1,198,716	1,251,066	1,310,322	87.52	4.74
South America		18,972	17,947	14,769	17,029	15,202	1.02	-10.73
Argentina		2,470	2,444	1,736	2,032	1,544	0.10	-24.02
Bolivia		183	271	151	108	114	0.01	5.56
Brazil		1,671	1,662	1,635	1,873	1,560	0.10	-16.71
Chile		920	1,525	1,367	912	830	0.06	-8.99
Colombia		2,645	3,230	3,131	3,377	2,771	0.19	-17.94
Ecuador		276	341	221	398	250	0.02	-37.19
French Guiana		16	5	11	22	17		-22.73
Guyana		28	11	4	8	6		-25.00
Paraguay		54	33	16	26	34		30.77
Peru		760	594	716	884	680	0.05	-23.08
Suriname		19	12	7	14	5		-64.29
Uruguay		115	243	65	125	104	0.01	-16.80
Venezuela		5,785	4,568	3,616	4,451	3,622	0.24	-18.63
Other countries of South America		4,030	3,008	2,093	2,799	3,665	0.24	30.94
EAST ASIA AND THE PACIFIC		2,936	3,735	4,382	4,873	4,351	0.29	-10.71
North-East Asia		1,155	1,091	1,099	1,259	1,547	0.10	22.88
China		193	278	188	146	236	0.02	61.64
Taiwan (Province of China)		44	36	35	22	52		136.36
Hong Kong, China		43	80	133	124	441	0.03	255.65
Japan		875	697	743	967	818	0.05	-15.41
South-East Asia		298	302	453	320	441	0.03	37.81
Philippines		269	232	366	289	389	0.03	34.60
Thailand		29	70	87	31	52		67.74
Australasia		947	1,551	2,119	2,064	1,579	0.11	-23.50
Australia		894	1,493	2,078	2,025	1,480	0.10	-26.91

PUERTO RICO

3. Arrivals of non-resident tourists in hotels and similar establishments, by country of residence

	2002	2003	2004	2005	2006	Market share 06	% Change 06-05
New Zealand	53	58	41	39	99	0.01	153.85
Other East Asia and the Pacific	**536**	**791**	**711**	**1,230**	**784**	**0.05**	**-36.26**
Other countries of Asia	536	791	711	1,230	784	0.05	-36.26
EUROPE	**32,202**	**27,345**	**30,045**	**44,530**	**43,539**	**2.91**	**-2.23**
Central/Eastern Europe	**352**	**411**	**534**	**561**	**382**	**0.03**	**-31.91**
Bulgaria	33	23	32	52	18		-65.38
Czech Republic/Slovakia	34	66	85	91	85	0.01	-6.59
Hungary	65	46	90	116	58		-50.00
Poland	43	65	64	78	47		-39.74
Romania	36	43	72	58	42		-27.59
Ussr (Former)	141	168	191	166	132	0.01	-20.48
Northern Europe	**7,458**	**7,272**	**7,802**	**7,787**	**9,449**	**0.63**	**21.34**
Denmark	840	211	416	494	484	0.03	-2.02
Finland	112	291	238	501	186	0.01	-62.87
Iceland	30	31	40	28	25		-10.71
Ireland	205	171	332	540	254	0.02	-52.96
Norway	272	225	305	315	303	0.02	-3.81
Sweden	478	640	739	685	596	0.04	-12.99
United Kingdom	5,521	5,703	5,732	5,224	7,601	0.51	45.50
Southern Europe	**8,938**	**9,961**	**10,764**	**14,150**	**13,027**	**0.87**	**-7.94**
Gibraltar		12	10	11	9		-18.18
Greece	173	120	141	82	92	0.01	12.20
Italy	1,679	1,827	2,358	2,709	1,934	0.13	-28.61
Malta	18	12	15	10	21		110.00
Portugal	233	268	375	302	242	0.02	-19.87
San Marino	2	18	15		4		
Spain	6,816	7,696	7,825	11,001	10,700	0.71	-2.74
Yugoslavia, Sfr (Former)	17	8	25	35	25		-28.57
Western Europe	**8,162**	**7,317**	**7,701**	**9,828**	**7,117**	**0.48**	**-27.58**
Austria	515	546	259	321	471	0.03	46.73
Belgium	453	486	451	450	491	0.03	9.11
France	1,957	1,775	2,009	2,705	1,897	0.13	-29.87
Germany	3,371	2,858	3,038	4,395	2,608	0.17	-40.66
Luxembourg	21	19	9	13	14		7.69
Netherlands	1,152	916	934	774	733	0.05	-5.30
Switzerland	693	717	1,001	1,170	903	0.06	-22.82
East Mediterranean Europe	**359**	**310**	**382**	**354**	**611**	**0.04**	**72.60**
Israel	241	242	285	234	540	0.04	130.77
Turkey	118	68	97	120	71		-40.83
Other Europe	**6,933**	**2,074**	**2,862**	**11,850**	**12,953**	**0.87**	**9.31**
Other countries of Europe	6,933	2,074	2,862	11,850	12,953	0.87	9.31
MIDDLE EAST	**72**	**197**	**210**	**150**	**78**	**0.01**	**-48.00**
Middle East	**72**	**197**	**210**	**150**	**78**	**0.01**	**-48.00**
Iraq	2			5	12		140.00
Saudi Arabia	22	154	168	101	50		-50.50
Egypt	48	43	42	44	16		-63.64
REGION NOT SPECIFIED	**43,730**	**53,298**	**40,483**	**30,620**	**38,228**	**2.55**	**24.85**
Not Specified	**43,730**	**53,298**	**40,483**	**30,620**	**38,228**	**2.55**	**24.85**
Other countries of the World (*)	23,243	32,880	31,320	18,788	21,917	1.46	16.65

PUERTO RICO

3. Arrivals of non-resident tourists in hotels and similar establishments, by country of residence

	2002	2003	2004	2005	2006	Market share 06	% Change 06-05
Nationals Residing Abroad	20,487	20,418	9,163	11,832	16,311	1.09	37.85

Source: World Tourism Organization (UNWTO)

QATAR

3. Arrivals of non-resident tourists in hotels and similar establishments, by country of residence

		2002	2003	2004	2005	2006	Market share 06	% Change 06-05
TOTAL	(*)	586,645	556,965	732,454	912,997	945,970	100.00	3.61
EAST ASIA AND THE PACIFIC		107,832	127,348	145,974	159,279	180,543	19.09	13.35
Other East Asia and the Pacific		107,832	127,348	145,974	159,279	180,543	19.09	13.35
All countries of Asia		107,832	127,348	145,974	159,279	180,543	19.09	13.35
EUROPE		102,983	88,620	195,732	233,315	201,187	21.27	-13.77
Other Europe		102,983	88,620	195,732	233,315	201,187	21.27	-13.77
All countries of Europe		102,983	88,620	195,732	233,315	201,187	21.27	-13.77
MIDDLE EAST		312,063	282,538	295,335	364,977	413,523	43.71	13.30
Middle East		312,063	282,538	295,335	364,977	413,523	43.71	13.30
All countries of Middle East		312,063	282,538	295,335	364,977	413,523	43.71	13.30
REGION NOT SPECIFIED		63,767	58,459	95,413	155,426	150,717	15.93	-3.03
Not Specified		63,767	58,459	95,413	155,426	150,717	15.93	-3.03
Other countries of the World		63,767	58,459	95,413	155,426	150,717	15.93	-3.03

Source: World Tourism Organization (UNWTO)

QATAR

5. Overnight stays of non-resident tourists in hotels and similar establishments, by country of residence

		2002	2003	2004	2005	2006	Market share 06	% Change 06-05
TOTAL	(*)	697,616	848,395	982,619	1,023,698	1,146,922	100.00	12.04
EAST ASIA AND THE PACIFIC		129,372	165,060	186,154	188,970	209,557	18.27	10.89
Other East Asia and the Pacific		129,372	165,060	186,154	188,970	209,557	18.27	10.89
All countries of Asia		129,372	165,060	186,154	188,970	209,557	18.27	10.89
EUROPE		155,321	165,335	243,446	260,095	260,892	22.75	0.31
Other Europe		155,321	165,335	243,446	260,095	260,892	22.75	0.31
All countries of Europe		155,321	165,335	243,446	260,095	260,892	22.75	0.31
MIDDLE EAST		327,458	405,781	419,185	419,532	511,475	44.60	21.92
Middle East		327,458	405,781	419,185	419,532	511,475	44.60	21.92
All countries of Middle East		327,458	405,781	419,185	419,532	511,475	44.60	21.92
REGION NOT SPECIFIED		85,465	112,219	133,834	155,101	164,998	14.39	6.38
Not Specified		85,465	112,219	133,834	155,101	164,998	14.39	6.38
Other countries of the World		85,465	112,219	133,834	155,101	164,998	14.39	6.38

Source: World Tourism Organization (UNWTO)

REPUBLIC OF MOLDOVA

2. Arrivals of non-resident visitors at national borders, by nationality

		2002	2003	2004	2005	2006	Market share 06	% Change 06-05
TOTAL	(*)	20,161	23,598	26,045	25,073	14,240	100.00	-43.21
AFRICA		40	45	71	15	10	0.07	-33.33
East Africa		4	8	11		1	0.01	
Kenya			4			1	0.01	
Rwanda			1	5				
Zimbabwe			1					
Uganda		2	2	5				
United Republic of Tanzania		1		1				
Zambia		1						
Central Africa		1	2	8	2			
Angola				3				
Cameroon			1	3	1			
Chad				1				
Congo		1	1	1	1			
North Africa		5	21	19	7	6	0.04	-14.29
Algeria			1					
Morocco			5	3				
Sudan		3	14	9	3	2	0.01	-33.33
Tunisia		2	1	7	4	4	0.03	
Southern Africa		1	6	16	4	2	0.01	-50.00
Botswana				10				
South Africa		1	6	6	4	2	0.01	-50.00
West Africa		29	8	17	2	1	0.01	-50.00
Guinea				2				
Liberia					1			
Mauritania		1		4				
Niger		1						
Nigeria		1	5	11	1	1	0.01	
Senegal			3					
Sierra Leone		26						
AMERICAS		1,788	2,556	2,564	3,161	1,123	7.89	-64.47
Caribbean			2	19	1	2	0.01	100.00
Cuba			1	17		2	0.01	
Dominican Republic			1	2				
Haiti					1			
Central America		11		3	1			
Costa Rica		11		3				
Panama					1			
North America		1,762	2,543	2,536	3,141	1,108	7.78	-64.72
Canada		52	49	31	52	36	0.25	-30.77
Greenland						1	0.01	
Mexico		3		1	1	5	0.04	400.00
United States		1,707	2,494	2,504	3,088	1,066	7.49	-65.48
South America		15	11	6	18	13	0.09	-27.78
Argentina		5	2	2	4	7	0.05	75.00
Bolivia		1						
Brazil			4	4	11	3	0.02	-72.73
Chile		1			2			
Colombia		3						
Ecuador					1			
Peru		2	2			3	0.02	

REPUBLIC OF MOLDOVA

2. Arrivals of non-resident visitors at national borders, by nationality

	2002	2003	2004	2005	2006	Market share 06	% Change 06-05
Suriname		1					
Venezuela	3	2					
EAST ASIA AND THE PACIFIC	**411**	**295**	**307**	**277**	**243**	**1.71**	**-12.27**
North-East Asia	**394**	**259**	**298**	**240**	**227**	**1.59**	**-5.42**
China	247	85	58	87	29	0.20	-66.67
Taiwan (Province of China)	13	14	89	56	14	0.10	-75.00
Hong Kong, China					1	0.01	
Japan	118	139	89	82	139	0.98	69.51
Korea, Dem. People's Republic of	1	2	13	1	4	0.03	300.00
Korea, Republic of	14	19	18	4	39	0.27	875.00
Mongolia	1		31	10	1	0.01	-90.00
South-East Asia	**3**	**12**	**2**	**13**	**4**	**0.03**	**-69.23**
Indonesia	1	7	1	8	1	0.01	-87.50
Malaysia	1	1	1	4			
Philippines				1	3	0.02	200.00
Singapore		2					
Viet Nam	1	1					
Thailand		1					
Australasia	**11**	**24**	**7**	**24**	**12**	**0.08**	**-50.00**
Australia	6	19	6	18	7	0.05	-61.11
New Zealand	5	5	1	6	5	0.04	-16.67
Melanesia	**3**						
New Caledonia	3						
EUROPE	**17,631**	**20,152**	**22,686**	**21,223**	**12,741**	**89.47**	**-39.97**
Central/Eastern Europe	**11,283**	**11,336**	**12,474**	**13,133**	**7,469**	**52.45**	**-43.13**
Azerbaijan	97	23	107	78	73	0.51	-6.41
Armenia	36	26	94	23	8	0.06	-65.22
Bulgaria	326	625	471	448	295	2.07	-34.15
Belarus	720	750	1,072	1,161	580	4.07	-50.04
Czech Republic	224	100	218	123	126	0.88	2.44
Estonia	27	75	27	71	15	0.11	-78.87
Georgia	88	35	107	46	66	0.46	43.48
Hungary	160	171	146	173	135	0.95	-21.97
Kazakhstan	85	45	87	88	26	0.18	-70.45
Kyrgyzstan	29	19	13	20	19	0.13	-5.00
Latvia	223	39	54	82	69	0.48	-15.85
Lithuania	83	115	128	125	110	0.77	-12.00
Poland	486	320	428	443	262	1.84	-40.86
Romania	1,929	2,381	2,350	3,496	2,787	19.57	-20.28
Russian Federation	3,758	3,270	3,952	3,294	1,353	9.50	-58.93
Slovakia	5	23	5	17	59	0.41	247.06
Tajikistan	16	4	30	8	6	0.04	-25.00
Turkmenistan	3	4		7			
Ukraine	2,947	3,283	3,173	3,406	1,472	10.34	-56.78
Uzbekistan	41	28	12	24	8	0.06	-66.67
Northern Europe	**518**	**664**	**3,407**	**815**	**693**	**4.87**	**-14.97**
Denmark	23	44	25	50	233	1.64	366.00
Finland	32	17	26	28	25	0.18	-10.71
Iceland	3	25	1		5	0.04	
Ireland	70	39	29	57	27	0.19	-52.63
Norway	44	69	156	179	62	0.44	-65.36
Sweden	156	251	116	136	50	0.35	-63.24

REPUBLIC OF MOLDOVA

2. Arrivals of non-resident visitors at national borders, by nationality

	2002	2003	2004	2005	2006	Market share 06	% Change 06-05
United Kingdom	190	219	3,054	365	291	2.04	-20.27
Southern Europe	**998**	**1,117**	**1,326**	**1,989**	**1,190**	**8.36**	**-40.17**
Albania	10	30	14	41	11	0.08	-73.17
Andorra	1						
Bosnia and Herzegovina	9	13	10	4	48	0.34	1,100.00
Croatia	17	9	9	20	39	0.27	95.00
Greece	120	103	88	177	215	1.51	21.47
Italy	491	702	1,019	1,141	663	4.66	-41.89
Malta	1		5	26			
Portugal	62	12	41	36	47	0.33	30.56
San Marino	2						
Slovenia	96	56	47	275	35	0.25	-87.27
Spain	118	58	65	98	64	0.45	-34.69
TFYR of Macedonia	16	18	22	53	9	0.06	-83.02
Serbia and Montenegro	55	116	6	118	59	0.41	-50.00
Western Europe	**1,033**	**2,400**	**1,472**	**1,877**	**1,504**	**10.56**	**-19.87**
Austria	63	451	153	205	147	1.03	-28.29
Belgium	43	39	64	70	81	0.57	15.71
France	179	305	319	464	266	1.87	-42.67
Germany	560	717	632	703	673	4.73	-4.27
Liechtenstein				1			
Luxembourg	2	2	1	55	3	0.02	-94.55
Netherlands	161	529	223	268	199	1.40	-25.75
Switzerland	25	357	80	111	135	0.95	21.62
East Mediterranean Europe	**3,799**	**4,635**	**4,007**	**3,409**	**1,885**	**13.24**	**-44.71**
Cyprus	514	266	62	75	49	0.34	-34.67
Israel	416	404	424	296	149	1.05	-49.66
Turkey	2,869	3,965	3,521	3,038	1,687	11.85	-44.47
MIDDLE EAST	**281**	**525**	**392**	**362**	**114**	**0.80**	**-68.51**
Middle East	**281**	**525**	**392**	**362**	**114**	**0.80**	**-68.51**
Bahrain					1	0.01	
Iraq	5		6	5			
Jordan	10	47	26	14	6	0.04	-57.14
Kuwait	3	10	20	6	3	0.02	-50.00
Lebanon	220	333	263	173	72	0.51	-58.38
Libyan Arab Jamahiriya		1					
Oman		2	3				
Qatar			1	1			
Saudi Arabia	8	15	10	13	4	0.03	-69.23
Syrian Arab Republic	19	86	44	129	16	0.11	-87.60
United Arab Emirates	4	5	6	4	2	0.01	-50.00
Egypt	5	26	10	15	10	0.07	-33.33
Yemen	7		3	2			
SOUTH ASIA	**10**	**25**	**25**	**35**	**9**	**0.06**	**-74.29**
South Asia	**10**	**25**	**25**	**35**	**9**	**0.06**	**-74.29**
Bangladesh	2						
Sri Lanka			4	2			
India	6	12	10	30	6	0.04	-80.00
Iran, Islamic Republic of	1	8	9	1	1	0.01	
Pakistan	1	5	2	2	2	0.01	

Source: World Tourism Organization (UNWTO)

REPUBLIC OF MOLDOVA

4. Arrivals of non-resident tourists in all types of accommodation establishments, by nationality

		2002	2003	2004	2005	2006	Market share 06	% Change 06-05
TOTAL	(*)			68,829	67,235	62,771	100.00	-6.64
AFRICA				130	96	80	0.13	-16.67
Other Africa				130	96	80	0.13	-16.67
All countries of Africa				130	96	80	0.13	-16.67
AMERICAS				7,504	6,599	5,012	7.98	-24.05
North America				7,408	6,524	4,954	7.89	-24.06
Canada				322	301	243	0.39	-19.27
United States				7,063	6,206	4,534	7.22	-26.94
Other countries of North America				23	17	177	0.28	941.18
South America				73	55	46	0.07	-16.36
All countries of South America				73	55	46	0.07	-16.36
Other Americas				23	20	12	0.02	-40.00
Other countries of the Americas				23	20	12	0.02	-40.00
EAST ASIA AND THE PACIFIC				1,337	1,158	1,265	2.02	9.24
North-East Asia				591	488	741	1.18	51.84
China				266	212	368	0.59	73.58
Japan				325	276	373	0.59	35.14
Other East Asia and the Pacific				746	670	524	0.83	-21.79
Other countries of Asia				593	527	327	0.52	-37.95
All countries of Oceania				153	143	197	0.31	37.76
EUROPE				59,858	59,382	56,414	89.87	-5.00
Central/Eastern Europe				31,221	36,233	33,499	53.37	-7.55
Azerbaijan				410	600	395	0.63	-34.17
Armenia				288	188	148	0.24	-21.28
Bulgaria				1,084	1,158	830	1.32	-28.32
Belarus				1,706	2,120	1,473	2.35	-30.52
Czech Republic				479	437	529	0.84	21.05
Estonia				111	221	296	0.47	33.94
Georgia				295	359	317	0.51	-11.70
Hungary				449	431	480	0.76	11.37
Kazakhstan				306	323	325	0.52	0.62
Kyrgyzstan				209	77	119	0.19	54.55
Latvia				130	177	293	0.47	65.54
Lithuania				293	461	516	0.82	11.93
Poland				844	1,502	1,220	1.94	-18.77
Romania				7,809	11,549	13,187	21.01	14.18
Russian Federation				8,347	8,134	5,904	9.41	-27.42
Slovakia				128	188	220	0.35	17.02
Tajikistan				82	43	42	0.07	-2.33
Turkmenistan				14	27	10	0.02	-62.96
Ukraine				8,152	8,121	7,066	11.26	-12.99
Uzbekistan				85	117	129	0.21	10.26
Northern Europe				5,394	3,869	3,254	5.18	-15.90
Denmark				226	240	385	0.61	60.42
Finland				196	218	200	0.32	-8.26
Ireland				227	232	251	0.40	8.19
Norway				332	583	188	0.30	-67.75
Sweden				727	663	506	0.81	-23.68
United Kingdom				3,686	1,933	1,724	2.75	-10.81

REPUBLIC OF MOLDOVA

4. Arrivals of non-resident tourists in all types of accommodation establishments, by nationality

	2002	2003	2004	2005	2006	Market share 06	% Change 06-05
Southern Europe			6,275	6,433	6,290	10.02	-2.22
Albania			151	122	77	0.12	-36.89
Bosnia and Herzegovina			133	115	147	0.23	27.83
Croatia			81	141	217	0.35	53.90
Greece			682	743	1,064	1.70	43.20
Italy			4,012	3,884	3,788	6.03	-2.47
Portugal			141	129	97	0.15	-24.81
Slovenia			277	412	223	0.36	-45.87
Spain			687	669	473	0.75	-29.30
Serbia and Montenegro			111	218	204	0.32	-6.42
Western Europe			6,193	6,591	6,808	10.85	3.29
Austria			530	710	812	1.29	14.37
Belgium			400	451	490	0.78	8.65
France			1,207	1,415	1,404	2.24	-0.78
Germany			2,692	2,581	2,872	4.58	11.27
Luxembourg			68	41	29	0.05	-29.27
Netherlands			884	977	790	1.26	-19.14
Switzerland			412	416	411	0.65	-1.20
East Mediterranean Europe			9,573	5,826	6,198	9.87	6.39
Israel			1,115	813	1,112	1.77	36.78
Turkey			8,458	5,013	5,086	8.10	1.46
Other Europe			1,202	430	365	0.58	-15.12
Other countries of Europe			1,202	430	365	0.58	-15.12

Source: World Tourism Organization (UNWTO)

REUNION

1. Arrivals of non-resident tourists at national borders, by country of residence

	2002	2003	2004	2005	2006	Market share 06	% Change 06-05
TOTAL	426,000	432,000	430,000	409,000	278,800	100.00	-31.83
AFRICA	30,625	27,367	26,222	24,815	20,109	7.21	-18.96
East Africa	30,625	27,367	26,222	24,815	20,109	7.21	-18.96
Mauritius	30,625	27,367	26,222	24,815	20,109	7.21	-18.96
EUROPE	356,828	366,725	370,474	349,113	224,065	80.37	-35.82
Southern Europe			3,176				
Italy			3,176				
Western Europe	334,255	347,219	356,379	329,938	209,500	75.14	-36.50
France	334,255	347,219	343,171	329,938	209,500	75.14	-36.50
Germany			8,491				
Switzerland			4,717				
Other Europe	22,573	19,506	10,919	19,175	14,565	5.22	-24.04
Other countries of Europe	22,573	19,506	10,919	19,175	14,565	5.22	-24.04
REGION NOT SPECIFIED	38,547	37,908	33,304	35,072	34,626	12.42	-1.27
Not Specified	38,547	37,908	33,304	35,072	34,626	12.42	-1.27
Other countries of the World	38,547	37,908	33,304	35,072	34,626	12.42	-1.27

Source: World Tourism Organization (UNWTO)

ROMANIA

2. Arrivals of non-resident visitors at national borders, by country of residence

	2002	2003	2004	2005	2006	Market share 06	% Change 06-05
TOTAL	4,793,722	5,594,828	6,600,115	5,839,374	6,036,999	100.00	3.38
AFRICA	4,984	5,461	6,585	6,992	9,274	0.15	32.64
East Africa	366	404	574	585	695	0.01	18.80
Burundi	1	6	8	3	32		966.67
Comoros	3	1	3	2	11		450.00
Ethiopia	28	28	38	31	28		-9.68
Eritrea	8	2	16	4	5		25.00
Djibouti	3	6	2	1	16		1,500.00
Kenya	31	66	124	94	77		-18.09
Madagascar	4	19	23	22	52		136.36
Mauritius	82	103	178	281	301		7.12
Mozambique	5	2	11	9	43		377.78
Rwanda	9	9	8	6	10		66.67
Somalia	80	62	27	18	9		-50.00
Zimbabwe	25	31	38	33	40		21.21
Uganda	34	19	17	20	9		-55.00
United Republic of Tanzania	45	29	54	35	50		42.86
Zambia	8	21	27	26	12		-53.85
Central Africa	257	310	423	356	645	0.01	81.18
Angola	46	67	64	42	73		73.81
Cameroon	41	56	81	66	105		59.09
Central African Republic	50	26	41	35	54		54.29
Chad		1	4	5	14		180.00
Congo	96	111	194	163	241		47.85
Democratic Republic of the Congo		2	2		5		
Equatorial Guinea	2	21			40		
Gabon	22	26	36	40	105		162.50
Sao Tome and Principe			1	1	8		700.00
Other countries of Central Africa				4			
North Africa	2,555	2,781	3,381	3,858	4,692	0.08	21.62
Algeria	314	355	539	573	628	0.01	9.60
Morocco	730	721	816	846	991	0.02	17.14
Sudan	302	292	279	200	219		9.50
Tunisia	1,209	1,413	1,747	2,239	2,854	0.05	27.47
Southern Africa	983	1,170	1,302	1,251	1,729	0.03	38.21
Botswana	1	9	5	23	30		30.43
Lesotho	1	2	9	3	4		33.33
Namibia	12	34	15	7	9		28.57
South Africa	969	1,125	1,273	1,218	1,686	0.03	38.42
West Africa	823	796	905	942	1,513	0.03	60.62
Cape Verde	23	26	22	19	31		63.16
Benin	17	8	17	18	73		305.56
Gambia	16	2	6	6	6		
Ghana	115	92	101	81	114		40.74
Guinea	68	61	45	58	123		112.07
Cote D'Ivoire	26	35	34	32	84		162.50
Liberia	11	7	5	12	4		-66.67
Mali	18	9	18	13	55		323.08
Mauritania	13	7	21	7	50		614.29
Niger	3	1	2	10	14		40.00
Nigeria	403	415	494	585	576	0.01	-1.54
Guinea-Bissau	2	9	1	1	1		
Senegal	81	92	91	61	226		270.49

ROMANIA

2. Arrivals of non-resident visitors at national borders, by country of residence

	2002	2003	2004	2005	2006	Market share 06	% Change 06-05
Sierra Leone	2	5	8	11	9		-18.18
Togo	12	8	23	17	54		217.65
Burkina Faso	13	19	17	11	93		745.45
AMERICAS	**102,481**	**115,373**	**139,463**	**154,244**	**171,930**	**2.85**	**11.47**
Caribbean	**148**	**244**	**273**	**340**	**332**	**0.01**	**-2.35**
Cuba	100	184	187	252	182		-27.78
Dominican Republic	13	36	47	45	55		22.22
Haiti		3	8	9	16		77.78
Jamaica	35	21	31	34	79		132.35
Central America	**308**	**301**	**371**	**396**	**490**	**0.01**	**23.74**
Belize	4	5	6	4	7		75.00
Costa Rica	126	123	116	120	126		5.00
El Salvador	14	11	40	34	32		-5.88
Guatemala	24	17	32	55	69		25.45
Honduras	58	88	108	128	172		34.38
Nicaragua	14	15	28	18	39		116.67
Panama	68	42	41	37	45		21.62
North America	**98,813**	**111,851**	**135,095**	**148,843**	**165,316**	**2.74**	**11.07**
Canada	16,347	19,091	23,553	27,591	33,637	0.56	21.91
Mexico	729	830	924	1,345	1,438	0.02	6.91
United States	81,737	91,930	110,618	119,907	130,241	2.16	8.62
South America	**3,212**	**2,977**	**3,724**	**4,665**	**5,792**	**0.10**	**24.16**
Argentina	493	551	804	1,080	1,455	0.02	34.72
Bolivia	56	57	69	78	86		10.26
Brazil	954	901	1,114	1,425	1,799	0.03	26.25
Chile	306	356	434	482	645	0.01	33.82
Colombia	527	305	309	344	383	0.01	11.34
Ecuador	219	188	300	265	364	0.01	37.36
Guyana	1	2	6	5	8		60.00
Paraguay	27	10	22	40	25		-37.50
Peru	225	247	288	328	381	0.01	16.16
Suriname	1	1	7	4	3		-25.00
Uruguay	91	40	78	141	82		-41.84
Venezuela	312	319	293	473	561	0.01	18.60
EAST ASIA AND THE PACIFIC	**41,703**	**41,610**	**49,309**	**57,028**	**61,921**	**1.03**	**8.58**
North-East Asia	**23,118**	**22,333**	**27,457**	**29,920**	**32,763**	**0.54**	**9.50**
China	7,854	6,807	8,708	10,310	11,402	0.19	10.59
Taiwan (Province of China)	334	463	533	733	612	0.01	-16.51
Hong Kong, China	95	133	263	348	477	0.01	37.07
Japan	10,391	10,615	13,019	13,736	14,185	0.23	3.27
Korea, Dem. People's Republic of	293	153	224	241	93		-61.41
Korea, Republic of	3,944	3,977	4,389	4,385	5,833	0.10	33.02
Mongolia	207	185	321	167	161		-3.59
South-East Asia	**12,006**	**13,478**	**14,772**	**18,922**	**20,323**	**0.34**	**7.40**
Myanmar	210	313	596	916	506	0.01	-44.76
Cambodia	3	1	8	10	11		10.00
Indonesia	517	867	923	1,333	2,459	0.04	84.47
Lao People's Democratic Republic	1	7	6	2	8		300.00
Malaysia	315	428	457	583	837	0.01	43.57
Philippines	9,778	10,518	11,323	14,313	14,661	0.24	2.43
Singapore	176	221	257	317	420	0.01	32.49
Viet Nam	463	543	551	700	788	0.01	12.57

ROMANIA

2. Arrivals of non-resident visitors at national borders, by country of residence

	2002	2003	2004	2005	2006	Market share 06	% Change 06-05
Thailand	543	580	651	748	633	0.01	-15.37
Australasia	**6,081**	**5,700**	**7,023**	**8,154**	**8,809**	**0.15**	**8.03**
Australia	5,010	4,725	5,913	6,859	7,448	0.12	8.59
New Zealand	1,071	975	1,110	1,295	1,361	0.02	5.10
Melanesia	**1**	**6**	**17**	**11**	**6**		**-45.45**
Fiji	1	6	17	11	6		-45.45
Other East Asia and the Pacific	**497**	**93**	**40**	**21**	**20**		**-4.76**
Other countries East Asia/Pacific	497	93	40	21	20		-4.76
EUROPE	**4,603,867**	**5,391,609**	**6,360,587**	**5,580,091**	**5,751,503**	**95.27**	**3.07**
Central/Eastern Europe	**3,071,413**	**3,663,122**	**4,875,674**	**3,930,759**	**3,967,390**	**65.72**	**0.93**
Azerbaijan	910	1,380	1,813	1,386	1,962	0.03	41.56
Armenia	542	506	516	812	649	0.01	-20.07
Bulgaria	362,660	340,291	375,426	389,460	399,286	6.61	2.52
Belarus	25,480	23,228	25,076	33,626	43,309	0.72	28.80
Czech Republic	77,890	64,881	60,680	50,159	51,509	0.85	2.69
Estonia	1,110	1,288	1,846	1,182	1,801	0.03	52.37
Georgia	1,074	803	1,394	1,751	2,497	0.04	42.60
Hungary	1,152,599	1,537,114	2,603,477	1,522,166	1,366,686	22.64	-10.21
Kazakhstan	409	485	745	583	623	0.01	6.86
Kyrgyzstan	50	97	60	76	66		-13.16
Latvia	1,664	2,495	2,423	2,572	2,090	0.03	-18.74
Lithuania	5,143	3,994	4,702	4,172	4,436	0.07	6.33
Republic of Moldova	856,723	1,058,636	1,212,752	1,435,221	1,489,691	24.68	3.80
Poland	112,888	108,729	132,934	62,015	74,556	1.23	20.22
Russian Federation	79,868	85,251	53,121	48,745	54,036	0.90	10.85
Slovakia	102,747	84,450	88,709	47,710	40,654	0.67	-14.79
Tajikistan	42	12	16	32	23		-28.13
Turkmenistan	33	27	78	56	38		-32.14
Ukraine	289,383	349,268	309,752	328,419	433,392	7.18	31.96
Uzbekistan	158	160	137	606	84		-86.14
Other countries Central/East Europ	40	27	17	10	2		-80.00
Northern Europe	**111,705**	**124,977**	**95,625**	**126,337**	**156,441**	**2.59**	**23.83**
Denmark	12,178	12,958	11,411	15,453	17,386	0.29	12.51
Finland	4,008	4,360	3,828	4,424	6,810	0.11	53.93
Iceland	238	279	436	393	716	0.01	82.19
Ireland	5,565	6,344	5,479	6,418	10,725	0.18	67.11
Norway	9,448	10,419	5,682	6,677	12,039	0.20	80.31
Sweden	20,641	21,956	14,178	16,463	18,361	0.30	11.53
United Kingdom	59,627	68,661	54,611	76,509	90,404	1.50	18.16
Southern Europe	**528,389**	**655,126**	**571,890**	**564,950**	**615,659**	**10.20**	**8.98**
Albania	2,411	2,514	2,683	2,483	2,575	0.04	3.71
Bosnia and Herzegovina	2,393	2,160	2,585	2,829	3,257	0.05	15.13
Croatia	19,810	20,277	25,630	27,534	29,059	0.48	5.54
Greece	59,338	59,942	45,749	61,362	64,073	1.06	4.42
Holy See	11	17	16	11	12		9.09
Italy	230,454	258,830	230,628	270,864	277,916	4.60	2.60
Malta	305	516	1,014	603	669	0.01	10.95
Portugal	3,658	4,291	3,606	6,544	9,238	0.15	41.17
San Marino	170	208	961	231	215		-6.93
Slovenia	7,572	8,212	11,298	9,382	12,396	0.21	32.13
Spain	17,356	21,328	20,321	29,355	42,606	0.71	45.14
TFYR of Macedonia	10,268	5,541	7,052	5,733	6,805	0.11	18.70
Serbia and Montenegro	174,643	271,290	220,347	148,019	166,838	2.76	12.71

ROMANIA

2. Arrivals of non-resident visitors at national borders, by country of residence

	2002	2003	2004	2005	2006	Market share 06	% Change 06-05
Western Europe	641,784	688,499	560,452	690,012	722,278	11.96	4.68
Austria	87,995	101,182	90,300	129,173	151,510	2.51	17.29
Belgium	24,098	26,798	24,473	27,155	26,672	0.44	-1.78
France	91,788	101,080	93,008	109,976	129,518	2.15	17.77
Germany	358,738	380,478	296,133	353,621	342,675	5.68	-3.10
Liechtenstein	135	129	232	107	515	0.01	381.31
Luxembourg	1,007	1,256	858	756	1,263	0.02	67.06
Monaco	11	9	16	14	22		57.14
Netherlands	56,490	58,277	39,407	53,074	50,486	0.84	-4.88
Switzerland	21,522	19,290	16,025	16,136	19,617	0.32	21.57
East Mediterranean Europe	250,576	259,885	256,946	268,033	289,735	4.80	8.10
Cyprus	6,318	6,840	6,830	8,606	8,845	0.15	2.78
Israel	52,811	47,850	54,794	58,568	61,777	1.02	5.48
Turkey	191,447	205,195	195,322	200,859	219,113	3.63	9.09
MIDDLE EAST	27,105	26,867	27,760	24,090	25,049	0.41	3.98
Middle East	27,105	26,867	27,760	24,090	25,049	0.41	3.98
Bahrain	40	77	39	38	41		7.89
Palestine	227	282	368	340	313	0.01	-7.94
Iraq	1,279	801	1,356	1,244	1,545	0.03	24.20
Jordan	2,048	1,792	1,980	1,838	1,906	0.03	3.70
Kuwait	1,251	1,144	810	670	553	0.01	-17.46
Lebanon	4,122	4,060	4,180	4,030	4,158	0.07	3.18
Libyan Arab Jamahiriya	383	288	237	256	278		8.59
Oman	59	36	92	48	74		54.17
Qatar	142	125	118	92	147		59.78
Saudi Arabia	1,314	873	707	692	458	0.01	-33.82
Syrian Arab Republic	11,570	12,328	12,248	9,743	10,452	0.17	7.28
United Arab Emirates	792	714	602	607	620	0.01	2.14
Egypt	3,720	4,214	4,891	4,392	4,391	0.07	-0.02
Yemen	158	133	132	100	113		13.00
SOUTH ASIA	12,423	12,856	15,344	15,566	15,774	0.26	1.34
South Asia	12,423	12,856	15,344	15,566	15,774	0.26	1.34
Afghanistan	23	39	37	30	50		66.67
Bangladesh	110	101	220	294	106		-63.95
Sri Lanka	507	420	374	456	349	0.01	-23.46
India	4,773	4,024	5,864	6,033	6,632	0.11	9.93
Iran, Islamic Republic of	5,709	7,149	7,182	6,429	6,332	0.10	-1.51
Maldives	99	36	181	122	84		-31.15
Nepal	22	16	32	28	38		35.71
Pakistan	1,180	1,071	1,454	2,174	2,183	0.04	0.41
REGION NOT SPECIFIED	1,159	1,052	1,067	1,363	1,548	0.03	13.57
Not Specified	1,159	1,052	1,067	1,363	1,548	0.03	13.57
Other countries of the World	1,159	1,052	1,067	1,363	1,548	0.03	13.57

Source: World Tourism Organization (UNWTO)

ROMANIA

3. Arrivals of non-resident tourists in hotels and similar establishments, by country of residence

		2002	2003	2004	2005	2006	Market share 06	% Change 06-05
TOTAL		981,797	1,085,569	1,332,132	1,406,514	1,363,012	100.00	-3.09
AFRICA		4,683	5,239	7,098	7,494	7,934	0.58	5.87
Other Africa		4,683	5,239	7,098	7,494	7,934	0.58	5.87
All countries of Africa	(*)	4,683	5,239	7,098	7,494	7,934	0.58	5.87
AMERICAS		70,540	78,853	110,548	115,946	122,313	8.97	5.49
Central America		2,015	1,790	2,049				
All countries of Central America	(*)	2,015	1,790	2,049				
North America		66,149	74,842	104,934	110,953	116,353	8.54	4.87
Canada		7,943	8,023	10,407	10,915	17,391	1.28	59.33
Mexico					1,676	921	0.07	-45.05
United States		58,206	66,819	94,527	98,362	98,041	7.19	-0.33
South America		2,376	2,221	3,565				
All countries of South America		2,376	2,221	3,565				
Other Americas					4,993	5,960	0.44	19.37
Other countries of the Americas					4,993	5,960	0.44	19.37
EAST ASIA AND THE PACIFIC		42,180	40,113	50,824	55,325	56,900	4.17	2.85
North-East Asia		22,698	22,002	28,133	28,557	25,353	1.86	-11.22
China		4,250	3,605	4,960	5,339	4,809	0.35	-9.93
Japan		18,448	18,397	23,173	23,218	20,544	1.51	-11.52
Other East Asia and the Pacific		19,482	18,111	22,691	26,768	31,547	2.31	17.85
Other countries of Asia		15,760	14,641	15,975	19,168	23,288	1.71	21.49
All countries of Oceania		3,722	3,470	6,716	7,600	8,259	0.61	8.67
EUROPE		864,394	961,364	1,163,662	1,222,261	1,168,381	85.72	-4.41
Central/Eastern Europe		141,095	165,898	208,763	202,024	197,385	14.48	-2.30
Bulgaria		8,677	10,550	12,233	13,486	15,103	1.11	11.99
Czech Republic		8,379	10,071	11,787	15,493	16,669	1.22	7.59
Hungary		61,313	77,638	95,891	87,789	79,340	5.82	-9.62
Republic of Moldova		28,934	28,765	35,631	28,752	27,607	2.03	-3.98
Poland		9,802	13,095	19,424	24,836	22,659	1.66	-8.77
Russian Federation		10,960	13,070	16,407	14,582	15,415	1.13	5.71
Slovakia		4,182	4,103	7,004	7,773	6,623	0.49	-14.79
Ukraine		8,848	8,606	10,386	9,313	13,969	1.02	49.99
Northern Europe		92,858	108,171	136,374	155,735	138,716	10.18	-10.93
Denmark		11,516	12,690	16,244	22,698	15,727	1.15	-30.71
Finland		4,141	3,670	10,760	14,365	7,946	0.58	-44.68
Ireland		4,099	4,909	5,116	5,300	8,286	0.61	56.34
Norway		7,423	8,939	10,607	11,923	13,676	1.00	14.70
Sweden		11,831	12,021	18,938	19,049	14,541	1.07	-23.67
United Kingdom		53,848	65,942	74,709	82,400	78,540	5.76	-4.68
Southern Europe		204,269	232,281	288,824	285,432	285,781	20.97	0.12
Greece		20,899	24,273	25,792	33,496	33,037	2.42	-1.37
Italy		138,747	159,319	198,956	193,872	181,845	13.34	-6.20
Montenegro						1,102	0.08	
Portugal		3,377	3,537	4,493	6,241	12,318	0.90	97.37
Serbia						4,966	0.36	
Slovenia		3,104	3,176	5,665	5,354	7,984	0.59	49.12
Spain		28,709	31,223	41,459	41,117	44,529	3.27	8.30
Serbia and Montenegro		9,433	10,753	12,459	5,352			

ROMANIA

3. Arrivals of non-resident tourists in hotels and similar establishments, by country of residence

	2002	2003	2004	2005	2006	Market share 06	% Change 06-05
Western Europe	313,263	344,335	394,846	426,677	423,610	31.08	-0.72
Austria	34,842	40,278	45,652	52,918	57,684	4.23	9.01
Belgium	16,105	15,273	19,607	20,689	19,990	1.47	-3.38
France	83,252	91,719	107,487	112,296	107,824	7.91	-3.98
Germany	128,628	147,900	166,324	183,095	184,535	13.54	0.79
Luxembourg	1,111	1,171	1,056	1,253	1,142	0.08	-8.86
Netherlands	31,616	30,687	35,650	39,782	35,070	2.57	-11.84
Switzerland	17,709	17,307	19,070	16,644	17,365	1.27	4.33
East Mediterranean Europe	95,484	90,209	112,415	105,197	81,886	6.01	-22.16
Israel	68,307	63,120	75,094	72,787	55,794	4.09	-23.35
Turkey	27,177	27,089	37,321	32,410	26,092	1.91	-19.49
Other Europe	17,425	20,470	22,440	47,196	41,003	3.01	-13.12
Other countries of Europe	17,425	20,470	22,440	47,196	41,003	3.01	-13.12
REGION NOT SPECIFIED				5,488	7,484	0.55	36.37
Not Specified				5,488	7,484	0.55	36.37
Other countries of the World				5,488	7,484	0.55	36.37

Source: World Tourism Organization (UNWTO)

ROMANIA

4. Arrivals of non-resident tourists in all types of accommodation establishments, by country of residence

		2002	2003	2004	2005	2006	Market share 06	% Change 06-05
TOTAL		999,208	1,104,975	1,359,494	1,429,911	1,379,832	100.00	-3.50
AFRICA		4,685	5,244	7,151	7,503	7,945	0.58	5.89
Other Africa		4,685	5,244	7,151	7,503	7,945	0.58	5.89
All countries of Africa	(*)	4,685	5,244	7,151	7,503	7,945 .	0.58	5.89
AMERICAS		70,861	79,110	111,458	116,149	122,444	8.87	5.42
Central America		2,028	1,791	2,062				
All countries of Central America	(*)	2,028	1,791	2,062				
North America		66,457	75,096	105,822	111,151	116,480	8.44	4.79
Canada		7,993	8,059	11,036	10,972	17,424	1.26	58.80
Mexico					1,677	921	0.07	-45.08
United States		58,464	67,037	94,786	98,502	98,135	7.11	-0.37
South America		2,376	2,223	3,574				
All countries of South America		2,376	2,223	3,574				
Other Americas					4,998	5,964	0.43	19.33
Other countries of the Americas					4,998	5,964	0.43	19.33
EAST ASIA AND THE PACIFIC		42,861	40,291	51,051	55,521	56,974	4.13	2.62
North-East Asia		22,714	22,028	28,151	28,597	25,370	1.84	-11.28
China		4,262	3,627	4,964	5,353	4,815	0.35	-10.05
Japan		18,452	18,401	23,187	23,244	20,555	1.49	-11.57
Other East Asia and the Pacific		20,147	18,263	22,900	26,924	31,604	2.29	17.38
Other countries of Asia		16,329	14,745	16,022	19,190	23,325	1.69	21.55
All countries of Oceania		3,818	3,518	6,878	7,734	8,279	0.60	7.05
EUROPE		880,801	980,330	1,189,834	1,245,194	1,184,984	85.88	-4.84
Central/Eastern Europe		144,767	171,223	215,421	206,810	192,150	13.93	-7.09
Bulgaria		8,722	10,692	12,352	13,543	4,755	0.34	-64.89
Czech Republic		8,666	10,425	12,310	16,144	16,901	1.22	4.69
Hungary		63,147	80,710	99,647	90,170	81,280	5.89	-9.86
Republic of Moldova		29,554	29,404	36,407	29,211	28,837	2.09	-1.28
Poland		10,411	13,799	20,355	25,681	23,155	1.68	-9.84
Russian Federation		10,993	13,218	16,698	14,860	16,373	1.19	10.18
Slovakia		4,247	4,171	7,087	7,849	6,711	0.49	-14.50
Ukraine		9,027	8,804	10,565	9,352	14,138	1.02	51.18
Northern Europe		94,473	109,573	139,278	157,416	139,125	10.08	-11.62
Denmark		12,429	13,200	17,414	23,311	15,782	1.14	-32.30
Finland		4,234	3,932	10,828	14,394	7,963	0.58	-44.68
Ireland		4,120	4,959	5,213	5,471	8,314	0.60	51.96
Norway		7,432	9,048	10,846	12,033	13,685	0.99	13.73
Sweden		12,053	12,091	19,339	19,493	14,649	1.06	-24.85
United Kingdom		54,205	66,343	75,638	82,714	78,732	5.71	-4.81
Southern Europe		205,679	234,272	291,639	286,593	286,886	20.79	0.10
Greece		20,920	24,341	25,925	33,539	33,062	2.40	-1.42
Italy		139,860	160,774	201,118	194,763	182,576	13.23	-6.26
Montenegro						1,102	0.08	
Portugal		3,395	3,612	4,534	6,258	12,331	0.89	97.04
Serbia						5,027	0.36	
Slovenia		3,158	3,212	5,744	5,386	8,014	0.58	48.79
Spain		28,814	31,400	41,797	41,274	44,774	3.24	8.48
Serbia and Montenegro		9,532	10,933	12,521	5,373			

ROMANIA

4. Arrivals of non-resident tourists in all types of accommodation establishments, by country of residence

	2002	2003	2004	2005	2006	Market share 06	% Change 06-05
Western Europe	322,181	354,297	407,072	441,750	433,321	31.40	-1.91
Austria	35,179	40,664	46,786	53,373	58,022	4.21	8.71
Belgium	16,331	15,702	20,063	21,490	20,312	1.47	-5.48
France	84,153	92,760	109,563	114,920	109,778	7.96	-4.47
Germany	134,963	154,242	172,830	191,738	189,890	13.76	-0.96
Luxembourg	1,156	1,172	1,057	1,255	1,142	0.08	-9.00
Netherlands	32,614	32,103	37,571	41,885	35,910	2.60	-14.27
Switzerland	17,785	17,654	19,202	17,089	18,267	1.32	6.89
East Mediterranean Europe	96,061	90,454	112,688	105,299	81,990	5.94	-22.14
Israel	68,535	63,222	75,176	72,843	55,859	4.05	-23.32
Turkey	27,526	27,232	37,512	32,456	26,131	1.89	-19.49
Other Europe	17,640	20,511	23,736	47,326	51,512	3.73	8.85
Other countries of Europe	17,640	20,511	23,736	47,326	51,512	3.73	8.85
REGION NOT SPECIFIED				5,544	7,485	0.54	35.01
Not Specified				5,544	7,485	0.54	35.01
Other countries of the World				5,544	7,485	0.54	35.01

Source: World Tourism Organization (UNWTO)

ROMANIA

5. Overnight stays of non-resident tourists in hotels and similar establishments, by country of residence

	2002	2003	2004	2005	2006	Market share 06	% Change 06-05
TOTAL	2,470,622	2,687,832	3,210,600	3,377,148	3,169,183	100.00	-6.16
AFRICA	12,075	14,691	22,429	21,876	21,814	0.69	-0.28
Other Africa	12,075	14,691	22,429	21,876	21,814	0.69	-0.28
All countries of Africa (*)	12,075	14,691	22,429	21,876	21,814	0.69	-0.28
AMERICAS	169,773	185,941	236,113	238,962	241,823	7.63	1.20
Central America	4,041	3,933	5,409				
All countries of Central America (*)	4,041	3,933	5,409				
North America	160,536	176,526	221,478	226,884	226,879	7.16	
Canada	18,214	19,113	21,496	21,518	36,124	1.14	67.88
Mexico				6,025	2,000	0.06	-66.80
United States	142,322	157,413	199,982	199,341	188,755	5.96	-5.31
South America	5,196	5,482	9,226				
All countries of South America	5,196	5,482	9,226				
Other Americas				12,078	14,944	0.47	23.73
Other countries of the Americas				12,078	14,944	0.47	23.73
EAST ASIA AND THE PACIFIC	92,858	84,465	110,501	110,449	114,031	3.60	3.24
North-East Asia	43,313	38,779	54,836	56,276	50,674	1.60	-9.95
China	8,323	7,101	10,867	10,339	10,312	0.33	-0.26
Japan	34,990	31,678	43,969	45,937	40,362	1.27	-12.14
Other East Asia and the Pacific	49,545	45,686	55,665	54,173	63,357	2.00	16.95
Other countries of Asia	42,617	38,969	43,843	41,682	49,074	1.55	17.73
All countries of Oceania	6,928	6,717	11,822	12,491	14,283	0.45	14.35
EUROPE	2,195,916	2,402,735	2,841,557	2,995,531	2,778,967	87.69	-7.23
Central/Eastern Europe	313,858	397,603	518,372	485,121	489,731	15.45	0.95
Bulgaria	16,575	21,537	26,906	28,574	30,383	0.96	6.33
Czech Republic	16,283	21,282	22,591	28,574	35,347	1.12	23.70
Hungary	123,159	159,453	200,870	196,026	172,200	5.43	-12.15
Republic of Moldova	74,029	75,005	85,776	73,781	72,741	2.30	-1.41
Poland	18,749	34,403	45,864	51,830	55,133	1.74	6.37
Russian Federation	33,914	54,442	90,358	55,318	69,573	2.20	25.77
Slovakia	9,542	10,233	17,413	15,893	15,393	0.49	-3.15
Ukraine	21,607	21,248	28,594	35,125	38,961	1.23	10.92
Northern Europe	261,954	298,271	422,996	473,667	350,489	11.06	-26.01
Denmark	31,602	37,750	63,613	81,283	48,296	1.52	-40.58
Finland	10,878	8,437	48,864	75,800	30,486	0.96	-59.78
Ireland	8,809	11,289	11,325	11,782	17,980	0.57	52.61
Norway	38,019	46,633	54,251	49,426	51,024	1.61	3.23
Sweden	36,949	37,540	71,087	72,650	39,842	1.26	-45.16
United Kingdom	135,697	156,622	173,856	182,726	162,861	5.14	-10.87
Southern Europe	449,167	495,014	604,815	599,691	618,637	19.52	3.16
Greece	47,935	52,612	58,053	67,253	65,566	2.07	-2.51
Italy	314,352	347,775	415,479	412,944	401,038	12.65	-2.88
Montenegro					2,593	0.08	
Portugal	8,824	9,338	12,998	16,930	41,625	1.31	145.87
Serbia					9,628	0.30	
Slovenia	6,593	6,574	17,699	15,984	18,573	0.59	16.20
Spain	51,573	56,283	74,079	74,952	79,614	2.51	6.22
Serbia and Montenegro	19,890	22,432	26,507	11,628			

ROMANIA

5. Overnight stays of non-resident tourists in hotels and similar establishments, by country of residence

	2002	2003	2004	2005	2006	Market share 06	% Change 06-05
Western Europe	880,626	929,885	981,103	1,033,145	974,275	30.74	-5.70
Austria	65,730	78,297	88,383	98,994	103,031	3.25	4.08
Belgium	40,538	38,376	44,340	43,090	40,077	1.26	-6.99
France	196,066	215,466	239,724	246,304	242,652	7.66	-1.48
Germany	463,660	493,827	492,567	528,920	481,034	15.18	-9.05
Luxembourg	3,935	3,793	3,208	2,887	2,816	0.09	-2.46
Netherlands	82,423	68,843	76,877	82,429	72,760	2.30	-11.73
Switzerland	28,274	31,283	36,004	30,521	31,905	1.01	4.53
East Mediterranean Europe	244,866	236,317	263,845	236,039	206,389	6.51	-12.56
Israel	186,711	175,220	185,371	174,816	146,621	4.63	-16.13
Turkey	58,155	61,097	78,474	61,223	59,768	1.89	-2.38
Other Europe	45,445	45,645	50,426	167,868	139,446	4.40	-16.93
Other countries of Europe	45,445	45,645	50,426	167,868	139,446	4.40	-16.93
REGION NOT SPECIFIED				10,330	12,548	0.40	21.47
Not Specified				10,330	12,548	0.40	21.47
Other countries of the World				10,330	12,548	0.40	21.47

Source: World Tourism Organization (UNWTO)

ROMANIA

6. Overnight stays of non-resident tourists in all types of accommodation establishments, by country of residence

		2002	2003	2004	2005	2006	Market share 06	% Change 06-05
TOTAL		2,534,225	2,765,500	3,333,005	3,464,134	3,242,105	100.00	-6.41
AFRICA		12,077	14,696	22,516	21,893	21,858	0.67	-0.16
Other Africa		12,077	14,696	22,516	21,893	21,858	0.67	-0.16
All countries of Africa	(*)	12,077	14,696	22,516	21,893	21,858	0.67	-0.16
AMERICAS		171,286	187,131	241,647	239,623	242,289	7.47	1.11
Central America		4,056	3,934	5,426				
All countries of Central America	(*)	4,056	3,934	5,426				
North America		162,034	177,713	226,986	227,539	227,341	7.01	-0.09
Canada		18,464	19,221	25,653	21,707	36,222	1.12	66.87
Mexico					6,032	2,000	0.06	-66.84
United States		143,570	158,492	201,333	199,800	189,119	5.83	-5.35
South America		5,196	5,484	9,235				
All countries of South America		5,196	5,484	9,235				
Other Americas					12,084	14,948	0.46	23.70
Other countries of the Americas					12,084	14,948	0.46	23.70
EAST ASIA AND THE PACIFIC		94,734	85,288	110,771	110,954	114,157	3.52	2.89
North-East Asia		43,346	38,823	54,868	56,564	50,699	1.56	-10.37
China		8,350	7,139	10,875	10,361	10,322	0.32	-0.38
Japan		34,996	31,684	43,993	46,203	40,377	1.25	-12.61
Other East Asia and the Pacific		51,388	46,465	55,903	54,390	63,458	1.96	16.67
Other countries of Asia		44,236	39,700	43,899	41,710	49,149	1.52	17.84
All countries of Oceania		7,152	6,765	12,004	12,680	14,309	0.44	12.85
EUROPE		2,256,128	2,478,385	2,958,071	3,081,252	2,851,246	87.94	-7.46
Central/Eastern Europe		320,953	413,870	542,281	497,607	512,671	15.81	3.03
Bulgaria		16,665	22,223	27,351	28,685	30,432	0.94	6.09
Czech Republic		17,916	22,432	25,400	29,199	36,086	1.11	23.59
Hungary		125,849	169,046	212,685	201,847	177,884	5.49	-11.87
Republic of Moldova		75,264	76,523	88,469	75,086	77,769	2.40	3.57
Poland		19,594	35,794	48,868	53,279	56,432	1.74	5.92
Russian Federation		34,006	55,291	92,866	58,179	78,959	2.44	35.72
Slovakia		9,676	10,407	17,559	16,000	15,509	0.48	-3.07
Ukraine		21,983	22,154	29,083	35,332	39,600	1.22	12.08
Northern Europe		269,803	304,113	444,419	484,405	351,459	10.84	-27.45
Denmark		37,660	40,936	73,579	86,500	48,436	1.49	-44.00
Finland		10,980	8,713	49,095	75,864	30,511	0.94	-59.78
Ireland		8,854	11,410	11,483	12,433	18,029	0.56	45.01
Norway		38,048	47,101	56,410	49,993	51,053	1.57	2.12
Sweden		38,012	37,890	74,368	76,186	39,997	1.23	-47.50
United Kingdom		136,249	158,063	179,484	183,429	163,433	5.04	-10.90
Southern Europe		452,095	499,029	612,653	602,034	622,150	19.19	3.34
Greece		47,962	53,090	58,344	67,342	65,602	2.02	-2.58
Italy		316,736	350,530	420,917	414,852	403,689	12.45	-2.69
Montenegro						2,593	0.08	
Portugal		8,854	9,429	13,161	16,954	41,699	1.29	145.95
Serbia						9,908	0.31	
Slovenia		6,663	6,671	17,818	16,056	18,645	0.58	16.12
Spain		51,729	56,548	75,715	75,164	80,014	2.47	6.45
Serbia and Montenegro		20,151	22,761	26,698	11,666			

ROMANIA

6. Overnight stays of non-resident tourists in all types of accommodation establishments, by country of residence

	2002	2003	2004	2005	2006	Market share 06	% Change 06-05
Western Europe	**921,685**	**978,744**	**1,037,270**	**1,091,484**	**1,018,171**	**31.40**	**-6.72**
Austria	67,191	79,237	92,337	100,346	103,941	3.21	3.58
Belgium	41,245	39,171	45,915	44,671	40,876	1.26	-8.50
France	197,683	218,771	249,901	257,240	253,088	7.81	-1.61
Germany	497,817	533,942	525,322	566,751	506,766	15.63	-10.58
Luxembourg	4,202	3,797	3,215	2,889	2,816	0.09	-2.53
Netherlands	84,863	71,790	84,091	87,611	74,509	2.30	-14.95
Switzerland	28,684	32,036	36,489	31,976	36,175	1.12	13.13
East Mediterranean Europe	**245,762**	**236,909**	**264,743**	**236,270**	**206,547**	**6.37**	**-12.58**
Israel	187,103	175,399	185,518	174,930	146,706	4.53	-16.13
Turkey	58,659	61,510	79,225	61,340	59,841	1.85	-2.44
Other Europe	**45,830**	**45,720**	**56,705**	**169,452**	**140,248**	**4.33**	**-17.23**
Other countries of Europe	45,830	45,720	56,705	169,452	140,248	4.33	-17.23
REGION NOT SPECIFIED				**10,412**	**12,555**	**0.39**	**20.58**
Not Specified				**10,412**	**12,555**	**0.39**	**20.58**
Other countries of the World				10,412	12,555	0.39	20.58

Source: World Tourism Organization (UNWTO)

RUSSIAN FEDERATION

2. Arrivals of non-resident visitors at national borders, by nationality

	2002	2003	2004	2005	2006	Market share 06	% Change 06-05
TOTAL	23,308,711	22,521,059	22,064,213	22,200,649	22,486,043	100.00	1.29
AFRICA	31,473	28,985	29,217	26,909	28,288	0.13	5.12
East Africa	3,586	3,145	3,367	3,188	3,717	0.02	16.59
British Indian Ocean Territory					13		
Burundi	50	126	81	44	57		29.55
Comoros	1	7	63	138	151		9.42
Ethiopia	542	457	285	236	390		65.25
Eritrea	953	69	73	64	42		-34.38
Djibouti	5	8	52	43	5		-88.37
Kenya	399	368	497	781	818		4.74
Madagascar	54	124	148	130	204		56.92
Malawi	6	36	226	40	47		17.50
Mauritius	493	389	442	493	434		-11.97
Mozambique	179	137	50	34	90		164.71
Rwanda	43	51	47	39	43		10.26
Seychelles	33	76	278	113	59		-47.79
Somalia	211	370	337	61	102		67.21
Zimbabwe	137	166	234	221	318		43.89
Uganda	79	299	111	178	116		-34.83
United Republic of Tanzania	196	241	231	328	574		75.00
Zambia	205	221	212	245	254		3.67
Central Africa	1,663	1,802	2,957	2,584	2,382	0.01	-7.82
Angola	722	925	1,022	963	904		-6.13
Cameroon	365	381	482	825	545		-33.94
Central African Republic	10	16	610	17	16		-5.88
Chad	78	80	318	78	119		52.56
Congo	288	309	330	490	606		23.67
Democratic Republic of the Congo				6	31		416.67
Equatorial Guinea	126	37	125	127	102		-19.69
Gabon	73	51	59	72	55		-23.61
Sao Tome and Principe	1	3	11	6	4		-33.33
North Africa	12,496	6,287	6,634	6,509	6,803	0.03	4.52
Algeria	7,862	1,713	1,602	1,362	1,911	0.01	40.31
Morocco	2,670	2,345	2,546	2,455	2,504	0.01	2.00
Western Sahara			5	3			
Sudan	452	656	934	906	665		-26.60
Tunisia	1,512	1,573	1,547	1,783	1,723	0.01	-3.37
Southern Africa	3,671	4,241	5,296	5,587	7,642	0.03	36.78
Botswana	8	24	16	40	36		-10.00
Lesotho	13	24	5	8	311		3,787.50
Namibia	129	162	156	170	181		6.47
South Africa	3,514	4,025	5,109	5,355	7,087	0.03	32.34
Swaziland	7	6	10	14	27		92.86
West Africa	10,057	13,510	10,963	9,041	7,744	0.03	-14.35
Cape Verde	176	135	169	192	248		29.17
Benin	145	154	155	155	138		-10.97
Gambia	52	59	31	32	39		21.88
Ghana	225	313	494	629	694		10.33
Guinea	190	265	1,210	291	209		-28.18
Cote D'Ivoire	131	193	181	239	230		-3.77
Liberia	7,680	10,919	5,806	5,403	3,814	0.02	-29.41
Mali	147	185	164	192	210		9.38
Mauritania	109	77	88	66	113		71.21

RUSSIAN FEDERATION

2. Arrivals of non-resident visitors at national borders, by nationality

	2002	2003	2004	2005	2006	Market share 06	% Change 06-05
Niger	14	36	20	16	44		175.00
Nigeria	848	843	1,370	1,348	1,554	0.01	15.28
Guinea-Bissau	76	76	85	97	98		1.03
Senegal	127	144	210	227	185		-18.50
Sierra Leone	55	64	294	54	82		51.85
Togo	68	40	661	48	37		-22.92
Burkina Faso	14	7	25	52	49		-5.77
AMERICAS	**342,594**	**420,857**	**477,338**	**457,301**	**532,991**	**2.37**	**16.55**
Caribbean	**42,632**	**76,111**	**84,560**	**90,305**	**74,694**	**0.33**	**-17.29**
Antigua and Barbuda	1,066	1,720	3,335	3,174	3,273	0.01	3.12
Bahamas	32,297	61,762	58,605	55,275	44,869	0.20	-18.83
Barbados	142	138	1,169	294	501		70.41
Bermuda	41	1,374	7,933	16,125	14,880	0.07	-7.72
British Virgin Islands					1		
Cayman Islands	1,456	1,642	724	683	457		-33.09
Cuba	2,453	3,518	4,649	6,499	5,166	0.02	-20.51
Dominica	36	275	278	501	531		5.99
Dominican Republic	238	106	115	135	254		88.15
Grenada	60	389	1,246	158	82		-48.10
Haiti	58	82	289	61	35		-42.62
Jamaica	1,804	851	770	482	222		-53.94
Martinique				1			
Netherlands Antilles	112	140	219	242	94		-61.16
Puerto Rico		2	2	17	12		-29.41
Saint Kitts and Nevis	4	3	1	9	71		688.89
Anguilla	56	6	2	18	12		-33.33
Saint Lucia	4	6	8	3	13		333.33
Saint Vincent and the Grenadines	2,750	4,035	5,086	6,504	3,752	0.02	-42.31
Trinidad and Tobago	55	62	129	124	469		278.23
Central America	**14,534**	**13,278**	**19,657**	**18,844**	**26,257**	**0.12**	**39.34**
Belize	1,137	617	1,905	2,305	3,296	0.01	42.99
Costa Rica	236	384	1,425	687	370		-46.14
El Salvador	122	136	73	75	1,065		1,320.00
Guatemala	169	251	227	236	422		78.81
Honduras	174	1,406	1,031	192	5,077	0.02	2,544.27
Nicaragua	187	134	138	98	145		47.96
Panama	12,509	10,350	14,858	15,251	15,882	0.07	4.14
North America	**272,337**	**316,510**	**349,187**	**322,540**	**404,654**	**1.80**	**25.46**
Canada	30,314	29,778	34,575	31,671	42,149	0.19	33.08
Greenland					34		
Mexico	6,327	5,884	6,340	9,943	11,210	0.05	12.74
United States	235,696	280,848	308,272	280,926	351,261	1.56	25.04
South America	**13,091**	**14,958**	**23,934**	**25,612**	**27,386**	**0.12**	**6.93**
Argentina	2,060	3,424	6,310	6,414	7,236	0.03	12.82
Bolivia	313	288	321	304	400		31.58
Brazil	4,068	4,685	8,196	10,829	9,424	0.04	-12.97
Chile	1,447	1,400	1,931	2,062	2,409	0.01	16.83
Colombia	1,298	1,685	2,427	1,577	2,312	0.01	46.61
Ecuador	1,035	752	940	1,125	1,069		-4.98
Falkland Islands (Malvinas)	1	64					
French Guiana			7	82			
Guyana		4	21	12	34		183.33
Paraguay	29	36	253	99	102		3.03
Peru	1,192	1,132	1,405	1,252	1,096		-12.46

RUSSIAN FEDERATION

2. Arrivals of non-resident visitors at national borders, by nationality

	2002	2003	2004	2005	2006	Market share 06	% Change 06-05
Suriname	3	4	2	4	2		-50.00
Uruguay	455	615	610	634	592		-6.62
Venezuela	1,190	869	1,511	1,218	2,710	0.01	122.50
EAST ASIA AND THE PACIFIC	**1,150,430**	**1,106,605**	**1,313,669**	**1,315,480**	**1,345,870**	**5.99**	**2.31**
North-East Asia	**1,056,682**	**1,006,310**	**1,173,096**	**1,158,853**	**1,158,642**	**5.15**	**-0.02**
China	725,825	679,608	813,142	798,661	765,336	3.40	-4.17
Taiwan (Province of China)	6,090	6,660	13,057	10,677	11,742	0.05	9.97
Hong Kong, China		3,585	3,547	3,018	3,317	0.01	9.91
Japan	73,734	86,764	92,326	87,642	97,648	0.43	11.42
Korea, Dem. People's Republic of	20,536	18,412	18,528	18,682	23,148	0.10	23.91
Korea, Republic of	96,010	94,563	108,808	111,221	110,788	0.49	-0.39
Macao, China	3	34	12	24	27		12.50
Mongolia	134,484	116,684	123,676	128,928	146,636	0.65	13.73
South-East Asia	**72,065**	**73,327**	**102,654**	**115,641**	**141,512**	**0.63**	**22.37**
Brunei Darussalam	14	18	32	70	68		-2.86
Myanmar	1,672	1,470	1,767	2,210	3,440	0.02	55.66
Cambodia	5,535	5,002	6,202	5,392	3,136	0.01	-41.84
Indonesia	4,413	4,931	12,439	6,544	8,047	0.04	22.97
Lao People's Democratic Republic	61	128	90	100	193		93.00
Malaysia	3,612	3,560	5,054	7,137	9,541	0.04	33.68
Philippines	23,327	26,082	32,604	43,993	57,595	0.26	30.92
Singapore	3,246	3,665	4,098	4,192	6,839	0.03	63.14
Viet Nam	26,614	23,911	33,427	37,388	37,395	0.17	0.02
Thailand	3,571	4,560	6,941	8,615	15,258	0.07	77.11
Australasia	**20,529**	**21,474**	**28,831**	**30,591**	**36,980**	**0.16**	**20.89**
Australia	16,672	16,961	23,546	24,932	31,066	0.14	24.60
New Zealand	3,857	4,513	5,285	5,659	5,914	0.03	4.51
Melanesia	**155**	**323**	**228**	**197**	**256**		**29.95**
Solomon Islands	31	14		1	4		300.00
Fiji	46	51	40	35	12		-65.71
New Caledonia	1		14		3		
Vanuatu	74	250	164	135	226		67.41
Norfolk Island			1				
Papua New Guinea	3	8	9	26	11		-57.69
Micronesia	**900**	**5,021**	**8,779**	**10,020**	**8,286**	**0.04**	**-17.31**
Kiribati	46	14	28	22	13		-40.91
Guam	6		3	14	4		-71.43
Nauru	1			1	1		
Northern Mariana Islands					2		
Micronesia (Federated States of)	2	7	2	1			
Marshall Islands	844	4,998	8,746	9,979	8,264	0.04	-17.19
Palau	1	2		3	2		-33.33
Polynesia	**99**	**150**	**81**	**178**	**194**		**8.99**
American Samoa					11		
French Polynesia					1		
Pitcairn					5		
Tokelau					9		
Tonga	1	21	1	4	5		25.00
Tuvalu	98	129	80	174	153		-12.07
Samoa					10		
EUROPE	**21,097,290**	**20,236,821**	**19,607,077**	**19,690,628**	**19,872,873**	**88.38**	**0.93**
Central/Eastern Europe	**18,366,351**	**17,336,497**	**16,470,798**	**16,578,364**	**16,731,514**	**74.41**	**0.92**

RUSSIAN FEDERATION

2. Arrivals of non-resident visitors at national borders, by nationality

	2002	2003	2004	2005	2006	Market share 06	% Change 06-05
Azerbaijan	844,318	825,974	823,496	824,627	935,546	4.16	13.45
Armenia	309,049	331,922	377,277	386,462	390,480	1.74	1.04
Bulgaria	28,997	31,718	33,709	34,091	36,612	0.16	7.39
Belarus	197,492	148,979	152,441	210,382	242,615	1.08	15.32
Czech Republic	28,140	30,212	32,198	32,958	36,846	0.16	11.80
Estonia	386,537	406,004	521,086	510,329	438,179	1.95	-14.14
Georgia	988,203	737,936	320,811	228,997	125,938	0.56	-45.00
Hungary	15,602	17,059	18,660	19,148	20,481	0.09	6.96
Kazakhstan	2,955,993	2,674,895	2,761,475	2,453,194	2,598,595	11.56	5.93
Kyrgyzstan	307,700	271,956	306,556	293,616	408,968	1.82	39.29
Latvia	292,629	344,971	371,093	709,258	380,690	1.69	-46.33
Lithuania	950,567	873,814	949,588	1,251,497	980,457	4.36	-21.66
Republic of Moldova	694,985	751,598	804,850	837,140	925,948	4.12	10.61
Poland	1,209,790	1,232,942	1,128,498	1,195,875	1,148,951	5.11	-3.92
Romania	14,097	12,474	10,876	11,723	14,410	0.06	22.92
Slovakia	13,032	14,687	14,909	14,497	17,973	0.08	23.98
Tajikistan	358,452	366,927	456,367	466,452	600,781	2.67	28.80
Turkmenistan	33,973	22,249	26,701	20,560	22,082	0.10	7.40
Ukraine	8,229,840	7,686,224	6,683,239	6,416,940	6,447,047	28.67	0.47
Uzbekistan	506,955	553,956	676,968	660,618	958,915	4.26	45.15
Northern Europe	**1,454,068**	**1,486,943**	**1,486,497**	**1,511,630**	**1,474,106**	**6.56**	**-2.48**
Denmark	30,105	33,388	38,021	32,053	33,218	0.15	3.63
Faeroe Islands	41	59	50	30	4		-86.67
Finland	1,161,233	1,154,129	1,092,326	1,115,513	1,078,231	4.80	-3.34
Iceland	2,072	1,906	2,040	2,089	1,983	0.01	-5.07
Ireland	11,960	12,093	14,097	10,615	14,449	0.06	36.12
Norway	43,621	45,254	51,345	47,997	48,568	0.22	1.19
Svalbard and Jan Mayen Islands					2		
Sweden	55,652	63,347	73,679	86,336	64,343	0.29	-25.47
United Kingdom	149,384	176,767	214,939	216,997	233,308	1.04	7.52
Southern Europe	**287,915**	**307,464**	**395,697**	**371,744**	**406,750**	**1.81**	**9.42**
Albania	1,210	914	852	965	1,497	0.01	55.13
Andorra	88	134	130	66	132		100.00
Bosnia and Herzegovina	3,900	5,007	5,851	5,947	7,757	0.03	30.44
Croatia	7,510	8,798	11,616	11,216	11,314	0.05	0.87
Gibraltar					2,269	0.01	
Greece	25,829	29,262	32,835	33,431	31,183	0.14	-6.72
Holy See	15	11	26	19	17		-10.53
Italy	154,319	169,730	192,024	193,156	187,878	0.84	-2.73
Malta	21,254	21,395	24,061	23,937	22,522	0.10	-5.91
Portugal	7,107	10,523	14,416	15,736	13,046	0.06	-17.09
San Marino	82	256	177	115	109		-5.22
Slovenia	8,018	8,109	9,130	10,845	11,999	0.05	10.64
Spain	58,557	52,205	69,096	76,311	70,227	0.31	-7.97
TFYR of Macedonia					4,033	0.02	
Serbia and Montenegro	26	1,120	35,483		42,767	0.19	
Western Europe	**792,573**	**887,910**	**999,443**	**950,225**	**974,386**	**4.33**	**2.54**
Austria	37,869	46,968	58,747	58,252	55,507	0.25	-4.71
Belgium	22,468	26,102	31,065	34,320	35,378	0.16	3.08
France	146,604	189,145	209,195	180,947	192,924	0.86	6.62
Germany	493,267	516,217	567,204	550,792	553,728	2.46	0.53
Liechtenstein	103	142	276	179	197		10.06
Luxembourg	2,712	3,258	4,213	3,628	2,539	0.01	-30.02
Monaco	80	244	240	165	77		-53.33
Netherlands	63,975	68,264	78,364	80,534	84,520	0.38	4.95

RUSSIAN FEDERATION

2. Arrivals of non-resident visitors at national borders, by nationality

	2002	2003	2004	2005	2006	Market share 06	% Change 06-05
Switzerland	25,495	37,570	50,139	41,408	49,516	0.22	19.58
East Mediterranean Europe	**196,383**	**218,007**	**254,642**	**278,665**	**286,117**	**1.27**	**2.67**
Cyprus	19,325	18,151	17,168	15,859	12,517	0.06	-21.07
Israel	58,358	60,111	59,131	64,655	60,294	0.27	-6.75
Turkey	118,700	139,745	178,343	198,151	213,306	0.95	7.65
MIDDLE EAST	**28,312**	**31,792**	**31,765**	**33,405**	**33,029**	**0.15**	**-1.13**
Middle East	**28,312**	**31,792**	**31,765**	**33,405**	**33,029**	**0.15**	**-1.13**
Bahrain	136	99	92	139	153		10.07
Palestine	388	384	619	587	593		1.02
Iraq	2,258	857	1,206	1,305	1,660	0.01	27.20
Jordan	2,675	3,147	2,603	2,358	2,497	0.01	5.89
Kuwait	413	400	223	253	252		-0.40
Lebanon	3,532	4,138	2,935	4,229	3,948	0.02	-6.64
Libyan Arab Jamahiriya	705	697	928	881	517		-41.32
Oman	278	318	350	356	326		-8.43
Qatar	98	621	129	138	131		-5.07
Saudi Arabia	844	1,220	701	668	835		25.00
Syrian Arab Republic	8,773	9,950	12,249	12,630	12,554	0.06	-0.60
United Arab Emirates	1,771	2,396	2,000	649	828		27.58
Egypt	5,317	6,848	6,792	8,066	7,973	0.04	-1.15
Yemen	1,124	717	938	1,146	762		-33.51
SOUTH ASIA	**57,708**	**58,804**	**62,927**	**68,421**	**71,917**	**0.32**	**5.11**
South Asia	**57,708**	**58,804**	**62,927**	**68,421**	**71,917**	**0.32**	**5.11**
Afghanistan	3,101	4,548	4,992	4,939	4,768	0.02	-3.46
Bangladesh	2,104	1,154	1,208	1,437	1,445	0.01	0.56
Bhutan	1		6	6	5		-16.67
Sri Lanka	1,664	1,541	1,603	1,853	1,765	0.01	-4.75
India	33,546	32,954	36,755	42,184	45,795	0.20	8.56
Iran, Islamic Republic of	13,481	13,983	13,499	13,528	13,489	0.06	-0.29
Maldives	119	165	151	147	107		-27.21
Nepal	662	773	867	897	1,298	0.01	44.70
Pakistan	3,030	3,686	3,846	3,430	3,245	0.01	-5.39
REGION NOT SPECIFIED	**600,904**	**637,195**	**542,220**	**608,505**	**601,075**	**2.67**	**-1.22**
Not Specified	**600,904**	**637,195**	**542,220**	**608,505**	**601,075**	**2.67**	**-1.22**
Other countries of the World	600,904	637,195	542,220	608,505	601,075	2.67	-1.22

Source: World Tourism Organization (UNWTO)

SABA

1. Arrivals of non-resident tourists at national borders, by country of residence

	2002	2003	2004	2005	2006	Market share 06	% Change 06-05
TOTAL	10,778	10,260	11,012	11,462			
AMERICAS	4,380	4,106	4,764	4,933			
North America	4,380	4,106	4,764	4,933			
Canada	639	450	592	645			
United States	3,741	3,656	4,172	4,288			
EUROPE	4,565	4,732	5,043	5,484			
Northern Europe	479	591	555				
United Kingdom	479	591	555				
Southern Europe		67					
Italy		67					
Western Europe	4,086	4,074	4,073				
France	573	551	753				
Germany	280	278					
Netherlands	3,233	3,245	3,320				
Other Europe			415	5,484			
Other countries of Europe			415				
All countries of Europe				5,484			
REGION NOT SPECIFIED	1,833	1,422	1,205	1,045			
Not Specified	1,833	1,422	1,205	1,045			
Other countries of the World	1,833	1,422	1,205	1,045			

Source: World Tourism Organization (UNWTO)

SAINT EUSTATIUS

1. Arrivals of non-resident tourists at national borders, by country of residence

		2002	2003	2004	2005	2006	Market share 06	% Change 06-05
TOTAL	(*)	9,781	10,451	11,056	10,355	9,584	100.00	-7.45
AMERICAS		3,403	3,483	3,732	3,457	3,177	33.15	-8.10
Caribbean		417	391	474	438	386	4.03	-11.87
Dominican Republic		417	391	474	438	386	4.03	-11.87
North America		2,563	2,562	2,674	2,503	2,344	24.46	-6.35
Canada		192	184	211	194	138	1.44	-28.87
United States		2,371	2,378	2,463	2,309	2,206	23.02	-4.46
South America		145	198	266	201	239	2.49	18.91
Guyana		145	198	266	201	239	2.49	18.91
Other Americas		278	332	318	315	208	2.17	-33.97
Other countries of the Americas		278	332	318	315	208	2.17	-33.97
EUROPE		4,600	5,272	5,505	5,400	4,851	50.62	-10.17
Western Europe		3,394	4,000	4,057	3,973	3,699	38.60	-6.90
Germany		89	70	68	69	69	0.72	
Netherlands		3,305	3,930	3,989	3,904	3,630	37.88	-7.02
Other Europe		1,206	1,272	1,448	1,427	1,152	12.02	-19.27
Other countries of Europe		1,206	1,272	1,448	1,427	1,152	12.02	-19.27
REGION NOT SPECIFIED		1,778	1,696	1,819	1,498	1,556	16.24	3.87
Not Specified		1,778	1,696	1,819	1,498	1,556	16.24	3.87
Other countries of the World		1,778	1,696	1,819	1,498	1,556	16.24	3.87

Source: World Tourism Organization (UNWTO)

SAINT KITTS AND NEVIS

1. Arrivals of non-resident tourists at national borders, by country of residence

		2002	2003	2004	2005	2006	Market share 06	% Change 06-05
TOTAL	(*)	68,998	90,599	117,638	127,728	132,970	100.00	4.10
AMERICAS		60,023		103,093	112,153	118,963	89.47	6.07
Caribbean		28,146		31,909	27,394	32,608	24.52	19.03
All countries of the Caribbean		28,146		31,909	27,394	32,608	24.52	19.03
North America		31,877		71,184	84,759	86,355	64.94	1.88
Canada		4,352		6,325	8,233	7,555	5.68	-8.24
United States		27,525		64,859	76,526	78,800	59.26	2.97
EUROPE		5,464		13,181	11,553	12,030	9.05	4.13
Northern Europe		5,464		11,004	9,536	9,890	7.44	3.71
United Kingdom		5,464		11,004	9,536	9,890	7.44	3.71
Other Europe				2,177	2,017	2,140	1.61	6.10
Other countries of Europe				2,177	2,017	2,140	1.61	6.10
REGION NOT SPECIFIED		3,511	90,599	1,364	4,022	1,977	1.49	-50.85
Not Specified		3,511	90,599	1,364	4,022	1,977	1.49	-50.85
Other countries of the World		3,511	90,599	1,364	4,022	1,977	1.49	-50.85

Source: World Tourism Organization (UNWTO)

SAINT LUCIA

1. Arrivals of non-resident tourists at national borders, by country of residence

		2002	2003	2004	2005	2006	Market share 06	% Change 06-05
TOTAL	(*)	253,463	276,948	298,431	317,939	302,510	100.00	-4.85
AMERICAS		175,390	183,349	197,433	214,621	213,405	70.54	-0.57
Caribbean		66,409	67,818	71,385	81,667	78,464	25.94	-3.92
Antigua and Barbuda		3,217	2,855	3,181	3,188			
Barbados		16,973	14,329	15,186	18,746			
Dominica		3,685	3,700	3,866	4,692			
Dominican Republic		134	135	122	68			
Grenada		2,401	3,770	3,494	3,823			
Haiti		134	201	162	154			
Jamaica		3,563	3,495	3,692	2,854			
Netherlands Antilles		775	504	606	566			
Puerto Rico		807	556	595	416			
Saint Kitts and Nevis		1,158	891	933	989			
Saint Vincent and the Grenadines		4,289	3,986	4,072	4,451			
Trinidad and Tobago		11,040	10,639	10,747	13,782			
United States Virgin Islands		1,618	1,009	810	797			
Other countries of the Caribbean		16,615	21,748	23,919	27,141			
All countries of the Caribbean						78,464	25.94	
North America		106,971	111,572	122,404	129,063	134,941	44.61	4.55
Canada		12,927	13,494	15,315	16,506	17,491	5.78	5.97
United States		94,044	98,078	107,089	112,557	117,450	38.83	4.35
South America		900	2,725	2,857	3,062			
Guyana		900	2,725	2,857	3,062			
Other Americas		1,110	1,234	787	829			
Other countries of the Americas		1,110	1,234	787	829			
EAST ASIA AND THE PACIFIC		278	373	282	260			
North-East Asia		278	373	282	260			
Japan		278	373	282	260			
EUROPE		76,199	90,193	96,793	101,790	85,565	28.29	-15.94
Northern Europe		63,702	75,820	82,041	85,200	73,312	24.23	-13.95
Sweden		425	394	671	475			
United Kingdom		63,277	75,426	81,370	84,725	73,312	24.23	-13.47
Southern Europe		910	884	990	1,230			
Italy		698	697	680	909			
Spain		212	187	310	321			
Western Europe		9,042	11,136	11,703	11,802	6,333	2.09	-46.34
Austria		402	431	293	315			
Belgium		225	194	156	161			
France		3,405	6,017	7,682	7,241	3,764	1.24	-48.02
Germany		3,929	3,582	3,289	3,318	2,569	0.85	-22.57
Netherlands		337	346	283	256			
Switzerland		744	566		511			
Other Europe		2,545	2,353	2,059	3,558	5,920	1.96	66.39
Other countries of Europe		2,545	2,353	2,059	3,558	5,920	1.96	66.39
REGION NOT SPECIFIED		1,596	3,033	3,923	1,268	3,540	1.17	179.18
Not Specified		1,596	3,033	3,923	1,268	3,540	1.17	179.18
Other countries of the World		1,596	3,033	3,923	1,268	3,540	1.17	179.18

Source: World Tourism Organization (UNWTO)

SAINT MAARTEN

1. Arrivals of non-resident tourists at national borders, by nationality

		2002	2003	2004	2005	2006	Market share 06	% Change 06-05
TOTAL	(*)	380,801	427,587	475,032	467,861	467,804	100.00	-0.01
AMERICAS		259,506	301,018	338,241	331,841	328,450	70.21	-1.02
Caribbean		33,371	39,913	44,907	40,426	39,034	8.34	-3.44
Antigua and Barbuda		6,072	6,382					
Dominican Republic		3,504	4,597					
Haiti		2,946	4,536					
Saint Kitts and Nevis		8,325	8,997					
Trinidad and Tobago		2,061	2,452					
Other countries of the Caribbean		10,463	12,949					
All countries of the Caribbean				44,907	40,426	39,034	8.34	-3.44
North America		215,368	251,792	282,822	281,364	276,710	59.15	-1.65
Canada		23,460	29,545	31,667	34,506	30,646	6.55	-11.19
United States		191,908	222,247	251,155	246,858	246,064	52.60	-0.32
South America		10,767	9,313	2,756	2,241	2,062	0.44	-7.99
Argentina		931	627					
Brazil		697	725					
Chile		152	163					
Venezuela		3,447	2,485	2,756	2,241	2,062	0.44	-7.99
Other countries of South America		5,540	5,313					
Other Americas				7,756	7,810	10,644	2.28	36.29
Other countries of the Americas				7,756	7,810	10,644	2.28	36.29
EUROPE		87,147	88,259	96,404	93,821	97,058	20.75	3.45
Central/Eastern Europe		215	191					
Russian Federation		215	191					
Southern Europe		4,178	4,842					
Italy		4,178	4,842					
Western Europe		71,644	71,719	15,554	15,441	15,842	3.39	2.60
France	(*)	62,457	58,801					
Netherlands		9,187	12,918	15,554	15,441	15,842	3.39	2.60
Other Europe		11,110	11,507	80,850	78,380	81,216	17.36	3.62
Other countries of Europe		11,110	11,507	80,850	78,380	81,216	17.36	3.62
REGION NOT SPECIFIED		34,148	38,310	40,387	42,199	42,296	9.04	0.23
Not Specified		34,148	38,310	40,387	42,199	42,296	9.04	0.23
Other countries of the World		20,673	23,568	40,387	42,199	42,296	9.04	0.23
Nationals Residing Abroad		13,475	14,742					

Source: World Tourism Organization (UNWTO)

SAINT VINCENT AND THE GRENADINES

1. Arrivals of non-resident tourists at national borders, by country of residence

		2002	2003	2004	2005	2006	Market share 06	% Change 06-05
TOTAL	(*)	**77,631**	**78,535**	**86,722**	**95,506**	**97,432**	**100.00**	**2.02**
AMERICAS		**58,465**	**60,315**	**66,871**	**74,173**	**74,193**	**76.15**	**0.03**
Caribbean		**30,229**	**32,776**	**36,013**	**39,944**	**38,219**	**39.23**	**-4.32**
Antigua and Barbuda		988	1,109	1,200	1,357	1,583	1.62	16.65
Barbados		10,217	9,906	11,205	12,824	12,293	12.62	-4.14
Grenada		2,001	2,667	3,175	3,268	2,501	2.57	-23.47
Netherlands Antilles		312	518	538	563	487	0.50	-13.50
Saint Lucia		2,127	2,862	3,470	3,450	3,294	3.38	-4.52
Trinidad and Tobago		8,975	9,654	10,194	11,683	11,002	11.29	-5.83
Other countries of the Caribbean		5,609	6,060	6,231	6,799	7,059	7.25	3.82
North America		**27,680**	**27,112**	**30,325**	**33,340**	**35,140**	**36.07**	**5.40**
Canada		5,268	4,918	5,219	6,187	6,542	6.71	5.74
United States		22,412	22,194	25,106	27,153	28,598	29.35	5.32
Other Americas		**556**	**427**	**533**	**889**	**834**	**0.86**	**-6.19**
Other countries of the Americas		556	427	533	889	834	0.86	-6.19
EUROPE		**17,997**	**17,201**	**18,652**	**19,928**	**21,961**	**22.54**	**10.20**
Northern Europe		**12,432**	**12,171**	**13,146**	**14,628**	**15,597**	**16.01**	**6.62**
Ireland		299	194	132	199	225	0.23	13.07
Norway		170	96	95	95	117	0.12	23.16
Sweden		332	334	309	393	418	0.43	6.36
United Kingdom		11,631	11,547	12,610	13,941	14,837	15.23	6.43
Southern Europe		**1,204**	**1,192**	**1,498**	**1,623**	**1,857**	**1.91**	**14.42**
Italy		985	1,030	1,249	1,435	1,634	1.68	13.87
Spain		219	162	249	188	223	0.23	18.62
Western Europe		**3,917**	**3,311**	**3,383**	**2,952**	**3,280**	**3.37**	**11.11**
Belgium		217	151	181	168	189	0.19	12.50
France		2,142	1,750	1,765	1,379	1,560	1.60	13.13
Germany		894	815	837	811	910	0.93	12.21
Netherlands		243	127	180	123	132	0.14	7.32
Switzerland		421	468	420	471	489	0.50	3.82
Other Europe		**444**	**527**	**625**	**725**	**1,227**	**1.26**	**69.24**
Other countries of Europe		444	527	625	725	1,227	1.26	69.24
REGION NOT SPECIFIED		**1,169**	**1,019**	**1,199**	**1,405**	**1,278**	**1.31**	**-9.04**
Not Specified		**1,169**	**1,019**	**1,199**	**1,405**	**1,278**	**1.31**	**-9.04**
Other countries of the World		1,169	1,019	1,199	1,405	1,278	1.31	-9.04

Source: World Tourism Organization (UNWTO)

SAINT VINCENT AND THE GRENADINES

2. Arrivals of non-resident visitors at national borders, by country of residence

		2002	2003	2004	2005	2006	Market share 06	% Change 06-05
TOTAL	(*)	90,693	92,231	99,657	104,433	106,463	100.00	1.94
AMERICAS		64,125	65,864	71,902	78,918	78,665	73.89	-0.32
Caribbean		33,989	36,748	39,424	43,556	41,533	39.01	-4.64
Antigua and Barbuda		1,101	1,180	1,265	1,450	1,676	1.57	15.59
Barbados		11,595	11,228	12,406	14,040	13,489	12.67	-3.92
Grenada		2,610	3,226	3,656	3,823	2,847	2.67	-25.53
Netherlands Antilles		321	590	552	587	510	0.48	-13.12
Saint Lucia		2,558	3,583	4,193	4,089	3,854	3.62	-5.75
Trinidad and Tobago		9,785	10,440	10,795	12,430	11,692	10.98	-5.94
Other countries of the Caribbean		6,019	6,501	6,557	7,137	7,465	7.01	4.60
North America		29,545	28,648	31,914	34,426	36,226	34.03	5.23
Canada		5,642	5,189	5,545	6,387	6,800	6.39	6.47
United States		23,903	23,459	26,369	28,039	29,426	27.64	4.95
Other Americas		591	468	564	936	906	0.85	-3.21
Other countries of the Americas		591	468	564	936	906	0.85	-3.21
EUROPE		25,271	25,241	26,507	24,041	26,443	24.84	9.99
Northern Europe		17,466	18,401	19,231	17,690	18,855	17.71	6.59
Ireland		424	319	215	246	288	0.27	17.07
Norway		213	111	103	98	128	0.12	30.61
Sweden		389	379	334	404	436	0.41	7.92
United Kingdom		16,440	17,592	18,579	16,942	18,003	16.91	6.26
Southern Europe		1,473	1,383	1,812	1,742	2,105	1.98	20.84
Italy		1,220	1,211	1,545	1,543	1,864	1.75	20.80
Spain		253	172	267	199	241	0.23	21.11
Western Europe		5,726	4,781	4,707	3,753	4,198	3.94	11.86
Belgium		284	166	203	184	213	0.20	15.76
France		3,371	2,654	2,670	1,880	2,083	1.96	10.80
Germany		1,251	1,236	1,143	1,064	1,210	1.14	13.72
Netherlands		297	167	203	133	138	0.13	3.76
Switzerland		523	558	488	492	554	0.52	12.60
Other Europe		606	676	757	856	1,285	1.21	50.12
Other countries of Europe		606	676	757	856	1,285	1.21	50.12
REGION NOT SPECIFIED		1,297	1,126	1,248	1,474	1,355	1.27	-8.07
Not Specified		1,297	1,126	1,248	1,474	1,355	1.27	-8.07
Other countries of the World		1,297	1,126	1,248	1,474	1,355	1.27	-8.07

Source: World Tourism Organization (UNWTO)

SAMOA

1. Arrivals of non-resident tourists at national borders, by country of residence

	2002	2003	2004	2005	2006	Market share 06	% Change 06-05
TOTAL	88,971	92,486	98,155	101,807	115,882	100.00	13.83
AMERICAS	9,095	8,959	8,311	9,682	9,067	7.82	-6.35
North America	9,095	8,959	8,311	9,682	9,067	7.82	-6.35
Canada	375	407	372	445	385	0.33	-13.48
United States	8,720	8,552	7,939	9,237	8,682	7.49	-6.01
EAST ASIA AND THE PACIFIC	74,833	78,155	84,882	87,217	101,915	87.95	16.85
North-East Asia	577	683	1,013	661	1,468	1.27	122.09
China					752	0.65	
Japan	577	683	1,013	661	716	0.62	8.32
Australasia	35,228	39,080	45,934	53,838	66,569	57.45	23.65
Australia	11,438	12,103	13,914	17,598	23,603	20.37	34.12
New Zealand	23,790	26,977	32,020	36,240	42,966	37.08	18.56
Melanesia	1,928	2,184	2,406	2,430	2,740	2.36	12.76
Fiji	1,928	2,184	2,406	2,430	2,740	2.36	12.76
Polynesia	31,917	30,481	28,159	23,638	26,367	22.75	11.54
American Samoa	31,806	30,326	27,959	23,433	26,183	22.59	11.74
Cook Islands	111	155	200	205	184	0.16	-10.24
Other East Asia and the Pacific	5,183	5,727	7,370	6,650	4,771	4.12	-28.26
Other countries of Asia	1,310	1,780	2,412	2,424	1,596	1.38	-34.16
Other countries of Oceania	3,873	3,947	4,958	4,226	3,175	2.74	-24.87
EUROPE	4,762	5,136	4,756	4,632	4,581	3.95	-1.10
Northern Europe	2,283	2,759	2,417	2,233	2,109	1.82	-5.55
United Kingdom	1,480	2,092	1,704	1,562	1,580	1.36	1.15
Scandinavia	803	667	713	671	529	0.46	-21.16
Western Europe	1,381	1,436	1,296	1,380	1,304	1.13	-5.51
Germany	1,196	1,207	1,140	1,212	1,094	0.94	-9.74
Benelux	185	229	156	168	210	0.18	25.00
Other Europe	1,098	941	1,043	1,019	1,168	1.01	14.62
Other countries of Europe	1,098	941	1,043	1,019	1,168	1.01	14.62
REGION NOT SPECIFIED	281	236	206	276	319	0.28	15.58
Not Specified	281	236	206	276	319	0.28	15.58
Other countries of the World	281	236	206	276	319	0.28	15.58

Source: World Tourism Organization (UNWTO)

SAN MARINO

2. Arrivals of non-resident visitors at national borders, by nationality

		2002	2003	2004	2005	2006	Market share 06	% Change 06-05
TOTAL	(*)	3,102,453	2,882,207	2,812,488	2,107,092	2,135,589	100.00	1.35
AFRICA					111	140	0.01	26.13
North Africa					68	106		55.88
Morocco					45	88		95.56
Tunisia					23	18		-21.74
Southern Africa					43	34		-20.93
South Africa					43	34		-20.93
AMERICAS					17,479	22,131	1.04	26.61
Caribbean					18			
Puerto Rico					18			
North America					15,700	18,731	0.88	19.31
Canada					3,434	3,145	0.15	-8.42
Mexico					180	110	0.01	-38.89
United States					12,086	15,476	0.72	28.05
South America					1,761	3,400	0.16	93.07
Argentina					464	1,397	0.07	201.08
Brazil					533	876	0.04	64.35
Chile					177	130	0.01	-26.55
Colombia					85	84		-1.18
Peru					36	52		44.44
Venezuela					128	229	0.01	78.91
Other countries of South America					338	632	0.03	86.98
EAST ASIA AND THE PACIFIC					53,328	36,340	1.70	-31.86
North-East Asia					48,593	32,087	1.50	-33.97
China					37,566	25,788	1.21	-31.35
Taiwan (Province of China)					46	79		71.74
Japan					10,535	6,019	0.28	-42.87
Korea, Republic of					280	201	0.01	-28.21
Mongolia					166			
South-East Asia					445	1,112	0.05	149.89
Indonesia					85			
Malaysia					167	520	0.02	211.38
Philippines					153	523	0.02	241.83
Viet Nam					26	28		7.69
Thailand					14	41		192.86
Australasia					4,290	3,141	0.15	-26.78
Australia					4,240	3,070	0.14	-27.59
New Zealand					50	71		42.00
EUROPE					2,035,386	2,075,681	97.19	1.98
Central/Eastern Europe					162,822	174,293	8.16	7.05
Bulgaria					4,966	4,805	0.22	-3.24
Belarus					1,292	1,432	0.07	10.84
Czech Republic					16,948	13,008	0.61	-23.25
Estonia					4,266	3,994	0.19	-6.38
Hungary					7,438	8,965	0.42	20.53
Latvia					1,788	2,679	0.13	49.83
Lithuania					4,920	6,601	0.31	34.17
Poland					49,717	46,955	2.20	-5.56
Romania					9,190	10,235	0.48	11.37

SAN MARINO

2. Arrivals of non-resident visitors at national borders, by nationality

	2002	2003	2004	2005	2006	Market share 06	% Change 06-05
Russian Federation				57,521	71,590	3.35	24.46
Slovakia				1,743	1,713	0.08	-1.72
Ukraine				1,235	1,374	0.06	11.26
Other countries Central/East Europ				1,798	942	0.04	-47.61
Northern Europe				**30,310**	**30,127**	**1.41**	**-0.60**
Denmark				1,435	3,650	0.17	154.36
Finland				6,899	5,734	0.27	-16.89
Iceland				264	511	0.02	93.56
Ireland				645	702	0.03	8.84
Norway				1,591	2,154	0.10	35.39
Sweden				6,771	5,217	0.24	-22.95
United Kingdom				11,886	11,659	0.55	-1.91
Other countries of Northern Europe				819	500	0.02	-38.95
Southern Europe				**1,508,271**	**1,512,496**	**70.82**	**0.28**
Albania				204	223	0.01	9.31
Andorra				71			
Bosnia and Herzegovina				1,022	715	0.03	-30.04
Croatia				6,582	5,341	0.25	-18.85
Greece				10,156	15,852	0.74	56.09
Italy				1,469,346	1,469,778	68.82	0.03
Malta				332	78		-76.51
Portugal				1,013	607	0.03	-40.08
Slovenia				7,848	7,951	0.37	1.31
Spain				3,412	3,500	0.16	2.58
TFYR of Macedonia				17	100		488.24
Serbia and Montenegro				7,706	8,157	0.38	5.85
Other countries Southern Europe				562	194	0.01	-65.48
Western Europe				**332,029**	**356,181**	**16.68**	**7.27**
Austria				22,688	26,084	1.22	14.97
Belgium				18,886	19,301	0.90	2.20
France				67,727	75,389	3.53	11.31
Germany				148,417	152,248	7.13	2.58
Luxembourg				1,332	1,373	0.06	3.08
Netherlands				32,308	34,090	1.60	5.52
Switzerland				40,671	47,696	2.23	17.27
East Mediterranean Europe				**1,954**	**2,584**	**0.12**	**32.24**
Cyprus				111			
Israel				1,069	1,452	0.07	35.83
Turkey				774	1,132	0.05	46.25
MIDDLE EAST				**270**	**88**		**-67.41**
Middle East				**270**	**88**		**-67.41**
Lebanon				164			
Saudi Arabia				18	14		-22.22
Syrian Arab Republic				88	74		-15.91
SOUTH ASIA				**436**			
South Asia				**436**			
Bangladesh				77			
Sri Lanka				76			
India				283			
REGION NOT SPECIFIED	**3,102,453**	**2,882,207**	**2,812,488**	**82**	**1,209**	**0.06**	**1,374.39**
Not Specified	**3,102,453**	**2,882,207**	**2,812,488**	**82**	**1,209**	**0.06**	**1,374.39**

SAO TOME AND PRINCIPE

1. Arrivals of non-resident tourists at national borders, by nationality

	2002	2003	2004	2005	2006	Market share 06	% Change 06-05
TOTAL	9,189	10,039	10,576	15,746	12,266	100.00	-22.10
AFRICA	1,938	2,550	2,076	4,361	2,751	22.43	-36.92
East Africa				78			
Mozambique				78			
Central Africa	1,337	1,517	1,269	2,576	1,659	13.53	-35.60
Angola	651	938	683	873	999	8.14	14.43
Cameroon	150	136	145	845	220	1.79	-73.96
Central African Republic				93			
Chad				97			
Congo				67			
Equatorial Guinea	140	143	126	106	89	0.73	-16.04
Gabon	396	300	315	495	351	2.86	-29.09
North Africa				68			
Morocco				68			
Southern Africa		120	104	182	192	1.57	5.49
South Africa		120	104	182	192	1.57	5.49
West Africa	601	913	703	1,457	900	7.34	-38.23
Cape Verde	189	233	242	442	432	3.52	-2.26
Benin				23			
Ghana				54			
Cote D'Ivoire				34			
Mali				18			
Nigeria	412	680	461	787	468	3.82	-40.53
Guinea-Bissau				38			
Senegal				61			
AMERICAS	251	638	710	580	525	4.28	-9.48
Caribbean				48			
Cuba				48			
North America	251	369	412	377	277	2.26	-26.53
Canada				50			
United States	251	369	412	327	277	2.26	-15.29
South America		269	298	155	248	2.02	60.00
Brazil		269	298	155	248	2.02	60.00
EAST ASIA AND THE PACIFIC				156			
North-East Asia				135			
China				35			
Taiwan (Province of China)				71			
Japan				29			
South-East Asia				21			
Philippines				21			
EUROPE	5,429	6,742	6,803	10,299	7,568	61.70	-26.52
Northern Europe	170	235	104	258	169	1.38	-34.50
Denmark				37			
Norway				20			
Sweden				21			
United Kingdom	170	235	104	180	169	1.38	-6.11
Southern Europe	3,069	5,158	5,332	7,650	5,632	45.92	-26.38
Italy	142	117	105	112	99	0.81	-11.61

SAO TOME AND PRINCIPE

1. Arrivals of non-resident tourists at national borders, by nationality

	2002	2003	2004	2005	2006	Market share 06	% Change 06-05
Portugal	2,630	4,674	4,841	7,028	5,138	41.89	-26.89
Spain	297	367	386	510	395	3.22	-22.55
Western Europe	**2,190**	**1,349**	**1,367**	**2,391**	**1,767**	**14.41**	**-26.10**
Austria				33			
Belgium	121	102	116	190	114	0.93	-40.00
France	1,066	1,058	1,132	1,578	1,186	9.67	-24.84
Germany	1,003	189	119	433	467	3.81	7.85
Netherlands				96			
Switzerland				61			
MIDDLE EAST				**35**			
Middle East				**35**			
Lebanon				35			
SOUTH ASIA				**23**			
South Asia				**23**			
India				23			
REGION NOT SPECIFIED	**1,571**	**109**	**987**	**292**	**1,422**	**11.59**	**386.99**
Not Specified	**1,571**	**109**	**987**	**292**	**1,422**	**11.59**	**386.99**
Other countries of the World	1,571	109	987	292	1,422	11.59	386.99

Source: World Tourism Organization (UNWTO)

SAUDI ARABIA

1. Arrivals of non-resident tourists at national borders, by nationality

	2002	2003	2004	2005	2006	Market share 06	% Change 06-05
TOTAL	7,511,299	7,332,233	8,599,430	8,036,613	8,620,465	100.00	7.26
AFRICA	606,791	525,045	675,441	436,292	488,751	5.67	12.02
East Africa	57,116	56,185	76,534	38,901	43,206	0.50	11.07
Burundi	39	33	55	87	70		-19.54
Comoros	1,316	1,941	841	134	1,014	0.01	656.72
Ethiopia	27,248	26,332	43,212	19,914	11,367	0.13	-42.92
Eritrea	3,699	3,555	5,514	3,507	5,401	0.06	54.01
Djibouti	1,381	1,284	1,607	369	1,522	0.02	312.47
Kenya	2,663	2,847	3,631	1,807	4,892	0.06	170.72
Madagascar	111	122	20	3	105		3,400.00
Malawi	135	134	118	87	186		113.79
Mauritius	2,536	2,420	3,078	2,477	2,796	0.03	12.88
Mozambique	419	364	387	195	409		109.74
Rwanda	28	27	59	11	95		763.64
Seychelles	65	47	103	53	51		-3.77
Somalia	14,854	14,546	14,844	9,139	12,020	0.14	31.52
Zimbabwe	179	95	144	141	160		13.48
Uganda	650	773	1,043	379	1,091	0.01	187.86
United Republic of Tanzania	1,639	1,524	1,658	495	1,814	0.02	266.46
Zambia	154	141	220	103	153		48.54
Other countries of East Africa					60		
Central Africa	14,345	11,981	15,450	8,926	10,010	0.12	12.14
Angola	7	14	19				
Cameroon	2,625	2,723	2,466	2,724	2,901	0.03	6.50
Central African Republic	763	459	551	516	453	0.01	-12.21
Chad	10,856	8,662	12,210	5,481	6,441	0.07	17.52
Congo	42	22	127	105	147		40.00
Democratic Republic of the Congo	6	1					
Equatorial Guinea	2	3	9				
Gabon	44	97	68	100	68		-32.00
North Africa	366,095	296,905	386,511	235,880	258,916	3.00	9.77
Algeria	92,788	85,352	112,924	23,465	69,520	0.81	196.27
Morocco	78,095	70,238	80,322	52,123	57,415	0.67	10.15
Sudan	156,342	108,742	157,548	130,098	111,961	1.30	-13.94
Tunisia	38,870	32,573	35,717	30,194	20,020	0.23	-33.70
Southern Africa	17,104	17,483	23,052	9,742	21,544	0.25	121.15
Botswana	20	24	63	27	57		111.11
Lesotho	38	22	47	44	41		-6.82
Namibia	7	11	18	36	18		-50.00
South Africa	17,012	17,388	22,913	9,625	21,390	0.25	122.23
Swaziland	27	38	11	10	38		280.00
West Africa	152,131	142,491	173,894	142,843	155,075	1.80	8.56
Benin	1,799	2,367	2,751	2,610	1,349	0.02	-48.31
Gambia	2,403	2,476	2,305	2,148	2,307	0.03	7.40
Ghana	2,546	2,495	3,363	3,029	3,734	0.04	23.28
Guinea	4,693	6,243	8,135	4,082	7,028	0.08	72.17
Cote D'Ivoire	2,765	1,616	3,065	2,891	3,274	0.04	13.25
Liberia	261	337	129	143	363		153.85
Mali	5,468	5,291	6,565	1,602	7,368	0.09	359.93
Mauritania	4,501	3,960	6,008	5,870	11,632	0.13	98.16
Niger	7,230	6,549	7,442	11,170	7,378	0.09	-33.95
Nigeria	109,316	99,028	119,553	96,671	94,239	1.09	-2.52
Guinea-Bissau	175	561	39				

SAUDI ARABIA

1. Arrivals of non-resident tourists at national borders, by nationality

	2002	2003	2004	2005	2006	Market share 06	% Change 06-05
Senegal	7,806	8,179	10,799	9,985	13,013	0.15	30.33
Sierra Leone	489	602	811	870	849	0.01	-2.41
Togo	856	1,071	1,235	126	624	0.01	395.24
Burkina Faso	1,823	1,716	1,694	1,646	1,917	0.02	16.46
AMERICAS	**51,981**	**46,496**	**53,190**	**70,196**	**66,464**	**0.77**	**-5.32**
Caribbean	**454**	**408**	**560**	**4,268**	**12,404**	**0.14**	**190.63**
Bahamas	23	13		590	2		-99.66
Barbados	119	81	104	1,156	65		-94.38
British Virgin Islands				61			
Cuba	6	9	19	7	15		114.29
Dominica	51	43	35	767	6,005	0.07	682.92
Dominican Republic	20	8	12				
Haiti	1				13		
Jamaica	9	16	7	1,583	5,848	0.07	269.43
Puerto Rico	2		2	1			
Trinidad and Tobago	223	238	381	103	456	0.01	342.72
Central America	**146**	**111**	**153**	**115**	**167**		**45.22**
Belize	13	24	19	2	7		250.00
Costa Rica	8	11	12	8	10		25.00
El Salvador	5		1	2	3		50.00
Guatemala	13	12	21	10	25		150.00
Honduras	57	22	22	10	21		110.00
Nicaragua		4	6	42			
Panama	50	38	72	41	101		146.34
North America	**49,920**	**44,668**	**51,904**	**62,085**	**49,866**	**0.58**	**-19.68**
Canada	9,972	9,081	12,591	13,405	10,896	0.13	-18.72
Mexico	179	178	217	182	164		-9.89
United States	39,756	35,405	39,096	48,498	38,756	0.45	-20.09
Other countries of North America	13	4			50		
South America	**1,461**	**1,309**	**573**	**3,728**	**4,027**	**0.05**	**8.02**
Argentina	235	193	345	1,916	272		-85.80
Bolivia	25	19	2	21	52		147.62
Brazil	623	637	105	960	859	0.01	-10.52
Chile	48	88	7	84	112		33.33
Colombia	74	83	9	150	1,549	0.02	932.67
Ecuador	60	19	1	61	49		-19.67
Guyana	30			4	13		225.00
Paraguay	8	5	9	43	14		-67.44
Peru	14	17	6	56	74		32.14
Suriname	48	53	55	5	77		1,440.00
Uruguay	112	21	2	44	41		-6.82
Venezuela	184	174	32	384	915	0.01	138.28
EAST ASIA AND THE PACIFIC	**660,329**	**612,340**	**752,905**	**439,021**	**595,438**	**6.91**	**35.63**
North-East Asia	**20,774**	**23,131**	**31,679**	**38,104**	**47,243**	**0.55**	**23.98**
China	11,552	15,136	21,398	22,837	30,658	0.36	34.25
Taiwan (Province of China)	230		1,305				
Hong Kong, China		20	52	92	469	0.01	409.78
Japan	6,291	5,466	5,342	10,214	9,850	0.11	-3.56
Korea, Dem. People's Republic of	193	201	205				
Korea, Republic of	2,488	2,284	3,372	4,961	6,263	0.07	26.24
Mongolia	20	24	5		3		
South-East Asia	**632,345**	**582,503**	**712,835**	**392,915**	**527,057**	**6.11**	**34.14**

SAUDI ARABIA

1. Arrivals of non-resident tourists at national borders, by nationality

	2002	2003	2004	2005	2006	Market share 06	% Change 06-05
Brunei Darussalam	5,655	2,617	3,132	3,397	2,206	0.03	-35.06
Myanmar	577	224	3,619	2,901	3,828	0.04	31.95
Cambodia	71	153	221	409	269		-34.23
Indonesia	418,704	396,709	486,869	226,037	373,027	4.33	65.03
Lao People's Democratic Republic		2					
Malaysia	105,000	84,473	98,608	101,206	73,847	0.86	-27.03
Philippines	78,863	79,490	98,707	35,253	50,948	0.59	44.52
Singapore	12,618	7,149	6,969	15,390	6,968	0.08	-54.72
Viet Nam	2		66	55	1,538	0.02	2,696.36
Thailand	10,855	11,686	14,644	8,267	14,426	0.17	74.50
Australasia	**7,152**	**6,609**	**8,226**	**7,996**	**10,003**	**0.12**	**25.10**
Australia	5,649	5,273	6,948	6,508	8,096	0.09	24.40
New Zealand	1,503	1,336	1,278	1,488	1,907	0.02	28.16
Melanesia	**57**	**96**	**152**	**6**	**173**		**2,783.33**
Fiji	57	96	152	6	173		2,783.33
Micronesia	**1**				**6**		
Kiribati					6		
Micronesia (Federated States of)	1						
Polynesia		**1**	**13**		**10,956**	**0.13**	
American Samoa					10,956	0.13	
French Polynesia		1	13				
EUROPE	**338,580**	**334,159**	**424,297**	**340,310**	**484,575**	**5.62**	**42.39**
Central/Eastern Europe	**21,686**	**20,307**	**29,180**	**37,759**	**26,484**	**0.31**	**-29.86**
Azerbaijan	1,206	1,358	2,340	2,591	3,778	0.04	45.81
Armenia	23	32	41	35	31		-11.43
Bulgaria	379	492	453	443	629	0.01	41.99
Belarus	327	168	165	238	86		-63.87
Czech Republic	450	377	530	407	320		-21.38
Estonia	13	49	30	63	28		-55.56
Georgia	35	53	65	19	66		247.37
Hungary	219	159	212	218	336		54.13
Kazakhstan	650	906	1,823	1,901	3,241	0.04	70.49
Kyrgyzstan	46	683	1,157	1,116			
Latvia	37	46	78	33	59		78.79
Lithuania	29	13	33	24	17		-29.17
Republic of Moldova	36	84	230	30	23		-23.33
Poland	432	460	746	748	1,192	0.01	59.36
Romania	577	479	638	693	1,182	0.01	70.56
Russian Federation	1,942	5,679	9,441	9,475	1,246	0.01	-86.85
Slovakia	136	113	149	150	145		-3.33
Tajikistan	5,525	3,292	4,240	4,706	4,334	0.05	-7.90
Turkmenistan	236	234	335	443	330		-25.51
Ukraine	500	621	647	542	574	0.01	5.90
Uzbekistan	5,733	5,009	4,563	6,797	8,476	0.10	24.70
Other countries Central/East Europ	3,155		1,264	7,087	391		-94.48
Northern Europe	**85,035**	**78,669**	**93,645**	**72,362**	**74,854**	**0.87**	**3.44**
Denmark	2,236	1,990	2,536	1,782	2,572	0.03	44.33
Finland	704	616	556	637	776	0.01	21.82
Iceland	82	150	144	30	298		893.33
Ireland	1,886	1,971	2,448	2,320	2,535	0.03	9.27
Norway	1,721	1,481	1,820	2,087	1,993	0.02	-4.50
Sweden	3,556	2,909	3,539	3,483	4,201	0.05	20.61
United Kingdom	74,850	69,552	82,602	62,023	62,479	0.72	0.74

SAUDI ARABIA

1. Arrivals of non-resident tourists at national borders, by nationality

	2002	2003	2004	2005	2006	Market share 06	% Change 06-05
Southern Europe	15,332	18,177	12,821	28,412	24,309	0.28	-14.44
Albania	269	568	530	566	473	0.01	-16.43
Bosnia and Herzegovina	1,405	1,521	1,849	2,095	1,991	0.02	-4.96
Croatia	320	397	396	444	471	0.01	6.08
Greece	1,435	1,367	1,543		1,805	0.02	
Italy	6,194	5,615	5,446	13,500	11,097	0.13	-17.80
Malta	51	56	33	66	106		60.61
Portugal	567	469	669	1,058	692	0.01	-34.59
San Marino	3		2	2	5		150.00
Slovenia	69	58	65	92	237		157.61
Spain	1,925	1,712	2,288	8,371	3,499	0.04	-58.20
Serbia and Montenegro	1				1,362	0.02	
Other countries Southern Europe	3,093	6,414		2,218	2,571	0.03	15.92
Western Europe	40,195	39,273	52,037	101,090	92,428	1.07	-8.57
Austria	1,569	1,824	2,406	2,169	4,353	0.05	100.69
Belgium	2,094	1,970	2,584	2,723	4,192	0.05	53.95
France	15,851	15,237	17,539	30,946	40,638	0.47	31.32
Germany	12,185	12,007	18,406	51,682	27,476	0.32	-46.84
Luxembourg	15	18	28	33	70		112.12
Monaco					6		
Netherlands	6,127	5,832	8,269	8,775	10,844	0.13	23.58
Switzerland	2,354	2,385	2,805	4,762	4,849	0.06	1.83
East Mediterranean Europe	176,332	177,733	236,614	100,687	266,500	3.09	164.68
Cyprus	344	266	347	520	428		-17.69
Turkey	175,988	177,467	236,267	100,167	266,072	3.09	165.63
MIDDLE EAST	4,212,598	3,923,873	4,752,257	5,607,356	5,515,980	63.99	-1.63
Middle East	4,212,598	3,923,873	4,752,257	5,607,356	5,515,980	63.99	-1.63
Bahrain	252,697	281,875	277,618	356,163	389,513	4.52	9.36
Palestine	52,034	46,301	47,342	8,822	25,163	0.29	185.23
Iraq	23,987	25,099	43,063	52,477	52,483	0.61	0.01
Jordan	263,592	240,356	306,495	279,288	322,548	3.74	15.49
Kuwait	1,010,943	971,341	1,238,382	1,462,879	1,681,843	19.51	14.97
Lebanon	61,977	63,793	74,591	68,703	70,054	0.81	1.97
Libyan Arab Jamahiriya	44,558	39,546	48,149	49,108	36,296	0.42	-26.09
Oman	126,976	136,389	118,695	137,562	221,623	2.57	61.11
Qatar	363,345	388,239	434,944	511,143	501,157	5.81	-1.95
Syrian Arab Republic	564,776	541,894	726,752	576,950	605,150	7.02	4.89
United Arab Emirates	177,581	189,471	238,536	1,043,076	800,059	9.28	-23.30
Egypt	1,015,078	787,277	976,931	799,665	609,831	7.07	-23.74
Yemen	255,054	212,292	220,759	261,520	200,260	2.32	-23.42
SOUTH ASIA	1,618,928	1,868,897	1,932,990	1,142,202	1,469,257	17.04	28.63
South Asia	1,618,928	1,868,897	1,932,990	1,142,202	1,469,257	17.04	28.63
Afghanistan	14,249	31,481	33,313	25,918	33,093	0.38	27.68
Bangladesh	221,447	209,560	255,402	52,633	92,088	1.07	74.96
Sri Lanka	75,847	81,695	98,403	42,445	56,910	0.66	34.08
India	373,636	362,609	474,467	117,101	345,431	4.01	194.99
Iran, Islamic Republic of	376,774	618,897	386,507	519,865	387,556	4.50	-25.45
Maldives	2,042	1,341	1,177	1,263	1,847	0.02	46.24
Nepal	25,091	23,843	29,662	31,305	41,883	0.49	33.79
Pakistan	529,842	539,471	654,059	351,672	510,449	5.92	45.15
REGION NOT SPECIFIED	22,092	21,423	8,350	1,236			
Not Specified	22,092	21,423	8,350	1,236			

SENEGAL

1. Arrivals of non-resident tourists at national borders, by nationality

	2002	2003	2004	2005	2006	Market share 06	% Change 06-05
TOTAL			666,616	769,489	866,154	100.00	12.56
AFRICA			209,226	265,113	429,955	49.64	62.18
North Africa			5,597	5,935	6,271	0.72	5.66
Morocco			3,784	4,108	4,582	0.53	11.54
Tunisia			1,813	1,827	1,689	0.19	-7.55
West Africa			191,215	244,156	346,375	39.99	41.87
Gambia			47,732	70,294	109,617	12.66	55.94
Guinea			40,908	43,274	40,996	4.73	-5.26
Cote D'Ivoire			17,249	17,677			
Mali			36,443	45,303	41,622	4.81	-8.13
Mauritania			34,044	37,417	44,781	5.17	19.68
Guinea-Bissau			8,554	24,199	109,359	12.63	351.92
Burkina Faso			6,285	5,992			
Other Africa			12,414	15,022	77,309	8.93	414.64
Other countries of Africa			12,414	15,022	77,309	8.93	414.64
AMERICAS			24,686	26,274	25,921	2.99	-1.34
North America			20,316	21,869	25,921	2.99	18.53
United States			20,316	21,869	25,921	2.99	18.53
Other Americas			4,370	4,405			
Other countries of the Americas			4,370	4,405			
EUROPE			348,852	392,767	323,721	37.37	-17.58
Southern Europe			30,594	34,519	28,283	3.27	-18.07
Italy			16,363	17,901	14,570	1.68	-18.61
Spain			14,231	16,618	13,713	1.58	-17.48
Western Europe			293,003	329,289	272,268	31.43	-17.32
France			255,048	287,454	232,043	26.79	-19.28
Germany			12,795	14,193	9,027	1.04	-36.40
Benelux			25,160	27,642	31,198	3.60	12.86
Other Europe			25,255	28,959	23,170	2.68	-19.99
Other countries of Europe			25,255	28,959	23,170	2.68	-19.99
REGION NOT SPECIFIED			83,852	85,335	86,557	9.99	1.43
Not Specified			83,852	85,335	86,557	9.99	1.43
Other countries of the World			83,852	85,335	86,557	9.99	1.43

Source: World Tourism Organization (UNWTO)

SENEGAL

3. Arrivals of non-resident tourists in hotels and similar establishments, by nationality

	2002	2003	2004	2005	2006	Market share 06	% Change 06-05
TOTAL	426,825	353,539	363,490	386,565	405,827	100.00	4.98
AFRICA	86,037	85,664	89,660	87,565	106,396	26.22	21.51
Other Africa	86,037	85,664	89,660	87,565	106,396	26.22	21.51
All countries of Africa	86,037	85,664	89,660	87,565	106,396	26.22	21.51
AMERICAS	9,536	10,025	12,431	13,989	14,684	3.62	4.97
North America	9,164	9,676	12,027	13,352	14,199	3.50	6.34
Canada	923	1,158	1,605	2,272	1,795	0.44	-20.99
United States	8,241	8,518	10,422	11,080	12,404	3.06	11.95
Other Americas	372	349	404	637	485	0.12	-23.86
Other countries of the Americas	372	349	404	637	485	0.12	-23.86
EAST ASIA AND THE PACIFIC	1,864	2,273	3,705	3,837	3,846	0.95	0.23
Other East Asia and the Pacific	1,864	2,273	3,705	3,837	3,846	0.95	0.23
All countries East Asia/Pacific	1,864	2,273	3,705	3,837	3,846	0.95	0.23
EUROPE	322,631	252,568	242,944	274,439	271,231	66.83	-1.17
Central/Eastern Europe	410	532	995	2,334	1,989	0.49	-14.78
All countries Central/East Europe	410	532	995	2,334	1,989	0.49	-14.78
Northern Europe	5,745	4,512	5,083	6,061	8,312	2.05	37.14
Denmark	167	639	298	374	496	0.12	32.62
Finland	159	119	136	390	409	0.10	4.87
Norway	152	415	219	257	515	0.13	100.39
Sweden	195	276	338	660	1,310	0.32	98.48
United Kingdom	5,072	3,063	4,092	4,380	5,582	1.38	27.44
Southern Europe	44,122	23,470	24,557	28,663	32,855	8.10	14.63
Italy	19,496	9,279	9,413	11,493	13,705	3.38	19.25
Portugal	1,402	1,511	1,729	1,817	2,129	0.52	17.17
Spain	23,224	12,680	13,415	15,353	17,021	4.19	10.86
Western Europe	255,057	207,955	198,782	224,420	218,774	53.91	-2.52
France	230,088	181,470	172,878	191,580	184,376	45.43	-3.76
Germany	8,458	7,985	8,374	9,615	8,708	2.15	-9.43
Switzerland	883	1,475	1,370	1,513	1,794	0.44	18.57
Benelux	15,628	17,025	16,160	21,712	23,896	5.89	10.06
Other Europe	17,297	16,099	13,527	12,961	9,301	2.29	-28.24
Other countries of Europe	17,297	16,099	13,527	12,961	9,301	2.29	-28.24
MIDDLE EAST	994	1,253	1,672	1,467	1,882	0.46	28.29
Middle East	994	1,253	1,672	1,467	1,882	0.46	28.29
All countries of Middle East	994	1,253	1,672	1,467	1,882	0.46	28.29
REGION NOT SPECIFIED	5,763	1,756	13,078	5,268	7,788	1.92	47.84
Not Specified	5,763	1,756	13,078	5,268	7,788	1.92	47.84
Other countries of the World	5,763	1,756	13,078	5,268	7,788	1.92	47.84

Source: World Tourism Organization (UNWTO)

SENEGAL

5. Overnight stays of non-resident tourists in hotels and similar establishments, by nationality

	2002	2003	2004	2005	2006	Market share 06	% Change 06-05
TOTAL	1,569,123	1,451,213	1,349,397	1,396,674	1,426,455	100.00	2.13
AFRICA	226,702	223,917	218,151	218,487	284,588	19.95	30.25
Other Africa	226,702	223,917	218,151	218,487	284,588	19.95	30.25
All countries of Africa	226,702	223,917	218,151	218,487	284,588	19.95	30.25
AMERICAS	20,150	58,624	33,509	45,272	41,576	2.91	-8.16
North America	19,313	57,771	32,148	43,418	39,968	2.80	-7.95
Canada	2,499	3,781	5,411	7,510	6,133	0.43	-18.34
United States	16,814	53,990	26,737	35,908	33,835	2.37	-5.77
Other Americas	837	853	1,361	1,854	1,608	0.11	-13.27
Other countries of the Americas	837	853	1,361	1,854	1,608	0.11	-13.27
EAST ASIA AND THE PACIFIC	4,278	7,146	9,576	11,697	11,144	0.78	-4.73
Other East Asia and the Pacific	4,278	7,146	9,576	11,697	11,144	0.78	-4.73
All countries East Asia/Pacific	4,278	7,146	9,576	11,697	11,144	0.78	-4.73
EUROPE	1,290,136	1,132,104	1,030,070	1,103,462	1,067,456	74.83	-3.26
Central/Eastern Europe	1,626	1,531	2,865	9,019	7,566	0.53	-16.11
All countries Central/East Europe	1,626	1,531	2,865	9,019	7,566	0.53	-16.11
Northern Europe	14,230	13,771	12,500	17,129	21,434	1.50	25.13
Denmark	516	1,205	904	1,072	1,376	0.10	28.36
Finland	309	331	390	952	1,024	0.07	7.56
Norway	529	1,015	781	715	1,463	0.10	104.62
Sweden	493	655	890	2,494	4,302	0.30	72.49
United Kingdom	12,383	10,565	9,535	11,896	13,269	0.93	11.54
Southern Europe	111,828	79,683	66,259	86,553	100,597	7.05	16.23
Italy	65,281	41,608	30,608	43,254	49,026	3.44	13.34
Portugal	3,962	5,372	5,249	5,808	7,504	0.53	29.20
Spain	42,585	32,703	30,402	37,491	44,067	3.09	17.54
Western Europe	1,114,890	988,345	910,353	953,058	912,929	64.00	-4.21
France	964,507	852,973	766,034	794,315	775,133	54.34	-2.41
Germany	68,610	41,608	47,493	50,475	37,805	2.65	-25.10
Switzerland	5,559	6,487	6,085	7,372	8,008	0.56	8.63
Benelux	76,214	87,277	90,741	100,896	91,983	6.45	-8.83
Other Europe	47,562	48,774	38,093	37,703	24,930	1.75	-33.88
Other countries of Europe	47,562	48,774	38,093	37,703	24,930	1.75	-33.88
MIDDLE EAST	2,543	2,928	7,358	5,808	6,096	0.43	4.96
Middle East	2,543	2,928	7,358	5,808	6,096	0.43	4.96
All countries of Middle East	2,543	2,928	7,358	5,808	6,096	0.43	4.96
REGION NOT SPECIFIED	25,314	26,494	50,733	11,948	15,595	1.09	30.52
Not Specified	25,314	26,494	50,733	11,948	15,595	1.09	30.52
Other countries of the World	25,314	26,494	50,733	11,948	15,595	1.09	30.52

Source: World Tourism Organization (UNWTO)

SERBIA

3. Arrivals of non-resident tourists in hotels and similar establishments, by nationality

	2002	2003	2004	2005	2006	Market share 06	% Change 06-05
TOTAL	294,382	320,814	374,005	433,636	447,669	100.00	3.24
AMERICAS	11,372	13,952	13,295	15,535	16,843	3.76	8.42
North America	11,372	13,952	13,295	15,535	16,843	3.76	8.42
Canada	1,840	2,329	2,537	3,077	3,413	0.76	10.92
United States	9,532	11,623	10,758	12,458	13,430	3.00	7.80
EAST ASIA AND THE PACIFIC	2,908	3,637	4,821	5,597	6,315	1.41	12.83
North-East Asia	1,504	1,615	1,926	1,968	2,562	0.57	30.18
Japan	1,504	1,615	1,926	1,968	2,562	0.57	30.18
Australasia	1,404	2,022	2,895	3,629	3,753	0.84	3.42
Australia	1,167	1,754	2,584	3,241	3,312	0.74	2.19
New Zealand	237	268	311	388	441	0.10	13.66
EUROPE	271,111	294,576	345,874	400,476	414,649	92.62	3.54
Central/Eastern Europe	60,756	61,045	64,792	68,659	75,121	16.78	9.41
Bulgaria	12,584	12,416	14,635	14,520	16,084	3.59	10.77
Czech Republic	4,401	4,325	4,762	6,239	6,293	1.41	0.87
Hungary	11,889	10,184	10,198	11,625	13,401	2.99	15.28
Poland	10,355	13,877	13,570	11,851	13,989	3.12	18.04
Romania	9,112	7,946	8,374	8,904	8,767	1.96	-1.54
Russian Federation	8,775	8,340	9,385	11,072	11,363	2.54	2.63
Slovakia	3,640	3,957	3,868	4,448	5,224	1.17	17.45
Northern Europe	17,728	22,680	24,757	28,443	31,364	7.01	10.27
Denmark	1,892	2,305	2,433	2,710	3,081	0.69	13.69
Finland	857	924	1,137	1,391	1,549	0.35	11.36
Iceland	209	237	446	535	610	0.14	14.02
Ireland	1,010	1,295	1,452	1,758	1,621	0.36	-7.79
Norway	1,950	2,605	2,476	2,843	2,990	0.67	5.17
Sweden	3,139	4,082	5,330	4,888	5,888	1.32	20.46
United Kingdom	8,671	11,232	11,483	14,318	15,625	3.49	9.13
Southern Europe	128,222	140,392	176,630	210,463	214,848	47.99	2.08
Bosnia and Herzegovina	34,503	31,027	41,851	45,654	49,813	11.13	9.11
Croatia	14,367	18,896	23,762	28,291	32,944	7.36	16.45
Greece	10,345	13,270	17,260	22,685	23,926	5.34	5.47
Italy	19,104	20,789	23,333	27,855	27,392	6.12	-1.66
Portugal	501	664	871	1,185	1,105	0.25	-6.75
Slovenia	21,158	27,009	38,740	52,709	51,136	11.42	-2.98
Spain	2,048	3,120	2,776	4,019	4,072	0.91	1.32
TFYR of Macedonia	26,196	25,617	28,037	28,065	24,460	5.46	-12.85
Western Europe	49,067	56,002	60,514	71,620	74,294	16.60	3.73
Austria	10,289	11,399	12,212	15,319	17,740	3.96	15.80
Belgium	2,732	2,596	3,064	3,244	3,497	0.78	7.80
France	7,182	8,443	9,993	12,748	12,806	2.86	0.45
Germany	21,363	23,891	24,871	28,600	27,468	6.14	-3.96
Luxembourg	201	198	308	266	345	0.08	29.70
Netherlands	4,339	5,840	5,771	6,908	7,851	1.75	13.65
Switzerland	2,961	3,635	4,295	4,535	4,587	1.02	1.15
East Mediterranean Europe	7,155	7,762	11,996	10,397	9,059	2.02	-12.87
Israel	2,039	2,264	2,755	3,124	2,759	0.62	-11.68
Turkey	5,116	5,498	9,241	7,273	6,300	1.41	-13.38
Other Europe	8,183	6,695	7,185	10,894	9,963	2.23	-8.55
Other countries of Europe	8,183	6,695	7,185	10,894	9,963	2.23	-8.55

SERBIA

3. Arrivals of non-resident tourists in hotels and similar establishments, by nationality

	2002	2003	2004	2005	2006	Market share 06	% Change 06-05
REGION NOT SPECIFIED	8,991	8,649	10,015	12,028	9,862	2.20	-18.01
Not Specified	8,991	8,649	10,015	12,028	9,862	2.20	-18.01
Other countries of the World	8,991	8,649	10,015	12,028	9,862	2.20	-18.01

Source: World Tourism Organization (UNWTO)

SERBIA

4. Arrivals of non-resident tourists in all types of accommodation establishments, by nationality

	2002	2003	2004	2005	2006	Market share 06	% Change 06-05
TOTAL	312,063	339,283	391,826	452,679	468,842	100.00	3.57
AMERICAS	11,587	14,155	13,483	15,789	17,038	3.63	7.91
North America	11,587	14,155	13,483	15,789	17,038	3.63	7.91
Canada	1,877	2,373	2,587	3,133	3,486	0.74	11.27
United States	9,710	11,782	10,896	12,656	13,552	2.89	7.08
EAST ASIA AND THE PACIFIC	2,966	3,680	4,879	5,675	6,402	1.37	12.81
North-East Asia	1,508	1,620	1,936	1,976	2,571	0.55	30.11
Japan	1,508	1,620	1,936	1,976	2,571	0.55	30.11
Australasia	1,458	2,060	2,943	3,699	3,831	0.82	3.57
Australia	1,213	1,792	2,628	3,308	3,372	0.72	1.93
New Zealand	245	268	315	391	459	0.10	17.39
EUROPE	288,380	312,666	363,345	419,058	435,400	92.87	3.90
Central/Eastern Europe	65,095	65,094	69,479	73,596	80,643	17.20	9.58
Bulgaria	13,399	13,537	16,284	16,330	18,071	3.85	10.66
Czech Republic	4,496	4,414	4,925	6,442	6,663	1.42	3.43
Hungary	12,248	10,426	10,451	11,802	13,669	2.92	15.82
Poland	10,471	13,973	13,875	12,019	14,404	3.07	19.84
Romania	11,575	10,263	10,408	11,220	10,799	2.30	-3.75
Russian Federation	9,156	8,491	9,615	11,249	11,711	2.50	4.11
Slovakia	3,750	3,990	3,921	4,534	5,326	1.14	17.47
Northern Europe	17,950	22,985	25,184	28,824	31,682	6.76	9.92
Denmark	1,936	2,337	2,458	2,737	3,107	0.66	13.52
Finland	861	936	1,160	1,409	1,562	0.33	10.86
Iceland	211	237	450	545	615	0.13	12.84
Ireland	1,023	1,306	1,466	1,782	1,638	0.35	-8.08
Norway	1,975	2,659	2,493	2,895	3,060	0.65	5.70
Sweden	3,176	4,153	5,417	4,982	5,969	1.27	19.81
United Kingdom	8,768	11,357	11,740	14,474	15,731	3.36	8.68
Southern Europe	136,219	148,879	187,649	222,016	227,582	48.54	2.51
Bosnia and Herzegovina	36,759	33,844	44,726	49,202	53,973	11.51	9.70
Croatia	14,989	19,239	24,507	28,685	33,617	7.17	17.19
Greece	11,892	14,868	19,447	24,975	26,618	5.68	6.58
Italy	19,777	21,500	23,723	28,122	27,738	5.92	-1.37
Portugal	521	676	880	1,220	1,126	0.24	-7.70
Slovenia	23,338	29,569	42,353	56,128	54,440	11.61	-3.01
Spain	2,059	2,436	2,811	4,050	4,124	0.88	1.83
TFYR of Macedonia	26,884	26,747	29,202	29,634	25,946	5.53	-12.45
Western Europe	53,234	60,874	61,663	73,002	75,767	16.16	3.79
Austria	12,606	13,998	12,408	15,531	17,936	3.83	15.49
Belgium	2,776	2,629	3,109	3,311	3,553	0.76	7.31
France	7,223	8,591	10,177	13,224	13,224	2.82	
Germany	21,665	24,316	25,356	29,021	27,970	5.97	-3.62
Luxembourg	203	199	320	277	345	0.07	24.55
Netherlands	4,419	5,937	5,877	7,033	8,046	1.72	14.40
Switzerland	4,342	5,204	4,416	4,605	4,693	1.00	1.91
East Mediterranean Europe	7,591	7,914	12,110	10,535	9,489	2.02	-9.93
Israel	2,045	2,270	2,772	3,138	2,784	0.59	-11.28
Turkey	5,546	5,644	9,338	7,397	6,705	1.43	-9.36
Other Europe	8,291	6,920	7,260	11,085	10,237	2.18	-7.65

SERBIA

4. Arrivals of non-resident tourists in all types of accommodation establishments, by nationality

	2002	2003	2004	2005	2006	Market share 06	% Change 06-05
Other countries of Europe	8,291	6,920	7,260	11,085	10,237	2.18	-7.65
REGION NOT SPECIFIED	**9,130**	**8,782**	**10,119**	**12,157**	**10,002**	**2.13**	**-17.73**
Not Specified	**9,130**	**8,782**	**10,119**	**12,157**	**10,002**	**2.13**	**-17.73**
Other countries of the World	9,130	8,782	10,119	12,157	10,002	2.13	-17.73

Source: World Tourism Organization (UNWTO)

SERBIA

5. Overnight stays of non-resident tourists in hotels and similar establishments, by nationality

	2002	2003	2004	2005	2006	Market share 06	% Change 06-05
TOTAL	687,369	736,070	797,810	932,697	949,323	100.00	1.78
AMERICAS	45,039	43,506	36,805	40,939	43,861	4.62	7.14
North America	45,039	43,506	36,805	40,939	43,861	4.62	7.14
Canada	5,537	6,469	7,331	7,839	9,811	1.03	25.16
United States	39,502	37,037	29,474	33,100	34,050	3.59	2.87
EAST ASIA AND THE PACIFIC	7,755	9,305	11,423	12,834	13,738	1.45	7.04
North-East Asia	3,918	3,867	4,707	4,569	5,561	0.59	21.71
Japan	3,918	3,867	4,707	4,569	5,561	0.59	21.71
Australasia	3,837	5,438	6,716	8,265	8,177	0.86	-1.06
Australia	3,230	4,763	5,807	7,301	7,300	0.77	-0.01
New Zealand	607	675	909	964	877	0.09	-9.02
EUROPE	605,391	658,047	718,534	846,261	857,349	90.31	1.31
Central/Eastern Europe	131,819	139,710	131,018	152,971	157,355	16.58	2.87
Bulgaria	23,464	23,394	27,464	27,077	28,777	3.03	6.28
Czech Republic	9,754	10,017	11,160	14,348	14,413	1.52	0.45
Hungary	21,559	17,321	18,907	20,580	25,023	2.64	21.59
Poland	20,408	33,303	20,395	24,643	21,940	2.31	-10.97
Romania	18,218	17,874	20,603	24,001	21,798	2.30	-9.18
Russian Federation	26,522	24,415	24,125	32,508	34,899	3.68	7.36
Slovakia	11,894	13,386	8,364	9,814	10,505	1.11	7.04
Northern Europe	50,210	59,246	63,373	76,075	83,527	8.80	9.80
Denmark	4,939	5,337	5,843	6,751	7,270	0.77	7.69
Finland	2,322	2,331	3,060	3,536	3,787	0.40	7.10
Iceland	731	638	1,090	1,400	1,380	0.15	-1.43
Ireland	2,610	3,311	3,657	4,735	4,089	0.43	-13.64
Norway	4,385	6,926	5,789	7,040	8,045	0.85	14.28
Sweden	7,785	9,700	12,202	12,155	13,291	1.40	9.35
United Kingdom	27,438	31,003	31,732	40,458	45,665	4.81	12.87
Southern Europe	269,034	294,978	351,660	408,891	415,153	43.73	1.53
Bosnia and Herzegovina	71,875	70,114	86,528	91,363	101,142	10.65	10.70
Croatia	30,532	36,191	44,061	54,580	61,345	6.46	12.39
Greece	25,150	28,301	33,169	42,977	45,203	4.76	5.18
Italy	44,856	48,604	50,787	64,833	58,548	6.17	-9.69
Portugal	1,214	2,211	2,080	3,015	2,821	0.30	-6.43
Slovenia	44,339	49,293	67,751	91,544	91,162	9.60	-0.42
Spain	5,552	6,012	7,321	10,676	10,634	1.12	-0.39
TFYR of Macedonia	45,516	54,252	59,963	49,903	44,298	4.67	-11.23
Western Europe	112,899	127,444	132,608	160,351	158,332	16.68	-1.26
Austria	20,772	21,449	23,542	30,508	34,418	3.63	12.82
Belgium	6,099	6,228	6,983	7,095	6,923	0.73	-2.42
France	17,727	19,976	23,194	29,678	27,899	2.94	-5.99
Germany	49,986	56,920	55,592	66,953	61,817	6.51	-7.67
Luxembourg	601	721	552	583	707	0.07	21.27
Netherlands	10,335	13,571	12,430	15,114	16,125	1.70	6.69
Switzerland	7,379	8,579	10,315	10,420	10,443	1.10	0.22
East Mediterranean Europe	17,079	17,826	21,818	20,602	19,879	2.09	-3.51
Israel	7,750	6,779	7,502	7,629	7,416	0.78	-2.79
Turkey	9,329	11,047	14,316	12,973	12,463	1.31	-3.93
Other Europe	24,350	18,843	18,057	27,371	23,103	2.43	-15.59

SERBIA

5. Overnight stays of non-resident tourists in hotels and similar establishments, by nationality

	2002	2003	2004	2005	2006	Market share 06	% Change 06-05
Other countries of Europe	24,350	18,843	18,057	27,371	23,103	2.43	-15.59
REGION NOT SPECIFIED	**29,184**	**25,212**	**31,048**	**32,663**	**34,375**	**3.62**	**5.24**
Not Specified	**29,184**	**25,212**	**31,048**	**32,663**	**34,375**	**3.62**	**5.24**
Other countries of the World	29,184	25,212	31,048	32,663	34,375	3.62	5.24

Source: World Tourism Organization (UNWTO)

SERBIA

6. Overnight stays of non-resident tourists in all types of accommodation establishments, by nationality

	2002	2003	2004	2005	2006	Market share 06	% Change 06-05
TOTAL	738,261	791,702	851,059	991,748	1,015,312	100.00	2.38
AMERICAS	45,646	44,079	37,276	41,902	44,639	4.40	6.53
North America	45,646	44,079	37,276	41,902	44,639	4.40	6.53
Canada	5,669	6,601	7,472	8,143	10,161	1.00	24.78
United States	39,977	37,478	29,804	33,759	34,478	3.40	2.13
EAST ASIA AND THE PACIFIC	7,896	9,436	11,634	13,035	14,103	1.39	8.19
North-East Asia	3,925	3,878	4,730	4,589	5,586	0.55	21.73
Japan	3,925	3,878	4,730	4,589	5,586	0.55	21.73
Australasia	3,971	5,558	6,904	8,446	8,517	0.84	0.84
Australia	3,333	4,883	5,979	7,469	7,600	0.75	1.75
New Zealand	638	675	925	977	917	0.09	-6.14
EUROPE	654,360	712,260	770,637	903,692	921,347	90.75	1.95
Central/Eastern Europe	139,553	145,984	139,653	160,398	166,885	16.44	4.04
Bulgaria	24,845	24,723	30,227	29,254	31,073	3.06	6.22
Czech Republic	10,022	10,138	11,335	14,614	14,836	1.46	1.52
Hungary	22,872	17,814	19,302	20,915	25,495	2.51	21.90
Poland	20,788	33,765	21,690	24,973	23,584	2.32	-5.56
Romania	21,440	20,890	23,101	27,466	24,302	2.39	-11.52
Russian Federation	27,521	25,199	25,516	33,215	36,906	3.63	11.11
Slovakia	12,065	13,455	8,482	9,961	10,689	1.05	7.31
Northern Europe	50,998	60,264	64,488	77,483	84,832	8.36	9.48
Denmark	5,082	5,505	5,895	6,845	7,342	0.72	7.26
Finland	2,338	2,352	3,111	3,571	3,835	0.38	7.39
Iceland	734	638	1,094	1,432	1,403	0.14	-2.03
Ireland	2,635	3,329	3,683	4,805	4,133	0.41	-13.99
Norway	4,449	7,063	5,810	7,215	8,269	0.81	14.61
Sweden	7,983	9,996	12,580	12,573	13,783	1.36	9.62
United Kingdom	27,777	31,381	32,315	41,042	46,067	4.54	12.24
Southern Europe	302,342	333,861	389,760	452,297	462,115	45.51	2.17
Bosnia and Herzegovina	94,525	95,864	110,042	117,819	130,831	12.89	11.04
Croatia	31,898	37,358	46,051	56,404	63,886	6.29	13.27
Greece	27,016	30,878	36,098	46,559	48,942	4.82	5.12
Italy	46,001	49,735	51,636	65,451	59,518	5.86	-9.06
Portugal	1,338	2,230	2,100	3,277	2,869	0.28	-12.45
Slovenia	47,020	52,337	71,996	96,200	95,484	9.40	-0.74
Spain	5,577	6,064	7,440	10,750	10,774	1.06	0.22
TFYR of Macedonia	48,967	59,395	64,397	55,837	49,811	4.91	-10.79
Western Europe	118,694	134,042	136,373	164,341	163,002	16.05	-0.81
Austria	23,448	24,278	23,980	31,144	35,445	3.49	13.81
Belgium	6,278	6,304	7,078	7,227	7,105	0.70	-1.69
France	17,879	20,492	23,880	30,940	29,037	2.86	-6.15
Germany	50,970	58,013	57,557	68,339	63,334	6.24	-7.32
Luxembourg	603	722	584	602	707	0.07	17.44
Netherlands	10,605	13,943	12,749	15,473	16,579	1.63	7.15
Switzerland	8,911	10,290	10,545	10,616	10,795	1.06	1.69
East Mediterranean Europe	17,556	18,043	22,139	20,979	20,523	2.02	-2.17
Israel	7,779	6,785	7,536	7,688	7,554	0.74	-1.74
Turkey	9,777	11,258	14,603	13,291	12,969	1.28	-2.42
Other Europe	25,217	20,066	18,224	28,194	23,990	2.36	-14.91

SERBIA

6. Overnight stays of non-resident tourists in all types of accommodation establishments, by nationality

	2002	2003	2004	2005	2006	Market share 06	% Change 06-05
Other countries of Europe	25,217	20,066	18,224	28,194	23,990	2.36	-14.91
REGION NOT SPECIFIED	**30,359**	**25,927**	**31,512**	**33,119**	**35,223**	**3.47**	**6.35**
Not Specified	**30,359**	**25,927**	**31,512**	**33,119**	**35,223**	**3.47**	**6.35**
Other countries of the World	30,359	25,927	31,512	33,119	35,223	3.47	6.35

Source: World Tourism Organization (UNWTO)

SEYCHELLES

1. Arrivals of non-resident tourists at national borders, by country of residence

	2002	2003	2004	2005	2006	Market share 06	% Change 06-05
TOTAL	132,246	122,038	120,765	128,654	140,627	100.00	9.31
AFRICA	13,819	13,578	12,598	12,478	13,408	9.53	7.45
East Africa	8,233	7,221	6,554	6,347	6,313	4.49	-0.54
Ethiopia	72	104	90	67	64	0.05	-4.48
Djibouti	12	21	21	20	47	0.03	135.00
Kenya	1,163	1,038	954	801	1,024	0.73	27.84
Madagascar	300	329	174	226	263	0.19	16.37
Malawi	41	29	14	15	15	0.01	
Mauritius	3,100	2,351	2,345	2,626	2,579	1.83	-1.79
Mozambique	45	56	29	36	96	0.07	166.67
Reunion	2,909	2,816	2,458	2,167	1,770	1.26	-18.32
Rwanda	30	32	37	14	9	0.01	-35.71
Somalia	1						
Zimbabwe	178	143	91	94	116	0.08	23.40
Uganda	153	103	131	121	118	0.08	-2.48
United Republic of Tanzania	155	97	137	105	160	0.11	52.38
Zambia	74	102	73	55	52	0.04	-5.45
Central Africa		15	21	15	17	0.01	13.33
Democratic Republic of the Congo		15	21	15	17	0.01	13.33
North Africa	32	51	96	89	69	0.05	-22.47
Algeria	9	7	22	23	23	0.02	
Sudan	23	44	74	66	46	0.03	-30.30
Southern Africa	4,265	5,087	5,209	5,454	6,366	4.53	16.72
Botswana	66	67	57	46	65	0.05	41.30
Lesotho	11	6	8	7	8	0.01	14.29
South Africa	4,173	5,003	5,130	5,395	6,277	4.46	16.35
Swaziland	15	11	14	6	16	0.01	166.67
West Africa	129	138	138	136	168	0.12	23.53
Ghana	36	34	33	21	47	0.03	123.81
Nigeria	93	104	105	115	121	0.09	5.22
Other Africa	1,160	1,066	580	437	475	0.34	8.70
Other countries of Africa	1,160	1,066	580	437	475	0.34	8.70
AMERICAS	3,670	3,477	4,030	3,867	3,398	2.42	-12.13
North America	3,331	3,169	3,630	3,506	3,003	2.14	-14.35
Canada	342	331	428	597	462	0.33	-22.61
Mexico	35	45	56	31	31	0.02	
United States	2,954	2,793	3,146	2,878	2,510	1.78	-12.79
South America	212	200	267	213	254	0.18	19.25
Argentina	99	120	171	135	103	0.07	-23.70
Brazil	113	80	96	78	151	0.11	93.59
Other Americas	127	108	133	148	141	0.10	-4.73
Other countries of the Americas	127	108	133	148	141	0.10	-4.73
EAST ASIA AND THE PACIFIC	2,678	1,977	2,135	2,647	2,996	2.13	13.18
North-East Asia	1,108	871	838	1,024	1,286	0.91	25.59
China	551	407	400	505	644	0.46	27.52
Taiwan (Province of China)	55	54	36	53	120	0.09	126.42
Hong Kong, China	119	79	94	68	95	0.07	39.71
Japan	362	306	300	368	377	0.27	2.45
Korea, Republic of	21	25	8	30	50	0.04	66.67

SEYCHELLES

1. Arrivals of non-resident tourists at national borders, by country of residence

	2002	2003	2004	2005	2006	Market share 06	% Change 06-05
South-East Asia	1,077	598	573	690	847	0.60	22.75
Indonesia	88	65	40	72	102	0.07	41.67
Malaysia	140	77	73	89	105	0.07	17.98
Philippines	143	115	151	224	205	0.15	-8.48
Singapore	442	254	231	197	324	0.23	64.47
Thailand	264	87	78	108	111	0.08	2.78
Australasia	441	488	695	899	839	0.60	-6.67
Australia	396	432	611	777	718	0.51	-7.59
New Zealand	45	56	84	122	121	0.09	-0.82
Other East Asia and the Pacific	52	20	29	34	24	0.02	-29.41
Other countries East Asia/Pacific	33	6	11	11	14	0.01	27.27
Other countries of Oceania	19	14	18	23	10	0.01	-56.52
EUROPE	108,246	99,961	98,654	103,581	114,211	81.22	10.26
Central/Eastern Europe	3,248	3,644	4,545	4,463	6,055	4.31	35.67
Poland	390	260	285	215	647	0.46	200.93
Commonwealth Independent State	2,858	3,384	4,260	4,248	5,408	3.85	27.31
Northern Europe	22,978	22,189	20,739	19,100	18,837	13.40	-1.38
Denmark	1,307	882	752	837	1,147	0.82	37.04
Finland	368	420	323	257	295	0.21	14.79
Ireland	446	374	322	299	472	0.34	57.86
Norway	744	717	717	533	569	0.40	6.75
Sweden	1,223	1,031	996	677	825	0.59	21.86
United Kingdom	18,890	18,765	17,629	16,497	15,529	11.04	-5.87
Southern Europe	23,799	20,740	20,463	22,444	28,166	20.03	25.49
Greece	171	144	174	654	717	0.51	9.63
Italy	20,000	17,778	17,099	18,377	23,217	16.51	26.34
Portugal	846	522	575	405	572	0.41	41.23
Spain	2,550	2,062	2,449	2,686	3,185	2.26	18.58
Yugoslavia, Sfr (Former)	232	234	166	322	475	0.34	47.52
Western Europe	53,594	51,076	50,861	54,263	57,753	41.07	6.43
Austria	2,275	1,889	2,221	2,438	2,961	2.11	21.45
Belgium	1,426	1,392	1,283	1,461	1,703	1.21	16.56
France	28,326	25,990	26,049	27,592	27,350	19.45	-0.88
Germany	15,145	15,903	15,509	17,011	19,265	13.70	13.25
Luxembourg	195	187	261	249	267	0.19	7.23
Netherlands	1,067	978	1,035	1,039	1,254	0.89	20.69
Switzerland	5,160	4,737	4,503	4,473	4,953	3.52	10.73
East Mediterranean Europe	2,625	309	267	199	202	0.14	1.51
Israel	2,495	149	180	199	202	0.14	1.51
Turkey	130	160	87				
Other Europe	2,002	2,003	1,779	3,112	3,198	2.27	2.76
Other countries of Europe	2,002	2,003	1,779	3,112	3,198	2.27	2.76
MIDDLE EAST	2,023	1,770	1,911	4,458	4,731	3.36	6.12
Middle East	2,023	1,770	1,911	4,458	4,731	3.36	6.12
Bahrain	193	182	146	207	227	0.16	9.66
Kuwait	111	77	110	147	107	0.08	-27.21
Libyan Arab Jamahiriya	2	5	17		7		
Oman	37	76	47	75	96	0.07	28.00
Qatar	19	24	105	403	498	0.35	23.57
Saudi Arabia	363	247	341	585	591	0.42	1.03
United Arab Emirates	1,040	888	924	2,767	2,920	2.08	5.53

SEYCHELLES

1. Arrivals of non-resident tourists at national borders, by country of residence

	2002	2003	2004	2005	2006	Market share 06	% Change 06-05
Egypt	49	51	39	72	71	0.05	-1.39
Yemen	3	33	6	15	9	0.01	-40.00
Other countries of Middle East	206	187	176	187	205	0.15	9.63
SOUTH ASIA	**1,810**	**1,275**	**1,437**	**1,623**	**1,883**	**1.34**	**16.02**
South Asia	**1,810**	**1,275**	**1,437**	**1,623**	**1,883**	**1.34**	**16.02**
Bangladesh	94	5	14				
Sri Lanka	205	212	183	187	267	0.19	42.78
India	1,271	893	1,012	981	1,132	0.80	15.39
Iran, Islamic Republic of	34	34	30	88	130	0.09	47.73
Pakistan	114	64	48	146	161	0.11	10.27
Other countries of South Asia	92	67	150	221	193	0.14	-12.67

Source: World Tourism Organization (UNWTO)

SIERRA LEONE

1. Arrivals of non-resident tourists at national borders, by country of residence

		2002	2003	2004	2005	2006	Market share 06	% Change 06-05
TOTAL	(*)	**28,463**	**38,107**	**43,560**	**40,023**	**33,704**	**100.00**	**-15.79**
AFRICA		**13,519**	**23,341**	**24,446**	**21,798**	**10,122**	**30.03**	**-53.56**
Other Africa		**13,519**	**23,341**	**24,446**	**21,798**	**10,122**	**30.03**	**-53.56**
All countries of Africa		13,519	23,341	24,446	21,798	10,122	30.03	-53.56
AMERICAS		**3,785**	**4,699**	**4,790**	**4,713**	**6,669**	**19.79**	**41.50**
Other Americas		**3,785**	**4,699**	**4,790**	**4,713**	**6,669**	**19.79**	**41.50**
All countries of the Americas		3,785	4,699	4,790	4,713	6,669	19.79	41.50
EAST ASIA AND THE PACIFIC		**2,134**	**1,995**	**2,257**	**2,343**	**4,898**	**14.53**	**109.05**
Other East Asia and the Pacific		**2,134**	**1,995**	**2,257**	**2,343**	**4,898**	**14.53**	**109.05**
All countries of Asia		2,134	1,995	2,257	2,343	4,898	14.53	109.05
EUROPE		**7,403**	**6,460**	**9,476**	**9,879**	**10,470**	**31.06**	**5.98**
Other Europe		**7,403**	**6,460**	**9,476**	**9,879**	**10,470**	**31.06**	**5.98**
All countries of Europe		7,403	6,460	9,476	9,879	10,470	31.06	5.98
MIDDLE EAST		**1,622**	**1,612**	**2,591**	**1,290**	**1,545**	**4.58**	**19.77**
Middle East		**1,622**	**1,612**	**2,591**	**1,290**	**1,545**	**4.58**	**19.77**
All countries of Middle East		1,622	1,612	2,591	1,290	1,545	4.58	19.77

Source: World Tourism Organization (UNWTO)

SIERRA LEONE

5. Overnight stays of non-resident tourists in hotels and similar establishments, by country of residence

	2002	2003	2004	2005	2006	Market share 06	% Change 06-05
TOTAL	142,315	190,535	217,800	280,161	235,928	100.00	-15.79
AFRICA	67,595	116,705	122,230	152,586	70,854	30.03	-53.56
Other Africa	67,595	116,705	122,230	152,586	70,854	30.03	-53.56
All countries of Africa	67,595	116,705	122,230	152,586	70,854	30.03	-53.56
AMERICAS	18,925	23,495	23,950	32,991	46,683	19.79	41.50
Other Americas	18,925	23,495	23,950	32,991	46,683	19.79	41.50
All countries of the Americas	18,925	23,495	23,950	32,991	46,683	19.79	41.50
EAST ASIA AND THE PACIFIC	10,670	9,975	11,285	16,401	34,286	14.53	109.05
Other East Asia and the Pacific	10,670	9,975	11,285	16,401	34,286	14.53	109.05
All countries of Asia	10,670	9,975	11,285	16,401	34,286	14.53	109.05
EUROPE	37,015	32,300	47,380	69,153	73,290	31.06	5.98
Other Europe	37,015	32,300	47,380	69,153	73,290	31.06	5.98
All countries of Europe	37,015	32,300	47,380	69,153	73,290	31.06	5.98
MIDDLE EAST	8,110	8,060	12,955	9,030	10,815	4.58	19.77
Middle East	8,110	8,060	12,955	9,030	10,815	4.58	19.77
All countries of Middle East	8,110	8,060	12,955	9,030	10,815	4.58	19.77

Source: World Tourism Organization (UNWTO)

SINGAPORE

2. Arrivals of non-resident visitors at national borders, by nationality

		2002	2003	2004	2005	2006	Market share 06	% Change 06-05
TOTAL	(*)	7,567,110	6,127,288	8,328,658	8,943,029	9,750,967	100.00	9.03
AFRICA		65,672	53,838	68,848	77,754	86,771	0.89	11.60
East Africa		11,854	8,282	10,284	10,118	9,075	0.09	-10.31
Mauritius		11,854	8,282	10,284	10,118	9,075	0.09	-10.31
Southern Africa		30,543	27,650	35,428	37,547	40,349	0.41	7.46
South Africa		30,543	27,650	35,428	37,547	40,349	0.41	7.46
Other Africa		23,275	17,906	23,136	30,089	37,347	0.38	24.12
Other countries of Africa		23,275	17,906	23,136	30,089	37,347	0.38	24.12
AMERICAS		460,247	355,293	470,711	525,506	568,123	5.83	8.11
Caribbean		3,241	2,141	2,810	3,396	3,908	0.04	15.08
All countries of the Caribbean		3,241	2,141	2,810	3,396	3,908	0.04	15.08
Central America		2,004	1,214	1,765	1,602	1,927	0.02	20.29
All countries of Central America		2,004	1,214	1,765	1,602	1,927	0.02	20.29
North America		442,567	342,562	451,911	504,238	542,176	5.56	7.52
Canada		90,901	71,388	93,555	104,073	112,329	1.15	7.93
Mexico		8,655	4,453	7,553	7,452	8,903	0.09	19.47
United States		343,011	266,721	350,803	392,713	420,944	4.32	7.19
South America		12,435	9,376	14,225	16,270	20,112	0.21	23.61
Argentina		1,599	1,319	2,139	2,520	2,896	0.03	14.92
Brazil		4,611	3,695	5,849	6,865	8,815	0.09	28.40
Chile		1,294	979	1,408	1,546	1,598	0.02	3.36
Colombia		2,191	1,556	2,069	2,174	2,957	0.03	36.02
Uruguay		177	111	202	167	240		43.71
Venezuela		931	686	946	1,142	1,480	0.02	29.60
Other countries of South America		1,632	1,030	1,612	1,856	2,126	0.02	14.55
EAST ASIA AND THE PACIFIC		5,176,210	4,207,352	5,805,942	6,148,911	6,706,639	68.78	9.07
North-East Asia		2,193,906	1,591,955	2,240,210	2,271,986	2,527,081	25.92	11.23
China		666,315	559,734	866,498	836,858	1,015,658	10.42	21.37
Taiwan (Province of China)		212,943	147,291	184,059	214,397	219,251	2.25	2.26
Hong Kong, China		154,643	133,982	164,497	195,110	170,592	1.75	-12.57
Japan		774,330	475,751	646,431	638,799	643,791	6.60	0.78
Korea, Dem. People's Republic of		301	377	354	270	220		-18.52
Korea, Republic of		380,170	269,825	371,235	377,239	467,780	4.80	24.00
Macao, China		3,308	2,987	3,640	3,719	3,478	0.04	-6.48
Mongolia		1,896	2,008	3,496	5,594	6,311	0.06	12.82
South-East Asia		2,368,145	2,160,738	2,913,402	3,158,388	3,391,020	34.78	7.37
Brunei Darussalam		43,816	29,544	33,879	35,539	33,555	0.34	-5.58
Myanmar		23,170	20,069	31,596	39,884	49,349	0.51	23.73
Cambodia		6,412	6,495	10,618	11,747	17,311	0.18	47.37
Indonesia		1,384,409	1,335,261	1,758,696	1,807,998	1,917,548	19.67	6.06
Lao People's Democratic Republic		833	750	1,377	1,604	1,974	0.02	23.07
Malaysia		434,136	333,444	409,555	440,026	490,565	5.03	11.49
Philippines		202,283	181,952	255,448	333,599	403,247	4.14	20.88
Viet Nam		35,651	40,043	99,942	142,872	156,101	1.60	9.26
Thailand		237,435	213,180	312,291	345,119	321,370	3.30	-6.88
Australasia		607,974	449,416	645,504	711,408	781,183	8.01	9.81
Australia		505,621	370,038	529,372	587,617	656,453	6.73	11.71
New Zealand		102,353	79,378	116,132	123,791	124,730	1.28	0.76
Melanesia		4,398	3,979	5,277	5,552	5,582	0.06	0.54

SINGAPORE

2. Arrivals of non-resident visitors at national borders, by nationality

	2002	2003	2004	2005	2006	Market share 06	% Change 06-05
Fiji	2,230	2,486	3,268	3,233	3,057	0.03	-5.44
New Caledonia	9	9	5	7	29		314.29
Papua New Guinea	2,159	1,484	2,004	2,312	2,496	0.03	7.96
Micronesia	**245**	**182**	**148**	**152**	**124**		**-18.42**
Guam	20	4	11	15	25		66.67
Nauru	225	178	137	137	99		-27.74
Other East Asia and the Pacific	**1,542**	**1,082**	**1,401**	**1,425**	**1,649**	**0.02**	**15.72**
Other countries of Oceania	1,542	1,082	1,401	1,425	1,649	0.02	15.72
EUROPE	**1,285,220**	**1,026,011**	**1,252,241**	**1,324,566**	**1,418,517**	**14.55**	**7.09**
Central/Eastern Europe	**38,132**	**33,224**	**44,495**	**54,306**	**72,686**	**0.75**	**33.85**
Czech Republic	4,062	3,112	4,214	3,643	4,672	0.05	28.25
Hungary	2,880	2,472	3,289	3,242	3,773	0.04	16.38
Poland	6,930	6,314	6,848	8,332	10,679	0.11	28.17
Commonwealth Independent State	24,260	21,326	30,144	39,089	53,562	0.55	37.03
Northern Europe	**700,744**	**584,860**	**696,449**	**720,664**	**750,660**	**7.70**	**4.16**
Denmark	31,046	25,392	30,687	34,625	32,673	0.34	-5.64
Finland	13,969	11,853	14,714	17,442	19,723	0.20	13.08
Ireland	31,252	24,639	30,983	32,467	35,397	0.36	9.02
Norway	24,739	19,620	24,638	25,454	27,752	0.28	9.03
Sweden	40,020	32,526	39,689	38,202	40,439	0.41	5.86
United Kingdom	559,718	470,830	555,738	572,474	594,676	6.10	3.88
Southern Europe	**78,913**	**49,703**	**67,582**	**71,091**	**82,066**	**0.84**	**15.44**
Greece	13,080	8,232	11,881	9,974	10,890	0.11	9.18
Italy	41,271	23,639	32,126	35,945	41,675	0.43	15.94
Portugal	6,466	4,491	5,595	6,642	7,235	0.07	8.93
Spain	16,677	12,099	16,297	16,571	20,063	0.21	21.07
Serbia and Montenegro	1,419	1,242	1,683	1,959	2,203	0.02	12.46
Western Europe	**425,674**	**324,487**	**397,768**	**430,942**	**461,003**	**4.73**	**6.98**
Austria	16,379	10,911	15,359	16,607	18,119	0.19	9.10
Belgium	21,548	14,756	15,874	16,575	17,298	0.18	4.36
France	90,579	69,699	95,812	101,544	113,926	1.17	12.19
Germany	170,956	132,883	156,798	172,590	181,217	1.86	5.00
Luxembourg	845	484	647	960	1,052	0.01	9.58
Netherlands	83,921	65,533	73,963	80,253	82,700	0.85	3.05
Switzerland	41,446	30,221	39,315	42,413	46,691	0.48	10.09
East Mediterranean Europe	**23,550**	**19,765**	**27,002**	**28,029**	**29,121**	**0.30**	**3.90**
Israel	10,548	8,050	11,102	11,290	10,700	0.11	-5.23
Turkey	13,002	11,715	15,900	16,739	18,421	0.19	10.05
Other Europe	**18,207**	**13,972**	**18,945**	**19,534**	**22,981**	**0.24**	**17.65**
Other countries of Europe	18,207	13,972	18,945	19,534	22,981	0.24	17.65
MIDDLE EAST	**20,906**	**12,598**	**28,708**	**27,744**	**31,856**	**0.33**	**14.82**
Middle East	**20,906**	**12,598**	**28,708**	**27,744**	**31,856**	**0.33**	**14.82**
Bahrain	1,480	861	1,900	2,246	1,959	0.02	-12.78
Jordan	751	338	748	848	1,084	0.01	27.83
Kuwait	5,925	2,667	6,991	3,894	3,433	0.04	-11.84
Lebanon	500	336	588	664	962	0.01	44.88
Libyan Arab Jamahiriya	106	75	122	220	300		36.36
Saudi Arabia	2,282	1,610	3,732	3,820	6,270	0.06	64.14
United Arab Emirates	4,672	3,281	7,620	8,036	8,922	0.09	11.03
Egypt	1,949	1,772	2,620	2,794	3,165	0.03	13.28
Other countries of Middle East	3,241	1,658	4,387	5,222	5,761	0.06	10.32

SINGAPORE

2. Arrivals of non-resident visitors at national borders, by nationality

	2002	2003	2004	2005	2006	Market share 06	% Change 06-05
SOUTH ASIA	556,742	470,721	700,695	831,778	930,265	9.54	11.84
South Asia	556,742	470,721	700,695	831,778	930,265	9.54	11.84
Afghanistan	64	65	104	144	200		38.89
Bangladesh	27,049	26,334	42,217	53,491	62,775	0.64	17.36
Sri Lanka	61,650	55,946	78,136	72,801	77,406	0.79	6.33
India	434,199	359,501	538,702	655,399	731,587	7.50	11.62
Iran, Islamic Republic of	2,901	3,301	5,731	7,555	10,076	0.10	33.37
Nepal	14,589	10,887	14,611	17,250	17,598	0.18	2.02
Pakistan	10,524	9,575	14,339	17,869	22,374	0.23	25.21
Other countries of South Asia	5,766	5,112	6,855	7,269	8,249	0.08	13.48
REGION NOT SPECIFIED	2,113	1,475	1,513	6,770	8,796	0.09	29.93
Not Specified	2,113	1,475	1,513	6,770	8,796	0.09	29.93
Other countries of the World	2,113	1,475	1,513	6,770	8,796	0.09	29.93

Source: World Tourism Organization (UNWTO)

SINGAPORE

2. Arrivals of non-resident visitors at national borders, by country of residence

	2002	2003	2004	2005	2006	Market share 06	% Change 06-05
TOTAL (*)	7,567,110	6,127,288	8,328,658	8,943,029	9,750,967	100.00	9.03
AFRICA	70,117	55,997	70,626	78,803	87,132	0.89	10.57
East Africa	13,927	9,363	11,986	11,997	10,883	0.11	-9.29
Mauritius	13,927	9,363	11,986	11,997	10,883	0.11	-9.29
Southern Africa	30,524	27,486	34,502	35,981	38,488	0.39	6.97
South Africa	30,524	27,486	34,502	35,981	38,488	0.39	6.97
Other Africa	25,666	19,148	24,138	30,825	37,761	0.39	22.50
Other countries of Africa	25,666	19,148	24,138	30,825	37,761	0.39	22.50
AMERICAS	416,375	314,728	422,167	470,493	509,771	5.23	8.35
Caribbean	2,019	1,464	1,897	2,667	3,033	0.03	13.72
All countries of the Caribbean	2,019	1,464	1,897	2,667	3,033	0.03	13.72
Central America	1,370	750	1,097	1,093	1,298	0.01	18.76
All countries of Central America	1,370	750	1,097	1,093	1,298	0.01	18.76
North America	403,220	305,750	408,541	454,652	490,578	5.03	7.90
Canada	67,970	51,257	68,877	76,924	83,404	0.86	8.42
Mexico	7,602	3,815	6,508	6,288	7,390	0.08	17.53
United States	327,648	250,678	333,156	371,440	399,784	4.10	7.63
South America	9,434	6,569	10,274	11,738	14,441	0.15	23.03
Argentina	1,162	876	1,459	1,692	1,946	0.02	15.01
Brazil	4,191	3,004	4,845	5,676	7,126	0.07	25.55
Chile	1,015	809	1,115	1,160	1,216	0.01	4.83
Colombia	1,325	858	1,262	1,325	1,776	0.02	34.04
Uruguay	169	87	169	155	225		45.16
Venezuela	621	393	553	657	947	0.01	44.14
Other countries of South America	951	542	871	1,073	1,205	0.01	12.30
Other Americas	332	195	358	343	421		22.74
Other countries of the Americas	332	195	358	343	421		22.74
EAST ASIA AND THE PACIFIC	5,426,216	4,426,234	6,072,654	6,445,012	7,012,090	71.91	8.80
North-East Asia	2,249,216	1,643,412	2,304,393	2,350,832	2,610,457	26.77	11.04
China	670,098	568,508	880,233	857,814	1,037,198	10.64	20.91
Taiwan (Province of China)	209,321	144,942	182,443	213,959	219,463	2.25	2.57
Hong Kong, China	265,970	226,260	271,691	313,831	291,474	2.99	-7.12
Japan	723,431	434,087	598,840	588,535	594,405	6.10	1.00
Korea, Dem. People's Republic of	1,076	1,068	1,115	987	881	0.01	-10.74
Korea, Republic of	371,050	261,403	361,083	364,206	454,721	4.66	24.85
Macao, China	6,315	5,149	5,274	5,977	6,051	0.06	1.24
Mongolia	1,955	1,995	3,714	5,523	6,264	0.06	13.42
South-East Asia	2,532,887	2,307,228	3,085,853	3,341,721	3,577,222	36.69	7.05
Brunei Darussalam	60,052	41,156	46,087	47,860	45,331	0.46	-5.28
Myanmar	22,340	19,531	29,933	37,871	46,647	0.48	23.17
Cambodia	7,710	7,640	11,991	13,009	19,160	0.20	47.28
Indonesia	1,393,020	1,341,747	1,765,312	1,813,569	1,922,138	19.71	5.99
Lao People's Democratic Republic	1,024	887	1,495	1,788	2,105	0.02	17.73
Malaysia	548,659	439,437	537,336	577,987	634,274	6.50	9.74
Philippines	195,564	176,584	245,914	319,971	386,096	3.96	20.67
Viet Nam	40,652	44,420	105,802	150,626	165,105	1.69	9.61
Thailand	263,866	235,826	341,983	379,040	356,366	3.65	-5.98
Australasia	632,523	466,403	670,278	739,744	811,697	8.32	9.73
Australia	538,408	392,906	561,163	620,255	691,632	7.09	11.51

SINGAPORE

2. Arrivals of non-resident visitors at national borders, by country of residence

	2002	2003	2004	2005	2006	Market share 06	% Change 06-05
New Zealand	94,115	73,497	109,115	119,489	120,065	1.23	0.48
Melanesia	**8,007**	**6,672**	**8,753**	**9,026**	**8,893**	**0.09**	**-1.47**
Fiji	2,195	2,351	3,056	2,895	2,692	0.03	-7.01
New Caledonia	1,080	913	1,343	1,353	1,354	0.01	0.07
Papua New Guinea	4,732	3,408	4,354	4,778	4,847	0.05	1.44
Micronesia	**1,041**	**830**	**1,053**	**1,105**	**1,133**	**0.01**	**2.53**
Guam	889	723	982	1,047	1,108	0.01	5.83
Nauru	152	107	71	58	25		-56.90
Other East Asia and the Pacific	**2,542**	**1,689**	**2,324**	**2,584**	**2,688**	**0.03**	**4.02**
Other countries of Oceania	2,542	1,689	2,324	2,584	2,688	0.03	4.02
EUROPE	**1,112,156**	**885,146**	**1,081,336**	**1,136,024**	**1,220,159**	**12.51**	**7.41**
Central/Eastern Europe	**37,455**	**32,681**	**43,391**	**52,234**	**70,272**	**0.72**	**34.53**
Czech Republic	3,775	3,057	3,982	3,562	4,474	0.05	25.60
Hungary	2,823	2,408	3,244	3,150	3,763	0.04	19.46
Poland	7,686	6,557	6,906	7,699	9,705	0.10	26.06
Commonwealth Independent State	23,171	20,659	29,259	37,823	52,330	0.54	38.35
Northern Europe	**577,985**	**484,015**	**576,344**	**592,705**	**619,803**	**6.36**	**4.57**
Denmark	25,706	21,176	25,744	29,158	27,045	0.28	-7.25
Finland	11,317	9,544	12,057	14,467	16,303	0.17	12.69
Ireland	23,202	17,828	22,740	24,728	26,625	0.27	7.67
Norway	22,820	18,003	22,882	23,591	26,140	0.27	10.80
Sweden	36,412	29,482	35,659	33,607	35,524	0.36	5.70
United Kingdom	458,528	387,982	457,262	467,154	488,166	5.01	4.50
Southern Europe	**71,087**	**43,777**	**60,348**	**62,786**	**73,557**	**0.75**	**17.16**
Greece	12,801	7,894	11,566	9,570	10,440	0.11	9.09
Italy	36,737	20,342	27,664	30,651	35,657	0.37	16.33
Portugal	3,008	1,917	2,987	3,698	4,360	0.04	17.90
Spain	17,324	12,527	16,632	17,181	21,232	0.22	23.58
Serbia and Montenegro	1,217	1,097	1,499	1,686	1,868	0.02	10.79
Western Europe	**382,934**	**290,293**	**355,136**	**380,362**	**404,879**	**4.15**	**6.45**
Austria	14,645	9,373	13,123	14,135	15,406	0.16	8.99
Belgium	20,357	14,059	14,895	15,389	16,329	0.17	6.11
France	72,153	55,763	77,884	80,924	90,197	0.93	11.46
Germany	157,510	121,376	142,371	154,779	161,122	1.65	4.10
Luxembourg	1,384	918	1,231	1,552	1,771	0.02	14.11
Netherlands	71,651	55,358	61,399	66,480	68,174	0.70	2.55
Switzerland	45,234	33,446	44,233	47,103	51,880	0.53	10.14
East Mediterranean Europe	**22,471**	**18,872**	**25,570**	**26,541**	**27,653**	**0.28**	**4.19**
Israel	10,288	7,779	10,546	10,670	10,148	0.10	-4.89
Turkey	12,183	11,093	15,024	15,871	17,505	0.18	10.30
Other Europe	**20,224**	**15,508**	**20,547**	**21,396**	**23,995**	**0.25**	**12.15**
Other countries of Europe	20,224	15,508	20,547	21,396	23,995	0.25	12.15
MIDDLE EAST	**46,770**	**29,844**	**55,449**	**56,165**	**65,923**	**0.68**	**17.37**
Middle East	**46,770**	**29,844**	**55,449**	**56,165**	**65,923**	**0.68**	**17.37**
Bahrain	2,676	1,654	3,227	3,698	3,687	0.04	-0.30
Jordan	741	288	559	669	677	0.01	1.20
Kuwait	7,113	3,174	8,160	4,977	4,635	0.05	-6.87
Lebanon	645	265	522	574	652	0.01	13.59
Libyan Arab Jamahiriya	96	43	102	179	231		29.05
Saudi Arabia	6,753	3,477	7,288	6,993	9,549	0.10	36.55
United Arab Emirates	20,784	15,686	25,157	28,062	34,013	0.35	21.21

SINGAPORE

2. Arrivals of non-resident visitors at national borders, by country of residence

	2002	2003	2004	2005	2006	Market share 06	% Change 06-05
Egypt	2,621	2,318	3,150	2,970	3,151	0.03	6.09
Other countries of Middle East	5,341	2,939	7,284	8,043	9,328	0.10	15.98
SOUTH ASIA	**490,262**	**415,151**	**626,153**	**751,437**	**849,798**	**8.72**	**13.09**
South Asia	**490,262**	**415,151**	**626,153**	**751,437**	**849,798**	**8.72**	**13.09**
Afghanistan	63	58	129	183	192		4.92
Bangladesh	27,552	26,384	41,544	54,353	63,765	0.65	17.32
Sri Lanka	54,690	51,406	73,201	68,024	73,281	0.75	7.73
India	375,659	309,466	471,196	583,543	658,893	6.76	12.91
Iran, Islamic Republic of	2,530	3,089	5,363	6,983	9,350	0.10	33.90
Nepal	13,202	10,015	13,011	14,674	15,161	0.16	3.32
Pakistan	10,569	9,398	14,311	15,945	20,526	0.21	28.73
Other countries of South Asia	5,997	5,335	7,398	7,732	8,630	0.09	11.61
REGION NOT SPECIFIED	**5,214**	**188**	**273**	**5,095**	**6,094**	**0.06**	**19.61**
Not Specified	**5,214**	**188**	**273**	**5,095**	**6,094**	**0.06**	**19.61**
Other countries of the World	5,214	188	273	5,095	6,094	0.06	19.61

Source: World Tourism Organization (UNWTO)

SLOVAKIA

4. Arrivals of non-resident tourists in all types of accommodation establishments, by nationality

	2002	2003	2004	2005	2006	Market share 06	% Change 06-05
TOTAL	1,398,740	1,386,791	1,401,189	1,514,980	1,611,808	100.00	6.39
AFRICA	2,960	2,581	2,482	2,252	2,726	0.17	21.05
East Africa	5	7	11	43	46		6.98
Kenya	5	7	11	43	46		6.98
North Africa	143	45	102	86	50		-41.86
Tunisia	143	45	102	86	50		-41.86
Southern Africa	404	330	326	616	804	0.05	30.52
South Africa	404	330	326	616	804	0.05	30.52
Other Africa	2,408	2,199	2,043	1,507	1,826	0.11	21.17
Other countries of Africa	2,408	2,199	2,043	1,507	1,826	0.11	21.17
AMERICAS	33,352	33,981	38,712	42,100	39,118	2.43	-7.08
Caribbean	14	23	135	27	35		29.63
Dominican Republic	14	23	135	27	35		29.63
North America	30,595	31,133	35,304	38,483	35,844	2.22	-6.86
Canada	4,958	5,542	6,082	5,358	5,579	0.35	4.12
Mexico	255	208	557	532	696	0.04	30.83
United States	25,382	25,383	28,665	32,593	29,569	1.83	-9.28
South America	773	614	774	1,091	1,036	0.06	-5.04
Argentina	394	295	248	417	235	0.01	-43.65
Brazil	379	319	526	674	801	0.05	18.84
Other Americas	1,970	2,211	2,499	2,499	2,203	0.14	-11.84
Other countries of the Americas	1,970	2,211	2,499	2,499	2,203	0.14	-11.84
EAST ASIA AND THE PACIFIC	34,130	32,258	42,249	55,992	69,102	4.29	23.41
North-East Asia	10,469	9,133	16,651	27,749	41,112	2.55	48.16
China	780	684	801	1,447	2,177	0.14	50.45
Japan	9,153	7,278	10,648	14,321	15,878	0.99	10.87
Korea, Republic of	536	1,171	5,202	11,981	23,057	1.43	92.45
South-East Asia	132	331	166	747	217	0.01	-70.95
Thailand	132	331	166	747	217	0.01	-70.95
Australasia	5,277	7,590	6,521	5,431	7,491	0.46	37.93
Australia	4,799	6,965	6,015	4,915	6,808	0.42	38.51
New Zealand	478	625	506	516	683	0.04	32.36
Other East Asia and the Pacific	18,252	15,204	18,911	22,065	20,282	1.26	-8.08
Other countries of Asia	18,252	15,204	18,911	22,065	20,282	1.26	-8.08
EUROPE	1,326,492	1,316,120	1,316,705	1,412,628	1,499,394	93.03	6.14
Central/Eastern Europe	869,216	857,005	777,405	824,491	896,432	55.62	8.73
Bulgaria	3,464	3,235	3,369	3,301	5,051	0.31	53.01
Belarus	1,578	1,985	1,796	1,947	3,030	0.19	55.62
Czech Republic	447,962	469,991	419,273	424,900	455,381	28.25	7.17
Estonia	3,034	2,979	2,431	3,308	3,012	0.19	-8.95
Hungary	88,268	100,546	111,065	121,615	121,981	7.57	0.30
Latvia	2,913	3,528	3,971	5,736	5,562	0.35	-3.03
Lithuania	9,452	9,789	11,366	14,477	16,264	1.01	12.34
Republic of Moldova	657	1,427	2,055	944	354	0.02	-62.50
Poland	266,911	215,383	179,078	198,479	224,159	13.91	12.94
Romania	5,123	5,776	6,692	7,972	11,344	0.70	42.30

SLOVAKIA

4. Arrivals of non-resident tourists in all types of accommodation establishments, by nationality

	2002	2003	2004	2005	2006	Market share 06	% Change 06-05
Russian Federation	20,313	22,681	18,074	19,779	19,509	1.21	-1.37
Ukraine	19,541	19,685	18,235	22,033	30,785	1.91	39.72
Northern Europe	**57,129**	**54,129**	**71,745**	**91,548**	**107,063**	**6.64**	**16.95**
Denmark	9,390	7,946	7,844	8,911	12,154	0.75	36.39
Finland	7,467	8,017	13,497	12,560	11,369	0.71	-9.48
Iceland	143	98	91	200	600	0.04	200.00
Ireland	1,847	2,059	3,331	3,738	5,575	0.35	49.14
Norway	3,213	3,301	3,762	5,092	5,678	0.35	11.51
Sweden	6,977	6,646	8,871	9,327	8,550	0.53	-8.33
United Kingdom	28,092	26,062	34,349	51,720	63,137	3.92	22.07
Southern Europe	**67,625**	**74,756**	**94,512**	**108,848**	**112,275**	**6.97**	**3.15**
Albania	447	831	1,587	506	492	0.03	-2.77
Bosnia and Herzegovina	486	852	780	545	711	0.04	30.46
Croatia	9,489	11,499	11,525	15,016	15,375	0.95	2.39
Greece	1,906	2,163	2,638	3,178	3,381	0.21	6.39
Italy	34,998	37,996	50,201	59,344	60,971	3.78	2.74
Malta	187	107	527	237	336	0.02	41.77
Portugal	981	894	1,268	2,330	1,722	0.11	-26.09
Slovenia	9,351	10,404	12,055	12,245	12,388	0.77	1.17
Spain	5,463	5,464	9,022	9,665	11,429	0.71	18.25
TFYR of Macedonia	227	203	286	330	238	0.01	-27.88
Serbia and Montenegro	4,090	4,343	4,623	5,452	5,232	0.32	-4.04
Western Europe	**305,437**	**301,617**	**333,510**	**347,600**	**344,279**	**21.36**	**-0.96**
Austria	47,072	51,365	55,609	55,630	60,560	3.76	8.86
Belgium	11,338	10,626	12,844	13,745	14,848	0.92	8.02
France	21,890	28,629	37,006	42,668	41,095	2.55	-3.69
Germany	188,733	175,746	188,067	194,158	190,422	11.81	-1.92
Liechtenstein				14	83	0.01	492.86
Luxembourg	254	217	284	380	506	0.03	33.16
Netherlands	23,945	24,487	27,114	28,838	26,238	1.63	-9.02
Switzerland	12,205	10,547	12,586	12,167	10,527	0.65	-13.48
East Mediterranean Europe	**8,188**	**9,831**	**18,069**	**10,764**	**11,437**	**0.71**	**6.25**
Cyprus	506	452	816	1,051	1,188	0.07	13.04
Israel	6,563	7,988	16,225	8,225	8,105	0.50	-1.46
Turkey	1,119	1,391	1,028	1,488	2,144	0.13	44.09
Other Europe	**18,897**	**18,782**	**21,464**	**29,377**	**27,908**	**1.73**	**-5.00**
Other countries of Europe	18,897	18,782	21,464	29,377	27,908	1.73	-5.00
MIDDLE EAST	**224**	**241**	**314**	**328**	**272**	**0.02**	**-17.07**
Middle East	**224**	**241**	**314**	**328**	**272**	**0.02**	**-17.07**
Egypt	224	241	314	328	272	0.02	-17.07
SOUTH ASIA	**1,437**	**1,305**	**384**	**603**	**443**	**0.03**	**-26.53**
South Asia	**1,437**	**1,305**	**384**	**603**	**443**	**0.03**	**-26.53**
India	1,437	1,305	384	603	443	0.03	-26.53
REGION NOT SPECIFIED	**145**	**305**	**343**	**1,077**	**753**	**0.05**	**-30.08**
Not Specified	**145**	**305**	**343**	**1,077**	**753**	**0.05**	**-30.08**
Other countries of the World	145	305	343	1,077	753	0.05	-30.08

Source: World Tourism Organization (UNWTO)

SLOVAKIA

6. Overnight stays of non-resident tourists in all types of accommodation establishments, by nationality

	2002	2003	2004	2005	2006	Market share 06	% Change 06-05
TOTAL	5,043,135	4,964,392	4,674,995	4,872,042	5,133,503	100.00	5.37
AFRICA	10,068	8,936	8,370	8,019	9,002	0.18	12.26
East Africa	17	14	24	274	389	0.01	41.97
Kenya	17	14	24	274	389	0.01	41.97
North Africa	521	147	407	273	148		-45.79
Tunisia	521	147	407	273	148		-45.79
Southern Africa	1,069	1,092	1,278	1,489	1,552	0.03	4.23
South Africa	1,069	1,092	1,278	1,489	1,552	0.03	4.23
Other Africa	8,461	7,683	6,661	5,983	6,913	0.13	15.54
Other countries of Africa	8,461	7,683	6,661	5,983	6,913	0.13	15.54
AMERICAS	102,281	95,994	104,217	105,222	101,509	1.98	-3.53
Caribbean	38	67	646	110	108		-1.82
Dominican Republic	38	67	646	110	108		-1.82
North America	91,440	85,262	93,944	92,400	91,506	1.78	-0.97
Canada	15,368	15,551	16,613	13,635	14,311	0.28	4.96
Mexico	1,456	630	2,495	1,806	1,921	0.04	6.37
United States	74,616	69,081	74,836	76,959	75,274	1.47	-2.19
South America	2,797	2,228	2,685	4,565	2,908	0.06	-36.30
Argentina	776	710	567	1,374	530	0.01	-61.43
Brazil	2,021	1,518	2,118	3,191	2,378	0.05	-25.48
Other Americas	8,006	8,437	6,942	8,147	6,987	0.14	-14.24
Other countries of the Americas	8,006	8,437	6,942	8,147	6,987	0.14	-14.24
EAST ASIA AND THE PACIFIC	98,758	90,426	111,940	129,165	164,402	3.20	27.28
North-East Asia	18,878	19,618	38,499	53,656	71,210	1.39	32.72
China	1,559	1,346	1,680	3,770	4,398	0.09	16.66
Japan	15,651	14,102	19,320	22,865	26,323	0.51	15.12
Korea, Republic of	1,668	4,170	17,499	27,021	40,489	0.79	49.84
South-East Asia	538	1,050	577	1,092	422	0.01	-61.36
Thailand	538	1,050	577	1,092	422	0.01	-61.36
Australasia	12,676	16,519	16,128	12,461	17,234	0.34	38.30
Australia	11,768	15,469	15,189	11,487	16,117	0.31	40.31
New Zealand	908	1,050	939	974	1,117	0.02	14.68
Other East Asia and the Pacific	66,666	53,239	56,736	61,956	75,536	1.47	21.92
Other countries of Asia	66,666	53,239	56,736	61,956	75,536	1.47	21.92
EUROPE	4,823,625	4,764,280	4,445,304	4,624,292	4,854,435	94.56	4.98
Central/Eastern Europe	2,936,097	2,937,754	2,558,741	2,600,457	2,927,008	57.02	12.56
Bulgaria	7,609	7,264	8,582	8,912	11,366	0.22	27.54
Belarus	9,127	12,171	11,716	13,147	22,346	0.44	69.97
Czech Republic	1,478,155	1,674,918	1,431,664	1,374,778	1,515,676	29.53	10.25
Estonia	8,226	7,373	5,808	8,473	8,200	0.16	-3.22
Hungary	268,066	295,686	307,786	321,832	327,311	6.38	1.70
Latvia	7,730	8,662	9,120	12,736	13,459	0.26	5.68
Lithuania	24,988	25,038	28,961	30,494	31,547	0.61	3.45
Republic of Moldova	1,421	3,244	3,685	2,313	1,052	0.02	-54.52
Poland	940,805	703,067	563,362	607,936	719,752	14.02	18.39
Romania	15,344	15,454	17,639	23,601	35,630	0.69	50.97

SLOVAKIA

6. Overnight stays of non-resident tourists in all types of accommodation establishments, by nationality

	2002	2003	2004	2005	2006	Market share 06	% Change 06-05
Russian Federation	87,250	96,873	87,116	98,642	97,045	1.89	-1.62
Ukraine	87,376	88,004	83,302	97,593	143,624	2.80	47.17
Northern Europe	**148,910**	**135,873**	**175,333**	**225,621**	**254,606**	**4.96**	**12.85**
Denmark	32,075	22,461	21,159	23,985	37,410	0.73	55.97
Finland	19,023	22,005	38,379	35,385	32,158	0.63	-9.12
Iceland	277	425	235	658	1,144	0.02	73.86
Ireland	4,701	4,696	7,429	8,749	11,963	0.23	36.74
Norway	8,397	8,564	9,661	12,707	13,655	0.27	7.46
Sweden	15,971	14,684	20,093	21,467	18,578	0.36	-13.46
United Kingdom	68,466	63,038	78,377	122,670	139,698	2.72	13.88
Southern Europe	**164,881**	**173,144**	**204,401**	**234,716**	**234,228**	**4.56**	**-0.21**
Albania	2,026	2,217	4,230	1,174	1,142	0.02	-2.73
Bosnia and Herzegovina	1,490	2,288	1,995	1,345	1,894	0.04	40.82
Croatia	28,084	30,370	31,535	39,310	36,799	0.72	-6.39
Greece	5,638	5,729	6,243	8,221	8,319	0.16	1.19
Italy	75,371	79,203	98,264	116,955	119,039	2.32	1.78
Malta	402	332	1,291	767	1,110	0.02	44.72
Portugal	2,744	2,972	2,608	6,379	3,805	0.07	-40.35
Slovenia	22,257	24,100	23,674	23,970	22,354	0.44	-6.74
Spain	13,909	11,755	20,356	22,732	23,858	0.46	4.95
TFYR of Macedonia	502	625	657	875	761	0.01	-13.03
Serbia and Montenegro	12,458	13,553	13,548	12,988	15,147	0.30	16.62
Western Europe	**1,463,075**	**1,407,062**	**1,385,493**	**1,422,769**	**1,295,645**	**25.24**	**-8.93**
Austria	160,328	176,115	176,337	172,310	172,924	3.37	0.36
Belgium	32,465	28,638	34,379	35,949	42,033	0.82	16.92
France	49,129	59,226	78,008	98,738	89,837	1.75	-9.01
Germany	1,111,066	1,037,062	987,075	1,004,824	893,988	17.41	-11.03
Liechtenstein				56	214		282.14
Luxembourg	627	490	629	1,018	954	0.02	-6.29
Netherlands	79,273	80,114	81,965	82,831	72,259	1.41	-12.76
Switzerland	30,187	25,417	27,100	27,043	23,436	0.46	-13.34
East Mediterranean Europe	**54,377**	**53,706**	**61,579**	**63,240**	**66,113**	**1.29**	**4.54**
Cyprus	3,553	2,616	5,025	5,721	6,236	0.12	9.00
Israel	48,442	48,156	53,779	53,740	54,553	1.06	1.51
Turkey	2,382	2,934	2,775	3,779	5,324	0.10	40.88
Other Europe	**56,285**	**56,741**	**59,757**	**77,489**	**76,835**	**1.50**	**-0.84**
Other countries of Europe	56,285	56,741	59,757	77,489	76,835	1.50	-0.84
MIDDLE EAST	**1,857**	**1,749**	**1,548**	**1,463**	**1,304**	**0.03**	**-10.87**
Middle East	**1,857**	**1,749**	**1,548**	**1,463**	**1,304**	**0.03**	**-10.87**
Egypt	1,857	1,749	1,548	1,463	1,304	0.03	-10.87
SOUTH ASIA	**5,993**	**1,957**	**2,968**	**2,320**	**1,703**	**0.03**	**-26.59**
South Asia	**5,993**	**1,957**	**2,968**	**2,320**	**1,703**	**0.03**	**-26.59**
India	5,993	1,957	2,968	2,320	1,703	0.03	-26.59
REGION NOT SPECIFIED	**553**	**1,050**	**648**	**1,561**	**1,148**	**0.02**	**-26.46**
Not Specified	**553**	**1,050**	**648**	**1,561**	**1,148**	**0.02**	**-26.46**
Other countries of the World	553	1,050	648	1,561	1,148	0.02	-26.46

Source: World Tourism Organization (UNWTO)

SLOVENIA

3. Arrivals of non-resident tourists in hotels and similar establishments, by nationality

	2002	2003	2004	2005	2006	Market share 06	% Change 06-05
TOTAL	1,005,567	1,052,847	1,125,120	1,192,460	1,246,581	100.00	4.54
AFRICA					1,223	0.10	
Southern Africa					409	0.03	
South Africa					409	0.03	
Other Africa					814	0.07	
Other countries of Africa					814	0.07	
AMERICAS	31,520	30,815	38,369	41,085	57,208	4.59	39.24
North America	31,520	30,815	38,369	41,085	51,368	4.12	25.03
Canada	5,046	5,237	5,755	5,405	6,277	0.50	16.13
United States	26,474	25,578	32,614	35,680	40,798	3.27	14.34
Other countries of North America					4,293	0.34	
South America					1,365	0.11	
Brazil					1,365	0.11	
Other Americas					4,475	0.36	
Other countries of the Americas					4,475	0.36	
EAST ASIA AND THE PACIFIC	12,263	11,925	16,666	21,628	43,560	3.49	101.41
North-East Asia	6,260	5,809	8,017	11,270	25,059	2.01	122.35
China					2,456	0.20	
Japan	6,260	5,809	8,017	11,270	18,570	1.49	64.77
Korea, Republic of					4,033	0.32	
Australasia	6,003	6,116	8,649	10,358	11,908	0.96	14.96
Australia	5,062	5,065	7,502	9,286	11,006	0.88	18.52
New Zealand	941	1,051	1,147	1,072	902	0.07	-15.86
Other East Asia and the Pacific					6,593	0.53	
Other countries of Asia					5,774	0.46	
Other countries of Oceania					819	0.07	
EUROPE	951,052	999,215	1,054,531	1,102,265	1,144,590	91.82	3.84
Central/Eastern Europe	89,750	93,643	91,989	94,853	114,217	9.16	20.41
Bulgaria	7,159	7,197	7,892	8,161	10,742	0.86	31.63
Belarus	504	512	523				
Czech Republic	13,335	14,615	14,006	15,131	17,912	1.44	18.38
Estonia					1,581	0.13	
Hungary	20,585	22,451	23,872	27,058	27,218	2.18	0.59
Latvia					2,558	0.21	
Lithuania					1,612	0.13	
Poland	14,202	12,630	11,545	11,682	14,842	1.19	27.05
Romania	6,768	7,080	6,252	6,296	8,361	0.67	32.80
Russian Federation	14,277	14,603	13,631	15,396	16,321	1.31	6.01
Slovakia	5,738	7,000	6,190	6,885	8,209	0.66	19.23
Ukraine	3,751	4,522	4,256	4,244	4,861	0.39	14.54
Baltic countries	3,431	3,033	3,822				
Northern Europe	61,576	69,528	91,655	110,374	114,288	9.17	3.55
Denmark	4,866	5,892	6,450	7,423	7,774	0.62	4.73
Finland	3,028	4,220	5,017	5,807	6,795	0.55	17.01
Iceland	757	791	1,200	3,769	4,940	0.40	31.07
Ireland	4,717	6,442	7,929	7,728	7,123	0.57	-7.83
Norway	4,181	4,584	4,570	5,772	5,295	0.42	-8.26
Sweden	7,638	8,360	9,597	10,642	12,610	1.01	18.49
United Kingdom	36,389	39,239	56,892	69,233	69,751	5.60	0.75

SLOVENIA

3. Arrivals of non-resident tourists in hotels and similar establishments, by nationality

	2002	2003	2004	2005	2006	Market share 06	% Change 06-05
Southern Europe	376,134	392,923	418,677	445,767	474,520	38.07	6.45
Bosnia and Herzegovina	24,590	24,803	21,440	18,164	19,012	1.53	4.67
Croatia	75,812	75,685	75,589	76,052	82,457	6.61	8.42
Greece	1,996	3,036	3,443	3,930	3,497	0.28	-11.02
Italy	238,534	247,668	270,030	294,465	308,546	24.75	4.78
Malta					541	0.04	
Portugal	1,512	2,445	2,748	3,706	5,298	0.43	42.96
Spain	6,489	8,553	10,189	12,338	16,378	1.31	32.74
TFYR of Macedonia	9,354	8,493	8,434	7,686	7,008	0.56	-8.82
Serbia and Montenegro	17,847	22,240	26,804	29,426	31,783	2.55	8.01
Western Europe	384,321	399,464	410,122	407,238	398,817	31.99	-2.07
Austria	152,134	161,138	162,429	162,746	164,902	13.23	1.32
Belgium	15,726	16,573	16,981	17,859	20,507	1.65	14.83
France	21,246	25,307	32,917	38,924	37,169	2.98	-4.51
Germany	161,418	159,077	158,481	147,205	136,498	10.95	-7.27
Luxembourg	701	756	686	1,028	960	0.08	-6.61
Netherlands	16,417	18,463	20,198	20,545	20,461	1.64	-0.41
Switzerland	16,679	18,150	18,430	18,931	18,320	1.47	-3.23
East Mediterranean Europe	35,100	39,469	35,916	35,159	36,203	2.90	2.97
Cyprus					710	0.06	
Israel	29,342	35,140	30,370	26,685	27,168	2.18	1.81
Turkey	5,758	4,329	5,546	8,474	8,325	0.67	-1.76
Other Europe	4,171	4,188	6,172	8,874	6,545	0.53	-26.25
Other countries of Europe	4,171	4,188	6,172	8,874	6,545	0.53	-26.25
REGION NOT SPECIFIED	10,732	10,892	15,554	27,482			
Not Specified	10,732	10,892	15,554	27,482			
Other countries of the World	10,732	10,892	15,554	27,482			

Source: World Tourism Organization (UNWTO)

SLOVENIA

4. Arrivals of non-resident tourists in all types of accommodation establishments, by nationality

	2002	2003	2004	2005	2006	Market share 06	% Change 06-05
TOTAL	1,302,019	1,373,137	1,498,852	1,554,969	1,616,650	100.00	3.97
AFRICA				1,546	1,409	0.09	-8.86
Southern Africa				649	511	0.03	-21.26
South Africa				649	511	0.03	-21.26
Other Africa				897	898	0.06	0.11
Other countries of Africa				897	898	0.06	0.11
AMERICAS	36,232	35,945	45,880	59,303	67,159	4.15	13.25
North America	36,232	35,945	45,880	53,313	59,916	3.71	12.39
Canada	6,129	6,298	7,376	7,089	8,095	0.50	14.19
United States	30,103	29,647	38,504	41,347	47,169	2.92	14.08
Other countries of North America				4,877	4,652	0.29	-4.61
South America				1,032	1,563	0.10	51.45
Brazil				1,032	1,563	0.10	51.45
Other Americas				4,958	5,680	0.35	14.56
Other countries of the Americas				4,958	5,680	0.35	14.56
EAST ASIA AND THE PACIFIC	17,430	17,141	24,237	39,626	52,371	3.24	32.16
North-East Asia	6,921	6,539	8,985	16,878	26,832	1.66	58.98
China				1,754	2,615	0.16	49.09
Japan	6,921	6,539	8,985	12,152	19,880	1.23	63.59
Korea, Republic of				2,972	4,337	0.27	45.93
Australasia	10,509	10,602	15,252	16,244	17,852	1.10	9.90
Australia	8,499	8,360	12,504	14,175	16,366	1.01	15.46
New Zealand	2,010	2,242	2,748	2,069	1,486	0.09	-28.18
Other East Asia and the Pacific				6,504	7,687	0.48	18.19
Other countries of Asia				5,462	6,756	0.42	23.69
Other countries of Oceania				1,042	931	0.06	-10.65
EUROPE	1,235,856	1,307,775	1,410,671	1,454,494	1,495,711	92.52	2.83
Central/Eastern Europe	136,590	141,165	139,303	146,346	165,194	10.22	12.88
Bulgaria	7,831	7,915	8,700	8,887	11,912	0.74	34.04
Belarus	1,036	572	779				
Czech Republic	30,030	31,314	32,135	31,660	35,830	2.22	13.17
Estonia				2,113	2,231	0.14	5.58
Hungary	32,774	37,111	37,954	41,873	42,843	2.65	2.32
Latvia				3,672	3,591	0.22	-2.21
Lithuania				2,488	2,543	0.16	2.21
Poland	24,805	20,360	18,650	18,145	22,507	1.39	24.04
Romania	7,596	8,080	7,251	7,351	9,966	0.62	35.57
Russian Federation	15,370	16,030	14,680	16,310	17,321	1.07	6.20
Slovakia	7,832	10,370	8,640	9,226	11,129	0.69	20.63
Ukraine	4,249	5,008	4,698	4,621	5,321	0.33	15.15
Baltic countries	5,067	4,405	5,816				
Northern Europe	81,281	91,556	126,333	148,180	150,388	9.30	1.49
Denmark	8,712	9,740	11,454	13,798	13,302	0.82	-3.59
Finland	3,844	5,568	7,012	7,856	8,695	0.54	10.68
Iceland	814	922	1,396	4,154	5,223	0.32	25.73
Ireland	6,496	8,624	11,596	10,314	9,661	0.60	-6.33
Norway	5,131	5,542	5,819	7,217	6,660	0.41	-7.72
Sweden	10,167	10,940	12,783	13,969	15,846	0.98	13.44

715

SLOVENIA

4. Arrivals of non-resident tourists in all types of accommodation establishments, by nationality

	2002	2003	2004	2005	2006	Market share 06	% Change 06-05
United Kingdom	46,117	50,220	76,273	90,872	91,001	5.63	0.14
Southern Europe	**441,014**	**463,687**	**494,246**	**524,329**	**559,377**	**34.60**	**6.68**
Bosnia and Herzegovina	27,770	27,644	23,549	20,382	21,523	1.33	5.60
Croatia	94,176	93,639	92,045	93,968	101,827	6.30	8.36
Greece	2,273	3,372	3,801	4,406	3,940	0.24	-10.58
Italy	274,792	288,507	313,448	338,274	357,101	22.09	5.57
Malta				985	654	0.04	-33.60
Portugal	2,264	3,222	4,208	5,363	6,624	0.41	23.51
Spain	9,860	12,951	17,726	20,091	24,578	1.52	22.33
TFYR of Macedonia	10,292	9,233	9,482	8,562	8,013	0.50	-6.41
Serbia and Montenegro	19,587	25,119	29,987	32,298	35,117	2.17	8.73
Western Europe	**534,313**	**560,873**	**602,621**	**584,001**	**569,691**	**35.24**	**-2.45**
Austria	193,422	201,367	205,674	201,852	203,520	12.59	0.83
Belgium	23,637	25,000	27,733	27,668	31,162	1.93	12.63
France	27,863	34,745	50,400	55,900	54,007	3.34	-3.39
Germany	229,211	229,372	237,870	219,257	204,813	12.67	-6.59
Luxembourg	872	1,113	953	1,357	1,112	0.07	-18.05
Netherlands	38,682	46,762	56,213	53,602	51,847	3.21	-3.27
Switzerland	20,626	22,514	23,778	24,365	23,230	1.44	-4.66
East Mediterranean Europe	**37,917**	**44,361**	**41,125**	**41,566**	**43,279**	**2.68**	**4.12**
Cyprus				916	752	0.05	-17.90
Israel	31,972	39,852	35,436	31,868	33,856	2.09	6.24
Turkey	5,945	4,509	5,689	8,782	8,671	0.54	-1.26
Other Europe	**4,741**	**6,133**	**7,043**	**10,072**	**7,782**	**0.48**	**-22.74**
Other countries of Europe	4,741	6,133	7,043	10,072	7,782	0.48	-22.74
REGION NOT SPECIFIED	**12,501**	**12,276**	**18,064**				
Not Specified	**12,501**	**12,276**	**18,064**				
Other countries of the World	12,501	12,276	18,064				

Source: World Tourism Organization (UNWTO)

SLOVENIA

5. Overnight stays of non-resident tourists in hotels and similar establishments, by nationality

	2002	2003	2004	2005	2006	Market share 06	% Change 06-05
TOTAL	3,049,389	3,165,602	3,258,408	3,322,043	3,400,715	100.00	2.37
AFRICA					3,355	0.10	
Southern Africa					1,238	0.04	
South Africa					1,238	0.04	
Other Africa					2,117	0.06	
Other countries of Africa					2,117	0.06	
AMERICAS	74,670	72,064	93,562	91,222	131,017	3.85	43.62
North America	74,670	72,064	93,562	91,222	116,282	3.42	27.47
Canada	13,248	14,190	15,750	13,372	14,851	0.44	11.06
United States	61,422	57,874	77,812	77,850	92,837	2.73	19.25
Other countries of North America					8,594	0.25	
South America					3,721	0.11	
Brazil					3,721	0.11	
Other Americas					11,014	0.32	
Other countries of the Americas					11,014	0.32	
EAST ASIA AND THE PACIFIC	28,885	26,906	33,409	38,125	75,860	2.23	98.98
North-East Asia	12,502	11,156	14,278	17,596	37,104	1.09	110.87
China					4,479	0.13	
Japan	12,502	11,156	14,278	17,596	27,708	0.81	57.47
Korea, Republic of					4,917	0.14	
Australasia	16,383	15,750	19,131	20,529	23,654	0.70	15.22
Australia	14,240	13,593	16,881	18,698	21,866	0.64	16.94
New Zealand	2,143	2,157	2,250	1,831	1,788	0.05	-2.35
Other East Asia and the Pacific					15,102	0.44	
Other countries of Asia					13,112	0.39	
Other countries of Oceania					1,990	0.06	
EUROPE	2,905,824	3,037,532	3,095,532	3,128,469	3,190,483	93.82	1.98
Central/Eastern Europe	276,466	306,131	287,436	290,816	341,107	10.03	17.29
Bulgaria	12,658	13,069	13,375	12,946	18,297	0.54	41.33
Belarus	2,073	2,030	2,250				
Czech Republic	29,712	33,734	31,729	34,043	40,338	1.19	18.49
Estonia					3,753	0.11	
Hungary	52,913	59,880	64,377	71,141	72,871	2.14	2.43
Latvia					5,122	0.15	
Lithuania					3,686	0.11	
Poland	29,991	30,100	28,771	27,939	31,942	0.94	14.33
Romania	14,935	16,196	14,857	14,320	17,131	0.50	19.63
Russian Federation	86,786	93,439	82,381	92,678	99,351	2.92	7.20
Slovakia	17,210	24,584	15,238	16,594	20,760	0.61	25.11
Ukraine	21,741	25,055	24,927	21,155	27,856	0.82	31.68
Baltic countries	8,447	8,044	9,531				
Northern Europe	233,046	255,722	318,530	375,178	378,300	11.12	0.83
Denmark	13,037	16,589	17,368	19,242	17,089	0.50	-11.19
Finland	7,540	11,956	12,724	13,272	17,444	0.51	31.43
Iceland	3,540	3,371	4,494	13,117	14,560	0.43	11.00
Ireland	18,635	25,307	34,231	30,742	26,348	0.77	-14.29
Norway	10,899	10,510	11,743	13,352	13,199	0.39	-1.15
Sweden	18,282	20,982	22,686	27,783	33,854	1.00	21.85

SLOVENIA

5. Overnight stays of non-resident tourists in hotels and similar establishments, by nationality

	2002	2003	2004	2005	2006	Market share 06	% Change 06-05
United Kingdom	161,113	167,007	215,284	257,670	255,806	7.52	-0.72
Southern Europe	**972,717**	**1,028,702**	**1,083,468**	**1,119,366**	**1,181,415**	**34.74**	**5.54**
Bosnia and Herzegovina	65,439	87,381	71,901	42,673	52,354	1.54	22.69
Croatia	195,848	204,996	205,653	200,836	216,795	6.37	7.95
Greece	4,955	7,995	9,054	11,012	7,770	0.23	-29.44
Italy	618,314	626,530	680,874	744,462	767,824	22.58	3.14
Malta					2,191	0.06	
Portugal	3,508	6,606	6,657	7,646	9,712	0.29	27.02
Spain	14,032	20,185	22,162	24,930	32,129	0.94	28.88
TFYR of Macedonia	19,677	18,051	20,454	15,199	14,242	0.42	-6.30
Serbia and Montenegro	50,944	56,958	66,713	72,608	78,398	2.31	7.97
Western Europe	**1,344,816**	**1,354,524**	**1,302,187**	**1,237,659**	**1,183,780**	**34.81**	**-4.35**
Austria	531,586	553,728	547,367	535,630	533,669	15.69	-0.37
Belgium	67,503	66,167	58,823	60,894	69,116	2.03	13.50
France	46,836	54,237	66,087	76,239	71,369	2.10	-6.39
Germany	599,993	572,161	522,032	460,926	411,363	12.10	-10.75
Luxembourg	2,711	2,262	2,090	3,031	2,473	0.07	-18.41
Netherlands	49,566	55,148	55,264	53,318	50,856	1.50	-4.62
Switzerland	46,621	50,821	50,524	47,621	44,934	1.32	-5.64
East Mediterranean Europe	**67,566**	**82,188**	**87,159**	**85,242**	**89,309**	**2.63**	**4.77**
Cyprus					2,710	0.08	
Israel	58,975	73,708	77,328	73,288	73,229	2.15	-0.08
Turkey	8,591	8,480	9,831	11,954	13,370	0.39	11.85
Other Europe	**11,213**	**10,265**	**16,752**	**20,208**	**16,572**	**0.49**	**-17.99**
Other countries of Europe	11,213	10,265	16,752	20,208	16,572	0.49	-17.99
REGION NOT SPECIFIED	**40,010**	**29,100**	**35,905**	**64,227**			
Not Specified	**40,010**	**29,100**	**35,905**	**64,227**			
Other countries of the World	40,010	29,100	35,905	64,227			

Source: World Tourism Organization (UNWTO)

SLOVENIA

6. Overnight stays of non-resident tourists in all types of accommodation establishments, by nationality

	2002	2003	2004	2005	2006	Market share 06	% Change 06-05
TOTAL	4,020,799	4,175,385	4,362,783	4,399,246	4,488,829	100.00	2.04
AFRICA				4,001	3,835	0.09	-4.15
Southern Africa				1,443	1,427	0.03	-1.11
South Africa				1,443	1,427	0.03	-1.11
Other Africa				2,558	2,408	0.05	-5.86
Other countries of Africa				2,558	2,408	0.05	-5.86
AMERICAS	85,816	84,407	110,148	129,777	153,758	3.43	18.48
North America	85,816	84,407	110,148	115,715	135,799	3.03	17.36
Canada	15,978	16,678	19,389	16,691	19,579	0.44	17.30
United States	69,838	67,729	90,759	89,407	106,992	2.38	19.67
Other countries of North America				9,617	9,228	0.21	-4.04
South America				2,422	4,175	0.09	72.38
Brazil				2,422	4,175	0.09	72.38
Other Americas				11,640	13,784	0.31	18.42
Other countries of the Americas				11,640	13,784	0.31	18.42
EAST ASIA AND THE PACIFIC	39,784	37,013	47,462	79,711	97,007	2.16	21.70
North-East Asia	13,834	12,554	15,951	27,341	39,960	0.89	46.15
China				3,862	4,874	0.11	26.20
Japan	13,834	12,554	15,951	19,110	29,667	0.66	55.24
Korea, Republic of				4,369	5,419	0.12	24.03
Australasia	25,950	24,459	31,511	32,256	36,075	0.80	11.84
Australia	21,766	20,116	26,706	28,611	33,067	0.74	15.57
New Zealand	4,184	4,343	4,805	3,645	3,008	0.07	-17.48
Other East Asia and the Pacific				20,114	20,972	0.47	4.27
Other countries of Asia				18,407	18,785	0.42	2.05
Other countries of Oceania				1,707	2,187	0.05	28.12
EUROPE	3,847,883	4,019,677	4,162,560	4,185,757	4,234,229	94.33	1.16
Central/Eastern Europe	403,325	429,108	409,289	418,742	471,889	10.51	12.69
Bulgaria	14,144	14,695	14,682	14,431	20,854	0.46	44.51
Belarus	11,680	2,394	5,758				
Czech Republic	62,401	64,834	67,253	67,155	77,844	1.73	15.92
Estonia				3,865	4,859	0.11	25.72
Hungary	91,048	102,671	105,223	114,370	118,530	2.64	3.64
Latvia				8,530	7,616	0.17	-10.72
Lithuania				4,863	5,556	0.12	14.25
Poland	56,018	50,378	47,239	45,135	51,176	1.14	13.38
Romania	17,283	18,980	17,471	17,142	22,429	0.50	30.84
Russian Federation	92,553	100,656	87,787	97,060	104,411	2.33	7.57
Slovakia	22,461	36,787	23,540	23,476	27,893	0.62	18.81
Ukraine	24,013	27,303	26,920	22,715	30,721	0.68	35.25
Baltic countries	11,724	10,410	13,416				
Northern Europe	294,567	321,136	411,246	481,294	485,682	10.82	0.91
Denmark	25,104	28,960	34,483	40,236	36,342	0.81	-9.68
Finland	9,149	14,908	17,679	17,697	22,357	0.50	26.33
Iceland	3,650	3,700	5,171	14,022	15,309	0.34	9.18
Ireland	23,064	30,633	41,893	37,430	33,478	0.75	-10.56
Norway	13,414	12,723	14,903	16,817	16,966	0.38	0.89
Sweden	26,165	28,031	30,124	36,371	41,932	0.93	15.29

SLOVENIA

6. Overnight stays of non-resident tourists in all types of accommodation establishments, by nationality

	2002	2003	2004	2005	2006	Market share 06	% Change 06-05
United Kingdom	194,021	202,181	266,993	318,721	319,298	7.11	0.18
Southern Europe	**1,168,095**	**1,226,894**	**1,283,363**	**1,337,455**	**1,417,547**	**31.58**	**5.99**
Bosnia and Herzegovina	80,475	98,970	79,753	55,984	65,794	1.47	17.52
Croatia	256,145	264,827	260,832	258,209	281,414	6.27	8.99
Greece	5,879	8,945	9,986	12,088	9,047	0.20	-25.16
Italy	718,384	729,181	786,549	855,796	889,147	19.81	3.90
Malta				3,546	2,730	0.06	-23.01
Portugal	5,107	8,295	9,143	11,449	12,162	0.27	6.23
Spain	21,158	29,458	36,996	40,962	49,440	1.10	20.70
TFYR of Macedonia	22,505	20,151	23,559	17,758	18,123	0.40	2.06
Serbia and Montenegro	58,442	67,067	76,545	81,663	89,690	2.00	9.83
Western Europe	**1,895,618**	**1,934,730**	**1,941,359**	**1,825,543**	**1,735,959**	**38.67**	**-4.91**
Austria	677,043	690,827	691,509	674,090	666,585	14.85	-1.11
Belgium	95,241	94,117	91,187	90,412	99,531	2.22	10.09
France	63,494	75,891	105,330	112,525	107,473	2.39	-4.49
Germany	848,418	813,241	771,747	693,371	624,490	13.91	-9.93
Luxembourg	3,157	3,133	2,749	4,059	2,826	0.06	-30.38
Netherlands	150,345	195,356	215,200	190,971	177,835	3.96	-6.88
Switzerland	57,920	62,165	63,637	60,115	57,219	1.27	-4.82
East Mediterranean Europe	**73,363**	**92,312**	**98,475**	**99,023**	**103,920**	**2.32**	**4.95**
Cyprus				2,150	2,896	0.06	34.70
Israel	64,142	83,339	88,257	83,947	86,410	1.93	2.93
Turkey	9,221	8,973	10,218	12,926	14,614	0.33	13.06
Other Europe	**12,915**	**15,497**	**18,828**	**23,700**	**19,232**	**0.43**	**-18.85**
Other countries of Europe	12,915	15,497	18,828	23,700	19,232	0.43	-18.85
REGION NOT SPECIFIED	**47,316**	**34,288**	**42,613**				
Not Specified	**47,316**	**34,288**	**42,613**				
Other countries of the World	47,316	34,288	42,613				

Source: World Tourism Organization (UNWTO)

SOLOMON ISLANDS

1. Arrivals of non-resident tourists at national borders, by country of residence

	2002	2003	2004	2005	2006	Market share 06	% Change 06-05
TOTAL (*)		6,595		9,400	11,482	100.00	22.15
AMERICAS		600		642	879	7.66	36.92
North America		600		642	879	7.66	36.92
Canada		69		59	86	0.75	45.76
United States		531		583	793	6.91	36.02
EAST ASIA AND THE PACIFIC		5,406		8,128	9,755	84.96	20.02
North-East Asia		346		404	390	3.40	-3.47
Hong Kong, China		95		9	18	0.16	100.00
Japan		251		395	372	3.24	-5.82
Australasia		3,204		4,984	6,062	52.80	21.63
Australia		2,740		4,374	5,279	45.98	20.69
New Zealand		464		610	783	6.82	28.36
Melanesia		1,099		1,658	1,868	16.27	12.67
Fiji		365		451	602	5.24	33.48
Vanuatu		123		409	408	3.55	-0.24
Papua New Guinea		611		798	858	7.47	7.52
Other East Asia and the Pacific		757		1,082	1,435	12.50	32.62
Other countries of Asia		645		832	1,069	9.31	28.49
Other countries of Oceania		112		250	366	3.19	46.40
EUROPE		464		545	708	6.17	29.91
Northern Europe		218		252	327	2.85	29.76
United Kingdom		218		252	327	2.85	29.76
Southern Europe		53		65	33	0.29	-49.23
Italy		53		65	33	0.29	-49.23
Western Europe		69		98	131	1.14	33.67
France		19		36	33	0.29	-8.33
Germany		26		40	66	0.57	65.00
Netherlands		24		22	32	0.28	45.45
Other Europe		124		130	217	1.89	66.92
Other countries of Europe		124		130	217	1.89	66.92
REGION NOT SPECIFIED		125		85	140	1.22	64.71
Not Specified		125		85	140	1.22	64.71
Other countries of the World		125		85	140	1.22	64.71

Source: World Tourism Organization (UNWTO)

SOUTH AFRICA

1. Arrivals of non-resident tourists at national borders, by country of residence

		2002	2003	2004	2005	2006	Market share 06	% Change 06-05
TOTAL	(*)	6,429,583	6,504,890	6,677,844	7,368,742	8,395,833	100.00	13.94
AFRICA		4,452,762	4,450,212	4,638,371	5,370,137	6,280,500	74.80	16.95
East Africa		1,410,188	1,247,051	1,175,691	1,663,631	2,244,419	26.73	34.91
Kenya		17,031	17,743	19,549	20,738	22,362	0.27	7.83
Malawi		95,117	88,942	89,205	106,674	124,260	1.48	16.49
Mauritius		15,738	15,235	13,806	13,921	13,984	0.17	0.45
Mozambique		527,028	421,201	355,840	596,462	917,308	10.93	53.79
Reunion		845	1,095	1,326	916	593	0.01	-35.26
Seychelles		4,170	3,913	2,595	2,318	2,191	0.03	-5.48
Zimbabwe		608,986	563,877	551,113	773,991	980,571	11.68	26.69
Uganda		8,361	9,484	9,882	9,761	10,620	0.13	8.80
United Republic of Tanzania		10,546	10,855	10,991	11,595	12,738	0.15	9.86
Zambia		122,366	114,706	121,384	127,255	159,792	1.90	25.57
Central Africa		35,585	34,765	39,490	43,263	49,278	0.59	13.90
Angola		30,769	28,872	28,543	27,801	28,349	0.34	1.97
Democratic Republic of the Congo		4,816	5,893	10,947	15,462	20,929	0.25	35.36
Southern Africa		2,935,224	3,093,737	3,348,726	3,581,094	3,892,137	46.36	8.69
Botswana		779,794	791,785	802,715	794,706	762,530	9.08	-4.05
Lesotho		1,157,930	1,284,953	1,470,953	1,657,119	1,914,061	22.80	15.51
Namibia		216,566	216,313	225,882	219,303	224,128	2.67	2.20
Swaziland		780,934	800,686	849,176	909,966	991,418	11.81	8.95
West Africa		30,074	30,866	31,752	37,308	45,163	0.54	21.05
Ghana		7,983	8,221	8,311	8,313	10,141	0.12	21.99
Nigeria		22,091	22,645	23,441	28,995	35,022	0.42	20.79
Other Africa		41,691	43,793	42,712	44,841	49,503	0.59	10.40
Other countries of Africa		41,691	43,793	42,712	44,841	49,503	0.59	10.40
AMERICAS		254,586	262,496	290,625	322,099	358,096	4.27	11.18
North America		218,884	224,882	248,334	277,527	306,944	3.66	10.60
Canada		33,684	34,692	37,170	40,818	48,860	0.58	19.70
Mexico		2,609	2,743	3,005	3,246	3,269	0.04	0.71
United States		182,591	187,447	208,159	233,417	254,757	3.03	9.14
Other countries of North America					46	58		26.09
South America		26,851	28,816	33,837	36,023	42,973	0.51	19.29
Argentina		5,131	7,744	9,225	8,938	8,751	0.10	-2.09
Brazil		18,187	17,452	21,137	23,529	29,888	0.36	27.03
Chile		2,628	2,982	2,682	2,528	3,011	0.04	19.11
Venezuela		905	638	793	1,028	1,323	0.02	28.70
Other Americas		8,851	8,798	8,454	8,549	8,179	0.10	-4.33
Other countries of the Americas		8,851	8,798	8,454	8,549	8,179	0.10	-4.33
EAST ASIA AND THE PACIFIC		229,128	224,610	238,829	238,885	257,666	3.07	7.86
North-East Asia		90,785	88,689	103,275	99,227	104,146	1.24	4.96
China	(*)	36,957	42,822	51,080	44,228	41,962	0.50	-5.12
Taiwan (Province of China)		16,012	13,401	15,792	12,900	13,397	0.16	3.85
Japan		26,239	21,311	23,091	27,284	31,989	0.38	17.24
Korea, Republic of		11,577	11,155	13,312	14,815	16,798	0.20	13.39
South-East Asia		39,854	33,210	29,658	28,766	29,550	0.35	2.73
Indonesia		4,662	3,980	3,119	3,468	3,148	0.04	-9.23
Malaysia		12,771	12,049	10,535	9,905	8,966	0.11	-9.48
Philippines		8,421	5,781	4,929	4,853	4,349	0.05	-10.39

SOUTH AFRICA

1. Arrivals of non-resident tourists at national borders, by country of residence

	2002	2003	2004	2005	2006	Market share 06	% Change 06-05
Singapore	6,456	5,337	5,390	5,738	6,452	0.08	12.44
Thailand	7,544	6,063	5,685	4,802	6,635	0.08	38.17
Australasia	**84,739**	**88,074**	**92,023**	**95,063**	**107,701**	**1.28**	**13.29**
Australia	69,832	71,687	75,675	77,238	89,396	1.06	15.74
New Zealand	14,907	16,387	16,348	17,825	18,305	0.22	2.69
Other East Asia and the Pacific	**13,750**	**14,637**	**13,873**	**15,829**	**16,269**	**0.19**	**2.78**
Other countries of Asia	12,714	13,649	12,886	15,074	15,545	0.19	3.12
Other countries of Oceania	1,036	988	987	755	724	0.01	-4.11
EUROPE	**1,274,365**	**1,338,976**	**1,306,389**	**1,328,521**	**1,402,643**	**16.71**	**5.58**
Central/Eastern Europe	**23,766**	**21,313**	**17,132**	**17,346**	**21,834**	**0.26**	**25.87**
Czech Republic	3,596	4,383					
Hungary	5,094	2,864	3,447	2,575	3,158	0.04	22.64
Poland	6,527	6,368	6,212	6,459	8,060	0.10	24.79
Russian Federation	8,549	7,698	7,473	8,312	10,616	0.13	27.72
Northern Europe	**534,202**	**564,252**	**572,651**	**590,491**	**620,670**	**7.39**	**5.11**
Denmark	16,726	19,292	20,126	21,027	24,892	0.30	18.38
Finland	6,135	7,099	7,415	7,676	9,351	0.11	21.82
Ireland	29,506	34,379	37,989	36,335	38,124	0.45	4.92
Norway	14,998	17,633	18,506	20,235	21,122	0.25	4.38
Sweden	23,927	29,381	32,247	35,619	39,149	0.47	9.91
United Kingdom	442,910	456,468	456,368	469,599	488,032	5.81	3.93
Southern Europe	**108,626**	**112,204**	**109,768**	**116,481**	**122,176**	**1.46**	**4.89**
Greece	7,527	7,869	7,479	8,175	9,002	0.11	10.12
Italy	47,756	49,818	50,429	51,464	53,605	0.64	4.16
Portugal	29,088	28,920	28,966	29,846	28,548	0.34	-4.35
Spain	24,255	25,597	22,894	26,996	31,021	0.37	14.91
Western Europe	**569,309**	**605,797**	**570,231**	**565,151**	**592,488**	**7.06**	**4.84**
Austria	21,633	21,711	20,602	20,693	21,766	0.26	5.19
Belgium	39,242	42,735	37,277	38,502	40,052	0.48	4.03
France	112,078	127,760	109,276	101,139	106,088	1.26	4.89
Germany	248,990	257,018	245,452	249,504	258,517	3.08	3.61
Netherlands	110,389	120,933	120,838	116,244	124,689	1.49	7.26
Switzerland	36,977	35,640	36,786	39,069	41,376	0.49	5.90
East Mediterranean Europe	**21,655**	**19,804**	**19,332**	**19,887**	**20,762**	**0.25**	**4.40**
Israel	16,445	15,025	15,442	15,414	15,163	0.18	-1.63
Turkey	5,210	4,779	3,890	4,473	5,599	0.07	25.17
Other Europe	**16,807**	**15,606**	**17,275**	**19,165**	**24,713**	**0.29**	**28.95**
Other countries of Europe	16,807	15,606	17,275	19,165	24,713	0.29	28.95
MIDDLE EAST	**14,955**	**15,048**	**16,037**	**17,194**	**19,806**	**0.24**	**15.19**
Middle East	**14,955**	**15,048**	**16,037**	**17,194**	**19,806**	**0.24**	**15.19**
Saudi Arabia	2,865	3,523	3,581	3,818	4,125	0.05	8.04
United Arab Emirates	1,439	1,788	1,800	2,467	2,582	0.03	4.66
Egypt	3,209	3,038	3,716	3,530	3,844	0.05	8.90
Other countries of Middle East	7,442	6,699	6,940	7,379	9,255	0.11	25.42
SOUTH ASIA	**34,062**	**41,018**	**36,172**	**36,045**	**44,337**	**0.53**	**23.00**
South Asia	**34,062**	**41,018**	**36,172**	**36,045**	**44,337**	**0.53**	**23.00**
India	34,062	41,018	36,172	36,045	44,337	0.53	23.00
REGION NOT SPECIFIED	**169,725**	**172,530**	**151,421**	**55,861**	**32,785**	**0.39**	**-41.31**
Not Specified	**169,725**	**172,530**	**151,421**	**55,861**	**32,785**	**0.39**	**-41.31**

SOUTH AFRICA

2. Arrivals of non-resident visitors at national borders, by country of residence

		2002	2003	2004	2005	2006	Market share 06	% Change 06-05
TOTAL	(*)	6,549,916	6,640,095	6,815,202	7,518,320	8,508,806	100.00	13.17
AFRICA		4,530,022	4,536,397	4,720,457	5,463,441	6,320,636	74.28	15.69
East Africa		1,480,109	1,321,128	1,249,564	1,742,837	2,285,368	26.86	31.13
Burundi		996	1,190	1,464	1,129	1,260	0.01	11.60
Comoros		178	199	152	244	206		-15.57
Ethiopia		3,395	4,873	5,234	6,340	7,978	0.09	25.84
Eritrea		691	565	423	468	690	0.01	47.44
Djibouti		74	66	79	65	79		21.54
Kenya		17,853	18,780	20,825	22,389	24,209	0.28	8.13
Madagascar		1,601	1,864	1,734	1,927	2,472	0.03	28.28
Malawi		95,518	89,469	89,743	107,258	124,914	1.47	16.46
Mauritius		15,962	15,468	14,009	14,103	14,233	0.17	0.92
Mozambique		579,768	474,790	405,579	648,526	926,496	10.89	42.86
Reunion		850	1,095	1,326	934	599	0.01	-35.87
Rwanda		2,928	2,855	2,741	2,699	3,003	0.04	11.26
Seychelles		4,192	3,923	2,607	2,342	2,215	0.03	-5.42
Somalia		746	653	1,330	691	1,839	0.02	166.14
Zimbabwe		612,543	568,626	558,093	783,100	989,614	11.63	26.37
Uganda		8,824	9,889	10,314	10,237	11,208	0.13	9.49
United Republic of Tanzania		10,909	11,173	11,399	11,995	13,369	0.16	11.45
Zambia		123,081	115,650	122,512	128,390	160,984	1.89	25.39
Central Africa		52,224	53,551	56,100	59,796	67,031	0.79	12.10
Angola		31,230	29,511	29,058	28,515	29,005	0.34	1.72
Cameroon		2,375	3,118	3,710	3,911	4,014	0.05	2.63
Central African Republic		102	117	81	88	148		68.18
Chad		112	108	101	174	260		49.43
Congo		10,469	10,515	7,630	7,110	8,888	0.10	25.01
Democratic Republic of the Congo		4,938	6,042	11,391	16,079	21,421	0.25	33.22
Equatorial Guinea		404	490	514	421	277		-34.20
Gabon		2,463	3,535	3,463	3,365	2,888	0.03	-14.18
Sao Tome and Principe		131	115	152	133	130		-2.26
North Africa		4,036	3,177	4,169	4,989	5,635	0.07	12.95
Algeria		1,697	1,129	1,775	2,107	2,060	0.02	-2.23
Morocco		1,011	613	754	859	915	0.01	6.52
Western Sahara		2	2	4	4	11		175.00
Sudan		760	845	1,034	1,312	1,808	0.02	37.80
Tunisia		566	588	602	707	841	0.01	18.95
Southern Africa		2,950,894	3,114,584	3,365,783	3,599,316	3,903,644	45.88	8.46
Botswana		782,189	797,315	806,820	798,455	765,705	9.00	-4.10
Lesotho		1,162,786	1,291,242	1,479,802	1,668,826	1,919,889	22.56	15.04
Namibia		217,077	216,978	226,525	220,045	225,020	2.64	2.26
Swaziland		788,842	809,049	852,636	911,990	993,030	11.67	8.89
West Africa		42,669	43,182	44,841	50,785	58,958	0.69	16.09
Cape Verde		1,040	911	764	655	609	0.01	-7.02
Benin		1,303	1,212	1,053	1,264	1,025	0.01	-18.91
Gambia		475	664	764	591	597	0.01	1.02
Ghana		8,392	8,700	8,887	8,970	10,926	0.13	21.81
Guinea		659	817	861	894	960	0.01	7.38
Cote D'Ivoire		2,723	2,100	1,821	2,175	2,168	0.03	-0.32
Liberia		344	323	368	332	448	0.01	34.94
Mali		605	745	786	898	796	0.01	-11.36
Mauritania		149	153	174	185	181		-2.16
Niger		226	149	159	173	211		21.97

SOUTH AFRICA

2. Arrivals of non-resident visitors at national borders, by country of residence

	2002	2003	2004	2005	2006	Market share 06	% Change 06-05
Nigeria	22,981	23,477	24,627	30,248	36,635	0.43	21.12
Guinea-Bissau	139	170	210	178	162		-8.99
Saint Helena	341	196	145	120	163		35.83
Senegal	1,915	2,300	2,674	2,660	2,578	0.03	-3.08
Sierra Leone	609	620	640	586	636	0.01	8.53
Togo	361	319	381	387	384		-0.78
Burkina Faso	407	326	527	469	479	0.01	2.13
Other Africa	**90**	**775**		**5,718**			
Other countries of Africa	90	775		5,718			
AMERICAS	**261,831**	**270,022**	**297,682**	**330,225**	**365,194**	**4.29**	**10.59**
Caribbean	**2,784**	**2,330**	**2,449**	**2,564**	**2,622**	**0.03**	**2.26**
Antigua and Barbuda	33	39	34	28	40		42.86
Bahamas	68	79	130	64	176		175.00
Barbados	202	256	162	132	129		-2.27
Bermuda	91	105	121	81	140		72.84
British Virgin Islands	40	38	36	121	41		-66.12
Cuba	1,327	1,232	940	954	876	0.01	-8.18
Dominica				17			
Dominican Republic	72	38	34	34	128		276.47
Grenada	32	30	26	23	35		52.17
Jamaica	498		559	543	533	0.01	-1.84
Saint Lucia	42	37	23	46	49		6.52
Saint Vincent and the Grenadines	27	33	43	43	39		-9.30
Trinidad and Tobago	333	438	337	473	422		-10.78
Turks and Caicos Islands	15	4	3	3	12		300.00
United States Virgin Islands	4	1	1	2	2		
Central America	**1,028**	**984**	**962**	**943**	**1,002**	**0.01**	**6.26**
Belize	75	99	55	38	93		144.74
Costa Rica	280	271	308	349	316		-9.46
El Salvador	89	99	94	56	98		75.00
Guatemala	168	164	173	178	175		-1.69
Honduras	129	85	94	99	106		7.07
Nicaragua	119	107	92	80	51		-36.25
Panama	168	159	146	143	163		13.99
North America	**225,030**	**231,073**	**254,630**	**284,118**	**312,989**	**3.68**	**10.16**
Canada	34,664	35,683	38,214	41,827	49,963	0.59	19.45
Greenland	44	42	39	42	24		-42.86
Mexico	2,641	2,787	3,055	3,315	3,328	0.04	0.39
United States	187,681	192,561	213,322	238,934	259,674	3.05	8.68
South America	**32,320**	**34,411**	**39,641**	**41,827**	**48,581**	**0.57**	**16.15**
Argentina	5,256	7,904	9,420	9,108	8,957	0.11	-1.66
Bolivia	302	439	383	425	355		-16.47
Brazil	18,460	17,883	21,562	24,090	30,424	0.36	26.29
Chile	2,697	3,085	2,825	2,673	3,155	0.04	18.03
Colombia	876	699	923	1,009	1,120	0.01	11.00
Ecuador	257	257	265	259	313		20.85
Falkland Islands (Malvinas)	4	6	8	7	11		57.14
French Guiana	113	91	72	61	84		37.70
Guyana	378	329	321	244	3		-98.77
Paraguay	392	366	378	346	310		-10.40
Peru	1,294	1,161	1,314	1,328	1,331	0.02	0.23
Suriname	56	46	58	67	44		-34.33
Uruguay	1,285	1,489	1,293	1,140	1,096	0.01	-3.86
Venezuela	950	656	819	1,070	1,378	0.02	28.79

SOUTH AFRICA

2. Arrivals of non-resident visitors at national borders, by country of residence

	2002	2003	2004	2005	2006	Market share 06	% Change 06-05
Other Americas	669	1,224		773			
Other countries of the Americas	669	1,224		773			
EAST ASIA AND THE PACIFIC	223,980	220,415	238,326	237,604	260,344	3.06	9.57
North-East Asia	95,088	94,021	110,164	107,527	114,632	1.35	6.61
China	25,849	33,128	45,934	41,704	40,327	0.47	-3.30
Taiwan (Province of China)	16,420	13,959	16,753	13,579	15,591	0.18	14.82
Hong Kong, China	12,776	12,132	8,744	7,671	7,543	0.09	-1.67
Japan	27,581	22,741	24,469	28,861	33,500	0.39	16.07
Korea, Dem. People's Republic of	43	40	70	110	99		-10.00
Korea, Republic of	12,096	11,737	13,935	15,391	17,405	0.20	13.09
Macao, China	172	169	186	127	104		-18.11
Mongolia	151	115	73	84	63		-25.00
South-East Asia	41,601	36,003	33,899	33,078	36,039	0.42	8.95
Brunei Darussalam	120	156	118	69	81		17.39
Myanmar	370	535	533	462	557	0.01	20.56
Cambodia	75	59	88	76	82		7.89
Indonesia	4,837	4,347	3,841	4,383	4,448	0.05	1.48
Lao People's Democratic Republic	132	72	53	51	25		-50.98
Malaysia	13,078	12,289	10,846	10,272	9,314	0.11	-9.33
Philippines	8,707	6,723	6,813	6,526	7,654	0.09	17.28
Singapore	6,583	5,497	5,697	6,137	6,762	0.08	10.18
Thailand	7,699	6,325	5,910	5,102	7,116	0.08	39.47
Australasia	86,084	89,362	93,274	96,272	108,966	1.28	13.19
Australia	70,871	72,728	76,712	78,233	90,419	1.06	15.58
New Zealand	15,213	16,634	16,562	18,039	18,547	0.22	2.82
Melanesia	317	273	286	225	202		-10.22
Solomon Islands	15	18	28	2	13		550.00
Fiji	241	188	190	155	143		-7.74
New Caledonia	11	1	1	7	2		-71.43
Norfolk Island	1	5	9	14	3		-78.57
Papua New Guinea	49	61	58	47	41		-12.77
Micronesia	250	268	253	170	161		-5.29
Christmas Island (Australia)	56	19	11	18	5		-72.22
Cocos (Keeling) Islands	14	50	46	19	43		126.32
Kiribati	40	29	33	40	35		-12.50
Guam	11	25	7	17	14		-17.65
Nauru	14	10	24	13	12		-7.69
Northern Mariana Islands	48	66	69	50	27		-46.00
Micronesia (Federated States of)	56	52	58	5	19		280.00
Marshall Islands	11	17	5	8	6		-25.00
Polynesia	473	457	450	332	344		3.61
American Samoa				2			
Cook Islands	1		2	2			
French Polynesia	268	319	223	172	225		30.81
Pitcairn	2	2	1	2	2		
Tokelau	4	7	9	5	13		160.00
Tonga	28	17	44	49	16		-67.35
Tuvalu	22	37	22	1	15		1,400.00
Samoa	148	75	149	99	73		-26.26
Other East Asia and the Pacific	167	31					
Other countries of Asia	155						
Other countries of Oceania	12	31					

SOUTH AFRICA

2. Arrivals of non-resident visitors at national borders, by country of residence

	2002	2003	2004	2005	2006	Market share 06	% Change 06-05
EUROPE	1,297,647	1,365,004	1,332,162	1,352,722	1,433,896	16.85	6.00
Central/Eastern Europe	35,098	33,754	32,690	32,382	46,699	0.55	44.21
Azerbaijan	64	55	65	92	92		
Armenia	61	53	52	29	64		120.69
Bulgaria	1,923	2,366	2,813	2,431	2,393	0.03	-1.56
Belarus	10	14	21	229	756	0.01	230.13
Czech Republic	3,700	4,482	2,967	1,804	5,877	0.07	225.78
Estonia	359	371	390	406	708	0.01	74.38
Hungary	5,157	2,940	3,535	2,671	3,248	0.04	21.60
Kazakhstan	210	264	228	255	399		56.47
Kyrgyzstan	94	62	53	47	87		85.11
Latvia	708	408	559	628	1,137	0.01	81.05
Lithuania	612	564	549	594	966	0.01	62.63
Republic of Moldova	88	80	51	82	124		51.22
Poland	6,648	6,694	6,869	7,100	8,754	0.10	23.30
Romania	1,136	1,295	1,196	1,358	2,528	0.03	86.16
Russian Federation	8,907	8,604	8,610	9,645	12,606	0.15	30.70
Slovakia	1,067	1,078	596	1,253	1,845	0.02	47.25
Tajikistan				20	22		10.00
Turkmenistan	14	16	3	24	25		4.17
Ukraine	4,297	4,307	4,101	3,646	4,957	0.06	35.96
Uzbekistan	43	101	32	68	111		63.24
Northern Europe	543,172	573,905	582,680	600,617	631,437	7.42	5.13
Denmark	17,217	19,888	20,684	21,450	25,324	0.30	18.06
Faeroe Islands	43	48	52	22	33		50.00
Finland	6,311	7,265	7,604	7,902	9,691	0.11	22.64
Iceland	633	765	672	688	1,011	0.01	46.95
Ireland	29,885	34,806	38,437	36,799	38,692	0.45	5.14
Norway	15,270	17,982	18,959	20,636	21,508	0.25	4.23
Sweden	24,590	30,053	32,987	36,408	40,106	0.47	10.16
United Kingdom	449,166	463,021	463,176	476,627	494,955	5.82	3.85
Channel Islands	21	44	31	45	46		2.22
Isle of Man	36	33	78	40	71		77.50
Southern Europe	114,739	118,220	114,519	121,274	127,698	1.50	5.30
Albania	212	233	203	175	244		39.43
Andorra	29	68	43	47	79		68.09
Croatia	1,704	1,293	1,299	1,356	1,631	0.02	20.28
Gibraltar	19	28	26	25	13		-48.00
Greece	7,734	8,159	7,892	8,541	9,372	0.11	9.73
Holy See	11						
Italy	48,342	50,403	51,059	52,172	54,214	0.64	3.91
Malta	388	304	298	396	476	0.01	20.20
Portugal	29,492	29,347	29,421	30,277	28,978	0.34	-4.29
San Marino	35	81	41	56	43		-23.21
Slovenia	968	837	596	640	988	0.01	54.38
Spain	24,446	26,167	23,638	27,587	31,659	0.37	14.76
Serbia and Montenegro	1,359	1,300	3	2	1		-50.00
Western Europe	580,938	617,338	581,019	576,447	604,960	7.11	4.95
Austria	21,910	21,960	20,808	20,935	22,052	0.26	5.34
Belgium	40,023	43,537	38,036	39,385	40,959	0.48	4.00
France	114,797	130,365	111,636	103,674	108,713	1.28	4.86
Germany	253,411	261,194	249,564	253,471	263,225	3.09	3.85
Liechtenstein	183	186	195	254	246		-3.15
Luxembourg	1,138	1,292	1,141	1,227	1,529	0.02	24.61

SOUTH AFRICA

2. Arrivals of non-resident visitors at national borders, by country of residence

	2002	2003	2004	2005	2006	Market share 06	% Change 06-05
Monaco	72	36	49	55	56		1.82
Netherlands	111,873	122,565	122,271	117,855	126,327	1.48	7.19
Switzerland	37,531	36,203	37,319	39,591	41,853	0.49	5.71
East Mediterranean Europe	**23,700**	**21,787**	**21,254**	**22,002**	**23,102**	**0.27**	**5.00**
Cyprus	1,497	1,343	1,347	1,304	1,446	0.02	10.89
Israel	16,837	15,427	15,877	15,864	15,634	0.18	-1.45
Turkey	5,366	5,017	4,030	4,834	6,022	0.07	24.58
MIDDLE EAST	**13,897**	**13,915**	**14,778**	**16,417**	**17,952**	**0.21**	**9.35**
Middle East	**13,897**	**13,915**	**14,778**	**16,417**	**17,952**	**0.21**	**9.35**
Bahrain	184	136	193	148	300		102.70
Palestine		209	142	120	138		15.00
Iraq	154	139	147	169	166		-1.78
Jordan	1,249	1,087	1,186	1,349	1,601	0.02	18.68
Kuwait	841	693	707	704	708	0.01	0.57
Lebanon	1,491	1,396	1,461	1,572	1,843	0.02	17.24
Libyan Arab Jamahiriya	1,116	617	509	702	632	0.01	-9.97
Oman	237	202	209	184	349		89.67
Qatar	233	142	164	493	407		-17.44
Saudi Arabia	2,946	3,595	3,629	3,940	4,243	0.05	7.69
Syrian Arab Republic	374	329	370	401	433	0.01	7.98
United Arab Emirates	1,469	1,820	1,841	2,499	2,637	0.03	5.52
Egypt	3,435	3,428	4,001	3,896	4,268	0.05	9.55
Yemen	168	122	219	240	227		-5.42
SOUTH ASIA	**48,777**	**57,275**	**49,606**	**55,612**	**65,879**	**0.77**	**18.46**
South Asia	**48,777**	**57,275**	**49,606**	**55,612**	**65,879**	**0.77**	**18.46**
Afghanistan	416	432	406	528	739	0.01	39.96
Bangladesh	2,240	1,983	1,803	2,930	2,550	0.03	-12.97
Bhutan	25	11	9	9	8		-11.11
Sri Lanka	1,580	1,834	1,474	1,608	1,962	0.02	22.01
India	35,402	42,954	36,069	39,906	49,674	0.58	24.48
Iran, Islamic Republic of	1,066	1,181	1,132	1,220	2,024	0.02	65.90
Maldives	101	57	64	81	90		11.11
Nepal	355	292	391	329	315		-4.26
Pakistan	7,592	8,531	8,258	9,001	8,517	0.10	-5.38
REGION NOT SPECIFIED	**173,762**	**177,067**	**162,191**	**62,299**	**44,905**	**0.53**	**-27.92**
Not Specified	**173,762**	**177,067**	**162,191**	**62,299**	**44,905**	**0.53**	**-27.92**
Other countries of the World	173,762	177,067	162,191	62,299	44,905	0.53	-27.92

Source: World Tourism Organization (UNWTO)

SPAIN

1. Arrivals of non-resident tourists at national borders, by country of residence

	2002	2003	2004	2005	2006	Market share 06	% Change 06-05
TOTAL	52,326,766	50,853,822	52,429,836	55,913,780	58,190,469	100.00	4.07
AMERICAS	2,079,643	1,893,950	2,079,065	2,232,851	2,383,760	4.10	6.76
North America	1,308,309	1,231,224	1,213,427	1,239,849	1,294,024	2.22	4.37
Canada	154,989	141,824	125,824	111,854	127,955	0.22	14.39
Mexico	213,266	184,359	193,246	244,472	245,326	0.42	0.35
United States	940,054	905,041	894,357	883,523	920,743	1.58	4.21
South America	507,308	421,967	542,895	647,506	657,418	1.13	1.53
Argentina	166,496	176,366	198,328	244,702	202,268	0.35	-17.34
Brazil	145,582	97,392	183,749	221,645	256,581	0.44	15.76
Chile	61,750	56,613	53,352	57,555	76,320	0.13	32.60
Venezuela	133,480	91,596	107,466	123,604	122,249	0.21	-1.10
Other Americas	264,026	240,759	322,743	345,496	432,318	0.74	25.13
Other countries of the Americas	264,026	240,759	322,743	345,496	432,318	0.74	25.13
EAST ASIA AND THE PACIFIC	240,637	237,392	150,583	181,050	257,200	0.44	42.06
North-East Asia	240,637	237,392	150,583	181,050	257,200	0.44	42.06
Japan	240,637	237,392	150,583	181,050	257,200	0.44	42.06
EUROPE	49,303,582	47,835,345	49,238,605	52,189,873	54,361,593	93.42	4.16
Central/Eastern Europe	270,039	203,964	251,631	297,793	342,577	0.59	15.04
Russian Federation	270,039	203,964	251,631	297,793	342,577	0.59	15.04
Northern Europe	18,806,836	19,233,493	19,784,174	20,321,145	20,775,096	35.70	2.23
Denmark	639,071	633,560	693,116	726,900	805,468	1.38	10.81
Finland	431,491	381,435	417,618	435,747	474,480	0.82	8.89
Ireland	1,129,239	1,289,081	1,409,060	1,365,078	1,507,086	2.59	10.40
Norway	771,160	752,724	743,054	786,763	804,368	1.38	2.24
Sweden	1,138,488	952,667	892,101	916,626	998,647	1.72	8.95
United Kingdom	14,697,387	15,224,026	15,629,225	16,090,031	16,185,047	27.81	0.59
Southern Europe	4,448,259	4,162,545	4,810,895	5,040,100	5,639,364	9.69	11.89
Greece	154,654	104,114	86,032	91,293	84,504	0.15	-7.44
Italy	2,532,055	2,433,979	2,800,709	2,956,892	3,362,091	5.78	13.70
Portugal	1,761,550	1,624,452	1,924,154	1,991,915	2,192,769	3.77	10.08
Western Europe	24,414,631	22,944,983	22,905,325	24,817,642	25,719,300	44.20	3.63
Austria	461,000	415,281	413,119	481,852	535,943	0.92	11.23
Belgium	1,774,970	1,761,869	1,736,388	1,821,667	1,824,901	3.14	0.18
France	8,143,463	7,959,196	7,735,764	8,874,747	9,220,376	15.85	3.89
Germany	10,211,494	9,303,290	9,536,621	9,917,619	10,117,917	17.39	2.02
Luxembourg	185,308	135,939	128,485	131,276	124,726	0.21	-4.99
Netherlands	2,415,193	2,347,875	2,301,252	2,434,990	2,514,569	4.32	3.27
Switzerland	1,223,203	1,021,533	1,053,696	1,155,491	1,380,868	2.37	19.50
Other Europe	1,363,817	1,290,360	1,486,580	1,713,193	1,885,256	3.24	10.04
Other countries of Europe	1,363,817	1,290,360	1,486,580	1,713,193	1,885,256	3.24	10.04
REGION NOT SPECIFIED	702,904	887,135	961,583	1,310,006	1,187,916	2.04	-9.32
Not Specified	702,904	887,135	961,583	1,310,006	1,187,916	2.04	-9.32
Other countries of the World	702,904	887,135	961,583	1,310,006	1,187,916	2.04	-9.32

Source: World Tourism Organization (UNWTO)

SPAIN

3. Arrivals of non-resident tourists in hotels and similar establishments, by country of residence

		2002	2003	2004	2005	2006	Market share 06	% Change 06-05
TOTAL	(*)	26,610,690	27,248,610	27,619,865	29,028,687	34,411,762	100.00	18.54
AFRICA		265,328	285,307	247,349	325,479	347,701	1.01	6.83
Other Africa		265,328	285,307	247,349	325,479	347,701	1.01	6.83
All countries of Africa		265,328	285,307	247,349	325,479	347,701	1.01	6.83
AMERICAS		2,754,604	2,627,163	2,665,121	2,696,630	3,156,633	9.17	17.06
North America		1,885,772	1,841,878	1,807,862	1,402,064	1,595,831	4.64	13.82
Canada		186,325	184,701	166,073				
Mexico		267,913	248,716	247,596				
United States		1,431,534	1,408,461	1,394,193	1,402,064	1,595,831	4.64	13.82
South America		428,534	412,215	462,170				
Argentina		212,708	210,852	230,999				
Brazil		148,933	142,331	164,372				
Venezuela		66,893	59,032	66,799				
Other Americas		440,298	373,070	395,089	1,294,566	1,560,802	4.54	20.57
Other countries of the Americas		440,298	373,070	395,089	1,294,566	1,560,802	4.54	20.57
EAST ASIA AND THE PACIFIC		961,481	919,579	970,839	604,176			
North-East Asia		596,382	545,653	575,868	604,176			
Japan		596,382	545,653	575,868	604,176			
Australasia		143,019	154,490	158,980				
Australia		117,996	126,677	131,064				
New Zealand		25,023	27,813	27,916				
Other East Asia and the Pacific		222,080	219,436	235,991				
Other countries of Asia		222,080	219,436	235,991				
EUROPE		22,080,020	22,856,178	23,130,322	24,407,350	28,906,791	84.00	18.43
Central/Eastern Europe		558,280	553,028	512,924	546,728	726,025	2.11	32.79
Czech Republic		138,408	147,887	104,905	138,222	154,560	0.45	11.82
Hungary		45,174	48,363	47,771				
Poland		128,964	110,216	111,055	139,040	192,103	0.56	38.16
Russian Federation		218,423	210,766	224,738	269,466	379,362	1.10	40.78
Slovakia		27,311	35,796	24,455				
Northern Europe		7,537,941	8,080,075	8,140,775	8,475,940	9,751,953	28.34	15.05
Denmark		203,191	210,770	221,067	264,535	322,586	0.94	21.94
Finland		128,466	131,196	128,559	143,365	173,624	0.50	21.11
Iceland		17,077	22,108	27,795				
Ireland		271,201	322,977	383,616	441,867	533,470	1.55	20.73
Norway		239,472	217,264	213,665	219,998	274,490	0.80	24.77
Sweden		399,355	367,267	362,112	387,723	467,787	1.36	20.65
United Kingdom		6,279,179	6,808,493	6,803,961	7,018,452	7,979,996	23.19	13.70
Southern Europe		2,848,857	2,817,563	2,963,517	3,242,447	3,851,314	11.19	18.78
Greece		92,757	82,751	72,739	82,865	118,570	0.34	43.09
Italy		1,788,290	1,741,685	1,868,598	2,083,244	2,483,812	7.22	19.23
Portugal		967,810	993,127	1,022,180	1,076,338	1,248,932	3.63	16.04
Western Europe		10,736,760	11,004,489	11,094,155	11,434,837	13,612,798	39.56	19.05
Austria		185,271	205,225	200,701	218,967	287,056	0.83	31.10
Belgium		906,991	931,155	886,859	855,214	1,015,059	2.95	18.69
France		2,856,615	2,970,755	2,921,362	3,037,376	3,387,318	9.84	11.52
Germany		5,215,352	5,390,488	5,620,921	5,858,612	7,106,809	20.65	21.31

SPAIN

3. Arrivals of non-resident tourists in hotels and similar establishments, by country of residence

	2002	2003	2004	2005	2006	Market share 06	% Change 06-05
Luxembourg	63,104	70,021	61,922	61,845	79,611	0.23	28.73
Netherlands	1,056,563	1,011,883	969,343	982,194	1,212,412	3.52	23.44
Switzerland	452,864	424,962	433,047	420,629	524,533	1.52	24.70
East Mediterranean Europe	**30,184**	**36,023**	**37,187**				
Turkey	30,184	36,023	37,187				
Other Europe	**367,998**	**365,000**	**381,764**	**707,398**	**964,701**	**2.80**	**36.37**
Other countries of Europe	367,998	365,000	381,764	707,398	964,701	2.80	36.37
REGION NOT SPECIFIED	**549,257**	**560,383**	**606,234**	**995,052**	**2,000,637**	**5.81**	**101.06**
Not Specified	**549,257**	**560,383**	**606,234**	**995,052**	**2,000,637**	**5.81**	**101.06**
Other countries of the World	549,257	560,383	606,234	995,052	2,000,637	5.81	101.06

Source: World Tourism Organization (UNWTO)

SPAIN

4. Arrivals of non-resident tourists in all types of accommodation establishments, by country of residence

		2002	2003	2004	2005	2006	Market share 06	% Change 06-05
TOTAL	(*)	36,038,355	36,643,764	36,297,326	37,407,144	43,114,325	100.00	15.26
AFRICA		280,001	298,098	261,587	349,747	374,474	0.87	7.07
Other Africa		280,001	298,098	261,587	349,747	374,474	0.87	7.07
All countries of Africa		280,001	298,098	261,587	349,747	374,474	0.87	7.07
AMERICAS		2,853,427	2,739,029	2,776,462	2,802,281	3,274,977	7.60	16.87
North America		1,472,392	1,458,359	1,442,152	1,455,436	1,654,123	3.84	13.65
United States		1,472,392	1,458,359	1,442,152	1,455,436	1,654,123	3.84	13.65
Other Americas		1,381,035	1,280,670	1,334,310	1,346,845	1,620,854	3.76	20.34
Other countries of the Americas		1,381,035	1,280,670	1,334,310	1,346,845	1,620,854	3.76	20.34
EAST ASIA AND THE PACIFIC		828,136	930,783	823,571				
Other East Asia and the Pacific		828,136	930,783	823,571				
All countries of Asia		828,136	930,783	823,571				
EUROPE		31,338,684	32,053,355	31,608,175	32,583,093	37,373,980	86.69	14.70
Northern Europe		12,362,334	12,784,757	12,533,706	12,672,252	13,998,835	32.47	10.47
Denmark		422,220	395,636	406,046	461,659	539,291	1.25	16.82
Finland		282,113	283,271	283,515	297,043	353,957	0.82	19.16
Ireland		589,789	681,277	757,922	811,621	948,925	2.20	16.92
Norway		475,358	415,496	402,400	414,951	475,716	1.10	14.64
Sweden		803,142	712,684	681,513	716,402	780,877	1.81	9.00
United Kingdom		9,789,712	10,296,393	10,002,310	9,970,576	10,900,069	25.28	9.32
Southern Europe		3,213,096	3,201,372	3,362,804	3,644,228	4,300,607	9.97	18.01
Greece		100,977	89,253	78,627	88,385	124,334	0.29	40.67
Italy		2,037,616	2,007,080	2,140,927	2,344,171	2,788,715	6.47	18.96
Portugal		1,074,503	1,105,039	1,143,250	1,211,672	1,387,558	3.22	14.52
Western Europe		14,007,146	14,340,037	14,026,203	14,276,916	16,523,638	38.33	15.74
Austria		239,208	256,830	258,683	273,533	336,873	0.78	23.16
Belgium		1,119,254	1,146,309	1,085,654	1,035,955	1,201,166	2.79	15.95
France		3,605,718	3,804,008	3,698,022	3,826,186	4,210,534	9.77	10.05
Germany		6,962,131	7,048,022	7,122,844	7,336,272	8,708,279	20.20	18.70
Luxembourg		70,089	77,310	71,836	81,556	103,705	0.24	27.16
Netherlands		2,010,746	2,007,558	1,789,164	1,723,414	1,963,081	4.55	13.91
Other Europe		1,756,108	1,727,189	1,685,462	1,989,697	2,550,900	5.92	28.21
Other countries of Europe		1,756,108	1,727,189	1,685,462	1,989,697	2,550,900	5.92	28.21
REGION NOT SPECIFIED		738,107	622,499	827,531	1,672,023	2,090,894	4.85	25.05
Not Specified		738,107	622,499	827,531	1,672,023	2,090,894	4.85	25.05
Other countries of the World		738,107	622,499	827,531	1,672,023	2,090,894	4.85	25.05

Source: World Tourism Organization (UNWTO)

SPAIN

5. Overnight stays of non-resident tourists in hotels and similar establishments, by country of residence

		2002	2003	2004	2005	2006	Market share 06	% Change 06-05
TOTAL	(*)	135,836,394	136,865,483	134,653,618	138,761,840	151,939,606	100.00	9.50
AFRICA		722,685	694,328	609,904	745,414	755,846	0.50	1.40
Other Africa		722,685	694,328	609,904	745,414	755,846	0.50	1.40
All countries of Africa		722,685	694,328	609,904	745,414	755,846	0.50	1.40
AMERICAS		6,525,878	6,147,464	6,161,370	6,352,796	6,789,959	4.47	6.88
North America		4,362,589	4,232,145	4,126,408	3,197,291	3,371,102	2.22	5.44
Canada		452,671	500,792	415,373				
Mexico		631,645	581,607	578,434				
United States		3,278,273	3,149,746	3,132,601	3,197,291	3,371,102	2.22	5.44
South America		1,102,165	993,724	1,106,116				
Argentina		571,147	524,673	552,514				
Brazil		358,451	317,803	372,585				
Venezuela		172,567	151,248	181,017				
Other Americas		1,061,124	921,595	928,846	3,155,505	3,418,857	2.25	8.35
Other countries of the Americas		1,061,124	921,595	928,846	3,155,505	3,418,857	2.25	8.35
EAST ASIA AND THE PACIFIC		1,795,394	1,778,783	1,843,650	999,664			
North-East Asia		985,750	963,535	973,654	999,664			
Japan		985,750	963,535	973,654	999,664			
Australasia		303,389	323,408	333,233				
Australia		254,775	267,747	276,890				
New Zealand		48,614	55,661	56,343				
Other East Asia and the Pacific		506,255	491,840	536,763				
Other countries of Asia		506,255	491,840	536,763				
EUROPE		125,351,926	126,840,401	124,489,217	128,300,958	140,334,079	92.36	9.38
Central/Eastern Europe		3,406,388	3,061,855	2,822,960	3,107,145	3,788,373	2.49	21.92
Czech Republic		919,974	872,895	615,014	783,767	841,409	0.55	7.35
Hungary		202,494	200,403	210,256				
Poland		637,889	482,487	481,798	619,035	802,929	0.53	29.71
Russian Federation		1,506,677	1,336,879	1,399,214	1,704,343	2,144,035	1.41	25.80
Slovakia		139,354	169,191	116,678				
Northern Europe		50,368,499	51,087,614	49,335,403	50,418,086	52,449,790	34.52	4.03
Denmark		966,702	987,754	1,055,596	1,299,848	1,490,009	0.98	14.63
Finland		646,350	623,288	629,635	690,309	775,091	0.51	12.28
Iceland		90,123	151,668	163,977				
Ireland		1,483,135	1,735,687	2,069,712	2,229,562	2,354,757	1.55	5.62
Norway		1,204,940	1,124,578	1,069,788	1,147,456	1,288,043	0.85	12.25
Sweden		2,315,221	2,060,669	1,978,895	2,012,347	2,250,886	1.48	11.85
United Kingdom		43,662,028	44,403,970	42,367,800	43,038,564	44,291,004	29.15	2.91
Southern Europe		9,573,579	9,432,002	9,793,657	10,525,646	11,790,942	7.76	12.02
Greece		224,258	217,447	181,773	199,780	267,738	0.18	34.02
Italy		6,790,623	6,608,280	6,999,667	7,534,699	8,204,104	5.40	8.88
Portugal		2,558,698	2,606,275	2,612,217	2,791,167	3,319,100	2.18	18.91
Western Europe		60,692,637	61,882,352	61,135,365	61,808,241	69,171,238	45.53	11.91
Austria		849,079	1,038,943	958,640	1,005,230	1,258,965	0.83	25.24
Belgium		5,533,379	5,615,284	5,115,308	4,764,859	5,357,656	3.53	12.44
France		9,003,762	9,174,828	8,526,684	8,864,514	9,220,823	6.07	4.02
Germany		37,206,735	38,160,674	38,977,852	39,968,005	44,877,209	29.54	12.28

SPAIN

5. Overnight stays of non-resident tourists in hotels and similar establishments, by country of residence

	2002	2003	2004	2005	2006	Market share 06	% Change 06-05
Luxembourg	381,405	418,851	371,417	371,045	425,362	0.28	14.64
Netherlands	5,538,314	5,378,812	5,089,630	5,010,427	5,845,289	3.85	16.66
Switzerland	2,179,963	2,094,960	2,095,834	1,824,161	2,185,934	1.44	19.83
East Mediterranean Europe	**83,290**	**92,116**	**114,170**				
Turkey	83,290	92,116	114,170				
Other Europe	**1,227,533**	**1,284,462**	**1,287,662**	**2,441,840**	**3,133,736**	**2.06**	**28.34**
Other countries of Europe	1,227,533	1,284,462	1,287,662	2,441,840	3,133,736	2.06	28.34
REGION NOT SPECIFIED	**1,440,511**	**1,404,507**	**1,549,477**	**2,363,008**	**4,059,722**	**2.67**	**71.80**
Not Specified	**1,440,511**	**1,404,507**	**1,549,477**	**2,363,008**	**4,059,722**	**2.67**	**71.80**
Other countries of the World	1,440,511	1,404,507	1,549,477	2,363,008	4,059,722	2.67	71.80

Source: World Tourism Organization (UNWTO)

SPAIN

6. Overnight stays of non-resident tourists in all types of accommodation establishments, by country of residence

		2002	2003	2004	2005	2006	Market share 06	% Change 06-05
TOTAL	(*)	220,707,302	217,851,793	209,081,380	209,518,388	224,066,652	100.00	6.94
AFRICA		818,264	794,014	704,379	884,513	905,195	0.40	2.34
Other Africa		818,264	794,014	704,379	884,513	905,195	0.40	2.34
All countries of Africa		818,264	794,014	704,379	884,513	905,195	0.40	2.34
AMERICAS		7,122,349	6,787,707	6,803,918	7,021,863	7,499,733	3.35	6.81
North America		3,481,056	3,410,561	3,381,771	3,481,836	3,678,551	1.64	5.65
United States		3,481,056	3,410,561	3,381,771	3,481,836	3,678,551	1.64	5.65
Other Americas		3,641,293	3,377,146	3,422,147	3,540,027	3,821,182	1.71	7.94
Other countries of the Americas		3,641,293	3,377,146	3,422,147	3,540,027	3,821,182	1.71	7.94
EAST ASIA AND THE PACIFIC		1,549,601	1,518,628	1,573,033				
Other East Asia and the Pacific		1,549,601	1,518,628	1,573,033				
All countries of Asia		1,549,601	1,518,628	1,573,033				
EUROPE		209,256,759	206,759,181	197,768,631	197,867,839	211,179,612	94.25	6.73
Northern Europe		96,026,773	94,672,916	89,176,885	87,468,713	89,667,129	40.02	2.51
Denmark		2,815,478	2,543,140	2,625,065	2,844,879	3,232,499	1.44	13.63
Finland		2,034,045	1,979,945	2,027,479	2,061,398	2,285,696	1.02	10.88
Ireland		4,584,868	4,797,124	5,311,400	5,751,900	6,054,835	2.70	5.27
Norway		3,542,615	2,997,812	2,886,690	3,004,384	3,355,196	1.50	11.68
Sweden		5,901,146	5,098,783	4,652,223	4,667,922	4,861,496	2.17	4.15
United Kingdom		77,148,621	77,256,112	71,674,028	69,138,230	69,877,407	31.19	1.07
Southern Europe		11,438,548	11,282,846	11,672,268	12,497,257	14,059,177	6.27	12.50
Greece		263,384	262,852	217,971	231,660	304,017	0.14	31.23
Italy		8,082,632	7,911,067	8,294,689	8,898,184	9,803,828	4.38	10.18
Portugal		3,092,532	3,108,927	3,159,608	3,367,413	3,951,332	1.76	17.34
Western Europe		92,139,870	91,628,417	88,124,643	88,117,505	95,807,264	42.76	8.73
Austria		1,225,980	1,392,331	1,356,866	1,374,263	1,612,656	0.72	17.35
Belgium		7,363,098	7,298,323	6,713,974	6,303,915	6,962,763	3.11	10.45
France		13,566,205	13,671,925	12,825,969	13,449,894	13,897,770	6.20	3.33
Germany		54,867,175	54,651,503	54,212,785	54,584,350	60,097,519	26.82	10.10
Luxembourg		439,596	477,918	457,320	489,043	593,501	0.26	21.36
Netherlands		14,677,816	14,136,417	12,557,729	11,916,040	12,643,055	5.64	6.10
Other Europe		9,651,568	9,175,002	8,794,835	9,784,364	11,646,042	5.20	19.03
Other countries of Europe		9,651,568	9,175,002	8,794,835	9,784,364	11,646,042	5.20	19.03
REGION NOT SPECIFIED		1,960,329	1,992,263	2,231,419	3,744,173	4,482,112	2.00	19.71
Not Specified		1,960,329	1,992,263	2,231,419	3,744,173	4,482,112	2.00	19.71
Other countries of the World		1,960,329	1,992,263	2,231,419	3,744,173	4,482,112	2.00	19.71

Source: World Tourism Organization (UNWTO)

SRI LANKA

1. Arrivals of non-resident tourists at national borders, by nationality

	2002	2003	2004	2005	2006	Market share 06	% Change 06-05
TOTAL (*)	393,171	500,642	566,202	549,309	559,603	100.00	1.87
AFRICA	1,545	1,925	1,759	2,337	3,163	0.57	35.34
Other Africa	1,545	1,925	1,759	2,337	3,163	0.57	35.34
All countries of Africa	1,545	1,925	1,759	2,337	3,163	0.57	35.34
AMERICAS	20,553	25,735	31,369	47,459	36,493	6.52	-23.11
North America	20,004	25,099	30,654	46,727	35,688	6.38	-23.62
Canada	8,337	11,109	14,974	21,335	14,863	2.66	-30.34
United States	11,667	13,990	15,680	25,392	20,825	3.72	-17.99
Other Americas	549	636	715	732	805	0.14	9.97
Other countries of the Americas	549	636	715	732	805	0.14	9.97
EAST ASIA AND THE PACIFIC	67,008	85,726	92,093	100,542	99,046	17.70	-1.49
North-East Asia	27,522	32,940	36,613	36,928	41,562	7.43	12.55
China	4,350	7,380	9,424	9,818	16,364	2.92	66.67
Taiwan (Province of China)	3,417	2,532	1,929	2,705	2,580	0.46	-4.62
Hong Kong, China	3,582	3,150	916	1,219	1,083	0.19	-11.16
Japan	13,566	17,178	19,747	17,163	16,217	2.90	-5.51
Korea, Republic of	2,607	2,700	4,597	6,023	5,318	0.95	-11.71
South-East Asia	24,234	27,524	26,247	31,872	30,380	5.43	-4.68
Indonesia	1,473	1,392	1,426	1,639	4,940	0.88	201.40
Malaysia	9,603	9,283	9,939	11,668	9,823	1.76	-15.81
Philippines	1,626	2,418	1,807	2,360	3,480	0.62	47.46
Singapore	7,578	8,423	7,866	10,796	6,662	1.19	-38.29
Thailand	3,954	6,008	5,209	5,409	5,475	0.98	1.22
Australasia	13,254	22,933	27,802	29,444	24,792	4.43	-15.80
Australia	11,334	20,075	24,471	25,836	21,665	3.87	-16.14
New Zealand	1,920	2,858	3,331	3,608	3,127	0.56	-13.33
Other East Asia and the Pacific	1,998	2,329	1,431	2,298	2,312	0.41	0.61
Other countries of Asia	1,941	2,195	1,293	2,167	2,204	0.39	1.71
Other countries of Oceania	57	134	138	131	108	0.02	-17.56
EUROPE	208,722	265,779	299,625	236,864	242,902	43.41	2.55
Central/Eastern Europe	8,046	10,600	14,259	9,305	14,236	2.54	52.99
Russian Federation	2,943	3,683	4,985	3,719	8,000	1.43	115.11
Other countries Central/East Europ	5,103	6,917	9,274	5,586	6,236	1.11	11.64
Northern Europe	76,053	104,734	124,111	107,667	101,951	18.22	-5.31
Denmark	1,980	2,732	3,496	3,793	3,540	0.63	-6.67
Finland	726	1,103	1,989	1,150	1,244	0.22	8.17
Norway	2,892	3,677	3,444	4,333	3,057	0.55	-29.45
Sweden	2,523	3,916	8,140	5,462	5,579	1.00	2.14
United Kingdom	67,932	93,306	107,042	92,929	88,531	15.82	-4.73
Southern Europe	14,520	18,449	20,971	11,929	14,722	2.63	23.41
Italy	12,171	15,648	17,984	10,148	12,353	2.21	21.73
Spain	2,349	2,801	2,987	1,781	2,369	0.42	33.02
Western Europe	107,067	128,445	135,871	104,591	108,238	19.34	3.49
Austria	6,144	7,337	8,625	4,148	4,677	0.84	12.75
Belgium	4,731	4,268	5,718	3,891	6,373	1.14	63.79
France	19,980	28,576	30,422	26,641	22,703	4.06	-14.78
Germany	55,137	58,875	58,932	46,320	47,296	8.45	2.11
Netherlands	11,763	18,212	21,487	15,252	19,460	3.48	27.59

SRI LANKA

1. Arrivals of non-resident tourists at national borders, by nationality

	2002	2003	2004	2005	2006	Market share 06	% Change 06-05
Switzerland	9,312	11,177	10,687	8,339	7,729	1.38	-7.32
Other Europe	**3,036**	**3,551**	**4,413**	**3,372**	**3,755**	**0.67**	**11.36**
Other countries of Europe	3,036	3,551	4,413	3,372	3,755	0.67	11.36
MIDDLE EAST	**6,462**	**6,759**	**9,486**	**10,230**	**10,191**	**1.82**	**-0.38**
Middle East	**6,462**	**6,759**	**9,486**	**10,230**	**10,191**	**1.82**	**-0.38**
All countries of Middle East	6,462	6,759	9,486	10,230	10,191	1.82	-0.38
SOUTH ASIA	**88,881**	**114,718**	**131,870**	**151,877**	**167,808**	**29.99**	**10.49**
South Asia	**88,881**	**114,718**	**131,870**	**151,877**	**167,808**	**29.99**	**10.49**
Bangladesh	1,518	1,851	1,760	2,325	2,466	0.44	6.06
India	69,996	90,639	104,390	113,023	128,520	22.97	13.71
Maldives	9,855	11,577	15,201	24,396	24,505	4.38	0.45
Nepal	786	977	890	1,077	1,152	0.21	6.96
Pakistan	6,726	9,674	9,629	11,056	11,165	2.00	0.99

Source: World Tourism Organization (UNWTO)

SRI LANKA

1. Arrivals of non-resident tourists at national borders, by country of residence

	2002	2003	2004	2005	2006	Market share 06	% Change 06-05
TOTAL (*)	393,171	500,642	566,202	549,308	559,603	100.00	1.87
AFRICA	1,611	1,991	1,855	2,340	3,235	0.58	38.25
Southern Africa	660	980	987	1,107	1,116	0.20	0.81
South Africa	660	980	987	1,107	1,116	0.20	0.81
Other Africa	951	1,011	868	1,233	2,119	0.38	71.86
Other countries of Africa	951	1,011	868	1,233	2,119	0.38	71.86
AMERICAS	20,421	25,744	30,500	47,162	36,098	6.45	-23.46
North America	19,869	25,110	29,759	46,457	35,323	6.31	-23.97
Canada	8,304	11,164	14,633	21,185	14,623	2.61	-30.97
United States	11,565	13,946	15,126	25,272	20,700	3.70	-18.09
Other Americas	552	634	741	705	775	0.14	9.93
Other countries of the Americas	552	634	741	705	775	0.14	9.93
EAST ASIA AND THE PACIFIC	66,084	84,145	91,076	99,736	98,476	17.60	-1.26
North-East Asia	27,747	32,697	36,705	36,661	41,299	7.38	12.65
China	4,338	7,251	9,088	9,668	16,274	2.91	68.33
Taiwan (Province of China)	3,432	2,547	1,907	2,720	2,565	0.46	-5.70
Hong Kong, China	3,759	3,075	1,538	1,069	973	0.17	-8.98
Japan	13,602	17,115	19,641	17,148	16,189	2.89	-5.59
Korea, Republic of	2,616	2,709	4,531	6,056	5,298	0.95	-12.52
South-East Asia	24,312	27,602	26,987	32,193	30,701	5.49	-4.63
Indonesia	1,476	1,395	1,466	1,669	5,042	0.90	202.10
Malaysia	9,651	9,331	10,132	11,578	9,713	1.74	-16.11
Philippines	1,641	2,433	1,808	2,366	3,474	0.62	46.83
Singapore	7,599	8,444	8,546	11,156	7,012	1.25	-37.15
Thailand	3,945	5,999	5,035	5,424	5,460	0.98	0.66
Australasia	13,137	22,816	26,431	29,603	24,996	4.47	-15.56
Australia	11,217	19,958	23,247	25,986	21,849	3.90	-15.92
New Zealand	1,920	2,858	3,184	3,617	3,147	0.56	-12.99
Other East Asia and the Pacific	888	1,030	953	1,279	1,480	0.26	15.72
Other countries of Asia	816	881	844	1,144	1,349	0.24	17.92
Other countries of Oceania	72	149	109	135	131	0.02	-2.96
EUROPE	208,374	265,802	298,776	236,481	242,666	43.36	2.62
Central/Eastern Europe	8,079	10,633	14,336	9,290	14,221	2.54	53.08
Russian Federation	2,946	3,686	5,000	3,704	7,985	1.43	115.58
Other countries Central/East Europ	5,133	6,947	9,336	5,586	6,236	1.11	11.64
Northern Europe	75,606	104,658	123,359	107,292	101,659	18.17	-5.25
Denmark	1,968	2,720	3,269	3,781	3,531	0.63	-6.61
Finland	729	1,106	1,989	1,150	1,244	0.22	8.17
Norway	2,889	3,674	3,477	4,330	3,054	0.55	-29.47
Sweden	2,487	3,880	7,979	5,402	5,524	0.99	2.26
United Kingdom	67,533	93,278	106,645	92,629	88,306	15.78	-4.67
Southern Europe	14,505	18,434	21,872	11,973	14,791	2.64	23.54
Italy	12,177	15,654	18,862	10,192	12,424	2.22	21.90
Spain	2,328	2,780	3,010	1,781	2,367	0.42	32.90
Western Europe	107,166	128,544	134,534	104,540	108,177	19.33	3.48
Austria	6,117	7,310	8,633	4,127	4,662	0.83	12.96
Belgium	4,767	4,304	5,582	3,855	6,333	1.13	64.28
France	19,989	28,585	29,996	26,653	22,693	4.06	-14.86

738

SRI LANKA

1. Arrivals of non-resident tourists at national borders, by country of residence

	2002	2003	2004	2005	2006	Market share 06	% Change 06-05
Germany	55,170	58,908	58,258	46,350	47,402	8.47	2.27
Netherlands	11,748	18,197	21,455	15,156	19,360	3.46	27.74
Switzerland	9,375	11,240	10,610	8,399	7,727	1.38	-8.00
Other Europe	**3,018**	**3,533**	**4,675**	**3,386**	**3,818**	**0.68**	**12.76**
Other countries of Europe	3,018	3,533	4,675	3,386	3,818	0.68	12.76
MIDDLE EAST	**6,492**	**6,789**	**10,463**	**10,236**	**10,345**	**1.85**	**1.06**
Middle East	**6,492**	**6,789**	**10,463**	**10,236**	**10,345**	**1.85**	**1.06**
All countries of Middle East	6,492	6,789	10,463	10,236	10,345	1.85	1.06
SOUTH ASIA	**90,189**	**116,171**	**133,532**	**153,353**	**168,783**	**30.16**	**10.06**
South Asia	**90,189**	**116,171**	**133,532**	**153,353**	**168,783**	**30.16**	**10.06**
Bangladesh	1,521	1,830	1,721	2,316	2,456	0.44	6.04
India	69,960	90,603	105,151	113,323	128,370	22.94	13.28
Maldives	9,861	11,583	15,013	24,576	24,831	4.44	1.04
Nepal	789	980	883	1,071	1,146	0.20	7.00
Pakistan	6,756	9,704	9,638	11,029	11,145	1.99	1.05
Other countries of South Asia	1,302	1,471	1,126	1,038	835	0.15	-19.56

Source: World Tourism Organization (UNWTO)

SRI LANKA

6. Overnight stays of non-resident tourists in all types of accommodation establishments, by nationality

	2002	2003	2004	2005	2006	Market share 06	% Change 06-05
TOTAL	3,989,058	5,092,782	5,742,427	4,754,087	5,793,590	100.00	21.87
AFRICA	14,987	18,288	16,535	17,102	31,168	0.54	82.25
Other Africa	14,987	18,288	16,535	17,102	31,168	0.54	82.25
All countries of Africa	14,987	18,288	16,535	17,102	31,168	0.54	82.25
AMERICAS	214,312	275,267	332,249	512,781	400,456	6.91	-21.91
North America	206,954	267,566	323,509	503,105	390,847	6.75	-22.31
Canada	82,700	123,380	164,874	238,995	163,684	2.83	-31.51
United States	124,254	144,186	158,635	264,110	227,163	3.92	-13.99
Other Americas	7,358	7,701	8,740	9,676	9,609	0.17	-0.69
Other countries of the Americas	7,358	7,701	8,740	9,676	9,609	0.17	-0.69
EAST ASIA AND THE PACIFIC	577,039	793,694	878,424	835,344	1,002,732	17.31	20.04
North-East Asia	222,707	278,022	318,749	302,587	409,171	7.06	35.22
China	30,015	59,040	74,450	73,635	145,640	2.51	97.79
Taiwan (Province of China)	23,724	15,952	12,731	26,504	42,705	0.74	61.13
Hong Kong, China	23,856	22,680	6,412	5,729	10,289	0.18	79.60
Japan	120,737	156,320	185,622	152,751	160,548	2.77	5.10
Korea, Republic of	24,375	24,030	39,534	43,968	49,989	0.86	13.69
South-East Asia	166,627	216,402	205,406	199,493	237,770	4.10	19.19
Indonesia	8,617	8,491	8,841	12,784	45,942	0.79	259.37
Malaysia	58,962	75,192	82,494	75,842	87,425	1.51	15.27
Philippines	9,984	14,508	12,649	15,812	29,928	0.52	89.27
Singapore	59,336	66,542	55,062	72,333	49,965	0.86	-30.92
Thailand	29,728	51,669	46,360	22,722	24,510	0.42	7.87
Australasia	164,926	271,017	334,112	309,622	291,769	5.04	-5.77
Australia	140,542	235,006	296,139	273,903	255,833	4.42	-6.60
New Zealand	24,384	36,011	37,973	35,719	35,936	0.62	0.61
Other East Asia and the Pacific	22,779	28,253	20,157	23,642	64,022	1.11	170.80
Other countries of Asia	22,089	26,645	18,556	22,384	63,460	1.10	183.51
Other countries of Oceania	690	1,608	1,601	1,258	562	0.01	-55.33
EUROPE	2,461,444	3,066,972	3,444,894	2,222,372	2,939,258	50.73	32.26
Central/Eastern Europe	81,827	108,710	161,061	86,974	166,050	2.87	90.92
Russian Federation	32,648	40,832	60,107	33,348	97,366	1.68	191.97
Other countries Central/East Europ	49,179	67,878	100,954	53,626	68,684	1.19	28.08
Northern Europe	833,012	1,078,464	1,266,484	955,253	1,167,455	20.15	22.21
Denmark	24,923	31,051	38,690	35,242	41,064	0.71	16.52
Finland	8,579	12,175	22,793	10,025	13,347	0.23	33.14
Norway	31,260	40,479	39,420	37,403	35,634	0.62	-4.73
Sweden	28,225	41,379	87,855	54,523	59,210	1.02	8.60
United Kingdom	740,025	953,380	1,077,726	818,060	1,018,200	17.57	24.47
Southern Europe	145,991	199,855	223,976	112,065	164,948	2.85	47.19
Italy	123,206	174,605	196,134	96,347	140,992	2.43	46.34
Spain	22,785	25,250	27,842	15,718	23,956	0.41	52.41
Western Europe	1,367,778	1,647,588	1,747,261	1,036,618	1,395,026	24.08	34.57
Austria	81,233	91,864	105,271	36,709	57,994	1.00	57.98
Belgium	52,484	49,140	65,469	33,412	74,592	1.29	123.25
France	213,898	292,084	307,658	247,934	247,463	4.27	-0.19
Germany	750,130	830,322	843,042	460,333	653,113	11.27	41.88

SRI LANKA

6. Overnight stays of non-resident tourists in all types of accommodation establishments, by nationality

	2002	2003	2004	2005	2006	Market share 06	% Change 06-05
Netherlands	152,116	242,924	293,648	166,907	265,203	4.58	58.89
Switzerland	117,917	141,254	132,173	91,323	96,661	1.67	5.85
Other Europe	**32,836**	**32,355**	**46,112**	**31,462**	**45,779**	**0.79**	**45.51**
Other countries of Europe	32,836	32,355	46,112	31,462	45,779	0.79	45.51
MIDDLE EAST	**51,050**	**54,836**	**74,996**	**70,614**	**82,768**	**1.43**	**17.21**
Middle East	**51,050**	**54,836**	**74,996**	**70,614**	**82,768**	**1.43**	**17.21**
All countries of Middle East	51,050	54,836	74,996	70,614	82,768	1.43	17.21
SOUTH ASIA	**670,226**	**883,725**	**995,329**	**1,095,874**	**1,337,208**	**23.08**	**22.02**
South Asia	**670,226**	**883,725**	**995,329**	**1,095,874**	**1,337,208**	**23.08**	**22.02**
Bangladesh	10,778	13,512	12,496	15,113			
India	531,970	716,048	803,803	836,370	1,015,308	17.52	21.39
Maldives	69,971	84,512	104,887	165,893	230,347	3.98	38.85
Pakistan	57,507	69,653	74,143	78,498	91,553	1.58	16.63

Source: World Tourism Organization (UNWTO)

SUDAN

1. Arrivals of non-resident tourists at national borders, by nationality

		2002	2003	2004	2005	2006	Market share 06	% Change 06-05
TOTAL	(*)	51,580	52,291	60,577	245,798	328,148	100.00	33.50
AFRICA		7,000	7,000	9,000	58,991	50,665	15.44	-14.11
Other Africa		7,000	7,000	9,000	58,991	50,665	15.44	-14.11
All countries of Africa		7,000	7,000	9,000	58,991	50,665	15.44	-14.11
AMERICAS					20,751	11,607	3.54	-44.07
Other Americas					20,751	11,607	3.54	-44.07
All countries of the Americas					20,751	11,607	3.54	-44.07
EAST ASIA AND THE PACIFIC		13,000	14,000	17,000	109,380	222,157	67.70	103.11
Other East Asia and the Pacific		13,000	14,000	17,000	109,380	222,157	67.70	103.11
All countries of Asia		13,000	14,000	17,000	109,380	222,157	67.70	103.11
EUROPE		12,000	14,000	17,000	55,796	43,719	13.32	-21.64
Other Europe		12,000	14,000	17,000	55,796	43,719	13.32	-21.64
All countries of Europe		12,000	14,000	17,000	55,796	43,719	13.32	-21.64
REGION NOT SPECIFIED		19,580	17,291	17,577	880			
Not Specified		19,580	17,291	17,577	880			
Other countries of the World		19,580	17,291	17,577	880			

Source: World Tourism Organization (UNWTO)

SURINAME

1. Arrivals of non-resident tourists at national borders, by nationality

		2002	2003	2004	2005	2006	Market share 06	% Change 06-05
TOTAL	(*)	60,223	82,298	74,887				
AFRICA		32	187	177				
Other Africa		32	187	177				
All countries of Africa		32	187	177				
AMERICAS		4,307	6,903	7,986				
Caribbean		510	448	1,244				
Dominican Republic		33	131	257				
Haiti		163	116	260				
Trinidad and Tobago		203	127	362				
Other countries of the Caribbean		111	74	365				
North America		858	1,629	1,800				
Canada		91	718	731				
United States		767	911	1,069				
South America		2,911	4,806	4,852				
Brazil		1,065	2,315	3,068				
Colombia		35	37	63				
Guyana		1,717	2,219	1,368				
Venezuela		66	151	161				
Other countries of South America		28	84	192				
Other Americas		28	20	90				
Other countries of the Americas		28	20	90				
EAST ASIA AND THE PACIFIC		1,306	998	2,522				
North-East Asia		1,042	776	2,114				
China		962	730	2,041				
Japan		31	20	39				
Korea, Republic of		49	26	34				
South-East Asia		87	95	80				
Indonesia		87	95	80				
Other East Asia and the Pacific		177	127	328				
Other countries of Asia		153	89	261				
All countries of Oceania		24	38	67				
EUROPE		54,477	74,153	64,011				
Northern Europe		51	137	190				
United Kingdom		51	137	190				
Western Europe		54,207	73,724	63,480				
Belgium		214	234	237				
France		291	440	652				
Germany		110	160	139				
Netherlands		53,592	72,890	62,452				
Other Europe		219	292	341				
Other countries of Europe		219	292	341				
SOUTH ASIA		68	55	165				
South Asia		68	55	165				
India		68	55	165				
REGION NOT SPECIFIED		33	2	26				
Not Specified		33	2	26				

SURINAME

1. Arrivals of non-resident tourists at national borders, by country of residence

	2002	2003	2004	2005	2006	Market share 06	% Change 06-05
TOTAL			137,808	160,022			
AFRICA				279			
Other Africa				279			
All countries of Africa				279			
AMERICAS			44,802	56,338			
Caribbean			8,621	9,662			
Dominican Republic				235			
Haiti				1,669			
Trinidad and Tobago				1,883			
Other countries of the Caribbean				5,875			
All countries of the Caribbean			8,621				
North America			4,465	6,169			
Canada				1,470			
United States			4,465	4,699			
South America			31,716	40,225			
Brazil			4,260	5,875			
Colombia				181			
French Guiana			1,840	20,211			
Guyana			13,573	13,218			
Venezuela				396			
Other countries of South America			12,043	344			
Other Americas				282			
Other countries of the Americas				282			
EAST ASIA AND THE PACIFIC				3,247			
North-East Asia				2,679			
China				2,536			
Japan				125			
Korea, Republic of				18			
South-East Asia				181			
Indonesia				181			
Other East Asia and the Pacific				387			
Other countries of Asia				155			
All countries of Oceania				232			
EUROPE			86,913	99,265			
Northern Europe				695			
United Kingdom				695			
Western Europe			82,215	97,570			
Belgium				794			
France				2,837			
Germany				499			
Netherlands			82,215	93,440			
Other Europe			4,698	1,000			
Other countries of Europe			4,698	1,000			
SOUTH ASIA				498			
South Asia				498			
India				498			
REGION NOT SPECIFIED			6,093	395			

SWAZILAND

2. Arrivals of non-resident visitors at national borders, by country of residence

	2002	2003	2004	2005	2006	Market share 06	% Change 06-05
TOTAL				1,182,141	1,199,858	100.00	1.50
AFRICA				1,043,248	1,056,388	88.04	1.26
East Africa				201,104	258,308	21.53	28.44
Kenya				1,398	1,668	0.14	19.31
Malawi				2,206	2,396	0.20	8.61
Mozambique				183,382	237,939	19.83	29.75
Zimbabwe				6,523	7,769	0.65	19.10
United Republic of Tanzania				2,440	3,023	0.25	23.89
Zambia				5,155	5,513	0.46	6.94
Southern Africa				833,819	788,083	65.68	-5.49
Botswana				3,497	3,390	0.28	-3.06
Lesotho				3,635	3,618	0.30	-0.47
South Africa				826,687	781,075	65.10	-5.52
West Africa				1,864	2,454	0.20	31.65
Nigeria				1,864	2,454	0.20	31.65
Other Africa				6,461	7,543	0.63	16.75
Other countries of Africa				6,461	7,543	0.63	16.75
AMERICAS				17,217	18,945	1.58	10.04
North America				16,475	17,874	1.49	8.49
Canada				2,470	3,175	0.26	28.54
United States				14,005	14,699	1.23	4.96
South America				343	470	0.04	37.03
Brazil				343	470	0.04	37.03
Other Americas				399	601	0.05	50.63
Other countries of the Americas				399	601	0.05	50.63
EAST ASIA AND THE PACIFIC				9,699	9,642	0.80	-0.59
North-East Asia				4,850	4,569	0.38	-5.79
China				2,381	1,975	0.16	-17.05
Taiwan (Province of China)				1,660	1,734	0.14	4.46
Korea, Republic of				809	860	0.07	6.30
South-East Asia				363	439	0.04	20.94
Philippines				363	439	0.04	20.94
Australasia				2,333	2,672	0.22	14.53
Australia				2,333	2,672	0.22	14.53
Other East Asia and the Pacific				2,153	1,962	0.16	-8.87
Other countries of Asia				2,153	1,962	0.16	-8.87
EUROPE				107,957	109,970	9.17	1.86
Northern Europe				24,799	24,673	2.06	-0.51
Norway				1,272	1,508	0.13	18.55
Sweden				2,244	2,692	0.22	19.96
United Kingdom				21,283	20,473	1.71	-3.81
Southern Europe				7,443	9,790	0.82	31.53
Italy				3,681	3,891	0.32	5.70
Portugal				3,762	5,899	0.49	56.80
Western Europe				67,930	65,917	5.49	-2.96
Belgium				4,539	4,896	0.41	7.87
France				16,880	16,428	1.37	-2.68

SWAZILAND

2. Arrivals of non-resident visitors at national borders, by country of residence

	2002	2003	2004	2005	2006	Market share 06	% Change 06-05
Germany				25,395	23,975	2.00	-5.59
Netherlands				17,703	16,696	1.39	-5.69
Switzerland				3,413	3,922	0.33	14.91
East Mediterranean Europe				**676**	**766**	**0.06**	**13.31**
Israel				676	766	0.06	13.31
Other Europe				**7,109**	**8,824**	**0.74**	**24.12**
Other countries of Europe				7,109	8,824	0.74	24.12
SOUTH ASIA				**4,020**	**4,913**	**0.41**	**22.21**
South Asia				**4,020**	**4,913**	**0.41**	**22.21**
India				2,396	3,071	0.26	28.17
Pakistan				1,624	1,842	0.15	13.42

Source: World Tourism Organization (UNWTO)

SWAZILAND

3. Arrivals of non-resident tourists in hotels and similar establishments, by country of residence

	2002	2003	2004	2005	2006	Market share 06	% Change 06-05
TOTAL	255,927	218,813	352,040	311,656	316,082	100.00	1.42
AFRICA	173,420	110,054	151,879	134,456	167,347	52.94	24.46
East Africa	17,304	11,642	17,619	15,597	11,702	3.70	-24.97
Mozambique	17,304	11,642	17,619	15,597	11,702	3.70	-24.97
Southern Africa	146,286	85,899	112,027	99,176	135,537	42.88	36.66
South Africa	146,286	85,899	112,027	99,176	130,783	41.38	31.87
Other countries of Southern Africa					4,754	1.50	
Other Africa	9,830	12,513	22,233	19,683	20,108	6.36	2.16
Other countries of Africa	9,830	12,513	22,233	19,683	20,108	6.36	2.16
AMERICAS	10,380	11,092	4,968	4,398	3,576	1.13	-18.69
Other Americas	10,380	11,092	4,968	4,398	3,576	1.13	-18.69
All countries of the Americas	10,380	11,092	4,968	4,398	3,576	1.13	-18.69
EAST ASIA AND THE PACIFIC	5,244	2,343	3,485	3,085	5,423	1.72	75.79
Australasia	1,496	701	1,725	1,527	4,192	1.33	174.53
Australia	1,496	701	1,725	1,527	4,192	1.33	174.53
Other East Asia and the Pacific	3,748	1,642	1,760	1,558	1,231	0.39	-20.99
Other countries of Asia	3,748	1,642	1,760	1,558	1,231	0.39	-20.99
EUROPE	40,483	87,999	110,709	98,009	114,249	36.15	16.57
Northern Europe	5,818	13,702	17,776	15,737	11,948	3.78	-24.08
United Kingdom	5,818	13,702	17,776	15,737	11,948	3.78	-24.08
Southern Europe	2,006	8,666	828	733	8,188	2.59	1,017.05
Portugal	2,006	8,666	828	733	8,188	2.59	1,017.05
Other Europe	32,659	65,631	92,105	81,539	94,113	29.77	15.42
Other countries of Europe	32,659	65,631	92,105	81,539	94,113	29.77	15.42
REGION NOT SPECIFIED	26,400	7,325	80,999	71,708	25,487	8.06	-64.46
Not Specified	26,400	7,325	80,999	71,708	25,487	8.06	-64.46
Other countries of the World	26,400	7,325	80,999	71,708	25,487	8.06	-64.46

Source: World Tourism Organization (UNWTO)

SWEDEN

5. Overnight stays of non-resident tourists in hotels and similar establishments, by country of residence

		2002	2003	2004	2005	2006	Market share 06	% Change 06-05
TOTAL	(*)	4,867,679	4,833,186	5,060,943	5,382,161	5,606,018	100.00	4.16
AMERICAS		445,191	394,864	415,569	465,231	468,379	8.35	0.68
North America		435,879	379,674	396,827	434,893	437,278	7.80	0.55
Canada		59,048	30,576	31,469	31,985	33,473	0.60	4.65
United States		376,831	349,098	365,358	402,908	403,805	7.20	0.22
Other Americas		9,312	15,190	18,742	30,338	31,101	0.55	2.51
Other countries of the Americas		9,312	15,190	18,742	30,338	31,101	0.55	2.51
EAST ASIA AND THE PACIFIC		213,441	183,273	269,518	339,407	350,647	6.25	3.31
North-East Asia		138,561	110,179	140,652	186,589	220,060	3.93	17.94
China				18,533	65,329	94,927	1.69	45.31
Japan		123,302	99,237	108,807	105,249	104,092	1.86	-1.10
Korea, Republic of		15,259	10,942	13,312	16,011	21,041	0.38	31.42
Australasia		25,242	22,821	30,881	41,133	35,519	0.63	-13.65
Australia		24,259	21,326	26,676	32,228	31,133	0.56	-3.40
New Zealand		983	1,495	4,205	8,905	4,386	0.08	-50.75
Other East Asia and the Pacific		49,638	50,273	97,985	111,685	95,068	1.70	-14.88
Other countries of Asia		49,638	50,273	97,985	111,685	95,068	1.70	-14.88
EUROPE		3,677,557	3,697,125	3,818,217	4,118,150	4,264,518	76.07	3.55
Central/Eastern Europe		192,300	193,439	219,258	241,210	292,051	5.21	21.08
Czech Republic		5,765	9,381	13,512	18,780	23,049	0.41	22.73
Estonia		17,143	14,620	13,686	13,492	14,913	0.27	10.53
Hungary		4,036	6,170	9,774	16,353	16,248	0.29	-0.64
Latvia		8,311	9,701	6,650	7,552	8,264	0.15	9.43
Lithuania		6,896	10,349	8,592	8,398	9,777	0.17	16.42
Poland		44,918	38,716	38,515	46,615	59,098	1.05	26.78
Russian Federation		103,696	102,871	123,668	123,064	156,579	2.79	27.23
Slovakia		1,535	1,631	4,861	6,956	4,123	0.07	-40.73
Northern Europe		1,956,075	2,011,374	1,985,375	2,123,033	2,180,384	38.89	2.70
Denmark		331,597	368,657	367,639	386,272	391,959	6.99	1.47
Finland		265,453	262,487	267,628	299,451	299,641	5.34	0.06
Iceland		3,840	7,401	9,963	15,508	17,553	0.31	13.19
Ireland		10,928	15,586	18,704	23,674	26,352	0.47	11.31
Norway		837,232	868,342	797,000	840,915	880,161	15.70	4.67
United Kingdom		507,025	488,901	524,441	557,213	564,718	10.07	1.35
Southern Europe		253,996	241,480	317,018	353,751	361,418	6.45	2.17
Greece		4,354	6,215	11,077	22,060	24,332	0.43	10.30
Italy		150,910	141,726	192,722	191,469	184,474	3.29	-3.65
Portugal		5,565	7,360	7,195	14,033	14,347	0.26	2.24
Spain		93,167	86,179	106,024	126,189	138,265	2.47	9.57
Western Europe		1,054,764	1,038,842	1,086,106	1,198,157	1,233,643	22.01	2.96
Austria		31,963	34,072	29,806	29,869	34,684	0.62	16.12
Belgium		50,247	56,098	63,922	63,479	70,102	1.25	10.43
France		153,231	141,441	146,017	155,573	152,658	2.72	-1.87
Germany		601,608	601,609	619,784	705,842	724,255	12.92	2.61
Luxembourg		1,245	3,323	3,637	4,231	4,847	0.09	14.56
Netherlands		126,101	124,824	143,717	149,389	159,169	2.84	6.55
Switzerland		90,369	77,475	79,223	89,774	87,928	1.57	-2.06
East Mediterranean Europe		3,232	6,984	6,231	10,350	12,828	0.23	23.94

SWEDEN

5. Overnight stays of non-resident tourists in hotels and similar establishments, by country of residence

	2002	2003	2004	2005	2006	Market share 06	% Change 06-05
Turkey	3,232	6,984	6,231	10,350	12,828	0.23	23.94
Other Europe	**217,190**	**205,006**	**204,229**	**191,649**	**184,194**	**3.29**	**-3.89**
Other countries of Europe	217,190	205,006	204,229	191,649	184,194	3.29	-3.89
REGION NOT SPECIFIED	**531,490**	**557,924**	**557,639**	**459,373**	**522,474**	**9.32**	**13.74**
Not Specified	**531,490**	**557,924**	**557,639**	**459,373**	**522,474**	**9.32**	**13.74**
Other countries of the World	531,490	557,924	557,639	459,373	522,474	9.32	13.74

Source: World Tourism Organization (UNWTO)

SWEDEN

6. Overnight stays of non-resident tourists in all types of accommodation establishments, by country of residence

	2002	2003	2004	2005	2006	Market share 06	% Change 06-05
TOTAL (*)	9,767,708	9,714,883	9,723,676	10,077,859	10,951,666	100.00	8.67
AMERICAS	467,468	418,587	442,142	494,548	497,481	4.54	0.59
North America	454,271	398,710	418,991	458,605	460,273	4.20	0.36
Canada	62,476	33,931	35,789	37,661	39,043	0.36	3.67
United States	391,795	364,779	383,202	420,944	421,230	3.85	0.07
Other Americas	13,197	19,877	23,151	35,943	37,208	0.34	3.52
Other countries of the Americas	13,197	19,877	23,151	35,943	37,208	0.34	3.52
EAST ASIA AND THE PACIFIC	243,763	209,612	299,069	372,966	386,389	3.53	3.60
North-East Asia	154,443	122,791	156,687	202,411	234,246	2.14	15.73
China			23,047	70,097	99,070	0.90	41.33
Japan	137,598	109,557	118,177	114,935	112,313	1.03	-2.28
Korea, Republic of	16,845	13,234	15,463	17,379	22,863	0.21	31.56
Australasia	33,571	31,635	40,090	53,345	48,579	0.44	-8.93
Australia	31,347	28,845	34,260	42,554	41,972	0.38	-1.37
New Zealand	2,224	2,790	5,830	10,791	6,607	0.06	-38.77
Other East Asia and the Pacific	55,749	55,186	102,292	117,210	103,564	0.95	-11.64
Other countries of Asia	55,749	55,186	102,292	117,210	103,564	0.95	-11.64
EUROPE	8,452,417	8,439,628	8,337,425	8,645,852	9,443,832	86.23	9.23
Central/Eastern Europe	297,354	279,049	305,059	345,080	425,667	3.89	23.35
Czech Republic	14,238	18,159	21,210	26,259	32,561	0.30	24.00
Estonia	30,183	23,318	19,066	21,937	27,853	0.25	26.97
Hungary	5,137	7,387	12,087	20,864	19,122	0.17	-8.35
Latvia	16,017	14,559	9,817	13,726	14,306	0.13	4.23
Lithuania	9,826	12,572	13,847	13,302	20,190	0.18	51.78
Poland	105,624	87,909	88,608	108,154	137,318	1.25	26.97
Russian Federation	114,054	113,137	132,016	132,536	167,128	1.53	26.10
Slovakia	2,275	2,008	8,408	8,302	7,189	0.07	-13.41
Northern Europe	4,625,562	4,527,873	4,513,629	4,541,147	4,870,352	44.47	7.25
Denmark	999,674	1,024,094	959,983	974,300	1,038,498	9.48	6.59
Finland	448,890	417,770	385,121	417,045	428,219	3.91	2.68
Iceland	5,250	9,081	11,142	16,851	19,818	0.18	17.61
Ireland	13,106	18,579	21,841	26,902	31,231	0.29	16.09
Norway	2,541,303	2,465,835	2,531,570	2,464,157	2,709,794	24.74	9.97
United Kingdom	617,339	592,514	603,972	641,892	642,792	5.87	0.14
Southern Europe	304,549	288,827	380,573	433,582	447,762	4.09	3.27
Greece	4,851	6,915	11,896	23,129	25,879	0.24	11.89
Italy	192,511	178,995	243,806	251,071	244,413	2.23	-2.65
Portugal	6,511	8,258	8,554	15,765	17,033	0.16	8.04
Spain	100,676	94,659	116,317	143,617	160,437	1.46	11.71
Western Europe	2,935,356	3,035,188	2,811,044	3,008,007	3,384,245	30.90	12.51
Austria	39,603	40,549	37,228	38,985	42,849	0.39	9.91
Belgium	56,074	61,283	73,704	73,105	79,257	0.72	8.42
France	215,766	200,845	208,891	224,989	238,919	2.18	6.19
Germany	1,913,612	2,012,896	1,753,518	1,942,223	2,123,566	19.39	9.34
Luxembourg	1,696	4,150	4,211	5,055	5,756	0.05	13.87
Netherlands	541,383	576,531	583,086	557,615	716,702	6.54	28.53
Switzerland	167,222	138,934	150,406	166,035	177,196	1.62	6.72
East Mediterranean Europe	3,457	7,476	6,779	11,015	13,790	0.13	25.19

SWEDEN

6. Overnight stays of non-resident tourists in all types of accommodation establishments, by country of residence

	2002	2003	2004	2005	2006	Market share 06	% Change 06-05
Turkey	3,457	7,476	6,779	11,015	13,790	0.13	25.19
Other Europe	**286,139**	**301,215**	**320,341**	**307,021**	**302,016**	**2.76**	**-1.63**
Other countries of Europe	286,139	301,215	320,341	307,021	302,016	2.76	-1.63
REGION NOT SPECIFIED	**604,060**	**647,056**	**645,040**	**564,493**	**623,964**	**5.70**	**10.54**
Not Specified	**604,060**	**647,056**	**645,040**	**564,493**	**623,964**	**5.70**	**10.54**
Other countries of the World	604,060	647,056	645,040	564,493	623,964	5.70	10.54

Source: World Tourism Organization (UNWTO)

SWITZERLAND

3. Arrivals of non-resident tourists in hotels and similar establishments, by country of residence

		2002	2003	2004	2005	2006	Market share 06	% Change 06-05
TOTAL	(*)	6,867,696	6,530,108		7,228,851	7,862,957	100.00	8.77
AFRICA		74,195	72,786		78,143	85,460	1.09	9.36
North Africa		18,747	16,921		20,311	23,003	0.29	13.25
All countries of North Africa	(*)	18,747	16,921		20,311	23,003	0.29	13.25
Southern Africa		21,836	21,517		26,444	29,063	0.37	9.90
South Africa		21,836	21,517		26,444	29,063	0.37	9.90
Other Africa		33,612	34,348		31,388	33,394	0.42	6.39
Other countries of Africa		33,612	34,348		31,388	33,394	0.42	6.39
AMERICAS		871,279	757,015		829,551	933,715	11.87	12.56
North America		758,404	663,819		733,057	814,228	10.36	11.07
Canada		69,584	65,773		75,997	88,731	1.13	16.76
United States		688,820	598,046		657,060	725,497	9.23	10.42
South America		72,455	59,442		65,903	80,302	1.02	21.85
Argentina		10,321	9,214		9,047	11,606	0.15	28.29
Brazil		34,447	27,961		34,458	44,668	0.57	29.63
Chile		3,526	3,280		3,476	3,961	0.05	13.95
Other countries of South America		24,161	18,987		18,922	20,067	0.26	6.05
Other Americas		40,420	33,754		30,591	39,185	0.50	28.09
Other countries of the Americas		40,420	33,754		30,591	39,185	0.50	28.09
EAST ASIA AND THE PACIFIC		865,244	727,005		846,703	896,031	11.40	5.83
North-East Asia		632,078	516,919		610,658	645,765	8.21	5.75
China		69,268	62,542		110,004	132,610	1.69	20.55
Taiwan (Province of China)		41,518	34,396		43,125	41,935	0.53	-2.76
Hong Kong, China		35,991	28,142		27,375	28,558	0.36	4.32
Japan		416,306	320,593		335,199	347,299	4.42	3.61
Korea, Republic of		68,995	71,246		94,955	95,363	1.21	0.43
South-East Asia		136,717	126,800		129,919	135,246	1.72	4.10
Indonesia		11,430	10,096		9,255	10,779	0.14	16.47
Malaysia		18,108	15,661		14,952	15,399	0.20	2.99
Philippines		3,895	3,685		3,678	3,462	0.04	-5.87
Singapore		20,215	18,879		21,173	23,306	0.30	10.07
Thailand		32,918	30,323		38,984	36,467	0.46	-6.46
Other countries of South-East Asia		50,151	48,156		41,877	45,833	0.58	9.45
Other East Asia and the Pacific		96,449	83,286		106,126	115,020	1.46	8.38
Other countries of Asia		16,444	14,792		19,359	23,209	0.30	19.89
All countries of Oceania		80,005	68,494		86,767	91,811	1.17	5.81
EUROPE		4,906,368	4,821,157		5,304,949	5,747,455	73.10	8.34
Central/Eastern Europe		177,217	183,853		225,117	270,503	3.44	20.16
Bulgaria		6,875	8,456		12,248	13,953	0.18	13.92
Belarus		2,896	2,832		3,305	3,852	0.05	16.55
Czech Republic		19,983	20,222		25,245	28,658	0.36	13.52
Hungary		22,213	21,071		21,913	27,739	0.35	26.59
Poland		27,371	26,451		31,012	38,351	0.49	23.67
Romania		8,396	9,696		19,235	23,108	0.29	20.14
Russian Federation		64,145	68,759		78,749	93,369	1.19	18.57
Slovakia		8,997	8,727		8,961	10,467	0.13	16.81
Ukraine		8,394	9,498		11,334	14,197	0.18	25.26
Baltic countries		7,947	8,141		13,115	16,809	0.21	28.17

752

SWITZERLAND

3. Arrivals of non-resident tourists in hotels and similar establishments, by country of residence

	2002	2003	2004	2005	2006	Market share 06	% Change 06-05
Northern Europe	802,023	800,374		919,804	1,027,477	13.07	11.71
Denmark	40,755	39,602		49,296	55,788	0.71	13.17
Finland	23,977	23,767		27,188	32,918	0.42	21.08
Iceland	6,275	5,363		5,065	6,375	0.08	25.86
Ireland	18,731	23,255		25,278	32,802	0.42	29.77
Norway	27,687	30,798		30,820	35,703	0.45	15.84
Sweden	65,285	65,154		73,002	78,928	1.00	8.12
United Kingdom	619,313	612,435		709,155	784,963	9.98	10.69
Southern Europe	671,827	663,715		724,064	801,880	10.20	10.75
Croatia	8,381	8,349		8,936	10,929	0.14	22.30
Greece	38,387	36,460		39,795	46,891	0.60	17.83
Italy	429,436	434,515		460,982	498,702	6.34	8.18
Portugal	27,269	25,375		30,689	35,434	0.45	15.46
Slovenia	8,363	7,583		8,292	9,290	0.12	12.04
Spain	145,149	137,904		163,981	189,121	2.41	15.33
Serbia and Montenegro	14,842	13,529		11,389	11,513	0.15	1.09
Western Europe	3,117,191	3,032,366		3,265,416	3,449,371	43.87	5.63
Austria	144,890	144,189		149,826	160,031	2.04	6.81
Belgium	197,957	191,463		207,644	218,743	2.78	5.35
France	488,817	488,468		542,502	585,472	7.45	7.92
Germany	1,952,214	1,881,932		2,007,203	2,106,860	26.79	4.96
Liechtenstein	8,961	9,019		10,386	11,566	0.15	11.36
Luxembourg	35,234	32,313		35,309	37,677	0.48	6.71
Netherlands	289,118	284,982		312,546	329,022	4.18	5.27
East Mediterranean Europe	89,438	85,174		85,472	90,559	1.15	5.95
Israel	66,015	60,539		59,062	62,150	0.79	5.23
Turkey	23,423	24,635		26,410	28,409	0.36	7.57
Other Europe	48,672	55,675		85,076	107,665	1.37	26.55
Other countries of Europe	48,672	55,675		85,076	107,665	1.37	26.55
MIDDLE EAST	70,180	67,460		76,033	85,241	1.08	12.11
Middle East	70,180	67,460		76,033	85,241	1.08	12.11
Egypt	11,325	11,624		9,412	9,889	0.13	5.07
Other countries of Middle East	58,855	55,836		66,621	75,352	0.96	13.11
SOUTH ASIA	80,430	84,685		93,472	115,055	1.46	23.09
South Asia	80,430	84,685		93,472	115,055	1.46	23.09
India	80,430	84,685		93,472	115,055	1.46	23.09

Source: World Tourism Organization (UNWTO)

SWITZERLAND

5. Overnight stays of non-resident tourists in hotels and similar establishments, by country of residence

		2002	2003	2004	2005	2006	Market share 06	% Change 06-05
TOTAL	(*)	17,767,537	16,964,160		18,321,316	19,644,449	100.00	7.22
AFRICA		242,468	242,269		239,997	256,644	1.31	6.94
North Africa		75,222	71,947		77,418	74,991	0.38	-3.13
All countries of North Africa	(*)	75,222	71,947		77,418	74,991	0.38	-3.13
Southern Africa		56,814	58,373		66,321	78,864	0.40	18.91
South Africa		56,814	58,373		66,321	78,864	0.40	18.91
Other Africa		110,432	111,949		96,258	102,789	0.52	6.78
Other countries of Africa		110,432	111,949		96,258	102,789	0.52	6.78
AMERICAS		2,057,695	1,827,312		1,942,692	2,189,216	11.14	12.69
North America		1,752,300	1,561,515		1,672,412	1,864,184	9.49	11.47
Canada		165,356	163,533		178,202	205,120	1.04	15.11
United States		1,586,944	1,397,982		1,494,210	1,659,064	8.45	11.03
South America		209,061	179,647		188,217	223,057	1.14	18.51
Argentina		31,637	27,022		25,495	31,121	0.16	22.07
Brazil		105,524	93,833		102,677	127,780	0.65	24.45
Chile		10,778	9,197		9,320	11,064	0.06	18.71
Other countries of South America		61,122	49,595		50,725	53,092	0.27	4.67
Other Americas		96,334	86,150		82,063	101,975	0.52	24.26
Other countries of the Americas		96,334	86,150		82,063	101,975	0.52	24.26
EAST ASIA AND THE PACIFIC		1,552,555	1,364,776		1,539,201	1,608,822	8.19	4.52
North-East Asia		1,030,819	870,174		1,002,884	1,048,950	5.34	4.59
China		119,261	106,037		171,793	205,355	1.05	19.54
Taiwan (Province of China)		63,336	51,526		62,515	59,234	0.30	-5.25
Hong Kong, China		59,217	49,069		48,043	53,121	0.27	10.57
Japan		690,452	558,222		584,923	594,951	3.03	1.71
Korea, Republic of		98,553	105,320		135,610	136,289	0.69	0.50
South-East Asia		288,889	280,615		286,743	288,980	1.47	0.78
Indonesia		25,079	22,046		22,047	24,462	0.12	10.95
Malaysia		41,876	39,619		39,586	35,633	0.18	-9.99
Philippines		12,525	12,823		10,818	11,253	0.06	4.02
Singapore		45,634	43,716		47,742	51,735	0.26	8.36
Thailand		57,103	57,086		70,769	67,169	0.34	-5.09
Other countries of South-East Asia		106,672	105,325		95,781	98,728	0.50	3.08
Other East Asia and the Pacific		232,847	213,987		249,574	270,892	1.38	8.54
Other countries of Asia		54,674	51,786		54,615	64,704	0.33	18.47
All countries of Oceania		178,173	162,201		194,959	206,188	1.05	5.76
EUROPE		13,390,553	13,048,429		14,065,505	14,979,513	76.25	6.50
Central/Eastern Europe		546,967	557,861		660,000	799,718	4.07	21.17
Bulgaria		19,508	21,600		30,656	34,923	0.18	13.92
Belarus		7,292	7,860		9,437	10,851	0.06	14.98
Czech Republic		53,085	53,446		63,346	74,595	0.38	17.76
Hungary		62,994	59,062		56,797	66,200	0.34	16.56
Poland		70,046	66,098		77,484	100,351	0.51	29.51
Romania		28,292	28,113		51,076	68,133	0.35	33.40
Russian Federation		231,816	239,511		276,322	327,918	1.67	18.67
Slovakia		23,025	23,352		23,602	27,055	0.14	14.63
Ukraine		28,584	34,577		38,409	47,934	0.24	24.80
Baltic countries		22,325	24,242		32,871	41,758	0.21	27.04

SWITZERLAND

5. Overnight stays of non-resident tourists in hotels and similar establishments, by country of residence

	2002	2003	2004	2005	2006	Market share 06	% Change 06-05
Northern Europe	**2,292,835**	**2,256,617**		**2,521,244**	**2,786,254**	**14.18**	**10.51**
Denmark	91,470	89,542		112,030	124,783	0.64	11.38
Finland	57,474	58,321		65,234	77,764	0.40	19.21
Iceland	17,397	12,988		11,702	14,428	0.07	23.30
Ireland	48,284	59,455		64,312	85,901	0.44	33.57
Norway	61,936	72,473		73,045	89,910	0.46	23.09
Sweden	149,816	150,762		170,354	191,144	0.97	12.20
United Kingdom	1,866,458	1,813,076		2,024,567	2,202,324	11.21	8.78
Southern Europe	**1,477,964**	**1,475,697**		**1,607,903**	**1,745,343**	**8.88**	**8.55**
Croatia	23,963	21,748		22,389	28,235	0.14	26.11
Greece	95,598	93,228		99,294	116,858	0.59	17.69
Italy	932,663	958,484		1,011,279	1,057,218	5.38	4.54
Portugal	69,489	64,036		81,046	92,109	0.47	13.65
Slovenia	18,757	16,632		18,938	20,254	0.10	6.95
Spain	304,108	292,185		348,245	403,460	2.05	15.86
Serbia and Montenegro	33,386	29,384		26,712	27,209	0.14	1.86
Western Europe	**8,705,200**	**8,393,686**		**8,863,520**	**9,168,836**	**46.67**	**3.44**
Austria	326,794	326,341		331,380	355,855	1.81	7.39
Belgium	714,817	699,452		775,687	767,640	3.91	-1.04
France	1,166,228	1,149,441		1,225,619	1,269,871	6.46	3.61
Germany	5,543,920	5,301,798		5,563,695	5,757,096	29.31	3.48
Liechtenstein	20,182	20,011		23,204	25,341	0.13	9.21
Luxembourg	115,638	109,404		115,046	121,761	0.62	5.84
Netherlands	817,621	787,239		828,889	871,272	4.44	5.11
East Mediterranean Europe	**240,145**	**228,071**		**224,373**	**241,769**	**1.23**	**7.75**
Israel	175,833	163,770		154,030	165,984	0.84	7.76
Turkey	64,312	64,301		70,343	75,785	0.39	7.74
Other Europe	**127,442**	**136,497**		**188,465**	**237,593**	**1.21**	**26.07**
Other countries of Europe	127,442	136,497		188,465	237,593	1.21	26.07
MIDDLE EAST	**324,114**	**284,505**		**284,851**	**325,864**	**1.66**	**14.40**
Middle East	**324,114**	**284,505**		**284,851**	**325,864**	**1.66**	**14.40**
Egypt	35,348	37,565		32,670	34,436	0.18	5.41
Other countries of Middle East	288,766	246,940		252,181	291,428	1.48	15.56
SOUTH ASIA	**200,152**	**196,869**		**249,070**	**284,390**	**1.45**	**14.18**
South Asia	**200,152**	**196,869**		**249,070**	**284,390**	**1.45**	**14.18**
India	200,152	196,869		249,070	284,390	1.45	14.18

Source: World Tourism Organization (UNWTO)

SYRIAN ARAB REPUBLIC

2. Arrivals of non-resident visitors at national borders, by nationality

	2002	2003	2004	2005	2006	Market share 06	% Change 06-05
TOTAL (*)	4,272,911	4,388,119	6,153,653	5,837,980	6,009,483	100.00	2.94
AFRICA	71,089	73,487	89,664	92,585	81,136	1.35	-12.37
North Africa	71,089	73,487	89,664	92,585	81,136	1.35	-12.37
Algeria	21,170	25,382	33,073	32,983	31,618	0.53	-4.14
Morocco	9,182	9,754	10,711	11,217	9,236	0.15	-17.66
Sudan	19,280	17,303	17,859	17,885	18,246	0.30	2.02
Tunisia	21,457	21,048	28,021	30,500	22,036	0.37	-27.75
AMERICAS	44,588	43,901	58,032	57,795	59,408	0.99	2.79
North America	39,895	38,887	52,510	51,817	50,640	0.84	-2.27
Canada	11,417	9,864	13,571	13,474	15,259	0.25	13.25
United States	28,478	29,023	38,939	38,343	35,381	0.59	-7.73
South America	4,693	5,014	5,522	5,978	8,768	0.15	46.67
Argentina	564	778	985	904	853	0.01	-5.64
Brazil	1,665	1,753	1,989	2,012	3,953	0.07	96.47
Venezuela	2,464	2,483	2,548	3,062	3,962	0.07	29.39
EAST ASIA AND THE PACIFIC	27,767	25,897	36,852	35,088	35,155	0.58	0.19
North-East Asia	6,491	4,787	5,751	6,715	5,841	0.10	-13.02
Japan	6,491	4,787	5,751	6,715	5,841	0.10	-13.02
South-East Asia	12,239	13,513	18,559	17,119	15,428	0.26	-9.88
Indonesia	12,239	13,513	18,559	17,119	15,428	0.26	-9.88
Australasia	9,037	7,597	12,542	11,254	13,886	0.23	23.39
Australia	9,037	7,597	12,542	11,254	13,886	0.23	23.39
EUROPE	645,942	651,800	933,239	946,853	709,697	11.81	-25.05
Central/Eastern Europe	36,539	42,157	52,440	60,117	59,292	0.99	-1.37
Bulgaria	3,939	4,232	5,015	3,426	3,981	0.07	16.20
Czech Republic/Slovakia	2,605	1,951	2,473	3,307	2,468	0.04	-25.37
Hungary	2,825	2,526	3,244	4,479	3,345	0.06	-25.32
Poland	1,880	1,399	2,671	3,022	2,087	0.03	-30.94
Romania	3,684	3,353	3,849	3,883	3,783	0.06	-2.58
Ussr (Former)	21,606	28,696	35,188	42,000	43,628	0.73	3.88
Northern Europe	38,104	37,802	52,505	49,696	48,067	0.80	-3.28
Denmark	5,041	5,616	9,188	8,770	8,564	0.14	-2.35
Norway	2,285	2,328	4,346	3,870	2,978	0.05	-23.05
Sweden	11,567	12,950	19,069	16,548	15,570	0.26	-5.91
United Kingdom	19,211	16,908	19,902	20,508	20,955	0.35	2.18
Southern Europe	24,091	24,300	31,923	39,481	29,514	0.49	-25.25
Greece	2,773	3,207	4,264	4,801	4,656	0.08	-3.02
Italy	9,607	8,859	11,729	13,898	10,431	0.17	-24.95
Spain	6,263	6,890	11,329	15,744	9,732	0.16	-38.19
Yugoslavia, Sfr (Former)	5,448	5,344	4,601	5,038	4,695	0.08	-6.81
Western Europe	73,806	70,014	95,627	96,591	85,693	1.43	-11.28
Austria	3,809	3,730	4,631	5,231	4,075	0.07	-22.10
Belgium	3,591	3,376	4,709	5,074	5,057	0.08	-0.34
France	28,586	26,910	33,599	31,191	27,151	0.45	-12.95
Germany	26,425	25,036	34,878	38,408	36,372	0.61	-5.30
Netherlands	7,426	7,862	12,880	11,790	8,952	0.15	-24.07
Switzerland	3,969	3,100	4,930	4,897	4,086	0.07	-16.56
East Mediterranean Europe	473,402	477,527	700,744	700,968	487,131	8.11	-30.51

SYRIAN ARAB REPUBLIC

2. Arrivals of non-resident visitors at national borders, by nationality

	2002	2003	2004	2005	2006	Market share 06	% Change 06-05
Cyprus	5,754	6,627	11,163	11,990	6,578	0.11	-45.14
Turkey	467,648	470,900	689,581	688,978	480,553	8.00	-30.25
MIDDLE EAST	**3,093,856**	**3,325,490**	**4,760,773**	**4,369,669**	**4,734,283**	**78.78**	**8.34**
Middle East	**3,093,856**	**3,325,490**	**4,760,773**	**4,369,669**	**4,734,283**	**78.78**	**8.34**
Bahrain	76,402	60,648	67,163	55,854	44,555	0.74	-20.23
Palestine	50,166	52,087	56,884	65,839	82,702	1.38	25.61
Iraq	278,934	253,120	804,131	913,266	1,289,250	21.45	41.17
Jordan	692,211	752,935	851,095	940,413	882,501	14.69	-6.16
Kuwait	99,906	72,693	105,715	103,474	98,892	1.65	-4.43
Lebanon	1,410,511	1,654,001	2,262,733	1,681,158	1,786,943	29.74	6.29
Libyan Arab Jamahiriya	19,101	18,230	20,102	22,957	22,156	0.37	-3.49
Qatar	8,362	9,883	14,411	17,126	16,075	0.27	-6.14
Saudi Arabia	371,601	361,758	461,035	469,118	408,186	6.79	-12.99
United Arab Emirates	18,984	24,274	30,538	28,188	26,192	0.44	-7.08
Egypt	31,010	31,423	44,533	36,398	46,026	0.77	26.45
Yemen	23,387	22,046	28,760	19,123	17,934	0.30	-6.22
Other countries of Middle East	13,281	12,392	13,673	16,755	12,871	0.21	-23.18
SOUTH ASIA	**340,457**	**228,357**	**217,947**	**268,952**	**289,658**	**4.82**	**7.70**
South Asia	**340,457**	**228,357**	**217,947**	**268,952**	**289,658**	**4.82**	**7.70**
Afghanistan	636	649	678	626	730	0.01	16.61
India	16,689	9,560	11,936	11,875	9,830	0.16	-17.22
Iran, Islamic Republic of	310,839	213,931	196,699	247,662	270,915	4.51	9.39
Pakistan	12,293	4,217	8,634	8,789	8,183	0.14	-6.89
REGION NOT SPECIFIED	**49,212**	**39,187**	**57,146**	**67,038**	**100,146**	**1.67**	**49.39**
Not Specified	**49,212**	**39,187**	**57,146**	**67,038**	**100,146**	**1.67**	**49.39**
Other countries of the World	49,212	39,187	57,146	67,038	100,146	1.67	49.39

Source: World Tourism Organization (UNWTO)

SYRIAN ARAB REPUBLIC

3. Arrivals of non-resident tourists in hotels and similar establishments, by nationality

	2002	2003	2004	2005	2006	Market share 06	% Change 06-05
TOTAL (*)	847,308	862,978	1,231,918	1,379,652	1,754,431	100.00	27.16
AFRICA	57,652	50,371	61,525	63,244	45,166	2.57	-28.58
North Africa	57,652	50,371	61,525	63,244	45,166	2.57	-28.58
Algeria	16,981	22,769	29,063	28,984	22,655	1.29	-21.84
Morocco	15,177	1,325	3,405	3,566	3,725	0.21	4.46
Sudan	11,585	13,335	10,743	10,759	6,901	0.39	-35.86
Tunisia	13,909	12,942	18,314	19,935	11,885	0.68	-40.38
AMERICAS	12,405	7,990	20,557	20,291	25,828	1.47	27.29
North America	11,485	5,746	17,936	17,715	18,630	1.06	5.17
Canada	3,691	4,420	6,633	6,585	7,935	0.45	20.50
United States	7,794	1,326	11,303	11,130	10,695	0.61	-3.91
South America	920	2,244	2,621	2,576	7,198	0.41	179.43
Argentina	273	491	803	737	708	0.04	-3.93
Brazil	647	1,753	1,818	1,839	3,518	0.20	91.30
Venezuela					2,972	0.17	
EAST ASIA AND THE PACIFIC	12,999	18,116	26,606	25,768	24,619	1.40	-4.46
North-East Asia	9,244	4,787	5,751	6,715	5,158	0.29	-23.19
Japan	9,244	4,787	5,751	6,715	5,158	0.29	-23.19
South-East Asia		8,532	13,539	12,488	12,651	0.72	1.31
Indonesia		8,532	13,539	12,488	12,651	0.72	1.31
Australasia	3,755	4,797	7,316	6,565	6,810	0.39	3.73
Australia	3,755	4,797	7,316	6,565	6,810	0.39	3.73
EUROPE	181,458	124,597	205,370	269,204	238,179	13.58	-11.52
Central/Eastern Europe	19,005	28,144	38,219	43,917	37,885	2.16	-13.74
Bulgaria	1,312	2,672	3,658	2,499	2,986	0.17	19.49
Czech Republic/Slovakia	1,850	1,827	2,283	3,052	2,221	0.13	-27.23
Hungary	1,828	2,526	1,622	2,240	2,576	0.15	15.00
Poland	2,199	883	1,948	2,204	1,461	0.08	-33.71
Romania		2,117	1,857	1,873	2,270	0.13	21.20
Ussr (Former)	11,816	18,119	26,851	32,049	26,371	1.50	-17.72
Northern Europe	29,856	20,714	28,023	26,536	33,100	1.89	24.74
Denmark	3,078	5,616	6,636	6,334	6,423	0.37	1.41
Norway	3,564	2,177	3,810	3,393	2,382	0.14	-29.80
Sweden	5,074	5,190	8,016	6,957	9,653	0.55	38.75
United Kingdom	18,140	7,731	9,561	9,852	14,642	0.83	48.62
Southern Europe	29,823	18,264	26,750	33,266	23,166	1.32	-30.36
Greece	2,085	2,005	3,465	3,901	2,975	0.17	-23.74
Italy	19,457	7,444	9,791	11,602	8,449	0.48	-27.18
Spain	7,748	5,441	10,138	14,088	8,033	0.46	-42.98
Yugoslavia, Sfr (Former)	533	3,374	3,356	3,675	3,709	0.21	0.93
Western Europe	83,570	46,095	67,560	68,351	57,039	3.25	-16.55
Austria	4,990	3,730	4,000	4,517	3,219	0.18	-28.74
Belgium	4,635	2,801	3,023	3,258	4,065	0.23	24.77
France	37,862	14,936	21,457	19,920	16,417	0.94	-17.59
Germany	29,589	16,564	24,204	26,654	25,181	1.44	-5.53
Netherlands		4,964	9,946	9,105	5,092	0.29	-44.07
Switzerland	6,494	3,100	4,930	4,897	3,065	0.17	-37.41
East Mediterranean Europe	19,204	11,380	44,818	97,134	86,989	4.96	-10.44

SYRIAN ARAB REPUBLIC

3. Arrivals of non-resident tourists in hotels and similar establishments, by nationality

	2002	2003	2004	2005	2006	Market share 06	% Change 06-05
Cyprus	6,904	4,312	9,213	9,895	3,289	0.19	-66.76
Turkey	12,300	7,068	35,605	87,239	83,700	4.77	-4.06
MIDDLE EAST	**425,181**	**447,151**	**753,590**	**801,665**	**1,146,820**	**65.37**	**43.05**
Middle East	**425,181**	**447,151**	**753,590**	**801,665**	**1,146,820**	**65.37**	**43.05**
Bahrain	3,063	13,097	16,331	15,353	11,209	0.64	-26.99
Palestine	9,108	13,875	10,021	11,598	19,021	1.08	64.00
Iraq	44,968	41,071	235,564	278,021	345,883	19.71	24.41
Jordan	118,606	129,367	167,108	212,407	330,602	18.84	55.65
Kuwait	9,984	7,715	15,627	17,272	14,273	0.81	-17.36
Lebanon	124,785	149,339	187,036	138,963	286,705	16.34	106.32
Libyan Arab Jamahiriya	12,672	12,073	9,448	10,790	13,086	0.75	21.28
Oman			1,960	2,507	2,227	0.13	-11.17
Qatar	1,960	275	475	637	3,054	0.17	379.43
Saudi Arabia	55,637	49,801	73,267	83,926	88,185	5.03	5.07
United Arab Emirates	4,309	4,831	6,223	6,490	6,417	0.37	-1.12
Egypt	16,889	8,088	18,349	14,997	18,022	1.03	20.17
Yemen	12,958	12,972	11,411	7,587	6,994	0.40	-7.82
Other countries of Middle East	10,242	4,647	770	1,117	1,142	0.07	2.24
SOUTH ASIA	**127,326**	**188,031**	**120,215**	**147,823**	**166,886**	**9.51**	**12.90**
South Asia	**127,326**	**188,031**	**120,215**	**147,823**	**166,886**	**9.51**	**12.90**
Afghanistan					584	0.03	
India	3,570	9,560	10,907	10,852	4,322	0.25	-60.17
Iran, Islamic Republic of	121,777	175,808	106,582	134,196	157,548	8.98	17.40
Pakistan	1,979	2,663	2,726	2,775	4,432	0.25	59.71
REGION NOT SPECIFIED	**30,287**	**26,722**	**44,055**	**51,657**	**106,933**	**6.10**	**107.01**
Not Specified	**30,287**	**26,722**	**44,055**	**51,657**	**106,933**	**6.10**	**107.01**
Other countries of the World	30,287	26,722	44,055	51,657	106,933	6.10	107.01

Source: World Tourism Organization (UNWTO)

SYRIAN ARAB REPUBLIC

4. Arrivals of non-resident tourists in all types of accommodation establishments, by nationality

		2002	2003	2004	2005	2006	Market share 06	% Change 06-05
TOTAL	(*)	1,657,779	2,084,956	3,029,964	3,367,935	4,422,482	100.00	31.31
AFRICA		63,008	73,487	89,664	92,585	71,796	1.62	-22.45
North Africa		61,348	73,487	89,664	92,585	71,796	1.62	-22.45
Algeria		19,716	25,382	33,073	32,983	29,422	0.67	-10.80
Morocco		4,114	9,754	10,711	11,217	8,467	0.19	-24.52
Sudan		18,669	17,303	17,859	17,885	16,430	0.37	-8.14
Tunisia		18,849	21,048	28,021	30,500	17,477	0.40	-42.70
West Africa		1,660						
Mauritania		1,660						
AMERICAS		16,577	43,901	57,032	57,795	54,583	1.23	-5.56
North America		14,949	38,887	52,510	51,817	45,815	1.04	-11.58
Canada		5,696	9,864	13,571	13,474	15,259	0.35	13.25
United States		9,253	29,023	38,939	38,343	30,556	0.69	-20.31
South America		1,628	5,014	4,522	5,978	8,768	0.20	46.67
Argentina			778	985	904	853	0.02	-5.64
Brazil		1,628	1,753	1,989	2,012	3,953	0.09	96.47
Venezuela			2,483	1,548	3,062	3,962	0.09	29.39
EAST ASIA AND THE PACIFIC		6,228	25,897	36,852	35,088	32,378	0.73	-7.72
North-East Asia		6,228	4,787	5,751	6,715	5,841	0.13	-13.02
Japan		6,228	4,787	5,751	6,715	5,841	0.13	-13.02
South-East Asia			13,513	18,559	17,119	15,428	0.35	-9.88
Indonesia			13,513	18,559	17,119	15,428	0.35	-9.88
Australasia			7,597	12,542	11,254	11,109	0.25	-1.29
Australia			7,597	12,542	11,254	11,109	0.25	-1.29
EUROPE		113,436	204,445	313,956	430,120	467,151	10.56	8.61
Central/Eastern Europe		5,072	42,157	52,440	60,117	57,994	1.31	-3.53
Bulgaria			4,232	5,015	3,426	3,981	0.09	16.20
Czech Republic/Slovakia		2,408	1,951	2,473	3,307	2,468	0.06	-25.37
Hungary		2,664	2,526	3,244	4,479	3,345	0.08	-25.32
Poland			1,399	2,671	3,022	2,087	0.05	-30.94
Romania			3,353	3,849	3,883	3,783	0.09	-2.58
Ussr (Former)			28,696	35,188	42,000	42,330	0.96	0.79
Northern Europe		23,418	37,802	52,505	49,696	45,607	1.03	-8.23
Denmark		5,041	5,616	9,188	8,770	8,564	0.19	-2.35
Norway			2,328	4,346	3,870	2,978	0.07	-23.05
Sweden		5,847	12,950	19,069	16,548	15,570	0.35	-5.91
United Kingdom		12,530	16,908	19,902	20,508	18,495	0.42	-9.82
Southern Europe		15,825	24,300	31,923	39,481	29,514	0.67	-25.25
Greece		2,166	3,207	4,264	4,801	4,656	0.11	-3.02
Italy		8,714	8,859	11,729	13,898	10,431	0.24	-24.95
Spain		4,945	6,890	11,329	15,744	9,732	0.22	-38.19
Yugoslavia, Sfr (Former)			5,344	4,601	5,038	4,695	0.11	-6.81
Western Europe		55,873	70,014	95,627	96,591	81,281	1.84	-15.85
Austria		3,809	3,730	4,631	5,231	4,075	0.09	-22.10
Belgium		2,979	3,376	4,709	5,074	5,057	0.11	-0.34
France		17,529	26,910	33,599	31,191	25,257	0.57	-19.02
Germany		20,161	25,036	34,878	38,408	34,973	0.79	-8.94

SYRIAN ARAB REPUBLIC

4. Arrivals of non-resident tourists in all types of accommodation establishments, by nationality

	2002	2003	2004	2005	2006	Market share 06	% Change 06-05
Netherlands	7,426	7,862	12,880	11,790	7,833	0.18	-33.56
Switzerland	3,969	3,100	4,930	4,897	4,086	0.09	-16.56
East Mediterranean Europe	**13,248**	**30,172**	**81,461**	**184,235**	**252,755**	**5.72**	**37.19**
Cyprus	3,743	6,627	11,163	11,990	6,578	0.15	-45.14
Turkey	9,505	23,545	70,298	172,245	246,177	5.57	42.92
MIDDLE EAST	**1,055,832**	**1,470,289**	**2,259,703**	**2,416,358**	**3,458,290**	**78.20**	**43.12**
Middle East	**1,055,832**	**1,470,289**	**2,259,703**	**2,416,358**	**3,458,290**	**78.20**	**43.12**
Bahrain	66,250	53,188	58,902	55,376	44,212	1.00	-20.16
Palestine	14,904	52,087	56,884	65,839	76,085	1.72	15.56
Iraq	158,332	189,840	619,040	730,613	1,152,943	26.07	57.80
Jordan	160,269	316,233	384,725	489,015	734,671	16.61	50.23
Kuwait	80,668	63,752	92,712	102,476	95,152	2.15	-7.15
Lebanon	186,525	363,880	497,801	369,855	819,157	18.52	121.48
Libyan Arab Jamahiriya	19,100	18,230	20,102	22,957	20,771	0.47	-9.52
Oman	23,420		8,390	10,730	7,681	0.17	-28.42
Qatar	6,834	8,667	12,638	16,934	16,075	0.36	-5.07
Saudi Arabia	284,650	317,262	404,328	463,152	400,839	9.06	-13.45
United Arab Emirates	15,163	21,288	26,782	27,934	25,668	0.58	-8.11
Egypt	13,361	31,423	44,533	36,398	41,911	0.95	15.15
Yemen	21,377	22,046	28,760	19,123	17,934	0.41	-6.22
Other countries of Middle East	4,979	12,393	4,106	5,956	5,191	0.12	-12.84
SOUTH ASIA	**293,628**	**228,357**	**217,947**	**268,952**	**264,998**	**5.99**	**-1.47**
South Asia	**293,628**	**228,357**	**217,947**	**268,952**	**264,998**	**5.99**	**-1.47**
Afghanistan		649	678	626	730	0.02	16.61
India	15,897	9,560	11,936	11,875	7,373	0.17	-37.91
Iran, Islamic Republic of	277,731	213,931	196,699	247,662	250,076	5.65	0.97
Pakistan		4,217	8,634	8,789	6,819	0.15	-22.41
REGION NOT SPECIFIED	**109,070**	**38,580**	**54,810**	**67,037**	**73,286**	**1.66**	**9.32**
Not Specified	**109,070**	**38,580**	**54,810**	**67,037**	**73,286**	**1.66**	**9.32**
Other countries of the World	109,070	38,580	54,810	67,037	73,286	1.66	9.32

Source: World Tourism Organization (UNWTO)

SYRIAN ARAB REPUBLIC

5. Overnight stays of non-resident tourists in hotels and similar establishments, by nationality

		2002	2003	2004	2005	2006	Market share 06	% Change 06-05
TOTAL	(*)	1,940,939	5,774,524	7,995,088	8,803,464	9,788,213	100.00	11.19
AFRICA		177,741	327,331	486,955	500,222	337,360	3.45	-32.56
North Africa		177,741	327,331	486,955	500,222	337,360	3.45	-32.56
Algeria		49,672	115,503	204,431	207,861	140,091	1.43	-32.60
Morocco		55,690	9,277	32,288	26,392	40,979	0.42	55.27
Sudan		30,853	105,705	96,099	99,462	81,427	0.83	-18.13
Tunisia		41,526	96,846	154,137	166,507	74,863	0.76	-55.04
AMERICAS		25,305	57,245	158,033	146,511	198,740	2.03	35.65
North America		23,355	36,326	132,045	119,280	167,663	1.71	40.56
Canada		7,648	21,736	48,100	36,561	71,411	0.73	95.32
United States		15,707	14,590	83,945	82,719	96,252	0.98	16.36
South America		1,950	20,919	25,988	27,231	31,077	0.32	14.12
Argentina		645	4,154	7,180	6,510	5,664	0.06	-13.00
Brazil		1,305	3,507	7,429	7,662	10,555	0.11	37.76
Venezuela			13,258	11,379	13,059	14,858	0.15	13.78
EAST ASIA AND THE PACIFIC		34,525	129,727	187,007	140,900	146,765	1.50	4.16
North-East Asia		27,235	17,010	22,345	26,089	25,792	0.26	-1.14
Japan		27,235	17,010	22,345	26,089	25,792	0.26	-1.14
South-East Asia			72,153	103,233	92,350	50,604	0.52	-45.20
Indonesia			72,153	103,233	92,350	50,604	0.52	-45.20
Australasia		7,290	40,564	61,429	22,461	70,369	0.72	213.29
Australia		7,290	40,564	61,429	22,461	70,369	0.72	213.29
EUROPE		381,728	1,037,338	1,434,517	1,658,392	1,442,674	14.74	-13.01
Central/Eastern Europe		91,156	216,005	239,927	252,768	344,274	3.52	36.20
Bulgaria		3,845	22,597	27,896	18,482	23,887	0.24	29.24
Czech Republic/Slovakia		3,320	7,740	10,407	13,932	19,991	0.20	43.49
Hungary		2,775	7,072	7,137	3,135	18,029	0.18	475.09
Poland		3,587	7,470	14,857	16,301	24,835	0.25	52.35
Romania			17,903	9,410	9,793	27,235	0.28	178.11
Ussr (Former)		77,629	153,223	170,220	191,125	230,297	2.35	20.50
Northern Europe		54,394	214,641	239,364	211,600	315,966	3.23	49.32
Denmark		6,349	31,339	40,710	40,831	70,656	0.72	73.04
Norway		4,513	9,685	20,705	16,670	16,677	0.17	0.04
Sweden		9,526	33,928	42,063	32,526	67,572	0.69	107.75
United Kingdom		34,006	139,689	135,886	121,573	161,061	1.65	32.48
Southern Europe		53,082	154,130	225,202	276,131	144,654	1.48	-47.61
Greece		4,120	13,630	27,235	27,752	19,515	0.20	-29.68
Italy		34,138	62,169	84,808	100,381	54,687	0.56	-45.52
Spain		13,614	49,797	87,566	120,820	48,197	0.49	-60.11
Yugoslavia, Sfr (Former)		1,210	28,534	25,593	27,178	22,255	0.23	-18.11
Western Europe		147,032	402,817	566,046	556,001	389,296	3.98	-29.98
Austria		9,782	52,841	35,246	41,032	19,035	0.19	-53.61
Belgium		7,706	14,564	26,185	32,214	24,390	0.25	-24.29
France		64,383	142,297	177,445	159,319	144,845	1.48	-9.08
Germany		53,299	128,557	209,965	213,725	151,083	1.54	-29.31
Netherlands			41,979	82,612	75,348	35,642	0.36	-52.70
Switzerland		11,862	22,579	34,593	34,363	14,301	0.15	-58.38
East Mediterranean Europe		36,064	49,745	163,978	361,892	248,484	2.54	-31.34

SYRIAN ARAB REPUBLIC

5. Overnight stays of non-resident tourists in hotels and similar establishments, by nationality

	2002	2003	2004	2005	2006	Market share 06	% Change 06-05
Cyprus	13,643	17,249	34,043	34,637	16,445	0.17	-52.52
Turkey	22,421	32,496	129,935	327,255	232,039	2.37	-29.10
MIDDLE EAST	**744,326**	**2,903,850**	**4,594,297**	**4,985,408**	**6,008,350**	**61.38**	**20.52**
Middle East	**744,326**	**2,903,850**	**4,594,297**	**4,985,408**	**6,008,350**	**61.38**	**20.52**
Bahrain	6,374	154,254	156,210	144,901	134,507	1.37	-7.17
Palestine	17,437	86,906	60,088	57,410	64,197	0.66	11.82
Iraq	83,384	373,922	1,626,703	2,013,112	2,075,298	21.20	3.09
Jordan	189,110	744,395	810,698	1,039,870	1,653,010	16.89	58.96
Kuwait	21,989	78,880	126,827	146,971	85,637	0.87	-41.73
Lebanon	199,126	745,768	763,089	568,376	860,114	8.79	51.33
Libyan Arab Jamahiriya	30,815	84,356	79,339	68,044	100,366	1.03	47.50
Qatar	5,295	4,072	8,313	11,082	33,598	0.34	203.18
Saudi Arabia	101,645	377,159	627,080	710,273	705,477	7.21	-0.68
United Arab Emirates	11,009	27,195	45,772	48,339	53,088	0.54	9.82
Egypt	39,011	44,443	144,476	81,343	126,154	1.29	55.09
Yemen	31,876	159,262	122,857	65,667	94,461	0.97	43.85
Other countries of Middle East	7,255	23,238	22,845	30,020	22,443	0.23	-25.24
SOUTH ASIA	**491,250**	**1,109,798**	**814,439**	**977,053**	**1,019,026**	**10.41**	**4.30**
South Asia	**491,250**	**1,109,798**	**814,439**	**977,053**	**1,019,026**	**10.41**	**4.30**
Afghanistan		3,465	3,771	3,377	2,336	0.02	-30.83
India	7,867	41,427	57,696	57,875	38,900	0.40	-32.79
Iran, Islamic Republic of	478,843	1,042,389	711,977	904,069	945,286	9.66	4.56
Pakistan	4,540	22,517	40,995	11,732	32,504	0.33	177.05
REGION NOT SPECIFIED	**86,064**	**209,235**	**319,840**	**394,978**	**635,298**	**6.49**	**60.84**
Not Specified	**86,064**	**209,235**	**319,840**	**394,978**	**635,298**	**6.49**	**60.84**
Other countries of the World	86,064	209,235	319,840	394,978	635,298	6.49	60.84

Source: World Tourism Organization (UNWTO)

SYRIAN ARAB REPUBLIC

6. Overnight stays of non-resident tourists in all types of accommodation establishments, by nationality

	2002	2003	2004	2005	2006	Market share 06	% Change 06-05
TOTAL (*)		20,699,978	27,929,913	30,948,331	48,482,398	100.00	56.66
AFRICA		693,651	857,722	920,863	602,447	1.24	-34.58
North Africa		693,651	857,722	920,863	602,447	1.24	-34.58
Algeria		167,752	278,502	285,956	195,014	0.40	-31.80
Morocco		154,655	134,721	140,184	82,720	0.17	-40.99
Sudan		188,490	203,221	249,714	191,203	0.39	-23.43
Tunisia		182,754	241,278	245,009	133,510	0.28	-45.51
AMERICAS		953,308	882,262	869,588	416,495	0.86	-52.10
North America		942,498	865,220	854,155	397,994	0.82	-53.40
Canada		153,288	149,892	145,908	121,154	0.25	-16.97
United States		789,210	715,328	708,247	276,840	0.57	-60.91
South America		10,810	17,042	15,433	18,501	0.04	19.88
Argentina		7,303	9,154	7,424	6,010	0.01	-19.05
Brazil		3,507	7,888	8,009	12,491	0.03	55.96
EAST ASIA AND THE PACIFIC		88,318	122,137	118,125	128,729	0.27	8.98
North-East Asia		17,010	22,345	26,089	28,181	0.06	8.02
Japan		17,010	22,345	26,089	28,181	0.06	8.02
Australasia		71,308	99,792	92,036	100,548	0.21	9.25
Australia		71,308	99,792	92,036	100,548	0.21	9.25
EUROPE		2,331,728	2,530,233	2,979,939	4,405,794	9.09	47.85
Central/Eastern Europe		337,388	305,657	318,547	514,208	1.06	61.42
Bulgaria		39,723	38,408	25,262	26,475	0.05	4.80
Czech Republic/Slovakia		8,112	10,891	14,255	20,485	0.04	43.70
Hungary		7,072	14,273	9,854	19,337	0.04	96.24
Poland		13,131	20,456	22,282	25,601	0.05	14.90
Ussr (Former)		269,350	221,629	246,894	422,310	0.87	71.05
Northern Europe		753,527	668,528	630,409	480,126	0.99	-23.84
Denmark		31,339	51,936	46,258	73,939	0.15	59.84
Norway		14,959	41,777	36,036	19,717	0.04	-45.29
Sweden		258,865	246,889	289,015	170,020	0.35	-41.17
United Kingdom		448,364	327,926	259,100	216,450	0.45	-16.46
Southern Europe		234,655	281,017	329,342	184,885	0.38	-43.86
Greece		35,277	39,290	35,855	23,491	0.05	-34.48
Italy		81,867	105,802	125,491	86,939	0.18	-30.72
Spain		67,350	100,687	130,847	51,092	0.11	-60.95
Yugoslavia, Sfr (Former)		50,161	35,238	37,149	23,363	0.05	-37.11
Western Europe		871,969	975,432	1,038,963	713,172	1.47	-31.36
Austria		52,841	52,589	48,403	22,824	0.05	-52.85
Belgium		38,141	50,145	75,045	32,566	0.07	-56.60
France		342,113	336,405	305,294	238,935	0.49	-21.74
Germany		342,500	385,252	472,836	344,356	0.71	-27.17
Netherlands		73,795	116,448	103,022	56,870	0.12	-44.80
Switzerland		22,579	34,593	34,363	17,621	0.04	-48.72
East Mediterranean Europe		134,189	299,599	662,678	2,513,403	5.18	279.28
Cyprus		33,460	44,926	41,969	54,542	0.11	29.96
Turkey		100,729	254,673	620,709	2,458,861	5.07	296.14
MIDDLE EAST		14,752,711	21,422,756	23,575,240	41,109,243	84.79	74.37

SYRIAN ARAB REPUBLIC

6. Overnight stays of non-resident tourists in all types of accommodation establishments, by nationality

	2002	2003	2004	2005	2006	Market share 06	% Change 06-05
Middle East		14,752,711	21,422,756	23,575,240	41,109,243	84.79	74.37
Bahrain		697,119	603,231	564,299	570,561	1.18	1.11
Palestine		521,597	623,010	699,949	779,131	1.61	11.31
Iraq		2,390,227	6,578,676	8,092,183	18,539,329	38.24	129.10
Jordan		2,218,165	2,723,439	3,480,155	5,546,766	11.44	59.38
Kuwait		822,373	1,116,028	1,245,163	1,586,191	3.27	27.39
Lebanon		2,609,589	2,979,153	2,320,422	7,357,829	15.18	217.09
Libyan Arab Jamahiriya		164,958	263,386	222,922	184,372	0.38	-17.29
Qatar		83,714	156,922	212,360	267,976	0.55	26.19
Saudi Arabia		3,771,679	4,865,628	5,542,138	4,584,038	9.46	-17.29
United Arab Emirates		262,644	378,733	378,257	342,628	0.71	-9.42
Egypt		505,060	493,714	345,281	851,222	1.76	146.53
Yemen		333,780	455,742	288,804	301,065	0.62	4.25
Other countries of Middle East		371,806	185,094	183,307	198,135	0.41	8.09
SOUTH ASIA		1,324,738	1,485,277	1,814,531	1,349,370	2.78	-25.64
South Asia		1,324,738	1,485,277	1,814,531	1,349,370	2.78	-25.64
India		41,427	61,258	59,922	54,260	0.11	-9.45
Iran, Islamic Republic of		1,243,729	1,279,890	1,650,128	1,249,854	2.58	-24.26
Pakistan		39,582	144,129	104,481	45,256	0.09	-56.68
REGION NOT SPECIFIED		555,524	629,526	670,045	470,320	0.97	-29.81
Not Specified		555,524	629,526	670,045	470,320	0.97	-29.81
Other countries of the World		555,524	629,526	670,045	470,320	0.97	-29.81

Source: World Tourism Organization (UNWTO)

TAIWAN (PROVINCE OF CHINA)

2. Arrivals of non-resident visitors at national borders, by country of residence

	2002	2003	2004	2005	2006	Market share 06	% Change 06-05
TOTAL	2,977,692	2,248,117	2,950,342	3,378,118	3,519,827	100.00	4.19
AFRICA	9,120	7,375	9,538	9,018	8,714	0.25	-3.37
East Africa	353	152					
Madagascar	17	9					
Mauritius	336	143					
Southern Africa	5,724	5,182	6,180	5,620	5,332	0.15	-5.12
South Africa	5,724	5,182	6,180	5,620	5,332	0.15	-5.12
West Africa	835	585					
Nigeria	835	585					
Other Africa	2,208	1,456	3,358	3,398	3,382	0.10	-0.47
Other countries of Africa	2,208	1,456	3,358	3,398	3,382	0.10	-0.47
AMERICAS	406,227	311,594	440,887	453,271	457,167	12.99	0.86
North America	398,421	305,609	432,245	443,990	447,326	12.71	0.75
Canada	42,815	33,873	49,891	53,838	53,225	1.51	-1.14
Mexico	2,195	1,213	2,144	1,999	2,097	0.06	4.90
United States	353,411	270,523	380,210	388,153	392,004	11.14	0.99
South America	2,758	2,261	3,387	3,471	3,680	0.10	6.02
Argentina	552	438	667	652	652	0.02	
Brazil	2,206	1,823	2,720	2,819	3,028	0.09	7.41
Other Americas	5,048	3,724	5,255	5,810	6,161	0.18	6.04
Other countries of the Americas	5,048	3,724	5,255	5,810	6,161	0.18	6.04
EAST ASIA AND THE PACIFIC	1,761,660	1,348,597	1,782,053	2,131,368	2,185,273	62.08	2.53
North-East Asia	1,142,128	801,381	1,100,815	1,378,431	1,429,603	40.62	3.71
Hong Kong, China	76,690	56,076	70,878	77,275	77,549	2.20	0.35
Japan	985,564	655,131	885,168	1,122,192	1,159,533	32.94	3.33
Korea, Republic of	79,874	90,174	144,769	178,964	192,521	5.47	7.58
South-East Asia	508,742	447,395	557,955	626,498	632,787	17.98	1.00
Indonesia	86,098	37,116	43,694	88,086	90,593	2.57	2.85
Malaysia	64,483	66,487	92,272	107,084	114,761	3.26	7.17
Philippines	74,022	75,851	82,319	87,205	75,240	2.14	-13.72
Singapore	107,069	78,300	116,445	165,666	183,511	5.21	10.77
Thailand	105,688	97,478	101,989	92,584	94,644	2.69	2.23
Other countries of South-East Asia	71,382	92,163	121,236	85,873	74,038	2.10	-13.78
Australasia	37,601	31,559	49,041	54,032	50,303	1.43	-6.90
Australia	31,477	26,287	41,529	46,017	42,114	1.20	-8.48
New Zealand	6,124	5,272	7,512	8,015	8,189	0.23	2.17
Other East Asia and the Pacific	73,189	68,262	74,242	72,407	72,580	2.06	0.24
Other countries of Asia	72,941	67,972	72,989	71,254	71,450	2.03	0.28
Other countries of Oceania	248	290	1,253	1,153	1,130	0.03	-1.99
EUROPE	146,730	118,273	164,032	171,665	171,816	4.88	0.09
Northern Europe	39,009	32,188	42,399	41,319	41,327	1.17	0.02
Sweden	4,927	3,872	5,486	5,571	5,533	0.16	-0.68
United Kingdom	34,082	28,316	36,913	35,748	35,794	1.02	0.13
Southern Europe	15,664	11,297	16,113	16,779	16,545	0.47	-1.39
Greece	1,174	856	1,444	1,287	1,257	0.04	-2.33
Italy	10,664	7,678	10,302	10,913	10,722	0.30	-1.75
Spain	3,826	2,763	4,367	4,579	4,566	0.13	-0.28

TAIWAN (PROVINCE OF CHINA)

2. Arrivals of non-resident visitors at national borders, by country of residence

	2002	2003	2004	2005	2006	Market share 06	% Change 06-05
Western Europe	**77,455**	**62,305**	**83,608**	**89,093**	**88,048**	**2.50**	**-1.17**
Austria	4,098	3,119	4,305	5,049	5,464	0.16	8.22
Belgium	3,833	3,014	3,801	4,208	3,832	0.11	-8.94
France	20,179	15,188	21,152	21,785	22,372	0.64	2.69
Germany	33,469	28,476	37,063	39,626	38,602	1.10	-2.58
Netherlands	10,237	8,022	11,173	12,084	11,418	0.32	-5.51
Switzerland	5,639	4,486	6,114	6,341	6,360	0.18	0.30
Other Europe	**14,602**	**12,483**	**21,912**	**24,474**	**25,896**	**0.74**	**5.81**
Other countries of Europe	14,602	12,483	21,912	24,474	25,896	0.74	5.81
MIDDLE EAST	**9,929**	**7,696**	**12,598**	**13,431**	**12,692**	**0.36**	**-5.50**
Middle East	**9,929**	**7,696**	**12,598**	**13,431**	**12,692**	**0.36**	**-5.50**
All countries of Middle East	9,929	7,696	12,598	13,431	12,692	0.36	-5.50
SOUTH ASIA	**13,945**	**12,405**	**16,255**	**17,475**	**18,020**	**0.51**	**3.12**
South Asia	**13,945**	**12,405**	**16,255**	**17,475**	**18,020**	**0.51**	**3.12**
India	13,945	12,405	16,255	17,475	18,020	0.51	3.12
REGION NOT SPECIFIED	**630,081**	**442,177**	**524,979**	**581,890**	**666,145**	**18.93**	**14.48**
Not Specified	**630,081**	**442,177**	**524,979**	**581,890**	**666,145**	**18.93**	**14.48**
Other countries of the World	6,406	6,094	2,934	1,982	1,947	0.06	-1.77
Nationals Residing Abroad	623,675	436,083	522,045	579,908	664,198	18.87	14.54

Source: World Tourism Organization (UNWTO)

TAIWAN (PROVINCE OF CHINA)

4. Arrivals of non-resident tourists in all types of accommodation establishments, by country of residence

	2002	2003	2004	2005	2006	Market share 06	% Change 06-05
TOTAL	2,236,936	1,813,814	2,476,374	2,902,003	3,056,108	100.00	5.31
AFRICA	6,549	4,940	6,932	6,766	6,837	0.22	1.05
East Africa	315	8					
Madagascar	18	7					
Mauritius	297	1					
Southern Africa	3,689	3,054	4,042	3,839	3,780	0.12	-1.54
South Africa	3,689	3,054	4,042	3,839	3,780	0.12	-1.54
West Africa	646	503					
Nigeria	646	503					
Other Africa	1,899	1,375	2,890	2,927	3,057	0.10	4.44
Other countries of Africa	1,899	1,375	2,890	2,927	3,057	0.10	4.44
AMERICAS	371,449	283,085	406,927	416,678	419,096	13.71	0.58
North America	364,514	277,857	398,979	408,403	410,570	13.43	0.53
Canada	35,872	27,298	42,523	46,664	45,848	1.50	-1.75
Mexico	1,946	1,082	2,009	1,804	1,790	0.06	-0.78
United States	326,696	249,477	354,447	359,935	362,932	11.88	0.83
South America	2,487	1,999	3,198	3,273	3,464	0.11	5.84
Argentina	479	353	647	584	639	0.02	9.42
Brazil	2,008	1,646	2,551	2,689	2,825	0.09	5.06
Other Americas	4,448	3,229	4,750	5,002	5,062	0.17	1.20
Other countries of the Americas	4,448	3,229	4,750	5,002	5,062	0.17	1.20
EAST ASIA AND THE PACIFIC	1,694,291	1,370,891	1,882,984	2,291,943	2,447,266	80.08	6.78
North-East Asia	1,273,802	1,004,488	1,382,197	1,676,463	1,724,512	56.43	2.87
Hong Kong, China	244,103	287,312	393,034	410,095	411,326	13.46	0.30
Japan	955,439	631,219	849,287	1,091,714	1,127,688	36.90	3.30
Korea, Republic of	74,260	85,957	139,876	174,654	185,498	6.07	6.21
South-East Asia	263,726	224,277	310,781	373,407	394,005	12.89	5.52
Indonesia	32,527	23,699	29,407	31,749	33,157	1.08	4.43
Malaysia	56,420	58,225	82,946	98,253	103,815	3.40	5.66
Philippines	23,155	22,257	27,772	28,382	26,402	0.86	-6.98
Singapore	105,056	76,118	112,656	161,394	179,280	5.87	11.08
Thailand	29,103	24,881	32,255	31,992	32,084	1.05	0.29
Other countries of South-East Asia	17,465	19,097	25,745	21,637	19,267	0.63	-10.95
Australasia	34,093	28,367	43,283	47,726	45,183	1.48	-5.33
Australia	28,833	23,814	36,694	40,557	37,727	1.23	-6.98
New Zealand	5,260	4,553	6,589	7,169	7,456	0.24	4.00
Other East Asia and the Pacific	122,670	113,759	146,723	194,347	283,566	9.28	45.91
Other countries of Asia	122,471	113,503	145,581	193,322	282,515	9.24	46.14
Other countries of Oceania	199	256	1,142	1,025	1,051	0.03	2.54
EUROPE	133,050	106,125	149,183	155,857	153,925	5.04	-1.24
Northern Europe	34,832	28,873	38,509	37,940	36,529	1.20	-3.72
Sweden	4,633	3,615	5,104	5,264	5,290	0.17	0.49
United Kingdom	30,199	25,258	33,405	32,676	31,239	1.02	-4.40
Southern Europe	14,280	10,099	14,764	15,526	15,128	0.50	-2.56
Greece	989	625	1,114	1,051	1,016	0.03	-3.33
Italy	9,782	6,952	9,591	10,142	9,976	0.33	-1.64

TAIWAN (PROVINCE OF CHINA)

4. Arrivals of non-resident tourists in all types of accommodation establishments, by country of residence

	2002	2003	2004	2005	2006	Market share 06	% Change 06-05
Spain	3,509	2,522	4,059	4,333	4,136	0.14	-4.55
Western Europe	**70,993**	**56,391**	**76,542**	**80,981**	**80,031**	**2.62**	**-1.17**
Austria	3,783	2,819	4,021	4,606	4,799	0.16	4.19
Belgium	3,484	2,771	3,524	3,823	3,511	0.11	-8.16
France	18,492	13,766	19,327	19,607	20,231	0.66	3.18
Germany	30,692	25,644	33,952	36,237	34,943	1.14	-3.57
Netherlands	9,219	7,139	9,841	10,624	10,586	0.35	-0.36
Switzerland	5,323	4,252	5,877	6,084	5,961	0.20	-2.02
Other Europe	**12,945**	**10,762**	**19,368**	**21,410**	**22,237**	**0.73**	**3.86**
Other countries of Europe	12,945	10,762	19,368	21,410	22,237	0.73	3.86
MIDDLE EAST	**9,320**	**7,186**	**11,993**	**12,877**	**12,051**	**0.39**	**-6.41**
Middle East	**9,320**	**7,186**	**11,993**	**12,877**	**12,051**	**0.39**	**-6.41**
All countries of Middle East	9,320	7,186	11,993	12,877	12,051	0.39	-6.41
SOUTH ASIA	**11,793**	**9,996**	**13,522**	**14,558**	**15,141**	**0.50**	**4.00**
South Asia	**11,793**	**9,996**	**13,522**	**14,558**	**15,141**	**0.50**	**4.00**
India	11,793	9,996	13,522	14,558	15,141	0.50	4.00
REGION NOT SPECIFIED	**10,484**	**31,591**	**4,833**	**3,324**	**1,792**	**0.06**	**-46.09**
Not Specified	**10,484**	**31,591**	**4,833**	**3,324**	**1,792**	**0.06**	**-46.09**
Other countries of the World	10,484	31,591	4,833	3,324	1,792	0.06	-46.09

Source: World Tourism Organization (UNWTO)

TAIWAN (PROVINCE OF CHINA)

6. Overnight stays of non-resident tourists in all types of accommodation establishments, by country of residence

	2002	2003	2004	2005	2006	Market share 06	% Change 06-05
TOTAL	16,856,168	14,460,852	18,838,367	20,593,095	21,157,033	100.00	2.74
AFRICA	81,135	71,214	85,554	79,070	77,543	0.37	-1.93
East Africa	3,308	38					
Madagascar	258	31					
Mauritius	3,050	7					
Southern Africa	49,841	45,151	53,630	48,598	47,320	0.22	-2.63
South Africa	49,841	45,151	53,630	48,598	47,320	0.22	-2.63
West Africa	12,333	12,844					
Nigeria	12,333	12,844					
Other Africa	15,653	13,181	31,924	30,472	30,223	0.14	-0.82
Other countries of Africa	15,653	13,181	31,924	30,472	30,223	0.14	-0.82
AMERICAS	3,790,449	2,929,600	4,271,758	4,301,258	4,306,740	20.36	0.13
North America	3,714,087	2,867,900	4,183,058	4,206,353	4,213,283	19.91	0.16
Canada	377,030	317,346	468,515	490,122	468,952	2.22	-4.32
Mexico	14,477	8,531	16,694	13,317	13,972	0.07	4.92
United States	3,322,580	2,542,023	3,697,849	3,702,914	3,730,359	17.63	0.74
South America	29,585	25,803	36,157	37,358	37,201	0.18	-0.42
Argentina	7,873	5,573	8,189	6,954	7,946	0.04	14.27
Brazil	21,712	20,230	27,968	30,404	29,255	0.14	-3.78
Other Americas	46,777	35,897	52,543	57,547	56,256	0.27	-2.24
Other countries of the Americas	46,777	35,897	52,543	57,547	56,256	0.27	-2.24
EAST ASIA AND THE PACIFIC	11,639,663	10,218,702	13,042,486	14,725,917	15,291,630	72.28	3.84
North-East Asia	6,236,387	5,432,610	7,150,428	8,179,384	8,042,613	38.01	-1.67
Hong Kong, China	1,321,527	1,400,068	1,826,165	1,856,452	1,862,656	8.80	0.33
Japan	4,506,849	3,591,033	4,643,185	5,477,583	5,331,205	25.20	-2.67
Korea, Republic of	408,011	441,509	681,078	845,349	848,752	4.01	0.40
South-East Asia	2,734,813	2,403,631	3,079,044	3,426,579	3,479,959	16.45	1.56
Indonesia	499,814	345,119	390,018	444,196	482,136	2.28	8.54
Malaysia	499,243	483,919	662,618	780,447	804,501	3.80	3.08
Philippines	285,725	321,357	368,937	361,528	329,646	1.56	-8.82
Singapore	762,479	528,789	789,964	1,085,330	1,162,505	5.49	7.11
Thailand	346,215	318,284	327,965	309,848	314,608	1.49	1.54
Other countries of South-East Asia	341,337	406,163	539,542	445,230	386,563	1.83	-13.18
Australasia	267,598	241,444	346,787	355,261	350,867	1.66	-1.24
Australia	219,083	194,369	282,443	287,810	283,478	1.34	-1.51
New Zealand	48,515	47,075	64,344	67,451	67,389	0.32	-0.09
Other East Asia and the Pacific	2,400,865	2,141,017	2,466,227	2,764,693	3,418,191	16.16	23.64
Other countries of Asia	2,398,400	2,138,423	2,457,096	2,755,832	3,409,407	16.11	23.72
Other countries of Oceania	2,465	2,594	9,131	8,861	8,784	0.04	-0.87
EUROPE	1,027,500	832,011	1,175,559	1,224,965	1,223,153	5.78	-0.15
Northern Europe	268,485	229,981	303,431	303,127	282,736	1.34	-6.73
Sweden	32,621	25,196	39,139	38,975	41,031	0.19	5.28
United Kingdom	235,864	204,785	264,292	264,152	241,705	1.14	-8.50
Southern Europe	90,339	63,998	91,329	97,707	99,995	0.47	2.34
Greece	6,060	3,273	5,285	5,188	6,512	0.03	25.52
Italy	61,625	42,544	55,979	60,313	61,992	0.29	2.78

TAIWAN (PROVINCE OF CHINA)

6. Overnight stays of non-resident tourists in all types of accommodation establishments, by country of residence

	2002	2003	2004	2005	2006	Market share 06	% Change 06-05
Spain	22,654	18,181	30,065	32,206	31,491	0.15	-2.22
Western Europe	**567,880**	**460,298**	**634,919**	**657,846**	**669,942**	**3.17**	**1.84**
Austria	37,844	27,112	39,908	41,384	45,482	0.21	9.90
Belgium	19,617	18,665	26,025	25,741	25,422	0.12	-1.24
France	154,739	119,653	162,964	169,686	179,439	0.85	5.75
Germany	254,570	212,808	289,761	295,197	293,268	1.39	-0.65
Netherlands	61,209	48,061	70,270	75,982	76,699	0.36	0.94
Switzerland	39,901	33,999	45,991	49,856	49,632	0.23	-0.45
Other Europe	**100,796**	**77,734**	**145,880**	**166,285**	**170,480**	**0.81**	**2.52**
Other countries of Europe	100,796	77,734	145,880	166,285	170,480	0.81	2.52
MIDDLE EAST	**63,202**	**50,807**	**83,515**	**88,472**	**79,802**	**0.38**	**-9.80**
Middle East	**63,202**	**50,807**	**83,515**	**88,472**	**79,802**	**0.38**	**-9.80**
All countries of Middle East	63,202	50,807	83,515	88,472	79,802	0.38	-9.80
SOUTH ASIA	**111,513**	**98,841**	**127,883**	**145,755**	**156,928**	**0.74**	**7.67**
South Asia	**111,513**	**98,841**	**127,883**	**145,755**	**156,928**	**0.74**	**7.67**
India	111,513	98,841	127,883	145,755	156,928	0.74	7.67
REGION NOT SPECIFIED	**142,706**	**259,677**	**51,612**	**27,658**	**21,237**	**0.10**	**-23.22**
Not Specified	**142,706**	**259,677**	**51,612**	**27,658**	**21,237**	**0.10**	**-23.22**
Other countries of the World	142,706	259,677	51,612	27,658	21,237	0.10	-23.22

Source: World Tourism Organization (UNWTO)

THAILAND

1. Arrivals of non-resident tourists at national borders, by nationality

		2002	2003	2004	2005	2006	Market share 06	% Change 06-05
TOTAL	(*)	10,872,976	10,082,109	11,737,413	11,567,341	13,821,802	100.00	19.49
AFRICA		98,290	74,285	91,505	85,736	110,511	0.80	28.90
Southern Africa		39,262	35,560	43,068	35,748	47,228	0.34	32.11
South Africa		39,262	35,560	43,068	35,748	47,228	0.34	32.11
Other Africa		59,028	38,725	48,437	49,988	63,283	0.46	26.60
Other countries of Africa		59,028	38,725	48,437	49,988	63,283	0.46	26.60
AMERICAS		730,402	679,210	823,957	833,814	923,382	6.68	10.74
North America		691,021	652,826	785,128	796,276	877,352	6.35	10.18
Canada		135,668	137,963	157,622	156,618	183,094	1.32	16.90
United States		555,353	514,863	627,506	639,658	694,258	5.02	8.54
South America		12,358	9,132	13,092	12,500	16,168	0.12	29.34
Argentina		3,398	2,348	3,979	3,487	4,327	0.03	24.09
Brazil		8,960	6,784	9,113	9,013	11,841	0.09	31.38
Other Americas		27,023	17,252	25,737	25,038	29,862	0.22	19.27
Other countries of the Americas		27,023	17,252	25,737	25,038	29,862	0.22	19.27
EAST ASIA AND THE PACIFIC		6,663,355	6,139,091	7,118,876	6,913,420	8,273,506	59.86	19.67
North-East Asia		3,752,228	3,257,112	3,871,000	3,429,919	4,205,640	30.43	22.62
China		797,976	606,635	729,848	776,792	949,117	6.87	22.18
Taiwan (Province of China)		674,366	501,573	540,803	365,664	475,117	3.44	29.93
Hong Kong, China		335,816	411,242	489,171	274,402	376,636	2.72	37.26
Japan		1,239,421	1,042,349	1,212,213	1,196,654	1,311,987	9.49	9.64
Korea, Republic of		704,649	695,313	898,965	816,407	1,092,783	7.91	33.85
South-East Asia		2,474,523	2,504,231	2,735,747	2,948,919	3,389,342	24.52	14.94
Brunei Darussalam		10,129	8,863	9,345	9,499	9,418	0.07	-0.85
Myanmar		36,111	32,702	42,017	53,769	62,769	0.45	16.74
Cambodia		70,187	65,502	88,694	105,367	117,100	0.85	11.14
Indonesia		164,645	168,568	193,222	186,259	219,783	1.59	18.00
Lao People's Democratic Republic		90,717	100,747	111,916	203,748	276,207	2.00	35.56
Malaysia		1,332,355	1,354,295	1,404,929	1,373,946	1,591,328	11.51	15.82
Philippines		139,364	140,371	171,655	186,529	198,443	1.44	6.39
Singapore		546,796	515,630	578,027	650,559	687,160	4.97	5.63
Viet Nam		84,219	117,553	135,942	179,243	227,134	1.64	26.72
Australasia		425,218	361,259	483,213	514,247	648,333	4.69	26.07
Australia		351,508	291,872	399,291	428,521	549,547	3.98	28.24
New Zealand		73,710	69,387	83,922	85,726	98,786	0.71	15.23
Other East Asia and the Pacific		11,386	16,489	28,916	20,335	30,191	0.22	48.47
Other countries of Asia		9,495	15,015	27,213	18,359	27,262	0.20	48.49
Other countries of Oceania		1,891	1,474	1,703	1,976	2,929	0.02	48.23
EUROPE		2,749,683	2,587,034	2,947,518	2,947,226	3,612,287	26.13	22.57
Central/Eastern Europe		143,585	152,312	192,985	174,174	297,771	2.15	70.96
Russian Federation		70,692	89,329	115,064	102,783	187,658	1.36	82.58
Other countries Central/East Europ		72,893	62,983	77,921	71,391	110,113	0.80	54.24
Northern Europe		1,152,169	1,161,748	1,230,054	1,271,745	1,501,623	10.86	18.08
Denmark		90,480	82,828	93,400	103,787	128,037	0.93	23.37
Finland		66,772	66,513	75,430	85,632	110,502	0.80	29.04
Norway		74,607	71,885	79,195	85,551	106,314	0.77	24.27
Sweden		215,894	204,002	224,761	222,932	306,085	2.21	37.30
United Kingdom		704,416	736,520	757,268	773,843	850,685	6.15	9.93

THAILAND

1. Arrivals of non-resident tourists at national borders, by nationality

	2002	2003	2004	2005	2006	Market share 06	% Change 06-05
Southern Europe	176,724	129,052	178,309	171,372	220,078	1.59	28.42
Italy	129,293	97,526	126,399	120,237	150,420	1.09	25.10
Spain	47,431	31,526	51,910	51,135	69,658	0.50	36.22
Western Europe	1,062,294	976,655	1,112,426	1,108,042	1,304,231	9.44	17.71
Austria	54,020	53,646	59,797	58,978	76,106	0.55	29.04
Belgium	56,865	52,052	56,283	57,466	68,617	0.50	19.40
France	271,395	237,690	274,049	276,840	321,278	2.32	16.05
Germany	411,049	386,532	455,170	441,827	516,659	3.74	16.94
Netherlands	150,138	138,839	146,961	152,493	180,830	1.31	18.58
Switzerland	118,827	107,896	120,166	120,438	140,741	1.02	16.86
East Mediterranean Europe	98,691	69,837	96,285	98,380	121,508	0.88	23.51
Israel	98,691	69,837	96,285	98,380	121,508	0.88	23.51
Other Europe	116,220	97,430	137,459	123,513	167,076	1.21	35.27
Other countries of Europe	116,220	97,430	137,459	123,513	167,076	1.21	35.27
MIDDLE EAST	147,131	117,792	176,154	194,182	270,908	1.96	39.51
Middle East	147,131	117,792	176,154	194,182	270,908	1.96	39.51
Kuwait	25,251	19,977	30,938	29,773	33,934	0.25	13.98
Saudi Arabia	6,886	4,849	7,202	10,474	20,804	0.15	98.63
United Arab Emirates	26,565	22,914	41,175	48,802	69,509	0.50	42.43
Egypt	7,719	5,264	8,545	7,887	11,882	0.09	50.65
Other countries of Middle East	80,710	64,788	88,294	97,246	134,779	0.98	38.60
SOUTH ASIA	410,206	407,041	492,693	542,558	631,208	4.57	16.34
South Asia	410,206	407,041	492,693	542,558	631,208	4.57	16.34
Bangladesh	35,928	53,421	54,178	42,739	40,281	0.29	-5.75
Sri Lanka	31,649	38,483	33,722	38,740	46,557	0.34	20.18
India	280,641	253,752	332,387	381,471	459,795	3.33	20.53
Nepal	19,933	19,909	20,356	23,081	21,180	0.15	-8.24
Pakistan	31,246	31,315	38,809	42,069	46,367	0.34	10.22
Other countries of South Asia	10,809	10,161	13,241	14,458	17,028	0.12	17.78
REGION NOT SPECIFIED	73,909	77,656	86,710	50,405			
Not Specified	73,909	77,656	86,710	50,405			
Nationals Residing Abroad	73,909	77,656	86,710	50,405			

Source: World Tourism Organization (UNWTO)

THAILAND

1. Arrivals of non-resident tourists at national borders, by country of residence

		2002	2003	2004	2005	2006	Market share 06	% Change 06-05
TOTAL	(*)	10,872,976	10,082,109	11,737,413	11,567,341	13,821,802	100.00	19.49
AFRICA		89,153	67,121	82,711	72,875	96,117	0.70	31.89
East Africa		19,753	13,403	19,811	21,346	28,576	0.21	33.87
Burundi		115	59	90	64	71		10.94
Comoros		2	1	1	3			
Ethiopia		3,757	1,039	2,150	1,488	2,527	0.02	69.83
Eritrea		3	3			2		
Djibouti		93	88	115	84	84		
Kenya		3,310	2,909	3,813	3,534	4,728	0.03	33.79
Madagascar		632	701	2,449	5,088	7,186	0.05	41.23
Malawi		352	202	289	120	160		33.33
Mauritius		3,611	2,478	3,179	3,444	3,169	0.02	-7.98
Mozambique		351	201	285	257	407		58.37
Reunion		224	2	21	76	123		61.84
Rwanda		106	145	97	91	195		114.29
Seychelles		706	528	600	1,168	2,592	0.02	121.92
Somalia		207	113	98	76	99		30.26
Zimbabwe		992	815	909	662	763	0.01	15.26
Uganda		1,503	1,235	1,742	1,908	2,060	0.01	7.97
United Republic of Tanzania		2,545	2,013	2,516	2,194	2,605	0.02	18.73
Zambia		1,244	871	1,457	1,089	1,805	0.01	65.75
Central Africa		3,694	2,188	2,053	2,032	2,396	0.02	17.91
Angola		371	348	316	309			
Cameroon		1,570	551	612	622	1,130	0.01	81.67
Central African Republic		6	5	13	1	2		100.00
Chad		23	18	20	18	22		22.22
Congo		1,433	959	960	963	1,098	0.01	14.02
Democratic Republic of the Congo		17	17	15	14			
Equatorial Guinea			1	1	5	6		20.00
Gabon		273	288	116	98	130		32.65
Sao Tome and Principe		1	1		2	8		300.00
North Africa		5,790	3,780	5,347	4,649	5,945	0.04	27.88
Algeria		1,010	906	981	984	999	0.01	1.52
Morocco		2,928	1,614	3,011	2,274	3,367	0.02	48.07
Western Sahara		1		1	6			
Sudan		488	497	628	681	913	0.01	34.07
Tunisia		1,363	763	726	704	666		-5.40
Southern Africa		39,083	35,692	44,043	34,242	44,793	0.32	30.81
Botswana		854	737	1,113	795	693	0.01	-12.83
Lesotho		60	80	91	51	46		-9.80
Namibia		254	261	251	191	231		20.94
South Africa		37,721	34,522	40,732	33,120	43,444	0.31	31.17
Swaziland		194	92	1,856	85	379		345.88
West Africa		20,444	12,031	11,396	10,553	14,407	0.10	36.52
Cape Verde		49	11	42	21	9		-57.14
Benin		311	222	190	137	262		91.24
Gambia		663	507	436	441	451		2.27
Ghana		1,334	1,076	1,597	1,992	2,644	0.02	32.73
Guinea		4,344	2,832	2,073	1,880	1,632	0.01	-13.19
Cote D'Ivoire		2,094	589	749	275	351		27.64
Liberia		1,398	419	558	398	552		38.69
Mali		4,196	1,994	1,463	1,464	1,653	0.01	12.91
Mauritania		211	145	152	120	3,169	0.02	2,540.83

THAILAND

1. Arrivals of non-resident tourists at national borders, by country of residence

	2002	2003	2004	2005	2006	Market share 06	% Change 06-05
Niger	305	130	128	101	57		-43.56
Nigeria	1,950	2,026	1,633	1,503	1,484	0.01	-1.26
Senegal	2,440	1,504	1,802	1,751	1,548	0.01	-11.59
Sierra Leone	270	93	75	103	104		0.97
Togo	737	415	377	242	390		61.16
Burkina Faso	142	68	121	125	101		-19.20
Other Africa	**389**	**27**	**61**	**53**			
Other countries of Africa	389	27	61	53			
AMERICAS	**640,142**	**576,587**	**692,792**	**739,703**	**825,079**	**5.97**	**11.54**
Caribbean	**1,335**	**1,046**	**1,103**	**1,960**	**985**	**0.01**	**-49.74**
Antigua and Barbuda	5	2	8	14	8		-42.86
Bahamas	194	148	161	718	79		-89.00
Barbados	40	29	42	46	54		17.39
Bermuda	99	142	81	119	53		-55.46
Cayman Islands	14	1					
Cuba	230	357	163	190	176		-7.37
Dominican Republic	170	95	152	226	148		-34.51
Grenada	9	4	5	4			
Guadeloupe	22	36	75	43	23		-46.51
Haiti	29	10	40	27	31		14.81
Jamaica	158	76	138	168	121		-27.98
Martinique	12	13	14	11	3		-72.73
Curacao	4	1	5	1	3		200.00
Puerto Rico	31	21	43	45	53		17.78
Saint Kitts and Nevis	4		1				
Saint Lucia	2		3	5			
Saint Vincent and the Grenadines			3	168			
Trinidad and Tobago	310	108	166	172	233		35.47
United States Virgin Islands	2	3	3	3			
Central America	**1,238**	**877**	**1,252**	**1,192**	**1,291**	**0.01**	**8.31**
Belize	165	159	99	67	62		-7.46
Costa Rica	425	329	536	466	596		27.90
El Salvador	126	59	71	103	75		-27.18
Guatemala	188	119	189	169	199		17.75
Honduras	58	38	108	50	56		12.00
Nicaragua	20	24	33	65	44		-32.31
Panama	256	149	216	272	259		-4.78
North America	**622,564**	**563,467**	**674,357**	**719,865**	**800,568**	**5.79**	**11.21**
Canada	101,369	97,616	107,293	125,310	149,924	1.08	19.64
Greenland	60	67	46	47	43		-8.51
Mexico	11,159	5,893	9,866	8,998	9,927	0.07	10.32
United States	509,841	459,862	557,098	585,476	640,674	4.64	9.43
Other countries of North America	135	29	54	34			
South America	**15,005**	**11,197**	**16,080**	**16,686**	**22,235**	**0.16**	**33.26**
Argentina	2,380	1,585	3,018	2,690	3,814	0.03	41.78
Bolivia	142	128	201	197	222		12.69
Brazil	5,535	4,656	6,270	6,609	8,926	0.06	35.06
Chile	2,052	1,580	2,383	1,990	2,850	0.02	43.22
Colombia	1,649	998	1,663	2,092	2,691	0.02	28.63
Ecuador	394	214	439	366	435		18.85
Guyana	14	12	49	29	29		
Paraguay	158	41	55	39	47		20.51
Peru	749	598	885	1,035	1,320	0.01	27.54
Suriname	101	44	80	51	62		21.57

THAILAND

1. Arrivals of non-resident tourists at national borders, by country of residence

	2002	2003	2004	2005	2006	Market share 06	% Change 06-05
Uruguay	909	293	292	384	492		28.13
Venezuela	921	1,048	741	1,204	1,347	0.01	11.88
Other countries of South America	1		4				
EAST ASIA AND THE PACIFIC	**6,955,363**	**6,510,375**	**7,500,966**	**7,194,866**	**8,568,558**	**61.99**	**19.09**
North-East Asia	**3,915,427**	**3,519,620**	**4,106,843**	**3,592,142**	**4,382,090**	**31.70**	**21.99**
China	763,139	624,214	779,070	761,904	1,033,305	7.48	35.62
Taiwan (Province of China)	673,652	521,941	556,341	375,299	472,851	3.42	25.99
Hong Kong, China	526,138	649,920	656,941	438,519	463,339	3.35	5.66
Japan	1,222,270	1,014,513	1,182,067	1,181,913	1,293,313	9.36	9.43
Korea, Dem. People's Republic of	53	43	122	48	26		-45.83
Korea, Republic of	716,725	694,297	909,667	815,814	1,101,499	7.97	35.02
Macao, China	12,031	12,966	20,872	16,771	15,224	0.11	-9.22
Mongolia	1,419	1,726	1,763	1,874	2,533	0.02	35.17
South-East Asia	**2,614,627**	**2,646,003**	**2,926,264**	**3,099,572**	**3,556,395**	**25.73**	**14.74**
Brunei Darussalam	13,755	17,244	13,905	15,124	12,662	0.09	-16.28
Myanmar	42,266	37,180	45,963	56,466	67,054	0.49	18.75
Cambodia	79,219	73,868	98,551	112,477	125,336	0.91	11.43
Indonesia	164,994	167,414	201,303	186,687	218,167	1.58	16.86
Lao People's Democratic Republic	94,052	104,468	116,357	208,097	282,239	2.04	35.63
Malaysia	1,296,109	1,338,624	1,388,981	1,341,535	1,578,632	11.42	17.67
Philippines	142,940	143,015	173,218	188,404	202,305	1.46	7.38
Timor-Leste			5	3			
Singapore	683,296	629,103	732,180	795,322	818,162	5.92	2.87
Viet Nam	97,996	135,087	155,801	195,457	251,838	1.82	28.85
Australasia	**420,300**	**341,366**	**463,992**	**498,945**	**625,193**	**4.52**	**25.30**
Australia	355,529	281,361	393,040	421,594	538,490	3.90	27.73
New Zealand	64,771	60,005	70,952	77,351	86,703	0.63	12.09
Melanesia	**2,523**	**2,063**	**2,213**	**1,990**	**1,587**	**0.01**	**-20.25**
Solomon Islands	74	44	150	48	57		18.75
Fiji	813	666	701	733	629		-14.19
New Caledonia	1,015	894	904	622	418		-32.80
Vanuatu	135	101	82	103	58		-43.69
Papua New Guinea	486	358	376	484	425		-12.19
Micronesia	**420**	**307**	**371**	**698**	**329**		**-52.87**
Kiribati	27	32	48	17	7		-58.82
Guam	281	180	178	252	205		-18.65
Nauru	77	58	65	96	84		-12.50
Northern Mariana Islands	12	14	49	13	8		-38.46
Micronesia (Federated States of)	7	3	9	6	5		-16.67
Marshall Islands				298			
Palau	16	20	22	16	20		25.00
Polynesia	**376**	**273**	**470**	**390**	**172**		**-55.90**
Cook Islands	7		2	12	4		-66.67
French Polynesia	165	69	80	175			
Tonga	88	81	242	120	87		-27.50
Tuvalu	6	3	1	4	1		-75.00
Samoa	110	120	145	79	80		1.27
Other East Asia and the Pacific	**1,690**	**743**	**813**	**1,129**	**2,792**	**0.02**	**147.30**
Other countries of Asia	1,690	743	813	1,129	2,792	0.02	147.30
EUROPE	**2,549,488**	**2,320,807**	**2,706,062**	**2,778,693**	**3,439,010**	**24.88**	**23.76**
Central/Eastern Europe	**132,240**	**147,757**	**189,706**	**171,577**	**287,597**	**2.08**	**67.62**

THAILAND

1. Arrivals of non-resident tourists at national borders, by country of residence

	2002	2003	2004	2005	2006	Market share 06	% Change 06-05
Azerbaijan	252	175	369	345	419		21.45
Armenia	242	178	107	145	193		33.10
Bulgaria	1,283	1,264	1,578	1,652	2,357	0.02	42.68
Belarus	781	755	979	676	1,795	0.01	165.53
Czech Republic/Slovakia	13	10	4	13	15		15.38
Czech Republic	13,020	12,382	12,980	10,316	13,128	0.09	27.26
Estonia	2,037	1,884	2,467	2,453	3,735	0.03	52.26
Georgia	146	245	156	128	126		-1.56
Hungary	8,048	9,258	11,719	11,240	16,328	0.12	45.27
Kazakhstan	5,058	5,131	7,031	5,000	10,537	0.08	110.74
Kyrgyzstan	800	611	379	693	391		-43.58
Latvia	1,080	925	1,248	1,639	3,248	0.02	98.17
Lithuania	683	575	951	887	1,639	0.01	84.78
Republic of Moldova	176	115	234	248	230		-7.26
Poland	9,378	8,524	10,618	8,308	12,945	0.09	55.81
Romania	2,333	2,148	2,051	2,180	3,048	0.02	39.82
Russian Federation	68,978	90,665	118,895	107,017	190,834	1.38	78.32
Slovakia	2,649	2,037	3,132	2,397	3,096	0.02	29.16
Tajikistan	132	123	116	192	160		-16.67
Turkmenistan	2,670	346	578	552	879	0.01	59.24
Ukraine	5,446	7,738	11,262	12,018	18,434	0.13	53.39
Uzbekistan	7,035	2,668	2,848	3,478	4,060	0.03	16.73
Other countries Central/East Europ			4				
Northern Europe	**1,054,785**	**1,005,331**	**1,137,206**	**1,218,491**	**1,450,161**	**10.49**	**19.01**
Denmark	84,617	78,587	87,603	98,554	124,151	0.90	25.97
Finland	64,115	62,509	71,476	80,558	112,006	0.81	39.04
Iceland	1,328	1,067	1,292	1,790	2,281	0.02	27.43
Ireland	39,100	38,030	49,870	50,006	56,994	0.41	13.97
Norway	74,947	70,694	77,009	84,308	101,920	0.74	20.89
Sweden	220,866	209,444	221,277	222,297	307,284	2.22	38.23
United Kingdom	569,812	545,000	628,679	680,978	745,525	5.39	9.48
Southern Europe	**208,090**	**146,033**	**199,563**	**193,391**	**253,891**	**1.84**	**31.28**
Albania	354	134	161	161	351		118.01
Andorra	128	76	129	151	306		102.65
Bosnia and Herzegovina	148	103	120	185	180		-2.70
Croatia	1,364	1,155	1,129	1,272	1,334	0.01	4.87
Greece	14,050	10,840	14,847	13,220	16,424	0.12	24.24
Holy See	12	16	11	19			
Italy	126,222	92,656	118,946	113,987	143,343	1.04	25.75
Malta	1,068	721	873	739	878	0.01	18.81
Portugal	11,799	4,598	8,028	7,276	11,526	0.08	58.41
San Marino	67	865	38	63	72		14.29
Slovenia	3,104	1,917	2,056	2,847	3,960	0.03	39.09
Spain	48,491	31,850	52,299	52,309	73,820	0.53	41.12
TFYR of Macedonia	190	144	174	122	217		77.87
Serbia and Montenegro	1,093	958	752	1,040	1,480	0.01	42.31
Western Europe	**1,031,767**	**941,221**	**1,059,824**	**1,081,525**	**1,297,393**	**9.39**	**19.96**
Austria	48,067	46,717	51,229	53,858	76,698	0.55	42.41
Belgium	56,179	50,772	53,321	55,730	66,835	0.48	19.93
France	253,463	219,227	250,995	260,704	319,910	2.31	22.71
Germany	403,240	378,642	438,238	436,552	507,942	3.67	16.35
Liechtenstein	393	281	565	440	922	0.01	109.55
Luxembourg	2,767	2,347	2,550	2,616	3,683	0.03	40.79
Monaco	461	430	668	466	1,490	0.01	219.74
Netherlands	140,966	129,211	135,515	145,350	174,266	1.26	19.89

THAILAND

1. Arrivals of non-resident tourists at national borders, by country of residence

	2002	2003	2004	2005	2006	Market share 06	% Change 06-05
Switzerland	126,217	113,581	126,670	125,694	145,647	1.05	15.87
Other countries of Western Europe	14	13	73	115			
East Mediterranean Europe	**122,606**	**80,460**	**119,755**	**113,699**	**149,968**	**1.09**	**31.90**
Cyprus	3,813	1,807	3,369	2,380	2,868	0.02	20.50
Israel	98,629	64,650	89,715	92,126	117,649	0.85	27.70
Turkey	20,164	14,003	26,671	19,193	29,451	0.21	53.45
Other Europe		**5**	**8**	**10**			
Other countries of Europe		5	8	10			
MIDDLE EAST	**151,180**	**118,339**	**172,699**	**178,718**	**239,171**	**1.73**	**33.83**
Middle East	**151,180**	**118,339**	**172,699**	**178,718**	**239,171**	**1.73**	**33.83**
Bahrain	10,698	9,815	13,491	11,249	11,292	0.08	0.38
Palestine	313	250	225	356	471		32.30
Iraq	4,078	953	412	1,056	1,237	0.01	17.14
Jordan	5,116	4,261	6,257	5,893	6,986	0.05	18.55
Kuwait	28,448	21,264	33,191	31,966	38,885	0.28	21.64
Lebanon	4,750	3,331	4,816	5,084	5,012	0.04	-1.42
Libyan Arab Jamahiriya	1,534	1,181	1,151	1,529	1,513	0.01	-1.05
Oman	18,121	14,104	19,397	22,441	33,305	0.24	48.41
Qatar	6,034	4,458	6,963	8,027	11,463	0.08	42.81
Saudi Arabia	14,254	9,886	11,658	13,152	23,870	0.17	81.49
Syrian Arab Republic	2,267	1,675	2,077	2,317	3,702	0.03	59.78
United Arab Emirates	43,549	39,317	61,093	65,081	87,006	0.63	33.69
Egypt	7,489	5,209	8,673	7,798	11,546	0.08	48.06
Yemen	4,529	2,634	3,126	2,716	2,883	0.02	6.15
Other countries of Middle East		1	169	53			
SOUTH ASIA	**413,741**	**411,224**	**495,473**	**552,081**	**653,867**	**4.73**	**18.44**
South Asia	**413,741**	**411,224**	**495,473**	**552,081**	**653,867**	**4.73**	**18.44**
Afghanistan	349	507	548	681	622		-8.66
Bangladesh	41,145	57,651	59,413	46,187	44,081	0.32	-4.56
Bhutan	6,428	6,069	7,316	8,180	8,763	0.06	7.13
Sri Lanka	32,441	38,309	34,226	39,348	47,448	0.34	20.59
India	253,110	230,316	300,163	352,766	429,732	3.11	21.82
Iran, Islamic Republic of	22,996	20,889	27,157	33,203	48,631	0.35	46.47
Maldives	4,369	4,192	5,505	6,169	6,263	0.05	1.52
Nepal	23,001	22,397	23,512	24,545	23,205	0.17	-5.46
Pakistan	29,902	30,894	37,633	41,002	45,122	0.33	10.05
REGION NOT SPECIFIED	**73,909**	**77,656**	**86,710**	**50,405**			
Not Specified	**73,909**	**77,656**	**86,710**	**50,405**			
Nationals Residing Abroad	73,909	77,656	86,710	50,405			

Source: World Tourism Organization (UNWTO)

THAILAND

3. Arrivals of non-resident tourists in hotels and similar establishments, by country of residence

	2002	2003	2004	2005	2006	Market share 06	% Change 06-05
TOTAL			11,338,252	10,653,623	12,818,616	100.00	20.32
AFRICA			81,064	68,272	88,842	0.69	30.13
Southern Africa			40,263	31,170	41,053	0.32	31.71
South Africa			40,263	31,170	41,053	0.32	31.71
Other Africa			40,801	37,102	47,789	0.37	28.80
Other countries of Africa			40,801	37,102	47,789	0.37	28.80
AMERICAS			662,649	642,957	723,082	5.64	12.46
North America			635,528	615,539	690,498	5.39	12.18
Canada			103,602	110,978	132,895	1.04	19.75
United States			531,926	504,561	557,603	4.35	10.51
South America			8,571	8,771	11,730	0.09	33.74
Argentina			2,719	2,419	3,657	0.03	51.18
Brazil			5,852	6,352	8,073	0.06	27.09
Other Americas			18,550	18,647	20,854	0.16	11.84
Other countries of the Americas			18,550	18,647	20,854	0.16	11.84
EAST ASIA AND THE PACIFIC			7,304,265	6,756,966	8,047,811	62.78	19.10
North-East Asia			4,029,717	3,402,378	4,156,197	32.42	22.16
China			769,824	729,437	990,939	7.73	35.85
Taiwan (Province of China)			549,043	353,241	448,412	3.50	26.94
Hong Kong, China			651,780	421,189	444,137	3.46	5.45
Japan			1,158,351	1,106,187	1,205,437	9.40	8.97
Korea, Republic of			900,719	792,324	1,067,272	8.33	34.70
South-East Asia			2,797,631	2,878,693	3,294,543	25.70	14.45
Brunei Darussalam			13,617	14,473	11,944	0.09	-17.47
Myanmar			42,756	46,049	54,275	0.42	17.86
Cambodia			90,857	101,356	108,881	0.85	7.42
Indonesia			196,000	175,657	203,781	1.59	16.01
Lao People's Democratic Republic			108,539	189,499	261,238	2.04	37.86
Malaysia			1,307,773	1,260,219	1,483,465	11.57	17.71
Philippines			166,653	163,684	174,606	1.36	6.67
Singapore			719,468	745,134	763,983	5.96	2.53
Viet Nam			151,968	182,622	232,370	1.81	27.24
Australasia			450,890	454,021	574,801	4.48	26.60
Australia			382,035	384,617	495,939	3.87	28.94
New Zealand			68,855	69,404	78,862	0.62	13.63
Other East Asia and the Pacific			26,027	21,874	22,270	0.17	1.81
Other countries of Asia			23,194	19,217	20,433	0.16	6.33
Other countries of Oceania			2,833	2,657	1,837	0.01	-30.86
EUROPE			2,642,062	2,504,000	3,122,948	24.36	24.72
Central/Eastern Europe			185,569	164,336	272,299	2.12	65.70
Russian Federation			116,989	104,285	184,065	1.44	76.50
Other countries Central/East Europ			68,580	60,051	88,234	0.69	46.93
Northern Europe			1,058,972	1,040,315	1,243,221	9.70	19.50
Denmark			85,014	89,201	112,376	0.88	25.98
Finland			70,321	75,085	106,216	0.83	41.46
Norway			75,625	75,336	89,797	0.70	19.20
Sweden			216,577	201,873	281,642	2.20	39.51

THAILAND

3. Arrivals of non-resident tourists in hotels and similar establishments, by country of residence

	2002	2003	2004	2005	2006	Market share 06	% Change 06-05
United Kingdom			611,435	598,820	653,190	5.10	9.08
Southern Europe			**166,951**	**151,506**	**200,762**	**1.57**	**32.51**
Italy			115,954	103,168	131,620	1.03	27.58
Spain			50,997	48,338	69,142	0.54	43.04
Western Europe			**1,031,089**	**965,544**	**1,167,381**	**9.11**	**20.90**
Austria			49,943	49,449	69,825	0.54	41.21
Belgium			51,870	48,994	60,756	0.47	24.01
France			244,388	230,022	285,487	2.23	24.11
Germany			429,021	394,860	462,632	3.61	17.16
Netherlands			132,022	129,850	157,572	1.23	21.35
Switzerland			123,845	112,369	131,109	1.02	16.68
East Mediterranean Europe			**87,872**	**86,937**	**112,838**	**0.88**	**29.79**
Israel			87,872	86,937	112,838	0.88	29.79
Other Europe			**111,609**	**95,362**	**126,447**	**0.99**	**32.60**
Other countries of Europe			111,609	95,362	126,447	0.99	32.60
MIDDLE EAST			**196,797**	**203,961**	**276,719**	**2.16**	**35.67**
Middle East			**196,797**	**203,961**	**276,719**	**2.16**	**35.67**
Kuwait			32,693	31,063	37,761	0.29	21.56
Saudi Arabia			11,454	12,512	23,089	0.18	84.53
United Arab Emirates			60,341	62,458	83,157	0.65	33.14
Egypt			8,584	7,452	10,898	0.09	46.24
Other countries of Middle East			83,725	90,476	121,814	0.95	34.64
SOUTH ASIA			**451,415**	**477,467**	**559,214**	**4.36**	**17.12**
South Asia			**451,415**	**477,467**	**559,214**	**4.36**	**17.12**
Bangladesh			57,844	42,991	40,606	0.32	-5.55
Sri Lanka			33,327	37,272	45,150	0.35	21.14
India			288,127	323,748	397,100	3.10	22.66
Nepal			22,685	22,015	20,826	0.16	-5.40
Pakistan			36,774	38,124	42,024	0.33	10.23
Other countries of South Asia			12,658	13,317	13,508	0.11	1.43

Source: World Tourism Organization (UNWTO)

THAILAND

5. Overnight stays of non-resident tourists in hotels and similar establishments, by nationality

	2002	2003	2004	2005	2006	Market share 06	% Change 06-05
TOTAL		81,931,465	94,665,934				
AFRICA		673,884	818,633				
Southern Africa		284,104	362,597				
South Africa		284,104	362,597				
Other Africa		389,780	456,036				
Other countries of Africa		389,780	456,036				
AMERICAS		6,933,253	8,130,466				
North America		6,676,362	7,791,319				
Canada		1,463,850	1,610,388				
United States		5,212,512	6,180,931				
South America		94,997	129,497				
Argentina		28,419	42,259				
Brazil		66,578	87,238				
Other Americas		161,894	209,650				
Other countries of the Americas		161,894	209,650				
EAST ASIA AND THE PACIFIC		34,845,007	40,510,704				
North-East Asia		19,608,857	22,454,145				
China		3,962,170	4,659,613				
Taiwan (Province of China)		3,156,836	3,465,006				
Hong Kong, China		1,763,868	2,057,139				
Japan		7,251,406	8,176,218				
Korea, Republic of		3,474,577	4,096,169				
South-East Asia		11,678,098	13,310,285				
Brunei Darussalam		38,369	41,125				
Myanmar		424,402	499,647				
Cambodia		375,401	469,510				
Indonesia		752,860	848,209				
Lao People's Democratic Republic		1,229,796	1,222,077				
Malaysia		4,886,776	5,709,098				
Philippines		984,096	1,166,407				
Singapore		2,312,057	2,561,083				
Viet Nam		674,341	793,129				
Australasia		3,418,154	4,504,284				
Australia		2,808,661	3,772,649				
New Zealand		609,493	731,635				
Other East Asia and the Pacific		139,898	241,990				
Other countries of Asia		126,069	227,047				
Other countries of Oceania		13,829	14,943				
EUROPE		35,357,911	40,169,138				
Central/Eastern Europe		1,817,052	2,338,590				
Russian Federation		1,041,545	1,401,896				
Other countries Central/East Europ		775,507	936,694				
Northern Europe		15,466,717	16,806,254				
Denmark		1,202,335	1,358,429				
Finland		930,620	1,057,768				
Norway		1,130,759	1,245,903				
Sweden		3,148,997	3,487,642				

THAILAND

5. Overnight stays of non-resident tourists in hotels and similar establishments, by nationality

	2002	2003	2004	2005	2006	Market share 06	% Change 06-05
United Kingdom		9,054,006	9,656,512				
Southern Europe		**1,591,698**	**2,085,503**				
Italy		1,288,173	1,610,055				
Spain		303,525	475,448				
Western Europe		**14,478,306**	**16,190,275**				
Austria		802,341	880,673				
Belgium		746,745	808,351				
France		2,887,377	3,297,512				
Germany		6,148,715	7,080,167				
Netherlands		2,183,587	2,249,413				
Switzerland		1,709,541	1,874,159				
East Mediterranean Europe		**937,799**	**1,301,499**				
Israel		937,799	1,301,499				
Other Europe		**1,066,339**	**1,447,017**				
Other countries of Europe		1,066,339	1,447,017				
MIDDLE EAST		**1,132,775**	**1,634,060**				
Middle East		**1,132,775**	**1,634,060**				
Kuwait		221,730	307,482				
Saudi Arabia		52,478	77,567				
United Arab Emirates		231,144	430,565				
Egypt		45,197	64,159				
Other countries of Middle East		582,226	754,287				
SOUTH ASIA		**2,988,635**	**3,402,933**				
South Asia		**2,988,635**	**3,402,933**				
Bangladesh		363,405	354,683				
Sri Lanka		193,697	187,690				
India		1,988,758	2,356,107				
Nepal		158,783	154,013				
Pakistan		215,453	260,202				
Other countries of South Asia		68,539	90,238				

Source: World Tourism Organization (UNWTO)

THE FORMER YUGOSLAV REP. OF MACEDONIA

3. Arrivals of non-resident tourists in hotels and similar establishments, by nationality

	2002	2003	2004	2005	2006	Market share 06	% Change 06-05
TOTAL	115,391	148,508	153,644	181,484	185,185	100.00	2.04
AMERICAS	7,704	8,209	8,231	8,193	8,962	4.84	9.39
North America	7,704	8,209	8,231	8,193	8,962	4.84	9.39
Canada	765	923	700	840	889	0.48	5.83
United States	6,939	7,286	7,531	7,353	8,073	4.36	9.79
EAST ASIA AND THE PACIFIC	1,540	2,289	2,125	2,635	3,238	1.75	22.88
North-East Asia	584	1,050	927	1,027	1,201	0.65	16.94
Japan	584	1,050	927	1,027	1,201	0.65	16.94
Australasia	956	1,239	1,198	1,608	2,037	1.10	26.68
Australia	832	1,146	1,102	1,473	1,815	0.98	23.22
New Zealand	124	93	96	135	222	0.12	64.44
EUROPE	103,525	134,549	139,822	167,184	169,929	91.76	1.64
Central/Eastern Europe	18,325	20,705	18,293	24,581	24,951	13.47	1.51
Bulgaria	10,510	12,375	11,110	15,894	15,548	8.40	-2.18
Belarus	153	156	116	184	118	0.06	-35.87
Czech Republic	921	1,129	883	1,182	1,794	0.97	51.78
Hungary	1,973	2,171	1,270	1,554	1,757	0.95	13.06
Poland	1,043	1,007	1,174	1,119	1,193	0.64	6.61
Romania	1,198	1,304	1,079	1,643	1,558	0.84	-5.17
Russian Federation	1,227	1,310	1,424	1,904	1,815	0.98	-4.67
Slovakia	481	558	552	520	575	0.31	10.58
Ukraine	819	695	685	581	593	0.32	2.07
Northern Europe	8,142	9,420	9,186	10,535	11,259	6.08	6.87
Denmark	780	1,002	1,328	1,151	976	0.53	-15.20
Finland	679	760	755	808	850	0.46	5.20
Iceland	152	157	117	125	136	0.07	8.80
Ireland	522	471	503	646	944	0.51	46.13
Norway	1,049	1,104	955	1,030	1,244	0.67	20.78
Sweden	1,059	1,464	1,540	1,799	1,890	1.02	5.06
United Kingdom	3,901	4,462	3,988	4,976	5,219	2.82	4.88
Southern Europe	56,107	78,664	86,739	102,862	102,307	55.25	-0.54
Albania	8,314	11,338	12,470	15,392	14,402	7.78	-6.43
Bosnia and Herzegovina	1,737	2,450	3,118	3,546	3,783	2.04	6.68
Croatia	3,647	4,754	5,767	6,770	7,976	4.31	17.81
Greece	14,200	26,514	28,661	31,504	28,868	15.59	-8.37
Italy	3,025	3,558	3,537	4,160	4,473	2.42	7.52
Portugal	308	412	317	355	503	0.27	41.69
Slovenia	3,576	4,094	4,848	6,754	8,156	4.40	20.76
Spain	833	1,354	880	1,169	1,114	0.60	-4.70
Serbia and Montenegro	20,467	24,190	27,141	33,212	33,032	17.84	-0.54
Western Europe	14,200	17,128	16,586	19,115	20,539	11.09	7.45
Austria	1,836	2,511	2,433	2,604	3,340	1.80	28.26
Belgium	947	1,196	941	1,090	1,279	0.69	17.34
France	2,508	3,429	2,785	2,881	2,987	1.61	3.68
Germany	5,986	6,159	6,337	6,762	7,412	4.00	9.61
Netherlands	1,973	2,380	2,524	3,995	3,653	1.97	-8.56
Switzerland	950	1,453	1,566	1,783	1,868	1.01	4.77
East Mediterranean Europe	5,249	6,024	6,686	7,953	8,239	4.45	3.60
Israel	429	526	676	1,158	1,066	0.58	-7.94
Turkey	4,820	5,498	6,010	6,795	7,173	3.87	5.56

THE FORMER YUGOSLAV REP. OF MACEDONIA

3. Arrivals of non-resident tourists in hotels and similar establishments, by nationality

	2002	2003	2004	2005	2006	Market share 06	% Change 06-05
Other Europe	**1,502**	**2,608**	**2,332**	**2,138**	**2,634**	**1.42**	**23.20**
Other countries of Europe	1,502	2,608	2,332	2,138	2,634	1.42	23.20
REGION NOT SPECIFIED	**2,622**	**3,461**	**3,466**	**3,472**	**3,056**	**1.65**	**-11.98**
Not Specified	**2,622**	**3,461**	**3,466**	**3,472**	**3,056**	**1.65**	**-11.98**
Other countries of the World	2,622	3,461	3,466	3,472	3,056	1.65	-11.98

Source: World Tourism Organization (UNWTO)

THE FORMER YUGOSLAV REP. OF MACEDONIA

4. Arrivals of non-resident tourists in all types of accommodation establishments, by nationality

	2002	2003	2004	2005	2006	Market share 06	% Change 06-05
TOTAL	122,861	157,692	165,306	197,216	202,357	100.00	2.61
AMERICAS	7,773	8,373	8,362	8,439	9,181	4.54	8.79
North America	7,773	8,373	8,362	8,439	9,181	4.54	8.79
Canada	776	970	704	851	906	0.45	6.46
United States	6,997	7,403	7,658	7,588	8,275	4.09	9.05
EAST ASIA AND THE PACIFIC	1,566	2,362	2,143	2,747	3,490	1.72	27.05
North-East Asia	594	1,076	931	1,041	1,212	0.60	16.43
Japan	594	1,076	931	1,041	1,212	0.60	16.43
Australasia	972	1,286	1,212	1,706	2,278	1.13	33.53
Australia	844	1,187	1,116	1,563	2,014	1.00	28.85
New Zealand	128	99	96	143	264	0.13	84.62
EUROPE	110,878	143,387	151,215	182,534	186,519	92.17	2.18
Central/Eastern Europe	19,754	22,608	19,720	26,772	27,760	13.72	3.69
Bulgaria	11,703	14,147	12,156	17,462	17,421	8.61	-0.23
Belarus	154	157	197	188	127	0.06	-32.45
Czech Republic	927	1,155	905	1,290	2,108	1.04	63.41
Hungary	1,985	2,173	1,320	1,582	1,835	0.91	15.99
Poland	1,095	1,029	1,233	1,254	1,332	0.66	6.22
Romania	1,255	1,330	1,144	1,733	1,662	0.82	-4.10
Russian Federation	1,246	1,352	1,487	2,092	1,998	0.99	-4.49
Slovakia	481	559	554	554	636	0.31	14.80
Ukraine	908	706	724	617	641	0.32	3.89
Northern Europe	8,204	9,585	9,408	10,788	11,563	5.71	7.18
Denmark	786	1,048	1,379	1,165	1,018	0.50	-12.62
Finland	683	768	782	835	885	0.44	5.99
Iceland	153	159	118	125	137	0.07	9.60
Ireland	525	482	522	659	991	0.49	50.38
Norway	1,059	1,108	962	1,051	1,277	0.63	21.50
Sweden	1,082	1,503	1,596	1,854	1,937	0.96	4.48
United Kingdom	3,916	4,517	4,049	5,099	5,318	2.63	4.29
Southern Europe	61,047	84,632	94,888	114,134	113,832	56.25	-0.26
Albania	9,086	12,088	13,452	16,868	16,188	8.00	-4.03
Bosnia and Herzegovina	1,885	2,687	3,648	4,021	4,240	2.10	5.45
Croatia	4,097	5,467	6,828	7,667	8,817	4.36	15.00
Greece	14,677	27,042	29,901	33,080	30,835	15.24	-6.79
Italy	3,076	3,626	3,618	4,259	4,651	2.30	9.20
Portugal	308	432	331	365	511	0.25	40.00
Slovenia	3,837	4,579	5,444	7,514	9,228	4.56	22.81
Spain	842	1,386	895	1,213	1,154	0.57	-4.86
Serbia and Montenegro	23,239	27,325	30,771	39,147	38,208	18.88	-2.40
Western Europe	14,496	17,592	17,116	19,968	21,429	10.59	7.32
Austria	1,919	2,564	2,503	2,736	3,490	1.72	27.56
Belgium	970	1,243	996	1,157	1,414	0.70	22.21
France	2,542	3,513	2,845	3,017	3,133	1.55	3.84
Germany	6,084	6,317	6,522	6,995	7,659	3.78	9.49
Netherlands	2,016	2,470	2,652	4,218	3,809	1.88	-9.70
Switzerland	965	1,485	1,598	1,845	1,924	0.95	4.28
East Mediterranean Europe	5,610	6,281	7,172	8,586	8,974	4.43	4.52
Israel	430	526	676	1,207	1,170	0.58	-3.07

THE FORMER YUGOSLAV REP. OF MACEDONIA

4. Arrivals of non-resident tourists in all types of accommodation establishments, by nationality

	2002	2003	2004	2005	2006	Market share 06	% Change 06-05
Turkey	5,180	5,755	6,496	7,379	7,804	3.86	5.76
Other Europe	**1,767**	**2,689**	**2,911**	**2,286**	**2,961**	**1.46**	**29.53**
Other countries of Europe	1,767	2,689	2,911	2,286	2,961	1.46	29.53
REGION NOT SPECIFIED	**2,644**	**3,570**	**3,586**	**3,496**	**3,167**	**1.57**	**-9.41**
Not Specified	**2,644**	**3,570**	**3,586**	**3,496**	**3,167**	**1.57**	**-9.41**
Other countries of the World	2,644	3,570	3,586	3,496	3,167	1.57	-9.41

Source: World Tourism Organization (UNWTO)

THE FORMER YUGOSLAV REP. OF MACEDONIA

5. Overnight stays of non-resident tourists in hotels and similar establishments, by nationality

	2002	2003	2004	2005	2006	Market share 06	% Change 06-05
TOTAL	249,463	320,932	329,327	390,693	392,359	100.00	0.43
AMERICAS	20,866	21,957	22,238	21,027	22,817	5.82	8.51
North America	20,866	21,957	22,238	21,027	22,817	5.82	8.51
Canada	1,752	2,142	1,582	2,024	2,074	0.53	2.47
United States	19,114	19,815	20,656	19,003	20,743	5.29	9.16
EAST ASIA AND THE PACIFIC	3,481	5,014	4,638	5,959	6,730	1.72	12.94
North-East Asia	1,209	2,187	1,846	2,090	2,362	0.60	13.01
Japan	1,209	2,187	1,846	2,090	2,362	0.60	13.01
Australasia	2,272	2,827	2,792	3,869	4,368	1.11	12.90
Australia	1,993	2,663	2,585	3,595	4,039	1.03	12.35
New Zealand	279	164	207	274	329	0.08	20.07
EUROPE	218,368	284,192	294,350	355,781	355,735	90.67	-0.01
Central/Eastern Europe	42,067	45,606	40,201	47,951	51,447	13.11	7.29
Bulgaria	21,398	24,631	21,631	28,752	30,196	7.70	5.02
Belarus	381	492	298	433	445	0.11	2.77
Czech Republic	2,673	3,157	2,030	2,310	3,382	0.86	46.41
Hungary	3,805	4,010	3,049	2,887	3,134	0.80	8.56
Poland	3,336	3,407	3,486	2,464	2,845	0.73	15.46
Romania	2,661	3,108	2,859	4,276	4,271	1.09	-0.12
Russian Federation	3,449	3,801	3,867	4,328	4,114	1.05	-4.94
Slovakia	1,783	1,267	1,215	1,187	1,488	0.38	25.36
Ukraine	2,581	1,733	1,766	1,314	1,572	0.40	19.63
Northern Europe	18,346	21,775	20,228	24,467	25,508	6.50	4.25
Denmark	1,473	2,312	2,611	2,781	2,109	0.54	-24.16
Finland	1,122	1,352	1,280	1,531	1,660	0.42	8.43
Iceland	288	287	243	181	340	0.09	87.85
Ireland	1,618	1,105	988	1,357	2,294	0.58	69.05
Norway	2,200	2,820	2,282	2,397	2,790	0.71	16.40
Sweden	2,404	3,294	3,333	4,093	3,856	0.98	-5.79
United Kingdom	9,241	10,605	9,491	12,127	12,459	3.18	2.74
Southern Europe	113,072	157,419	178,723	209,661	208,150	53.05	-0.72
Albania	17,476	22,232	22,948	28,584	25,968	6.62	-9.15
Bosnia and Herzegovina	3,752	5,050	6,885	8,972	8,466	2.16	-5.64
Croatia	8,005	10,278	11,741	14,135	15,901	4.05	12.49
Greece	29,694	51,995	61,078	65,442	62,367	15.90	-4.70
Italy	6,620	7,928	7,428	8,767	9,209	2.35	5.04
Portugal	620	888	690	664	961	0.24	44.73
Slovenia	6,883	8,431	9,975	14,164	15,940	4.06	12.54
Spain	1,506	2,536	1,874	2,569	2,546	0.65	-0.90
Serbia and Montenegro	38,516	48,081	56,104	66,364	66,792	17.02	0.64
Western Europe	31,848	43,039	39,121	52,626	48,775	12.43	-7.32
Austria	2,875	4,606	5,222	5,119	6,053	1.54	18.25
Belgium	1,795	2,613	1,922	2,319	2,570	0.66	10.82
France	5,906	9,848	6,183	6,113	5,862	1.49	-4.11
Germany	14,509	15,829	16,184	15,753	17,709	4.51	12.42
Netherlands	4,791	6,590	6,419	19,316	12,493	3.18	-35.32
Switzerland	1,972	3,553	3,191	4,006	4,088	1.04	2.05
East Mediterranean Europe	10,176	11,742	12,147	16,465	16,304	4.16	-0.98
Israel	829	1,176	1,522	2,268	2,733	0.70	20.50

THE FORMER YUGOSLAV REP. OF MACEDONIA

5. Overnight stays of non-resident tourists in hotels and similar establishments, by nationality

	2002	2003	2004	2005	2006	Market share 06	% Change 06-05
Turkey	9,347	10,566	10,625	14,197	13,571	3.46	-4.41
Other Europe	**2,859**	**4,611**	**3,930**	**4,611**	**5,551**	**1.41**	**20.39**
Other countries of Europe	2,859	4,611	3,930	4,611	5,551	1.41	20.39
REGION NOT SPECIFIED	**6,748**	**9,769**	**8,101**	**7,926**	**7,077**	**1.80**	**-10.71**
Not Specified	**6,748**	**9,769**	**8,101**	**7,926**	**7,077**	**1.80**	**-10.71**
Other countries of the World	6,748	9,769	8,101	7,926	7,077	1.80	-10.71

Source: World Tourism Organization (UNWTO)

THE FORMER YUGOSLAV REP. OF MACEDONIA

6. Overnight stays of non-resident tourists in all types of accommodation establishments, by nationality

	2002	2003	2004	2005	2006	Market share 06	% Change 06-05
TOTAL	274,720	346,200	360,589	442,988	442,845	100.00	-0.03
AMERICAS	21,154	22,251	22,732	22,005	23,618	5.33	7.33
North America	21,154	22,251	22,732	22,005	23,618	5.33	7.33
Canada	1,791	2,238	1,586	2,049	2,108	0.48	2.88
United States	19,363	20,013	21,146	19,956	21,510	4.86	7.79
EAST ASIA AND THE PACIFIC	3,546	5,278	4,663	6,519	7,505	1.69	15.13
North-East Asia	1,219	2,345	1,852	2,133	2,382	0.54	11.67
Japan	1,219	2,345	1,852	2,133	2,382	0.54	11.67
Australasia	2,327	2,933	2,811	4,386	5,123	1.16	16.80
Australia	2,044	2,763	2,604	4,089	4,742	1.07	15.97
New Zealand	283	170	207	297	381	0.09	28.28
EUROPE	243,206	308,453	324,483	406,467	404,291	91.29	-0.54
Central/Eastern Europe	45,901	50,136	45,836	55,439	58,247	13.15	5.07
Bulgaria	24,413	28,772	25,262	32,678	34,184	7.72	4.61
Belarus	382	493	1,084	448	467	0.11	4.24
Czech Republic	2,687	3,202	2,091	3,255	3,830	0.86	17.67
Hungary	3,825	4,014	3,226	2,947	3,244	0.73	10.08
Poland	3,600	3,543	3,754	3,081	3,125	0.71	1.43
Romania	2,852	3,144	3,083	4,665	4,604	1.04	-1.31
Russian Federation	3,488	3,936	4,164	5,617	5,292	1.20	-5.79
Slovakia	1,783	1,272	1,218	1,327	1,642	0.37	23.74
Ukraine	2,871	1,760	1,954	1,421	1,859	0.42	30.82
Northern Europe	18,469	22,295	20,893	25,451	26,468	5.98	4.00
Denmark	1,483	2,497	2,713	2,800	2,208	0.50	-21.14
Finland	1,132	1,376	1,392	1,593	1,760	0.40	10.48
Iceland	289	291	252	181	341	0.08	88.40
Ireland	1,629	1,119	1,042	1,394	2,461	0.56	76.54
Norway	2,220	2,832	2,295	2,451	2,922	0.66	19.22
Sweden	2,442	3,472	3,523	4,500	4,149	0.94	-7.80
United Kingdom	9,274	10,708	9,676	12,532	12,627	2.85	0.76
Southern Europe	130,894	174,262	195,486	245,850	242,205	54.69	-1.48
Albania	20,665	24,095	26,117	34,787	32,214	7.27	-7.40
Bosnia and Herzegovina	4,091	5,494	7,676	10,754	10,270	2.32	-4.50
Croatia	8,537	11,313	13,371	15,605	17,476	3.95	11.99
Greece	30,730	53,447	63,834	68,825	66,417	15.00	-3.50
Italy	6,694	8,120	7,593	9,019	9,693	2.19	7.47
Portugal	620	1,028	745	676	981	0.22	45.12
Slovenia	7,546	9,262	10,837	16,283	17,873	4.04	9.76
Spain	1,515	2,704	1,898	2,776	2,768	0.63	-0.29
Serbia and Montenegro	50,496	58,799	63,415	87,125	84,513	19.08	-3.00
Western Europe	33,272	44,424	40,727	55,443	51,732	11.68	-6.69
Austria	3,715	4,704	5,423	5,857	6,702	1.51	14.43
Belgium	1,850	2,746	2,104	2,534	3,090	0.70	21.94
France	5,986	10,115	6,385	6,459	6,343	1.43	-1.80
Germany	14,849	16,390	16,805	16,342	18,247	4.12	11.66
Netherlands	4,876	6,874	6,772	20,001	12,981	2.93	-35.10
Switzerland	1,996	3,595	3,238	4,250	4,369	0.99	2.80
East Mediterranean Europe	11,445	12,426	13,393	19,039	18,513	4.18	-2.76
Israel	830	1,176	1,522	2,318	2,980	0.67	28.56

THE FORMER YUGOSLAV REP. OF MACEDONIA

6. Overnight stays of non-resident tourists in all types of accommodation establishments, by nationality

	2002	2003	2004	2005	2006	Market share 06	% Change 06-05
Turkey	10,615	11,250	11,871	16,721	15,533	3.51	-7.10
Other Europe	**3,225**	**4,910**	**8,148**	**5,245**	**7,126**	**1.61**	**35.86**
Other countries of Europe	3,225	4,910	8,148	5,245	7,126	1.61	35.86
REGION NOT SPECIFIED	**6,814**	**10,218**	**8,711**	**7,997**	**7,431**	**1.68**	**-7.08**
Not Specified	**6,814**	**10,218**	**8,711**	**7,997**	**7,431**	**1.68**	**-7.08**
Other countries of the World	6,814	10,218	8,711	7,997	7,431	1.68	-7.08

Source: World Tourism Organization (UNWTO)

TOGO

3. Arrivals of non-resident tourists in hotels and similar establishments, by country of residence

	2002	2003	2004	2005	2006	Market share 06	% Change 06-05
TOTAL	**57,539**	**60,592**	**82,686**	**80,763**	**94,096**	**100.00**	**16.51**
AFRICA	**28,636**	**31,334**	**43,842**	**45,967**	**52,549**	**55.85**	**14.32**
West Africa	**20,104**	**19,935**	**27,159**	**25,130**	**25,120**	**26.70**	**-0.04**
Benin	5,371	5,111	7,434	5,909	6,495	6.90	9.92
Ghana	1,755	1,585	2,161	1,880	2,438	2.59	29.68
Cote D'Ivoire	3,071	4,134	5,860	5,916	6,181	6.57	4.48
Nigeria	3,919	3,152	3,572	3,356	3,598	3.82	7.21
Burkina Faso (*)	5,988	5,953	8,132	8,069	6,408	6.81	-20.58
Other Africa	**8,532**	**11,399**	**16,683**	**20,837**	**27,429**	**29.15**	**31.64**
Other countries of Africa	8,532	11,399	16,683	20,837	27,429	29.15	31.64
AMERICAS	**1,975**	**1,785**	**2,738**	**2,633**	**3,314**	**3.52**	**25.86**
North America	**1,895**	**1,699**	**2,540**	**2,539**	**3,187**	**3.39**	**25.52**
Canada	269	315	443	398	484	0.51	21.61
United States	1,626	1,384	2,097	2,141	2,703	2.87	26.25
Other Americas	**80**	**86**	**198**	**94**	**127**	**0.13**	**35.11**
Other countries of the Americas	80	86	198	94	127	0.13	35.11
EAST ASIA AND THE PACIFIC	**1,125**	**1,452**	**3,492**	**2,627**	**3,205**	**3.41**	**22.00**
North-East Asia	**47**	**60**	**97**	**141**	**286**	**0.30**	**102.84**
Japan	47	60	97	141	286	0.30	102.84
Other East Asia and the Pacific	**1,078**	**1,392**	**3,395**	**2,486**	**2,919**	**3.10**	**17.42**
Other countries of Asia	1,078	1,392	3,395	2,486	2,919	3.10	17.42
EUROPE	**24,097**	**24,484**	**30,018**	**27,092**	**33,266**	**35.35**	**22.79**
Central/Eastern Europe	**147**	**79**	**567**	**168**	**55**	**0.06**	**-67.26**
Ussr (Former)	147	79	567	168	55	0.06	-67.26
Northern Europe	**554**	**679**	**949**	**653**	**912**	**0.97**	**39.66**
United Kingdom	526	655	879	619	859	0.91	38.77
Scandinavia	28	24	70	34	53	0.06	55.88
Southern Europe	**527**	**570**	**960**	**674**	**857**	**0.91**	**27.15**
Italy	527	570	960	674	857	0.91	27.15
Western Europe	**15,048**	**15,767**	**20,041**	**21,417**	**27,165**	**28.87**	**26.84**
France	12,764	14,154	17,674	16,511	24,753	26.31	49.92
Germany	991	830	879	1,092	1,102	1.17	0.92
Switzerland	393	274	464	297	237	0.25	-20.20
Benelux	900	509	1,024	3,517	1,073	1.14	-69.49
Other Europe	**7,821**	**7,389**	**7,501**	**4,180**	**4,277**	**4.55**	**2.32**
Other countries of Europe	7,821	7,389	7,501	4,180	4,277	4.55	2.32
MIDDLE EAST	**1,680**	**1,495**	**2,500**	**2,371**	**1,635**	**1.74**	**-31.04**
Middle East	**1,680**	**1,495**	**2,500**	**2,371**	**1,635**	**1.74**	**-31.04**
All countries of Middle East	1,680	1,495	2,500	2,371	1,635	1.74	-31.04
REGION NOT SPECIFIED	**26**	**42**	**96**	**73**	**127**	**0.13**	**73.97**
Not Specified	**26**	**42**	**96**	**73**	**127**	**0.13**	**73.97**
Other countries of the World	26	42	96	73	127	0.13	73.97

Source: World Tourism Organization (UNWTO)

TOGO

5. Overnight stays of non-resident tourists in hotels and similar establishments, by country of residence

	2002	2003	2004	2005	2006	Market share 06	% Change 06-05
TOTAL	117,079	136,422	182,628	157,003	208,869	100.00	33.04
AFRICA	70,154	70,552	94,440	87,755	97,814	46.83	11.46
West Africa	47,357	42,551	57,559	47,801	44,941	21.52	-5.98
Benin	9,122	8,293	12,410	9,521	10,012	4.79	5.16
Ghana	4,026	3,181	3,977	3,687	3,921	1.88	6.35
Cote D'Ivoire	9,561	11,373	16,321	12,167	11,698	5.60	-3.85
Nigeria	7,983	5,961	8,147	6,519	6,479	3.10	-0.61
Burkina Faso (*)	16,665	13,743	16,704	15,907	12,831	6.14	-19.34
Other Africa	22,797	28,001	36,881	39,954	52,873	25.31	32.33
Other countries of Africa	22,797	28,001	36,881	39,954	52,873	25.31	32.33
AMERICAS	4,689	6,024	7,410	6,152	9,473	4.54	53.98
North America	4,359	4,755	6,458	5,950	9,131	4.37	53.46
Canada	724	1,015	1,323	1,215	1,020	0.49	-16.05
United States	3,635	3,740	5,135	4,735	8,111	3.88	71.30
Other Americas	330	1,269	952	202	342	0.16	69.31
Other countries of the Americas	330	1,269	952	202	342	0.16	69.31
EAST ASIA AND THE PACIFIC	2,363	3,072	5,795	4,855	4,992	2.39	2.82
North-East Asia	230	263	213	440	441	0.21	0.23
Japan	230	263	213	440	441	0.21	0.23
Other East Asia and the Pacific	2,133	2,809	5,582	4,415	4,551	2.18	3.08
Other countries of Asia	2,133	2,809	5,582	4,415	4,551	2.18	3.08
EUROPE	37,600	54,700	71,961	54,962	94,464	45.23	71.87
Central/Eastern Europe	236	373	256	574	294	0.14	-48.78
Ussr (Former)	236	373	256	574	294	0.14	-48.78
Northern Europe	1,072	2,122	2,944	1,762	1,670	0.80	-5.22
United Kingdom	1,009	2,114	2,873	1,696	1,561	0.75	-7.96
Scandinavia	63	8	71	66	109	0.05	65.15
Southern Europe	1,386	1,538	1,857	1,453	1,779	0.85	22.44
Italy	1,386	1,538	1,857	1,453	1,779	0.85	22.44
Western Europe	21,691	33,141	48,701	41,339	80,398	38.49	94.48
France	16,268	27,765	41,652	30,778	73,795	35.33	139.77
Germany	2,155	2,199	3,080	2,363	3,343	1.60	41.47
Switzerland	962	1,350	1,212	638	1,032	0.49	61.76
Benelux	2,306	1,827	2,757	7,560	2,228	1.07	-70.53
Other Europe	13,215	17,526	18,203	9,834	10,323	4.94	4.97
Other countries of Europe	13,215	17,526	18,203	9,834	10,323	4.94	4.97
MIDDLE EAST	2,177	1,779	2,809	3,142	1,902	0.91	-39.47
Middle East	2,177	1,779	2,809	3,142	1,902	0.91	-39.47
All countries of Middle East	2,177	1,779	2,809	3,142	1,902	0.91	-39.47
REGION NOT SPECIFIED	96	295	213	137	224	0.11	63.50
Not Specified	96	295	213	137	224	0.11	63.50
Other countries of the World	96	295	213	137	224	0.11	63.50

Source: World Tourism Organization (UNWTO)

TONGA

1. Arrivals of non-resident tourists at national borders, by country of residence

		2002	2003	2004	2005	2006	Market share 06	% Change 06-05
TOTAL	(*)	36,588	40,110	41,208	41,862	39,451	100.00	-5.76
AFRICA		92						
Southern Africa		59						
South Africa		59						
Other Africa		33						
Other countries of Africa		33						
AMERICAS		7,860	7,930	8,202	8,147	6,345	16.08	-22.12
North America		7,801	7,930	8,202	8,147	6,345	16.08	-22.12
Canada		328	365	279	286	255	0.65	-10.84
United States		7,473	7,565	7,923	7,861	6,090	15.44	-22.53
Other Americas		59						
Other countries of the Americas		59						
EAST ASIA AND THE PACIFIC		24,477	27,932	28,972	30,424	29,720	75.33	-2.31
North-East Asia		1,254	790	874	946	1,074	2.72	13.53
Taiwan (Province of China)		414		307	285	352	0.89	23.51
Hong Kong, China		44						
Japan		796	790	567	661	722	1.83	9.23
Australasia		19,199	22,954	24,407	26,349	26,155	66.30	-0.74
Australia		6,261	8,272	8,023	8,854	8,710	22.08	-1.63
New Zealand		12,938	14,682	16,384	17,495	17,445	44.22	-0.29
Melanesia		2,112	2,012	1,837	1,535	1,400	3.55	-8.79
Fiji		2,112	2,012	1,837	1,535	1,400	3.55	-8.79
Polynesia		898						
American Samoa		114						
Samoa		784						
Other East Asia and the Pacific		1,014	2,176	1,854	1,594	1,091	2.77	-31.56
Other countries of Asia		352	765	322	283	319	0.81	12.72
Other countries of Oceania		662	1,411	1,532	1,311	772	1.96	-41.11
EUROPE		4,082	4,131	3,408	2,908	2,875	7.29	-1.13
Northern Europe		1,303	1,385	1,157	943	970	2.46	2.86
Sweden		212						
United Kingdom		1,091	1,385	1,157	943	970	2.46	2.86
Southern Europe		322						
Italy		322						
Western Europe		1,723	979	900	868	708	1.79	-18.43
Austria		137						
France		271						
Germany		1,188	979	900	868	708	1.79	-18.43
Switzerland		127						
Other Europe		734	1,767	1,351	1,097	1,197	3.03	9.12
Other countries of Europe		734	1,767	1,351	1,097	1,197	3.03	9.12
SOUTH ASIA		77						
South Asia		77						
India		77						
REGION NOT SPECIFIED			117	626	383	511	1.30	33.42
Not Specified			117	626	383	511	1.30	33.42

TRINIDAD AND TOBAGO

1. Arrivals of non-resident tourists at national borders, by country of residence

	2002	2003	2004	2005	2006	Market share 06	% Change 06-05
TOTAL (*)	384,212	409,069	442,596	463,191	457,434	100.00	-1.24
AFRICA	997	935	1,017	1,299	1,389	0.30	6.93
East Africa	178	141	180	159	205	0.04	28.93
British Indian Ocean Territory	4		5	5	6		20.00
Burundi		3	3	1	1		
Comoros		2					
Ethiopia	4	4	18	5	5		
Eritrea	1						
Djibouti	3						
Kenya	49	41	61	41	37	0.01	-9.76
Madagascar	3		1				
Malawi	3	3	6	5	7		40.00
Mauritius	11	9	20	21	22		4.76
Mozambique	2	2	6	4			
Reunion	1				4		
Rwanda	3	4		2	4		100.00
Seychelles	7	2	8	7	7		
Somalia			2		1		
Zimbabwe	38	15	12	13	47	0.01	261.54
Uganda	15	9	6	6	10		66.67
United Republic of Tanzania	16	22	21	27	19		-29.63
Zambia	18	25	11	22	35	0.01	59.09
Central Africa	27	37	39	36	50	0.01	38.89
Angola	2	3	11	12	24	0.01	100.00
Cameroon	13	3	6	5	12		140.00
Central African Republic		3	2	1	1		
Chad	1				1		
Congo	4	7	6	5	4		-20.00
Democratic Republic of the Congo	2		2	1	1		
Equatorial Guinea	2	18	8	6	4		-33.33
Gabon	1	3	1	3			
Sao Tome and Principe	2		3	3	3		
North Africa	26	17	44	25	36	0.01	44.00
Algeria	7	2	20	4	4		
Morocco	6	4	3	3	6		100.00
Sudan	7	3	8	10	16		60.00
Tunisia	6	8	13	8	10		25.00
Southern Africa	386	373	430	647	668	0.15	3.25
Botswana	67	112	79	102	109	0.02	6.86
Lesotho	1	1			1		
Namibia	3	3	10	3	7		133.33
South Africa	303	249	327	477	380	0.08	-20.34
Swaziland	12	8	14	65	171	0.04	163.08
West Africa	380	367	324	432	430	0.09	-0.46
Cape Verde		3	3		1		
Benin	1		3		1		
Gambia	8	4	6	13	4		-69.23
Ghana	37	44	36	67	58	0.01	-13.43
Guinea	5	13	2	2	2		
Cote D'Ivoire	1	2	2	4	4		
Liberia	4		9	8	10		25.00
Mali	1			1	1		
Mauritania	2	8	10	2			

TRINIDAD AND TOBAGO

1. Arrivals of non-resident tourists at national borders, by country of residence

	2002	2003	2004	2005	2006	Market share 06	% Change 06-05
Niger	4	1	1		7		
Nigeria	300	258	226	300	316	0.07	5.33
Guinea-Bissau	2		3	4	1		-75.00
Saint Helena	2	1	1	2			
Senegal	2	24	7	9	7		-22.22
Sierra Leone	9	7	15	13	12		-7.69
Togo	2	1		2	4		100.00
Burkina Faso		1		5	2		-60.00
AMERICAS	**308,018**	**324,175**	**347,181**	**365,311**	**364,888**	**79.77**	**-0.12**
Caribbean	**91,792**	**100,690**	**100,854**	**105,701**	**98,826**	**21.60**	**-6.50**
Antigua and Barbuda	4,233	4,334	4,351	4,692	4,805	1.05	2.41
Bahamas	1,179	1,343	1,226	1,560	1,745	0.38	11.86
Barbados	33,989	37,320	35,456	35,319	31,218	6.82	-11.61
Bermuda	522	575	580	813	649	0.14	-20.17
British Virgin Islands	981	960	1,133	1,342	1,624	0.36	21.01
Cayman Islands	464	556	546	528	662	0.14	25.38
Cuba	231	227	406	236	296	0.06	25.42
Dominica	1,277	1,535	1,564	1,777	2,141	0.47	20.48
Dominican Republic	525	574	876	858	881	0.19	2.68
Grenada	16,539	19,220	19,575	19,501	14,814	3.24	-24.03
Guadeloupe	668	712	798	625	655	0.14	4.80
Haiti	174	184	183	203	228	0.05	12.32
Jamaica	6,044	6,186	6,210	7,848	8,663	1.89	10.38
Martinique	1,005	1,076	900	1,016	972	0.21	-4.33
Montserrat	209	220	205	231	251	0.05	8.66
Netherlands Antilles	563	466	356	502	605	0.13	20.52
Aruba	403	437	373	446	444	0.10	-0.45
Curacao	1,003	1,060	885	989	965	0.21	-2.43
Puerto Rico	1,479	1,616	1,582	1,576	1,740	0.38	10.41
Saint Kitts and Nevis	1,280	1,438	1,493	1,779	1,730	0.38	-2.75
Anguilla	330	254	311	353	485	0.11	37.39
Saint Lucia	6,892	7,423	8,192	8,823	8,902	1.95	0.90
Saint Vincent and the Grenadines	9,636	11,041	11,747	12,658	12,288	2.69	-2.92
Turks and Caicos Islands	127	143	163	186	198	0.04	6.45
United States Virgin Islands	2,039	1,790	1,743	1,840	1,865	0.41	1.36
Central America	**1,433**	**1,592**	**1,936**	**2,580**	**2,292**	**0.50**	**-11.16**
Belize	280	360	356	381	373	0.08	-2.10
Costa Rica	403	516	683	836	626	0.14	-25.12
El Salvador	64	37	61	126	141	0.03	11.90
Guatemala	113	115	160	415	253	0.06	-39.04
Honduras	104	98	127	164	203	0.04	23.78
Nicaragua	18	21	44	37	47	0.01	27.03
Panama	451	445	505	621	649	0.14	4.51
North America	**175,873**	**182,677**	**204,000**	**216,989**	**221,654**	**48.46**	**2.15**
Canada	41,506	43,036	43,565	47,702	49,242	10.76	3.23
Greenland	1			3	1		-66.67
Mexico	801	703	967	1,297	1,517	0.33	16.96
Saint Pierre and Miquelon		3	1	2	1		-50.00
United States	133,565	138,935	159,467	167,985	170,893	37.36	1.73
South America	**38,920**	**39,216**	**40,391**	**40,041**	**42,116**	**9.21**	**5.18**
Argentina	437	429	442	612	596	0.13	-2.61
Bolivia	42	70	57	29	33	0.01	13.79
Brazil	974	836	986	1,251	1,233	0.27	-1.44
Chile	103	188	230	259	299	0.07	15.44

TRINIDAD AND TOBAGO

1. Arrivals of non-resident tourists at national borders, by country of residence

	2002	2003	2004	2005	2006	Market share 06	% Change 06-05
Colombia	923	1,353	1,589	1,717	2,178	0.48	26.85
Ecuador	109	116	212	220	232	0.05	5.45
Falkland Islands (Malvinas)	1	3		45	96	0.02	113.33
French Guiana	433	536	90	133	159	0.03	19.55
Guyana	22,299	22,783	22,328	22,208	23,673	5.18	6.60
Paraguay	7	8	17	30	14		-53.33
Peru	88	187	302	332	393	0.09	18.37
Suriname	2,344	2,354	3,547	2,926	3,212	0.70	9.77
Uruguay	53	80	63	88	92	0.02	4.55
Venezuela	11,107	10,273	10,528	10,191	9,906	2.17	-2.80
EAST ASIA AND THE PACIFIC	**2,670**	**3,313**	**2,925**	**3,046**	**4,082**	**0.89**	**34.01**
North-East Asia	**1,123**	**1,170**	**1,258**	**1,444**	**1,933**	**0.42**	**33.86**
China	278	377	431	604	859	0.19	42.22
Taiwan (Province of China)	109	66	83	68	86	0.02	26.47
Hong Kong, China	70	81	72	92	108	0.02	17.39
Japan	578	599	566	521	634	0.14	21.69
Korea, Dem. People's Republic of	31	13	49	87	162	0.04	86.21
Korea, Republic of	56	29	54	64	82	0.02	28.13
Macao, China	1	1	2	1			
Mongolia		4	1	7	2		-71.43
South-East Asia	**496**	**418**	**522**	**623**	**1,000**	**0.22**	**60.51**
Brunei Darussalam				4	4		
Myanmar	15	23	15	8	17		112.50
Cambodia	1	3	5	4			
Indonesia	43	67	59	45	51	0.01	13.33
Malaysia	111	95	199	224	330	0.07	47.32
Philippines	163	110	153	171	443	0.10	159.06
Singapore	102	93	58	100	92	0.02	-8.00
Viet Nam	5	3	2	7	11		57.14
Thailand	56	24	31	60	52	0.01	-13.33
Australasia	**1,005**	**1,679**	**1,034**	**876**	**1,104**	**0.24**	**26.03**
Australia	799	1,516	870	705	908	0.20	28.79
New Zealand	206	163	164	171	196	0.04	14.62
Melanesia	**16**	**14**	**32**	**59**	**9**		**-84.75**
Solomon Islands	2	7	4	1			
Fiji	8	5	14	19	4		-78.95
New Caledonia	1				2		
Vanuatu	1	2	10	13	3		-76.92
Norfolk Island	2						
Papua New Guinea	2		4	26			
Micronesia	**25**	**19**	**40**	**20**	**25**	**0.01**	**25.00**
Guam	1		9	3	2		-33.33
Nauru	20	12	15	11	14		27.27
Northern Mariana Islands	1	6			4		
Micronesia (Federated States of)			2		5		
Marshall Islands	1		10	3			
Wake Island	2	1	4	3			
Polynesia	**5**	**13**	**39**	**24**	**11**		**-54.17**
American Samoa	1		1		3		
Cook Islands			11	2	2		
French Polynesia	3	2	5	14	1		-92.86
Niue		1		1			
Pitcairn		1			1		

TRINIDAD AND TOBAGO

1. Arrivals of non-resident tourists at national borders, by country of residence

	2002	2003	2004	2005	2006	Market share 06	% Change 06-05
Tonga			6				
Tuvalu		1	5	1	2		100.00
Wallis and Futuna Islands	1	4	3	5	1		-80.00
Samoa		4	8	1	1		
EUROPE	**71,133**	**79,236**	**89,512**	**91,424**	**84,243**	**18.42**	**-7.85**
Central/Eastern Europe	**326**	**432**	**556**	**767**	**882**	**0.19**	**14.99**
Azerbaijan	6	9	23	34	32	0.01	-5.88
Armenia	3	1	3	2			
Bulgaria	5	6	15	27	37	0.01	37.04
Belarus	6	4	5	5	35	0.01	600.00
Czech Republic/Slovakia	11	2	3		3		
Czech Republic	19	60	52	80	95	0.02	18.75
Estonia	9	4	12	26	43	0.01	65.38
Georgia		3	23	4	1		-75.00
Hungary	30	38	32	73	83	0.02	13.70
Kazakhstan	12	5	4	10	21		110.00
Kyrgyzstan		2		3			
Latvia	19	49	39	57	31	0.01	-45.61
Lithuania	16	12	11	12	21		75.00
Republic of Moldova	1				1		
Poland	75	79	113	127	192	0.04	51.18
Romania	20	16	35	52	47	0.01	-9.62
Russian Federation	43	79	76	145	132	0.03	-8.97
Slovakia	8	11	30	40	30	0.01	-25.00
Tajikistan	3	6	12	12	6		-50.00
Turkmenistan		2		7	9		28.57
Ukraine	21	10	33	22	51	0.01	131.82
Uzbekistan	19	34	35	29	12		-58.62
Northern Europe	**56,115**	**61,840**	**70,730**	**68,999**	**64,895**	**14.19**	**-5.95**
Denmark	803	811	931	1,016	1,417	0.31	39.47
Faeroe Islands	2	1			1		
Finland	194	141	161	222	193	0.04	-13.06
Iceland	7	14	26	27	14		-48.15
Ireland	1,059	1,103	928	1,233	1,283	0.28	4.06
Norway	1,155	1,019	1,100	1,210	1,329	0.29	9.83
Sweden	1,187	1,167	1,471	1,720	2,016	0.44	17.21
United Kingdom	51,688	57,566	66,090	63,523	58,612	12.81	-7.73
Isle of Man	20	18	23	48	30	0.01	-37.50
Southern Europe	**1,977**	**1,812**	**1,837**	**1,952**	**2,360**	**0.52**	**20.90**
Albania	6	6	8	7	8		14.29
Andorra	2	4	2	1	2		100.00
Bosnia and Herzegovina	2		2	2	4		100.00
Croatia	34	19	24	36	76	0.02	111.11
Gibraltar	1	2		1	3		200.00
Greece	51	45	85	104	91	0.02	-12.50
Holy See		1		6	2		-66.67
Italy	1,099	1,028	1,048	1,038	1,224	0.27	17.92
Malta	36	12	19	17	30	0.01	76.47
Portugal	82	129	70	87	152	0.03	74.71
San Marino	1		2	1			
Slovenia	9	12	38	52	53	0.01	1.92
Spain	640	543	539	600	715	0.16	19.17
Serbia and Montenegro	14	11					
Western Europe	**12,504**	**14,966**	**16,157**	**19,454**	**15,887**	**3.47**	**-18.34**

TRINIDAD AND TOBAGO

1. Arrivals of non-resident tourists at national borders, by country of residence

	2002	2003	2004	2005	2006	Market share 06	% Change 06-05
Austria	546	850	1,318	3,121	1,234	0.27	-60.46
Belgium	441	401	397	440	387	0.08	-12.05
France	2,194	2,203	1,942	1,960	2,306	0.50	17.65
Germany	5,659	7,491	8,178	8,666	6,706	1.47	-22.62
Liechtenstein	2	4	2				
Luxembourg	22	11	22	28	27	0.01	-3.57
Monaco	19	9	5	15	12		-20.00
Netherlands	2,591	2,817	3,232	3,966	4,051	0.89	2.14
Switzerland	1,030	1,180	1,061	1,258	1,164	0.25	-7.47
East Mediterranean Europe	**211**	**186**	**232**	**252**	**219**	**0.05**	**-13.10**
Cyprus	15	33	21	18	32	0.01	77.78
Israel	165	135	177	183	130	0.03	-28.96
Turkey	31	18	34	51	57	0.01	11.76
MIDDLE EAST	**219**	**239**	**221**	**338**	**363**	**0.08**	**7.40**
Middle East	**219**	**239**	**221**	**338**	**363**	**0.08**	**7.40**
Bahrain	1	4	5	83	10		-87.95
Iraq	2	3	1	2			
Jordan	4	16	12	8	5		-37.50
Kuwait	9	13	13	17	17		
Lebanon	8	9	13	16	18		12.50
Libyan Arab Jamahiriya	2	4	1	5	4		-20.00
Oman	13	11	20	12	15		25.00
Qatar	11	16	6	18	19		5.56
Saudi Arabia	56	46	51	37	18		-51.35
Syrian Arab Republic	41	38	36	28	27	0.01	-3.57
United Arab Emirates	25	29	31	47	159	0.03	238.30
Egypt	47	49	31	65	67	0.01	3.08
Yemen		1	1		4		
SOUTH ASIA	**1,164**	**1,136**	**1,411**	**1,632**	**2,365**	**0.52**	**44.91**
South Asia	**1,164**	**1,136**	**1,411**	**1,632**	**2,365**	**0.52**	**44.91**
Afghanistan	14	13	32	18	18		
Bangladesh	30	49	68	37	22		-40.54
Sri Lanka	27	40	27	20	53	0.01	165.00
India	962	931	1,188	1,465	2,199	0.48	50.10
Iran, Islamic Republic of	24	30	18	24	3		-87.50
Nepal	8	2	9	6			
Pakistan	99	71	69	62	70	0.02	12.90
REGION NOT SPECIFIED	**11**	**35**	**329**	**141**	**104**	**0.02**	**-26.24**
Not Specified	**11**	**35**	**329**	**141**	**104**	**0.02**	**-26.24**
Other countries of the World	11	35	329	141	104	0.02	-26.24

Source: World Tourism Organization (UNWTO)

TUNISIA

1. Arrivals of non-resident tourists at national borders, by nationality

		2002	2003	2004	2005	2006	Market share 06	% Change 06-05
TOTAL	(*)	5,063,538	5,114,304	5,997,918	6,378,430	6,549,549	100.00	2.68
AFRICA		786,053	872,251	984,538	993,378	1,010,195	15.42	1.69
North Africa		767,784	847,157	950,735	961,665	978,594	14.94	1.76
Algeria		728,309	811,463	914,064	930,715	945,324	14.43	1.57
Morocco		38,865	35,003	35,897	29,912	32,386	0.49	8.27
Sudan		610	691	774	1,038	884	0.01	-14.84
West Africa		5,788	6,962	8,111	7,871	8,258	0.13	4.92
Mauritania		5,788	6,962	8,111	7,871	8,258	0.13	4.92
Other Africa		12,481	18,132	25,692	23,842	23,343	0.36	-2.09
Other countries of Africa		12,481	18,132	25,692	23,842	23,343	0.36	-2.09
AMERICAS		21,920	23,217	30,347	35,202	33,947	0.52	-3.57
North America		21,920	22,192	29,008	32,776	31,562	0.48	-3.70
Canada		10,339	11,913	15,803	17,039	15,278	0.23	-10.34
United States		11,581	10,279	13,205	15,737	16,284	0.25	3.48
South America			1,025	1,339	2,426	2,385	0.04	-1.69
Brazil			1,025	1,339	2,426	2,385	0.04	-1.69
EAST ASIA AND THE PACIFIC		7,167	9,389	10,784	13,710	15,442	0.24	12.63
North-East Asia		7,167	7,899	8,872	11,307	12,985	0.20	14.84
China			1,066	1,763	1,874	2,138	0.03	14.09
Japan		7,167	6,833	7,109	9,433	10,847	0.17	14.99
Australasia			1,490	1,912	2,403	2,457	0.04	2.25
Australia			1,490	1,912	2,403	2,457	0.04	2.25
EUROPE		2,918,526	2,840,307	3,482,041	3,869,030	3,956,274	60.41	2.25
Central/Eastern Europe		195,113	305,734	401,140	477,229	509,983	7.79	6.86
Bulgaria		1,728	1,791	2,449	4,414	4,798	0.07	8.70
Czech Republic		58,813	90,038	128,404	145,881	153,927	2.35	5.52
Hungary		30,468	55,532	52,895	58,546	48,534	0.74	-17.10
Poland		36,720	54,443	75,133	122,627	135,402	2.07	10.42
Romania		4,133	8,656	8,120	9,620	20,070	0.31	108.63
Russian Federation		47,207	73,376	99,406	96,175	111,705	1.71	16.15
Slovakia		16,044	21,898	34,733	39,966	35,547	0.54	-11.06
Northern Europe		354,648	316,283	402,329	460,728	456,690	6.97	-0.88
Denmark		9,392	10,487	17,266	36,982	12,447	0.19	-66.34
Finland		12,759	11,009	13,942	19,902	17,139	0.26	-13.88
Ireland		30,320	22,713	20,736	21,163	23,186	0.35	9.56
Norway		23,703	25,599	15,273	18,711	13,144	0.20	-29.75
Sweden		20,675	23,286	34,328	36,428	40,081	0.61	10.03
United Kingdom		257,799	223,189	300,784	327,542	350,693	5.35	7.07
Southern Europe		498,169	523,304	642,527	708,416	687,203	10.49	-2.99
Greece		8,086	8,381	12,162	12,615	13,512	0.21	7.11
Italy		375,160	379,773	448,292	472,768	464,323	7.09	-1.79
Malta		8,288	14,311	14,095	15,619	5,995	0.09	-61.62
Portugal		24,912	28,197	35,795	38,901	37,913	0.58	-2.54
Serbia				17,312	22,109	25,205	0.38	14.00
Spain		74,325	78,223	114,871	146,404	140,255	2.14	-4.20
Yugoslavia, Sfr (Former)		7,398	14,419					
Western Europe		1,846,492	1,660,193	1,973,977	2,148,430	2,226,560	34.00	3.64
Austria		77,168	70,065	84,383	86,412	92,034	1.41	6.51

TUNISIA

1. Arrivals of non-resident tourists at national borders, by nationality

	2002	2003	2004	2005	2006	Market share 06	% Change 06-05
Belgium	122,111	132,596	140,790	155,082	164,301	2.51	5.94
France	885,167	833,989	1,020,810	1,170,100	1,234,735	18.85	5.52
Germany	613,666	488,481	569,475	571,934	547,403	8.36	-4.29
Luxembourg	5,558	4,807	5,719	6,040	6,421	0.10	6.31
Netherlands	48,885	44,490	53,683	66,096	78,542	1.20	18.83
Switzerland	93,937	85,765	99,117	92,766	103,124	1.57	11.17
East Mediterranean Europe	**8,509**	**11,520**	**11,931**	**9,624**	**11,542**	**0.18**	**19.93**
Turkey	8,509	11,520	11,931	9,624	11,542	0.18	19.93
Other Europe	**15,595**	**23,273**	**50,137**	**64,603**	**64,296**	**0.98**	**-0.48**
Other countries of Europe	15,595	23,273	50,137	64,603	64,296	0.98	-0.48
MIDDLE EAST	**1,310,607**	**1,355,878**	**1,471,752**	**1,440,387**	**1,507,155**	**23.01**	**4.64**
Middle East	**1,310,607**	**1,355,878**	**1,471,752**	**1,440,387**	**1,507,155**	**23.01**	**4.64**
Bahrain	869	504	611	644	489	0.01	-24.07
Palestine	1,778	2,352	2,593	2,477	2,059	0.03	-16.88
Iraq	1,434	939	1,113	1,175	1,100	0.02	-6.38
Jordan	1,846	2,208	2,745	2,637	2,528	0.04	-4.13
Kuwait	1,093	1,095	1,199	1,292	1,128	0.02	-12.69
Lebanon	2,589	3,007	4,289	4,379	3,877	0.06	-11.46
Libyan Arab Jamahiriya	1,280,733	1,325,660	1,435,785	1,404,007	1,472,411	22.48	4.87
Oman	448	862	740	750	875	0.01	16.67
Qatar	768	543	773	1,013	911	0.01	-10.07
Saudi Arabia	6,506	5,657	6,890	7,179	7,207	0.11	0.39
Syrian Arab Republic	2,729	3,352	3,638	3,083	3,759	0.06	21.93
United Arab Emirates	543	857	863	963	1,161	0.02	20.56
Egypt	8,575	8,277	9,642	10,037	8,895	0.14	-11.38
Yemen	696	565	871	751	755	0.01	0.53
REGION NOT SPECIFIED	**19,265**	**13,262**	**18,456**	**26,723**	**26,536**	**0.41**	**-0.70**
Not Specified	**19,265**	**13,262**	**18,456**	**26,723**	**26,536**	**0.41**	**-0.70**
Other countries of the World	19,265	13,262	18,456	26,723	26,536	0.41	-0.70

Source: World Tourism Organization (UNWTO)

TUNISIA

3. Arrivals of non-resident tourists in hotels and similar establishments, by nationality

	2002	2003	2004	2005	2006	Market share 06	% Change 06-05
TOTAL	4,244,985	4,064,176	4,900,172	5,442,410	5,415,192	100.00	-0.50
AFRICA	232,139	245,376	250,756	269,827	280,736	5.18	4.04
North Africa	215,876	220,638	223,436	241,316	253,074	4.67	4.87
Algeria	197,100	202,759	205,130	225,977	237,059	4.38	4.90
Morocco	18,776	17,879	18,306	15,339	16,015	0.30	4.41
Other Africa	16,263	24,738	27,320	28,511	27,662	0.51	-2.98
Other countries of Africa	16,263	24,738	27,320	28,511	27,662	0.51	-2.98
AMERICAS	38,015	41,102	58,549	64,521	63,748	1.18	-1.20
North America	38,015	41,102	58,421	63,911	63,242	1.17	-1.05
Canada	24,253	29,509	42,842	45,945	42,993	0.79	-6.43
United States	13,762	11,593	15,579	17,966	20,249	0.37	12.71
South America			128	610	506	0.01	-17.05
Brazil			128	610	506	0.01	-17.05
EAST ASIA AND THE PACIFIC	22,272	20,899	21,764	36,317	47,242	0.87	30.08
North-East Asia	22,272	20,899	21,308	35,239	45,513	0.84	29.16
China			350	1,087	1,123	0.02	3.31
Japan	22,272	20,899	20,958	34,152	44,390	0.82	29.98
Australasia			456	1,078	1,729	0.03	60.39
Australia			456	1,078	1,729	0.03	60.39
EUROPE	3,704,079	3,512,217	4,307,586	4,778,814	4,705,853	86.90	-1.53
Central/Eastern Europe	245,663	381,813	508,599	611,205	635,732	11.74	4.01
Bulgaria	1,274	1,421	1,792	3,021	3,153	0.06	4.37
Czech Republic	71,835	114,233	149,862	170,957	170,351	3.15	-0.35
Hungary	34,810	57,010	62,565	61,752	53,528	0.99	-13.32
Poland	49,748	66,050	94,512	156,027	166,377	3.07	6.63
Romania	2,168	3,718	8,086	6,195	13,758	0.25	122.08
Russian Federation	70,438	119,448	159,993	170,811	184,006	3.40	7.72
Slovakia	15,390	19,933	31,789	42,442	44,559	0.82	4.99
Northern Europe	410,699	373,469	462,219	519,368	506,389	9.35	-2.50
Ireland	6,673	6,615	4,900	4,693	8,136	0.15	73.36
United Kingdom	331,987	287,872	364,430	388,144	405,606	7.49	4.50
Scandinavia	72,039	78,982	92,889	126,531	92,647	1.71	-26.78
Southern Europe	771,233	776,938	980,111	1,077,317	990,847	18.30	-8.03
Greece	22,292	17,913	31,385	29,158	31,915	0.59	9.46
Italy	469,164	467,888	542,345	555,717	506,021	9.34	-8.94
Malta	7,086	10,122	11,052	15,688	5,976	0.11	-61.91
Portugal	26,201	20,503	30,134	26,722	27,691	0.51	3.63
Serbia			19,546	23,224	19,723	0.36	-15.07
Spain	237,087	245,757	345,649	426,808	399,521	7.38	-6.39
Yugoslavia, Sfr (Former)	9,403	14,755					
Western Europe	2,235,831	1,934,552	2,291,845	2,495,866	2,515,139	46.45	0.77
Austria	67,339	55,400	66,153	61,313	69,091	1.28	12.69
Belgium	134,011	149,898	163,572	176,422	200,153	3.70	13.45
France	1,144,750	1,010,428	1,221,501	1,406,549	1,406,688	25.98	0.01
Germany	716,393	560,033	664,606	686,244	653,303	12.06	-4.80
Luxembourg	12,839	16,328	23,152	20,223	20,593	0.38	1.83
Netherlands	57,881	51,814	54,348	66,119	74,071	1.37	12.03
Switzerland	102,618	90,651	98,513	78,996	91,240	1.68	15.50
East Mediterranean Europe	7,010	11,742	10,608	8,605	10,068	0.19	17.00

TUNISIA

3. Arrivals of non-resident tourists in hotels and similar establishments, by nationality

	2002	2003	2004	2005	2006	Market share 06	% Change 06-05
Turkey	7,010	11,742	10,608	8,605	10,068	0.19	17.00
Other Europe	**33,643**	**33,703**	**54,204**	**66,453**	**47,678**	**0.88**	**-28.25**
Other countries of Europe	33,643	33,703	54,204	66,453	47,678	0.88	-28.25
MIDDLE EAST	**171,200**	**161,260**	**161,984**	**171,416**	**180,066**	**3.33**	**5.05**
Middle East	**171,200**	**161,260**	**161,984**	**171,416**	**180,066**	**3.33**	**5.05**
Libyan Arab Jamahiriya	144,597	131,770	126,155	131,352	142,742	2.64	8.67
Other countries of Middle East	26,603	29,490	35,829	40,064	37,324	0.69	-6.84
REGION NOT SPECIFIED	**77,280**	**83,322**	**99,533**	**121,515**	**137,547**	**2.54**	**13.19**
Not Specified	**77,280**	**83,322**	**99,533**	**121,515**	**137,547**	**2.54**	**13.19**
Other countries of the World	77,280	80,316	95,979	115,018	126,551	2.34	10.03
Nationals Residing Abroad		3,006	3,554	6,497	10,996	0.20	69.25

Source: World Tourism Organization (UNWTO)

TUNISIA

5. Overnight stays of non-resident tourists in hotels and similar establishments, by nationality

	2002	2003	2004	2005	2006	Market share 06	% Change 06-05
TOTAL	25,897,226	25,301,322	30,664,500	33,587,183	34,086,092	100.00	1.49
AFRICA	606,880	726,309	732,914	769,590	862,899	2.53	12.12
North Africa	547,921	633,256	618,589	675,219	753,765	2.21	11.63
Algeria	497,832	581,137	564,544	630,719	707,768	2.08	12.22
Morocco	50,089	52,119	54,045	44,500	45,997	0.13	3.36
Other Africa	58,959	93,053	114,325	94,371	109,134	0.32	15.64
Other countries of Africa	58,959	93,053	114,325	94,371	109,134	0.32	15.64
AMERICAS	140,131	184,757	243,122	255,531	240,147	0.70	-6.02
North America	140,131	184,757	242,710	254,586	238,592	0.70	-6.28
Canada	91,973	132,463	195,352	200,195	176,584	0.52	-11.79
United States	48,158	52,294	47,358	54,391	62,008	0.18	14.00
South America			412	945	1,555		64.55
Brazil			412	945	1,555		64.55
EAST ASIA AND THE PACIFIC	40,397	40,275	43,929	61,252	80,435	0.24	31.32
North-East Asia	40,397	40,275	42,948	58,239	70,809	0.21	21.58
China			1,426	3,070	2,957	0.01	-3.68
Japan	40,397	40,275	41,522	55,169	67,852	0.20	22.99
Australasia			981	3,013	9,626	0.03	219.48
Australia			981	3,013	9,626	0.03	219.48
EUROPE	24,417,881	23,669,982	28,873,046	31,670,111	31,980,900	93.82	0.98
Central/Eastern Europe	1,748,381	2,886,959	3,848,190	4,492,934	4,760,618	13.97	5.96
Bulgaria	3,853	8,470	5,819	14,072	15,378	0.05	9.28
Czech Republic	583,142	984,417	1,288,584	1,432,338	1,439,104	4.22	0.47
Hungary	187,747	357,055	388,071	375,856	304,422	0.89	-19.01
Poland	353,216	524,725	748,308	1,135,783	1,229,867	3.61	8.28
Romania	9,702	19,203	18,320	29,021	67,493	0.20	132.57
Russian Federation	502,600	859,273	1,181,314	1,210,330	1,381,964	4.05	14.18
Slovakia	108,121	133,816	217,774	295,534	322,390	0.95	9.09
Northern Europe	3,308,966	2,970,758	3,654,225	4,180,850	4,006,961	11.76	-4.16
Denmark		78,565	123,591	284,395	111,092	0.33	-60.94
Finland		114,222	142,074	184,770	161,695	0.47	-12.49
Ireland	60,929	56,737	44,378	42,163	63,213	0.19	49.93
Norway		237,582	122,271	133,971	90,521	0.27	-32.43
Sweden		193,718	258,070	301,314	306,014	0.90	1.56
United Kingdom	2,678,069	2,289,934	2,963,841	3,234,237	3,274,426	9.61	1.24
Scandinavia	569,968						
Southern Europe	3,491,269	3,607,281	4,508,632	4,952,947	4,670,549	13.70	-5.70
Greece	42,832	37,824	59,464	57,755	58,567	0.17	1.41
Italy	2,678,635	2,711,719	3,251,102	3,393,580	3,199,817	9.39	-5.71
Malta	32,933	51,515	61,872	95,060	34,015	0.10	-64.22
Portugal	102,833	88,140	143,148	116,162	147,891	0.43	27.31
Serbia			129,266	151,120	137,502	0.40	-9.01
Spain	581,673	626,072	863,780	1,139,270	1,092,757	3.21	-4.08
Yugoslavia, Sfr (Former)	52,363	92,011					
Western Europe	15,750,501	13,995,618	16,570,590	17,676,887	18,207,803	53.42	3.00
Austria	553,312	465,220	544,331	515,557	572,471	1.68	11.04
Belgium	1,102,259	1,267,594	1,395,542	1,492,812	1,696,519	4.98	13.65
France	6,066,662	5,671,187	6,835,348	7,798,901	8,196,616	24.05	5.10

TUNISIA

5. Overnight stays of non-resident tourists in hotels and similar establishments, by nationality

	2002	2003	2004	2005	2006	Market share 06	% Change 06-05
Germany	6,805,286	5,498,718	6,535,380	6,641,427	6,372,459	18.70	-4.05
Luxembourg	113,484	113,472	155,952	179,088	185,475	0.54	3.57
Netherlands	351,656	329,628	364,455	443,862	527,910	1.55	18.94
Switzerland	757,842	649,799	739,582	605,240	656,353	1.93	8.45
East Mediterranean Europe	**27,225**	**41,976**	**39,511**	**29,592**	**33,561**	**0.10**	**13.41**
Turkey	27,225	41,976	39,511	29,592	33,561	0.10	13.41
Other Europe	**91,539**	**167,390**	**251,898**	**336,901**	**301,408**	**0.88**	**-10.54**
Other countries of Europe	91,539	167,390	251,898	336,901	301,408	0.88	-10.54
MIDDLE EAST	**384,706**	**370,980**	**385,215**	**391,681**	**416,244**	**1.22**	**6.27**
Middle East	**384,706**	**370,980**	**385,215**	**391,681**	**416,244**	**1.22**	**6.27**
Libyan Arab Jamahiriya	283,701	256,658	247,209	242,810	268,658	0.79	10.65
Other countries of Middle East	101,005	114,322	138,006	148,871	147,586	0.43	-0.86
REGION NOT SPECIFIED	**307,231**	**309,019**	**386,274**	**439,018**	**505,467**	**1.48**	**15.14**
Not Specified	**307,231**	**309,019**	**386,274**	**439,018**	**505,467**	**1.48**	**15.14**
Other countries of the World	307,231	301,983	373,946	421,779	464,807	1.36	10.20
Nationals Residing Abroad		7,036	12,328	17,239	40,660	0.12	135.86

Source: World Tourism Organization (UNWTO)

TURKEY

1. Arrivals of non-resident tourists at national borders, by nationality

	2002	2003	2004	2005	2006	Market share 06	% Change 06-05
TOTAL	12,789,827	13,340,956	16,826,062	20,272,877	18,916,436	100.00	-6.69
AFRICA	130,758	119,122	131,148	154,489	152,983	0.81	-0.97
North Africa	105,436	102,174	113,018	130,903	118,966	0.63	-9.12
Algeria	39,490	39,945	42,500	43,089	36,351	0.19	-15.64
Morocco	12,548	13,704	15,903	24,754	30,307	0.16	22.43
Sudan	2,209	1,911	2,371	2,884	4,376	0.02	51.73
Tunisia	51,189	46,614	52,244	60,176	47,932	0.25	-20.35
Southern Africa	15,193	7,270	7,309	10,216	12,077	0.06	18.22
South Africa	15,193	7,270	7,309	10,216	12,077	0.06	18.22
Other Africa	10,129	9,678	10,821	13,370	21,940	0.12	64.10
Other countries of Africa	10,129	9,678	10,821	13,370	21,940	0.12	64.10
AMERICAS	253,804	213,136	282,586	390,884	458,898	2.43	17.40
Central America	1,614	918	1,277	5,111	1,931	0.01	-62.22
All countries of Central America	1,614	918	1,277	5,111	1,931	0.01	-62.22
North America	235,723	197,491	260,439	351,102	414,375	2.19	18.02
Canada	28,686	27,732	36,503	49,395	58,838	0.31	19.12
Mexico	8,171	6,395	9,551	12,216	12,893	0.07	5.54
United States	197,402	162,198	212,774	283,836	326,652	1.73	15.08
Other countries of North America	1,464	1,166	1,611	5,655	15,992	0.08	182.79
South America	16,467	14,727	20,870	34,671	42,592	0.23	22.85
Argentina	2,371	2,769	4,281	7,624	8,096	0.04	6.19
Brazil	6,040	5,072	7,675	14,500	18,617	0.10	28.39
Chile	2,480	2,171	3,040	4,105	4,494	0.02	9.48
Colombia	1,396	983	1,285	2,237	2,598	0.01	16.14
Venezuela	1,321	865	1,318	2,250	3,211	0.02	42.71
Other countries of South America	2,859	2,867	3,271	3,955	5,576	0.03	40.99
EAST ASIA AND THE PACIFIC	280,607	241,996	288,326	421,643	471,280	2.49	11.77
North-East Asia	164,917	137,127	152,444	246,304	281,187	1.49	14.16
China	31,637	26,506	34,666	43,157	54,783	0.29	26.94
Japan	91,153	64,664	61,911	112,396	119,391	0.63	6.22
Korea, Republic of	42,127	45,957	55,867	90,751	107,013	0.57	17.92
South-East Asia	33,534	31,317	42,729	58,220	60,339	0.32	3.64
Indonesia	8,080	5,324	6,558	7,996	8,444	0.04	5.60
Malaysia	8,070	6,828	14,036	18,887	17,797	0.09	-5.77
Philippines	9,253	11,044	10,272	12,691	15,909	0.08	25.36
Singapore	4,959	5,802	8,237	12,855	11,216	0.06	-12.75
Thailand	3,172	2,319	3,626	5,791	6,973	0.04	20.41
Australasia	64,272	54,020	68,515	90,538	95,365	0.50	5.33
Australia	52,551	45,289	57,693	76,012	81,144	0.43	6.75
New Zealand	11,721	8,731	10,822	14,526	14,221	0.08	-2.10
Other East Asia and the Pacific	17,884	19,532	24,638	26,581	34,389	0.18	29.37
Other countries of Asia	17,432	19,252	24,377	26,048	34,221	0.18	31.38
Other countries of Oceania	452	280	261	533	168		-68.48
EUROPE	11,359,447	11,871,694	14,946,162	17,663,077	16,268,842	86.00	-7.89
Central/Eastern Europe	2,935,932	3,501,961	4,523,765	5,603,934	5,644,149	29.84	0.72
Azerbaijan	162,503	192,698	329,532	411,075	379,012	2.00	-7.80
Armenia	17,519	23,104	33,007	36,637	41,684	0.22	13.78
Bulgaria	832,220	1,005,684	1,309,396	1,621,113	1,177,083	6.22	-27.39

TURKEY

1. Arrivals of non-resident tourists at national borders, by nationality

	2002	2003	2004	2005	2006	Market share 06	% Change 06-05
Belarus	36,271	43,607	62,234	77,029	85,197	0.45	10.60
Czech Republic	61,446	46,341	57,390	86,303	90,033	0.48	4.32
Estonia					15,835	0.08	
Georgia	161,095	167,551	234,301	367,122	548,749	2.90	49.47
Hungary	49,920	46,767	60,060	74,771	73,346	0.39	-1.91
Kazakhstan	43,749	64,968	83,272	106,166	135,439	0.72	27.57
Kyrgyzstan	10,379	13,793	24,705	31,015	41,426	0.22	33.57
Latvia					34,055	0.18	
Lithuania					48,099	0.25	
Republic of Moldova	45,772	54,828	71,395	90,736	108,887	0.58	20.00
Poland	148,836	100,538	134,790	177,254	185,193	0.98	4.48
Romania	177,397	184,366	168,702	201,827	244,914	1.29	21.35
Russian Federation	937,298	1,272,140	1,593,647	1,855,918	1,842,248	9.74	-0.74
Slovakia	33,064	23,597	31,269	34,133	34,788	0.18	1.92
Tajikistan	1,526	3,557	4,917	6,814	11,947	0.06	75.33
Turkmenistan	21,317	15,784	26,617	34,282	48,856	0.26	42.51
Ukraine	175,247	223,619	277,943	367,105	468,787	2.48	27.70
Uzbekistan	20,373	19,019	20,588	24,634	28,571	0.15	15.98
Northern Europe	**1,487,981**	**1,470,435**	**2,004,174**	**2,682,095**	**2,424,964**	**12.82**	**-9.59**
Denmark	159,795	147,730	209,730	299,285	229,867	1.22	-23.19
Finland	76,728	55,354	75,394	90,397	73,671	0.39	-18.50
Iceland	1,168	1,137	2,061	3,826	6,488	0.03	69.58
Ireland	49,412	54,055	74,502	95,175	85,072	0.45	-10.62
Norway	85,827	81,670	115,708	156,687	160,064	0.85	2.16
Sweden	197,179	194,724	278,047	398,382	320,286	1.69	-19.60
United Kingdom	917,872	935,765	1,248,732	1,638,343	1,549,516	8.19	-5.42
Southern Europe	**930,210**	**988,234**	**1,222,593**	**1,432,724**	**1,320,125**	**6.98**	**-7.86**
Albania	29,075	32,206	43,948	50,513	49,891	0.26	-1.23
Bosnia and Herzegovina	32,482	34,618	41,629	44,501	40,434	0.21	-9.14
Croatia	14,045	14,861	20,128	22,173	21,590	0.11	-2.63
Greece	255,867	364,571	454,572	548,177	388,745	2.06	-29.08
Italy	193,669	144,095	220,871	282,619	314,726	1.66	11.36
Malta					3,348	0.02	
Portugal	12,233	9,179	12,940	16,208	14,743	0.08	-9.04
Slovenia	10,488	15,078	21,882	22,558	21,365	0.11	-5.29
Spain	73,379	68,415	97,965	151,593	183,276	0.97	20.90
TFYR of Macedonia	120,945	119,299	115,996	119,144	118,376	0.63	-0.64
Serbia and Montenegro	188,027	185,912	192,662	175,238	163,631	0.87	-6.62
Western Europe	**5,600,689**	**5,448,832**	**6,699,100**	**7,330,694**	**6,348,206**	**33.56**	**-13.40**
Austria	369,866	370,306	447,304	476,114	422,066	2.23	-11.35
Belgium	306,911	299,583	419,147	493,166	448,102	2.37	-9.14
France	510,381	444,142	514,443	660,812	624,699	3.30	-5.46
Germany	3,421,112	3,231,115	3,880,892	4,166,430	3,674,107	19.42	-11.82
Luxembourg	3,983	3,111	4,772	7,740	4,719	0.02	-39.03
Netherlands	848,771	921,704	1,173,809	1,231,930	972,315	5.14	-21.07
Switzerland	139,665	178,871	258,733	294,502	202,198	1.07	-31.34
East Mediterranean Europe	**357,900**	**407,296**	**403,007**	**500,636**	**508,168**	**2.69**	**1.50**
Cyprus	94,033	104,376	121,662	140,888	172,578	0.91	22.49
Israel	263,867	302,920	281,345	359,748	335,590	1.77	-6.72
Other Europe	**46,735**	**54,936**	**93,523**	**112,994**	**23,230**	**0.12**	**-79.44**
Other countries of Europe	46,735	54,936	93,523	112,994	23,230	0.12	-79.44
MIDDLE EAST	**303,860**	**359,281**	**498,095**	**625,686**	**630,140**	**3.33**	**0.71**
Middle East	**303,860**	**359,281**	**498,095**	**625,686**	**630,140**	**3.33**	**0.71**

TURKEY

1. Arrivals of non-resident tourists at national borders, by nationality

	2002	2003	2004	2005	2006	Market share 06	% Change 06-05
Bahrain	4,567	4,122	3,146	4,178	4,230	0.02	1.24
Iraq	14,261	24,725	111,472	107,952	123,110	0.65	14.04
Jordan	33,099	37,365	39,946	43,591	46,490	0.25	6.65
Kuwait	6,972	8,164	7,167	10,958	11,766	0.06	7.37
Lebanon	30,903	34,710	35,847	38,506	35,027	0.19	-9.03
Libyan Arab Jamahiriya	29,959	27,882	27,842	29,275	31,492	0.17	7.57
Oman	1,204	1,298	941	761	230		-69.78
Qatar	824	1,209	1,414	1,950	2,579	0.01	32.26
Saudi Arabia	25,593	23,244	24,940	36,029	38,679	0.20	7.36
Syrian Arab Republic	125,711	153,787	192,835	287,317	276,380	1.46	-3.81
United Arab Emirates	4,964	6,717	7,191	8,778	12,133	0.06	38.22
Egypt	21,155	29,667	34,114	42,723	41,930	0.22	-1.86
Yemen	1,809	2,138	2,221	2,513	2,931	0.02	16.63
Other countries of Middle East	2,839	4,253	9,019	11,155	3,163	0.02	-71.65
SOUTH ASIA	**450,787**	**522,054**	**660,787**	**994,620**	**917,360**	**4.85**	**-7.77**
South Asia	**450,787**	**522,054**	**660,787**	**994,620**	**917,360**	**4.85**	**-7.77**
Bangladesh	858	2,050	2,731	2,888	3,111	0.02	7.72
India	9,626	12,756	19,154	22,864	33,924	0.18	48.37
Iran, Islamic Republic of	432,083	497,189	628,667	957,171	865,731	4.58	-9.55
Pakistan	8,220	10,059	10,235	11,697	14,594	0.08	24.77
REGION NOT SPECIFIED	**10,564**	**13,673**	**18,958**	**22,478**	**16,933**	**0.09**	**-24.67**
Not Specified	**10,564**	**13,673**	**18,958**	**22,478**	**16,933**	**0.09**	**-24.67**
Other countries of the World	10,564	13,673	18,958	22,478	16,933	0.09	-24.67

Source: World Tourism Organization (UNWTO)

807

TURKEY

2. Arrivals of non-resident visitors at national borders, by nationality

		2002	2003	2004	2005	2006	Market share 06	% Change 06-05
TOTAL	(*)	13,256,028	14,029,558	17,516,908	21,124,886	19,819,833	100.00	-6.18
AFRICA		134,029	122,912	135,559	160,665	158,722	0.80	-1.21
North Africa		107,597	104,569	114,963	133,758	121,319	0.61	-9.30
Algeria		41,473	42,140	44,124	44,854	38,542	0.19	-14.07
Morocco		12,643	13,794	15,987	24,914	30,410	0.15	22.06
Sudan		2,210	1,917	2,382	2,897	4,383	0.02	51.29
Tunisia		51,271	46,718	52,470	61,093	47,984	0.24	-21.46
Southern Africa		16,168	8,494	9,430	13,315	15,131	0.08	13.64
South Africa		16,168	8,494	9,430	13,315	15,131	0.08	13.64
Other Africa		10,264	9,849	11,166	13,592	22,272	0.11	63.86
Other countries of Africa		10,264	9,849	11,166	13,592	22,272	0.11	63.86
AMERICAS		323,759	304,088	388,126	593,289	725,751	3.66	22.33
Central America		2,143	1,721	1,820	5,992	3,127	0.02	-47.81
All countries of Central America		2,143	1,721	1,820	5,992	3,127	0.02	-47.81
North America		299,665	278,463	359,244	540,475	666,988	3.37	23.41
Canada		38,999	42,019	52,870	81,229	97,925	0.49	20.55
Mexico		11,297	12,163	13,417	17,801	20,000	0.10	12.35
United States		247,629	222,918	291,102	434,991	532,419	2.69	22.40
Other countries of North America		1,740	1,363	1,855	6,454	16,644	0.08	157.89
South America		21,951	23,904	27,062	46,822	55,636	0.28	18.82
Argentina		2,890	6,509	5,796	10,265	11,474	0.06	11.78
Brazil		8,332	7,346	9,934	20,077	24,222	0.12	20.65
Chile		3,315	3,070	3,759	5,415	5,644	0.03	4.23
Colombia		2,259	1,797	2,088	3,277	4,175	0.02	27.40
Venezuela		1,832	1,460	1,680	3,202	4,545	0.02	41.94
Other countries of South America		3,323	3,722	3,805	4,586	5,576	0.03	21.59
EAST ASIA AND THE PACIFIC		297,779	265,150	307,552	449,853	508,912	2.57	13.13
North-East Asia		169,039	141,836	156,583	252,643	290,218	1.46	14.87
China		31,951	27,557	35,339	44,077	56,323	0.28	27.78
Japan		94,514	67,874	64,318	116,969	125,755	0.63	7.51
Korea, Republic of		42,574	46,405	56,926	91,597	108,140	0.55	18.06
South-East Asia		39,202	36,330	46,035	61,498	66,845	0.34	8.69
Indonesia		9,609	5,928	7,083	8,269	8,893	0.04	7.55
Malaysia		8,159	6,975	14,373	19,183	18,084	0.09	-5.73
Philippines		13,123	15,100	12,422	15,072	21,115	0.11	40.09
Singapore		5,068	5,915	8,432	13,066	11,577	0.06	-11.40
Thailand		3,243	2,412	3,725	5,908	7,176	0.04	21.46
Australasia		71,455	67,125	79,965	108,723	117,448	0.59	8.02
Australia		58,678	56,854	67,413	91,107	99,580	0.50	9.30
New Zealand		12,777	10,271	12,552	17,616	17,868	0.09	1.43
Other East Asia and the Pacific		18,083	19,859	24,969	26,989	34,401	0.17	27.46
Other countries of Asia		17,628	19,572	24,702	26,450	34,221	0.17	29.38
Other countries of Oceania		455	287	267	539	180		-66.60
EUROPE		11,731,327	12,438,301	15,510,661	18,277,378	16,854,388	85.04	-7.79
Central/Eastern Europe		2,974,370	3,536,498	4,637,734	5,731,841	5,695,644	28.74	-0.63
Azerbaijan		163,133	193,410	330,042	411,652	380,133	1.92	-7.66
Armenia		17,530	23,118	33,034	36,648	41,692	0.21	13.76
Bulgaria		834,073	1,006,612	1,310,082	1,621,918	1,177,906	5.94	-27.38

TURKEY

2. Arrivals of non-resident visitors at national borders, by nationality

	2002	2003	2004	2005	2006	Market share 06	% Change 06-05
Belarus	36,371	43,746	62,374	77,183	85,336	0.43	10.56
Czech Republic	63,223	48,768	59,112	88,739	94,450	0.48	6.44
Estonia			13,016	16,710	15,952	0.08	-4.54
Georgia	161,375	167,911	234,937	367,338	549,328	2.77	49.54
Hungary	51,336	48,216	62,102	78,115	78,275	0.39	0.20
Kazakhstan	43,793	65,092	83,404	106,196	135,637	0.68	27.72
Kyrgyzstan	10,379	13,796	24,717	31,023	41,455	0.21	33.63
Latvia			24,985	24,467	34,177	0.17	39.69
Lithuania			37,607	50,481	48,458	0.24	-4.01
Republic of Moldova	46,091	55,385	71,985	91,178	109,206	0.55	19.77
Poland	150,949	102,347	138,327	181,021	190,774	0.96	5.39
Romania	180,203	185,174	169,398	202,860	245,941	1.24	21.24
Russian Federation	946,511	1,281,407	1,605,006	1,864,682	1,853,442	9.35	-0.60
Slovakia	33,507	24,127	31,931	35,448	36,151	0.18	1.98
Tajikistan	1,526	3,559	4,922	6,814	11,950	0.06	75.37
Turkmenistan	21,317	15,785	26,620	34,282	48,857	0.25	42.52
Ukraine	192,661	238,962	293,459	380,397	487,917	2.46	28.27
Uzbekistan	20,392	19,083	20,674	24,689	28,607	0.14	15.87
Northern Europe	**1,635,710**	**1,658,843**	**2,168,891**	**2,828,160**	**2,580,840**	**13.02**	**-8.74**
Denmark	164,979	154,350	214,948	304,621	235,755	1.19	-22.61
Finland	80,739	59,753	80,908	95,730	78,766	0.40	-17.72
Iceland	1,273	1,355	2,114	3,934	6,667	0.03	69.47
Ireland	53,036	58,913	78,884	98,316	88,973	0.45	-9.50
Norway	94,528	88,863	120,143	161,760	165,580	0.84	2.36
Sweden	203,648	204,205	284,086	405,956	326,254	1.65	-19.63
United Kingdom	1,037,507	1,091,404	1,387,808	1,757,843	1,678,845	8.47	-4.49
Southern Europe	**992,602**	**1,138,346**	**1,381,075**	**1,654,796**	**1,496,233**	**7.55**	**-9.58**
Albania	29,221	32,439	44,423	51,296	50,328	0.25	-1.89
Bosnia and Herzegovina	32,490	34,642	41,685	44,701	40,489	0.20	-9.42
Croatia	14,826	15,291	20,748	22,923	22,321	0.11	-2.63
Greece	280,033	393,517	491,627	593,444	418,158	2.11	-29.54
Italy	210,657	236,931	318,097	401,852	402,568	2.03	0.18
Malta			2,146	2,831	4,596	0.02	62.35
Portugal	16,559	12,185	14,909	21,013	18,148	0.09	-13.63
Slovenia	10,889	15,701	22,898	23,737	23,139	0.12	-2.52
Spain	88,811	92,326	115,764	198,462	234,334	1.18	18.07
TFYR of Macedonia	120,989	119,305	116,009	119,150	118,387	0.60	-0.64
Serbia and Montenegro	188,127	186,009	192,769	175,387	163,765	0.83	-6.63
Western Europe	**5,715,854**	**5,623,353**	**6,885,485**	**7,507,157**	**6,523,065**	**32.91**	**-13.11**
Austria	377,036	379,830	455,863	486,051	429,709	2.17	-11.59
Belgium	313,585	308,118	426,971	503,821	459,824	2.32	-8.73
France	522,740	470,582	548,858	701,190	657,859	3.32	-6.18
Germany	3,481,671	3,332,451	3,983,899	4,243,584	3,762,475	18.98	-11.34
Luxembourg	4,172	3,432	7,125	9,676	5,365	0.03	-44.55
Netherlands	873,278	940,098	1,191,382	1,254,153	997,556	5.03	-20.46
Switzerland	143,372	188,842	271,387	308,682	210,277	1.06	-31.88
East Mediterranean Europe	**364,406**	**425,590**	**420,857**	**534,863**	**535,180**	**2.70**	**0.06**
Cyprus	94,143	104,438	121,685	140,920	172,679	0.87	22.54
Israel	270,263	321,152	299,172	393,943	362,501	1.83	-7.98
Other Europe	**48,385**	**55,671**	**16,619**	**20,561**	**23,426**	**0.12**	**13.93**
Other countries of Europe	48,385	55,671	16,619	20,561	23,426	0.12	13.93
MIDDLE EAST	**306,947**	**362,333**	**494,298**	**622,801**	**633,625**	**3.20**	**1.74**
Middle East	**306,947**	**362,333**	**494,298**	**622,801**	**633,625**	**3.20**	**1.74**

TURKEY

2. Arrivals of non-resident visitors at national borders, by nationality

	2002	2003	2004	2005	2006	Market share 06	% Change 06-05
Bahrain	4,569	4,133	3,154	4,201	4,254	0.02	1.26
Iraq	15,765	24,727	111,475	107,968	123,118	0.62	14.03
Jordan	33,130	37,449	39,985	43,700	46,518	0.23	6.45
Kuwait	6,989	8,210	7,198	11,086	11,823	0.06	6.65
Lebanon	31,298	35,285	36,298	41,074	35,995	0.18	-12.37
Libyan Arab Jamahiriya	29,970	28,185	27,846	29,327	31,497	0.16	7.40
Oman	1,206	1,298	944	763	233		-69.46
Qatar	824	1,210	1,414	1,955	2,585	0.01	32.23
Saudi Arabia	25,657	23,676	25,197	36,328	38,890	0.20	7.05
Syrian Arab Republic	126,323	154,447	193,961	288,625	277,779	1.40	-3.76
United Arab Emirates	4,977	6,717	7,213	8,814	12,153	0.06	37.88
Egypt	21,583	30,556	34,454	43,149	42,686	0.22	-1.07
Yemen	1,810	2,141	2,221	2,529	2,931	0.01	15.90
Other countries of Middle East	2,846	4,299	2,938	3,282	3,163	0.02	-3.63
SOUTH ASIA	**451,623**	**523,101**	**661,753**	**998,418**	**919,148**	**4.64**	**-7.94**
South Asia	**451,623**	**523,101**	**661,753**	**998,418**	**919,148**	**4.64**	**-7.94**
Bangladesh	866	2,055	2,735	2,939	3,128	0.02	6.43
India	10,122	13,667	20,003	26,480	35,379	0.18	33.61
Iran, Islamic Republic of	432,282	497,282	628,725	957,244	865,941	4.37	-9.54
Pakistan	8,353	10,097	10,290	11,755	14,700	0.07	25.05
REGION NOT SPECIFIED	**10,564**	**13,673**	**18,959**	**22,482**	**19,287**	**0.10**	**-14.21**
Not Specified	**10,564**	**13,673**	**18,959**	**22,482**	**19,287**	**0.10**	**-14.21**
Other countries of the World	10,564	13,673	18,959	22,482	19,287	0.10	-14.21

Source: World Tourism Organization (UNWTO)

TURKEY

3. Arrivals of non-resident tourists in hotels and similar establishments, by nationality

		2002	2003	2004	2005	2006	Market share 06	% Change 06-05
TOTAL	(*)	9,859,459	8,983,199	10,962,053	12,936,651	11,882,836	100.00	-8.15
AFRICA		35,528	25,505	32,528	56,065	59,755	0.50	6.58
North Africa		24,583	18,255	22,960	39,927	42,900	0.36	7.45
Algeria		12,502	5,938	9,061	13,942	16,544	0.14	18.66
Morocco		2,903	3,987	4,441	7,831	9,448	0.08	20.65
Sudan		718	1,051	1,428	1,835	2,352	0.02	28.17
Tunisia		8,460	7,279	8,030	16,319	14,556	0.12	-10.80
Southern Africa		9,641	6,023	7,709	10,093	9,964	0.08	-1.28
South Africa		9,641	6,023	7,709	10,093	9,964	0.08	-1.28
Other Africa		1,304	1,227	1,859	6,045	6,891	0.06	14.00
Other countries of Africa		1,304	1,227	1,859	6,045	6,891	0.06	14.00
AMERICAS		381,698	231,566	321,152	430,703	553,417	4.66	28.49
Central America		178	106	90	573	761	0.01	32.81
All countries of Central America		178	106	90	573	761	0.01	32.81
North America		348,196	220,131	304,977	407,390	515,208	4.34	26.47
Canada		36,446	14,453	21,286	32,929	41,228	0.35	25.20
Mexico		7,247	6,264	11,986	11,014	11,106	0.09	0.84
United States		303,797	198,528	264,575	361,655	460,744	3.88	27.40
Other countries of North America		706	886	7,130	1,792	2,130	0.02	18.86
South America		33,324	11,329	16,085	22,740	37,448	0.32	64.68
Argentina		24,773	6,117	6,954	7,883	13,178	0.11	67.17
Brazil		4,292	2,849	5,162	10,096	15,659	0.13	55.10
Chile		1,363	844	1,890	1,901	2,134	0.02	12.26
Colombia		467	356	537	949	2,086	0.02	119.81
Venezuela		552	270	897	859	1,503	0.01	74.97
Other countries of South America		1,877	893	645	1,052	2,888	0.02	174.52
EAST ASIA AND THE PACIFIC		524,576	391,934	439,998	802,082	721,455	6.07	-10.05
North-East Asia		419,305	331,306	340,198	672,757	591,700	4.98	-12.05
China		23,670	21,538	29,821	41,933	49,893	0.42	18.98
Japan		332,168	233,847	207,891	458,862	363,354	3.06	-20.81
Korea, Republic of		63,467	75,921	102,486	171,962	178,453	1.50	3.77
South-East Asia		24,960	14,362	30,906	42,787	43,351	0.36	1.32
Indonesia		1,079	373	1,102	1,654	1,726	0.01	4.35
Malaysia		6,871	4,771	12,457	18,297	19,162	0.16	4.73
Philippines		1,904	3,536	3,609	3,698	5,140	0.04	38.99
Singapore		14,037	5,249	12,621	16,928	13,778	0.12	-18.61
Thailand		1,069	433	1,117	2,210	3,545	0.03	60.41
Australasia		77,060	44,970	64,609	82,639	81,622	0.69	-1.23
Australia		69,543	41,829	59,644	74,645	72,311	0.61	-3.13
New Zealand		7,517	3,141	4,965	7,994	9,311	0.08	16.47
Other East Asia and the Pacific		3,251	1,296	4,285	3,899	4,782	0.04	22.65
Other countries of Asia		2,547	1,173	3,029	2,707	4,192	0.04	54.86
All countries of Oceania		704	123	1,256	1,192	590		-50.50
EUROPE		8,425,209	7,912,376	9,703,060	10,949,945	9,938,550	83.64	-9.24
Central/Eastern Europe		1,477,550	1,603,975	2,021,034	2,246,255	3,112,396	26.19	38.56
Bulgaria		65,690	53,805	63,521	70,718	77,755	0.65	9.95
Czech Republic		44,641	29,833	47,409	64,712	63,013	0.53	-2.63
Hungary		31,016	21,970	32,954	43,035	37,942	0.32	-11.83

TURKEY

3. Arrivals of non-resident tourists in hotels and similar establishments, by nationality

	2002	2003	2004	2005	2006	Market share 06	% Change 06-05
Poland	77,222	129,778	75,081	115,282	93,382	0.79	-19.00
Romania	58,076	56,776	60,051	69,750	86,418	0.73	23.90
Commonwealth Independent State	1,200,905	1,311,813	1,742,018	1,882,758	2,753,886	23.18	46.27
Northern Europe	**689,585**	**624,030**	**876,254**	**1,334,667**	**1,191,266**	**10.03**	**-10.74**
Iceland	3,189	1,561	3,180	8,754	10,816	0.09	23.55
Ireland	52,894	75,388	66,535	46,515	50,787	0.43	9.18
United Kingdom	459,013	406,644	582,970	911,356	799,334	6.73	-12.29
Scandinavia	174,489	140,437	223,569	368,042	330,329	2.78	-10.25
Southern Europe	**735,810**	**595,257**	**667,440**	**918,643**	**703,468**	**5.92**	**-23.42**
Albania	10,842	15,279	21,031	22,074	22,626	0.19	2.50
Greece	108,818	124,318	162,825	266,765	113,714	0.96	-57.37
Italy	293,648	182,975	203,234	273,867	213,338	1.80	-22.10
Portugal	18,551	11,407	14,266	13,770	10,752	0.09	-21.92
Spain	186,582	163,857	168,419	239,339	239,162	2.01	-0.07
Yugoslavia, Sfr (Former)	117,369	97,421	97,665	102,828	103,876	0.87	1.02
Western Europe	**5,244,075**	**4,834,032**	**5,900,661**	**6,123,215**	**4,549,868**	**38.29**	**-25.69**
Austria	256,600	227,714	212,052	222,893	167,298	1.41	-24.94
France	593,557	437,108	477,409	598,386	429,807	3.62	-28.17
Germany	3,312,540	3,147,411	3,741,566	3,856,154	2,894,641	24.36	-24.93
Switzerland	145,632	155,304	217,701	210,288	117,555	0.99	-44.10
Benelux	935,746	866,495	1,251,933	1,235,494	940,567	7.92	-23.87
East Mediterranean Europe	**259,867**	**247,865**	**220,014**	**303,265**	**342,603**	**2.88**	**12.97**
Cyprus	17,602	21,691	23,715	70,101	108,126	0.91	54.24
Israel	242,265	226,174	196,299	233,164	234,477	1.97	0.56
Other Europe	**18,322**	**7,217**	**17,657**	**23,900**	**38,949**	**0.33**	**62.97**
Other countries of Europe	18,322	7,217	17,657	23,900	38,949	0.33	62.97
MIDDLE EAST	**223,860**	**214,991**	**245,695**	**306,114**	**343,612**	**2.89**	**12.25**
Middle East	**223,860**	**214,991**	**245,695**	**306,114**	**343,612**	**2.89**	**12.25**
Bahrain	2,107	2,258	2,785	2,272	4,007	0.03	76.36
Iraq	12,504	13,974	26,393	40,033	49,537	0.42	23.74
Jordan	20,462	20,301	23,707	25,130	29,794	0.25	18.56
Kuwait	7,415	9,182	10,221	13,090	12,271	0.10	-6.26
Lebanon	52,077	34,455	27,155	31,820	22,226	0.19	-30.15
Libyan Arab Jamahiriya	13,641	11,636	13,510	14,397	13,453	0.11	-6.56
Oman	407	472	661	673	1,727	0.01	156.61
Qatar	480	826	2,070	1,976	2,197	0.02	11.18
Saudi Arabia	41,779	44,649	39,605	49,027	79,204	0.67	61.55
Syrian Arab Republic	35,309	32,566	46,306	51,637	55,397	0.47	7.28
United Arab Emirates	11,069	18,106	17,971	25,571	31,437	0.26	22.94
Egypt	17,395	19,164	24,235	36,581	32,052	0.27	-12.38
Yemen	582	838	784	3,216	2,325	0.02	-27.71
Other countries of Middle East	8,633	6,564	10,292	10,691	7,985	0.07	-25.31
SOUTH ASIA	**114,857**	**106,882**	**133,266**	**160,852**	**176,547**	**1.49**	**9.76**
South Asia	**114,857**	**106,882**	**133,266**	**160,852**	**176,547**	**1.49**	**9.76**
Bangladesh	544	742	487	687	857	0.01	24.75
India	4,998	6,893	10,835	17,263	22,861	0.19	32.43
Iran, Islamic Republic of	104,956	94,735	116,853	136,562	143,996	1.21	5.44
Pakistan	4,359	4,512	5,091	6,340	8,833	0.07	39.32
REGION NOT SPECIFIED	**153,731**	**99,945**	**86,354**	**230,890**	**89,500**	**0.75**	**-61.24**
Not Specified	**153,731**	**99,945**	**86,354**	**230,890**	**89,500**	**0.75**	**-61.24**
Other countries of the World	153,731	99,945	86,354	230,890	89,500	0.75	-61.24

TURKEY

4. Arrivals of non-resident tourists in all types of accommodation establishments, by nationality

		2002	2003	2004	2005	2006	Market share 06	% Change 06-05
TOTAL	(*)	9,871,594	8,991,456	10,981,763	12,952,616	11,896,571	100.00	-8.15
AFRICA		35,530	25,506	32,528	56,087	59,755	0.50	6.54
North Africa		24,583	18,255	22,960	39,949	42,900	0.36	7.39
Algeria		12,502	5,938	9,061	13,942	16,544	0.14	18.66
Morocco		2,903	3,987	4,441	7,831	9,448	0.08	20.65
Sudan		718	1,051	1,428	1,835	2,352	0.02	28.17
Tunisia		8,460	7,279	8,030	16,341	14,556	0.12	-10.92
Southern Africa		9,643	6,024	7,709	10,093	9,964	0.08	-1.28
South Africa		9,643	6,024	7,709	10,093	9,964	0.08	-1.28
Other Africa		1,304	1,227	1,859	6,045	6,891	0.06	14.00
Other countries of Africa		1,304	1,227	1,859	6,045	6,891	0.06	14.00
AMERICAS		382,266	231,898	321,156	430,809	553,424	4.65	28.46
Central America		178	106	90	573	761	0.01	32.81
All countries of Central America		178	106	90	573	761	0.01	32.81
North America		348,679	220,463	304,981	407,496	515,215	4.33	26.43
Canada		36,456	14,453	21,286	32,929	41,228	0.35	25.20
Mexico		7,247	6,387	11,986	11,028	11,106	0.09	0.71
United States		304,270	198,737	264,579	361,747	460,751	3.87	27.37
Other countries of North America		706	886	7,130	1,792	2,130	0.02	18.86
South America		33,409	11,329	16,085	22,740	37,448	0.31	64.68
Argentina		24,855	6,117	6,954	7,883	13,178	0.11	67.17
Brazil		4,295	2,849	5,162	10,096	15,659	0.13	55.10
Chile		1,363	844	1,890	1,901	2,134	0.02	12.26
Colombia		467	356	537	949	2,086	0.02	119.81
Venezuela		552	270	897	859	1,503	0.01	74.97
Other countries of South America		1,877	893	645	1,052	2,888	0.02	174.52
EAST ASIA AND THE PACIFIC		524,613	391,959	439,999	802,173	721,462	6.06	-10.06
North-East Asia		419,324	331,306	340,199	672,812	591,702	4.97	-12.06
China		23,670	21,538	29,821	41,937	49,893	0.42	18.97
Japan		332,174	233,847	207,892	458,901	363,356	3.05	-20.82
Korea, Republic of		63,480	75,921	102,486	171,974	178,453	1.50	3.77
South-East Asia		24,961	14,362	30,906	42,787	43,351	0.36	1.32
Indonesia		1,079	373	1,102	1,654	1,726	0.01	4.35
Malaysia		6,871	4,771	12,457	18,297	19,162	0.16	4.73
Philippines		1,904	3,536	3,609	3,698	5,140	0.04	38.99
Singapore		14,038	5,249	12,621	16,928	13,778	0.12	-18.61
Thailand		1,069	433	1,117	2,210	3,545	0.03	60.41
Australasia		77,077	44,995	64,609	82,641	81,627	0.69	-1.23
Australia		69,556	41,852	59,644	74,647	72,312	0.61	-3.13
New Zealand		7,521	3,143	4,965	7,994	9,315	0.08	16.52
Other East Asia and the Pacific		3,251	1,296	4,285	3,933	4,782	0.04	21.59
Other countries of Asia		2,547	1,173	3,029	2,741	4,192	0.04	52.94
All countries of Oceania		704	123	1,256	1,192	590		-50.50
EUROPE		8,436,556	7,919,946	9,722,765	10,965,669	9,951,567	83.65	-9.25
Central/Eastern Europe		1,478,515	1,604,478	2,025,018	2,257,096	3,119,461	26.22	38.21
Bulgaria		65,718	53,806	63,521	70,769	77,757	0.65	9.87
Czech Republic		44,754	29,913	47,487	64,801	63,093	0.53	-2.64

TURKEY

4. Arrivals of non-resident tourists in all types of accommodation establishments, by nationality

	2002	2003	2004	2005	2006	Market share 06	% Change 06-05
Hungary	31,173	22,014	32,954	43,035	37,965	0.32	-11.78
Poland	77,306	129,787	75,240	115,312	93,391	0.79	-19.01
Romania	58,241	56,778	60,051	69,852	86,422	0.73	23.72
Commonwealth Independent State	1,201,323	1,312,180	1,745,765	1,893,327	2,760,833	23.21	45.82
Northern Europe	**690,037**	**624,255**	**876,733**	**1,334,953**	**1,191,294**	**10.01**	**-10.76**
Iceland	3,189	1,561	3,180	8,754	10,816	0.09	23.55
Ireland	52,898	75,388	66,535	46,515	50,796	0.43	9.20
United Kingdom	459,181	406,735	582,981	911,404	799,341	6.72	-12.30
Scandinavia	174,769	140,571	224,037	368,280	330,341	2.78	-10.30
Southern Europe	**736,543**	**595,690**	**667,484**	**918,777**	**703,489**	**5.91**	**-23.43**
Albania	10,844	15,279	21,031	22,074	22,626	0.19	2.50
Greece	108,824	124,318	162,825	266,786	113,716	0.96	-57.38
Italy	294,090	183,296	203,255	273,904	213,347	1.79	-22.11
Portugal	18,557	11,509	14,289	13,770	10,752	0.09	-21.92
Spain	186,613	163,857	168,419	239,360	239,164	2.01	-0.08
Yugoslavia, Sfr (Former)	117,615	97,431	97,665	102,883	103,884	0.87	0.97
Western Europe	**5,253,263**	**4,840,431**	**5,915,859**	**6,127,678**	**4,555,771**	**38.29**	**-25.65**
Austria	256,859	227,724	212,058	222,921	167,394	1.41	-24.91
France	593,993	440,041	483,717	598,600	429,844	3.61	-28.19
Germany	3,320,142	3,149,203	3,748,651	3,860,070	2,900,021	24.38	-24.87
Switzerland	145,711	155,434	217,781	210,317	117,638	0.99	-44.07
Benelux	936,558	868,029	1,253,652	1,235,770	940,874	7.91	-23.86
East Mediterranean Europe	**259,876**	**247,875**	**220,014**	**303,265**	**342,603**	**2.88**	**12.97**
Cyprus	17,602	21,691	23,715	70,101	108,126	0.91	54.24
Israel	242,274	226,184	196,299	233,164	234,477	1.97	0.56
Other Europe	**18,322**	**7,217**	**17,657**	**23,900**	**38,949**	**0.33**	**62.97**
Other countries of Europe	18,322	7,217	17,657	23,900	38,949	0.33	62.97
MIDDLE EAST	**223,866**	**215,135**	**245,695**	**306,127**	**344,316**	**2.89**	**12.47**
Middle East	**223,866**	**215,135**	**245,695**	**306,127**	**344,316**	**2.89**	**12.47**
Bahrain	2,107	2,258	2,785	2,272	4,007	0.03	76.36
Iraq	12,504	13,974	26,393	40,033	49,537	0.42	23.74
Jordan	20,462	20,301	23,707	25,130	30,498	0.26	21.36
Kuwait	7,415	9,182	10,221	13,090	12,271	0.10	-6.26
Lebanon	52,079	34,455	27,155	31,820	22,226	0.19	-30.15
Libyan Arab Jamahiriya	13,641	11,636	13,510	14,397	13,453	0.11	-6.56
Oman	407	472	661	673	1,727	0.01	156.61
Qatar	480	826	2,070	1,976	2,197	0.02	11.18
Saudi Arabia	41,783	44,670	39,605	49,027	79,204	0.67	61.55
Syrian Arab Republic	35,309	32,566	46,306	51,637	55,397	0.47	7.28
United Arab Emirates	11,069	18,106	17,971	25,571	31,437	0.26	22.94
Egypt	17,395	19,287	24,235	36,581	32,052	0.27	-12.38
Yemen	582	838	784	3,216	2,325	0.02	-27.71
Other countries of Middle East	8,633	6,564	10,292	10,704	7,985	0.07	-25.40
SOUTH ASIA	**115,032**	**107,067**	**133,266**	**160,861**	**176,547**	**1.48**	**9.75**
South Asia	**115,032**	**107,067**	**133,266**	**160,861**	**176,547**	**1.48**	**9.75**
Bangladesh	585	742	487	687	857	0.01	24.75
India	5,132	6,893	10,835	17,263	22,861	0.19	32.43
Iran, Islamic Republic of	104,956	94,740	116,853	136,571	143,996	1.21	5.44
Pakistan	4,359	4,692	5,091	6,340	8,833	0.07	39.32
REGION NOT SPECIFIED	**153,731**	**99,945**	**86,354**	**230,890**	**89,500**	**0.75**	**-61.24**

TURKEY

5. Overnight stays of non-resident tourists in hotels and similar establishments, by nationality

		2002	2003	2004	2005	2006	Market share 06	% Change 06-05
TOTAL	(*)	43,224,611	40,818,839	49,614,062	55,995,884	46,587,820	100.00	-16.80
AFRICA		109,022	72,239	82,295	122,907	135,059	0.29	9.89
North Africa		68,682	55,718	62,735	90,423	96,636	0.21	6.87
Algeria		36,199	18,822	26,932	29,297	32,530	0.07	11.04
Morocco		7,992	9,804	13,845	18,270	21,181	0.05	15.93
Sudan		1,908	2,961	3,969	5,720	6,218	0.01	8.71
Tunisia		22,583	24,131	17,989	37,136	36,707	0.08	-1.16
Southern Africa		34,568	13,611	15,491	20,967	20,930	0.04	-0.18
South Africa		34,568	13,611	15,491	20,967	20,930	0.04	-0.18
Other Africa		5,772	2,910	4,069	11,517	17,493	0.04	51.89
Other countries of Africa		5,772	2,910	4,069	11,517	17,493	0.04	51.89
AMERICAS		1,002,342	664,387	851,620	983,788	1,261,069	2.71	28.19
Central America		294	167	139	1,293	2,067		59.86
All countries of Central America		294	167	139	1,293	2,067		59.86
North America		907,952	634,266	804,881	928,331	1,170,343	2.51	26.07
Canada		82,540	36,100	56,018	76,415	100,135	0.21	31.04
Mexico		17,373	13,533	22,361	21,603	23,944	0.05	10.84
United States		805,804	582,668	713,556	825,272	1,041,306	2.24	26.18
Other countries of North America		2,235	1,965	12,946	5,041	4,958	0.01	-1.65
South America		94,096	29,954	46,600	54,164	88,659	0.19	63.69
Argentina		69,073	16,974	26,178	19,373	37,251	0.08	92.28
Brazil		15,290	6,933	11,316	22,844	32,783	0.07	43.51
Chile		2,741	2,428	3,245	4,889	4,792	0.01	-1.98
Colombia		1,710	1,123	1,573	1,986	3,942	0.01	98.49
Venezuela		1,410	935	2,618	2,013	3,199	0.01	58.92
Other countries of South America		3,872	1,561	1,670	3,059	6,692	0.01	118.76
EAST ASIA AND THE PACIFIC		925,914	670,110	749,210	1,225,121	1,128,143	2.42	-7.92
North-East Asia		606,045	489,849	497,368	939,964	840,932	1.81	-10.54
China		46,270	42,927	61,122	76,034	105,137	0.23	38.28
Japan		460,711	334,053	290,301	601,465	490,514	1.05	-18.45
Korea, Republic of		99,064	112,869	145,945	262,465	245,281	0.53	-6.55
South-East Asia		49,270	29,037	52,614	76,862	78,381	0.17	1.98
Indonesia		1,956	973	1,850	3,274	3,565	0.01	8.89
Malaysia		15,328	8,983	22,672	33,437	29,823	0.06	-10.81
Philippines		5,358	9,029	8,874	6,570	12,918	0.03	96.62
Singapore		24,452	9,218	17,310	29,468	25,870	0.06	-12.21
Thailand		2,176	834	1,908	4,113	6,205	0.01	50.86
Australasia		263,203	148,713	185,862	199,773	198,973	0.43	-0.40
Australia		248,222	141,071	176,032	180,025	178,137	0.38	-1.05
New Zealand		14,981	7,642	9,830	19,748	20,836	0.04	5.51
Other East Asia and the Pacific		7,396	2,511	13,366	8,522	9,857	0.02	15.67
Other countries of Asia		6,007	2,226	5,459	5,155	8,922	0.02	73.07
All countries of Oceania		1,389	285	7,907	3,367	935		-72.23
EUROPE		39,909,628	38,229,461	46,639,042	51,945,955	42,461,863	91.14	-18.26
Central/Eastern Europe		6,274,021	7,509,465	9,327,221	10,138,364	11,790,909	25.31	16.30
Bulgaria		188,152	162,941	152,264	198,303	199,416	0.43	0.56
Czech Republic		223,087	184,081	249,270	322,521	279,002	0.60	-13.49

TURKEY

5. Overnight stays of non-resident tourists in hotels and similar establishments, by nationality

	2002	2003	2004	2005	2006	Market share 06	% Change 06-05
Hungary	115,243	95,608	149,523	196,728	135,629	0.29	-31.06
Poland	327,378	256,764	279,465	364,606	336,996	0.72	-7.57
Romania	182,677	173,623	202,643	232,330	305,516	0.66	31.50
Commonwealth Independent State	5,237,484	6,636,448	8,294,056	8,823,876	10,534,350	22.61	19.38
Northern Europe	**3,439,295**	**3,201,007**	**4,577,839**	**6,724,891**	**5,748,171**	**12.34**	**-14.52**
Iceland	6,262	3,998	6,552	23,477	26,709	0.06	13.77
Ireland	188,743	280,965	215,222	218,272	173,864	0.37	-20.35
United Kingdom	2,314,599	2,238,953	3,156,772	4,496,033	3,960,345	8.50	-11.91
Scandinavia	929,691	677,091	1,199,293	1,987,109	1,587,253	3.41	-20.12
Southern Europe	**1,953,309**	**1,687,633**	**1,818,294**	**2,359,616**	**1,780,505**	**3.82**	**-24.54**
Albania	31,241	41,736	71,078	74,151	77,615	0.17	4.67
Greece	238,240	292,947	357,097	543,766	230,249	0.49	-57.66
Italy	819,279	480,726	532,156	783,730	555,996	1.19	-29.06
Portugal	39,758	26,332	35,730	29,958	23,325	0.05	-22.14
Spain	414,057	386,339	387,842	528,657	515,905	1.11	-2.41
Yugoslavia, Sfr (Former)	410,734	459,553	434,391	399,354	377,415	0.81	-5.49
Western Europe	**27,415,171**	**25,004,581**	**30,177,895**	**31,718,680**	**22,129,226**	**47.50**	**-30.23**
Austria	1,689,332	1,427,588	1,226,801	1,225,267	855,664	1.84	-30.17
France	2,370,769	1,511,173	1,641,962	2,617,336	1,626,803	3.49	-37.85
Germany	17,788,271	16,283,624	19,317,114	20,136,102	14,370,879	30.85	-28.63
Switzerland	684,540	623,512	958,326	858,056	456,133	0.98	-46.84
Benelux	4,882,259	5,158,684	7,033,692	6,881,919	4,819,747	10.35	-29.97
East Mediterranean Europe	**742,519**	**787,189**	**650,905**	**871,378**	**814,933**	**1.75**	**-6.48**
Cyprus	38,025	46,997	49,096	138,037	205,591	0.44	48.94
Israel	704,494	740,192	601,809	733,341	609,342	1.31	-16.91
Other Europe	**85,313**	**39,586**	**86,888**	**133,026**	**198,119**	**0.43**	**48.93**
Other countries of Europe	85,313	39,586	86,888	133,026	198,119	0.43	48.93
MIDDLE EAST	**601,135**	**615,695**	**656,066**	**783,348**	**868,394**	**1.86**	**10.86**
Middle East	**601,135**	**615,695**	**656,066**	**783,348**	**868,394**	**1.86**	**10.86**
Bahrain	7,387	6,165	8,147	6,281	8,458	0.02	34.66
Iraq	40,492	48,162	80,398	143,560	116,925	0.25	-18.55
Jordan	57,475	65,842	63,430	64,709	81,383	0.17	25.77
Kuwait	20,885	24,726	26,895	29,613	32,275	0.07	8.99
Lebanon	97,608	88,193	73,494	79,329	51,400	0.11	-35.21
Libyan Arab Jamahiriya	46,112	32,470	40,989	37,151	34,014	0.07	-8.44
Oman	985	1,187	1,678	1,744	4,473	0.01	156.48
Qatar	1,472	2,423	5,690	6,099	6,115	0.01	0.26
Saudi Arabia	134,618	119,461	109,584	122,664	192,257	0.41	56.73
Syrian Arab Republic	85,491	79,519	99,594	109,935	124,843	0.27	13.56
United Arab Emirates	32,837	64,724	50,136	70,802	112,612	0.24	59.05
Egypt	59,053	62,802	73,111	89,367	79,705	0.17	-10.81
Yemen	1,433	2,191	2,040	5,421	5,224	0.01	-3.63
Other countries of Middle East	15,287	17,830	20,880	16,673	18,710	0.04	12.22
SOUTH ASIA	**339,592**	**314,812**	**424,118**	**460,658**	**469,486**	**1.01**	**1.92**
South Asia	**339,592**	**314,812**	**424,118**	**460,658**	**469,486**	**1.01**	**1.92**
Bangladesh	1,397	2,614	1,331	1,742	2,063		18.43
India	14,621	21,408	33,067	43,732	55,114	0.12	26.03
Iran, Islamic Republic of	313,215	278,994	376,745	398,686	391,755	0.84	-1.74
Pakistan	10,359	11,796	12,975	16,498	20,554	0.04	24.58
REGION NOT SPECIFIED	**336,978**	**252,135**	**211,711**	**474,107**	**263,806**	**0.57**	**-44.36**

TURKEY

6. Overnight stays of non-resident tourists in all types of accommodation establishments, by nationality

		2002	2003	2004	2005	2006	Market share 06	% Change 06-05
TOTAL	(*)	43,312,498	40,866,002	49,727,905	56,108,453	46,640,460	100.00	-16.87
AFRICA		109,024	72,242	82,295	122,929	135,059	0.29	9.87
North Africa		68,682	55,718	62,735	90,445	96,636	0.21	6.85
Algeria		36,199	18,822	26,932	29,297	32,530	0.07	11.04
Morocco		7,992	9,804	13,845	18,270	21,181	0.05	15.93
Sudan		1,908	2,961	3,969	5,720	6,218	0.01	8.71
Tunisia		22,583	24,131	17,989	37,158	36,707	0.08	-1.21
Southern Africa		34,570	13,614	15,491	20,967	20,930	0.04	-0.18
South Africa		34,570	13,614	15,491	20,967	20,930	0.04	-0.18
Other Africa		5,772	2,910	4,069	11,517	17,493	0.04	51.89
Other countries of Africa		5,772	2,910	4,069	11,517	17,493	0.04	51.89
AMERICAS		1,010,626	669,497	851,631	983,899	1,261,082	2.70	28.17
Central America		294	167	139	1,293	2,067		59.86
All countries of Central America		294	167	139	1,293	2,067		59.86
North America		915,235	639,376	804,892	928,442	1,170,356	2.51	26.06
Canada		82,566	36,100	56,018	76,415	100,135	0.21	31.04
Mexico		17,373	15,273	22,361	21,621	23,944	0.05	10.74
United States		813,061	586,038	713,567	825,365	1,041,319	2.23	26.16
Other countries of North America		2,235	1,965	12,946	5,041	4,958	0.01	-1.65
South America		95,097	29,954	46,600	54,164	88,659	0.19	63.69
Argentina		70,061	16,974	26,178	19,373	37,251	0.08	92.28
Brazil		15,303	6,933	11,316	22,844	32,783	0.07	43.51
Chile		2,741	2,428	3,245	4,889	4,792	0.01	-1.98
Colombia		1,710	1,123	1,573	1,986	3,942	0.01	98.49
Venezuela		1,410	935	2,618	2,013	3,199	0.01	58.92
Other countries of South America		3,872	1,561	1,670	3,059	6,692	0.01	118.76
EAST ASIA AND THE PACIFIC		925,986	670,440	749,211	1,225,214	1,128,158	2.42	-7.92
North-East Asia		606,082	489,849	497,369	940,019	840,934	1.80	-10.54
China		46,270	42,927	61,122	76,038	105,137	0.23	38.27
Japan		460,720	334,053	290,302	601,504	490,516	1.05	-18.45
Korea, Republic of		99,092	112,869	145,945	262,477	245,281	0.53	-6.55
South-East Asia		49,274	29,037	52,614	76,862	78,381	0.17	1.98
Indonesia		1,956	973	1,850	3,274	3,565	0.01	8.89
Malaysia		15,328	8,983	22,672	33,437	29,823	0.06	-10.81
Philippines		5,358	9,029	8,874	6,570	12,918	0.03	96.62
Singapore		24,456	9,218	17,310	29,468	25,870	0.06	-12.21
Thailand		2,176	834	1,908	4,113	6,205	0.01	50.86
Australasia		263,234	149,043	185,862	199,777	198,986	0.43	-0.40
Australia		248,244	141,395	176,032	180,029	178,140	0.38	-1.05
New Zealand		14,990	7,648	9,830	19,748	20,846	0.04	5.56
Other East Asia and the Pacific		7,396	2,511	13,366	8,556	9,857	0.02	15.21
Other countries of Asia		6,007	2,226	5,459	5,189	8,922	0.02	71.94
All countries of Oceania		1,389	285	7,907	3,367	935		-72.23
EUROPE		39,984,737	38,267,172	46,752,873	52,058,276	42,506,769	91.14	-18.35
Central/Eastern Europe		6,285,833	7,511,460	9,362,897	10,205,534	11,817,536	25.34	15.80
Bulgaria		188,271	162,942	152,264	198,362	199,430	0.43	0.54
Czech Republic		223,456	184,712	249,435	322,622	279,093	0.60	-13.49

TURKEY

6. Overnight stays of non-resident tourists in all types of accommodation establishments, by nationality

	2002	2003	2004	2005	2006	Market share 06	% Change 06-05
Hungary	115,533	95,656	149,523	196,728	135,708	0.29	-31.02
Poland	327,570	256,796	280,652	364,660	337,006	0.72	-7.58
Romania	183,854	173,625	202,643	232,723	305,552	0.66	31.29
Commonwealth Independent State	5,247,149	6,637,729	8,328,380	8,890,439	10,560,747	22.64	18.79
Northern Europe	**3,444,547**	**3,203,371**	**4,583,239**	**6,727,217**	**5,748,350**	**12.32**	**-14.55**
Iceland	6,262	3,998	6,552	23,477	26,709	0.06	13.77
Ireland	188,752	280,965	215,222	218,272	173,876	0.37	-20.34
United Kingdom	2,315,991	2,240,123	3,156,994	4,496,319	3,960,422	8.49	-11.92
Scandinavia	933,542	678,285	1,204,471	1,989,149	1,587,343	3.40	-20.20
Southern Europe	**1,958,412**	**1,689,753**	**1,818,374**	**2,360,045**	**1,780,565**	**3.82**	**-24.55**
Albania	31,247	41,736	71,078	74,151	77,615	0.17	4.67
Greece	238,256	292,947	357,097	543,787	230,255	0.49	-57.66
Italy	822,933	482,628	532,195	784,002	556,018	1.19	-29.08
Portugal	39,770	26,519	35,771	29,958	23,325	0.05	-22.14
Spain	414,530	386,339	387,842	528,684	515,907	1.11	-2.42
Yugoslavia, Sfr (Former)	411,676	459,584	434,391	399,463	377,445	0.81	-5.51
Western Europe	**27,468,096**	**25,035,710**	**30,250,570**	**31,761,076**	**22,147,266**	**47.49**	**-30.27**
Austria	1,690,622	1,427,612	1,226,807	1,225,419	855,933	1.84	-30.15
France	2,374,963	1,520,130	1,653,379	2,619,400	1,626,864	3.49	-37.89
Germany	17,830,614	16,301,447	19,371,393	20,174,818	14,387,151	30.85	-28.69
Switzerland	685,049	623,799	958,526	858,137	456,444	0.98	-46.81
Benelux	4,886,848	5,162,722	7,040,465	6,883,302	4,820,874	10.34	-29.96
East Mediterranean Europe	**742,536**	**787,292**	**650,905**	**871,378**	**814,933**	**1.75**	**-6.48**
Cyprus	38,025	46,997	49,096	138,037	205,591	0.44	48.94
Israel	704,511	740,295	601,809	733,341	609,342	1.31	-16.91
Other Europe	**85,313**	**39,586**	**86,888**	**133,026**	**198,119**	**0.42**	**48.93**
Other countries of Europe	85,313	39,586	86,888	133,026	198,119	0.42	48.93
MIDDLE EAST	**601,150**	**617,898**	**656,066**	**783,361**	**876,100**	**1.88**	**11.84**
Middle East	**601,150**	**617,898**	**656,066**	**783,361**	**876,100**	**1.88**	**11.84**
Bahrain	7,387	6,165	8,147	6,281	8,458	0.02	34.66
Iraq	40,492	48,162	80,398	143,560	116,925	0.25	-18.55
Jordan	57,475	65,842	63,430	64,709	89,089	0.19	37.68
Kuwait	20,885	24,726	26,895	29,613	32,275	0.07	8.99
Lebanon	97,610	88,193	73,494	79,329	51,400	0.11	-35.21
Libyan Arab Jamahiriya	46,112	32,470	40,989	37,151	34,014	0.07	-8.44
Oman	985	1,187	1,678	1,744	4,473	0.01	156.48
Qatar	1,472	2,423	5,690	6,099	6,115	0.01	0.26
Saudi Arabia	134,631	119,564	109,584	122,664	192,257	0.41	56.73
Syrian Arab Republic	85,491	79,519	99,594	109,935	124,843	0.27	13.56
United Arab Emirates	32,837	64,724	50,136	70,802	112,612	0.24	59.05
Egypt	59,053	64,902	73,111	89,367	79,705	0.17	-10.81
Yemen	1,433	2,191	2,040	5,421	5,224	0.01	-3.63
Other countries of Middle East	15,287	17,830	20,880	16,686	18,710	0.04	12.13
SOUTH ASIA	**343,997**	**316,618**	**424,118**	**460,667**	**469,486**	**1.01**	**1.91**
South Asia	**343,997**	**316,618**	**424,118**	**460,667**	**469,486**	**1.01**	**1.91**
Bangladesh	2,344	2,614	1,331	1,742	2,063		18.43
India	18,079	21,408	33,067	43,732	55,114	0.12	26.03
Iran, Islamic Republic of	313,215	279,004	376,745	398,695	391,755	0.84	-1.74
Pakistan	10,359	13,592	12,975	16,498	20,554	0.04	24.58
REGION NOT SPECIFIED	**336,978**	**252,135**	**211,711**	**474,107**	**263,806**	**0.57**	**-44.36**

TURKMENISTAN

1. Arrivals of non-resident tourists at national borders, by nationality

	2002	2003	2004	2005	2006	Market share 06	% Change 06-05
TOTAL	10,791	8,214	14,799	11,611			
AFRICA				1			
Other Africa				1			
All countries of Africa				1			
AMERICAS	249	207	374	384			
North America	236	187	373	380			
Canada	19	4	30	48			
Mexico		2					
United States	217	181	343	332			
South America	13	20	1	4			
Brazil	13	20	1	4			
EAST ASIA AND THE PACIFIC	545	466	1,053	753			
North-East Asia	468	423	986	563			
China	42	24	73	41			
Taiwan (Province of China)	95	57	2				
Japan	203	269	770	428			
Korea, Republic of	127	73	141	94			
Mongolia	1						
South-East Asia	32	6	2	47			
Malaysia				42			
Philippines				2			
Singapore	7			3			
Thailand	25	6	2				
Australasia	45	37	65	143			
Australia	33	32	46	101			
New Zealand	12	5	19	42			
EUROPE	2,344	1,855	3,915	3,284			
Central/Eastern Europe	384	230	494	82			
Azerbaijan		3	2				
Armenia	20	5	1				
Bulgaria		5	1	1			
Belarus	3			3			
Czech Republic	10	2	9	21			
Georgia	4		1				
Hungary	10	2	7	15			
Kazakhstan	45	44	47	3			
Kyrgyzstan	12	8	11				
Latvia	7	1	2	1			
Republic of Moldova	2		2	1			
Poland	4		8	3			
Romania	4	2	9				
Russian Federation	145	115	318	13			
Tajikistan			2				
Ukraine	27	35	48	20			
Uzbekistan	91	8	26	1			
Northern Europe	247	100	415	362			
Denmark	2	1	1	13			
Finland	6	5	10	18			
Iceland				10			
Ireland	13	2	8	6			

TURKMENISTAN

1. Arrivals of non-resident tourists at national borders, by nationality

	2002	2003	2004	2005	2006	Market share 06	% Change 06-05
Norway	10	5	12	4			
Sweden	1	14	31	21			
United Kingdom	215	73	353	290			
Southern Europe	**339**	**442**	**481**	**299**			
Albania	1						
Bosnia and Herzegovina	6		2				
Croatia	6	4	1				
Greece				4			
Italy	286	337	320	234			
Portugal	1			1			
Slovenia		35	52	4			
Spain	39	64	106	56			
Serbia and Montenegro		2					
Western Europe	**1,124**	**963**	**2,384**	**2,422**			
Austria	43	21	104	95			
Belgium	8	30	42	39			
France	302	298	636	683			
Germany	546	466	1,191	1,028			
Luxembourg			1	1			
Netherlands	106	84	324	453			
Switzerland	119	64	86	123			
East Mediterranean Europe	**250**	**120**	**141**	**119**			
Israel	72	50	24				
Turkey	178	70	117	119			
MIDDLE EAST	**22**	**37**	**32**	**4**			
Middle East	**22**	**37**	**32**	**4**			
Iraq	2						
Jordan	1						
Kuwait			2	2			
Qatar	2						
Saudi Arabia	3	2					
Syrian Arab Republic	4						
United Arab Emirates	10	35	20	2			
Egypt			10				
SOUTH ASIA	**7,631**	**5,649**	**9,425**	**7,185**			
South Asia	**7,631**	**5,649**	**9,425**	**7,185**			
Bangladesh				11			
India	36	24	55	1			
Iran, Islamic Republic of	7,592	5,623	9,341	7,173			
Nepal			29				
Pakistan	3	2					

Source: World Tourism Organization (UNWTO)

TURKS AND CAICOS ISLANDS

1. Arrivals of non-resident tourists at national borders, by country of residence

	2002	2003	2004	2005	2006	Market share 06	% Change 06-05
TOTAL	154,961	164,100	173,081	176,130	248,343	100.00	41.00
AMERICAS	139,901	149,072	148,711	156,674	221,372	89.14	41.29
Caribbean	5,017	5,398	8,273	12,192	21,908	8.82	79.69
Antigua and Barbuda	27						
Bahamas	1,955						
Barbados	129						
Bermuda	92						
British Virgin Islands	12						
Cayman Islands	228						
Cuba	24						
Dominica	2						
Dominican Republic	266						
Guadeloupe	5						
Haiti	345						
Jamaica	1,482						
Martinique	5						
Montserrat	5						
Aruba	4						
Bonaire	1						
Puerto Rico	101						
Saint Kitts and Nevis	7						
Anguilla	7						
Saint Lucia	42						
Saint Maarten	3						
Saint Vincent and the Grenadines	25						
Trinidad and Tobago	156						
United States Virgin Islands	12						
Other countries of the Caribbean	82						
All countries of the Caribbean		5,398	8,273	12,192	21,908	8.82	79.69
Central America	20						
Belize	20						
North America	134,274	143,674	140,438	144,482	199,464	80.32	38.05
Canada	14,721	14,689	19,793	21,136	29,802	12.00	41.00
United States	119,553	128,985	120,645	123,346	169,662	68.32	37.55
South America	590						
Argentina	172						
Brazil	87						
Guyana	62						
Venezuela	74						
Other countries of South America	195						
EAST ASIA AND THE PACIFIC	35						
North-East Asia	35						
Japan	35						
EUROPE	10,548	12,626	13,807	17,613	24,834	10.00	41.00
Northern Europe	6,898						
Denmark	21						
Ireland	67						
Norway	32						
Sweden	136						
United Kingdom	6,642						
Southern Europe	1,161						

TURKS AND CAICOS ISLANDS

1. Arrivals of non-resident tourists at national borders, by country of residence

	2002	2003	2004	2005	2006	Market share 06	% Change 06-05
Greece	9						
Italy	1,082						
Portugal	18						
Spain	52						
Western Europe	**2,479**						
Austria	104						
Belgium	119						
France	1,569						
Germany	357						
Luxembourg	10						
Switzerland	320						
Other Europe	**10**	**12,626**	**13,807**	**17,613**	**24,834**	**10.00**	**41.00**
Other countries of Europe	10						
All countries of Europe		12,626	13,807	17,613	24,834	10.00	41.00
REGION NOT SPECIFIED	**4,477**	**2,402**	**10,563**	**1,843**	**2,137**	**0.86**	**15.95**
Not Specified	**4,477**	**2,402**	**10,563**	**1,843**	**2,137**	**0.86**	**15.95**
Other countries of the World	4,477	2,402	10,563	1,843	2,137	0.86	15.95

Source: World Tourism Organization (UNWTO)

TUVALU

1. Arrivals of non-resident tourists at national borders, by nationality

	2002	2003	2004	2005	2006	Market share 06	% Change 06-05
TOTAL	1,313	1,377	1,290	1,085	1,135	100.00	4.61
AMERICAS	92	130	79	101	63	5.55	-37.62
North America	92	130	79	101	63	5.55	-37.62
Canada	14	17	11	18	7	0.62	-61.11
United States	78	113	68	83	56	4.93	-32.53
EAST ASIA AND THE PACIFIC	1,075	1,101	1,043	828	858	75.59	3.62
North-East Asia	152	109	137	118	250	22.03	111.86
Japan	152	109	137	118	250	22.03	111.86
Australasia	362	352	331	303	283	24.93	-6.60
Australia	187	207	184	186	136	11.98	-26.88
New Zealand	175	145	147	117	147	12.95	25.64
Melanesia	336	336	332	223	197	17.36	-11.66
Fiji	336	336	332	223	197	17.36	-11.66
Micronesia		162	54	33	28	2.47	-15.15
Kiribati		162	54	33	28	2.47	-15.15
Other East Asia and the Pacific	225	142	189	151	100	8.81	-33.77
Other countries of Asia	68	58	89	73	80	7.05	9.59
All countries of Oceania	157	84	100	78	20	1.76	-74.36
EUROPE	108	97	108	104	120	10.57	15.38
Northern Europe	34	46	49	37	55	4.85	48.65
United Kingdom	34	46	49	37	55	4.85	48.65
Western Europe	39	28	34	26	33	2.91	26.92
France	13	16	9	12	8	0.70	-33.33
Germany	26	12	25	14	25	2.20	78.57
Other Europe	35	23	25	41	32	2.82	-21.95
Other countries of Europe	35	23	25	41	32	2.82	-21.95
REGION NOT SPECIFIED	38	49	60	52	94	8.28	80.77
Not Specified	38	49	60	52	94	8.28	80.77
Other countries of the World	38	49	60	52	94	8.28	80.77

Source: World Tourism Organization (UNWTO)

UGANDA

1. Arrivals of non-resident tourists at national borders, by country of residence

	2002	2003	2004	2005	2006	Market share 06	% Change 06-05
TOTAL	254,212	304,656	512,379	467,728	538,586	100.00	15.15
AFRICA	192,278	233,043	405,706	337,188	397,031	73.72	17.75
East Africa	158,039	196,006	355,727	272,545	324,877	60.32	19.20
Ethiopia	1,509	1,811	2,482	2,954	3,075	0.57	4.10
Kenya	80,516	113,681	220,062	138,346	160,306	29.76	15.87
Rwanda	52,431	50,107	65,298	80,522	111,385	20.68	38.33
United Republic of Tanzania	23,583	30,407	67,885	50,723	50,111	9.30	-1.21
Central Africa	7,586	5,890	3,998	6,277	4,653	0.86	-25.87
Democratic Republic of the Congo	7,586	5,890	3,998	6,277	4,653	0.86	-25.87
North Africa	3,969	5,606	5,535	2,819	6,433	1.19	128.20
Sudan	3,969	5,606	5,535	2,819	6,433	1.19	128.20
Southern Africa				10,423	11,135	2.07	6.83
South Africa				10,423	11,135	2.07	6.83
Other Africa	22,684	25,541	40,446	45,124	49,933	9.27	10.66
Other countries of Africa	22,684	25,541	40,446	45,124	49,933	9.27	10.66
AMERICAS	14,785	16,409	23,438	28,557	35,749	6.64	25.18
North America	14,139	15,683	22,567	27,163	34,243	6.36	26.06
Canada	2,216	2,507	3,669	5,195	6,123	1.14	17.86
United States	11,923	13,176	18,898	21,968	28,120	5.22	28.00
Other Americas	646	726	871	1,394	1,506	0.28	8.03
Other countries of the Americas	646	726	871	1,394	1,506	0.28	8.03
EAST ASIA AND THE PACIFIC	4,188	4,845	8,150	10,046	12,003	2.23	19.48
North-East Asia	1,616	1,842	2,695	3,691	4,463	0.83	20.92
China	1,036	1,181	1,798	2,177	2,951	0.55	35.55
Japan	580	661	897	1,514	1,512	0.28	-0.13
Australasia	1,325	1,555	2,405	3,502	4,469	0.83	27.61
Australia	1,100	1,349	2,132	3,190	3,846	0.71	20.56
New Zealand	225	206	273	312	623	0.12	99.68
Other East Asia and the Pacific	1,247	1,448	3,050	2,853	3,071	0.57	7.64
Other countries of Asia	1,247	1,448	3,050	2,853	3,071	0.57	7.64
EUROPE	33,850	39,207	48,847	62,312	71,131	13.21	14.15
Central/Eastern Europe	312	349	621	859	1,510	0.28	75.79
Czech Republic/Slovakia	39	63	135	236	259	0.05	9.75
Russian Federation	273	286	486	623	1,251	0.23	100.80
Northern Europe	20,711	23,277	30,006	37,289	41,771	7.76	12.02
Denmark	1,499	1,642	1,891	2,509	2,974	0.55	18.53
Finland	227	224	354	411	596	0.11	45.01
Ireland	700	863	1,139	1,422	1,243	0.23	-12.59
Norway	1,480	1,528	1,749	2,262	2,343	0.44	3.58
Sweden	1,637	1,844	2,471	2,458	3,120	0.58	26.93
United Kingdom	15,168	17,176	22,402	28,227	31,495	5.85	11.58
Southern Europe	1,842	2,009	2,406	3,335	4,485	0.83	34.48
Italy	1,735	1,924	2,406	3,301	4,075	0.76	23.45
Serbia and Montenegro	107	85		34	410	0.08	1,105.88
Western Europe	9,888	12,246	13,615	17,111	19,556	3.63	14.29
Austria	262	349	500	396	420	0.08	6.06
Belgium	1,438	1,748	1,914	2,675	3,433	0.64	28.34

UGANDA

1. Arrivals of non-resident tourists at national borders, by country of residence

	2002	2003	2004	2005	2006	Market share 06	% Change 06-05
France	1,353	3,022	2,079	2,351	2,956	0.55	25.73
Germany	3,280	3,519	4,241	4,972	5,683	1.06	14.30
Netherlands	2,339	2,474	3,313	4,751	5,162	0.96	8.65
Switzerland	1,216	1,134	1,568	1,966	1,902	0.35	-3.26
Other Europe	**1,097**	**1,326**	**2,199**	**3,718**	**3,809**	**0.71**	**2.45**
Other countries of Europe	1,097	1,326	2,199	3,718	3,809	0.71	2.45
MIDDLE EAST	**1,836**	**1,976**	**3,133**	**3,766**	**4,111**	**0.76**	**9.16**
Middle East	**1,836**	**1,976**	**3,133**	**3,766**	**4,111**	**0.76**	**9.16**
Egypt	609	583	1,038	1,035	1,021	0.19	-1.35
Other countries of Middle East	1,227	1,393	2,095	2,731	3,090	0.57	13.15
SOUTH ASIA	**6,439**	**7,647**	**12,139**	**13,879**	**14,339**	**2.66**	**3.31**
South Asia	**6,439**	**7,647**	**12,139**	**13,879**	**14,339**	**2.66**	**3.31**
India	5,708	6,623	9,366	10,691	11,829	2.20	10.64
Pakistan	731	1,024	2,773	3,188	2,510	0.47	-21.27
REGION NOT SPECIFIED	**836**	**1,529**	**10,966**	**11,980**	**4,222**	**0.78**	**-64.76**
Not Specified	**836**	**1,529**	**10,966**	**11,980**	**4,222**	**0.78**	**-64.76**
Other countries of the World	836	1,529	10,966	11,980	4,222	0.78	-64.76

Source: World Tourism Organization (UNWTO)

UKRAINE

1. Arrivals of non-resident tourists at national borders, by country of residence

	2002	2003	2004	2005	2006	Market share 06	% Change 06-05
TOTAL	10,516,665	12,513,883	15,629,213	17,630,760	18,900,263	100.00	7.20
AFRICA	4,748	12,367	6,586	7,259	10,696	0.06	47.35
East Africa	340	5,251	725	2,588	903		-65.11
Burundi	20	6	24	9	6		-33.33
Ethiopia	108	1,800	63	72	104		44.44
Eritrea	6	16	10	459	18		-96.08
Kenya	22	69	127	157	163		3.82
Madagascar	9	10	18	32	17		-46.88
Malawi		1		4	29		625.00
Mauritius	62	197	230	200	188		-6.00
Mozambique	2	2	23	22	6		-72.73
Rwanda	6	2,885	9	21	40		90.48
Somalia	47	88	26	397	60		-84.89
Zimbabwe	15	33	36	262	36		-86.26
Uganda	16	114	96	118	88		-25.42
United Republic of Tanzania	27	18	39	108	130		20.37
Zambia		5	24	727	18		-97.52
Other countries of East Africa		7					
Central Africa	297	2,469	1,159	314	376		19.75
Angola	78	2,204	895	62	104		67.74
Cameroon	83	117	143	242	228		-5.79
Chad	8	16	12	7	7		
Congo	108	102	107				
Democratic Republic of the Congo					35		
Sao Tome and Principe	3	1	2	3	2		-33.33
Other countries of Central Africa	17	29					
North Africa	2,775	3,082	3,413	3,194	3,592	0.02	12.46
Algeria	650	339	401	451	457		1.33
Morocco	800	1,316	1,277	1,457	1,378	0.01	-5.42
Sudan	332	274	315	352	367		4.26
Tunisia	993	1,153	1,420	934	1,390	0.01	48.82
Southern Africa	491	715			984	0.01	
South Africa	485	702			984	0.01	
Other countries of Southern Africa	6	13					
West Africa	845	850	1,289	1,163	4,841	0.03	316.25
Cape Verde	5	29	39	12	681		5,575.00
Benin	80	16	57	16	16		
Ghana	159	76	86	211	290		37.44
Guinea	62	16	60	49	45		-8.16
Liberia	122	154	24	9	2,745	0.01	*********
Mali	13	20	9	14	42		200.00
Mauritania	10	28	18	21	17		-19.05
Nigeria	254	393	506	688	926		34.59
Guinea-Bissau	42	8	3	15	3		-80.00
Senegal	35	17	17	36	17		-52.78
Sierra Leone	1	19	436	14	9		-35.71
Togo	24	20	16	64	27		-57.81
Burkina Faso	31	12	18	14	23		64.29
Other countries of West Africa	7	42					
AMERICAS	52,632	83,451	99,135	95,540	140,633	0.74	47.20
Caribbean	694	1,655	730	811	791		-2.47
Antigua and Barbuda		462	1		95		

UKRAINE

1. Arrivals of non-resident tourists at national borders, by country of residence

	2002	2003	2004	2005	2006	Market share 06	% Change 06-05
Bahamas	33	47	19	38	70		84.21
Bermuda		22		1	1		
British Virgin Islands		419					
Cayman Islands		21	125		2		
Cuba	426	513	507	717	554		-22.73
Dominican Republic	9	30	48	27	38		40.74
Jamaica	11	41	15	8	15		87.50
Aruba			3				
Saint Lucia	176	1	1	2			
Saint Vincent and the Grenadines	35	77					
Trinidad and Tobago	4	4	11	18	16		-11.11
Other countries of the Caribbean		18					
Central America	**1,359**	**1,148**	**273**	**182**	**337**		**85.16**
Belize	1,145	9	9	25	23		-8.00
Costa Rica	38	43	31	53	176		232.08
El Salvador	14	42	8	35	37		5.71
Guatemala	4	11	25	19	56		194.74
Honduras	7	28	6	3	8		166.67
Nicaragua	5	556	136	23	21		-8.70
Panama	146	459	58	24	16		-33.33
North America	**48,140**	**78,392**	**95,333**	**91,812**	**135,830**	**0.72**	**47.94**
Canada	9,567	11,530	15,072	17,986	23,474	0.12	30.51
Greenland			795	1	13		1,200.00
Mexico	203	523	582	779	897		15.15
United States	38,370	66,339	78,884	73,046	111,446	0.59	52.57
South America	**2,439**	**2,256**	**2,799**	**2,735**	**3,675**	**0.02**	**34.37**
Argentina	681	588	788	838	994	0.01	18.62
Bolivia	41	270	104	42	42		
Brazil	1,119	685	911	1,001	1,271	0.01	26.97
Chile	95	94	158	95	201		111.58
Colombia	81	104	113	99	117		18.18
Ecuador	119	76	134	165	198		20.00
Guyana		4	1	1	290		*********
Paraguay	4	4	28	20	21		5.00
Peru	179	251	304	274	246		-10.22
Uruguay	18	26	23	60	68		13.33
Venezuela	90	136	235	140	227		62.14
Other countries of South America	12	18					
EAST ASIA AND THE PACIFIC	**21,900**	**26,362**	**32,494**	**34,946**	**40,956**	**0.22**	**17.20**
North-East Asia	**13,500**	**17,520**	**21,352**	**24,752**	**28,904**	**0.15**	**16.77**
China	8,451	8,332	11,037	12,756	14,414	0.08	13.00
Taiwan (Province of China)	80	230	390	883	614		-30.46
Hong Kong, China	26	158	53	54	57		5.56
Japan	2,109	4,526	4,507	5,295	6,660	0.04	25.78
Korea, Dem. People's Republic of	236	163	109	1,035	1,329	0.01	28.41
Korea, Republic of	1,137	3,304	3,654	2,989	3,712	0.02	24.19
Mongolia	1,461	806	1,602	1,740	2,118	0.01	21.72
Other countries of North-East Asia		1					
South-East Asia	**3,686**	**6,305**	**6,746**	**6,088**	**6,193**	**0.03**	**1.72**
Brunei Darussalam	6	4	49		12		
Myanmar	19	49	52	70	2		-97.14
Cambodia	51	96	51	8	49		512.50
Indonesia	142	359	197	291	204		-29.90
Lao People's Democratic Republic		36	14	13	7		-46.15

UKRAINE

1. Arrivals of non-resident tourists at national borders, by country of residence

	2002	2003	2004	2005	2006	Market share 06	% Change 06-05
Malaysia	637	1,723	2,339	2,300	2,284	0.01	-0.70
Philippines	398	1,509	388	431	287		-33.41
Singapore	95	176	236	141	391		177.30
Viet Nam	2,173	2,125	3,133	2,565	2,549	0.01	-0.62
Thailand	165	228	287	269	408		51.67
Australasia	**4,714**	**2,518**	**4,395**	**4,105**	**5,859**	**0.03**	**42.73**
Australia	4,440	2,189	3,956	3,564	5,275	0.03	48.01
New Zealand	274	329	439	541	584		7.95
Melanesia		**19**	**1**	**1**			
Fiji		19	1	1			
EUROPE	**10,408,714**	**12,345,396**	**15,450,129**	**17,442,407**	**18,655,155**	**98.70**	**6.95**
Central/Eastern Europe	**10,065,891**	**11,974,308**	**15,021,154**	**16,909,073**	**17,998,052**	**95.23**	**6.44**
Azerbaijan	10,445	13,510	57,472	44,226	58,351	0.31	31.94
Armenia	16,475	21,640	33,756	30,295	42,950	0.23	41.77
Bulgaria	13,573	12,817	15,014	16,083	15,246	0.08	-5.20
Belarus	1,045,093	1,595,369	1,768,081	1,841,783	2,126,839	11.25	15.48
Czech Republic	15,579	17,503	21,983	35,338	45,179	0.24	27.85
Estonia	9,751	10,199	12,462	14,381	17,169	0.09	19.39
Georgia	15,687	18,335	28,006	29,341	39,406	0.21	34.30
Hungary	776,241	1,181,959	2,011,315	1,957,708	1,158,771	6.13	-40.81
Kazakhstan	18,625	20,658	29,177	30,144	35,910	0.19	19.13
Kyrgyzstan	3,871	11,687	4,604	4,848	7,281	0.04	50.19
Latvia	23,787	19,414	20,492	25,760	33,210	0.18	28.92
Lithuania	26,098	30,058	33,062	38,685	46,111	0.24	19.20
Republic of Moldova	2,259,446	2,556,999	2,898,375	2,780,880	3,055,833	16.17	9.89
Poland	555,998	1,239,195	1,793,213	3,489,033	3,977,938	21.05	14.01
Romania	43,195	68,102	97,872	161,948	348,157	1.84	114.98
Russian Federation	5,170,280	5,026,201	5,994,823	6,043,829	6,423,850	33.99	6.29
Slovakia	42,529	105,056	162,921	321,977	505,480	2.67	56.99
Tajikistan	3,053	2,052	3,973	4,310	11,723	0.06	172.00
Turkmenistan	2,775	4,594	5,886	11,137	3,385	0.02	-69.61
Uzbekistan	13,390	18,960	28,667	27,367	45,263	0.24	65.39
Northern Europe	**52,701**	**48,611**	**58,963**	**69,873**	**97,307**	**0.51**	**39.26**
Denmark	7,687	4,846	5,458	7,930	9,543	0.05	20.34
Finland	1,737	2,922	4,143	4,967	6,304	0.03	26.92
Iceland	45	152	208	346	473		36.71
Ireland	1,282	1,637	1,842	3,265	4,600	0.02	40.89
Norway	2,794	3,187	3,813	3,636	6,596	0.03	81.41
Sweden	4,283	6,606	7,519	9,415	13,711	0.07	45.63
United Kingdom	34,873	29,261	35,980	40,314	56,080	0.30	39.11
Southern Europe	**42,384**	**60,806**	**66,834**	**83,534**	**115,496**	**0.61**	**38.26**
Albania	346	356	469	382	379		-0.79
Andorra	8	6	25	40	44		10.00
Bosnia and Herzegovina	571	532	447	467	1,143	0.01	144.75
Croatia	1,363	1,814	2,003	2,174	2,660	0.01	22.36
Greece	9,665	10,553	8,602	11,561	14,551	0.08	25.86
Holy See	155	33	138	12			
Italy	19,031	30,444	36,062	47,082	62,943	0.33	33.69
Malta	186	740	103	252	296		17.46
Portugal	649	1,281	1,496	2,164	2,408	0.01	11.28
San Marino	14	31	43	23	56		143.48
Slovenia	1,464	1,951	2,233	3,684	4,795	0.03	30.16
Spain	4,828	6,766	8,229	7,637	12,451	0.07	63.04
TFYR of Macedonia	722	1,092	1,069	1,311	1,688	0.01	28.76

UKRAINE

1. Arrivals of non-resident tourists at national borders, by country of residence

	2002	2003	2004	2005	2006	Market share 06	% Change 06-05
Serbia and Montenegro	3,382	5,207	5,915	6,745	12,082	0.06	79.13
Western Europe	**141,613**	**188,003**	**213,764**	**280,136**	**330,310**	**1.75**	**17.91**
Austria	13,446	11,966	13,696	20,306	25,495	0.13	25.55
Belgium	2,627	5,606	6,243	7,730	10,181	0.05	31.71
France	16,636	25,396	27,370	34,066	42,408	0.22	24.49
Germany	94,986	118,513	141,534	189,546	214,389	1.13	13.11
Liechtenstein	103	54	43	53	70		32.08
Luxembourg	260	504	451	587	739		25.89
Monaco	78	937	1,088	47	27		-42.55
Netherlands	8,287	18,235	15,342	17,043	24,638	0.13	44.56
Switzerland	5,190	6,792	7,997	10,758	12,363	0.07	14.92
East Mediterranean Europe	**106,125**	**73,668**	**89,414**	**99,791**	**113,990**	**0.60**	**14.23**
Cyprus	3,045	1,823	2,238	3,087	3,105	0.02	0.58
Israel	80,813	39,995	44,481	51,186	51,699	0.27	1.00
Turkey	22,267	31,850	42,695	45,518	59,186	0.31	30.03
MIDDLE EAST	**14,777**	**18,720**	**20,130**	**25,501**	**22,209**	**0.12**	**-12.91**
Middle East	**14,777**	**18,720**	**20,130**	**25,501**	**22,209**	**0.12**	**-12.91**
Bahrain	46	89	115	198	325		64.14
Palestine	726	505	546	279	525		88.17
Iraq	196	111	411	623	1,188	0.01	90.69
Jordan	2,910	3,078	3,344	3,561	4,130	0.02	15.98
Kuwait	235	271	668	1,303	1,410	0.01	8.21
Lebanon	3,149	4,298	4,086	4,609	3,667	0.02	-20.44
Libyan Arab Jamahiriya	1,318	2,259	2,610	3,079	2,745	0.01	-10.85
Oman	40	38	44	54	24		-55.56
Qatar	10	32	61	40	41		2.50
Saudi Arabia	133	289	413	667	1,061	0.01	59.07
Syrian Arab Republic	3,632	5,367	5,043	7,817	4,363	0.02	-44.19
United Arab Emirates	231	342	292	493	411		-16.63
Egypt	2,053	1,902	2,304	2,622	2,094	0.01	-20.14
Yemen	98	139	193	156	225		44.23
SOUTH ASIA	**9,866**	**13,978**	**13,434**	**14,544**	**14,490**	**0.08**	**-0.37**
South Asia	**9,866**	**13,978**	**13,434**	**14,544**	**14,490**	**0.08**	**-0.37**
Afghanistan	595	407	453	602	563		-6.48
Bangladesh	412	235	251	230	182		-20.87
Sri Lanka	378	221	539	142	145		2.11
India	4,103	6,249	5,240	5,918	6,169	0.03	4.24
Iran, Islamic Republic of	3,222	5,824	5,822	6,298	6,120	0.03	-2.83
Maldives	6	5	16	107	26		-75.70
Nepal	63	66	76	91	96		5.49
Pakistan	1,087	971	1,037	1,156	1,189	0.01	2.85
REGION NOT SPECIFIED	**4,028**	**13,609**	**7,305**	**10,563**	**16,124**	**0.09**	**52.65**
Not Specified	**4,028**	**13,609**	**7,305**	**10,563**	**16,124**	**0.09**	**52.65**
Other countries of the World	4,028	13,609	7,305	10,563	16,124	0.09	52.65

Source: World Tourism Organization (UNWTO)

UNITED ARAB EMIRATES

3. Arrivals of non-resident tourists in hotels and similar establishments, by nationality

	2002	2003	2004	2005	2006	Market share 06	% Change 06-05
TOTAL	5,445,367	5,871,023	6,195,006				
AFRICA	310,722	306,872	315,418				
North Africa	31,211	35,347	36,260				
Sudan	31,211	35,347	36,260				
Other Africa	279,511	271,525	279,158				
Other countries of Africa	279,511	271,525	279,158				
AMERICAS	238,749	254,362	285,627				
North America	218,990	230,413	250,666				
Canada	95,878	55,297	57,718				
United States	123,112	175,116	192,948				
Other Americas	19,759	23,949	34,961				
Other countries of the Americas	19,759	23,949	34,961				
EAST ASIA AND THE PACIFIC	395,061	427,506	444,575				
North-East Asia	32,876	37,549	50,272				
Japan	32,876	37,549	50,272				
Other East Asia and the Pacific	362,185	389,957	394,303				
Other countries of Asia	293,751	305,550	293,677				
All countries of Oceania	68,434	84,407	100,626				
EUROPE	1,468,015	1,584,792	2,007,600				
Central/Eastern Europe	267,655	324,484	340,716				
Russian Federation	267,655	324,484	340,716				
Northern Europe	491,604	496,147	644,688				
United Kingdom	491,604	496,147	644,688				
Western Europe	364,574	371,334	492,325				
France	90,735	98,624	112,429				
Germany	236,660	235,147	337,594				
Netherlands	37,179	37,563	42,302				
Other Europe	344,182	392,827	529,871				
Other countries of Europe	344,182	392,827	529,871				
MIDDLE EAST	1,556,533	1,583,258	1,544,557				
Middle East	1,556,533	1,583,258	1,544,557				
Palestine	15,042	13,946	12,941				
Iraq	18,521	18,401	23,789				
Jordan	73,140	76,553	76,308				
Lebanon	74,225	83,137	90,409				
Syrian Arab Republic	53,836	60,104	59,033				
Egypt	111,822	121,221	131,635				
Yemen	47,383	36,912	31,055				
Other countries of Middle East	1,162,564	1,172,984	1,119,387				
SOUTH ASIA	807,094	921,698	909,339				
South Asia	807,094	921,698	909,339				
Bangladesh	45,987	45,580	43,007				
India	336,046	357,941	356,446				
Iran, Islamic Republic of	270,350	334,453	336,734				
Pakistan	154,711	183,724	173,152				
REGION NOT SPECIFIED	669,193	792,535	687,890				

830

UNITED ARAB EMIRATES

3. Arrivals of non-resident tourists in hotels and similar establishments, by nationality

		2002	2003	2004	2005	2006	Market share 06	% Change 06-05
Not Specified		669,193	792,535	687,890				
Nationals Residing Abroad	(*)	669,193	792,535	687,890				

Source: World Tourism Organization (UNWTO)

UNITED ARAB EMIRATES

5. Overnight stays of non-resident tourists in hotels and similar establishments, by nationality

	2002	2003	2004	2005	2006	Market share 06	% Change 06-05
TOTAL	12,359,593	14,191,984	16,345,395				
AFRICA	806,365	872,745	975,247				
North Africa	73,597	84,742	90,641				
Sudan	73,597	84,742	90,641				
Other Africa	732,768	788,003	884,606				
Other countries of Africa	732,768	788,003	884,606				
AMERICAS	524,020	602,103	755,763				
North America	472,341	536,106	663,214				
Canada	180,558	134,588	141,939				
United States	291,783	401,518	521,275				
Other Americas	51,679	65,997	92,549				
Other countries of the Americas	51,679	65,997	92,549				
EAST ASIA AND THE PACIFIC	824,890	956,483	1,025,604				
North-East Asia	82,536	102,956	137,827				
Japan	82,536	102,956	137,827				
Other East Asia and the Pacific	742,354	853,527	887,777				
Other countries of Asia	612,347	685,930	671,847				
All countries of Oceania	130,007	167,597	215,930				
EUROPE	4,399,671	4,826,954	6,595,033				
Central/Eastern Europe	910,063	1,054,744	1,383,992				
Russian Federation	910,063	1,054,744	1,383,992				
Northern Europe	1,451,979	1,574,331	1,997,754				
United Kingdom	1,451,979	1,574,331	1,997,754				
Western Europe	1,018,541	1,065,598	1,581,819				
France	236,050	249,386	316,013				
Germany	673,823	699,367	1,124,622				
Netherlands	108,668	116,845	141,184				
Other Europe	1,019,088	1,132,281	1,631,468				
Other countries of Europe	1,019,088	1,132,281	1,631,468				
MIDDLE EAST	2,941,737	3,345,105	3,437,245				
Middle East	2,941,737	3,345,105	3,437,245				
Palestine	29,928	29,346	28,302				
Iraq	48,319	50,513	79,838				
Jordan	158,968	175,979	179,264				
Lebanon	165,598	195,412	219,137				
Syrian Arab Republic	121,456	136,658	140,777				
Egypt	254,026	296,319	321,934				
Yemen	99,859	79,599	75,709				
Other countries of Middle East	2,063,583	2,381,279	2,392,284				
SOUTH ASIA	1,690,591	2,106,343	2,246,757				
South Asia	1,690,591	2,106,343	2,246,757				
Bangladesh	92,326	89,090	85,340				
India	717,049	819,990	871,583				
Iran, Islamic Republic of	580,214	816,580	906,313				
Pakistan	301,002	380,683	383,521				

UNITED ARAB EMIRATES

5. Overnight stays of non-resident tourists in hotels and similar establishments, by nationality

		2002	2003	2004	2005	2006	Market share 06	% Change 06-05
REGION NOT SPECIFIED		1,172,319	1,482,251	1,309,746				
Not Specified		1,172,319	1,482,251	1,309,746				
Nationals Residing Abroad	(*)	1,172,319	1,482,251	1,309,746				

Source: World Tourism Organization (UNWTO)

UNITED KINGDOM

2. Arrivals of non-resident visitors at national borders, by country of residence

	2002	2003	2004	2005	2006	Market share 06	% Change 06-05
TOTAL	24,181,000	24,715,000	27,754,000	29,970,000	32,712,919	100.00	9.15
AFRICA	631,000	569,000	639,000	654,000	701,468	2.14	7.26
East Africa	127,000	107,000	119,000	100,000	96,250	0.29	-3.75
Zimbabwe	28,000	17,000	25,000	21,000	14,830	0.05	-29.38
Other countries of East Africa	99,000	90,000	94,000	79,000	81,420	0.25	3.06
North Africa	42,000	33,000	32,000	39,000	43,739	0.13	12.15
All countries of North Africa	42,000	33,000	32,000	39,000	43,739	0.13	12.15
Southern Africa	276,000	266,000	269,000	308,000	351,312	1.07	14.06
South Africa	276,000	266,000	269,000	308,000	351,312	1.07	14.06
West Africa	158,000	139,000	189,000	182,000	186,510	0.57	2.48
Nigeria	111,000	102,000	141,000	141,000	146,314	0.45	3.77
Other countries of West Africa	47,000	37,000	48,000	41,000	40,196	0.12	-1.96
Other Africa	28,000	24,000	30,000	25,000	23,657	0.07	-5.37
Other countries of Africa	28,000	24,000	30,000	25,000	23,657	0.07	-5.37
AMERICAS	4,619,000	4,326,000	4,692,000	4,597,000	5,166,674	15.79	12.39
Caribbean	109,000	90,000	112,000	107,000	109,282	0.33	2.13
All countries of the Caribbean	109,000	90,000	112,000	107,000	109,282	0.33	2.13
North America	4,342,000	4,074,000	4,423,000	4,316,000	4,851,644	14.83	12.41
Canada	660,000	652,000	740,000	803,000	867,575	2.65	8.04
Mexico	71,000	76,000	67,000	77,000	87,689	0.27	13.88
United States	3,611,000	3,346,000	3,616,000	3,436,000	3,896,380	11.91	13.40
South America	119,000	108,000	119,000	124,000	157,923	0.48	27.36
Argentina	19,000	29,000	32,000	27,000	37,128	0.11	37.51
Brazil	83,000	70,000	78,000	91,000	112,068	0.34	23.15
Venezuela	17,000	9,000	9,000	6,000	8,727	0.03	45.45
Other Americas	49,000	54,000	38,000	50,000	47,825	0.15	-4.35
Other countries of the Americas	49,000	54,000	38,000	50,000	47,825	0.15	-4.35
EAST ASIA AND THE PACIFIC	1,854,000	1,809,000	2,086,000	2,190,000	2,310,449	7.06	5.50
North-East Asia	721,000	660,000	768,000	744,000	791,887	2.42	6.44
China	64,000	68,000	95,000	92,000	107,276	0.33	16.60
Taiwan (Province of China)	39,000	38,000	43,000	35,000	35,167	0.11	0.48
Hong Kong, China	158,000	131,000	145,000	144,000	154,432	0.47	7.24
Japan	368,000	314,000	347,000	326,000	341,932	1.05	4.89
Korea, Republic of	92,000	109,000	138,000	147,000	153,080	0.47	4.14
South-East Asia	205,000	200,000	259,000	221,000	242,103	0.74	9.55
Malaysia	80,000	74,000	105,000	85,000	84,702	0.26	-0.35
Singapore	84,000	79,000	87,000	84,000	99,401	0.30	18.33
Thailand	41,000	47,000	67,000	52,000	58,000	0.18	11.54
Australasia	839,000	867,000	961,000	1,124,000	1,178,608	3.60	4.86
Australia	702,000	723,000	787,000	915,000	956,057	2.92	4.49
New Zealand	137,000	144,000	174,000	209,000	222,551	0.68	6.48
Other East Asia and the Pacific	89,000	82,000	98,000	101,000	97,851	0.30	-3.12
Other countries of Asia	89,000	82,000	98,000	101,000	97,851	0.30	-3.12
EUROPE	16,409,000	17,371,000	19,582,000	21,742,000	23,541,245	71.96	8.28
Central/Eastern Europe	778,000	1,017,000	1,481,000	2,307,000	2,896,299	8.85	25.54
Czech Republic	122,000	202,000	274,000	294,000	322,630	0.99	9.74
Hungary	132,000	111,000	188,000	267,000	278,418	0.85	4.28

UNITED KINGDOM

2. Arrivals of non-resident visitors at national borders, by country of residence

	2002	2003	2004	2005	2006	Market share 06	% Change 06-05
Poland	188,000	325,000	528,000	1,027,000	1,325,925	4.05	29.11
Russian Federation	117,000	138,000	148,000	174,000	241,316	0.74	38.69
Other countries Central/East Europ	219,000	241,000	343,000	545,000	728,010	2.23	33.58
Northern Europe	**3,956,000**	**4,064,000**	**4,389,000**	**4,970,000**	**5,064,357**	**15.48**	**1.90**
Denmark	431,000	425,000	477,000	542,000	527,560	1.61	-2.66
Finland	121,000	122,000	156,000	172,000	190,494	0.58	10.75
Iceland	38,000	63,000	83,000	77,000	85,229	0.26	10.69
Ireland	2,439,000	2,488,000	2,578,000	2,824,000	2,909,295	8.89	3.02
Norway	397,000	433,000	510,000	627,000	637,515	1.95	1.68
Sweden	530,000	533,000	585,000	728,000	714,264	2.18	-1.89
Southern Europe	**2,465,000**	**2,894,000**	**3,452,000**	**3,581,000**	**4,140,651**	**12.66**	**15.63**
Gibraltar	32,000	22,000	42,000	31,000	50,241	0.15	62.07
Greece	169,000	185,000	203,000	199,000	178,716	0.55	-10.19
Italy	977,000	1,168,000	1,348,000	1,189,000	1,477,190	4.52	24.24
Malta	36,000	50,000	58,000	54,000	57,155	0.17	5.84
Portugal	170,000	193,000	213,000	221,000	242,432	0.74	9.70
Spain	1,010,000	1,206,000	1,465,000	1,773,000	1,980,678	6.05	11.71
Yugoslavia, Sfr (Former)	71,000	70,000	123,000	114,000	154,239	0.47	35.30
Western Europe	**8,874,000**	**9,038,000**	**9,901,000**	**10,537,000**	**11,002,486**	**33.63**	**4.42**
Austria	219,000	263,000	295,000	289,000	300,094	0.92	3.84
Belgium	966,000	936,000	1,104,000	1,120,000	997,072	3.05	-10.98
France	3,077,000	3,073,000	3,254,000	3,333,000	3,693,215	11.29	10.81
Germany	2,556,000	2,611,000	2,968,000	3,318,000	3,411,404	10.43	2.82
Luxembourg	44,000	42,000	63,000	51,000	65,160	0.20	27.76
Netherlands	1,419,000	1,549,000	1,620,000	1,729,000	1,790,980	5.47	3.58
Switzerland	593,000	564,000	597,000	697,000	744,561	2.28	6.82
East Mediterranean Europe	**336,000**	**358,000**	**359,000**	**347,000**	**437,452**	**1.34**	**26.07**
Cyprus	80,000	104,000	105,000	110,000	122,176	0.37	11.07
Israel	191,000	162,000	159,000	140,000	163,950	0.50	17.11
Turkey	65,000	92,000	95,000	97,000	151,326	0.46	56.01
MIDDLE EAST	**360,000**	**346,000**	**384,000**	**380,000**	**471,855**	**1.44**	**24.17**
Middle East	**360,000**	**346,000**	**384,000**	**380,000**	**471,855**	**1.44**	**24.17**
Saudi Arabia	78,000	63,000	64,000	59,000	65,493	0.20	11.01
United Arab Emirates	109,000	113,000	147,000	134,000	177,705	0.54	32.62
Egypt	32,000	41,000	34,000	30,000	43,623	0.13	45.41
Other countries of Middle East	141,000	129,000	139,000	157,000	185,034	0.57	17.86
SOUTH ASIA	**308,000**	**294,000**	**371,000**	**407,000**	**521,228**	**1.59**	**28.07**
South Asia	**308,000**	**294,000**	**371,000**	**407,000**	**521,228**	**1.59**	**28.07**
Bangladesh	18,000	12,000	10,000	17,000	9,725	0.03	-42.79
India	205,000	199,000	255,000	269,000	366,745	1.12	36.34
Iran, Islamic Republic of	23,000	26,000	30,000	31,000	31,205	0.10	0.66
Pakistan	62,000	57,000	76,000	90,000	113,553	0.35	26.17

Source: World Tourism Organization (UNWTO)

UNITED KINGDOM

6. Overnight stays of non-resident tourists in all types of accommodation establishments, by country of residence

	2002	2003	2004	2005	2006	Market share 06	% Change 06-05
TOTAL	199,283,000	203,431,000	227,406,000	247,586,000	273,416,648	100.00	10.43
AFRICA	12,163,000	11,119,000	11,280,000	12,784,000	13,160,439	4.81	2.94
East Africa	2,880,000	2,390,000	2,479,000	1,966,000	1,836,171	0.67	-6.60
Zimbabwe	536,000	622,000	698,000	480,000	372,350	0.14	-22.43
Other countries of East Africa	2,344,000	1,768,000	1,781,000	1,486,000	1,463,821	0.54	-1.49
North Africa	865,000	873,000	568,000	1,045,000	763,962	0.28	-26.89
All countries of North Africa	865,000	873,000	568,000	1,045,000	763,962	0.28	-26.89
Southern Africa	5,100,000	4,668,000	4,266,000	4,887,000	5,756,743	2.11	17.80
South Africa	5,100,000	4,668,000	4,266,000	4,887,000	5,756,743	2.11	17.80
West Africa	2,939,000	2,813,000	3,631,000	4,588,000	4,434,885	1.62	-3.34
Nigeria	1,746,000	1,776,000	2,119,000	3,262,000	3,204,657	1.17	-1.76
Other countries of West Africa	1,193,000	1,037,000	1,512,000	1,326,000	1,230,228	0.45	-7.22
Other Africa	379,000	375,000	336,000	298,000	368,678	0.13	23.72
Other countries of Africa	379,000	375,000	336,000	298,000	368,678	0.13	23.72
AMERICAS	43,645,000	41,921,000	46,284,000	40,677,000	46,975,548	17.18	15.48
Caribbean	2,458,000	2,583,000	1,690,000	2,110,000	1,259,022	0.46	-40.33
All countries of the Caribbean	2,458,000	2,583,000	1,690,000	2,110,000	1,259,022	0.46	-40.33
North America	38,341,000	36,024,000	42,075,000	36,104,000	42,017,862	15.37	16.38
Canada	7,810,000	7,351,000	9,027,000	8,950,000	9,304,735	3.40	3.96
Mexico	794,000	537,000	2,599,000	811,000	931,654	0.34	14.88
United States	29,737,000	28,136,000	30,449,000	26,343,000	31,781,473	11.62	20.64
South America	1,886,000	2,666,000	1,980,000	1,926,000	2,913,496	1.07	51.27
Argentina	507,000	382,000	383,000	315,000	370,457	0.14	17.61
Brazil	1,159,000	1,744,000	1,529,000	1,579,000	2,421,552	0.89	53.36
Venezuela	220,000	540,000	68,000	32,000	121,487	0.04	279.65
Other Americas	960,000	648,000	539,000	537,000	785,168	0.29	46.21
Other countries of the Americas	960,000	648,000	539,000	537,000	785,168	0.29	46.21
EAST ASIA AND THE PACIFIC	28,687,000	30,888,000	30,545,000	29,364,000	30,631,714	11.20	4.32
North-East Asia	8,950,000	9,986,000	9,510,000	8,875,000	8,490,839	3.11	-4.33
China	1,216,000	1,770,000	2,157,000	1,555,000	1,375,595	0.50	-11.54
Taiwan (Province of China)	1,029,000	1,955,000	619,000	570,000	1,001,056	0.37	75.62
Hong Kong, China	1,804,000	1,466,000	2,501,000	1,839,000	1,454,017	0.53	-20.93
Japan	3,931,000	3,406,000	3,228,000	3,723,000	3,099,167	1.13	-16.76
Korea, Republic of	970,000	1,389,000	1,005,000	1,188,000	1,561,004	0.57	31.40
South-East Asia	3,228,000	3,289,000	3,699,000	2,559,000	3,194,690	1.17	24.84
Malaysia	1,683,000	1,694,000	1,919,000	815,000	1,156,722	0.42	41.93
Singapore	906,000	981,000	802,000	827,000	957,028	0.35	15.72
Thailand	639,000	614,000	978,000	917,000	1,080,940	0.40	17.88
Australasia	14,436,000	15,534,000	15,356,000	16,010,000	17,001,739	6.22	6.19
Australia	11,678,000	13,125,000	12,239,000	12,659,000	13,490,170	4.93	6.57
New Zealand	2,758,000	2,409,000	3,117,000	3,351,000	3,511,569	1.28	4.79
Other East Asia and the Pacific	2,073,000	2,079,000	1,980,000	1,920,000	1,944,446	0.71	1.27
Other countries of Asia	2,073,000	2,079,000	1,980,000	1,920,000	1,944,446	0.71	1.27
EUROPE	101,739,000	105,831,000	122,722,000	145,629,000	161,250,979	58.98	10.73
Central/Eastern Europe	9,583,000	16,999,000	23,773,000	38,423,000	40,445,859	14.79	5.26
Czech Republic	770,000	1,940,000	1,971,000	2,568,000	3,712,857	1.36	44.58

UNITED KINGDOM

6. Overnight stays of non-resident tourists in all types of accommodation establishments, by country of residence

	2002	2003	2004	2005	2006	Market share 06	% Change 06-05
Hungary	985,000	1,709,000	1,875,000	2,658,000	2,634,061	0.96	-0.90
Poland	3,870,000	7,993,000	11,539,000	20,515,000	22,293,103	8.15	8.67
Russian Federation	1,395,000	1,548,000	2,024,000	1,940,000	2,930,406	1.07	51.05
Other countries Central/East Europ	2,563,000	3,809,000	6,364,000	10,742,000	8,875,432	3.25	-17.38
Northern Europe	**18,433,000**	**17,875,000**	**18,258,000**	**21,437,000**	**21,251,693**	**7.77**	**-0.86**
Denmark	2,558,000	1,944,000	2,349,000	3,024,000	2,479,704	0.91	-18.00
Finland	958,000	795,000	841,000	1,199,000	1,080,088	0.40	-9.92
Iceland	445,000	407,000	424,000	343,000	412,171	0.15	20.17
Ireland	9,927,000	9,675,000	9,217,000	10,172,000	10,248,499	3.75	0.75
Norway	1,829,000	1,948,000	2,245,000	3,073,000	3,289,372	1.20	7.04
Sweden	2,716,000	3,106,000	3,182,000	3,626,000	3,741,859	1.37	3.20
Southern Europe	**21,091,000**	**22,582,000**	**26,853,000**	**30,043,000**	**34,531,879**	**12.63**	**14.94**
Greece	2,015,000	1,715,000	1,917,000	1,626,000	2,396,355	0.88	47.38
Italy	7,749,000	8,048,000	9,597,000	9,560,000	9,768,546	3.57	2.18
Portugal	1,439,000	1,206,000	1,502,000	2,126,000	1,754,058	0.64	-17.49
Spain	9,348,000	10,957,000	12,968,000	15,974,000	18,550,863	6.78	16.13
Yugoslavia, Sfr (Former)	540,000	656,000	869,000	757,000	2,062,057	0.75	172.40
Western Europe	**48,448,000**	**44,378,000**	**49,303,000**	**51,477,000**	**59,257,333**	**21.67**	**15.11**
Austria	1,761,000	1,813,000	1,835,000	2,069,000	2,051,510	0.75	-0.85
Belgium	2,999,000	2,667,000	2,925,000	3,155,000	3,129,863	1.14	-0.80
France	17,735,000	13,765,000	17,283,000	16,699,000	21,092,817	7.71	26.31
Germany	15,392,000	15,435,000	16,603,000	18,120,000	20,886,917	7.64	15.27
Luxembourg	167,000	152,000	245,000	193,000	168,286	0.06	-12.81
Netherlands	6,276,000	7,032,000	6,377,000	7,134,000	7,444,942	2.72	4.36
Switzerland	4,118,000	3,514,000	4,035,000	4,107,000	4,482,998	1.64	9.16
East Mediterranean Europe	**2,298,000**	**2,168,000**	**2,344,000**	**2,264,000**	**3,579,171**	**1.31**	**58.09**
Israel	1,452,000	1,166,000	1,330,000	1,181,000	1,190,511	0.44	0.81
Turkey	846,000	1,002,000	1,014,000	1,083,000	2,388,660	0.87	120.56
Other Europe	**1,886,000**	**1,829,000**	**2,191,000**	**1,985,000**	**2,185,044**	**0.80**	**10.08**
Other countries of Europe	1,886,000	1,829,000	2,191,000	1,985,000	2,185,044	0.80	10.08
MIDDLE EAST	**6,063,000**	**5,523,000**	**6,093,000**	**5,720,000**	**6,793,030**	**2.48**	**18.76**
Middle East	**6,063,000**	**5,523,000**	**6,093,000**	**5,720,000**	**6,793,030**	**2.48**	**18.76**
Saudi Arabia	1,325,000	1,209,000	966,000	1,043,000	1,023,246	0.37	-1.89
United Arab Emirates	1,831,000	1,626,000	2,116,000	1,747,000	2,442,773	0.89	39.83
Egypt	536,000	614,000	443,000	533,000	582,696	0.21	9.32
Other countries of Middle East	2,371,000	2,074,000	2,568,000	2,397,000	2,744,315	1.00	14.49
SOUTH ASIA	**6,986,000**	**8,149,000**	**10,482,000**	**13,412,000**	**14,604,938**	**5.34**	**8.89**
South Asia	**6,986,000**	**8,149,000**	**10,482,000**	**13,412,000**	**14,604,938**	**5.34**	**8.89**
Bangladesh	206,000	382,000	438,000	683,000	214,028	0.08	-68.66
India	4,753,000	5,054,000	6,800,000	7,709,000	9,601,006	3.51	24.54
Iran, Islamic Republic of	445,000	972,000	772,000	894,000	833,662	0.30	-6.75
Pakistan	1,582,000	1,741,000	2,472,000	4,126,000	3,956,242	1.45	-4.11

Source: World Tourism Organization (UNWTO)

UNITED REPUBLIC OF TANZANIA

2. Arrivals of non-resident visitors at national borders, by country of residence

	2002	2003	2004	2005	2006	Market share 06	% Change 06-05
TOTAL	575,296	576,198	582,807	612,754	644,124	100.00	5.12
AFRICA	249,601	267,940	256,455	275,718	293,440	45.56	6.43
East Africa	200,295	216,086	215,942	228,417	248,031	38.51	8.59
Burundi	6,951	11,907	3,157	5,767	10,631	1.65	84.34
Comoros	2,656	1,346	5,740	4,467	4,211	0.65	-5.73
Ethiopia	1,628	1,465	877	1,234	1,170	0.18	-5.19
Eritrea	241	125	96	236	135	0.02	-42.80
Djibouti	423	176	60	701	46	0.01	-93.44
Kenya	112,036	119,406	124,967	112,766	127,016	19.72	12.64
Madagascar	717	332	235	294	26		-91.16
Malawi	17,531	14,267	16,868	19,999	17,247	2.68	-13.76
Mauritius	1,021	781	612	307	293	0.05	-4.56
Mozambique	1,149	3,340	1,562	1,530	1,679	0.26	9.74
Rwanda	4,090	12,061	6,089	17,037	13,056	2.03	-23.37
Seychelles	618	204	190	221	139	0.02	-37.10
Somalia	1,040	1,547	512	481	698	0.11	45.11
Zimbabwe	8,480	3,795	5,319	8,884	5,031	0.78	-43.37
Uganda	28,618	34,664	24,253	25,373	35,521	5.51	40.00
Zambia	13,096	10,670	25,405	29,120	31,132	4.83	6.91
Central Africa	15,369	8,972	9,006	10,925	11,100	1.72	1.60
Angola	261	386	600	550	286	0.04	-48.00
Cameroon	1,009	806	315	810	407	0.06	-49.75
Central African Republic	18	363	16	13	39	0.01	200.00
Chad	20	27	11	22	19		-13.64
Congo	377	140	9	32	530	0.08	1,556.25
Democratic Republic of the Congo	12,784	6,850	8,030	9,479	9,792	1.52	3.30
Gabon	900	400	25	19	27		42.11
North Africa	1,955	674	562	582	568	0.09	-2.41
Algeria	52	81	64	57	46	0.01	-19.30
Morocco	74	66	61	50	73	0.01	46.00
Sudan	1,493	442	367	398	365	0.06	-8.29
Tunisia	336	85	70	77	84	0.01	9.09
Southern Africa	25,369	37,099	27,821	31,659	30,650	4.76	-3.19
Botswana	781	632	773	1,299	658	0.10	-49.35
Lesotho	519	288	233	177	233	0.04	31.64
Namibia	845	598	615	780	527	0.08	-32.44
South Africa	22,916	35,071	25,849	28,922	28,961	4.50	0.13
Swaziland	308	510	351	481	271	0.04	-43.66
West Africa	6,613	5,109	3,124	4,135	3,091	0.48	-25.25
Cape Verde	10	4	8	3	7		133.33
Benin	410	406	154	129	98	0.02	-24.03
Gambia	190	219	188	259	139	0.02	-46.33
Ghana	1,993	1,303	603	832	633	0.10	-23.92
Guinea	183	199	110	140	124	0.02	-11.43
Cote D'Ivoire	578	306	147	446	134	0.02	-69.96
Liberia	111	95	62	92	119	0.02	29.35
Mali	206	158	155	170	160	0.02	-5.88
Mauritania	234	124	152	285	176	0.03	-38.25
Niger	84	86	38	181	27		-85.08
Nigeria	1,428	1,214	763	803	837	0.13	4.23
Guinea-Bissau		1		9	1		-88.89
Senegal	394	496	393	370	260	0.04	-29.73
Sierra Leone	211	193	155	197	108	0.02	-45.18

UNITED REPUBLIC OF TANZANIA

2. Arrivals of non-resident visitors at national borders, by country of residence

	2002	2003	2004	2005	2006	Market share 06	% Change 06-05
Togo	186	173	88	93	99	0.02	6.45
Burkina Faso	395	132	108	126	169	0.03	34.13
AMERICAS	**59,077**	**49,781**	**53,437**	**61,604**	**71,278**	**11.07**	**15.70**
Caribbean	**974**	**532**	**374**	**410**	**333**	**0.05**	**-18.78**
Antigua and Barbuda	16	43	3		10		
Bahamas	2		12	4	12		200.00
Barbados	24		12	15	14		-6.67
Cuba	183	39	39	37	50	0.01	35.14
Dominica	51	18	13	40	14		-65.00
Grenada	24		11	1			
Haiti	31	36	33	26	22		-15.38
Jamaica	538	283	141	145	120	0.02	-17.24
Saint Lucia		16	9	11	17		54.55
Saint Vincent and the Grenadines			1	2			
Trinidad and Tobago	105	97	88	87	61	0.01	-29.89
Other countries of the Caribbean			12	42	13		-69.05
Central America	**644**	**465**	**164**	**342**	**169**	**0.03**	**-50.58**
Belize			13	5	7		40.00
Costa Rica	353	132	76	53	49	0.01	-7.55
El Salvador	4	79	6	38	34	0.01	-10.53
Guatemala		46	40	48	27		-43.75
Honduras	32	5	9	14	7		-50.00
Nicaragua	227	31	8	170	17		-90.00
Panama	28	172	12	14	28		100.00
North America	**50,994**	**47,429**	**51,397**	**59,201**	**68,877**	**10.69**	**16.34**
Canada	12,042	10,354	10,613	10,922	12,536	1.95	14.78
Mexico	793	656	536	658	654	0.10	-0.61
United States	38,159	36,419	40,248	47,621	55,687	8.65	16.94
South America	**6,465**	**1,355**	**1,502**	**1,651**	**1,899**	**0.29**	**15.02**
Argentina	281	199	319	200	552	0.09	176.00
Bolivia	50	14	21	80	40	0.01	-50.00
Brazil	4,476	408	454	714	651	0.10	-8.82
Chile	142	99	183	116	135	0.02	16.38
Colombia	523	320	100	171	185	0.03	8.19
Ecuador	47	31	26	90	48	0.01	-46.67
Guyana	44	36	48	31	28		-9.68
Paraguay	25	3	9	6	21		250.00
Peru	125	141	138	107	135	0.02	26.17
Suriname		43	9	7	1		-85.71
Uruguay	160	32	141	64	23		-64.06
Venezuela	592	29	54	65	80	0.01	23.08
EAST ASIA AND THE PACIFIC	**30,087**	**27,208**	**22,928**	**24,714**	**28,222**	**4.38**	**14.19**
North-East Asia	**11,919**	**12,949**	**10,694**	**11,976**	**12,359**	**1.92**	**3.20**
China	3,163	4,007	3,602	4,289	4,798	0.74	11.87
Taiwan (Province of China)	470	221	259	273	1,218	0.19	346.15
Hong Kong, China	281	22	82	56			
Japan	5,574	5,936	4,504	4,534	3,989	0.62	-12.02
Korea, Dem. People's Republic of		59	30	509	267	0.04	-47.54
Korea, Republic of	2,428	2,690	2,210	2,304	2,079	0.32	-9.77
Mongolia	3	14	7	11	8		-27.27
South-East Asia	**4,221**	**2,228**	**1,908**	**2,241**	**1,977**	**0.31**	**-11.78**
Brunei Darussalam		170	4	2	5		150.00

UNITED REPUBLIC OF TANZANIA

2. Arrivals of non-resident visitors at national borders, by country of residence

	2002	2003	2004	2005	2006	Market share 06	% Change 06-05
Myanmar	214	20	10	19	21		10.53
Cambodia	28	102	36	104	52	0.01	-50.00
Indonesia	734	322	255	290	125	0.02	-56.90
Malaysia	926	366	377	339	339	0.05	
Philippines	1,058	655	522	651	578	0.09	-11.21
Singapore	589	217	315	318	320	0.05	0.63
Viet Nam	51	19	30	43	82	0.01	90.70
Thailand	621	357	359	475	455	0.07	-4.21
Australasia	**13,748**	**11,989**	**10,162**	**10,460**	**13,864**	**2.15**	**32.54**
Australia	9,715	9,698	8,161	8,270	12,162	1.89	47.06
New Zealand	4,033	2,291	2,001	2,190	1,702	0.26	-22.28
Melanesia	**199**	**42**	**154**	**36**	**21**		**-41.67**
Solomon Islands			137				
Fiji	199	42	14	35	21		-40.00
Papua New Guinea			3	1			
Polynesia			**10**	**1**	**1**		
Samoa			10	1	1		
EUROPE	**191,982**	**191,025**	**221,865**	**220,255**	**229,048**	**35.56**	**3.99**
Central/Eastern Europe	**5,679**	**6,850**	**4,554**	**5,803**	**6,495**	**1.01**	**11.92**
Azerbaijan		57	22	11	204	0.03	1,754.55
Armenia	16	28	16	16	12		-25.00
Bulgaria	352	1,220	175	142	167	0.03	17.61
Belarus	447	39	30	307	52	0.01	-83.06
Czech Republic	672	539	500	610	1,067	0.17	74.92
Estonia	56	22	59	67	153	0.02	128.36
Hungary	359	389	400	912	1,022	0.16	12.06
Kazakhstan	3	36	55	37	31		-16.22
Latvia	250	117	79	81	169	0.03	108.64
Lithuania	84	61	98	54	129	0.02	138.89
Republic of Moldova			5	9			
Poland	1,382	2,181	976	1,422	1,297	0.20	-8.79
Romania	150	425	287	236	234	0.04	-0.85
Russian Federation	1,404	1,385	1,569	1,451	1,415	0.22	-2.48
Slovakia	79	44	47	98			
Tajikistan			4	2	76	0.01	3,700.00
Ukraine	422	307	224	251	336	0.05	33.86
Uzbekistan	3		4	20	19		-5.00
Other countries Central/East Europ			4	77	112	0.02	45.45
Northern Europe	**68,792**	**71,226**	**81,894**	**76,731**	**94,724**	**14.71**	**23.45**
Denmark	5,524	5,210	4,813	4,848	5,425	0.84	11.90
Finland	2,630	4,163	2,104	2,649	2,419	0.38	-8.68
Iceland	469	35	60	361	89	0.01	-75.35
Ireland	3,508	4,145	3,484	3,295	4,082	0.63	23.88
Norway	4,984	5,590	4,674	5,172	5,207	0.81	0.68
Sweden	8,408	8,427	7,212	7,964	8,342	1.30	4.75
United Kingdom	43,269	43,656	59,547	52,442	69,160	10.74	31.88
Southern Europe	**42,474**	**38,127**	**57,771**	**64,334**	**64,320**	**9.99**	**-0.02**
Albania	10	25	3	37	38	0.01	2.70
Andorra	10	7	30	20	42	0.01	110.00
Bosnia and Herzegovina	56	15	77	24	17		-29.17
Croatia	190	139	191	166	149	0.02	-10.24
Greece	410	775	505	620	378	0.06	-39.03
Holy See		14					

UNITED REPUBLIC OF TANZANIA

2. Arrivals of non-resident visitors at national borders, by country of residence

	2002	2003	2004	2005	2006	Market share 06	% Change 06-05
Italy	23,459	24,675	44,045	49,829	50,287	7.81	0.92
Malta	52	84	80	113	59	0.01	-47.79
Portugal	1,486	2,288	1,294	1,199	1,265	0.20	5.50
San Marino	20	43			31		
Slovenia	464	176	367	422	423	0.07	0.24
Spain	16,054	9,565	11,168	11,709	11,575	1.80	-1.14
TFYR of Macedonia	66	46					
Serbia and Montenegro	197	275	11	195	56	0.01	-71.28
Western Europe	**71,278**	**73,169**	**75,619**	**70,744**	**60,663**	**9.42**	**-14.25**
Austria	3,101	2,908	4,025	2,405	3,241	0.50	34.76
Belgium	6,203	6,497	8,378	5,466	5,680	0.88	3.92
France	22,059	22,103	21,849	23,547	19,643	3.05	-16.58
Germany	17,855	19,222	20,209	18,170	19,651	3.05	8.15
Liechtenstein		8	23	27	37	0.01	37.04
Luxembourg	127	100	176	182	143	0.02	-21.43
Monaco	73	76	5	1	21		2,000.00
Netherlands	15,891	15,272	14,594	15,805	262	0.04	-98.34
Switzerland	5,969	6,983	6,360	5,141	11,985	1.86	133.13
East Mediterranean Europe	**3,759**	**1,653**	**2,027**	**2,643**	**2,846**	**0.44**	**7.68**
Cyprus	84	104	108	278	125	0.02	-55.04
Israel	3,360	1,188	1,512	1,835	2,131	0.33	16.13
Turkey	315	361	407	530	590	0.09	11.32
MIDDLE EAST	**16,682**	**13,742**	**11,594**	**10,528**	**6,815**	**1.06**	**-35.27**
Middle East	**16,682**	**13,742**	**11,594**	**10,528**	**6,815**	**1.06**	**-35.27**
Bahrain	308	118	60	2,951	32		-98.92
Palestine	10	280	8	23	10		-56.52
Iraq	330	559	12	23	12		-47.83
Jordan	405	302	134	129	76	0.01	-41.09
Kuwait	449	947	65	67	42	0.01	-37.31
Lebanon	505	387	222	326	232	0.04	-28.83
Libyan Arab Jamahiriya	169	163	80	93	94	0.01	1.08
Oman	7,728	5,225	7,601	4,488	4,104	0.64	-8.56
Qatar		34	17	17	23		35.29
Saudi Arabia	384	249	191	140	159	0.02	13.57
Syrian Arab Republic	700	263	82	55	40	0.01	-27.27
United Arab Emirates	1,425	884	1,581	1,222	1,155	0.18	-5.48
Egypt	1,120	1,145	671	423	406	0.06	-4.02
Yemen	3,149	3,186	870	571	430	0.07	-24.69
SOUTH ASIA	**27,867**	**26,502**	**16,528**	**19,935**	**15,321**	**2.38**	**-23.15**
South Asia	**27,867**	**26,502**	**16,528**	**19,935**	**15,321**	**2.38**	**-23.15**
Afghanistan			12	9	18		100.00
Bangladesh	141	277	153	207	432	0.07	108.70
Bhutan			9		22		
Sri Lanka	3,670	1,695	304	318	275	0.04	-13.52
India	21,973	22,215	14,804	17,598	13,020	2.02	-26.01
Iran, Islamic Republic of	385	272	217	222	348	0.05	56.76
Nepal	165	362	225	334	252	0.04	-24.55
Pakistan	1,533	1,681	804	1,247	954	0.15	-23.50

Source: World Tourism Organization (UNWTO)

UNITED STATES

1. Arrivals of non-resident tourists at national borders, by country of residence

	2002	2003	2004	2005	2006	Market share 06	% Change 06-05
TOTAL (*)	43,580,707	41,218,213	46,086,257	49,205,528	50,977,532	100.00	3.60
AFRICA	241,011	236,067	240,488	251,654	251,841	0.49	0.07
East Africa	43,257	39,674	40,770	40,909	44,185	0.09	8.01
Burundi	289	181	294	506	720		42.29
Comoros	19	10	6	8	18		125.00
Ethiopia	4,749	5,582	4,975	4,707	6,444	0.01	36.90
Eritrea	1,025	1,034	1,039	915	789		-13.77
Djibouti	127	191	136	117	145		23.93
Kenya	17,275	13,913	14,979	14,118	14,909	0.03	5.60
Madagascar	500	499	454	593	655		10.46
Malawi	1,212	1,098	1,092	1,238	1,055		-14.78
Mauritius	846	701	836	1,245	1,458		17.11
Mozambique	710	623	689	783	737		-5.87
Reunion	81	174	127	229	130		-43.23
Rwanda	657	674	945	1,132	1,218		7.60
Seychelles	266	246	164	189	167		-11.64
Somalia	23	22	35	55	30		-45.45
Zimbabwe	5,457	5,223	5,138	4,796	4,535	0.01	-5.44
Uganda	3,326	3,215	3,622	3,764	4,147	0.01	10.18
United Republic of Tanzania	3,530	3,506	3,357	3,621	4,015	0.01	10.88
Zambia	3,165	2,782	2,882	2,893	3,013	0.01	4.15
Central Africa	10,973	10,550	10,123	12,148	13,189	0.03	8.57
Angola	2,912	2,781	3,060	3,651	4,418	0.01	21.01
Cameroon	5,003	5,214	4,366	4,759	4,958	0.01	4.18
Central African Republic	169	47	49	341	390		14.37
Chad	229	230	222	349	335		-4.01
Congo	1,432	1,111	1,223	1,449	1,267		-12.56
Democratic Republic of the Congo	81	76	70	156	418		167.95
Equatorial Guinea	83	78	43	72	119		65.28
Gabon	1,031	980	1,062	1,341	1,250		-6.79
Sao Tome and Principe	33	33	28	30	34		13.33
North Africa	17,294	16,179	17,888	20,082	20,726	0.04	3.21
Algeria	1,988	1,631	1,802	2,409	2,894	0.01	20.13
Morocco	12,464	11,857	12,538	13,430	13,270	0.03	-1.19
Western Sahara	1	1		8	14		75.00
Sudan	852	670	628	669	1,066		59.34
Tunisia	1,989	2,020	2,920	3,566	3,482	0.01	-2.36
Southern Africa	77,381	75,206	82,186	93,043	92,721	0.18	-0.35
Botswana	2,116	1,873	2,273	2,269	2,038		-10.18
Lesotho	272	201	232	269	233		-13.38
Namibia	883	912	1,033	1,004	1,076		7.17
South Africa	73,910	72,029	78,433	89,102	89,017	0.17	-0.10
Swaziland	200	191	215	399	357		-10.53
West Africa	92,106	94,458	89,521	85,472	81,020	0.16	-5.21
Cape Verde	1,744	1,211	1,208	1,559	1,562		0.19
Benin	669	698	795	1,045	1,260		20.57
Gambia	3,382	2,910	2,055	1,868	1,288		-31.05
Ghana	18,957	20,760	18,679	15,155	12,710	0.02	-16.13
Guinea	3,589	3,958	3,528	2,822	2,707	0.01	-4.08
Cote D'Ivoire	2,514	1,649	1,638	1,463	2,132		45.73
Liberia	1,400	848	1,038	669	976		45.89
Mali	2,743	2,705	1,480	1,688	2,668	0.01	58.06
Mauritania	558	564	582	625	496		-20.64

UNITED STATES

1. Arrivals of non-resident tourists at national borders, by country of residence

	2002	2003	2004	2005	2006	Market share 06	% Change 06-05
Niger	4,930	1,720	3,614	2,903	2,194		-24.42
Nigeria	40,128	46,938	45,606	47,397	44,999	0.09	-5.06
Guinea-Bissau	30	15	12	24	23		-4.17
Senegal	7,762	6,830	5,689	4,804	4,445	0.01	-7.47
Sierra Leone	765	882	919	858	925		7.81
Togo	1,801	1,695	1,549	1,099	943		-14.19
Burkina Faso	1,134	1,075	1,129	1,493	1,692		13.33
AMERICAS	**28,035,856**	**26,368,298**	**29,195,830**	**31,178,408**	**33,128,737**	**64.99**	**6.26**
Caribbean	**1,052,576**	**998,266**	**1,094,908**	**1,134,886**	**1,198,027**	**2.35**	**5.56**
Antigua and Barbuda	16,317	16,479	18,585	19,966	20,949	0.04	4.92
Bahamas	262,469	253,229	265,681	237,140	243,300	0.48	2.60
Barbados	41,934	41,558	49,198	51,233	54,096	0.11	5.59
Bermuda	6,227	13,382	15,996	16,120	13,230	0.03	-17.93
British Virgin Islands	14,497	14,748	16,902	19,487	20,266	0.04	4.00
Cayman Islands	35,069	37,160	49,191	46,353	47,534	0.09	2.55
Cuba	26,880	18,543	22,762	18,847	20,356	0.04	8.01
Dominica	17,271	6,792	8,831	5,765	6,096	0.01	5.74
Dominican Republic	153,586	153,019	180,048	221,449	236,622	0.46	6.85
Grenada	7,161	7,509	8,691	8,083	8,182	0.02	1.22
Guadeloupe	6,290	6,019	6,623	7,844	6,486	0.01	-17.31
Haiti	59,444	59,756	60,521	63,970	58,918	0.12	-7.90
Jamaica	183,903	159,484	163,059	175,351	204,912	0.40	16.86
Martinique	6,021	5,902	5,531	5,755	4,751	0.01	-17.45
Montserrat	650	696	810	782	858		9.72
Netherlands Antilles	58,043	54,170	56,179	59,126	62,412	0.12	5.56
Saint Kitts and Nevis	7,917	7,897	9,863	11,403	11,112	0.02	-2.55
Anguilla	3,050	3,451	4,104	5,090	5,655	0.01	11.10
Saint Lucia	12,530	12,007	13,846	13,879	15,022	0.03	8.24
Saint Vincent and the Grenadines	4,992	4,928	5,724	5,939	6,544	0.01	10.19
Trinidad and Tobago	118,336	111,820	121,158	128,392	133,906	0.26	4.29
Turks and Caicos Islands	9,989	9,717	11,605	12,912	16,820	0.03	30.27
Central America	**704,050**	**655,841**	**691,580**	**696,207**	**693,821**	**1.36**	**-0.34**
Belize	22,327	22,074	21,430	20,533	21,968	0.04	6.99
Costa Rica	124,993	112,880	127,112	133,820	130,702	0.26	-2.33
El Salvador	197,159	177,240	181,209	164,492	153,835	0.30	-6.48
Guatemala	162,367	151,891	161,983	170,076	173,793	0.34	2.19
Honduras	85,322	82,099	85,506	89,718	92,445	0.18	3.04
Nicaragua	36,387	37,244	38,308	38,713	39,720	0.08	2.60
Panama	75,495	72,413	76,032	78,855	81,358	0.16	3.17
North America	**24,464,000**	**23,192,000**	**25,764,000**	**27,527,000**	**29,309,242**	**57.49**	**6.47**
Canada	13,024,000	12,666,000	13,857,000	14,862,000	15,992,242	31.37	7.60
Mexico	11,440,000	10,526,000	11,907,000	12,665,000	13,317,000	26.12	5.15
South America	**1,815,230**	**1,522,191**	**1,645,342**	**1,820,315**	**1,927,647**	**3.78**	**5.90**
Argentina	164,658	150,719	167,726	188,865	212,096	0.42	12.30
Bolivia	25,011	22,307	22,843	21,786	22,785	0.04	4.59
Brazil	405,094	348,945	384,734	485,373	525,271	1.03	8.22
Chile	115,359	95,389	101,171	101,550	110,143	0.22	8.46
Colombia	321,439	280,259	295,371	325,398	348,388	0.68	7.07
Ecuador	139,094	119,737	133,046	143,073	147,173	0.29	2.87
Falkland Islands (Malvinas)	106	94	74	76	79		3.95
French Guiana	94	102	181	233	269		15.45
Guyana	19,358	15,991	14,777	16,091	14,195	0.03	-11.78
Paraguay	12,069	9,754	9,716	10,326	9,218	0.02	-10.73
Peru	164,482	154,324	151,409	151,823	133,398	0.26	-12.14

UNITED STATES

1. Arrivals of non-resident tourists at national borders, by country of residence

	2002	2003	2004	2005	2006	Market share 06	% Change 06-05
Suriname	5,237	5,346	5,812	5,665	5,266	0.01	-7.04
Uruguay	47,316	34,801	28,197	29,741	30,329	0.06	1.98
Venezuela	395,913	284,423	330,285	340,315	369,037	0.72	8.44
EAST ASIA AND THE PACIFIC	**5,888,710**	**5,192,366**	**6,086,708**	**6,518,211**	**6,427,817**	**12.61**	**-1.39**
North-East Asia	**4,917,373**	**4,299,930**	**5,000,150**	**5,316,266**	**5,191,409**	**10.18**	**-2.35**
China	225,565	157,326	202,544	270,272	320,450	0.63	18.57
Taiwan (Province of China)	288,032	238,999	297,684	318,886	300,382	0.59	-5.80
Hong Kong, China	135,409	114,112	123,335	135,108	137,278	0.27	1.61
Japan	3,627,264	3,169,682	3,747,620	3,883,906	3,672,584	7.20	-5.44
Korea, Dem. People's Republic of	29	29	6	15	36		140.00
Korea, Republic of	638,697	617,573	626,595	705,093	757,721	1.49	7.46
Macao, China	2,377	2,209	2,366	2,986	2,958	0.01	-0.94
South-East Asia	**442,246**	**367,837**	**426,805**	**465,105**	**480,182**	**0.94**	**3.24**
Brunei Darussalam	762	702	696	763	958		25.56
Myanmar	1,461	829	945	760	1,039		36.71
Cambodia	2,575	3,115	3,480	3,056	2,425		-20.65
Indonesia	45,811	40,744	45,905	51,566	53,133	0.10	3.04
Lao People's Democratic Republic	1,190	955	1,192	1,724	1,837		6.55
Malaysia	40,750	34,274	45,396	51,442	50,597	0.10	-1.64
Philippines	173,203	134,338	143,962	153,821	153,887	0.30	0.04
Timor-Leste	27	8	14	10	7		-30.00
Singapore	97,259	87,525	106,527	115,939	122,995	0.24	6.09
Viet Nam	12,360	9,463	12,401	19,191	24,068	0.05	25.41
Thailand	66,848	55,884	66,287	66,833	69,236	0.14	3.60
Australasia	**516,710**	**512,912**	**647,349**	**721,553**	**741,761**	**1.46**	**2.80**
Australia	407,130	405,698	519,955	581,773	603,275	1.18	3.70
New Zealand	109,580	107,214	127,394	139,780	138,486	0.27	-0.93
Melanesia	**6,178**	**5,238**	**5,607**	**7,012**	**6,764**	**0.01**	**-3.54**
Solomon Islands	159	99	93	74	81		9.46
Fiji	4,112	3,408	3,685	4,893	4,811	0.01	-1.68
New Caledonia	1,025	961	1,116	1,273	1,139		-10.53
Vanuatu	214	184	176	184	184		
Papua New Guinea	668	586	537	588	549		-6.63
Micronesia	**580**	**583**	**488**	**362**	**187**		**-48.34**
Christmas Island (Australia)	14	15	11	6	5		-16.67
Cocos (Keeling) Islands	11	3	5	9	7		-22.22
Kiribati	516	547	453	325	161		-50.46
Nauru	39	18	19	22	14		-36.36
Polynesia	**5,623**	**5,866**	**6,309**	**7,913**	**7,514**	**0.01**	**-5.04**
Cook Islands	244	456	469	355	215		-39.44
French Polynesia	2,176	2,434	2,831	3,973	3,857	0.01	-2.92
Niue	11	6	3	11	7		-36.36
Pitcairn	2		4	5			
Tonga	2,112	1,713	1,915	2,288	2,127		-7.04
Tuvalu	41	23	31	29	12		-58.62
Wallis and Futuna Islands	31	26	41	79	38		-51.90
Samoa	1,006	1,208	1,015	1,173	1,258		7.25
EUROPE	**8,964,202**	**8,981,711**	**10,055,657**	**10,701,847**	**10,530,566**	**20.66**	**-1.60**
Central/Eastern Europe	**360,881**	**349,781**	**384,774**	**437,485**	**467,028**	**0.92**	**6.75**
Azerbaijan	1,322	1,508	1,563	1,587	2,207		39.07
Armenia	4,453	3,244	3,664	3,633	3,668	0.01	0.96
Bulgaria	13,858	13,868	14,639	16,565	18,123	0.04	9.41

UNITED STATES

1. Arrivals of non-resident tourists at national borders, by country of residence

	2002	2003	2004	2005	2006	Market share 06	% Change 06-05
Belarus	4,451	5,033	4,751	5,225	5,982	0.01	14.49
Czech Republic/Slovakia	16,473	7,535	8,132	6,874	5,911	0.01	-14.01
Czech Republic	26,209	33,174	30,944	35,341	36,659	0.07	3.73
Estonia	5,630	5,569	5,919	6,625	7,547	0.01	13.92
Georgia	2,618	3,106	2,811	2,360	2,583	0.01	9.45
Hungary	35,001	31,984	32,694	37,308	37,257	0.07	-0.14
Kazakhstan	3,602	3,355	3,784	4,992	5,629	0.01	12.76
Kyrgyzstan	765	600	641	608	837		37.66
Latvia	5,870	5,280	5,787	6,981	7,693	0.02	10.20
Lithuania	9,482	7,539	6,997	6,959	7,373	0.01	5.95
Republic of Moldova	1,177	1,427	1,661	2,186	2,549	0.01	16.61
Poland	108,707	107,892	123,003	134,430	137,588	0.27	2.35
Romania	26,440	25,058	30,270	37,627	39,775	0.08	5.71
Russian Federation	64,228	62,330	72,419	84,780	94,681	0.19	11.68
Slovakia	12,235	10,677	11,641	13,800	14,965	0.03	8.44
Tajikistan	295	250	231	341	477		39.88
Turkmenistan	185	176	334	363	378		4.13
Ukraine	12,169	15,098	18,822	24,164	30,125	0.06	24.67
Ussr (Former)	177	171	182	271	533		96.68
Uzbekistan	5,534	4,907	3,885	4,465	4,488	0.01	0.52
Northern Europe	**4,595,440**	**4,729,636**	**5,288,742**	**5,460,565**	**5,337,367**	**10.47**	**-2.26**
Denmark	118,716	125,435	150,839	174,581	185,337	0.36	6.16
Finland	64,860	67,761	78,612	89,125	87,904	0.17	-1.37
Iceland	18,692	21,389	26,777	38,929	42,139	0.08	8.25
Ireland	259,687	254,320	345,119	383,400	414,423	0.81	8.09
Norway	112,593	113,233	130,400	139,043	145,359	0.29	4.54
Sweden	204,156	211,386	254,258	290,530	285,994	0.56	-1.56
United Kingdom	3,816,736	3,936,112	4,302,737	4,344,957	4,176,211	8.19	-3.88
Southern Europe	**822,594**	**830,396**	**953,014**	**1,098,312**	**1,126,234**	**2.21**	**2.54**
Albania	4,405	4,101	4,160	5,986	4,850	0.01	-18.98
Andorra	777	800	866	1,180	1,133		-3.98
Bosnia and Herzegovina	4,068	4,154	4,656	4,700	4,753	0.01	1.13
Croatia	9,676	9,685	11,176	11,722	12,290	0.02	4.85
Gibraltar	690	841	1,336	1,674	1,573		-6.03
Greece	44,839	40,993	43,208	49,835	49,923	0.10	0.18
Holy See	8	13	7	14	8		-42.86
Italy	406,160	408,633	470,805	545,546	532,829	1.05	-2.33
Malta	4,482	4,080	5,157	5,206	4,346	0.01	-16.52
Portugal	56,012	54,572	60,930	68,111	71,406	0.14	4.84
San Marino	281	284	362	429	514		19.81
Slovenia	7,300	9,420	11,045	12,566	12,762	0.03	1.56
Spain	269,520	284,031	333,432	385,640	424,224	0.83	10.01
TFYR of Macedonia	3,404	3,119	2,633	2,656	3,181	0.01	19.77
Serbia and Montenegro	10,972	5,670	3,241	3,047	2,442		-19.86
Western Europe	**2,834,150**	**2,738,152**	**3,068,263**	**3,327,043**	**3,216,711**	**6.31**	**-3.32**
Austria	97,930	99,924	112,950	117,688	117,191	0.23	-0.42
Belgium	159,052	151,069	175,997	191,596	188,311	0.37	-1.71
France	734,260	688,887	775,274	878,648	789,815	1.55	-10.11
Germany	1,189,856	1,180,212	1,319,904	1,415,530	1,385,520	2.72	-2.12
Liechtenstein	1,248	1,099	1,235	1,287	1,468		14.06
Luxembourg	9,646	9,522	10,709	12,243	12,202	0.02	-0.33
Monaco	3,851	3,707	4,136	4,671	4,848	0.01	3.79
Netherlands	384,367	373,690	424,872	448,650	446,785	0.88	-0.42
Switzerland	253,940	230,042	243,186	256,730	270,571	0.53	5.39
East Mediterranean Europe	**351,137**	**333,746**	**360,864**	**378,442**	**383,226**	**0.75**	**1.26**

UNITED STATES

1. Arrivals of non-resident tourists at national borders, by country of residence

	2002	2003	2004	2005	2006	Market share 06	% Change 06-05
Cyprus	9,378	9,485	9,087	9,698	9,215	0.02	-4.98
Israel	263,097	249,034	275,373	284,310	283,889	0.56	-0.15
Turkey	78,662	75,227	76,404	84,434	90,122	0.18	6.74
MIDDLE EAST	**126,613**	**110,111**	**137,259**	**144,131**	**164,283**	**0.32**	**13.98**
Middle East	**126,613**	**110,111**	**137,259**	**144,131**	**164,283**	**0.32**	**13.98**
Bahrain	3,802	3,745	4,148	5,176	5,630	0.01	8.77
Iraq	541	442	1,046	1,131	993		-12.20
Jordan	12,339	11,798	12,265	14,656	14,714	0.03	0.40
Kuwait	14,204	13,775	15,247	18,367	20,866	0.04	13.61
Lebanon	14,517	12,981	15,074	15,543	15,880	0.03	2.17
Libyan Arab Jamahiriya	212	199	264	542	719		32.66
Oman	3,468	2,911	3,221	3,447	3,422	0.01	-0.73
Qatar	2,842	2,698	3,203	4,250	5,650	0.01	32.94
Saudi Arabia	25,588	18,727	18,573	25,119	31,511	0.06	25.45
Syrian Arab Republic	5,194	3,843	3,901	4,015	4,030	0.01	0.37
United Arab Emirates	19,080	18,353	22,571	26,883	32,633	0.06	21.39
Egypt	24,315	20,225	20,772	24,048	27,129	0.05	12.81
Yemen	445	388	562	937	1,078		15.05
Other countries of Middle East	66	26	16,412	17	28		64.71
SOUTH ASIA	**324,315**	**329,660**	**370,315**	**411,277**	**474,288**	**0.93**	**15.32**
South Asia	**324,315**	**329,660**	**370,315**	**411,277**	**474,288**	**0.93**	**15.32**
Afghanistan	135	227	304	671	678		1.04
Bangladesh	9,585	8,434	8,384	9,637	8,288	0.02	-14.00
Bhutan	154	188	187	188	183		-2.66
Sri Lanka	6,613	7,622	7,512	9,024	10,432	0.02	15.60
India	257,271	272,161	308,845	344,926	406,845	0.80	17.95
Iran, Islamic Republic of	4,996	3,454	4,311	5,330	5,940	0.01	11.44
Maldives	72	82	93	150	176		17.33
Nepal	6,047	6,270	6,446	8,117	9,768	0.02	20.34
Pakistan	39,442	31,222	34,233	33,234	31,978	0.06	-3.78

Source: World Tourism Organization (UNWTO)

UNITED STATES VIRGIN ISLANDS

3. Arrivals of non-resident tourists in hotels and similar establishments, by nationality

	2002	2003	2004	2005	2006	Market share 06	% Change 06-05
TOTAL	585,684	623,394	603,944	617,603	701,023	100.00	13.51
AFRICA	828	134	289	162	59	0.01	-63.58
Other Africa	828	134	289	162	59	0.01	-63.58
All countries of Africa	828	134	289	162	59	0.01	-63.58
AMERICAS	494,324	531,270	560,581	568,908	648,824	92.55	14.05
Caribbean	26,893	28,790	31,515	29,270	36,050	5.14	23.16
Bahamas	110	112	172	152	599	0.09	294.08
Barbados	247	325	268	523	466	0.07	-10.90
British Virgin Islands	3,289	2,926	4,102	4,907	7,514	1.07	53.13
Dominican Republic	90	50	114	229	109	0.02	-52.40
Jamaica	218	147	292	607	1,404	0.20	131.30
Puerto Rico	21,859	23,792	24,717	21,452	24,823	3.54	15.71
Trinidad and Tobago	207	145	248	153	173	0.02	13.07
Other countries of the Caribbean	873	1,293	1,602	1,247	962	0.14	-22.85
Central America	192	239	919	954	339	0.05	-64.47
Costa Rica	81	125	769	754	222	0.03	-70.56
El Salvador	2	1	1	3			
Guatemala	6		5	26	1		-96.15
Honduras	1	6	11		13		
Nicaragua		1	2		20		
Panama	77	104	131	164	28		-82.93
Other countries of Central America	25	2		7	55	0.01	685.71
North America	466,279	501,235	526,897	537,397	611,150	87.18	13.72
Canada	4,372	4,822	5,239	5,372	5,267	0.75	-1.95
Mexico	169	245	394	316	137	0.02	-56.65
United States	461,738	496,168	521,264	531,709	605,746	86.41	13.92
South America	960	1,006	1,250	1,287	1,285	0.18	-0.16
Argentina	232	171	386	356	547	0.08	53.65
Bolivia	51	90	25	80	31		-61.25
Brazil	266	296	335	360	233	0.03	-35.28
Chile	96	87	88	171	107	0.02	-37.43
Colombia	54	146	61	40	41	0.01	2.50
Ecuador	12	1	20	1	7		600.00
Guyana	6	21	11				
Paraguay	3						
Peru	20	36	76	87	3		-96.55
Uruguay	49	10	6	17	49	0.01	188.24
Venezuela	162	144	233	101	264	0.04	161.39
Other countries of South America	9	4	9	74	3		-95.95
EAST ASIA AND THE PACIFIC	333	363	379	501	350	0.05	-30.14
North-East Asia	204	185	230	306	160	0.02	-47.71
Taiwan (Province of China)	13	58	71	94			
Japan	191	127	159	212	160	0.02	-24.53
Australasia	129	178	149	195	190	0.03	-2.56
Australia	109	175	118	168	178	0.03	5.95
New Zealand	20	3	31	27	12		-55.56
EUROPE	6,144	7,747	15,819	18,821	15,076	2.15	-19.90
Northern Europe	3,341	4,153	11,638	12,575	9,582	1.37	-23.80
Denmark	1,282	2,082	8,883	10,480	7,604	1.08	-27.44
Finland	42	68	94	48	52	0.01	8.33

UNITED STATES VIRGIN ISLANDS

3. Arrivals of non-resident tourists in hotels and similar establishments, by nationality

	2002	2003	2004	2005	2006	Market share 06	% Change 06-05
Norway	113	117	178	247	234	0.03	-5.26
Sweden	98	142	202	192	49	0.01	-74.48
United Kingdom	1,806	1,744	2,281	1,608	1,643	0.23	2.18
Southern Europe	**1,150**	**1,462**	**1,501**	**3,265**	**2,983**	**0.43**	**-8.64**
Greece	68	135	223	1,550	256	0.04	-83.48
Italy	895	1,035	1,048	1,129	2,639	0.38	133.75
Portugal	11	30	16	87	3		-96.55
Spain	176	262	214	499	85	0.01	-82.97
Western Europe	**1,547**	**1,898**	**2,105**	**2,407**	**1,306**	**0.19**	**-45.74**
Austria	58	69	106	150	93	0.01	-38.00
France	414	440	848	535	295	0.04	-44.86
Germany	763	748	603	1,100	467	0.07	-57.55
Netherlands	20	213	267	192	174	0.02	-9.38
Switzerland	292	428	281	430	277	0.04	-35.58
Other Europe	**106**	**234**	**575**	**574**	**1,205**	**0.17**	**109.93**
Other countries of Europe	106	234	575	574	1,205	0.17	109.93
REGION NOT SPECIFIED	**84,055**	**83,880**	**26,876**	**29,211**	**36,714**	**5.24**	**25.69**
Not Specified	**84,055**	**83,880**	**26,876**	**29,211**	**36,714**	**5.24**	**25.69**
Other countries of the World	84,055	83,880	26,876	29,211	36,714	5.24	25.69

Source: World Tourism Organization (UNWTO)

URUGUAY

2. Arrivals of non-resident visitors at national borders, by nationality

	2002	2003	2004	2005	2006	Market share 06	% Change 06-05
TOTAL	1,353,872	1,508,055	1,870,858	1,917,049	1,824,340	100.00	-4.84
AMERICAS	1,030,738	1,159,580	1,457,944	1,497,756	1,402,957	76.90	-6.33
North America	34,961	49,667	64,485	86,630	87,318	4.79	0.79
Canada	2,835	3,409	5,062	7,335	8,223	0.45	12.11
Mexico	6,317	10,567	13,051	17,008	16,261	0.89	-4.39
United States	25,809	35,691	46,372	62,287	62,834	3.44	0.88
South America	981,181	1,084,704	1,372,482	1,388,716	1,288,270	70.62	-7.23
Argentina	813,304	866,570	1,108,592	1,107,514	975,027	53.45	-11.96
Bolivia	1,803	2,442	2,521	2,752	2,409	0.13	-12.46
Brazil	118,400	151,383	187,744	197,672	228,353	12.52	15.52
Chile	18,690	32,751	38,662	42,154	43,800	2.40	3.90
Paraguay	18,015	17,716	19,227	20,155	21,670	1.19	7.52
Peru	8,460	10,749	11,346	12,609	10,975	0.60	-12.96
Venezuela	2,509	3,093	4,390	5,860	6,036	0.33	3.00
Other Americas	14,596	25,209	20,977	22,410	27,369	1.50	22.13
Other countries of the Americas	14,596	25,209	20,977	22,410	27,369	1.50	22.13
EAST ASIA AND THE PACIFIC	5,618	6,230	7,221	11,686	12,877	0.71	10.19
North-East Asia	3,321	2,833	2,875	4,707	6,269	0.34	33.18
Japan	1,871	1,847	2,385	2,547	2,833	0.16	11.23
Other countries of North-East Asia	1,450	986	490	2,160	3,436	0.19	59.07
Australasia	2,087	2,665	4,051	5,679	6,606	0.36	16.32
Australia	1,630	2,063	3,093	4,466	5,096	0.28	14.11
New Zealand	457	602	958	1,213	1,510	0.08	24.48
Other East Asia and the Pacific	210	732	295	1,300	2		-99.85
Other countries East Asia/Pacific	210	732	295	1,300	2		-99.85
EUROPE	56,159	73,230	97,223	119,553	124,215	6.81	3.90
Northern Europe	9,877	13,454	17,739	22,780	27,250	1.49	19.62
Denmark	540	813	1,171	1,375	1,468	0.08	6.76
Finland	358	761	978	1,537	2,120	0.12	37.93
Ireland	641	1,045	1,621	2,362	2,494	0.14	5.59
Norway	594	956	1,105	1,422	1,644	0.09	15.61
Sweden	1,269	1,699	2,328	3,461	3,840	0.21	10.95
United Kingdom	6,475	8,180	10,536	12,623	15,684	0.86	24.25
Southern Europe	21,765	28,341	38,705	49,193	50,569	2.77	2.80
Greece	376	584	1,028	1,117	1,272	0.07	13.88
Italy	7,549	9,607	12,129	15,335	15,334	0.84	-0.01
Portugal	893	1,456	2,120	2,527	2,631	0.14	4.12
Spain	12,947	16,694	23,428	30,214	31,332	1.72	3.70
Western Europe	21,902	26,309	34,315	37,984	38,665	2.12	1.79
Austria	883	1,302	1,552	1,844	1,792	0.10	-2.82
Belgium	1,117	1,344	1,761	2,054	1,985	0.11	-3.36
France	7,517	9,095	12,211	12,661	13,019	0.71	2.83
Germany	7,981	9,584	12,724	14,187	14,421	0.79	1.65
Luxembourg	22	26	52	75	61		-18.67
Netherlands	1,964	2,180	2,645	3,416	3,756	0.21	9.95
Switzerland	2,418	2,778	3,370	3,747	3,631	0.20	-3.10
East Mediterranean Europe	2,000	2,325	3,041	3,635	3,552	0.19	-2.28
Israel	2,000	2,325	3,041	3,635	3,552	0.19	-2.28
Other Europe	615	2,801	3,423	5,961	4,179	0.23	-29.89

URUGUAY

2. Arrivals of non-resident visitors at national borders, by nationality

	2002	2003	2004	2005	2006	Market share 06	% Change 06-05
Other countries of Europe	615	2,801	3,423	5,961	4,179	0.23	-29.89
MIDDLE EAST	**170**	**131**	**489**	**182**	**172**	**0.01**	**-5.49**
Middle East	**170**	**131**	**489**	**182**	**172**	**0.01**	**-5.49**
All countries of Middle East	170	131	489	182	172	0.01	-5.49
REGION NOT SPECIFIED	**261,187**	**268,884**	**307,981**	**287,872**	**284,119**	**15.57**	**-1.30**
Not Specified	**261,187**	**268,884**	**307,981**	**287,872**	**284,119**	**15.57**	**-1.30**
Other countries of the World	2,679	4,067	6,793	3,051	3,245	0.18	6.36
Nationals Residing Abroad	258,508	264,817	301,188	284,821	280,874	15.40	-1.39

Source: World Tourism Organization (UNWTO)

UZBEKISTAN

1. Arrivals of non-resident tourists at national borders, by country of residence

	2002	2003	2004	2005	2006	Market share 06	% Change 06-05
TOTAL	331,500	231,000	261,600				
AFRICA	1,000	1,000	1,000				
Other Africa	1,000	1,000	1,000				
All countries of Africa	1,000	1,000	1,000				
AMERICAS	4,100	2,000	12,000				
Other Americas	4,100	2,000	12,000				
All countries of the Americas	4,100	2,000	12,000				
EAST ASIA AND THE PACIFIC	195,100	145,000	140,000				
Other East Asia and the Pacific	195,100	145,000	140,000				
All countries of Asia	195,100	145,000	140,000				
EUROPE	99,800	51,000	68,600				
Other Europe	99,800	51,000	68,600				
All countries of Europe	99,800	51,000	68,600				
MIDDLE EAST	23,500	24,000	30,000				
Middle East	23,500	24,000	30,000				
All countries of Middle East	23,500	24,000	30,000				
SOUTH ASIA	8,000	8,000	10,000				
South Asia	8,000	8,000	10,000				
All countries of South Asia	8,000	8,000	10,000				

Source: World Tourism Organization (UNWTO)

VANUATU

1. Arrivals of non-resident tourists at national borders, by country of residence

	2002	2003	2004	2005	2006	Market share 06	% Change 06-05
TOTAL	49,462	50,400	61,453	62,123	68,179	100.00	9.75
AMERICAS	1,438	1,625	1,954	1,625	1,896	2.78	16.68
North America	1,438	1,625	1,954	1,625	1,896	2.78	16.68
All countries of North America	1,438	1,625	1,954	1,625	1,896	2.78	16.68
EAST ASIA AND THE PACIFIC	44,256	44,876	55,027	55,894	61,023	89.50	9.18
North-East Asia	731	570	591	583	656	0.96	12.52
Japan	731	570	591	583	656	0.96	12.52
Australasia	36,993	37,222	44,627	45,727	50,206	73.64	9.80
Australia	29,730	29,493	36,407	38,075	40,385	59.23	6.07
New Zealand	7,263	7,729	8,220	7,652	9,821	14.40	28.35
Melanesia	4,704	5,050	6,630	6,848	7,480	10.97	9.23
New Caledonia	4,704	5,050	6,630	6,848	7,480	10.97	9.23
Other East Asia and the Pacific	1,828	2,034	3,179	2,736	2,681	3.93	-2.01
Other countries of Oceania	1,828	2,034	3,179	2,736	2,681	3.93	-2.01
EUROPE	2,948	3,003	3,388	3,504	4,021	5.90	14.75
Other Europe	2,948	3,003	3,388	3,504	4,021	5.90	14.75
All countries of Europe	2,948	3,003	3,388	3,504	4,021	5.90	14.75
REGION NOT SPECIFIED	820	896	1,084	1,100	1,239	1.82	12.64
Not Specified	820	896	1,084	1,100	1,239	1.82	12.64
Other countries of the World	820	896	1,084	1,100	1,239	1.82	12.64

Source: World Tourism Organization (UNWTO)

VENEZUELA

1. Arrivals of non-resident tourists at national borders, by nationality

	2002	2003	2004	2005	2006	Market share 06	% Change 06-05
TOTAL	431,677	336,974	486,401	706,103	747,930	100.00	5.92
AFRICA	518	438	640	787	914	0.12	16.14
Southern Africa				464	612	0.08	31.90
South Africa				464	612	0.08	31.90
West Africa				323	302	0.04	-6.50
Nigeria				323	302	0.04	-6.50
Other Africa	518	438	640				
All countries of Africa	518	438	640				
AMERICAS	185,276	154,334	217,699	374,460	411,772	55.05	9.96
Caribbean	11,728	9,137	13,324	40,445	43,262	5.78	6.97
Barbados	2,948	2,300	3,357	1,297	906	0.12	-30.15
Cuba	669	581	827	11,224	11,848	1.58	5.56
Dominican Republic	1,501	1,267	1,770	9,599	9,231	1.23	-3.83
Grenada				624	624	0.08	
Haiti				795	963	0.13	21.13
Jamaica				416	360	0.05	-13.46
Puerto Rico				193	189	0.03	-2.07
Saint Lucia				763	459	0.06	-39.84
Trinidad and Tobago	5,454	4,113	6,120	15,534	18,682	2.50	20.27
Other countries of the Caribbean	1,156	876	1,250				
Central America	2,983	2,531	3,592	12,421	12,404	1.66	-0.14
Costa Rica	1,717	1,398	1,984	3,426	3,317	0.44	-3.18
El Salvador				796	894	0.12	12.31
Guatemala				1,819	1,748	0.23	-3.90
Honduras				853	837	0.11	-1.88
Nicaragua				1,064	1,052	0.14	-1.13
Panama	690	627	890	4,463	4,556	0.61	2.08
Other countries of Central America	576	506	718				
North America	117,835	94,746	118,340	131,742	134,850	18.03	2.36
Canada	29,106	20,588	31,794	25,527	28,014	3.75	9.74
Mexico	8,722	7,447	10,344	16,514	18,011	2.41	9.07
United States	80,007	66,711	76,202	89,701	88,825	11.88	-0.98
South America	52,730	47,920	82,443	189,852	221,256	29.58	16.54
Argentina	15,133	14,108	18,708	26,596	26,287	3.51	-1.16
Bolivia				2,217	2,243	0.30	1.17
Brazil	11,022	9,929	13,404	18,574	45,438	6.08	144.63
Chile	6,786	6,345	8,402	15,872	15,020	2.01	-5.37
Colombia	11,855	10,576	32,030	74,497	84,293	11.27	13.15
Ecuador	1,357	1,222	1,734	18,576	14,630	1.96	-21.24
Guyana				503	618	0.08	22.86
Paraguay				691	699	0.09	1.16
Peru	3,120	2,707	3,847	28,202	27,671	3.70	-1.88
Uruguay	1,892	1,773	2,518	4,124	4,357	0.58	5.65
Other countries of South America	1,565	1,260	1,800				
EAST ASIA AND THE PACIFIC	3,756	3,201	4,475	16,360	17,106	2.29	4.56
North-East Asia	3,015	2,646	3,681	14,359	14,966	2.00	4.23
China	676	615	892	8,403	8,517	1.14	1.36
Taiwan (Province of China)				547	532	0.07	-2.74
Japan	2,090	1,835	2,511	4,050	4,329	0.58	6.89
Korea, Dem. People's Republic of				174	331	0.04	90.23

VENEZUELA

1. Arrivals of non-resident tourists at national borders, by nationality

	2002	2003	2004	2005	2006	Market share 06	% Change 06-05
Korea, Republic of				1,185	1,257	0.17	6.08
Other countries of North-East Asia	249	196	278				
South-East Asia	**215**	**176**	**252**				
All countries of South-East Asia	215	176	252				
Australasia	**526**	**379**	**542**	**2,001**	**2,140**	**0.29**	**6.95**
Australia				1,594	1,698	0.23	6.52
New Zealand				407	442	0.06	8.60
Australia, New Zealand	526	379	542				
EUROPE	**237,250**	**175,159**	**258,178**	**296,310**	**297,601**	**39.79**	**0.44**
Central/Eastern Europe	**1,613**	**1,156**	**1,635**	**11,019**	**11,993**	**1.60**	**8.84**
Bulgaria				504	508	0.07	0.79
Czech Republic	248	182	259	3,774	4,067	0.54	7.76
Hungary				728	635	0.08	-12.77
Lithuania				588	1,530	0.20	160.20
Poland	773	536	758	2,327	2,384	0.32	2.45
Romania				1,119	983	0.13	-12.15
Russian Federation	348	271	382	1,715	1,648	0.22	-3.91
Ukraine				264	238	0.03	-9.85
Other countries Central/East Europ	244	167	236				
Northern Europe	**41,661**	**30,793**	**40,844**	**43,699**	**49,038**	**6.56**	**12.22**
Denmark	8,636	6,325	9,573	5,795	7,052	0.94	21.69
Finland				2,371	3,782	0.51	59.51
Ireland				860	801	0.11	-6.86
Norway	2,607	1,977	2,810	2,221	2,870	0.38	29.22
Sweden	2,666	2,149	3,051	6,462	10,476	1.40	62.12
United Kingdom	26,880	19,624	24,399	25,990	24,057	3.22	-7.44
Other countries of Northern Europe	872	718	1,011				
Southern Europe	**41,566**	**34,787**	**48,832**	**143,412**	**140,032**	**18.72**	**-2.36**
Croatia				248	294	0.04	18.55
Greece				1,111	1,106	0.15	-0.45
Italy	23,396	20,166	27,867	56,521	53,177	7.11	-5.92
Portugal	3,558	2,967	4,174	19,351	19,561	2.62	1.09
Spain	14,288	11,389	16,429	66,181	65,894	8.81	-0.43
Other countries Southern Europe	324	265	362				
Western Europe	**151,603**	**107,740**	**165,866**	**95,766**	**94,210**	**12.60**	**-1.62**
Austria	4,419	3,566	5,071	4,724	4,269	0.57	-9.63
Belgium	11,300	7,660	12,130	3,171	3,594	0.48	13.34
France	18,526	14,362	21,041	25,464	23,487	3.14	-7.76
Germany	60,426	42,320	65,733	38,797	37,089	4.96	-4.40
Netherlands	52,310	36,039	56,521	16,892	18,129	2.42	7.32
Switzerland	4,320	3,588	5,096	6,718	7,642	1.02	13.75
Other countries of Western Europe	302	205	274				
East Mediterranean Europe	**621**	**551**	**808**	**2,414**	**2,328**	**0.31**	**-3.56**
Israel	621	551	808	1,979	1,884	0.25	-4.80
Turkey				435	444	0.06	2.07
Other Europe	**186**	**132**	**193**				
Other countries of Europe	186	132	193				
MIDDLE EAST	**432**	**371**	**492**	**9,957**	**10,324**	**1.38**	**3.69**
Middle East	**432**	**371**	**492**	**9,957**	**10,324**	**1.38**	**3.69**
Jordan				640	572	0.08	-10.63
Lebanon				5,041	5,148	0.69	2.12

VENEZUELA

1. Arrivals of non-resident tourists at national borders, by nationality

	2002	2003	2004	2005	2006	Market share 06	% Change 06-05
Libyan Arab Jamahiriya				430	387	0.05	-10.00
Syrian Arab Republic				3,661	3,872	0.52	5.76
Egypt				185	345	0.05	86.49
All countries of Middle East	432	371	492				
SOUTH ASIA	**302**	**270**	**344**	**1,801**	**1,931**	**0.26**	**7.22**
South Asia	**302**	**270**	**344**	**1,801**	**1,931**	**0.26**	**7.22**
India				1,338	1,287	0.17	-3.81
Iran, Islamic Republic of				463	644	0.09	39.09
All countries of South Asia	302	270	344				
REGION NOT SPECIFIED	**4,143**	**3,201**	**4,573**	**6,428**	**8,282**	**1.11**	**28.84**
Not Specified	**4,143**	**3,201**	**4,573**	**6,428**	**8,282**	**1.11**	**28.84**
Other countries of the World	4,143	3,201	4,573	6,428	8,282	1.11	28.84

Source: World Tourism Organization (UNWTO)

VIET NAM

2. Arrivals of non-resident visitors at national borders, by country of residence

	2002	2003	2004	2005	2006	Market share 06	% Change 06-05
TOTAL	2,627,988	2,428,735	2,927,873	3,467,757	3,583,488	100.00	3.34
AMERICAS	303,519	258,991	326,286	396,997	459,398	12.82	15.72
North America	303,519	258,991	326,286	396,997	459,398	12.82	15.72
Canada	43,552	40,063	53,813	63,431	73,744	2.06	16.26
United States	259,967	218,928	272,473	333,566	385,654	10.76	15.62
EAST ASIA AND THE PACIFIC	1,694,624	1,669,541	2,008,366	2,365,222	2,361,258	65.89	-0.17
North-East Asia	1,320,286	1,241,095	1,538,806	1,680,532	1,600,785	44.67	-4.75
China	724,385	693,423	778,431	752,576	516,286	14.41	-31.40
Taiwan (Province of China)	211,072	207,866	256,906	286,324	274,663	7.66	-4.07
Hong Kong, China			3,264	3,814	4,199	0.12	10.09
Japan	279,769	209,730	267,210	320,605	383,896	10.71	19.74
Korea, Republic of	105,060	130,076	232,995	317,213	421,741	11.77	32.95
South-East Asia	269,448	327,050	330,410	525,464	573,792	16.01	9.20
Brunei Darussalam	434	592	532				
Myanmar	1,131	1,369	1,441	2,423	1,877	0.05	-22.53
Cambodia	69,538	84,256	90,839	186,543	154,956	4.32	-16.93
Indonesia	13,456	16,799	18,500	21,830	21,315	0.59	-2.36
Lao People's Democratic Republic	37,237	75,396	34,215	44,462	33,980	0.95	-23.58
Malaysia	46,086	48,662	55,717	76,755	105,558	2.95	37.53
Philippines	25,306	22,983	24,542	31,675	27,355	0.76	-13.64
Singapore	35,261	36,870	50,942	77,676	104,947	2.93	35.11
Thailand	40,999	40,123	53,682	84,100	123,804	3.45	47.21
Australasia	104,890	101,396	139,150	159,226	186,681	5.21	17.24
Australia	96,624	93,292	128,661	145,359	172,519	4.81	18.68
New Zealand	8,266	8,104	10,489	13,867	14,162	0.40	2.13
EUROPE	343,360	293,636	354,735	425,774	480,585	13.41	12.87
Central/Eastern Europe	7,964	8,604	12,249	23,796	28,776	0.80	20.93
Russian Federation	7,964	8,604	12,249	23,796	28,776	0.80	20.93
Northern Europe	108,676	98,095	112,836	126,378	139,156	3.88	10.11
Denmark	11,815	10,432	12,172	14,740	18,050	0.50	22.46
Finland	4,149	4,312	5,625	4,659	5,342	0.15	14.66
Norway	8,586	7,404	8,435	9,229	12,684	0.35	37.44
Sweden	14,444	12,599	15,588	16,866	18,816	0.53	11.56
United Kingdom	69,682	63,348	71,016	80,884	84,264	2.35	4.18
Southern Europe	22,527	14,827	22,645	36,411	37,877	1.06	4.03
Italy	12,221	8,976	11,305	16,449	15,746	0.44	-4.27
Portugal	10,306	5,851					
Spain			11,340	19,962	22,131	0.62	10.87
Western Europe	204,193	172,110	207,005	239,189	274,776	7.67	14.88
Austria	4,476	4,387	5,371		7,725	0.22	
Belgium	10,325	9,017	10,427	11,654	14,770	0.41	26.74
France	111,546	86,791	104,025	126,402	132,304	3.69	4.67
Germany	46,327	44,609	56,561	64,448	76,745	2.14	19.08
Netherlands	18,125	16,079	17,664	22,318	26,546	0.74	18.94
Switzerland	13,394	11,227	12,957	14,367	16,686	0.47	16.14
REGION NOT SPECIFIED	286,485	206,567	238,486	279,764	282,247	7.88	0.89
Not Specified	286,485	206,567	238,486	279,764	282,247	7.88	0.89
Other countries of the World	286,485	206,567	238,486	279,764	282,247	7.88	0.89

Source: World Tourism Organization (UNWTO)

YEMEN

3. Arrivals of non-resident tourists in hotels and similar establishments, by nationality

	2002	2003	2004	2005	2006	Market share 06	% Change 06-05
TOTAL	98,020	154,667	273,732	336,070	382,332	100.00	13.77
AFRICA	3,045	8,627	10,853	12,628	13,025	3.41	3.14
East Africa			4,706	7,017	7,693	2.01	9.63
Ethiopia			3,182	5,259	5,388	1.41	2.45
Kenya			774	1,065	1,072	0.28	0.66
United Republic of Tanzania			750	693	1,233	0.32	77.92
North Africa	1,472	1,875	3,055	2,179	2,821	0.74	29.46
Sudan	1,472	1,875	3,055	2,179	2,821	0.74	29.46
Southern Africa			773	1,675	918	0.24	-45.19
South Africa			773	1,675	918	0.24	-45.19
Other Africa	1,573	6,752	2,319	1,757	1,593	0.42	-9.33
Other countries of Africa	1,573	6,752	2,319	1,757	1,593	0.42	-9.33
AMERICAS	4,429	12,932	17,099	18,253	18,771	4.91	2.84
North America	3,527	3,860	15,758	12,327	16,882	4.42	36.95
Canada			3,586	2,700	3,423	0.90	26.78
United States	3,527	3,860	12,172	9,627	13,459	3.52	39.80
Other Americas	902	9,072	1,341	5,926	1,889	0.49	-68.12
Other countries of the Americas	902	9,072	1,341	5,926	1,889	0.49	-68.12
EAST ASIA AND THE PACIFIC	11,303	15,966	22,512	24,437	18,839	4.93	-22.91
North-East Asia	1,262	628	4,403	3,192	6,703	1.75	109.99
China			2,872	1,947	3,414	0.89	75.35
Japan	1,262	628	1,531	1,245	2,408	0.63	93.41
Korea, Republic of					881	0.23	
South-East Asia			11,120	6,428	7,362	1.93	14.53
Indonesia			3,110	2,782	3,514	0.92	26.31
Malaysia			1,413	1,056	1,076	0.28	1.89
Philippines			6,597	2,590	2,772	0.73	7.03
Australasia	468	377	733	1,177	996	0.26	-15.38
Australia	468	377	733	1,177	996	0.26	-15.38
Other East Asia and the Pacific	9,573	14,961	6,256	13,640	3,778	0.99	-72.30
Other countries of Asia	9,573	14,961	6,256	13,640	3,778	0.99	-72.30
EUROPE	15,828	13,733	28,608	26,456	32,788	8.58	23.93
Northern Europe	1,951	4,640	7,061	4,348	9,230	2.41	112.28
United Kingdom	1,951	4,640	7,061	4,348	9,230	2.41	112.28
Southern Europe	2,352	1,731	2,332	3,054	2,436	0.64	-20.24
Italy	2,352	1,731	2,332	3,054	2,436	0.64	-20.24
Western Europe	6,911	4,806	7,312	7,330	10,910	2.85	48.84
Austria					631	0.17	
France	2,792	1,882	3,101	3,078	5,465	1.43	77.55
Germany	2,772	1,894	2,757	2,975	2,705	0.71	-9.08
Netherlands	693	801	1,117	932	1,543	0.40	65.56
Switzerland	654	229	337	345	566	0.15	64.06
East Mediterranean Europe					3,888	1.02	
Turkey					3,888	1.02	
Other Europe	4,614	2,556	11,903	11,724	6,324	1.65	-46.06
Other countries of Europe	4,614	2,556	11,903	11,724	6,324	1.65	-46.06

YEMEN

3. Arrivals of non-resident tourists in hotels and similar establishments, by nationality

	2002	2003	2004	2005	2006	Market share 06	% Change 06-05
MIDDLE EAST	**63,415**	**103,409**	**175,679**	**238,524**	**278,385**	**72.81**	**16.71**
Middle East	**63,415**	**103,409**	**175,679**	**238,524**	**278,385**	**72.81**	**16.71**
Bahrain					3,032	0.79	
Iraq	1,691	2,846	3,945	1,687	3,464	0.91	105.33
Jordan	2,385	2,689	5,129	3,483	6,060	1.59	73.99
Lebanon					2,149	0.56	
Oman					24,998	6.54	
Qatar					3,584	0.94	
Saudi Arabia	38,254	59,669	123,799	162,160	178,670	46.73	10.18
Syrian Arab Republic	3,727	6,780	7,307	7,622	11,044	2.89	44.90
United Arab Emirates					19,327	5.06	
Egypt	2,509	3,677	8,464	6,947	10,915	2.85	57.12
Other countries of Middle East	14,849	27,748	27,035	56,625	15,142	3.96	-73.26
SOUTH ASIA			**18,981**	**15,772**	**20,524**	**5.37**	**30.13**
South Asia			**18,981**	**15,772**	**20,524**	**5.37**	**30.13**
India			15,260	11,420	14,522	3.80	27.16
Pakistan			3,721	4,352	6,002	1.57	37.91

Source: World Tourism Organization (UNWTO)

YEMEN

5. Overnight stays of non-resident tourists in hotels and similar establishments, by nationality

	2002	2003	2004	2005	2006	Market share 06	% Change 06-05
TOTAL	588,120	928,002	1,642,392	2,017,497	2,293,992	100.00	13.70
AFRICA	38,658	51,762	65,118	69,777	78,150	3.41	12.00
East Africa					46,158	2.01	
Ethiopia					32,328	1.41	
Kenya					6,432	0.28	
United Republic of Tanzania					7,398	0.32	
North Africa	7,933	11,250	18,330	13,074	16,926	0.74	29.46
Sudan	7,933	11,250	18,330	13,074	16,926	0.74	29.46
Southern Africa					5,508	0.24	
South Africa					5,508	0.24	
Other Africa	30,725	40,512	46,788	56,703	9,558	0.42	-83.14
Other countries of Africa	30,725	40,512	46,788	56,703	9,558	0.42	-83.14
AMERICAS	61,486	77,592	102,594	126,179	112,626	4.91	-10.74
North America	36,734	23,160	73,032	75,358	101,292	4.42	34.41
Canada					20,538	0.90	
United States	36,734	23,160	73,032	75,358	80,754	3.52	7.16
Other Americas	24,752	54,432	29,562	50,821	11,334	0.49	-77.70
Other countries of the Americas	24,752	54,432	29,562	50,821	11,334	0.49	-77.70
EAST ASIA AND THE PACIFIC	87,989	95,796	248,958	238,971	113,034	4.93	-52.70
North-East Asia	3,996	3,768	9,186	8,039	40,218	1.75	400.29
China					20,484	0.89	
Japan	3,996	3,768	9,186	8,039	14,448	0.63	79.72
Korea, Republic of					5,286	0.23	
South-East Asia					44,172	1.93	
Indonesia					21,084	0.92	
Malaysia					6,456	0.28	
Philippines					16,632	0.73	
Australasia	981	2,262	4,398	6,636	5,976	0.26	-9.95
Australia	981	2,262	4,398	6,636	5,976	0.26	-9.95
Other East Asia and the Pacific	83,012	89,766	235,374	224,296	22,668	0.99	-89.89
Other countries of Asia	83,012	89,766	235,374	224,296	22,668	0.99	-89.89
EUROPE	113,246	82,398	171,648	161,196	196,728	8.58	22.04
Northern Europe	30,336	27,840	42,366	33,559	55,380	2.41	65.02
United Kingdom	30,336	27,840	42,366	33,559	55,380	2.41	65.02
Southern Europe	8,531	10,386	13,992	17,668	14,616	0.64	-17.27
Italy	8,531	10,386	13,992	17,668	14,616	0.64	-17.27
Western Europe	26,652	28,836	43,872	42,938	65,460	2.85	52.45
Austria					3,786	0.17	
France	9,614	11,292	18,606	17,264	32,790	1.43	89.93
Germany	11,970	11,364	16,542	17,094	16,230	0.71	-5.05
Netherlands	2,546	4,806	6,702	6,580	9,258	0.40	40.70
Switzerland	2,522	1,374	2,022	2,000	3,396	0.15	69.80
East Mediterranean Europe					23,328	1.02	
Turkey					23,328	1.02	
Other Europe	47,727	15,336	71,418	67,031	37,944	1.65	-43.39

YEMEN

5. Overnight stays of non-resident tourists in hotels and similar establishments, by nationality

	2002	2003	2004	2005	2006	Market share 06	% Change 06-05
Other countries of Europe	47,727	15,336	71,418	67,031	37,944	1.65	-43.39
MIDDLE EAST	**286,741**	**620,454**	**1,054,074**	**1,421,374**	**1,670,310**	**72.81**	**17.51**
Middle East	**286,741**	**620,454**	**1,054,074**	**1,421,374**	**1,670,310**	**72.81**	**17.51**
Bahrain					18,192	0.79	
Iraq	28,287	17,076	23,670	10,122	20,784	0.91	105.33
Jordan	32,299	16,134	30,774	20,898	36,360	1.59	73.99
Lebanon					12,894	0.56	
Oman					149,988	6.54	
Qatar					21,504	0.94	
Saudi Arabia	85,167	358,014	742,794	973,860	1,072,020	46.73	10.08
Syrian Arab Republic	32,455	40,680	43,842	45,730	66,264	2.89	44.90
United Arab Emirates					115,962	5.06	
Egypt	34,514	22,062	50,784	55,782	65,490	2.85	17.40
Other countries of Middle East	74,019	166,488	162,210	314,982	90,852	3.96	-71.16
SOUTH ASIA					**123,144**	**5.37**	
South Asia					**123,144**	**5.37**	
India					87,132	3.80	
Pakistan					36,012	1.57	

Source: World Tourism Organization (UNWTO)

ZAMBIA

1. Arrivals of non-resident tourists at national borders, by country of residence

		2002	2003	2004	2005	2006	Market share 06	% Change 06-05
TOTAL	(*)	565,073	412,675	515,000	668,862	756,860	100.00	13.16
AFRICA		363,783	298,485	366,918	461,000	510,270	67.42	10.69
East Africa		183,640	184,155	178,380	243,504	295,830	39.09	21.49
Kenya		2,611	9,064	7,087	11,738	11,669	1.54	-0.59
Zimbabwe		143,872	138,288	123,573	148,436	194,639	25.72	31.13
United Republic of Tanzania		33,735	30,776	33,502	65,881	74,039	9.78	12.38
Other countries of East Africa		3,422	6,027	14,218	17,449	15,483	2.05	-11.27
Central Africa		53,190	24,736	23,087	47,780	63,588	8.40	33.08
All countries of Central Africa		53,190	24,736	23,087	47,780	63,588	8.40	33.08
North Africa		654	2,806	2,533	2,752	1,509	0.20	-45.17
All countries of North Africa		654	2,806	2,533	2,752	1,509	0.20	-45.17
Southern Africa		124,902	82,883	159,161	161,157	144,063	19.03	-10.61
South Africa		87,578	62,604	110,710	110,272	100,286	13.25	-9.06
Other countries of Southern Africa		37,324	20,279	48,451	50,885	43,777	5.78	-13.97
West Africa		1,397	3,905	3,757	5,807	5,280	0.70	-9.08
All countries of West Africa		1,397	3,905	3,757	5,807	5,280	0.70	-9.08
AMERICAS		33,935	22,667	29,053	37,580	52,457	6.93	39.59
North America		30,929	20,566	26,728	35,125	50,345	6.65	43.33
Canada		9,295	4,687	6,181	11,230	11,545	1.53	2.80
United States		21,634	15,879	20,547	23,895	38,800	5.13	62.38
Other Americas		3,006	2,101	2,325	2,455	2,112	0.28	-13.97
Other countries of the Americas		3,006	2,101	2,325	2,455	2,112	0.28	-13.97
EAST ASIA AND THE PACIFIC		34,230	17,297	23,107	39,912	38,171	5.04	-4.36
North-East Asia		2,799	1,703	1,683	5,204	4,317	0.57	-17.04
Japan		2,799	1,703	1,683	5,204	4,317	0.57	-17.04
Australasia		24,396	9,617	11,887	23,971	19,999	2.64	-16.57
Australia		19,508	5,957	7,490	16,336	14,617	1.93	-10.52
New Zealand		4,888	3,660	4,397	7,635	5,382	0.71	-29.51
Other East Asia and the Pacific		7,035	5,977	9,537	10,737	13,855	1.83	29.04
Other countries of Asia		7,035	5,977	9,537	10,737	13,855	1.83	29.04
EUROPE		130,218	71,363	91,863	121,712	143,304	18.93	17.74
Northern Europe		82,784	41,960	51,086	62,359	84,437	11.16	35.40
Denmark		5,036	3,256	4,256	4,142	3,196	0.42	-22.84
Sweden		4,530	2,941	4,395	5,738	10,366	1.37	80.66
United Kingdom		63,570	31,072	37,520	44,369	57,119	7.55	28.74
Scandinavia		9,648	4,691	4,915	8,110	13,756	1.82	69.62
Southern Europe		2,960	6,659	5,460	7,698	8,499	1.12	10.41
Italy		2,960	6,659	5,460	7,698	8,499	1.12	10.41
Western Europe		9,469	15,059	18,508	25,784	19,502	2.58	-24.36
France		3,963	8,380	9,123	8,024	3,832	0.51	-52.24
Germany		5,506	6,679	9,385	17,760	15,670	2.07	-11.77
Other Europe		35,005	7,685	16,809	25,871	30,866	4.08	19.31
Other countries of Europe		35,005	7,685	16,809	25,871	30,866	4.08	19.31
SOUTH ASIA		2,907	2,863	4,059	8,658	12,658	1.67	46.20
South Asia		2,907	2,863	4,059	8,658	12,658	1.67	46.20
India		2,907	2,863	4,059	8,658	12,658	1.67	46.20

ZIMBABWE

2. Arrivals of non-resident visitors at national borders, by country of residence

	2002	2003	2004	2005	2006	Market share 06	% Change 06-05
TOTAL	2,041,202	2,256,205	1,854,488	1,558,501	2,286,572	100.00	46.72
AFRICA	1,760,097	1,942,052	1,523,090	1,356,384	2,082,724	91.08	53.55
East Africa	494,598	706,445	628,025	466,137	374,447	16.38	-19.67
Kenya		12,311	14,189	17,696	19,344	0.85	9.31
Malawi		71,968	81,247	55,965	78,039	3.41	39.44
Mauritius		3,580	3,806	4,122	1,037	0.05	-74.84
Mozambique	242,154	313,954	299,122	183,792	114,988	5.03	-37.44
Uganda		3,363	3,554	1,792	3,361	0.15	87.56
United Republic of Tanzania		6,166	6,047	8,459	11,535	0.50	36.36
Zambia	224,302	295,103	220,060	194,311	146,143	6.39	-24.79
Other countries of East Africa	28,142						
Central Africa		38,974	36,384	27,555	17,193	0.75	-37.60
Angola		19,630	18,423	18,133	5,056	0.22	-72.12
Democratic Republic of the Congo		19,344	17,961	9,422	12,137	0.53	28.82
Southern Africa	1,183,064	1,141,128	804,962	833,851	1,656,183	72.43	98.62
Botswana		242,750	135,860	189,751	86,117	3.77	-54.62
Lesotho		6,065	5,175	2,075	9,051	0.40	336.19
Namibia		5,880	6,764	11,103	16,709	0.73	50.49
South Africa		882,726	653,352	626,677	1,516,135	66.31	141.93
Swaziland		3,707	3,811	4,245	28,171	1.23	563.63
All countries of Southern Africa	1,183,064						
West Africa		6,770	10,039	4,159	2,924	0.13	-29.69
Ghana		1,059	1,162	792	1,127	0.05	42.30
Nigeria		5,711	8,877	3,367	1,797	0.08	-46.63
Other Africa	82,435	48,735	43,680	24,682	31,977	1.40	29.56
Other countries of Africa	82,435	48,735	43,680	24,682	31,977	1.40	29.56
AMERICAS	65,194	61,181	75,161	43,976	44,746	1.96	1.75
Caribbean		415	3,002	475	1,961	0.09	312.84
All countries of the Caribbean		415	3,002	475	1,961	0.09	312.84
North America	55,180	55,160	61,122	40,184	37,449	1.64	-6.81
Canada		7,375	10,185	9,069	3,887	0.17	-57.14
Mexico		588	1,029	405	594	0.03	46.67
United States		47,197	49,908	30,710	32,968	1.44	7.35
Canada, United States	55,180						
South America		1,687	4,261	1,177	1,664	0.07	41.38
Argentina		617	657	449	596	0.03	32.74
Brazil		1,070	3,604	728	1,068	0.05	46.70
Other Americas	10,014	3,919	6,776	2,140	3,672	0.16	71.59
Other countries of the Americas	10,014	3,919	6,776	2,140	3,672	0.16	71.59
EAST ASIA AND THE PACIFIC	65,916	68,414	90,405	38,767	53,908	2.36	39.06
North-East Asia		24,307	49,894	20,836	27,131	1.19	30.21
Hong Kong, China		8,199	25,974	7,146	9,583	0.42	34.10
Japan		9,648	17,406	10,481	12,124	0.53	15.68
Korea, Republic of		6,460	6,514	3,209	5,424	0.24	69.02
South-East Asia		1,446	4,056	2,297	1,779	0.08	-22.55
Malaysia		1,134	3,709	1,456	1,039	0.05	-28.64
Singapore		312	347	841	740	0.03	-12.01
Australasia	36,841	40,141	28,540	13,369	20,023	0.88	49.77

ZIMBABWE

2. Arrivals of non-resident visitors at national borders, by country of residence

	2002	2003	2004	2005	2006	Market share 06	% Change 06-05
Australia		25,054	18,962	8,993	13,605	0.59	51.28
New Zealand		15,087	9,578	4,376	6,418	0.28	46.66
Australia, New Zealand	36,841						
Other East Asia and the Pacific	**29,075**	**2,520**	**7,915**	**2,265**	**4,975**	**0.22**	**119.65**
Other countries of Asia		1,970	3,390	1,820	3,925	0.17	115.66
All countries of Asia	29,075						
Other countries of Oceania		550	4,525	445	1,050	0.05	135.96
EUROPE	**149,995**	**169,938**	**155,767**	**112,608**	**96,849**	**4.24**	**-13.99**
Northern Europe	**77,262**	**68,896**	**55,012**	**52,904**	**30,157**	**1.32**	**-43.00**
United Kingdom		58,354	42,260	42,525	22,045	0.96	-48.16
United Kingdom/Ireland	77,262						
Scandinavia		10,542	12,752	10,379	8,112	0.35	-21.84
Southern Europe		**33,971**	**36,605**	**15,037**	**18,564**	**0.81**	**23.46**
Italy		18,682	5,630	5,245	5,624	0.25	7.23
Portugal		11,398	26,930	6,086	8,023	0.35	31.83
Spain		3,891	4,045	3,706	4,917	0.22	32.68
Western Europe	**44,455**	**61,541**	**52,283**	**39,560**	**41,036**	**1.79**	**3.73**
Austria		1,922	4,091	1,951	2,045	0.09	4.82
France		12,504	12,331	12,197	11,834	0.52	-2.98
Germany	21,333	25,902	11,863	6,851	10,104	0.44	47.48
Netherlands	17,465	12,928	20,052	14,842	14,467	0.63	-2.53
Switzerland	5,657	8,285	3,946	3,719	2,586	0.11	-30.47
Other Europe	**28,278**	**5,530**	**11,867**	**5,107**	**7,092**	**0.31**	**38.87**
Other countries of Europe	28,278	5,530	11,867	5,107	7,092	0.31	38.87
MIDDLE EAST		**2,209**	**3,749**	**1,989**	**4,145**	**0.18**	**108.40**
Middle East		**2,209**	**3,749**	**1,989**	**4,145**	**0.18**	**108.40**
Egypt		1,552	601	321	293	0.01	-8.72
Other countries of Middle East		657	3,148	1,668	3,852	0.17	130.94
SOUTH ASIA		**12,411**	**6,316**	**4,777**	**4,200**	**0.18**	**-12.08**
South Asia		**12,411**	**6,316**	**4,777**	**4,200**	**0.18**	**-12.08**
India		10,424	5,476	3,623	3,316	0.15	-8.47
Pakistan		1,987	840	1,154	884	0.04	-23.40

Source: World Tourism Organization (UNWTO)

1. Arrivals of non-resident tourists at national borders, by nationality

ARGENTINA	TOTAL	2005-2006: provisional data. Starting 2004, as a result of the importance of the "Survey on International Tourism", the estimates of the series of the "travel" item of the balance of payments were modified. For this reason, the data are not rigorously comparable with those of previous years.
BELARUS	TOTAL	Organized tourism.
BRUNEI DARUSSALAM	TOTAL	Air arrivals.
BURUNDI	TOTAL	Including nationals residing abroad.
CENTRAL AFRICAN REPUBLIC	TOTAL	Arrivals by air to Bangui only. 2006: Estimates.
COMOROS	TOTAL	Air arrivals.
DEMOCRATIC REPUBLIC OF THE CONGO	TOTAL	2002-2004: arrival by air only. 2005-2006: provisional data.
ETHIOPIA	TOTAL	Arrivals through all ports of entry.
GAMBIA	TOTAL	Charter tourists only.
GREECE	TFYROM	2005 included in "other countries of Europe".
	UKRAINE	From 2005, included in "other countries of Europe".
	EGYPT	Including Sudan.
	LEBANON	Including Syria.
	TOTAL	Information based on administrative data.
GUINEA	TOTAL	2003,2005,2006: air arrivals at Conakry Airport.
GUINEA-BISSAU	TOTAL	Arrivals at "Osvaldo Vieira" Airport.
INDIA	TOTAL	Excluding nationals residing abroad.
ITALY	TOTAL	Seasonal and border workers are excluded.
JORDAN	OTH.WORLD	U.N. passport.
KIRIBATI	TOTAL	Air arrivals. 2002,2003,2006: Tarawa and Christmas Island. 2004,2005: Tarawa only.
LEBANON	TOTAL	Excluding Syrian nationals, Palestinians and students.
MALDIVES	TOTAL	Arrivals by air.
MALTA	TOTAL	2004-2006: data based on departures by air and by sea.
MARSHALL ISLANDS	TOTAL	2002,2003,2006: air arrivals. 2004,2005: air and sea arrivals.
MEXICO	USA	Including the tourists of the border zone: 2005: 9,381,000 2006: 8,745,000
	TOTAL	Including nationals residing abroad. 2006: preliminary data.
MYANMAR	TOTAL	Including tourist arrivals through border entry points to Yangon.
NEPAL	GREECE	Including Cyprus.
NICARAGUA	TOTAL	2006: Preliminary estimates.
NORWAY	TOTAL	Figures are based on "The Guest Survey" carried out by "Institute of Transport Economics".
PARAGUAY	TOTAL	Excluding nationals residing abroad and crew members. E/d cards in the "Silvio Petirossi" airport and passenger counts at the national border crossings - National Police and SENATUR.
PERU	TOTAL	From 2002, new estimated series including tourists with identity document other than a passport. 2004-2006: preliminary estimates.

NOTES: 2002 - 2006

1. Arrivals of non-resident tourists at national borders, by nationality

PORTUGAL	**TOTAL**	2002-2003: Excluding arrivals of nationals residing abroad. 2004-2006: Including arrivals of nationals residing abroad. Due to a change in the methodology, from 2004 the data are not comparable with those of previous years.
SAINT MAARTEN	**FRANCE**	Including residents of the French West Indies.
	TOTAL	Arrivals at Princess Juliana International Airport. Including visitors to St. Maarten (the French side of the island).
SRI LANKA	**TOTAL**	Excluding nationals residing abroad.
SUDAN	**TOTAL**	2005-2006: including nationals residing abroad.
SURINAME	**TOTAL**	Arrivals at Zanderij Airport.
THAILAND	**TOTAL**	2002-2005: Including nationals residing abroad.
TUNISIA	**TOTAL**	Excluding nationals residing abroad.

NOTES: 2002 - 2006

1. Arrivals of non-resident tourists at national borders, by country of residence

ANGUILLA	TOTAL	Excluding nationals residing abroad.
ANTIGUA AND BARBUDA	TOTAL	Air arrivals. Excluding nationals residing abroad.
BARBADOS	TOTAL	2006: Provisional data.
BENIN	TOTAL	2003-2006: estimates.
BERMUDA	TOTAL	Air arrivals.
CAMBODIA	OTH.WORLD	2004-2006: including arrivals in the Preah Vihear Province: 2004: 67,843 2005: 88,615 2006: 108,691
CAYMAN ISLANDS	TOTAL	Air arrivals.
COOK ISLANDS	TOTAL	Air and sea arrivals. 2006: provisional data.
CURACAO	TOTAL	Arrivals by air.
DOMINICAN REPUBLIC	TOTAL	Arrivals by air. 2002: excluding passengers at Herrera Airport. 2006: provisional data.
FIJI	TOTAL	Excluding nationals residing abroad.
FRANCE	TOTAL	Estimated based on surveys at national borders (1996-2004). 2005: revised data. Break in the series, data not comparable with previous years. 2006: provisional data.
	AUST/N.ZLND	Australia, Oceania.
FRENCH POLYNESIA	TOTAL	Air arrivals. Excluding nationals residing abroad.
	SAMOA	Including American Samoa.
GUINEA	TOTAL	Air arrivals at Conakry Airport.
GUYANA	TOTAL	Arrivals to Timehri Airport only.
IRELAND	UK	Including Northern Ireland resident arrivals.
	GREECE	Including Turkey.
ISRAEL	TOTAL	Excluding nationals residing abroad and including 1 day visitors.
JAMAICA	TOTAL	Air arrivals. Including nationals residing abroad.
	USA	Including Puerto Rico.
KYRGYZSTAN	TOTAL	2003-2006 new data source: Department of Customs Control.
MALAWI	TOTAL	Departures.
MALAYSIA	TOTAL	Includes Singapore residents crossing the frontier by road through Johore Causeway.
MARSHALL ISLANDS	TOTAL	2002,2003,2006: air arrivals. 2004,2005: air and sea arrivals.
MARTINIQUE	TOTAL	Including French overseas departments and territories.
MEXICO	TOTAL	Including nationals residing abroad. 2006: preliminary data.
MICRONESIA (FEDERATED STATES OF)	TOTAL	Arrivals in the States of Kosrae, Chuuk, Pohnpei and Yap.
NEPAL	GREECE	Including Cyprus.
NEW CALEDONIA	TOTAL	Including nationals residing abroad.
	ALL CO CARIB	Martinique, Guadeloupe and Guyana.
NIUE	TOTAL	Arrivals by air, including Niuans residing usually in New Zealand.

NOTES: 2002   -   2006

1. Arrivals of non-resident tourists at national borders, by country of residence

PALAU	**TOTAL**	Air arrivals (Palau International Airport).
PHILIPPINES	**N RESID ABRO**	Philippine passport holders permanently residing abroad; excludes overseas Filipino workers.
PORTUGAL	**TOTAL**	2002-2003: Excluding arrivals of nationals residing abroad. 2004-2006: Including arrivals of nationals residing abroad. Due to a change in the methodology, from 2004 the data are not comparable with those of previous years.
PUERTO RICO	**TOTAL**	Arrivals by air. Fiscal year July to June. Source: "Junta de Planificación de Puerto Rico".
SAINT EUSTATIUS	**TOTAL**	Excluding Netherlands Antillean residents.
SAINT KITTS AND NEVIS	**TOTAL**	Air arrivals.
SAINT LUCIA	**TOTAL**	Excluding nationals residing abroad.
SAINT VINCENT AND THE GRENADINES	**TOTAL**	Arrivals by air.
SIERRA LEONE	**TOTAL**	Arrivals by air.
SOLOMON ISLANDS	**TOTAL**	2005: without 1st quarter.
SOUTH AFRICA	**TOTAL** **CHINA**	Excluding arrivals by work and contract workers. Including Hong Kong, China.
SRI LANKA	**TOTAL**	Excluding nationals residing abroad.
THAILAND	**TOTAL**	2002-2005: Including nationals residing abroad.
TONGA	**TOTAL**	Arrivals by air.
TRINIDAD AND TOBAGO	**TOTAL**	Arrivals by air.
UNITED STATES	**TOTAL**	Data include Mexicans staying one night or longer in the United States.
ZAMBIA	**TOTAL**	2002: provisional data.

NOTES: 2002 - 2006

2. Arrivals of non-resident visitors at national borders, by nationality

ALGERIA	TOTAL	Including nationals residing abroad.
BAHRAIN	TOTAL	Excluding nationals residing abroad.
BELIZE	TOTAL	Including transit passengers and border permits.
COLOMBIA	TOTAL	Source: "Dirección de Extranjería - Departamento Administrativo de Seguridad (DAS)". 2006: provisional data.
ECUADOR	TOTAL	Excluding nationals residing abroad.
EGYPT	TOTAL	Excluding nationals residing abroad.
HUNGARY	TOTAL	Departures.
ITALY	TOTAL	Border survey of the "Ufficio Italiano dei Cambi". Seasonal and border workers are excluded.
JAPAN	TOTAL	Excluding nationals residing abroad.
KOREA, REPUBLIC OF	TOTAL	Including nationals residing abroad and crew members.
LIBYAN ARAB JAMAHIRIYA	TOTAL	Travellers. Preliminary data.
MACAO, CHINA	TOTAL	Including arrivals by sea, land and by air. Included stateless and Chinese people who do not have permanent residency in Hong Kong, China.
PORTUGAL	TOTAL	2002-2003: Excluding arrivals of nationals residing abroad. 2004-2006: Including arrivals of nationals residing abroad. Due to a change in the methodology, from 2004 the data are not comparable with those of previous years.
REPUBLIC OF MOLDOVA	TOTAL	Visitors who enjoyed the services of the economic agents officially registered under tourism activity and accommodation. Excluding the left side of the river Nistru and the municipality of Bender.
SAN MARINO	TOTAL	New methodology from 2005.
SINGAPORE	TOTAL	Excluding Malaysian citizens arriving by land.
SYRIAN ARAB REPUBLIC	TOTAL	Excluding arrivals of nationals residing abroad. Data source: the survey of the incoming tourism in 2002 and 2004.
TURKEY	TOTAL	Travellers, including temporary immigrants, diplomats, consular representatives and members of the armed forces. Excluding arrivals of crew members, transit passengers and nationals of the country residing abroad.

2. Arrivals of non-resident visitors at national borders, by country of residence

AUSTRALIA	**TOTAL**	Excluding nationals residing abroad and crew members.
CANADA	**CHINA**	Including Mongolia and Tibet.
	FRANCE	Including Andorra and Monaco.
	ITALY	Including San Marino and the Holy See.
	SWITZERLAND	Including Liechtenstein.
	DENMARK	Including Faeroe Islands.
	BULGARIA	Including Albania and Romania.
	ESTONIA	Including Latvia and Lithuania.
FINLAND	**TOTAL**	Border survey.
HONG KONG, CHINA	**FRANCE**	Including New Caledonia and French Polynesia.
	USA	Including Guam.
	NEW ZEALAND	Including Cook Islands.
ISRAEL	**TOTAL**	Excluding nationals residing abroad.
KENYA	**TOTAL**	Excluding nationals residing abroad. All data are estimates, projected using 1989 market shares. Source: Economic Survey various years.
LATVIA	**TOTAL**	Non-resident departures. Survey of persons crossing the state border.
NEW ZEALAND	**TOTAL**	Data regarding to short term movements are compiled from a random sample of passenger declarations. Including nationals residing abroad. Source: Statistics New Zealand, External Migration.
PANAMA	**TOTAL**	Total number of visitors broken down by permanent residence who arrived in Panama at Tocumen International Airport.
PORTUGAL	**TOTAL**	2002-2003: Excluding arrivals of nationals residing abroad. 2004-2006: Including arrivals of nationals residing abroad. Due to a change in the methodology, from 2004 the data are not comparable with those of previous years.
SAINT VINCENT AND THE GRENADINES	**TOTAL**	Arrivals by air.
SINGAPORE	**TOTAL**	Excluding Malaysian citizens arriving by land.
SOUTH AFRICA	**TOTAL**	Excluding nationals residing abroad. Including arrivals by purpose of holiday, business, study, work, transit, border traffic and contract workers.

NOTES: 2002 - 2006

3. Arrivals of non-resident tourists in hotels and similar establishments, by nationality

BOLIVIA	**TOTAL**	Hotel arrivals in the regional capitals.
EL SALVADOR	**TOTAL**	Provisional data under revision.
ITALY	**TOTAL**	Arrivals at hotels only.
MALTA	**TOTAL**	2002 source: Malta Tourism Authority. 2003-2006: tourist departures by air, compiled by country of residence. Source: National Statistics Office.
MOROCCO	**TOTAL**	Arrivals in classified hotels, holiday villages and tourist residences.
PERU	**TOTAL**	2003-2006: preliminary estimates.
SYRIAN ARAB REPUBLIC	**TOTAL**	Data source: the survey of the incoming tourism in 2002 and 2004.
TURKEY	**TOTAL**	Arrivals at licensed establishments including: hotels, motels, boarding houses, inns, apartment hotels, holiday villages, spa hotels and special hotels. Results of a monthly survey carried out among accommodation establishments licensed by the Ministry of Tourism.
UNITED ARAB EMIRATES	**N RESID ABRO**	Including domestic tourism.

NOTES: 2002 - 2006

3. Arrivals of non-resident tourists in hotels and similar establishments, by country of residence

AUSTRIA	TOTAL	Hotels only.
CAPE VERDE	BELGIUM	Including Netherlands.
DENMARK	TOTAL	New methodology from 2004.
FRANCE	TOTAL	Only hotels 0 to 4 stars. 2004-2006: including unclassified hotels. 2006: renewal of the survey, data not comparable with previous years.
FRENCH POLYNESIA	TOTAL	Hotels only.
GERMANY	CHINA	Including Hong Kong, China.
GUADELOUPE	TOTAL	2003,2004: estimates for continental Guadeloupe (without Saint-Martin and Saint-Barthelemy). 2005: data based on a survey conducted at Guadeloupe Airport.
GUINEA	TOTAL	Hotels only.
ISRAEL	ALL SOUTH AM	Including central America.
	TOTAL	Arrivals at tourist hotels and not yet listed hotels.
LITHUANIA	TOTAL	Hotels only.
LUXEMBOURG	TOTAL	Arrivals in hotels, guest houses and inns.
NETHERLANDS	TOTAL	Hotels and boarding houses.
NEW CALEDONIA	TOTAL	It refers to hotels in Noumea.
PHILIPPINES	N RESID ABRO	Philippine passport holders permanently residing abroad; excludes overseas Filipino workers.
	TOTAL	Air arrivals.
PORTUGAL	TOTAL	Since 2002, new methodology. 2006: provisional data.
PUERTO RICO	OTH CARIBBE	As from fiscal year 2001, aggregated data of tourists coming from minor Antilles who did not specify their country of origin are included.
	OTH.WORLD	Including crew members.
	TOTAL	Fiscal year July to June. Hotels registered by the "Compañía de Turismo de Puerto Rico".
QATAR	TOTAL	Arrivals at hotels only.
ROMANIA	ALL CENT AME	Including Mexico.
	ALL AFRICA	Including Egypt and Libya.
SPAIN	TOTAL	Arrivals at hotels and "hostales" (accommodation establishments providing limited services).
SWITZERLAND	TOTAL	2001-2003: hotels, motels and inns. 2005-2006: hotels and health establishments.
	ALL NORT AFR	Algeria, Libya, Morocco and Tunisia.
TOGO	BURKINA FASO	Including Mali and Niger.

NOTES: 2002   -   2006

4. Arrivals of non-resident tourists in all types of accommodation establishments, by nationality

HUNGARY	**TOTAL**	Collective accommodation establishments.
MALTA	**TOTAL**	2002 source: Malta Tourism Authority. 2003-2006: tourist departures by air, compiled by country of residence. Source: National Statistics Office.
REPUBLIC OF MOLDOVA	**TOTAL**	Excluding the left side of the river Nistru and the municipality of Bender.
SYRIAN ARAB REPUBLIC	**TOTAL**	Excluding private accommodation. Data source: the survey of the incoming tourism in 2002 and 2004.
TURKEY	**TOTAL**	Results of a monthly survey carried out among accommodation establishments licensed by the Ministry of Tourism.

NOTES: 2002   -   2006

4. Arrivals of non-resident tourists in all types of accommodation establishments, by country of residence

AUSTRIA	TOTAL	Including private accommodation.
BELGIUM	TOTAL	Hotel establishments, campings, holiday centres, holiday villages and specific categories of accommodation.
CROATIA	TOTAL	Including arrivals in ports of nautical tourism.
DENMARK	TOTAL	New methodology from 2004.
FINLAND	TOTAL	Due to a change in the methodology, data for 2004 are not comparable to previous years.
GERMANY	CHINA	Including Hong Kong, China.
LUXEMBOURG	TOTAL	Hotels, inns, guest houses, youth hostels, private tourist lodgings, camping sites and others.
PHILIPPINES	TOTAL	Air arrivals.
	N RESID ABRO	Philippine passport holders permanently residing abroad; excludes overseas Filipino workers.
PORTUGAL	TOTAL	Since 2002, new methodology. 2006: provisional data.
ROMANIA	ALL AFRICA	Including Egypt and Libya.
	ALL CENT AME	Including Mexico.
SPAIN	TOTAL	Arrivals at hotels, "hostales", camping, tourism apartments and rural dwellings.

5. Overnight stays of non-resident tourists in hotels and similar establishments, by nationality

BOLIVIA	TOTAL	Hotel nights in the regional capitals.
EL SALVADOR	TOTAL	Provisional data under revision.
ITALY	TOTAL	Nights in hotels only.
MADAGASCAR	TOTAL	All star-establishments (registered and non-registered).
MALTA	TOTAL	2002 source: Malta Tourism Authority. 2003-2006: tourist departures by air, compiled by country of residence. Source: National Statistics Office.
MOROCCO	TOTAL	Overnight stays in classified hotels, holiday villages and tourist residences.
NORWAY	TOTAL	Nights in registered establishments. Figures relate to establishments with 20 or more beds.
PERU	TOTAL	2003-2006: preliminary estimates.
SYRIAN ARAB REPUBLIC	TOTAL	Data source: the survey of the incoming tourism in 2002 and 2004.
TURKEY	TOTAL	Classified hotels, motels, boarding houses, inns, apartment hotels, holiday villages, spa hotels and special hotels. Results of a monthly survey carried out among accommodation establishments licensed by the Ministry of Tourism.
UNITED ARAB EMIRATES	N RESID ABRO	Including domestic tourism.

5. Overnight stays of non-resident tourists in hotels and similar establishments, by country of residence

AUSTRIA	TOTAL	Hotels only.
BULGARIA	TOTAL	The data cover mainly former state owned and public sector in accommodation.
CAPE VERDE	BELGIUM	Including Netherlands.
DENMARK	TOTAL	New methodology from 2004.
FINLAND	TOTAL	Due to a change in the methodology, data for 2004 are not comparable to previous years.
FRANCE	TOTAL	Only hotels 0 to 4 stars. 2004-2006: including unclassified hotels. 2006: renewal of the survey, data not comparable with previous years.
FRENCH POLYNESIA	TOTAL	Hotels only.
GERMANY	CHINA	Including Hong Kong, China.
ISRAEL	TOTAL	Nights in tourist hotels and apartment hotels.
	ALL SOUTH AM	Including central America.
KENYA	TOTAL	Source: Economic Survey various years.
LITHUANIA	TOTAL	Hotels only.
LUXEMBOURG	TOTAL	Nights in hotels, guest houses and inns.
NETHERLANDS	TOTAL	Hotels and boarding houses.
NEW CALEDONIA	TOTAL	It refers to hotels in Noumea.
PORTUGAL	TOTAL	Since 2002, new methodology. 2006: provisional data.
QATAR	TOTAL	Nights in hotels only.
ROMANIA	ALL CENT AME	Including Mexico.
	ALL AFRICA	Including Egypt and Libya.
SPAIN	TOTAL	Nights in hotels and "hostales" (accommodation establishments providing limited services).
SWEDEN	TOTAL	Nights in hotels only.
SWITZERLAND	TOTAL	2001-2003: hotels, motels and inns. 2005-2006: hotels and health establishments.
	ALL NORT AFR	Algeria, Libya, Morocco and Tunisia.
TOGO	BURKINA FASO	Including Mali and Niger.

NOTES: 2002 - 2006

6. Overnight stays of non-resident tourists in all types of accommodation establishments, by nationality

BERMUDA	TOTAL	Including overnight stays at private homes.
HUNGARY	TOTAL	Collective accommodation establishments.
MALTA	TOTAL	2002 source: Malta Tourism Authority. 2003-2006: tourist departures by air, compiled by country of residence. Source: National Statistics Office.
SYRIAN ARAB REPUBLIC	TOTAL	Data source: the survey of the incoming tourism in 2002 and 2004.
TURKEY	TOTAL	Results of a monthly survey carried out among accommodation establishments licensed by the Ministry of Tourism.

6. Overnight stays of non-resident tourists in all types of accommodation establishments, by country of residence

AUSTRIA	**TOTAL**	Including private accommodation.
BAHAMAS	**TOTAL**	Nights in all forms of commercial accommodation.
BELGIUM	**TOTAL**	Hotel establishments, campings, holiday centres, holiday villages and specific categories of accommodation.
BULGARIA	**TOTAL**	The data cover mainly former state owned and public sector in accommodation.
CANADA	**CHINA**	Including Mongolia and Tibet.
	SWITZERLAND	Including Liechtenstein.
	ITALY	Including San Marino and the Holy See.
	ESTONIA	Including Latvia and Lithuania.
	BULGARIA	Including Albania and Romania.
	DENMARK	Including Faeroe Islands.
	FRANCE	Including Andorra and Monaco.
CROATIA	**TOTAL**	Including nights in ports of nautical tourism.
DENMARK	**TOTAL**	New methodology from 2004.
FINLAND	**TOTAL**	Due to a change in the methodology, data for 2004 are not comparable to previous years.
FRANCE	**AUST/N.ZLND**	Australia, Oceania.
	TOTAL	Estimated based on surveys at national borders (1996-2004). 2005: revised data. Break in the series, data not comparable with previous years. 2006: provisional data.
GERMANY	**CHINA**	Including Hong Kong, China.
IRELAND	**SCANDINAVIA**	Denmark, Norway, Sweden, Finland, Iceland.
	UK	Including Northern Ireland residents.
	TOTAL	Including nights spent in private homes and holiday homes where no payment is made.
JAMAICA	**ALL EUROPE**	United Kingdom and rest of Europe.
	OTH AMERICA	Latin America.
	TOTAL	Information obtained by multiplying the average length of stay by the number of stop-overs of each country origin.
MALAWI	**TOTAL**	2004: provisional data.
NETHERLANDS	**TOTAL**	Excluding overnight stays at fixed pitches (hired on a yearly or seasonal basis).
PORTUGAL	**TOTAL**	Since 2002, new methodology. 2006: provisional data.
ROMANIA	**ALL CENT AME**	Including Mexico.
	ALL AFRICA	Including Egypt and Libya.
SPAIN	**TOTAL**	Nights in hotels, "hostales", camping, tourism apartments and rural dwellings.
SWEDEN	**TOTAL**	Nights in hotels, youth hostels, holiday villages and camping.

NOTES: 2002 - 2006

1. Arrivées de touristes non résidents aux frontières nationales, par nationalité

ARGENTINE	TOTAL	2005-2006: données provisoires. A partir de 2004, vu l'importance de l' "Enquête sur le Tourisme International", des modifications ont été apportées aux estimations de la série du poste "voyages" de la balance des paiements. C'est la raison pour laquelle les données ne sont pas rigoureusement comparables avec celles des années précédentes.
BELARUS	TOTAL	Tourisme organisé.
BRUNEI DARUSSALAM	TOTAL	Arrivées par voie aérienne.
BURUNDI	TOTAL	Y compris les nationaux résidant à l¿étranger.
COMORES	TOTAL	Arrivées par voie aérienne.
ETHIOPIE	TOTAL	Arrivées à travers tous les ports d'entrée.
GAMBIE	TOTAL	Arrivées en vols à la demande seulement.
GRECE	TFYROM UKRAINE EGYPTE LIBAN TOTAL	2005 inclus dans "autres pays d'Europe". A partir de 2005, inclus dans "autres pays d'Europe". Y compris le Soudan. Y compris la Syrie. Information tirée de données administratives.
GUINEE	TOTAL	2003,2005,2006: arrivées par voie aérienne à l'aéroport de Conakry.
GUINEE-BISSAU	TOTAL	Arrivées à l'aéroport "Osvaldo Vieira".
ILES MARSHALL	TOTAL	2002,2003,2006: arrivées par voie aérienne. 2004,2005: arrivées par voies aérienne et maritime.
INDE	TOTAL	À l'exclusion des nationaux résidant à l'étranger.
ITALIE	TOTAL	À l¿exclusion des travailleurs saisonniers et frontaliers.
JORDANIE	AUT.MONDE	Passeport de l'ONU.
KIRIBATI	TOTAL	Arrivées par voie aérienne. 2002,2003,2006: Tarawa et Île Christmas. 2004,2005: Tarawa uniquement.
LIBAN	TOTAL	À l'exclusion des ressortissants syriens, palestiniens et sous-études.
MALDIVES	TOTAL	Arrivées par voie aérienne.
MALTE	TOTAL	2004-2006: données tirées des départs par voies aérienne et maritime.
MEXIQUE	EU TOTAL	Y compris les touristes de la frange frontalière: 2005: 9.381.000 2006: 8.745.000 Y compris les nationaux résidant à l'étranger. 2006: données préliminaires.
MYANMAR	TOTAL	Comprenant les arrivées de touristes aux postes-frontières de Yangon.
NEPAL	GRECE	Y compris Chypre.
NICARAGUA	TOTAL	2006: Estimations préliminaires.
NORVEGE	TOTAL	Les chiffres se fondent sur "l'Enquête auprès de la clientèle" de l'Institut d'Économie des Transports.
PARAGUAY	TOTAL	À l'exclusion des nationaux résidant à l'étranger et des membres des équipages. Cartes d'embarquement et de débarquement à l'aéroport Silvio Petirossi et comptages des passagers lors du franchissement des frontières nationales - Police nationale et SENATUR.
PEROU	TOTAL	À partir de 2002, nouvelle série estimée comprenant les touristes avec une pièce d'identité autre qu'un passeport. 2004-2006: estimations préliminaires.
PORTUGAL	TOTAL	2002-2003: Sont exclues les arrivées de nationaux résidant à l'étranger. 2004-2006: Sont incluses les arrivées de nationaux résidant à l'étranger. La méthodologie a été modifiée et pour cela, à partir de 2004 les données ne sont pas comparables avec celles des années précédentes.

878

NOTES: 2002 - 2006

1. Arrivées de touristes non résidents aux frontières nationales, par nationalité

REPUBLIQUE CENTRAFRICAINE	TOTAL	Arrivées par voie aérienne à Bangui uniquement. 2006: Estimations.
REPUBLIQUE DEMOCRATIQUE DU CONGO	TOTAL	2002-2004: arrivées par voie aérienne uniquement. 2005-2006: données provisoires.
SAINT-MARTIN	FRANCE	Y compris les résidents des Antilles françaises.
	TOTAL	Arrivées à l'aéroport international "Princess Juliana". Y compris les visiteurs à St. Martin (partie française de l'île).
SOUDAN	TOTAL	2005-2006: y compris les nationaux résidant à l'étranger.
SRI LANKA	TOTAL	À l'exclusion des nationaux résidant à l'étranger.
SURINAME	TOTAL	Arrivées à l'aéroport de Zanderij.
THAILANDE	TOTAL	2002-2005: Y compris les nationaux résidant à l'étranger.
TUNISIE	TOTAL	À l'exclusion des nationaux résidant à l'étranger.

1. Arrivées de touristes non résidents aux frontières nationales, par nationalité

NOTES: 2002 - 2006

1. Arrivées de touristes non résidents aux frontières nationales, par pays de résidence

AFRIQUE DU SUD	TOTAL	À l'exclusion des arrivées par travail et les travailleurs contractuels.
	CHINE	Y compris Hong-Kong, Chine.
ANGUILLA	TOTAL	À l'exclusion des nationaux résidant à l¿étranger.
ANTIGUA-ET-BARBUDA	TOTAL	Arrivées par voie aérienne. A l'exclusion des nationaux résidant à l'étranger.
BARBADE	TOTAL	2006: Données provisoires.
BENIN	TOTAL	2003-2006: estimations.
BERMUDES	TOTAL	Arrivées par voie aérienne.
CAMBODGE	AUT.MONDE	2004-2006: y compris les arrivées dans la région "Phreah Vihear": 2004: 67.843 2005: 88.615 2006: 108.691
CURACAO	TOTAL	Arrivées par voie aérienne.
ETATS-UNIS	TOTAL	Les donnés comprennent les Mexicains qui passent une ou plusieurs nuits aux États-Unis.
FIDJI	TOTAL	À l'exclusion des nationaux résidant à l'étranger.
FRANCE	TOTAL	Estimations à partir d'enquêtes aux frontières (1996-2004). 2005: données révisées. Rupture de série, données non comparables aux années antérieures. 2006: données provisoires.
	AUSTR/N.ZEA	Australie, Océanie.
GUINEE	TOTAL	Arrivées par voie aérienne à l'aéroport de Conakry.
GUYANE	TOTAL	Arrivées à l'aéroport de Timehri seulement.
ILES CAIMANES	TOTAL	Arrivées par voie aérienne.
ILES COOK	TOTAL	Arrivées par voies aérienne et maritime. 2006: données provisoires.
ILES MARSHALL	TOTAL	2002,2003,2006: arrivées par voie aérienne. 2004,2005: arrivées par voies aérienne et maritime.
ILES SALOMON	TOTAL	2005: à l¿exclusion du 1er trimestre.
IRLANDE	ROYAUME-UNI	Y compris les arrivées des résidents de l'Irlande du nord.
	GRECE	Y compris la Turquie.
ISRAEL	TOTAL	À l'exclusion des nationaux résidant à l'étranger et y compris visiteurs de la journée.
JAMAIQUE	TOTAL	Arrivées par voie aérienne. À l'inclusion des nationaux résidant à l'étranger.
	EU	Y compris Porto Rico.
KIRGHIZISTAN	TOTAL	2003-2006 nouvelle source d'information: Département du Contrôle Douanier.
MALAISIE	TOTAL	Y compris les résidents de Singapour traversant la frontière par voie terrestre à travers le Johore Causeway.
MALAWI	TOTAL	Départs.
MARTINIQUE	TOTAL	Y compris les départements et territoires français d¿outremer.
MEXIQUE	TOTAL	Y compris les nationaux résidant à l'étranger. 2006: données préliminaires.
MICRONESIE, ETATS FEDERES DE	TOTAL	Arrivées dans les États de Kosrae, Chuuk, Pohnpei et Yap.
NEPAL	GRECE	Y compris Chypre.
NIOUE	TOTAL	Arrivées par voie aérienne, y compris les nationaux de Niue résidant habituellement en Nouvelle-Zélande.

NOTES: 2002 - 2006

1. Arrivées de touristes non résidents aux frontières nationales, par pays de résidence

NOUVELLE-CALEDONIE	TOTAL	Y compris les nationaux résidant à l'étranger.
	T.CARAIBES	Martinique, Guadeloupe et Guyane.
PALAOS	TOTAL	Arrivées par voie aérienne (aéroport international de Palaos).
PHILIPPINES	N RESID ETRA	Titulaires d'un passeport philippin résidant en permanence à l'étranger; travailleurs philippins exclus.
POLYNESIE FRANCAISE	TOTAL	Arrivées par voie aérienne. À l'exclusion des nationaux résidant à l'étranger.
	SAMOA	Y compris les Samoa américaines.
PORTO RICO	TOTAL	Arrivées par voie aérienne. Année fiscale de juillet à juin. Source: "Junta de Planificación de Puerto Rico".
PORTUGAL	TOTAL	2002-2003: Sont exclues les arrivées de nationaux résidant à l'étranger. 2004-2006: Sont incluses les arrivées de nationaux résidant à l'étranger. La méthodologie a été modifiée et pour cela, à partir de 2004 les données ne sont pas comparables avec celles des années précédentes.
REPUBLIQUE DOMINICAINE	TOTAL	Arrivées par voie aérienne. 2002: à l'exclusion des passagers de l'aéroport de Herrera. 2006: données provisoires.
SAINT-EUSTACHE	TOTAL	À l'exclusion des résidents des Antilles néerlandaises.
SAINT-KITTS-ET-NEVIS	TOTAL	Arrivées par voie aérienne.
SAINT-VINCENT-ET-LES-GRENADINES	TOTAL	Arrivées par voie aérienne.
SAINTE-LUCIE	TOTAL	À l'exclusion des nationaux résidant à l'étranger.
SIERRA LEONE	TOTAL	Arrivées par voie aérienne.
SRI LANKA	TOTAL	À l'exclusion des nationaux résidant à l'étranger.
THAILANDE	TOTAL	2002-2005: Y compris les nationaux résidant à l'étranger.
TONGA	TOTAL	Arrivées par voie aérienne.
TRINITE-ET-TOBAGO	TOTAL	Arrivées par voie aérienne.
ZAMBIE	TOTAL	2002: données provisoires.

NOTES: 2002 - 2006

2. Arrivées de visiteurs non résidents aux frontières nationales, par nationalité

ALGERIE	**TOTAL**	Y compris les nationaux résidant à l'étranger.
BAHREIN	**TOTAL**	A l'exclusion des nationaux résidant à l'étranger.
BELIZE	**TOTAL**	Y compris passagers en transit et passagers à la frontière.
COLOMBIE	**TOTAL**	Source: "Dirección de Extranjería - Departamento Administrativo de Seguridad (DAS)". 2006: données provisoires.
COREE, REPUBLIQUE DE	**TOTAL**	Y compris les nationaux résidant à l'étranger et les membres des équipages.
EGYPTE	**TOTAL**	À l'exclusion des nationaux résidant à l'étranger.
EQUATEUR	**TOTAL**	À l'exclusion des nationaux résidant à l'étranger.
HONGRIE	**TOTAL**	Départs.
ITALIE	**TOTAL**	Enquête aux frontières de l' "Ufficio Italiano dei Cambi". À l'exclusion des travailleurs saisonniers et frontaliers.
JAMAHIRIYA ARABE LIBYENNE	**TOTAL**	Voyageurs. Données préliminaires.
JAPON	**TOTAL**	À l'exclusion des nationaux résidant à l'étranger.
MACAO, CHINE	**TOTAL**	Y compris les arrivées par mer, terre et air. Y compris les apatrides et les Chinois qui ne résident pas de manière permanente à Hong-Kong, Chine.
PORTUGAL	**TOTAL**	2002-2003: Sont exclues les arrivées de nationaux résidant à l'étranger. 2004-2006: Sont incluses les arrivées de nationaux résidant à l'étranger. La méthodologie a été modifiée et pour cela, à partir de 2004 les données ne sont pas comparables avec celles des années précédentes.
REPUBLIQUE ARABE SYRIENNE	**TOTAL**	À l'exclusion des arrivées de nationaux résidant à l'étranger. Source des données: enquête du tourisme récepteur en 2002 et 2004.
REPUBLIQUE DE MOLDOVA	**TOTAL**	Visiteurs qui ont bénéficié des services des agents économiques officiellement enregistrés avec le type d'activité tourisme et des unités d'hébergement qui leur appartiennent. À l'exception de la rive gauche de la rivière Nistru et de la municipalité de Bender.
SAINT-MARIN	**TOTAL**	Nouvelle méthodologie à partir de 2005.
SINGAPOUR	**TOTAL**	À l'exclusion des arrivées de Malaisiens par voie terrestre.
TURQUIE	**TOTAL**	Voyageurs, y compris les immigrants temporaires, diplomates, représentant consulaires et membres des forces armées. Sont exclues les arrivées des membres des équipages, des passagers en transit et des nationaux résidant à l'étranger.

2. Arrivées de visiteurs non résidents aux frontières nationales, par pays de résidence

AFRIQUE DU SUD	**TOTAL**	À l'exclusion des nationaux résidant à l'étranger. Y compris les arrivées par motif de vacances, affaires, études, travail, transit, trafic frontalier et travailleurs contractuels.
AUSTRALIE	**TOTAL**	A l'exclusion des nationaux résidant à l'étranger et les membres des équipages.
CANADA	**CHINE**	Y compris la Mongolie et le Tibet.
	SUISSE	Y compris le Liechtenstein.
	FRANCE	Y compris Andorre et Monaco.
	DANEMARK	Y compris les Îles Féroé.
	BULGARIE	Y compris l'Albanie et la Roumanie.
	ESTONIE	Y compris la Lettonie et la Lituanie.
	ITALIE	Y compris Saint-Marin et le Saint Siège.
FINLANDE	**TOTAL**	Enquête aux frontières.
HONG-KONG, CHINE	**FRANCE**	Y compris la Nouvelle-Calédonie et la Polynésie française.
	NOUV-ZELANDE	Y compris les Îles Cook.
	EU	Y compris Guam.
ISRAEL	**TOTAL**	À l'exclusion des nationaux résidant à l'étranger.
KENYA	**TOTAL**	À l'exclusion des nationaux résidant à l'étranger. Toutes les données représentent des estimations, dont la projection à été faite sur la base des taux de marché de l'année 1989. Source: Enquête Économique de diverses années.
LETTONIE	**TOTAL**	Départs des non-résidents. Enquête auprès des personnes qui traversent les frontières du pays.
NOUVELLE-ZELANDE	**TOTAL**	Les données relatives aux mouvements de courte durée sont obtenues à partir d'un échantillon aléatoire de déclarations des passagers. Y compris les nationaux résidant à l'étranger. Source: Statistiques de la Nouvelle Zélande, Immigration.
PANAMA	**TOTAL**	Nombre total de visiteurs arrivés au Panama par l'aéroport international de Tocumen, classés selon leur résidence permanente.
PORTUGAL	**TOTAL**	2002-2003: Sont exclues les arrivées de nationaux résidant à l'étranger. 2004-2006: Sont incluses les arrivées de nationaux résidant à l'étranger. La méthodologie a été modifiée et pour cela, à partir de 2004 les données ne sont pas comparables avec celles des années précédentes.
SAINT-VINCENT-ET-LES-GRENADINES	**TOTAL**	Arrivées par voie aérienne.
SINGAPOUR	**TOTAL**	À l'exclusion des arrivées de Malaisiens par voie terrestre.

NOTES: 2002 - 2006

3. Arrivées de touristes non résidents dans les hôtels et établissements assimilés, par nationalité

BOLIVIE	**TOTAL**	Mouvement hôtelier dans les capitales de département.
EL SALVADOR	**TOTAL**	Données provisoires en révision.
EMIRATS ARABES UNIS	**N RESID ETRA**	Y compris le tourisme interne.
ITALIE	**TOTAL**	Arrivées dans les hôtels uniquement.
MALTE	**TOTAL**	2002 source: "Malta Tourism Authority". 2003-2006: départs de touristes par voie aérienne, compilées par pays de résidence. Source: "National Statistics Office".
MAROC	**TOTAL**	Arrivées dans les hôtels homologués, villages de vacances et résidences touristiques.
PEROU	**TOTAL**	2003-2006: estimations préliminaires.
REPUBLIQUE ARABE SYRIENNE	**TOTAL**	Source des données: enquête du tourisme récepteur en 2002 et 2004.
TURQUIE	**TOTAL**	Arrivées dans les établissements homologues y compris: hôtels, motels, pensions, auberges, hôtels-appartements, villages de vacances, hôtels stations thermales et hôtels spéciaux. Résultats de l'enquête mensuelle réalisée auprès des établissements d'hébergement classés par le Ministère du Tourisme.

3. Arrivées de touristes non résidents dans les hôtels et établissements assimilés, par pays de résidence

ALLEMAGNE	**CHINE**	Y compris Hong-Kong, Chine.
AUTRICHE	**TOTAL**	Hôtels uniquement.
CAP-VERT	**BELGIQUE**	Y compris les Pays-Bas.
DANEMARK	**TOTAL**	Nouvelle méthodologie à partir de 2004.
ESPAGNE	**TOTAL**	Arrivées dans les hôtels et les "hostales" (établissements d'hébergement offrant des services limités).
FRANCE	**TOTAL**	Uniquement hôtels 0 à 4 étoiles. 2004-2006: y compris hôtels non homologués. 2006: rénovation de l'enquête, données non comparables aux années antérieures.
GUADELOUPE	**TOTAL**	2003,2004: estimations pour la Guadeloupe continentale (sans Saint-Martin et Saint-Barthélemy). 2005: données tirées d'une enquête réalisée à l'aéroport de Guadeloupe.
GUINEE	**TOTAL**	Hôtels uniquement.
ISRAEL	**T.AMER SUD**	Y compris l'Amérique centrale.
	TOTAL	Arrivées dans les hôtels de tourisme et les hôtels non encore enregistrés.
LITUANIE	**TOTAL**	Hôtels uniquement.
LUXEMBOURG	**TOTAL**	Arrivées dans les hôtels, pensions de famille et auberges.
NOUVELLE-CALEDONIE	**TOTAL**	Il s¿agit des hôtels de Nouméa.
PAYS-BAS	**TOTAL**	Hôtels et pensions.
PHILIPPINES	**N RESID ETRA**	Titulaires d'un passeport philippin résidant en permanence à l'étranger; travailleurs philippins exclus.
	TOTAL	Arrivées par voie aérienne.
POLYNESIE FRANCAISE	**TOTAL**	Hôtels uniquement.
PORTO RICO	**AUT CARAIBES**	À partir de l'année fiscale 2001, les données agrégées des touristes en provenance des petites Antilles qui n'ont pas spécifié leur pays d'origine son inclues.
	AUT.MONDE	Y compris les membres des équipages.
	TOTAL	Année fiscale de juillet à juin. Hôtels enregistrés par la "Compañia de Turismo de Puerto Rico".
PORTUGAL	**TOTAL**	Depuis 2002, nouvelle méthodologie. 2006: données provisoires.
QATAR	**TOTAL**	Arrivées dans les hôtels uniquement.
ROUMANIE	**T.AMER.CENTR**	Y compris le Mexique.
	TOUTES AFRIC	Y compris l'Égypte et la Libye.
SUISSE	**TOTAL**	2001-2003: hôtels, motels et auberges. 2005-2006: hôtels et établissements de cure.
	T.AFR.NORD	Algérie, Libye, Maroc et Tunisie.
TOGO	**BURKINA FASO**	Y compris le Mali et le Niger.

NOTES: 2002 - 2006

4. Arrivées de touristes non résidents dans tous les types d'établissements d'hébergement, par nationalité

HONGRIE	TOTAL	Établissements d'hébergement collectif.
MALTE	TOTAL	2002 source: "Malta Tourism Authority". 2003-2006: départs de touristes par voie aérienne, compilées par pays de résidence. Source: "National Statistics Office".
REPUBLIQUE ARABE SYRIENNE	TOTAL	À l'exclusion de l'hébergement chez des particuliers. Source des données: enquête du tourisme récepteur en 2002 et 2004.
REPUBLIQUE DE MOLDOVA	TOTAL	À l'exception de la rive gauche de la rivière Nistru et de la municipalité de Bender.
TURQUIE	TOTAL	Résultats de l'enquête mensuelle réalisée auprès des établissements d'hébergement classés par le Ministère du Tourisme.

NOTES: 2002 - 2006

4. Arrivées de touristes non résidents dans tous les types d'établissements d'hébergement, par pays de résidence

ALLEMAGNE	**CHINE**	Y compris Hong-Kong, Chine.
AUTRICHE	**TOTAL**	Y compris hébergement privé.
BELGIQUE	**TOTAL**	Etablissements hôteliers, terrains de camping, centres de vacances, villages de vacances et catégories spécifiques d'hébergement.
CROATIE	**TOTAL**	Y compris les arrivées dans des ports à tourisme nautique.
DANEMARK	**TOTAL**	Nouvelle méthodologie à partir de 2004.
ESPAGNE	**TOTAL**	Arrivées dans hôtels, "hostales", camping, appartements touristiques et logements ruraux.
FINLANDE	**TOTAL**	Dû à un changement dans la méthodologie, l'information de 2004 n'est pas comparable à celle des années précédentes.
LUXEMBOURG	**TOTAL**	Hôtels, auberges, pensions de famille, auberges de jeunesse, logements touristiques privés, terrains de camping et autres.
PHILIPPINES	**TOTAL**	Arrivées par voie aérienne.
	N RESID ETRA	Titulaires d'un passeport philippin résidant en permanence à l'étranger; travailleurs philippins exclus.
PORTUGAL	**TOTAL**	Depuis 2002, nouvelle méthodologie. 2006: données provisoires.
ROUMANIE	**TOUTES AFRIC**	Y compris l'Égypte et la Libye.
	T.AMER.CENTR	Y compris le Mexique.

NOTES: 2002 - 2006

5. Nuitées de touristes non résidents dans les hôtels et établissements assimilés, par nationalité

BOLIVIE	**TOTAL**	Nuitées dans les capitales de département.
EL SALVADOR	**TOTAL**	Données provisoires en révision.
EMIRATS ARABES UNIS	**N RESID ETRA**	Y compris le tourisme interne.
ITALIE	**TOTAL**	Nuitées dans les hôtels uniquement.
MADAGASCAR	**TOTAL**	Établissements de classe étoile (classés et non classés).
MALTE	**TOTAL**	2002 source: "Malta Tourism Authority". 2003-2006: départs de touristes par voie aérienne, compilées par pays de résidence. Source: "National Statistics Office".
MAROC	**TOTAL**	Nuitées dans les hôtels homologués, villages de vacances et résidences touristiques.
NORVEGE	**TOTAL**	Nuitées dans les établissements homologués. Les données ne couvrent que les établissements avec une capacité d'au moins 20 lits.
PEROU	**TOTAL**	2003-2006: estimations préliminaires.
REPUBLIQUE ARABE SYRIENNE	**TOTAL**	Source des données: enquête du tourisme récepteur en 2002 et 2004.
TURQUIE	**TOTAL**	Hôtels classés, motels, pensions de familles, auberges, aparthôtels, villages de vacances, stations thermales et hôtels spéciaux. Résultats de l'enquête mensuelle réalisée auprès des établissements d'hébergement classés par le Ministère du Tourisme.

5. Nuitées de touristes non résidents dans les hôtels et établissements assimilés, par pays de résidence

ALLEMAGNE	CHINE	Y compris Hong-Kong, Chine.
AUTRICHE	TOTAL	Hôtels uniquement.
BULGARIE	TOTAL	Les données couvrent principalement l'ancien hébergement du secteur public et celui propriété de l'État.
CAP-VERT	BELGIQUE	Y compris les Pays-Bas.
DANEMARK	TOTAL	Nouvelle méthodologie à partir de 2004.
ESPAGNE	TOTAL	Nuitées dans les hôtels et les "hostales" (établissements d'hébergement offrant des services limités).
FINLANDE	TOTAL	Dû à un changement dans la méthodologie, l'information de 2004 n'est pas comparable à celle des années précédentes.
FRANCE	TOTAL	Uniquement hôtels 0 à 4 étoiles. 2004-2006: y compris hôtels non homologués. 2006: rénovation de l'enquête, données non comparables aux années antérieures.
ISRAEL	TOTAL	Nuitées dans les hôtels de tourisme et aparthôtels.
	T.AMER SUD	Y compris l'Amérique centrale.
KENYA	TOTAL	Source: Enquête Économique de diverses années.
LITUANIE	TOTAL	Hôtels uniquement.
LUXEMBOURG	TOTAL	Nuitées dans les hôtels, pensions de famille et auberges.
NOUVELLE-CALEDONIE	TOTAL	Il s¿agit des hôtels de Nouméa.
PAYS-BAS	TOTAL	Hôtels et pensions.
POLYNESIE FRANCAISE	TOTAL	Hôtels uniquement.
PORTUGAL	TOTAL	Depuis 2002, nouvelle méthodologie. 2006: données provisoires.
QATAR	TOTAL	Nuitées dans les hôtels uniquement.
ROUMANIE	T.AMER.CENTR	Y compris le Mexique.
	TOUTES AFRIC	Y compris l'Égypte et la Libye.
SUEDE	TOTAL	Nuitées dans les hôtels uniquement.
SUISSE	TOTAL	2001-2003: hôtels, motels et auberges. 2005-2006: hôtels et établissements de cure.
	T.AFR.NORD	Algérie, Libye, Maroc et Tunisie.
TOGO	BURKINA FASO	Y compris le Mali et le Niger.

NOTES: 2002 - 2006

6. Nuitées de touristes non résidents dans tous les types d'établissements d'hébergement, par nationalité

BERMUDES	TOTAL	Sont comprises les nuitées dans les maisons privées.
HONGRIE	TOTAL	Établissements d'hébergement collectif.
MALTE	TOTAL	22002 source: "Malta Tourism Authority". 2003-2006: départs de touristes par voie aérienne, compilées par pays de résidence. Source: "National Statistics Office".
REPUBLIQUE ARABE SYRIENNE	TOTAL	Source des données: enquête du tourisme récepteur en 2002 et 2004.
TURQUIE	TOTAL	Résultats de l'enquête mensuelle réalisée auprès des établissements d'hébergement classés par le Ministère du Tourisme.

6. Nuitées de touristes non résidents dans tous les types d'établissements d'hébergement, par pays de résidence

ALLEMAGNE	**CHINE**	Y compris Hong-Kong, Chine.
AUTRICHE	**TOTAL**	Y compris hébergement privé.
BAHAMAS	**TOTAL**	Nuitées dans tout moyen d'hébergement commercial.
BELGIQUE	**TOTAL**	Etablissements hôteliers, terrains de camping, centres de vacances, villages de vacances et catégories spécifiques d'hébergement.
BULGARIE	**TOTAL**	Les données couvrent principalement l'ancien hébergement du secteur public et celui propriété de l'État.
CANADA	**CHINE**	Y compris la Mongolie et le Tibet.
	ITALIE	Y compris Saint-Marin et le Saint Siège.
	ESTONIE	Y compris la Lettonie et la Lituanie.
	BULGARIE	Y compris l'Albanie et la Roumanie.
	DANEMARK	Y compris les Îles Féroé.
	FRANCE	Y compris Andorre et Monaco.
	SUISSE	Y compris le Liechtenstein.
CROATIE	**TOTAL**	Y compris les nuitées dans des ports à tourisme nautique.
DANEMARK	**TOTAL**	Nouvelle méthodologie à partir de 2004.
ESPAGNE	**TOTAL**	Nuitées dans hôtels, "hostales", camping, appartements touristiques et logements ruraux.
FINLANDE	**TOTAL**	Dû à un changement dans la méthodologie, l'information de 2004 n'est pas comparable à celle des années précédentes.
FRANCE	**AUSTR/N.ZEA**	Australie, Océanie.
	TOTAL	Estimations à partir d'enquêtes aux frontières (1996-2004). 2005: données révisées. Rupture de série, données non comparables aux années précédentes. 2006: données provisoires.
IRLANDE	**SCANDINAVIE**	Danemark, Norvège, Suède, Finlande, Islande.
	TOTAL	Y compris nuitées dans hébergement privé non payant (maisons privées et maisons de vacances).
	ROYAUME-UNI	Y compris les résidents de l'Irlande du Nord.
JAMAIQUE	**TOUTE EUROPE**	Royaume-Uni et le reste de l'Europe.
	AUT AMERIQUE	Amérique latine.
	TOTAL	L'information à été obtenue en multipliant la durée moyenne de séjour par le nombre de touristes (stop-over) provenant de chaque pays d'origine.
MALAWI	**TOTAL**	2004: données provisoires.
PAYS-BAS	**TOTAL**	À l'exclusion des nuitées dans des installations fixes (louées sur une base annuelle ou saisonnière).
PORTUGAL	**TOTAL**	Depuis 2002, nouvelle méthodologie. 2006: données provisoires.
ROUMANIE	**T.AMER.CENTR**	Y compris le Mexique.
	TOUTES AFRIC	Y compris l'Égypte et la Libye.
SUEDE	**TOTAL**	Nuitées dans les hôtels, auberges de jeunesse, villages de vacances et camping.

NOTAS: 2002 - 2006

1. Llegadas de turistas no residentes en las fronteras nacionales, por nacionalidad

ARGENTINA	TOTAL	2005-2006: datos provisionales. A partir del año 2004, como resultado de la importancia de la "Encuesta de Turismo Internacional" se modificaron las estimaciones de la serie de la cuenta "viajes" de la balanza de pagos. Por este motivo, los datos no son rigurosamente comparables con los años anteriores.
BELARUS	TOTAL	Turismo organizado.
BRUNEI DARUSSALAM	TOTAL	Llegadas por vía aérea.
BURUNDI	TOTAL	Incluidos los nacionales residentes en el extranjero.
COMORAS	TOTAL	Llegadas por vía aérea.
ETIOPIA	TOTAL	Llegadas a través de todos los puestos fronterizos.
GAMBIA	TOTAL	Llegadas en vuelos fletados únicamente.
GRECIA	TFYROM UCRANIA EGIPTO LIBANO TOTAL	2005 incluido en "otros países de Europa". A partir de 2005, incluido en "otros países de Europa". Incluido Sudán. Incluido Siria. Información procedente de datos administrativos.
GUINEA	TOTAL	2003,2005,2006: llegadas por vía aérea al aeropuerto de Conakry.
GUINEA-BISSAU	TOTAL	Llegadas al aeropuerto "Osvaldo Vieira".
INDIA	TOTAL	Excluidos los nacionales residentes en el extranjero.
ISLAS MARSHALL	TOTAL	2002,2003,2006: llegadas por vía aérea. 2004,2005: llegadas por vías aérea y marítima.
ITALIA	TOTAL	Excluidos los trabajadores estacionales y fronterizos.
JORDANIA	OTR.MUNDO	Pasaporte de la ONU.
KIRIBATI	TOTAL	Llegadas por vía aérea. 2002,2003,2006: Tarawa e Isla Christmas. 2004,2005: Tarawa únicamente.
LIBANO	TOTAL	Excluidos nacionales de Siria, Palestina y estudiantes.
MALDIVAS	TOTAL	Llegadas por vía aérea.
MALTA	TOTAL	2004-2006: datos procedentes de las salidas por vías aérea y marítima.
MEXICO	EEUU	Incluidos los turistas de la franja fronteriza: 2005: 9.381.000 2006: 8.745.000
	TOTAL	Incluidos los nacionales residentes en el extranjero. 2006: datos preliminares.
MYANMAR	TOTAL	Incluidas las llegadas de turistas a través de los puntos de entrada fronterizos a Yangon.
NEPAL	GRECIA	Incluido Chipre.
NICARAGUA	TOTAL	2006: Estimaciones preliminares.
NORUEGA	TOTAL	Las cifras se basan en "The Guest Survey", un estudio realizado por el "Institute of Transport Economics".
PARAGUAY	TOTAL	Excluidos los nacionales residentes en el extranjero y los miembros de tripulaciones. Tarjetas E/D en el aeropuerto Silvio Petirossi y planillas de pasajeros en los puestos terrestres - Policía Nacional y SENATUR.
PERU	TOTAL	A partir de 2002, nueva serie estimada incluyendo a los turistas con un documento de identidad diferente al pasaporte. 2004-2006: estimaciones preliminares.
PORTUGAL	TOTAL	2002-2003: Excluidas las llegadas de nacionales residentes en el extranjero. 2004-2006: Incluidas las llegadas de nacionales residentes en el extranjero. Debido a un cambio de metodología, a partir de 2004 los datos no son comparables con los años anteriores.

NOTAS: 2002 - 2006

1. Llegadas de turistas no residentes en las fronteras nacionales, por nacionalidad

REPUBLICA CENTROAFRICANA	TOTAL	Llegadas por vía aérea a Bangui únicamente. 2006: Estimationes.
REPUBLICA DEMOCRATICA DEL CONGO	TOTAL	2002-2004: llegadas por vía aérea únicamente. 2005-2006: datos provisionales.
SAN MARTIN	FRANCIA	Incluidos los residentes de las Antillas Francesas.
	TOTAL	Llegadas al aeropuerto internacional "Princess Juliana". Incluidos los visitantes a San Martín (parte francesa de la isla).
SRI LANKA	TOTAL	Excluidos los nacionales residentes en el extranjero.
SUDAN	TOTAL	2005-2006: incluidos los nacionales residentes en el extranjero.
SURINAME	TOTAL	Llegadas al aeropuerto de Zanderij.
TAILANDIA	TOTAL	2002-2005: Incluidos los nacionales residentes en el extranjero.
TUNEZ	TOTAL	Excluidos los nacionales residentes en el extranjero.

NOTAS: 2002 - 2006

1. Llegadas de turistas no residentes en las fronteras nacionales, por país de residencia

ANGUILA	TOTAL	Excluidos los nacionales residentes en el extranjero.
ANTIGUA Y BARBUDA	TOTAL	Llegadas por vía aérea. Excluidos los nacionales residentes en el extranjero.
BARBADOS	TOTAL	2006: Datos provisionales.
BENIN	TOTAL	2003-2006: estimaciones.
BERMUDA	TOTAL	Llegadas por vía aérea.
CAMBOYA	OTR.MUNDO	2004-2006: incluidas las llegadas a la provincia "Phreah Vihear": 2004: 67.843 2005: 88.615 2006: 108.691
CURACAO	TOTAL	Llegadas por vía aérea.
ESTADOS UNIDOS	TOTAL	Los datos comprenden a los mexicanos que pasan una o más noches en los Estados Unidos.
FIJI	TOTAL	Excluidos los nacionales residentes en el extranjero.
FILIPINAS	N RESID EXTR	Titulares de pasaportes filipino que residen permanentemente en el extranjero; están excluidos los trabajadores filipinos.
FRANCIA	TOTAL	Estimaciones basadas en encuestas en fronteras (1996-2004). 2005: datos revisados. Ruptura de serie, datos no comparables con años anteriores. 2006: datos provisionales.
	AUSTR/N.ZEAL	Australia, Oceanía.
GUINEA	TOTAL	Llegadas por vía aérea al aeropuerto de Conakry.
GUYANA	TOTAL	Llegadas al aeropuerto de Timehri únicamente.
IRLANDA	REINO UNIDO GRECIA	Incluidas las llegadas de los residentes de Irlanda del Norte. Incluido Turquía.
ISLAS CAIMAN	TOTAL	Llegadas por vía aérea.
ISLAS COOK	TOTAL	Llegadas por vías aérea y marítima. 2006: datos provisionales.
ISLAS MARSHALL	TOTAL	2002,2003,2006: llegadas por vía aérea. 2004,2005: llegadas por vías aérea y marítima.
ISLAS SALOMON	TOTAL	2005: excluido el 1er trimestre.
ISRAEL	TOTAL	Excluidos los nacionales residentes en el extranjero e incluidos los visitantes del día.
JAMAICA	TOTAL	Llegadas por vía aérea. Incluidos los nacionales residentes en el extranjero.
	EEUU	Incluido Puerto Rico.
KIRGUISTAN	TOTAL	2003-2006 nueva fuente de información: Departamento de Control Aduanero.
MALASIA	TOTAL	Incluidos residentes de Singapur que atraviesan la frontera por vía terrestre a través de Johore Causeway.
MALAWI	TOTAL	Salidas.
MARTINICA	TOTAL	Incluidos los departamentos y territorios franceses de ultramar.
MEXICO	TOTAL	Incluidos los nacionales residentes en el extranjero. 2006: datos preliminares.
MICRONESIA (ESTADOS FEDERADOS DE)	TOTAL	Llegadas en los Estados de Kosrae, Chuuk, Pohnpei y Yap.
NEPAL	GRECIA	Incluido Chipre.
NIUE	TOTAL	Llegadas por vía aérea, incluidos los nacionales de Niue que residen habitualmente en Nueva Zelandia.
NUEVA CALEDONIA	TOTAL TODOS CARIBE	Incluidos los nacionales residentes en el extranjero. Martinica, Guadalupe y Guyana.

NOTAS: 2002 - 2006

1. Llegadas de turistas no residentes en las fronteras nacionales, por país de residencia

PALAU	**TOTAL**	Llegadas por vía aérea (aeropuerto internacional de Palau).
POLINESIA FRANCESA	**TOTAL**	Llegadas por vía aérea. Excluidos los nacionales residentes en el extranjero.
	SAMOA	Incluida Samoa americana.
PORTUGAL	**TOTAL**	2002-2003: Excluidas las llegadas de nacionales residentes en el extranjero. 2004-2006: Incluidas las llegadas de nacionales residentes en el extranjero. Debido a un cambio de metodología, a partir de 2004 los datos no son comparables con los años anteriores.
PUERTO RICO	**TOTAL**	Llegadas por vía aérea. Año fiscal de julio a junio. Fuente: Junta de Planificación de Puerto Rico.
REPUBLICA DOMINICANA	**TOTAL**	Llegadas por vía aérea. 2002: excluidos los pasajeros del aeropuerto de herrera. 2006: datos provisionales.
SAINT KITTS Y NEVIS	**TOTAL**	Llegadas por vía aérea.
SAN EUSTAQUIO	**TOTAL**	Excluidos los residentes de las Antillas neerlandesas.
SAN VICENTE Y LAS GRANADINAS	**TOTAL**	Llegadas por vía aérea.
SANTA LUCIA	**TOTAL**	Excluidos los nacionales residentes en el extranjero.
SIERRA LEONA	**TOTAL**	Llegadas por vía aérea.
SRI LANKA	**TOTAL**	Excluidos los nacionales residentes en el extranjero.
SUDAFRICA	**TOTAL**	Excluidas las llegadas por trabajo y los trabajadores con contrato.
	CHINA	Incluye Hong Kong, China.
TAILANDIA	**TOTAL**	2002-2005: Incluidos los nacionales residentes en el extranjero.
TONGA	**TOTAL**	Llegadas por vía aérea.
TRINIDAD Y TABAGO	**TOTAL**	Llegadas por vía aérea.
ZAMBIA	**TOTAL**	2002: datos provisionales.

NOTAS: 2002 - 2006

2. Llegadas de visitantes no residentes en las fronteras nacionales, por nacionalidad

ARGELIA	TOTAL	Incluidos los nacionales residentes en el extranjero.
BAHREIN	TOTAL	Excluidos los nacionales residentes en el extranjero.
BELICE	TOTAL	Incluidos pasajeros en tránsito y cruce de fronteras.
COLOMBIA	TOTAL	Fuente: "Dirección de Extranjería - Departamento Administrativo de Seguridad (DAS)". 2006: datos provisionales.
COREA, REPUBLICA DE	TOTAL	Incluidos los nacionales residentes en el extranjero y los miembros de las tripulaciones.
ECUADOR	TOTAL	Excluidos los nacionales residentes en el extranjero.
EGIPTO	TOTAL	Excluidos los nacionales residentes en el extranjero.
HUNGRIA	TOTAL	Salidas.
ITALIA	TOTAL	Encuesta en fronteras del "Ufficio Italiano dei Cambi". Excluidos los trabajadores estacionales y fronterizos.
JAMAHIRIYA ARABE LIBIA	TOTAL	Viajeros. Datos preliminares.
JAPON	TOTAL	Excluidos los nacionales residentes en el extranjero.
MACAO, CHINA	TOTAL	Incluidas las llegadas por mar, tierra y aire. Incluye apátridas y personas de origen chino que no residen de forma permanente en Hong Kong, China.
PORTUGAL	TOTAL	2002-2003: Excluidas las llegadas de nacionales residentes en el extranjero. 2004-2006: Incluidas las llegadas de nacionales residentes en el extranjero. Debido a un cambio de metodología, a partir de 2004 los datos no son comparables con los años anteriores.
REPUBLICA ARABE SIRIA	TOTAL	Excluidas las llegadas de nacionales residentes en el extranjero. Fuente de los datos: encuesta del turismo receptor en 2002 y 2004.
REPUBLICA DE MOLDOVA	TOTAL	Visitantes que se beneficiaron de los servicios de los agentes económicos registrados oficialmente en la actividad turística y en el alojamiento. Excluido el margen izquierdo del río Nistru y la municipalidad de Bender.
SAN MARINO	TOTAL	Nueva metodología a partir de 2005.
SINGAPUR	TOTAL	Excluidas llegadas de los malasios por vía terrestre.
TURQUIA	TOTAL	Viajeros, incluidos inmigrantes temporeros, diplomáticos, representantes consulares y miembros de las fuerzas armadas. Excluidas las llegadas de miembros de tripulaciones, de pasajeros en tránsito y de nacionales del país residentes en el extranjero.

NOTAS: 2002 - 2006

2. Llegadas de visitantes no residentes en las fronteras nacionales, por país de residencia

AUSTRALIA	**TOTAL**	Excluidos los nacionales residentes en el extranjero y los miembros de tripulaciones.
CANADA	**CHINA**	Incluido Mongolia y Tibet.
	FRANCIA	Incluido Andorra y Mónaco.
	ITALIA	Incluido San Marino y la Santa Sede.
	SUIZA	Incluido Liechtenstein.
	DINAMARCA	Incluido las Islas Feroe.
	BULGARIA	Incluido Albania y Rumania.
	ESTONIA	Incluido Letonia y Lituania.
FINLANDIA	**TOTAL**	Encuesta en las fronteras.
HONG KONG, CHINA	**FRANCIA**	Incluidas Nueva Caledonia y la Polinesia Francesa.
	EEUU	Incluido Guam.
	NUEVA ZELAND	Incluidas las Islas Cook.
ISRAEL	**TOTAL**	Excluidos los nacionales residentes en el extranjero.
KENYA	**TOTAL**	Excluidos los nacionales residentes en el extranjero. Todos los datos corresponden a estimaciones, cuya proyección se basa en la cuota de mercado del año 1989. Fuente: Encuesta Económica realizada en diferentes años.
LETONIA	**TOTAL**	Salidas de no residentes. Encuesta realizada en los puestos fronterizos del país.
NUEVA ZELANDIA	**TOTAL**	Los datos relativos a los movimientos de corta duración se obtienen de una muestra aleatoria de declaraciones de los pasajeros. Incluidos los nacionales residentes en el extranjero. Fuente: Estadísticas Nueva Zelandia, Inmigración.
PANAMA	**TOTAL**	Total de visitantes ingresados a Panamá por el aeropuerto internacional de Tocumen según domicilio permanente.
PORTUGAL	**TOTAL**	2002-2003: Excluidas las llegadas de nacionales residentes en el extranjero. 2004-2006: Incluidas las llegadas de nacionales residentes en el extranjero. Debido a un cambio de metodología, a partir de 2004 los datos no son comparables con los años anteriores.
SAN VICENTE Y LAS GRANADINAS	**TOTAL**	Llegadas por vía aérea.
SINGAPUR	**TOTAL**	Excluidas llegadas de los malasios por vía terrestre.
SUDAFRICA	**TOTAL**	Excluidos los nacionales residentes en el extranjero. Incluidas las llegadas por motivo de vacaciones, negocios, estudios, trabajo, tránsito, tráfico fronterizo y trabajadores con contrato.

NOTAS: 2002 - 2006

3. Llegadas de turistas no residentes a los hoteles y establecimientos asimilados, por nacionalida

BOLIVIA	**TOTAL**	Movimiento hotelero en las capitales de departamento.
EL SALVADOR	**TOTAL**	Datos provisionales en proceso de revisión.
EMIRATOS ARABES UNIDOS	**N RESID EXTR**	Incluido el turismo interno.
ITALIA	**TOTAL**	Llegadas a los hoteles únicamente.
MALTA	**TOTAL**	2002 fuente: "Malta Tourism Authority". 2003-2006: salidas de turistas por vía aérea, compiladas por país de residencia. Fuente: "National Statistics Office".
MARRUECOS	**TOTAL**	Llegadas en hoteles homologados, ciudades de vacaciones y residencias turísticas.
PERU	**TOTAL**	2003-2006: estimaciones preliminares.
REPUBLICA ARABE SIRIA	**TOTAL**	Fuente de los datos: encuesta del turismo receptor en 2002 y 2004.
TURQUIA	**TOTAL**	Llegadas a los establecimientos homologados incluidos: hoteles, moteles, pensiones, albergues, apartahoteles, ciudades de vacaciones, estaciones termales y hoteles especiales. Resultados de la encuesta mensual realizada en ciertos establecimientos de alojamiento clasificados por el Ministerio de Turismo.

NOTAS: 2002 - 2006

3. Llegadas de turistas no residentes a los hoteles y establecimientos asimilados, por país de residencia

ALEMANIA	**CHINA**	Incluido Hong Kong, China.
AUSTRIA	TOTAL	Hoteles únicamente.
CABO VERDE	**BELGICA**	Incluido los Países Bajos.
DINAMARCA	TOTAL	Nueva metodología a partir de 2004.
ESPAÑA	TOTAL	Llegadas a hoteles y hostales.
FILIPINAS	**N RESID EXTR**	Titulares de pasaportes filipinos que residen permanentemente en el extranjero; están excluidos los trabajadores filipinos.
	TOTAL	Llegadas por vía aérea.
FRANCIA	TOTAL	Únicamente hoteles 0 a 4 estrellas. 2004-2006: incluidos hoteles sin clasificar. 2006: renovación de la encuesta, datos no comparables con años anteriores.
GUADALUPE	TOTAL	2003,2004: estimaciones para Guadalupe continental (sin San Martín y San Barthelemy). 2005: datos obtenidos en una encuesta realizada en el aeropuerto de Guadalupe.
GUINEA	TOTAL	Hoteles únicamente.
ISRAEL	**T.AMER SUR**	Incluida América Central.
	TOTAL	Llegadas a los hoteles de turismo en aquellos aun no homologados.
LITUANIA	TOTAL	Hoteles únicamente.
LUXEMBURGO	TOTAL	Llegadas en hoteles, casas de huéspedes y albergues.
NUEVA CALEDONIA	TOTAL	Corresponde a los hoteles de Noumea.
PAISES BAJOS	TOTAL	Hoteles y pensiones.
POLINESIA FRANCESA	TOTAL	Hoteles únicamente.
PORTUGAL	TOTAL	Desde 2002, nueva metodología. 2006: datos provisionales.
PUERTO RICO	**OTROS CARIBE**	A partir del año fiscal 2001, se incluyen cifras agregadas de los turistas procedentes de las Antillas menores que no especificaron su país de procedencia.
	TOTAL	Año fiscal de julio a junio. Hoteles endosados por la Compañía de Turismo de Puerto Rico.
	OTR.MUNDO	Incluye a los miembros de las tripulaciones.
QATAR	TOTAL	Llegadas a los hoteles únicamente.
RUMANIA	**T.AMER.CENTR**	Incluido México.
	TODOS AFRICA	Incluido Egipto y Libia.
SUIZA	TOTAL	2001-2003: hoteles, moteles y posadas. 2005-2006: hoteles y establecimientos de cura.
	T.AFR.NORTE	Argelia, Libia, Marruecos y Túnez.
TOGO	**BURKINA FASO**	Incluidos Malí y Níger.

NOTAS: 2002 - 2006

4. Llegadas de turistas no residentes en todo tipo de establecimientos de alojamiento, por nacionalidad

HUNGRIA	TOTAL	Establecimientos de alojamiento colectivo.
MALTA	TOTAL	2002 fuente: "Malta Tourism Authority". 2003-2006: salidas de turistas por vía aérea, compiladas por país de residencia. Fuente: "National Statistics Office".
REPUBLICA ARABE SIRIA	TOTAL	Se excluye el alojamiento privado. Fuente de los datos: encuesta del turismo receptor en 2002 y 2004.
REPUBLICA DE MOLDOVA	TOTAL	Excluido el margen izquierdo del río Nistru y la municipalidad de Bender.
TURQUIA	TOTAL	Resultados de la encuesta mensual realizada en ciertos establecimientos de alojamiento clasificados por el Ministerio de Turismo.

NOTAS: 2002 - 2006

4. Llegadas de turistas no residentes en todo tipo de establecimientos de alojamiento, por país de residencia

ALEMANIA	**CHINA**	Incluido Hong Kong, China.
AUSTRIA	**TOTAL**	Incluido alojamiento privado.
BELGICA	**TOTAL**	Establecimientos hoteleros, terrenos de camping, centros vacacionales, ciudades de vacaciones y categorías específicas de alojamiento.
CROACIA	**TOTAL**	Incluidas las llegadas a puertos de turismo náutico.
DINAMARCA	**TOTAL**	Nueva metodología a partir de 2004.
ESPAÑA	**TOTAL**	Llegadas en hoteles, hostales, camping, apartamentos turísticos y alojamientos/casas rurales.
FILIPINAS	**TOTAL**	Llegadas por vía aérea.
	N RESID EXTR	Titulares de pasaportes filipinos que residen permanentemente en el extranjero; están excluidos los trabajadores filipinos.
FINLANDIA	**TOTAL**	Debido a un cambio en la metodología, la información de 2004 no es comparable con años anteriores.
LUXEMBURGO	**TOTAL**	Hoteles, albergues, casas de huéspedes, albergues de juventud, alojamientos turísticos privados, terrenos de camping y otros.
PORTUGAL	**TOTAL**	Desde 2002, nueva metodología. 2006: datos provisionales.
RUMANIA	**TODOS AFRICA**	Incluido Egipto y Libia.
	T.AMER.CENTR	Incluido México.

NOTAS: 2002 - 2006

5. Pernoctaciones de turistas no residentes en hoteles y establecimientos asimilados, por nacionalidad

BOLIVIA	**TOTAL**	Pernoctaciones en las capitales de departamento.
EL SALVADOR	**TOTAL**	Datos provisionales en proceso de revisión.
EMIRATOS ARABES UNIDOS	**N RESID EXTR**	Incluido el turismo interno.
ITALIA	**TOTAL**	Pernoctaciones en los hoteles únicamente.
MADAGASCAR	**TOTAL**	Todos los establecimientos categorizados por estrellas (homologados y no homologados).
MALTA	**TOTAL**	2002 fuente: "Malta Tourism Authority". 2003-2006: salidas de turistas por vía aérea, compiladas por país de residencia. Fuente: "National Statistics Office".
MARRUECOS	**TOTAL**	Pernoctaciones en hoteles homologados, ciudades de vacaciones y residencias turísticas.
NORUEGA	**TOTAL**	Pernoctaciones en los establecimientos homologados. Los datos cubren solamente los establecimientos con una capacidad de 20 o más camas.
PERU	**TOTAL**	2003-2006: estimaciones preliminares.
REPUBLICA ARABE SIRIA	**TOTAL**	Fuente de los datos: encuesta del turismo receptor en 2002 y 2004.
TURQUIA	**TOTAL**	Hoteles homologados, moteles, pensiones, albergues, apartahoteles, ciudades de vacaciones, estaciones termales y hoteles especiales. Resultados de la encuesta mensual realizada en ciertos establecimientos de alojamiento clasificados por el Ministerio de Turismo.

NOTAS: 2002 - 2006

5. Pernoctaciones de turistas no residentes en hoteles y establecimientos asimilados, por país de residencia

ALEMANIA	CHINA	Incluido Hong Kong, China.
AUSTRIA	TOTAL	Hoteles únicamente.
BULGARIA	TOTAL	Los datos cubren prácticamente el antiguo alojamiento del sector público y de propiedad del estado.
CABO VERDE	BELGICA	Incluido los Países Bajos.
DINAMARCA	TOTAL	Nueva metodología a partir de 2004.
ESPAÑA	TOTAL	Pernoctaciones en hoteles y hostales.
FINLANDIA	TOTAL	Debido a un cambio en la metodología, la información de 2004 no es comparable con años anteriores.
FRANCIA	TOTAL	Únicamente hoteles 0 a 4 estrellas. 2004-2006: incluidos hoteles sin clasificar. 2006: renovación de la encuesta, datos no comparables con años anteriores.
ISRAEL	TOTAL T.AMER SUR	Pernoctaciones en hoteles de turismo y apartahoteles. Incluida América Central.
KENYA	TOTAL	Fuente: Encuesta Económica realizada en diferentes años.
LITUANIA	TOTAL	Hoteles únicamente.
LUXEMBURGO	TOTAL	Pernoctaciones en hoteles, casas de huéspedes y albergues.
NUEVA CALEDONIA	TOTAL	Corresponde a los hoteles de Noumea.
PAISES BAJOS	TOTAL	Hoteles y pensiones.
POLINESIA FRANCESA	TOTAL	Hoteles únicamente.
PORTUGAL	TOTAL	Desde 2002, nueva metodología. 2006: datos provisionales.
QATAR	TOTAL	Pernoctaciones en los hoteles únicamente.
RUMANIA	T.AMER.CENTR TODOS AFRICA	Incluido México. Incluido Egipto y Libia.
SUECIA	TOTAL	Pernoctaciones en los hoteles únicamente.
SUIZA	TOTAL T.AFR.NORTE	2001-2003: hoteles, moteles y posadas. 2005-2006: hoteles y establecimientos de cura. Argelia, Libia, Marruecos y Túnez.
TOGO	BURKINA FASO	Incluidos Malí y Níger.

NOTAS: 2002 - 2006

6. Pernoctaciones de turistas no residentes en todo tipo de establecimientos de alojamiento, por nacionalidad

BERMUDA	TOTAL	Incluidas las pernoctaciones en casas particulares.
HUNGRIA	TOTAL	Establecimientos de alojamiento colectivo.
MALTA	TOTAL	2002 fuente: "Malta Tourism Authority". 2003-2006: salidas de turistas por vía aérea, compiladas por país de residencia. Fuente: "National Statistics Office".
REPUBLICA ARABE SIRIA	TOTAL	Fuente de los datos: encuesta del turismo receptor en 2002 y 2004.
TURQUIA	TOTAL	Resultados de la encuesta mensual realizada en ciertos establecimientos de alojamiento clasificados por el Ministerio de Turismo.

NOTAS: 2002 - 2006

6. Pernoctaciones de turistas no residentes en todo tipo de establecimientos de alojamiento, por país de residencia

ALEMANIA	**CHINA**	Incluido Hong Kong, China.
AUSTRIA	**TOTAL**	Incluido alojamiento privado.
BAHAMAS	**TOTAL**	Pernoctaciones en todo tipo de alojamiento comercial.
BELGICA	**TOTAL**	Establecimientos hoteleros, terrenos de camping, centros vacacionales, ciudades de vacaciones y categorías específicas de alojamiento.
BULGARIA	**TOTAL**	Los datos cubren prácticamente el antiguo alojamiento del sector público y de propiedad del estado.
CANADA	**CHINA**	Incluido Mongolia y Tibet.
	ITALIA	Incluido San Marino y la Santa Sede.
	ESTONIA	Incluido Letonia y Lituania.
	BULGARIA	Incluido Albania y Rumania.
	DINAMARCA	Incluido las Islas Feroe.
	FRANCIA	Incluido Andorra y Mónaco.
	SUIZA	Incluido Liechtenstein.
CROACIA	**TOTAL**	Incluidas las pernoctaciones en puertos de turismo náutico.
DINAMARCA	**TOTAL**	Nueva metodología a partir de 2004.
ESPAÑA	**TOTAL**	Pernoctaciones en hoteles, hostales, camping, apartamentos turísticos y alojamientos/casas rurales.
FINLANDIA	**TOTAL**	Debido a un cambio en la metodología, la información de 2004 no es comparable con años anteriores.
FRANCIA	**AUSTR/N.ZEAL**	Australia, Oceanía.
	TOTAL	Estimaciones basadas en encuestas en fronteras (1996-2004). 2005: datos revisados. Ruptura de serie, datos no comparables con años anteriores. 2006: datos provisionales.
IRLANDA	**ESCANDINAVIA**	Dinamarca, Noruega, Suecia, Finlandia, Islandia.
	TOTAL	Incluidas pernoctaciones en alojamiento privado gratuito (casas de huéspedes y casas particulares).
	REINO UNIDO	Incluidos los residentes de Irlanda del Norte.
JAMAICA	**TODO EUROPA**	Reino unido y resto de Europa.
	OTR AMERICA	América Latina.
	TOTAL	Se ha obtenido la información multiplicando la duración media de estancia por el numero de turistas (stop-overs) procedentes de cada país de origen.
MALAWI	**TOTAL**	2004: datos provisionales.
PAISES BAJOS	**TOTAL**	Excluidas las pernoctaciones en instalaciones fijas (alquiladas anualmente o por temporada).
PORTUGAL	**TOTAL**	Desde 2002, nueva metodología. 2006: datos provisionales.
RUMANIA	**T.AMER.CENTR**	Incluido México.
	TODOS AFRICA	Incluido Egipto y Libia.
SUECIA	**TOTAL**	Pernoctaciones en hoteles, albergues juveniles, poblados de vacaciones y camping.